University Casebook Series

October, 1986

ACCOUNTING AND THE LAW, Fourth Edition (1978), with Problems Pamphlet (Successor to Dohr, Phillips, Thompson & Warren)

George C. Thompson, Professor, Columbia University Graduate School of Business.
Robert Whitman, Professor of Law, University of Connecticut.
Ellis L. Phillips, Jr., Member of the New York Bar.
William C. Warren, Professor of Law Emeritus, Columbia University.

ACCOUNTING FOR LAWYERS, MATERIALS ON (1980)

David R. Herwitz, Professor of Law, Harvard University.

ADMINISTRATIVE LAW, Eighth Edition (1987), with 1983 Problems Supplement (Supplement edited in association with Paul R. Verkuil, Dean and Professor of Law, Tulane University)

Walter Gellhorn, University Professor Emeritus, Columbia University.
Clark Byse, Professor of Law, Harvard University.
Peter L. Strauss, Professor of Law, Columbia University.
Todd D. Rakoff, Professor of Law, Harvard University.

ADMIRALTY, Third Edition (1987), with Statute and Rule Supplement

Jo Desha Lucas, Professor of Law, University of Chicago.

ADVOCACY, see also Lawyering Process

AGENCY, see also Enterprise Organization

AGENCY—PARTNERSHIPS, Third Edition (1982)

Abridgement from Conard, Knauss & Siegel's Enterprise Organization, Third Edition.

ANTITRUST: FREE ENTERPRISE AND ECONOMIC ORGANIZATION, Sixth Edition (1983), with 1983 Problems in Antitrust Supplement and 1986 Case Supplement

Louis B. Schwartz, Professor of Law, University of Pennsylvania.
John J. Flynn, Professor of Law, University of Utah.
Harry First, Professor of Law, New York University.

BANKRUPTCY (1985)

Robert L. Jordan, Professor of Law, University of California, Los Angeles.
William D. Warren, Professor of Law, University of California, Los Angeles.

BUSINESS ORGANIZATION, see also Enterprise Organization

BUSINESS PLANNING, Temporary Second Edition (1984)

David R. Herwitz, Professor of Law, Harvard University.

BUSINESS TORTS (1972)

Milton Handler, Professor of Law Emeritus, Columbia University.

i

CHILDREN IN THE LEGAL SYSTEM (1983)

Walter Wadlington, Professor of Law, University of Virginia.
Charles H. Whitebread, Professor of Law, University of Southern California.
Samuel Davis, Professor of Law, University of Georgia.

CIVIL PROCEDURE, see Procedure

CLINIC, see also Lawyering Process

COMMERCIAL LAW (1983) with 1986 Bankruptcy Supplement

Robert L. Jordan, Professor of Law, University of California, Los Angeles.
William D. Warren, Professor of Law, University of California, Los Angeles.

COMMERCIAL LAW, CASES & MATERIALS ON, Fourth Edition (1985)

E. Allan Farnsworth, Professor of Law, Columbia University.
John Honnold, Professor of Law, University of Pennsylvania.

COMMERCIAL PAPER, Third Edition (1984)

E. Allan Farnsworth, Professor of Law, Columbia University.

COMMERCIAL PAPER (1983) (Reprinted from COMMERCIAL LAW)

Robert L. Jordan, Professor of Law, University of California, Los Angeles.
William D. Warren, Professor of Law, University of California, Los Angeles.

COMMERCIAL PAPER AND BANK DEPOSITS AND COLLECTIONS (1967), with Statutory Supplement

William D. Hawkland, Professor of Law, University of Illinois.

COMMERCIAL TRANSACTIONS—Principles and Policies (1982)

Alan Schwartz, Professor of Law, University of Southern California.
Robert E. Scott, Professor of Law, University of Virginia.

COMPARATIVE LAW, Fourth Edition (1980)

Rudolf B. Schlesinger, Professor of Law, Hastings College of the Law.

COMPETITIVE PROCESS, LEGAL REGULATION OF THE, Third Edition (1986), with 1986 Selected Statutes Supplement

Edmund W. Kitch, Professor of Law, University of Virginia.
Harvey S. Perlman, Dean of the Law School, University of Nebraska.

CONFLICT OF LAWS, Eighth Edition (1984), with 1986 Case Supplement

Willis L. M. Reese, Professor of Law, Columbia University.
Maurice Rosenberg, Professor of Law, Columbia University.

CONSTITUTIONAL LAW, Seventh Edition (1985), with 1986 Supplement

Edward L. Barrett, Jr., Professor of Law, University of California, Davis.
William Cohen, Professor of Law, Stanford University.

CONSTITUTIONAL LAW, CIVIL LIBERTY AND INDIVIDUAL RIGHTS, Second Edition (1982), with 1985 Supplement

William Cohen, Professor of Law, Stanford University.
John Kaplan, Professor of Law, Stanford University.

CONSTITUTIONAL LAW, Eleventh Edition (1985), with 1986 Supplement (Supplement edited in association with Frederick F. Schauer, Professor of Law, University of Michigan)

Gerald Gunther, Professor of Law, Stanford University.

UNIVERSITY CASEBOOK SERIES—Continued

CONSTITUTIONAL LAW, INDIVIDUAL RIGHTS IN, Fourth Edition (1986), (Reprinted from CONSTITUTIONAL LAW, Eleventh Edition), with 1986 Supplement (Supplement edited in association with Frederick F. Schauer, Professor of Law, University of Michigan)

Gerald Gunther, Professor of Law, Stanford University.

CONSUMER TRANSACTIONS (1983), with Selected Statutes and Regulations Supplement and 1987 Case Supplement

Michael M. Greenfield, Professor of Law, Washington University.

CONTRACT LAW AND ITS APPLICATION, Third Edition (1983)

The late Addison Mueller, Professor of Law, University of California, Los Angeles.
Arthur I. Rosett, Professor of Law, University of California, Los Angeles.
Gerald P. Lopez, Professor of Law, University of California, Los Angeles.

CONTRACT LAW, STUDIES IN, Third Edition (1984)

Edward J. Murphy, Professor of Law, University of Notre Dame.
Richard E. Speidel, Professor of Law, Northwestern University.

CONTRACTS, Fourth Edition (1982)

John P. Dawson, Professor of Law Emeritus, Harvard University.
William Burnett Harvey, Professor of Law and Political Science, Boston University.
Stanley D. Henderson, Professor of Law, University of Virginia.

CONTRACTS, Third Edition (1980), with Statutory Supplement

E. Allan Farnsworth, Professor of Law, Columbia University.
William F. Young, Professor of Law, Columbia University.

CONTRACTS, Second Edition (1978), with Statutory and Administrative Law Supplement (1978)

Ian R. Macneil, Professor of Law, Cornell University.

COPYRIGHT, PATENTS AND TRADEMARKS, see also Competitive Process; see also Selected Statutes and International Agreements

COPYRIGHT, PATENT, TRADEMARK AND RELATED STATE DOCTRINES, Second Edition (1981), with 1985 Case Supplement, 1986 Selected Statutes Supplement and 1981 Problem Supplement

Paul Goldstein, Professor of Law, Stanford University.

COPYRIGHT, Unfair Competition, and Other Topics Bearing on the Protection of Literary, Musical, and Artistic Works, Fourth Edition (1985), with 1985 Statutory Supplement

Ralph S. Brown, Jr., Professor of Law, Yale University.
Robert C. Denicola, Professor of Law, University of Nebraska.

CORPORATE ACQUISITIONS, The Law and Finance of (1986)

Ronald J. Gilson, Professor of Law, Stanford University.

CORPORATE FINANCE, Second Edition (1979), with 1984 Supplement

Victor Brudney, Professor of Law, Harvard University.
Marvin A. Chirelstein, Professor of Law, Columbia University.

CORPORATE READJUSTMENTS AND REORGANIZATIONS (1976)

Walter J. Blum, Professor of Law, University of Chicago.
Stanley A. Kaplan, Professor of Law, University of Chicago.

EQUITY, see also Remedies

EQUITY, RESTITUTION AND DAMAGES, Second Edition (1974)

Robert Childres, late Professor of Law, Northwestern University.
William F. Johnson, Jr., Professor of Law, New York University.

ESTATE PLANNING, Second Edition (1982), with 1985 Case, Text and Documentary Supplement

David Westfall, Professor of Law, Harvard University.

ETHICS, see Legal Profession, and Professional Responsibility

ETHICS AND PROFESSIONAL RESPONSIBILITY (1981) (Reprinted from THE LAWYERING PROCESS)

Gary Bellow, Professor of Law, Harvard University.
Bea Moulton, Legal Services Corporation.

EVIDENCE, Fifth Edition (1984)

John Kaplan, Professor of Law, Stanford University.
Jon R. Waltz, Professor of Law, Northwestern University.

EVIDENCE, Seventh Edition (1983) with Rules and Statute Supplement (1984)

Jack B. Weinstein, Chief Judge, United States District Court.
John H. Mansfield, Professor of Law, Harvard University.
Norman Abrams, Professor of Law, University of California, Los Angeles.
Margaret Berger, Professor of Law, Brooklyn Law School.

FAMILY LAW, see also Domestic Relations

FAMILY LAW Second Edition (1985)

Judith C. Areen, Professor of Law, Georgetown University.

FAMILY LAW AND CHILDREN IN THE LEGAL SYSTEM, STATUTORY MATERIALS (1981)

Walter Wadlington, Professor of Law, University of Virginia.

FEDERAL COURTS, Seventh Edition (1982), with 1986 Supplement

Charles T. McCormick, late Professor of Law, University of Texas.
James H. Chadbourn, late Professor of Law, Harvard University.
Charles Alan Wright, Professor of Law, University of Texas.

FEDERAL COURTS AND THE FEDERAL SYSTEM, Hart and Wechsler's Second Edition (1973), with 1981 Supplement

Paul M. Bator, Professor of Law, Harvard University.
Paul J. Mishkin, Professor of Law, University of California, Berkeley.
David L. Shapiro, Professor of Law, Harvard University.
Herbert Wechsler, Professor of Law, Columbia University.

FEDERAL PUBLIC LAND AND RESOURCES LAW, Second Edition (1987), with 1984 Statutory Supplement

George C. Coggins, Professor of Law, University of Kansas.
Charles F. Wilkinson, Professor of Law, University of Oregon.

FEDERAL RULES OF CIVIL PROCEDURE, 1986 Edition

FEDERAL TAXATION, see Taxation

FOOD AND DRUG LAW (1980), with Statutory Supplement

Richard A. Merrill, Dean of the School of Law, University of Virginia.
Peter Barton Hutt, Esq.

UNIVERSITY CASEBOOK SERIES—Continued

FUTURE INTERESTS (1958)

Philip Mechem, late Professor of Law Emeritus, University of Pennsylvania.

FUTURE INTERESTS (1970)

Howard R. Williams, Professor of Law, Stanford University.

FUTURE INTERESTS AND ESTATE PLANNING (1961), with 1962 Supplement

W. Barton Leach, late Professor of Law, Harvard University.
James K. Logan, formerly Dean of the Law School, University of Kansas.

GOVERNMENT CONTRACTS, FEDERAL, Successor Edition (1985)

John W. Whelan, Professor of Law, Hastings College of the Law.

GOVERNMENT REGULATION: FREE ENTERPRISE AND ECONOMIC ORGANI-ZATION, Sixth Edition (1985)

Louis B. Schwartz, Professor of Law, University of Pennsylvania.
John J. Flynn, Professor of Law, University of Utah.
Harry First, Professor of Law, New York University.

HINCKLEY JOHN W., TRIAL OF: A Case Study of the Insanity Defense

Peter W. Low, Professor of Law, University of Virginia.
John C. Jeffries, Jr., Professor of Law, University of Virginia.
Richard C. Bonnie, Professor of Law, University of Virginia.

INJUNCTIONS, Second Edition (1984)

Owen M. Fiss, Professor of Law, Yale University.
Doug Rendleman, Professor of Law, College of William and Mary.

INSTITUTIONAL INVESTORS, 1978

David L. Ratner, Professor of Law, Cornell University.

INSURANCE, Second Edition (1985)

William F. Young, Professor of Law, Columbia University.
Eric M. Holmes, Professor of Law, University of Georgia.

INTERNATIONAL LAW, see also Transnational Legal Problems, Transnational Business Problems, and United Nations Law

INTERNATIONAL LAW IN CONTEMPORARY PERSPECTIVE (1981), with Essay Supplement

Myres S. McDougal, Professor of Law, Yale University.
W. Michael Reisman, Professor of Law, Yale University.

INTERNATIONAL LEGAL SYSTEM, Second Edition (1981), with Documentary Supplement

Joseph Modeste Sweeney, Professor of Law, Tulane University.
Covey T. Oliver, Professor of Law, University of Pennsylvania.
Noyes E. Leech, Professor of Law, University of Pennsylvania.

INTRODUCTION TO LAW, see also Legal Method, On Law in Courts, and Dynamics of American Law

INTRODUCTION TO THE STUDY OF LAW (1970)

E. Wayne Thode, late Professor of Law, University of Utah.
Leon Lebowitz, Professor of Law, University of Texas.
Lester J. Mazor, Professor of Law, University of Utah.

UNIVERSITY CASEBOOK SERIES—Continued

JUDICIAL CODE and Rules of Procedure in the Federal Courts with Excerpts from the Criminal Code, 1984 Edition

Henry M. Hart, Jr., late Professor of Law, Harvard University.
Herbert Wechsler, Professor of Law, Columbia University.

JURISPRUDENCE (Temporary Edition Hardbound) (1949)

Lon L. Fuller, Professor of Law Emeritus, Harvard University.

JUVENILE, see also Children

JUVENILE JUSTICE PROCESS, Third Edition (1985)

Frank W. Miller, Professor of Law, Washington University.
Robert O. Dawson, Professor of Law, University of Texas.
George E. Dix, Professor of Law, University of Texas.
Raymond I. Parnas, Professor of Law, University of California, Davis.

LABOR LAW, Tenth Edition (1986), with 1986 Statutory Supplement

Archibald Cox, Professor of Law, Harvard University.
Derek C. Bok, President, Harvard University.
Robert A. Gorman, Professor of Law, University of Pennsylvania.

LABOR LAW, Second Edition (1982), with Statutory Supplement

Clyde W. Summers, Professor of Law, University of Pennsylvania.
Harry H. Wellington, Dean of the Law School, Yale University.
Alan Hyde, Professor of Law, Rutgers University.

LAND FINANCING, Third Edition (1985)

The late Norman Penney, Professor of Law, Cornell University.
Richard F. Broude, Member of the California Bar.
Roger Cunningham, Professor of Law, University of Michigan.

LAW AND MEDICINE (1980)

Walter Wadlington, Professor of Law and Professor of Legal Medicine, University of Virginia.
Jon R. Waltz, Professor of Law, Northwestern University.
Roger B. Dworkin, Professor of Law, Indiana University, and Professor of Biomedical History, University of Washington.

LAW, LANGUAGE AND ETHICS (1972)

William R. Bishin, Professor of Law, University of Southern California.
Christopher D. Stone, Professor of Law, University of Southern California.

LAW, SCIENCE AND MEDICINE (1984), with 1987 Supplement

Judith C. Areen, Professor of Law, Georgetown University.
Patricia A. King, Professor of Law, Georgetown University.
Steven P. Goldberg, Professor of Law, Georgetown University.
Alexander M. Capron, Professor of Law, Georgetown University.

LAWYERING PROCESS (1978), with Civil Problem Supplement and Criminal Problem Supplement

Gary Bellow, Professor of Law, Harvard University.
Bea Moulton, Professor of Law, Arizona State University.

LEGAL METHOD (1980)

Harry W. Jones, Professor of Law Emeritus, Columbia University.
John M. Kernochan, Professor of Law, Columbia University.
Arthur W. Murphy, Professor of Law, Columbia University.

UNIVERSITY CASEBOOK SERIES—Continued

LEGAL METHODS (1969)

Robert N. Covington, Professor of Law, Vanderbilt University.
E. Blythe Stason, late Professor of Law, Vanderbilt University.
John W. Wade, Professor of Law, Vanderbilt University.
Elliott E. Cheatham, late Professor of Law, Vanderbilt University.
Theodore A. Smedley, Professor of Law, Vanderbilt University.

LEGAL PROFESSION, THE, Responsibility and Regulation (1985)

Geoffrey C. Hazard, Jr., Professor of Law, Yale University.
Deborah L. Rhode, Professor of Law, Stanford University.

LEGISLATION, Fourth Edition (1982) (by Fordham)

Horace E. Read, late Vice President, Dalhousie University.
John W. MacDonald, Professor of Law Emeritus, Cornell Law School.
Jefferson B. Fordham, Professor of Law, University of Utah.
William J. Pierce, Professor of Law, University of Michigan.

LEGISLATIVE AND ADMINISTRATIVE PROCESSES, Second Edition (1981)

Hans A. Linde, Judge, Supreme Court of Oregon.
George Bunn, Professor of Law, University of Wisconsin.
Fredericka Paff, Professor of Law, University of Wisconsin.
W. Lawrence Church, Professor of Law, University of Wisconsin.

LOCAL GOVERNMENT LAW, Second Revised Edition (1986)

Jefferson B. Fordham, Professor of Law, University of Utah.

MASS MEDIA LAW, Third Edition (1987)

Marc A. Franklin, Professor of Law, Stanford University.

MENTAL HEALTH PROCESS, Second Edition (1976), with 1981 Supplement

Frank W. Miller, Professor of Law, Washington University.
Robert O. Dawson, Professor of Law, University of Texas.
George E. Dix, Professor of Law, University of Texas.
Raymond I. Parnas, Professor of Law, University of California, Davis.

MUNICIPAL CORPORATIONS, see Local Government Law

NEGOTIABLE INSTRUMENTS, see Commercial Paper

NEGOTIATION (1981) (Reprinted from THE LAWYERING PROCESS)

Gary Bellow, Professor of Law, Harvard Law School.
Bea Moulton, Legal Services Corporation.

NEW YORK PRACTICE, Fourth Edition (1978)

Herbert Peterfreund, Professor of Law, New York University.
Joseph M. McLaughlin, Dean of the Law School, Fordham University.

OIL AND GAS, Fifth Edition (1987)

Howard R. Williams, Professor of Law, Stanford University.
Richard C. Maxwell, Professor of Law, University of California, Los Angeles.
Charles J. Meyers, Dean of the Law School, Stanford University.
Stephen F. Williams, Professor of Law, University of Colorado.

ON LAW IN COURTS (1965)

Paul J. Mishkin, Professor of Law, University of California, Berkeley.
Clarence Morris, Professor of Law Emeritus, University of Pennsylvania.

UNIVERSITY CASEBOOK SERIES—Continued

PATENTS AND ANTITRUST (Pamphlet) (1983)

Milton Handler, Professor of Law Emeritus, Columbia University.
Harlan M. Blake, Professor of Law, Columbia University.
Robert Pitofsky, Professor of Law, Georgetown University.
Harvey J. Goldschmid, Professor of Law, Columbia University.

PERSPECTIVES ON THE LAWYER AS PLANNER (Reprint of Chapters One through Five of Planning by Lawyers) (1978)

Louis M. Brown, Professor of Law, University of Southern California.
Edward A. Dauer, Professor of Law, Yale University.

PLANNING BY LAWYERS, MATERIALS ON A NONADVERSARIAL LEGAL PROCESS (1978)

Louis M. Brown, Professor of Law, University of Southern California.
Edward A. Dauer, Professor of Law, Yale University.

PLEADING AND PROCEDURE, see Procedure, Civil

POLICE FUNCTION, Fourth Edition (1986), with 1986 Case Supplement

Reprint of Chapters 1–10 of Miller, Dawson, Dix and Parnas's CRIMINAL JUSTICE ADMINISTRATION, Third Edition.

PREPARING AND PRESENTING THE CASE (1981) (Reprinted from THE LAW-YERING PROCESS)

Gary Bellow, Professor of Law, Harvard Law School.
Bea Moulton, Legal Services Corporation.

PREVENTIVE LAW, see also Planning by Lawyers

PROCEDURE—CIVIL PROCEDURE, Second Edition (1974), with 1979 Supplement

The late James H. Chadbourn, Professor of Law, Harvard University.
A. Leo Levin, Professor of Law, University of Pennsylvania.
Philip Shuchman, Professor of Law, Cornell University.

PROCEDURE—CIVIL PROCEDURE, Fifth Edition (1984), with 1986 Supplement

Richard H. Field, late Professor of Law, Harvard University.
Benjamin Kaplan, Professor of Law Emeritus, Harvard University.
Kevin M. Clermont, Professor of Law, Cornell University.

PROCEDURE—CIVIL PROCEDURE, Fourth Edition (1985)

Maurice Rosenberg, Professor of Law, Columbia University.
Hans Smit, Professor of Law, Columbia University.
Harold L. Korn, Professor of Law, Columbia University.

PROCEDURE—PLEADING AND PROCEDURE: State and Federal, Fifth Edition (1983), with 1986 Supplement

David W. Louisell, late Professor of Law, University of California, Berkeley.
Geoffrey C. Hazard, Jr., Professor of Law, Yale University.
Colin C. Tait, Professor of Law, University of Connecticut.

PROCEDURE—FEDERAL RULES OF CIVIL PROCEDURE, 1986 Edition

PRODUCTS LIABILITY (1980)

Marshall S. Shapo, Professor of Law, Northwestern University.

PRODUCTS LIABILITY AND SAFETY (1980), with 1985 Case and Documentary Supplement

W. Page Keeton, Professor of Law, University of Texas.
David G. Owen, Professor of Law, University of South Carolina.
John E. Montgomery, Professor of Law, University of South Carolina.

PROFESSIONAL RESPONSIBILITY, Third Edition (1984), with 1986 Selected National Standards Supplement

Thomas D. Morgan, Dean of the Law School, Emory University.
Ronald D. Rotunda, Professor of Law, University of Illinois.

PROPERTY, Fifth Edition (1984)

John E. Cribbet, Dean of the Law School, University of Illinois.
Corwin W. Johnson, Professor of Law, University of Texas.

PROPERTY—PERSONAL (1953)

S. Kenneth Skolfield, late Professor of Law Emeritus, Boston University.

PROPERTY—PERSONAL, Third Edition (1954)

Everett Fraser, late Dean of the Law School Emeritus, University of Minnesota.
Third Edition by Charles W. Taintor, late Professor of Law, University of Pittsburgh.

PROPERTY—INTRODUCTION, TO REAL PROPERTY, Third Edition (1954)

Everett Fraser, late Dean of the Law School Emeritus, University of Minnesota.

PROPERTY—REAL AND PERSONAL, Combined Edition (1954)

Everett Fraser, late Dean of the Law School Emeritus, University of Minnesota.
Third Edition of Personal Property by Charles W. Taintor, late Professor of Law, University of Pittsburgh.

PROPERTY—FUNDAMENTALS OF MODERN REAL PROPERTY, Second Edition (1982), with 1985 Supplement

Edward H. Rabin, Professor of Law, University of California, Davis.

PROPERTY—PROBLEMS IN REAL PROPERTY (Pamphlet) (1969)

Edward H. Rabin, Professor of Law, University of California, Davis.

PROPERTY, REAL (1984)

Paul Goldstein, Professor of Law, Stanford University.

PROSECUTION AND ADJUDICATION, Third Edition (1986), with 1986 Case Supplement

Reprint of Chapters 11–26 of Miller, Dawson, Dix and Parnas's CRIMINAL JUSTICE ADMINISTRATION, Third Edition.

PSYCHIATRY AND LAW, see Mental Health, see also Hinckley, Trial of

PUBLIC REGULATION OF DANGEROUS PRODUCTS (paperback) (1980)

Marshall S. Shapo, Professor of Law, Northwestern University.

PUBLIC UTILITY LAW, see Free Enterprise, also Regulated Industries

REAL ESTATE PLANNING (1980), with 1980 Problems, Statutes and New Materials Supplement

Norton L. Steuben, Professor of Law, University of Colorado.

UNIVERSITY CASEBOOK SERIES—Continued

REAL ESTATE TRANSACTIONS, Second Edition (1985), with 1985 Statute, Form and Problem Supplement

Paul Goldstein, Professor of Law, Stanford University.

RECEIVERSHIP AND CORPORATE REORGANIZATION, see Creditors' Rights

REGULATED INDUSTRIES, Second Edition, 1976

William K. Jones, Professor of Law, Columbia University.

REMEDIES (1982), with 1984 Case Supplement

Edward D. Re, Chief Judge, U. S. Court of International Trade.

RESTITUTION, Second Edition (1966)

John W. Wade, Professor of Law, Vanderbilt University.

SALES, Second Edition (1986)

Marion W. Benfield, Jr., Professor of Law, University of Illinois.
William D. Hawkland, Chancellor, Louisiana State Law Center.

SALES AND SALES FINANCING, Fifth Edition (1984)

John Honnold, Professor of Law, University of Pennsylvania.

SALES LAW AND THE CONTRACTING PROCESS (1982)

Reprint of Chapters 1–10 of Schwartz and Scott's Commercial Transactions.

SECURED TRANSACTIONS IN PERSONAL PROPERTY (1983) (Reprinted from COMMERCIAL LAW)

Robert L. Jordan, Professor of Law, University of California, Los Angeles.
William D. Warren, Professor of Law, University of California, Los Angeles.

SECURITIES REGULATION, Fifth Edition (1982), with 1986 Cases and Releases Supplement and 1986 Selected Statutes, Rules and Forms Supplement

Richard W. Jennings, Professor of Law, University of California, Berkeley.
Harold Marsh, Jr., Member of California Bar.

SECURITIES REGULATION (1982), with 1985 Supplement

Larry D. Soderquist, Professor of Law, Vanderbilt University.

SECURITY INTERESTS IN PERSONAL PROPERTY (1984)

Douglas G. Baird, Professor of Law, University of Chicago.
Thomas H. Jackson, Professor of Law, Stanford University.

SECURITY INTERESTS IN PERSONAL PROPERTY (1985) (Reprinted from Sales and Sales Financing, Fifth Edition)

John Honnold, Professor of Law, University of Pennsylvania.

SENTENCING AND THE CORRECTIONAL PROCESS, Second Edition (1976)

Frank W. Miller, Professor of Law, Washington University.
Robert O. Dawson, Professor of Law, University of Texas.
George E. Dix, Professor of Law, University of Texas.
Raymond I. Parnas, Professor of Law, University of California, Davis.

SOCIAL SCIENCE IN LAW, Cases and Materials (1985)

John Monahan, Professor of Law, University of Virginia.
Laurens Walker, Professor of Law, University of Virginia.

UNIVERSITY CASEBOOK SERIES—Continued

SOCIAL WELFARE AND THE INDIVIDUAL (1971)

Robert J. Levy, Professor of Law, University of Minnesota.
Thomas P. Lewis, Dean of the College of Law, University of Kentucky.
Peter W. Martin, Professor of Law, Cornell University.

TAX, POLICY ANALYSIS OF THE FEDERAL INCOME (1976)

William A. Klein, Professor of Law, University of California, Los Angeles.

TAXATION, FEDERAL INCOME, Successor Edition (1985)

Michael J. Graetz, Professor of Law, Yale University.

TAXATION, FEDERAL INCOME, Fifth Edition (1985)

James J. Freeland, Professor of Law, University of Florida.
Stephen A. Lind, Professor of Law, University of Florida.
Richard B. Stephens, Professor of Law Emeritus, University of Florida.

TAXATION, FEDERAL INCOME, Volume I, Personal Income Taxation, Successor Edition (1986), Volume II, Taxation of Partnerships and Corporations, Second Edition (1980), with 1985 Legislative Supplement

Stanley S. Surrey, late Professor of Law, Harvard University.
Paul R. McDaniel, Professor of Law, Boston College Law School.
Hugh J. Ault, Professor of Law, Boston College Law School.
Stanley A. Koppelman, Boston University

TAXATION, FEDERAL WEALTH TRANSFER, Second Edition (1982) with 1985 Legislative Supplement

Stanley S. Surrey, late Professor of Law, Harvard University.
William C. Warren, Professor of Law Emeritus, Columbia University.
Paul R. McDaniel, Professor of Law, Boston College Law School.
Harry L. Gutman, Instructor, Harvard Law School and Boston College Law School.

TAXATION, FUNDAMENTALS OF CORPORATE, Cases and Materials (1985)

Stephen A. Lind, Professor of Law, University of Florida.
Stephen Schwarz, Professor of Law, University of California, Hastings.
Daniel J. Lathrope, Professor of Law, University of California, Hastings.
Joshua Rosenberg, Professor of Law, University of San Francisco.

TAXATION, FUNDAMENTALS OF PARTNERSHIP, Cases and Materials (1985)

Stephen A. Lind, Professor of Law, University of California, Hastings.
Stephen Schwarz, Professor of Law, University of California, Hastings.
Daniel J. Lathrope, Professor of Law, University of California, Hastings.
Joshua Rosenberg, Professor of Law, University of San Francisco.

TAXATION, PROBLEMS IN THE FEDERAL INCOME TAXATION OF PARTNERSHIPS AND CORPORATIONS, Second Edition (1986)

Norton L. Steuben, Professor of Law, University of Colorado.
William J. Turnier, Professor of Law, University of North Carolina.

TAXATION, PROBLEMS IN THE FUNDAMENTALS OF FEDERAL INCOME, Second Edition (1985)

Norton L. Steuben, Professor of Law, University of Colorado.
William J. Turnier, Professor of Law, University of North Carolina.

TAXES AND FINANCE—STATE AND LOCAL (1974)

Oliver Oldman, Professor of Law, Harvard University.
Ferdinand P. Schoettle, Professor of Law, University of Minnesota.

UNIVERSITY CASEBOOK SERIES—Continued

TORT LAW AND ALTERNATIVES, Third Edition (1983)

Marc A. Franklin, Professor of Law, Stanford University.
Robert L. Rabin, Professor of Law, Stanford University.

TORTS, Seventh Edition (1982)

William L. Prosser, late Professor of Law, University of California, Hastings College.
John W. Wade, Professor of Law, Vanderbilt University.
Victor E. Schwartz, Professor of Law, American University.

TORTS, Third Edition (1976)

Harry Shulman, late Dean of the Law School, Yale University.
Fleming James, Jr., Professor of Law Emeritus, Yale University.
Oscar S. Gray, Professor of Law, University of Maryland.

TRADE REGULATION, Second Edition (1983), with 1985 Supplement

Milton Handler, Professor of Law Emeritus, Columbia University.
Harlan M. Blake, Professor of Law, Columbia University.
Robert Pitofsky, Professor of Law, Georgetown University.
Harvey J. Goldschmid, Professor of Law, Columbia University.

TRADE REGULATION, see Antitrust

TRANSNATIONAL BUSINESS PROBLEMS (1986)

Detlev F. Vagts, Professor of Law, Harvard University.

TRANSNATIONAL LEGAL PROBLEMS, Third Edition (1986) with Documentary Supplement

Henry J. Steiner, Professor of Law, Harvard University.
Detlev F. Vagts, Professor of Law, Harvard University.

TRIAL, see also Evidence, Making the Record, Lawyering Process and Preparing and Presenting the Case

TRIAL ADVOCACY (1968)

A. Leo Levin, Professor of Law, University of Pennsylvania.
Harold Cramer, of the Pennsylvania Bar.
Maurice Rosenberg, Professor of Law, Columbia University, Consultant.

TRUSTS, Fifth Edition (1978)

George G. Bogert, late Professor of Law Emeritus, University of Chicago.
Dallin H. Oaks, President, Brigham Young University.

TRUSTS AND SUCCESSION (Palmer's), Fourth Edition (1983)

Richard V. Wellman, Professor of Law, University of Georgia.
Lawrence W. Waggoner, Professor of Law, University of Michigan.
Olin L. Browder, Jr., Professor of Law, University of Michigan.

UNFAIR COMPETITION, see Competitive Process and Business Torts

UNITED NATIONS LAW, Second Edition (1967), with Documentary Supplement (1968)

Louis B. Sohn, Professor of Law, Harvard University.

WATER RESOURCE MANAGEMENT, Second Edition (1980), with 1983 Supplement

Charles J. Meyers, Dean of the Law School, Stanford University.
A. Dan Tarlock, Professor of Law, Indiana University.

UNIVERSITY CASEBOOK SERIES—Continued

WILLS AND ADMINISTRATION, Fifth Edition (1961)

Philip Mechem, late Professor of Law, University of Pennsylvania.
Thomas E. Atkinson, late Professor of Law, New York University.

WORLD LAW, see United Nations Law

University Casebook Series

FEDERAL PUBLIC LAND

AND

RESOURCES LAW

SECOND EDITION

By

GEORGE CAMERON COGGINS
Tyler Professor of Law, University of Kansas

and

CHARLES F. WILKINSON
Professor of Law
University of Oregon

Mineola, New York
THE FOUNDATION PRESS, INC.
1987

Library of Congress Cataloging in Publication Data

Coggins, George Cameron, 1941–
    Federal land and resources law.

    (University casebook series)
    Includes index.
    1. United States—Public lands—Cases. 2. Natural
resources—Law and legislation—United States—Cases.
I. Wilkinson, Charles F., 1941–   . II. Title.
III. Series.
KF5604.C64   1986   343.73'0256   86–14960
ISBN 0–88277–345–3

Coggins & Wilkinson—Fed.Land & Res.Law 2nd Ed. UCB

TO

JEAN COGGINS

and

ANN AMUNDSON

*

PREFACE

Public land and resources law has been basically reordered in modern times. Among other developments, discussed more fully in chapter one, doctrines involving resources that traditionally have been treated separately are coalescing, and a variety of concerns reflecting the public interest are being infused into the legal process.

We have attempted to synthesize these developments in this book. It has been customary to treat some public land issues in separate courses, such as water law or mining law; this volume is not an attempt to supercede any of those specialized subjects. Rather, in our view, modern public land law demands a coordinated treatment of the various legal doctrines applicable to all public resources and their interrelationships.

We believe that this book, though a considerable departure, nevertheless is the logical extension of previous casebooks on natural resources. In 1951, Clyde Martz published CASES ON NATURAL RESOURCES, the first comprehensive effort to organize and integrate teaching materials on that subject. The Martz casebook was succeeded and updated in 1965 by Professors Trelease, Bloomenthal, and Geraud in the publication of CASES AND MATERIALS ON NATURAL RESOURCES. These pioneering casebooks included some public issues, but both were largely devoted to "private law;" that is, they dealt primarily with issues relating to whether a private entity could use or acquire ownership of federal land or resources. In each, heavy emphasis was placed on the fields of water law, mining law, and oil and gas law. That neither work paid much attention to "public law" or "public interest litigation" is not a criticism because, for all practical purposes, such public law issues had not yet surfaced on the public lands. We have made a determined effort to outline the historical context of recent disputes, but the great bulk of cases reprinted in this volume were decided since 1970. The legal doctrines that they represent have supplemented or replaced prior law.

This book's approach to federal land and resources law is the product of many years' development. Each of these editors independently concluded that major public resource themes were related and could be grouped around the concept of federal land ownership. Each of us taught courses in 1975 that sought to investigate federal regulation of the federal resources. Those crude efforts gradually evolved through the development of separate classroom materials until several colleagues familiar with our efforts urged us to pool our resources, natural and otherwise. With assistance from the Rocky Mountain Mineral Law Foundation, we did so, making available the first edition of this casebook in 1980.

The more that we study this field, the more it becomes apparent that public land law has been fundamentally altered and that changes are accelerating. Even so, there is a commonality in the usual issues that cuts across traditional subject matter lines. Federal vs. state regulatory power, federal reserved rights or interests, multiple use management problems, withdrawals and reservations, judicial review notions—all of these are common threads running through legal consideration of all of the major resources. Recent enactments recognize and further the unification of federal natural resources law.

The first four chapters are devoted to the historical background, the constitutional underpinnings, and the administrative systems governing public land policy. Chapter one is an overview of federal lands and resources; it concludes with several perspectives on the bases of federal land policy. The history of public land law, treated in chapter two, remains a matter of vital interest today because ancient notions, doctrines, and problems refuse to be relegated to molding archives: several sections conclude with recent Supreme Court decisions and another outlines the contemporary "Sagebrush Rebellion," a movement rooted in history whereby some states have sought to divest federal ownership of lands within their borders. The chapter is lengthy, reflecting our view that history is a fundamental component of modern public land law.

Chapter three follows by analyzing the respective constitutional powers of the federal and state governments over activities on the public lands. Although the federal government usually can preempt state authority, the more difficult question to be investigated is whether, in any particular instance, Congress intended to do so. The fourth chapter introduces the student to several basic problems that permeate all that follows: executive withdrawals and reservations; judicial review of land management agency decisions; and administrative planning mandated by novel statutes, especially the National Environmental Policy Act of 1969.

The remaining seven chapters take up the law of the seven major federal resources in this order: water, minerals, timber, range, wildlife, recreation, and preservation. Case selection and placement is necessarily arbitrary to some degree, for resource conflicts almost always involve more than one resource or value. Thus, a case in which a timber contract is enjoined because it would alter the wilderness characteristics of an area could as well go into the Timber Resource chapter as the Preservation chapter, and so forth on down the line. The second maxim of ecology, that everything is related to everything else, is both trite and true.

We have strived to make this treatment as readable and enjoyable as we think it is worthwhile. It is, of course, just a casebook and subject to all of the limitations of that art form, so complete success is virtually impossible. But the subject matter itself, from the exciting Gold Rush to the progress of settlement by homesteading, from the great railroad land grabs to the episodic range wars, from the Alaska Pipeline to the Snail Darter, cannot help but interest and delight all but the most jaded of students.

A word about the editing form and style used throughout. We have sought to be rigorous in eliminating irrelevant or tangential matters. Discussions of repetitive procedural defenses, common statements of law (particularly boilerplate recitations on NEPA), and string citations were more often than not axed. Thus, any case or article reproduced below is not necessarily complete—it probably is not—and the researching student is advised to consult the original.

Most original footnotes have also been omitted. Where footnotes are retained, they still bear the court's or author's original number. Footnotes inserted by the editors are preceded by a lower case letter instead of a number. Textual deletions are indicated by "* * *," but omissions of authorities have not been signalled.

We of course accept full responsibility for the inevitable errors, omissions, and lack of foresight commonly associated with these ventures. We would caution that some selectivity on the part of the instructor is assumed; the materials in these pages are more than is necessary for a normal one-semester course.

Expressing gratitude to those who have assisted an endeavor such as this is a dangerous business, for often one is left out who should be included. With a blanket "thanks" to the many who have contributed, we single out first our research assistants. Debra Arnett, Michael Axline, Kurt Burkholder, Derb Carter, Susan Driver, Parthenia Blessing Evans, and Martin Miller all contributed to the first edition. At that time, we predicted that all would make their own marks on public land law and, six years later, our forecast has proved to be accurate. We give our thanks and our similar high regard to those students who worked on this edition: Alexandra Callam, Jeremy Firestone, Sandy Hoffman, Stephanie Matthews, Doris Nagel, and Matt Selby. The typing was done by Marcea Metzler, Joan Wellman, and Mary Jo Guy. Dean Mike Davis of the University of Kansas has provided us with invaluable support over the years. Dean Chapin Clark of Oregon walked the extra mile to provide us with resources for the first edition. Professor Wilkinson was a visiting professor at the University of Michigan Law School during the preparation of this second edition and both of us extend our appreciation for the inordinately generous assistance provided by Associate Dean Edward H. Cooper and Dean Terrance Sandalow. We are also grateful to the Rocky Mountain Mineral Law Foundation for its support, and the advice of its members, on both the first and second editions. Finally, we appreciate the helpful suggestions of several colleagues, including Gail L. Achterman, Harrison C. Dunning, Kent Frizzell, David H. Getches, Arthur D. Smith, Sally K. Fairfax, H. Michael Anderson, Maryanne Chambers, Cameron LaFollette, and Darius M. Adams.

GEORGE CAMERON COGGINS
CHARLES F. WILKINSON

October, 1986

SUMMARY OF CONTENTS

SUMMARY OF CONTENTS

TABLE OF CONTENTS

TABLE OF CONTENTS

TABLE OF CONTENTS

Page

TABLE OF CASES

The principal cases are in italic type. The cases cited or discussed are in roman type. References are to pages.

xl

*

TABLE OF STATUTES

TABLE OF STATUTES

FEDERAL PUBLIC LAND

AND

RESOURCES LAW

*

Chapter One

PUBLIC LAND LAW: AN INTRODUCTION

A. THE FIELD OF PUBLIC LAND LAW

Most citizens are unaware of the full extent to which the United States government owns or controls land. Many are generally familiar with some of the national parks, the "crown jewels" of the federal land holdings. Those who have gazed into the Grand Canyon, or marvelled at the natural wonders of Yellowstone, or found incomparable beauty in Yosemite Valley may have breathed a prayer of thanksgiving that some of our predecessors had the wisdom to preserve those unique areas intact for the awe of generations then unborn. But the national parks are merely the tip of the federal iceberg: they account for only a part of the lands managed by the National Park Service, which in turn are less than 15% of the Nation's total federal land. Other people may have frequented a national forest, perhaps not realizing that national forests are in a management system separate from the national parks, in the charge of a different agency in a different department. Only in the West and in Alaska are the existence and activities of the Bureau of Land Management (BLM) common knowledge, but this little-publicized agency controls about one-seventh of the total national land surface, nearly as much acreage as all other federal lands categories together. Most citizens also are at least vaguely aware that a variety of federal agencies own land for some purpose, from post offices to reservoirs, from military forts to wildlife refuges, and from atomic reactor sites to office buildings. In all, the United States owns in fee some 732 million acres, or about one-third of all land in the country.

Public land law is at the core of the history of national economic development, but it encompasses far more than mundane legalities. Federal land policy impelled the homesteaders to seek new lives, validated the Gold Rush mining claims, brought about the range wars, and built the massive dams in the West. Even today the livelihoods of pipeline roughnecks, subsistence hunters, loggers, cattle barons, mineral prospectors, and other latterday rugged individualists are intimately affected by the constraints of public land law. Contemporary concern over the uses and abuses of the public lands and natural resources goes much deeper than interest in romantic exploits. Lord Macauley long ago noted that the true test of American institutions would come when the free public domain was exhausted and an increased population competed for ownership of the land and its depleted resources. That time has arrived, and the competition is intense. The controversies, large and small, that contribute to growth and direction of the new and

1

emerging body of federal land and resources law provide one of the most fascinating studies in all of legal literature.

This book is organized around the concepts that the public lands and the resources they contain are, indeed, public, and that public land law is an expression of and is guided by the public interest. Society through its legislatures professes to see virtue in many products and values; it wishes to have both energy production and wilderness preservation. On these and other questions, an overall balance must be sought that will guide individual decisions as to individual public land parcels. The issues and particulars and forums of public land disputes have changed over the years as the nature of public land law has changed. The one enduring element is the argument over what course of action will best serve the public interest, but the premises used in the argument have radically shifted.

1. TRADITIONAL PUBLIC LAND LAW: PRIVATE RIGHTS IN CONFLICT

That federal lands should be retained in federal ownership and managed by federal agencies for the general public interest is a fairly modern phenomenon. For the better part of 200 years, public land law existed to facilitate and make more profitable transfers of federal lands and resources into private hands. Traditional public land law, however, was never an organized, coherent body of rules or knowledge. In 1880, for instance, there were an estimated 3500 federal statutes governing the disposition and use of federal lands; by 1964 the number was still close to 3000. Considering the vast judicial common law that has grown from single, succinct laws, together with the thousands upon thousands of pages of administrative regulations and rulings, it is not difficult to see that the practice of natural resources law can approach the arcane. Further, through most of American history, it has been common practice to ignore, evade, circumvent, or violate the laws on the books governing the public lands. The Teapot Dome scandal in the 1920's was not an isolated incident; defrauding the government already had been a national sport for over a century.

"Public Land Law" always has been a somewhat ambiguous phrase, more descriptive than definitive. In general, it has meant those statutes, rules, practices, and common law doctrines that define who has a right to own or use a parcel of federal land or its tangible resources. Fairly discrete bodies of law—including oil and gas, water rights, and mining law—have grown up within it. The typical controversies in the traditional formulation involved individuals or entities contesting between themselves or with the government for private right or privilege. Examples are the now-legendary contests between cattle and sheep ranchers over priority to graze the public domain, mining claim-jumping and resultant litigation, disputes between agricultural surface owners and holders of subsurface mineral rights, the efforts of the government to eject squatters on public lands, and scores of similar controversies. The resolution of these derivative "private" disputes likely will continue to be a main business of practicing lawyers, and this volume presents the basic legal doctrines governing private interests in the public resources.

2. MODERN FEDERAL LANDS AND RESOURCES LAW: THE SEARCH FOR THE PUBLIC INTEREST

During the last generation, the central place of private rights, private disputes, and private law as components of overall public land law has been partly superceded by overriding public considerations. Whether viewed as a new direction in traditional public land management, or as another instance of counterproductive federal overregulation, modern federal and land resources law encompasses far more than questions of property rights. The natural resources lawyer now must be conversant with such subjects as zoning, pollution control, land use planning, reclamation requirements, environmental impact statements, public trust duties, competing recreational and preservational values, wildlife protection, pesticide restrictions, and other limitations on economic activity. These, in the aggregate, have come to be as important to public land users as questions of prior appropriation or oil lease interpretation.

Modern public land law is somewhat broader in dimension and more diverse in concept than the classic private contests. New disputants bringing different philosophies have entered oldtime controversies; Congress has changed the statutory framework drastically; winds of reform sweep through land management agencies; formerly disregarded aspects assume new importance. There is an elusive unity concerning treatment of the public land which for want of a more definitive phrase can be called the public interest in the public resources.

In the search for the public interest, no one simple answer in any concrete situation ordinarily suffices. The changing nature of private interest and public emphasis necessarily dictates that the public interest is but an ambiguous goal, always sought but never ultimately found. Whether a particular tract is better suited for timber cutting or wildlife propagation or recreation, for instance, is a question that is seldom finally resolved. Virtually every controversy recounted herein is relevant to the central question. A dispute may be phrased in terms such as:

- should cattle or wild horses be removed from an overgrazed tract in Idaho?
- have all procedural steps been completed in the grant of a timber cutting contract?
- does a hunter have a right of access over an unpatented mining claim?
- should off-road vehicles be banned from certain areas?
- should creation of a wilderness area impliedly override state water laws?

— should a road to a potentially valuable mineral deposit be cut through an area used by grizzly bears for denning?

But, in every such case, the initial inquiries are the same: Where lies the public interest? Who decides where it lies in particular situations? What are the legal and practical consequences of the choice? Only after the "public" questions are answered do the "private" questions become relevant.

Preconceptions of the public interest are hazardous to mental health. To many, wilderness preservation is one of the highest endeavors of organized society. They sometimes forget that potential wilderness areas may have supplied the lumber that built their houses, the iron that formed their cars, and the oil that makes them go. Few of those who complain of pollution from the local utility generating plant would readily give up air conditioning altogether. On the other hand, those who espouse production over all else have an equally narrow perspective. There are limits to growth. There are points of diminishing returns: it is inescapable that the oil burned now or even the old growth timber cut now will not be available ten or twenty years from now to fuel even more expansion for us and for our descendants. Further, the societal upheaval of the 1960's and 1970's should have taught us that there are values beyond the economic that society prizes more than gold. More people prefer, for instance, to watch birds than to hunt them. The legislature has reflected these public preferences. More and more preservation and recreation lands systems have been created in the past two decades, and more and more lands have been set aside for special, non-economic purposes. This is not to say that the "preservationists" have "won" or should win. The Nation needs energy, it needs food, it needs minerals, it needs timber; unless the American way of life is to change, some national requirements must be filled from national lands. Few heroes or villains are prominent in modern public land controversies, only people with differing conceptions of the public interest.

This book attempts to provide students with both sides of the public policy argument on particular questions to the extent possible. Little is gained by adhering rigidly to preconceptions or by thinking only in terms of absolutist maxims. The debate over the wise use and management of the Nation's natural heritage is not enhanced by name-calling or ideological rigidity. Fortunately, the recent history of legal and political strife seems to have calmed the ardor of zealots in many respects. Most state and local politicians now concede that not all federal environmental regulation or public interest litigation is necessarily bad. Preservationists will admit that economic development of some natural resources must be pursued if in an environmentally sound manner. Industry is resigned to the new fabric of legal constraint and frequently seeks accommodation rather than evasion. Government has opened itself to new concerns expressed by new organizations, and has in the process gradually but radically reformed agency procedures and outlooks. The efforts of James G. Watt to swing back the pendulum of public land law apparently failed in Congress and the courts.

The cast of characters in traditional public land law dramas was usually rather limited; most involved relatively simple private property disputes. Could a new upstream appropriator of stream-flow reduce the water available to prior downstream users? Did Jones jump Smith's gold mining claim? To what extent could Monumental Oil Company disrupt the surface use of Black's Acre in pursuing its right to subsurface resources? In these private fights, the government and the direct public interest became involved only indirectly, when the courts were called upon to resolve them. The presence and participation of a new element in the decisional equation, the self-styled "public interest" organization, is largely responsible for a new emphasis. Because much of the change in federal land and resources law has resulted from the efforts of non-traditional lobbyists and litigators, it is appropriate to introduce the newcomers to the dramatis personnae of public land controversy.

Even though the conservation movement won some notable victories in the late 19th century, it is fair to say that non-economically oriented interests (non-Hofeldian plaintiffs, in legal conceptualization) did not achieve an equal, or even significant, voice until the late 1960's. Nowadays, the main public land controversies, many of which are examined in later chapters, virtually always involve the degree to which the interest of the public, or segments of it, is translated into the eventual decision. Most such modern disputes tend to be three- or four-cornered, or more, and the private rights tend to be subordinated to or contingent upon the initial determination of the public rights in the decisional process. This has been brought about by changes in legal doctrines, by the growth and new-found aggressiveness of environmental organizations and individuals, by new legislation, and by other factors, but the most important cause of change in public land law is the change in general public attitudes and awareness. No longer is the question whether a ski resort should be developed on public land one solely between the developer and the federal agency, as the Disney Company learned to its expense and sorrow. No longer is a timbercutting contract in a national forest automatically granted on the rationale that the nation needs lumber. No longer is the condition of BLM grazing lands of concern to ranchers alone. No longer can wildlife and recreation values be ignored in multiple use management. In these and many other disputes over use of public lands, a new class of disputants has successfully challenged all of the old assumptions and ushered in a new era.

It is not possible to delineate precisely just who the new parties are or what they represent. In some cases, private landowners have rejected economic benefit to themselves by various forms of development on or adjacent to their property. They have, for instance, risen up in litigation against forms of the condemnation power. In terms of public lands, adjacent private landowners frequently do not accept new mines, new energy facilities, new logging operations, and the like as unalloyed blessings, and they have demonstrated a willingness to go to court to halt them. Allied to new landowner attitudes is a new aggressiveness on the part of non-consumptive economic users of public lands. Resorts, guides, river outfitters, backpacking equipment manufacturers, and so forth have resisted development of a resource valuable to them as primitive real estate. Growing numbers of economists and political conservatives are calling into question the many federal subsidies afforded to developers of public lands and resources.

Many of the largest changes have come about through institutional strategies and actions by established and new environmental organizations. Among the most active and effective organizations are the oldline Sierra Club and Wilderness Society, and three newcomers, the Environmental Defense Fund (EDF), the Natural Resources Defense Council (NRDC), and the National Wildlife Federation. Even the traditionally apolitical Audubon Society has found itself lobbying and litigating. These organizations alone—and there are dozens of similar if less visible groups—have wrought legislative change, pursued hundreds of successful lawsuits—NRDC v. EPA cases alone are legion—and mobilized considerable public support. Overlap and coalitions among organizations are common.

Defining the goals of conservation organizations is difficult, as they cover a broad spectrum. In general, they are striving to achieve their vision of a higher quality of life, a more "natural" or environmentally compatible existence. That scarcely enhances semantic definition, but it is understandable to many on some level. Slightly more specifically, and realizing that each group professes a somewhat different group of aims, one common denominator appears to be a disdain for profits at the expense of less tangible values. While there are ideological relationships between "conservationist" and "conservative," the former tend to be politically liberal in the sense of preferring government control over unfettered private enterprise in public land management. Preservation of fauna, flora, and the land in their primeval state is often high on priority lists of conservationists.

Modern public land law, like politics, often makes strange bedfellows: there is a tendency toward coalitions of otherwise divergent entities. In the lawsuit and the lobbying over Locks and Dam 26, for instance, the lamb lay down with the lion: the Sierra Club and the railroads were joint plaintiffs. See Atchison, T. & S.F. Ry. v. Calloway, 382 F.Supp. 610 (D.D.C.1974). In the 1980's, when ETSI proposed a coal slurry pipeline between Wyoming and Louisiana, common cause was joined by environmentalists (fearing the shipment of scarce western water) and the railroads (fearing the loss of lucrative shipping contracts). It is likely that more such coalitions will form as corporate self-interest overcomes corporate distaste at cooperating with the erstwhile enemy, as conservationists become more realistic on goals and methods, and as the "sides" more fully comprehend the areas of common interest where joint action can be mutually beneficial.

The emergence of so-called public interest guardians has not lessened the role of the traditional economically oriented disputants. To the contrary, new emphases in the legal processes affecting public land use and management have caused extractive and consumptive industries to redouble their efforts in courts, Congress, and agencies. Beginning with the Pacific Legal Foundation, industries and individuals have financed their own versions of public interest law firms to present the corporate view of the public interest in resource litigation. James Watt, irrepressible Interior Secretary during the early Reagan years, earned his spurs with the Mountain States Legal Foundation.

Some of the most powerful economic interests in the country have large stakes in the direction of public land policy. Oil companies have paid billions of dollars for the privilege of drilling on offshore and other federal lands. Those same oil companies and many other entities own or have leased from the government billions of tons of coal underlying hundreds of thousands of acres. Public utilities not only rely upon federal coal and federal dams for hydroelectric power, but are also desirous of locating new generating facilities on federal lands. Mining companies jealously guard their statutory right to extract any mineral locatable on the public domain. While the prospector with a pan and mule may be a thing of the past, not all modern mining is done by corporate giants. The public lands have yielded immense stores of mineral wealth, and most remaining domestic ore bodies will probably be located on federal lands in the West, including Alaska. Timber companies, too, find it necessary to cut a large share of their requirements from national forests because private lands do not yield sufficient lumber to meet national and international demand. Many small communities are dependent on the local timber harvest from national forests. The nuclear energy industry relies heavily on the public land uranium reserves. Most of the politically powerful cattle and sheep ranchers of the West use public lands for grazing their stock.

Direct users frequently have strong views as to the proper means and degree of public land utilization, and they are supported by other indirect users and their colleagues. Many business people and others, some not directly associated with extractive industry, hold as a philosophic tenet that land and water are commodities to be used like any other; correlatively, they feel that the federal government has an obligation to develop its resources to the fullest for the sake of the Nation's economic health while accepting as inevitable any unfortunate environmental byproducts. In the western states generally, it is a widely held view that states, not the federal agencies, should have the final say on resource development, that federal agencies and environmental organizations are bureaucratic intermeddlers into matters of local concern, and that the public interest is best served by full development of the economic potential of the public domain.

Federal land management agencies are frequently caught in the middle of modern federal land use controversies. Historical missions and practices have been severely eroded by new statutes, and new missions have been charted, but congressional directives often have held out little concrete guidance in concrete situations, and procedural requisites have proliferated. Interests over a wide spectrum forcibly argue that their conception of the public interest should prevail in the circumstances, and all sides are willing to resort to higher forums if dissatisfied with decisional results. Federal budget deficits both decrease administrative resources and focus unwanted attention on the many subsidies available to public land users. The land manager's role is increasingly a hard one.

It is as necessary to understand how public land law is made as it is to know what the law currently provides. There are interactions in and among the main components of the legal process that are not always clearly perceived. Neither statutes nor regulations nor judicial opinions are sufficient in themselves for an understanding of the broader context in which the broader questions are resolved. Any limited approach is fundamentally fallacious, for it assumes that "law" is a given when in fact public land law is an everchanging complex of rules derived from and altered by different sources. Although the final determination usually resides in Congress, each of the three branches of government has and uses the power to alter or upset the result reached in another branch. Throughout this volume are scattered "non-legal" or "quasi-legal" materials affording a glimpse into the interactive and interdisciplinary nature of public land law.

One other seldom-noted facet of lawmaking that pervades these materials is that the federal government is by no means a monolithic, homogeneous entity. Often the main dispute is between two agencies, and the private parties who may have initiated the legal challenge become passive or active bystanders. In TVA v. Hill, 437 U.S. 153 (1978) (the *Snail Darter* case), for instance, the federal Fish and Wildlife Service (FWS) joined with the environmentalist plaintiffs against the federal Tennessee Valley Authority. The Justice Department opted for the TVA position in argument before the Supreme Court, but counterpressure from higher up forced Justice to file a "split" brief appending FWS's argument against the conclusions in the main body. In that controversy, like many others, the litigation was but the prelude to ultimate resolution of the problem by Congress. There has always been a certain amount of interagency competition, but openly taking opposing sides in litigation and like proceedings is a relatively recent development. Whether or not it is a good thing from the standpoint of governmental efficiency may be debated, but it does serve the function of bringing issues into clearer focus.

In retrospect, it is apparent that a time of unparalleled change and ferment in federal land and resources law began about 1964. Old truths were challenged, and many have fallen. Hundreds of old United States Code sections were swept away at a stroke. Congress suddenly commanded long-advocated planning, inventorying, and other modern management techniques. Wildlife protection achieved an unanticipated degree of priority in a few short years. The Bureau of Land

Management finally received a statutory mission in the sweeping Federal Land Policy and Management Act of 1976. Thoroughgoing reform came to the Forest Service, the oldest federal land agency, in the National Forest Management Act of 1976. The Alaska National Interest Lands Conservation Act of 1980 allocated more than 100 million federal acres in Alaska to various conservation systems. Excluding Alaska, Congress conferred wilderness status on more than 20 million acres between the mid-1970's and the mid-1980's.

In 1981, Secretary Watt brought his brand of development-oriented reform to the Interior Department. Among other things, Mr. Watt attempted to open huge tracts of onshore and offshore tracts to mineral development as one solution to the energy crisis. The new emphasis at Interior spawned a wave of litigation and public outcry. The outcry died down with Watt's resignation in 1983, but the litigation continues.

Legislative, judicial, and administrative developments in this modern era have redefined some first principles. The Public Land Law Review Commission Report of 1970, addressing one of the fundamental issues throughout the history of public land policy, found that retention, not disposition, of federal lands, should be the guiding principle for the future. Congress then adopted the concept of retention as a policy declaration in the first provision of the comprehensive Federal Land Policy and Management Act of 1976: "The Congress declares that it is the policy of the United States that the public lands be retained in Federal ownership, unless as a result of the land use planning procedure provided for in this Act, it is determined that disposition of a particular parcel will serve the national interest." 43 U.S.C.A. § 1701(a)(1). This policy statement was among the political and legal developments that prompted the "Sagebrush Rebellion" of the late 1970's. The Rebels, with fervor equalling or exceeding that of earlier efforts to achieve a large-scale transfer of public lands, called for a sell-off of most federal lands to the states or private developers. The Sagebrush Rebellion now has receded, but it has left in its wake an intensified focus on the proper relationship between the state and federal governments in relation to public lands and resources.

3. THE FUTURE

The ferment in public land law is bound to continue. Recent legislative developments are sweeping, but it is naive to suppose that legislative activity will cease. The public and institutional recognition of the failure of some federal management agencies to achieve a balanced resource policy will not be cured by statutory innovation alone. The extensive planning efforts called for by the modern statutes governing the Bureau of Land Management and the Forest Service have helped create vastly improved resource inventories and long-range plans, but planning efforts to date have been sharply criticized on various grounds, including costs. It is likely, at least in the short term, that the new organic acts will engender considerable litigation, in turn creating bodies of common law, leading in turn to corrective legislative

action. Students now in law school will in coming years be in positions
to influence the directions those changes will take.

Developments, problems, crises, and attitudes are already apparent, the intersections of which will determine future land law policy.
In spite of the 1980 Alaska Lands Act, a host of issues remain unresolved concerning Alaska's lands, minerals, and animals. Mineral
development, whether for coal in the upper Great Plains or for oil and
gas in the Overthrust Belt in the heart of the Rockies, will continue to
present hard choices between energy requirements and the protection
of non-commodity resources. Proposals by the Forest Service to build
roads into virgin forestlands to accelerate timber harvests are being
fought in Congress and the courts. Federal land policy will be heavily
influenced by federal water allocation and development policies now in
a state of flux if not confusion. Pressure to discard the century-old law
governing mineral claim location wanes and waxes. The growing
public appetite for recreation will engender new and continuing conflicts with preservation as well as with extraction. Whether large, wild
mammals can survive on this continent will largely be determined by
future public land policy. Much of the western livestock industry faces
curtailment or bankruptcy. The stakes are enormous, and the times
are fluid. In the future of federal land and resources law lies a good
part of the Nation's future welfare.

B. THE FEDERAL LANDS AND RESOURCES

Except for the area of the original thirteen colonies, Texas, and
Hawaii, the United States government once owned nearly all of the
land within its present borders. The real estate comprising this original "public domain" is probably the richest in the variety and extent of
its natural resources of all comparable areas in the world. The forests,
the farmlands, the rivers and harbors, the mineral wealth, and the
scenic wonders are of literally inestimable economic, social, and aesthetic value. Most of the original national legacy has passed out of
national ownership as the public lands were opened for settlement and
development.

Easy availability of land was the primary incentive for pioneers,
then settlers, to move west and populate the Nation. Each wave of
settlers chose the available lands that were then thought to be the most
economically valuable. New cities grew up around the ports and many
of the strategic river junctions. The heart of public land policy was to
promote the small family farm: after the best agricultural lands in the
Midwest were settled, the homesteaders moved to the Willamette
Valley in Oregon, the Central Valley in California, and other verdant
agricultural areas. Prospectors and mining firms claimed the land
over the fabulous gold, silver, iron, and copper deposits in areas such as
the California Mother Lode country, the Comstock Lode in Nevada, the
Mesabi Range in Minnesota, and Butte in Montana. The timber
industry obtained prime timber lands throughout the country; their
relatively low-lying lands in the Pacific Northwest remain especially

valuable. In this century, reclamation projects were built to irrigate otherwise arid homesteads in the Great Plains, the Great Basin between the Sierra Nevada and Rocky Mountains, and elsewhere.

In the mid-19th century, Congresses and presidents withdrew a few public land parcels from the various programs for disposition into private hands and dedicated—or "reserved"—them for some specific purpose. Reservation for other than military or Indian purposes began haltingly with establishment of Yellowstone National Park in 1872, and "conservation" momentum grew until large scale homesteading ended in 1934. Retention instead of disposition became official federal public land policy. Land selection by the State of Alaska and Alaska Natives will take approximately 148 million acres out of federal ownership, and some minor sales or exchanges of lands especially suited for certain forms of non-federal ownership are still authorized. Conversely, some acquisitions of private lands by the federal government likely will continue. But, as of the mid-1980's, the outlines of the federal landed estate seem reasonably stable.

The United States now owns in fee roughly 732 million acres or, as is commonly said, about one-third of the Nation's total land area of 2.3 billion acres. Although federal public lands are located in all states, they are heavily concentrated in the "eleven western states" (Arizona, California, Colorado, Idaho, Montana, Nevada, New Mexico, Oregon, Utah, Washington, and Wyoming) and especially in Alaska, which has one-half of all public lands. Breaking down the "one-third of the Nation's land" characterization, public lands constitute 47.9% of the land in the eleven western states, 87.9% of the land in Alaska, and 4.3% of the land in the remaining 38 states.

The federal government also owns major less-than-fee interests. In addition to such holdings as acquired waterfowl easements, the United States retains subsurface mineral interests under some 60 million acres in the West. The federal government asserts sovereignty over the resources of the outer continental shelf, an area of about 860,000 square miles extending from 3 miles offshore (3 marine leagues off the Florida and Texas coasts) seaward to the edge of the geographic shelf, and also controls fisheries out to 200 miles.

Because of the historical pattern of national disposition, the remaining federal lands have relatively less economic potential than the other two-thirds of the United States land area. The public lands tend to be relatively arid and infertile, high in elevation, low in population, and remote from major transportation systems. Nevertheless, such generalizations may prove too much: in fact, immense riches of many kinds remain in federal ownership. Further, just as lands containing uranium were of no interest to our forebears, it is likely that other forms of wealth necessary for 21st century needs will be located on the federal lands.

In 1964, as a part of the compromise whereby the Wilderness Act became law, Congress created a body to study the federal laws and recommend more coherent courses for their disposition or management.

After years of debate, massive studies, and political compromises, the Public Land Law Review Commission issued its Report in 1970. The Commission recognized that Congress and federal land management agencies will always be challenged by the difficulty of structuring general policies to govern the munificent national potpourri of lands and resources:

One of the most important characteristics of the public lands is their great diversity. Because of their great range— they are found from the northern tip of Alaska to the southern end of Florida—all kinds of climate conditions are found on them. Arctic cold, rain forest torrents, desert heat, mountain snows, and semitropical littoral conditions are all characteristic of public lands in one area or another.

Great differences in terrain are also typical. The tallest mountain in North America, Mount McKinley in Alaska, is on public lands, as is the tallest mountain in the 48 contiguous states, Mount Whitney in California. But the lowest point in the United States, Death Valley, is also on public lands, as are most of the highest peaks in the White Mountains of New Hampshire and the Appalachians of the southeastern states.

Not all of these lands are mountains and valleys, however. Vast areas of tundra and river deltas in Alaska are flat, marked only with an incredible number of small lakes. Other vast areas in the Great Basin area of Nevada and Oregon are not marked with lakes, but with desert shrubs. Still other areas of rolling timber-covered mountains extend for mile after mile, both in the Pacific Northwest and the Inland Empire of Idaho, eastern Washington, and western Montana, and in the Allegheny, Green, and Ouachita Mountains of Pennsylvania, Vermont, and Arkansas. And still other vast areas are range-lands used for grazing domestic livestock.

However, not all of these public lands can be characterized as vast wild or semideveloped expanses. In many instances, Federal ownership is scattered in relatively small tracts among largely privately owned lands. The condition of the land may still be undeveloped, but our consideration of how the land should be used is necessarily influenced by the scattered nature of the Federal ownership. In some cases, public lands are found almost in the midst of urban areas and here again we must view the use of the lands in relation to the surrounding lands.

The great diversity of these lands is a resource in itself. As needs of the Nation have changed, the public lands have been able to play a changing role in meeting these needs. Whether the demand is for minerals, crop production, timber, or recreation, and whether it is national or regional, the public lands are able to play a role in meeting them.

Comparison of Federal Land With Total Acreage of States as of September 30, 1983

State	Acreage owned by the Federal Government			Acreage not owned by Federal Govt	Acreage of state [1]	Percent owned by Government [2]
	Public domain	Acquired by other methods	Total			
Alabama	29,365.6	1,112,775.2	1,142,140.8	31,536,259.2	32,678,400	3.495
Alaska	321,491,080.3	36,466.6	321,527,546.9	43,954,053.1	365,481,600	87.974
Arizona	30,996,063.3	1,071,208.3	32,067,271.6	40,620,728.4	72,688,000	44.116
Arkansas	1,073,225.3	2,401,238.0	3,474,463.3	30,124,896.7	33,599,360	10.341
California	44,095,839.2	1,794,055.3	45,689,894.5	54,316,825.5	100,206,720	45.795
Colorado	22,820,123.6	1,099,108.7	23,919,232.3	42,566,527.7	66,485,760	35.977
Connecticut	.0	10,464.0	10,464.0	3,124,896.0	3,135,360	.334
Delaware	.0	40,744.8	40,744.8	1,225,175.2	1,265,920	3.219
Dist of Columbia	17.5	12,542.3	12,559.8	26,480.2	39,040	32.172
Florida	354,549.0	3,802,772.4	4,157,321.4	30,563,958.6	34,721,280	11.973
Georgia	.0	2,291,219.3	2,291,219.3	35,004,140.7	37,295,360	6.143
Hawaii	331,648.8	359,404.4	691,053.6	3,414,546.4	4,105,600	16.832
Idaho	33,613,644.5	867,241.6	34,480,886.1	18,452,233.9	52,933,120	65.141
Illinois	442.6	622,180.6	622,423.2	35,172,576.8	35,795,200	1.739
Indiana	432.0	501,444.1	501,876.1	22,656,523.9	23,158,400	2.167
Iowa	340.8	227,707.9	228,048.7	35,632,431.3	35,860,480	.636
Kansas	26,092.8	707,080.0	733,172.8	51,777,547.2	52,510,720	1.396
Kentucky	.0	1,419,314.3	1,419,314.3	24,093,005.7	25,512,320	5.563
Louisiana	12,881.4	1,153,415.2	1,166,296.6	27,701,543.4	28,867,840	4.040
Maine	3.0	135,949.9	135,952.9	19,711,727.1	19,847,680	.685
Maryland	.3	186,199.7	186,200.0	6,133,160.0	6,319,360	2.947
Massachusetts	.0	85,743.4	85,743.4	4,949,136.4	5,034,880	1.703
Michigan	307,843.4	3,305,805.8	3,613,649.2	32,878,510.8	36,492,160	9.903
Minnesota	1,184,305.8	2,266,118.0	3,450,423.8	47,755,336.2	51,205,760	6.738
Mississippi	2,442.1	1,756,644.1	1,759,086.2	28,463,633.8	30,222,720	5.820
Missouri	2,925.4	2,174,636.5	2,177,561.9	42,070,758.1	44,248,320	4.921
Montana	25,121,983.0	2,287,220.2	27,409,203.2	65,861,836.8	93,271,040	29.387
Nebraska	244,173.0	406,563.6	650,736.6	48,380,943.4	49,031,680	1.327
Nevada	59,859,158.5	190,515.8	60,049,674.3	10,214,645.7	70,264,320	85.463
New Hampshire	.0	738,227.3	738,227.3	5,030,732.7	5,768,960	12.797
New Jersey	.0	150,639.3	150,639.3	4,662,800.7	4,813,440	3.130
New Mexico	23,977,543.1	1,943,035.3	25,920,578.4	51,845,821.6	77,766,400	33.331
New York	.0	247,599.8	247,599.8	30,433,360.2	30,680,960	.807
North Carolina	.0	2,158,585.7	2,158,585.7	29,244,294.3	31,402,880	6.874
North Dakota	208,360.0	2,038,585.5	2,246,945.5	42,205,534.5	44,452,480	5.055
Ohio	219.2	365,346.2	365,565.4	25,856,514.6	26,222,080	1.394
Oklahoma	141,878.1	1,459,069.4	1,600,947.5	42,486,732.5	44,087,680	3.631
Oregon	30,865,456.1	1,369,850.6	32,235,306.7	29,363,413.3	61,598,720	52.331
Pennsylvania	.0	694,724.5	694,724.5	28,109,755.5	28,804,480	2.412
Rhode Island	.0	5,804.9	5,804.9	671,315.1	677,120	.857
South Carolina	.0	1,198,295.7	1,198,295.7	18,175,784.3	19,374,080	6.185
South Dakota	1,591,445.9	1,556,647.3	3,148,093.2	45,733,826.8	48,881,920	6.440
Tennessee	.0	1,862,629.0	1,862,629.0	24,865,051.0	26,727,680	6.969
Texas	230.8	3,549,179.6	3,549,410.4	164,668,189.6	168,217,600	2.110
Utah	32,859,287.9	513,647.5	33,372,935.4	19,324,024.6	52,696,960	63.330
Vermont	.0	319,700.2	319,700.2	5,616,939.8	5,936,640	5.385
Virginia	.0	2,429,066.4	2,429,066.4	23,067,253.4	25,496,320	9.527
Washington	11,073,011.9	1,081,690.5	12,154,702.4	30,539,057.4	42,693,760	28.470
West Virginia	.0	1,117,425.0	1,117,425.0	14,293,135.0	15,410,560	7.251
Wisconsin	10,471.4	1,889,449.0	1,899,920.4	33,111,279.6	35,011,200	5.427
Wyoming	30,139,135.3	591,772.4	30,730,927.7	31,612,112.3	62,343,040	49.293
Total	672,435,666.9	59,806,751.3	732,042,392.4	1,539,300,967.6	2,271,343,360	32.230

1. Does not include inland waters
2. Excludes trust properties
SOURCE: General Services Administration

ONE THIRD OF THE NATION'S LAND—A REPORT TO THE PRESI-
DENT AND TO THE CONGRESS BY THE PUBLIC LAND LAW
REVIEW COMMISSION 22 (1970) (PLLRC Report).

Because the federal government now intends to retain ownership of
almost all its lands (with the exception of the ongoing transfers in
Alaska), the basic public land legal conflicts are over use, not disposition, of the public resources. In some instances, use of a parcel for
development of one resource can be entirely compatible with a different
use: timber harvesting can benefit some wildlife and recreation resources by creating meadows beneficial for deer habitat; a wilderness
area can provide watershed protection for downstream development; a
reclamation project for irrigation purposes can also produce electrical
energy and recreation. The theory that uses should be allowed in
compatible combinations is at the heart of much modern land management law. But often the development of one resource is detrimental,
even devastating, to others: the creation of a wilderness area eliminates timber harvesting and curtails mineral development; an open pit
mine preempts all other uses in the area, at least until the area is
reclaimed; the designation of a minimum stream flow can restrict the
use of water for grazing and mining. Avoiding or resolving such
resource conflicts is the overriding problem of modern land law. The
seven major resources of the federal lands, water, minerals, timber,
range, wildlife, recreation, and preservation, each deserves its own
introduction.

———

Water is the resource most often involved in the tough resource use
choices. Availability of water has always been the limiting factor for
development in many Trans-Mississippi regions. Wallace Stegner, one
of the most respected contemporary commentators on the American
West, has observed that the region's aridity and large concentration of
public lands are the two most distinctive features of western society.
See W. Stegner, THE SOUND OF MOUNTAIN WATER 33 (1969).
Justice Rehnquist, who has joined Justices Field, Van Devanter, and
McKenna as one of the most prolific public land law opinion writers,
commented in California v. United States, 438 U.S. 645, 648–50 (1978):

> * * * The final expansion of our Nation in the 19th
> century into the arid lands beyond the hundredth meridian of
> longitude, which had been shown on early maps as the "Great
> American Desert," brought the participants in that expansion
> face to face with the necessity for irrigation in a way that no
> previous territorial expansion had.

> * * * "[T]he afternoon of July 23, 1847, was the true
> date of the beginning of modern irrigation. It was on that
> afternoon that the first band of Mormon pioneers built a small
> dam across City Creek near the present site of the Mormon
> Temple and diverted sufficient water to saturate some five

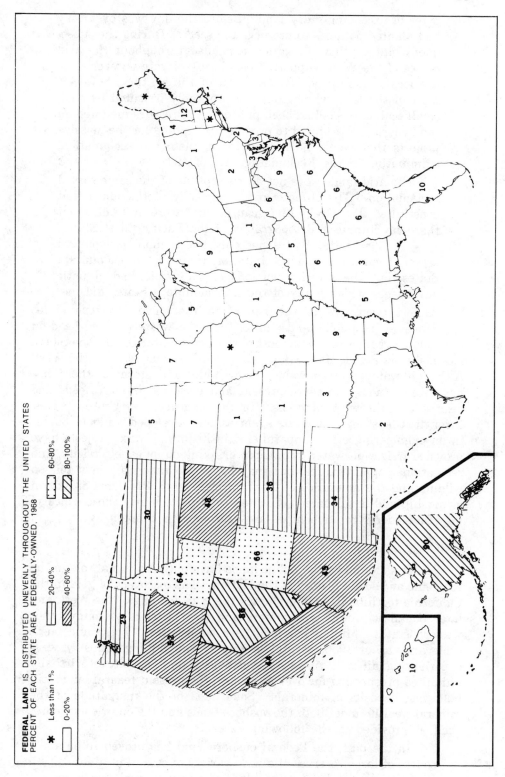

FEDERAL LAND IS DISTRIBUTED UNEVENLY THROUGHOUT THE UNITED STATES
PERCENT OF EACH STATE AREA FEDERALLY-OWNED. 1968

* Less than 1%

☐ 0-20%

☐ 20-40%

☐ 40-60%

☐ 60-80%

☐ 80-100%

acres of exceedingly dry land. Before the day was over they had planted potatoes to preserve the seed." During the subsequent half century, irrigation expanded throughout the arid States of the West, supported usually by private enterprise or the local community. By the turn of the century, however, most of the land which could be profitably irrigated by such small scale projects had been put to use. Pressure mounted on the Federal Government to provide the funding for the massive projects that would be needed to complete the reclamation, culminating in the Reclamation Act of 1902.

The arid lands were not all susceptible of the same sort of reclamation. The climate and topography of the lands that constituted the "Great American Desert" were quite different than the climate and topography of the Pacific Coast States. * * * [T]he latter States not only had a more pronounced seasonal variation and precipitation than the intermountain States, but the interior portions of California had climatic advantages which many of the intermountain States did not.

Almost two-thirds of the run-off in the eleven western states originates on the public lands: all of the great western rivers head on public lands, which comprise most of the Continental Divide, the Sierra Nevada, the Cascade Range, and other mountainous areas in the West. Although water is "renewable," recyclable, and storable, there has never been enough to serve present and projected human needs and desires in most western areas. In this century, the United States, through at least eight separate agencies, has developed water resources in an engineering effort unparalleled in history. These projects have provided irrigation water, municipal drinking supplies, electricity, and recreational opportunities, but they have also taken a heavy toll on wildlife and the amenities of free-flowing rivers. Problems of federal ownership and development of water—and particularly those concerning state-federal relationships—are examined in chapter five.

––––––––

Minerals found on the public lands have played a signal role in the economic and social history of the Nation. The discovery of gold in the California foothills in 1848 prompted the true opening of the West, and later bonanzas would lead miners and then settlers to many other western states. Mining has long been subject to a "boom and bust" cycle and, as of 1986, several sectors of the mining industry were experiencing difficult times. Nevertheless, and in spite of virtually unlimited prospecting for over a century, the present federal lands still hold vast deposits of minerals. Some idea of the magnitude of the mineral wealth, under both the onshore lands and the outer continental shelf, is provided in the following excerpts.

In the past, the Federal onshore land has proven to be a source of large reserves of a wide variety of essential minerals. In addition, for some minerals (for example, coal) large resources on Federal onshore land can be predicted on the basis of current knowledge, while for some other minerals (for example, copper) a large potential can be inferred on the basis of past experience and geologic evidence.

* * *

In 1975, petroleum and natural gas production from about 5.5 million acres of producing leases on Federal onshore land amounted to approximately 6 percent of the national total and was valued at over $1.64 billion. Large areas of the Federal onshore land not yet thoroughly drilled are considered favorable for the occurrence of petroleum and natural gas. In 1975, more than 84 million acres were under lease for petroleum and natural gas exploration and development. More than 90 percent of the leased acreage was in the 11 Western States and Alaska.

Substantial deposits of coal, phosphate, and sodium compounds are also known to exist on Federal onshore land, and large resources of these minerals are under lease. The value of production at the mine or wellhead of all leasable minerals on Federal onshore land in 1975 was more than $2.21 billion. Their cumulative production value for 1920 through 1975 was more than $22.5 billion.

Detailed records are not kept for production of hardrock minerals on Federal land unless they are produced from leases on Federal *acquired* land. * * * Nevertheless, some idea of the importance of Federal land for hardrock mineral production can be obtained from the data on mineral production in the Western States because * * * most hardrock mines on what is now private land in the Western States have passed into private ownership through location on Federal land under the Mining Law. In 1975, the Western States produced the following approximate amounts of the Nation's domestic primary mineral supply: 92 percent of the copper, 84 percent of the silver, and almost 100 percent of the nickel. In fact, the bulk of the known domestic resources of a majority of the metallic minerals is situated in the West.

* * * Of the 14 [representative essential] mineral commodities, 7 (coal, copper, nickel, phosphate rock, silver, sodium carbonate, and uranium) have a relatively high potential for occurrence on Federal onshore land, 6 (geothermal steam, fluorspar, lead, natural gas, petroleum, and potash) have a more moderate potential, and 1 (iron ore) has only limited, but possibly locally important, potential. Even minerals with lesser Federal land potential may take on added significance when viewed within the context of national needs and the reliability of imports.

Office of Technology Assessment, MANAGEMENT OF FUEL AND NON–FUEL MINERALS IN FEDERAL LAND 41–46 (R. Wright, ed., 1979).

Using the Department of the Interior's definition of the outer continental shelf [OCS], it constitutes an area of approximately 1 billion acres. Although 56% lies off the coast of Alaska, Louisiana has historically been the major OCS oil and gas producer. Although the area is vast and largely unexplored, its oil and gas potential is impressive. The OCS is estimated to contain somewhere between 26 and 41% of the nation's undiscovered recoverable crude oil reserves and 25 to 28% of the undiscovered recoverable natural gas reserves. This amounts to between 17 and 44 billion barrels of oil and between 117 and 230 trillion cubic feet of gas. Although these estimates are variable and likely to change, OCS production currently accounts for a significant proportion of our national totals. Since the inception of leasing in the 1950's, OCS natural gas production has been rising at a rate of roughly 1% annually. The OCS share of domestic output totalled 24% in 1981 * * *.

S. Fairfax & C. Yale, THE FINANCIAL INTEREST OF WESTERN STATES IN NON–TAX REVENUES FROM THE FEDERAL PUBLIC LANDS 87 (1985).

Hardrock minerals are freely available to private prospectors, and fuel minerals can be leased to bidders, but only on the lands that have not been withdrawn for other purposes. Such withdrawals pose a fundamental policy dilemma. Some argue that when national parks, wilderness areas, wildlife refuges, and other special reservations by their terms prohibit or limit mineral exploration, an inadvertent national sacrifice can occur because the extent of underground resources is not always known when the designation is made. Others respond that the resource is being saved for the future, not sacrificed to present consumption, while other and equally important resources are being protected at the same time. The legal regimes governing mineral extraction and the problems they create vis-a-vis other resources are taken up in chapter six.

The public timber resource has become increasingly important to American forestry as private stands of timber have been depleted. Expanding demand for housing, paper, plastics, fuel, and other uses has dictated great demand for timber production on the public lands. The federal government owns about 18% of the nearly 500 million acres of commercial timber lands in the United States. Six-sevenths of federal commercial timber is in national forests. Before World War II, federal timber holdings managed by the Forest Service and the Bureau of Land Management were managed conservatively, producing only about five percent of the national total timber harvest. One result of that former conservatism is that the federal lands still hold a comparatively large amount of old-growth, virgin timber of great economic value, especially in the Pacific Northwest. Over half of the national softwood timber inventory is located on national forests, roughly three times the amount owned by the forest industry, with small private owners and other public entities controlling the rest. Many of the lands containing timber, particularly the extraordinary stands of old-growth Douglas fir, redwood, and pine, also contain unique scenic and aesthetic values. A central policy issue in public timber management is the rate at which old-growth stands will be liquidated to make way for new, faster-growing forests. "Below-cost" sales of national forest timber (in which timber sales fail to return the government's full cost of growing and selling the trees) is an issue that also promises to bedevil forest planners. Below-cost sales benefit the timber industry and some local communities but are sharply criticized by resource economists, who believe that sales of federal timber should be subjected to the full rigors of the market, and by environmentalists, who oppose timber harvesting in remote roadless areas. The timber resource is explored in chapter seven.

More acres of federal lands are used for domestic livestock grazing than for any other single use except recreation. The number of animals on the federal range has declined substantially, but ranchers still graze cattle and sheep on some 170 million acres of BLM lands and 101 million acres within the National Forests. The public lands supply 12% of the total forage in the West. Historically, the public domain was a "commons" where grazing was allowed with no federal regulation whatsoever, a situation that took a great toll on the forage resource. In spite of some federal regulations since the 1930's (and earlier, in the case of national forests), the public range is largely in "fair" or "poor" condition, overgrazing by modern standards is still common, and some assert that land conditions continue to deteriorate. As the following excerpt from Phillip Foss' classic study shows, federal officials and western ranchers face a complex task in reducing erosion and resuscitating the range resource:

> * * * Competition for water and the scant grass and browse of this free land was chiefly responsible for the range wars and the "romantic" legend of the guntoting cowboy.

> Stockmen attempted to reserve grazing rights for themselves by homesteading waterholes, by acquiring land along creeks, by checkerboard patterns of ownership, and by various other devices. These schemes all had as their objective the free and exclusive use of parts of the public domain. This kind of finagling does not necessarily imply that the early stockmen were rogues or possessed of any particularly sinister or wicked intent. Most of the land so manipulated was of such low productivity that homestead tracts were too small to provide a reasonable living. Consequently, stockmen and farmers were forced to supplement their homestead with "free land" or go bankrupt.

* * *

There were two general results of this "free land" situation. First, squabbles over range and water continued intermi-
nably and even the most powerful operators lived an uncertain
economic existence. Second, the "free land" *had* to result in
overgrazing. Cattlemen and sheepmen could not be expected
to withhold stock from government range to prevent overgrazing when they knew that other stockmen would get the grass
they left. Overgrazing permitted an accelerated rate of erosion by removing the forage that held moisture and soil.
Erosion of soil led to still greater erosion with the result that
the carrying capacity of the range decreased and floods and
desert land increased.

Overgrazing caused millions of acres of grassland to become desert. Lands which produced native grasses "up to your
stirrups" within the lifetime of persons now living became, and
remain today, virtual deserts. The Department of Agriculture
reported in 1936, "a range once capable of supporting 22.5
million animal units [an animal unit was one cow or horse or
five sheep or goats] can now carry only 10.8 million." This
meant that the forage capacity of the western range had been
reduced by more than one half.

To remedy the evils of unrestricted competition for the
range and consequent overgrazing and soil erosion, Congress
passed the Taylor Grazing Act in 1934. By that year all of the
most desirable land had become privately owned, but there still
remained approximately 170,000,000 acres of government land.
In 1934 this was still open range—the open range of cutthroat
competition and extreme overgrazing.

* * *

An area of 142,000,000 acres is 221,875 square miles. This
is 9,000 square miles larger than the republic of France. It is
almost twice the area of Japan. Naturally, in such a large
area there exist wide diversities in topography, climate, soils,
and vegetation. Probably the most uniform feature of these
lands is the low precipitation rate. According to F. R. Carpenter, 95 per cent of the public lands are within a zone of less
than fifteen inches of annual rainfall. * * *

P. Foss, POLITICS AND GRASS 3–4, 74, 77 (1960).

Today about 7.6 million domestic animals spend part of their lives
on federal rangeland. The forage on the public range, however, is also
used by an estimated 60,000 wild horses and burros and by uncounted
millions of antelope, deer, moose, and mountain sheep. Regulation to
reconcile the competition among those uses and to increase the productivity of grazing lands is the dominant theme of chapter eight.

The federal lands contain some of the most valuable wildlife
habitat in the world. Maintenance of wildlife in the wild is valuable to

hunters, to industries that depend upon wildlife products or that support recreational pursuits, to people who only watch wildlife, and to those who simply believe that wild animals should remain free and wild. The native ranges of certain species, such as wild turkeys, moose, elk, and mountain sheep, correspond closely to public land holdings. Even in many eastern states, big game species depend heavily on public land habitat. The Public Land Law Review Commission reported, for example, that 21% of big game populations in Arkansas, Florida, Michigan, Minnesota, New Hampshire, North Carolina, South Dakota, Virginia, and West Virginia occurred on public lands. In some instances, the public lands offer the last refuge for species in danger.

A number of species of American wildlife owe their very survival to the preservation of their habitat on public lands. The Whooping Crane, for instance, would have been extinct by now, except for a few specimens in zoos, if it had not been for the protection of their wintering ground on the Aransas National Wildlife Refuge and on their nesting grounds in the Wood Buffalo National Park in Canada. The most successful Bald Eagle population in the contiguous states is in the Chippewa National Forest in Minnesota, where 78 young were produced in 1976.

Grizzly Bears and Grey Wolves could not have survived in the lower 48 states except for the National Forests and National Parks which provided them the required habitat and protection. These are wide-ranging species which need vast areas of relatively undisturbed land—areas so large that only the government could provide them. Grizzly Bears, for example, range so widely that it is questionable whether viable populations could continue even in areas as large as Yellowstone Park (2.2 million acres) or Glacier Park (1 million acres) which form the nucleus of the lower 48 Grizzly Bear population habitat. * * *

For some species of wildlife, then, a sine qua non is large tracts of undisturbed or relatively undisturbed lands, and only the public lands provide them. For other species, illustrated by the Kirtland's Warbler, it is not size of the area which is important, for each pair of warblers uses a breeding territory of only about 30 acres; it is the nature of the management of the area which is critical. These warblers, for reasons unknown, will nest only in young pine lands (primarily Jack Pine) where the scattered trees are 8 to 20 years old. Before forest fires were fought and controlled, wildfires created the conditions ideal for the Jack Pine; management measures required for maintenance of this unique and beautiful songbird include prescribed burning on the state and National Forests in certain areas of northern Michigan. Again the public lands are a prerequisite. In the 1976 census, 162 males were found on state lands, 32 on the National Forests, and only 6 on private lands.

*   *   *

The increasing public interest in wildlife over the past half century has resulted in numerous changes, sometimes by legislation, often through executive decisions. Through the first decades of this century, the public accepted narrow single use policies of management for vast areas of public lands which ignored or neglected the now widely accepted fact that wildlife and public recreation could be enjoyed on many of these lands without serious interference with other uses.

G. Swanson, Wildlife on the Public Lands, in WILDLIFE IN AMERICA 428, 432–33 (H. Brokaw, ed., 1978). Management and protection of the wildlife resource on public lands under new legal guidelines is the subject of chapter nine.

Minerals, timber, water, forage, and even wildlife are commonly considered the conventional resources on the public lands. Nothing better symbolizes the recent evolution of public land policy than the emergence of recreation and preservation as co-equal and competing resources.

Americans with their leisure time, affluence, new philosophies, and means of transportation desire recreational opportunities in myriad forms, and they demand that such opportunities be made available on the public lands. Congress and federal land management agencies have hastened to obey the popular will. Every major federal land system offers something of a recreational nature to somebody, from hiking to powerboating to resorts. One can tour a national park by car, shoot the rapids on a wild river, fish, swim, and boat in federal reservoirs, ride jeeps through grazing districts, and collect rocks in national forests. These opportunities have been considered "givens," unchallenged rights available to all citizens. But, as in the case of all resources, the underlying productivity of the recreation resource can be threatened by human overuse. The novel legal questions arising from conflicts between recreational use and other resources are addressed in chapter ten.

American society was indelibly marked in 1868 when John Muir stepped on the wharf in San Francisco, and said, "Take me anywhere that is wild." Because of the work of Muir and others, Congress was moved to set aside numerous national parks in the late 19th and early 20th centuries. National parks were and are an important part of the preservation resource, but government officials came to recognize the need to preserve truly wild areas without roads, lodges, or restaurants. Before wilderness was fashionable, Aldo Leopold, at one time a forester in the Forest Service, commented:

Like winds and sunsets, wild things were taken for granted until progress began to do away with them. Now we face the question whether a still higher 'standard of living' is worth its cost in things natural, wild, and free. For us of the minority, the opportunity to see geese is more important than television, and the chance to find a pasque-flower is a right as inalienable as free speech.

These wild things, I admit, had little human value until mechanization assured us of a good breakfast, and until science disclosed the drama of where they come from and how they live. The whole conflict thus boils down to a question of degree. We of the minority see a law of diminishing returns in progress: our opponents do not.

A. Leopold, A SAND COUNTY ALMANAC vii (1949).

From obscure philosophical beginnings, the movement to preserve wild areas has succeeded in persuading Congress to create a new public land system, the dominant purpose of which is preservation. Shortly after passage of the Wilderness Act in 1964, one of the most articulate wilderness advocates, the late Justice William O. Douglas, made the following observations on the place of preservation in national resource priorities:

* * * The islands of wilderness, even if they never shrink in acreage, shrink *per capita*. For the pressure of population is ever and ever greater; and the year is drawing near when one who wants to backpack or travel by pack train into the High Sierras, the Northern Cascades, the Wind River Range, or the Tetons must get a permit—just as he does today for picnicking along Rock Creek Park, Washington, D.C.

* * *

The wilderness areas [in 1965] plus the primitive areas amount to 14,617,461 wilderness-type acres which represent 8.02 per cent of total national forest lands. This 8.02 per cent, however, is largely at high altitudes where the timber production potential is relatively low. That means that no more than 2 to 3 per cent of the long-range timber production potential of the Forest Service is in wilderness-type acreage. Nationally that is the equivalent of a fraction of a per cent of the total sustainable wood production.

* * *

There are inside the national park areas roads, accommodations, and installations deemed necessary "for the enjoyment of the parks" as the law provides, but yet not compatible with wilderness *per se*. National parks have indeed been greatly developed. Ideally the development should take place on the perimeter, leaving the park untouched except for trails, campgrounds, and the like. A few—the Great Smokies for example—have done that in large part.

Other national parks have often become huge building sites. Yellowstone has about 2 million visitors and needs accommodations for 15,000 people. That makes up into a "small city" or into several "small cities." It means long avenues cut through thick forests to bring power lines to these new communities. It means the debris of civilization inside the sanctuary.

The Grand Canyon has a glorious rim that is already cluttered with buildings, including a church. As if the majesty and grandeur of the rim could be improved by man!

W. Douglas, A WILDERNESS BILL OF RIGHTS 61–70 (1965).*

There is no longer an open "public domain" where ranchers can graze without regulation and citizens can obtain land by homesteading. But the phrase "public domain" is still commonly used, and those who know the public lands have a mental image of the public domain. It is high desert or plains country, uncluttered and quiet. The colors are not dramatic—it is a land of pastels. There is a growing awareness that this land, too, has preservation values:

For years, the public domain—especially outside Alaska— has suffered from a bad press; even those who have fought for its preservation have frequently assumed that it consisted of little more than godforsaken wastelands, bleak alkali flats, smelly sumps, and monotonous stretches of sand and sage-brush. In fact, it is quite as varied in all its characteristics as the West itself (not too surprising, since in many respects the public domain *is* the West), and is neither bleak nor forsaken by God. If a good deal of it is desert (and it might be useful to remember that the Son of God once walked in deserts), it also includes grasslands and prairie and tundra; mountain peaks as sheer and rock-ribbed as anything in Rocky Mountain National Park; swamps, lakes, streams, rivers, tarns, marsh-lands, hot springs, and geysers; forests of chaparral, oak, juniper, redwood, western red cedar, white pine, yellow pine, and bristlecone pine; flattopped mesas that float in the dis-tance like mirages, spectacular canyons that look as if they had been sliced into the earth with a knife yesterday after-noon, and balancing rocks, toadstool rocks, caves, caverns, sandstone arches, and all the other geological formations carved by the hand of time; a zoological index of deer, antelopes, elk, caribou, moose, bears—black, brown, and griz-zly—beaver, otters, coyotes, wolves, mountain lions, golden eagles and bald eagles, pelicans, peregrine falcons, and ospreys, and hundreds more, including such rare fish as the desert pupfish and the Utah cutthroat trout; and the marks of twenty thousand years of human history, from the delicate petroglyphs of prehistoric Indians to the axle-grease scrawls of wagontrain pioneers, from the cliff dwellings of the Anasazi and Moqui to the prospect holes of the new Jasons of the nineteenth century.

T. Watkins & C. Watson, Jr., THE LAND NO ONE KNOWS 138 (1975).

These, then, are the primary resources of the public lands. For every proposed use there are phalanxes of disparate advocates and opponents. Many claim that if the United States were literally to "lock up" for preservation even one of the major economic resources, catastrophic social and economic consequences would follow. On the other hand, opening all federal lands for wholesale, unregulated development would irreparably wound a special part of the national spirit. Because of the compulsion to compromise inherent in our political, legal, and administrative mechanisms, resource decisions mostly fall in the middle of the two extremes. It is within this diverse and emotional context that legislators, land management officials, lawyers, and judges must operate in making and reviewing decisions affecting the national resources.

It is difficult to locate a common legal denominator among the many diverse instances of present federal ownership. The federal purposes behind construction of a post office and creation of a wilderness area are so different that comparison in legal terms is nearly impossible. One writer has divided all federal holdings into three broad classifications: resource preservation lands; multiple resource use lands; and lands used for specific non-resource oriented purposes. Muys, The Federal Lands, in FEDERAL ENVIRONMENTAL LAW 495 (1974). The "resource preservation" lands include the National Park System (which includes Monuments, Preserves, Recreation Areas, Seashores, Lakeshores, Trails, and Rivers), Wilderness Areas, and the National Wildlife Refuge System. The "multiple use" category includes National Forests (including the National Grasslands), the BLM lands (the traditional "public domain"), outer continental shelf lands, and the lands administered for power, irrigation, or flood control purposes by the Federal Energy Regulatory Commission, the Army Corps of Engineers, and the Bureau of Reclamation. The final "non-resource oriented" category is a catchall for all other forms of federal land ownership. That category is not necessarily negligible—the Department of Defense administers nearly 23 million acres—but the focus of this volume is on the vast bulk of the federal lands in the two "resource" categories.

A number of recent books deal with public lands policy. In addition to the authorities excerpted in the following section—designed to introduce various perspectives on the field—see, e.g., RETHINKING THE FEDERAL LANDS (S. Brubaker, ed. 1984); R. Nash, WILDERNESS AND THE AMERICAN MIND (3d ed. 1983); P. Fradkin, A RIVER NO MORE: THE COLORADO RIVER AND THE WEST (1981); P. Wiley & R. Gottlieb, EMPIRES IN THE SUN: THE RISE OF THE

NEW AMERICAN WEST (1982); W. Wyant, WESTWARD IN EDEN: THE PUBLIC LANDS AND THE CONSERVATION MOVEMENT (1982); P. Culhane, PUBLIC LANDS POLITICS: INTEREST GROUP INFLUENCE ON THE FOREST SERVICE AND THE BUREAU OF LAND MANAGEMENT (1981); WESTERN PUBLIC LANDS (J. Francis & R. Ganzel eds, 1984); M. Clawson, THE PUBLIC LANDS REVISITED (1983); B. Shanks, THIS LAND IS YOUR LAND (1984); R. Lamm & M. McCarthy, THE ANGRY WEST (1982); P. Truluck, PRIVATE RIGHTS AND PUBLIC LANDS (1983).

C. PERSPECTIVES ON PUBLIC LAND AND RESOURCES LAW

GARRETT HARDIN, THE TRAGEDY OF THE COMMONS
162 Science 1243 (1968).

The tragedy of the commons develops in this way. Picture a pasture open to all. It is to be expected that each herdsman will try to keep as many cattle as possible on the commons. Such an arrangement may work reasonably satisfactorily for centuries because tribal wars, poaching, and disease keep the numbers of both man and beast well below the carrying capacity of the land. Finally, however, comes the day of reckoning, that is, the day when the long-desired goal of social stability becomes a reality. At this point, the inherent logic of the commons remorselessly generates tragedy.

* * *

Adding together the component partial utilities, the rational herdsman concludes that the only sensible course for him to pursue is to add another animal to his herd. And another; and another. * * * But this is the conclusion reached by each and every rational herdsman sharing a commons. Therein is the tragedy. Each man is locked into a system that compels him to increase his herd without limit—in a world that is limited. Ruin is the destination toward which all men rush, each pursuing his own best interest in a society that believes in the freedom of the commons. Freedom in a commons brings ruin to all.

* * *

In an approximate way, the logic of the commons has been understood for a long time, perhaps since the discovery of agriculture or the invention of private property in real estate. But it is understood mostly only in special cases which are not sufficiently generalized. Even at this late date, cattlemen leasing national land on the western ranges demonstrate no more than an ambivalent understanding, in constantly pressuring federal authorities to increase the head count to the point where overgrazing produces erosion and weed-dominance.

* * *

The National Parks present another instance of the working out of the tragedy of the commons. At present, they are open to all, without limit. The parks themselves are limited in extent—there is only one Yosemite Valley—whereas population seems to grow without limit.

The values that visitors seek in the parks are steadily eroded. Plainly, we must soon cease to treat the parks as commons or they will be of no value to anyone.

What shall we do? We have several options. We might sell them off as private property. We might keep them as public property, but allocate the right to enter them. The allocation might be on the basis of wealth, by the use of an auction system. It might be on the basis of merit, as defined by some agreed upon standards. It might be by lottery. Or it might be on a first-come, first-served basis, administered to long queues. These, I think, are all the reasonable possibilities. They are all objectionable. But we must choose—or acquiesce in the destruction of the commons that we call our National Parks.

NOTE, MANAGING FEDERAL LANDS: REPLACING THE MULTIPLE USE SYSTEM *
82 Yale L.J. 787 (1973).

The land agencies are directed by statute to manage most federal lands for "multiple use," which in practice means that they have nearly unlimited discretion in the allocation of land to particular uses. The statutory definition of the term "multiple use" is a collection of vacuous platitudes, providing authority for the "judicious use" of land resources, "periodic adjustments in use to conform to changing needs and conditions," and consideration of the "relative value of the various resources" in case of conflict. The Forest Service act lists five contemplated uses of National Forest lands: "outdoor recreation, range, timber, watershed, and wildlife and fish purposes." A special provision states that "the establishment and maintenance of areas of wilderness are consistent with the purposes and provisions" of the act. None of these possible uses * * * is given priority status.

* * *

* * * At the same time, ample opportunity is provided for informal pressure on agency planners and decisionmakers at the local level, since present agency procedures give local officials critical decisionmaking responsibility. Local users have the best opportunity to exert such pressure; those located in other parts of the country, many of them having strong recreational or conservationist concerns, are virtually unrepresented. Among local users, commercial interests appear to have an advantage over others, as a result of their financial and organizational strength.

* * *

This influence takes three principal forms. First, the line officer's friends and neighbors are the same local people who make demands on the resources under his control. There is understandable social pressure to conform to their wishes. Second, these same local users are likely to sit on the advisory boards with which the line officer deals. Even without real authority, such boards can assume the role of

organized lobbies for the common interests of their members. Finally,
the agency adjudication process is used heavily by local persons to
challenge decisions about the use of particular lands. The decisions of
agency officials at both the local and regional levels may reflect the
desire to placate such interests in order to minimize time-consuming
appeals.

* * *

Similarly, at the national level, commercial users have an advantage over recreation advocates, for two reasons. First, persons and
firms interested in obtaining exploitation rights on public lands are
much fewer in number than the potential recreational users. This
alone makes the cost of organizing a collective pressure group much
smaller for the commercial interests than for recreationists. Second,
conservationists labor under the "free rider" problem; their members'
incentives are undercut by the fact that, even when they win favorable
planning decisions, they do not gain exclusive use of the benefits of
their victory.

ONE THIRD OF THE NATION'S LANDS—A REPORT TO THE CONGRESS BY THE PUBLIC LAND LAW REVIEW COMMISSION
1–7 (1970).

[The Commission's 289 page Report (exclusive of appendices and
the many voluminous supporting studies) may be the most prominent
and comprehensive investigation into public land law ever undertaken.
It has been analyzed, discussed, dissected, criticized, and cited more
than any other like document, and it is a primary research resource for
the serious student. Although some provisions of some recent statutes
are consistent with recommendations in the Report, it has never been
acted on as such by Congress. The following excerpts are the main
general policy recommendations from the first chapter of the Report,
each of which was preceded by: "We, therefore, recommend that:"]

* * *

An immediate review should be undertaken of all lands not
previously designated for any specific use, and of all existing
withdrawals, set asides, and classifications of public domain
lands that were effected by Executive action to determine the
type of use that would provide the maximum benefit for the
general public in accordance with standards set forth in this
report.

* * *

Congress should establish national policy in all public land
laws by prescribing the controlling standards, guidelines, and
criteria for the exercise of authority delegated to executive
agencies.

* * *

Congress assert its constitutional authority by enacting legislation reserving unto itself exclusive authority to withdraw or

otherwise set aside public lands for specified limited-purpose uses and delineating specific delegation of authority to the Executive as to the types of withdrawals and set asides that may be effected without legislative action.

* * *

Statutory goals and objectives should be established as guidelines for land-use planning under the general principle that within a specific unit, consideration should be given to all possible uses and the maximum number of compatible uses permitted. This should be subject to the qualification that where a unit, within an area managed for many uses, can contribute maximum benefit through one particular use, that use should be recognized as the dominant use, and the land should be managed to avoid interference with fulfillment of such dominant use.

* * *

Statutory guidelines be established providing generally that the United States receive full value for the use of the public lands and their resources retained in Federal ownership, except that monetary payment need not represent full value, or so-called market value, in instances where there is no consumptive use of the land or its resources.

* * *

Fundamental premises are beliefs set forth in the foregoing underlying principles as well as in the implementing recommendations that follow. These are:

1. *Functioning of Government in a manner that reflects the principles set forth in the Constitution.*

In adhering to this principle, we seek to give recognition particularly to these specific principles:

— Congress, elected by and responsive to the will of the people, makes policy; the executive branch administers the policy.

— Maintenance of a strong Federalism. The Federal Government not only recognizes the importance of state and local governments in the Federal system but affirmatively supports and strengthens their roles to the maximum extent possible.

— The Federal Government protects the rights of individual citizens and assures that each one is dealt with fairly and equitably.

2. *Balancing of all major interests in order to assure maximum benefit for the general public.*

— No one of the interests we have identified should benefit to the unreasonable detriment of

another unless there is an overriding national
interest present.

3. *Providing responsible stewardship of the public lands
and their resources.*

* * *

— Guidelines must be established to provide for priorities in reducing conflicts among users and
resolving conflicts when they arise.

4. *In addition to serving national requirements, the public
lands must serve regional and local needs.*

— In many areas, consideration must be given to
dependence of regional and local social and economic growth upon public lands and land policy.

— In planning the use of public lands, the uses of
nonpublic lands must be given consideration.

RICHARD L. STROUP & JOHN A. BADEN, NATURAL RESOURCES: BUREAUCRATIC MYTHS AND ENVIRONMENTAL MANAGEMENT *

118–27 (1983).

When well-trained economists look at the [Forest Service] planning
process, they see many problems in the way values are assigned, in the
way criteria are set, and in the lack of distinction between the two.
These problems can be easily explained. They are caused by the lack of
good data inherent in a failure to price outputs as well as inputs, in a
failure to recognize the opportunity cost of capital, and to the pressures
that must come to bear when decision makers are held accountable
only through the political system. The wonder is that the national
forests have been managed as well as they have.

Privatizing the national forests should end many of the obstacles to
good management. Not only would decision makers be given larger
amounts of validated and continuously updated information, but political obstacles to efficient management would largely disappear. Perhaps just as important, environmentalists, timber producers, miners,
recreationists, and others who make demands on the Forest Service
would quickly move away from their carping and faultfinding toward
positive and constructive accommodation.

Whenever someone owns a piece of land, everyone with a potential
interest in it begins to act *as if* they cared about everyone else. Each
party's goals can best be reached by close, constructive, and even
imaginative cooperation with all other parties. This results whenever
trade occurs by the rule of willing consent, for such trade must be
mutually beneficial. This process contrasts sharply with debates over
public land, where the name of the game is discrediting the other side's

* Reprinted with the permission of the
Pacific Institute for Public Policy Research.

views and rejecting compromises unless defeat appears imminent. When the price is zero, each side naturally wants it all.

* * *

* * * We believe that it does not matter very much who owns a resource when it comes to determining how that resource will be used. Any owner, whatever his goals, will find those goals frequently met more fully by cooperation with others through trade. Since dollars, additional wilderness lands, buffer zones for existing wilderness, and other items attainable through trade are desired by any potential owner, it follows that even a zealot who owns the land can gain by listening carefully and discussing constructively the alternatives proposed by nonowners who desire wilderness, mineral, or other values from the landowner. Until all rights are (for the moment) optimally allocated among competing and compatible uses and users, further trade can make all parties to the trade better off in the pursuit of their various goals.

* * *

The point is that if a mining company bought an entire forest, it would have every incentive to maximize the value of the 98 percent that it didn't really want by carefully considering the amenity effects of its exploration and mining operations. Similarly, if the Audubon Society submitted the high bid on ecologically critical portions of all the resold part of the forest, it would carefully consider its information and preferences. Demanding more only increases the required bid. The major reason we expect improvement in forest management is that a market system holds every private owner accountable to the rest of society by having to outbid everyone else—or reject others' bids—for every alternative forgone (or destroyed) on the land.

* * * But what about the individual who does not want to buy a part of the national forest but still wants access? Consider what people from Montana do when they want to use facilities in New York City but do not want to purchase real estate there. Just as some of the living space in New York is rented by the day or by the month, some of the private land in our country is leased by the hour, the week, or the year. Some people will pay a higher price for vacations filled with amenities, and many owners of the world's resources are happy to accommodate such vacationers. Access to a unique ecological site may be compared with access to a Rembrandt painting. In both cases, the admission fee can make it worthwhile for the owner to share the asset and, indeed, take elaborate precautions against its depreciation.

A key feature of our proposal is that the immense forest wealth of our nation would be more broadly shared among all citizens. Instead of a few favored firms and individuals enjoying the benefits of the forest, everyone would benefit from the revenues. Those revenues would capture the high bidder's estimate of the present capitalized value of all future benefits that could be derived from the land.

How large would the revenues from the sale of the national forests be? No one really knows. But it is not the *average* person's value that would determine the sale price of any tract. It is, rather, the most optimistic view, shared by the minimum number of people necessary to win the auction for a piece of land. * * *

Marion Clawson estimated that the national forests were worth $42 billion in 1976. Since then there have been large increases in timber prices, in the value of strategic minerals, and in the value of oil and gas potential. In addition, the demand for recreation opportunities and amenity values continues to increase. With reduced opportunities for "free" forest services, we would expect prices to rise significantly. Note, however, that this does *not* mean that the average citizen, or even the forest user, is necessarily disadvantaged. Currently, every citizen is a member of one of the most expensive clubs in the world: the U.S. Forest Service. Our club dues are measured in tax dollars paid and in productivity values forgone. With the constructive attitudes and imaginative entrepreneurship unleashed by implementation of our proposal, the national forests could be sold for several hundred billion dollars.

* * *

* * * Making the pie bigger is what efficiency is all about; but it is also the only way to make everyone better off. Increased efficiency— that is, movement toward the production possibility frontier—is the only real source of a "free lunch." Efficient use of resources requires that decision makers have both the authority and the responsibility for the resources about which decisions are being made. * * * When the worst cases of externalities can be controlled, private and transferable property rights are the best way to link responsibility and authority consistently.

Our proposal would help the American productivity problem * * *. [I]t would make better use of the mineral, timber, recreation, and amenity values found in the public forests. * * * Perhaps as important to the future of the nation would be a fundamental change in attitude. From the fierce and never-ending battles of lobbyist pressures and alarmist rhetoric would emerge a positive sum game. Rewards would be given for imaginative and constructive solutions to resource conflicts rather than for carefully articulated pleas and raw political clout. The formidable power of American entrepreneurs would be shifted from the negative sum political arena to the positive sum private arena, where every change must be mutually beneficial.

WILLIAM H. RODGERS, JR., BUILDING THEORIES OF JUDICIAL REVIEW IN NATURAL RESOURCE LAW *
53 U.Colo.L.Rev. 213 (1982).

By necessity, legal academics are in the perpetual presence of normative values and are called upon regularly to adjudge a particular outcome "right" or "wrong." This presupposes a baseline from which we measure compliance, and this baseline is accepted as the governing ethical arrangement. It seems inescapable that we are thus forced into

* Reprinted with permission of the University of Colorado Law Review.

a consideration of ethical theories. There are many candidates, and only some of these theories are derived from human preferences expressed biologically, culturally, or economically.

Moral philosophy may offer some guidance, but hardly in the detail satisfactory for the particularized needs of the law. Philosophical theories like those of John Rawls, moreover, exude confidence in the power of human rationality to prescribe just outcomes; there is much to be said for the contrary view that many seemingly nonrational cultural practices reflect an unarticulated wisdom presumptively deserving respect. Also, moral philosophy does not purport to be an empirical science, and for this lawyer at least, that stance gives the arguments a suspiciously hypothetical character. Rawls' fairminded soul, hiding behind the veil of ignorance, resembles nobody I ever knew, and in that respect is quite like the calculating rational person of economic theory. These twin caricatures are hardly the full measure of human nature, although legal theorists sometimes act as if they were.

Let me use as an illustration the case of Mr. Bryznowski, the northern Minnesota farmer, who had the misfortune to lose one, perhaps two, head of livestock to a pack of hungry wolves.[39] Bryznowski then persuaded the Fish and Wildlife Service to assign a trapper, full time, to hang around his farm and repulse the advances of the hungry wolves. This conflict fits the classical nuisance pattern, and resource law teachers could be expected to turn to the popular economic analyses for suggested solutions. Coase points out that through exchange the parties can be expected to achieve the most efficient combination of wolf-raising and cow-rearing.[40] The idea of Bryznowski negotiating with a pack of wolves troubles me not at all. In fact, it might be easier to strike an understanding with wolves than the operators of the chemical plants, pulp mills, and smelters commonly invoked in Coasian analyses. Whatever may be said of wolves, they keep their word, by which I mean behavior and needs are predictable and consistent.

What is the least costly means of averting this wolf damage? Indulge me further by assuming that Bryznowski, with the aid of the Fish and Wildlife Service, can go forth and suppress or exterminate the invaders at a cost of $400 a month; he can do nothing and accept the loss, randomly inflicted against his stock, of $200 a month; or he can select his puniest cow, at a cost of $100 per month, and stake it out in the woods as a bribe to the pack. This bribe turns out to be the efficient means of loss-avoidance. After all, in the causation-neutral world of economics the loss can be attributed as much to the tastiness of cows as to the hunger of wolves.

Will Bryznowski settle for the efficient outcome? Not likely under a psychological or biological model of human behavior which accepts people as they are, not as the reasonable economic beings they are

39. Fund for Animals v. Andrus (Minnesota Wolf Kill), 11 E.R.C. 2189 (1978). [Excerpted infra at page 805.]

40. Coase, *The Problem of Social Cost,* 3 J.Law & Econ. 1 (1960).

supposed to be. Bryznowski, under this view, would pursue the absolutist line of complete defense because he perceives injustice in this random misfortune, or because his genes recall the days before the technology of firearms, or because he lives in a house of straw. In the reported case, Bryznowski not only adhered to the absolutist line but the Fish and Wildlife Service agreed with him. While there may be no absolute rights to work or to eat, the right to be free of wolves is decidedly nonutilitarian.

Nor would I expect Bryznowski to be any better as a philosopher than as an economist. How far would you get persuading him to retreat behind the Rawlsian veil of ignorance with one of the wolves to talk things over on the assumption that either one might emerge as farmer or wolf? [41] It seems that any way the situation is hypothecized, Bryznowski's biological vote, and probably the cultural vote of his neighbors, is unlikely to be favorable to the wolves. In this case, I would be unwilling to accept the local biological and cultural preference, which is a reminder that the search for a governing ethic in law is ongoing and demanding. It is tempting to invoke the rights of wolves, or of people present and future who care about wolves, to condemn Bryznowski's conviction as prejudice and his neighbors' support as superstition. There is nothing central to his existence as a farmer in northern Minnesota that turns on recognition of a continuing right to exterminate wolves. Professors Coggins and Wilkinson would compensate Bryznowski for loss of the right to be free of wolves, pointing out that a payoff would be a tiny fraction of the cost of trapper protection.[42] Wolf damage, in my opinion, is merely another form of just loss not unlike that inflicted by a wide variety of natural hazards.

125 CONG. REC. S11665–66

(daily ed. Aug. 8, 1979) (remarks of Sen. Orrin G. Hatch).

Mr. HATCH. Mr. President, I have introduced today a comprehensive bill which will correct a longstanding inequity in the adjudication of rights and privileges to the various States of the Union. This bill, entitled "Western Lands Distribution and Regional Equalization Act of 1979," establishes a mechanism by which States west of the 100th meridian may obtain rightful title to certain public lands within their respective boundaries.

In recent years, citizens of these Western States have experienced abnormally high levels of apprehension toward the Federal Establishment. This concern has directly resulted from the enactment of the Federal Land Management and Policy Act of 1976 and other, similar legislative and administrative measures that effectuated absolute control over many aspects of the public domain by Federal land managers. More specifically, it has been observed that in the absence of some form of external restraint, Federal land managers have interpreted discre-

41. J. Rawls, A Theory of Justice (1971).   42. See G.C. Coggins & C.F. Wilkinson, Federal Public Land & Resources Law 671 (1980). [Eds.: see note 1 infra at page 814.]

tionary legislative mandates to extremes with devastating effects on economic, social, and political institutions in those Western States where lands are preponderantly of Federal ownership.

Mr. President, no conceivable benefit to the American public can be derived from extreme and inflexible management of the national resource lands. This kind of management benefits only the politicians who have chosen to use the public lands as political cannon fodder in the battle for the votes of indignant dogmatists. Perhaps of greater significance, it benefits and fertilizes the inflationary growth of a Federal bureaucracy; the only true function of which is to preserve and proliferate itself at the public's expense.

I ask you, Mr. President, is it in the Nation's best interest, at a time when shortages of energy resources are causing civil strife and catastrophic economic disorder, to have precious resources, so abundant in the West, subjected to the whims and vagaries of the politically and bureaucratically inspired? I ask you—is it just to subject the unfortunate citizenship of a few of these United States to a degree of Federal involvement in their lives that most, if not all Americans, would find intolerable? Can you not imagine how BLM district managers might be likened to the sheriff of Nottingham, or colonial magistrates, by westerners?

The common solution to these critical problems is clear: The transferral of the unappropriated public lands to States' jurisdiction. The various Western States have repeatedly demonstrated the capability to manage public resources in an evenhanded, dynamic and effective fashion. They have, for decades, managed wildlife resources in such a manner that the resource has flourished and the harvest by all Americans has been abundant. The States have for decades, managed and regulated the most complex and technical aspects of oil and gas production and development on all lands within their borders. These activities by States clearly refute the argument that State control of the public domain would be dominated by parochial interests.

* * *

I believe, Mr. President, that if this country is to overcome the crisis facing it today, it must utilize all of its resources; including the vast amount of natural resources in Western States. These resources will never be fully developed while the Government subjugates the Western States. We must act now to provide all States with equality. I urge my colleagues to support this concept.

JOHN D. LESHY, UNRAVELING THE SAGEBRUSH REBELLION: LAW, POLITICS AND FEDERAL LANDS *

14 U.C.D.L.Rev. 317 (1980).

The "sagebrush rebellion" burst onto the Western scene in 1979, when the Nevada legislature began considering a bill to claim owner-

* Reprinted with permission of the University of California at Davis Law Review.

ship of the "unappropriated" federally controlled public lands in the state. Since that measure was enacted in June 1979, other Western states have passed similar bills. Thus the stage appears to be set for a legal test of continued federal management of much of the land in the West. [ed: That legal test eventuated. See page 80, infra.]

Dissatisfaction in Nevada with federal policies goes back at least as far as 1861, when the young Mark Twain accompanied his brother Orion to the newly created territory, where Orion had been appointed Secretary to the territorial government. Twain poked fun at the inability of the distant federal bureaucracy to govern an area 2,500 miles away. For example, he described the difficulty of obtaining sufficient federal money to pay for running the territorial government. The Secretary's instructions were to print the territorial legislature's journals at a particular cost. Things being expensive in the territory, this could not be done, so the Secretary entreatied his superiors in Washington for an increase, calling attention to the fact that

> even hay was two hundred and fifty dollars a ton. The United States responded by subtracting the printing bill from the Secretary's suffering salary—and moreover remarked with dense gravity that he would find nothing in his "instructions" requiring him to purchase hay!

> Nothing in this world is palled in such impenetrable obscurity as a U.S. Treasury Comptroller's understanding. The very fires of the hereafter could get up nothing more than a fitful glimmer in it.

But Washington was not the only object of Twain's acerbic pen. The first Nevada territorial legislature also received his jibes:

> That was a fine collection of sovereigns, that first Nevada legislature. They levied taxes to the amount of thirty or forty thousand dollars and ordered expenditures to the extent of about a million.   *   *   *

> The legislature sat sixty days, and passed private toll road franchises all the time. When they adjourned it was estimated that every citizen owned about three franchises, and it was believed that unless Congress gave the territory another degree of longitude there would not be room enough to accommodate the toll roads. The ends of them were hanging over the boundary line everywhere like a fringe.

Twain's observations foreshadowed the differences in perception which are reflected in rhetoric heard today about the sagebrush rebellion. Does it represent a genuinely inspired effort to replace distant, inefficient and unresponsive federal land management with better, local governmental control? Or is it instead merely a land grab, with states fronting for certain interest groups who seek exclusive rights to exploit the resources of these lands free from any regulation?

*   *   *

[T]he rebellion has several disparate roots which are not easily reconciled with each other, but which can teach us several things about politics and values in the modern West.

First, the rebellion obviously feeds at the trough of national disaffection with government regulations and bureaucracy. With its extensive landholdings giving it a highly visible, pervasive presence throughout the West, the federal government naturally feels the brunt of anti-government feeling there.

* * *

Also at work here is the increasing realization that man's abilities to make nature over in his own image are not unbounded. Natural limitations in the West, most obviously its aridness, have long been obstacles to development. But in many areas they have been, at least for the time being, successfully surmounted by man's ingenuity, often aided by federal funds. But now Westerners find themselves facing resource shortages which are not only fractious but, more important, appear to defy the solutions of the past. Part of the frustration provoked by that realization has undoubtedly tarnished the image of the federal government as problem-solver. At the same time, ironically, the resources of federal lands are increasingly being viewed as providing a safety net to help solve local or regional problems in the West.

Another factor is an idea long basic to the Western system of values—that man not only can but *must* exploit and tame nature into submission in order to survive and prosper in the sometimes harsh Western environment. Part of the FLPMA's regulatory scheme is designed to achieve environmental restoration and protection on all the public lands and, beyond that, to preserve parts of the public lands in their natural condition. This does not go down easily with those who, by experience or cultural inculcation, regard the natural environment as their enemy.

A fourth root of the rebellion is found in the greatly increased competition for public lands and resources. "Multiple use" is the well worn phrase which describes the fundamental management principle for most public lands in this country. Yet until recently, overt competition for use of specific areas of public lands was the exception rather than the rule. Livestock graziers, miners, lumbermen, hunters and fishermen generally coexisted peacefully, and few other demands were placed on these lands. Now, however, growing numbers of off-road vehicle fanciers, wilderness advocates, endangered species and other wildlife protectionists, white-water enthusiasts, cultural and archaeological resource investigators, hikers, campers, skiers, photography buffs and rockhounds have combined with the sometimes increasing demands of more traditional users (especially those seeking to exploit domestic energy resources) to place unprecedented strains on the poor land managers who must give concrete meaning to the lordly dictate of "multiple use." Increasing competition inevitably means increasing regulation and red tape for all public lands users, most dramatically illustrated, perhaps, by the increasing need to require permits for foot access into wilderness areas. Needless to say, such regulation does not please those whose private pursuits are regulated in order that the public's resources may be preserved for use by others, including future generations. It takes a certain maturity or breadth of perspective to appreciate the common good which flows from this kind of regulation, and at least the initial reaction to its imposition is likely to be hostility.

* * *

Another factor which explains why the rebellion has advanced as far as it has and as fast as it has is the lag between demographic changes and political power shifts. Many are surprised to learn that the modern West has become, by generally accepted standards of measurement, the most urban region in the country.[95] The availability of nearby public lands for recreation and the value that open spaces provide the human spirit are important parts of the lifestyle that most Westerners lead from their urban oases. Recreation and tourism are major sectors in the economies of most Western states, sometimes even outstripping more traditional pursuits such as mining, grazing and farming. But in many areas of the West, the interests of urbanites and suburbanites have not yet been effectively translated into political power in state legislatures. Where public lands are concerned, traditional agricultural, stock-raising and mining interests still tend to hold sway, though the situation is changing.

* * *

* * * I believe that the sagebrush rebellion will ultimately be viewed as representing not the beginnings of a second American Revolution, but instead a last gasp of a passing era, a poignant effort to turn back the clock to the days when competition among uses of federal lands was rare, when resources seemed inexhaustible, and when a consensus existed for exploitation. Yet there are reasons to welcome it. For one thing, it will focus attention on positive as well as negative attributes of federal land ownership, out of which may ultimately emerge an even stronger consensus for sound land management. Although concern about such management and support for federal land managers exists, it is often latent. A frontal assault like the sagebrush rebellion can be the catalyst to mobilize it. Those calling for state or private ownership will, I would suggest, ultimately find that they are a minority—that the public lands have friends and supporters in numbers greater than the rebels imagined. These supporters are not limited simply to effete eastern liberals but embrace many of diverse political persuasions in the West as well. If I am correct in surmising that these people constitute a large, if largely silent, majority, their organization around the sagebrush rebellion could prove to be a powerful force indeed.

* * *

95. * * * [I]n 1970 82.9% of the people in the West were urban, compared to a national average of 73.5%. * * *

The rebellion might also prompt a reexamination of federal financial assistance to those states with large amounts of federal lands, including the wisdom of continuing the heavy subsidies for western agriculture embodied in the federal reclamation program, the special "revenue sharing" of the Payments in Lieu of Taxes Act, and the existing schemes for sharing with the states the revenues generated from the sale and lease of federal lands and resources. Because the theory on which the rebels seek transfer of federal lands is bottomed on equity, the rebellion inevitably implicates questions of fairness among regions in the distribution of federal benefits, as well as the ownership of federal lands. Such questions have recently surfaced in federal water project funding, and ongoing efforts to bring the federal budget into balance might well make this a propitious time for scrutiny of such federal programs. If such an examination shows that the states with large amounts of federal land obtain more federal funds than other states, of course, the rebels' case is weakened. Measurements that are readily available, while admittedly crude, might give the rebels pause.

* * *

As constitutional theory, the sagebrush rebellion is fatally flawed. The rebels are surely fighting the wrong battle—for absolute ownership of all public lands rather than for more limited transfers and a greater state and local voice in federal land management. And they are fighting in the wrong place—the courts rather than in Congress and the executive land-management agencies.

Despite its legal veneer, the rebellion is, like its predecessors, a political movement. Accepting it as such, as raising questions about federal, and indeed all governmental land management, the rebellion is not wholly undesirable. I suspect, however, that the ultimate outcome will be largely counter to the rebels' objective. * * *

RICHARD W. BEHAN, RPA/NFMA—TIME TO PUNT *
79 Journal of Forestry 802 (1981).

The controversies over the management of the national forests in the 1970s—the now historic battles on the Bitterroot and Monongahela national forests—clearly called for reforms in the ways we were doing business.

During that decade, we hammered out a piece of legislation, the Resources Planning Act of 1974 as amended by the National Forest Management Act of 1976, to effect those reforms. We used the vehicle of statute to reform the management of the national forests, and I believe now, altogether after the fact, we made a serious mistake in doing so. I believe the Resources Planning Act, as amended by the National Forest Management Act, should be repealed.

* * *

I offer this opinion not as flippant iconoclasm but as a sincerely sad commentary on our contemporary fixation with legislation (and the

* Reprinted with the permission of the
Journal of Forestry.

litigation that always follows) as the main approach to public problems. I believe there are other ways and will suggest one shortly.

It is fashionable, and I think accurate, to see the Resources Planning Act as one piece of policy and the National Forest Management Act as another. * * * The Forest Service, however, is trying valiantly to cement them together, to come up with a single, smooth, up-and-down planning process. I will yield to the agency's attempt and speak of the legislation in the singular.

What do we have in general and abstract terms? A planning process as close to the classic rational and comprehensive model, and as close to perfection, as human imagination can design and implement. The legislation is long and detailed; the regulations added much specificity; the adopted procedures and FORPLAN, the analytical model that the agency insisted upon, are rational and comprehensive and at least theoretically rigorous and invincible; and the training manual for planning teams highlights and prescribes the very latest in mathematical, conceptual, and analytical elegance.

RPA/NFMA mandates with the force of law that forest plans will be rational, comprehensive, and essentially perfect. We have adopted an idealized planning process and blessed it with all the force and power and rigor of statute that a law-based society can muster.

Superficially, I suppose that's fine. I was genuinely enthusiastic as we all worked in various ways on the legislation. But a corollary of statutory perfection has become apparent lately, and it is sobering, indeed: an imperfect plan is an illegal plan, and if there is a fir tree in Oregon that will mean litigation later. And that means, ultimately, forest management by court decisions, instead of the considered judgment of professional land managers.

Without a law, you can't litigate, and that's one reason to repeal RPA/NFMA. From the land manager's point of view, repealing the law is a guaranteed way to help get forest management decisions out of the courtroom and back into the forest.

From the perspective of the various forest users, repealing the law removes the necessity for litigation. They can then pursue their several objectives with means and tactics that are certainly less expensive and potentially more effective. I refer to various species of negotiated on-the-ground settlements. When you "settle out of court," everybody wins; in litigation, only half the parties do.

But there are at least three other reasons to repeal RPA/NFMA.

One is that the requirements of legal proceedings impose a distortion on the planning process. Documentation, consistency, and correct procedure become far more important than a land manager's solid, professional, experienced judgment—the essence of resource planning, in my view. * * * And so the viability of any plan becomes more tenuous still; not only does it need to be comprehensive and perfect, but it cannot deviate from strict legal procedure. It is jeopardized from another direction.

Another reason to repeal the law is the matter of cost-effectiveness. At enormous costs in money, manpower, political energy, and activity (and legal fees), we are achieving very, very little. Neither the 1975 nor the 1980 RPA *Program* has had much, if any, effect on long-range appropriations—or even annual appropriations—for the Forest Service. That was the original intent of the act, as I recall.

And the final reason, I believe, is the most serious of all. Because it is mandated in law, the forest planning process now has the capability of paralyzing or displacing completely the management and production responsibilities of the agency.

* * *

Origin and Irony of RPA/NFMA

RPA/NFMA is an enormously costly program without visible or tangible benefit, and certainly no one wanted that. How did we get it? There is much irony in the story; we got RPA/NFMA by the dedicated, continuous, often brilliant hard work of the various actors in the process, all of whom did exactly the jobs their roles called for.

There was a group of hell raisers who drew attention to the issue. There was a group of policy professionals who fashioned and passed two successive pieces of legislation—a demanding and difficult task. And there was group of technical hotshots who fleshed out the details and provided some tools. Each group performed magnificently, but at each stage there emerged a major error that can't be attributed, in my mind, to any particular person, organization, or institution. "Sinister forces"? Maybe. Or just the random glitches and hassles that characterize human enterprise? In any case, the errors are apparent with a clarity that is altogether retroactive.

* * *

The irony that I mentioned earlier is indeed extreme. All the way through the story of developing and implementing RPA/NFMA, everyone did his or her best. And most of the time that was very good. But we lost control of the process somehow and somewhere; it got away from us. Every step seemed logical and competently accomplished at the time, and singly the steps still do; only in the aggregate, and only at the end, has the product become intolerable.

* * *

RPA/NFMA is a monster on the landscape, and I am compelled to suggest an axiom: Idealized, perfect planning that is mandated in law, and constrained only by an agency's budget, will exhaust that budget. And, given manpower ceilings, planning efforts can expand only at the expense of other activities. There will come a time when the Forest Service can do nothing but plan, and all its management, production, and protection activities will cease.

There are some Forest Service people who think that day is very near at hand. The morale problem that RPA/NFMA caused in the agency is real, acute, and growing. It is easy, reflecting on the heritage of the Forest Service, to see why; The agency has a long tradition of hard work, dedication, and "can-do" accomplishment; but we have given it, this time, an impossible task.

RPA/FMA cannot be made to work. Its flaw is fundamental: it is a *law*, and it needs to be repealed. We failed, in our collective problem solving, by placing too much faith in planning and by placing far too much faith in statute. It is time to punt.

* * *

SALLY K. FAIRFAX, BARBARA T. ANDREWS & ANDREW P. BUCHSBAUM, FEDERALISM AND THE WILD AND SCENIC RIVERS ACT: NOW YOU SEE IT, NOW YOU DON'T *

59 Wash.L.Rev. 417 (1984).

In July 1980, then Governor Edmund Brown, Jr. nominated 4000 miles of California's North Coast rivers for inclusion in the National Wild and Scenic River System. It seemed an obvious ploy: in signing separate legislation that would complete the California Water Project by building a long-debated canal across the Sacramento-San Joaquin River Delta, Governor Brown had offended the environmental community. He hoped that his proposal for additional protection for the North Coast rivers would placate environmentalists, while simultaneously giving the state a broader opportunity to administer federal lands adjacent to the rivers.

By 1984, after expensive litigation and extensive campaigning, the North Coast river designations have stalled and the canal has at least temporarily evaporated. What looked like a casebook example of federal-state cooperation to achieve long-standing and well-defined state and national goals has turned into an unpredictable stewpot of shifting economic interests, changing government personnel, and conflicting public policies. As the laws and regulations have evolved, so have the alliances, their goals, and their tactics.

Governor Brown's 1980 proposal was based on an unfamiliar provision of the Wild and Scenic Rivers Act (WSRA) that allows governors to request federal protection for state-protected rivers. * * * The governor's request came near the close of the Carter Administration; working in great haste and in close cooperation with the California State Resources Agency, the Department of the Interior completed its review of the request in January, 1981. Interior Secretary Andrus had literally but a few hours to act on Governor Brown's request before turning his office over to the incoming Reagan Administration. The tight timing suggested procedural irregularity and invited numerous court challenges.

A major congressional purpose behind WSRA was to control water development. However, water issues only partially motivated Governor Brown's request. A state effort to control federal land management was a major impetus behind his rather extraordinary use of the

* Reprinted with permission of the University of Washington Law Review.

statute. This was particularly true regarding the Smith River, the most pristine of the North Coast streams and the only one running almost entirely through national forest lands. Because the federal Act gives the state a role in managing federally designated rivers, inclusion of the Smith River in the system could enhance California's effort to push North Coast forest management more towards fisheries and aesthetic management and away from timber harvest. If all 3100 miles of the Smith and its tributaries were included in the national system, huge acreages of forest land would be affected.

Secretary Andrus' cliff-hanger decision, while appearing responsive to Governor Brown's initiative, left most of the Smith River out of the national system. As a result, Governor Brown's effort to use WSRA to influence federal land management was deflected. The implications of the program for future state sorties into federal land management are still unclear, and will continue to evolve on the North Coast with implications for similar state efforts elsewhere in the nation.

* * * The shifting legal framework and changing economic and political interests in the North Coast controversy are particularly enlightening to students of federalism. Lawyers are among those who may be tempted to view the North Coast controversy in terms of federal-state conflict or intergovernmental cooperation run amuck, and to view the courts as an umpire in a dispute over authority.

Unfortunately, such an approach would reveal very little that is useful about what has occurred. The details of the story challenge familiar notions: (1) that the federal-state conflict is the core of federalism; (2) that cooperation between governments is preferable to confrontation; and (3) that the role of the courts is to act (or to refrain from acting) as umpires in the conflict.

The traditional federal-state conflict model suggests implacable, clearly identifiable foes locked in battle over authority and control. The North Coast story is one of complex and shifting alliances that does not, except for temporary convenience, form around identifiable—let alone permanent—ties to a particular level of government or an institutional configuration. *Part* of the state—particularly the Resources Agency and the Governor—was initially at odds with *part* of the federal government—the United States Forest Service—over priorities for North Coast river management. There was, however, great cooperation between the Resources Agency and other federal entities, agencies in the Department of the Interior, in pressing for the controversial river designations. Neither the cooperation nor the conflict has been stable largely because the players are not stable. Moreover, the Forest Service, target of the initial action, regularly cooperates on other issues with the Resources Agency and with many other state agencies, who frequently sue their North Coast partners in the Department of the Interior. Changing coalitions of affected groups reflect the incomplete divisions between and among timber, fisheries, mineral, water, recreation, and aesthetic interest groups and their various state and county government allies. Evolving conditions shift alliances and alter both the "state" and the "federal" positions. This volatility is enhanced by the changing of administrations in both Washington and Sacramento. The insufficiency of the traditional federal conflict model is underscored by the tension between the designation controversy, which could be forced to fit fleetingly into the format, and the larger and more durable controversy about resource management priorities which involves significantly different players, issues, and interactions.

Cooperative federalism theorists will likewise find little succor in the North Coast controversy. Cooperation in the North Coast situation is less obviously a public virtue than standard theories of cooperative federalism would indicate, or than the elated environmental groups, thrilled by Governor Brown's flashy proposal, might lead one to believe. Moreover, the concept applies only momentarily to a small subset of the complex pattern of interactions which comprise the policy field.

Finally, the role of the courts in this controversy is neither so pivotal nor so profound as one might anticipate on the basis of the "court as the umpire of federalism" concept. Very few instances of litigated federal-state conflict actually involve state and federal parties or major constitutional principles. The North Coast situation is not an exception. Although it is possible that the state could become a plaintiff in a suit against the Secretary of the Interior, they began litigation as not-wholly-comfortable allies defending the designations. The basic dispute was among competing private groups. The litigants are a typical garden-crop of special interests seeking to defend an advantage or prevent a barrier to their own positions. Interestingly, it was a fragile coalition of California *counties* which initially challenged Governor Brown's proposal. The legal issues include a rather confusing National Environmental Policy Act (NEPA) compliance question, and an important but only slightly weightier statutory interpretation. Both are critical in the designation issue but are largely unrelated to the resource management disputes that are the heart of the conflict.

JOSEPH L. SAX, MOUNTAINS WITHOUT HANDRAILS: REFLECTIONS ON THE NATIONAL PARKS *
103–09 (1980).

It must seem curious that a book about the national parks talks so little about nature for its own sake, and may even seem to denigrate ecosystem preservation as central to the mission of the parks. My only explanation is that most conflict over national park policy does not really turn on whether we ought to have nature reserves (for that is widely agreed), but on the uses that people will make of those places— which is neither a subject of general agreement nor capable of resolution by reference to ecological principles. The preservationists are really moralists at heart, and people are very much at the center of their concerns. They encourage people to immerse themselves in

* Reprinted with permission from the University of Michigan Press.

natural settings and to behave there in certain ways, because they believe such behavior is redeeming.

Moreover, the preservationists do not merely aspire to persuade individuals how to conduct their personal lives. With the exception of Thoreau, who predated the national park era, they have directed their prescriptions to government. The parks are, after all, public institutions which belong to everyone, not just to wilderness hikers. The weight of the preservationist view, therefore, turns not only on its persuasiveness for the individual as such, but also on its ability to garner the support—or at least the tolerance—of citizens in a democratic society to bring the preservationist vision into operation as official policy. It is not enough to accept the preservationists simply as a minority, speaking for a minority, however impressive. For that reason I have described them as secular prophets, preaching a message of secular salvation. I have attempted to articulate their views as a public philosophy, rather than treating them merely as spokesmen for an avocation of nature appreciation, because the claims they make on government oblige them to bear the weightier burden.

This is not to say that what they preach cannot be rejected as merely a matter of taste, of elitist sentiment or as yet another reworking of pastoral sentimentalism. It is, however, to admit that their desire to dominate a public policy for public parks cannot prevail if their message is taken in so limited a compass. If they cannot persuade a majority that the country needs national parks of the kind they propose, much as it needs public schools and libraries, then the role they have long sought to play in the governmental process cannot be sustained. The claim is bold, and it has often been concealed in a pastiche of argument for scientific protection of nature, minority rights, and sentimental rhetoric. I have tried to isolate and make explicit the political claim, as it relates to the fashioning of public policy, and leave it to sail or sink on that basis.

It may also seem curious that I have put the preservationists into the foreground, rather than the Congress or the National Park Service. Of course Congress has the power to be paternalistic if it wishes, and it often is. It thinks a lot of things are good for us, from free trade and a nuclear defense system to public statuary and space exploration. But no unkindness is intended by the observation that Congress doesn't really think at all. At best it responds to the ideas that thinkers put before it, considers the merits of those thoughts, tests them against its sense of the larger themes that give American society coherence, and asks whether the majority will find them attractive or tolerable. The fundamental question then—and the question I have tried to address here—is whether the ideas of nature preservationists meet these tests. If they do, Congress will ultimately reflect them.

The National Park Service, and other bureaucracies that manage nature reserves, are also basically reflective institutions. Strictly speaking, they enforce the rules Congress makes, doing what they are told. But no administrative agency is in fact so mechanical in its operation. It has its own sense of mission, an internal conception of what it ought to be doing, and that sense of mission also harks back to what thinkers have persuaded it, institutionally, to believe. If the Park Service is basically dominated by the ideology of the preservationists, it will act in certain ways, given the opportunity. If, on the other hand, it has come to believe in the commodity-view of the parks, it will behave quite differently. Thus, again, the capacity of the preservationist view to persuade is the essential issue.

At the same time, no bureaucracy behaves simply according to its own sense of mission. It lives in a political milieu, with constituencies of users and neighbors who impose strong, and at times irresistable, pressures on it. What the general public believes about the appropriate mission of the national parks is also essential. If the preservationist is to prevail, he must gain at least the passive support of the public, which will indirectly be felt by the Park Service in the decisions it makes in day to day management.

* * *

To those for whom wilderness values and the symbolic message of the parks has never been of more than peripheral importance, this book asks principally for tolerance: a willingness to entertain the suggestion that the parks are more valuable as artifacts of culture than as commodity resources; a willingness to try a new departure in the use of leisure more demanding than conventional recreation; a sympathetic ear tuned to the claim for self-paternalism.

[T]o the preservationists themselves, in whose ranks I include myself, the message is that the parks are not self-justifying. Your vision is not necessarily one that will commend itself to the majority. It rests on a set of moral and aesthetic attitudes whose force is not strengthened either by contemptuous disdain of those who question your conception of what a national park should be, or by taking refuge in claims of ecological necessity. Tolerance is required on all sides, along with a certain modesty. "I have gone a-fishing while others were struggling and groaning and losing their souls in the great social or political or business maelstrom," the nature writer John Burroughs observed late in his life. "I know too I have gone a-fishing while others have labored in the slums and given their lives to the betterment of their fellows. But I have been a good fisherman, and I should have made a poor reformer. * * * My strength is my calm, my serenity."

Chapter Two

HISTORY OF PUBLIC LAND LAW

The policy of the United States toward the lands it acquired has changed drastically over the course of two centuries. Until 1976, the official federal policy was to sell or give away the public lands and resources to private owners and to states in order that the Nation would be tamed, farmed, and developed. Grants to individuals were made by credit or cash sale and later by homesteading and special purpose homesteading. Outright land grants to new and admitted states were made to further education, transportation, and other purposes. A vast amount of land was granted to railroads in return for construction of the rails that opened up the West. Other laws allowed the private acquisition of timber and mineral resources essentially for free. By these means, approximately one and a quarter billion acres became private land.

From the beginning, federal policy favored the small farmer, and, from the beginning, various means were used by private claimants to circumvent legal restrictions aimed at preventing "monopoly" and aggrandizement. But the chicanery, fraud, and perjury that permeated public land administration also contributed to sentiment for various reform proposals. Toward the end of the 19th century, the policy emphasis began shifting. At first, a few parcels were "withdrawn" from the operation of the disposition laws; some were "reserved" by the federal government for specific purposes. A classification process evolved by which certain federal lands were deemed chiefly valuable for one or more specific uses. Reserved public lands required protection from private trespassers; the public land management machinery grew up first to meet that need and later to enhance the productivity of the public lands. Depletion of mineral, timber, and forage resources in the first third of the 20th century led to further restrictions on federal largess and accentuated the trend toward permanent ownership and active management. Large scale disposition ended in 1934, but several states have claimed title to some federal lands within their borders, and the current Administration has tried to sell off some federal holdings. Despite those movements, the likely future trend is in the direction of continued retention of federal lands and reacquisition of lands by the United States for primarily non-economic uses such as recreation and wildlife protection. Public land law history is a complicated and intricate mosaic, many pieces of which often appear unrelated or internally inconsistent, but some themes constantly recur.

It is impossible to comprehend contemporary public land controversies fully without an understanding of public land law history. The standard terms still in current use, such as "withdrawal," "entry," "location," "patent," or "in lieu selection," are foreign to those not versed in historical development. Modern public land litigation frequently hinges on interpretation of century-old statutes or cases. From a recitation of how the United States became the owner of its continental territory, this chapter will proceed to the ways in which the Nation disposed of two-thirds of its conquests and purchases. The disposition policies and the actions taken to further them are grouped according to the main beneficiaries: states; farmers and ranchers; miners; railroads; irrigators; and loggers. The rise of the conservation movement and the change in policy from disposition to retention are highlighted thereafter, and the final sections introduce the developments leading to present federal land systems.

This chapter was compiled from many sources. The primary authorities include P. Gates, HISTORY OF PUBLIC LAND LAW DEVELOPMENT (1968); L. Peffer, THE CLOSING OF THE PUBLIC DOMAIN (1951); B.H. Hibbard, A HISTORY OF PUBLIC LAND POLICIES (1924, U.Wis.ed.1965); S.T. Dana, FOREST AND RANGE POLICY (1956); S. Dana & S. Fairfax, FOREST AND RANGE POLICY (2d Ed. 1980). For popular but highly instructive works that bear upon the history of the public lands, see, e.g., W. Stegner, BEYOND THE HUNDREDTH MERIDIAN: JOHN WESLEY POWELL AND THE SECOND OPENING OF THE WEST (1953); B. Devoto, 1946: YEAR OF DECISION (1942); M. Twain, ROUGHING IT (1872); A. Leopold, A SAND COUNTY ALMANAC WITH ESSAYS ON CONSERVATION FROM ROUND VALLEY (1966); T.H. Watkins & C. Watson, THE LANDS NO ONE KNOWS: AMERICA AND THE PUBLIC DOMAIN (1975).

A. ACQUISITION OF THE PUBLIC DOMAIN

All of the land the United States has acquired on the North American continent was previously "owned" both by foreign nations and by Indian tribes. Federal acquisition came about by a combination of purchase and conquest.

Upon ratification of the Constitution, the infant United States gained title to the lands between the Alleghenies and the Mississippi. It had taken more than 170 years for settlement to begin in this New West, an area larger than the original thirteen colonies. Such a huge area might have been expected to satisfy even the most voracious land hunger for many years; opportunity and opportunism so coincided in the next eighty years, however, that national land ownership expanded another fourfold.

1. FROM FOREIGN NATIONS

At the time of the Revolution, only England, Spain, and Russia had claims to land in North America. Dutch and Swedish claims had long been extinguished and the French government had been defeated and ejected from the continent a generation before. The British settlements in Canada attracted the continuing but unsuccessful attention of

American expansionists. Other lands claimed by the English and the Spanish (and later the Mexicans) gradually succumbed to Manifest Destiny. Acquisition of the tenuous Russian claims was last and easiest.

In the 1790's, the population of the United States expanded 35%, three new states were admitted, and national economic policies brought about stability, prosperity, and new settlement. Beyond the Alleghenies, trade was necessarily funnelled through New Orleans and other Spanish-held ports on the Mississippi. Ill-feeling and annoyance from trade restrictions and runaway slave havens abounded, even though the Pinckney Treaty of 1795 confirmed the right of navigation on the Mississippi. When Spain ceded its Louisiana lands to France in 1800, the greatest menace yet to the new Republic was created.

a. LOUISIANA PURCHASE

The negotiations that Jefferson began with Napoleon for the purchase of New Orleans were greatly aided by the decimation of a French expeditionary force in Santo Domingo. Although doubtful that he could accept without constitutional amendment, Jefferson could not refuse Napoleon's unexpected and unparalleled offer to sell the entire Louisiana Territory. A grave danger was turned into a great political victory, and 523 million acres were added to the public domain in 1803 for three cents an acre, doubling the American territory.

New England Federalists were unhappy with Western prospects, fearing the growing influence of the radical Republican representatives from the frontiers. Lewis and Clark presently penetrated the new territory and beyond, but settlement proceeded mostly east of the Mississippi. Louisiana was admitted to statehood in 1812 and Missouri in 1821, however. The slavery question began to loom larger.

b. FLORIDA ACQUISITION

Irritations on remaining borders with Spanish territory did not cease after unfettered commerce was established. Indians raided Georgia from the Spanish holdings and slaves sought freedom in them. In 1817–19, Indian conflicts became acute in Florida, whereupon Andrew Jackson crossed into Florida and defeated the Creeks. He also summarily executed their leaders and two accused British instigators, all of which Spanish officials were powerless to prevent. Spain accepted the inevitable and agreed to surrender East and West Florida and its claims to the Oregon Territory in exchange for only a guarantee of its Texas border and United States payment of claims. In 1818, Great Britain agreed to extend the Canadian border along the 49th parallel from Minnesota to the Rocky Mountains; the United States thus gained undisputed title to the rich Red River Valley. A similar dispute over the boundary of Maine was not settled until 1842.

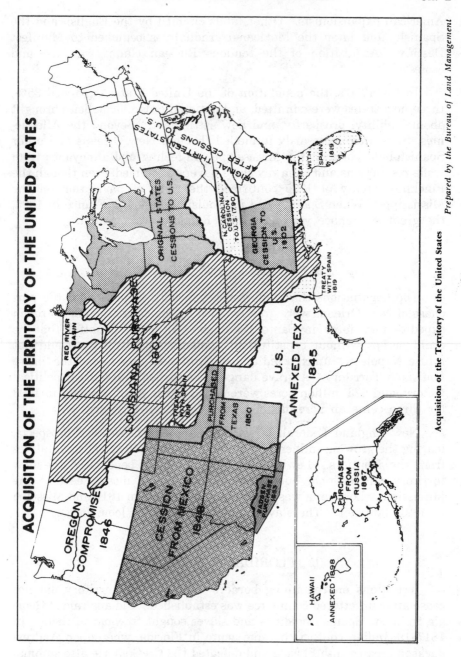

Acquisition of the Territory of the United States

Prepared by the Bureau of Land Management

c. TEXAS, THE TREATY OF GUADALOUPE HIDALGO, AND THE GADSDEN PURCHASE

Hundreds of millions of acres of productive land remained unsettled in the first half of the 19th century, but the insatiable American land hunger led explorers and settlers further afield. The storied Mountain Men, with the indomitable Jedidiah Smith in the vanguard, explored most of the unknown West while decimating the beaver in the

Rockies. Stephan Austin established colonies in Texas, Marcus Whitman led settlers to Oregon, and Brigham Young took the Mormon Saints to the inhospitable "place" that became Utah. Then, between 1845 and 1853, the United States acquired another 781 million acres, of which 613 million acres were added to the public domain.

After Mexico gained its independence, it made the mistake of contracting with promoters such as Austin to bring in American settlers. The generous grant terms offered to Texas immigrants were taken up by 20,000 Americans and their 1000 slaves by 1830. The Mexican officials quickly regretted their invitation, however, and the Americans quickly resented Mexican rule, especially efforts to outlaw slavery and to require Catholicism. The Alamo and Texas independence ensued in 1835–36.

But the newly independent "nation" was unexpectedly refused admission into the United States for another nine years because of the slavery question. Under the Missouri Compromise of 1820, northern legislators had anticipated only two more slave states; they were now unwilling to admit an area (46 times the size of Massachusetts) in which five or six additional "slavocracies" could be created. Manifest Destiny eventually won out: the 1844 election of James K. Polk was a victory for expansion, and Texas was annexed and then admitted the following year.

Admission, however, was on different terms than admission of other new states. During its Independence, Texas had granted away some 30 million acres but still had a huge debt, fueled by many questionable tricks of finance to which the Texans had been compelled to resort. The United States left the remaining lands in the possession of the new State to avoid investigating prior practices and to avoid assuming the Texas debt financing. After annexation, Texas sold 79 million acres of its western lands (now parts of New Mexico, Oklahoma, Wyoming, Colorado, and Kansas) to the federal government, the only Texas acreage initially to enter the public domain.

Boundary and other disputes with Mexico continued, and negotiations failed while feeling ran high. A Mexican incursion into the disputed territory gave President Polk a pretext for declaring war, and the Mexicans were soundly defeated. In the 1848 Treaty of Guadaloupe Hidalgo, Mexico ceded most of the Southwest including California to the United States for $15 million. For a pittance, the Nation gained title to spectacular scenic resources including the Grand Canyon, San Francisco Bay, and the Uinta Mountains, as well as to the vast mineral wealth in the arid mountains.

But shortly thereafter, with railroads being projected or promoted in all directions, it was seen that a New Orleans to San Diego line would require additional land for a favorable route. In 1853, James Gadsden negotiated the purchase of Arizona below the Gila River from Mexico for $10 million, completing the acquisition of contiguous territory.

d. THE OREGON COMPROMISE

In the meantime, the United States had agreed with Great Britain on the northwest boundary. The area around the Columbia had long been used by the Hudson's Bay Company in its trapping operations, but the British were overwhelmed by the influx of American settlers in the 1840's, and the beaver had virtually disappeared. Recognizing the inevitable, England agreed to a boundary fixed at the 49th parallel, except that Vancouver Island below that line was retained for Canada. The settlement of the Oregon question added 180 million acres north of California to the public domain.

e. THE ALASKA PURCHASE

The surprising acquisition of Alaska had not been preceded by public demand or even public discussion. The Russians were anxious to sell, however, and Secretary of State Seward wanted to buy, so the transaction was quickly consummated. For $7.2 million, the United States purchased an enormous unsurveyed area only slightly touched by human habitation.

Alaska was the last purchase or conquest that increased the federal public domain lands. Later acquisitions of Hawaii, Puerto Rico, the Philippines, Guam, Samoa, the Virgin Islands, and smaller Pacific islands made no addition to the public lands except for buildings, parks, and minor reservations.

The lands acquired from foreign nations between 1789 and 1867 were also subject to the claims of their inhabitants, the American Indians.

2. FROM INDIAN TRIBES

The American Indians did not have highly developed notions of private property but nevertheless fiercely resisted white intrusions into their ancestral tribal lands. They were, of course, subdued eventually, and tribal members were assimilated, killed, or removed to "reservations." All foreign claims to present United States territory were extinguished over a century ago, but questions of Indian title and of reparations for 18th and 19th century transactions are still being litigated.

The following opinion by Chief Justice John Marshall is a landmark in public land law. It reconciled the property rights of the United States, American Indian tribes, foreign nations, and the settlers anxious to obtain title to real property on the frontier. In doing so, the Court laid the legal predicates for the federal disposition program and the westward expansion.

JOHNSON v. M'INTOSH

Supreme Court of the United States, 1823.
21 U.S. (8 Wheat.) 543.

[The litigation involved title to land within what is now the State of Illinois. Plaintiffs claimed title based on grants in 1773 and 1775 from chiefs of the Illinois and Piankeshaw tribes. In 1795, the tribes entered into treaties with the United States, retaining certain lands as reservations but ceding to the federal government the lands earlier transferred to the plaintiffs' predecessors in title. In 1818, the United States granted to defendant M'Intosh a patent to the parcels in question. Plaintiffs then brought this quiet title action.]

MARSHALL, Ch.J., delivered the opinion of the court. * * *
The inquiry, therefore, is, in a great measure, confined to the power of Indians to give, and of private individuals to receive, a title, which can be sustained in the courts of this country.

* * *

On the discovery of this immense continent, the great nations of Europe were eager to appropriate to themselves so much of it as they could respectively acquire. Its vast extent offered an ample field to the ambition and enterprise of all; and the character and religion of its inhabitants afforded an apology for considering them as a people over whom the superior genius of Europe might claim an ascendency. The potentates of the old world found no difficulty in convincing themselves that they made ample compensation to the inhabitants of the new, by bestowing on them civilization and Christianity, in exchange for unlimited independence. But as they were all in pursuit of nearly the same object, it was necessary, in order to avoid conflicting settlements, and consequent war with each other, to establish a principle, which all should acknowledge as the law by which the right of acquisition, which they all asserted, should be regulated, as between themselves. This principle was, that discovery gave title to the government by whose subjects, or by whose authority, it was made, against all other European governments, which title might be consummated by possession.

The exclusion of all other Europeans, necessarily gave to the nation making the discovery the sole right of acquiring the soil from the natives, and establishing settlements upon it. It was a right with which no Europeans could interfere. It was a right which all asserted for themselves, and to the assertion of which, by others, all assented.
* * *

* * *

In the establishment of these relations, the rights of the original inhabitants were, in no instance, entirely disregarded; but were, necessarily, to a considerable extent, impaired. They were admitted to be the rightful occupants of the soil, with a legal as well as just claim to retain possession of it, and to use it according to their own discretion; but their rights to complete sovereignty, as independent nations, were necessarily diminished, and their power to dispose of the soil, at their own will, to whomsoever they pleased, was denied by the original fundamental principle, that discovery gave exclusive title to those who made it.

While the different nations of Europe respected the right of the natives, as occupants, they asserted the ultimate dominion to be in themselves; and claimed and exercised, as a consequence of this ultimate dominion, a power to grant the soil, while yet in possession of the natives. These grants have been understood by all, to convey a title to the grantees, subject only to the Indian right of occupancy.

The history of America, from its discovery to the present day, proves, we think, the universal recognition of these principles.

[The opinion then discussed various competing claims, many dating to the 15th and 16th centuries, to the New World by Spain, Great Britain, Portugal, France, and Holland.]

* * *

The contests between the cabinets of Versailles and Madrid, respecting the territory on the northern coast of the gulf of Mexico, were fierce and bloody; and continued, until the establishment of a Bourbon on the throne of Spain, produced such amicable dispositions in the two crowns, as to suspend or terminate them.

Between France and Great Britain, whose discoveries as well as settlements were nearly contemporaneous, contests for the country, actually covered by the Indians, began as soon as their settlements approached each other * * *.

* * *

These conflicting claims produced a long and bloody war, which was terminated by the conquest of the whole country east of the Mississippi. In the treaty of 1763, France ceded and guaranteed to Great Britain, all Nova Scotia, or Acadie, and Canada, with their dependencies; and it was agreed, that the boundaries between the territories of the two nations, in America, should be irrevocably fixed by a line drawn from the source of the Mississippi, through the middle of that river and the lakes Maurepas and Ponchartrain, to the sea. This treaty expressly cedes, and has always been understood to cede, the whole country, on the English side of the dividing line, between the two nations, although a great and valuable part of it was occupied by the Indians. Great Britain, on her part, surrendered to France all her pretensions to the country west of the Mississippi. It has never been supposed that she surrendered nothing, although she was not in actual possession of a foot of land. She surrendered all right to acquire the country; and any after attempt to purchase it from the Indians, would have been considered and treated as an invasion of the territories of France.

By the 20th article of the same treaty, Spain ceded Florida, with its dependencies, and all the country she claimed east or southeast of the Mississippi, to Great Britain. Great part of this territory also was in possession of the Indians.

By a secret treaty, which was executed about the same time, France ceded Louisiana to Spain; and Spain has since retroceded the same country to France. At the time both of its cession and retrocession, it was occupied, chiefly, by the Indians.

Thus, all the nations of Europe, who have acquired territory on this continent, have asserted in themselves, and have recognised in others, the exclusive right of the discoverer to appropriate the lands occupied by the Indians. Have the American States rejected or adopted this principle?

By the treaty which concluded the war of our revolution, Great Britain relinquished all claim, not only to the government, but to the "propriety and territorial rights of the United States," whose boundaries were fixed in the second article. By this treaty, the powers of government, and the right to soil, which had previously been in Great Britain, passed definitively to these States. * * *

* * *

After these States became independent, a controversy subsisted between them and Spain respecting boundary. By the treaty of 1795, this controversy was adjusted, and Spain ceded to the United States the territory in question. This territory, though claimed by both nations, was chiefly in the actual occupation of Indians.

The magnificent purchase of Louisiana, was the purchase from France of a country almost entirely occupied by numerous tribes of Indians, who are in fact independent. Yet, any attempt of others to intrude into that country, would be considered as an aggression which would justify war.

Our late acquisitions from Spain are of the same character; and the negotiations which preceded those acquisitions, recognise and elucidate the principle which has been received as the foundation of all European title in America.

The United States, then, have unequivocally acceded to that great and broad rule by which its civilized inhabitants now hold this country. They hold, and assert in themselves, the title by which it was acquired. They maintain, as all others have maintained, that discovery gave an exclusive right to extinguish the Indian title of occupancy, either by purchase or by conquest; and gave also a right to such a degree of sovereignty, as the circumstances of the people would allow them to exercise.

* * *

* * * Conquest gives a title which the courts of the conqueror cannot deny, whatever the private and speculative opinions of individuals may be, respecting the original justice of the claim which has been successfully asserted. The British government, which was then our government, and whose rights have passed to the United States, asserted a title to all the lands occupied by Indians, within the chartered limits of the British colonies. It asserted also a limited sovereignty over them, and the exclusive right of extinguishing the titles which occupancy gave to them. These claims have been maintained and

established as far west as the river Mississippi, by the sword. The title to a vast portion of the lands we now hold, originates in them. It is not for the courts of this country to question the validity of this title, or to sustain one which is incompatible with it.

* * *

[T]he tribes of Indians inhabiting this country were fierce savages, whose occupation was war, and whose subsistence was drawn chiefly from the forest. To leave them in possession of their country, was to leave the country a wilderness; to govern them as a distinct people, was impossible, because they were as brave and as high-spirited as they were fierce, and were ready to repel by arms every attempt on their independence.

* * *

Frequent and bloody wars, in which the whites were not always the aggressors, unavoidably ensued. European policy, numbers and skill prevailed. As the white population advanced, that of the Indians necessarily receded. The country in the immediate neighbourhood of agriculturists became unfit for them. The game fled into thicker and more unbroken forests, and the Indians followed. The soil, to which the crown originally claimed title, being no longer occupied by its ancient inhabitants, was parcelled out according to the will of the sovereign power, and taken possession of by persons who claimed immediately from the crown, or mediately, through its grantees or deputies.

* * *

However extravagant the pretension of converting the discovery of an inhabited country into conquest may appear; if the principle has been asserted in the first instance, and afterwards sustained; if a country has been acquired and held under it; if the property of the great mass of the community originates in it, it becomes the law of the land, and cannot be questioned. So too, with respect to the concomitant principle, that the Indian inhabitants are to be considered merely as occupants, to be protected, indeed, while in peace, in the possession of their lands, but to be deemed incapable of transferring the absolute title to others. However this restriction may be opposed to natural right, and to the usages of civilized nations, yet, if it be indispensible to that system under which the country has been settled, and be adapted to the actual condition of the two people, it may, perhaps, be supported by reason, and certainly cannot be rejected by Courts of justice.

* * *

[The Court affirmed the judgment of the District Court of Illinois in favor of defendant M'Intosh.]

NOTES

1. Johnson v. M'Intosh was the major early opinion dealing with Indian title (also called aboriginal title or Indian right of occupancy). Indian title was created by the doctrine of discovery: when a European nation planted a flag and claimed a vast region in the New World, the

absolute possession of Indians was transmuted into Indian title. Among other things, this unique property interest allows Indian tribes to reside, hunt, and fish upon their aboriginal lands; transfer title only to the United States; and sue trespassing parties for damages. Indian title is not a compensable property interest under the Fifth Amendment, and can be taken by the United States without payment of just compensation, but Indian title cannot be affected by the actions of states or private parties. On Indian title, see F. Cohen, HANDBOOK OF FEDERAL INDIAN LAW 486–93 (1982 ed.).

Although Johnson v. M'Intosh acknowledged the right of the United States to obtain Indian title by conquest, the federal government has usually dealt with tribes by treaty. Congress ended treaty-making with Indian tribes in 1871, but the United States continued the process of clearing Indian title and establishing reservations by other means, primarily statutes and executive orders. A leading authority estimates that these transactions resulted in the payment to tribes of between 500 million and one billion dollars. See generally Cohen, Original Indian Title, 32 Minn.L.Rev. 28 (1947). In other cases, takings of Indian lands were not compensated at the time; in 1946, Congress passed the Indian Claims Commission Act to allow payment to some of those tribes. 25 U.S.C.A. §§ 70–70v–1. See generally Friedman, Interest on Indian Claims: Judicial Protection of the Fisc, 5 Valparaiso L.Rev. 26 (1970).

The creation of the Indian reservation system has in most instances eliminated Indian title. Most tribes, by treaty or otherwise, have transferred the majority of their aboriginal lands to the United States and reserved some of the remaining lands to themselves. These transactions had the effect of resolving Indian title: tribes own their reservation lands, which are protected by the Fifth Amendment and held in trust by the United States; Indian title was cleared as to the ceded lands, which the United States was free to open for homesteading or devote to other purposes.

2. Indian title has had continuing importance in three respects. First, as Johnson v. M'Intosh held, Indian land transactions are valid only if approved by the United States. This rule, codified in the Indian Trade and Intercourse Act of 1790, 25 U.S.C.A. § 177, regularized frontier property dealings and allowed reasonably orderly homesteading. Second, some old transactions, thought to be valid, were flawed because they had never been sanctioned by the United States, as required by Johnson v. M'Intosh and the Trade and Intercourse Act. This has resulted in a number of Indian land claims, most notably in the East and Alaska. Recently, the Supreme Court held invalid a 1795 land transfer from the Oneida Nation to the State of New York, never approved by Congress, and ruled that the tribe's suit for possession was not barred by the statute of limitations or other defenses based on the passage of time. See Oneida County v. Oneida Indian Nation, 105 S.Ct. 1245 (1985). See generally Clinton & Hotopp, Judicial Enforcement of the Federal Restraints on Alienation of Indian Land: The Origins of the Eastern Land Claims, 31 Maine L. Rev. 17 (1979). Several Indian

land claims have been settled, with the tribes receiving title to part of their aboriginal lands. See, e.g., Maine Claims Settlement Act of 1980, 25 U.S.C.A. §§ 1721–35; Alaska Native Claims Settlement Act of 1971, 43 U.S.C. §§ 1601–28.

Third, federal land agencies are limited in their ability to dispose of or manage lands where Congress has not extinguished Indian title. Thus a land patent involving lands to which Indian title had not been cleared was held invalid in Cramer v. United States, 261 U.S. 219 (1923). See also United States v. Santa Fe Pacific R. Co., 314 U.S. 339 (1941). More recently, Western Shoshone Indians argued that certain BLM grazing leases were unauthorized because Indian title to 13 million acres in western Nevada had never been extinguished. The Court held in United States v. Dann, 105 S.Ct. 1058 (1985), that title had been extinguished because the tribe had been compensated in a money damages case brought pursuant to the Indian Claims Commissions Act of 1946. In most areas, it is assumed that Indian title has been extinguished to lands administered by federal agencies, but, as *Dann* shows, there remain some situations in which congressional action—by treaty or otherwise—may not have occurred or may be disputed.

3. Today, some 53 million acres of Indian reservation lands are held in trust by the United States for Indian tribes and individuals. They are not properly public lands, because they must be managed for the benefit of specific beneficiaries. Thus an additional decision-maker, the tribal government, is involved when resource development is considered. Nevertheless, Indian lands cannot be completely disassociated from modern public land policy because the Bureau of Indian Affairs is located in the Department of Interior, because some public works projects are located partially or completely on Indian lands, and because private parties seek to develop tribal resources under Department of Interior leasing and contracting procedures that in some cases resemble procedures employed on the public lands. See generally F. Cohen, HANDBOOK OF FEDERAL INDIAN LAW (1982 ed.); P. Maxfield, M. Dieterich & F. Trelease, NATURAL RESOURCES LAW ON AMERICAN INDIAN LANDS (1977).

4. What kind of title to real estate did the United States receive from the European nations when it executed treaties with them? What steps did the United States need to take in order to "clear" title obtained from foreign nations so that the United States could dispose of land for settlement? What is the chain of title to the public domain?

B. DISPOSITION OF THE PUBLIC DOMAIN

1. EARLY PUBLIC LAND POLICY AND PROBLEMS

Before the Revolution, speculation in the unsettled western lands and squatting upon them were already common habits of the colonists. Other colonial practices that became entrenched in public policy or tradition included rewarding war veterans with a grant of lands, the

failure to survey before allowing settlement, and the recurrent shady
dealing that sometimes erupted into public scandal. Several colonies
had charters extending their borders to the Mississippi, and the colonial
patrons, governors, and legislatures encouraged expansion in that direction by various means, some legal. After the Revolution, as a part of
the agreement on the new federal Constitution, the original states
ceded to the United States most of their claims to the lands beyond
their present boundaries. The original states then, together with
Vermont, Maine, Tennessee and Kentucky (and, later, Texas and Hawaii), were never considered "public land" states, because the federal
government never had appreciable ownership of lands within their
borders. The sharp contrast in the amount of federal land holdings
was the beginning of a rift between eastern and western states over
public land policy that continues today. As early as 1776, Maryland
demanded some of the western lands for its own benefit, and in 1821 it
was still calling for a share of the territory won "by the common sword,
purse, and blood of all the States, united in a common effort." Also
evident from the beginning was the conflict between those who sought
the Jeffersonian ideal of an agrarian society dominated by small,
independent farmers having a "natural right" to uncultivated lands in
the public domain, and those to whom land was a commodity to be
developed to the highest use as fast as possible for the benefit of the
entrepreneur.

The Congress of Confederation enacted the Land Ordinance of
1785; its enduring contribution to public land law was the rectangular
survey system by which the lands were divided into square townships of
36 numbered sections, each section containing 640 acres.[a] The lands
surveyed were to be offered at auction for a minimum price of one
dollar an acre, and section 16 in each township was reserved for public
education. No limitations on speculation were imposed, and no provisions for the protection of squatters, then numerous and obnoxious,
were made. Little settlement was accomplished under the Ordinance,
for surveying had to be completed, Indian resistance in the Ohio
Territory was strong, and largescale speculators were attempting to
make private deals with the Congress of Confederation. That body
viewed land sales as an important revenue source, but it forsook the
profit motive when it rewarded Revolutionary War veterans and refu-
gees with bounty warrants or scrip entitling them to select lands from
the Military Reserves in Ohio. The Congress of Confederation also
enacted the Northwest Ordinance of 1787, which defined a three-stage
process whereby territories could become co-equal states.

Doubts about the constitutionality of the Northwest Ordinance
were in part a motivating factor behind the drafting of the United
States Constitution. In Article I, section 8, clause 17 (the "Enclave"
Clause), the framers gave Congress exclusive authority over the seat of
government and "other needful Buildings." Article IV, section 3,

---

a. The same survey system has been
followed ever since. Even though the
United States Geological Survey has continued the work of its predecessors—going
back at least to George Washington—the
survey has not yet been completed.

provided for the admission of new states, and Article IV, section 3, clause 2 (the Property Clause) set out the fundamental grant of power to Congress over the public lands:

> The Congress shall have Power to dispose of and make all needful Rules and Regulations respecting the Territory or other Property belonging to the United States.

One of the first tasks of the new federal Congress was to determine which lands were "Property belonging to the United States," for predecessor governments had made various grants to individuals of lands over which the American government eventually gained sovereignty. Beginning with the Jay Treaty of 1794, the young Nation agreed in all treaties of cession that foreign grantees could retain title to their property and could become citizens. In fact, it took generations for the courts and Congress to decide the validity and extent of prior grants made by the governments of Great Britain, Spain, France, and Mexico. The claims ranged from the size of town lots in Detroit to a 1.5 million acre grant in Florida. The disputes were widespread and long-lasting; 126 such cases were decided by the Supreme Court before 1860, and many more thereafter. As in other areas of public land law, "incredible forgeries, fraud, subornation, and perjuries" were all too common. Territorial administrators as well as the likes of Johnstone Amerson (a "poor wandering wretch, equally destitute of morality or character willing to testify, on moderate terms, for any man who would pay him for it") participated in the purchase and fabrication of prior land grants. Corruption was so common that one historian felt compelled to protest that "[n]ot all public officials participated in the grab and by no means all of the claims acquired by officers were improperly obtained or tainted with fraud." P. Gates, supra, at 228. Language difficulties, political patronage appointments of land officials, incomplete foreign records, abandonment of grants, and similar factors complicated the process.

Congress was extremely patient with dilatory claimants and generous in recognizing questionable claims, and Boards of Land Commissioners and other administrators struggled with questions of title for generations. Emotions on such questions ran high: a United States Senator killed the son of a federal judge in a Missouri duel caused by disputes over the validity of Spanish land grants, and another federal judge was later impeached but not convicted for incidents arising out of similar squabbles. The Presidential Proclamation of December 12, 1815 declared that "uninformed or evil-disposed persons" occupying Spanish land grants in violation of the 1807 Anti-Intrusion Act would be forcibly removed. However, the federal marshall of the same Territory responded by warning that not "five Militia men of this Territory would * * * march against the intruders on public lands."

The claimants of large tracts generally prevailed in the end because of their persistence, congressional sympathy, and superior representation before Congress, courts, and commissioners. (Daniel Webster and Thomas Hart Benton represented claimants while serving in Congress.) The resulting validation of estates aggregating hundreds of thousands and even millions of acres led to such bitter indictments of land policy as Henry George's single tax proposal. Ultimately, 34 million acres in 19 states were confirmed to grantees of former governments, and these lands were usually the most desirable acreage that otherwise would have been available to settlers. In the protracted disputes, the primary beneficiaries were, of course, the lawyers.

2. GRANTS TO STATES

a. STATEHOOD GRANTS

After ordinary settler-farmers, new states upon admission were the primary beneficiaries of the federal largess in land disposition. Over the course of years, the federal policy also favored special purpose grants to states for transportation, education, and other purposes.

The creation of new "public land" states, each to be on an "equal footing" with the others, was a complicated process. The admission of Ohio in 1803 served as a model for later federal land grants to new states. After considerable wrangling, Congress agreed to grant the new State of Ohio four percent of its land area for the benefit of its schools, five percent of the net proceeds of land sales within the state to provide a road-building fund, and all of its salt springs for lease. While the non-public land states felt that proceeds from lands conquered by the older states should also benefit the older as well as the new states, the Ohio statehood grant pattern was generally followed (with numerous deviations) in the admission of Louisiana, Indiana, Illinois, Mississippi, Alabama, Missouri, Michigan, Arkansas, Florida, and Iowa. Later enabling acts sometimes granted the new states lands for the support of a university, and some received lands for internal improvements other than roads. The question of admission later was complicated by the debate on slavery and by the territories' continual demand for more landed concessions, but the terms of later statehood admissions were substantially similar—although a slow liberalization, particularly with grants for education, was perceptible. In the latter part of the century, grants to new states varied widely in purpose and acreage. For example, Nevada received the expanded school grants plus 25,000 acres for public buildings and a jail, while Arizona later received the school sections plus over two million acres for various public purposes. All in all, state education was greatly benefitted by the federal largess: 77 million acres for schools and 21 million acres for higher education were eventually granted to the states.

The terms and effect of the school grants, like other types of grants, are not yet finally settled.

ANDRUS v. UTAH

Supreme Court of the United States, 1980.
446 U.S. 500.

Mr. Justice STEVENS delivered the opinion of the Court.

The State of Utah claims the right to select extremely valuable oil shale lands located within federal grazing districts in lieu of and as indemnification for original school land grants of significantly lesser value that were frustrated by federal preemption, or private entry, prior to survey. The question presented is whether the Secretary of the Interior is obliged to accept Utah's selections of substitute tracts of the same size as the originally designated sections even though there is a gross disparity between the value of the original grants and the selected substitutes. We hold that the Secretary's "grossly disparate value" policy is a lawful exercise of the broad discretion vested in him by § 7 of the Taylor Grazing Act of 1934, as amended in 1936, 43 U.S.C.A. § 315f, and is a valid ground for refusing to accept Utah's selections.

Utah became a State in 1896. In the Utah Enabling Act of 1894, Congress granted Utah, upon admission, four numbered sections in each township for the support of public schools. The statute provided that if the designated sections had already "been sold or otherwise disposed of" pursuant to another act of Congress, "other lands equivalent thereto * * * are hereby granted." The substitute grants, denominated "indemnity lands" were "to be selected within [the] State in such manner as [its] legislature may provide with the approval of the Secretary of the Interior."

Because much of the State was not surveyed until long after its admission to the Union, its indemnity or "in lieu" selections were not made promptly. On September 10, 1965, Utah filed the first of 194 selection lists with the Bureau of Land Management of the Department of the Interior covering the land in dispute in this litigation. The 194 indemnity selections include 157,255.90 acres in Uintah County, Utah, all of which are located within federal grazing districts created pursuant to the Taylor Grazing Act.

In January 1974, before Utah's selection lists had been approved or disapproved, the Governor of Utah agreed that the Secretary of the Interior could include two tracts comprising 10,240 acres of selected indemnity lands in an oil shale leasing program, on the understanding that the rental proceeds would ultimately be paid to the State if its selections were approved. The proceeds of the leases are of substantial value.[2]

In February 1974, the Secretary advised the Governor that he would not approve any indemnity applications that involved "grossly disparate values."[3] He wrote:

2. The District Court found that as of May 25, 1976, $48,291,840 had been accumulated. It should be noted that these proceeds were derived from only 10,240 acres out of the total area selected comprising over 157,000 acres.

3. Suggested guidelines of the Department of the Interior provide that the policy

* * * In January 1967, the then Secretary of the Interior adopted the policy that in the exercise of his discretion under, *inter alia*, Section 7 of the Taylor Grazing Act, he would refuse to approve indemnity applications that involve grossly disparate values. That policy remains in effect.

"In the present case, although the land values are not precisely determined, it appears that the selections involve lands of grossly disparate values, within the meaning of the Department's policy. While the Department is not yet prepared to adjudicate the State's applications, I feel it is appropriate at this time to advise you that we will apply the above-mentioned policy in that adjudication."

The State promptly filed this action in United States District Court for the Southern District of Utah. The facts were stipulated, and Judge Ritter entered summary judgment in favor of the State. He held that if Utah's selections satisfy all of the statutory criteria governing indemnity selections when filed,[5] the Secretary has no discretion to refuse them pursuant to a "grossly disparate value" policy. The Court of Appeals for the Tenth Circuit affirmed, 586 F.2d 756 (1978), holding that § 7 of the Taylor Grazing Act gave the Secretary no authority to classify land as eligible for selection and that the State had a right to select indemnity land of equal acreage without regard to the relative values of the original grants and the indemnity selections.

Because the dispute between the parties involves a significant issue regarding the disposition of vast amounts of public lands,[6] we granted certiorari. We believe that the Court of Appeals and the District Court failed to give proper effect to the congressional policy underlying the provision for indemnity selection, and specifically misconstrued § 7 of the Taylor Grazing Act as amended in 1936. We therefore reverse.

I

The Enabling Act of each of the public land States admitted into the Union since 1802 has included grants of designated sections of federal lands for the purpose of supporting public schools. Whether the Enabling Act contained words of present or future grant, title to the numbered sections did not vest in the State until completion of an official survey. Prior to survey, the Federal Government remained free

will not be applied unless the estimated value of the selected lands exceeds that of the base lands by more than $100 per acre or 25% whichever is greater. If the values are grossly disparate using those criteria, the case will be submitted to the Washington office for evaluation of all the circumstances.

5. [43 U.S.C.A. §§ 851–53].

6. "Because the western states are the ones most recently admitted to the Union and because Utah and Arizona are two of the three states that received particularly large grants the remaining indemnity selection rights are concentrated in seven western states. Utah and Arizona alone hold nearly 70% of the outstanding indemnity rights. The approximate number of acres still to be selected in each state (and thus the approximate number of acres potentially affected by this lawsuit) is as follows: Arizona, 170,000 acres; California, 108,000 acres; Colorado, 17,000 acres; Idaho, 27,000 acres; Montana, 22,900 acres; Utah, 225,000 acres; and Wyoming, 1,100 acres."

to dispose of the designated lands "in any manner and for any purpose consistent with applicable federal statutes." In recognition of the fact that the essentially random grants in place might therefore be unavailable at the time of survey for a variety of reasons, Congress authorized grants of indemnity or "lieu" lands of equal acreage.

As Utah correctly emphasizes, the school land grant was a "solemn agreement" which in some ways may be analogized to a contract between private parties. The United States agreed to cede some of its land to the State in exchange for a commitment by the State to use the revenues derived from the land to educate the citizenry.

The State's right to select indemnity lands may be viewed as the remedy stipulated by the parties for the Federal Government's failure to perform entirely its promise to grant the specific numbered sections. The fact that the Utah Enabling Act used the phrase "lands equivalent thereto" and described the substituted land as "indemnity lands" implies that the purpose of the substitute selections was to provide the State with roughly the same resources with which to support its schools as it would have had had it actually received all of the granted sections in place.[10] Thus, as is typical of private contract remedies, the purpose of the right to make indemnity selections was to give the State the benefit of the bargain.

The history of the general statutes relating to land grants for school purposes confirms this view. Thus, for example, in 1859, when confronted with the fact that many settlers had occupied unsurveyed lands that had been included in school grants, Congress confirmed the settlers' claims and granted to the States "other lands of like quantity." 11 Stat. 385. The substitution of an equal quantity of land provided the States a rough measure of equal value.

The school land grants gave the States a random selection of public lands subject, however, to one important exception. The original school land grants in general, and Utah's in particular, did not include any numbered sections known to be mineral in character by the time of survey. United States v. Sweet, 245 U.S. 563. This Court so held even though the Utah Enabling Act "neither expressly includes mineral lands nor expressly excludes them." The Court's opinion stressed "the practice of Congress to make a distinction between mineral lands and other lands, to deal with them along different lines, and to withhold mineral lands from disposal save under laws specially including them." Mineral lands were thus excluded not only from the original grants in place but also from the indemnity selections.[11] Since mineral resources provide both the most significant potential source of value and the

---

10. See Heydenfeldt v. Daney Gold and Silver Mining Co., 93 U.S. 634, 639–640:

"Until the *status* of the lands was fixed by a survey, and they were capable of identification, Congress reserved absolute power over them; and if in exercising it the whole or any part of a 16th or 36th section had been disposed of, the State was to be compensated by other lands equal in quantity, and *as near as may be in quality*." (Emphasis added.)

11. Under the 1891 general indemnity selection statute then in effect, selections were limited to "unappropriated, surveyed public lands, not mineral in character." 26 Stat. 796–797.

greatest potential for variation in value in the generally arid western lands, the total exclusion of mineral lands from the school land grants is consistent with an intent that the States' indemnity selections of equal acreage approximate the value of the numbered sections lost.

In 1927, some nine years after the decision in United States v. Sweet, supra, Congress changed its policy to allow grants of school lands to embrace numbered sections that were mineral in character. But the 1927 statute did not expand the kinds of land available for indemnity selections. Thus, after 1927 even if the lost school lands were mineral in character, a State was prohibited from selecting mineral lands as indemnity. It was not until 1958 that Congress gave the States the right to select mineral lands to replace lost school lands, and that right was expressly conditioned on a determination that the lost lands were also mineral in character. 43 U.S.C.A. § 852. For 30 years, then, States were not even permitted to select lands roughly equivalent in value to replace lost mineral lands. The condition in the 1958 statute, that the lost lands be mineral in character before mineral lands could be selected as indemnity, rather clearly reflects an intention to restore the character of the indemnity selection as a substitute of roughly equal value.

Throughout the history of congressional consideration of school land grants and related subjects—a history discussed at great length in the voluminous briefs submitted to us—we find no evidence whatever of any congressional desire to have the right to select indemnity lands do anything more than make the States whole for the loss of value resulting from the unavailability of the originally designated cross section of lands within the State. There is certainly no suggestion of a purpose at any time, including 1958, to allow the States to obtain substantially greater values through the process of selecting indemnity land.

Thus, viewing the program in this broad historical perspective, it is difficult to identify any sensible justification for Utah's position that it is entitled to select any mineral lands it chooses regardless of the value of the school sections lost. Nevertheless, Utah is quite correct in arguing that the Secretary has no power to reject its selections unless Congress has given it to him. We have no doubt that it has.

II

Prior to the 1930's, cases in this Court had made it perfectly clear that the Federal Government retained the power to appropriate public lands embraced within school grants for other purposes if it acted in a timely fashion. On the other hand, it was equally clear that the States' title to unappropriated land in designated sections could not be defeated after survey, and that their right to indemnity selections could not be rejected if they satisfied the statutory criteria when made, and if the selections were filed before the lands were appropriated for other purposes. The authority of the Secretary of the Interior was limited to determining whether the States' indemnity selections met the relevant statutory criteria. See Wyoming v. United States, 255 U.S. 489; Payne v. New Mexico, 255 U.S. 367, 371.

In the 1930's, however, dissatisfaction with the rather loose regime' governing use and disposition of unappropriated federal lands, prompted mostly by the waste caused by unregulated stock grazing, led to a series of congressional and executive actions that are critical to this case. By means of these actions, all unappropriated federal lands were withdrawn from every form of entry or selection. The withdrawal did not affect the original school land grants in place, whether or not surveyed, but did include all lands then available for school indemnity selections. The lands thus withdrawn were thereafter available for indemnity selections only as permitted by the Secretary of the Interior in the exercise of his discretion.

The sequence of events was as follows. In 1934, Congress enacted the Taylor Grazing Act "[t]o stop injury to the public grazing lands by preventing overgrazing and soil deterioration, to provide for their orderly use, improvement, and development, to stabilize the livestock industry dependent upon the public range, and for other purposes." 48 Stat. 1269. Section 1 authorized the Secretary of the Interior to establish grazing districts in up to 80 million acres of unappropriated federal lands; the establishment of such a district had the effect of withdrawing all lands within its boundaries "from all forms of entry of settlement." That section also expressly provided that "Nothing in this Act shall be construed in any way * * * to affect any land heretofore or hereafter surveyed which, except for the provisions of this Act, would be a part of any grant to any State * * *." Thus, § 1 preserved the original school land grants, whether or not the designated sections had already been identified by survey, but the statute made no provision for school indemnity selections.

Because the Taylor Grazing Act as originally passed in 1934 applied to less than half of the federal lands in need of more orderly regulation, President Roosevelt promptly issued Executive Order 6910 withdrawing all of the unappropriated and unreserved public lands in 12 western States, including Utah, from "settlement, location, sale or entry" pending a determination of the best use of the land. The withdrawal affected the land covered by the Taylor Grazing Act as well as land not covered by the statute. The President's authority to issue Executive Order 6910 was expressly conferred by the Pickett Act.

Congress responded to Executive Order No. 6910 by amending the Taylor Grazing Act in 1936 in two respects that are relevant to this case. First, it expanded the acreage subject to the Act. Second, it revised § 7 of the Act, to give the Secretary the authority, in his discretion, to classify both lands within grazing districts and lands withdrawn by the recent Executive order as proper not only for homesteading, but also, for the first time, for satisfaction of any outstanding "lieu" rights, and to open such lands to "selection." The section [43 U.S.C.A. § 315f], thus amended, provided in pertinent part:

"The Secretary of the Interior is authorized, in his discretion, to examine and classify any lands withdrawn or reserved by Executive order * * * or within a grazing district, which are * * * proper for acquisition in satisfaction of any outstanding lieu, exchange or script rights or land grant, and to open such lands to entry, selection or location for disposal in accordance with * * * applicable public-land laws. * * * *Such lands shall not be subject to disposition* * * * *until after the same have been classified* * * *." (Emphasis added.)

The changes in this section were apparently prompted in part by the fact that while the Taylor Grazing Act withdrawal preserved the States' school grants in place, no provision had been made in the 1934 version for the States' indemnity selections from land within grazing districts even though the States had expressed the concern that "the establishment of a grazing district would restrict the State in its indemnity selections." While this omission may not have been critical in 1934 when the Act was passed—since only about half of the unappropriated federal land was then affected—by 1936, as a consequence of Executive Order No. 6910, no land at all was available in the public domain for indemnity selections. It is therefore reasonable to infer that the amendments to § 7 were at least in part a response to the complaint expressed in congressional hearings in 1935, that there was no land available under current law for indemnity selections.

The 1936 amendment to § 7 rectified that problem, but did not give the States a completely free choice in making indemnity selections. Rather, Congress decided to route the States' selections through § 7, and thereby to condition their acceptance on the Secretary's discretion. That decision was consistent with the dominant purpose of both the Act and Executive Order No. 6910, to exert firm control over the Nation's land resources through the Department of the Interior. In sum, the Taylor Grazing Act, coupled with the withdrawals by Executive order, "locked up" all of the federal lands in the western States pending further action by Congress or the President, except as otherwise permitted in the discretion of the Secretary of the Interior for the limited purposes specified in § 7.

This was Congress' understanding of the Taylor Grazing Act in 1958 when it amended the school land indemnity selection statute to permit selection of mineral lands. * * * Since Congress was specifically dealing with school indemnity selections, the reports make it perfectly clear that Congress deemed school indemnity selections to be subject to § 7 of the Taylor Grazing Act. And since the congressional decision in 1958 to allow school land indemnity selections to embrace mineral lands was expressly conditioned on a determination that the lost school lands were also mineral in character, it is manifest that Congress did not intend to grant the States any windfall. It only intended to restore to the States a rough approximation of what was lost.

We therefore hold that the 1936 amendment to the Taylor Grazing Act conferred on the Secretary the authority in his discretion to classify lands within a federal grazing district as proper for school indemnity selection. And we find no merit in the argument that the Secretary's "grossly disparate value" policy constitutes an abuse of the broad discretion thus conferred. On the contrary, that policy is wholly faithful to Congress' consistent purpose in providing for indemnity selections, to give the States a rough equivalent of the school land grants in place that were lost through pre-emption or private entry prior to survey. Accordingly, the judgment of the Court of Appeals is reversed.

Mr. Justice POWELL, with whom THE CHIEF JUSTICE, Mr. Justice BLACKMUN, and Mr. Justice REHNQUIST join, dissenting.

Since the early days of the Republic, the Federal Government's compact with each new State has granted the State land for the support of education and allowed the State to select land of equal acreage as indemnity for deficiencies in the original grant. Today, the Court holds that the Taylor Grazing Act abrogated those compacts by approving selection requirements completely at odds with the equal acreage principle. Nothing in the Court's opinion persuades me that Congress meant so lightly to breach compacts that it has respected and enforced throughout our Nation's history. I therefore dissent.

The Court's decision rests on three fundamental misconceptions. First, the Court reasons from the accepted proposition that indemnity lands compensate the States for gaps in the original grants to the mistaken conclusion that the States have no right to lands of equal acreage. This argument ignores the clear meaning of statutes spanning about two centuries in which Congress specifically adopted an equal acreage principle as the standard for making compensation. Second, the Court believes that the establishment of grazing districts under the Taylor Grazing Act has the same effect as a withdrawal of lands under the Pickett Act. This belief manifests a serious misunderstanding of both the history of federal land management and the language of the Taylor Grazing Act. Third, the Court assumes— without discussion—that the Taylor Grazing Act gives the Secretary of the Interior discretion to reject indemnity selections under standards inconsistent with the criteria set out in the statutes authorizing the selections. Every federal court that has considered the Secretary's authority under the Taylor Grazing Act has rejected this assumption.

* * *

Utah has selected land in satisfaction of grants made to support the public education of its citizens. Those grants are part of the bilateral compact under which Utah was admitted to the Union. They guarantee the State a specific quantity of the public lands within its borders. * * * Nothing in the Taylor Grazing Act empowers the Secretary to review Utah's selections under a comparative value standard explicitly at odds with principles consistently respected since the early days of our Republic.

* * *

NOTES

1. The circuit court opinion in Andrus v. Utah and other questions of state ownership and selection are discussed in Dragoo, The Impact of the Federal Land Policy and Management Act Upon Statehood Grants and Indemnity Land Selections, 21 Ariz.L.Rev. 395 (1979).

2. The "solemn compact" has been adhered to very closely in other instances. Where the federal land grant to the state was for a specific purpose, courts have held the state strictly to the original terms. New Mexico received 100,000 acres, for instance, the proceeds to be put in trust for "miners' hospitals for disabled miners." In 1968, New Mexico consolidated its hospitals and changed its Miners' Hospital into a more limited facility, with disabled miners eligible to receive care at other institutions. The Tenth Circuit ruled that the original conditions overrode the modern medical administration program. In United States v. New Mexico, 536 F.2d 1324, 1326–27 (10th Cir.1976), the court opined:

> A main area of contention in this litigation centers on the purpose for which Congress granted the trust lands to New Mexico. New Mexico argues that Congress granted the 100,000 acres for the primary purpose of promoting the public welfare by attending to the health needs of disabled miners and that the trust terms should be liberally construed to effectuate this purpose. On the other hand the United States and the intervenors assert that the Enabling Act must be strictly construed and that the purpose of the trust is plainly stated in the Enabling Act—that of establishing and maintaining a "miners' hospital."

> In construing the Enabling Act the Supreme Court citing the restrictions placed on the use of the trust lands has consistently applied a narrow interpretation to the terms of the Enabling Act. Ervien v. United States, 251 U.S. 41. Because of previous abuses of federal lands granted in trust to the states, the Court observed that it had been Congress' intent "[t]o preclude any license of construction or liberties of inference" when construing the Enabling Act. Ervien v. United States, supra, at 47.

> Therefore applying a narrow interpretation of the terms of the Enabling Act, we cannot agree with New Mexico's broad construction. While the underlying motivation for the trust may have been a desire on the part of Congress generally to provide for the health care of miners the specific purpose of the trust was the establishment and maintenance of a "miners' hospital." The wording of the Enabling Act evidences a determination by Congress that the health needs of New Mexico miners could best be provided by a separate hospital for miners. To imply a more expansive purpose for the trust than that stated

in the Enabling Act is to indulge in a license of construction which Congress intended to prevent.

Will the proceeds from these lands still be devoted to the care of injured miners when there are no more miners in New Mexico? Are there good reasons why ancient grant purposes cannot be reinterpreted in light of modern conditions? Assuming that, as a matter of societal judgment, it is wiser to consolidate the hospital system in the manner that New Mexico undertook, is there any remedy? Why should the United States Congress decide how New Mexico's hospitals are to be organized?

3. The *Ervien* case referred to in the excerpt also arose from the New Mexico enabling Act. The New Mexico legislature had authorized the use of 3% of the proceeds from sales of land granted to the State in trust "for making known the resources and advantages of this State generally and particularly to homeseekers and investors." The Supreme Court did not countenance such a radical deviation from the trust terms:

> The dedication * * * was special and exact, precluding any supplementary or aiding sense, in prophetic realization, it may be, that the state might be tempted to do that which it has done, lured from the patient methods to speculative advertising in the hope of a speedy prosperity.

251 U.S. at 47–48.

4. In Andrus v. Idaho, 445 U.S. 715 (1980), the Supreme Court held that the Carey Act, 43 U.S.C.A. § 641, which authorized the Interior Secretary to grant lands to states for reclamation purposes, did not "reserve any specific number of acres of desert land for any State," and that the Secretary was free to devote lands sought by the State to other purposes, even after the state application is filed.

b. OTHER GRANTS

The grants to states upon admission were not considered sufficient to fulfill state goals, so other general land grants to states were also made. Before railroads were invented, the federal government had become heavily involved in promoting internal transportation improvements. The Cumberland Road was a federal project that eventually encouraged further land grants to western states for turnpike construction. As in the case of Ohio, new states received lands to be devoted to road-building funds. The Erie Canal, the first and most successful canal project, was a state venture, but development of New York in its wake led to a series of proposals from new states, many of which were undertaken with the proceeds from federal lands. In 1827–28, Congress gave land to Ohio, Indiana, Illinois, and Alabama for the building of canals to connect the Great Lakes with the Ohio and Mississippi Rivers, and to improve navigation on the Tennessee River. The Canal Era passed quickly but, before it had, Congress had granted more than six million acres for canals and river improvements, and more than three million acres for roads. The procedure of selecting alternate sections along the right-of-way began with the canals but was carried to unprecedented lengths by the railroads.

By the Act of 1841, every public land state was granted outright 500,000 acres for internal improvements, less acreage that had already been received for those purposes. Diversion of funds to other purposes by recipient states helped influence Congress to end the general grant system in 1889 in favor of specific trust grants such as that in United States v. New Mexico, supra. Meanwhile, Congress had also determined to give states the unclaimed, seemingly useless swampland within their borders. After an experimental grant to Louisiana, the General Swamp Land Act of 1850 allowed states to select and acquire such lands under certain criteria; administrative implementation was so lacking, however, that erroneous and fraudulent selections were common. It was intended that five or six million acres would pass by this method, but over 80 million acres of purported swamplands were ultimately selected, though not all selections were approved for fee title. With the connivance of state officials, a predecessor of the giant Kern County Land Company received over 80,000 valuable acres through this process. Conflicts with other grants, notably to the railroads, abounded. See Work v. Louisiana, 269 U.S. 250 (1925); Martin v. Marks, 97 U.S. (7 Otto) 345 (1877). Remedial legislation was passed, and contests were initiated, but many conflicts were not resolved until this century, and several state patent applications were confirmed as late as 1963. "Despite Congress' unmistakable intention to benefit the states, the titles it created have proved extremely unstable." Shearer, Federal Land Grants to the States: An Advocate's Dream; A Title Examiner's Nightmare, 14 Rocky Mtn. Min.L.Inst. 185, 188 (1968).

By the Morrill Act of 1862, each state received the rights to 30,000 acres for each of its senators and representatives, to be used for support of an agricultural and mechanical college. These grants differed from the norm in that states could not select such lands within their boundaries but rather were given "scrip" for the acreage, entitling them to sell the rights to public lands elsewhere. Many evaded the conditions, and great landed estates grew out of speculation in scrip, but Morrill's purpose of providing free, practical higher education has been realized in some measure by the establishment of such schools as Cornell and Michigan State Universities.

The Morrill Act was one of the few disposition laws that allowed the non-public land states to share in the proceeds from sale of public domain land. The controversy between East and West had raged for decades with inconclusive results. "Distribution," "deposit," and similar revenue sharing schemes from which eastern states would benefit either never passed or were short-lived due to economic exigencies. The eastern desire for a share of the proceeds from western lands was almost universally thwarted, but losing that battle led the East to fight and win a new war: beginning in 1872 and continuing to the present day, pressure from the East has been mainly responsible for the withdrawal and reservation of millions of acres from availability for development or settlement. New national purposes thus were served in the face of consistent western opposition to such public "conservation" and "preservation."

c. STATEHOOD AND EQUAL FOOTING

From the admission of Ohio in 1803 to that of Alaska in 1959, the state-making procedure involved Congress and the people of the territories in complicated and lengthy political disputes. The parties hammered out agreements concerning the management and sharing of the public lands, the basis for the fundamental law of each state, and limitations on their taxing powers. In the process, the states were brought, with some reluctance, to give up plans entertained by some of their leaders for either acquiring or controlling and managing the public lands as the Original Thirteen and Texas did. By a curious quirk of constitutional law, however, the states did receive by implication a part of their territories, the lands underlying navigable waters within their boundaries.

POLLARD v. HAGAN
Supreme Court of the United States, 1845.
44 U.S. (3 How.) 212.

[Plaintiffs claimed title to land formerly covered by high tide under a patent from the United States; defendants claimed title under a prior Spanish land grant. The trial court charged that if the land was below high tide when Alabama became a state then the United States could not later grant title. The Supreme Court affirmed the judgment for defendant. In the course of his lengthy opinion, Mr. Justice McKIN-LEY made the following comments about state admission on an equal footing and the corresponding powers and duties of the United States.]

We think a proper examination of this subject will show, that the United States never held any municipal sovereignty, jurisdiction, or right of soil in and to the territory, of which Alabama or any of the new states were formed; except for temporary purposes, and to execute the trusts created by the acts of the Virginia and Georgia legislatures, and the deeds of cession executed by them to the United States, and the trust created by the treaty with the French republic, of the 30th of April, 1803, ceding Louisiana.

* * *

* * * Taking the legislative acts of the United States, and the states of Virginia and Georgia, and their deeds of cession to the United States, and giving to each, separately, and to all jointly, a fair interpretation, we must come to the conclusion that it was the intention of the parties to invest the United States with the eminent domain of the country ceded, both national and municipal, for the purposes of temporary government, and to hold it in trust for the performance of the stipulations and conditions expressed in the deeds of cession and the legislative acts connected with them. To a correct understanding of the rights, powers, and duties of the parties to these contracts, it is necessary to enter into a more minute examination of the rights of eminent domain, and the right to the public lands. When the United States accepted the cession of the territory, they took upon themselves the trust to hold the municipal eminent domain for the new states, and to invest them with it, to the same extent, in all respects, that it was held by the states ceding the territories.

The right which belongs to the society, or to the sovereign, of disposing, in case of necessity, and for the public safety, of all the wealth contained in the state, is called the *eminent domain*. It is evident that this right is, in certain cases, necessary to him who governs, and is, consequently, a part of the empire, or sovereign power.
*   *   *

*   *   *

When Alabama was admitted into the union, on an equal footing with the original states, she succeeded to all the rights of sovereignty, jurisdiction, and eminent domain which Georgia possessed at the date of the cession, except so far as this right was diminished by the public lands remaining in the possession and under the control of the United States, for the temporary purposes provided for in the deed of cession and the legislative acts connected with it. Nothing remained to the United States, according to the terms of the agreement, but the public lands. And, if an express stipulation had been inserted in the agreement, granting the municipal right of sovereignty and eminent domain to the United States, such stipulation would have been void and inoperative; because the United States have no constitutional capacity to exercise municipal jurisdiction, sovereignty, or eminent domain, within the limits of a state or elsewhere, except in the cases in which it is expressly granted.

By the 16th clause of the 8th section of the 1st article of the Constitution, power is given to Congress "to exercise exclusive legislation in all cases whatsoever, over such district (not exceeding ten miles square) as may by cession of particular states, and the acceptance of Congress, become the seat of government of the United States, and to exercise like authority over all places purchased, by the consent of the legislature of the state in which the same may be, for the erection of forts, magazines, arsenals, dock-yards, and other needful buildings." Within the District of Columbia, and the other places purchased and used for the purposes above mentioned, the national and municipal powers of government, of every description, are united in the government of the union. And these are the only cases, within the United States, in which all the powers of government are united in a single government, except in the cases already mentioned of the temporary territorial governments, and there a local government exists. The right of Alabama and every other new state to exercise all the powers of government, which belong to and may be exercised by the original states of the union, must be admitted, and remain unquestioned, except so far as they are, temporarily, deprived of control over the public lands.

We will now inquire into the nature and extent of the right of the United States to these lands, and whether that right can in any manner affect or control the decision of the case before us. This right originated in voluntary surrenders, made by several of the old states, of their waste and unappropriated lands, to the United States, under a resolution of the old Congress, of the 6th of September, 1780, recommending such surrender and cession, to aid in paying the public debt, incurred by the war of the Revolution. The object of all the parties to these contracts of cession, was to convert the land into money for the payment of the debt, and to erect new states over the territory thus ceded; and as soon as these purposes could be accomplished, the power of the United States over these lands, as property, was to cease.

Whenever the United States shall have fully executed these trusts, the municipal sovereignty of the new states will be complete, throughout their respective borders, and they, and the original states, will be upon an equal footing, in all respects whatever. We, therefore, think the United States hold the public lands within the new states by force of the deeds of cession, and the statutes connected with them, and not by any municipal sovereignty which it may be supposed they possess, or have reserved by compact with the new states, for that particular purpose. The provision of the Constitution above referred to shows that no such power can be exercised by the United States within a state. Such a power is not only repugnant to the Constitution, but it is inconsistent with the spirit and intention of the deeds of cession. The argument so much relied on by the counsel for the plaintiffs, that the agreement of the people inhabiting the new states, "that they for ever disclaim all right and title to the waste or unappropriated lands lying within the said territory; and that the same shall be and remain at the sole and entire disposition of the United States," cannot operate as a contract between the parties, but is binding as a law. Full power is given to Congress "to make all needful rules and regulations respecting the territory or other property of the United States." This authorized the passage of all laws necessary to secure the rights of the United States to the public lands, and to provide for their sale, and to protect them from taxation.

* * *

This supposed compact is, therefore, nothing more than a regulation of commerce, to that extent, among the several states, and can have no controlling influence in the decision of the case before us. This right of eminent domain over the shores and the soils under the navigable waters, for all municipal purposes, belongs exclusively to the states within their respective territorial jurisdictions, and they, and they only, have the constitutional power to exercise it. To give to the United States the right to transfer to a citizen the title to the shores and the soils under the navigable waters, would be placing in their hands a weapon which might be wielded greatly to the injury of state sovereignty, and deprive the states of the power to exercise a numerous and important class of police powers. But in the hands of the states this power can never be used so as to affect the exercise of any national right of eminent domain or jurisdiction with which the United States have been invested by the Constitution. For, although the territorial limits of Alabama have extended all her sovereign power into the sea, it is there, as on the shore, but municipal power, subject to the Constitution of the United States, "and the laws which shall be made in pursuance thereof."

By the preceding course of reasoning we have arrived at these general conclusions: First, The shores of navigable waters, and the soils under them, were not granted by the Constitution to the United States, but were reserved to the states respectively. Secondly, The new states have the same rights, sovereignty, and jurisdiction over this subject as the original states. Thirdly, The right of the United States to the public lands, and the power of Congress to make all needful rules and regulations for the sale and disposition thereof, conferred no power to grant to the plaintiffs the land in controversy in this case. The judgment of the Supreme Court of the state of Alabama is, therefore, affirmed.

Mr. Justice CATRON dissented.

* * *

NOTES

1. Article IV, section 3, clause 1 of the Constitution provides that "New States may be admitted by the Congress into this Union." As explained in Coyle v. Oklahoma, 221 U.S. 559, 566–67 (1911), the "equal footing doctrine" assures those new states that they will possess governmental authority equal to all other states:

> But what is this power? It is not to admit political organizations which are less or greater, or different in dignity or power, from those political entities which constitute the Union. It is, as strongly put by counsel, a "power to admit States."

> The definition of "a State" is found in the powers possessed by the original States which adopted the Constitution, a definition emphasized by the terms employed in all subsequent acts of Congress admitting new States into the Union. The first two States admitted into the Union were the States of Vermont and Kentucky, one as of March 4, 1791, and the other as of June 1, 1792. No terms or conditions were exacted from either. Each act declares that the State is admitted "as a new and *entire member* of the United States of America." 1 Stat. 189, 191. Emphatic and significant as is the phrase admitted as "an entire member," even stronger was the declaration upon the admission in 1796 of Tennessee, as the third new State, it being declared to be "one of the United States of America," "on an equal footing with the original States in all respects whatsoever," phraseology which has ever since been

substantially followed in admission acts, concluding with the Oklahoma act, which declares that Oklahoma shall be admitted "on an equal footing with the original States."

The power is to admit "new States into *this* Union."

"This Union" was and is a union of States, equal in power, dignity and authority, each competent to exert that residuum of sovereignty not delegated to the United States by the Constitution itself. To maintain otherwise would be to say that the Union, through the power of Congress to admit new States, might come to be a union of States unequal in power, as including States whose powers were restricted only by the Constitution, with others whose powers had been further restricted by an act of Congress accepted as a condition of admission. Thus it would result, first, that the powers of Congress would not be defined by the Constitution alone, but in respect to new States, enlarged or restricted by the conditions imposed upon new States by its own legislation admitting them into the Union; and, second, that such new States might not exercise all of the powers which had not been delegated by the Constitution, but only such as had not been further bargained away as conditions of admission.

See also Hanna, Equal Footing in the Admission of States, 3 Baylor L.Rev. 519 (1951). In Arizona v. California, 373 U.S. 546, 596–97 (1962), the Court noted:

Arizona's contention that the Federal Government had no power, after Arizona became a State, to reserve waters for the use and benefit of federally reserved lands rests largely upon statements in Pollard's Lessee v. Hagan, 3 How. 212 (1845), and Shively v. Bowlby, 152 U.S. 1 (1894). Those cases and others that followed them gave rise to the doctrine that lands underlying navigable waters within territory acquired by the Government are held in trust for future States and that title to such lands is automatically vested in the States upon admission to the Union. But those cases involved only the shores of and lands beneath navigable waters. They do not determine the problem before us and cannot be accepted as limiting the broad powers of the United States to regulate navigable waters under the Commerce Clause and to regulate government lands under Art. IV, § 3, of the Constitution.

2. Pollard v. Hagan enunciated the doctrine that upon statehood new states acquired title to the beds of navigable streams and lakes to the high-water mark. A uniform federal test is used to determine navigability, United States v. Holt State Bank, 270 U.S. 49 (1926). See R. Clark, 1 WATERS AND WATER RIGHTS 250–51 (1967):

On the public domain within states created out of territories, the states acquired title to the beds and banks up to high-water mark of that water which was navigable under the federal test on the date of admission of each such state. In these states, the federal government continued to hold nearly all of the remaining land as public domain, the newly admitted states acquiring only thin ribbons of land comprising the beds and banks of navigable waters. That may sound ridiculous, but it is true.

3. The Court in Pollard v. Hagan did not resolve questions of title to offshore lands. A century later, the Court in United States v. California, 332 U.S. 19 (1947), held that the United States owned the latter, not the states. The federal government then returned title to the states in the Submerged Lands Act of 1953, 43 U.S.C.A. §§ 1301–15.

4. In what some regard as another quirk, the lands thus acquired by the states at statehood came with strings attached. An opinion by the Supreme Court in 1892 (which recently has been resurrected and expanded in various contexts) holds that lands underlying navigable waters are subject to the public trust doctrine.

ILLINOIS CENTRAL RAILROAD CO. v. ILLINOIS
Supreme Court of the United States, 1892.
146 U.S. 387.

Mr. Justice FIELD delivered the opinion of the court.

[The State of Illinois granted to the Illinois Central Railroad a large part of Chicago's waterfront on Lake Michigan, including the submerged lands in Chicago's harbor. The grant was made under highly dubious circumstances, the Illinois Legislature later attempted to revoke it, and the Illinois Attorney General brought suit to invalidate it. The Court first recited the *Pollard v. Hagan* rule that the State succeeded to ownership of lands beneath navigable water and held that Illinois acquired title to the lands in dispute upon statehood.]

The question, therefore, to be considered is whether the legislature was competent to thus deprive the State of its ownership of the submerged lands in the harbor of Chicago, and of the consequent control of its waters; or, in other words, whether the railroad corporation can hold the lands and control the waters by the grant, against any future exercise of power over them by the State.

That the State holds the title to the lands under the navigable waters of Lake Michigan, within its limits, in the same manner that the State holds title to soils under tide water, by the common law, we have already shown, and that title necessarily carries with it control over the waters above them whenever the lands are subjected to use. But it is a title different in character from that which the State holds in lands intended for sale. It is different from the title which the United States hold in the public lands which are open to preemption and sale. It is a title held in trust for the people of the State that they may enjoy the navigation of the waters, carry on commerce over them, and have liberty of fishing therein freed from the obstruction or interference of private parties. The interest of the people in the navigation of the waters and in commerce over them may be improved in many instances by the erection of wharves, docks and piers therein, for which purpose the State may grant parcels of the submerged lands; and, so long as their disposition is made for such purpose, no valid objections can be made to the grants. It is grants of parcels of lands under navigable waters, that may afford foundation for wharves, piers, docks and other structures in aid of commerce, and grants of parcels which, being occupied, do not substantially impair the public interest in the lands and waters remaining, that are chiefly considered and sustained in the adjudged cases as a valid exercise of legislative power consistently with the trust to the public upon which such lands are held by the State. But that is a very different doctrine from the one which would sanction the abdication of the general control of the State over lands under the navigable waters of an entire harbor or bay, or of a sea or lake. Such abdication is not consistent with the exercise of that trust which requires the government of the State to preserve such waters for the use of the public. The trust devolving upon the State for the public, and which can only be discharged by the management and control of property in which the public has an interest, cannot be relinquished by a transfer of the property. The control of the State for the purposes of the trust can never be lost, except as to such parcels as are used in promoting the interests of the public therein, or can be disposed of without any substantial impairment of the public interest in the lands and waters remaining. It is only by observing the distinction between a grant of such parcels for the improvement of the public interest, or which when occupied do not substantially impair the public interest in the lands and waters remaining, and a grant of the whole property in which the public is interested, that the language of the adjudged cases can be reconciled. General language sometimes found in opinions of the courts, expressive of absolute ownership and control by the State of lands under navigable waters, irrespective of any trust as to their use and disposition, must be read and construed with reference to the special facts of the particular cases. A grant of all the lands under the navigable waters of a State has never been adjudged to be within the legislative power; and any attempted grant of the kind would be held, if not absolutely void on its face, as subject to revocation. The State can no more abdicate its trust over property in which the whole people are interested, like navigable waters and soils under them, so as to leave them entirely under the use and control of private parties, except in the instance of parcels mentioned for the improvement of the navigation and use of the waters, or when parcels can be disposed of without impairment of the public interest in what remains, than it can abdicate its police powers in the administration of government and the preservation of the peace. In the administration of government the use of such powers may for a limited period be delegated to a municipality or other body, but there always remains with the State the right to revoke those powers and exercise them in a more direct manner, and one more conformable to its wishes. So with trusts connected with public property, or property of a special character, like lands under navigable waters, they cannot be placed entirely beyond the direction and control of the State.

The harbor of Chicago is of immense value to the people of the State of Illinois in the facilities it affords to its vast and constantly increasing commerce; and the idea that its legislature can deprive the State of control over its bed and waters and place the same in the hands of a private corporation created for a different purpose, one limited to transportation of passengers and freight between distant points and the city, is a proposition that cannot be defended.

The area of the submerged lands proposed to be ceded by the act in question to the railroad company embraces something more than 1,000 acres, being, as stated by counsel, more than three times the area of the outer harbor, and not only including all of that harbor, but embracing adjoining submerged lands, which will, in all probability, be hereafter included in the harbor. It is as large as that embraced by all the merchandise docks along the Thames at London; is much larger than that included in the famous docks and basins at Liverpool; is twice that of the port of Marseilles, and nearly, if not quite, equal to the pier area along the water front of the city of New York. And the arrivals and clearings of vessels at the port exceed in number those of New York, and are equal to those of New York and Boston combined. Chicago has nearly 25 per cent. of the lake carrying trade, as compared with the arrivals and clearings of all the leading ports of our great inland seas.

* * *

Any grant of the kind is necessarily revocable, and the exercise of the trust by which the property was held by the State can be resumed at any time. Undoubtedly there may be expenses incurred in improvements made under such a grant which the State ought to pay; but, be that as it may, the power to resume the trust whenever the State judges best is, we think, incontrovertible. The position advanced by the railroad company in support of its claim to the ownership of the submerged lands and the right to the erection of wharves, piers and docks at its pleasure, or for its business in the harbor of Chicago, would place every harbor in the country at the mercy of a majority of the legislature of the State in which the harbor is situated.

We cannot, it is true, cite any authority where a grant of this kind has been held invalid, for we believe that no instance exists where the harbor of a great city and its commerce have been allowed to pass into the control of any private corporation. But the decisions are numerous which declare that such property is held by the State, by virtue of its sovereignty, in trust for the public. The ownership of the navigable waters of the harbor and of the lands under them is a subject of public concern to the whole people of the State. The trust with which they are held, therefore, is governmental and cannot be alienated, except in those instances mentioned of parcels used in the improvement of the interest thus held, or when parcels can be disposed of without detriment to the public interest in the lands and waters remaining.

* * *

NOTES

1. See Sax, The Public Trust Doctrine in Natural Resources Law: Effective Judicial Intervention, 68 Mich.L.Rev. 471 (1970); Symposium on the Public Trust Doctrine, 14 U.C.D.L.Rev. 180 (1980).

2. The public trust is assuming increasing importance as a limitation on state management of state lands, and it has been applied to resources and amenities other than the kinds of lands at issue in *Illinois Central*. See infra at page 303.

NOTE: THE SAGEBRUSH REBELLION

Political interests in the western states have always resented federal ownership of lands within their borders, and some state officials professed shock and despair when Congress in 1976 made explicit what had long been implicit: the United States was going to retain its remaining land base substantially intact (except for those lands still being granted as a result of the statehood acts, most notably to the State and Native Corporations in Alaska). The resulting movement to force the federal government to give its lands, or at least some of them, to the western states was called the "Sagebrush Rebellion." Some termed it the "Great Terrain Robbery." Led by disgruntled ranchers whose grazing rights on public lands were being reduced, the Rebellion inspired widespread publicity and much overblown rhetoric. Prominent officials, such as Utah's Senator Hatch, perhaps succumbing to oratorical excess, saw the local federal land manager as akin to the Sheriff of Nottingham. See supra at page 34.

The Sagebrush Rebels claimed legal as well as political justifications. In 1977, Utah distributed to the Western Conference of Attorneys General a proposal for litigation to wrest title to the public lands from the United States. After reciting that "Congress has chosen a policy of colonialism with respect to the western states" and that federal policy showed an "arrogant attitude typical of the federal government's lack of commitment to important and traditional state and local interests in the western states." Utah concluded:

> It appears that the fundamental unfairness of the present federal system of western energy and public land management might best be attacked in terms of a combination of traditional legal theories, including denial of equal protection; denial of equal footing and violation of the Tenth Amendment.

In June, 1979, the Nevada legislature passed a law claiming title to 69% of the State's land area (why Nevada exempted wildlife refuges and Indian reservations was not entirely clear), instructing a state board to manage the new holdings, and appropriating $250,000 for the Attorney General's Office to protect Nevada's interest in the public lands. Relying primarily on Pollard v. Hagan, supra, the Nevada Attorney General used a pending lawsuit as the vehicle to assert the State's Sagebrush claims.

NEVADA EX REL. NEVADA STATE BOARD OF
AGRICULTURE v. UNITED STATES

United States District Court, District of Nevada, 1981.
512 F.Supp. 166, aff'd, 699 F.2d 486 (9th Cir.1983).

EDWARD C. REED, Jr., District Judge.

* * *

This litigation commenced with the filing of a Complaint for Mandamus, Injunctive and Declaratory Relief, on April 25, 1978. It alleged that on June 4, 1964, the then Secretary of the Interior of the United States, Stewart L. Udall, had published in the Federal Register an order which placed a moratorium upon consideration of applications for agricultural entries within the State of Nevada under the Homestead and Desert Land Acts. The Complaint asserted that the defendants had refused even to process applications since June 4, 1964. It is contended that the moratorium constituted invidious discrimination against Nevadans. Further, the plaintiff alleged that its Tenth Amendment rights were interfered with by reason of the defendants' policy of perpetual retention of public lands, when the law requires disposal of those lands by the United States.

* * *

On December 14, 1978, Secretary of the Interior Cecil D. Andrus rescinded the moratorium order of June 4, 1964. The plaintiff State, with leave of Court then filed an Amended Complaint for Mandamus, Injunctive and Declaratory Relief. This is the pleading that is the subject of the instant motion to dismiss. It contends that the United States holds Nevada's public lands in trust temporarily, for the purpose of disposal to the State and its citizens. The plaintiff alleges that Nevada was admitted into the Union on an "equal footing" with the original thirteen states, which had ceded their unappropriated lands to the federal government with the understanding they would be sold for the benefit of the people of all the states. The Amended Complaint further alleges that The Federal Land Policy and Management Act of 1976, 43 U.S.C. §§ 1701 et seq. (hereinafter referred to as FLPMA), unconstitutionally infringes upon Nevada's Tenth Amendment and "equal footing" rights by declaring a new and different policy that public lands shall be retained in federal ownership unless, as a result of the comprehensive land use planning procedure provided for in the FLPMA, " * * * it is determined that disposal of a particular parcel will serve the national interest * * *." 43 U.S.C. § 1701(a)(1). The State also asks for a declaratory judgment adjudicating whether the defendants may constitutionally impose a moratorium on the disposal of public lands and whether the United States "may maintain a policy of permanent and perpetual retention of the public lands."

* * *

The position of the plaintiff *vis a vis* the motion to dismiss has been stated clearly * * *:

"In summary, the State's arguments advanced against the defendants' motion to dismiss have been as follows: The State contends that she and all of the public land states had an expectancy upon admission into the Union that the unappropriated, unreserved and vacant lands within their borders would be disposed of by patents to private individuals or by grants to the States. This expectancy was supported by two legal theories: First, that the United States held the public lands in trust, the conditions of which were established by the early deeds of cessions by which certain of the original states ceded their western lands and by subsequent treaties and understandings associated with later acquisitions of territory now a part of the United States; disposal was one of the conditions. Second, that the new states would not be in an equal footing until the disposal contemplated by the deeds of cession and the temporary land holding trusts was accomplished; and that equal footing is a constitutional condition of all of the states of the Union."

Pollard's Lessee v. Hagan:

The keystone of the State of Nevada's argument is the case of Pollard's Lessee v. Hagan, 44 U.S. (3 How.) 212 (1845). * * *

* * *

Pollard's Lessee discusses the agreement by the legislatures of territories seeking admission into the Union that they disclaim all right and title to the unappropriated lands lying within their respective territories. (Section 4 of the Nevada Admission Act [1864], found in Volume 29 of Nevada Revised Statutes, contains such a provision.) It states that such an agreement, in combination with the Property Clause of the U.S. Constitution (Art. 4, § 3, cl. 2) which reads that Congress is given the power to make all needful rules and regulations respecting the territory or other property belonging to the United States, results merely in the federal government having the right to pass laws protecting public lands from taxation and providing for their sale.

* * *

"Equal Footing" Doctrine:

Unfortunately for the plaintiff herein, the U.S. Supreme Court has greatly weakened the *Pollard's Lessee* case as precedent supportive of the plaintiff's arguments. In Dred Scott v. Sandford, 60 U.S. (19 How.) 393 (1856), said Court discussed the reasons for insertion of the Property Clause in the Constitution. The federal government was to be one of carefully limited powers, and it had no grant of authority to receive and administer the unappropriated lands and other properties, such as military equipment and supplies, which the thirteen original sovereign states wished to cede to it for the common good. The raising of money to pay the public debt by selling the lands was the main object of the cessions. The Property Clause provided the United States Government with the power to take possession of the properties and protect them, so that they could be disposed of in an orderly fashion. "It applied only to the property which the States held in common at that time, and has no reference whatever to any territory or other property which the new sovereignty might afterwards itself acquire." To the same effect is the opinion in United States v. Gratiot, 39 U.S. (14 Pet.) 526 (1840), which declares that the limitations on what the federal government can do with its property, by reason of the origin of the Property Clause, apply only to lands within the original thirteen states; there are no such limitations on territory subsequently acquired by the federal government by treaty or conquest.

Thus, it can be seen that the trust (to sell the public lands) found in *Pollard's Lessee* would not apply to such lands owned by the United States within the borders of Nevada.

In addition, the U.S. Supreme Court has stated that *Pollard's Lessee* involved only the shores of and lands beneath navigable waters. Arizona v. California, 373 U.S. 546 (1963). As a result, its broad discussions seemingly covering unappropriated lands could be dismissed as dicta.

Federal regulation which is otherwise valid is not a violation of the "equal footing" doctrine merely because its impact may differ between various states because of geographic or economic reasons. The doctrine applies only to political rights and sovereignty; it does not cover economic matters, for there never has been equality among the states in that sense. United States v. Texas, 339 U.S. 707 (1950). Said case points out that, when they entered the Union, some states contained large tracts of land belonging to the federal government, whereas others had none. "The requirement of equal footing was designed not to wipe out these diversities but to create parity as respects political standing and sovereignty." Accordingly, Congress may cede property to one state without a corresponding cession to all states. The equal footing doctrine does not affect Congress' power to dispose of federal property.

Federal Power over Public Lands:

The public domain passes to the United States upon the admission of a state to the Union; this is implicit in the acts of admission. Regulations dealing with the care and disposition of public lands within the boundaries of a new state may properly be embraced in its act of admission, as within the sphere of the plain power of Congress. United States v. Sandoval, 231 U.S. 28 (1913). No state legislation may interfere with Congress' power over the public domain; to prevent any attempt at interference, the act of admission usually contains an agreement by the state not to interfere. Gibson v. Chouteau, 80 U.S. (13 Wall.) 92 (1871); Van Brocklin v. State of Tennessee, 117 U.S. 151 (1886). Nevada was admitted to the Union subject to such an agreement.

[The Property Clause] entrusts Congress with power over the public land without limitations; it is not for the courts to say how that trust shall be administered, but for Congress to determine. Necessarily, then, the U.S. Government may sell public land or withhold it from sale. Light v. United States, 220 U.S. 523, 570 (1911); Camfield v. United States, 167 U.S. 518 (1897). Thus, the consent of the state is not required for Congress to withdraw large bodies of land from settlement. Light v. United States, supra. That a power may be injuriously exercised is no reason for a misconstruction of the scope and extent of that power. Stearns v. Minnesota, 179 U.S. 223 (1900).

The responsibility of Congress to utilize the country's assets in a way that it decides is best for the future of the nation is a sort of trust, but not in the sense that a private trustee holds for the benefit of the trust's beneficiaries.

It appearing beyond doubt that the plaintiff can prove no set of facts which would entitle it to judicial relief, the defendants' motion to dismiss for failure to state a claim upon which relief can be granted, must be granted.

* * *

NOTES

1. In February 1983 the Ninth Circuit affirmed the foregoing decision, but on different grounds:

* * *

In December of 1978 Acting Assistant Secretary of the Interior Wicks rescinded the moratorium order of 1964. Nevada filed an amended complaint after the rescission further elaborating its philosophy on federal landholding, but the amended complaint sought no additional or alternative relief to that sought in the original complaint. In this appeal from the district court's dismissal of the action, Nevada has not asked for any judicial relief other than an injunction against a similar moratorium in the future; nor has Nevada indicated what legal rights, apart from issues relating to the moratorium, it would ask the district court to determine if the case were remanded.

Nevada agrees that this case does not involve a claim of title to land. Rather, Nevada in one of its own publications appended to its brief in this appeal, has said that the case involves the "narrower" issue of "whether federal proprietary discretion over the public lands is essentially unlimited or instead must be exercised in a manner that will result in effective rather than simply formalistic legal equality among the states." This formulation may outline public policy objectives; but it does not describe a controversy susceptible to judicial determination.

Nevada ex rel. Nevada State Board of Agriculture v. United States, 699 F.2d 486 (9th Cir.1983).

2. The Nevada Attorney General's Office informed the editors that the litigation is not necessarily over, but that its reinstitution must await a concrete dispute that amounts to a case or controversy. On the

litigation and the motivating forces behind it, see generally Leshy, Unraveling the Sagebrush Rebellion: Law, Politics, and Federal Lands, 14 U.C.D. L.Rev. 317 (1980); Clayton, The Sagebrush Rebellion: Who Should Control the Public Lands?, 1980 Utah L.Rev. 505; Titus, The Nevada "Sagebrush Rebellion" Act: A Question of Constitutionality, 23 Ariz.L.Rev. 263 (1981). The Supreme Court's subsequent decision in Block v. North Dakota, 461 U.S. 273 (1983), may spell a procedural death knell for Nevada's attempt to win title to the public lands through litigation. In *Block,* lower courts had agreed that North Dakota was entitled to certain disputed lands, but the Supreme Court held that the statute of limitations in the Quiet Title Act, 28 U.S.C.A. § 2409a, barred the state's suit because it was not brought within twelve years. As Nevada's claims, if any, accrued at statehood, if at all, the period of limitations may have lapsed long ago.

3. President Reagan and Secretary of the Interior Watt both pledged allegiance to the Sagebrush Rebellion prior to the 1980 election. What is the obligation of government officials who find themselves defending against claims that they agree with philosophically? Mr. Watt stated in his confirmation hearings that his new "good neighbor" policy would make wholesale divestiture unnecessary. The western ardor for federal disposition apparently was already cooling at that time as states realized that the costs of divestiture might outweigh benefits. See [Arizona Governor] Babbitt, Federalism and the Environment: An Intergovernmental Perspective of the Sagebrush Rebellion, 12 Envtl.L. 847 (1982).

Professor Leshy, in his insightful chapter on "Sharing Federal Multiple-Use Lands" in RETHINKING THE FEDERAL LANDS 235, 272 (S. Brubaker, ed., 1984), persuasively demonstrates that the various economic and other interests in the West will oppose any radical change for fear of losing the considerable benefits they now enjoy:

> The key interests concerned with federal multiple-use land management are relatively numerous these days and, perhaps more important, each interest commands enough political power to exercise veto power against proposals for major change which it finds unacceptable. As a result, existing arrangements for use of these lands have grown up largely incrementally, by piecemeal, transitory compromise. Though my purpose here has not been to serve as an apologist for the status quo, in a sense that is the burden of my presentation. By leaving federal land management to the vagaries of the political process, we have erected a patchwork structure which is, like the tax code and the political process they both reflect, full of inertia and Byzantine interrelationships.

> The result is likely to be a stalemate on bold proposals for reform, and continuing incremental change. It usually has been this way, although the dramatically increased political power wielded by recreationists and preservationists and the enlarged role of the courts in recent years have further dif-

fused the power to influence federal land management policies, and have enlarged the dimensions of the balancing of interests which shapes those policies. And, I believe, it will continue to be so until the right combination of ideas, people, and triggering events can be found to dramatically shift political power among those diffused interests. Perhaps "privatization," Ronald Reagan, and the Sagebrush Rebellion are such a combination, but the signs are not, I think, particularly favorable to their cause.

"Privatization," an offshoot of the Sagebrush Rebellion, was a program to sell public lands to reduce the federal budget deficit in the early days of the Reagan Administration; it, too, apparently has passed into oblivion. See infra at page 273.

4. The historic drama of state creation, with its inevitable federal/state friction, is being reenacted on a larger scale in Alaska. See infra page 165. But while some western states are agitating for less federal restrictions on public land developments, other states are fighting federal developments deemed by them to be harmful to their environment. See, e.g., California v. Block, 690 F.2d 753 (9th Cir.1982), infra at page 1001. In other instances, the ownership of certain lands is still being disputed between state and federal governments. See, e.g., Block v. North Dakota, 461 U.S. 273 (1983). Our unique federal system ensures a constant tension among levels of government that is frequently focused on uses and abuses of the federal lands.

———

The outright land grants to states were not the only implementation of the federal policy of assisting states through public land revenues. Beginning with the Reclamation Act of 1902, 43 U.S.C.A. § 371 et seq., a series of federal statutes has provided that revenues accruing from uses of the retained public lands will be shared with the states in which the lands are located. These continuing federal programs under the Reclamation Act, the Mineral Leasing Act of 1920, 30 U.S.C.A. § 181 et seq., the Federal Power Act of 1920, 16 U.S.C.A. §§ 791a–825r, the Taylor Grazing Act of 1934, 43 U.S.C.A. § 315 et seq., and the Submerged Lands Act of 1953, 43 U.S.C.A. § 1301 et seq., among others, will be discussed below. Attention now reverts to the various forms of individual homesteading by which the bulk of the country was settled.

3. GRANTS TO SETTLERS

Official national public land policy for 150 years was directed primarily at getting the lands into the hands of the pioneer, the small farmer seeking a new life on the frontier. The official policy was undercut from many directions, it resulted in as much individual heartbreak as eventual happy prosperity, and it both succeeded and failed. It succeeded in that millions were able to build new lives on cheap or free land, there to develop communities, commerce, and other attributes of civilization. The country was developed and unified; the lands and resources nurtured and sustained the characteristic American ingenuity and industry; and the Nation rapidly rose to pinnacles of wealth and power. But the national policy also failed in many respects. Disdain for legal requirements bred widespread lawlessness. The development of individual and corporate monopoly ownerships operated to exclude the small farmer. Many could not make a go of it; the berserk Colorado farmwife in Michener's *Centennial* had many models from real life.

The following account of how individual settlers could and did acquire title to public lands is painted with a broad brush and necessarily omits most nuances and details. As an introduction, consider these excerpts from B.H. Hibbard, A HISTORY OF THE PUBLIC LAND POLICIES * 136, 138–39 (1924, U.Wis.ed. 1965):

> No doubt the leading men in Congress, and out, during the period of attempted use of the public domain as a source of revenue would have insisted that they were undertaking to promote national development through their land policies. In the perspective of a century and a half, however, it appears that a much clearer and more comprehensive outlook upon national development characterized the actions of 1841 than had been discernible a half century before. True, this outlook was not gained by the instantaneous falling of the scales from the eyes of the men in charge of affairs at that time. Washington and Jefferson had held progressive and liberal ideas. Benton and John Quincy Adams, in different ways, had tried to link the new West to the older settlements by internal improvements, fostered and supported by federal liberality and expenditure. The long succession of preemption acts were but the premonitions of a free land policy, a policy destined to come, but hindered by sectional interests and differences for many years.

*   *   *

> For a half century, or more, following 1841 the policy of using the public domain in the promotion of settlement, the very basis of national strength and security, of civilization itself, was accepted and furthered in the disposition of the western lands. It was the fruition of the work and teachings of such men as Gallatin, Jefferson and Benton. In 1826 Benton had said regarding a liberal treatment of the western pioneer: "I speak to Senators who know this to be a Republic, not a Monarchy, who know that the public lands belong to the People and not to the Federal Government." Thus debts were to be forgiven, preemption was to be granted, land was to be made easy of access and of acquisition, indeed free as soon as the East could be converted to the view.

Every new Territory and State wanted people to take up and use the vacant lands. Immigration agents were employed by the state. Advertising campaigns were adroitly conducted by the railroads. The private land agent became an institution, offering to conduct land seekers to the best locations. All forces combined to get the land into the hands of settlers. The government helped the campaign along. With the transportation lines established, the ownership of land assumed a new aspect; values were expected to increase. In the early years of the development of farms on the frontier the settler was looking for room, for a chance to support himself and family. With a market assured, not by going around half a continent by water, taking weeks for the trip, but going with speed directly toward the eastern seaboard with its cities, meant a price for product which would soon reflect itself in land values of the West. Thus the farmer, not altogether for the first time, but with a new emphasis, began to look upon the land as a prize in itself, easily obtained, and likely to increase rapidly in value. With this optimism permeating the imaginations of the oncoming waves of settlers it was inevitable that more enterprising adventurers should precede them and profit by the optimism by taking the first advance in price over the government minimum. The Preemption Act was designed to preclude, at least to restrict this practice.

a. PREEMPTION

Since before the Revolution, the common practice—as epitomized in the exploits of Daniel Boone—was to stake out a claim on the edge of the frontier and later, perhaps, pay whoever turned out to be the patent holder. Squatting has had a long if less than honorable history; in the early days of the Republic, troops were called out on several occasions to remove squatters from land owned by the government or speculators. As Jefferson noted in 1776, "they will settle the lands in spite of everybody." The United States struggled with the problem for a century, and while the right of "preemption" usually prevailed, the dilemma between the desire to accommodate the actual settlers and protection of actual or potential purchasers was never finally resolved.

Preemption was the preferential right of settler-squatters to buy their claims at modest prices without competitive bidding. The squatters alternatively desired compensation for any improvements they had made. From 1790 onward, Congress received numerous impassioned petitions and memorials asking for confirmation of title to those who had illegally braved the frontier hazards. To quiet settler resentment of prevailing policy, 24 special acts were adopted before 1820 granting preemption privileges to special groups or within certain territories and states. Payment was usually required, but liberal credit was extended—and extended again. Since the squatters had often ranged beyond the surveyors and land offices, title questions long remained unsettled.

A uniform policy was hard to come by: eastern congressmen criticized the Westerners for being greedy, lawless, disloyal landgrabbers who had no respect for order, absentee owners, or Indian rights; western representatives, however, presented the squatters as loyal people who had exhausted their resources in reaching the West and who had defended the frontier against the marauding Indians.

In 1830, a retroactive, one-year general preemption measure was passed (because it was ignored in the heat of more pressing matters), but abuses by those claiming under it retarded progress toward a permanent preemption law. Nevertheless, and despite acute difficulties in administration, another series of limited preemption acts was passed up to 1840, and several million acres were eventually patented for $1.25 per acre under this method. Some thought that preemption rights had become unnecessary because "claims associations" of settlers had sprung up to keep competition out of bidding by threats of violence, as speculators had done by illegal agreement. Until 1841, all preemption statutes had been retroactive; i.e., they validated previous claims but did not authorize future squatting.

The General Preemption Act of 1841 finally authorized prospective preemption as part of a package of provisions engineered by Henry Clay, including the 500,000 acre grants to states and other pot sweeteners. The Act abandoned the view that all settlement on unoffered public land was illegal but sanctioned further settlement only on surveyed land. A maximum of 160 acres could be obtained by occupying settlers for $1.25 per acre, and a number of eligibility conditions were imposed. Abuses under the Act were notable not only for speculation and fraud, the common sports of the day, but also for the practice of squatting on timberland, stripping it bare, and then abandoning the claim for another. It was estimated in 1849 that "not three of a hundred" preemption declarations went to patent (documentary fee title). Before 1862, many national benefits in terms of settlement and title security accrued from preemption in spite of its many problems, but after that date, it was subject to major and obvious abuse that led to its repeal in 1891. The more usual homesteading methods had proceeded concurrently with preemption.

b.   CREDIT AND CASH SALES

The young Nation had a legacy of debt and but two sources of revenue: tariffs and land sales. After some years of inconclusive debate over revenue versus settlement, and cash versus credit, and small versus large holdings, Congress passed the Land Act of 1796. It adopted the 36 section rectangular system of survey and provided for land auctions at minimum prices of $2.00 per acre (Hamilton had advocated 20 cents), but with only five percent of the purchase price down, the balance in a year. The important distinction (for preemption) between offered and unoffered tracts was also created. Requirements of administration led to the organization of the General Land

Office in 1812, which remained in business until it was absorbed into the BLM in 1946.

The 1796 Act did not produce the revenue anticipated, and the Congress in ensuing years progressively liberalized the credit terms and other conditions. Sales greatly increased, but speculation became common and many settlers could not make payments. That led to a series of relief acts by which delinquents were relieved of forfeiture threats under the original law. Relief only increased speculation and indebtedness; by the end of 1819, over 22 million dollars was owed the federal government, most in arrears. While continuing its liberality toward hard-pressed settlers into the next decades, Congress in 1820 ended the credit sale experiment.

Under the Act of April 24, 1820, cash at time of purchase at auction was required; lands offered but unsold were then open to private entry at a lower price. Settlers detested auction sales and urged their postponement year after year to spite the cash-rich speculators. The activities of speculators' and claims' associations grew more fraudulent and more violent, and the claims clubs did not end with grant of prospective preemption in 1841. An act of 1830 prohibiting combinations to prevent competition at land auctions accomplished little, even though the Westerners professed themselves totally against "Monopoly." Even after the great land boom of the 1830's, less than half of the 190 million acres of surveyed, offered lands had been purchased by cash sale, preemption, or otherwise. Fraud and speculation had become so virulent, and large monopolistic land companies so prevalent, that in the Specie Circular of 1836, President Jackson, himself no mean speculator, placed severe limitations on future sales and recommended that only actual bona fide settlers be allowed to purchase and patent. Due to the Panic of 1837 and the ensuing depression, land sales fell off drastically until 1845. Public policy was riven by the now traditional East-West split, and was further confused by acute ambiguity in the settlers' policy desires. But with preemption, veteran's bounties, and grants to states, a new land rush commenced that was not abated until President Pierce withdrew 31 million acres from entry in 1853. Uncertain of the constitutionality of that action, Pierce then restored the lands the following year. Railroad and canal grants opened even more land at this time.

In the great rush westward, vast acreage considered undesirable remained unsold in the older public land states. In 1854 the Graduation Act was passed, providing that the price for land long unclaimed would be reduced in proportion to the time unsold, down to $1.00 after 10 years, and down to 12½ cents an acre after 30 years ("one-bit" land). As in earlier and later legislation, a limit of 320 acres per claimant was imposed. As in the other legislation, it was easily circumvented. The Graduation Act triggered another land rush; e.g., in Missouri, 64 percent of the 14 million acres of "graduated" land had been taken by 1862. Coupled with sales under other statutes, an unprecedented amount of land passed out of the public domain in the 1850's, causing endless confusion and antagonism. States, railroads, miners, speculators, and settlers all disputed with the federal government and each other. Ferment for land reform grew side by side with political ferment over slavery.

Although the federal policy of disposing of the public domain almost as fast as possible frequently was accomplished by dubious means, it did achieve in large measure its end of providing land for small farmers. The speculators and money lenders may have been despised, but their self-interest also contributed greatly to the development of the Trans-Appalachian West. Jefferson's goal of a dominant agrarian "yeomanry" was largely realized—but, at the same time, an alarming increase in tenant farming was also taking place.

c. HOMESTEADING

By the time of the Civil War, revenues from land sales as a percentage of the federal budget had declined drastically. Emigration and industrialization had created a class of landless, unemployed eastern workers. The government had resorted to "donation" acts, essentially giving away to actual settlers lands it wished quickly settled, such as Oregon. The cash requirement favored speculators and was thought to retard settlement. An Illinois Representative, arguing for free land, emoted:

> Unless the government shall grant head rights * * * prairies, with their gorgeous growth of flowers, their green carpeting, their lovely lawns and gentle slopes, will for centuries continue to be the home of the wild deer and wolf; their stillness will be undisturbed by the jocund song of the farmer, and their deep and fertile soil unbroken by the ploughshare. Something must be done to remedy this evil. [Quoted in P. Foss, POLITICS AND GRASS 20 (1960)].

Public land reform became a national crusade, resulting in the great Homestead Act of 1862, 43 U.S.C.A. § 161 et seq. (repealed 1976). The South had previously opposed land policy liberalization, correctly fearing that new antislavery states would be created. But secession opened the way for the northern legislators to push through the statute that would govern agrarian disposition for 114 years. It authorized entry onto 160 acres of any land subject to preemption, later extended to unsurveyed lands where Indian title was extinguished. To those who met the requirements, the land was free, except for filing fees. A settler was allowed six months to establish actual residence after application. Thereafter, actual settlement and cultivation were required for five years, after which a patent would issue upon affidavit. Only one homestead was allowed, but a homesteader could also claim a preemption of another 160 acres—though not at the same time. The Act, however, contained few safeguards, and the preemption, cash sales, state grants, and railroad grants remained in effect. In 1862, the states, railroads, and Indians controlled 440 million acres of the West. Over 600 million acres remained, but relatively little was arable. After the Civil War, the incongruous disposal laws of the United States combined to produce the "Great American Barbeque," a generation's unparalleled plunder of the Nation's natural resources. Less than a third of the new farms created in the 1860's were by homesteading, and not until the 1880's did homesteads constitute a majority of new farms.

Homesteading became the national preoccupation, but difficulties in its administration multiplied. Many chose not to wait the five years but "commuted" their claim by payment. Homesteads and preemption claims were used to strip timber lands without any payment. Perjury became universal as speculators again surmounted legal barriers such as the 160 acre limitation. The semi-arid lands beyond the 100th meridian were not sufficiently productive to support small farming units. Surveying was fragmented (in 1877 there were 16 surveyors general), incomplete, and often fraudulent. Litigation proliferated, as legislation already had done. Publication of the voluminous reports of a public land law review commission effected little change. More specialized land grant acts, summarized below, complicated the overall picture. Indian reservations were broken up both by treaty and by allotment to individual tribal members. In either case, the lands soon passed into white hands. Settlement proceeded apace—one half million farms were created between 1880 and 1900. Range wars between settlers, sheepmen, and cattle ranchers periodically erupted. Foreign owners gained title to immense tracts: a company owned by a Scot was said to have fenced in over a million acres. Even though the famous inclosure order of 1885 was enforced strictly at first, President Roosevelt 15 years later had to start removing the unlawful fences all over again. Whenever a federal official made a proposal for radical, effective reform, or made a point of decrying abuses under the land laws, or tried to do something about it, his job was in jeopardy.

Notwithstanding the fraud, politics, and other problems, much of the West was settled under the Homestead and cognate acts. True, often the final farm size was far in excess of the legal limits, but often conditions dictated larger farming units. Hostility to large holdings was directed at aliens, and in 1887 alien ownership was severely restricted. Many of the more abused laws were repealed in 1891, but the Homestead Act survived. From 1868 to 1904, when much remaining land was withdrawn from entry, nearly 100 million acres were homesteaded, many if not most by the yeoman tillers of the soil that the expressed national policy was intended to benefit.

d. DESERT LANDS

The liberal terms of the Homestead Act and available means to circumvent its acreage limitations did not stem the pressure for more specialized disposition laws under which larger tracts could pass legally. Lands east of the 100th meridian were settled quickly, and those beyond went begging for lack of suitability to conventional farming. By 1877, much of the remaining unclaimed land was in the arid and semi-arid regions of the West. Settlement was difficult because the irrigation necessary was thought to require large capital and larger blocks of land. One solution, large grants to corporations, was in bad odor in the wake of the railroad abuses. To better open those lands, Congress in the Desert Lands Act of 1877, 43 U.S.C.A. §§ 321–39 (as amended), provided for entry on 640 acres at only 25 cents an acre, with patent to follow upon proof that the land had been irrigated. Although over 33 million acres would eventually be entered and over ten million acres patented under the Desert Lands Act, it failed entirely to accomplish its purposes. Large corporations got the bulk of the available lands through dummies. Some people received patents after hauling a can of water to the claim and swearing that irrigation had been achieved. Very little land ever became irrigated; most claims were used for stock grazing. Concern about the misuse of the Act led Congress in 1888 to provide for reservation from entry of lands found by the Geological Survey to be necessary for reservoirs and irrigation works. Effective administration of the proviso, however, removed so much land from entry that in 1890 the withdrawn land was restored to the public domain—although new claims were limited to 320 acres. The failure of private irrigation efforts led more or less directly to the Reclamation Act of 1902, infra at page 128.

e. VETERAN'S BOUNTIES

Individuals serving the armed forces in time of war also received the benefit of special disposition laws. Land grants to military veterans have ancient origins and serve the functions of rewarding the aggressive conquerors while removing them from the civilized vicinity. The practice was followed by the United States after the Revolution, and for as long thereafter as the Nation was land rich and cash poor. Because the early grants were commonly made in scrip, ownership concentration became common, and absentee ownership generated disputes with squatters and others. It is not known how many acres were granted to veterans over the past 200 years, but bounty warrants for over 60 million acres were issued between 1847 and 1906. The practice ended after the Spanish-American War, but scrip and warrants were still dribbling into government land offices in the mid-20th century. By a 1955 statute, scrip of all descriptions had to be recorded within two years, and any unsatisfied existing rights were to be extinguished by purchase thereafter.

f. STOCK–RAISING HOMESTEADS

With the repeal of preemption and the end of the true frontier by 1890, it might seem that entry for homesteading and other purposes would have declined if not ceased by 1900. As the accompanying chart shows, that was not to be the case, for Congress was still determined to create settlement opportunities and dispose of the federal lands. In Nebraska, almost nine million acres open to entry had gone unclaimed by 1903. In the Kinkaid Act of 1904, 43 U.S.C.A. § 224 (repealed 1976) Congress allowed entry (for the benefit of cattle raisers) on 640 acres in

Western Nebraska for $1.25 per acre. By 1920 nearly all the land in Nebraska had been claimed. The purpose of encouraging small stock-raising homesteads was not achieved, however, because by the usual devices nearly all of the land passed to the large ranchers, and the small operators were wiped out by weather and less neutral means. In one county by 1928 the average ranch was 6,681 acres, or more than ten times the allowable homestead size.

Another 20th century disposition measure was the Enlarged Homestead Act of 1909, 43 U.S.C.A. §§ 218–21 (repealed 1976). The 1909 Act allowed entry upon 320 instead of 160 acres west of the 100th meridian. The rush to take up enlarged homesteads abated with a drought, and most entries ended in failure for the same reason: in one area, 247 out of 250 claims had been abandoned. In large part, enlarged homesteads also ended up in the hands of large ranchers, even after later liberalization of settlement conditions. Dry farming was and is an extremely hazardous occupation financially.

Total Disposals

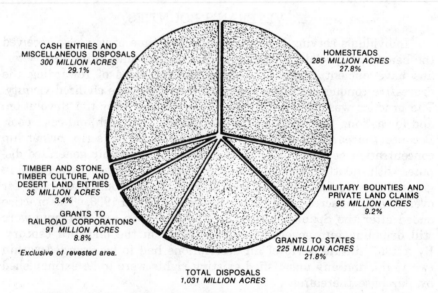

Approximate Area of the Public Domain Disposed of Under the Public Land Laws

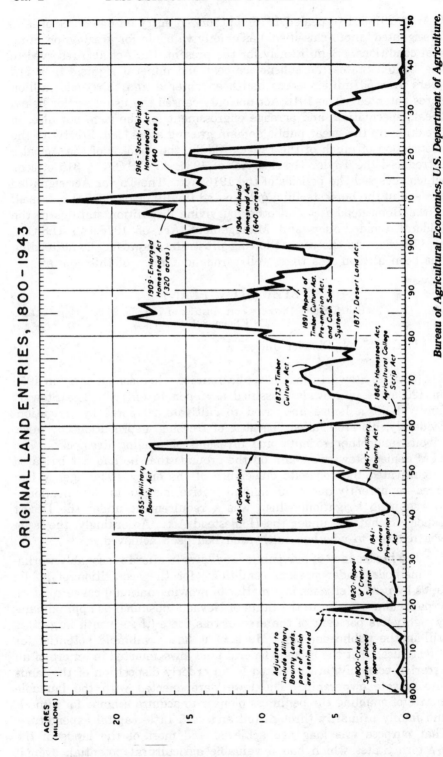

ORIGINAL LAND ENTRIES, 1800–1943

Bureau of Agricultural Economics, U.S. Department of Agriculture.

If prior experience furnished a lesson, it had not yet been learned by Congress. In spite of a growing sentiment for a leasing system, even among cattlemen, the Stock-Raising Homestead Act of 1916, 43 U.S.

C.A. §§ 291–301 (repealed 1976), authorized entry on 640 acres of land "designated" (not "classified") as chiefly valuable for grazing, on minimal conditions. Significantly for the present, the Act also reserved to the United States the subsurface coal and mineral rights. In a few years over 50 million acres had been entered and thirty-odd million acres patented. The 1916 Act not only caused the usual settler heartbreak, speculation, and acreage engrossment for the rich, but also, in breaking up the great public domain grazing areas, led directly to the destruction of much of the range. Oddly, the sponsor of the Act also introduced the Taylor Grazing Act of 1934, 43 U.S.C.A. § 315 et seq., which reversed the policies of the 1916 Act. The Taylor Act signalled the end of the homesteading era, an end finally made official by repeal of the Homestead Act and other surviving disposition statutes in the Federal Land Policy and Management Act of 1976, 43 U.S.C.A. §§ 1701–84. As the case following illustrates, however, homesteading has been alive if less than well throughout most of this century.

STEWART v. PENNY

United States District Court, District of Nevada, 1965.
238 F.Supp. 821.

THOMPSON, District Judge.

* * *

[Charles Stewart filed an application for a homestead entry in 1953 on 120 acres in Nevada classified as "open to entry." The Stewart family built a house and tried to cultivate 20 acres by irrigation. Evidently, his crop failed "because of freezing, depredations by mice, rabbits, and other rodents, and invasions of ranging livestock." The BLM denied Stewart's claim on the grounds that he had not irrigated or cultivated the requisite one-eighth of the entry. The agency had erred—apparently due to an administrative mistake in classification—by requiring irrigation, which was a requirement under the Desert Lands Act but not under the Homestead Act. Accordingly, the issue was reduced to whether cultivation had been achieved.]

The inadequacy of our public land laws to afford reasonably workable methods, under present conditions, for the acquisition of public lands by private citizens is a matter of growing national concern. It is of particular concern to the State of Nevada inasmuch as approximately eighty-five per cent of the area of this State (the seventh largest) is still in the public domain. Much of it has a valuable potential for private use. Yet the archaic federal land laws, enacted in an era of an agrarian economy, are ill-suited to an orderly disposition of the lands into private ownership. The laws were enacted with the laudable motive of enabling the penniless pioneer to acquire a home for himself and family primarily through toil and with little capital expenditure. That purpose was long ago achieved and most of the lands of the Western States which had a valuable agricultural potential, even if only marginally so, have been patented to individuals under the beneficent laws to the exclusion of the wealthy who, under a different policy, might have acquired large blocks of public lands by purchase. The inapplicability of this policy to modern conditions has, during the past quarter-century, accomplished a virtual deep-freeze of public lands in federal ownership. * * *

* * *

SCOPE OF REVIEW

The Government has filed an excellent brief in which it argues, in part, that the decision of the Secretary finding non-compliance with the statutory requirements for valid homestead entry is conclusive and binding upon the courts. We recognize the peculiar and specialized knowledge of the officials of the Department of the Interior respecting the interpretation of the multifarious laws and regulations relating to public lands, and that Congress has entrusted the guardianship of the public domain to the Department of the Interior. We have relied upon that knowledge and expertise in reaching our conclusions. We cannot, however, accept without limitation a contention that a high administrative official in Washington, D.C. is better qualified than others to analyze and draw conclusive fact inferences from a cold record produced at an evidentiary hearing three thousand miles away and relating to physical conditions with which he has questionable familiarity, conditions normally deemed to be within the realm of judicial notice. We deem the correct rule of judicial review to be that announced in Foster v. Seaton, 1959, 106 U.S.App.D.C. 253, 271 F.2d 836: "Thus the case really comes down to a question whether the Secretary's finding was supported by substantial evidence on the record as a whole."

* * *

The omnipotence of the Department of the Interior as guardian of the public domain is exhibited when the Department acts affirmatively and grants patents under the public land laws. The converse is not true. An entry or application for patent which is contested or rejected by the Secretary presents issues regarding the legal rights of the entryman under the public land laws. These are rights established by Congress which the Secretary of the Interior may not arbitrarily or capriciously ignore and which must be determined within the due process safeguards of the Administrative Procedure Act.

* * *

GOOD FAITH

The Director of the Bureau placed his decision of April 11, 1961 upon the ground that the applicant had not shown good faith. This was not an issue presented by the contest complaint. The Secretary discarded the issue of good faith, saying:

"Hence, I am unable to find, on the basis of the evidence adduced at the hearing, that there was a total want of the type of cultivation reasonably calculated to produce profitable results. If this were the only pertinent factor in the case, it would be necessary to remand the case for the taking of further evidence. However, I believe that this is unnecessary

since, after a careful examination of the evidence, I am obliged
to conclude that the entryman did not apply the processes of
cultivation which he employed to the required ⅛ of the acreage
of the entry so that he failed to meet the cultivation requirement of the homestead law for this reason."

The good faith requirement stems from 43 U.S.C.A. § 162 requiring
the applicant to make oath "that such application is honestly and in
good faith made for the purpose of actual settlement and cultivation,
and not for the benefit of any other person, persons or corporation, and
that he or she will faithfully and honestly endeavor to comply with all
the requirements of law as to settlement, residence and cultivation
necessary to acquire title to the land applied for."   *   *   *   An
appropriate statement of the meaning of good faith in this context is
found in Carr v. Fife (CC Wash.1891), 44 F. 713:

> " *   *   * whether he (the applicant) had actually, within
> the time limited by law, established his residence upon the
> land, with the intention of acquiring it for a home; whether he
> had continued to actually reside upon the land; whether he
> was really engaged in improving the land, or in good faith
> intending to do so; or whether he was only making a *colorable
> pretense* of residing upon and improving the land for the
> purpose of stripping it of its valuable timber, and acquiring it
> for *speculative purposes,* without complying with the terms of
> the homestead law."   (Emphasis added)

The words "colorable pretense" and "speculative purposes" are
operative and characterize the meaning of good faith in fulfilling the
specific requirements of residence and cultivation under the homestead
law.   They refer to the intent and motive of the applicant.

In the light of what Stewart did on the land, it is inconceivable to
this Court that there could be found the slightest semblance of an issue
of good faith.   *   *   *   He was seventy-eight years old when final proof
was filed, about four years after homestead entry was approved.   There
is not the least intimation that the land is valuable for anything other
than grazing and agriculture, so there is no basis for speculating about
"speculative purposes".

*   *   *

That the homestead laws should be liberally applied in favor of the
entryman is established by law and is not a matter of the whim or
predisposition of the particular Secretary of the Interior who graces the
office.   The Supreme Court of the United States has established the
principle.   Ard v. Brandon, 1895, 156 U.S. 537:

> "The law deals tenderly with one who, in good faith, goes
> upon the public lands, with a view of making a home thereon.
> If he does all that the statute prescribes as the condition of
> acquiring rights, the law protects him in those rights, and does
> not make their continued existence depend alone upon the
> question whether or not he takes an appeal from an adverse

decision of the officers charged with the duty of acting upon his application."

* * *

ACREAGE CULTIVATED

On the issue of the acreage cultivated, the Hearing Examiner stated that he could not find that 20 acres were cultivated, as alleged by contestee Stewart, but that "neither can I find that less than one-eighth of the entry (15 acres) was cultivated as alleged by contestant." The Examiner then volunteered the opinion that the burden of proof was on the Government. We do not agree. The Administrative Procedure Act imposes the burden of proof on "the proponent of a rule or order" (5 U.S.C.A. § 1006[c]). In our case, Stewart's Homestead Entry Final Proof, filed January 14, 1959, was an application for patent. Procedurally, the Contest Complaint filed by the Department was, in effect, an Answer to the Final Proof affirmatively specifying the alleged deficiencies. * * * The true proponent of the rule or order is the applicant for patent or other right to public lands claiming compliance with the public land laws. The government "bears only the burden of going forward with sufficient evidence to establish a prima facie case, and the burden then shifts to the claimant to show by a preponderance of the evidence that his claim is valid."

* * *

[The court found, based on surveys and aerial photographs, that Stewart had in fact cultivated 15 acres, even if the crop failed.]

We have related the administrative history of this case at some length. The varying approaches to decision adopted in the administrative hierarchy seem to us to stem from a basic feeling that the area was not properly classified for homestead entry. This may or may not be so. Perhaps it would have been more prudent to classify less than the entire 120 acres covered by the amended application as suitable for homestead entry. Once the entry was allowed, however, all the entryman had to do was comply with the statutory requirements to be entitled to patent. The photographs, maps and testimony prove that he did so, taking into consideration "the degree and condition in life" of the entryman and the obstacles of nature and environment with which he contended.

* * *

NOTES

1. In Falkner v. Watt, 661 F.2d 809 (9th Cir.1981), plaintiffs claimed that their applications to open land for entry under the Desert Lands Act, 43 U.S.C.A. §§ 321–23, pursuant to the procedure in the Taylor Grazing Act, 43 U.S.C.A. § 315f, required the Secretary to accept the applications, to reclassify the lands, and to give them a preference right to enter. The Department had earlier classified the land as unsuitable for agriculture and was holding all proposed reclassifications in abeyance pending completion of a general land use plan.

Relying on Nelson v. Andrus, 591 F.2d 1265 (9th Cir.1978), and Bleamaster v. Morton, 448 F.2d 1289 (9th Cir.1971), the court rejected all of plaintiffs' claims. The Ninth Circuit held that the Secretary's duty to classify extends only to unclassified lands, and not to reclassification upon application, and that, when reclassified for entry, the prior applicants are not entitled to preference. Since no final reclassification decision has been made, review was premature.

2.   What about the psychological effect of the end of the frontier? Is the Nation better or worse off for the lack of an area where society's poor, dispossessed, and criminal elements can start anew on the land? Are the dilapidated central cities the new frontier? Is it coincidental that new housing rehabilitation programs are called "urban homesteading"? Programs for reinvigoration of rural homesteading have also been proposed. See Stuck, Modern Innovations to the Homestead Concept, 21 S.Dak.L.Rev. 542 (1976).

4. GRANTS TO MINERS

Homesteading, railroad grants, and military bounties have ceased on the public lands, but mining is a different story: it is still governed by an act that was ancient before the frontier was closed. Only a few historical developments will be touched on in this section.

Although the Congress of Confederation had reserved to the Nation one-third of the precious metals on public lands, that measure died with ratification of the Constitution, and Congress did not consider mining at all until 1807. From then until 1846, the government attempted to lease the lead mines of Indiana, Illinois, and Missouri for revenue and to insure ammunition, but failure of administration, fraud, and uncertainty caused the experiment to be abandoned. Cases arising under the leasing system, however, established two fundamental land law principles: Congress has the constitutional power to lease public lands, United States v. Gratiot, 39 U.S. (14 Pet.) 526 (1840); and unauthorized mining on the public domain is an actionable trespass, United States v. Gear, 44 U.S. (3 How.) 120 (1845).

From 1847 to 1872, and later, most of the mineral land east of the Mississippi, including the immensely valuable iron and copper ore in Michigan and Minnesota, went for $1.25 an acre via preemption, cash purchase, or homestead. The government was unable or unwilling to check this seeming perversion of the public land acts, and the local people found nothing strange in homestead entries on claims virtually worthless for agriculture.

During the great California Gold Rush, the only law governing miners was the "law of the mining camps." A great deal of nonsense has been written about the customary mining camp law as a distinctive contribution to American jurisprudence. In fact, it was conceived out of necessity, it was simple, it followed the general public land law precept of first in time, first in right, and it was enforced at the end of a rope. Mining law proceeded from the same premises as the preemption and prior appropriation doctrines, although it did contain some specifics such as discovery, marking of claims, and so forth. That "law" also governed the camps that mushroomed and died all over the West in the next several decades, because Congress took no action until 1866.

a. THE CALIFORNIA GOLD RUSH

RODMAN W. PAUL, CALIFORNIA GOLD *
20–25 (1947).

In the history of almost any of the American states one can find a few events and trends that in significance stand out from the purely local as sharply as a single tree upon a desert plain. The Gold Rush is an instance. Within California the Gold Rush was a revolution that changed forever the character of the state. Beyond California's boundaries it was a magnetic force that sent its lines of attraction into every nation.

Within two years of Marshall's discovery every civilized country knew the name "California," although at that time few persons in Europe, or Asia, or Latin America could have identified Illinois, or Massachusetts, or Georgia. In all parts of the world men made ready to seek the Golden Fleece, or to venture their money in the expeditions organized by those more daring than themselves, or to invest in the expansion of trade and shipping to which the Gold Rush was giving rise.

Even if cautious men decided to remain at home and keep their capital with them, still they could not escape entirely the effects of the train of events set in motion at Coloma. * * * Presently the basic medium in the world's currency began to increase, more rapidly than in any previous period of which there is record. In the United States alone, gold production multiplied seventy-three times during the six years that began in 1848, and from a position of insignificance among the gold producing nations, the United States climbed upward so rapidly that during the period from 1851 to 1855 it contributed nearly 45 per cent of the world's total output. The result was an inflation that affected all the countries on the earth's surface.

More dramatic and more immediately obvious was the functioning of the Gold Rush as a population movement. Here the first phase was confined to California itself. It consisted of a tumultuous stampede to the Sierra foothills by the people already in the province. * * *

Until midsummer, 1848, California's own population had sole possession of the mines. Then commenced the rush from outside the province. In June the great news reached the Hawaiian Islands, and in July crowded vessels began ferrying gold seekers—white, Kanaka, and half-breed—across the Pacific. In early August Oregon heard of the discovery and began sending delegations southward. Mexico learned of it somewhat later, and apparently did not contribute until October. Peru and Chile knew of it as early as September, and sent several

* Reprinted from CALIFORNIA GOLD by Rodman W. Paul, by permission of University of Nebraska Press. Copyright © 1947 by Rodman W. Paul.

thousand men northward in the closing months of 1848 and the early part of 1849.

Rumors of the discovery reached the Atlantic seaboard of the United States in August, but did not attract much attention until mid-September, and they were not established as fact until confirmed by the President's message to Congress on December 5. For that reason no Americans save those from Oregon and Hawaii reached California during 1848. The first to arrive were those who sailed into San Francisco harbor on February 28, 1849, at the conclusion of the voyage which inaugurated steam communication between New York and the Pacific Coast, via the Isthmus of Panama.

The bulk of the American immigration did not reach California until the vanguard of the Cape Horn sailing vessels had made port in June, July, and August, 1849, or until the overland caravans had begun to straggle in during August and September. Direct immigration from Europe was even later, and can hardly be placed much before the close of the year. Indirectly, a considerable number of Europeans of dubious background came to California during 1849 and 1850 from England's Australian penal colony.

How many joined in the rush of "forty-eight," "forty-nine," and the early fifties will never be known with any degree of accuracy, but it is clear that the influx of 1848 was comparatively so small that it was no more than a prelude to the stampede of 1849 and the subsequent years. Apparently the number of persons in the province, other than Indians, increased from about 14,000 in the summer of 1848 to somewhat less than 20,000 at the end of the year. At the latter time there must have been between 6,000 and 8,000 Americans, and several thousand Latin Americans, Europeans, and Pacific Islanders, in addition to the Spanish Californians.

Twelve months later, at the close of 1849, the population, exclusive of Indians, was probably several thousand short of 100,000, with Americans forming between one-half and two-thirds of the total. When the United States census was taken in the middle of 1850, amidst turbulent conditions that made accuracy impossible, it returned a total of only 92,597, but this figure was at least 19,000 less than the true number, since the returns were lost for San Francisco and for two other counties.

Because of the imperfect nature of the United States census of 1850, the state of California took a census of its own two years later. By that time the state had felt the full force of the Gold Rush. A host of eager gold seekers had come hurrying to El Dorado over the routes pioneered by the forty-eighters and forty-niners. There had been losses along with the gains, for some of the very dissatisfied and the very successful had soon left California, and the death-rate had been very high. The state had, however, doubled its population. Its total in 1852 seems to have been 223,856. One may summarize these several sets of figures by saying that California's population jumped from 14,000 in

1848 to something less than 100,000 at the close of 1849, and that it then advanced to 223,000 by the latter part of 1852.

MORTON v. SOLAMBO COPPER MINING CO.
Supreme Court of California, 1864.
26 Cal. 527.

[Joseph Dejon located a lode claim which he posted with his name and the names of plaintiffs' assignors without their knowledge. This quadrupled the permissible size of the claim. A few days later Dejon tore down the original location notice and replaced it with one bearing the names of defendant's assignors. The trial court instructed that if the claim was validly located, plaintiffs' assignors acquired a right to it as tenants in common, notwithstanding their lack of knowledge or consent. After reciting these facts, the California Supreme Court, per Sanderson, C.J., discussed the law of the camps.]

* * *

The six hundred and twenty-first section of the Practice Act provides that: "In actions respecting 'mining claims' proof shall be admitted of the customs, usages or regulations established and in force at the bar or diggings embracing such claims; and such customs, usages or regulations, when not in conflict with the Constitution and laws of this State, shall govern the decision of the action."

At the time the foregoing became a part of the law of the land there had sprung up throughout the mining regions of the State local customs and usages by which persons engaged in mining pursuits were governed in the acquisition, use, forfeiture or loss of mining ground. (We do not here use the word forfeiture in its common law sense, but in its mining law sense as used and understood by the miners who are the framers of our mining codes.) These customs differed in different localities and varied to a greater or less extent according to the character of the mines. They prescribed the acts by which the right to mine a particular piece of ground could be secured and its use and enjoyment continued and preserved and by what non-action on the part of the appropriator such right should become forfeited or lost and the ground become, as at first, *publici juris* and open to the appropriation of the next comer. They were few, plain and simple, and well understood by those with whom they originated. They were well adapted to secure the end designed to be accomplished, and were adequate to the judicial determination of all controversies touching mining rights. And it was a wise policy on the part of the Legislature not only not to supplant them by legislative enactments, but on the contrary to give them the additional weight of a legislative sanction. These usages and customs were the fruit of the times, and demanded by the necessities of communities who, though living under the common law, could find therein no clear and well defined rules for their guidance applicable to the new conditions by which they were surrounded, but were forced to depend upon remote analogies of doubtful application and unsatisfactory results. Having received the sanction of the Legislature, they have become as much a part of the law of the land as the common law itself, which was not adopted in a more solemn form. And it is to be regretted that the wisdom of the Legislature in thus leaving mining controversies to the arbitrament of mining laws has not always been seconded by the Courts and the legal profession, who seem to have been too long tied down to the treadmill of the common law to readily escape its thraldom while engaged in the solution of a mining controversy. These customs and usages have, in progress of time, become more general and uniform, and in their leading features are now the same throughout the mining regions of the State, and however it may have been heretofore, there is no reason why Judges or lawyers should wander, with counsel for the appellant in this case, back to the time when Abraham dug his well, or explore with them the law of agency or the Statute of Frauds in order to solve a simple question affecting a mining right, for a more convenient and equally legal solution can be found nearer home, in the "customs and usages of the bar or diggings embracing the claim" to which such right is asserted or denied.

The only question for us to determine in the present case is whether the instruction of the Court contains a correct exposition of the mining rule or custom under which the Solambo Claim was located, for that custom contains all the law applicable to the question before us, and by it the question is to be solved, whether the custom is written or unwritten, without any reference to the Statute of Frauds, or the law of agency, except as declared in the custom itself.

The custom provides that any person who has discovered a vein or lode and desires to locate a mining claim upon it for himself, or for himself and others, may do so by putting up a notice, with his own name and the names of those whom he may choose to associate with him appended thereto, to that effect, designating the extent of his claim, which may amount to three hundred feet for himself and one hundred and fifty feet for each of his associates. Thus the law itself makes the discoverer the agent of those for whom he chooses to act, and makes his act their act regardless of the fact whether they have any knowledge of it or not. The discoverer can only locate three hundred feet for himself; and if he locates more he can only do so as the agent of another; and having located for another his power as agent ceases, for beyond the act of location the custom does not authorize him to proceed as agent, and he can thereafter make no change without power to do so from the person whose name he has so used. The act of location being accomplished in the manner designated, the discoverer becomes vested with a mining right to the extent of an undivided three hundred feet and no more, and each of his associates with an undivided one hundred and fifty feet, and thereafter they hold the claim as tenants in common, provided that the discoverer or some of them enter upon and work the same. It follows that the instruction was correct, and the judgment must be affirmed.

b. THE GENERAL MINING LAW OF 1872

Between 1850 and 1866, various bills to regulate mining activities were introduced in Congress, particularly when conflicts between miners and other settlers became acute, but discussion bogged down over such questions as ways in which to exclude the Chinese from the harvest of metals. But pressure grew, and, after much maneuvering, Congress reported out the 1866 Act under the title: "An Act granting the Right of Way to Ditch and Canal Owners over the Public Lands," with which it was concerned not at all. Opponents were concerned about the "little miner," but mining already had become dominated by engineers, corporate investors, and large mines. The Mining Act of 1866 has been called the "miners' Magna Carta" because it legalized existing trespasses. The Act declared that "mineral lands are free and open to exploration and occupation" under local usage and custom. 30 U.S.C.A. § 22. Lode claims, which are veins of ore, could be patented— fee title obtained—if the miner expended $1,000 in labor or improvements and filed a description with the local land office. Existing claims were retroactively validated. The area of the claim was limited, and the cost for a patent was $5 per acre. Surface rights and extralateral rights were flexible, depending upon where the vein went.

In order to accommodate holders of worked out gold claims in California, Congress next passed the Placer Act of 1870. The earlier law had ignored placer claims, now defined as "all forms of deposit, excepting veins of quartz, or other rock in place"; these chiefly encompassed deposits in the nature of gravel. Placer locations were limited to 160 acres, to be purchased for $2.50 an acre.

The Mining Law of 1872, 30 U.S.C.A. §§ 22–39, still the main statutory provision for hardrock mining, consolidated and codified the 1866 and 1870 laws, and made several substantive changes. It qualified coverage by referring to "valuable" minerals, it increased the size of permissible lode claims and reduced the size of placer claims, it required $100 worth of annual development work for either type, and it indicated rights and liabilities in related situations. From 1872 to the present, mining law exclusive of fuel minerals and a few special problems, has concerned itself primarily with interpretation of the short and not overly specific Mining Act of 1872.

The traditional view of the principal interest granted by the 1872 Act—the unpatented mining claim—was described in Belk v. Meagher, 104 U.S. 279, 283–84 (1881):

> A mining claim perfected under the law is property in the highest sense of that term, which may be bought, sold, and conveyed, and will pass by descent. There is nothing in the act of Congress which makes actual possession any more necessary for the protection of the title acquired to such a claim by a valid location, than it is for any other grant from the United States. The language of the act is that the locators "shall have the exclusive right of possession and enjoyment of all the

surface included within the lines of their locations," which is to continue until there shall be a failure to do the requisite amount of work within the prescribed time. Congress has seen fit to make the possession of that part of the public lands which is valuable for minerals separable from the fee, and to provide for the existence of an exclusive right to the possession, while the paramount title to the land remains in the United States. * * *

In recent years, the 1872 Act has been supplemented or limited by various statutes including the Common Varieties Act, 30 U.S.C.A. § 611, the Surface Resources Act, 30 U.S.C.A. § 612, and the Federal Land Policy and Management Act, 43 U.S.C.A. §§ 1701–1784. The Forest Service and the BLM have recently adopted administrative rules regulating hardrock mining for the first time. The requirements of the National Environmental Policy Act have had some impact, as have regulatory initiatives by the states. See chapter six, § A(7), infra. All of these developments have impinged on former prerogatives of hardrock miners in some respect. Even greater changes have been wrought, however, by the segregation of fuel and chemical minerals out of the location system into a leasing regime in 1920, and by shifts in other public land policies.

5. GRANTS TO RAILROADS

By the mid-19th century, the West wanted railroads. Congress had been granting railroads rights-of-way up to 100 feet wide through the public lands since 1835, and in 1852 it adopted a general law to that effect which also authorized the use of earth, stone, and timber from adjacent public lands. In 1850, the bill to assist the Chicago to Mobile line granted Illinois, Mississippi, and Alabama the even numbered sections within six miles of the line. The states assigned the land to the builder, and the rush was on. (Thereafter, odd-numbered sections were granted so the railroads would not lose sections 16 and 36, reserved for schools.)

By 1852, seven states had submitted proposals to Congress involving 14 million acres. President Pierce, who vetoed land grants for the care of the insane, signed bills granting nearly 20 million acres to eight states for railroads by the end of his term. These were all more or less local roads. The pace of giving slowed considerably during the Buchanan Administration, but by 1860 eight roads were building or operating beyond the Mississippi. Sentiment for one or more lines to the Pacific was getting stronger.

It is not necessary to chronicle fully the splendid indifference to the common public good in the matter of transcontinental railroads. When the Great Barbeque was over, Congress had given over 90 million acres to the railroads directly and another 35–40 million acres to states to be used by the railroads (in addition to another 200 million acres for other internal improvements, some of which were also granted to railroads)

The progress of the first transcontinental line is somewhat typical of the problems generated.

The Union Pacific and the Central Pacific were financed by the Act of July 1, 1862, ch. 120, 12 Stat. 489, (liberalized in 1864). It provided the railroads construction loans and a 400 foot right of way, together with their choice of 20 odd-numbered sections within a 40 mile belt for every mile built. In furtherance of homesteading, the Act required the railroads to dispose of their lands within three years at $1.25 per acre, but the Supreme Court upheld the device of "disposing" of the lands by mortgaging them to affiliates. Platt v. Union Pacific R.R. Co., 99 U.S. 48 (1878). A provision for reversion to federal ownership if conditions were not met was also watered down by courts, Schulenberg v. Harriman, 88 U.S. (21 Wall.) 44 (1874), and only a few isolated forfeitures, declared by Congress, ever resulted from the widespread failures to comply. The timber-rich "O & C" (Oregon and California) lands were returned to the public domain in that fashion. While the roads were building, enormous quantities of land were withdrawn from settlement, and the railroads frequently delayed selection to avoid taxes. The West, which had pressed for railroad land grants, quickly became hostile to the railroads because the supply of free land dried up. From 1871 on, most efforts were directed at redressing real and imagined grievances stemming from railroad ownership and practices, but few effective remedies were ever instituted.

The Gilded Age was one of the low points of public morality in the United States, but its effects were not uniformly bad. As promoters, the railroads encouraged and directed immigration. The West was developed, and towns sprang up in the railroads' wake. Opposition to the worst abuses was noteworthy and led to some worthwhile reforms. The railroad enterprise effectively ended the frontier. Pressure to force return of the railroad lands to the public domain has continued all through this century and has not yet died out completely. Compare Greene, Promised Land: A Contemporary Critique of Distribution of Public Land by the United States, 5 Ecology L.Q. 707, 750–51 (1976):

> The economic interests of large landowners and railroads have prevented a broad-based distribution of public lands without proper regard for the public interest. Although 70 years have passed since the bulk of our public lands were transferred to private ownership, the original distributive goal of the land laws remains unfulfilled. Yet, despite the lapse of time, it is still realistic to seek to attain this objective.
>
> There are a number of approaches which can restore to the public much of the interest in lands lost to predatory economic interests in the 19th century. These include the return of the railroad lands to the public domain, the establishment of regional public land banks and trusts, the adoption of a tax policy which gives the public a greater share in the unearned increment in land value and discourages the speculative use of land, and the implementation of increased regional

and national land use planning. As the American nation enters its third century, the recognition that the reallocation of some of our existing resources can provide a new initiative and impulse for growth, should assist the country in realizing its potential for all of its people. The bicentennial year is a good time to renew the Jeffersonian ideal.

Prior and subsequent federal reservations of land within railroads' grant areas raised in lieu selection problems analogous to those faced by Utah in Andrus v. Utah, 446 U.S. 500 (1980), supra at page 62. The Forest Lieu Exchange Act of 1897 allowed the railroads to exchange their inholdings in reserved lands for other lands outside the federal reservations; the Transportation Act of 1940, 49 U.S.C.A. § 65(b), released railroads from rate limitations in exchange for their relinquishment of in lieu rights. See Neuhoff v. Secretary of the Interior, 578 F.2d 810 (9th Cir.1978).

An historical hangover from the railroad grants is the "checkerboard" problem. Well over 100 million acres, *in alternate odd-numbered sections,* were granted to the railroads, directly and indirectly, between 1850 and 1871. When the even-numbered sections were not homesteaded or claimed by other means, and the era of disposition faded, a strange pattern of ownership was consolidated whereby neither private nor public owner could gain access to its property without at least nominal trespass upon the property of the other. Some but by no means all of these conflicts were worked out by agreement over the years, but fundamental public land law issues remained.

CAMFIELD v. UNITED STATES
United States Supreme Court, 1897.
167 U.S. 518.

[The Unlawful Inclosure Act provided that it was unlawful for any person without "claim or color of title acquired in good faith" to enclose the public lands. District courts were vested with jurisdiction to order offending fences destroyed.

This diagram of one township, from the 9th Circuit opinion, will serve to illustrate the manner in which the fence was constructed on Camfield's odd-numbered sections so as to enclose the even-numbered sections that remained in federal ownership. The fence is indicated by the dotted lines.]

6	5	4	3	2	1
7	8	9	10	11	12
18	17	16	15	14	13
19	20	21	22	23	24
30	29	28	27	26	25
31	32	33	34	35	36

Mr. Justice BROWN delivered the opinion of the court.

This case involves the construction and application of the act of Congress of February 25, 1885, c. 149, entitled "An act to prevent unlawful occupancy of the public lands." 23 Stat. 321. * * *

* * *

Defendants are certainly within the letter of this statute. They did enclose public lands of the United States to the amount of 20,000 acres, and there is nothing tending to show that they had any claim or color of title to the same, or any asserted right thereto under a claim made in good faith under the general laws of the United States. The defence is in substance that, if the act be construed so as to apply to fences upon private property, it is unconstitutional.

There is no doubt of the general proposition that a man may do what he will with his own, but this right is subordinate to another, which finds expression in the familiar maxim: *Sic utere tuo ut alienum non loedas.* His right to erect what he pleases upon his own land will not justify him in maintaining a nuisance, or in carrying on a business or trade that is offensive to his neighbors. Ever since *Aldred's case,* 9 Coke, 57, it has been the settled law, both of this country and of England, that a man has no right to maintain a structure upon his own land, which, by reason of disgusting smells, loud or unusual noises, thick smoke, noxious vapors, the jarring of machinery or the unwarrantable collection of flies, renders the occupancy of adjoining property dangerous, intolerable or even uncomfortable to its tenants. No person maintaining such a nuisance can shelter himself behind the sanctity of private property.

* * *

* * * [T]he evil of permitting persons, who owned or controlled the alternate sections, to enclose the entire tract, and thus to exclude or frighten off intending settlers, finally became so great that Congress passed the act of February 25, 1885, forbidding all enclosures of public lands, and authorizing the abatement of the fences. If the act be construed as applying only to fences actually erected upon public lands, it was manifestly unnecessary, since the Government as an ordinary proprietor would have the right to prosecute for such a trespass. It is only by treating it as prohibiting all "enclosures" of public lands, by whatever means, that the act becomes of any avail. The device to which defendants resorted was certainly an ingenious one, but it is too clearly an evasion to permit our regard for the private rights of defendants as landed proprietors to stand in the way of an enforcement of the statute. So far as the fences were erected near the outside line of the odd-numbered sections, there can be no objection to them; but so far as they were erected immediately outside the even-numbered sections, they are manifestly intended to enclose the Government's lands, though, in fact, erected a few inches inside the defendants' line. Considering the obvious purposes of this structure, and the necessities of preventing the enclosure of public lands, we think the fence is clearly a nuisance, and that it is within the constitutional power of Congress to order its abatement, notwithstanding such action may involve an entry upon the lands of a private individual. The general Government doubtless has a power over its own property analogous to the police power of the several States, and the extent to which it may go in the exercise of such power is measured by the exigencies of the particular case. * * * While we do not undertake to say that Congress has the unlimited power to legislate against nuisances within a State, which it would have within a Territory, we do not think the admission of a Territory as a State deprives it of the power of legislating for the protection of the public lands, though it may thereby involve the exercise of what is ordinarily known as the police power, so long as such power is directed solely to its own protection. A different rule would place the public domain of the United States completely at the mercy of state legislation.

We are not convinced by the argument of counsel for the railway company, who was permitted to file a brief in this case, that the fact that a fence, built in the manner indicated, will operate incidentally or indirectly to enclose public lands, is a necessary result, which Congress must have foreseen when it made the grants, of the policy of granting odd sections and retaining the even ones as public lands; and that if such a result inures to the damage of the United States it must be ascribed to their improvidence and carelessness in so surveying and laying off the public lands, that the portion sold and granted by the Government cannot be enclosed by the purchasers without embracing also in such enclosure the alternate sections reserved by the United States. Carried to its logical conclusion, the inference is that, because Congress chose to aid in the construction of these railroads by donating to them all the odd-numbered sections within certain limits, it thereby intended incidentally to grant them the use for an indefinite time of all the even-numbered sections. It seems but an ill return for the generosity of the Government in granting these roads half its lands to claim that it thereby incidentally granted them the benefit of the whole.

* * *

NOTES

1. Is the holding in *Camfield* derived more from congressional intent or from notions of "equitable considerations"? Can *Camfield* be read as holding that the United States has inherent power to regulate land use on private lands if it affects the use or quality of the public lands? Compare United States v. Alford, 274 U.S. 264 (1927). If so, what are the limits of such a power? Whether it is a "needful" Rule or Regulation, U.S. Const., Art. IV, § 3? Could the United States prohibit, for instance, snowmobiles near a wildlife refuge? Or unsightly curio shops or hot dog stands near a national park? Or is the United States merely in the same position as any landowner with a "nuisance" next door? (Is a fence a nuisance?) See generally Sax, Helpless Giants: The National Parks and the Regulation of Private Lands, 75 Mich.L.Rev. 239 (1976). The twin themes of federal power under the Constitution to control the public lands and of the jurisdictional relationship between the federal and state governments in various contexts permeate federal lands and resources law; they are treated extensively in chapter three.

2. In Mackay v. Uinta Development Co., 219 F. 116 (8th Cir.1914), the question was whether a nomadic sheepherder was liable for the damage done by his sheep as he trailed them across checkerboarded private lands while going to and from summer and winter pastures on public lands. Relying on the similar case of Buford v. Houtz, 133 U.S. 320 (1890), in which the Court held that congressional acquiescence in their trespasses gave all nomadic herders an implied license to graze their animals on the public lands, and on the Unlawful Enclosures Act as construed in *Camfield,* the court reversed a judgment for the private landowner. The opinion noted:

> This case illustrates the conflict between the rights of private property and the public welfare under exceptional conditions. It is difficult to say that a man may not inclose his own land, regardless of the effect upon others; but the Camfield Case, supra, has been recognized as sustaining the doctrine that "wholesome legislation" may be constitutionally enacted, though it lessens in a moderate degree what are frequently regarded as absolute rights of private property. This large body of land, with the odd-numbered sections of the company and the even-numbered sections of the public domain located alternately like the squares of a checker-board, remains open as nature left it. Its appearance is that of a common, and the company is so using the contained public

portions. In such use it makes no distinction between them and its own holdings. It has not attempted physically to separate the latter for exclusive private use. It admits that Mackay had the right in common with the public to pass over the public lands. But the right admitted is a theoretical one, without utility, because practically it is denied except on terms it prescribes. Contrary to the prevailing rule of construction, it seeks to cast upon the government and its licensees all the disadvantages of the interlocking arrangement of the odd and even numbered sections because the grant in aid of the railroad took that peculiar form. It could have lawfully fenced its own without obstructing access to the public lands. That would have lessened the value of the entire tract as a great grazing pasture, but it cannot secure for itself that value, which includes as an element the exclusive use of the public lands, by warnings and actions in trespass.

LEO SHEEP CO. v. UNITED STATES
Supreme Court of the United States, 1979.
440 U.S. 668.

Mr. Justice REHNQUIST delivered the opinion of the Court.

This is one of those rare cases evoking episodes in this country's history that, if not forgotten, are remembered as dry facts and not as adventure. Admittedly the issue is mundane: Whether the Government has an implied easement to build a road across land that was originally granted to the Union Pacific Railroad under the Union Pacific Act of 1862—a grant that was part of a governmental scheme to subsidize the construction of the transcontinental railroad. But that issue is posed against the backdrop of a fascinating chapter in our history. As this Court noted in another case involving the Union Pacific Railroad, "courts, in construing a statute, may with propriety recur to the history of the times when it was passed; and this is frequently necessary, in order to ascertain the reason as well as the meaning of particular provisions in it." United States v. Union Pacific Railroad Co., 91 U.S. 72, 79 (1875). In this spirit we relate the events underlying passage of the Union Pacific Act of 1862.

I

The early 19th Century—from the Louisiana Purchase in 1803 to the Gadsden Purchase in 1853—saw the acquisition of the territory we now regard as the American West. During those years, however, the area remained a largely untapped resource, for the settlers on the Eastern Seaboard of the United States did not keep pace with the rapidly expanding western frontier. A vaguely delineated area forbiddingly referred to as "The Great American Desert" can be found on more than one map published before 1850, embracing much of the United States' territory west of the Missouri River. As late as 1860, for example, the entire population of the State of Nebraska was less than

30,000 persons, which represented one person for every five square miles of land area within the State.

With the discovery of gold at Sutter's Mill in California in 1849, the California gold rush began and with it a sharp increase in settlement of the West. Those in the East with visions of instant wealth, however, confronted the unenviable choice among an arduous four-month overland trek, risking yellow fever on a 35-day voyage via the Isthmus of Panama, and a better than four-month voyage around Cape Horn. They obviously yearned for another alternative, and interest focused on the transcontinental railroad.

The idea of a transcontinental railroad predated the California gold rush. From the time that Asa Whitney had proposed a relatively practical plan for its construction in 1844, it had, in the words of one of this century's leading historians of the era, "engaged the eager attention of promoters and politicians until dozens of schemes were in the air." The building of the railroad was not to be the unalloyed product of the free enterprise system. There was indeed the inspiration of men like Thomas Durant and Leland Stanford and the perspiration of a generation of immigrants, but animating it all was the desire of the Federal Government that the West be settled. This desire was intensified by the need to provide a logistical link with California in the heat of the Civil War. That the venture was much too risky and much too expensive for private capital alone was evident in the years of fruitless exhortation; private investors would not move without tangible governmental inducement.

In the mid-19th Century there was serious disagreement as to the forms that inducement could take. Justice Story, in his Commentaries on the Constitution, described one extant school of thought which argued that "internal improvements," such as railroads, were not within the enumerated constitutional powers of Congress. Under such a theory, the direct subsidy of a transcontinental railroad was constitutionally suspect—an uneasiness aggravated by President Andrew Jackson's 1830 veto of a bill appropriating funds to construct a road from Maysville to Lexington within the State of Kentucky.

The response to this constitutional "gray" area, and source of political controversy, was the "checkerboard" land grant scheme. The Union Pacific Act of 1862 granted public land to the Union Pacific Railroad for each mile of track that it laid. Land surrounding the railway right-of-way was divided into "checkerboard" blocks. Odd-numbered lots were granted to the Union Pacific; even-numbered lots were reserved by the Government. As a result, Union Pacific land in the area of the right-of-way was usually surrounded by public land, and vice versa. The historical explanation for this peculiar disposition is that it was apparently an attempt to disarm the "internal improvement" opponents by establishing a grant scheme with "demonstrable" benefits. * * *

In 1850 this technique was first explicitly employed for the subsidization of a railroad when the Illinois delegation in Congress, which included Stephen A. Douglas, secured the enactment of a bill that granted public lands to aid the construction of the Illinois Central Railroad. * * * Before this line was constructed, public lands had gone begging at the Government's minimum price; within a few years after its completion, the railroad had disposed of more than one million acres and was rapidly selling more at prices far above those at which land had been originally offered by the Government.

The "internal improvements" theory was not the only obstacle to a transcontinental railroad. In 1853 Congress had appropriated monies and authorized Secretary of War Jefferson Davis to undertake surveys of various proposed routes for a transcontinental railroad. Congress was badly split along sectional lines on the appropriate location of the route—so badly split that Stephen A. Douglas, now a Senator from Illinois, in 1854 suggested the construction of a northern, central, and southern route, each with connecting branches in the East. That proposal, however, did not break the impasse.

The necessary impetus was provided by the Civil War. Senators and Representatives from those States which seceded from the Union were no longer present in Congress, and therefore the sectional over-tones of the dispute as to routes largely disappeared. Although there were no major engagements during the Civil War in the area between the Missouri River and the West Coast which would be covered by any transcontinental railroad, there were two minor engagements which doubtless made some impression upon Congress of the necessity for being able to transport readily men and materials into that area for military purposes.

* * *

* * * As is often the case, war spurs technological development, and Congress enacted the Union Pacific Act in May 1862. Perhaps not coincidentally, the Homestead Act was passed the same month.

The 1862 Act specified a route west from the 100th meridian, between a site in the Platte River Valley near the cities of Kearney and North Platte, Neb., to California. The original plan was for five eastern terminals located at various points on or near the Missouri River; but in fact Omaha was the only terminal built according to the plan.

The land grants made by the 1862 Act included all the odd-numbered lots within 10 miles on either side of the track. When the Union Pacific's original subscription drive for private investment proved a failure, the land grant was doubled by extending the checker-board grants to 20 miles on either side of the track. Private invest-ment was still sluggish, and construction did not begin until July 1865, three months after the cessation of Civil War hostilities.[13] Thus began

---

13. Construction would not have begun then without the Credit Mobilier, a limited liability company that was essentially owned by the promoters and investors of the Union Pacific. One of these investors, Oakes Ames, a wealthy New England shov-el maker, was a substantial investor in Credit Mobilier and also a Member of Congress. Credit Mobilier contracted with the Union Pacific to build portions of the road, and by 1866 several individuals were large investors in both corporations. Allegations

a race with the Central Pacific Railroad, which was laying track eastward from Sacramento, for the government land grants which went with each mile of track laid. The race culminated in the driving of the golden spike at Promontory Point, Utah, on May 10, 1869.

II

This case is the modern legacy of these early grants. Petitioners, the Leo Sheep Company and the Palm Livestock Company, are the Union Pacific Railroad's successors in fee to specific odd-numbered sections of land in Carbon County, Wyo. These sections lie to the east and south of the Seminoe Reservoir, an area that is used by the public for fishing and hunting. Because of the checkerboard configuration, it is physically impossible to enter the Seminoe Reservoir sector from this direction without some minimum physical intrusion upon private land. In the years immediately preceding this litigation, the Government had received complaints that private owners were denying access over their lands to the reservoir area or requiring the payment of access fees. After negotiation with these owners failed, the Government cleared a dirt road extending from a local county road to the Reservoir across both public domain lands and fee lands of the Leo Sheep Company. It also erected signs inviting the public to use the road as a route to the Reservoir.[a]

Petitioners initiated this action pursuant to 28 U.S.C.A. § 2409a to quiet title against the United States. The District Court granted petitioners' motion for summary judgment, but was reversed on appeal by the Court of Appeals for the Tenth Circuit. The latter court concluded that when Congress granted land to the Union Pacific Railroad, it implicitly reserved an easement to pass over the odd-numbered sections in order to reach the even-numbered sections that were held by the Government. Because this holding affects property rights in 150 million acres of land in the Western United States, we granted certiorari and now reverse.

The Government does not claim that there is any express reservation of an easement in the Union Pacific Act that would authorize the construction of a public road on the Leo Sheep Company's property. Section 3 of the 1862 Act sets out a few specific reservations to the

of improper use of funds and bribery of Members of the House of Representatives led to the appointment of a special congressional investigatory committee that during 1872 and 1873 looked into the affairs of Credit Mobilier. These investigations revealed improprieties on the part of more than one Member of Congress, and the committee recommended that Ames be expelled from Congress. The investigation also touched on the career of a future President. See M. Leech & H. Brown, The Garfield Orbit (1978).

In 1872 the House of Representatives enacted a resolution condemning the policy

of granting subsidies of public lands to railroads. Cong. Globe, 42d Cong., 2d Sess., 1585 (1872); see Great Northern R. Co. v. United States, 315 U.S. 262, 273–274 (1942). Of course, the reaction of the public or of Congress a decade after the enactment of the Union Pacific Act to the conduct of those associated with the Union Pacific cannot influence our interpretation of that Act today.

a. A map of the area, from the Tenth Circuit opinion, is found at page 121 infra.

"checkerboard" grant. The grant was not to include land "sold, reserved, or otherwise disposed of by the United States," such as land to which there were homestead claims. 12 Stat., at 492. Mineral lands were also excepted from the operation of the Act. Ibid. Given the existence of such explicit exceptions, this Court has in the past refused to add to this list by divining some "implicit" congressional intent. In Missouri K. & T.R. Co. v. Kansas P.R. Co., 97 U.S. 491, 497 (1878), for example, this Court in an opinion by Justice Field noted that the intent of Congress in making the Union Pacific grants was clear: "It was to aid in the construction of the road by a gift of lands along its route, without reservation of rights, except such as were specifically mentioned. * * *" The Court held that although a railroad right-of-way under the grant may not have been located until years after 1862, by the clear terms of the Act only claims established prior to 1862 overrode the railroad grant; conflicting claims arising after that time could not be given effect. To overcome the lack of support in the Act itself, the Government here argues that the implicit reservation of the asserted easement is established by "settled principles of property law" and by the Unlawful Inclosures of Public Lands Act of 1885.

Where a private landowner conveys to another individual a portion of his lands in a certain area and retains the rest, it is presumed at common law that the grantor has reserved an easement to pass over the granted property if such passage is necessary to reach the retained property. These rights of way are referred to as "easements by necessity." There are two problems with the Government's reliance on that notion in this case. First of all, whatever right of passage a private landowner might have, it is not at all clear that it would include the right to construct a road for public access to a recreational area.[15] More importantly, the easement is not actually a matter of necessity in this case because the Government has the power of eminent domain. Jurisdictions have generally seen eminent domain and easements by necessity as alternative ways to effect the same result. For example, the State of Wyoming no longer recognizes the common-law easement by necessity in cases involving landlocked estates. It provides instead for a procedure whereby the landlocked owner can have an access route condemned on his behalf upon payment of the necessary compensation to the owner of the servient estate.[16] For similar reasons other state courts have held that the "easement by necessity" doctrine is not available to the sovereign.

15. It is very unlikely that Congress in 1862 contemplated this type of intrusion, and it could not reasonably be maintained that failure to provide access to the public at large would render the Seminoe Reservoir land useless. Yet these are precisely the considerations that define the scope of easements by necessity. * * *

16. Wyo.Stat.Ann. §§ 24–9–101 to 24–9–104 (1977); see Snell v. Ruppert, 541 P.2d 1042, 1046 (Wyo.1975) (statute "offers complete relief to the shut-in landowner and covers the whole subject matter"; "[i]f a statute covers a whole subject matter, the abrogation of the common law on the same subject will necessarily be implied.") See also, e.g., Quinn v. Holly, 244 Miss. 808, 146 So.2d 357 (1962). In light of the history of public land grants related in Part I of this opinion, it is not surprising that "private" eminent domain statutes like that of Wyoming are most prevalent in the Western United States.

The applicability of the doctrine of easement by necessity in this case is, therefore, somewhat strained, and ultimately of little significance. The pertinent inquiry in this case is the intent of Congress when it granted land to the Union Pacific in 1862. The 1862 Act specifically listed reservations to the grant, and we do not find the tenuous relevance of the common-law doctrine of ways of necessity sufficient to overcome the inference prompted by the omission of any reference to the reserved right asserted by the Government in this case. It is possible that Congress gave the problem of access little thought; but it is at least as likely that the thought which was given focused on negotiation, reciprocity considerations, and the power of eminent domain as obvious devices for ameliorating disputes.[18] So both as matter of common-law doctrine and as a matter of construing congressional intent, we are unwilling to imply rights of way, with the substantial impact that such implication would have on property rights granted over 100 years ago, in the absence of a stronger case for their implication than the Government makes here.

The Government would have us decide this case on the basis of the familiar canon of construction that when grants to federal lands are at issue, any doubts "are resolved for the Government not against it." Andrus v. Charlestone Stone Products Co., 436 U.S. 604, 617 (1978). But this Court long ago declined to apply this canon in its full vigor to grants under the railroad acts. In 1885 this Court observed that:

> "The solution of [ownership] questions [involving the railroad grants] depends, of course, upon the construction given to the acts making the grants; and they are to receive such a construction as will carry out the intent of Congress, however difficult it might be to give full effect to the language used if the grants were by instruments of private conveyance. To

18. The intimations that can be found in the Congressional Globe are that there was no commonly understood reservation by the Government of the right to enter upon granted lands and construct a public road. Representative Cradlebaugh of Nevada offered an amendment to what became the Union Pacific Act of 1862 that would have reserved the right to the public to enter granted land and prospect for valuable minerals upon the payment of adequate compensation to the owner. The proposed amendment was defeated. The only representative other than Cradlebaugh who spoke to it, Representative Sargent of California, stated:

"The amendment of the gentleman proposes to allow the public to enter upon the lands of any man, whether they be mineral lands or not, and prospect for gold and silver, and as compensation proposes some loose method of payment for the injuries inflicted. Now, sir, it may turn out that the man who thus commits the injuries may be utterly insolvent, not

able to pay a dollar, and how is the owner of the property to be compensated for tearing down his dwellings, rooting up his orchards, and destroying his crops?" Cong.Globe, 37th Cong., 2d Sess., 1910 (1862).

In debates on an earlier Pacific Railroad Bill it was explicitly suggested that there be "a reservation in every grant of land that [the Government] shall have a right to go through it, and take it at proper prices to be paid thereafter." The author of this proposal, Senator Simmons of Rhode Island, lamented the lack of such a reservation in the bill under consideration. Cong. Globe, 35th Cong., 2d Sess., 579 (1859). Apparently the intended purpose of this proposed reservation was to permit railroads to obtain rights of way through granted property at the Government's behest. Senator Simmons' comments are somewhat confused, but they certainly do not evince any prevailing assumption that the Government implicitly reserved a right-of-way through granted lands.

ascertain that intent we must look to the condition of the
country when the acts were passed, as well as to the purpose
declared on their face, and read all parts of them together."
Winona and St. Peter R. Co. v. Barney, 113 U.S. 618, 625
(1885).

The Court harmonized the longstanding rule enunciated most recently
in *Andrus,* supra, with the doctrine of *Winona* in United States v.
Denver and Rio Grande R. Co., 150 U.S. 1, 14 (1893) when it said:

"It is undoubtedly, as urged by the plaintiffs in error, the
well-settled rule of this court that public grants are construed
strictly against the grantees, but they are not to be so construed as to defeat the intent of the legislature, or to withhold
what is given either expressly or by necessary or fair implication. * * *

" * * * When an act, operating as a general law, and
manifesting clearly the intention of Congress to secure public
advantages, or to subserve the public interests and welfare by
means of benefits more or less valuable, offers individuals or to
corporations as an inducement to undertake and accomplish
great and expensive enterprises or works of a *quasi* public
character in or through an immense and undeveloped public
domain, such legislation stands upon a somewhat different
footing from merely a private grant, and should receive at the
hands of the court a more liberal construction in favor of the
purposes for which it was enacted."

Thus invocation of the canon reiterated in *Andrus* does little to advance
the Government's position in this case.

Nor do we find the Unlawful Inclosures of Public Lands Act of 1885
of any significance in this controversy. That Act was a response to the
"range wars," the legendary struggle between cattlemen and farmers
during the last half of the 19th Century. Cattlemen had entered
Kansas, Nebraska, and the Dakota Territory before other settlers, and
they grazed their herds freely on public lands with the Federal Government's acquiescence. To maintain their dominion over the ranges,
cattlemen used homestead and pre-emption laws to gain control of
water sources in the range lands. With monopoly control of such
sources, the cattlemen found that ownership over a relatively small
area might yield effective control of thousands of acres of grassland.
Another exclusionary technique was the illegal fencing of public lands
which was often the product of the checkerboard pattern of railroad
grants. By placing fences near the borders of their parts of the
checkerboard, cattlemen could fence in thousands of acres of public
lands. Reports of the Secretary of Interior indicated that vast areas of
public grazing land had been preempted by such fencing patterns. In
response Congress passed the Unlawful Inclosures Act of 1885.

Section 1 of the Unlawful Inclosures Act states that "[a]ll inclosures of any public lands * * * constructed by any person * * *
to any of which land included within the inclosure the person * * *

had no claim or color of title made or acquired in good faith ∗ ∗ ∗ are hereby declared to be unlawful."   43 U.S.C.A. § 1061.   Section 3 further provides that:

> "[n]o person, by force, threats, intimidation, or by any fencing or inclosing, or any other unlawful means, shall prevent or obstruct, or shall combine and confederate with others to prevent or obstruct, any person from peaceably entering upon or establishing a settlement or residence on any tract of public land subject to settlement or entry under the public land laws of the United States, or shall prevent or obstruct free passage or transit over or through the public lands: *Provided,* This section shall not be held to affect the right or title of persons, who have gone upon, improved or occupied said lands under the land laws of the United States, claiming title thereto, in good faith."   43 U.S.C.A. § 1063.

The Government argues that the prohibitions of this Act should somehow be read to include the Leo Sheep Company's refusal to acquiesce in a public road over its property, and that such a conclusion is supported by this Court's opinion in Camfield v. United States, 167 U.S. 518 (1897).   We find, however, that *Camfield* does not afford the support that the Government seeks.   That case involved a fence that was constructed on odd-numbered lots so as to enclose 20,000 acres of public land, thereby appropriating it to the exclusive use of Camfield and his associates.   This Court analyzed the fence from the perspective of nuisance law, and concluded that the Unlawful Inclosures Act was an appropriate exercise of the police power.

There is nothing, however, in the *Camfield* opinion to suggest that the Government has the authority asserted here.   In fact, the Court affirmed the grantee's right to fence completely his own land.

> "So long as the individual proprietor confines his enclosure to his own land, the Government has no right to complain, since he is entitled to the complete and exclusive enjoyment of it, regardless of any detriment to his neighbor; but when, under the guise of enclosing his own land, he builds a fence which is useless for that purpose, and can only have been intended to enclose the lands of the Government, he is plainly within the statute, and is guilty of an unwarrantable appropriation of that which belongs to the public at large."   167 U.S., at 528.

Obviously if odd-numbered lots are individually fenced, the access to even-numbered lots is obstructed.   Yet the *Camfield* Court found that this was not a violation of the Unlawful Inclosures Act.   In that light we cannot see how the Leo Sheep Company's unwillingness to entertain a public road without compensation can be a violation of that Act.   It is certainly true that the problem we confront today was not a matter of great concern during the time the 1862 railroad grants were made. The order of the day was the open range—barbed wire had not made its presence felt—and the type of incursions on private property necessary to reach public land was not such an interference that litigation would serve any motive other than spite. Congress obviously believed that when development came, it would occur in a parallel fashion on adjoining public and private lands and that the process of subdivision, organization of a polity and the ordinary pressures of commercial and social intercourse would work itself into a pattern of access roads.[23] The *Camfield* case expresses similar sentiments. After the passage quoted above conceding the authority of a private landowner to fence the entire perimeter of his odd-numbered lot, the Court opined that such authority was of little practical significance "since a separate enclosure of each section would only become desirable when the country had been settled, and roads had been built which would give access to each section." Ibid. It is some testament to common sense that the present case is virtually unprecedented, and that in the 117 years since the grants were made, litigation over access questions generally has been rare.

Nonetheless, the present times are litigious ones and the 37th Congress did not anticipate our plight. Generations of land patents have issued without any express reservation of the right now claimed by the Government. Nor has a similar right been asserted before.[24] When the Secretary of Interior has discussed access rights, his discussion has been colored by the assumption that those rights had to be purchased.[25] This Court has traditionally recognized the special need for certainty and predictability where land titles are concerned, and we are unwilling to upset settled expectations to accommodate some ill-defined power to construct public thoroughfares without compensation. The judgment of the Court of Appeals of the Tenth Circuit is accordingly

Reversed.

23. This expectation was fostered by the general land grants scheme. Each block in the checkerboard was a square mile—640 acres. The public lots were open to homesteading, with 160 acres the maximum allowable claim under the Homestead Act. Act of May 20, 1862, ch. 75, 12 Stat. 392. The Union Pacific was required by the 1862 Act to sell or otherwise dispose of the land granted to it within three years after completion of the entire road, with lands not so disposed of within that period subject to homesteading and pre-emption. Thus in 1862 the process of subdivision was perceived, to a great degree, as inevitable.

24. This distinguishes the instant case from Buford v. Houtz, 133 U.S. 320 (1890). The appellants there were a group of cattle ranchers seeking, *inter alia,* an injunction against sheep ranchers who moved their herds across odd-numbered lots held by the appellants in order to graze their sheep on even-numbered public lots. This Court denied the requested relief because it was contrary to a century-old grazing custom.

The Court also was influenced by the sheep ranchers' lack of any alternative.

"Upon the whole, we see no equity in the relief sought by the appellants in this case, which undertakes to deprive the defendants of this recognized right to permit their cattle to run at large over the lands of the United States and feed upon the grasses found in them, while, under pretence of owning a small proportion of the land which is the subject of controversy, they themselves obtain the monopoly of this valuable privilege." Id., at 332. Here neither custom nor necessity supports the Government.

25. In 1887 the Secretary of Interior recommended that Congress enact legislation providing for a public road around each section of public land to provide access to the various public lots in the checkerboard scheme. The Secretary also recommended that to the extent building these roads required the taking of property that had passed to private individuals, "the bill should provide for necessary compensation."

Mr. Justice WHITE took no part in the consideration or decision of this case.

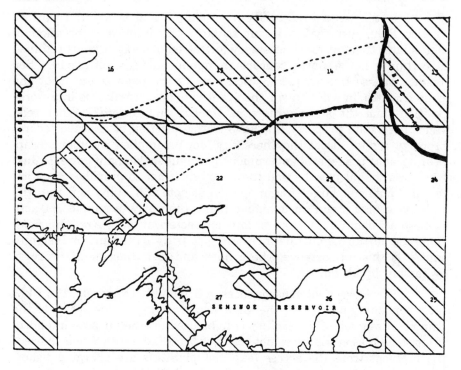

Area Near Seminoe Dam, Carbon County, Wyoming

.Odd-numbered sections granted to railroad in 1862 and now owned by plaintiff

Even-numbered sections of public domain

---- Pre-existing dirt road

==== Pre-existing dirt road improved by B.L.M. December 1973

—— Dirt road relocated by B.L.M. December 1973

NOTES

1. The Circuit Court opinion in *Leo Sheep* had relied upon *Camfield, Mackay,* and Buford v. Houtz, cited in the main opinion at note 24, in finding that "Congress, by its 1862 grant to the railroad of the odd-numbered sections, did by implication intend to reserve a right of access to the inter-locking even-numbered sections not conveyed to the railroad." "To hold to the contrary would be to ascribe to Congress a degree of carelessness or lack of foresight which in our view would be unwarranted." 570 F.2d 881, 885 (10th Cir.1977). Clyde Martz, the experienced attorney for plaintiffs, told one of these editors that this passage inspired him to seek certiorari even though only a few square feet of land were involved. For, he said, the Supreme Court sits in

Washington and has a much closer and realistic view of the "careless-ness" of which Congress is capable.

2. Is the issue in *Leo Sheep* as simple and straightforward as Justice Rehnquist makes it out to be? The implied reservation of rights later thought to be necessary for the enjoyment of lands retained is certainly not a novel concept in public land jurisprudence. See chapter six, section C, infra. Does the Court mean to say that the United States (in whose favor the grant is to be construed) is in a worse position than the sheepherders in *Mackay* and *Buford*? What rele-vance does state property law have to the question of asserted federal property rights? Does the "necessity" for an implied easement disap-pear because the federal government has eminent domain power? Just what was the purpose behind the reservoir if not to provide recreation for the "public at large" (main opinion at note 15)? Why is it that the railroad grants stand on a higher plane than, say, a simple 160-acre homestead claim? Is that a fair characterization? Are *Camfield, Buford,* and the Unlawful Enclosure Act truly irrelevant or insignifi-cant? Is this an instance where hard and fast concepts of property ownership break down?

3. What practical consequences will follow? Obviously, the BLM must condemn and pay for the lands necessary to provide access to the Seminoe Reservoir if the facility is to be used for the purpose intended. If for some reason that does not occur, is the BLM entitled to a share of the proceeds from the access fees that plaintiffs are charging fisher-men? Short of condemnation, can the local BLM manager now reach Seminoe Reservoir without paying an access fee? Does it depend on whether the manager walks or drives a jeep?

4. Consider the converse of *Leo Sheep:* could the BLM close its lands to plaintiffs, cutting off their access to their property? Sauce for the goose. * * * If you were a BLM official, would you recommend such retaliation? Why? Would it work? Is there, ultimately, any "fair" resolution to this controversy available?

5. Litigation over access questions has proliferated since the *Leo Sheep* decision and, given the pattern of federal landholdings, no end is in sight. See Note, Public Access to Federal Lands: Dilemma, 3 Pub. Land L.Rev. 194 (1982). Several decisions have affirmed BLM determi-nations to ban offroad vehicles from some areas. See chapter ten, § D infra. In Humboldt County v. United States, 684 F.2d 1276 (9th Cir. 1982), the court upheld BLM closure of two roads to protect natural values pending a study of the area's wilderness characteristics. In Southern Appalachian Multiple Use Council v. Berglund, 11 ELR 20679 (W.D.N.C.1981), however, the court ruled that

> the acts of the Secretary in designating the lands surrounding the lands of Will Orr as "wilderness study" areas or "further planning" areas and the closing of the access road to his lands constituted a taking of his lands without due process of law in violation of the Fifth Amendment. The Court concludes that unless the access road leading to Mr. Orr's property is re-

opened to him and his bona fide guests within sixty (60) days from the date of the order in this cause an order will be entered directing the Secretary to withdraw his designation of the surrounding lands as "wilderness study" or "further planning" areas and to resume the "multiple-use" management of said areas forthwith.

Id. at 20683. See also Foundation for North American Wild Sheep v. United States, 681 F.2d 1172 (9th Cir.1982), infra at page 877 (Forest Service must prepare an EIS before approving permit to reopen a road that might adversely affect "sensitive" wildlife species).

6.   In United States v. 82.46 Acres of Land, More or Less, Situate in Carbon County, Wyoming, 691 F.2d 474 (10th Cir.1982), the BLM sought to condemn 100 foot wide easements on preexisting private roadways for public access to public lands. BLM condemnation authority is limited by a provision in FLPMA: "with respect to the public lands, the Secretary may exercise the power of eminent domain only if necessary to secure access to public lands, and then only if the lands so acquired are confined to as narrow a corridor as is necessary to serve such a purpose." 43 U.S.C.A. § 1715(a). After a brief hearing, the district court vacated the government's declaration of taking on some of the roads after finding that access was already provided by other existing roads. The lower court also held that 100 feet was too wide because existing roads were only 22 to 39 feet wide. The appellate court reversed, holding the record insufficient to sustain either determination.

UNITED STATES EX REL. BERGEN v. LAWRENCE
United States District Court, District of Wyoming, 1985.
620 F.Supp. 1414, Appeal Pending.

BRIMMER, Chief Judge.

This case arises from the contentions of the United States and plaintiff-intervenors Wyoming Wildlife Federation and National Wildlife Federation (Wildlife Federations), that defendant has wrongfully fenced in federal land in violation of the Unlawful Inclosures of Public Lands Act, 43 U.S.C. §§ 1061–1066.   *   *   *

*   *   *

Defendant owns a cattle ranch in the vicinity of Rawlins, Wyoming, and in the spring and summer months for about 60 days grazes his cattle on a combination of private, federal and state lands in the area of south central Wyoming known as Red Rim. Red Rim is an escarpment and uplifting plateau of approximately 22,000 acres, fifteen miles southwest of Rawlins, Wyoming, which lies just south of the railroad right-of-way granted to the Union Pacific Railroad in 1862. Red Rim contains an abundance of Wyoming big sagebrush, which, as testified to by Mr. Moody and Dr. Alldredge, is not eaten by cattle, but constitutes the major part of an antelope's diet, especially during winter. Due to Red Rim's geological features, winter winds blow the snow off this sagebrush, allowing the antelope to find food here when their other grazing areas are covered over with deep snow. The Wyoming Game and Fish Department has declared that portions of Red Rim constitute critical winter habitat for pronghorn antelope. The Baggs antelope herd which uses Red Rim for winter range is estimated to number 2,000 or more, and those 2,000 antelope have virtually no other alternative winter feeding grounds.

Red Rim, and defendant's Daley Ranch, are the legacy of a checkerboard ownership plan arising from the Union Pacific Railroad Act of July 1, 1862.

* * * Defendant now has fee title or permission to fence from the title owner, to the Union Pacific sections in question, and has grazing permits on the odd-numbered federal and state sections. Defendant's fence, which covers 28 miles, is physically located on private land, except where it crosses at the common corners of state and federal sections, * * *.

The matter in issue is quite simple. Defendant Lawrence contends that since the fence is located on his land, and that he can construct it in any manner he chooses, without having to comply with Bureau of Land Management (BLM) requirements. Plaintiff-intervenors counter that since the fence encloses public lands, it violates the Unlawful Inclosures Act, unless the fence conforms with BLM standards promulgated pursuant to the Taylor Grazing Act, 43 U.S.C. § 315 et seq. Those BLM standards require that fences for cattle operations provide a gap of at least sixteen inches at the bottom, with a bottom strand of smooth wire, so that antelope can crawl underneath, and with a top wire only thirty-eight inches high, to allow antelope to jump the fence when snow drifts block passage beneath the bottom strand. Defendant's fence on the other hand, is made of woven wire with no gap at the bottom, and is topped off with barbed wire at a height of five feet, making it, as defendant admits, antelope-proof.

In 1897 the United States Supreme Court dealt with an identical situation in Camfield v. United States, 167 U.S. 518 (1897). * * *

Finally, the Court concluded that defendant's intent, whether to irrigate the public lands or use them for pasturage, was unimportant. The only matter at issue was whether or not the fence violated the statute.

> The device to which defendants resorted was certainly an ingenious one, but it is too clearly an envasion (sic) to permit our regard for the private rights of defendants as landed proprietors to stand in the way of an enforcement of the statute. * * * Considering the obvious purposes of this structure, and the necessities of preventing the enclosure of public lands, we think the fence is clearly a nuisance, and that it is within the constitutional power of Congress to order its abatement, notwithstanding such action may involve an entry upon the lands of a private individual. *Camfield* at 525.

The situation in this matter is virtually identical to that dealt with by the Supreme Court in *Camfield.* Although written in 1897, *Camfield* is still good law, and in fact was relied upon by the Supreme Court as recently as 1983 in North Dakota v. United States, 460 U.S. 300, 319 (1983). While the defendant relies on four major arguments in an attempt to distinguish *Camfield,* the Court is convinced that none of these arguments take the facts of this case beyond the scope of *Camfield.*

Defendant first contends that *Camfield* is inapplicable because *Camfield* relies for its holding on the Unlawful Inclosures Act, (UIA), 43 U.S.C. § 1061 et seq., [and] the UIA does not apply to antelope. * * * Because the UIA says no person shall "prevent or obstruct any person", defendant says that the act only applies to humans, and that it is permissible for him to prevent antelope from crossing his fence. This argument might be valid except for the second clause of § 1063, which continues "or shall prevent or obstruct free passage or transit over or through the public lands." That clause does not contain the word "person", and neither does the Court believe that "person" from the preceding clause should be read into it. Had Congress intended only to protect people, the first clause would have accomplished that purpose without necessity of the second clause.

In Mackay v. Uinta Development Co., 219 F. 116 (1914), a Wyoming case decided by the Eighth Circuit Court of Appeals before the Tenth Circuit was created, the court held that there must be reasonable access for livestock to reach enclosed federal lands. Moreover, in Stoddard v. United States, 214 F. 566 (8th Cir.1914), the Eighth Circuit specifically rejected the argument that defendant now presses this Court to embrace. In holding that the UIA did not apply only to humans, the Court held that the act

> was intended to prevent the obstruction of free passage or transit for any or all lawful purposes over public lands. Id. at 568–69.

Surely, the free passage of hunters and their quarry is a lawful purpose for which the public may seek access to public lands. In light of these precedents the Court is hardpressed to understand how the UIA could apply to cattle, but not to antelope. In the words of the *Stoddard* Court, "[w]e think this is a forced and unwarrantable construction of the language employed." *Stoddard* at 568.

In the years since the 1885 passage of the UIA, the then-pressing concerns of settlement and range wars have faded. But, new present-day concerns have arisen. In the Federal Land Policy and Management Act (FLPMA), 43 U.S.C. § 1701 et seq., Congress set out new goals for the public lands, one of which is that

> the public lands be managed in a manner * * * that will provide food and habitat for fish and wildlife and domestic animals. * * * 43 U.S.C. § 1701(a)(8).

* * * At the Hearing on Preliminary Injunction the Court was thoroughly convinced by the undisputed testimony of Mr. Moody and Dr. Alldredge that not only is the enclosed portion of Red Rim critical winter range for the Baggs antelope herd, but that if the fence remains standing, the herd may very probably be decimated by winter starvation. The Court cannot accept as the intent of Congress that the UIA would allow that outcome, when it is clear that defendant could not build his fence to prevent humans from undertaking mere recreational pastimes, such as hiking or fishing.

Defendant next contends that *Camfield* and the UIA do not apply to his fence because of the Taylor Grazing Act, 43 U.S.C. § 315 et seq. Defendant argues that since § 315c allows fencing directly on public lands under permit issued by the Secretary of the Interior, the UIA was implicitly repealed. This argument must fail. First, "repeals by implication are not favored, * * * [t]he intention of the legislature to repeal must be 'clear and manifest.'" [citations omitted]. Watt v. Alaska, 451 U.S. 259, 267 (1981). There is no indication that Congress intended to repeal the UIA through passage of the Taylor Grazing Act, particularly when the UIA was amended as recently as 1984. * * *

* * *

As an adjunct to this argument, defendant contends that the Bureau of Land Management (BLM) tacitly approved the fence, and that the Government should not now be allowed to complain. Although the Government waited almost two years before commencing this suit, the Court is not convinced that mere inaction constitutes approval. Moreover, the BLM's inaction was based not on approval, but on a mistaken belief that BLM lacked the power to prevent defendant from building the fence.

* * *

Neither is the fact that the fence is broken by 28 gates, 19 of which are unlocked, enough to take defendant's fence outside the scope of the UIA. Some of the locked gates have "No Trespassing" signs on them; and certainly none of the gates invite the public to come in. The Court is not entirely convinced that all of these gates provide adequate access for humans. However, the question at issue here is access by antelope. The testimony of Mr. Moody and Dr. Alldredge convinces the Court that gates, even if left open, make little or no difference to the antelope, which are creatures of habit that encounter a fence and will trail along it, totally missing small openings such as gates. It is not the fence itself, but its effect which constitutes the UIA violation. McKelvey v. United States, 260 U.S. 353 (1922). The clear, admitted, and intended effect of this fence is to exclude antelope. The presence of gates in it is unimportant.

Finally, defendant contends that *Camfield* and the UIA do not outlaw his fence because of the Supreme Court's decision in Leo Sheep Co. v. United States, 440 U.S. 668 (1979). * * * [T]he Court stated:

Nor do we find the Unlawful Inclosures [of Public Lands Act] of 1885 of any significance in this controversy. That Act was a response to the "range wars," the legendary struggle between cattlemen and farmers during the last half of the 19th century.

Defendant concludes that the Supreme Court held by this language that the UIA's purpose was to prevent the continuation of "range wars", and that it should not be extended beyond this purpose. That is not what the Court meant. The UIA indeed was a response to the range wars, but nothing in the act or its history limits its application in such a manner. If the UIA was only meant for such a limited purpose, the Court would have said so in *Camfield,* and Congress should have repealed it in 1934 when the Taylor Grazing Act was passed to end public lands disputes. Certainly Congress would not have amended the UIA in 1984 if the act was not useless.

Because *Leo Sheep* involved the Government's claim to an implied easement at the common corners of a checkerboard tract, the Court only concluded that *Camfield* and the UIA did not "suggest that the Government had the authority asserted here." That does not mean that *Camfield* now has no applicability in this matter. As the *Leo Sheep* Court stated, "[t]hat case [*Camfield*] involved a fence that was constructed on odd-numbered lots so as to enclose 20,000 acres of public land. * * *" Id. at 683. Defendant has erected the same type of fence. Certainly *Camfield* is not applicable to a road question, but it clearly has much to say on the subject of defendant's fence. The Court finds that while *Leo Sheep* has no applicability in this matter, *Camfield* is dispositive of it.

* * * The fence was built ostensibly to protect defendant's crop of crested wheat grass; but, in eight years the defendant has never planted that crop. The Court believes that he does not intend to, either. The fence has an ulterior purpose, and since the parties assured the Court that the mineral rights of that area were not involved, the only reason left for it is the exclusion of antelope from their winter range, which will result in decimation of that herd. The antelope grazed on the Wyoming big sagebrush at Red Rim long before the Daley Ranch was ever built, and unless driven to extinction, will graze there long after it is gone. * * * Therefore, it is

ORDERED that the Defendant, Taylor Lawrence, shall within 10 days from and after October 29, 1985 remove the 48″ woven wire from the fence at the places in the fence where it has been removed and laid down in the past two winters, in accord with the Order of this Court dated October 29, 1985. It is

FURTHER ORDERED that defendant Lawrence, within 60 days from the date of this Order, shall remove the 48″ woven wire from all 28 miles of his Red Rim fence and conform the fence to BLM standards, for enclosure of cattle, or remove it altogether. It is further

ORDERED that if defendant fails to comply with this Order and modify or remove the fence, he shall be in contempt of Court, and subject, from the sixty-first day on until compliance, to a fine of $1,000 [1] per day. It is further

ORDERED that in the event defendant desires to appeal this decision, this Order may be stayed upon his filing of a supersedeas bond, cash or surety, in the amount of $120,000 [2] but that if the defendant demonstrates to the Court that he has complied, and will continue to comply with the October 29, 1985 Order on Preliminary Injunction instructing him to remove the woven wire from those sections of the fence he has laid down in past years in agreement with the State of Wyoming, then this Order may be stayed upon filing of a supersedeas bond, cash or surety, in the amount of $1,000.

NOTES

1. The more things change * * *.

2. Is *Camfield* "identical"? Did Congress in 1885 intend to safeguard access by wildlife? Does the court adequately distinguish *Leo Sheep*?

3. Private access to inholdings within all national forests is now assured, oddly enough, by the Alaska National Interest Lands Conservation Act as construed in Montana Wilderness Ass'n v. United States Forest Service, 655 F.2d 951 (9th Cir.1981), cert. denied, 455 U.S. 989 (1982), infra at page 1016. Most access questions on the BLM lands and national forests are governed by the Federal Land Policy and Management Act of 1976, 43 U.S.C.A. §§ 1761–65, which provides, among other things, that terms and conditions in rights-of-way across public lands shall "minimize damage to scenic and aesthetic values in fish and wildlife habitat and otherwise protect the environment." Id. § 1765(a). See Martz, Love & Kaiser, Access to Mineral Interests by Right, Permit, Condemnation, or Purchase, 28 Rocky Mtn. Min.L.Inst. 1075 (1983).

6. GRANTS FOR RECLAMATION

The beginnings of fundamental changes in the national policy of disposition can be seen retrospectively in the federal treatment of renewable resources, notably water and timber. The Desert Lands Act had opened the arid lands, and state water laws (the prior appropriation system) allowed the taking and use of water, but the laws did nothing to solve the physical problem of water scarcity. Many lands were still available for homesteading, but they would go unclaimed until largescale water diversion and storage capacity was developed. Neither the states nor private entrepreneurs were able to meet this widely perceived need. When it became apparent that the Desert Lands Act had failed to achieve its sponsors' aim of increased productivity through private irrigation efforts, Congress finally decided to go into

1. Based on an estimate of 2000 antelope in the Baggs herd, at $.50 per head per day.

2. Based on the median of $60 per head from the $15 charged for an in-state antelope hunting permit and the $105 charged for an out-of-state antelope hunting permit by the Wyoming Game and Fish Department.

the water business. By the Reclamation Act of 1902, 43 U.S.C.A. § 371 et seq., called the Newlands Act after its sponsor, the federal government embarked on an unprecedented water resources program to irrigate the West. The Reclamation Act, which proved to be a major impetus to settlement, involves federal construction, ownership, and operation of facilities. Farmers receiving reclamation water apply it to their private lands, but reclamation law also assumes some continuing federal control over the water rights accruing to the beneficiaries. The projects were to be financed by the proceeds from land sales in the 16 states affected, and it was contemplated that water user charges would repay the cost of project construction and maintenance. In many cases the costs have never been repaid; the Act as administered and amended has provided extensive subsidies to western agricultural interests. See, e.g., Sax, Selling Reclamation Water Rights: A Case Study in Federal Subsidy Policy, 64 Mich.L.Rev. 13 (1965).

The constitutional validity of federal reclamation activity was in doubt for some time. The Supreme Court in Kansas v. Colorado, 206 U.S. 46 (1907), an original action between states for apportionment of an interstate river, went out of its way to declare that Congress could exercise no reclamation powers within states contrary to state laws. Congress thereafter attempted to justify reclamation projects, notably the massive California Valley Project (CVP), on the specious ground of improving navigation. The need for pretense was obviated by the decision in United States v. Gerlach Livestock Co., 339 U.S. 725, 738 (1950), holding that "the power of Congress to promote the general welfare through large-scale projects for reclamation, irrigation, or other internal improvement, is now as clear and ample as its power to accomplish the same results indirectly through resort to strained interpretation of the power over navigation." The CVP is the subject of a fascinating study in C. Meyers & A.D. Tarlock, WATER RESOURCE MANAGEMENT 322–81 (2d ed. 1980).

Reclamation in this century has grown beyond the wildest hopes of its sponsors. By 1906 the Reclamation Service had commenced projects in 15 states for the irrigation of 2½ million acres. Still to come were such huge undertakings as Hoover Dam. The course of diverted water under the Reclamation Act never did run smooth; many technical and economic problems were encountered, not the least of which was the ever-present trend toward speculation and monopoly. A serious problem, never yet resolved, has been repayment of costs through user fees. By a series of Extension Acts beginning in 1914, terms of repayment were extended, liberalized, and extended again. In spite of all of the legal and practical difficulties, over nine million acres were irrigated by Bureau of Reclamation projects in 1964. Naturally, with continued federal financing and involvement came continuing attempts at federal control, even of those parcels that passed out of federal ownership. Federal development in tandem with disposition was an important departure in public land law.

Until 1982 controversy still revolved around the meaning of the section requiring that:

> No right to the use of water for land in private ownership shall be sold for a tract exceeding one hundred and sixty acres to any one landowner, and no such sale shall be made to any landowner unless he be an actual bona fide resident on such land * * *. 43 U.S.C.A. § 431.

This "excess lands" provision had not been enforced by the Department of Interior until recently; thus, large agribusinesses, some with holdings in excess of 100,000 acres, have received subsidized irrigation water from the Bureau of Reclamation.

One of the strongest advocates for strict enforcement of the 1902 Act's excess land provisions was Paul S. Taylor, Professor of Economics Emeritus at the University of California at Berkeley, who argued that there are both historical and modern policy reasons for enforcing the 160-acre maximum:

> A generation ago a government study in California's Central Valley compared two rural communities: one, Arvin, was surrounded by large-scale farms and the other, Dinuba, was surrounded by smaller family-size farms. Proportionately, Dinuba had twice as many business, professional, and white collar workers; three times as many farm operators; slightly more skilled, semi-skilled, and service laborers; and fewer than half as many agricultural laborers. Per dollar of agricultural production, the family-size farms of Dinuba supported a larger number of persons in the local community at a higher average living standard than did the large-scale farms of Arvin. Similar contrasts were found between the two communities in the quality of civic life—Dinuba had more parks, schools, churches, recreational opportunities, local newspapers, etc.

> More recently, in 1969, another study found that Imperial County, California, was a "two-class" polarized community consisting of 4.4 percent "upper class" farm persons and 87.3 percent "mass of laborers." More than half of the farmed land was in holdings in excess of 160 acres, the ceiling on individual water deliveries set by federal reclamation law. By contrast, Livingston County, Illinois, was found to be an overwhelmingly "middle class" community, where only 1.3 percent of "farm personnel" was "upper class" and only 11.7 percent "lower class."

> Today, ownership of California agricultural land is heavily concentrated. This concentration is largely an inheritance from early eras of railroad land grants, Spanish and Mexican land grants, and speculative acquisition of large blocks of public lands.

* * *

As it was emerging, this pattern of concentrated landownership was sharply contested. Debate came to a particularly sharp focus at the State's 1879 Constitutional Convention. Ultimately, it was decided that future grants of state lands should be limited to 320 acres per individual. In the same year, Major John Wesley Powell, explorer of the Colorado River, wrote that in the water-short West, "The question for legislators to solve is to devise some practical means by which water rights may be distributed among individual farmers and water monopolies prevented." [12]

This issue was not confined within the boundaries of any one state. It spread steadily throughout the West and arrived eventually at the national Capitol. A popular movement sprang up in the 1890's seeking development of Western waters. The minutes of the nearly annual sessions of the National Irrigation Congress reflect two principal concerns: (1) to find a public source of financing Western water development and (2) to prevent the building of water monopoly upon the foundations of existing land monopoly.

Both these purposes were embodied in a bill introduced in Congress in 1902. Congressman Francis G. Newlands of Nevada, author of the bill, explained that President Theodore Roosevelt

> was somewhat in doubt as to whether the bill was sufficiently guarded in the interest of homeseekers. It was a question simply of construction * * *. We all wanted to prevent monopoly and concentration of ownership, and the result was that certain changes were made absolutely satisfactory both to the Executive and to the Irrigation Committee * * *.
>
> * * *

Although the words "ecology" and "environment" were not used during Congressional debate on the Reclamation Bill, it is clear that the relevance of environmental considerations to the issue of concentrated versus dispersed landownership was understood. * * *

* * *

Thus the principles of the homestead tradition of giving actual settlers access to land, enacted six years earlier in the acreage and residency provisions of reclamation law, were recognized officially by the governors of the states as being vital to the nation's conservation of natural resources. A half century later, in the form of acreage limitation, this policy was challenged in the courts. The U.S. Supreme Court rejected the challenge in a unanimous decision declaring that reclamation projects were "designed to benefit people, not land," and to

12. J. Powell, Report on the Lands of the Arid Region of the United States 41 (2d ed. 1879). * * *

distribute benefits "in accordance with the greatest good to the greatest number of individuals."

Taylor, California Water Project: Law and Politics,* 5 Ecol.L.Q. 1, 2–6 (1975). Other of Professor Taylor's writings on the same subject are at 52 Calif.L.Rev. 978 (1964); 9 U.C.L.A. L.Rev. 1 (1962); 47 Calif.L.Rev. 499 (1959); 64 Yale L.J. 477 (1955).

The last quotation in Professor Taylor's article is from Ivanhoe Irrigation Dist. v. McCracken, 357 U.S. 275 (1958), which upheld the 160-acre maximum in the 1902 Act. In *Ivanhoe*, the Court rejected the argument that the United States could not include excess lands provisions in contracts with irrigation districts because the provision was contrary to state law.

The original Reclamation Act residency and acreage requirements often were honored only in the breach, in spite of the ruling in *Ivanhoe*. In California v. United States, 438 U.S. 645 (1978), the Court departed from *Ivanhoe* and other cases indicating that state law was inapplicable except to determine federal water rights to unappropriated waters. It held instead that states could impose any conditions not expressly precluded by federal statute on the operation of federal reclamation projects. Although it "disavowed dictum" in *Ivanhoe* contrary to its holding, the *California* Court apparently approved *Ivanhoe's* conclusion that the 160 acre maximum prevailed over different state law.

The spate of litigation in the 1970's over enforcement of the acreage limitation was slowed by the 1980 decision of Bryant v. Yellen, 447 U.S. 352 (1980) and stopped by amendments to the Reclamation Act in 1982. In *Bryant*, the Court of Appeals ruled that prospective purchasers of land in Imperial Valley, California, were entitled to judgment forcing the owners of excess lands to sell or lose their reclamation water. The Supreme Court agreed that plaintiffs had standing, but reversed on the merits. It held that the Boulder Canyon Project Act of 1926, as construed by the Interior Department, exempted from the acreage limitation owners in Imperial Valley whose water rights predated the federal reclamation project.

Congress finally revised the reclamation laws in the Reclamation Reform Act of 1982, 43 U.S.C.A. §§ 390aa to 390zz–1. Among other things, the Act loosened acreage limitations: "qualified applicants" (individuals, or entities of fewer than 26 persons) cannot receive project irrigation water for lands in excess of 960 acres; "limited applicants" (entities of more than 25 persons) are restricted to 640 acres. Congress abolished the residency requirement. Under the Act, lands using project water may be leased without acreage limit for up to ten years (25 years for perennial crops). Holders of excess lands can receive project water at contract rates if they execute recordable contracts to dispose of the excess lands within five years; under prior law, excess land holders could receive water at the subsidized rate for ten years if recordable contracts were executed. These provisions apply only to

* Copyright © 1975 by the Ecology   Berkeley, California. Reprinted by permis-
Law Quarterly, University of California,   sion of the Ecology Law Quarterly.

contracts entered into by irrigation districts and the Bureau of Reclamation after the passage of the Act, but many districts are expected to enter into amended contracts.

The Reclamation Reform Act exempts most Army Corps of Engineers irrigation projects from the reclamation laws. This important exemption apparently overrules cases holding some irrigators to the acreage limitations. Thus, for example, the Act seems to supersede the result in the litigation over the Pine Flat Project in California. See United States v. Tulare Lake Canal Co., 535 F.2d 1093 (9th Cir.1976); United States v. Tulare Lake Canal Co., 677 F.2d 713 (9th Cir.1982), vacated as moot, 459 U.S. 1095 (1983). See generally the symposium on irrigation districts at 1982 Ariz.St.L.J. 345; Kelley, Staging a Comeback—Section 8 of the Reclamation Act, 18 U.C.D. L.Rev. 97 (1984).

7. GRANTS OF TIMBER

Another fundamental shift in public land policy can be traced through successive congressional treatments of lands chiefly valuable for timber. For centuries, of course, the forest was the enemy, the wilderness standing between the pioneer and agrarian productivity. It has been conservatively estimated that by 1900, 600 billion board feet of lumber were destroyed in clearing the land. Early on, however, it was recognized that certain timber was necessary for the new national navy, and in 1799 and later certain tracts were acquired or set aside for that purpose. The early naval timber reservations were eventually returned to the public domain because the age of the wooden sailing ships passed, depredations of adjoining settlers had denuded the tracts, and little replanting had ever been accomplished.

Elsewhere on the public domain, timber was cleared from agricultural claims and pilfered or plundered from public land for use on the claims. Demand for lumber from the growing midwestern cities created vast logging industries in Michigan, Wisconsin, and other forested states. Woodburning steamboats and railroad engines added to demand. The public lands supplied most of the insatiable market by fraudulent preemption, use of the shifting "rubber forty" claim, and outright theft. By the use of their own "claim clubs," lumbermen seldom paid more than the minimum $1.25 per acre price, if they paid at all. Sawmills operated in Minnesota for eleven years before an acre of public land was sold. A few weak efforts to prosecute trespassers were bitterly and successfully fought. Absentee owners were similarly plundered. No remedy was effective because people on the timber frontier were united against any regulation, and they carried the day. When some prosecutions had been initiated by the reformer Carl Schurz in the 1870's, Congress in 1878 refused to appropriate funds for regulating timber cutting on public lands. Ironically, in 1872 Congress had enacted the Timber Culture Act, which gave settlers a third quarter-section if they would plant and cultivate trees on 40 acres. A few groves on the Plains have survived, but the main use of the Act was preemptive: a settler could control the Timber Culture land claimed for

13 years without payment; three-quarters of the claims ultimately lapsed, but over ten million acres went to patent.

In spite of the known abuses of timber resources, the Timber and Stone Act of 1878 allowed one to appropriate lands in named western states "chiefly valuable for timber (or stone)" for $2.50 an acre, but not for speculation. One purpose of the Act was to do away with the need for false swearing, but it succeeded only in fueling the fires of perjury. The Timber Cutting Act, also of 1878, was similar in effect, giving residents of other states rights to cut on unentered mining lands. Efforts at control waxed and waned with Administrations: the lonely efforts of Commissioner Sparks to preserve the public timber resources in the late 1880's are noteworthy, but they too had little effect except to stir up western antagonism. The century-long misuse of the forests had several lasting effects, not the least of which were the rise of the conservation movement and the retention policy. Depletion of the forest resources set in motion the trend toward federal retention and management.

C. RESERVATION AND WITHDRAWAL

During the 19th century, unprecedented growth, expansion, and development had taken place, and the United States had truly become the haven for the oppressed—save Indians—and a world power. The widespread abuses of the public land laws, however, gave rise to sentiments and movements that would bring about the end of the public land disposal policy. In its place, a federal retention and management policy would evolve, and conservation would become a critical national concern.

The origins of new federal policy can be traced to the early post-Civil War period. The conservation-oriented writings of George Perkins Marsh in 1864 gave a rationale to aggressive federal officials such as Schurz and Sparks. The vast Yellowstone reservation was set aside as a "pleasuring ground" in 1872 (but did not become a true national park until many years later when the U.S. Army ejected the squatters, hunters, loggers, and miners still exploiting its resources). The classification process slowly got underway with laws distinguishing among coal lands, timber lands, desert lands, and so forth. Reaction to the excesses of land barons led to counterpressures and the formation of new organizations, such as that of the Sierra Club in 1892. The use of executive withdrawal of land from entry grew.

The creation of Yellowstone National Park is rightly regarded as the beginning of the modern federal lands systems, but a more significant milestone was passage of the General Revision Act of 1891, 16 U.S. C.A. § 471. In addition to repealing the Preemption and Timber Culture Acts, the Forest Reservation provision, buried in an amendment, authorized the President to "set apart and reserve * * * any part of the public lands wholly or in part covered with timber or undergrowth, whether of commercial value or not, as public reservations." While five more national parks had been set aside by 1900, the

General Revision Act resulted in the reservation of millions of acres from which future parks and the national forest system would be created. The Organic Act of 1897, 16 U.S.C.A. §§ 473–481 (repealed in part, 1976), authorized protective management of the retained Forest Reserves. By 1901, some 50 million acres had been withdrawn from the exploitable public domain, and President Theodore Roosevelt (working in concert with Gifford Pinchot, his chief forester) withdrew another 150 or so million acres for forest reservations with a few strokes. Great controversies raged, and still do, over those and subsequent withdrawals, but a new age in public land law had irrevocably dawned.

1. THE PINCHOT ERA

Federal policy in the 19th century was not solely one of disposition. There was also a nascent impulse to segregate and preserve for the common good or interest those lands deemed of unique national importance. The executive regularly withdrew certain lands from the public domain for specific purposes, usually for military or Indian reservations. In some instances, the United States purchased land from private owners to serve public needs, and if the acquisition could not be agreed to, it was occasionally made involuntarily. A significant legal principle emerges in roundabout fashion from the following case, which arose when the United States attempted to acquire by condemnation a symbolically important parcel that had always been in private ownership.

UNITED STATES v. GETTYSBURG ELEC. RY. CO.

Supreme Court of the United States, 1896.
160 U.S. 668.

[The United States sought to condemn the Railroad's land for inclusion in what was to be Gettysburg National Military Park.]

Mr. Justice PECKHAM, after stating the case, delivered the opinion of the court.

The really important question to be determined in these proceedings is, whether the use to which the petitioner desires to put the land described in the petitions is of that kind of public use for which the government of the United States is authorized to condemn land.

It has authority to do so whenever it is necessary or appropriate to use the land in the execution of any of the powers granted to it by the Constitution.

*   *   *

In [the relevant acts] of Congress *   *   * the intended use of this land is plainly set forth. It is stated in the second volume of Judge Dillon's work on Municipal Corporations, (4th ed. § 600) that when the legislature has declared the use or purpose to be a public one, its judgment will be respected by the courts, unless the use be palpably without reasonable foundation. Many authorities are cited in the note, and, indeed, the rule commends itself as a rational and proper one.

*   *   *

Upon the question whether the proposed use of this land is a public one, we think there can be no well founded doubt. And also, in our judgment, the government has the constitutional power to condemn the land for the proposed use. It is, of course, not necessary that the power of condemnation for such purpose be expressly given by the Constitution. The right to condemn at all is not so given. It results from the powers that are given, and it is implied because of its necessity, or because it is appropriate in exercising those powers. Congress has power to declare war and to create and equip armies and navies. It has the great power of taxation to be exercised for the common defence and general welfare. Having such powers, it has such other and implied ones as are necessary and appropriate for the purpose of carrying the powers expressly given into effect. Any act of Congress which plainly and directly tends to enhance the respect and love of the citizen for the institutions of his country and to quicken and strengthen his motives to defend them, and which is germane to and intimately connected with and appropriate to the exercise of some one or all of the powers granted by Congress must be valid. This proposed use comes within such description. * * *

The end to be attained by this proposed use, as provided for by the act of Congress, is legitimate, and lies within the scope of the Constitution. The battle of Gettysburg was one of the great battles of the world. The numbers contained in the opposing armies were great; the sacrifice of life was dreadful; while the bravery and, indeed, heroism displayed by both the contending forces rank with the highest exhibition of those qualities ever made by man. The importance of the issue involved in the contest of which this great battle was a part cannot be overestimated. The existence of the government itself and the perpetuity of our institutions depended upon the result. Valuable lessons in the art of war can now be learned from an examination of this great battlefield in connection with the history of the events which there took place. Can it be that the government is without power to preserve the land, and properly mark out the various sites upon which this struggle took place? Can it not erect the monuments provided for by these acts of Congress, or even take possession of the field of battle in the name and for the benefit of all the citizens of the country for the present and for the future? Such a use seems necessarily not only a public use, but one so closely connected with the welfare of the republic itself as to be within the powers granted Congress by the Constitution for the purpose of protecting and preserving the whole country. * * *

No narrow view of the character of this proposed use should be taken. Its national character and importance, we think, are plain. The power to condemn for this purpose need not be plainly and unmistakably deduced from any one of the particularly specified powers. Any number of those powers may be grouped together, and an inference from them all may be drawn that the power claimed has been conferred.

* * *

This, we think, completes the review of the material questions presented by the record. The first and important question in regard to whether the proposed use is public or not, having been determined in favor of the United States, we are not disposed to take any very technical view of the other questions which might be subject to amendment or to further proof upon the hearing below.

NOTES

1. The notion of what constitutes "public purposes" has changed considerably since the Constitution was drafted. In Buffalo River Conservation & Recreation Council v. National Park Service, 558 F.2d 1342 (8th Cir.1977), cert. denied, 435 U.S. 924 (1978), the court agreed with the district court that a challenge to federal condemnation of land for the Buffalo National River in Arkansas did not raise a substantial constitutional question.

2. Many recent federal land acquisition statutes apparently only authorize the government to acquire lands by donation, exchange, or purchase with appropriated funds. In United States v. 16.92 Acres of Land, 670 F.2d 1369 (7th Cir.1982), the condemnee claimed that the Apostle Islands National Lakeshore Act, 16 U.S.C.A. § 460w–2, which was phrased in that consensual fashion, did not allow the Interior Department to condemn his land. The court affirmed the condemnation award on the basis of the General Condemnation Act of 1888, 40 U.S.C.A. § 257, which provides:

> In every case in which * * * any other officer of the Government has been * * * authorized to procure real estate * * * for public purposes, he may acquire the same for the United States by condemnation, under judicial process, whenever in his opinion it is necessary or advantageous to do so * * *.

Federal condemnation procedures are summarized in Kirby Forest Industries, Inc. v. United States, 467 U.S. 1 (1984), involving a Park Service acquisition to expand Big Thicket National Park in Texas.

Creation of the forest reserves by withdrawing public land from private entry and settlement was unpopular in the West. Some hoped or feared that it was unconstitutional. The following classic public land law decision, a test case instituted by the Pinchot administration, crushed the grazers' hopes and laid the conservationists' fears to rest.

LIGHT v. UNITED STATES
Supreme Court of the United States, 1911.
220 U.S. 523.

Mr. Justice LAMAR delivered the opinion of the court.

The defendant was enjoined from pasturing his cattle on the Holy Cross Forest Reserve, because he had refused to comply with the regulations adopted by the Secretary of Agriculture, under the authority conferred by the act of June 4, 1897, (30 Stat. 35), to make rules and regulations as to the use, occupancy and preservation of forests. The validity of the rule is attacked on the ground that Congress could not delegate to the Secretary legislative power. We need not discuss that question in view of the opinion in United States v. Grimaud, 220 U.S. 506 [(1911)] [infra at page 238].

The bill alleged, and there was evidence to support the finding, that the defendant, with the expectation and intention that they would do so, turned his cattle out at a time and place which made it certain that they would leave the open public lands and go at once to the Reserve, where there was good water and fine pasturage. When notified to remove the cattle, he declined to do so and threatened to resist if they should be driven off by a forest officer. He justified this position on the ground that the statute of Colorado provided that a landowner could not recover damages for trespass by animals unless the property was enclosed with a fence of designated size and material. Regardless of any conflict in the testimony, the defendant claims that unless the Government put a fence around the Reserve it had no remedy, either at law or in equity, nor could he be required to prevent his cattle straying upon the Reserve from the open public land on which he had a right to turn them loose.

At common law the owner was required to confine his live stock, or else was held liable for any damage done by them upon the land of third persons. That law was not adapted to the situation of those States where there were great plains and vast tracts of unenclosed land, suitable for pasture. And so, without passing a statute, or taking any affirmative action on the subject, the United States suffered its public domain to be used for such purposes. There thus grew up a sort of implied license that these lands, thus left open, might be used so long as the Government did not cancel its tacit consent. Buford v. Houtz, 133 U.S. 326. Its failure to object, however, did not confer any vested right on the complainant, nor did it deprive the United States of the power of recalling any implied license under which the land had been used for private purposes. Steele v. United States, 113 U.S. 130; Wilcox v. Jackson, 13 Pet. 513.

It is contended, however, that Congress cannot constitutionally withdraw large bodies of land from settlement without the consent of the State where it is located; and it is then argued that the act of 1891 providing for the establishment of reservations was void, so that what is nominally a Reserve is, in law, to be treated as open and unenclosed land, as to which there still exists the implied license that it may be used for grazing purposes. * * *

The United States can prohibit absolutely or fix the terms on which its property may be used. As it can withhold or reserve the land it can do so indefinitely, Stearns v. Minnesota, 179 U.S. 243. It is true that the "United States do not and cannot hold property as a monarch may for private or personal purposes." * * *

"All the public lands of the nation are held in trust for the people of the whole country." United States v. Trinidad Coal Co., 137 U.S. 160. And it is not for the courts to say how that trust shall be administered. That is for Congress to determine. The courts cannot compel it to set aside the lands for settlement; or to suffer them to be used for agricultural or grazing purposes; nor interfere when, in the exercise of its discretion, Congress establishes a forest reserve for what it decides to be national and public purposes. In the same way and in the exercise of the same trust it may disestablish a reserve, and devote the property to some other national and public purpose. These are rights incident to proprietorship, to say nothing of the power of the United States as a sovereign over the property belonging to it. Even a private owner would be entitled to protection against willful trespasses, and statutes providing that damage done by animals cannot be recovered, unless the land had been enclosed with a fence of the size and material required, do not give permission to the owner of cattle to use his neighbor's land as a pasture. They are intended to condone trespasses by straying cattle; they have no application to cases where they are driven upon unfenced land in order that they may feed there.

Fence laws do not authorize wanton and willful trespass, nor do they afford immunity to those who, in disregard of property rights, turn loose their cattle under circumstances showing that they were intended to graze upon the lands of another.

* * *

NOTES

1. How does the Court characterize the powers of the federal government over the public lands? As a sovereign? As a proprietor? Compare Pollard v. Hagan, 44 U.S. (3 How.) 212 (1845), supra at page 72. Can the difference between the formulations in the two cases be explained by the evolution in congressional policy between 1845 and 1911?

2. Nineteenth century policies had served their intended goals, but the problems they created in the altered circumstances demanded some fundamental changes. The public supply of productive farm land had all but disappeared; private irrigation was but a drop in the bucket; western grazing lands were in poor condition; wildlife resources were at historical lows; and timber resources were severely depleted. Scandal was endemic, reforms had been repeatedly thwarted, and the trend toward large holdings and monopoly grew. Some national leaders had long advocated new methods of dealing with public domain, but the foremost architect of radical revision in public land policy was Gifford Pinchot.

STEWART T. UDALL, THE QUIET CRISIS
97–108 (1963).

Gifford Pinchot saw the climax of the Big Raids in the 1890's, and he described the scene with both candor and color:

Out in the Great Open Spaces where Men were Men the domination of concentrated wealth over mere human beings was something to make you shudder. I saw it and fought it, and I know. * * * Big money was King in the Great Open Spaces, and no mistake. * * * The powers and principalities which controlled the politics and the people of the West began to emerge from the general landscape. Principalities like the Homestake Mine in the Black Hills, the Anaconda Mine in the Rockies, Marcus Daly's feudal overlordship of the Bitterroot Valley, and Miller and Lux's vast holdings of flocks and herds and control of grazing lands on the Pacific slope—these and others showed their hands or their teeth. So did powers like the Northern and Southern Pacific and the Great Northern Railroads, the irrigation interests of California, and the great cattle and sheep stock growers' association.

* * *

By any standards, Gifford Pinchot was a magnificent bureaucrat. In his time the Forest Service was the most exciting organization in Washington. It was more a family than a bureau. In the field, around campfires, and in his home GP discussed the next moves and gave his associates the feeling that they served on the general staff in a national crusade. A natural leader, he chose his men well, gave them authority, aroused an *esprit de corps* and sent them forth to save the forests. The rule book he wrote for his men was filled with crisp, common-sense guidelines. Typical Pinchot maxims were: "The public good comes first," and "Local questions will be decided by local officers on local grounds." In a matter of months his new "forest rangers" were winning over the West.

* * *

What was needed now was a word, a name—to sum up the concept. A conversation with forester Overton Price brought up the fact that government forests in India were called "conservancies." Pinchot and Price liked the ring of the word, and thus a concept that had originated in the seminal thinking of such men as Thoreau and Marsh now had an expressive name—conservation.

* * *

The conservation movement was a river of many tributaries, and if GP was not, as he liked to believe in his later years, its fountainhead, he was nevertheless one of its vital sources. He was a key man of a key decade, and his leadership was crucial in persuading the American people to turn from flagrant waste of resources to programs of wise stewardship.

* * *

The classic encounter that embroiled him and other dedicated conservationists involved the first head-on collision between the Pinchot idea of conservation-for-use and the park concept of scenic preservation. The controversy was known by an improbable name: Hetch Hetchy. Pinchot's chief opponent, a friend who knew even more

about the American out-of-doors than he, was an improbable person—
John Muir.

————

One key to reform of public land policy was the process of classification. A de facto classification system of sorts had existed since the
birth of the Republic: certain lands had been set aside for military
purposes, Indian reservations had been created, and some lands were
deemed "mineral in character." For our purposes, the first modern
category of public lands was the national parks. Since the withdrawal
and reservation of Yellowstone, Congress had created national parks at
irregular intervals, many preceding the founding of the Forest Service.
Not until 1916, however, was the National Park Service (NPS)
chartered, with organic authority to administer the new National Park
System. The quietly revolutionary statute directed NPS to "conserve
the scenery and the natural and historic objects and the wild life [in
national parks] and to provide for the enjoyment of the same in such
manner and by such means as will leave them unimpaired for the
enjoyment of future generations." 16 U.S.C.A. § 1. Thus, early in this
century there had developed a trichotomy of resource philosophies,
described roughly as uncontrolled extraction, regulated use, and preservation.

HAROLD W. WOOD, JR., PINCHOT AND MATHER: HOW THE FOREST SERVICE AND PARK SERVICE GOT THAT WAY *

Not Man Apart, December 1976.

Gifford Pinchot was the person most responsible for establishing
the US Forest Service and dedicating it to utilitarian uses of natural
resources. Stephen Mather was the person most responsible for organizing the National Park Service, dedicated to the preservation of
natural features in the undisturbed state. The conflicts epitomized by
these agencies have continued into the present day, so an understanding of the contrasting viewpoints of these two architects of policy may
help us understand some of the land-use conflicts we still have to deal
with.

* * *

Pinchot's fundamental attitude toward the environment was utilitarian. He consistently favored resource development over mere preservation, as illustrated by two controversies of his day—issues we are
still struggling with. One contest was over the Adirondack Forest
Preserve in New York, where voters had passed an amendment to the
state constitution that prohibited any timber from the area being sold,
removed, or destroyed. Pinchot felt that the prohibition was tremen-

dous waste and said forestry had nothing to do with decoration of public places, "that scenery is altogether outside its province." * * *

But by far the most famous episode in the utilitarian/aesthetic battle was the controversy over Hetch Hetchy Valley in Yosemite National Park. The preservationists, led by John Muir and the Sierra Club, believed that the park should not be violated. San Francisco, however, wanted to build a dam to provide a water supply for the city. Pinchot sided with the city and used his influence in Washington on its behalf.

Pinchot was adamant in his position: "I am fully persuaded that * * * the injury * * * by substituting a lake for the present swampy floor of the [Hetch Hetchy] valley. * * * is altogether unimportant compared with the benefits to be derived from its use as a reservoir." * * * Pinchot, like others, ignored the fact that alternative sites were available, if at a higher cost of construction.

John Muir's view on Hetch Hetchy was just as succinctly put: "Dam Hetch Hetchy! As well dam for water-tanks the people's cathedrals and churches, for no holier temple has ever been consecrated by the heart of man."

The Sierra Club and its allies lost Hetch Hetchy to the dam-builders in 1913. It is probable that the controversy, with all its publicity, helped generate public support in 1916 for the National Park Service Act, which would better protect National Parks from such encroachment.

Pinchot expanded his philosophy of forestry into a full-scale political ideology in 1905 when he became Chief Forester of the newly established US Forest Service, which had jurisdiction over the forest reserves. In his instructions from Agriculture Secretary James Wilson in 1905 (which Pinchot wrote himself), he was told: "All the resources of forest reserves are for *use* * * * where conflicting interests must be reconciled, the question will always be decided from the standpoint of the greatest good for the greatest number in the long run." With this last phrase, Pinchot thought he had found an unbeatable formula for success.

* * *

His utilitarian attitude led him to believe that national parks, and not just national forests, should be open to such development as grazing and lumbering. As early as 1904 he recommended to Congress that the national parks be transferred to the Forest Service for administration. He opposed bills to create a separate National Park Service by saying it was "no more needed than two tails to a cat."

The Forest Service consistently opposed bills to create new parks and reliably suggested national forest status instead. When the bill to establish Glacier National Park appeared in Congress, Pinchot objected because the only commercial use to be allowed was removal of dead, down, or decaying timber by settlers. He prepared a rival measure to permit timber cutting, water power development, and railroad construction within the park.

Stephen Mather was every bit as energetic as Pinchot and just as dedicated to his own cause. * * *

* * *

Some of Mather's biggest struggles in protecting the parks came during World War I, at the beginning of his administration. Secretary Lane was a "hawk" on the President's cabinet and favored using all resources in the war effort. It is reported that after Mather had failed to keep cattle out of Yosemite legally, he had some of the cows caught and staked near trails, hoping to incite hikers into denouncing the business to their Representatives. (Mather always denied this; he said it was too good an idea to be his own.)

* * *

While the National Park Service is usually considered preservationist, Mather was not a complete purist. He believed that the national parks should be opened up to development to provide visitors' accommodations. Much of his effort went into having roads constructed and improved, having inns and hotels built, and encouraging railroads to bring people to the parks.

He did all of this, however, within certain limits. For example, he refused to allow railroad lines *within* Yellowstone Park, although he had gone out of his way to encourage railroad lines *to* the Park.

While he believed in providing inns and hotels, he wouldn't allow such concessions unwarranted power. When the Great Northern Railroad set up a sawmill to construct a hotel in Glacier National Park, Mather watched the progress carefully. When the hotel was finished, he reminded the company that the sawmill and its sawdust must go. The company asked for a little more lumber, which Mather reluctantly let it have. The stay expired on August 10, 1925, and the railroad company again asked for more time, although the hotel was already taking in tourists. Mather was in the park on business at the time, so that afternoon he rounded up the Park Service trail crews and had the sawmill blown up.

* * *

It might seem that Mather's attitude was ambivalent. The parks were dedicated to preservation, but also to the people's enjoyment. Translating this dualistic approach into workable policies is much more difficult than interpreting a simple utilitarianism such as Pinchot's. Nevertheless, Stephen Mather had criteria and sound reasoning with which to provide suitable development compatible with preservation. Considering the enormous pressure to commercialize the parks, Mather did an admirable job of keeping preservation foremost.

It cannot be said that Mather objected to sustained-yield forestry, and he did not think that national park standards and management practices should be applied to national forests. In contrast, Pinchot implacably felt that national parks should be managed just as the national forests were.

* * *

It is ironic that Pinchot had such a comprehensive view of managing natural resources, even speaking of conserving human resources, and yet entirely neglected aesthetic values. Mather certainly did not attempt to enlarge his ideas on preservation into a political philosophy, as Pinchot did, but he still accepted the need for both preservation and utilitarian conservation—as long as the utilization wasn't in the national parks.

If it were not for Pinchot's recalcitrant opposition to the preservationists, the utilitarian and aesthetic schools of conservation probably would not have become so split. For many years, agency rivalry between the Forest Service and the National Park Service created ugly moods. The squabbling was often as much over jurisdiction as philosophy. But, partly in response to the Park Service's carving new parks and monuments out of national forests, the Forest Service began its own program of recreational development and safeguards for scenic resources. With the help of men such as Arthur Carhart, Robert Marshall, and Aldo Leopold of the Forest Service, a system of wilderness areas began developing in the 1930's. Without the competition, it is likely that this would not have been done for a long time.

2. JOHN MUIR AND THE MODERN CONSERVATION MOVEMENT

Pinchot and Mather were men of affairs, personally wealthy, influential, and highly placed in the national government. Their accomplishments were great and their philosophies were advanced. Their names will long live in public land annals. Their fame is eclipsed, however, by the memory of John Muir. Muir never held an important position except, perhaps, President of the young Sierra Club, of which he was a founder. He was a philosopher, a traveller, a nature lover, and a writer. He lived in and for the mountains. His contribution to public land and resources law was spiritual, a lasting legacy of love for the land and its creatures. He was the archetypal preservationist whose ironbound, indomitable will more than matched those of the "timber barons" and other largescale users of the land whom he so despised.

Muir inspired a new ethic that has been absorbed into the American consciousness, an ethic that is not less real for its lack of precise definition. Its most important manifestation has been the formation of groups composed of private citizens who, like Muir, are willing to devote their time and money to causes that have no advocates in the community of money and development.

Muir's lasting contribution to public land law is incapable of measurement. But the esteem that he has inspired in later generations is reflected in the fact that more place names in California, from Muir Woods to the John Muir Trail (not to mention the USS *John Muir*), are named after him than after any other individual. In 1976, a citizen poll named Muir the "single greatest Californian" in history.

E.W. TEALE, THE WILDERNESS WORLD OF JOHN MUIR
XIV, XIX–XX (1954).

Before his first book came from the press John Muir was already famous as a writer. His sequence of "Sierra Studies" in the old *Overland Monthly* and his articles in the *Century Magazine* had had wide influence and had given him a national reputation. * * * An exactness and depth of firsthand observation characterizes all his pages. He was by turn a scientist, a poet, a mystic, a philosopher, a humorist. Because he saw everything, mountains and streams and landscapes, as evolving, unfinished, in the process of creation, there is a pervading sense of vitality in all he wrote. Even his records of scientific studies read like adventure stories.

* * *

Considerable as was John Muir's contribution to science, even greater was his stature in the long fight for conservation. During those critical years around the turn of the century, his was the most eloquent and powerful voice raised in defense of nature. He was the spearhead of the western movement to preserve wild beauty, a prime mover in the national park system so valued today. Beside a campfire at Soda Springs on the Tuolumne Meadows in 1889, he and Robert Underwood Johnson mapped the seventeen-year battle that preserved Yosemite as a national park. Beside other campfires under sequoias, while on a three-day outing with Theodore Roosevelt in 1903, he presented the case for the preservation of numerous wilderness areas with moving effect. Major credit for saving the Grand Canyon and the Petrified Forest, in Arizona, is ascribed to John Muir. He was president of the Sierra Club from the formation of that militant conservation organization in 1892 until the time of his death in 1914. His last long battle to save Hetch Hetchy, the beautiful Yosemite Park valley flooded to form a reservoir for San Francisco water—water that could have been obtained elsewhere—ended only the year before he died. It represents one of the great heroic struggles of conservation, no less heroic because the cause was lost.

Near the end of his life Muir said to a close friend, "I have lived a bully life. I have done what I set out to do." Rich in time, rich in enjoyment, rich in appreciation, rich in enthusiasm, rich in understanding, rich in expression, rich in friends, rich in knowledge, John Muir lived a full and rounded life, a life unique in many ways, admirable in many ways, valuable in many ways. "A man in his books," he once wrote, "may be said to walk the earth long after he had gone." In his writings and in his conservation achievements, Muir seems especially present in a world that is better because he lived here. His finest monument is the wild beauty he called attention to and helped preserve—beauty, however, that is never entirely safe, beauty that needs as vigilant protection today and tomorrow as it needed yesterday.

———————

Muir was the catalyst, but workaday legislators brought about conservationist reforms through law. In the Mineral Leasing Act of 1920, 30 U.S.C.A. §§ 181 et seq., Congress asserted a new form of public control over the disposition of fuel minerals. And in the Taylor Grazing Act of 1934, 43 U.S.C.A. §§ 315 et seq., Congress for practical purposes ended the national disposition policy.

3. MINERAL LEASING

The Mining Act of 1872 was as subject to abuse as the other disposition statutes, but it has survived because mineral development has been seen in every generation as a necessary requisite to national growth and development. It became evident in the late 19th and early 20th centuries, however, that one category of minerals deserved separate treatment because of its increasing importance in the national economy and to the national well-being. The new system for fuel mineral development that evolved was a significant departure from prior law and practice.

Fuel minerals, primarily coal, oil, and gas, differ greatly from hardrock minerals in characteristics and usage, and their legal treatment has also come to be significantly different. Legislation for disposition of coal lands was first passed in 1865; it evolved into an Act of 1873, which provided for entry and patent in a fashion similar to agricultural entry, but at a higher price (in contrast to the free mining policy for metals). The usual abuses led President Roosevelt in 1906 to withdraw from all forms of entry 66 million acres where "workable coal is known to occur," and to call for a leasing system. Much of the land was later returned to the public domain, but the attention created helped pass several statutes in ensuing years that severed the rights to underlying coal from the surface estate, reserving the former for the United States. The 30-odd million acres patented under the Stock-Raising Homestead Act, for instance, overlay more energy in the form of coal than Saudi Arabia has as oil.

In the meantime, petroleum had been discovered and had gone from a curiosity to a highly valuable resource. Oil strikes all over the country caused fevers reminiscent of the Gold Rush. The legal status of petroleum was unclear, however, until Congress in 1897 confirmed an understanding that petroleum locations were to be governed by the placer mining laws. Thus, under the General Mining Law of 1872, drillers were able to enter public lands without obtaining government approval and obtain a vested property right to a deposit at the moment a discovery was made. Fearing that all oil lands would soon pass into private ownership, forcing the Navy to buy back the oil that was being given away, President Taft in 1909 stunned the Nation by withdrawing from all forms of entry three million acres valuable for oil in Wyoming and California. Uncertain of the constitutional basis for his action, Taft requested congressional validation, which was forthcoming by the ambiguous Pickett Act of 1910, 43 U.S.C.A. §§ 141–143 (repealed 1976). The Act granted a "temporary" withdrawal power, but it was silent as to prior reservations, and it stipulated that lands subsequently withdrawn would still be open to hardrock mineral entry. See infra at page 242. In 1915, the Supreme Court reviewed the validity of Taft's prior withdrawals.

UNITED STATES v. MIDWEST OIL CO.
Supreme Court of the United States, 1915.
236 U.S. 459.

Mr. Justice LAMAR delivered the opinion of the court.

All public lands containing petroleum or other mineral oils and chiefly valuable therefor, have been declared by Congress to be "free and open to occupation, exploration and purchase by citizens of the United States * * * under regulations prescribed by law." Act of February 11, 1897, c. 216, 29 Stat. 526; R.S. 2319, 2329.

As these regulations permitted exploration and location without the payment of any sum, and as title could be obtained for a merely nominal amount, many persons availed themselves of the provisions of the statute. Large areas in California were explored; and petroleum having been found, locations were made, not only by the discoverer but by others on adjoining land. And, as the flow through the well on one lot might exhaust the oil under the adjacent land, the interest of each operator was to extract the oil as soon as possible so as to share what would otherwise be taken by the owners of nearby wells.

The result was that oil was so rapidly extracted that on September 17, 1909, the Director of the Geological Survey made a report to the Secretary of the Interior which, with enclosures, called attention to the fact that, while there was a limited supply of coal on the Pacific coast and the value of oil as a fuel had been fully demonstrated, yet at the rate at which oil lands in California were being patented by private parties it would "be impossible for the people of the United States to continue ownership of oil lands for more than a few months. After that the Government will be obliged to repurchase the very oil that it has practically given away. * * * " "In view of the increasing use of fuel by the American Navy there would appear to be an immediate necessity for assuring the conservation of a proper supply of petroleum for the Government's own use * * * " and "pending the enactment of adequate legislation on this subject, the filing of claims to oil lands in the State of California should be suspended."

This recommendation was approved by the Secretary of the Interior. Shortly afterwards he brought the matter to the attention of the President who, on September 27, 1909, issued the following Proclamation:

"Temporary Petroleum Withdrawal No. 5."

"In aid of proposed legislation affecting the use and disposition of the petroleum deposits on the public domain, all public lands in the accompanying lists are hereby temporarily withdrawn from all forms of location, settlement, selection, filing, entry, or disposal under the mineral or nonmineral public-land laws. All locations or claims existing and valid on this date may proceed to entry in the usual manner after field investigation and examination."

The list attached described an area aggregating 3,041,000 acres in California and Wyoming—though, of course, the order only applied to the public lands therein, the acreage of which is not shown.

On March 27, 1910, six months after the publication of the Proclamation, William T. Henshaw and others entered upon a quarter section of this public land in Wyoming so withdrawn. They made explorations, bored a well, discovered oil and thereafter assigned their interest to the Appellees, who took possession and extracted large quantities of oil. On May 4, 1910, they filed a location certificate.

As the explorations by the original claimants, and the subsequent operation of the well, were both long after the date of the President's Proclamation, the Government filed, in the District Court of the United States for the District of Wyoming, a Bill in Equity against the Midwest Oil Company and the other Appellees, seeking to recover the land and to obtain an accounting for 50,000 barrels of oil alleged to have been illegally extracted. * * *

* * * On the part of the Government it is urged that the President, as Commander-in-Chief of the Army and Navy, had power to make the order for the purpose of retaining and preserving a source of supply of fuel for the Navy, instead of allowing the oil land to be taken up for a nominal sum, the Government being then obliged to purchase at a great cost what it had previously owned. It is argued that the President, charged with the care of the public domain, could, by virtue of the executive power vested in him by the Constitution (Art. 2, § 1), and also in conformity with the tacit consent of Congress, withdraw, in the public interest, any public land from entry or location by private parties.

The Appellees, on the other hand, insist that there is no dispensing power in the Executive and that he could not suspend a statute or withdraw from entry or location any land which Congress had affirmatively declared should be free and open to acquisition by citizens of the United States. They further insist that the withdrawal order is absolutely void since it appears on its face to be a mere attempt to suspend a statute—supposed to be unwise,—in order to allow Congress to pass another more in accordance with what the Executive thought to be in the public interest.

1. We need not consider whether, as an original question, the President could have withdrawn from private acquisition what Congress had made free and open to occupation and purchase. The case can be determined on other grounds and in the light of the legal consequences flowing from a long continued practice to make orders like the one here involved. For the President's proclamation of September 27, 1909, is by no means the first instance in which the Executive, by a special order, has withdrawn land which Congress, by

general statute, had thrown open to acquisition by citizens. [The Presidents have] during the past 80 years, without express statutory authority—but under the claim of power so to do—made a multitude of Executive Orders which operated to withdraw public land that would otherwise have been open to private acquisition. They affected every kind of land—mineral and nonmineral. The size of the tracts varied from a few square rods to many square miles and the amount withdrawn has aggregated millions of acres. The number of such instances cannot, of course, be accurately given, but the extent of the practice can best be appreciated by a consideration of what is believed to be a correct enumeration of such Executive Orders mentioned in public documents.

They show that prior to the year 1910 there had been issued

> 99 Executive Orders establishing or enlarging Indian Reservations;

> 109 Executive Orders establishing or enlarging Military Reservations and setting apart land for water, timber, fuel, hay, signal stations, target ranges and rights of way for use in connection with Military Reservations;

> 44 Executive Orders establishing Bird Reserves.

In the sense that these lands may have been intended for public use, they were reserved for a public purpose. But they were not reserved in pursuance of law or by virtue of any general or special statutory authority. For, it is to be specially noted that there was no act of Congress providing for Bird Reserves or for these Indian Reservations. There was no law for the establishment of these Military Reservations or defining their size or location. There was no statute empowering the President to withdraw any of these lands from settlement or to reserve them for any of the purposes indicated.

But when it appeared that the public interest would be served by withdrawing or reserving parts of the public domain, nothing was more natural than to retain what the Government already owned. And in making such orders, which were thus useful to the public, no private interest was injured. For prior to the initiation of some right given by law the citizen had no enforceable interest in the public statute and no private right in land which was the property of the people. The President was in a position to know when the public interest required particular portions of the people's lands to be withdrawn from entry or location; his action inflicted no wrong upon any private citizen, and being subject to disaffirmance by Congress, could occasion no harm to the interest of the public at large. Congress did not repudiate the power claimed or the withdrawal orders made. On the contrary it uniformly and repeatedly acquiesced in the practice and, as shown by these records, there had been, prior to 1910, at least 252 Executive Orders making reservations for useful, though non-statutory purposes.

This right of the President to make reservations,—and thus withdraw land from private acquisition,—was expressly recognized in Grisar

v. McDowell, 6 Wall. 364, 381 (1867), where it was said that "from an early period in the history of the Government it has been the practice of the President to order, from time to time, as the exigencies of the public service required, parcels of land belonging to the United States to be reserved from sale and set apart for public uses."

* * *

2. It may be argued that while these facts and rulings prove a usage they do not establish its validity. But government is a practical affair intended for practical men. Both officers, law-makers and citizens naturally adjust themselves to any long-continued action of the Executive Department—on the presumption that unauthorized acts would not have been allowed to be so often repeated as to crystallize into a regular practice. That presumption is not reasoning in a circle but the basis of a wise and quieting rule that in determining the meaning of a statute or the existence of a power, weight shall be given to the usage itself—even when the validity of the practice is the subject of investigation.

* * *

3. These decisions do not, of course, mean that private rights could be created by an officer withdrawing for a Rail Road more than had been authorized by Congress in the land grant act. Southern Pacific v. Bell, 183 U.S. 685; Brandon v. Ard, 211 U.S. 21. Nor do these decisions mean that the Executive can by his course of action create a power. But they do clearly indicate that the long-continued practice, known to and acquiesced in by Congress, would raise a presumption that the withdrawals had.been made in pursuance of its consent or of a recognized administrative power of the Executive in the management of the public lands. This is particularly true in view of the fact that the land is property of the United States and that the land laws are not of a legislative character in the highest sense of the term (Art. 4, § 3) "but savor somewhat of mere rules prescribed by an owner of property for its disposal." Bulle City Water Co. v. Baker, 196 U.S. 126.

These rules or laws for the disposal of public land are necessarily general in their nature. Emergencies may occur, or conditions may so change as to require that the agent in charge should, in the public interest, withhold the land from sale; and while no such express authority has been granted, there is nothing in the nature of the power exercised which prevents Congress from granting it by implication just as could be done by any other owner of property under similar conditions. The power of the Executive, as agent in charge, to retain that property from sale need not necessarily be expressed in writing.

For it must be borne in mind that Congress not only has a legislative power over the public domain, but it also exercises the powers of the proprietor therein. Congress "may deal with such lands precisely as a private individual may deal with his farming property. It may sell or withhold them from sale." Camfield v. United States, 167 U.S. 524; Light v. United States, 220 U.S. 536. Like any other owner it may provide when, how and to whom its land can be sold. It can permit it to be withdrawn from sale. Like any other owner, it can waive its strict rights, as it did when the valuable privilege of grazing cattle on this public land was held to be based upon an "implied license growing out of the custom of nearly a hundred years." Buford v. Houtz, 133 U.S. 326. So too, in the early days the "Government, by its silent acquiescence, assented to the general occupation of the public lands for mining." Atchison v. Peterson, 20 Wall. 512. If private persons could acquire a privilege in public land by virtue of an implied congressional consent, then for a much stronger reason, an implied grant of power to preserve the public interest would arise out of like congressional acquiescence.

The Executive, as agent, was in charge of the public domain; by a multitude of orders extending over a long period of time and affecting vast bodies of land, in many States and Territories, he withdrew large areas in the public interest. These orders were known to Congress, as principal, and in not a single instance was the act of the agent disapproved. Its acquiescence all the more readily operated as an implied grant of power in view of the fact that its exercise was not only useful to the public but did not interfere with any vested right of the citizen.

4. The appellees, however, argue that the practice thus approved, related to Reservations—to cases where the land had been reserved for military or other special public purposes—and they contend that even if the President could reserve land for a public purpose or for naval uses, it does not follow that he can withdraw land in aid of legislation.

When analyzed, this proposition, in effect, seeks to make a distinction between a Reservation and a Withdrawal—between a Reservation for a purpose, not provided for by existing legislation, and a Withdrawal made in aid of future legislation. It would mean that a Permanent Reservation for a purpose designated by the President, but not provided for by a statute, would be valid, while a merely Temporary Withdrawal to enable Congress to legislate in the public interest would be invalid. It is only necessary to point out that, as the greater includes the less, the power to make permanent reservations includes power to make temporary withdrawals. For there is no distinction in principle between the two. The character of the power exerted is the same in both cases. In both, the order is made to serve the public interest and in both the effect on the intending settler or miner is the same.

* * *

[T]hat the existence of [withdrawal] power was recognized and its exercise by the Executive assented to by Congress, is emphasized by [a] Report which the Secretary of the Interior made in 1902, in response to a resolution of the Senate calling for information "as to what, if any, of the public lands have been withdrawn from disposition under the settlement or other laws by order of the Commissioner of the General Land Office and *what, if any, authority of law exists for such order of withdrawal.*"

The answer to this specific inquiry was returned March 3, 1902, (Senate Doc. 232, 57th Cong., 1st Sess., Vol. 17). On that date the

Secretary transmitted to the Senate the elaborate and detailed report of the Commissioner of the Land Office, who in response to the inquiry as to the authority by which withdrawals had been made, answered that:

> "the power of the Executive Department of the Government to make reservations of land for public use, and to temporarily withdraw lands from appropriation by individuals as exigencies might demand, to prevent fraud, to aid in proper administration and in aid of pending legislation is one that has been long recognized both in the acts of Congress and the decisions of the court; * * * that this power has been long exercised by the Commissioner of the General Land Office is shown by reference to the date of some of the withdrawals enumerated. * * * The attached list embraces only such lands as were withdrawn by this office, acting on its own motion, in cases where the emergencies appeared to demand such action in furtherance of public interest and does not include lands withdrawn under express statutes so directed."

> * * *

This report refers to *Withdrawals* and not to *Reservations*. It is most important in connection with the present inquiry as to whether Congress knew of the practice to make temporary withdrawals and knowingly assented thereto. It will be noted that the Resolution called on the Department to state the extent of such withdrawals and the authority by which they were made. The officer of the Land Department in his answer shows that there have been a large number of withdrawals made for good but for non-statutory reasons. He knows that these 92 orders had been made by virtue of a long-continued practice and under claim of a right to take such action in the public interest "as exigencies might demand. * * *" Congress with notice of this practice and of this claim of authority, received the Report. Neither at that session nor afterwards did it ever repudiate the action taken or the power claimed. Its silence was acquiescence. Its acquiescence was equivalent to consent to continue the practice until the power was revoked by some subsequent action by Congress.

* * *

Reversed.

DAY, McKENNA, and VAN DEVANTER, JJ., dissenting.

* * *

NOTES

1. The Court did not reach the question whether the President had authority to withdraw lands under his power as Commander in Chief, Article II, § 2, cl. 1, or under the basic executive authority, Article II, § 1, cl. 1 ("The executive Power shall be vested in a president * * *.") Would presidential power to make these withdrawals from mineral entry have been upheld on either of these two bases if no longstanding executive practice had existed? See generally L. Tribe, AMERICAN CONSTITUTIONAL LAW 172–84 (1978), discussing both

provisions and referring to the "decline of 'inherent' power." Were these withdrawals within the scope of implied authority created by the earlier kinds of withdrawals described in the opinion? Would the President be upheld if a withdrawal were made for a new purpose, such as a wilderness area, unrelated to those kinds of withdrawals to which Congress had given its "longstanding acquiescence"?

2. The subject of withdrawals and reservations is critical to public land law; chapter four, § A addresses it in far more detail.

3. *Midwest Oil* did not end the considerable confusion as to the status of mining claims on oil lands. In 1920, Congress enacted the Mineral Leasing Act, 30 U.S.C.A. § 181 et seq., which remains a cornerstone of natural resources law. It withdrew from location all fuel minerals, and it ended the governmental policy of outright sale or grant of these resources. In essence, the Act requires competitive bidding for leases of lands known to hold valuable reserves. For other lands, the Secretary may issue prospecting permits for up to 2560 acres; a discoverer is then entitled to a preference (non-competitive) lease for a fixed term. Lease proceeds go to the Reclamation Fund, the states, and the federal treasury. The leasing system was later extended to the offshore lands and to geothermal resources. See chapter six, § B infra.

4. THE TAYLOR GRAZING ACT

The reality of the tragedy of the commons is nowhere more evident than in the history of grazing on the public domain. After the lands chiefly valuable for farming, timber, mining, townsites, etc. had been claimed by successive waves of settlers and entrepreneurs, most of the public lands remaining were useful only for grazing. Naturally, it was to the economic benefit of ranchers to take for their own herds and flocks all of the free forage available before someone else did. Naturally, millions of acres of marginal, semi-arid lands were turned into wastelands by the resulting overgrazing. The disputes—sometimes violent range wars—involving the differing interests of homesteaders, ranchers, and sheepmen in the settling of the West have ascended into the mists of legend. As the following case shows, state law—that is, almost no law—applied on the open range because there had been no federal efforts to regulate grazing outside of the national parks and forests.

OMAECHEVARRIA v. IDAHO
Supreme Court of the United States, 1918.
246 U.S. 343.

Mr. Justice BRANDEIS delivered the opinion of the court.

For more than forty years the raising of cattle and sheep have been important industries in Idaho. The stock feeds in part by grazing on the public domain of the United States. This is done with the Government's acquiescence, without the payment of compensation, and without federal regulation. Buford v. Houtz, 133 U.S. 320, 326. Experience has demonstrated, says the state court, that in arid and semi-arid regions cattle will not graze, nor can they thrive, on ranges where sheep are allowed to graze extensively; that the encroachment of sheep upon ranges previously occupied by cattle results in driving out the cattle and destroying or greatly impairing the industry; and that this conflict of interests led to frequent and serious breaches of the peace and the loss of many lives. Efficient policing of the ranges is impossible; for the State is sparsely settled and the public domain is extensive, comprising still more than one-fourth of the land surface. To avert clashes between sheep herdsmen and the farmers who customarily allowed their few cattle to graze on the public domain near their dwellings, the territorial legislature passed in 1875 the so-called "Two Mile Limit Law." It was enacted first as a local statute applicable to three counties, but was extended in 1879 and again in 1883 to additional counties, and was made a general law in 1887. After the admission of Idaho to the Union, the statute was reenacted and its validity sustained by this court in Bacon v. Walker, 204 U.S. 311. To avert clashes between the sheep herdsmen and the cattle rangers, further legislation was found necessary; and in 1883 the law (now § 6872 of the Revised Codes,) was enacted which prohibits any person having charge of sheep from allowing them to graze on a range previously occupied by cattle. For violating this statute the plaintiff in error, a sheep herdsman, was convicted in the local police court and sentenced to pay a fine. The judgment was affirmed by an intermediate appellate court and also by the Supreme Court of Idaho. 27 Idaho, 797. On writ of error from this court the validity of the statute is assailed on the ground that the statute is inconsistent both with the Fourteenth Amendment and with the Act of Congress of February 25, 1885, c. 149, 23 Stat. 321, entitled, "An act to prevent unlawful occupancy of the public lands."

First: It is urged that the statute denies rights guaranteed by the Fourteenth Amendment, namely: Privileges of citizens of the United States, in so far as it prohibits the use of the public lands by sheep owners; and equal protection of the laws, in that it gives to cattle owners a preference over sheep owners. These contentions are, in substance, the same as those made in respect to the "Two Mile Limit Law," and the answer made there is applicable here. The police power of the State extends over the federal public domain, at least when there is no legislation by Congress on the subject. We cannot say that the measure adopted by the State is unreasonable or arbitrary. It was found that conflicts between cattle rangers and sheep herders on the public domain could be reconciled only by segregation. In national forests, where the use of land is regulated by the Federal Government, the plan of segregation is widely adopted. And it is not an arbitrary discrimination to give preference to cattle owners in prior occupancy without providing for a like preference to sheep owners in prior occupancy. For experience shows that sheep do not require protection against encroachment by cattle, and that cattle rangers are not likely to encroach upon ranges previously occupied by sheep herders. The propriety of treating sheep differently than cattle has been generally recognized. That the interest of the sheep owners of Idaho received due consideration is indicated by the fact that in 1902 they opposed the abolition by the Government of the free ranges.

* * *

Third: It is further contended that the statute is in direct conflict with the Act of Congress of February 25, 1885. That statute which was designed to prevent the illegal fencing of public lands, contains at the close of § 1 the following clause with which the Idaho statute is said to conflict: "and the assertion of a right to the exclusive use and occupancy of any part of the public lands of the United States in any State or any of the Territories of the United States, without claim, color of title, or asserted right as above specified as to inclosure, is likewise declared unlawful, and hereby prohibited."

An examination of the federal act in its entirety makes it clear that what the clause quoted from § 1 sought to prohibit was merely the assertion of an exclusive right to use or occupation by force or intimidation or by what would be equivalent in effect to an enclosure. That this was the intent of Congress is confirmed by the history of the act. The reports of the Secretary of the Interior upon whose recommendation the act was introduced, the reports of the committees of Congress, and the debates thereon indicate that this alone was the evil sought to be remedied, and to such action only does its prohibition appear to have been applied in practice. * * *

The Idaho statute makes no attempt to grant a right to use public lands. McGinnis v. Friedman, 2 Idaho, 393. The State, acting in the exercise of its police power, merely excludes sheep from certain ranges under certain circumstances. Like the forcible entry and detainer act of Washington, which was held in Denee v. Ankeny [246 U.S. 208 (1918)], not to conflict with the homestead laws, the Idaho statute was enacted primarily to prevent breaches of the peace. The incidental protection which it thereby affords to cattle owners does not purport to secure to any of them, or to cattle owners collectively, "the exclusive use and occupancy of any part of the public lands." For every range from which sheep are excluded remains open not only to *all* cattle, but also to horses, of which there are many in Idaho. This exclusion of sheep owners under certain circumstances does not interfere with any rights of a citizen of the United States. Congress has not conferred upon citizens the right to graze stock upon the public lands. The Government has merely suffered the lands to be so used. Buford v. Houtz, supra. It is because the citizen possesses no such right that it was held by this court that the Secretary of Agriculture might, in the exercise of his general power to regulate forest reserves, exclude sheep and cattle therefrom. United States v. Grimaud, 220 U.S. 506; Light v. United States, 220 U.S. 523.

All the objections urged against the validity of the statute are unsound. The judgment of the Supreme Court of Idaho is

Affirmed.

Mr. Justice VAN DEVANTER and Mr. Justice McREYNOLDS dissent.

By 1934, overgrazing and drought had reduced the public grazing lands, never very productive, to a state of crisis. Neither free access nor enlarged homesteads contributed to betterment of range conditions. Even the ranchers agreed that drastic action was necessary. The result was the Taylor Grazing Act of 1934, 43 U.S.C.A. § 315 et seq.

E.L. PEFFER, THE CLOSING OF THE PUBLIC DOMAIN *
214–224 (1951).

The great success of the Mizpah-Pumpkin Creek grazing district in Montana was responsible for keeping the issue alive. It put into effect many of the points which the grazing industry of the West considered desirable. Although the supervisory power over the district was vested in the Secretary of the Interior, most of the business, such as the allotment of quotas, the counting in and out of stock, charges, policing against trespass, and the construction and maintenance of improvements, was conducted by an executive committee chosen from among the members of an association of qualified graziers within the district.

* * *

* * *

The Taylor grazing bill was truly Taylor's own measure and his campaign for its passage was completely under his generalship. When called before Congressional committees to explain and defend his bill, he did not resemble the usual witness at such hearings. He dominated them. On the floor of the House, he parried all arguments skillfully. He knew the rocks upon which earlier attempts at regulation had foundered. The jurisdictional question raised its head; he urged the prior necessity of control. The usual tribute to the homesteader appeared and the lament was heard that the Taylor bill would banish him from the American scene. Mr. Taylor had an answer for that:

> * * * The praises and eulogies upon the American homesteader will continue as long as our Republic survives. The West was built, and its present proud development rests most largely upon the courage, privations, and frightfully hard work of the pioneer homesteaders. * * *

> But my dear sirs, if those hardy pioneers had had to go onto the kind of land that is contemplated within this bill, the West would still be a barren wilderness.

* * *

FACTORS CONTRIBUTING TO PASSAGE

Other factors eased the way for the passage of the bill. President Roosevelt wanted it. Secretary of the Interior Harold L. Ickes jumped into the fight, scolding the stockmen for having interposed obstacles in the way of the passage of a law which would work so materially for their benefit. When Congress did not pass the Taylor bill during the first session of the 73d Congress, Ickes inquired into his authority under the Pickett Act of 1910 to withdraw the remaining public lands, pending passage of a law for their protection. He was advised that he had the authority; nevertheless, he concluded that it would be best to postpone recourse to this action. At the same time, however, he let it be known that he had this expedient in mind should Congress delay action much longer.

* * *

The debates leading to the passage of the Taylor bill in Congress differed little in content from debates on previous public land bills. The ethical claim of the Western states to the lands within their borders was reasserted. The tribute to the homesteader was heard again. There were familiar protests against turning over the large acreage involved to the big cattlemen. They were all there—all the old, familiar strains. But they were like faint echoes of all the other debates which had gone before, diluted by time and the hopelessness of the cause they represented.

* * *

The Taylor Grazing Act passed the House of Representatives on April 11, 1934 and the Senate on June 12. Between these dates occurred what was later considered the most devastating of conceivable condemnations of past land policy. The dust storms of May 11 carried sands from Western deserts to the sidewalks of New York and sifted them down around the dome of the Capitol in Washington. They provided what Senator Gore of Oklahoma later called "the most tragic, the most impressive lobbyist, that have ever come to this Capital."

* * *

* * *

PROVISIONS OF THE TAYLOR GRAZING ACT

The Taylor Grazing Act vests in the Secretary of the Interior authority to create grazing districts in areas "which in his opinion are chiefly valuable for grazing and raising forage crops," but not until local reactions, gained through public hearings, had been ascertained. The Secretary is empowered to make all necessary regulations to carry out the purposes of the act and to grant grazing permits for periods up to ten years, with preference to settlers and landowners within or near the respective districts. He is instructed to enter into co-operative agreements with other departments of the government, with state land officials, and users of the districts. He may accept gifts of land or make exchanges of public land outside of grazing districts for private or state-owned lands within their limits. * * * Section 15 of the bill provides that isolated or disconnected tracts or parcels of 640 acres or more of grazing land, not capable of being included within grazing districts, may be leased to owners of contiguous property. (These have come to be known as Section 15 lands.)

* * *

The amendment to the Taylor Grazing Act passed Congress on June 20, 1936, and was approved by the President on June 26. It increased the area to which the law applies to 142,000,000 acres and created the post of Director of Grazing, which appointment was to be made by the Secretary of the Interior and approved by the Senate. * * * Western interests were considered in the further stipulation that "No Director of Grazing, Assistant Director, or grazier shall be appointed who at the time of appointment or selection has not been for one year a bona-fide citizen or resident of the State or of one of the States in which such Director, Assistant Director, or grazier is to serve."

* * *

SUBSEQUENT WITHDRAWALS

At long last the government was able to care for its grazing lands. The Taylor Grazing Act did not itself do, however, what has been claimed for it—"close the public domain to further entry by homesteaders and [bury] a policy which had been slowly dying." That was accomplished, in effect, but with no express intention of permanence, by two executive orders of the President, those of November 26, 1934 and February 5, 1935. In November, acting under the authority of the Taylor Grazing Act, he withdrew for classification all public land in the twelve Western states. Then, in February, he withdrew all remaining parcels in all other states for use in connection with Federal Emergency Relief Administration.

The President by these withdrawals implemented the classification feature of the Taylor Grazing Act and made certain that it would apply to all remaining Western public lands. Thus it was that the classification which for more than fifty years had been urgently recommended by the land specialists of the country was finally authorized. It was not done until the results of nature's own classification had become disastrously apparent.

If the Taylor Grazing Act and supporting measures did not completely close the public domain, they at least were a signpost pointing to a radical change in direction of public land policy. They represented official admission of the exhaustion of the values which had made the public domain a dynamic force in the building of the country. There was still land in plenty, but such opportunity as it might have represented had literally "gone with the wind." Overgrazed, wind-eroded expanses, interspersed with rocky peaks and barren slopes, were all that remained of the public domain in 1934. The days of its greatness, * * * had long since passed. The open public domain of the future was to be more a sentimental and political issue than an active factor in American life.

Just as the Forest Reservation Provision in the 1891 legislation had accidentally created the National Forest System, so too did the Taylor Act create a new federal land system by indirection, now variously called the "BLM lands" or the "national resource lands" or the "public lands." The Taylor Grazing Act did not immediately improve actual range conditions; in fact, the majority of BLM lands in the 1970s were in less than good condition. The grazing lands before 1934 had not been "managed" in the modern sense, and the changeover to a new system embodying a new philosophy was not made without pain. The following remarks made in 1974 by Ferry Carpenter, the first director of the Grazing Service, [quoted in Conklin, PLLRC Revisited—A Potpourri of Memories, 54 Denver L.J. 445, 446–47 (1977)], illustrate some of the practical difficulties of implementation.

Well, I feel like the man from Mars. How did I ever get in here? What have I been listening to this morning? What is this problem that brings you here and furls your brow when you think about it? I don't belong here, but 40 years ago to a day, I belonged very much here in Grand Junction because that was the first meeting ever held under the recently passed Taylor Grazing Act to see whether they could put the show on the road or not.

I got my appointment on September 7 and on the 12th I was here, with no instructions what to do, and this is what I found: Grand Junction was packed with stockmen. The cattle boys had the LaCourt Hotel and the woolgrowers had the LaHarpe Hotel, and neither would speak to the other.

There were so many of them and the next morning when we looked around for a hall, we couldn't begin to get them in any hall. We adjourned and went out on the city park here and took over the exhibition building. The cowboys sat on one side with Frank Delaney and the sheepherders on the other with Dan Hughes and Wilson McCarthy and we got ready for business like a peace talk between two nations that had been fighting—and they had been fighting and I knew they had been fighting. What were they there to talk about? Why did Congress wake up and say they should have to drag grass into the conservation program? They put water in under the Reclamation Act; put trees under the Forest Act; put minerals and oils under the Mineral Reserve Act. But not the grass. Everybody could get the grass if you knew how to get it. All of a sudden they passed the Taylor Grazing Act. The boys out here didn't know the Act existed but they were there to see that they got their share of the grass. There were two factions and they were ready to continue the war they had been having for fifty years to fight over it. That's the woolgrowers and the cowboys.

I didn't get any help from Washington on what to do. There wasn't anybody in the whole Department that knew which end of the cow got up first. I went to the Land Office. I said "You want me to straighten out this land—give me a map of it." "Oh! We haven't got any map. There is filing on it day and night all over 27 local land offices, but we haven't got any map." "Well, how in the hell can I find the land if I haven't got a map!" "That's for you." That was for me. So, when I came here, I said I'm supposed to set up grazing districts. I don't know whether you want them or not and I wouldn't know where they go and Washington doesn't know where they would go and nobody knows where they would go. But you fellows have been fighting over this thing, you know every blessed acre there is and the poorer the acre, the harder you fight for it. I found that out, too. But I had one little piece of advice that I followed—and I am going to follow it until the end of my days—and it was a little saying by Justice Cardozo on the Supreme Court. "When the task is to clean house, it is sensible and usual to first consult with the inhabitants." There I was and there were the inhabitants—cowboys ready to jump and sheepherders ready to jump—everybody at each other's throat. But they were the inhabitants.

Well, they read a message from President Roosevelt. He said it was a great day for the West. Read a message from Secretary Ickes; he said he was the Lord's anointed! And now we got down to business and they began asking me questions about the Act, like how near was near. I didn't know how near was near. I didn't know the answer to them but I did know what to do with them. So, I said, all right; you woolgrowers go out there and caucus and pick five men to speak for you. You cowboys do the same.

D. PERMANENT RETENTION AND MANAGEMENT

In theory, the Taylor Act was an interim measure: the range management it authorized was to control "pending final disposition." In fact, the creation of grazing districts marked the "closing of the public domain," even though a few small tracts were claimed as homesteads thereafter.

The federal government now owns retained and acquired lands for many diverse purposes, but the focus of this volume is on the federal lands classified as national forests, BLM or public lands, national parks and monuments, national wildlife refuges, and wilderness areas. This section traces in brief the origins and growth of the modern federal lands systems.

The key to public land classification is allowable use. With the "use" of disposition by sale or grant now mostly a nostalgic memory, the primary public land uses are for mining, grazing, logging, recreation, watershed, wildlife, and preservation. The system or classification into which Congress places a particular parcel determines whether and to what extent specific uses can or must be made or allowed by the land management agency. The National Forests and the BLM lands are commonly termed the multiple use lands, but in fact every category of federal lands accommodates more than one use to greater or lesser extent, and the official multiple use lands have been devoted de facto to dominant uses in many instances. All of this is by way of saying that federal land classification is not an exact science. No classification of public lands is exclusive or immutable (even classifications chosen expressly by Congress), and overlapping functions and common problems are more of a rule than an exception. The interactions between use and classification can be intricate, complex, and confusing; in some respects, sorting out the possibilities is a main task of this book.

This section preliminarily describes the divisions of the four principal federal land management agencies. It also discusses preservation lands—wilderness areas and wild and scenic rivers—some of which are managed by each of those four agencies. Finally, this section introduces the major federal legal entities, other than courts, that contribute to public land law development.

1. THE NATIONAL FORESTS

The withdrawals of the Forest Reserves beginning in 1891, the creation of Pinchot's Forest Service in the Department of Agriculture, and the transfer of the Forest Reserves to Agriculture in 1905, all combined to create the present National Forest System. Some of the original reservations were later returned to the public domain, and other national forest land has been transferred to the Department of the Interior, but National Forests still contain 192 million acres, the second largest system by acreage. Moves to transfer the National Forests back to Interior have surfaced at least once every decade, but none has yet succeeded.

The National Forest System was the beneficiary of the initial impetus for federal reacquisition of lands from private owners. During the period 1912–30, the Forest Service purchased several million acres of agriculturally depressed or abandoned land east of the Mississippi; it also manages the National Grasslands, acquired by purchase from bankrupt dirt farmers in drought-ridden Depression years under its Submarginal Land Retirement Program. Consequently, the Forest Service has widely dispersed holdings in nearly every state, while BLM lands are concentrated in the eleven western states and Alaska.

The Forest Reserves that became the National Forests were established "to improve and protect the forest * * * [and] for the purpose of securing favorable conditions of water flows, and to furnish a continuous supply of timber." 16 U.S.C.A. § 475. The Organic Act of

1897, 16 U.S.C.A. §§ 473–481 (partially repealed 1976), directed the managing agency to promulgate regulations for protection of the Reserves from fire and depredation, and authorized the sale of "dead, matured, or large growth of trees" at appraised value. For decades, the management of the Forests was primarily custodial: before World War II they supplied less than five percent of the annual timber harvests. See Huffman, A History of Forest Policy in the United States, 8 Envtl.L. 239 (1978). With the post-war housing boom and the relative depletion of privately-owned commercial forests, pressure on the National Forests to produce more sawtimber led first to a refinement of Pinchot's utilitarian philosophy and then to the enactment of the multiple use mandate into law. Multiple-Use, Sustained-Yield Act of 1960, 16 U.S.C.A. §§ 528–531. National forest resource allocation is now controlled in large part by the National Forest Management Act of 1976 (NFMA), 16 U.S.C.A. § 1601 et seq., discussed in detail in chapter seven.

2. THE BLM PUBLIC LANDS

The lands subject to the Taylor Grazing Act were administered by the Department of Interior's Grazing Service until 1946, when it was merged with the General Land Office to form the Bureau of Land Management. In the contiguous states, the BLM is responsible for the management of 174 or so million acres of the Nation's least economically productive land. In Alaska, the BLM retains jurisdiction over about 167 million acres, even after the reclassifications and disposals mandated by Congress in 1971 and 1980. See infra at page 165. BLM stewardship has not, for the most part, undone the damage wrought before the agency existed. Like the Forest Service, the BLM evolved internally a multiple use philosophy over the years, but with emphasis on grazing and mining instead of logging. Statutory authority for such management was provided first by the Classification and Multiple Use Act of 1964, 43 U.S.C.A. §§ 1411–18, which expired in 1970, and then by permanent, comprehensive legislation, the Federal Land Policy and Management Act of 1976 (FLPMA), 43 U.S.C.A. §§ 1701–84. The BLM administers several fragile tracts classified as "Conservation Areas," and under FLPMA, it is required to identify "areas of critical environmental concern" and potential wilderness areas.

The FLPMA of 1976 caused a semantic problem by defining BLM lands as "public lands." 43 U.S.C.A. § 1702(e). This narrow definition must, of course, be used in construing FLPMA. Nevertheless, the traditional meaning of public lands (such as employed by the Public Land Law Review Commission in its 1970 Report) to describe all federally-owned areas continues to be found in other statutes and in common usage.

Throughout its relatively short history, the BLM has been assigned difficult management tasks without the wherewithal to accomplish them. Some of its programs long have been dominated by the private interests the BLM was supposed to regulate; congressional ignorance and indifference allowed the BLM lands to deteriorate further, and resource crises on the formerly open range are coming to a head in litigation. Whether the BLM can cope with the ire of old land users while implementing new and more restrictive statutory authority is one of the major problems dealt with in chapters six, on mining, and eight, on grazing.

3. THE NATIONAL WILDLIFE REFUGES

The present National Wildlife Refuge System began when President Roosevelt set aside Pelican Island off the Florida coast for the benefit of wildlife in 1903. Congress and the President purchased and withdrew miscellaneous parcels over the years under various authorities until, in conjunction with the first Endangered Species Act, the National Wildlife Refuge System was created in 1966. See National Wildlife Refuge Administration Act of 1966, 16 U.S.C.A. § 668dd et seq. The system is administered by the Fish and Wildlife Service in the Department of Interior, and comprises 85 million acres in fee ownership, together with lesser interests such as waterfowl easements in other property. Seventy-five million acres of the Refuge System are in Alaska.

The National Wildlife Refuge System is the only category of federal lands administered primarily for the conservation of wildlife, although states have wildlife areas and wildlife management is a concern of greater or lesser magnitude on all federal lands. Additions to the system are funded through special segregated tax revenues such as duck stamps, but the refuges have suffered from underfunding, political neglect, and popular overuse. Although wildlife conservation is the main criterion in refuge management under the relevant statutes, almost every other common use is allowed to some extent on some refuges. See chapter nine.

4. THE NATIONAL PARK SYSTEM

Among the uses allowed and encouraged on the foregoing three systems are forms of recreation from bird watching to camping to hunting to motorcycling; to that extent they can be considered "recreational lands." On the other hand, the various categories of lands within the National Park System are devoted primarily to recreation, and, in some cases, to preservation.

The National Park System has grown to over 77 million acres, 57 million of which are in Alaska. The system has units in most states, and its growth continues. An orientation toward preservation has characterized the Park Service since its inception in 1916, but its mission has been broadened in recent years by assignment of responsibility for recreation areas, urban parks, cultural areas, and the like. The 38 National Parks, the most famous units in the System, are still managed for the "enjoyment of future generations" as best the overburdened Park Service can manage, but more intensive recreation is typical on other land designations within the System.

The Park Service manages another federal lands category that was created, perhaps inadvertently, by passage of the 1906 Antiquities Act, 16 U.S.C.A. §§ 431–433. Under it, the President is authorized to designate by proclamation National Monuments on federal lands if the area contains "historic landmarks, historic and prehistoric structures, and other objects of historic or scientific interest." Although only the smallest area compatible with preservation is to be so reserved, huge areas such as Death Valley and Glacier Bay have been proclaimed monuments. Many monuments were created in the early years, some of which later became national parks, but congressional resistance to unilateral designation had all but eliminated sizable proclamations since the 1930's. In 1978, however, to prevent economic use of federal lands in Alaska until Congress acted on a pending bill to classify lands in Alaska, President Carter unilaterally designated over 50 million acres as national monuments, breeding further controversy and litigation. See infra at page 249.

The recreation opportunities inherent in the reservoir created by Hoover Dam inspired Congress to designate the lake and surrounding shoreline as the Lake Mead National Recreation Area. The concept was popular and has since been followed at Lake Powell, Flaming Gorge, Ross Lake, and other impoundments. Congress also experimented with National Parkways such as Blue Ridge in the 1930's; the incongruence of parks and roads, however, led to the formation of the Wilderness Society in protest and to abandonment of the concept. Recreation continued to grow as an important facet of public land policy. Congressional desires to satisfy demand for outdoor recreation resulted in an explosion of new land categories, all under NPS jurisdiction. There are now National Seashores (e.g., Point Reyes in California), National Lakeshores (e.g., Sleeping Bear in Michigan), National Rivers (e.g., the Buffalo in Arkansas), the Boundary Water Canoe Area in Minnesota, National Wild and Scenic Rivers (e.g. the Allegash in Maine), National Trails (e.g., the Pacific Crest), National Gateway Parks, (e.g. Golden Gate in and near San Francisco), and the Big Thicket and Big Cypress National Preserves. The Park Service also manages historical memorials, battlefield monuments, the Washington, D.C. parks, and the Wolf Trap Cultural Area. Chapter ten illustrates that a main problem with units of the Park System has been their popularity for outdoor recreation.

5. THE PRESERVATION LANDS

The national park lands are to be managed for preservation as well as recreation, but many felt that park resources alone were too few and too vulnerable for national needs. In 1964 Congress created yet another lands category by passage of the Wilderness Act, 16 U.S.C.A. §§ 1131–36, under which lands so designated are to be devoted primarily to preservation. Some nine million acres, in roadless areas of over 5,000 acres "untrammelled by man," were set aside initially, and the Wilderness Preservation System has continued to grow. Additions to the new System, now encompassing some 88 million acres, have been and are being carved out of other federal lands by a longterm process of selection, inventory, presidential recommendation, and congressional designation. A wilderness area is managed by the agency under whose jurisdiction the area fell before designation.

6. THE LEGAL OFFICES

An agency with special pertinence to public land law is the Office of the Solicitor in the Department of the Interior. The Solicitor is general counsel to the Secretary; the Office is an entity separate from the resource agencies. Lawyers in the Solicitor's Office write opinions, draft regulations, and render continuing legal advice to the land management agencies. The Solicitor's Office does not, however, represent the Department in court, a task that is left to the Department of Justice. Although General Counsel in the Department of Agriculture serves a similar function for the Forest Service, the concentration of resource issues in Interior and the wealth of Solicitor's Opinions (collected in Interior Decisions) mean that the Interior Solicitor's Office is a primary source of law on the public lands.

Another important entity for lawyers involved in public land law is the Interior Board of Land Appeals (IBLA), the major organ of the Interior Department's Office of Hearings and Appeals. Decisions of BLM officials that before 1970 were appealed to the Solicitor's Office now go to the IBLA. It possesses broad authority to decide finally for the Department appeals from decisions relating to the use and disposition of public lands and resources. IBLA jurisdiction also extends to land selections under the Alaska Native Claims Settlement Act of 1971 and to issues arising under the Surface Mining Control and Reclamation Act of 1977. Many of the roughly 1000 appeals filed each year with the IBLA involve mineral resources, but the agency's jurisdiction also encompasses a wide variety of subjects including grazing, patent issuance, wilderness review, and wild horses and burros. The IBLA is comprised of nine administrative law judges who sit in three-judge panels, but some en banc decisions are issued. See generally 43 C.F.R. Part 4.

E. ALASKA REPRISE

The public land law eras that played themselves out over the course of two centuries in the Lower 48 States were recreated, compressed, and intensified in Alaska during the last thirty years. The high-stakes events in the largest public lands state—"The Last Pork Chop," as one writer has dubbed it—are summarized here and will recur throughout.

The word Alaska means "Great Land," but the territory was known as "Seward's Folly" after the United States purchased it from Russia in 1867. Because of Alaska's daunting remoteness and clime, the new sovereign long did little with it. Alaska became a federal judicial district in 1884 and a territory in 1912. Alaskans, like other territorial residents before them, chafed under rule from Washington, D.C. but their cries of "colonialism" were perhaps even stronger. When statehood came to Alaska in 1959, the lands remained almost completely in federal ownership because of the small amount of land suitable for homesteading in the State. Significantly, Congress had given almost no attention to Alaska Natives: no treaties with them had been negotiated and only a handful of reservations had been established by statute or executive order.

Alaskans drove the most successful statehood bargain of all. Under the Alaska Enabling Act, the new state government won the right to select 104 million acres of the state's 365 million acres. State officials promptly ordered surveys to determine the choicest parcels. At about the same time, rumors of extensive oil and gas deposits were bruited about as the mineral companies made resource explorations. In the mid-1960's, Alaska Natives began to protest in earnest, taking the position that their aboriginal title had never been disturbed and that any administrative transfers of title to the state or the mining industry would violate Native property rights. On Indian title, see supra at page 52. Accordingly, in 1966, Interior Secretary Stewart Udall suspended the issuance of almost all patents and mineral leases. The pressure heightened in 1968 when the discovery of massive oil deposits at Prudhoe Bay was confirmed. Udall then withdrew all unreserved lands in Alaska from all forms of entry by means of Public Land Order 4582, the 1968 "Superfreeze."

The logjam was broken by the passage of the Alaska Native Claims Settlement Act of 1971, 43 U.S.C.A. §§ 1601–1624. ANCSA paved the way for the Alaska Pipeline; extinguished all Indian title; granted Alaska Natives the right to select 44 million acres; provided Natives a fund of nearly $1 billion; and allowed state selections to resume. Further, the 1971 Act reflected the lobbying efforts of the newly-constituted environmental movement. ANCSA's "d(2)" provision, 43 U.S.C.A. § 1616(d)(2), authorized the Secretary of the Interior to withdraw up to 80 million acres of land that might merit inclusion in the four "national interest" systems (national parks, forests, wildlife refuges, and wild rivers). Thus, after ANCSA, four major potential sets of landowners—the state, Alaska Native corporations, the mineral companies, and the United States—were undergoing overlapping and conflicting selection processes involving hundreds of millions of acres. In particular, the d(2) "national interest" selections frustrated Alaskans, who believed that the process impeded mineral development. See, e.g., Rudd, Who Owns Alaska?—Mineral Rights Acquisition Amid Rapidly Changing Land Ownership, 20 Rocky Mtn.Min.L.Inst. 109 (1975). On the passage of ANCSA, see M. Berry, THE ALASKA PIPELINE (1979).

The d(2) withdrawals were due to expire on December 16, 1978. Congress did not act by then but, in historic actions, President Carter and Secretary Andrus executed massive, overlapping withdrawals that effectively extended the d(2) withdrawals and staved off mineral development on the proposed "national interest" lands. See infra at page 249.

On December 2, 1980, President Carter signed the Alaska National Interest Lands Conservation Act (ANILCA) into law. This major and complex legislation (it encompasses 181 pages in statutes-at-large) is found at 16 U.S.C.A. §§ 3101–33 and in scattered sections of titles 16 and 43.

ANILCA allocated more than 103 million acres, mostly former BLM lands, to the federal conservation systems. The Act added 43.5 million acres to the National Park System, 53.7 million acres to the National Wildlife Refuge System, and 56.4 million acres to the National Wilderness Preservation System. Thirteen rivers were added to the National Wild and Scenic Rivers System. Congress made two special designations for BLM lands, the 1.2 million acre Steese Conservation Area, and the 1 million acre White Mountain National Recreation Area. The total of the acres allocated to specific preservation systems, as just described, far exceeds the 103 million acres actually affected by the Act because there are some double classifications; for example, large amounts of the new national parks and wildlife refuges are also designated as wilderness.

ANILCA has multiplied several times over the size of the major preservation systems. The national parklands were more than doubled, wildlife refuges were almost tripled, and wilderness lands were quadrupled. Similarly, ANILCA made significant alterations in the amount of lands administered by federal agencies nationally. The following changes in total agency land holdings, according to the most recent available figures, have been wrought primarily by ANILCA and by state and Native selections of BLM lands in Alaska:

Federal Agency Land Holdings (by millions of acres)

Agency	1978	1983
Bureau of Land Management	480.5	341.1
Forest Service	188.9	192.1
Fish and Wildlife Service	31.3	84.9
National Park Service	26.6	77.3
Department of Defense	33.9	22.9
All other agencies	14.7	13.7
TOTAL PUBLIC LANDS	775.9	732.0

Sources: Bureau of Land Management, U.S. Department of the Interior, PUBLIC LAND STATISTICS (1978); id. (1983).

ANILCA is omnibus legislation that includes many provisions dealing with Alaska public lands generally, not just lands added to the preservation systems. Among other things, ANILCA implements a preference for subsistence hunting and fishing, including traditional uses of snowmobiles and motorboats, on federal lands in Alaska. The Act allows many existing uses in the new wilderness areas, including cabins and access by airplanes and motorboats, to continue. Detailed provisions govern mineral development on ANILCA lands. See generally Sagalkin & Panitch, Mineral Development Under the Alaska Lands Act, 10 UCLA–Alaska L.Rev. 117 (1981); Southeast Alaska Conservation Council, Inc. v. Watson, 526 F.Supp. 202 (D.Alaska 1981) and 535 F.Supp. 653 (D.Alaska 1982); Trustees for Alaska v. Watt, 524 F.Supp. 1303 (D.Alaska 1981), aff'd, 690 F.2d 1279 (9th Cir.1982). ANILCA rescinded and superseded the Carter Administration withdrawals of 1978 and 1979. The timber industry succeeded in obtaining a provision that "the Secretary of the Treasury shall make available" to the Forest Service at least $40 million annually to maintain the timber harvest for the Tongass National Forest at 4.5 billion board feet per decade. See 16 U.S.C.A. § 439d. The access provisions in ANILCA have been interpreted to govern access to private inholdings in all national forests, not just those in Alaska. See Montana Wilderness Association v. United States Forest Service, 655 F.2d 951 (9th Cir.1981), infra at page 1016.

Senator Paul Tsongas called ANILCA "perhaps the greatest conservation achievement of the century." Environmentalists have both harkened back to the poet Horace (ANILCA is "a monument more lasting than bronze", Sierra 5 (Jan./Dec.1981)) and bemoaned its limitations (ANILCA "has hardly stopped the development pressures on at least one major portion of the state's rich but fragile environment, the 15.4 million acre Tongass National Forest in southeast Alaska," Sierra 53 (July/August 1982)). Senator Mike Gravel, speaking for many Alaskans, argued that "the massive conservation system designations" will cause the state to be "throttled down economically over the next decade." See generally R. Cahn, THE FIGHT TO SAVE WILD ALASKA (1982); Alaska Geographic Society, ALASKA NATIONAL INTEREST LANDS (1981); 4 Alaska Geographic; Cravez, ANILCA, Directing the Great Lands Future, 10 UCLA–Alaska L.Rev. 33 (1980); Comment, Preservation and Strategic Mineral Development in Alaska: Congress Writes a New Equation, 12 Envtl.L. 137 (1981).

———

In sum, federal public land policy has been gradually but thoroughly revised in the Nation's second century. The age of wholesale disposition is over; the age of retention and management is middle-aged; and the age of federal reacquisition is haltingly underway. Wilderness, the enemy of the settler, has become a prominent goal of national policy. Many more changes are in the offing, especially with respect to remaining energy resources on public lands.

The foregoing recitation of public land law history was intended for more than general information. Two centuries of legal development cannot be ignored, even if the area is undergoing a continuing revolution. The rights, interests, and liabilities created in two hundred years are established, and modern systems must recognize them. Century-old cases still are persuasive precedent. And some century-old statutes, enacted with a view of the future that did not always prove out, continue to pose legal problems in modern public land management.

Chapter Three

AUTHORITY ON THE PUBLIC LANDS: CONGRESS AND THE STATES

One problem inherent in many contemporary resource disputes is the allocation of jurisdictional power between federal and state governments. In spite of frequent federal expressions of intent to defer to state law and policy, state preeminence has steadily eroded. The conflict among governments on the public lands has a history nearly as colorful as the storied wars carried on by individual miners, homesteaders, ranchers, and conservationists. The disputes are bound to continue apace; the "Sagebrush Rebellion" was only one part of a larger problem frequently thought to be a political powder keg. The federal government clearly owns the federal lands, but the question of which sovereign's law rules must be analyzed on a case-by-case basis. Students of public land law generations hence may conclude that the subject of jurisdictional allocation on the public lands was just beginning to mature in the 1980's.

The starting point for analysis is the constitutional power of Congress. The Commerce, Treaty, and General Welfare Clauses of the United States Constitution have all had some relevance to the public lands. The Commerce Power includes federal control of navigation, which has been held sufficient to support federal hydropower licenses issued in contravention of state law. First Iowa Hydro-Elec. Coop. v. FPC, 328 U.S. 152 (1946). The Treaty Power supports a general exercise of federal power off as well as on public lands. Missouri v. Holland, 252 U.S. 416 (1920). Federal reclamation projects are proper as means to advance the general welfare. United States v. Gerlach Livestock Co., 339 U.S. 725 (1950).

In recent times, disputes have turned mainly on three other constitutional provisions. The first is the Enclave Clause, Article I, § 8, cl. 17:

> Congress shall have power to exercise *exclusive Legislation* in all Cases whatsoever over such District (not exceeding ten Miles square) as may, by Cession of particular States, and the Acceptance of Congress, become the Seat of the Government of the United States, and *to exercise like Authority* over all Places *purchased* by the *Consent* of the Legislature of the State in which the Same shall be, for the Erection of Forts, Magazines, Arsenals, dock-Yards, and *other needful Buildings.* (emphasis supplied)

The "exclusive legislation" reference has always been interpreted as meaning "exclusive jurisdiction," e.g., United States v. Bevans, 16 U.S. (3 Wheat.) 336, 387 (1818); thus it has come to be known as the

Jurisdiction or Enclave Clause. Lands under federal control pursuant to the Enclave Clause, which by definition must be acquired with state consent, are commonly called "federal enclaves." Examples are some but not all military bases, post offices, and national parks.

Several strict interpretations of the Enclave Clause have been rejected. Voluntary transactions with states are not the sole means by which the United States can obtain state and private lands: Congress possesses an inherent power of eminent domain as an attribute of its sovereignty, derived indirectly from the Fifth Amendment. See, e.g., United States v. Gettysburg Elec. Ry., 160 U.S. 668 (1896), supra at page 135. Federal jurisdiction on acquired lands need not be exclusive. States are free to attach conditions or to retain some jurisdictional powers in making cessions to the federal government. They have often done so, with the result that mutual, divided crazyquilts of jurisdiction on enclaves are common. More importantly, the Enclave Clause is not the exclusive mechanism for the assertion of federal jurisdiction, and federal sovereign authority under the Property Clause has been upheld over federal lands that do not qualify as enclaves. The Enclave Clause is now overshadowed by the Property Clause for most practical purposes. Nevertheless, roughly 5% of all public lands are classified as enclaves, and a special body of law still governs activities on them.

Second, the doctrine of intergovernmental immunities bars some state regulation on the federal lands. In McCulloch v. Maryland, 17 U.S. (4 Wheat.) 316 (1819), the Court held that the Supremacy Clause, Article VI, § 2, prohibited states from imposing taxes on the Bank of the United States. That immunity from state regulation has been narrowed over the years, but it explains the tax-exempt status of the public lands and remains vital in some situations.

Third, the Property Clause, Article IV, § 3, cl. 2, recites simply that:

> The Congress shall have Power to dispose of and make all needful Rules and Regulations respecting the Territory or other Property belonging to the United States * * *.

Early cases established the right of the federal government, pursuant to Article IV, to establish territorial governments and to manage public lands during the era when such lands were outside state boundaries. E.g., United States v. Gratiot, 39 U.S. (14 Pet.) 526 (1840). Before statehood, Congress was the source of all law in the territories. When states were carved out of public lands, however, difficult questions arose. The first was one of title: did the state obtain title to all or part of those unsold public lands? Pollard v. Hagan, 44 U.S. (3 How.) 212 (1845), supra at page 72, held that the states did come into title of lands underlying navigable waters, but all other public lands continued in federal ownership. As to those non-enclave federal lands, it was disputed whether federal Property Clause authority could be squared with the reserved Tenth Amendment rights of states: did the federal government have only the proprietary powers of an ordinary private owner, or could it assert the far more expansive power of a sovereign?

In spite of a succession of cases such as Camfield v. United States, 167 U.S. 518 (1897), supra at page 108, and Light v. United States, 220 U.S. 523 (1911), supra at page 137, which stated that the federal government was more than a mere proprietor, the issue remained alive until 1976, when the Court in Kleppe v. New Mexico, 426 U.S. 529 (1976), infra at page 194, definitively resolved it in favor of federal sovereign power. The confirmation of sovereign federal power over public lands is anathema to some because the exercise of federal power preempts and invalidates inconsistent state law. See Engdahl, State and Federal Power over Federal Property, 18 Ariz.L.Rev. 283 (1976).

This chapter analyzes the three principal barriers to state jurisdiction on the public lands. Section A examines the law applicable to those comparatively few acres held in enclave status, while Section B treats the relatively narrow scope of federal intergovernmental immunity. Section C then follows the cases that raised the Property Clause from obscure beginnings to a plenary federal power to preempt state law over one-third of the Nation's land (and over some private lands adjoining federal lands). That section concludes with a series of recent cases raising the most important jurisdiction issue at this time, the extent to which Congress intended to override state law in particular situations.

A. JURISDICTION WITHIN FEDERAL ENCLAVES

The 1970 Public Land Law Review Commission Report, at 277, identified four categories of public lands for jurisdictional purposes:

1. *Exclusive*—the Federal Government possesses all of the authority of the state, the only reservation being the right of the state to serve criminal and civil process in the area for activities occurring outside the area;

2. *Concurrent*—the state grants to the Federal Government what would otherwise be exclusive jurisdiction, but reserves to itself the right to exercise concurrently the same powers;

3. *Partial*—the Federal Government has been granted the right to exercise certain of the state's authority, with the state reserving the right to exercise by itself, or concurrently, other authority beyond the mere right to serve process;

4. *Proprietorial*—the United States has acquired some right or title to an area within a state but no measure of the state's authority over the area.

Where there has been piecemeal acquisition, more than one category of jurisdiction may be applicable in the same area.

Of the 730 or so million acres of public lands owned by the United States, only about six million are Enclave Clause holdings under "exclusive" federal control. The great majority of these lands are in either national parks or military installations. The Park Service also has holdings in each of the other three categories. Almost all Forest Service land is held in "proprietorial" status, although the Forest Service has some holdings that are exclusive jurisdiction and some that are partial jurisdiction. Except for three parcels, all of the land administered by the Bureau of Land Management is held proprietorially. An important exception is Navy Petroleum Reserve Number 4 on the North Slope of Alaska where massive oil discoveries have been made; the BLM has concurrent jurisdiction with the State of Alaska. A total of about 36.5 million acres are held by various agencies under "concurrent" or "partial" jurisdiction. Lands for national wildlife refuges have been reserved or purchased under various authorities; acquisition pursuant to the Migratory Bird Conservation Act of 1929, 16 U.S.C.A. § 715f required state consent, but these lands are not enclaves. See generally U.S. Department of Justice, FEDERAL LEGISLATIVE JURISDICTION (PLLRC Study, 1969). The result is that almost 700 million acres of federal land are held in "proprietorial" status.

Those four categories can be reduced to two. Lands subject to "concurrent," "partial," or "exclusive" jurisdiction are all federal enclaves, governed by jurisdictional cessions from the states, normally under the Enclave Clause. All three are controlled by a single broad principle: the states and the federal government may make agreements as to jurisdiction and the courts will enforce them. Most of the public lands are not governed by state cessions of jurisdiction. They constitute the second category, although the description "proprietorial" is no longer appropriate since the Court in Kleppe v. New Mexico, 426 U.S. 529 (1976), infra at page 194, found that federal power under the Property Clause far exceeds that of a proprietor.

By its terms, the Enclave Clause is very limited. If it had ever been interpreted literally, jurisdictional arrangements on enclaves would be very rigid, creating states within states, and the writ of a state would stop dead at the enclave borders. This would be undesirable from many perspectives, not the least of which is the state's need for tax revenue. Recognizing this, the United States Supreme Court has upheld arrangements not within the literal terms of the Clause to accommodate legitimate state interests.

FORT LEAVENWORTH R.R. v. LOWE
Supreme Court of the United States, 1885.
114 U.S. 525.

Mr. Justice FIELD delivered the opinion of the court.

The plaintiff, a corporation organized under the laws of Kansas, was in 1880, and has ever since been, the owner of a railroad in the reservation of the United States in that State, known as the Fort Leavenworth Military Reservation. In that year its track, right of way, franchises, road-bed, telegraph line and instruments connected therewith on the Reservation, were assessed by the board of assessors of the State, and a tax of $394.40 levied thereon, which was paid by the railroad company under protest, in order to prevent a sale of the property. The present action is brought to recover back the money thus paid, on the ground that the property, being entirely within the Reservation, was exempt from assessment and taxation by the State.

The land constituting the Reservation was part of the territory acquired in 1803 by cession from France, and, until the formation of the State of Kansas, and her admission into the Union, the United States possessed the rights of a proprietor, and had political dominion and sovereignty over it. For many years before that admission it had been reserved from sale by the proper authorities of the United States for military purposes, and occupied by them as a military post. The jurisdiction of the United States over it during this time was necessarily paramount. But in 1861 Kansas was admitted into the Union upon an equal footing with the original States, that is, with the same rights of political dominion and sovereignty, subject like them only to the Constitution of the United States. Congress might undoubtedly, upon such admission, have stipulated for retention of the political authority, dominion and legislative power of the United States over the Reservation, so long as it should be used for military purposes by the government; that is, it could have excepted the place from the jurisdiction of Kansas, as one needed for the uses of the general government. But from some cause, inadvertence perhaps, or over-confidence that a recession of such jurisdiction could be had whenever desired, no such stipulation or exception was made. The United States, therefore, retained, after the admission of the State, only the rights of an ordinary proprietor; except as an instrument for the execution of the powers of the general government, that part of the tract, which was actually used for a fort or military post, was beyond such control of the State, by taxation or otherwise, as would defeat its use for those purposes. So far as the land constituting the Reservation was not used for military purposes, the possession of the United States was only that of an individual proprietor. The State could have exercised, with reference to it, the same authority and jurisdiction which she could have exercised over similar property held by private parties. This defect in the jurisdiction of the United States was called to the attention of the government in 1872. * * * The Attorney General replied * * * that to restore the federal jurisdiction over the land included in the Reservation, it would be necessary to obtain from the State of Kansas a cession of jurisdiction, which he had no doubt would upon application be readily granted by the State Legislature. 14 Opin. Attorneys General, 33. It does not appear from the record before us that such application was ever made; but, on the 22d of February, 1875, the Legislature of the State passed an act entitled "An Act to cede jurisdiction to the United States over the territory of the Fort Leavenworth Military Reservation," the first section of which is as follows:

"That exclusive jurisdiction be, and the same is hereby ceded to the United States over and within all the territory owned by the United States, and included within the limits of the United States military reservation known as the Fort Leavenworth Reservation in said State, as declared from time to time by the President of the United States, saving, however, to the said State the right to serve civil or criminal process within said Reservation, in suits or prosecutions for or on account of rights acquired, obligations incurred, or crimes committed in said State, but outside of said cession and Reservation; and saving further to said State the right to tax railroad, bridge, and other corporations, their franchises and property, on said Reservation." Laws of Kansas, 1875, p. 95.

The question as to the right of the plaintiff to recover back the taxes paid depends upon the validity and effect of the last saving clause in this act. As we have said, there is no evidence before us that any application was made by the United States for this legislation, but, as it conferred a benefit, the acceptance of the act is to be presumed in the absence of any dissent on their part. The contention of the plaintiff is that the act of cession operated under the Constitution to vest in the United States exclusive jurisdiction over the Reservation, and that the last saving clause, being inconsistent with that result, is to be rejected. The Constitution provides that "Congress shall have power to *exercise exclusive legislation in all cases whatsoever* over such district, (not exceeding ten miles square,) as may, by cession of particular States and the acceptance of Congress, become the seat of the government of the United States, and *to exercise like authority* over all places purchased by the consent of the Legislature of the State in which the same shall be, for the erection of forts, magazines, arsenals, dock-yards, and other needful buildings." Art. 1, sec. 8.

The necessity of complete jurisdiction over the place which should be selected as the seat of government was obvious to the framers of the Constitution.

* * *

Upon the second part of the clause in question, giving power to "exercise like authority," that is, of exclusive legislation "over all places purchased by the consent of the Legislature of the State in which the same shall be, for the erection of forts, magazines, arsenals, dock-yards, and other needful buildings," the Federalist observes that the necessity of this authority is not less evident. "The public money expended on such places," it adds, "and the public property deposited in them, require that they should be exempt from the authority of the particular State. Nor would it be proper for the places on which the security of the entire Union may depend to be in any degree dependent on a particular member of it. All objections and scruples are here also obviated by requiring the concurrence of the States concerned in every such establishment." "The power," says Mr. Justice Story, repeating the substance of Mr. Madison's language, "is wholly unexceptionable, since it can only be exercised at the will of the State, and therefore it is placed beyond all reasonable scruple."

This power of exclusive legislation is to be exercised, as thus seen, over places purchased, by consent of the Legislatures of the States in which they are situated, for the specific purposes enumerated. It would seem to have been the opinion of the framers of the Constitution that, without the consent of the States, the new government would not be able to acquire lands within them.   *   *   *.

But not only by direct purchase have the United States been able to acquire lands they needed without the consent of the States, but it has been held that they possess the right of eminent domain within the States, using those terms, not as expressing the ultimate dominion or title to property, but as indicating the right to take private property for public uses when needed to execute the powers conferred by the Constitution; and that the general government is not dependent upon the caprice of individuals or the will of State Legislatures in the acquisition of such lands as may be required for the full and effective exercise of its powers.   *   *   *

Besides these modes of acquisition, the United States possessed, on the adoption of the Constitution, an immense domain lying north and west of the Ohio River, acquired as the result of the Revolutionary War from Great Britain, or by cessions from Virginia, Massachusetts and Connecticut; and, since the adoption of the Constitution, they have by cession from foreign countries, come into the ownership of a territory still larger, lying between the Mississippi River and the Pacific Ocean, and out of these territories several States have been formed and admitted into the Union. The proprietorship of the United States in large tracts of land within these States has remained after their admission. There has been, therefore, no necessity for them to purchase or to condemn lands within those States, for forts, arsenals, and other public buildings, unless they had disposed of what they afterwards needed. Having the title, they have usually reserved certain portions of their lands from sale or other disposition, for the uses of the government.

This brief statement as to the different modes in which the United States have acquired title to lands upon which public buildings have been erected will serve to explain the nature of their jurisdiction over such places, and the consistency with each other of decisions on the subject by Federal and State tribunals, and of opinions of the Attorneys General.

When the title is acquired by purchase by consent of the Legislatures of the States, the federal jurisdiction is exclusive of all State authority. This follows from the declaration of the Constitution that Congress shall have "like authority" over such places as it has over the district which is the seat of government; that is, the power of "exclusive legislation in all cases whatsoever." Broader or clearer language could not be used to exclude all other authority than that of Congress; and that no other authority can be exercised over them has been the uniform opinion of Federal and State tribunals, and of the Attorneys General.

The reservation which has usually accompanied the consent of the States that civil and criminal process of the State courts may be served in the places purchased, is not considered as interfering in any respect with the supremacy of the United States over them; but is admitted to

prevent them from becoming an asylum for fugitives from justice.
*   *   *

These authorities are sufficient to support the proposition which follows naturally from the language of the Constitution, that no other legislative power than that of Congress can be exercised over lands within a State purchased by the United States with her consent for one of the purposes designated; and that such consent under the Constitution operates to exclude all other legislative authority.

But with reference to lands owned by the United States, acquired by purchase without the consent of the State, or by cessions from other governments, the case is different. Story, in his Commentaries on the Constitution, says: "If there has been no cession by the State of the place, although it has been constantly occupied and used under purchase, or otherwise, by the United States for a fort or arsenal, or other constitutional purpose, the State jurisdiction still remains complete and perfect;" and in support of this statement he refers to People v. Godfrey, 17 Johns. 225. *   *   *

Where, therefore, lands are acquired in any other way by the United States within the limits of a State than by purchase with her consent, they will hold the lands subject to this qualification: that if upon them forts, arsenals, or other public buildings are erected for the uses of the general government, such buildings, with their appurtenances, as instrumentalities for the execution of its powers, will be free from any such interference and jurisdiction of the State as would destroy or impair their effective use for the purposes designed. Such is the law with reference to all instrumentalities created by the general government. Their exemption from State control is essential to the independence and sovereign authority of the United States within the sphere of their delegated powers. But, when not used as such instrumentalities, the legislative power of the State over the places acquired will be as full and complete as over any other places within her limits.

As already stated, the land constituting the Fort Leavenworth Military Reservation was not purchased, but was owned by the United States by cession from France many years before Kansas became a State; and whatever political sovereignty and dominion the United States had over the place comes from the cession of the State since her admission into the Union. It not being a case where exclusive legislative authority is vested by the Constitution of the United States, that cession could be accompanied with such conditions as the State might see fit to annex not inconsistent with the free and effective use of the fort as a military post. *   *   *

The Military Reservation of Fort Leavenworth was not, as already said, acquired by purchase with the consent of Kansas. And her cession of jurisdiction is not of exclusive legislative authority over the land, except so far as that may be necessary for its use as a military post; and it is not contended that the saving clause in the act of cession interferes with such use. There is, therefore, no constitutional prohibition against the enforcement of that clause. The right of the State to subject the railroad property to taxation exists as before the cession. The invalidity of the tax levied not being asserted on any other ground than the supposed exclusive jurisdiction of the United States over the reservation notwithstanding the saving clause, the judgment of the court below must be

Affirmed.

NOTES

1. If the Enclave Clause were the sole basis for the adjustment of jurisdiction on public lands, would this cession have been void? The land was not purchased and the cession did not provide for "exclusive" jurisdiction.

2. Colorado v. Toll, 268 U.S. 228 (1925), was a suit by the State against the Superintendent of Rocky Mountain National Park in which Colorado alleged that the Park Service was trying to monopolize the "car-for-hire" business on state roads within the Park contrary to the Acts of Cession. The bill had been dismissed below for want of equity. The Supreme Court reversed, holding that the State could attempt to prove that jurisdiction had been retained by the State in the cession process: "[T]he defendant is undertaking to assert exclusive control and to establish a monopoly in a manner as to which, if the allegations of the bill are maintained, the State has not surrendered its legislative power, a cause of action is disclosed if we do not look beyond the bill, and it was wrongly dismissed." The Court then refused to look beyond the bill "because the terms of cession were not in the record."

The rather inconclusive result was often subsequently relied upon as an affirmation of general state predominance over federal land in the absence of specific cession, but the Court in 1976 laid that notion to rest: "at most the case stands for the proposition that where Congress does not purport to override state power over public lands under the Property Clause and where there has been no cession, a federal officer lacks power to regulate contrary to state law." Kleppe v. New Mexico, 426 U.S. 529, 544–45 n. 12 (1976).

3. James v. Dravo Contracting Co., 302 U.S. 134 (1937), involved questions of state jurisdiction over locks and dams that had been constructed to improve navigation. The Court read the Enclave Clause broadly in two respects. First, such structures were "other needful buildings" within the meaning of article I, which the Court found was broad enough to include "whatever structures are found to be necessary in the performance of the functions of the Federal Government." Second, the Court rejected the notion that acquired lands must always be subject to exclusive federal jurisdiction. The cession in *James* provided for a reservation of concurrent state jurisdiction and the Court found that such a qualified cession could be agreed to by the two sovereigns in spite of the Enclave Clause language referring only to "exclusive" federal jurisdiction.

Later in the same Term, the Court dealt with an even more difficult "arrangement" between a state and the federal government.

In Collins v. Yosemite Park & Curry Co., 304 U.S. 518 (1938), the Court reviewed the complex series of statutes creating the country's second national park, Yosemite National Park. The Park was comprised of both federal public domain land and acquired land (the United States had conveyed to California "the 'Cleft' or 'Gorge' known as Yosemite" in 1864 and later reacquired it). The case presented an issue similar to that in *Fort Leavenworth*—California had reserved the right to tax specified transactions—but the Park could not possibly fit within the "other needful buildings" reference in the Enclave Clause. The Court found that "this clause has never been strictly construed," upheld the "arrangements" between California and the federal government, and made it clear that the states and the federal government were free to adjust jurisdiction wholly outside of the strictures of the Enclave Clause:

> The United States has large bodies of public lands. These properties are used for forests, parks, ranges, wild life sanctuaries, flood control, and other purposes which are not covered by Clause 17. In Silas Mason Co. v. Tax Commission of Washington, 302 U.S. 186, we upheld in accordance with the arrangements of the State and National Governments the right of the United States to acquire private property for use in "the reclamation of arid and semiarid lands" and to hold its purchases subject to state jurisdiction. In other instances, it may be deemed important or desirable by the National Government and the State Government in which the particular property is located that exclusive jurisdiction be vested in the United States by cession or consent. No question is raised as to the authority to acquire land or provide for national parks. As the National Government may, "by virtue of its sovereignty" acquire lands within the borders of states by eminent domain and without their consent, the respective sovereignties should be in a position to adjust their jurisdictions. There is no constitutional objection to such an adjustment of rights.

The *Collins* Court found that the Enclave Clause was not the "sole authority" for the acquisition of jurisdiction and that "by virtue of its sovereignty" the United States may exercise jurisdiction over land not covered by the Enclave Clause and make "arrangements" providing for less than exclusive jurisdiction. What enumerated constitutional power is the basis for these conclusions? The eminent domain power included in the Fifth Amendment? The Property Clause?

NOTE: ASSIMILATION OF STATE LAW IN FEDERAL ENCLAVES

State consent to exclusive federal jurisdiction was once thought essential to the protection of federal interests within certain federal installations. Today, the doctrine of intergovernmental immunities and Congress' unilateral power to enact protective legislation under the Property Clause provide ample security to the United States. Nevertheless, the historic practice of providing for federal enclaves, coupled with patchwork federal legislation, has created what the Public Land Law Review Commission called "a jumbled condition." PLLRC Report, supra, at 278.

An 1841 statute required the states to consent to exclusive jurisdiction whenever the United States acquired property on which improvements would be placed. In 1940, that law, 40 U.S.C.A. § 255, was amended to make future cessions of exclusive jurisdiction discretionary with federal officials, but the status of existing enclaves was left undisturbed. Several laws have been enacted since then to adjust equities within enclaves. The Buck Act, 4 U.S.C.A. §§ 104–10, allows states to collect uniform income, gasoline, sales, and use taxes within enclaves, although direct taxation of the United States and federal instrumentalities (such as officers' clubs, United States v. State Tax Comm'n, 412 U.S. 363 (1973)), is barred. State unemployment and workers' compensation laws apply to persons who live and work within federal enclaves. 26 U.S.C.A. § 3305(d); 40 U.S.C.A. § 290. State property taxes do not reach federal property, but federal Impact Aid payments are made to local school districts with federal employees living on federal property within enclaves. 20 U.S.C.A. §§ 236–44, 631–47. In the area of civil liberties, the Supreme Court, in Evans v. Cornman, 398 U.S. 419 (1970), held that the Fourteenth Amendment requires states to allow enclave residents to vote in state elections.

In 1825 Congress passed the first Assimilative Crimes Act to provide a body of criminal laws for federal enclaves. The Act, now codified at 18 U.S.C.A. § 13, "assimilates" criminal laws of the host state when no federal law applies and provides for prosecution in federal court according to state substantive law:

> Whoever within or upon any of the places now existing or hereafter reserved or acquired as provided in section 7 of this title, is guilty of any act or omission which, although not made punishable by any enactment of Congress, would be punishable if committed or omitted within the jurisdiction of the State, Territory, Possession, or District in which such place is situated, by the laws thereof in force at the time of such act or omission, shall be guilty of a like offense and subject to a like punishment.

18 U.S.C.A. § 7, referred to in the Assimilative Crimes Act, defines lands covered by the Act as follows:

> "(3) Any lands reserved or acquired for the use of the United States, and under the exclusive or concurrent jurisdiction thereof, or any place purchased or otherwise acquired by the United States by consent of the legislature of the State in which the same shall be, for the erection of a fort, magazine, arsenal, dockyard, or other needful building."

The Assimilative Crimes Act has been challenged on the ground that it is beyond Congress' power to incorporate state laws passed after the Act's effective date. In United States v. Sharpnack, 355 U.S. 286

(1958), for example, the prosecution was based upon sex crimes as defined in a 1950 Texas statute, but the most recent reenactment of the Assimilative Crimes Act had been in 1948. The Court upheld the legislative power to provide for a modern criminal justice system by assimilation.

In a few instances, federal agencies have assimilated state laws selectively by administrative action. A notable example of such "administrative assimilation" is the Park Service's incorporation of state fishing laws: there are many Park Service fishing regulations, but "nonconflicting State Laws are adopted as a part of these regulations." 36 C.F.R. § 2.3(a) (1985). Violators of the incorporated state laws are then prosecuted before federal magistrates.

Anomalies remain. In Arlington Hotel Co. v. Fant, 278 U.S. 439 (1929), plaintiffs sued to recover the value of their property lost when the hotel in Hot Springs National Park burned down. The small Hot Springs reservation had been reserved by the United States for medicinal purposes prior to Arkansas statehood and Arkansas in 1903 ceded, and the United States in 1904 accepted, "sole and exclusive jurisdiction" over the resort. In 1904 the Arkansas common law made the innkeeper an insurer of guests' property, but in 1913 the Arkansas law was changed to afford liability only for negligence. Plaintiffs claimed and the Arkansas courts held that the cession effectively "froze" the law applicable to Hot Springs as of 1904, making the innkeeper strictly liable without proof of negligence in the conceded absence of contrary federal law. The Supreme Court, without discussion, agreed. Defendant was thus reduced to claiming that the cession was invalid because the purpose of the reservation was not one of those in the Jurisdiction Clause. The Court found that this particular reservation came within the Jurisdiction Clause because the "healing waters" were appropriate for the reservation's original use as a military hospital.

Modern state wrongful death laws have been made applicable within enclaves by statute, 16 U.S.C.A. § 457, see Morgan v. United States, 709 F.2d 580 (9th Cir.1983), but, under *Arlington Hotel*, most other state civil laws at the time of the jurisdiction transfer remain in effect until altered by Congress. E.g., James Stewart & Co. v. Sadrakula, 309 U.S. 94 (1940); Pacific Coast Dairy, Inc. v. Department of Agriculture, 318 U.S. 285 (1943). The rationale is a principle of international law that "whenever political jurisdiction and legislative power over any territory are transferred from one nation or sovereign to another, the municipal laws of the country, that is, laws which are intended for the protection of private rights, continue in force until abrogated or changed by the new government or sovereign." Chicago, Rock Island & Pac. R.R. Co. v. McGlinn, 114 U.S. 542, 546 (1885). Does this make sense in this context, where the "new" sovereign, the United States, does not normally pass laws implementing the full range of police powers? Should litigation between two private citizens over an automobile accident in a federal enclave under exclusive jurisdiction be governed by state statutory and common law that existed when the cession was made (before autos were invented)? Should Congress pass a comprehensive "Assimilative Civil Law Act" to eliminate the problem raised by Arlington Hotel v. Fant? Congress took a preliminary step in 1976 by granting the Interior Department authority to cede all or part of federal jurisdiction within units of the National Park System, 16 U.S. C.A. § 1a–3, but the authority has been employed sparingly.

B. INTERGOVERNMENTAL IMMUNITIES

The Court generally described the effect of the doctrine of intergovernmental immunities in *Fort Leavenworth,* supra: federal lands and buildings must be "free from * * * such interference * * * as would destroy or impair their effective use * * *." The doctrine, derived from the Supremacy Clause, is also the basis of the immunity of federal property from state tax laws. See Van Brocklin v. Anderson, 117 U.S. 151 (1886).

UTAH POWER & LIGHT CO. v. UNITED STATES
Supreme Court of the United States, 1917.
243 U.S. 389.

Mr. Justice VAN DEVANTER delivered the opinion of the court.

We are concerned here with three suits by the United States to enjoin the continued occupancy and use, without its permission, of certain of its lands in forest reservations in Utah as sites for works employed in generating and distributing electric power, and to secure compensation for such occupancy and use in the past. The reservations were created by executive orders and proclamations with the express sanction of Congress. Almost all the lands therein belong to the United States and before the reservations were created were public lands subject to disposal and acquisition under the general land laws. The works in question consist of diversion dams, reservoirs, pipe lines, power houses, transmission lines and some subsidiary structures. In the aggregate these are used in collecting water from mountain streams, in conducting it for considerable distances to power houses where the force arising. from its descent through the pipe lines is transmuted into electric energy, and in transmitting that energy to places beyond the reservations, where it is sold to whoever has occasion to use it for power, lighting or heating. In each case some part of the works is on private lands, but much the greater part is on lands of the United States. Part was constructed before and part after the reservation was created, but all after 1896 and nearly all after 1901. The entire works are conducted in each instance as a commercial enterprise, and not as an incident to or in aid of any other business in which the defendant is engaged.

In occupying and using the government lands as sites for these works the defendants have proceeded upon the assumption that they were entitled so to do without seeking or securing any grant or license from the Secretary of the Interior or the Secretary of Agriculture under the legislation of Congress, and, in truth, they have neither applied for nor received such a grant or license from either. But, notwithstanding this, they assert that they have acquired and are invested with rights to occupy and use permanently, for the purposes indicated, the government lands upon which the works are located.

The principal object of the suits, as is said in one of the briefs, is to test the validity of these asserted rights and, if they be found invalid, to require the defendants to conform to the legislation of Congress or, at their option, to remove from the government lands. The District Court ruled against the defendants upon the main question, * * * but refused the Government's prayer for pecuniary relief. Cross appeals were then taken directly to this court.

The first position taken by the defendants is that their claims must be tested by the laws of the State in which the lands are situate rather than by the legislation of Congress, and in support of this position they say that lands of the United States within a State, when not used or needed for a fort or other governmental purpose of the United States, are subject to the jurisdiction, powers and laws of the State in the same way and to the same extent as are similar lands of others. To this we cannot assent. Not only does the Constitution (Art. IV, § 3, cl. 2) commit to Congress the power "to dispose of and make all needful rules and regulations respecting" the lands of the United States, but the settled course of legislation, congressional and state, and repeated decisions of this court have gone upon the theory that the power of Congress is exclusive and that only through its exercise in some form can rights in lands belonging to the United States be acquired. True, for many purposes a State has civil and criminal jurisdiction over lands within its limits belonging to the United States, but this jurisdiction does not extend to any matter that is not consistent with full power in the United States to protect its lands, to control their use and to prescribe in what manner others may acquire rights in them. Thus while the State may punish public offenses, such as murder or larceny, committed on such lands, and may tax private property, such as live stock, located thereon, it may not tax the lands themselves or invest others with any right whatever in them. United States v. McBratney, 104 U.S. 621, 624; Van Brocklin v. Tennessee, 117 U.S. 151, 168; Wisconsin Central R.R. Co. v. Price Co., 133 U.S. 496, 504. From the earliest times Congress by its legislation, applicable alike in the States and Territories, has regulated in many particulars the use by others of the lands of the United States, has prohibited and made punishable various acts calculated to be injurious to them or to prevent their use in the way intended, and has provided for and controlled the acquisition of rights of way over them for highways, railroads, canals, ditches, telegraph lines and the like. The States and the public have almost uniformly accepted this legislation as controlling, and in the instances where it has been questioned in this court its validity has been upheld and its supremacy over state enactments sustained. Wilcox v. Jackson, 13 Pet. 498, 516; Jourdan v. Barrett, 4 How. 168, 185; Gibson v. Chouteau, 13 Wall. 92, 99; Camfield v. United States, 167 U.S. 518; Light v. United States, 220 U.S. 523, 536–537. And so we are of opinion that the inclusion within a State of lands of the United States does not take from Congress the power to control their occupancy and use, to protect them from trespass and injury and to prescribe the conditions upon which others may obtain rights in them, even though this may involve the exercise in some measure of what commonly is known as the police power. "A different rule," as was said in Camfield v. United States, supra, "would place the public domain of the United States completely at the mercy of state legislation."

It results that state laws, including those relating to the exercise of the power of eminent domain, have no bearing upon a controversy such as is here presented, save as they may have been adopted or made applicable by Congress.

* * *

In their answers some of the defendants assert that when the forest reservations were created an understanding and agreement was had between the defendants, or their predecessors, and some unmentioned officers or agents of the United States to the effect that the reservations would not be an obstacle to the construction or operation of the works in question; that all rights essential thereto would be allowed and granted under the Act of 1905; that consistently with this understanding and agreement and relying thereon the defendants, or their predecessors, completed the works and proceeded with the generation and distribution of electric energy, and that in consequence the United States is estopped to question the right of the defendants to maintain and operate the works. Of this it is enough to say that the United States is neither bound nor estopped by acts of its officers or agents in entering into an arrangement or agreement to do or cause to be done what the law does not sanction or permit.

* * * And, if it be assumed that the rule is subject to exceptions, we find nothing in the cases in hand which fairly can be said to take them out of it as heretofore understood and applied in this court. A suit by the United States to enforce and maintain its policy respecting lands which it holds in trust for all the people stands upon a different plane in this and some other respects from the ordinary private suit to regain the title to real property or to remove a cloud from it. Causey v. United States, 240 U.S. 399, 402.

* * *

As the defendants have been occupying and using reserved lands of the United States without its permission and contrary to its laws, we think it is entitled to have appropriate compensation therefor included in the decree. The compensation should be measured by the reasonable value of the occupancy and use, considering its extent and duration, and not by the scale of charges named in the regulations as prayed in the bill. However much this scale of charges may bind one whose occupancy and use are under a license or permit granted under the statute, it cannot be taken as controlling what may be recovered from an occupant and user who has not accepted or assented to the regulations in any way.

It follows that the decrees are right and must be affirmed, save as they deny the Government's right to compensation for the occupancy and use in the past, and in that respect they must be reversed.

It is so ordered.

NOTES

1. Congress has since issued a limited waiver of its immunity from state adverse possession laws. Among other provisions, the Color of Title Act, 43 U.S.C.A. §§ 1068–1068b, requires either (a) good faith adverse possession for more than 20 years and either cultivation or erection of valuable improvements, or (b) continuous good faith possession since January 1, 1901. Knowledge of federal ownership is a bar. See, e.g., Day v. Hickel, 481 F.2d 473 (9th Cir.1973). Congress has passed some private bills to alleviate inequities in individual cases where claimants cannot meet the terms of the Act.

The United States has also waived immunity, on specified terms, as to those who claim title based on a valid conveyance rather than on adverse possession. See the Quiet Title Act of 1972, 28 U.S.C.A. §§ 2409a, 1346(f), 1402(d). Many private and state claims are barred by its 12-year statute of limitations, which begins to run on the date a plaintiff knew or should have known of the opposing claim to title by the United States. States with claims to submerged lands as of statehood are subject to that statute of limitations. In Block v. North Dakota, 461 U.S. 273 (1983), the Quiet Title Act is described in detail. See also, e.g., California v. Yuba Goldfields, Inc., 752 F.2d 393 (9th Cir. 1985), appeal pending. On difficulties caused by resurveys of public lands, see Picone, Resurveys of Public Lands, 30 Rocky Mtn.Min.L.Inst. 20–1 (1985).

Should the United States be subject to adverse possession and quiet title laws in the same manner as any other landowner?

2. The *Utah Power & Light* formulation continues to be the law on the application of estoppel based on the conduct of federal employees. Some courts have suggested, however, that they may be willing to allow estoppel against the United States in unusual cases. In United States v. Wharton, 514 F.2d 406 (9th Cir.1975), the Ninth Circuit held that the BLM was estopped by its conduct to eject a family that had resided on a federal parcel since 1919. The same court discussed the law in United States v. Ruby Co., 588 F.2d 697 (9th Cir.1978), cert. denied, 442 U.S. 917 (1979); it noted that the *Utah Power & Light* rule was "no longer absolute" but found no estoppel because there had been no "affirmative misconduct" by federal employees. For extended discussions on the issue, see City & County of Denver v. Bergland, 517 F.Supp. 155, 194–97 (D.Colo.1981), modified on other grounds, 695 F.2d 465 (10th Cir.1982) (refusing to find an estoppel resulting in a right-of-way across BLM and Forest Service lands); Tosco Corp. v. Hickel, 611 F.Supp. 1130, 1201–09 (D.Colo.1985) (finding estoppel based on affirmative governmental misconduct toward oil shale claimants). See also Alaska Limestone Corp. v. Hodel, 614 F.Supp. 642, 647–48 (D.Alaska

1985) (no estoppel). Outside of the public lands context, the Supreme
Court recently denied a claim based on estoppel, stating "though the
arguments the Government advances for the rule [that estoppel can
never run against the United States] are substantial, we are hesitant,
when it is unnecessary to decide this case, to say that there are *no cases*
in which the public interest in insuring that the Government can
enforce the law free from estoppel might be outweighed by the countervailing interest of citizens in some minimum standard of decency,
honor and reliability in their dealings with their Government." Heckler v. Community Health Services of Crawford County, 467 U.S. 51, 58
(1984) (emphasis in original). See generally Note, Estopping the Federal Government: Still Waiting for the Right Case, 53 Geo.Wash.L.Rev.
191 (1985). Could or should estoppel against the government be confined in the public lands field?

UNITED STATES v. COUNTY OF FRESNO
Supreme Court of the United States, 1977.
429 U.S. 452.

Mr. Justice WHITE delivered the opinion of the Court.

The issue in this case is whether, consistent with the Federal
Government's immunity from state taxation inherent in the Supremacy
Clause of the United States Constitution, see McCulloch v. Maryland, 4
Wheat. 316 (1819), the State of California may tax federal employees on
their possessory interests in housing owned and supplied to them by the
Federal Government as part of their compensation. We hold that it
may.

I

The individual appellants in this case are employees of the Forest
Service, a branch of the United States Department of Agriculture
responsible for administering the national forests. Petitioners work in
the Sierra, Sequoia, and Stanislaus National Forests which are located
in Fresno and Tuolumne Counties in California. During the year 1967
each appellant lived with his family in a house which was built and
owned by the Forest Service in one of these national forests. Appellants were required by the Forest Service to live in these houses so that
they would be nearer to the place where they performed their duties
and so that they would be better able to perform those duties. Struc-
turally, the houses were very similar to residential houses of the same
size available in the private sector. The Forest Service viewed the
occupancy of these houses as partial compensation for the services of its
employees, and made a deduction from the salary of the employee for
each two-week pay period in which the employee occupied such a house.
The Forest Service fixed the amount of the deduction by estimating the
fair rental value of a similar house in the private sector and then
discounting that figure to take account of the distance between the
Forest Service house and the nearest established community and the

absence, if any, of any customary amenities in or near the house.[2] Adjustment was also made for the fact that the Forest Service reserved the right to remove employees from their houses at any time, to enter the houses with or without notice for inspection purposes, and to use part or all of the houses for official purposes in an emergency.

Pursuant to 16 U.S.C.A. § 480, the States retain civil and criminal jurisdiction over the national forests notwithstanding the fact that the national forests are owned by the Federal Government. Under the California Revenue and Taxation Code, §§ 104, 107 and § 21(b) of Title 18 of the California Administrative Code, counties in California are authorized to impose an annual use or property tax on possessory interests in improvements on tax-exempt land. The counties of Fresno and Tuolumne imposed such a tax on the appellants—Forest Service employees who live in the federally owned houses in the national forests located in those counties. In computing the value of the possessory interests on which the tax is imposed, the counties used the annual estimated fair rental value of the houses, discounted to take into account essentially the same factors considered by the Forest Service in computing the amount that it deducted from the salaries of employees who used the houses.

Appellants paid the taxes under protest and they, together with the United States, sued for a refund in California courts in Fresno and Tuolumne Counties. They claimed, *inter alia,* that the tax interfered with a federal function—i.e., the running of the Forest Service—that it discriminated against employees of the Federal Government and that it was therefore forbidden by the Supremacy Clause of the United States Constitution. E.g., McCulloch v. Maryland, supra. * * *

* * *

[The California Court of Appeals upheld the tax and the Supreme Court of California denied review.]

II

The Government relies principally on the landmark case of McCulloch v. Maryland, supra. There the State of Maryland imposed a tax on notes issued by "any Bank * * * established without authority from the State." The only such bank in Maryland was the Bank of the United States, created and incorporated by Act of Congress in order to carry out Congress' enumerated powers. No similar tax was imposed on the issuance of notes by any other bank in Maryland. The Court held the tax to violate that part of the Federal Constitution which declares that the laws of the United States are the "supreme law of the

---

2. Examples of the amenities considered are, according to the testimony of a Forest Service official:

"Paved streets, street lighting at least at intersections, sidewalks, lawns, trees and landscaping, general attractiveness of the neighborhood, community sanitation services, reliability and adequacy of water safe for household use, reliability of adequacy of electrical service, reliability and adequacy of telephone service, reliability and adequacy of fuel for heating, hot water and cooking, police protection, fire protection, unusual design features of a dwelling, absence of disturbing noises or offensive odors and standards of maintenance."

land." An Act of Congress had created the bank in order to carry out functions of the National government enumerated in the United States Constitution. The Court noted that the power to tax the bank "by the States may be exercised so as to destroy it," id., 4 Wheat., at 427, and consequently that the power to tax, if admitted, could be exercised so as effectively to repeal the Act of Congress which created the bank. If the State's power to tax the bank were recognized in principle, the Court doubted the ability of federal courts to review each exercise of such power to determine whether the tax would or would not destroy a federal function. Finally, the Court rejected the State's argument that the power to tax involves the power to destroy only where the taxing power is abused, and that the Court should simply trust the States not to abuse their power to tax a federal function just as it must trust a State not to abuse its power to tax its own citizens. The Court rejected the argument because the political check against abuse of the power to tax a State's constituents is absent when the State taxes only a federal function. A State's constituents can be relied on to vote out of office any legislature that imposes an abusively high tax on them. They cannot be relied upon to be similarly motivated when the tax is instead solely on a federal function.

The Court was careful to limit the reach of its decision. It stated that its opinion does not

> "extend to a tax * * * imposed on the interest which the citizens of Maryland may hold in this institution [the bank], *in common with other property of the same description throughout the State. * * *"* Id., at 436. (Emphasis added.)

Since *McCulloch,* this Court has adhered to the rule that States may not impose taxes directly on the Federal Government, nor may they impose taxes the legal incidence of which falls on the Federal Government. The decisions of this Court since *McCulloch* have been less uniform on the question whether taxes, the economic but not the legal incidence of which falls in part or in full on the Federal Government, are invalid.

For many years the Court read the decision in *McCulloch* as forbidding taxes on those who had contractual relationships with the Federal Government or with its instrumentalities whenever the effect of the tax was or might be to increase the cost to the Federal Government of performing its functions. In later years, however, the Court departed from this interpretation of *McCulloch.* * * *

The rule to be derived from the Court's more recent decisions, then, is that the economic burden on a federal function of a state tax imposed on those who deal with the Federal Government does not render the tax unconstitutional so long as the tax is imposed equally on the other similarly situated constituents of the State. This rule returns to the original intent of McCulloch v. Maryland, supra. The political check against abuse of the taxing power found lacking in *McCulloch,* where the tax was imposed solely on the Bank of the United States, is present where the State imposes a nondiscriminatory tax only on its constituents or their artificially owned entities; and *McCulloch* foresaw the unfairness in forcing a State to exempt private individuals with beneficial interests in federal property from taxes imposed on similar interests held by others in private property. Accordingly, *McCulloch* expressly excluded from its rule a tax on "interests which the citizens of Maryland may hold [in a federal instrumentality] in common with other property of the same description throughout the State."

III

Applying the rule set forth above, decision of this case is relatively simple. The "legal incidence" of the tax involved in this case falls neither on the Federal Government nor on federal property. The tax is imposed solely on private citizens who work for the Federal Government. The tax threatens to interfere with federal laws relating to the functions of the Forest Service *only* insofar as it may impose an economic burden on the Forest Service—causing it to reimburse its employees for the taxes legally owned by them or, failing reimbursement, removing an advantage otherwise enjoyed by the Federal Government in the employment market.[12] There is no other respect in which the tax involved in this case threatens to obstruct or burden a federal function. The tax can be invalidated, then, only if it discriminates against the Forest Service or other federal employees, which it does not do.

Although the tax is imposed by the appellee counties on renters of real property only if the owner is exempt from taxation—and consequently is not imposed on the vast majority of renters of real property in California—the tax is not for that reason discriminatory. * * *

* * *

Affirmed.

NOTES

1. As *County of Fresno* demonstrates, the doctrine of intergovernmental immunities has waned in public land law, as elsewhere, and extensions are highly unlikely. See generally United States v. New Mexico, 455 U.S. 720 (1982); L. Tribe, AMERICAN CONSTITUTIONAL LAW 391–401 (1978). As a policy matter, narrow federal immunity still leaves Congress with virtually unfettered authority to enact protective legislation by preempting state law under the Property Clause. See section C infra.

2. The tax exempt status of federal lands has caused Congress, as a matter of equity, to adopt methods in lieu of taxation providing revenues from federal lands to state and local governments. A common device is the payment of a percentage of proceeds from resource development. For example, counties receive 25% of stumpage sales

---

12. The Federal Government would otherwise have had the power—enjoyed by no other employer—of giving its employees housing on which no property tax is paid by them either directly or indirectly as rent paid to a landlord who himself paid a property tax.

receipts from timber harvesting on national forests. 16 U.S.C.A. § 500.
Nineteen counties in western Oregon receive over $100 million annual-
ly as their 50% share of the proceeds from stumpage sales on the
timber-rich "Oregon & California" (O & C) lands administered by the
BLM. See 43 U.S.C.A. § 1181f; P. Gates, HISTORY OF PUBLIC
LAND LAW DEVELOPMENT 602–04 (1968). The state of origin
receives 50% of revenues from oil and gas leases under the provisions of
the Mineral Leasing Act—except Alaska, which receives 90% of such
revenues. 30 U.S.C.A. § 191. A number of other acts provide for such
in lieu payments when federal resources are developed. In Watt v.
Alaska, 451 U.S. 259 (1981), the Court upheld Alaska's favored position
in the receipt of revenues from mineral leasing on national wildlife
refuges. The Mineral Leasing Act provides that Alaska will receive
90% of all revenues produced by federal oil and gas leasing in the state.
In 1964, the Wildlife Refuge Revenue Sharing Act was amended to add
the word "minerals" to the list of refuge resources; 25% of the
revenues from such resources are paid to counties, and 75% are
retained by the United States. The Court, with three justices dissenting, invoked the rule that implied repeals are not favored and ruled
that Alaska's 90% share had not been affected. See generally S.
Fairfax & C. Yates, THE FINANCIAL INTEREST OF WESTERN
STATES IN NON–TAX REVENUES FROM THE PUBLIC LANDS
(1985); Leshy, Sharing the Federal Multiple-Use Lands—Historic Lessons and Speculations for the Future, in RETHINKING THE PUBLIC
LANDS 235 (1984).

In 1976, Congress enacted the Payment In Lieu of Taxes Act, 31
U.S.C.A. § 6901 et seq., which provides that a minimum payment of 75
cents per acre will be made to local governments regardless of development revenues, and reduces the tax loss to local governments in other
ways. In Lawrence County v. Lead-Deadwood School Dist., 469 U.S.
256 (1985), the Court held that counties are free to spend funds received
under the 1976 Act for any governmental purposes and that the states
cannot place restrictions on such county expenditures:

> The Payment in Lieu of Taxes Act was passed in response
> to a comprehensive review of the policies applicable to the use,
> management, and disposition of federal lands. Public Land
> Law Review Commission, One Third of the Nation's Land
> (1970). The Federal Government had for many years been
> providing payments to partially compensate state and local
> governments for revenues lost as a result of the presence of
> tax-exempt federal lands within their borders. But the Public
> Land Law Review Commission and Congress identified a num-
> ber of flaws in the existing programs. Prominent among
> congressional concerns was that, under systems of direct pay-
> ment to the States, local governments often received funds that
> were insufficient to cover the full cost of maintaining the
> federal lands within their jurisdictions. Where these lands
> consisted of wilderness or park areas, they attracted thousands
> of visitors each year. State governments might benefit from

this federally inspired tourism through the collection of income or sales taxes, but these revenues would not accrue to local governments, who were often restricted to raising revenue from property taxes. Yet it was the local governments that bore the brunt of the expenses associated with federal lands, such as law enforcement, road maintenance, and the provision of public health services.

Revenue sharing raises a number of difficult issues. It is a generally accepted principle that states and counties should be fairly compensated for net financial burdens caused by tax-exempt lands within their boundaries. On the other hand, the approach of tying those revenues to receipts from resource development is seen by many as an inducement to development divorced from the intrinsic merits of the proposal. See, e.g., D. Barney, THE LAST STAND 118–19 (1974); Muys, The Federal Lands, in FEDERAL ENVIRONMENTAL LAW 532–35 (1974). A good case can be made for the proposition that the western states receive far more economic benefits from federal land ownership than detriments. See Leshy, supra. At this writing, Congress is debating the question whether states should get a share of federal offshore oil and gas lease revenues.

In addition to direct federal payments, states often can obtain substantial direct revenues by taxing private development activities on federal lands. See, e.g., Commonwealth Edison Co. v. Montana, 453 U.S. 609 (1981), infra at page 230, upholding a state coal severance tax.

3. Federal lands are not subject to state land use planning requirements, but federal agencies are directed in various statutes to coordinate with local land use planners to the extent practicable. See infra at page 229.

C. FEDERAL PREEMPTION

The modern test to determine whether state or federal law governs a particular problem occurring on federal lands is roughly this. If the area is an enclave, start from the proposition that federal law governs and go on to seek reservations of state jurisdiction in the cession arrangement or subsequent retrocession of jurisdiction to the state by Congress. Second, if the situation comes within the narrow ambit of federal immunity, the state law will be struck down. In all other situations, however, the beginning premise is that state law controls, and the search is for federal law that might preempt state authority—the ultimate criterion is the intent of Congress.

As the following materials show, it has not always been conceded that the ultimate sovereign power over federal non-enclave lands reposed in the federal legislature.

HICKS v. BELL
Supreme Court of California, 1853.
3 Cal. 219.

[A jury, having been instructed on principles of state law, found that appellees had been wrongfully dispossessed of their mining claims.]

* * *

The main reliance in this case of the appellants is, that the land in question is the public land of the United States, and therefore the statutes of this State, which recognize the possessions of miners, which provide for their protection, and require mining claims to be decided according to the rules and regulations of bodies of miners, at each particular mining locality, are mere police regulations, and are invalid to confer any right, such as that of possession, or to enable the recovery thereof.

This position involves the decision of the question, to whom do the mines of gold and silver belong? To arrive at a satisfactory solution, it is only necessary to examine a few of the leading authorities.

* * *

It is hardly necessary at this period of our history to make an argument to prove that the several States of the Union, in virtue of their respective sovereignties, are entitled to the jura regalia which pertained to the king at common law.

An analogous question to the one under consideration was fully discussed in the Supreme Court of the United States in the case of Pollard's Lessee v. Hagan, 3 Howard. It was there held, in the case of a new State, that she was admitted into the Union upon the same footing as the original States, and possessed the right of eminent domain. Numerous other cases can be cited in which the decisions are uniform that the United States has no municipal sovereignty within the limits of the States.

In reference to the ownership of the public lands, the United States only occupied the position of any private proprietor, with the exception of an express exemption from State taxation. The mines of gold and silver on the public lands are as much the property of this State, by virtue of her sovereignty, as are similar mines in the lands of private citizens. She has, therefore, solely the right to authorize them to be worked; to pass laws for their regulation; to license miners; and to affix such terms and conditions as she may deem proper, to the freedom of their use. In her legislation upon this subject, she has established the policy of permitting all who desire it to work her mines of gold and silver, with or without conditions; and she has wisely provided that their conflicting claims shall be adjudicated by the rules and customs which may be established by bodies of them working in the same vicinity.

According to this enactment, the case under consideration has been tried and decided, and for aught that is disclosed by the record, the decision is consonant with right and justice.

Judgment is affirmed.

The narrow reading of federal power under the Property Clause in Pollard v. Hagan, 44 U.S. (3 How.) 212 (1845), supra at page 72, in several other nineteenth century Supreme Court cases, and in state cases like Hicks v. Bell, seemed to indicate that on the public lands the United States could exercise only its enumerated powers and not the full range of sovereign powers. See Engdahl, State and Federal Power over Federal Property, 18 Ariz.L.Rev. 283, 308–09 (1976).

Contrary language began to appear in Supreme Court cases. In 1897, the Court in Camfield v. United States, 167 U.S. 518 (1897), supra at page 108, found that the United States "doubtless has a power over its own property analogous to the police power of the several states, and the extent to which it may go in the exercise of such power is measured by the exigencies of the particular case." 167 U.S. at 525. In Light v. United States, 220 U.S. 523 (1911), supra at page 137, the United States was granted an injunction against a private person who willfully allowed his livestock to graze on the public lands without federal permission. The Court could have upheld the injunction solely on the grounds that the United States as a proprietor is entitled to be protected against willful trespass, but it went further:

> "All the public lands of the nation are held in trust for the people of the whole country." United States v. Trinidad Coal Co., 137 U.S. 160. And it is not for the courts to say how that trust shall be administered. That is for Congress to determine. The courts cannot compel it to set aside the lands for settlement; or to suffer them to be used for agricultural or grazing purposes; nor interfere when, in the exercise of its discretion, Congress establishes a forest reserve for what it decides to be national and public purposes. In the same way and in the exercise of the same trust it may disestablish a reserve, and devote the property to some other national and public purpose. These are rights incident to proprietorship, to say nothing of the power of the United States as a sovereign over the property belonging to it.

220 U.S. at 537.

The Court confronted the issue more directly six years later in *Utah Power & Light*, supra, but questions of federal power on federal lands reached the Supreme Court only occasionally over the next 60 years, leaving many potential conflicts unresolved. In McKelvey v. United States, 260 U.S. 353 (1922), sheepherders had been denied passage over public lands by defendant cattle ranchers who, after warning and threatening the sheep owner's employees, then "shot and seriously injured one of the employees, threatened to finish him, and did other things calculated to put all three in terror." Defendants were convicted of violating the Unlawful Enclosures Act, 23 Stat. 321 ("no person, by force, threats, intimidation ＊ ＊ ＊ or any other unlawful means, shall prevent or obstruct ＊ ＊ ＊ any person from peaceably entering upon ＊ ＊ ＊ any tract of public land ＊ ＊ ＊"). On appeal, they claimed that if the statute were construed to punish their conduct, it was beyond the power of Congress and an encroachment on the state police power. Mr. Justice Van Devanter would have none of it:

> It is firmly settled that Congress may prescribe rules respecting the use of the public lands. It may sanction some uses and prohibit others, and may forbid interference with such as are sanctioned. The provision now before us is but an exertion of that power. ＊ ＊ ＊

> It also is settled that the states may prescribe police regulations applicable to public-land areas, so long as the regulations are not arbitrary or inconsistent with applicable congressional enactments.

In Hunt v. United States, 278 U.S. 96 (1928), the Court summarily brushed aside state law objections to a federal deer population control program, deeming the program one necessary for the protection of public lands. In United States v. San Francisco, 310 U.S. 16, 29 (1940), the Court emphasized that Congress has broad powers to determine what rules are "needful" for public land management: "The power over the public land thus entrusted to Congress [by the Property Clause] is without limitations."

Between 1917 and 1976, society, law, and public land policy changed considerably. The Depression and the New Deal led to the expansion of the Commerce Clause. Management replaced disposition as fundamental national public land policy. New values, such as protecting pests like wild burros, were incorporated into the statutes.

KLEPPE v. NEW MEXICO
Supreme Court of the United States, 1976.
426 U.S. 529.

Mr. Justice MARSHALL delivered the opinion of the Court.

At issue in this case is whether Congress exceeded its powers under the Constitution in enacting the Wild Free-Roaming Horses and Burros Act.

I

The Wild Free-Roaming Horses and Burros Act (the Act), 16 U.S. C.A. §§ 1331–1340, was enacted in 1971 to protect "all unbranded and unclaimed horses and burros on public lands of the United States," § 2(b) of the Act, 16 U.S.C.A. § 1332(b), from "capture, branding, harassment, or death." § 1 of the Act, 16 U.S.C.A. § 1331. The Act provides that all such horses and burros on the public lands administered by the Secretary of the Interior through the Bureau of Land

Management (BLM) or by the Secretary of Agriculture through the Forest Service are committed to the jurisdiction of the respective Secretaries, who are "directed to protect and manage [the animals] as components of the public lands * * * in a manner that is designed to achieve and maintain a thriving natural ecological balance on the public lands." § 3(a) of the Act, 16 U.S.C.A. § 1333(a). If protected horses or burros "stray from public lands onto privately owned land, the owners of such land may inform the nearest Federal marshall or agent of the Secretary, who shall arrange to have the animals removed." [1] § 4 of the Act, 16 U.S.C.A. 1334.

Section 6 of the Act, 16 U.S.C.A. § 1336, authorizes the Secretaries to promulgate regulations, see 36 CFR § 231.11 (1975) (Agriculture); 43 CFR pt. 4710 (1975) (Interior), and to enter into cooperative agreements with other landowners and with state and local governmental agencies in furtherance of the Act's purposes. On August 7, 1973, the Secretaries executed such an agreement with the New Mexico Livestock Board (the Livestock Board), the agency charged with enforcing the New Mexico Estray Law, N.Mex.Stat.Ann. § 47 14 1 et seq. (1953).[2] The agreement acknowledged the authority of the Secretaries to manage and protect the wild free-roaming horses and burros on the public lands of the United States within the State and established a procedure for evaluating the claims of private parties to ownership of such animals.

The Livestock Board terminated the agreement three months later. Asserting that the Federal Government lacked power to control wild horses and burros on the public lands of the United States unless the animals were moving in interstate commerce or damaging the public lands and that neither of these bases of regulation was available here, the Board notified the Secretaries of its intent

> "to exercise all regulatory impoundment and sale powers which it derives from the New Mexico Estray Law, over all estray horses, mules or asses found running at large upon public or private lands within New Mexico * * *. This includes the right to go upon Federal or State lands to take possession of said horses or burros, should the Livestock Board so desire." App. 67, 72.

The differences between the Livestock Board and the Secretaries came to a head in February 1974. On February 1, 1974, a New Mexico

---

1. The landowner may elect to allow straying wild free-roaming horses and burros to remain on his property, in which case he must so notify the relevant Secretary. He may not destroy any such animals, however. § 4 of the Act, 16 U.S.C.A. § 1334.

2. Under the New Mexico law, an estray is defined as:

"Any bovine animal, horse, mule or ass, found running at large upon public or private lands, either fenced or unfenced, in the state of New Mexico, whose owner is unknown in the section where found, or which shall be fifty [50] miles or more from the limits of its usual range or pasture, or that is branded with a brand which is not on record in the office of the cattle sanitary board of New Mexico * * *." N.Mex.Stat.Ann. 47 14 1 (Repl.1966).

It is not disputed that the animals regulated by the Wild Free-Roaming Horses and Burros Act are estrays within the meaning of this law.

rancher, Kelley Stephenson, was informed by BLM that several un-branded burros had been seen near Taylor Well, where Stephenson watered his cattle. Taylor Well is on federal property, and Stephenson had access to it and some 8,000 surrounding acres only through a grazing permit issued pursuant to the Taylor Grazing Act. After BLM made it clear to Stephenson that it would not remove the burros and after he personally inspected the Taylor Well area, Stephenson com-plained to the Livestock Board that the burros were interfering with his livestock operation by molesting his cattle and eating their feed.

Thereupon the Board rounded up and removed 19 unbranded and unclaimed burros pursuant to the New Mexico Estray Law. Each burro was seized on the public lands of the United States and, as the director of the Board conceded, each burro fit the definition of a wild free-roaming burro under § 2(b) of the Act. App. 43. On February 18, 1974, the Livestock Board, pursuant to its usual practice, sold the burros at a public auction. After the sale, BLM asserted jurisdiction under the Act and demanded that the Board recover the animals and return them to the public lands.

On March 4, 1974, appellees filed a complaint in the United States District Court for the District of New Mexico seeking a declaratory judgment that the Wild Free-Roaming Horses and Burros Act is uncon-stitutional and an injunction against its enforcement. A three-judge court was convened pursuant to 28 U.S.C.A. § 2282.

Following an evidentiary hearing, the District Court held the Act unconstitutional and permanently enjoined the Secretary of the Interi-or (the Secretary) from enforcing its provisions. The court found that the Act "conflicts with * * * the traditional doctrines concerning wild animals," 406 F.Supp. 1237, 1238 (1975), and is in excess of Congress' power under the Property Clause of the Constitution, Art. IV, § 3, cl. 2. That Clause, the court found, enables Congress to regulate wild animals found on the public land only for the "*protection* of the public lands from damage of some kind." 406 F.Supp., at 1239 (empha-sis in original). Accordingly, this power was exceeded in this case because "[t]he statute is aimed at protecting the wild horses and burros, not at protecting the land they live on." Ibid.[6] We noted probable jurisdiction, 423 U.S. 818 (1975), and we now reverse.

II

The Property Clause of the Constitution provides that "Congress shall have Power to dispose of and make all needful Rules and Regula-tions respecting the Territory or other Property belonging to the United

---

6. The Court also held that the Act could not be sustained under the Com-merce Clause because "all the evidence establishes that the wild burros in question here do not migrate across state lines" and "Congress made no findings to indicate that it was in any way relying on the Commerce Clause in enacting this statute." While the Secretary argues in this Court that the Act is sustainable under the Com-merce Clause, we have no occasion to ad-dress this contention since we find the Act, as applied, to be permissible exercise of congressional power under the Property Clause.

States." U.S.Const., Art. IV, § 3, cl. 2. In passing the Wild Free-Roaming Horses and Burros Act, Congress deemed the regulated animals "an integral part of the natural system of the public lands" of the United States, § 1 of the Act, 16 U.S.C.A. § 1331, and found that their management was necessary "for achievement of an ecological balance on the public lands." According to Congress, these animals, if preserved in their native habitats, "contribute to the diversity of life forms within the Nation and enrich the lives of the American people." § 1 of the Act, 16 U.S.C.A. § 1331. Indeed, Congress concluded, the wild free-roaming horses and burros "are living symbols of the historic and pioneer spirit of the West." § 1 of the Act, 16 U.S.C.A. § 1331. Despite their importance, the Senate Committee found that these animals

> "have been cruelly captured and slain and their carcasses used in the production of pet food and fertilizer. They have been used for target practice and harassed for 'sport' and profit. In spite of public outrage, this bloody traffic continues unabated, and it is the firm belief of the committee that this senseless slaughter must be brought to an end." S.Rep. No. 92–242, 92d Cong., 1st Sess., 2 (1971), U.S.Code Cong. & Admin.News 1971, p. 2149.

For these reasons, Congress determined to preserve and protect the wild free-roaming horses and burros on the public lands of the United States. The question under the Property Clause is whether this determination can be sustained as a "needful" regulation "respecting" the public lands. In answering this question, we must remain mindful that, while courts must eventually pass upon them, determinations under the Property Clause are entrusted primarily to the judgment of Congress. United States v. San Francisco, 310 U.S. 16, 29–30 (1940); Light v. United States, 220 U.S. 523, 537 (1911); United States v. Gratiot, 14 Pet. 526, 537–538 (1841).

Appellees argue that the Act cannot be supported by the Property Clause. They contend that the Clause grants Congress essentially two kinds of power: (1) the power to dispose of and make incidental rules regarding the use of federal property; and (2) the power to protect federal property. According to appellees, the first power is not broad enough to support legislation protecting wild animals that live on federal property; and the second power is not implicated since the Act is designed to protect the animals, which are not themselves federal property, and not the public lands. As an initial matter, it is far from clear that the Act was not passed in part to protect the public lands of the United States [7] or that Congress cannot assert a property interest in the regulated horses and burros superior to that of the State.[8] But we

---

7. Congress expressly ordered that the animals were to be managed and protected in order "to achieve and maintain a thriving natural ecological balance on the public lands." § 3(a), 16 U.S.C.A. § 1333(a).

8. The Secretary makes no claim here, however, that the United States owns the wild free-roaming horses and burros found on public land.

need not consider whether the Act can be upheld on either of these grounds, for we reject appellees' narrow reading of the Property Clause.

Appellees ground their argument on a number of cases that, upon analysis, provide no support for their position. Like the District Court, appellees cite Hunt v. United States, 278 U.S. 96 (1928), for the proposition that the Property Clause gives Congress only the limited power to regulate wild animals in order to protect the public lands from damage. But *Hunt,* which upheld the Government's right to kill deer that were damaging foliage in the national forests, only holds that damage to the land is a sufficient basis for regulation; it contains no suggestion that it is a necessary one.

Next appellees refer to Kansas v. Colorado, 206 U.S. 46, 89 (1907). The referenced passage in that case states that the Property Clause "clearly * * * does not grant to Congress any legislative control over the states, and must, so far as they are concerned, be limited to authority over the property belonging to the United States within their limits." But this does no more than articulate the obvious: that the Property Clause is a grant of power only over federal property. It gives no indication of the kind of "authority" the Clause gives Congress over its property.

Camfield v. United States, 167 U.S. 518 (1897), is of even less help to appellees. Appellees rely upon the following language from *Camfield:*

> "While we do not undertake to say that Congress has the unlimited power to legislate against nuisances within a state which it would have within a territory, we do not think the admission of a territory as a state deprives it of the power of legislating for the protection of the public lands, though it may thereby involve the exercise of what is ordinarily known as the 'police power,' *so long as such power is directed solely to its own protection.*" Id., at 525–526 (emphasis added).

Appellees mistakenly read this language to limit Congress' power to regulate activity on the public lands; in fact, the quoted passage refers to the scope of congressional power to regulate conduct on *private* land that affects the public lands. And *Camfield* holds that the Property Clause is broad enough to permit federal regulation of fences built on private land adjoining public land when the regulation is for the protection of the federal property. *Camfield* contains no suggestion of any limitation on Congress' power over conduct on its own property; its sole message is that the power granted by the Property Clause is broad enough to reach beyond territorial limits.

Lastly, appellees point to dicta in two cases to the effect that, unless the State has agreed to the exercise of federal jurisdiction, Congress' rights in its land are "only the rights of an ordinary proprietor * * *." Fort Leavenworth R. Co. v. Lowe, 114 U.S. 525, 527 (1885). See also Paul v. United States, 371 U.S. 245 (1963). In neither case was the power of Congress under the Property Clause at issue or considered and, as we shall see, these dicta fail to account for the raft of cases in which the Clause has been given a broader construction.[9]

In brief, beyond the *Fort Leavenworth* and *Paul* dicta, appellees have presented no support for their position that the Clause grants Congress only the power to dispose of, to make incidental rules regarding the use of, and to protect federal property. This failure is hardly surprising, for the Clause, in broad terms, gives Congress the power to determine what are "needful" rules "respecting" the public lands. And while the furthest reaches of the power granted by the Property Clause have not yet been definitively resolved, we have repeatedly observed that "[t]he power over the public land thus entrusted to Congress is without limitations." United States v. San Francisco, 310 U.S., at 29.

* * *

The decided cases have supported this expansive reading. It is the Property Clause, for instance, that provides the basis for governing the territories of the United States. And even over public land within the States, "[t]he general government doubtless has a power over its own property analogous to the police power of the several states, and the extent to which it may go in the exercise of such power is measured by the exigencies of the particular case." Camfield v. United States, 167 U.S. 518, 525 (1897). We have noted, for example, that the Property Clause gives Congress the power over the public lands "to control their occupancy and use, to protect them from trespass and injury, and to prescribe the conditions upon which others may obtain rights in them * * *." Utah Power & Light Co. v. United States, 243 U.S. 389, 405 (1917). And we have approved legislation respecting the public lands "[i]f it be found to be necessary, for the protection of the public or of intending settlers [on the public lands]." Camfield v. United States, 167 U.S., at 525. In short, Congress exercises the powers both of a proprietor and of a legislature over the public domain. Although the Property Clause does not authorize "an exercise of a general control over public policy in a State," it does permit "an exercise of the complete power which Congress has over particular public property entrusted to it." United States v. San Francisco, 310 U.S., at 30 (footnote omitted). In our view, the "complete power" that Congress has over public lands necessarily includes the power to regulate and protect the wildlife living there.[10]

9. Indeed, Hunt v. United States, 278 U.S. 96 (1928), and Camfield v. United States, 167 U.S. 518 (1897), both relied upon by appellees, are inconsistent with the notion that the United States has only the rights of an ordinary proprietor with respect to its land. An ordinary proprietor may not, contrary to state law, kill game that is damaging his land, as the Government did in *Hunt;* nor may he prohibit the fencing in of his property without the assistance of state law, as the Government was able to do in *Camfield.*

10. Appellees ask us to declare that the Act is unconstitutional because the ani-

mals are not, as Congress found, "fast disappearing from the American scene." § 1 of the Act, 16 U.S.C.A. § 1331. At the outset, no reason suggests itself why Congress' power under the Property Clause to enact legislation to protect wild free-roaming horses and burros "from capture, branding, harassment, or death," ibid., must depend on a finding that the animals are decreasing in number. But responding directly to appellees' contention, we note that the evidence before Congress on this question was conflicting and that Congress weighed the evidence and made a judgment. What appellees ask is that we re-

III

Appellees argue that if we approve the Wild Free-Roaming Horses and Burros Act as a valid exercise of Congress' power under the Property Clause, then we have sanctioned an impermissible intrusion on the sovereignty, legislative authority and police power of the State and have wrongly infringed upon the State's traditional trustee powers over wild animals. The argument appears to be that Congress could obtain exclusive legislative jurisdiction over the public lands in the State only by state consent, and that in the absence of such consent Congress lacks the power to act contrary to state law. This argument is without merit.

Appellees' claim confuses Congress' derivative legislative powers, which are not involved in this case, with its powers under the Property Clause. Congress may acquire derivative legislative power from a state pursuant to Art. I, § 8, cl. 17, of the Constitution by consensual acquisition of land, or by nonconsensual acquisition followed by the State's subsequent cession of legislative authority over the land. Paul v. United States, 371 U.S. 245, 264 (1963); Fort Leavenworth R. Co. v. Lowe, 114 U.S. 525, 541–542 (1885).[11] In either case, the legislative jurisdiction acquired may range from exclusive federal jurisdiction with no residual state police power, to concurrent, or partial, federal legislative jurisdiction, which may allow the State to exercise certain authority.

But while Congress can acquire exclusive or partial jurisdiction over lands within a State by the State's consent or cession, the presence or absence of such jurisdiction has nothing to do with Congress' powers under the Property Clause. Absent consent or cession a State undoubtedly retains jurisdiction over federal lands within its territory, but Congress equally surely retains the power to enact legislation respecting those lands pursuant to the Property Clause. And when Congress so acts, the federal legislation necessarily overrides conflicting state laws under the Supremacy Clause. U.S.Const., Art. VI, cl. 2. See Hunt v. United States, 278 U.S., at 100; McKelvey v. United States, 260 U.S. 353, at 359. As we said in Camfield v. United States, 167 U.S., at 526, in response to a somewhat different claim, "A different rule would place the public domain of the United States completely at the mercy of state legislation."

Thus, appellees' assertion that "[a]bsent state consent by complete cession of jurisdiction of lands to the United States, exclusive jurisdiction does not accrue to the federal landowner with regard to federal lands within the borders of the state," is completely beside the point; and appellees' fear that the Secretary's position is that "the Property Clause totally exempts federal lands within state borders from state

weigh the evidence and substitute our judgment for that of Congress. This we must decline to do.

11. * * * The Clause has been broadly construed, and the acquisition by con-

sent or cession of exclusive or partial jurisdiction over properties for any legitimate governmental purpose beyond those itemized is permissible. Collins v. Yosemite Park Co., 304 U.S. 518, 528–530 (1938).

legislative powers, state police powers, and all rights and powers of local sovereignty and jurisdiction of the states," is totally unfounded. The Federal Government does not assert exclusive jurisdiction over the public lands in New Mexico, and the State is free to enforce its criminal and civil laws on those lands. But where those state laws conflict with the Wild Free-Roaming Horses and Burros Act, or with other legislation passed pursuant to the Property Clause, the law is clear: the state laws must recede.

Again, none of the cases relied upon by appellees are to the contrary. * * *

In short, these cases do not support appellees' claim that upholding the Act would sanction an impermissible intrusion upon state sovereignty. The Act does not establish exclusive federal jurisdiction over the public lands in New Mexico; it merely overrides the New Mexico Estray Law insofar as it attempts to regulate federally protected animals. And that is but the necessary consequence of valid legislation under the Property Clause.

Appellees' contention that the Act violates traditional state power over wild animals stands on no different footing. Unquestionably the States have broad trustee and police powers over wild animals within their jurisdictions. But as Geer v. Connecticut cautions, those powers exist only "in so far as [their] exercise may be not incompatible with, or restrained by, the rights conveyed to the federal government by the constitution." 161 U.S., at 528. "No doubt it is true that as between a State and its inhabitants the State may regulate the killing and sale of [wildlife], but it does not follow that its authority is exclusive of paramount powers." Missouri v. Holland, 252 U.S. 416, 434 (1920). * * * We hold today that the Property Clause also gives Congress the power to protect wildlife on the public lands, state law notwithstanding.

IV

In this case, the New Mexico Livestock Board entered upon the public lands of the United States and removed wild burros. These actions were contrary to the provisions of the Wild Free-Roaming Horses and Burros Act. We find that, as applied to this case, the Act is a constitutional exercise of congressional power under the Property Clause. We need not, and do not, decide whether the Property Clause would sustain the Act in all of its conceivable applications.

Appellees are concerned that the Act's extension of protection to wild free-roaming horses and burros that stray from public land onto private land, § 4 of the Act, 16 U.S.C.A. § 1334, will be read to provide federal jurisdiction over every wild horse or burro that at any time sets foot upon federal land. While it is clear that regulations under the Property Clause may have some effect on private lands not otherwise under federal control, Camfield v. United States, 167 U.S. 518 (1897), we do not think it appropriate in this declaratory judgment proceeding to determine the extent, if any, to which the Property Clause empowers

Congress to protect animals on private lands or the extent to which such regulation is attempted by the Act. * * *

For the reasons stated, the judgment of the District Court is reversed and the case is remanded for further proceedings consistent with this opinion.

It is so ordered.

NOTES

1. Can Kleppe v. New Mexico be reconciled with either the results or the reasoning of Pollard v. Hagan, 44 U.S. (3 How.) 212 (1845), supra at page 72, or of Hicks v. Bell, 3 Cal. 219 (1853), supra at page 192?

2. If, as *Kleppe* states, the federal power over proprietorial lands is plenary and preemptive, what does that say about the limitations in the Enclave Clause? Could Congress unilaterally establish a federal enclave with exclusive jurisdiction? Could it declare that federal jurisdiction will be exclusive on all federal lands? Could Congress by legislation abrogate the right of Kansas to tax railroad property within military reservations and thus undo the reserved jurisdiction in *Fort Leavenworth?* Have the decline of the Enclave Clause and the ascent of the Property Clause in the Supreme Court roughly followed congressional policy as the United States moved from a vendor to a custodian to an active manager? In terms of federal power, has the Property Clause swallowed the Enclave Clause? See generally Gaetke, Refuting the "Classic" Property Clause Theory, 63 N.C.L.Rev. 617 (1985).

3. The Court in *Kleppe* declined to decide whether Congress may regulate the wild burros during those times when they are off federal property. Leaving aside possible sources of federal authority in the Commerce and Treaty Clauses, see Coggins & Hensley, Constitutional Limits on Federal Power to Protect and Manage Wildlife: Is the Endangered Species Act Endangered?, 61 Iowa L.Rev. 1099 (1976), does the Property Clause give Congress authority to regulate activities on private lands if the activities affect the public lands? For an argument in favor of such a power, see Sax, Helpless Giants: The National Parks and the Regulation of Private Lands, 75 Mich.L.Rev. 239 (1976). See also Note, Protecting National Parks From Developments Beyond Their Borders, 132 U.Pa.L.Rev. 1189 (1984), and the authorities cited infra at page 208. No conclusive answer is provided by the decided Supreme Court cases (in part because the United States has rarely asserted any such authority), but ancient and recent opinions offer some conceptual support.

In Camfield v. United States, 167 U.S. 518 (1897) supra at page 108, a federal power to abate fences on adjacent land was confirmed. *Camfield* was followed by United States v. Alford, 274 U.S. 264 (1927). The Act of June 25, 1910, 36 Stat. 855, prohibited leaving unextinguished a fire "in or near" any public forest. Defendant's contention that Congress cannot bar activities on private lands was swept away in typically Holmesian fashion:

The danger depends upon the nearness of the fire, not upon the ownership of the land where it is built. * * *

The statute is constitutional. Congress may prohibit the doing of acts upon privately owned lands that imperil the publicly owned forests.

Then, after *Kleppe* had revived interest in the question, Congress resolved difficult preservation issues in northern Minnesota but did so in a manner that squarely raised the question whether Congress could regulate private inholdings under the Property Clause.

MINNESOTA v. BLOCK

United States Court of Appeals, Eighth Circuit, 1981.
660 F.2d 1240.
Cert. denied, 455 U.S. 1007 (1982).

BRIGHT, Circuit Judge.

These appeals arise from three consolidated cases involving multiple challenges to provisions of the Boundary Waters Canoe Area Wilderness Act of 1978, Pub.L. No. 95–495, 92 Stat. 1649 (BWCAW Act or the Act). On cross motions for summary judgment, the * * * District Court * * * upheld all portions of the Act. In this opinion, we will consider separately two groups of appeals. In Case No. 1, appellants allege that Congress unconstitutionally applied federal controls on the use of motorboats and snowmobiles to land and waters not owned by the United States. In Case No. 2, appellants assert that certain provisions of the legislation violate the Constitution and conflict with preexisting treaties and statutes.

Case No. 1

The State of Minnesota, joined by the National Association of Property Owners (NAPO) and numerous individuals, businesses, and organizations, brought suit against the United States, challenging the constitutionality of the BWCAW Act as applied to lands and waters that the federal government does not own. A group of organizations concerned with the environmental and wilderness aspects of the boundary waters intervened in support of the United States.

The challenged portion of the statute,[4] section 4, prohibits the use of motorboats in the BWCAW in all but a small number of lakes. The Act also limits snowmobiles to two routes. The United States owns ninety percent of the land within the borders of the BWCAW area. The State of Minnesota, in addition to owning most of the remaining ten percent of the land, owns the beds of all the lakes and rivers within the BWCAW.

Appellants assert that Congress had no power to enact the motor vehicle restriction as applied to nonfederal lands and waters. We reject this contention and conclude that Congress, in passing this

---

4. In addition to the provisions challenged here, the Act, *inter alia*, prohibits mining, phases out timber harvesting, and expands the area an additional 45,000 acres. * * *

legislation, acted within its authority under the property clause of the United States Constitution and that such action did not contravene the tenth amendment of the Constitution. Accordingly, we affirm.

I. Background

The Boundary Waters Canoe Area Wilderness (BWCAW), a part of the Superior National Forest, consists of approximately 1,075,000 acres of land and waterways along the Minnesota-Canadian border. * * *

* * *

Beginning with the federal government's first reservation of forest land in 1902, up to the present, both the United States and the State of Minnesota have sought to protect the boundary waters area. Increasingly through the century, the governments have sought to preserve the primitive character of the area. These efforts resulted in the designation of the boundary waters as part of the national wilderness system established under the Wilderness Act of 1964, *as amended*, 16 U.S.C. §§ 1131–36 (1976).

The Wilderness Act of 1964 prohibited use of motorized vehicles in any national wilderness area. That Act, however, provided a specific exception for the Boundary Waters Canoe Area * * *.

In response to the confusion and litigation generated by the proviso, as well as in reaction to threatened deterioration of the wilderness from excessive use, Congress enacted the Boundary Waters Canoe Area Wilderness Act of 1978. At issue here are portions of section 4 of the Act, the provision barring the use of motorized craft in all but designated portions of the wilderness.[9] Section 4(c) limits motorboat use to

9. Section 4 of the Act provides:

Sec. 4. (a) The Secretary shall administer the wilderness under the provisions of this Act, the Act of January 3, 1975 (88 Stat. 2096; 16 U.S.C. 1132 note), the Wilderness Act of 1964 (78 Stat. 890, 16 U.S.C. 1131–1136), and in accordance with other laws, rules and regulations generally applicable to areas designated as wilderness.

(b) Paragraph (5) of section 4(d) of the Wilderness Act of 1964 is hereby repealed * * *.

(c) Effective on January 1, 1979, the use of motorboats is prohibited within the wilderness designated by this Act, and that portion within the wilderness of all lakes which are partly within the wilderness, except for the following:

[listing the lakes where and times when limited powerboating is allowed].

* * *

(f) The Secretary is directed to develop and implement, as soon as practical, entry point quotas for use of motorboats within the wilderness portions of the lakes listed in subsection c, the quota levels to be based on such criteria as the size and configuration of each lake, and the amount of use on that lake: *Provided,* That the quota established for any one year shall not exceed the average actual annual motorboat use of the calendar years 1976, 1977, and 1978 for each lake, and shall take into account the fluctuation in use during different times of the year: *Provided further,* That on each lake homeowners and their guests and resort owners and their guests on that particular lake shall have access to that particular lake and their entry shall not be counted in determining such use.

* * *

(i) *Except for motorboats, snowmobiles, and mechanized portaging, as authorized and defined herein, no other motorized use of the wilderness shall be permitted.* Nothing in this Act shall prohibit the use of aircraft, motorboats, snowmobiles, or other mechanized uses in emergencies, or for the administration of the wilderness area by Federal, State, and local governmental officials or their deputies, only where the Secretary finds that such use is essential. [92 Stat. 1650–52 (emphasis added).]

Appellants specifically challenge subparagraphs (c), (e), (f), and (i).

designated lakes and rivers, allowing a maximum of either ten or twenty-five horsepower motors on these waters. Section 4(g) permits certain limited mechanized portages. Section 4(e) restricts the use of snowmobiles to two designated trails. With these exceptions, the Act as construed by the federal government and by the district court, prohibits all other motorized transportation on land and water falling within the external boundaries of the wilderness area.

The boundaries of the BWCAW circumscribe a total surface area of approximately 1,080,300 acres—920,000 acres of land and 160,000 of water. The United States owns approximately 792,000 acres of land surface, while the State of Minnesota owns approximately 121,000 acres of land,[12] in addition to the beds under the 160,000 acres of navigable water. Congress recognized that Minnesota would retain jurisdiction over the waters, but provided that the State could not regulate in a manner less stringent than that mandated by the Act.

* * *

On appeal, Minnesota and the intervening plaintiffs renew their assertions (1) that Congress acted in excess of its authority under the property clause by curtailing the use of motor-powered boats and other motorized vehicles on lands and waters not owned by the United States; and (2) that the tenth amendment of the United States Constitution bars the application of section 4 to "state-owned" lands and waters.

II. *Property Clause*

* * * In a recent unanimous decision, the Supreme Court upheld an expansive reading of Congress' power under the property clause. See Kleppe v. New Mexico, 426 U.S. 529 (1976). * * *

With this guidance, we must decide the question left open in *Kleppe*—the scope of Congress' property clause power as applied to activity occurring off federal land. Without defining the limits of the power, the Court in *Kleppe*, relying on its decision in Camfield v. United States, 167 U.S. 518 (1897), acknowledged that "it is clear the regulations under the Property Clause may have some effect on private lands not otherwise under federal control." * * *.

Under this authority to protect public land, Congress' power must extend to regulation of conduct on or off the public land that would threaten the designated purpose of federal lands. Congress clearly has the power to dedicate federal land for particular purposes. As a necessary incident of that power, Congress must have the ability to insure that these lands be protected against interference with their intended purposes. As the Supreme Court has stated, under the property clause "[Congress] may sanction some uses and prohibit others, and *may forbid interference with such as are sanctioned.*" McKelvey v. United States, 260 U.S. 353, 359 (1922) (emphasis added).

* * *

12. Private parties own approximately 7,300 acres of land.

Having established that Congress may regulate conduct off federal land that interferes with the designated purpose of that land, we must determine whether Congress acted within this power in restricting the use of motorboats and other motor vehicles in the BWCAW. In reviewing the appropriateness of particular regulations, "we must remain mindful that, while courts must eventually pass upon them, determinations under the Property Clause are entrusted primarily to the judgment of Congress." Kleppe v. New Mexico, supra, 426 U.S. at 536. Thus, if Congress enacted the motorized use restrictions to protect the fundamental purpose for which the BWCAW had been reserved, and if the restrictions in section 4 reasonably relate to that end, we must conclude that Congress acted within its constitutional prerogative.

Congress passed the BWCAW Act with the clear intent of insuring that the area would remain as wilderness and could be enjoyed as such. Specifically concerning the motor use regulations, Congressman Fraser, in introducing the 1978 Act, stated:

> The bill has four major thrusts. First, and most important, it seeks to end those activities that threaten the integrity of the BWCA's wilderness character by expressly prohibiting the following uses:
>
> * * *
>
> Recreational uses of motorized watercraft and snowmobiles * * *.

Congress based its conclusions on certain statutory findings:

> SECTION 1. The Congress finds that it is necessary and desirable to provide for the protection, enhancement, and preservation of the natural values of the lakes, waterways, and associated forested areas known (before the date of enactment of this Act) as the Boundary Waters Canoe Area, and for the orderly management of public use and enjoyment of that area as wilderness, and of certain contiguous lands and waters, while at the same time protecting the special qualities of the area as a natural forest-lakeland wilderness ecosystem of major esthetic, cultural, scientific, recreational and educational value to the Nation. [92 Stat. 1649.]

Hearings and other evidence provided ample support for Congress' finding that use of motorboats and snowmobiles must be limited in order to preserve the area as a wilderness. Testimony established that the sight, smell, and sound of motorized vehicles seriously marred the wilderness experience of canoeists, hikers, and skiers and threatened to destroy the integrity of the wilderness.

As a result of considerable testimony and debate and a series of compromises, Congress enacted section 4 in an attempt to accommodate all interests, determining the extent of motorized use the area might tolerate without serious threat to its wilderness values.[22]

22. We find no merit in appellants' argument that Congress should have banned all motorized travel if it were serious about protecting the wilderness. Congress retains the freedom, as well as the obligation and ability, to balance competing interests.

The motor use restrictions form only a small part of an elaborate system of regulations considered necessary to preserve the BWCAW as a wilderness. The United States owns close to ninety percent of the land surrounding the waters at issue. Congress concluded that motorized vehicles significantly interfere with the use of the wilderness by canoeists, hikers, and skiers and that restricted motorized use would enhance and preserve the wilderness values of the area. From the evidence presented, Congress could rationally reach these conclusions. We hold, therefore, that Congress acted within its power under the Constitution to pass needful regulations respecting public lands.[24]

III. *Tenth Amendment*

*   *   *

[The opinion concluded that the restrictions on motorized vehicles did not contravene the Tenth Amendment under the rationale of National League of Cities v. Usery, 426 U.S. 833 (1976), since overruled in Garcia v. San Antonio Metropolitan Transit Auth., 469 U.S. 528 (1985).]

Case No. 2

In case two, we consider appeals from two consolidated lawsuits brought by the National Association of Property Owners (NAPO) against the United States and the Secretary of Agriculture. *   *   *

*   *   * [A]ppellants allege that section 5 of the Act, which gives the United States a right of first refusal in certain property in the area, violates the takings clause and the due process clause of the fifth amendment. *   *   *

I. *Section 5 Challenge*

*   *   *

A. *Fifth Amendment Taking*

Appellants assert that section 5(c), by establishing in the federal government a right of first refusal on designated property, constitutes a "taking" of property without just compensation. The Local Appellants claim that the statute in and of itself creates a cloud on the title of any property affected, and that the one hundred-day waiting period especially serves to diminish the value of the land by deterring potential buyers. Minnesota argues that the statute automatically creates an option in real property and, therefore, "takes" private property without compensation.

*   *   *

In our view, the mere conditioning of the sale of property, as done with section 5, similarly cannot rise to the level of a taking. Even if some diminution in value results from the passage of section 5(c), any

---

Courts should not lightly set aside the resulting compromises.

24. Like the district court, we need not decide whether Congress could have enacted these regulations pursuant to its commerce clause or treaty making powers.

effect on the landowner's aggregate property rights would be minimal. Section 5(c) does not interfere with the owner's use or enjoyment of his property; it does not compel the surrender of the land or any portion thereof; it does not affect the owner's ability to give his property or to transfer it in any manner to members of his immediate family. Section 5(c) may affect slightly an owner's ability to alienate property, but it has little effect on even that "strand" in the bundle of property rights. We hold, therefore, that section 5(c), on its face, does not unlawfully take property in violation of the fifth amendment.

* * *

Affirmed.

NOTES

1. Should the same rules that apply to federal preemption of state law governing activities on private lands within or adjacent to federal lands also apply to federal laws affecting activities on state lands? Does Congress have constitutional power to regulate subject matter such as signs and noise on private inholdings within federal reservations? On adjacent lands outside of federal boundaries? Can Congress use the Property Clause to prohibit all hunting of migrating animals whose habitat is on the public lands only during certain seasons of the year?

2. Did the restrictions in Minnesota v. Block constitute a "taking"? How great a diminution in value need private property owners show in order to compel government compensation? Are the prohibitions against snowmobile and motorboat use significant encumbrances on the alienability of private property? For a general discussion of environmental regulation and "taking," see W. Rodgers, ENVIRONMENTAL LAW § 2.17 (1977).

3. See generally Gaetke, The Boundary Waters Canoe Area Wilderness Act of 1978: Regulating Non-Federal Property Under the Property Clause, 60 Or.L.Rev. 157 (1981).

4. Other recent decisions affirm the principle that the Property Clause empowers federal regulation of private activity on private or state lands to protect federal interests in public lands. In United States v. Brown, 552 F.2d 817 (8th Cir.1977), cert. denied, 431 U.S. 949 (1977), Congress had not spoken directly to the question of hunting in Voyageurs National Park in Minnesota. The Park Service regulations, however, prohibited possession of firearms. The defendant, who was duck hunting at a time when hunting was allowed by state law, was found guilty by a federal magistrate and fined $150. The Eighth Circuit held that Minnesota had ceded jurisdiction over the waters overlying submerged lands that passed to Minnesota at statehood. Then, in dictum, the court assumed arguendo that Minnesota had not ceded such jurisdiction. The opinion cited *Kleppe* and *Camfield* in upholding the exercise of federal power over the state-owned inholdings:

The National Park Service Act allows the Secretary of the Interior to promulgate "such rules and regulations as he may deem necessary or proper for the use and management of the parks." 16 U.S.C.A. § 3. The regulations prohibiting hunting and possession of a loaded firearm were promulgated pursuant to that authority, 36 C.F.R. §§ 2.11 and 2.32, and are valid prescriptions designed to promote the purposes of the federal lands within the national park. Under the Supremacy Clause the federal law overrides the conflicting state law allowing hunting within the park.

A direct holding to the same effect was handed down two years later in United States v. Lindsey, 595 F.2d 5 (9th Cir.1979). Defendant built a campfire without permission on state land within the boundaries of Hells Canyon National Recreation Area contrary to a Forest Service regulation. Citing *Alford* and *Kleppe,* the court summarily disposed of defendant's jurisdictional arguments by stating it to be "well established" that the Property Clause "grants to the United States power to regulate conduct on non-federal land when reasonably necessary to protect adjacent federal property or navigable waters." In United States v. Arbo, 691 F.2d 862 (9th Cir.1982), defendant claimed that the federal court had no jurisdiction over a charge of interfering with Forest Service officers because the offense took place on state lands. Relying on *Lindsey,* the court held that the actual location was immaterial because the inspection interfered with would determine if conditions on defendant's claim threatened adjacent federal property. The decision in Free Enterprise Canoe Renters Association v. Watt, 549 F.Supp. 252 (E.D.Mo.1982), aff'd, 711 F.2d 852 (8th Cir.1983), has apparently ended a decade of litigation over nonpermitted rental canoe use in the Ozark National Scenic Riverways. On the basis of Minnesota v. Block, above, the court reversed earlier holdings and held that the National Park Service could prohibit the use of state roads within the federal reservation for canoe pickups by canoe renters without a Park Service permit. See also United States v. Richard, 636 F.2d 236 (8th Cir.1980).

Kleppe, Brown, and Minnesota v. Block all involve inholdings. Should a different test be employed if the federal government seeks to regulate conduct outside the boundaries of a federal installation?

Federal preemption occurs when a state law conflicts with a valid exercise of an enumerated congressional power. The federal law overrides any contrary state laws pursuant to the Supremacy Clause of Article VI. Federal preemption is not always directly implemented by a statute. In United States v. Brown, supra, for example, state law was preempted by a valid administrative regulation; the relevant act of Congress did not expressly prohibit the hunting. The Court has recognized that "agency regulations implementing federal statutes have been held to pre-empt state law under the Supremacy Clause," Chrysler

Corp. v. Brown, 441 U.S. 281, 295–296 (1979), but the agency must be acting within its delegated authority. Should courts scrutinize more strictly when, as in *Brown,* the preemption stems from an agency regulation rather then a statute?

Sometimes Congress states its intention to preempt state law with some certainty and the results are easy to predict. See, e.g., Fouke Co. v. Brown, 463 F.Supp. 1142 (E.D.Cal.1979). More often, the assertedly preemptive federal statute and its legislative history fail to provide a clear indication whether Congress intended to preempt state law or to what extent. The Supreme Court has been quick to find preemption in traditionally federal areas or areas where uniform national regulation is important. Examples are the regulation of aliens, navigation, Indians, labor, and civil rights. See generally L. Tribe, AMERICAN CONSTITUTIONAL LAW 376–401 (1978); Note, The Preemption Doctrine: Shifting Perspectives on Federalism and the Burger Court, 75 Colum.L.. Rev. 623 (1975). In many other areas, where there is no tradition of pervasive federal action or other compelling federal need, the Court has, in effect, developed a presumption that Congress did not intend to preempt state law; the presumption will be overcome only by a reasonably clear showing of congressional intent to preempt. Cf. Pacific Gas & Electric Co. v. State Energy Resources Conservation & Development Comm'n, 461 U.S. 190, 206, 216 (1983).

Congress, as the legislature of a government with enumerated powers, is not ordinarily in the business of enacting laws to implement a police power. Although the federal legislative program has been vastly expanded in the past half century, it is, nevertheless, only the states that have used the full panoply of sovereign police powers in enacting laws dealing with business transactions, crimes, motor vehicle traffic, transaction and property taxes, health and safety, building codes, zoning, wildlife, education, and so forth. In addition, important rights and privileges derive from state laws, including the right to vote, to attend elementary and secondary schools, and to receive sewer service and fire protection, to name only a few. A comprehensive, ordered legal system on the public lands, therefore, must of necessity draw heavily on state law. State law continues to govern private activities on the public lands until it is preempted by supreme federal law.

The conflict between state and federal law in Kleppe v. New Mexico was irreconcilable: New Mexico law provided that the burros could be rounded up, sold, and killed, while federal law prohibited harassment, sale, or killing. Seldom is the incompatibility so clear cut. In most cases, Congress has been solicitous of state sensibilities when enacting federal regulatory programs, and the existence or extent of incompatibility between federal and state law becomes more difficult to determine. Questions of ultimate federal power were conclusively resolved in *Kleppe:* Congress can preempt state authority on the public lands. The more frequent and vexing question is whether, in particular contexts, Congress intended to do so. The following cases explore that question.

STATE EX REL. COX v. HIBBARD
Supreme Court of Oregon, 1977.
31 Or.App. 269, 570 P.2d 1190.

THORNTON, Judge.

Defendants appeal from a decree enjoining them from removing in excess of 50 cubic yards of material in any calendar year from Forest Creek in Jackson County, Oregon, without obtaining a permit from the Director of the Division of State Lands pursuant to ORS. 541.615(1).

Plaintiff's complaint for mandatory injunction alleged that defendants "removed the top layer of soil in and near Forest Creek by causing a trench to be dug approximately 200 feet long and from 6 to 10 feet wide, which soil was left to form a vertical unstable bank" and sought a decree requiring defendants to restore Forest Creek to its original condition and "[f]or such other relief as may deem to the Court to be reasonable and proper."

Defendants advance nine assignments of error. The first three assignments all arise out of a trial court order sustaining a demurrer to defendants' second affirmative defense. Defendants' second affirmative defense is a federal preemption claim in which it is alleged that "defendants have been and now are the owners of the Gold Dust placer unpatented mining claims Nos. 1 through 8, in Section 31, Township 17 South, Range 3 West, W.M., in the Upper Applegate Mining District, Jackson County, Oregon, subject only to the paramount title of the United States. Said ground was duly and regularly located on public domain land of the United States." Defendants then invoke the Property Clause of the United States Constitution, Art. IV, § 3, clause 2, the Supremacy Clause of the United States Constitution, Art. VI, clause 2, federal mining laws, 30 U.S.C.A. § 21 et seq. and an "Acceptance by Oregon of Propositions Offered by Congress in Admission Act" approved by the Oregon Legislative Assembly June 3, 1859, and assert the unconstitutionality of ORS 541.605 to 541.695 as applied to federal lands.

By way of background we should state that there are four general kinds of federal jurisdiction over federal lands: exclusive legislative jurisdiction, concurrent legislative jurisdiction, partial legislative jurisdiction and proprietorial legislative jurisdiction.

Exclusive, concurrent and partial legislative jurisdiction are dependent on the Jurisdiction Clause, Art. 1, § 8, clause 17, United States Constitution, and specific agreements between the state and federal governments with respect to a particular parcel of land. Since the defendants in this case have not asserted a Jurisdiction Clause claim, have not asserted that the Admission Act of 1859 applies to the land on which they mine their claim [5] and have not indicated in this record the nature or extent of the United States' interest in the land, we assume that interest is proprietorial.

The Supreme Court of Idaho has recently rejected a claim similar to that advanced here, finding no express or implied federal preemption. The defendants in State ex rel. Andrus v. Click, 97 Idaho 791, 554 P.2d 969 (1976), like the defendants in this case, asserted that federal preemption of state environmental regulation on federal land based on the Property Clause, the Supremacy Clause and federal mining laws, 30 U.S.C.A. § 21 et seq., prohibited the state from requiring defendants to obtain a permit prior to mining their claim. In rejecting defendants' preemption claim, the Idaho Supreme Court noted:

"* * * [W]e find nothing in the federal statute or its legislative history to indicate an intent to preempt state regulation. Indeed, the federal statute specifically recognizes the state's right to impose additional requirements in some areas. For example, even where standards are set for the location of mining claims, nonconflicting state requirements are upheld. 30 U.S.C. § 26; I.C. § 47–601 et seq.

"Nor can the federal statute be characterized as a pervasive regulatory scheme. If anything, the federal statute is characterized by its absence of regulation. Although the Forest Service recently promulgated regulations which purport to give them a greater part in the control of mining operations, 39 Fed.Reg. 31317 21, both these regulations and the statutes authorizing their promulgation specifically recognize the viability of existing state regulations. 16 U.S.C. §§ 551, 551a.

"We also fail to find preemptive qualities in the nature of the subject matter regulated. * * * Indeed, the preservation of the environmental quality of its lands is a subject particularly suited to administration by the states. Congress has recognized that even where extensive federal environmental legislation exists, the primary responsibility for implementing environmental policy rests with state and local governments. 42 U.S.C. § 4371(b)(2); see also 42 U.S.C. § 4331(a)." 97 Idaho at 798, 554 P.2d at 976.

We likewise conclude that federal mining laws do not indicate an intent to preempt state regulation and we find no conflict between any particular provision of the federal mining laws and ORS 541.605 to 541.695. See, Kleppe v. New Mexico, 426 U.S. 529 (1976); Omaechevarria v. Idaho, 246 U.S. 343 (1918);

* * *

In summary, neither the United States Constitution, the Admission Act nor the federal mining laws preempts the state's authority to require defendants to obtain a state permit prior to digging a water

---

5. * * *

We note that both parties in this case appear to have confused Jurisdiction Clause claims and Property Clause claims. See, Kleppe v. New Mexico, 426 U.S. 529 (1976).

diversion trench in and near Forest Creek; the Oregon Fill and Removal Law (ORS 541.605 et seq.) and the actions taken by plaintiff pursuant to the same did not constitute an unconstitutional impairment of contract either with the federal government or the state government pursuant to the federal and state mining and water laws; * * * Lastly, we see no conflict between the Fill and Removal Law, the state mining laws and the provisions governing the authority of the Rogue River Coordination Board. Each performs a separate function.

Ventura County v. Gulf Oil Corporation, et al., No. CV76–1723–ALS (CD Cal., filed April 7, 1977), cited by defendants, is distinguishable. There the county by its zoning ordinance was attempting to prohibit Gulf Oil from conducting any and all oil exploration and extraction activities. Requiring the holder of a permit to mine on federal lands to obtain a permit under a state environmental protection law as in the case at bar is not the same as the banning of all mining activity as was the case in *Ventura*. See Texas Oil and Gas Corp. v. Phillips Petroleum Co., 277 F.Supp. 366 (WD Okl.1967), aff'd 406 F.2d 1303 (10th Cir.), cert. denied 396 U.S. 829 (1969).

Affirmed.

VENTURA COUNTY v. GULF OIL CORP.

United States Court of Appeals, Ninth Circuit, 1979.
601 F.2d 1080, affirmed without opinion, 445 U.S. 947 (1980).

HUFSTEDLER, Circuit Judge.

The question on appeal is whether the County of Ventura ("Ventura") can require the federal Government's lessee, Gulf Oil Corporation ("Gulf"), to obtain a permit from Ventura in compliance with Ventura's zoning ordinances governing oil exploration and extraction activities before Gulf can exercise its rights under the lease and drilling permits acquired from the Government. The district court denied Ventura's motion for a preliminary injunction, and dismissed Ventura's second amended complaint. Ventura appeals. * * *

On January 1, 1974, the Department of the Interior, Bureau of Land Management, pursuant to the Mineral Lands Leasing Act of 1920 (30 U.S.C.A. §§ 181 et seq.), leased 120 acres located within the Los Padres National Forest in Ventura for purposes of oil exploration and development. A subsequent assignment of this lease to Gulf was approved by the Department of the Interior, effective April 1, 1974. On February 25, 1976, the United States Department of the Interior, Geological Survey, issued a permit approving Gulf's proposal to drill an oil well pursuant to its lease. On March 8, 1976, and April 15, 1976, the United States Department of Agriculture, Forest Service, also granted its permission, and on March 8, 1976, the California Resources Agency, Division of Oil and Gas, approved the proposed exploration. After drilling operations were commenced on April 28, 1976, Gulf pursued activities related to oil exploration and extraction on the leased property, and it intends to continue development of both its present and other drill sites.

Throughout this period the leased property has been zoned Open Space ("O–S") by Ventura. Under its zoning ordinance, oil exploration and extraction activities are prohibited on O–S property unless an Open Space Use Permit is obtained from the Ventura County Planning Commission in accordance with Articles 25 and 43 of the Ventura County Ordinance Code. The O–S Use Permits are granted for such time and upon such conditions as the Planning Commission considers in the public interest. The permits contain 11 mandatory conditions and additional conditions are committed to the Planning Board's discretion.

On May 5, 1976, Ventura advised Gulf that it must obtain an O–S Use Permit if it wished to continue its drilling operations. Gulf refused to comply, and on May 20, 1976, Ventura brought suit * * *.

* * *

Although Ventura and amicus argue extensively that congressional enactments under the Property Clause generally possess no preemptive capability, we believe that Kleppe v. New Mexico (1976) 426 U.S. 529, is dispositive. * * *

* * * In light of *Kleppe,* the renewed attempt to restrict the scope of congressional power under the Property Clause in the present case is legally frivolous.

Ventura next contends that even if Congress had the power to enact overriding legislation, there is no evidence of either a congressional intent to preempt local regulation or a conflict between local and federal law that can be resolved only by exclusion of local jurisdiction. We need not consider the extent to which local regulation of any aspect of oil exploration and extraction upon federal lands is precluded by federal legislation; the local ordinances impermissibly conflict with the Mineral Lands Leasing Act of 1920 and on this basis alone they cannot be applied to Gulf.

The extensive regulation of oil exploration and drilling under the Mineral Leasing Act is evident from the present record. The basic lease assigned to Gulf in 1974 contains approximately 45 paragraphs including requirements of diligence and protection of the environment as well as reservation of a one-eighth royalty interest in the United States. Because the lands lie within a National Forest, the lease requires Gulf's acceptance of additional Department of Agriculture conditions designed to combat the environmental hazards normally incident to mining operations. Specific drilling permits were also required from the Department of the Interior, Geological Survey, and the Department of Agriculture, Forest Service. The Geological Survey, which has formalized its procedures in accordance with the National Environmental Policy Act of 1969, approved the proposed drilling on February 25, 1976, subject to 10 conditions which assure continued and detailed supervision of Gulf's activities. And on March 8, and April 15, 1976, the Forest Service issued a drilling permit subject to conditions focusing upon protection of the National Forest. Finally, Gulf is subject to the extensive regulations governing oil and gas leasing (43

C.F.R., Part 3100) and both sub-surface and surface operations (30 C.F.R., Part 221) promulgated by the Secretary of the Interior under his authority "to prescribe necessary and proper rules and regulations to do any and all things necessary to carry out and accomplish the purposes" of the act. (30 U.S.C.A. § 189.) And since the lease concerns lands within a National Forest, Secretary of Agriculture regulations governing oil and gas development are also applicable. (36 C.F.R., Part 252.)

Despite this extensive federal scheme reflecting concern for the local environment as well as development of the nation's resources, Ventura demands a right of final approval. Ventura seeks to prohibit further activity by Gulf until it secures an Open Space Use Permit which may be issued on whatever conditions Ventura determines appropriate, or which may never be issued at all. The federal Government has authorized a specific use of federal lands, and Ventura cannot prohibit that use, either temporarily or permanently, in an attempt to substitute its judgment for that of Congress.

The present conflict is no less direct than that in Kleppe v. New Mexico, supra. Like *Kleppe,* our case involves a power struggle between local and federal governments concerning appropriate use of the public lands. That the New Mexico authorities wished to engage in activity that Congress prohibited, while the Ventura authorities wish to regulate conduct which Congress has authorized is a distinction without a legal difference.

*   *   *

Federal Power Commission v. Oregon [infra at page 370] presented a similar question. *   *   *

Ventura attempts to distinguish Federal Power Commission v. Oregon on the basis of reservations of local jurisdiction contained in sections 30 and 32 of the Mineral Lands Leasing Act (30 U.S.C.A. §§ 187, 189).[4] It contends that although preemption was perhaps

---

4. Before its 1978 amendment, section 30 provided in pertinent part:

"Each lease shall contain provisions for the purpose of insuring the exercise of reasonable diligence, skill, and care in the operation of said property; a provision that such rules for the safety and welfare of the miners and for the prevention of undue waste as may be prescribed by said Secretary shall be observed, including a restriction of the workday to not exceeding eight hours in any one day for underground workers except in cases of emergency; provisions prohibiting the employment of any boy under the age of sixteen or the employment of any girl or woman, without regard to age, in any mine below the surface; provisions securing the workmen complete freedom of purchase; provisions requiring the payment of wages at least twice a month in lawful money of the United States, and

providing proper rules and regulations to insure the fair and just weighing or measurement of the coal mined by each miner, and such other provisions as he may deem necessary to insure the sale of the production of such leased lands to the United States and to the public at reasonable prices, for the protection of the interests of the United States, for the prevention of monopoly, and for the safeguarding of the public welfare. None of such provisions shall be in conflict with the laws of the states in which the leased property is situated."

Section 32 provides:

"The Secretary of the Interior is authorized to prescribe necessary and proper rules and regulations and to do any and all things necessary to carry out and accomplish the purposes of this chapter, also to fix and determine the boundary

appropriate in light of the narrow reservations of local jurisdiction in the Federal Power Act, a similar finding in the present case is unwarranted given the broad savings provisions contained in the Mineral Lands Leasing Act.

The proviso in § 187 provides that "[n]one of *such provisions* shall be in conflict with the laws of the states in which the leased property is situated." (30 U.S.C.A. § 187.) But, as Gulf points out, by the use of the language "such provisions," the proviso relates only to the provisions of the preceding sentence. These provisions relate to employment practices, prevention of undue waste and monopoly, and diligence requirements. There is no mention of land use planning controls. Moreover, the proviso assures only that the Secretary of the Interior shall observe state standards in drafting the lease's terms. It is not a recognition of concurrent state jurisdiction.

Nor is the savings clause in § 189 of any avail. After delegating to the Secretary of the Interior broad authority to prescribe rules and regulations necessary to effect the purposes of the act, the section continues:

> "Nothing in this chapter shall be construed or held to affect the rights of the States or other local authority to exercise any rights which they may have, including the right to levy and collect taxes upon improvements, output of mines, or other rights, property, or assets of any lessee of the United States." (30 U.S.C.A. § 189.)

The proviso preserves to the states only "any rights which they may have." While this is an express recognition of the right of the states to tax activities of the Government's lessee pursuant to its lease and has been relied upon in part to uphold forced pooling and well spacing of federal mineral lessee operations (Texas Oil & Gas Corp. v. Phillips Petroleum Co. (W.D.Okl.1967) 277 F.Supp. 366, 371, aff'd (10th Cir.1969) 406 F.2d 1303, 1304), the proviso cannot give authority to the state which it does not already possess. Although state law may apply where it presents "no significant threat to any identifiable federal policy or interest" (Texas Oil & Gas Corp. v. Phillips Petroleum Co., supra, at 371), the states and their subdivisions have no right to apply local regulations impermissibly conflicting with achievement of a congressionally approved use of federal lands and the proviso of § 189 does not alter this principle.

Finally, we are reassured in the correctness of our decision by policy considerations implicitly reflected in the structure and operation of the Mineral Lands Leasing Act of 1920 and the National Environmental Policy Act of 1969 (42 U.S.C.A. §§ 4321 et seq.). As Ventura recognized in filing its second amended complaint, the National Environmental Protection Act ("NEPA") and the guidelines, regulations,

lines of any structure, or oil or gas field, for the purposes of this chapter. Nothing in this chapter shall be construed or held to affect the rights of the States or other local authority to exercise any rights which they may have, including the right to levy and collect taxes upon improvements, output of mines, or other rights, property, or assets of any lessee of the United States."

and Executive Orders issued in pursuance of that act, mandate extensive federal consideration and federal-local cooperation concerning the local, environmental impact of federal action under the Mineral Lands Leasing Act. If federal officials fail to comply with these requirements, Ventura has a remedy against those officials.

Our decision does not mean that local interests will be unheard or unprotected. In rejecting a local veto power while simultaneously guarding local concerns under NEPA, local interests can be represented, the integrity of the federal leases and drilling permits reconciling national energy needs and local environmental interests can be protected, and the ultimate lessee will be responsible to a single master rather than conflicting authority.

Although we recognize that federal incursions upon the historic police power of the states are not to be found without good cause we must affirm because "under the circumstances of this particular case, [the local ordinances] stand as an obstacle to the accomplishment and execution of the full purposes and objectives of Congress." "[W]here those state laws conflict ＊　＊　＊ with other legislation passed pursuant to the Property Clause, the law is clear: The state laws must recede." (Kleppe v. New Mexico, supra, 426 U.S. at 543).

Affirmed.

BRUBAKER v. BOARD OF COUNTY COMMISSIONERS, EL PASO COUNTY

Supreme Court of Colorado, 1982.
652 P.2d 1050.

LOHR, Justice.

The appellants, Earl J. Brubaker, Rexford L. Mitchell and Valco, Inc., are holders of unpatented mining claims located on federal land in Teller and El Paso Counties.

＊　＊　＊

I.

＊　＊　＊

In 1966, 25 mining claims, known as the Avenger Claims, were located in the Pike National Forest in a scenic area visible from U.S. Highway No. 24 west of Colorado Springs.

＊　＊　＊

The appellants duly submitted a proposed operating plan to the [Forest Service] District Ranger, who prepared an Environmental Assessment Report concerning the core drilling operations. This report considered the effect of the proposed activities on the environment and was based on consultation with federal and local officials and concerned private parties. Finding that there would not be a significant effect upon the quality of the human environment as a result of the proposed operations, the Ranger concluded that an environmental impact statement would not be necessary. Some modifications to the plan, however, were imposed by the Ranger in order to minimize the adverse environmental impact of the drilling activity, and the plan was approved as modified. The approved plan called for the drilling of eleven holes, six in El Paso County and five in Teller County. Each hole was to be approximately an inch and seven-eighths in diameter. The operating plan also required the appellants to post a $1500 reclamation bond to guarantee performance of their obligation to restore the land following the drilling operations. The plan further provided that "[t]he operator, while conducting operations authorized by this Operating Plan, shall comply with the regulations of the U.S. Department of Agriculture and all Federal, State, County, and Municipal laws, ordinances, or regulations which are applicable to the area or operations covered by this plan."

The appellants then applied to the Board [of County Commissioners] for a special use permit authorizing drilling of the proposed test holes in El Paso County. El Paso County considered the permit necessary because the appellants' mining claims in the County are located within an A–2 Agricultural zoning district, and "mineral and natural resources extraction" is a permitted use only if such a permit is obtained. Following hearings before the El Paso County Planning Commission and the Board, the permit application was denied by the Board, primarily on the bases that the proposed drilling operations were inconsistent with the long-range plans adopted for El Paso County and were incompatible with the existing and permitted uses on surrounding properties.

The appellants then filed a complaint in the El Paso County District Court for review of the Board's action. [The trial court upheld the County's action.]

* * *

II.

The underlying rationale of the preemption doctrine is that the Supremacy Clause invalidates state laws that "interfere with, or are contrary to, the laws of Congress."

* * *

The appellants do not contend that the Mining Law of 1872 precludes all state legislation concerning mining activities on federal lands. Rather, they assert that the particular action of the Board in this case "stands as an obstacle to the accomplishment and execution of the full purposes and objectives of Congress," and that, for this reason, it is impermissible. We agree.

Federal mining law has its foundation in the Mining Law of 1872. The act declares that:

> Except as otherwise provided, all valuable mineral deposits in lands belonging to the United States * * * shall be free and open to exploration and purchase. * * *

30 U.S.C. § 22 (1976).

As evidenced by this statute, the underlying purpose of the mining laws is to encourage exploration for and development of mineral resources on public lands. See, e.g., United States v. Weiss, 642 F.2d 296 (9th Cir.1981). "The system envisaged by the mining law was that the prospector could go out into the public domain, search for minerals and upon discovery establish a claim to the lands upon which the discovery was made." United States v. Curtis-Nevada Mines, Inc., 611 F.2d 1277, 1281 (9th Cir.1980). However, the Mining Law of 1872 also leaves room for operation of non-conflicting state requirements in this area. Thus, 30 U.S.C. § 22 further provides that the right to explore and purchase lands of the United States is to be exercised "under regulations prescribed by law, and according to the local customs or rules of miners in the several mining districts, so far as the same are applicable and not inconsistent with the laws of the United States." And 30 U.S.C. § 26 qualifies the locator's right of possession and enjoyment upon compliance with "laws of the United States, and with State, territorial, and local regulations not in conflict with the laws of the United States. * * *"

Pursuant to the above provisions, the appellants seek to conduct drilling operations necessary to establish their discovery of valuable mineral deposits on the contested claims. This activity has been subjected to the necessary federal review and approvals, but the Board asserts that it may now deny the appellants the right to use the land in this manner. The Board seeks not merely to supplement the federal scheme, but to prohibit the very activities contemplated and authorized by federal law. Such a veto power is not consistent with the Supremacy Clause.

A similar issue was presented in Ventura County v. Gulf Oil Corp., 601 F.2d 1080 (9th Cir.1979), aff'd without opinion, 445 U.S. 947 (1980) (Ventura County).

* * *

Similarly, the attempt by the Board to prohibit the appellants' drilling operations because they are inconsistent with the long-range plan of the County and with existing, surrounding uses reflects an attempt by the County to substitute its judgment for that of Congress concerning the appropriate use of these lands. Such a veto power does not relate to a matter of peripheral concern to federal law, but strikes at the central purpose and objectives of the applicable federal law. The core drilling program is directed to obtaining information vital to a determination of the validity of the appellants' mining claims. Recognition of a power in the Board to prohibit that activity would contravene the Congressional determination that the lands are "free and open to exploration and purchase," 30 U.S.C. § 22, and so would "stand as an obstacle to the accomplishment and execution of the full purposes and objectives of Congress" under the mining laws.

The trial court concluded that *Ventura County* was distinguishable because the federal law at issue in that case, the Mineral Lands Leasing Act of 1920, 30 U.S.C. §§ 181–263, is more pervasive than the federal scheme embodied in the Mining Law of 1872. Based on this premise it reasoned that, unlike in *Ventura County,* state and local regulations were not precluded here. However, that observation is relevant primarily to the question of whether Congress has occupied an entire field and thereby preempted *all* state and local regulation. Even if Congress has not preempted an entire field, specific state or local laws that conflict with the purposes and objectives of Congressional enactments are nevertheless preempted. Since it is the specific conflict between the Mining Law of 1872 and the application of the Board's zoning ordinance that is at issue in this case, the absence of a pervasive federal scheme is not controlling.

The trial court also concluded that *Ventura County* was distinguishable because, in the present case, the appellants' federally approved operating plan provided an explicit basis for local jurisdiction in stating that: "[t]he operator, while conducting operations authorized by this Operating Plan, shall comply with the regulations of the U.S. Department of Agriculture and all Federal, State, County, and Municipal laws, ordinances, or regulations applicable to the area or operations covered by this plan." We find this distinction unpersuasive. First, the provision only allows for the operation of "applicable" state and local regulations. Since a state law is not applicable if it is preempted, the scope of the provision is dependent upon, rather than determinative of, the proper resolution of the preemption issue. Second, even if this provision were construed as an attempt to preserve state and local laws that otherwise would be preempted, such a savings clause would be void as beyond the power of the Forest Service Ranger issuing the permit. Indeed, the Forest Service regulations governing such operating plans recognize that those plans may not be used to prohibit legislatively authorized mining activities. 36 C.F.R. 252.1 * * *.

Nor is the Board's action saved from preemption by the provisions of 30 U.S.C. §§ 22 and 26 recognizing a role for state and local regulations with respect to mining claims. Both of these statutes provide that such state and local regulations are applicable only to the extent that they are not "inconsistent with" or "in conflict with" the laws of the United States. Thus, the statutes merely recognize a role for nonconflicting state and local laws; they do not authorize state regulations that would bar the very activities authorized by the mining laws.

* * *

In the present case, we are not presented with a challenge to the facial validity of the El Paso zoning ordinances or with the question of whether the appellants could be required to apply for a permit under those ordinances. Rather, we are faced with the issue reserved by the court in State ex rel. Andrus v. Click, 97 Idaho 791, 554 P.2d 969 (1976) [upholding Idaho's right to require hardrock miners on federal lands to apply for permits under the Idaho Dredge and Placer Mining Protection Act.] That is, we consider a specific application of the local regulations so as to prohibit activities authorized by federal legislation.

It is established that state or local regulation supplementing the mining laws is permissible. State and local laws that merely impose reasonable conditions upon the use of federal lands may be enforceable, particularly where they are directed to environmental protection concerns. Indeed, the appellants concede that such regulation is proper. In this case, however, the Board seeks not to regulate but to prohibit the appellants' core drilling activities. In the resolution denying the application the Board stated that its reasons for this action were inconsistency of the appellants' proposed activities with the long-range land use plans of El Paso County and with existing, surrounding uses. This is not denial of a permit because of failure to comply with reasonable regulations supplementing the federal mining laws, but reflects simply a policy judgment as to the appropriate use of the land. That judgment cannot override the conflicting directive of federal legislation. As stated in *Ventura County,* "The federal Government has authorized a specific use of federal lands, and [the county] cannot prohibit that use, either temporarily or permanently, in an attempt to substitute its judgment for that of Congress."

* * *

In the present case, the Board has applied its zoning regulations so as to prohibit a use of federal lands authorized by federal legislation. That action conflicts with the objectives and purposes of Congress reflected in the federal mining laws, and, as stated by the United States Supreme Court, "The State laws must recede."

* * *

GULF OIL CORPORATION v. WYOMING OIL AND GAS CONSERVATION COMMISSION
Supreme Court of Wyoming, 1985.
693 P.2d 227.

ROSE, Justice.

This petition for review concerns the authority of the respondent Wyoming Oil and Gas Conservation Commission (Commission or WOGCC) to impose certain restrictions on the drilling activities of petitioner Gulf Oil Corporation (Gulf) on federal land within this state. The Commission granted Gulf's application for a permit to drill a well on national forest land, subject to the condition that Gulf refrain from using its preferred access route through the village of Story, Wyoming. At issue is whether federal mining and environmental protection laws preempt this state's statutes and rules which allow the Commission to condition federally authorized drilling activities on the basis of identified environmental concerns. Gulf also asserts that, the federal preemption question aside, the Commission's order in this case is not supported by substantial evidence. * * *

FACTS

In compliance with state and federal regulations Gulf sought permission from both WOGCC and the United States Department of the

Interior, Bureau of Land Management (BLM) to drill a wildcat well in the Granite Ridge Field of Sheridan County. The proposed well concerns federally owned minerals in the Big Horn National Forest and is one of several exploratory drillings planned by Gulf in this field. Gulf proposed to obtain access to the well site via state highway and county road through Story. This proposed access, designated the southern route, would require extending the existing county road west of Story for about 3.8 miles over national forest land and property owned jointly by Gulf and Texaco, Inc.

Respondent Story Oil Impact Committee (STOIC), composed of citizens of Story, filed a protest with WOGCC concerning the environmental consequences of Gulf's proposed well and access route. STOIC contended that the drilling and related activities would violate Rule 326 of the Rules and Regulations of the Wyoming Oil and Gas Conservation Commission, which provides in part:

"The owner shall not pollute streams, underground water, or unreasonably damage the surface of the leased premises or other lands."

* * *

The testimony and other evidence presented at the hearing focused on the feasibility and environmental impact of various means of reaching the well site. Representatives from Gulf testified concerning five alternative means of access:

1. The proposed southern access road through Story;

2. The northern access route—an extension of roadway from Gulf's existing well site on private property across national forest land, part of which is subject to Roadless Area Review and Evaluation (RARE II) by the United States Department of Agriculture, Forest Service;

3. The North Piney Creek route which would require the improvement of an existing county bridge;

4. Directional drilling from private property; and

5. Helicopter mobilization.

* * * *

After considering the evidence presented at the hearing, WOGCC, on November 23, 1983, issued its findings of fact and conclusions of law. Findings 9 through 12 describe the consequences of using the proposed southern road:

"9. * * * [The southern road] will go from an elevation of about 5,250 feet to 6,960 feet in a little over two air miles and about 3.8 road miles. To state the obvious, it will be a very steep grade.

"10. Much of this road goes along a limestone cliff. There is a minimal amount of vegetation on it now and there is not likely to be more in the future. About 700 feet of this will be visible from 80 percent of Story, and an additional 1,000 feet of road will be visible from various points in the area. Much would be visible from Interstate Highway 90.

"11. The road will also run close to the Story Penrose Trail, as shown on Gulf Exhibit 2. This trail is a major access route for recreational purposes (hiking, birdwatching, hunting, and fishing) to various lakes, creeks, and the Cloud Peak Primitive Area in the Big Horn National Forest.

"12. Due to the extreme grade of the road and its crossing of the limestone cliff, it will be impossible to reclaim a considerable portion of the road. Some parts will be a permanent scar on the landscape."

* * *

The Commission concluded that the proposed southern access road to the drill site would leave a nonreclaimable scar on the side of the mountain and, therefore, constituted unreasonable land surface damage. The Commission further concluded that Gulf had failed to prove a lack of any reasonable alternative to the southern road:

"It appears there are other feasible alternatives discussed in the Environmental Assessment. We prefer to let the Bureau of Land Management, the Forest Service, and Gulf consider these alternatives in the future. Before a permit would be granted for a route that would cause surface damage such as the southern route, the owner must prove to this Commission that there is no reasonable alternative. Gulf has failed to meet this burden of proof."

* * *

FEDERAL PREEMPTION

* * *

Gulf takes the position that federal regulation of the environmental consequences of its proposed well and access route is extensive and, therefore, exclusive. Since federally owned minerals are involved, the Mineral Lands Leasing Act of 1920, 30 U.S.C. § 181 et seq., and associated regulations promulgated by the Secretary of the Interior, 43 C.F.R. Part 3100, govern Gulf's activities. The United States Forest Service, Department of Agriculture, has jurisdiction over any surface disturbance caused by Gulf's drilling activities and road construction on national forest land. 16 U.S.C. §§ 478 and 551; 36 C.F.R. Part 228. Further, the National Environmental Policy Act of 1969 mandates that all federal laws and regulations be interpreted and administered in accordance with the policy of environmental protection. 42 U.S.C. § 4332. See Cabinet Mountains Wilderness/Scotchman's Peak Grizzly Bears v. Peterson, 685 F.2d 678 (D.C.Cir.1982). This comprehensive scheme of federal regulation leaves no room for the states to regulate the environmental effects of drilling activities on federal property, Gulf urges.

Our examination of the federal legislation cited by Gulf compels a contrary conclusion. We find that Congress, far from excluding state participation, has prescribed a significant role for local governments in the regulation of the environmental impact of mineral development on federal land.

We note at the outset that a state retains jurisdiction over national forest land within its boundaries and that the state is free to enforce its criminal and civil laws on that land. State police power extends over the public domain unless preempted by federal legislation enacted pursuant to the property clause.

Two specific provisions in the Mineral Lands Leasing Act, 30 U.S.C. §§ 187 and 189, indicate an absence of congressional intent to assert exclusive control over federal lands leased for mineral development. Section 187 provides in pertinent part:

> " * * * Each lease shall contain provisions for the purpose of insuring the exercise of reasonable diligence, skill, and care in the operation of said property * * *. None of such provisions shall be in conflict with the laws of the State in which the leased property is situated."

Section 189 protects the traditional rights of the states over federal land:

> " * * * Nothing in this chapter shall be construed or held to affect the rights of the States or other local authority to exercise any rights which they may have, including the right to levy and collect taxes upon improvements, output of mines, or other rights, property, or assets of any lessee of the United States."

The Tenth Circuit Court of Appeals relied upon these provisions in Texas Oil & Gas Corp. v. Phillips Petroleum Company, 406 F.2d 1303 (10th Cir.1969), cert. denied 396 U.S. 829, in upholding well spacing and forced pooling orders issued to federal lessees by the Oklahoma Corporation Commission. The court concluded that the act itself refuted the lessees' argument that the federal government, by statutes and regulations, had effectively asserted exclusive jurisdiction to regulate the exploration, development, and conservation of federal lands for oil and gas.

Gulf contends that the myriad administrative regulations respecting the development of minerals on public property support its claim of exclusive federal jurisdiction over the matter. However, these regulations emphasize the viability of pertinent state rules. The Department of Interior requires that:

> "All operations * * * shall be conducted to prevent unnecessary or undue degradation of the Federal lands and shall comply with all pertinent Federal and State laws * * *." 43 C.F.R. § 3809.2–2.

The Department of Agriculture specifies that compliance with state mining laws can satisfy the federal requirement that all mining activities be conducted so as to minimize adverse environmental activities on national forest land. 36 C.F.R. § 228.8(h).

The National Environmental Policy Act of 1969, supra, and the Environmental Quality Improvement Act of 1970, 42 U.S.C. § 4371 et seq., expressly designate state and local governments as the principal protectors of environmental values.

* * *

In contrast to the zoning ordinances at issue in *Ventura County* and *Brubaker,* mining permit requirements designed to safeguard the environment have received favorable treatment in the courts. These latter regulations constitute legitimate means of guiding mineral development without prohibiting it.

* * *

The reasoning in these cases concerning local environmental regulation applies to the restrictions imposed on Gulf by WOGCC pursuant to Rule 326, supra. The Commission has neither prohibited mineral development authorized by Congress nor mandated the use of a particular means of access. Instead, the Commission has granted Gulf a conditional permit to drill, based on its dual findings that the southern route inflicts unreasonable surface damage and feasible alternatives apparently exist. This action by WOGCC under Rule 326 implements the national policy of environmental protection by assuring that mineral development on federal property will be conducted so as to minimize the harm to surface resources.

In summary, we find no intent by Congress to exclude states from regulating mining activities on federal land so as to safeguard environmental values. Neither do we find a direct conflict between Rule 326 and federal laws or objectives. We hold, therefore, that federal mining and environmental protection laws do not preempt WOGCC Rule 326, supra, or the enabling statute. These state enactments provide valid authority for the Commission to condition Gulf's permit to drill on national forest land for federally owned minerals.

* * *

SUBSTANTIAL EVIDENCE TO SUPPORT THE COMMISSION'S ORDER

* * *

Although Gulf representatives testified as to the impossibility of reaching the proposed drill site by either helicopter mobilization or the northern route, federal reports before the Commission indicate the feasibility of these means of access. We conclude, therefore, that substantial evidence in the record supports the Commission's finding that Gulf failed to prove the absence of reasonable alternatives to the objectionable southern access road. We will not set aside the Commission's order based on that legally valid finding.

The order of the Commission granting permission to drill, provided Gulf not use its proposed southern access route, is affirmed.

ROONEY, Justice, dissenting, with whom BROWN, Justice, joins.

I believe the majority opinion reaches beyond the stars in its effort to find existence of authority in the Wyoming Oil and Gas Conservation

Commission to decide where access roads shall be constructed over privately or publicly owned lands *under the guise of environmental control.*

Because the word "conservation" is in the name of the Commission, the majority opinion now gives the job of protecting the environment to the Commission. Quite a reach! First, the Commission's job is to "conserve" oil and gas and protect correlative rights—nothing else. And second, another agency is charged with environmental protection.

* * *

I do not believe that we need to address the federal preemption issue. The Oil and Gas Conservation Commission had no jurisdiction over the question of whether or not an access road was improper on the basis of environmental injury.

* * *

NOTES

1. Can these four cases be reconciled? Should the Ninth Circuit in *Ventura County* have reviewed the actual workings of the local ordinances in the manner that the Wyoming Supreme Court in *Gulf Oil* reviewed the state administrative procedures in order to see if the ordinances amounted to a veto of mineral development on the public lands? Can attorneys for states and counties draft regulations that will afford substantial environmental protection but not run afoul of the federal hardrock mining laws? Of the federal mineral leasing laws?

Another major case on these issues is Granite Rock Co. v. California Coastal Comm'n, 768 F.2d 1077 (9th Cir.1985), 106 S.Ct. 1489 (1986) (postponing question of jurisdiction until hearing of case on the merits), excerpted in the materials on hardrock mining, infra at page 490. See also, e.g., Elliott v. Oregon International Mining Co., 60 Or.App. 474, 654 P.2d 663 (1982), involving facts and law similar to *Brubaker,* and Kirkpatrick Oil and Gas Co. v. United States, 675 F.2d 1122 (10th Cir. 1982), holding that federal law preempted state-forced commutization of a federal oil and gas lease.

2. Two cases only tangentially related to public land law are relevant to these preemption questions. The Clean Air Act of 1970, 42 U.S.C.A. § 1857(f) (1976) (since amended), provided that all federal facilities "shall comply with federal, state, interstate, and local requirements respecting control and abatement of air pollution to the same extent that any person is subject to such requirements." In Hancock v. Train, 426 U.S. 167 (1976), the Court held that this language did not mean that the United States had to obtain a state permit as all other polluters did. The statute was deemed ambiguous, and the court found that the federal government is immune from state regulation in the absence of clear congressional waiver:

> Taken with the "old and well-known rule that statutes which in general terms divest pre-existing rights or privileges will not be applied to the sovereign" [citing, inter alia, United States v. Knight, 14 Pet. 301, 315 (1840)] "without a clear expression or

implication to that effect," this immunity means that where "Congress does not affirmatively declare its instrumentalities or property subject to regulation," "the federal function must be left free" of regulation. (footnotes omitted). Id. at 179.

The "clear expression" rule in *Hancock* was not cited two years later when the Court decided California v. United States, 438 U.S. 645 (1978). The Bureau of Reclamation sought to build the New Melones Dam on the Stanislaus River in California as part of the massive Central Valley Project. Much of the water was to be used for irrigation purposes. The Bureau applied to the State Water Resources Control Board for a permit to appropriate water, i.e., to obtain water rights. The Board approved the application but attached 25 conditions, including measures to protect fish and wildlife and a requirement that there could be no full impoundment until firm commitments were made for the use of the water. The Bureau of Reclamation then sought a declaration in federal court that it was entitled to impound unappropriated water without complying with the conditions imposed pursuant to state law.

The majority opinion, written by Justice Rehnquist, held that the Bureau was bound by state law. The Court based its decision on Section 8 of the Reclamation Act of 1902, 43 U.S.C.A. § 383, providing that "nothing in this Act shall be construed * * * to in any way interfere with the laws of any state relating to the use or distribution of water used in irrigation * * *." In a lengthy opinion tracing the longstanding deference of Congress to state water law and the legislative history of the 1902 Act, the Court found that "if the term 'cooperative federalism' had been in vogue in 1902, the Reclamation Act of that year would certainly have qualified as a leading example of it."

In concluding that state law had not been preempted, the majority distinguished a line of cases, many of which also involved the Central Valley Project. The earlier opinions had seemed to indicate that state law governed only the acquisition of rights to unappropriated water, a point the Bureau of Reclamation did not dispute. In Ivanhoe Irrigation Dist. v. McCracken, 357 U.S. 275, 291–92 (1958), for example, the Court had stated that "as we read § 8, it merely requires the United States to comply with state law when * * * it becomes necessary for it to acquire water rights or vested rights therein. * * * We read nothing in § 8 that compels the United States to deliver water on conditions imposed by the State." The majority in California v. United States stated that "we disavow the dictum" in *Ivanhoe* and other cases.

The sharply-worded dissent by three Justices argued that state law had been preempted by the 1902 Act and that the earlier cases were binding: "only the revisionary zeal of the present majority can explain its misreading of our cases and its evident willingness to disregard them." 438 U.S. at 693. In any event, the majority seemed willing to go out of its way to find that state law was applicable. See, e.g., Kelley, Staging a Comeback—Section 8 of the Reclamation Act, 18 U.C.D.L. Rev. 97 (1984); Neeley-Kvarne, Federal Water Projects After California

v. United States: What Rights do the State and Federal Governments Have in the Water?, 11 U.C.D.L.Rev. 401 (1978).

After California v. United States, could a state totally frustrate the purposes of the federal reclamation program? Could it, for instance declare that industrial uses or in-stream flow have a higher priority to the water impounded by the federal project than agricultural uses? Could it require the Bureau of Reclamation to conform to California dam construction and safety standards? Could the state effectively reject the dam altogether?

On remand in California v. United States, the district court upheld most of the state's conditions but invalidated seven of them on grounds that they conflicted with congressional aims or intent. On appeal, the Ninth Circuit ruled the federal government had failed to show that any of the conditions was inconsistent with the federal Act. The court remanded the case for consideration of whether the future exercise of certain conditions could run afoul of congressional intent. United States v. California, 509 F.Supp. 867 (E.D.Cal.1981), affirmed in part, reversed in part, 694 F.2d 1171 (9th Cir.1982).

3. Where title to land is concerned, a federal "common law" may override state law in some instances. In United States v. Little Lake Misere Land Co. 412 U.S. 580 (1973), the Court held that federal land purchases for refuge purposes were not necessarily defined by state law. That holding was extended in United States v. Albrecht, 496 F.2d 906 (8th Cir.1974). The defendants' assignors had sold a "waterfowl easement" to the FWS, which included a prohibition against draining the prairie potholes on the land. A "stealthy ditchdigger" caused the area to be drained, and suit was brought to force defendants to fill in the ditches. Defendants argued that North Dakota did not recognize the easement at issue and it was therefore invalid. The court replied:

> *   *   * under the context of this case, while the determination of North Dakota law in regard to the validity of the property right conveyed to the United States would be useful, it is not controlling, particularly if viewed as aberrant or hostile to federal property rights. Assuming *arguendo* that North Dakota law would not permit the conveyance of the right to the United States in this case, the specific federal governmental interest in acquiring rights to property for waterfowl production areas is stronger than any possible "aberrant" or "hostile" North Dakota law that would preclude the conveyance granted in this case. *Little Lake,* supra at 595, 596. We fully recognize that laws of real property are usually governed by the particular states; yet the reasonable property right conveyed to the United States in this case effectuates an important national concern, the acquisition of necessary land for waterfowl production areas, and should not be defeated by any possible North Dakota law barring the conveyance of this property right. To hold otherwise would be to permit the possibility that states could rely on local property laws to

defeat the acquisition of reasonable rights to their citizens' property pursuant to 16 U.S.C. § 718(c) and to destroy a national program of acquiring property to aid in the breeding of migratory birds. We, therefore, specifically hold that the property right conveyed to the United States in this case, whether or not deemed a valid easement or other property right under North Dakota law, was a valid conveyance under federal law and vested in the United States the rights as stated therein. Section 718d(c) specifically allows the United States to acquire wetland and pothole areas and the "interests therein."

North Dakota v. United States, 460 U.S. 300 (1983), also dealt with federal acquisition of waterfowl easements. Under the Migratory Bird Conservation Act, land acquisitions by the United States Fish and Wildlife Service must receive the consent of the state, 16 U.S.C.A. § 715f. The Supreme Court held that North Dakota could not revoke its consent after acquisitions had been made. Further, citing *Little Lake Misere Land Co.*, the Court struck down a state statute authorizing land owners to drain wetlands created after the negotiation of federal waterfowl agreements insofar as the law was contrary to existing easement agreements. The statute was "hostile to federal interests" because "the United States is authorized to incorporate into easement agreements such rules and regulations as the Secretary of Interior deems necessary for the protection of wildlife, 16 U.S.C.A. § 715e, and these regulations may include restrictions on land outside the legal description of the easement."

4. The intergovernmental immunities doctrine and the broad-based federal power to preempt state law on the public lands give the federal government virtually total protection against the imposition of state law. The United States, however, can waive those protections. In California v. United States, supra, the Court held state law applicable to a federal irrigation project because it thought Congress had explicitly so directed. Several recent statutes have employed the notion of "cooperative federalism" to require federal land management agencies to comply with state and local law "to the maximum extent practicable" in various contexts. FLPMA imposes such a requirement on the BLM in its land use planning. 43 U.S.C.A. § 1712. See also id. §§ 1720, 1721(c), 1733(d), 1747, 1765(a); National Forest Management Act, 16 U.S.C.A. § 1612; Fish and Wildlife Coordination Act, 16 U.S. C.A. § 661; Intergovernmental Cooperation Act, 42 U.S.C.A. §§ 4231–33; American Motorcyclist Ass'n v. Watt, 534 F.Supp. 923 (C.D.Cal. 1981), aff'd, 714 F.2d 962 (9th Cir.1983), infra at page 739.

5. In Citizens and Landowners Against the Miles City/New Underwood Powerline v. Secretary of Energy, 683 F.2d 1171 (8th Cir.1982), plaintiffs challenged the construction of a federal power line. FLPMA provides that "each right-of-way shall [comply] with state standards for public health and safety, environmental protection, and siting, construction, operation, and maintenance of or for rights-of-way * * * if

those standards are more stringent than applicable federal standards."
43 U.S.C.A. § 1765(a).   A non-profit citizens group insisted that the
quoted FLPMA provision required the federal government to obtain a
state permit.   The court disagreed, holding that the project had to meet
state-imposed substantive powerline siting guidelines, but that the
federal agency need not obtain a state permit.   For similar holdings,
see Montana v. Johnson, 738 F.2d 1074 (9th Cir.1984); Columbia Basin
Land Protection Association v. Schlesinger, 643 F.2d 585, 602–06 (9th
Cir.1981).

COMMONWEALTH EDISON CO. v. MONTANA
Supreme Court of the United States, 1981.
453 U.S. 609.

Justice MARSHALL delivered the opinion of the Court.

Montana, like many other States, imposes a severance tax on
mineral production in the State.   In this appeal, we consider whether
the tax Montana levies on each ton of coal mined in the State, Mont.
Code § 15–35–101 et seq. (1979), violates the Commerce and Supremacy
Clauses of the United States Constitution.

I

Buried beneath Montana are large deposits of low sulfur coal, most
of it on federal land.   Since 1921, Montana has imposed a severance tax
on the output of Montana coal mines, including coal mined on federal
land.   After commissioning a study of coal production taxes in 1974, in
1975, the Montana Legislature enacted the tax schedule at issue in this
case.   Mont.Code § 15–35–103 (1979).   The tax is levied at varying rates
depending on the value, energy content, and method of extraction of
the coal, and may equal at a maximum, 30% of the "contract sales
price."[1]   *   *   *

Appellants, 4 Montana coal producers and 11 of their out-of-state
utility company customers, filed these suits in Montana state court in
1978.   They sought refunds of over $5.4 million in severance taxes paid
under protest, a declaration that the tax is invalid under the Supremacy and Commerce Clauses, and an injunction against further collection
of the tax.   Without receiving any evidence the court upheld the tax
and dismissed the complaints.

On appeal, the Montana Supreme Court affirmed the judgment of
the trial court.

*   *   *

[In Part II A of its opinion, the Court disapproved language in
Heisler v. Thomas Colliery Co., 260 U.S. 245 (1922), which had stated

---

1. Under   Mont.Code   § 15–35–103
(1979), the value of the coal is determined
by the "contract sales price" which is defined as "the price of coal extracted and
prepared for shipment f. o. b. mine, excluding the amount charged by the seller to
pay taxes paid on production *   *   *."

§ 15–35–102(1) (1979).   Taxes paid on production are defined in § 15–35–102(6)
(1979).   Because production taxes are excluded from the computation of the value
of the coal, the effective rate of the tax is
lower than the statutory rate.

that a tax imposed before the goods enter the stream of interstate commerce is immune from Commerce Clause scrutiny. In Part II B, the Court upheld the tax under the test in Complete Auto Transit, Inc. v. Brady, 430 U.S. 274 (1977), whereby a tax will be sustained if it "is applied to an activity with a substantial nexus with the taxing state, is fairly apportioned, does not discriminate against interstate commerce, and is fairly related to services provided by the state." The Court found that basing the tax on a percentage of total production met the fourth prong of the test: "When a tax is assessed in proportion to a taxpayer's activities or presence in a State, the taxpayer is shouldering its fair share of supporting the State's provision of 'police and fire protection, the benefit of a trained work force,' and 'the advantages of a civilized society.'" The majority opinion also found that the level of taxation was not normally a matter for the courts: "Under our federal system, the determination is to be made by state legislatures in the first instance and, if necessary, by Congress, when particular state taxes are thought to be contrary to federal interests."

In Part III of the opinion, the Court turned to the public lands issues.]

A

Appellants contend that the Montana tax, as applied to mining of federally owned coal, is invalid under the Supremacy Clause because it "substantially frustrates" the purposes of the Mineral Lands Leasing Act of 1920, 30 U.S.C. § 181 et seq. (1920 Act), as amended by the Federal Coal Leasing Amendments Act of 1975, 90 Stat. 1083 (1975 Amendments). Appellants argue that under the 1920 Act, the "economic rents" attributable to the mining of coal on federal land—i.e., the difference between the cost of production (including a reasonable profit) and the market price of the coal—are to be captured by the Federal Government in the form of royalty payments from federal lessees. The payments thus received are then to be divided between the States and the Federal Government according to a formula prescribed by the Act.[19] In appellants' view the Montana tax seriously undercuts and disrupts the 1920 Act's division of revenues between the federal land state governments by appropriating directly to Montana a major portion of the "economic rents." Appellants contend the Montana tax will alter the statutory scheme by causing potential coal producers to reduce the amount they are willing to bid in royalties on federal leases.

As an initial matter, we note that this argument rests on a factual premise—that the principal effect of the tax is to shift a major portion of the relatively fixed "economic rents" attributable to the extraction of federally owned coal from the Federal Treasury to the State of Montana—that appears to be inconsistent with the premise of appellants'

---

19. ✱ ✱ ✱ Section 35 was amended by § 9(a) of the Federal Coal Leasing Amendments Act of 1975, to provide for a new statutory formula which is currently in effect. Under this formula, the State in which the mining occurs receives 50% of the revenues, the reclamation fund receives 40%, and the United States Treasury the remaining 10%. 30 U.S.C. § 191.

Commerce Clause claims. In pressing their Commerce Clause arguments, appellants assert that Montana tax increases the cost of Montana coal, thereby *increasing* the total amount of "economic rents," and that the burden of the tax is borne by out-of-state consumers, not the Federal Treasury.[20] But even assuming that the Montana tax may reduce royalty payments to the Federal Government under leases executed in Montana, this fact alone hardly demonstrates that the tax is inconsistent with the 1920 Act. Indeed, appellants' argument is substantially undermined by the fact that in § 32 of the 1920 Act, 30 U.S.C. § 189, Congress expressly authorized the States to impose severance taxes on federal lessees without imposing any limits on the amount of such taxes. Section 32 provides in pertinent part:

> "Nothing in this chapter shall be construed or held to affect the rights of the States or other local authority to exercise any rights which they may have, including the right to levy and collect taxes upon improvements, outputs of mines, or other rights, property, or assets of any lessee of the United States."

This Court had occasion to construe § 32 soon after it was enacted. The Court explained that

> "Congress * * * meant by the proviso to say in effect that, although the act deals with the letting of public lands and the relations of the [federal] government to the lessees thereof, nothing in it shall be so construed as to affect the right of the states, in respect of such private persons and corporations, to *levy and collect taxes as though the government were not concerned.* * *
>
> * * *
>
> "We think the proviso plainly discloses the intention of Congress that *persons and corporations contracting with the United States under the act, should not, for that reason, be exempt from any form of state taxation otherwise lawful.*" Mid-Northern Oil Co. v. Walker, 268 U.S. 45, 48–50 (1925) (emphasis added).

It necessarily follows that if the Montana tax is "otherwise lawful," the 1920 Act does not forbid it.

Appellants contend that the Montana tax is not "otherwise lawful" because it conflicts with the very purpose of the 1920 Act. We do not agree. There is nothing in language or legislative history of either the 1920 Act or the 1975 Amendments to support appellants' assertion that Congress intended to maximize and capture *all* "economic rents" from the mining of federal coal, and then to distribute the proceeds in accordance with the statutory formula. The House Report on the 1975 Amendments, for example, speaks only in terms of a congressional

---

20. Indeed, appellants alleged in their complaints that the contracts between appellant coal producers and appellant utility companies *require* the utility companies to reimburse the coal producers for their severance tax payments, and that the ultimate incidence of the tax primarily falls on the utilities' out-of-state customers. Presumably, with regard to these contracts, the Federal Government's receipts will be unaffected by the Montana tax.

intent to secure a "fair return to the public." H.R.Rep. No. 94–681, at 17–18 (1975). Moreover, appellants' argument proves too much. By definition, any state taxation of federal lessees reduces the "economic rents" accruing to the Federal Government, and appellants' argument would preclude any such taxes despite the explicit grant of taxing authority to the States by § 32. Finally, appellants' contention necessarily depends on inferences to be drawn from §§ 7 and 35 of the 1920 Act, 30 U.S.C. §§ 207 and 191, which, as amended, prescribe the statutory formula for the division of the payments received by the Federal Government. Yet § 32 of the 1920 Act states that "[n]othing in this chapter"—which includes §§ 7 and 35—"shall be construed or held to affect the rights of the States * * * to levy and collect taxes upon * * * output of mines * * * of any lessee of the United States." 30 U.S.C. § 189. And if, as the Court has held, the States may "levy and collect taxes as though the [federal] government were not concerned," Mid-Northern Oil Co. v. Walker, supra, at 49, the manner in which the Federal Government collects receipts from its lessees and then shares them with the States has no bearing on the validity of a state tax. We therefore reject appellants' contention that the Montana tax must be invalidated as inconsistent with the Mineral Lands Leasing Act.

B

The final issue we must consider is appellants' assertion that the Montana tax is unconstitutional because it substantially frustrates national energy policies, reflected in several federal statutes, encouraging the production and use of coal, particularly low sulphur coal such as is found in Montana. Appellants insist that they are entitled to a hearing to explore the contours of these national policies and to adduce evidence supporting their claim that the Montana tax substantially frustrates and impairs the policies.

We cannot quarrel with appellants' recitation of federal statutes encouraging the use of coal. Appellants correctly note that § 2(6) of the Energy Policy and Conservation Act of 1975, 42 U.S.C. § 6201(6), declares that one of the Act's purposes is "to reduce the demand for petroleum products and natural gas through programs designed to provide greater availability and use of this Nation's abundant coal resources." And § 102(b)(3) of the Powerplant and Industrial Fuel Use Act of 1978 (PIFUA), 42 U.S.C. § 8301(b)(3), recites a similar objective "to encourage and foster the greater use of coal and other alternative fuels, in lieu of natural gas and petroleum, as a primary energy source." We do not, however, accept appellants' implicit suggestion that these general statements demonstrate a congressional intent to pre-empt all state legislation that may have an adverse impact on the use of coal. * * *

* * *

* * * The legislative history of § 601(a)(2) thus confirms what seems evident from the face of the statute—that Montana's severance

tax is not pre-empted by PIFUA. Since PIFUA is the only federal statute that even comes close to providing a specific basis for appellants' claims that the Montana statute "substantially frustrates" federal energy policies, this aspect of appellants' Supremacy Clause argument must also fail.[22]

IV

In sum, we conclude that appellants have failed to demonstrate either that the Montana tax suffers from any of the constitutional defects alleged in their complaints, or that a trial is necessary to resolve the issue of the constitutionality of the tax. Consequently, the judgment of the Supreme Court of Montana is affirmed.

So ordered.

Justice WHITE, concurring.

This is a very troublesome case for me, and I join the Court's opinion with considerable doubt and with the realization that Montana's levy on consumers in other States may in the long run prove to be an intolerable and unacceptable burden on commerce. Indeed, there is particular force in the argument that the tax is here and now unconstitutional. Montana collects most of its tax from coal lands owned by the Federal Government and hence by all of the people of this country, while at the same time sharing equally and directly with the Federal Government all of the royalties reserved under the leases the United States has negotiated on its land in the State of Montana. This share is intended to compensate the State for the burdens that coal mining may impose upon it. Also, as Justice Blackmun cogently points out, another 40% of the federal revenue from mineral leases is indirectly returned to the States through a reclamation fund. In addition, there is statutory provision for federal grants to areas affected by increased coal production.

But this very fact gives me pause and counsels withholding our hand, at least for now. Congress has the power to protect interstate commerce from intolerable or even undesirable burdens. It is also very much aware of the Nation's energy needs, of the Montana tax and of the trend in the energy-rich States to aggrandize their position and perhaps lessen the tax burdens on their own citizens by imposing unusually high taxes on mineral extraction. Yet, Congress is so far content to let the matter rest.

* * *

Justice BLACKMUN, with whom Justice POWELL and Justice STEVENS join, dissenting.

* * *

22. Appellants' assertion that the Montana tax is pre-empted by the Clean Air Act, 42 U.S.C. § 7401 et seq. (1976 ed., Supp. III), merits little discussion. The Clean Air Act does not mandate the use of coal; it merely prescribes standards governing the emission of sulphur dioxide when coal is used. Any effect those standards might have on the use of high or low sulphur coal is incidental.

The State of Montana has approximately 25% of all known United States coal reserves, and more than 50% of the Nation's low-sulfur coal reserves.[1] Approximately 70–75% of Montana's coal lies under land owned by the Federal Government in the State. The great bulk of the coal mined in Montana—indeed, allegedly as much as 90%—is exported to other States pursuant to long-term purchase contracts with out-of-state utilities. Those contracts typically provide that the costs of state taxation shall be passed on to the utilities; in turn, fuel adjustment clauses allow the utilities to pass the cost of taxation along to their consumers. Because federal environmental legislation has increased the demand for low-sulfur coal, and because the Montana coal fields occupy a "pivotal" geographic position in the midwestern and north-western energy markets, Montana has supplied an increasing percentage of the Nation's coal.[2]

* * *

As the Montana Legislature foresaw, the imposition of this severance tax has generated enormous revenues for the State. Montana collected $33.6 million in severance taxes in fiscal year 1978, and appellants alleged that it would collect not less than $40 million in fiscal year 1979. It has been suggested that by the year 2010, Montana will have collected more than $20 billion through the implementation of this tax.

No less remarkable is the increasing percentage of total revenue represented by the severance tax. In 1972, the then current flat rate severance tax on coal provided only 0.4% of Montana's total tax revenue; in contrast, in the year following the 1975 amendment, the coal severance tax supplied 11.4% of the State's total tax revenue. Appellants assert that the tax now supplies almost 20% of the State's total revenue. Indeed, the funds generated by the tax have been so large that, beginning in 1980, at least 50% of the severance tax is to be transferred and dedicated to a permanent trust fund, the principal of which must "forever remain inviolate" unless appropriated by a vote of three-fourths of the members of each house of the legislature. Mont. Const., Art. IX, § 5. Moreover, in 1979, Montana passed legislation providing property and income tax relief for state residents.

Appellants' complaint alleged that Montana's severance tax is ultimately borne by out-of-state consumers, and for the purposes of this appeal that allegation is to be treated as true. Appellants further alleged that the tax bears no reasonable relationship to the services or protection provided by the State. The issue here, of course, is whether they are entitled to a trial on that claim, not whether they will succeed on the merits. It should be noted, however, that Montana imposes numerous other taxes upon coal mining.[8] In addition, because 70% to

---

1. Montana and Wyoming together contain 40% of all United States coal reserves and 68% of all reserves of low-sulfur coal.

2. Together with Wyoming, Montana supplied 10% of the United States' demand for coal in 1977; it is estimated that Mon-

tana and Wyoming will supply 33% of the Nation's coal by 1990.

8. In addition to the severance tax on coal, Montana imposes a gross proceeds tax, Mont.Code Ann. § 15–6–132 (1979), a resource indemnity trust tax, § 15–38–104,

75% of the coal-bearing land in Montana is owned by the Federal Government, Montana derives a large amount of coal mining revenue from the United States as well. In light of these circumstances, the Interstate and Foreign Commerce Committee of the United States House of Representatives concluded that Montana's coal severance tax results in revenues "far in excess of the direct and indirect impact costs attributable to the coal production." Several commentators have agreed that Montana and other similarly situated western States have pursued a policy of "OPEC-like revenue maximization," and that the Montana tax accordingly bears no reasonable relationship to the services and protection afforded by the State. These findings, of course, are not dispositive of the issue whether the Montana severance tax is "fairly related" to the services provided by the State within the meaning of our prior cases. They do suggest, however, that appellants' claim is a substantial one. The failure of the Court to acknowledge this stems, it seems to me, from a misreading of our prior cases.

* * *

Because I believe that appellants are entitled to an opportunity to prove that, in Holmes' words, Montana's severance tax "embodies what the Commerce Clause was meant to end," I dissent.[21]

NOTE

The repercussions of *Commonwealth Edison* will continue to reverberate. Economists have had a field day; eastern politicians have warily considered legislative reform to protect their "have-not" region; and Sagebrush Rebels have had difficulty responding to the question, "please explain to me once more how you folks are so burdened by these public lands?" The voluminous commentary includes Browde & DuMars, State Taxation of Natural Resource Extraction and the Commerce Clause: Federalism's Modern Frontier, 60 Or.L.Rev. 7 (1981); Symposium, The Taxation of Natural Resources, 22 Nat.Resources J. 511 (1982); Golden, The Constitutionality of State Taxation of Energy Resources, 46 Alb.L.Rev. 805 (1982); Williams, Severance Taxes and Federalism: The Role of the Supreme Court in Preserving a National Common Market for Energy Supplies, 53 U.Colo.L.Rev. 281 (1982); Shurtz, State Taxation of Energy Resources: Are Consuming States Getting Burned?, 36 Vand.L.Rev. 55 (1983).

NOTE: FUTURE DIRECTIONS OF PREEMPTION LAW ON THE PUBLIC LANDS

It remains unclear whether general rules can fairly be applied to resolve preemption questions in public land law. As noted above, the

a property tax on mining equipment, § 15–6–138(b), and a corporation license tax, § 15–31–101. Furthermore, all costs of reclamation must be borne by the coal companies under both federal and state law, and Montana requires each company to purchase a reclamation bond prior to the commencement of mining operations. § 82–4–338.

21. I agree with the Court that appellants' Supremacy Clause claims are without merit.

Court tends not to rely upon a single approach to preemption cases. Rather, it examines the general traditions and context of the specific subject matter area and sometimes develops presumptions to resolve the close cases where congressional intent is unclear.

Is it possible in public land law to identify a general tradition either to defer or not to defer to state law? Is the tradition sufficiently specific to justify a presumption or a "clear expression" rule that would operate in favor of state or federal law to assist in resolving close cases when congressional intent in a specific instance is ambiguous? If a tradition cannot be identified for the field as a whole, are there special traditions attached to specific resources that would justify such an approach? Water allocation has largely been left to state law and discretion and, until recently, state law was dispositive on the procedural aspects of mining claim location. Wildlife management on the public lands has been an area of congressional deference, but the extent of such generalized deference is less certain when conflicts with federal resource goals occur. Matters involving timber harvesting, grazing, and preservation have typically been confided to exclusive federal regulation.

It may be that preemption questions or, conversely, questions of the extent of state power, in public land law cannot be decided in the abstract. Perhaps each case depends on the particular statute and the particular circumstances. But, as is evident from the preceding cases and from many others in subsequent chapters, the development (or lack) of general rules by which to analyze federal preemption could be central to resolution of the extent of state power on the public lands. See generally Hubbard, Dredge Mining and Wild Burros—A Tale of Two Cases and the Issue of State Versus Federal Regulation of Mineral Development on Public Domain Lands, 23 Rocky Mtn.Min.L.Inst. 71 (1977); Shapiro, Energy Development on the Public Domain: Federal/ State Cooperation and Conflict Regarding Environmental Land Use Control, 9 Nat.Res.Law. 397 (1976); Barry, Reclamation of Strip-Mined Federal Land: Preemptive Capability of Federal Standards over State Controls, 18 Ariz.L.Rev. 385 (1976); Wilkinson, The Field of Public Land Law: Some Connecting Threads and Future Directions, 1 Public Land L.Rev. 1, 7–23 (1980); Williams, Federal Preemption of State Conservation Laws After the National Gas Policy Act: A Preliminary Look, 56 U.Colo.L.Rev. 521 (1985); Wilkinson, Cross-Jurisdictional Conflicts: An Analysis of Legitimate State Interests on Federal and Indian Lands, 2 U.C.L.A. J.Envtl.L. & Policy 145 (1982); Skillern, Constitutional and Statutory Issues of Federation in the Development of Energy Resources, XVII Nat.Res.Law. 533 (1985); Note, State and Local Control of Energy Development on Federal Lands, 32 Stan.L.Rev. 373 (1980).

Chapter Four

AUTHORITY ON THE PUBLIC LANDS: THE EXECUTIVE AND THE COURTS

The power to manage the public lands under the Property Clause is vested in Congress, not the executive branch. Normally, therefore, any power exercised over federal property by the President or administrative agencies must be delegated by Congress. One of the early leading cases on constitutional delegation issues was a test case planned by Gifford Pinchot to establish expansive Forest Service authority under the 1897 Organic Act. United States v. Grimaud, 220 U.S. 506 (1911), involved a prosecution for grazing sheep on a forest reserve without having obtained the permit required by the regulations of the Forest Service. The Forest Service was acting pursuant to a broad provision in the 1897 Act, which delegated authority to make rules and regulations concerning use of the forest reserves. See 16 U.S.C.A. § 551. The Court upheld the delegation:

> In the nature of things it was impracticable for Congress to provide general regulations for these various and varying details of management. Each reservation had its peculiar and special features; and in authorizing the Secretary of Agriculture to meet these local conditions Congress was merely conferring administrative functions upon an agent, and not delegating to him legislative power. The authority actually given was much less than what has been granted to municipalities by virtue of which they make bylaws, ordinances and regulations for the government of towns and cities. Such ordinances do not declare general rules with reference to rights of persons and property, nor do they create or regulate obligations and liabilities, nor declare what shall be crimes nor fix penalties therefor. * * *

> From the beginning of the Government various acts have been passed conferring upon executive officers power to make rules and regulations—not for the government of their departments, but for administering the laws which did govern. None of these statutes could confer legislative power. But when Congress had legislated and indicated its will, it could give to those who were to act under such general provisions "power to fill up the details" by the establishment of administrative rules and regulations, the violation of which could be punished by fine or imprisonment fixed by Congress, or by penalties fixed by Congress or measured by the injury done.

A general delegation of authority to a cabinet-level officer or to an agency head is normally construed to include an implied power to subdelegate authority down through the department or agency. K.

238

Davis, ADMINISTRATIVE LAW 215–18 (1972). Subdelegations, however, must be express: in United States v. Gemmill, 535 F.2d 1145 (9th Cir.1976), for example, trespass convictions were overturned because power to close a part of a national forest had not been administratively subdelegated to the field official who had ordered the closure.

In modern public land and resources law, agency actions can be judicially restricted on jurisdictional, substantive, and procedural grounds. Recent litigation frequently involves a question whether Congress has delegated sufficient authority for the agency to take the action in issue. If the action is beyond the agency's delegated authority (or jurisdiction), the action can be set aside. Section A of this chapter examines executive withdrawals, reservations, and transfers, all of which raise questions about the scope of congressionally delegated power. Substantive problems arise when it is alleged that the agency action, although within delegated powers, has nevertheless violated a statute or regulation, or is "arbitrary or capricious." These determinations are central to judicial review, treated in the second section below. Section C explains the public trust doctrine as it may apply to public land law. Reversal of administrative action also may ensue if the agency has neglected to follow required procedures. Since 1970 a pervasive influence in public land law has been the procedure imposed across-the-board by the National Environmental Policy Act of 1969; NEPA is introduced in the final section of this chapter.

A. EXECUTIVE WITHDRAWALS, RESERVATIONS, AND TRANSFERS

A "withdrawal" of land is a generic term referring to a statute, an executive order, or an administrative order that changes the designation of a described parcel from "available" to "unavailable" for homesteading or resource exploitation. It is a permanent or temporary protective measure to preserve the status quo. It can be made "in aid of legislation" (e.g., a temporary measure pending the outcome of a bill to include the parcel in a wildlife refuge or a reclamation project) or for other reasons, and it can remove the parcel from some or all of the remaining disposition or use laws, including the mining laws.

A withdrawal is a negative act that prohibits some uses of specified land without affirmatively prescribing future use, but a "reservation" in this context means a dedication of the withdrawn land to a specified purpose, more or less permanently. (The word reservation is also used in public land law in a different sense, referring to bilateral transactions. For example, where a state cedes land or jurisdiction to the United States, it may "reserve" the right to tax activities on the granted land, or the United States may "reserve" subsurface mineral rights in a homestead patent. "Reservation" is also used in other senses, but for these purposes a reservation is a unilateral act resulting in the reclassification of a tract.) All public lands of the United States have now been withdrawn from operation of the homesteading and similar disposition laws and most have been reserved at least generally for various purposes. Whether a particular parcel remains open to mining, mineral leasing, logging, grazing, hunting and fishing, or intensive recreation is the key to many modern disputes on the federal public lands. See generally Getches, Managing the Public Lands: The Authority of the Executive to Withdraw Lands, 22 Nat.Res.J. 279 (1982); C. Wheatly, Jr., STUDY OF WITHDRAWALS AND RESERVATIONS OF PUBLIC DOMAIN LANDS (1969); Wheatly, Withdrawals Under the Federal Land Policy Management Act of 1976, 21 Ariz.L. Rev. 311 (1979).

In addition to the terms withdrawal and reservation, the term "classification" is also relevant here. Although the lines between these three processes cannot always be drawn brightly, the word classification is often used to describe the actions of land management agencies, operating pursuant to broad statutory authority, in categorizing (and recategorizing) lands according to their most beneficial use. Withdrawals and reservations, in other words, are usually large-scale and accomplished by Congress or the President, while classifications tend to be administrative fine-tuning on a parcel-by-parcel basis. Examples of classifications include the Interior Department's designations of lands available for in lieu selection by states, Andrus v. Utah, 446 U.S. 500 (1980), supra at page 62; the Interior Department's categorization of lands for specific uses according to the Classification and Multiple Use Act of 1964, 45 U.S.C.A. §§ 1411–18 (expired 1970), and later attempted revision of those decisions according to FLPMA, National Wildlife Federation v. Burford, 23 ERC 1609 (D.D.C.1985), infra at page 265; and the identification of land areas for various uses pursuant to the ongoing planning procedures of the NFMA, chapter seven, § C(3), and FLPMA, chapter eight, § C(3).

Various causes have given rise to classifications, withdrawals, and reservations, and the sources of authority and means of their exercise are also diverse. A rough division of authority between Congress and the President has grown up around specific statutes and long-term understandings. First, in some cases Congress has itself retained the sole power to withdraw and reserve certain lands. National parks, for instance, may be created only by an Act of Congress. The same is true of other—but not all—elements of the National Park System such as national preserves, national seashores, national lakeshores, and national recreation areas. Wilderness areas and wild or scenic river corridors also require explicit congressional designation, but designation is ordinarily preceded by administrative studies and evaluations and Presidential recommendations. See chapter eleven, §§ B and C infra. Congress also may reserve lands for other purposes, as it has in cases of some national wildlife refuges, and it always possesses the power to undo whatever it or the President has done.

A second, and more common, method of withdrawal and reservation is the delegation to the President by Congress of power to withdraw and reserve lands for certain purposes using certain criteria. In the Forest Reserve Amendment of 1891, the President was authorized to withdraw and reserve public lands covered with timber or undergrowth. The grant was repealed as to most western states, and some acreage returned to the public domain in 1907, but not before the Presidents from Cleveland through Theodore Roosevelt had set aside most of the lands that now are in the National Forest System. In the Antiquities Act of 1906, 16 U.S.C.A. §§ 431–433, Congress authorized the President to reserve lands containing scenic and scientific curiosities. The present network of national monuments has grown from this modest grant. In the Pickett Act of 1910, 43 U.S.C.A. §§ 141–142 (repealed 1976), Congress delegated a general withdrawal power to the President, relatively unbounded by selection criteria ("public purposes"), but which operated only against non-metalliferous entry: that is, lands withdrawn under the authority of the Pickett Act remained open to hardrock entry. Further, Pickett Act withdrawals were to be temporary, but many such orders are still in effect, fifty or sixty years later. Other ad hoc statutes over the years have delegated withdrawal powers to the President and his delegatees for more limited purposes.

A third category of withdrawal, unaccompanied by reservation, is withdrawal from disposition of a resource wherever it is found. By the Mineral Leasing Act of 1920, 30 U.S.C.A. § 181 et seq., for example, Congress purported to "withdraw" oil, gas, coal, and like minerals on all public lands from the operation of the mining location laws. That course was followed by withdrawals of common varieties of minerals, petrified wood, and geothermal resources. Their disposition thereafter was only by lease or sale.

Yet another type of withdrawal can be termed a "general congressional withdrawal." Thus, in the Taylor Grazing Act of 1934, 43 U.S.C.A. § 315 et seq., as amended, Congress effectively withdrew upwards of 140 million acres from the operation of the homesteading laws "pending final disposition," although land orders issued by the executive branch were necessary to carry out the congressional intent. Similarly, the Alaska Native Claims Settlement Act of 1971, 43 U.S.C.A. § 1601 et seq., effectively withdrew much of Alaska from availability for resource use or development pending ultimate congressional disposition and classification of Alaska lands.

All of the foregoing withdrawals and reservations have resulted from unilateral legislative action or from the President acting pursuant to congressionally delegated authority. Despite the clear constitutional delegation of authority over public lands to Congress, and the lack of a similar grant to the Executive, Presidents have long claimed and exercised an inherent power to withdraw—and in some cases, to reserve—public lands in the public interest. From the beginning Presidents carved military reservations out of the public domain by executive order, arguably in accordance with the President's role as Commander-in-Chief of the Armed Forces. Between 1855 and 1919, Presidents also set aside some 23 million acres of public lands for Indian reservations. Inevitably a situation arose where the executive action could not be justified by extension of a delegated power.

UNITED STATES v. MIDWEST OIL CO.
Supreme Court of the United States, 1915.
236 U.S. 459.

[The opinion is reproduced supra at page 147. The Court upheld President Taft's massive withdrawals of oil lands in 1909, made in order to prevent appropriation of most known federally-owned oil by energy companies, on the ground that the longtime "congressional acquiescence" to executive withdrawals amounted to an implied delegation of authority under the Property Clause.]

NOTES

1. The reasoning of *Midwest Oil* was later applied to validate executive withdrawals for Indian reservations. Arizona v. California, 373 U.S. 546, 594–601 (1963).

2. Shortly after the Taft withdrawals, Congress attempted to restrict presidential withdrawal power by passing the Pickett Act of 1910. See 43 U.S.C.A. §§ 141–142. The Pickett Act was repealed by FLMPA in 1976, but the many withdrawals between 1910 and 1976 are affected by the uncertain terms of the 1910 Act:

> The President may, at any time in his discretion, temporarily withdraw from settlement, location, sale, or entry any of the public lands of the United States, including Alaska, and reserve the same for water-power sites, irrigation, classification of lands, or other public purposes to be specified in the orders of withdrawals, and such withdrawals or reservations shall remain in force until revoked by him or by an Act of Congress. 43 U.S.C.A. § 141.

> All lands withdrawn under the provisions of this section and section 141 of this title shall at all times be open to exploration, discovery, occupation, and purchase under the mining laws of the United States, so far as the same apply to metalliferous minerals: *Provided,* That the rights of any person who, at the date of any order of withdrawal, is a bona fide occupant or claimant of oil- or gas-bearing lands and who, at such date, is in the diligent prosecution of work leading to the discovery of oil or gas, shall not be affected or impaired by such order so long as such occupant or claimant shall continue in diligent prosecution of said work * * *. 43 U.S.C.A. § 142.

Presidents continued to make withdrawals under the implied power recognized in *Midwest Oil*, but, by World War II, the question of the Pickett Act's effect on presidential power to withdraw had not been resolved. C. Wheatly, Jr., STUDY OF WITHDRAWALS AND RESERVATIONS OF PUBLIC DOMAIN LANDS 5 (1969):

> In 1940 and 1941, a debate developed in the executive branch as to the authority of the President to make a withdrawal of land from operation of the mining law, an action for

which no statutory authority existed. The Pickett Act had expressly provided that all withdrawals thereunder were to be open to mining for metalliferous minerals. Attorney General Jackson, when he first considered the matter in 1940, reached the opinion that Congress in the Pickett Act had circumscribed the entire field of the President's authority to withdraw lands except for the other specific delegations in particular areas, and that therefore no nonstatutory withdrawal authority remained in the Executive. This opinion was, however, not published. Secretary of the Interior Harold Ickes and various other government agencies vigorously sought to have the Attorney General change his opinion. Even after review of their opinions, the Attorney General persisted in his original views. Subsequently, however, a memorandum was prepared in the Justice Department under the supervision of Assistant Attorney General Fahy, who reported to the Attorney General that the matter was indeed very close but that in Fahy's opinion the nonstatutory authority of the President should be affirmed. Subsequently, Attorney General Jackson issued a new opinion in 1941 affirming the nonstatutory authority of the President to make "permanent" withdrawals of public lands as contrasted with the alleged "temporary" withdrawals of public lands to which the Pickett Act was then construed as limited.

No court has ever affirmed any inherent withdrawal authority in the Executive, or the asserted nonstatutory authority of the Executive to withdraw lands contained in the 1941 opinion of the Attorney General.

PORTLAND GEN. ELEC. CO. v. KLEPPE
United States District Court, District of Wyoming, 1977.
441 F.Supp. 859.

KERR, District Judge.

This case presents the question of the validity of 1,740 uranium mining claims located by plaintiff Portland General Electric (P.G.E.) on lands located in the State of Wyoming and purportedly withdrawn by Order of the Secretary of the Interior. The validity of these claims hinges upon the authority of the withdrawal Order and the propriety of such withdrawal.

Defendants filed their Motion for Judgment on the Pleadings. Plaintiffs responded by filing a Motion for Summary Judgment. The parties agree that there is no dispute as to any genuine issue of fact and the question to be resolved is one of law.

In April, 1968, the Secretary of the Interior issued Public Land Order (PLO) 4522, 35 Fed.Reg. 3057, which withdrew 3,000,000 acres of public lands in Wyoming, Colorado and Utah from appropriation under the mining laws relating to metalliferous minerals. Uranium is a metalliferous mineral. The authorization for this withdrawal consisted solely of a statement that the Order was issued under the authority vested in the President.

In 1975, P.G.E. located uranium mining claims on public lands in the Kinney Rim area of Wyoming, which lands were included in the withdrawal Order. Discovery was halted when the Federal Government threatened to bring a trespass action against P.G.E. The plaintiffs assert that no Presidential authority to make such withdrawal of public lands exists and, therefore, the withdrawal was invalid. P.G.E. seeks to have the withdrawal Order declared invalid so that it can establish title to the mineral claims on the lands in question.

The withdrawal of the lands in question from the operation of the mining laws was made more than six years before P.G.E. located its mining claims. P.G.E. contends it was unaware of the withdrawal. Publication of the withdrawal Order in 35 Fed.Reg. 3057 was sufficient notice. The lack of knowledge was due entirely to the plaintiffs' failure to investigate and the plaintiffs' lack of knowledge is of no effect.

* * * [Public Land Order 4522] provides in part:

COLORADO, UTAH, AND WYOMING

Withdrawal for Oil Shale

By virtue of the authority vested in the President and pursuant to Executive Order No. 10355 of May 26, 1952 (17 F.R. 4831), it is ordered as follows:

1. Subject to valid existing rights, the deposits of oil shale and lands containing such deposits, owned by the United States and under the administrative jurisdiction of the Department of the Interior in the following described areas, are hereby withdrawn (1) from appropriation under the United States mining laws relating to metalliferous minerals, and (2) from sodium leasing except as hereafter provided, for protection of the multiple development of the minerals and other resources in the lands.

The plaintiffs contend, and the Court agrees, that Congress has not expressly granted to the Executive the authority to withdraw public lands from the operation of the mining laws. However, the Court does not accept the contention that the Pickett Act, 43 U.S.C.A. §§ 141–142, prohibits such withdrawals under the provisions of 43 U.S.C.A. § 142:

All lands withdrawn under the provisions of this section and section 141 of this title shall at all times be open to exploration, discovery, occupation, and purchase under the mining laws of the United States, so far as the same apply to metalliferous minerals.

The President's power to make temporary withdrawals of lands from mineral entry was not destroyed by this Act. U.S. v. Midwest Oil Co., 236 U.S. 459 (1915). The President is authorized to withdraw and reserve public lands for public uses free of the operation of the mining laws notwithstanding the provisions of 43 U.S.C.A. § 142, 40 Op.Att'y

Gen. 71 (1941). Such withdrawals are made under the President's inherent power to withdraw public lands. See P & G Mining Company, 67 I.D. 217 (1960). This inherent authority extends to permit the President to withdraw lands from all forms of appropriation. Noel Teuscher, 62 I.D. 210 (1955).

The acquiescence or approval of Congress to the practice of withdrawing lands operates as an implied grant of the power to make such withdrawals. * * *

U.S. v. Midwest Oil Co. concerned a withdrawal made prior to the enactment of the Pickett Act whereby Congress expressly authorized the President to make temporary withdrawals of public lands. Even assuming that the Pickett Act did supersede the implied authority of the President to make withdrawals, Congress has, by its acquiescence, restored that power.

In 1941, Attorney General Robert H. Jackson issued an opinion holding that, notwithstanding the provision of the Pickett Act, the President had the "implied authority" to withdraw public lands through the acquiescence of Congress. He concluded that this implied authority permitted the President to withdraw public lands free of the operation of the mining laws. 40 Op.Att'y Gen. 73 (1941).

In 1957, in legislation limiting the Executive's authority to withdraw lands for military use, 43 U.S.C.A. §§ 155–158, Congress expressly acknowledged that its acquiescence had again given rise to a grant of implied authority. The legislative history for this act states:

> Congress—applying the Midwest Oil yardstick—has perhaps, since 1941 remained silent, and has therefore indulged in a practice—* * * equivalent to acquiescence and consent that the practice be continued until the power exercised is revoked.
>
> H.R. 5538 is specifically aimed at breaking that silence * * * with respect to the Federal property embraced by its terms, and for the reasons hereinafter set out, and to that extent signaling an end to the implied consent by direct congressional enactment limiting the power exercised. S.Rep. 857, 85th Cong., 2nd Sess. (1958), U.S.Code, Cong. & Admin. News 1958, p. 2238.

The Executive's implied authority over non-military withdrawals remained uncurtailed.

In 1968, the Secretary of the Interior presented a detailed statement supporting his oil shale program, including the withdrawal questioned here, to the Senate Committee on Interior and Insular Affairs. Congress was, therefore, aware of the proposed withdrawal and, by making no effort to prevent such action by the Secretary acquiesced in the Secretary's action.

Finally, in 1971 Congress directed the Secretary of the Interior to exercise the implied authority to withdraw lands from the operation of the mining laws. Section 17 of the Alaska Native Claims Settlement

Act, 43 U.S.C.A. § 1616(d)(2) directed the Secretary to withdraw 80 million acres from all forms of appropriation including location under the mining laws under the authority provided for in existing law. The only authority for withdrawal from mineral location was the implied Presidential authority which had been delegated to the Secretary of Interior pursuant to Executive Order No. 10355 of May 26, 1952.

It is obvious from the foregoing that Congress had knowledge of and acquiesced in repeated assertions of the implied authority under which the oil shale lands in question were withdrawn. The withdrawal, therefore, was valid and effective prior to the entry by P.G.E.

* * *

* * * Judgment shall be entered accordingly.

NOTES

1. Has the court gutted the Pickett Act? Could Congress in 1910 have intended anything other than to bar such withdrawals?

2. Reservations of federal land for purposes that exclude one or more economic uses, particularly hardrock mining and mineral leasing, have been the subject of ardent debate at least since the creation of Yellowstone National Park. Reservation of the national forests did not affect the availability of land for hardrock mineral exploration, but most subsequent withdrawals have decreased the amount of exploitable land. Consequently, the establishment of parks, monuments, wilderness areas, and other special purpose categories on which mining is forbidden or restricted have not been met with universal acclaim. In 1975 the debate over how much land should be withdrawn was touched off anew with publication of Bennethum & Lee, Is Our Account Overdrawn, 61 Am.Mining Cong.J. 33 (1975).

The authors, both of whom were BLM employees, undertook an "audit" of the "assets" (available land) in the national inventory. As of 1974, they concluded, there were 824 million acres of federal land or federal reserved subsurface rights under private land theoretically available for mineral leasing and 742 million acres theoretically available for hardrock mining locations. Their ultimate conclusions were that lands withdrawn (and they include what they call "de facto withdrawals," where administrative policies discourage mining but do not prohibit it) from the operation of the mineral leasing laws rose from 17 percent in 1968 to 73 percent in 1974, and that lands open to hardrock mining decreased from 83 to 27 percent in the same period. Bennethum & Lee began with these premises:

> * * * Lands which have been put off limits to mineral exploration can no longer be considered as assets in our account. History has shown that, after lands have been withdrawn for certain uses, only rarely are they reopened by a revocation of the withdrawal specifically to allow mineral exploration and development to again occur. Realistically, nothing short of a national emergency will provide the incentive for reopening many of these withdrawn lands to mineral

development. In the vast majority of cases the lands were withdrawn without any realistic evaluation of their mineral potential. Thus, the minerals in these lands cannot be considered to be available in a national emergency since there is no way of knowing which withdrawn lands should come back into our account should a serious shortage of a mineral commodity occur. * * *

The authors concluded that, while their numbers could not be exact and the ultimate question (how much is too much?) is not answerable, serious consequences nevertheless bode. They rejected the possibility of governmental exploitation of the public mineral resources, and noted that the implication of foreign mineral cartels on national security could be "staggering." "Intelligent land use decisions must be very finely balanced. Such a balance in tradeoff decisions is not possible if we do not know what the mineral side of the scale contains."

The mining industry enthusiastically endorsed the Bennethum & Lee prognosis, but elsewhere it has been the subject of serious criticism. An obvious difficulty is the inclusion of lands withdrawn pursuant to the Alaska Native Claims Settlement Act, which account for the great bulk of the decrease in land availability (about 270 million acres). Most of these lands were released from the freeze on development when the Alaska National Interest Lands Conservation Act was passed in 1980, and full release will occur upon completion of State and Native land selections. See supra at page 165. Excluding ANCSA lands, the Office of Technology Assessment later estimated that, as of 1975, 11.7% of federal lands were closed to mineral leasing, 9.9% were "highly restricted," and 45.4% had "slight" or "moderate" restrictions. For hardrock exploration, OTA estimated that 15.9% of the public lands were closed, 6.1% severely restricted, and 44% moderately or slightly restricted. OTA claimed that its "audit" was more complete and sophisticated than its predecessor. Office of Technology Assessment, MANAGEMENT OF FUEL AND NONFUEL MINERALS IN FEDERAL LAND 215–19 (R. Wright, ed. 1979).

The methodology of Bennethum & Lee was more sharply attacked in an unpublished paper, "Is Our Account Overdrawn: Revisited" by M.B. Paul in 1979. Bennethum & Lee's reliance on "judgment calls" was conceded necessary in light of informational inadequacies, but said nevertheless to be a source of error. Criticism also was expressed over failure to take account of "overlapping" withdrawals; Paul quotes one BLM employee who found a single parcel subject to a dozen different withdrawal orders. As "de facto" withdrawals were defined in the B & L study by "unacceptable risk," these unsegregated numbers were thought to be inaccurate, subjective, and excessive. Because of data unreliability, subjectivity, and the framing of the conclusion "in the politically symbolic construct of national security," Paul concludes that "both the political conclusions and the audit itself should not be treated as authoritative."

NOTE: FLPMA WITHDRAWAL PROCEDURES

Preservationists and conservationists had long believed that a vigorous executive withdrawal authority is essential to protection of land and resources from excessive development. They argued that the executive branch must have the wherewithal both to make long-term set asides and to react quickly to emergency situations when imminent development threatens important wildlife and recreation resources. The minerals industries sought strict limitations on executive discretion to withdraw. The result of this philosophical struggle was the complex, carefully-tuned compromise embodied in the 1976 FLPMA, which tried to reconcile legitimate economic and environmental concerns.

In the 1976 FLPMA, Congress sought to abolish the President's implied withdrawal powers in section 704 of FLPMA, 90 Stat. 2792: "the implied authority of the President to make withdrawals and reservations resulting from acquiescence of the Congress (U.S. v. Midwest Oil Co. * * *) [is] repealed." Some doubt remains, however, as to whether this "inartful repealer" can accomplish its intended purpose. If the President continues to withdraw land without other authority, and Congress with knowledge takes no action, has not the "power by acquiescence" been recreated?

Congress has long been hostile to unilateral executive actions of this nature, and FLPMA went beyond the repealer of *Midwest Oil* by establishing comprehensive procedures for the withdrawal of Interior and Forest Service lands. FLPMA, 43 U.S.C.A. § 1701(a)(4) sets general policy:

> The Congress declares that it is the policy of the United States that * * * the Congress exercise its constitutional authority to withdraw or otherwise designate or dedicate Federal lands for specified purposes and that Congress delineate the extent to which the Executive may withdraw lands without legislative action.

The Act allows the Secretary to make withdrawals of less than 5000 acres for resource purposes. 43 U.S.C.A. § 1714(d). Most withdrawals in excess of 5000 acres are subject to a "congressional veto" within 90 days under complex procedures, including detailed reports to Congress, set out in section 1714(c); the only exception to the statute's allowance for legislative override is that the Secretary may make "emergency" withdrawals of any size for three years. See 43 U.S.C.A. § 1714(e).

FLPMA repealed numerous older statutes dealing with withdrawals, including the Pickett Act. See section 704, 90 Stat. 2792. Further, FLPMA requires a secretarial review of all withdrawals and a report to Congress with an eye toward lifting withdrawals for which the original purpose may long since have passed. Id. § 1714(*l*). Attempts by the Reagan Administration to terminate protective classifications and revoke withdrawals on some 170 million acres were struck down in

National Wildlife Federation v. Burford, 23 ERC 1609 (D.D.C.1985), infra at page 265.

Procedurally, a withdrawal is accomplished by the issuance of a public land order. Executive Order 10355, referred to in *Midwest Oil,* is still in effect. Current procedure vests the authority to issue public land orders withdrawing land only in the Secretary of Interior, the Under Secretary, and the Assistant Secretaries. Under FLPMA, withdrawal authority can be subdelegated within Interior only to presidential appointees in the Office of the Secretary. 43 U.S.C.A. § 1714(a). Therefore, withdrawals made by line agencies such as the BLM or by officials in field offices are void. See City of Kotzebue, 26 IBLA 264 (1976). Regulations governing withdrawals are found at 43 CFR Part 2300 (1985).

The sweeping nature of FLPMA's reform of withdrawal policy in the Department of Interior should not obscure the fact that the Act is prospective only, 43 U.S.C.A. § 1714(a), and that millions of acres of withdrawn land are still subject to pre-FLPMA law. Thus the issues relating to withdrawals made between the Pickett Act in 1910 and FLPMA in 1976 remain alive, as Portland General Electric Co. v. Kleppe, supra, demonstrates.

Several aspects of the FLPMA withdrawal procedures are of doubtful constitutionality after the Court in Immigration and Naturalization Service v. Chadha, 462 U.S. 919 (1983), struck down a "legislative veto" provision on the grounds that it violated the bicameral requirement and the Presentment Clause. Those issues are taken up infra at page 257. First, however, it is useful to see the manner in which executive withdrawals, based on FLPMA and other sources, influenced the passage of the Alaska National Interest Lands Conservation Act of 1980.

The events after Alaska statehood have already been recounted. See supra at page 165. Most notably, Secretary Udall issued the "superfreeze" in 1968 to block state selections and mineral leases until questions of Alaska Native title were resolved. In 1971, Congress enacted ANCSA, which, among many other things, provided for secretarial withdrawal of 80 million acres to evaluate their suitability for inclusion in the "national interest" systems. The "d(2)" withdrawals of national interest lands were about to expire in 1978 when a new form of superfreeze took hold. Subsequent events are recounted in Congressional Stall Prompts Administrative Actions to Protect the Alaska National Interest Lands,* 8 E.L.R. 10245 (Dec. 1978):

> In a dramatic announcement on December 1, 1978, President Carter made good on his pledge that protection of the environmental values of the vast "national interest" lands in Alaska is the most important environmental goal of his administration. By setting aside 56 million acres of Alaska as national monuments and affirming the Secretary of the Interi-

* Reprinted with permission of the Environmental Law Institute. Copyright © 1978.

or's temporary withdrawal two weeks earlier of 105 million acres from state selection and resource exploitation, the President brought to a close a major phase in the struggle over the disposition of the vast federal domain in the 49th state, a struggle which has pitted those who view the Alaskan wilderness in terms of its potential for economic development against those who see Alaska as the last opportunity to preserve and protect wildlife and wilderness values that have all but vanished from the lower 48 states.

In 1971, Congress assigned to itself the task of settling the fate of the public domain lands in Alaska by authorizing the temporary withdrawal of up to 80 million acres from private or state claims while it chose which areas to place in permanent, federally protected reserves. Congress failed to meet its self-imposed deadline of December 16, 1978, however, necessitating executive branch action to ensure continued protection. The net result of the actions of the President and Secretary Andrus is to overlay several different protective classifications and thereby establish multiple mechanisms to preserve the Alaskan lands while congressional debate continues. * * * Despite the permanent nature of national monument designations, no administrative solution can be characterized as more than temporary because of continuing congressional deliberation over the ultimate disposition of these lands. As President Carter indicated, his action and those taken by Secretary Andrus were aimed only at preserving for Congress all options on the ultimate fate of the "national interest" lands in Alaska.

* * *

In 1973, as the first step in this process, Secretary of the Interior Morton withdrew 83.5 million acres pursuant to [43 U.S.C.A. § 1616(d)(1)]. Simultaneously, 67 million of those acres were also withdrawn under § 17(d)(2). Because of the statutory limitation, the § 17(d)(2) withdrawals would expire at midnight, December 16, 1978, while the § 17(d)(1) protection would continue indefinitely, although it had not been tested whether this provision would protect the lands so withdrawn from state selection and mineral entry. When the 95th Congress convened in January 1977, the vehicle for legislative action to settle the Alaskan lands issue became H.R. 39, a bill introduced by Congressman Udall (D.Ariz.), chairman of the House Committee on Interior and Insular Affairs. Later that year, Secretary of the Interior Andrus submitted, on behalf of the Carter Administration, recommendations that would have placed 92.6 million acres in the four conservation systems described in § 17(d)(2).[10] This past May, the House overwhelmingly passed H.R. 39, which provided for 101 million acres to be

---

10. According to the Interior Department, this still left 70 percent of hard rock minerals and 90 percent of high potential oil and gas areas outside the federally drawn boundaries. Also, 90 percent of the state was left open to sport hunting.

apportioned among the four conservation systems. In early October, the Senate Energy and Natural Resources Committee reported out a bill covering 98.8 million acres, but lack of time before the end of the session and the staunch opposition of Senator Gravel (D.Alas.) blocked final legislative action. Congress adjourned on October 15, having thus failed to adhere to its self-imposed timetable. Barring further action by the executive branch, the untested strength of § 17(d)(1) withdrawal would have been the only protection for the Alaska national interest lands from private claims for mineral exploration and development rights under the public land laws and state selection under the Alaska Statehood Act.

STATE OF ALASKA v. CARTER

United States District Court, District of Alaska, 1978.
462 F.Supp. 1155.

VON DER HEYDT, Chief Judge.

THIS CAUSE comes before the court on the State of Alaska's motion for a preliminary injunction enjoining the defendants from closing the comment period on a draft environmental supplement issued October 25, 1978, by the Department of the Interior. The draft supplement considers several alternative administrative actions proposed for classification of Alaska's "National Interest Lands". The court is requested to enjoin defendants from closing the comment period prior to 45 days from October 30, 1978, the date the draft supplement generally was available in the State of Alaska, and to enjoin defendants from taking any final administrative actions on the Alaska National Interest Lands until at least 90 days have elapsed from October 30, 1978. * * *

Factual Background

In 1971 the Congress included in the Alaska Native Claims Settlement Act (ANCSA) a provision which directed the Secretary of Interior

> "to withdraw from all forms of appropriation under the public land laws, including the mining and mineral leasing laws, and from selection under the Alaska Statehood Act, and from selection by the Regional Corporations * * * up to, but not to exceed, eighty million acres of unreserved public lands in the State of Alaska, including previously classified lands, which the Secretary deems are suitable for addition to or creation as units of the National Park, Forest, Wildlife Refuge, and Wild and Scenic Rivers Systems * * * "

Section 17(d)(2)(A), 43 U.S.C.A. § 1616(d)(2)(A). Section 17(d)(1) also authorized the Secretary of Interior to withdraw, under existing authority, lands needed to protect the public interest. Beginning in March, 1972, the Secretary issued a series of public land orders which withdrew millions of acres of public lands in Alaska. Lands withdrawn under section 17(d)(2) were simultaneously withdrawn under 17(d)(1). The "d–

2" withdrawals expire on December 16, 1978, while the "d–1" withdrawals have no time limit.

On December 17, 1973, Secretary of Interior Morton submitted recommendations for the legislative protection and classification of approximately 83 million acres of federal public land in Alaska. A draft environmental impact statement was released to the public at that time and after a period of public comment a 28-volume final environmental statement was issued on the Alaska lands legislative proposals. These procedures fully complied with the requirements of the National Environmental Policy Act.

In September, 1977, Interior Secretary Andrus submitted the current Administration's proposals for legislation at the request of the Chairman of the House Committee on Interior and Insular Affairs. The House passed an Alaska lands bill in May, 1978, but the bill failed in the Senate during the final hours of the Congressional session. [Interior issued a supplement to the EIS in 1978.] * * *

After conferring with the Council on Environmental Quality regarding the proper procedures to be employed, the Department of Interior released the draft supplement on October 25, 1978, with the 25-day public comment period scheduled to end on November 20. By agreement of the parties the comment period was extended to November 22.

During the comment period the State of Alaska filed this suit challenging the length of the comment period and the legality of the various administrative actions proposed. The only issue before the court on this motion is the length of the comment period. On November 14, 1978, the State filed land selections on 41 million acres of land including 9 million acres within the national interest lands areas discussed in the draft supplement. On November 16, 1978, after receiving a letter from the House Committee on Interior and Insular Affairs the previous day,[5] the Secretary of Interior determined that an emergency existed and exercised his power under section 204(e) of the Federal Land Policy and Management Act, 43 U.S.C.A. § 1714(e), withdrawing in excess of 100 million acres from the federal public domain in Alaska.

* * *

5. The letter from Chairman Udall stated in part:

[I]n view of the most recent selections filed by the State of Alaska, its new lawsuit and its threat to seek immediate judicial remedies to prevent administrative actions to protect these lands, I must emphasize to you, on behalf of the Committee on Interior and Insular Affairs of the U.S. House of Representatives, that an emergency exists with respect to the national interest lands. Extraordinary measures must be taken now to assure the preservation of the important values in these lands, which will be lost if such measures are not promptly effected. We urge you to exercise your authority under section 204(e) of the Federal Land Policy and Management Act of 1976 immediately, to assure that these significant values are saved.

Likelihood of Success on the Merits

In determining whether the State of Alaska has shown a probability of success on the merits on the issue of the legality of the shortened comment period, the court must decide whether the impact statement requirement of NEPA applies to the various Presidential and Secretarial actions proposed in the environmental supplement and whether, assuming NEPA applies, the comment period is in accordance with NEPA and the CEQ Guidelines, 40 C.F.R. Part 1500 (1977).

The Application of NEPA

* * *

The government contends that Presidential actions under the Antiquities Act are not subject to the impact statement requirements of NEPA because NEPA applies only to "federal agencies" and the President is not a federal agency. The court finds this argument persuasive. The Antiquities Act authorizes the President "in his discretion" to declare objects that have scientific interest, and are situated upon the public lands, to be national monuments. The Act authorizes only the President to declare these reservations and apparently this authority cannot be delegated.

* * * Moreover, the doctrine of separation of powers prevents this court from lightly inferring a Congressional intent to impose such a duty on the President. For these reasons the court holds that the President is not subject to the impact statement requirement of NEPA when exercising his power to proclaim national monuments under the Antiquities Act.

* * *

The court now turns to the issue of NEPA's application to the Secretary's emergency withdrawal powers. * * * Section 204(e) of FLPMA, 43 U.S.C.A. § 1714(e) [11] requires the Secretary to "immediately make a withdrawal" of public lands when he determines or is notified by either of the appropriate Congressional committees that an emergency exists. To require the Secretary to file an impact statement and impose its prescribed comment period would frustrate the mandate of the statute that the withdrawal be "immediate." The need for haste is emphasized by the provision in FLPMA which exempts these emergency withdrawals from the requirement of a public hearing. 43 U.S.C.A. § 1714(h). The court holds that an emergency withdrawal under

---

11. 43 U.S.C.A. § 1714(e) states:

(e) When the Secretary determines, or when the Committee on Interior and Insular Affairs of either the House of Representatives or the Senate notifies the Secretary, that an emergency situation exists and that extraordinary measures must be taken to preserve values that would otherwise be lost, the Secretary notwithstanding the provisions of subsections (c)(1) and (d) of this section, shall immediately make a withdrawal and file notice of such emergency withdrawal with the Committees on Interior and Insular Affairs of the Senate and the House of Representatives. Such emergency withdrawal shall be effective when made but shall last only for a period not to exceed three years and may not be extended except under the provisions of subsection (c)(1) or (d) of this section, whichever is applicable, and (b)(1) of this section. The information required in subsection (c)(2) of this subsection shall be furnished the committees within three months after filing such notice.

§ 204(e) of FLPMA does not require a NEPA environmental impact statement.

While the government contends that the other alternative withdrawal powers are also not covered by NEPA, the court finds the argument that they are "major federal actions significantly affecting the quality of the human environment" so substantial that the remaining issue of whether the comment period was adequate in these circumstances will have to be decided.

The Adequacy of the Comment Period

As discussed earlier, the October, 1978, report of the Department of the Interior was a supplement to an earlier multi-volume environmental impact statement (EIS) issued in 1974. The earlier EIS had considered the impact of a legislative withdrawal of 83 million acres for inclusion into the National Park System, the Wildlife Refuge System, the Forest System, and the Wild and Scenic Rivers System (known collectively as the National Conservation Systems).

The supplement was designed to add to this 83 million acre area sufficient acreages to cover all the possible withdrawals raised during the last Congressional session by either of the two Houses and by the President, and to evaluate the additional impact, if any, of proposed administrative and presidential withdrawals. The supplement was also designed to consider substantial changes in impacts since the date of the original EIS. An example of such a change was the consideration in the supplement of the impact on subsistence lifestyle and/or sport hunting if these activities were prohibited in National Park Service administered areas. With regard to the additional acreages involved, the Department of the Interior noted that

> Our review demonstrated that any portion of an administrative study area outside the boundaries discussed in the 1974 EIS merely shifted the geographical locus of the impacts of environmentally protective action. *The environmental impacts of administrative action on those portions remained substantially similar to those reported in the 1974 EIS.*

The Department's overall conclusion was that aside from certain boundary changes,

> The major area where anticipated environmental impacts resulting from the Administrative actions would substantially differ from the environmental impacts discussed in the 1974 EIS is the impact of disallowing subsistence and sport hunting in National Park Service-administered areas. The 1974 EIS did not discuss the impacts of disallowing such activities.

After careful review of the record the court agrees with the Government's characterization of the October, 1978, document as a supplement to the earlier EIS and not itself an independent statement. This is so because the supplement considered either environmental impacts omitted from what would be, in 1978, a deficient EIS, or discussed changes in the earlier EIS which are more properly characterized as modifications of a major federal action earlier considered in a final EIS rather than independent major federal actions.   *   *   *

Assuming that the provisions of NEPA required that a NEPA evaluation accompany the proposed administrative land withdrawal actions, the next issue presented is how much time, if any, should have been required for notice and comment on the proposed supplement to the earlier EIS.

*   *   *

The court concludes that establishment of the 25-day comment period on a draft supplement to an EIS was a reasonable interpretation and application of the guidelines and constituted a responsible exercise of discretion, not an abuse thereof.

*   *   *

In conclusion, the court finds that the State of Alaska has demonstrated little probability of success on the merits on any of its proffered legal theories.

*   *   *

NOTES

1. Did the emergency withdrawal meet the requirements of section 204(e) of FLPMA (quoted at note 11 of the opinion)? How can Congress' choice not to continue the withdrawal executed under ANCSA create an "emergency" within the meaning of the statute? Does a letter from the Committee Chairman to the Secretary constitute notice from the Committee? Were withdrawals of this magnitude contemplated by FLPMA? See DeStefano, The Federal Land Policy and Management Act and the State of Alaska, 21 Ariz.L.Rev. 417, 418–22 (1979), who concludes: "while recognizing the broad leeway accorded Congress in dealing with the public lands, the courts, as a logical check on this potential, must be willing to exercise a level of review which will assure at least a reasonable use of section 204(e) power."

2. As to the withdrawals under the Antiquities Act of 1906, this argument was made in Congressional Stall Prompts Administrative Actions to Protect Alaska National Interest Lands, 8 E.L.R. 10245 (Dec. 1978):

> Use of the Antiquities Act of 1906 to provide permanent protection to 56 million acres of Alaska land was likewise viewed as another prudent overlay for particularly valuable areas. Under [16 U.S.C.A. § 431]:
>
> > The President of the United States is authorized, in his discretion, to declare by public proclamation historic landmarks, historic and prehistoric structures, and other objects of historic or scientific interest that are situated upon the lands owned or controlled by the Government of the United States to be national monuments, and may reserve as a part thereof parcels of land, the limits of which in all cases shall be confined to the smallest area

compatible with the proper care and management of the objects to be protected.

The Antiquities Act has been used 66 times in the past by every President beginning with Theodore Roosevelt. First used to create the Devils Tower National Monument in Wyoming, it has also been the basis for establishing the Grand Canyon National Monument (271,145 acres), Death Valley (1,601,800 acres), Glacier Bay in Alaska (1,164,800 acres), and Katmai National Monument in Alaska (1,088,000 acres).

Because the creation of national monuments is left to the President's discretion under the Act, President Carter's December 1 reservation appears subject to legal challenge only on the ground that it violated the scope of discretion conferred by the statute. In a suit challenging the creation of the Jackson Hole National Monument, a court rejected this argument, finding that the action had not been shown to be arbitrary.[29] Another basis for such a challenge might be that the environmental and conservation motives behind the designations do not comport with the objectives permissible under the statute: preservation of "objects of historic or scientific interest." This argument is similarly unlikely to succeed in view of Supreme Court decisions upholding use of the Antiquities Act to protect the Grand Canyon [30] and, more recently, the addition of Devil's Hole in Nevada to the Death Valley National Monument to protect the rare pupfish.[31] Finally, an argument could be made that the announced boundaries of the Alaskan monuments exceed the statutory limitation to the "smallest area compatible with the proper care and management of the objects to be protected." The best response to this would be, however, that the matter lies within the President's discretion.

How do the withdrawals square with the statutory mandate that the national monuments "shall be confined to the smallest area compatible" with proper management? Can it be argued that, under *Midwest Oil,* congressional acquiescence to the earlier withdrawals helped define the scope of delegated authority under the Act? Are these withdrawals totalling 56 million acres within the delegated authority? Or should the presidential action be analyzed as 17 separate withdrawals, each involving a separate monument? A detailed record was made, with separate proclamations, each going to great pains to describe the areas and the facts justifying each withdrawal on the basis of "historic or scientific interest." For the texts of the proclamations, which make surprisingly good reading, see 43 Fed.Reg. 57009–57131 (Dec. 1, 1978). Maps of the withdrawals are included.

29. Wyoming v. Franke, 58 F.Supp. 890 (D.Wyo.1945).

30. Cameron v. United States, 252 U.S. 450 (1920).

31. Cappaert v. United States, 426 U.S. 128 (1976).

3. The merits of President Carter's withdrawals were reached, and the withdrawals upheld, in Anaconda Copper Co. v. Andrus, 14 ERC 1853 (D.Alaska 1980). During oral argument Judge Fitzgerald advised counsel for Anaconda, who was seeking to establish mining claims on the ground that the withdrawals were invalid, that "you had a most difficult position to advance, and it might have been * * * easier if we were at 1906. But too much has happened since, including Grand Canyon, Katmai, Glacier Park, many, many others." Id. at 1855. See also Getches, Managing the Public Lands: The Authority of the Executive to Withdraw Lands, 22 Nat.Resources J. 279, 300–08 (1982). The Alaska National Interest Lands Conservation Act of 1980 rescinded the Carter Administration withdrawals, effective on December 2, 1980, the date of the passage of the Act. See 16 U.S.C.A. § 3209. Most of the affected lands were included within various preservation systems.

NOTE: CONSTITUTIONALITY OF FLPMA WITHDRAWALS AFTER *CHADHA*

The decision in Immigration & Naturalization Service v. Chadha, 462 U.S. 919 (1983), has jeopardized the delicate balance struck in FLPMA concerning executive withdrawals. Chadha, an alien, had been admitted to the United States on a student visa. After the visa expired, an administrative hearing was held to determine whether he should be deported. The immigration judge ordered that the deportation be suspended, reasoning that Chadha had resided in the United States for seven years, was of good moral character, and would suffer "extreme hardship" if deported. The Attorney General then also recommended suspension of deportation. Pursuant to Section 244(c)(1) of the Immigration and Nationality Act, the Attorney General reported the suspension of the deportation to Congress where, in accordance with the Act, the House of Representatives vetoed the suspension order. No action was taken by the Senate or the President. After the House veto, the immigration judge reopened the deportation proceedings and ordered Chadha deported.

The Supreme Court held that the legislative veto provisions of the Act were unconstitutional because they failed to meet the requirements of bicameralism and presentment, U.S. Const. Art. I, § 7, cl. 2 (requiring that every "Bill" must pass both houses and be presented to the President). The Court was not inclined to recognize pragmatic arrangements or the maxim that "government is a practical affair intended for practical men" [*Midwest Oil*, supra at page 147]:

> The Constitution sought to divide the delegated powers of the new federal government into three defined categories, legislative, executive and judicial, to assure, as nearly as possible, that each Branch of government would confine itself to its assigned responsibility. The hydraulic pressure inherent within each of the separate Branches to exceed the outer limits of

its power, even to accomplish desirable objectives, must be resisted.

Although not "hermetically" sealed from one another, the powers delegated to the three Branches are functionally identifiable. When any Branch acts, it is presumptively exercising the power the Constitution has delegated to it. When the Executive acts, it presumptively acts in an executive or administrative capacity as defined in Art. II. And when, as here, one House of Congress purports to act, it is presumptively acting within its assigned sphere.

Beginning with this presumption, we must nevertheless establish that the challenged action under § 244(c)(2) is of the kind to which the procedural requirements of Art. I, § 7 apply. Not every action taken by either House is subject to the bicameralism and presentment requirements of Art. I. Whether actions taken by either House are, in law and fact, an exercise of legislative power depends not on their form but upon "whether they contain matter which is properly to be regarded as legislative in its character and effect."

Examination of the action taken here by one House pursuant to § 244(c)(2) reveals that it was essentially legislative in purpose and effect. In purporting to exercise power defined in Art. I, § 8, cl. 4 to "establish an uniform Rule of Naturalization," the House took action that had the purpose and effect of altering the legal rights, duties and relations of persons, including the Attorney General, Executive Branch officials and Chadha, all outside the legislative branch. Section 244(c)(2) purports to authorize one House of Congress to require the Attorney General to deport an individual alien whose deportation otherwise would be cancelled under § 244. The one-House veto operated in this case to overrule the Attorney General and mandate Chadha's deportation; absent the House action, Chadha would remain in the United States. Congress has *acted* and its action has altered Chadha's status.

The legislative character of the one-House veto in this case is confirmed by the character of the Congressional action it supplants. Neither the House of Representatives nor the Senate contends that, absent the veto provision in § 244(c)(2), either of them, or both of them acting together, could effectively require the Attorney General to deport an alien once the Attorney General, in the exercise of legislatively delegated authority, had determined the alien should remain in the United States. Without the challenged provision in § 244(c)(2), this could have been achieved, if at all, only by legislation requiring deportation. Similarly, a veto by one House of Congress under § 244(c)(2) cannot be justified as an attempt at amending the standards set out in § 244(a)(1), or as a repeal of

§ 244 as applied to Chadha. Amendment and repeal of statutes, no less than enactment, must conform with Art. I.

* * *

The veto authorized by § 244(c)(2) doubtless has been in many respects a convenient shortcut; the "sharing" with the Executive by Congress of its authority over aliens in this manner is, on its face, an appealing compromise. In purely practical terms, it is obviously easier for action to be taken by one House without submission to the President; but it is crystal clear from the records of the Convention, contemporaneous writings and debates, that the Framers ranked other values higher than efficiency. The records of the Convention and debates in the States preceding ratification underscore the common desire to define and limit the exercise of the newly created federal powers affecting the states and the people. There is unmistakable expression of a determination that legislation by the national Congress be a step-by-step, deliberate and deliberative process.

The choices we discern as having been made in the Constitutional Convention impose burdens on governmental processes that often seem clumsy, inefficient, even unworkable, but those hard choices were consciously made by men who had lived under a form of government that permitted arbitrary governmental acts to go unchecked. There is no support in the Constitution or decisions of this Court for the proposition that the cumbersomeness and delays often encountered in complying with explicit Constitutional standards may be avoided, either by the Congress or by the President. See Youngstown Sheet & Tube Co. v. Sawyer, 343 U.S. 579 (1952). With all the obvious flaws of delay, untidiness, and potential for abuse, we have not yet found a better way to preserve freedom than by making the exercise of power subject to the carefully crafted restraints spelled out in the Constitution.

* * *

In part because the Immigration Act had a severability clause, the Court found that the provisions of section 244 were severable and that those other than the one-House veto provision would remain in force. Thus the administrative authority to suspend deportations was preserved, as was the duty of the Attorney General to report all suspensions to Congress: "clearly, § 244 survives as a workable administrative mechanism without the one-House veto." In dictum, the Court approved "report and wait" provisions whereby proposed administrative action is reported to Congress and does not take effect until the end of a specified waiting period, 462 U.S. at 935 n. 9.

The leading treatment of these issues in the public lands context is Glicksman, Severability and the Realignment of the Balance of Power Over the Public Lands: The Federal Land Policy and Management Act of 1976 After the Legislative Veto Decisions, 36 Hast.L.J. 1 (1984). See also Sullivan, The Power of Congress Under the Property Clause: A

Potential Check on the Effect of the *Chadha* Decision on Public Land Legislation, 6 Pub.Land L.Rev. 65 (1985); Gaetke, Separation of Powers, Legislative Vetoes, and the Public Lands, 56 U.Colo.L.Rev. 559 (1985).

Two courts have confronted *Chadha*-type issues in public lands contexts. One of the first conflicts between Congress and the Interior Secretary Watt gave rise to Pacific Legal Foundation v. Watt, 529 F.Supp. 982 (D.Mont.1981), handed down after the Ninth Circuit decision in *Chadha* but before the Supreme Court ruling. The Wilderness Act allowed mining location and mineral leasing in wilderness areas to continue through December 31, 1983, at which time the areas would be withdrawn from availability for mining and mineral leasing, subject to existing rights. 16 U.S.C.A. § 1133(d)(3). In early 1981, Secretary Watt announced plans to issue mineral leases in the Bob Marshall, Scapegoat, and Great Bear Wilderness Areas in Montana. In May, the House Interior Committee, by a vote of 23–18, invoked the "emergency withdrawal" provision of FLPMA, 43 U.S.C.A. § 1714(e) (quoted supra at page 253), and directed the Secretary to withdraw the areas in question from mineral leasing. Secretary Watt stated his doubts about the constitutionality of section 1714(e) but issued a public land order making the withdrawals in accordance with the Committee directive. Pacific Legal Foundation, Mountain States Legal Foundation, and several individual miners challenged the withdrawal. The court thought the issue was close, but it upheld the emergency withdrawal provisions on the ground that the Secretary still had flexibility to set the duration of the withdrawal:

> If section 204(e) were interpreted to authorize the Committee to dictate the scope and duration of an emergency withdrawal, I would be compelled by [the Ninth Circuit decision in *Chadha*] to declare it unconstitutional. * * *
>
> [I]f section 204(e) is viewed as a device for correcting executive misapplication of a statute, the Committee "is performing a role ordinarily a judicial or an internal administrative responsibility." As with section 244(c)(2) of the INA, this would disrupt the relationship between the judiciary and persons who could otherwise invoke its jurisdiction to review agency decisions. Individuals would no longer be "guaranteed the constraints of articulated reasons and stare decisis in the interpretation" of wilderness, mining and mineral leasing, and other public lands legislation. Moreover, the integrity of the third branch would be undermined by the Committees' power under section 204(e) to prevent the Judiciary's review of Executive action under these statutes. There would be "virtually no procedural constraints on the ultimate [committee] decision nor any provision for review of [its] legal or factual conclusions." * * *
>
> Since the scope and duration of all emergency withdrawals must be determined by the Secretary, "legislative interference" could not "be exercised in any given case without a change in

the general standards the legislation decreed." The "case-by-case * * * law enforcement," would be performed by the Executive branch, as it should be.

Finally, this interpretation of section 204(e) is properly described as allowing the "exercise of a residual legislative power * * *". Since an emergency withdrawal is implemented and can be revoked by the Secretary, acting pursuant to the guidelines of the FLPMA, the Committee's action does not amount to a statutory amendment.

Obviously, the authority vested in the Committee under even this limited interpretation is somewhat unique. It still requires the Executive branch to take affirmative action at the request of a single congressional committee. But since the Secretary is allowed to exercise his discretion in implementing that request, the Committee's authority is sufficiently similar to traditional committee powers, and to proper report and wait provisions to pass constitutional muster.

* * *

The *Pacific Legal Foundation* litigation, which included a brief subsequent opinion at 539 F.Supp. 1194 (D.Mont.1982), triggered a series of executive and congressional actions resulting in the withdrawal of all wilderness areas from mineral leasing through December 31, 1983. At that point, the statutory withdrawal in the Wilderness Act took effect.

The second case raising the constitutionality of section 1714(e) involved the largescale proposed sale of mineral leases in the Upper Great Plains. The court expedited the litigation and issued the following opinion in support of its preliminary injunction.

NATIONAL WILDLIFE FEDERATION v. WATT

United States District Court, District of Columbia, 1983.
571 F.Supp. 1145.

OBERDORFER, District Judge.

* * *

MEMORANDUM WITH RESPECT TO PRELIMINARY INJUNCTION

* * * Plaintiffs seek a declaratory judgment holding illegal the Secretary's plan to lease for coal mining certain tracts of federal lands in the Fort Union Federal Coal Production Region in eastern Montana and western North Dakota. Plaintiffs also seek appropriate injunctive relief. They filed the suit after defendant gave notice of his intention to receive and accept bids for the sale of coal leases in the region despite a Resolution adopted by the Interior and Insular Affairs Committee of the House of Representatives on August 3, 1983, pursuant to section 204(e) of the Federal Land Policy and Management Act of 1976, 43 U.S.C. § 1714(e). That Resolution directed the Secretary to withdraw the Fort Union lands from coal leasing temporarily.

* * *

The Secretary's decision to bid and lease the Fort Union land for coal mining was preceded by an elaborate administrative process beginning in the late 1970's with the Federal Coal Management Program. The Program proceeded through several stages, including an environmental impact statement. * * *

* * *

In the year before the sale at issue, the Secretary auctioned leases for 1.5 billion tons of coal on approximately 32,000 acres in Montana and Wyoming. In May 1983, the General Accounting Office (GAO) reported that the Interior Department had issued those leases for $100 million less than the GAO's estimates of fair market value. See Comptroller General, Report to the Congress: Analysis of the Powder River Basin Federal Coal Lease Sale: Economic Valuation Improvements and Legislative Changes Needed (May 11, 1983). On July 30, 1983, Congress passed, and the President signed, an Act that ordered the Secretary to appoint a commission to review coal leasing procedures. The Commission was obligated to report to the Congress by January 1984 on methods to insure that fair market value is received for leases. * * *

The immediate actions leading up the current litigation began with an exchange of letters on August 2, 1983, between the Secretary and Chairman Udall. In his letter, the Secretary stated that he did not plan to postpone the sale of Fort Union leases previously scheduled for September 14. The Chairman replied with a request for postponement pending committee review. The Secretary then stated that any Committee resolution passed pursuant to section 204(e) would be treated as a request, not a directive. On August 3, the Committee adopted a Resolution pursuant to which the Chairman notified the Secretary that an emergency situation existed and that the Fort Union tracts "are to be immediately withdrawn" from coal leasing. Nevertheless, in two subsequent notices in the Federal Register, the Secretary continued preparations for the September 14 sale.

On September 9, 1983, the Secretary acknowledged by letter to Chairman Udall that he had received "the August 3, 1983 Resolution voted out of your Committee by a partisan vote." The Secretary stated that he was respectfully declining to comply with the Committee's directive because section 204(e) and the Committee Resolution were unconstitutional under Immigration and Naturalization Service v. Chadha, 462 U.S. 919 (1983). * * *

On the basis of the limited briefing and research which the schedule has afforded counsel and the Court, it appears to be unlikely that plaintiffs' original, nonconstitutional theory for distinguishing *Chadha* can succeed. If Congress' authority to enact the procedure at issue here derives solely from Article I of the Constitution, or if the *Chadha* rationale applies to Article IV, Section 3, the Committee resolution will probably be held to be impermissible legislative activity. Plaintiffs' attempt to distinguish a section 204(e) withdrawal from a legislative veto on the grounds that the withdrawal is only temporary is unconvincing. A forced withdrawal, whether temporary or permanent, alters the legal rights and duties of the Secretary of the Interior, and this cannot be done, according to *Chadha*, without bicameral passage and presidential presentment. The holding in *Pacific Legal Foundation* [supra] which plaintiffs cite as support, seems susceptible to similar criticism. If section 204(e) is read to give the Secretary total discretion over the duration of the withdrawal, then the section would lose all force. Yet once the section is interpreted to mandate withdrawal for any length of time, it alters the Secretary's legal rights and duties.

Finally, section 204(e) does not seem analogous, as plaintiffs claim, to the "report and wait" provisions that passed constitutional muster in *Chadha*. * * * This grace period, uniformly applied to every new rule, allows Congress time to amend or reject the rule if it desires. There is no similar rule of postponement universally applied to coal leases so that each lease can be reviewed by Congress as a whole. Rather, the House Committee may pick and choose to delay leases that may or may not become the subject of action by Congress. *Chadha* will probably be interpreted as holding that this sort of selective review of executive action by less than the full Congress is not a permissible exercise of its legislative power under Article I.

[The Interior Department had adopted the following regulation in order to implement section 1714(e) of FLPMA:

> When the Secretary determines, or when either one of the two Committees of the Congress that are specified in section 204(e) of the act (43 U.S.C. 1714(e)) notifies the Secretary, that an emergency exists * * * the Secretary shall immediately make a withdrawal which shall be limited in its scope and duration to the emergency. 43 CFR § 2310.5(a)].

Defendant's failure to follow his own regulation, or to rescind it after notice, comment, and reasoned determination, raises a more serious question. On the day after the Supreme Court decided *Chadha*, it announced its decision in Motor Vehicle Manufacturers Association v. State Farm Mutual Automobile Insurance Company, 463 U.S. 29 (1983). That decision reiterated the high standard set by Congress in the Administrative Procedure Act for Executive Department decisions which withdraw regulations, a standard not satisfied in that case even though there had been full compliance with APA notice and comment rules. *A fortiori*, it will probably be held that defendant's decision not to follow his regulation, on the basis of informal, *ex parte*, unpublished legal opinions that the parallel provision of section 204(e) was void, violated those notice requirements. Reliance on such *ex parte* opinions without minimal testing by other interested persons does not satisfy the notice and comment requirements of APA. * * *

Neither the material furnished by the parties nor that otherwise available to the Court in this brief time establishes with the certainty perceived by the defendant's legal advisers that section 204(e) of the

1976 Act, the Committee resolution, and the regulation are, as defendant asserts, "patently unconstitutional." * * *

It may well be that when this Court, the Court of Appeals, or the Supreme Court has had comprehensive briefs and an adequate opportunity to consider all the relevant historical evidence about the drafting and context of Article IV, Section 3, as well as its application over the years, they will reach a conclusion contrary to the opinions relied upon by the defendant here. The Supreme Court has stated that Congress' proprietary interest in public lands gives it constitutional prerogatives which transcend those which it enjoys in its purely legislative role in respect of immigration. See, e.g., United States v. California, 332 U.S. 19, 27 (1947). Moreover, it is common historical knowledge that in the years before the Constitution was adopted (and for many years thereafter) Congress was in session for only brief periods and in recess for many months at a time. Public lands were matters of even greater public and political interest than they are now. It is not inconceivable that courts will decide from the text and context of Article IV, Section 3, that its Framers contemplated that Congress' proprietary power to "dispose of" public lands included the power to delegate power to dispose of public land to the Executive as a trustee. The Framers may well have contemplated that such an Article IV delegation might be subject to an express and narrow condition that a specified Committee of Congress could, during or in anticipation of a congressional recess, temporarily suspend that delegation in the manner now provided for in section 204(e) of the 1976 Act. Such a condition would be analogous to limitations traditionally imposed by settlors under familiar principles of trust law.

* * *

[The court, reasoning that there was a probability that the plaintiffs would prevail on the merits, issued a preliminary injunction. Later, the court granted plaintiffs' motion for summary judgment. 577 F.Supp. 825 (D.D.C.1984).]

NOTES

1. Should an injunction issue to require compliance with a regulation adopted to implement an unconstitutional statutory provision? The regulation, it should be noted, was still in force several years later. See 43 CFR § 2310.5(a) (1985). Does the Court's reading of the Property Clause in the *Fort Union* case mean that FLPMA can be distinguished from the statute at issue in *Chadha*? Can the analysis of section 1714(e) in *Pacific Legal Foundation* to provide for durational limits on secretarial discretion be squared with the Supreme Court's decision in *Chadha*? Leaving aside section 1714(e), is the one-House veto in section 1714(c) for withdrawals in excess of 5000 acres constitutional? The commentators mostly conclude that both provisions probably violate the *Chadha* rationale. See, e.g., Glicksman, supra, 36 Hast. L.J. at 33–51. But see Sullivan, supra, 6 Pub.Land L.Rev. at 98–102, who argues that § 1714(e) may survive *Chadha*.

2. Assuming that FLPMA is constitutionally infirm, how should the courts deal with the key question of severability? What are the alternatives? Regarding section 1714(c), should all authority to make withdrawals in excess of 5000 acres be struck down? Should the right to make withdrawals in excess of 5000 acres be left in place, with no secretarial obligation to Congress? Should section 1714(c) be construed so that only the veto is severed, leaving in place the duty to report large withdrawals to Congress? See Glicksman, 36 Hast.L.J. at 65–90. Given the uncertainties surrounding the FLPMA withdrawal provisions, what, if anything, should Congress do to affirm and implement its supervisory powers in a constitutional fashion?

NATIONAL WILDLIFE FEDERATION v. BURFORD

United States District Court, District of Columbia, 1985.
23 E.R.C. 1609.

PRATT, J.

* * *

Background

This litigation focuses on defendants' termination of protective classifications and revocation of withdrawals on approximately 170 million acres of public lands since 1981. The Federal Land Policy and Management Act, 43 U.S.C. §§ 1701 et seq. (1982) (FLPMA), establishes comprehensive rules for the management of federal lands. The FLPMA includes two systems for preserving land in the public domain and thereby for protecting it from private ownership and development. "Classifications" allow the Department of the Interior to categorize lands according to their proper use. "Withdrawals" directly remove lands from private development and exploitation. Subject to certain procedural controls, the Secretary of the Interior may open land to private development by terminating the applicable classification or withdrawal. See 43 U.S.C. §§ 1712(d), 1714. Since the passage of the FLPMA in 1976, defendants have terminated classifications on 160.8 million acres of land, and revoked withdrawals for 20 million acres.

Plaintiff contends that in lifting these restrictions, defendants improperly ignored certain requirements of the FLPMA. Among plaintiff's claims are that defendants failed to review land status actions in the context of land use planning, to submit to the President and Congress withdrawal revocation recommendations, to promulgate rules and regulations governing withdrawal revocations, to provide for public participation, and to prepare environmental impact statements. Plaintiff ultimately seeks a declaration that defendants' land withdrawal program violates applicable law and regulations; an order both reinstating all withdrawals, classifications or other designations in effect on January 1, 1981[1] and enjoining defendants from taking any action inconsistent with these designations until they comply with their statu-

---

1. Although the figures in this case focus on events since 1976, it appears that most if not all of the contested terminations occurred since January 1, 1981.

tory obligations; and an order mandating that defendants rescind all directives, instructive memoranda, manuals or other documents regarding classification or withdrawal terminations until they have promulgated certain rules and regulations.

Plaintiff now moves for a preliminary injunction. The claim for relief here is more narrow than that in the Complaint. Specifically, plaintiff requests this court, *inter alia,* to enjoin defendants from modifying, terminating or altering any withdrawal, classification or other land use designation in effect on January 1, 1981, and to enjoin them from taking any action inconsistent with the 1981 status quo. It "does not seek to invalidate existing mining claims or mineral leases nor does it seek to overturn completely sales or exchanges of previously withdrawn lands."

In the meantime, defendants have moved to dismiss the entire action * * *.

* * *

II.　*Motion to Dismiss*

A.　*Failure to Join Indispensible Parties*

While the holders of mining claims and mineral leases are necessary parties, their absence does not compel dismissal. Defendants assert that plaintiff should have joined as defendants all third parties who hold mining claims or mineral leases to the lands at issue. Federal Rule of Civil Procedure 19 requires a two-step analysis for such compulsory joinder claims. First, the court must determine if the absent party falls within the category of persons "to be joined if feasible." Second, the court must determine whether, in equity and good conscience, the case should proceed without the third party or be dismissed.

The mining claimants and lessees meet the first requirement of compulsory joinder, as set out in Rule 19(a). They all claim an interest in the lands that are the subject of this action. In the case of the mining claimants, this interest may even amount to exclusive possession and enjoyment. 30 U.S.C. § 26 (1982).

Furthermore, disposition of the action in their absence could impair or impede the ability of these parties to protect their interests. If plaintiff's injunction is granted, such relief could suspend development of the third parties' interests. Until as late as 1991, defendants would be unable to issue patents, approve lease activities—in short, to authorize any commercial activity on these lands. Furthermore, if Congress rejects the Secretary's recommendations to revoke the withdrawals, those parties who now hold mining claims or mineral leases could lose their interest altogether. The fact that plaintiff does not directly seek to void these interests is irrelevant. What matters is the effect of ultimate disposition of the case.

The third parties here could suffer harm not just by disposition of the action but by disposition in their absence. To be sure, the present defendants share the interest of these parties in resisting plaintiff's proposed injunction. In fact, the intervention by the Mountain States Legal Foundation, which represents a group of mining and milling lessees, ensures advocacy of at least some of the third parties' claims. However, only the absent parties can accurately measure the full value of the interests that they now hold and the extent to which that value could be impaired or lessened. Their absence weakens defendants' ability precisely to articulate the harm that plaintiff's requested relief would cause. In sum, it cannot be denied that these holders of mining claims and leases have legitimate interests.

Our finding that the mining claimants and lessees are necessary parties under Rule 19(a), however, does not end the inquiry. In determining whether or not to dismiss, we must consider and weigh (1) the extent of potential prejudice to these parties, (2) the possibility of avoiding this prejudice by shaping alternative measures of relief, (3) the adequacy of judgment in these parties' absence, and (4) the adequacy of plaintiff's remedy if we dismiss. Balancing these factors, we conclude that the action may proceed without the mining claimants and lessees. Our reasoning may be summed up in the discussion which follows.

The fact that dismissal of plaintiff's claims for relief in this court would effectively foreclose plaintiff from relief elsewhere outweighs the more speculative harm to the absent parties. As we discussed, supra, plaintiff's proposed injunction would suspend development of and, depending on plaintiff's success in obtaining permanent relief, could possibly revoke existing claims or leases. Thus, if the case proceeds without the presence of the claimants or lessees, these third parties would suffer temporary hardship; the possibility of permanent harm, however, is only a matter of speculation.

In contrast, dismissal for failure to join would deny plaintiff an adequate forum in which ever to prosecute its claim. The availability of an alternative forum represents a "critical consideration" in deciding joinder questions. The lands involved in this case lie in seventeen different states. The absent parties probably cover an even broader geographical range. Because of problems of jurisdiction and venue, plaintiff could never join all defendants in one forum. Requiring it to bring seventeen separate lawsuits or even to combine actions through the device of multidistrict litigation would create enormous administrative disorder and delay. Dismissal, therefore, would effectively discourage and, for all practical purposes, put an end to this litigation. Balanced against the merely temporary or speculative harm to the absentees, this harsh result supports denial of the defendants' motion to dismiss.

The two other factors listed in Rule 19(b) do not influence our determination. If, as plaintiff contends, defendants have illegally terminated classifications and withdrawals, it may well be necessary to grant the injunction requested. Any lesser relief that sought to provide protection for the interest of third parties would have the effect of permitting defendants' actions to continue without further challenge. The third factor—adequacy of judgment in the third parties' absence—

also does not enter into our decision, since their presence is not essential to shape the judgment.

The "public rights" exception provides further support for denial of the motion to dismiss. This doctrine derives from the teaching of National Licorice Co. v. NLRB, 309 U.S. 350 (1940), where the Supreme Court held that the NLRB could order an employer not to enforce certain illegal contracts with its employees, even though the employees, who had a vital interest in the matter, had not been joined. As the Court reasoned, "[i]n a proceeding so narrowly restricted to the protection and enforcement of public rights, there is little scope or need for the traditional rules governing the joinder of parties in litigation determining private rights." Id. at 363. Here, as in *National Licorice,* the plaintiff's cause of action is grounded in the assertion of public rather than private rights. The public's interest in disposition of federal lands, and more concretely, in participating in the management of these lands is a matter of transcending importance. It extends this case far beyond the boundaries of private dispute.

* * *

III. *Motion for a Preliminary Injunction*

* * *

A. *Likelihood of Success on the Merits*

1. *Failure to Review Land Status Actions in the Context of Land Use Planning*

In considering the likelihood of success on the merits of plaintiff's several claims, we consider only two of the more important. The first is plaintiff's claim that defendants improperly terminated land classifications without first preparing Resource Management Plans. We hold that there is a likelihood that plaintiff will succeed on the merits.

Section 202 of the FLPMA, concerning classifications, directs the Secretary of the Interior to develop "land use plans," which establish the use of the public lands. 43 U.S.C. § 1712(a). Subsection (d) further provides:

> Any classification of public lands or any land use plan in effect on October 21, 1976, is subject to review in the land use planning process conducted under this section, and all public lands, regardless of classification, are subject to inclusion in any land use plan developed pursuant to this section. The Secretary may *modify or terminate any such classification consistent with such land use plan.*

42 U.S.C. § 1712(d) (emphasis supplied). Since 1976, defendants have terminated classifications affecting approximately 160 million acres of land. Yet, as plaintiff alleges and defendants do not deny, defendants have completed only a fraction of the land use plans for these areas. Thus, the vast majority of classification terminations have occurred outside the context of land use planning.

Defendants' reliance on "Management Framework Plans" (MFP's) is misplaced and does not satisfy the statutory expectations of "land use plans." As section 202(a) evidences, Congress sought a comprehensive system of land use plans. In its regulations, the Interior Department identifies these land use plans as "Resource Management Plans" (RMP's). 43 C.F.R. § 1601.0–5(k) (1984). It is true that Congress did not reject altogether existing MFP's. It recognized that RMP's would not be ready immediately, see 43 U.S.C. § 1732(a) (referring to land use plans "when they are available"), and it noted that BLM's pre-FLPMA system of land planning was consistent in general principles and practices with the objectives of the Act. H.Rep. No. 1163, 94th Cong., 2d Sess. 5 (1976), *reprinted in* 1976 U.S.Code Cong. & Ad.News 6175, 6179.

However, looking at the matter in its totality, it is clear to us that Congress approved only temporary reliance on MFP's. It never authorized the vast scale of classification terminations without land use plans which we see today, more than nine years after the passage in 1976 of the FLPMA. MFP's may conform to the general principles of the FLPMA, but they are not identical substitutes to RMP's. The land use plans Congress envisioned would modify existing plans in several aspects, including public participation. By terminating classifications for 160 million acres of land outside the context of land use planning, defendants have simply evaded the statute's directive that land use plans "shall be developed" and that the Secretary terminate classifications "consistent with such land use plans."

Defendants' obligation to review land status actions in the context of land use planning, however, does not extend beyond classification terminations. Plaintiff reads section 202(d) also to apply to withdrawal revocations, and it argues that defendants' failure to tie withdrawal revocations to land use planning thus violates the FLPMA. We disagree with plaintiff's reading of the statute. Classification terminations and withdrawal revocations are separate and distinct. Section 202(d) links land use planning to classification terminations. It never mentions withdrawal revocations, which appear in a separate section of the statute. See 43 U.S.C. § 1714. The history of classifications and withdrawals further contradicts plaintiff's equation of the two procedures. Classifications derive from the Classification and Multiple Use Act of 1964, Pub.L. No. 88–607, 78 Stat. 986, which expired in 1970. Withdrawals, on the other hand, date back to the nineteenth century and were executed by the Secretary largely without statutory guidance. Having developed along distinct paths, classification terminations and withdrawal revocations do not now merge in section 202(d), particularly since the statute separates the two terms. Therefore, plaintiff's likely success on its first claim applies only to defendants' terminations of land classifications.

2. *Lack of Public Participation*

Despite the statutory command, defendants have failed to provide for public participation in their withdrawal revocation decisions. Section 309(e) of the Act, 43 U.S.C. § 1739(e), requires the Secretary to establish procedures to give the public an opportunity "to comment upon the formulation of standards and criteria for, and to participate in, the preparation and execution of plans and programs for, *and the management of,* the public lands" (emphasis supplied). Defendants apparently have not permitted public input into their decisions to revoke land withdrawals. This lack of public participation both violates the text of the statute and frustrates Congress' intent that "[p]lanning decisions are to be made only after full opportunity for public involvement in the planning process." H.Rep. No. 1163 at 2. Defendants protest that they offer numerous avenues for public participation in land use planning. Yet the statute calls for participation also in the "management" of public lands. Withdrawal revocations fall into this "management" category. We find, therefore, that plaintiff is likely to succeed on this claim.

If plaintiff ultimately prevails on the two counts discussed, it could obtain the permanent injunction it seeks. Thus, in light of our conclusion that plaintiff will likely succeed on these counts, we do not need to reach the merits of plaintiff's other claims, including its claim that defendants failed to submit withdrawal recommendations to the President and the Congress as required by § 204(*l*) of the Act.

B. *Irreparable Injury*

We have no problem in holding that defendants' actions in lifting protective land restrictions will irreparably injure plaintiff's members unless enjoined. In ordering classification terminations and withdrawal revocations, defendants removed the only absolute shield against private exploitation of these federal lands. It is true, as defendants contend, that the classification terminations and withdrawal revocations do not immediately open the lands to mining and mineral leasing. They merely trigger the operation of certain discretionary land laws. Yet, as defendants also concede, some of the backup safeguards are optional. For example, the Secretary may choose whether or not to prepare an environmental impact assessment or statement. Moreover, neither the statutes nor the regulations can prohibit all development: they can only regulate its process.

If defendants have improperly terminated classifications or withdrawals to begin with, *any* allowance of mining or leasing can cause irreparable harm. Such activity can permanently destroy wildlife habitat, air and water quality, natural beauty and other environmental values. Defendants' suggestion that plaintiff's members can still hike, fish and otherwise enjoy these lands ignores both aesthetic interests and the process whereby a holder of a mining claim can gain the right to exclusive possession. Similarly, defendants' calculations limiting the acres that have actually been leased or mined [6] demonstrates nothing about the future impact of their actions. Without the preliminary

---

6. Defendants claim that only 845 acres are being mined. As the discussion of harm to private parties indicates, this is an axe that cuts both ways.

injunction, defendants' termination of classifications and withdrawals could lead to the permanent loss of lands to public use and enjoyment—an injury we feel would be irreparable.

C. *Harm to Interested Parties*

While we acknowledge that the preliminary injunction would harm third parties, we do not view this injury as so serious as to outweigh the other factors supporting the injunction. The preliminary injunction would bar present holders of mining claims and mineral leases from developing their interests. To the extent they have made investments in obtaining their claims or leases or in beginning development, the delay in their investment return would represent financial injury. However, the preliminary injunction alone would not sever these parties' interests. If defendants prevail on the merits, it would only delay their realization. Furthermore, the injunction is not likely to reduce the ultimate value of the ore to be mined.

D. *The Public Interest*

The public interest clearly favors granting the preliminary injunction. In section 102 of the FLPMA, Congress declared "it is the policy of the United States that—(1) the public lands be retained in Federal ownership, unless as a result of the land use planning procedure provided for in this Act, it is determined that disposal of a particular parcel will serve the national interest." 43 U.S.C. § 1701(a)(1). This statement of policy, which provides the basis for plaintiff's claims for relief, underscores the public interest in ensuring orderly procedures for removing certain federal controls over government-owned lands. If defendants have violated the FLPMA in the process of terminating classifications and revoking withdrawals, the preliminary injunction will protect against further illegal actions pending resolution of the merits.

Furthermore, the preliminary injunction would serve the public by protecting the environment from any threat of permanent damage. Defendants' scenario of administrative havoc invokes a limited version of the public interest. While granting the preliminary injunction would inconvenience defendants and those parties holding specific interests in the lands at issue, denying the motion could ruin some of the country's great environmental resources—and not just for now but for generations to come.

For these reasons, we grant the plaintiff's motion for a preliminary injunction.

Orders consistent with the foregoing have been entered this day.

ORDER

* * *

Finding that issuance of the requested injunction would serve the public interest, it is by the court this 4th day of December, 1985:

ORDERED that plaintiff's motion for a preliminary injunction is granted, and it is

* * *

ORDERED that the defendants, their officers, agents, servants, employees, and attorneys, and those persons in active concert or participation with them are hereby enjoined from:

1. Modifying, terminating or altering any withdrawal, classification, or other designation governing the protection of lands in the public domain that was in effect on January 1, 1981, or

2. Taking any action inconsistent with any withdrawal, classification, or other designation governing the protection of lands in the public domain that was in effect on January 1, 1981, including, but not limited to, the issuance of leases, the sale, exchange or disposal of land or interests in land, the grant of rights-of-way, or the approval of any plan of operations; and it is

ORDERED that all persons holding interests, including but not limited to, ownership, possession, mining claims and their development, leases and rights-of-way, in lands that were the subject of classification terminations or withdrawal revocations since January 1, 1981 are hereby enjoined from taking any action inconsistent with the present status quo of these lands, including but not limited to, the staking of additional mining claims, obtaining new leases, mining, timber removal, land clearing, construction, or other forms of development.

* * *

NOTES

1. Does the BLM have flexibility under the court's order in *Buford* to respond to individual problems of its lessees and mineral claimants on the now "rewithdrawn" lands? Cf. FLPMA § 1714(*l*), requiring the Secretary to report to Congress on recommendations for lifting withdrawals of lands from the operation of the mining and mineral leasing laws.

2. What exactly is the difference between a withdrawal and a classification?

3. Caution should be exercised in predicting the implications of a preliminary decision by a district court on a matter of fundamental importance to a great number and variety of interests. Nevertheless, who wins and who loses if the decision in the principal case is affirmed?

4. Between 1977 and 1980 the Forest Service and the BLM withheld action on applications for oil and gas leases in national forest roadless areas while the lands were being studied for possible inclusion in the wilderness system. The court in Mountain States Legal Foundation v. Andrus, 499 F.Supp. 383 (D.Wyo.1980), held this inaction a "de facto withdrawal" of those lands, stating:

the combined actions of the Department of the Interior and the Department of Agriculture fit squarely within the foregoing definition of withdrawal found in 43 U.S.C. § 1702(j). The combined actions of the Secretaries have (1) effectively removed large areas of federal land from oil and gas leasing and the operation of the Mineral Leasing Act of 1920, (2) in order to maintain other public values in the area, namely those of wilderness preservation. That's the plain meaning of Congress' definition of "withdrawal". * * *

We conclude that it was the intent of Congress with the passage of FLPMA to limit the ability of the Secretary of the Interior to remove large tracts of public land from the operation of the public land laws by generalized use of his discretion authorized under such laws.

We cannot allow the Defendants to accomplish by inaction what they could not do by formal administrative order. Id. at 391, 395, 397.

Because the Secretary of the Interior failed to follow the FLPMA withdrawal procedures, the court found his inaction on the applications illegal. Is the Secretary's decision to withhold leasing pending a study of wilderness suitability more accurately characterized as land use planning or as a withdrawal? How is the inaction described in *Mountain States* (the inaction by the Interior Department from 1977 until 1980) any different than the decision by Secretary Watt after the *Pacific Legal Foundation* litigation not to issue leases in the wilderness areas? Is withdrawal the only method for implementing land management decisions such as withholding leases? For a negative answer, see Rowe v. United States, 464 F.Supp. 1060, 1074 (D.Alaska 1979), affirmed in part, 633 F.2d 799 (9th Cir.1980). For an argument that the *Mountain States* court erred, see Getches, Managing the Public Lands: The Authority of the Executive to Withdraw Lands, 22 Nat. Resources J. 279, 326 n. 267 (1982). Reagan Administration officials dismissed the appeal in *Mountain States*.

NOTE: LAND EXCHANGES AND SALES

All of the major federal land management agencies traditionally have held delegated power to exchange lands under their control for private lands; each empowering statute contains various conditions such as an "equal value" standard to prevent profiteering. Most such exchanges are undertaken to consolidate federal land holdings. When they also divest public land users of their interest, however, they resemble withdrawals. The BLM, given the checkerboard character of many of its lands, is naturally the most active agency in promoting land exchanges. BLM authority vs. the rancher's interest in continuation of grazing was litigated in Red Canyon Sheep Co. v. Ickes, 98 F.2d 308 (D.C.Cir.1938), and LaRue v. Udall, 324 F.2d 428 (D.C.Cir.1963), infra at page 683. See also Lewis v. Hickel, 427 F.2d 673 (9th Cir.1970), cert. denied, 400 U.S. 992 (1971). Compare Payne v. New Mexico, 255 U.S. 367 (1921). A completed exchange between the Fish and Wildlife Service and a utility, pursuant to 16 U.S.C.A. § 668dd(b)(3), to facilitate construction of a nuclear generating complex, was unsuccessfully challenged in Sierra Club v. Hickel, 467 F.2d 1048 (6th Cir.1972), cert. denied, 411 U.S. 920 (1973); the court held that the exchange was unreviewable because it was discretionary and barred by the doctrine of sovereign immunity. Before the passage of FLPMA, Forest Service exchange authority was contained in the General Exchange Act of 1922, 16 U.S.C.A. § 485, and miscellaneous statutes usually involving individual national forests. One of the few cases construing the 1922 Act, which was not repealed by FLPMA, is National Forest Preservation Group v. Butz, 485 F.2d 408 (9th Cir.1973); the decision thwarted, at least temporarily, an attempted exchange between the Forest Service and the Big Sky Resort interests in Montana. On pre-FLPMA exchange law, see generally Anderson, Public Land Exchanges, Sales, and Purchases Under the Federal Land Policy and Management Act of 1976, 1979 Utah L.Rev. 657, 661–69.

FLPMA did not repeal all of the scattered exchange statutes, but the 1976 Act did include a general exchange section governing both BLM and Forest Service lands. See 43 U.S.C.A. § 1716. The provision expanded BLM powers and may prove to be of particular assistance to the agency: the BLM "should be able to rid itself of difficult-to-manage parcels, consolidate the checkerboard of public land holdings into more efficient units, and accommodate private desires for land transactions with the BLM." Anderson, supra, 1979 Utah L.Rev. at 658. States are also involved because their lands are often checkerboarded with BLM lands. Perhaps the most notable example is in Utah, where the State has been negotiating with the Interior Department over "Project Bold," which would involve a swap of as much as 2.5 million acres of state land for equivalent federal acreage. See, e.g., 10 Public Land News 6 (July 11, 1985).

FLPMA includes an "equal value" requirement and a mandate that exchange transactions be in the public interest:

> when considering public interest the Secretary concerned shall give full consideration to better Federal land management and the needs of State and local people, including needs for lands for the economy, community expansion, recreation areas, food, fiber, minerals, and fish and wildlife and the Secretary concerned finds that the values and the objectives which Federal lands or interests to be conveyed may serve if retained in Federal ownership are not more than the values of the non-Federal lands or interests and the public objectives they could serve if acquired. 43 U.S.C.A. § 1716(a).

Does this definition of the public interest call for stringent judicial review? See generally National Coal Ass'n v. Hodel, 617 F.Supp. 584 (D.D.C.1985), upholding a complex three-way exchange among the National Park Service, Princeton University and other non-profit institutions, and Rocky Mountain Energy Company. The arrangement allowed the Park Service, which had no acquisition funds for the transaction, to obtain an inholding in Grand Teton National Park, formerly owned by Princeton and others; the energy company pur-

chased BLM coal lands of equivalent value and paid the purchase price
to Princeton.   In National Audubon Society v. Clark, 21 E.R.C. 2069
(D.Alaska 1984), infra at page 837, the court strictly construed a broad
"public interest" provision in ANILCA, 16 U.S.C.A. § 3192(h), and
struck down an exchange involving St. Matthew Island, a wilderness
area in a national wildlife refuge.   The "equal value" provision of the
Park Service exchange statute, the Land and Water Conservation Fund
Act of 1976, 16 U.S.C.A. § 461*l*–22(b), was construed as follows in
Committee of 100 on the Federal City v. Hodel, 777 F.2d 711, 720 n. 11
(D.C.Cir.1985):

> We need not here detail the basis for our conclusion that
> the Park Service reasonably concluded that the properties to
> be exchanged were approximately equal in value.   We may,
> however, sketch the contours of our review of this matter.   We
> begin with the premise that the standard for review on this
> issue is highly deferential.   Appellees concede that the Park
> Service determination may only be overturned if it is arbitrary
> and capricious.   Great deference is due also because the matter
> is one largely within the technical expertise of the agency.
> Finally, § 22(b) does not require that the agency establish that
> it has calculated the values of the properties to the last penny;
> the values need only be "approximately equal."   With this
> standard in mind, we have reviewed the record materials to
> determine whether the Park Service has ignored any relevant
> issues and we have retraced its basic calculations.   We have
> not, however, substituted our judgments on the merits of
> competing appraisals or required the agency to justify every
> underlying assumption.

> While the Park Service calculations may not be the model
> of completeness or accuracy that appellees would wish, we are
> satisfied that it is reasonable.   The issues appellees raise on
> this appeal have all, at some point, been addressed in the
> administrative proceedings before the Park Service and other
> agencies.   The Park Service estimated, moreover, that the
> proposed exchange would provide a net advantage to the Unit-
> ed States of $102,144.   This estimate did not reflect additional
> benefits to the United States, including WHA maintenance
> obligations worth some $150,000 in the first year alone, and a
> commitment to provide a $1 million park on the site.   The
> Park Service estimate was surely reasonable.

It could be argued that land exchanges should be exempt from
judicial review because the government is acting in a solely proprietary
capacity.   No court would review an exchange by private owners, at
least at the behest of third parties not directly involved or affected.
Further, effective review is often difficult due to the complexity of the
transactions.   Perhaps the answer is that the sovereign cannot act
other than as a sovereign, so that sovereignty circumscribes the government's proprietary interests.   The more important question may be

whether such exchanges serve a general federal purpose. Federal land exchanges often involve commercial interests: does the government have a right or obligation to assist private developers?

Sales of federal lands have been even more controversial than exchanges because they reduce the total amount of federal land. Federal lands may be acquired by private individuals in some limited circumstances under the Isolated Tracts Act, 43 U.S.C.A. § 1171 et seq.; see Lewis v. Udall, 374 F.2d 180 (9th Cir.1967); Ferry v. Udall, 336 F.2d 706 (9th Cir.1964). Under the Federal Property and Administrative Services Act of 1949, 40 U.S.C.A. § 471 et seq., as amended (FPAS), the General Services Administration (GSA) may dispose of excess or surplus government real estate to federal agencies, other public bodies, or private enterprises, in that order, for various purposes. The duties imposed on GSA by FPAS remain obscure. See Rhode Island Committee on Energy v. GSA, 397 F.Supp. 41 (D.R.I.1975), aff'd in part, rev'd in part, 561 F.2d 397 (1st Cir.1977). One use of the FPAS principle has been the creation of urban "gateway" parks. In and around San Francisco, for instance, a variety of surplus military forts and reservations were turned over to the National Park Service for management as the Golden Gate National Recreation Area. Forest Service and public domain lands are expressly excluded from disposition under the FPAS. 40 U.S.C.A. § 472(d)(1).

Federal law sharply circumscribes the sale of Forest Service lands. Disposition laws affecting the national forests include 16 U.S.C.A. § 519 (sale of "small areas of land chiefly valuable for agriculture"), and 16 U.S.C.A. § 478a (sales of no more than 640 acres for townsites).

FLPMA governs BLM land sales. Section 1720 authorizes limited transfers of lands to state and local governments, and § 1713 governs sales to private parties. The statute provides that a sale of more than 2500 acres cannot be made for 90 days, during which time either House may veto such a sale. 43 U.S.C.A. § 1713(c). This legislative veto provision may well violate *Chadha,* and the severability issues are similar to those involving withdrawals. See supra page 257; Glicksman, supra, 36 Hast.L.J. at 43–44, 87–88. All sales must be for fair market value. 43 U.S.C.A. § 1713(d). Other substantive provisions for land sales are set out in § 1713(a):

> (a) A tract of the public lands [a] (except land in units of the National Wilderness Preservation System, National Wild and Scenic Rivers Systems, and National System of Trails) may be sold under this Act where, as a result of land use planning required under section 1712 of this title, the Secretary determines that the sale of such tract meets the following disposal criteria:

a. [Ed.] In FLPMA "public lands" does not carry its traditional meaning but rather is defined as "any land and interest in land * * * administered by the Secretary of the Interior through the Bureau of Land Management. * * *" 43 U.S.C.A. § 1702(e).

(1) such tract because of its location or other characteristics is difficult and uneconomic to manage as part of the public lands, and is not suitable for management by another Federal department or agency; or

(2) such tract was acquired for a specific purpose and the tract is no longer required for that or any other Federal purpose; or

(3) disposal of such tract will serve important public objectives, including but not limited to, expansion of communities and economic development, which cannot be achieved prudently or feasibly on land other than public land and which outweigh other public objectives and values, including, but not limited to, recreation and scenic values, which would be served by maintaining such tract in Federal ownership.

(b) Where the Secretary determines that land to be conveyed under clause (3) of subsection (a) of this section is of agricultural value and is desert in character, such land shall be conveyed either under the sale authority of this section or in accordance with other existing law.

* * *

(e) The Secretary shall determine and establish the size of tracts of public lands to be sold on the basis of the land use capabilities and development requirements of the lands; and, where any such tract which is judged by the Secretary to be chiefly valuable for agriculture is sold, its size shall be no larger than necessary to support a family-sized farm.

* * *

Does this section provide any substantial basis for judicial review of individual land sales?

On February 25, 1982, President Reagan issued Executive Order No. 12348, 47 Fed.Reg. 8547 (1982), which established the Property Review Board to implement the Administration's "privatization" program. The Board's purpose was to "review real property holdings of the federal government, * * * expedite the sale of unneeded property so that it can be put to more productive use, [and] use the proceeds from property sales to begin retiring the national debt."

At one point, the Administration projected land sales returning $4 billion annually over a five-year period. Approximately half of the proceeds would come from Department of Defense lands and half from BLM and Forest Service lands combined. The Administration also considered, but did not introduce, legislation to broaden its authority to make sales of national forest lands. Secretary Watt planned to sell, within five years, some 35 million acres of federally owned land (most of which would be BLM land), an area the size of Iowa. See Note, Sales of Public Land: A Problem in Legislative and Judicial Control of Administrative Action, 96 Harv.L.Rev. 927 (1983). See generally F.

Gregg, FEDERAL LAND TRANSFERS: THE CASE FOR A WESTWIDE PROGRAM BASED ON THE FLPMA (1982).

The controversial land sales program never got off the ground, and the Property Review Board was formally disbanded in 1984. The General Accounting Office, noting a lack of demand for the scattered, isolated BLM parcels offered for sale, found that in fiscal years 1982 and 1983 the BLM had offered 68,676 acres, sold 18,296 acres, and received approximately $15.4 million. U.S. General Accounting Office, The Bureau of Land Management's Efforts to Identify Land for Disposal (1985). See also Conservation Law Foundation v. Harper, 587 F.Supp. 357 (D.Mass.1984), discussing the sale program and dismissing most of the legal challenges made against it.

The Administration, as a wholly separate program, has also proposed an interagency land exchange between the Forest Service and the BLM. In January, 1985, it requested Congress to authorize a trade involving some 35 million acres. Legislative action is required because the Transfer Act of 1905, moving the forest reserves from Interior to Agriculture, provides that the Agriculture Secretary shall execute all laws relating to national forest lands. See 16 U.S.C.A. § 472. The plan was to consolidate large blocks of land under each agency in order to eliminate the costs resulting from virtually side-by-side BLM and Forest Service offices found in many regions. Also, the exchange would transfer most timber lands to the Forest Service and most grazing lands to the BLM to allow for greater specialization. In Washington state, for example, all BLM lands would be transferred to the Forest Service, while in Nevada nearly all Forest Service lands would go to the BLM. The maps describing the proposal thus portrayed neat, consolidated agency ownerships. There was one exception: a long, narrow tongue of Forest Service land extending down into western New Mexico, designed to be mainly a BLM area. The reason? Forest Service Chief Max Peterson, ever jealous of hallowed agency traditions, was unyielding in his refusal to relinquish the place in Lincoln National Forest where Smokey the Bear was found clinging to a charred tree in 1947.

Nearly everyone agreed with the concept of the swap, and nearly everyone objected to the particulars. Local ranchers, timber companies, and mine operators were unwilling to begin doing business with a new agency. Environmentalists opposed swaps of numerous parcels, often because they feared BLM management. Goodly numbers of field employees in both agencies resented a transfer to a new agency. As a result, in February 1986, the agencies announced a scaled-down version involving 24 million acres. Still, the complex proposal faces rough sledding in Congress. See generally 10 Public Land News 1 (Feb. 7, 1985); Two U.S. Agencies Plan Land Exchange, New York Times, p. 14 (Feb. 20, 1986).

B. JUDICIAL REVIEW

Intensive judicial review is a recent phenomenon in public land management. The Forest Service, for example, appeared in the Supreme Court in Light v. United States, 220 U.S. 523 (1911), supra at page 137, and in Hunt v. United States, 278 U.S. 96 (1928), but those were constitutional challenges to federal power. The Service did not return to the Court on anything approaching a major management issue until the Sierra Club joined it as a defendant to set aside the development of Mineral King in the 1972 decision in Sierra Club v. Morton, 405 U.S. 727 (1972). No lower court struck down any important Forest Service action until a district court in 1970 enjoined issuance of a timber contract for violations of the Wilderness Act. Parker v. United States, 309 F.Supp. 593 (D.Colo.1970), aff'd, 448 F.2d 793 (10th Cir.1971), infra at page 995. The BLM historically has had a reasonably large litigation load, but its cases almost always arose out of essentially private disputes involving adjudication of mining claims, mineral leases, and homestead applications.

The boom in public land litigation involving public issues that occurred during the 1970's can be traced to several factors. First, private foundation funding helped to spawn several "public interest law firms" at the beginning of the decade. Congress has enacted much more hard statutory law: it is far easier to sue over violations of specific statutory commands, such as those in the Wilderness Act, the National Environmental Policy Act, the Endangered Species Act, or the National Forest Management Act, than it is to challenge an action taken pursuant to a vague, discretionary mandate such as that in the Multiple-Use, Sustained-Yield Act. Finally, the expanded role of the courts in public land litigation has coincided with the more aggressive approach of courts in reviewing administrative actions of all kinds.

The so-called "hard look" doctrine of judicial review, stemming from Citizens to Preserve Overton Park, Inc. v. Volpe, 401 U.S. 402 (1971), means that judges will give much closer scrutiny to the substantive and procedural grounds for federal agency decisions. It remains to be seen whether tight judicial control will continue in the wake of Vermont Yankee Nuclear Power Corp. v. NRDC, 435 U.S. 519 (1978). The Supreme Court there overturned a ruling by the Court of Appeals for the District of Columbia—the most active court on administrative law matters in the country—and termed its ruling below as "border[ing] on the Kafkaesque. * * * Time may prove wrong the decision to develop nuclear energy, but it is Congress or the States within their appropriate agencies which must eventually make that judgment. In the meantime courts should perform their appointed function." If *Vermont Yankee* has a generalized impact far beyond its facts, the result will be greater agency authority vis-a-vis the courts. Compare Stewart, *Vermont Yankee* and the Evolution of Administrative Procedure, 91 Harv.L.Rev. 1804 (1978), with Rodgers, A Hard Look at *Vermont Yankee:* Environmental Law Under Close Scrutiny, 67 Geo.

L.J. 699 (1979), and Davis, Administrative Common Law and the *Vermont Yankee* Decision, 1980 Utah L.Rev. 3.   On judicial review in natural resources law, see generally Rodgers, Building Theories of Judicial Review in Natural Resources Law, 53 U.Colo.L.Rev. 213 (1981); Marcel, The Role of the Courts in a Legislative and Administrative Legal System—The Use of Hard Look Review in Federal Environmental Litigation, 62 Or.L.Rev. 403 (1983).

Almost all public land law litigation involves principles of administrative law in some fashion, partly because nearly all major litigation is against or by the government.   The typical law suit is brought by a private party against a federal agency, and the federal defendant then raises a host of procedural objections—standing, exhaustion of remedies, mootness, sovereign immunity, jurisdiction, reviewability, and others.   Those procedural defenses infrequently result in dismissal nowadays, so the court then must turn to an examination of the substantive statute or regulation on which administrative action is premised.   Such examination must proceed in the context of administrative law principles that define the court's scope of review.   See generally B. Schwartz, ADMINISTRATIVE LAW (2d ed., 1984); K. Davis, ADMINISTRATIVE LAW TREATISE (2d ed., 1983).   Professor William H. Rodgers, Jr. has published a valuable source book on environmental law containing a summary of judicial review in the field generally.   W. Rodgers, ENVIRONMENTAL LAW 16–49 (1977).

Federal land and resources law is deeply imprinted with a tradition of judicial deference to actions taken by land management agencies. The reasons for this tradition appear to be that many important decisions were handed down in a time of less aggressive judicial review, that western courts are less receptive to expanded review notions than the District of Columbia courts, and, most particularly, that public land management decisions often are seen as involving complex factual and technological questions with which the courts have little or no expertise.   That tradition has been modified, not just by the greater scrutiny that today's courts apply to administrative conduct generally, but also by the nature of modern congressional and administrative lawmaking: statutes and regulations have become many times more detailed concerning proper resource management so that plaintiffs are increasingly able to challenge land agencies on legal violations where, as opposed to fact issues, court oversight is most appropriate.   Further, judicial review has burgeoned simply because there are many new classes of plaintiffs.   The public has for the first time asserted itself in the judicial forum, and, as a result, public land law has been revolutionized.

Some aspects and doctrines of administrative law figure prominently in the context of litigation over federal lands and resources questions.   Before a litigant can obtain a ruling on the merits of a suit against the agency, plaintiff must run a procedural obstacle course.

1.   *Standing.*   The leading case on standing in public land law is Sierra Club v. Morton, 405 U.S. 727 (1972).   The Sierra Club sought to enjoin an extensive ski resort development by private interests in the

Mineral King Valley, basing its standing upon an allegation that it had "a special interest in the conservation and sound maintenance of the national parks, game refuges and forests of the country." The Court held that this allegation was insufficient to establish standing but in the process it expanded traditional standing doctrine so that organizations such as the Sierra Club would have little future difficulty on that score. It was pointedly noted that the Club had failed to allege that "its members would be affected in any of their activities or pastimes by the Disney development. Nowhere in the pleadings or affidavits did the Club state that its members use Mineral King for any purpose * * *." On remand, the Sierra Club was able to allege such use by its members, and the lawsuit continued. The Court also validated the representation by an organization of its members, and held that once standing is found, the substantive challenge to agency action is not confined to the grounds for standing. See also United States v. Students Challenging Regulatory Agency Procedures, 412 U.S. 669 (1973). More restrictive opinions on standing have since been rendered, e.g., Warth v. Seldin, 422 U.S. 490 (1975); Simon v. Eastern Kentucky Welfare Rights Organization, 426 U.S. 26 (1976), but not in public land cases, where use of the land or resource can usually be pleaded and proved by plaintiffs without difficulty. See generally Parker and Stone, Standing and Public Law Remedies, 78 Colum.L.Rev. 771 (1978); K. Davis, 4 ADMINISTRATIVE LAW TREATISE 208–348 (2d ed. 1983).

2. *Exhaustion of Remedies, Primary Jurisdiction, the Foreclosure Rule, and Laches.* A variety of doctrines operate to further the policy of requiring litigants to seek relief in the agencies before resorting to the courts.

The doctrine of primary jurisdiction is closely related to that of exhaustion of administrative remedies. Both are essentially doctrines of comity between courts and agencies. They are two sides of the timing coin: Each determines whether an action may be brought in a court or whether an agency proceeding, or further agency proceeding, is necessary. The basic difference is that primary jurisdiction determines whether a court or an agency has *initial* jurisdiction; exhaustion determines whether *review* may be had of agency action that is not the last agency word in the matter. The difference was pointed out by the Supreme Court in United States v. Western Pacific Railroad: [4] " 'Exhaustion' applies where a claim is cognizable in the first instance by an administrative agency alone; judicial interference is withheld until the administrative process has run its course. 'Primary jurisdiction,' on the other hand, applies where a claim is originally cognizable in the courts, and comes into play whenever enforcement of the claim requires the resolution of issues which, under a regulatory scheme, have been placed within the special competence of an administrative body; in such a case the judicial process is

4. 352 U.S. 59 (1956).

suspended pending referral of such issues to the administrative body for its views."

The exhaustion doctrine prevents premature judicial interference with administrative proceedings, while the primary jurisdiction doctrine denies jurisdiction where agency proceedings have not yet begun. Exhaustion applies where an agency alone has exclusive jurisdiction over the case; primary jurisdiction where both a court and an agency have the legal capacity to deal with the matter. In the typical case the original jurisdiction of the court is invoked to decide the merits of the case. If not for primary jurisdiction, the court would possess original jurisdiction over the case and be able to grant the relief requested.

B. Schwartz, ADMINISTRATIVE LAW 485–86 (2d ed., 1984). Primary jurisdiction has been invoked to require further factual determinations by the Forest Service before the courts would resolve legal questions involving the Wilderness Act. See Izaak Walton League v. St. Clair, 497 F.2d 849 (8th Cir.1974). An integral aspect of the exhaustion of remedies doctrine is the notion that there must be actual, formal procedures established in the agency where the plaintiff can raise the issue. See, e.g., United States v. Anthony Grace & Sons, Inc., 384 U.S. 424, 429–30 (1966). Both doctrines are flexible, involving balancing tests in which a wide variety of equities can be considered. McKart v. United States, 395 U.S. 185 (1969).

An adjunct to the exhaustion doctrine is the requirement that a plaintiff must normally raise all factual and legal issues in the agency: otherwise, the plaintiff may be "foreclosed" from raising those issues on review. The foreclosure doctrine is also flexible and is not rigidly applied if extenuating circumstances are shown. K. Davis, 3 ADMINISTRATIVE LAW TREATISE 92 (2d ed. 1983). Courts can, for example, permit the consideration of newly discovered evidence under proper circumstances. See Sierra Club v. Butz, 3 ELR 20292 (9th Cir.1973), infra at page 614. See generally Gelpe, Exhaustion of Administrative Remedies Lessons from Environmental Cases, 53 Geo.Wash.L.Rev. 1 (1985). Somewhat similarly, laches is disfavored in environmental cases because it often takes on-the-ground construction to "galvanize" citizen groups, Steubing v. Brinegar, 511 F.2d 489 (2d Cir.1975), and because courts are reluctant to decide public issues on the basis of delay by individual plaintiffs. See generally National Wildlife Federation v. United States Forest Service, 592 F.Supp. 931, 943–44 (D.Or.1984), appeal pending; Coalition for Canyon Preservation v. Bowers, 632 F.2d 774, 779 (9th Cir.1980). Among the few public lands cases dismissing an action based on delay are Sierra Club v. Block, 576 F.Supp. 959, 964–67 (D.Or.1983) (collateral estoppel barred plaintiffs from raising issues in unappealed administrative proceeding); Park County Resource Council v. USDA, 613 F.Supp. 1182 (D.Wyo.1985) (statute of limitations in Mineral Leasing Act bars NEPA claim).

3. *Sovereign Immunity.* The doctrine of sovereign immunity has been a confused and inconsistent body of law from the beginning. See Byse, Proposed Reforms in Federal "Non-Statutory" Judicial Review, 75 Harv.L.Rev. 1479 (1962). Confusion was often accompanied by inequity: the Common Law policy that "the King can do no wrong" was turned around in sovereign immunity cases, which proved conclusively that the sovereign can do wrong. The doctrine existed to shield such wrongs, and it had been employed with some frequency in public lands cases. See, e.g., Malone v. Bowdoin, 369 U.S. 643 (1962); Dugan v. Rank, 372 U.S. 609 (1963). See generally Scalia, Sovereign Immunity and Nonstatutory Review of Federal Administrative Action: Some Conclusions from the Public-Lands Cases, 68 Mich.L.Rev. 867 (1970).

In standard litigation challenging agency actions, the sovereign immunity rule had long been largely swallowed by its exceptions before Congress applied the coup de grace in 1976. An amendment to the Administrative Procedure Act (APA), 5 U.S.C.A. § 702, abolished sovereign immunity for most purposes:

> An action in a court of the United States seeking relief other than money damages and stating a claim that an agency or an officer or employee thereof acted or failed to act in an official capacity or under color of legal authority shall not be dismissed or relief therein be denied on the ground that it is against the United States or that the United States is an indispensible party.

See Jacoby, Roads to the Demise of the Doctrine of Sovereign Immunity, 29 Admin.L.Rev. 265 (1977). The 1976 amendment is not, however, a complete waiver of sovereign immunity. First, the amendment applies only to suits for "other than money damages," which are governed by the Federal Tort Claims Act, 28 U.S.C.A. §§ 1346(b), 2671 et seq. [see chapter ten, § B infra], and the Tucker Act, 28 U.S.C.A. §§ 1346(a), 1391. In addition, specific statutes limiting the waiver of sovereign immunity will prevail over the more general waiver in 5 U.S. C.A. § 702. The most important examples in the public lands field appear to be the Color of Title Act and the Quiet Title Act, supra at page 185; these and related statutes amount to narrow waivers of sovereign immunity when persons seek to quiet title to public lands.

4. *Committed to Agency Discretion by Law.* The Administrative Procedure Act, 5 U.S.C.A. § 701(a), provides:

> This chapter [of the APA as it relates to judicial review] applies, according to the provisions thereof, except to the extent that—
>
> (1) statutes preclude judicial review; or
>
> (2) agency action is committed to agency discretion by law.

The first exception has little or no application in public land law as statutes expressly precluding judicial review are rare. The second exception can cut off judicial review entirely, even in the absence of a statute precluding review; section 701(a)(2) has limited coverage but it occasionally operates in federal land and resources law.

The "committed to agency discretion" exception raises two interrelated problems: reviewability and scope of review. In every case challenging an action of a public land management agency, the reviewing court is required to determine whether the action is reviewable at all, and, if so, to what extent. In Citizens to Preserve Overton Park, Inc. v. Volpe, 401 U.S. 402 (1971), the Court emphasized that the total exemption from review was very narrow, applicable only where there was no "law to apply," and that there is a "basic presumption in favor of judicial review." In recent cases, review has been avoided altogether only (a) when the agency has made a factual determination under a wholly opaque statute and the context is so complex that the court has no reasonable basis for setting aside the action had it gone either way, e.g., Curran v. Laird, 420 F.2d 122 (D.C.Cir.1969), or (b) when a plaintiff seeks to require an agency to bring an enforcement action, thus invoking the doctrine of prosecutorial discretion and reversing the presumption of reviewability, e.g., Heckler v. Chaney, 105 S.Ct. 1649 (1985). See generally Saferstein, Nonreviewability: A Functional Analysis of "Committed to Agency Discretion," 82 Harv.L.Rev. 367 (1968). Comment, The Conservationists and the Public Lands: Administrative and Judicial Remedies Relating to the Use and Disposition of the Public Lands Administered by the Department of the Interior, 68 Mich.L.Rev. 1200, 1236–42 (1970), analyzes the doctrine in the public lands context.

Some argue that resource decisions are appropriate for no—or minimal—judicial review because some public land statutes by their lack of specificity confer great discretion on land management agencies, and because it is presumed that resource management requires technical expertise beyond judicial understanding. Congress, however, appears generally content with judicial review and frequently has broadened its availability in recent statutes, many of which explicitly authorize "citizen suits." Still, Federal land agencies sometimes cling to the notion that their actions should be beyond the law. A former BLM director concluded, in Landstrom, An Operational View of the BLM Organic Act, 54 Den.L.J. 455, 458 (1977):

> A policy declaration in the Act states that public land adjudication decisions should be subjected to judicial review as a matter of policy.[a] The word "adjudication" is not defined. This policy statement, along with others in the Act, has been heaped upon other relevant policy declarations contained in preexisting statutes.
>
> My difficulty with the policy statement is that it might be interpreted as furthering the proposition, urged on the Congress in earlier versions of the legislation, that not only "adjudicative" decisions but also "discretionary" decisions should be

---

a. [Ed.] The Federal Land Management and Policy Act of 1976, provides: "The Congress declares that it is the policy of the United States that ∗ ∗ ∗ judicial review of public land adjudication decisions be provided by law ∗ ∗ ∗." 43 U.S.C.A. § 701(a)(6).

subjected to judicial review. Plainly, such a method is not required by current administrative law. Such a review provision would be in derogation of the long line of precedent establishing that agency decisions, when discretionary, are not subject to review by the courts. Moreover, judicial review of discretionary land use decisions would appear to be contrary to the intent of Congress pursuant to section 10 of the Administrative Procedure Act.

It is to be hoped that when Congress implements this policy, it does nothing to restrict the current scope of discretion vested in public agencies. Otherwise, substantial delays may occur in the governmental decisionmaking process, and the authority and independence of executive agencies will be undermined.

As the above authorities and several cases in this volume show, Mr. Landstrom considerably overstates the present status of "nonreviewability." The real question is the scope of judicial review.

5. *Scope of Review.* It has been said that all of administrative law can be loosely summarized in the notion that "factual questions are for the agency and legal questions are for the court." Certainly that describes the basic positions typically taken by advocates in public land litigation. Government lawyers argue that the case turns on factual determinations with which management officials have expertise. Lawyers attacking management decisions contend that the case depends on legal analysis of statutes, regulations, or the Constitution—matters within the special qualifications of courts. The statute that defines the scope of review in public lands cases is normally the Administrative Procedure Act, 5 U.S.C.A. § 706:

> To the extent necessary to decision and when presented, the reviewing court shall decide all relevant questions of law, interpret constitutional and statutory provisions, and determine the meaning or applicability of the terms of an agency action. The reviewing court shall—
>
> (1) compel agency action unlawfully withheld or unreasonably delayed; and
>
> (2) hold unlawful and set aside agency action, findings, and conclusions found to be—
>
>> (A) arbitrary, capricious, an abuse of discretion, or otherwise not in accordance with law;
>>
>> (B) contrary to constitutional right, power, privilege, or immunity;
>>
>> (C) in excess of statutory jurisdiction, authority, or limitations, or short of statutory right;
>>
>> (D) without observance of procedure required by law;

(E) unsupported by substantial evidence in a case subject to sections 556 and 557 of this title or otherwise reviewed on the record of an agency hearing provided by statute; or

(F) unwarranted by the facts to the extent that the facts are subject to trial de novo by the reviewing court.

In making the foregoing determinations, the court shall review the whole record or those parts of it cited by a party, and due account shall be taken of the rule of prejudicial error.

The appropriate scope and depth of judicial review in any set of circumstances causes almost as much disputation among commentators as confusion in courts.

The scope of judicial review of administrative action ranges from zero to one hundred per cent. An example of scope of review at zero is the State Department's action on a typical problem of dealing with a foreign government. An example of something approaching one hundred per cent substitution of judgment is a tax case handled by the Internal Revenue Service in absence of the kind of problem on which a court pays deference to the views of the Service. Yet the dominant tendency in both federal and state courts is toward the middle position known as the substantial-evidence rule. Under this rule, the court decides questions of law but it limits itself to the test of reasonableness in reviewing findings of fact. Broadly, questions of law include not only common law, statutory interpretation, and constitutional law, but also questions of administrative jurisdiction, of fair administrative procedure, and of protection against arbitrary or capricious action or abuse of discretion.

K. Davis, CASES ON ADMINISTRATIVE LAW 75 (1977).

What then is the proper role for the courts to play? The baseline responsibility for environmental protection belongs to the administrative agency. The questions are complex and value-laden, and as many parties as possible must be heard to insure that conflicting points of view are considered in arriving at the final decision. The solutions may require deployment of monitoring equipment and manpower and establishment of administrative schemes. In many cases, government must assist by conducting basic research or building treatment plants. All of these actions can only be taken by an administrative agency. But the agencies must not be trusted to operate without vigilant supervision. Whenever they ignore duties thrust upon them by Congress (by missing deadlines, for example), or fail to take relevant factors (and only relevant factors) into account in making their decisions, or become "captive" to the interests which they purport to control, the courts must be open to correct individual abuses and to direct general compliance with environmental statutes and with procedures to guarantee fairness and openness. In difficult cases this careful scrutiny of procedure shades close to substantive review of the decision being made, both because the procedure is so intertwined with substance that they cannot be separated and because the issues being treated are so fundamental to life and health. But such delving into substance will be unusual. The customary version of the "new era" which Judge Bazelon envisioned [b] will be administrative agencies operating under the watchful, vigilant eye of courts quick to pick up errors of procedure or statutory interpretation, but still permitting discretion within those guidelines.

Thompson, The Role of the Courts, in FEDERAL ENVIRONMENTAL LAW 236–37 (1974).

Professor Rodgers has developed an inventive typology that he terms "the central premise of judicial review." When there is a "vague mandate" from Congress, the substantive decision will often be left to the agency but the courts will scrutinize the procedures followed by the agencies, and may determine whether the agency considered all relevant factors and whether it based its decision on irrelevant factors. When the controlling legislation provides a "specific mandate," the courts will also analyze the substance of the decision by determining whether it conformed to the statutory intent. W. Rodgers, ENERGY AND NATURAL RESOURCES LAW 190–240 (2d ed. 1983).

6. *Procedure.* In 1976 Congress greatly simplified the process for reaching the merits in administrative litigation. It amended 28 U.S. C.A. § 1331 to eliminate the $10,000 minimum amount in controversy for review of federal agency decisions. Compare Califano v. Sanders, 430 U.S. 99 (1977). No longer is it necessary to name specific agency officials as defendants; a complaint may name as defendant the United States, the agency, or the appropriate officer. 5 U.S.C.A. § 703. If an injunction is issued, it may be directed to a specified officer, even if not originally named as a defendant in the action. 5 U.S.C.A. § 702. Sovereign immunity is waived. Id. The APA has always allowed for injunctive or declaratory relief, 5 U.S.C.A. § 703, both of which are normally requested by plaintiffs. Mandamus-style relief is authorized by 5 U.S.C.A. § 706, which authorizes reviewing courts to "compel agency action unlawfully withheld or unreasonably delayed." In Weinberger v. Romero-Barcelo, 456 U.S. 305 (1982), the Court ruled that the issuance of an injunction for a violation of the Clean Water Act was within the equitable discretion of the trial judge. Accord: Kleppe v. Sierra Club, 427 U.S. 390 (1976); infra at page 323; but cf. TVA v. Hill, 437 U.S. 153 (1978), infra at page 785.

The following classic opinions demonstrate different approaches and emphases of judicial review in this field.

b. [Ed.] Environmental Defense Fund v. Ruckelshaus, 439 F.2d 584 (D.C.Cir.1971).

UDALL v. TALLMAN
Supreme Court of the United States, 1965.
380 U.S. 1.

Mr. Chief Justice WARREN delivered the opinion of the court.

At issue in this case is the effect of Executive Order No. 8979 and Public Land Order No. 487 upon the Secretary of the Interior's authority to issue oil and gas leases.

Between October 15, 1954, and January 28, 1955, D.J. Griffin and other persons—hereinafter collectively referred to as the Griffin lessees—filed applications for oil and gas leases on approximately 25,000 acres located in the Kenai National Moose Range in Alaska. On August 14, 1958, the respondents filed offers to lease the same lands. Section 17 of the Mineral Leasing Act of 1920 provides, in relevant part, that "the person first making application for the lease who is qualified to hold a lease * * * shall be entitled to a lease of such lands without competitive bidding. * * *" 30 U.S.C.A. § 226. The Bureau of Land Management of the Department of the Interior determined that the Griffin lessees were the persons who had applied first, and issued to them leases on the tracts, effective September 1, 1958. Respondents' applications were reached for processing in October 1959, and were rejected on the ground that the lands had been leased to prior applicants.

* * *

[The district court held for the Griffin lessees, but the circuit court reversed on the ground that the lands had been withdrawn from mineral leasing at the time of the Griffin applications, "rendering the leases issued on them nullities."]

We conclude that the District Court correctly refused to issue a writ of mandamus, and accordingly reverse the decision of the Court of Appeals. Since their promulgation, the Secretary has consistently construed both orders not to bar oil and gas leases; moreover, this interpretation has been made a repeated matter of public record. While the Griffin leases and others located in the Moose Range have been developed in reliance upon the Secretary's interpretation, respondents do not claim to have relied to their detriment upon a contrary construction. The Secretary's interpretation may not be the only one permitted by the language of the orders, but it is quite clearly a reasonable interpretation; courts must therefore respect it.

I

The Mineral Leasing Act of 1920, 30 U.S.C.A. § 181 et seq., gave the Secretary of the Interior broad power to issue oil and gas leases on public lands not within any known geological structure of a producing oil and gas field. Although the Act directed that if a lease was issued on such a tract, it had to be issued to the first qualified applicant, it left the Secretary discretion to refuse to issue any lease at all on a given tract. United States ex rel. McLennan v. Wilbur, 283 U.S. 414. The

Act excluded from its application certain designated lands, but did not exclude lands within wildlife refuge areas.

The Kenai National Moose Range was created in 1941 by Executive Order No. 8979, 6 Fed.Reg. 6471, by which approximately two million acres of the public domain were set aside "as a refuge and breeding ground for moose." The order provided that "[n]one of the above-described lands excepting [a defined area] shall be subject to settlement, location, sale, or entry, or other disposition (except for fish trap sites) under any of the public-land laws applicable to Alaska * * *." On November 8, 1947, the Secretary promulgated the first general regulation dealing with the issuance of oil and gas leases within wildlife refuges. It provided simply that such leases had to be subjected to an approved unit plan and contain a provision prohibiting drilling or prospecting without the advance consent of the Secretary. 12 Fed.Reg. 7334.

On June 16, 1948, the Secretary issued Public Land Order No. 487, 13 Fed.Reg. 3462:

> "[T]he public lands within the following-described areas in Alaska [including most of that portion of the Moose Range which had been excepted from Executive Order No. 8979] are hereby temporarily withdrawn from settlement, location, sale or entry, for classification and examination, and in aid of proposed legislation:
>
>   * * *
>
> "This order shall take precedence over, but shall not modify * * * the reservation for the Kenai National Moose Range made by Executive Order No. 8879 of December 16, 1941 * * *."

Thus neither Executive Order No. 8979 nor Public Land Order No. 487 expressly withdrew the lands to which it applied from oil and gas leasing. In 1951, however, the Secretary set aside, for uses inconsistent with mineral leasing, minor portions of the lands covered by Public Land Order No. 487:

> "[T]he following-described public lands in Alaska are hereby withdrawn from all forms of appropriation under the public-land laws, including the mining laws and the mineral-leasing laws * * *."

Had the Secretary thought that Public Land Order No. 487 had already withdrawn the lands covered by it from appropriation under the mineral-leasing laws, his reference to such laws in the 1951 orders would have been superfluous.

               * * *

On December 8, 1955, [a] revision of the 1947 refuge-leasing regulation was promulgated. 20 Fed.Reg. 9009. It was more restrictive than the old regulation, and gave increased power to the Fish and Wildlife Service to approve or disapprove oil and gas development of refuges.

* * *

               * * *

[T]he controversy over the leasing policies to be followed in wildlife refuges was resolved by the adoption, on January 8, 1958, of another complete revision of the regulation. 23 Fed.Reg. 227, 43 CFR § 192.9. The revision represented a near-total victory for the conservationists. It altogether prohibited oil and gas leasing, unless necessary to prevent draining, in wildlife refuges—with two exceptions: lands withdrawn for a dual purpose, and wildlife refuges located in Alaska. As to lands falling within these two excepted categories, the Bureau of Land Management and the Fish and Wildlife Service were to reach agreements specifying the lands which "shall not be subject to oil and gas leasing" and to decide on provisions to be required in leases issued on the remaining lands. * * *

Pursuant to the regulation, there was published in the Federal Register on August 2, 1958, an order of the Secretary announcing the agreement reached with respect to the Moose Range. 23 Fed.Reg. 5883. The order decreed that certain lands within the Range (essentially the southern half) "are hereby closed to oil and gas leasing because such activities would be incompatible with management thereof for wildlife purposes." It then provided:

> "The balance of the lands within the Kenai National Moose Range are subject to the filing of oil and gas lease offers * * *. Offers to lease covering any of these lands which have been pending and upon which action was suspended in accordance with the regulation 43 CFR 192.9(d) will now be acted upon and adjudicated in accordance with the regulations.

> * * *

> " * * * [L]ease offers for lands which have not been excluded from leasing will not be accepted for filing until the tenth day after the agreement and map are noted on the records of the land office * * *."

The agreement was noted in the Anchorage land office on August 4, 1958, and 10 days later respondents filed their applications.

Soon after the issuance of the regulation and the implementing order, the pending applications were acted upon; within the next two months, 294 leases covering 621,234 acres were issued in the area subject to Executive Order No. 8979, in response to applications (including those of the Griffin lessees) filed in 1954 and 1955. When these figures are added to those covering leases issued prior to 1958 (primarily those in the Swanson River area), it appears that in the area subject to Executive Order No. 8979, the Secretary issued a total of 331 leases covering 696,680 acres on applications filed during the period the Court of Appeals held that the area was closed to leasing. Thus, prior to the commencement of the instant suit, the Secretary had leased substantially the entire area in controversy; the Solicitor General further assures us that the lessees and their assignees had, in turn, expended tens of millions of dollars in the development of the leases.

II

When faced with a problem of statutory construction, this Court shows great deference to the interpretation given the statute by the officers or agency charged with its administration. "To sustain the Commission's application of this statutory term, we need not find that its construction is the only reasonable one, or even that it is the result we would have reached had the question arisen in the first instance in judicial proceedings." Unemployment Comm'n v. Aragon, 329 U.S. 143, 153. See also, e.g., Gray v. Powell, 314 U.S. 402; Universal Battery Co. v. United States, 281 U.S. 580, 583. "Particularly is this respect due when the administrative practice at stake 'involves a contemporaneous construction of a statute by the men charged with the responsibility of setting its machinery in motion, of making the parts work efficiently and smoothly while they are yet untried and new.'" Power Reactor Co. v. Electricians, 367 U.S. 396, 408. When the construction of an administrative regulation rather than a statute is in issue, deference is even more clearly in order.

> "Since this involves an interpretation of an administrative regulation a court must necessarily look to the administrative construction of the regulation if the meaning of the words used is in doubt. * * * [T]he ultimate criterion is the administrative interpretation, which becomes of controlling weight unless it is plainly erroneous or inconsistent with the regulation." Bowles v. Seminole Rock Co., 325 U.S. 410, 413–414.

In the instant case, there is no statutory limitation involved. While Executive Order No. 8979 was issued by the President, he soon delegated to the Secretary full power to withdraw lands or to modify or revoke any existing withdrawals. Public Land Order No. 487 was issued by the Secretary himself.

Moreover, as the discussion in Section I of this opinion demonstrates, the Secretary has consistently construed Executive Order No. 8979 and Public Land Order No. 487 not to bar oil and gas leases.

> "It may be argued that while these facts and rulings prove a usage they do not establish its validity. But government is a practical affair intended for practical men. Both officers, lawmakers and citizens naturally adjust themselves to any long-continued action of the Executive Department—on the presumption that unauthorized acts would not have been allowed to be so often repeated as to crystallize into a regular practice. That presumption is not reasoning in a circle but the basis of a wise and quieting rule that in determining the meaning of a statute or the existence of a power, weight shall be given to the usage itself—even when the validity of the practice is the subject of investigation." United States v. Midwest Oil Co., 236 U.S. 459, 472–473.

The Secretary's interpretation had, long prior to respondents' applications, been a matter of public record and discussion. * * * Finally, almost the entire area covered by the orders in issue has been developed, at very great expense, in reliance upon the Secretary's interpretation. In McLaren v. Fleischer, 256 U.S. 477, 480–481, it was held:

> "In the practical administration of the act the officers of the land department have adopted and given effect to the latter view. They adopted it before the present controversy arose or was thought of, and, except for a departure soon reconsidered and corrected, they have adhered to and followed it ever since. Many outstanding titles are based upon it and much can be said in support of it. If not the only reasonable construction of the act, it is at least an admissible one. It therefore comes within the rule that the practical construction given to an act of Congress, fairly susceptible of different constructions, by those charged with the duty of executing it is entitled to great respect and, if acted upon for a number of years, will not be disturbed except for cogent reasons."

If, therefore, the Secretary's interpretation is not unreasonable, if the language of the orders bears his construction, we must reverse the decision of the Court of Appeals.

III

Executive Order No. 8979, 6 Fed.Reg. 6471, provided:

> "None of the above-described lands excepting [a described area] shall be subject to settlement, location, sale, or entry, or other disposition (except for fish trap sites) under any of the public-land laws applicable to Alaska, or to classification and lease under the provisions of the act of July 3, 1926, entitled 'An Act to provide for the leasing of public lands in Alaska for fur farming, and for other purposes', 44 Stat. 821, U.S.C., title 48, secs. 360–361, or the act of March 4, 1927, entitled 'An Act to provide for the protection, development, and utilization of the public lands in Alaska by establishing an adequate system for grazing livestock thereon', 44 Stat. 1452, U.S.C., title 48, secs. 471–471o * * *."

"Settlement," "location," "sale" and "entry" are all terms contemplating transfer of title to the lands in question. It was therefore reasonable for the Secretary to construe "or other disposition" to encompass only dispositions which, like the four enumerated, convey or lead to the conveyance of the title of the United States—for example, "grants" and "allotments." Cf. Opinion of the Solicitor, 48 I.D. 459 (1921). An oil and gas lease does not vest title to the lands in the lessee. See Boesche v. Udall, 373 U.S. 472, 477–478. Moreover, the term "public-land laws" is ordinarily used to refer to statutes governing the alienation of public land, and generally is distinguished from both "mining laws," referring to statutes governing the mining of hard minerals on public lands, and "mineral leasing laws," a term used to designate that group of statutes governing the leasing of public lands for gas and oil.

The reference in Executive Order No. 8979 to the 1926 and 1927 statutes also lends support to the Secretary's interpretation. For both statutes relate to leasing rather than alienation of title; it would be reasonable to infer from their specific addition that "disposition" was not intended to encompass leasing. The Secretary also might reasonably have been influenced by a belief that in view of his overriding discretionary authority to refuse to issue an oil and gas lease on a given tract whenever he thought that granting a lease would undercut the purposes of the withdrawal, inclusion of such leases in the withdrawal order would have been unnecessary. Cf. Haley v. Seaton, 281 F.2d 620 (1960).

* * *

The placement of the fish trap exception—"(except for fish trap sites)"—a phrase admittedly not relating to alienation of title to land, does tend to cut against the Secretary's interpretation of Executive Order No. 8979. However, it appears that the exception was designed to assure the Alaskans, whose livelihood is largely dependent on the salmon catch, that they could continue—despite the order—to use fish traps. Since it was a reassurance not technically necessary and therefore not functionally related to any part of the regulation, it is no surprise to find it carelessly placed. Compare Executive Order No. 8857, 6 Fed.Reg. 4287, establishing the Kodiak National Wildlife Refuge. We do not think the position of the fish trap exception is sufficient to justify a court's overturning the Secretary's construction as unreasonable.

Public Land Order No. 487 withdrew the lands it covered from "settlement, location, sale or entry," but contained no reference to "other disposition." Nor did it contain anything analogous to the fish trap exception. The reasonableness of the Secretary's interpretation of Public Land Order No. 487 therefore follows *a fortiori* from the reasonableness of his construction of Executive Order No. 8979.

Reversed.

NOTES

1. The Court found that no "disposition" was involved and that the mining laws were not "public land laws." Does a land order that withdraws lands "from settlement and entry, or other form of appropriation" remove the lands from the operation of the hardrock mining laws? In Mason v. United States, 260 U.S. 545 (1923), it was argued that "other form of appropriation" meant forms akin to "settlement" (at a time when homesteading was still active), and that mining claims were acquired by "location." The Supreme Court held against the mining claimant:

> Here the supposed specific words are sufficiently comprehensive to exhaust the genus and leave nothing essentially similar upon which the general words may operate. If the appropriation of mineral lands by location and development be not akin to settlement and entry, what other form of appropriation can

be so characterized? None has been suggested, and we can think of none.

Mason was not cited in Udall v. Tallman. On whether mineral leases are "dispositions," is it relevant that the first section in the Mineral Leasing Act, 30 U.S.C.A. § 181, states that "deposits of ＊ ＊ ＊ oil ＊ ＊ ＊ shall be subject to disposition in the form and manner provided by this chapter"? Is the Mineral Leasing Act a "public land law"?

2. Udall v. Tallman is often cited for the general proposition that courts should defer to administrative interpretations of regulations and statutes than for its holding on withdrawals. The "deference" issue is frequently involved in public lands litigation because of the large number of administrative interpretations, especially by the Solicitor of the Department of Interior. But agency interpretations often involve legal issues and "reviewing courts are not obliged to stand aside and rubber-stamp their affirmance of administrative decisions that they deem inconsistant with a statutory mandate or that frustrate the congressional policy underlying a statute." NLRB v. Brown, 380 U.S. 278, 290–92 (1965). See also, e.g., Skidmore v. Swift & Co., 323 U.S. 134, 139–40 (1944).

3. In the light of the authority and statute in notes 1 and 2 above, did the Udall v. Tallman court "rubberstamp" the agency interpretation?

WILDERNESS SOCIETY v. MORTON
United States Court of Appeals, District of Columbia Circuit, 1973 (en banc).
479 F.2d 842.
Cert. denied, 411 U.S. 917 (1973).

J. SKELLY WRIGHT, Circuit Judge:

The question before us in these cases is whether a permanent injunction should issue barring appellee Secretary of the Interior from carrying out his stated intention of granting rights-of-way and special land use permits necessary for construction by appellee Alyeska Pipeline Service Company (Alyeska), across lands owned by the United States, of a 48-inch-wide oil pipeline which would stretch some 789 miles from Prudhoe Bay on the North Slope of the State of Alaska to the Port of Valdez on the southern Pacific coast of Alaska. ＊ ＊ ＊ The District Court, on April 23, 1970, granted a preliminary injunction against issuance of the permits and rights-of-way. See Wilderness Society v. Hickel, D.D.C., 325 F.Supp. 422 (1970). When the question of a permanent injunction came before the District Court on August 15, 1972, the court, in a brief unreported opinion, dissolved the preliminary injunction, denied a permanent injunction, and dismissed the complaints. This expedited appeal followed. We reverse.

While the parties to this action have managed to produce a record and a set of briefs commensurate with the multi-billion-dollar project at stake, the basic contentions of the parties, and our views with respect thereto, may be summarized quite briefly. Appellants contend that issuance of certain rights-of-way and special land use permits by the

Secretary of the Interior to Alyeska and to the State of Alaska would violate Section 28 of the Mineral Leasing Act of 1920, 30 U.S.C.A. § 185, by exceeding the width limitation of that section. ∗ ∗ ∗

∗ ∗ ∗

Appellees respond that all of the rights-of-way to be issued to the State of Alaska and some of the rights-of-way to be issued to Alyeska are authorized under statutes other than Section 28, that the Secretary's authority to issue the other rights-of-way to Alyeska may be implied under Section 28, and that the special land use permits to be issued to Alyeska are not rights-of-way within the meaning of Section 28 and are thus exempt from Section 28's width limitation. ∗ ∗ ∗

∗ ∗ ∗

In brief, it is our view that the legislative history clearly indicates that when Congress enacted Section 28 it intended that all construction work take place within the confines of the width limitation of the section—that is, within the area covered by the pipe itself (4 feet) and 25 feet on either side. In addition, the relevant regulations require that all special land use permits be revocable, and we hold that the permit in this case does not meet the requirement as it has previously been construed. Since all parties agree that construction of the proposed 48-inch diameter pipeline is impossible if all construction work must take place within the width limitation of Section 28, we must enjoin issuance of this special land use permit until Congress changes the applicable law, either by amending Section 28's width limitation or by exempting this project from its provisions.

∗ ∗ ∗

The main lesson of this legislative history is that the presumptions upon which our maxims of statutory interpretation are built are not always borne out. These presumptions, like most others in the law, are rebuttable. And while our maxims of statutory construction might have led us to conclude that Congress "must have intended" that those building pipelines could make use of land outside the statutory right-of-way for construction purposes, the legislative history simply indicates otherwise. One might have expected the Congress of the United States to exercise foresight in a situation in which it was expressly warned that the statute it was enacting was then, or might in the future become, ineffective. But such foresight was notably lacking. Foresight no doubt would have been the wisest choice in this instance, since after the passage of the Mineral Leasing Act pipeline technology developed to permit construction of larger pipelines needing greater amounts of construction space. It might fairly be said that Congress overreacted to the prior excesses of railroad rights-of-way. But it is not our function, when we pass on either the constitutionality of statutes or their interpretation, to substitute our opinion as to what is wise for that of Congress. Congress chose not to be foresightful; it chose to retain control of the width of pipeline rights-of-way over public land itself, and that decision and its consequences must stand until Congress chooses otherwise.

Appellees have placed their primary reliance on the administrative practice with respect to SLUPs.ᶜ While we find it unnecessary to review the administrative history in great detail, looking at that history in the light most favorable to appellees it indicates (1) that ever since the Mineral Leasing Act was passed the informal policy of the Bureau of Land Management has been to permit those constructing pipelines to use land for construction purposes outside the statutory right-of-way; (2) that since 1960 this informal practice has begun to become formalized through the procedure of granting SLUPs for construction space to supplement the statutory right-of-way; and (3) that the Department of the Interior and other agencies have granted SLUPs for a multitude of purposes other than pipeline purposes for the last 100 years, oftentimes in situations where the SLUP "supplemented" a limited statutory right-of-way. Appellees argue that this administrative practice should be accorded great weight and deference in the interpretation of the effect of Section 28 on SLUPs for construction purposes, and should lead us to conclude that Section 28 does not affect the Secretary's authority to issue SLUPs.

Before discussing the administrative history of SLUPs any further, it would be best to state at the outset our general approach to the area of executive interpretation of statutes. We do not question the settled principle that administrative interpretations of statutes are entitled to great weight. Udall v. Tallman, 380 U.S. 1 (1965). But it is our firm belief that a line must be drawn between according administrative interpretations deference and the proposition that administrative agencies are entitled to violate the law if they do it often enough. Not to draw this line is to make a mockery of the judicial function. "[T]he courts are the final authorities on issues of statutory construction * * * and 'are not obliged to stand aside and rubber-stamp their affirmance of administrative decisions that they deem inconsistent with a statutory mandate or that frustrate the congressional policy underlying a statute.' * * * 'The deference owed to an expert tribunal cannot be allowed to slip into a judicial inertia * * *.'" Volkswagenwerk Aktiengesellschaft v. F.M.C., supra, 390 U.S. at 272. Administrative construction of a statute "is only one input in the interpretational equation." Zuber v. Allen, supra, 396 U.S. at 192. A court should not "abdicate its ultimate responsibility to construe the language employed by Congress," id. at 193, but rather should defer to an administrative construction only if there are no "compelling indications that it is wrong." Red Lion Broadcasting Co. v. F.C.C., supra, 395 U.S. at 381. It has a duty to ignore that construction should it determine that it is "in conflict with the plain intent of the legislature." "Administrative interpretations are not absolute rules of law which must necessarily be followed in every instance, but are only helpful guides to aid courts in their task of statutory construction." Sims v. United States, 4 Cir., 252 F.2d 434, 438 (1958), affirmed, 359 U.S. 108 (1959). Judge Hand summarized the principle very succinctly when he said, "[I]n the end, after whatever reserve, upon the courts rests the ultimate responsibili-

c. [Ed.] "Special Land Use Permit."

ty of declaring what a statute means * * *." Fishgold v. Sullivan Drydock & Repair Corp., 2 Cir., 154 F.2d 785, 790, affirmed, 328 U.S. 275 (1946). An administrative practice which is plainly contrary to the legislative will may be overturned no matter how well settled and how long standing.

Balancing the maxim of deference to administrative interpretations with the principle that the courts remain the final arbiter of the meaning of the law is unquestionably a difficult process. It would seem, however, that a sensible way of meeting this task would be to analyze the rationales behind the doctrine of deference and to ask if they apply in this case. For if they do not, the maxim of deference must inevitably bow before the principle of judicial supremacy in matters of statutory construction. Application of that methodology to the instant case leads us to conclude that "[t]hose props that serve to support a disputable administrative construction are absent here." Zuber v. Allen, supra, 396 U.S. at 193.

Perhaps the primary rationale behind the doctrine of deference is the idea of administrative expertise. Thus it has been said that special deference is due when the administrators were involved in the drafting and passage of the statutory language. See ibid. "Administrative construction is less potent than it otherwise would be where it does not rest upon matters peculiarly within the administrator's field of expertise." Thompson v. Clifford, 408 F.2d 154, 167 (1968).

There can be no doubt that there is no need for administrative expertise in resolving the question of the meaning of Section 28. Expertise might be needed to decide what is a reasonable pipeline construction area, but it is not needed to decide whether Section 28 precludes construction outside the statutory right-of-way.

> " * * * [S]ince the only or principal dispute relates to the meaning of the statutory term, the controversy must ultimately be resolved, not on the basis of matters within the special competence of the Secretary, but by judicial application of canons of statutory construction. * * * 'The role of the courts should, in particular, be viewed hospitably where * * * the question sought to be reviewed does not significantly engage the agency's expertise. "[W]here the only or principal dispute relates to the meaning of the statutory term" * * * [the controversy] presents issues on which courts, and not [administrators], are relatively more expert.' * * * "

Barlow v. Collins, 397 U.S. 159, 166 (1970), *quoting* Hardin v. Kentucky Utilities Co., 390 U.S. 1, 14 (1968) (Mr. Justice Harlan, dissenting).

The second basic rationale for the doctrine of deference is the concept of congressional acquiescence in the administrative interpretation. "Under some circumstances, Congress' failure to repeal or revise [a statute] in the face of such administrative interpretation has been held to constitute persuasive evidence that that interpretation is the one intended by Congress." Zemel v. Rusk, 381 U.S. 1, 11 (1965). Thus in actual cases courts have to analyze whether there is any reason to believe that the particular administrative interpretation in question came to the attention of Congress so that it might reasonably be said that Congress, by failing to take any action with respect thereto, approved the interpretation. As we have had occasion to note, "Legislative silence cannot mean ratification unless, as a minimum, the existence of the administrative practice is brought home to the legislature." Thompson v. Clifford, supra, 408 F.2d at 164.

Applying the rationale to the present case, there is absolutely no indication that the practice of granting SLUPs for pipeline construction purposes has ever been brought to the attention of Congress, either through testimony at a congressional hearing or by any other means.[54] Nor is the practice of granting SLUPs for pipeline construction purposes of such public knowledge that it is reasonable to assume that congressmen, as members of the general public, knew of the practice. Indeed, it is ironic that the very oil companies which now claim that it was settled and well known administrative practice to grant pipeline construction SLUPs apparently did not know about the practice when they first made application for rights-of-way for the trans-Alaska pipeline. The first application, as noted in the factual introduction, requested an additional permanent right-of-way for construction purposes. Likewise, we note that in its Preliminary Report to the President in 1969 the North Slope Task Force organized by the Department of the Interior had not yet figured out how the additional space was to be acquired. In fact, the Interior Department's own version of

---

54. Compare Power Reactor Development Co. v. Int. U. of Elec., Radio & Mach. Wkrs, 367 U.S. at 408, where the Court found that the administrative interpretation had "time and again been brought to the attention" of the responsible congressional committee.

Not only do appellees argue that Congress has acquiesced in the practice of granting SLUP's for pipeline purposes. They also claim that Congress has specifically authorized the Secretary of the Interior to issue SLUPs for any and all purposes in his discretion. But an examination of the relevant statutes shows no such authorization. The 3 statutes cited by appellees are 43 U.S.C.A. §§ 2, 1201 & 1457. Section 2 provides that the Secretary of the Interior "shall perform all executive duties * * * in anywise respecting [the public lands of the United States] * * *." Section 1201 authorizes him "to enforce and carry into execution, by appropriate regulations, every part of the provisions of [Title 43] * * *." Section 1457 charges the Secretary "with the supervision of public business relating to the following subjects and agencies: * * * 12. Petroleum conservation. 13. Public lands, including mines." We cannot find an authorization to issue SLUPs in these statutes. There is no question, of course, that

the Secretary of the Interior, as the executive in charge of federal lands, has some power to authorize entry upon federal lands; otherwise every entry on such lands would be a trespass absent specific statutory authority. And we recognize that technically a special land use permit is nothing but a formal document permitting what would otherwise be a trespass. But to reason from the fact that the Secretary has some authority under these broad statutes to permit entry upon federal land to the conclusion that any and all special land use permits are congressionally authorized, no matter how permanent the intended use, no matter how inconsistent with other more specific legislation, requires a leap of faith we cannot make. This is an instance where a difference in degree constitutes a difference in kind, and although we might imagine cases in which it would be difficult to draw the line between uses which may be authorized under the Secretary's broad executive authority and those that must rest on specific statutory authority, given the express proviso in the Mineral Leasing Act and the Act's legislative history we are confident that the SLUP in this case is not authorized under these broad and vague delegations of administrative responsibility.

the development of the practice of granting pipeline construction SLUPs makes it highly unlikely that any but a small handful of prior recipients would know of the practice. The agency admits that until 1960 the practice was completely informal. That is, those building pipelines did not request use of additional space; they merely used what space they needed while project supervisors from the Bureau of Land Management silently looked on. It was not until 1960 that SLUPs were granted, and even then the main purpose of the SLUPs was not to authorize formally what otherwise would be a trespass on federal lands. Rather, the Bureau's desire to issue SLUPs stemmed from the Bureau's view that some builders of pipelines were using more construction space than was in fact reasonably necessary, or were refusing to attempt to return the construction space to its original condition. It was therefore felt that in those cases where there was a risk of such behavior a SLUP would be desirable either as a means of limiting, but not eliminating, encroachments on property outside the statutory right-of-way or as a means of providing a vehicle in which stipulations about returning the land to satisfactory condition could be placed. For all that appears from the administrative record before us, SLUPs are still not granted in every case of pipeline construction, but only in those cases where the Bureau's rationales are applicable. Even today the Bureau's policy is not publicized through a formal rule or through any other "expressly articulated position at the administrative level." We are constrained to conclude, therefore, that the practice of granting pipeline construction SLUPs has never come to the attention of Congress, and that there can be no finding of congressional acquiescence.[58]

*   *   *

We need not rest our decision holding the SLUP here to be illegal on Section 28 alone, for appellants have also demonstrated that this SLUP violates the agency's own regulations governing the granting of special land use permits.

Appellees have based their request for a SLUP on 43 C.F.R. § 2920.0–2(a) (1972):

"*   *   * It is the policy of the Secretary of the Interior, in the administration of the lands under the jurisdiction of the Bureau of Land Management, to permit the beneficial use thereof, where practical, for special purposes not specifically provided for by existing law. Permits for such special use will not be issued, however, in any case where the provisions of any law may be invoked. Permits will not be issued where such issuance would be inconsistent with the objectives of the regu-

---

58. *   *   *

More importantly, we reject any approach whereby congressional silence with respect to particular administrative action is used, not merely to show congressional acquiescence in that action, but to prove congressional acquiescence in the adminis- trative *reasoning* behind that action. It is common knowledge that in Congress, just as in the judicial system and elsewhere in life, individuals often agree on a particular result while disagreeing as to the reasoning that leads toward that result.

lations in this chapter or would be in conflict with any Federal
or State laws."

In addition, 43 C.F.R. § 2920.3(a)(1) (1972) provides: "A special land-use
permit will be revocable in the discretion of the authorized officer at
any time, upon notice, if in his judgment the lands should be devoted to
another use, or the conditions of the permit have been breached."
Appellants contend, first, that the SLUP in this case violates Section
2929.0–2(a), which only permits special land use permits for "purposes
not specifically provided for by existing law," and the similar proviso in
the same section that "[p]ermits for such special use will not be issued,
however, in any case where the provisions of any law may be invoked."
Also, it is argued that the SLUP violates Section 2920.3(a)(1) because it
is not "revocable in the discretion of the authorized officer at any time"
as that phrase has been construed in prior cases.

* * *

The analysis of whether the regulation is violated is thus identical
with our previous analysis of whether Section 28 was violated. Congressional intent to confine construction activities to the pipeline right-
of-way authorized in the statute represents a congressional intent to
preclude construction SLUPs for land outside the statutory right-of-
way. Thus the SLUP constitutes a violation of the regulation in this
regard.

Turning then to the regulation's requirement that the SLUP be
revocable, past administrative interpretation of the revocability requirement has produced two very different tests. * * *

Though the parties to this case have debated which of these tests is
proper, we find it unnecessary to approve one or the other, for we find
that the SLUP to be issued in the present case fails both tests.

* * *

[The Interior Solicitor had rendered two different interpretations of
"revocability." But the court found that this permit could not be truly
"revocable" because under either test the installation (a thick gravel
pad) must be "removable" in the sense that the land will be in suitable
condition for government use after removal:]

* * * Alyeska obviously has no intention of removing the pad
and the Interior Department will never require removal. The construction pad, a gravel roadway up to five feet deep, will be built with about
34 million cubic yards of gravel, taken from 234 gravel pits located
along the pipeline route. The Department clearly is not going to
require Alyeska to bear the great cost of breaking up this improvement
and returning the gravel to its source. As explained more fully below,
once the pad is constructed, it is environmentally more detrimental to
remove it than to keep it in place. We cannot believe, in light of all the
effort the Department has expended in developing stipulations to minimize detrimental environmental effects, that the Department will ever
force Alyeska affirmatively to degrade the environment.

We therefore conclude that the SLUP to be issued for pipeline construction violates the Bureau's own requirement of revocability, regardless of which interpretation of revocability we apply.

Having examined the regulations of the Bureau of Land Management as they pertain to the SLUP to be issued in this case, we need not resolve any purported conflict between the terms of the statute and the Bureau's historic authority to permit temporary special land use through permits. For the historic authority to issue permits applies only if the uses to be made thereunder are really temporary and revocable. If the use is really not temporary or occasional, but is permanent (or at least long-lasting), the matter cannot be papered over merely by designating it as "revocable" when it is not intended to be revocable and, in the nature of things, is not in fact revocable.

In addition to this inherent limitation on SLUPs, recognized in the Bureau's own regulations and many Attorney General opinions, it is obvious that SLUPs cannot be used as a means of avoiding the provisions of Section 28. Indeed, Alyeska concedes in its brief that it could not have avoided the legal dispute by not applying for any permanent right-of-way at all under Section 28, and obtaining all necessary land under a SLUP. The same result follows when a person is seeking a SLUP which is revocable in theory only to obtain authority for a use which Congress plainly contemplated would be obtained solely by application under, and subject to the limitations of, Section 28.

These two principles are both operative here. This case involves not only an attempt to avoid the width limitation of Section 28, but an attempt to do so in a manner inconsistent with the Bureau's own regulations. These two factors are interrelated and reinforcing and together they serve to invalidate the SLUP proposed to be issued by the Secretary of the Interior for construction of the Alaska pipeline.

CONCLUSION

"[G]reat cases are called great," Mr. Justice Holmes said 70 years ago, "not by reason of their real importance in shaping the law of the future, but because of some accident of immediate overwhelming interest * * *." Northern Securities Co. v. United States, 193 U.S. 197, 400 (1904) (dissenting opinion). The same may be said about the present litigation over the Alaska pipeline. These cases are indeed "great" because of the obvious magnitude and current importance of the interest at stake: billions of gallons of oil at a time when the nation faces an energy crisis of serious proportions; hundreds of millions of dollars in revenue for the State of Alaska at a time when financial support for important social programs is badly needed; industrial development and pollution of one of the last major unblemished wilderness areas in the world, at a time when we are all becoming increasingly aware of the delicate balance between man and his natural environment.

But despite these elements of greatness, the principles of law controlling these cases are neither complex nor revolutionary. Although the first part of this opinion went to great lengths to demonstrate that special land use permits for construction purposes were illegal under the Mineral Leasing Act, at the heart of that discussion is the following very simple point. Congress, by enacting Section 28, allowed pipeline companies to use a certain amount of land to construct their pipelines. These companies have now come into court, accompanied by the executive agency authorized to administer the statute, and have said, "This is not enough land; give us more." We have no more power to grant their request, of course, than we have the power to increase congressional appropriations to needy recipients.

* * *

Those who would attempt to avoid congressional restrictions have, in the past, argued that the conditions and limitations believed important by Congress in fact served no legitimate purpose. But the response of courts then was the same as our own. "It is not the office of the courts to pass upon the justification for that belief or the efficacy of the measures chosen for putting it into effect. Selection of the emphatically expressed purpose embodied in this Act was the appropriate business of the legislative body." United States v. City and County of San Francisco, supra, 310 U.S. at 26. In the past, also, parties sought to rationalize, or evoke sympathy for, their positions by demonstrating a settled administrative practice to ignore the law. The answer then was the same as our answer today. "We cannot accept the contention that administrative rulings—such as those here relied on—can thwart the plain purpose of a valid law." Id. at 31–32.

* * *

In the last analysis, it is an abiding function of the courts, in the course of decision of cases and controversies, to require the Executive to abide by the limitations prescribed by the Legislature. The scrupulous vindication of that basic principle of law, implicit in our form of government, its three branches and its checks and balances, looms more important in the abiding public interest than the embarkation on any immediate or specific project, however desirable in and of itself, in contravention of that principle. We think it plain that the Executive Branch, when confronted with the legal problems attendant upon the Alaska pipeline, should have taken note of the limitations that had been prescribed by Congress, and should have presented to Congress the case for revision of the basic statute.

* * *

It is so ordered.

NOTES

1. Is Wilderness Society v. Morton consistent with Udall v. Tallman on the deference accorded to administrative interpretations?

2. The requirement that agencies must follow their own regulations, like other laws, is likely to be of increasing importance as federal administrative rulemaking proliferates. E.g., United States v. Nixon, 418 U.S. 683 (1974); VanderMolen v. Stetson, 571 F.2d 617, 624 (D.C.

Cir.1977); Note, Violations by Agencies of Their Own Regulations, 87 Harv.L.Rev. 629 (1974). Land management agencies all have manuals that greatly exceed their regulations in length. Unlike regulations, manual provisions are not published in the Federal Register and there is little law on the subject, but the policy reasons for binding agencies to their policies and procedures in regulations seem to apply to manual provisions as well. United States v. Heffner, 420 F.2d 809, 811–13 (4th Cir.1969).

3. On November 16, 1973, seven months after the Supreme Court denied certiorari in Wilderness Society v. Morton, Congress eliminated the width limitation in 30 U.S.C.A. § 185, and exempted the Alaska Pipeline from further NEPA evaluation or review. Environmentalists were able to obtain additional provisions in the new section 185 dealing with environmental protection and public hearings.

C. THE PUBLIC TRUST DOCTRINE IN PUBLIC LAND LAW

The public trust doctrine, which has ancient roots in Roman and English law, was announced as part of federal common law in Illinois Central Railroad v. Illinois, 146 U.S. 387 (1892), supra at page 77. In *Illinois Central,* the Court imposed trust duties on the State, forbidding it to alienate beds of navigable watercourses that the State received by implication at statehood. The public trust doctrine lay dormant until the 1960's, when it was employed in several state court opinions. In 1970, the doctrine was the subject of one of the most influential articles in modern natural resources law, Sax, The Public Trust Doctrine in Natural Resources Law: Effective Judicial Introduction, 68 Mich.L.Rev. 471 (1970). Sax traced the trust's origins and explicated bases for its contemporary application; he emphasized its use as a mechanism for imposing limits on administrative discretion through judicial review, which would force debate on major resource questions in the legislative arena.

The public trust doctrine is ultimately premised on the notion that public access to important public resources is so fundamental to society that courts should imply restrictions when private development threatens to destroy public use. The doctrine has developed several branches in addition to the navigable stream bed context of *Illinois Central.* Courts have upheld public access to dry sand beaches. See, e.g., Van Ness v. Bay Head Improvement Ass'n, 95 N.J. 306, 471 A.2d 355 (1984). The trust has been invoked to require strict judicial review when state parklands are leased for private use, e.g., Gould v. Greylock Reservation Comm'n, 350 Mass. 410, 215 N.E.2d 114 (1966) and to demand payment of full market value when state lands are leased, e.g., Jerke v. State Dept. of Lands, 182 Mont. 294, 597 P.2d 49 (1979). Recent opinions also have applied the public trust doctrine to appropriations of water under state law. In the leading case, National Audubon Society v. Superior Court, 33 Cal.3d 419, 189 Cal.Rptr. 346, 658 P.2d 709 (1983), the City of Los Angeles had established appropriative rights in 1940 under state law to the waters of four tributaries to Mono Lake. The diversions from these streams, which were the only source of water for the lake, dropped the level of the lake markedly, adversely affecting dependent wildlife. Although rights established under the prior appropriation doctrine have been commonly thought to be near-absolute, the California Supreme Court ruled that the public trust doctrine subjects appropriative water rights to the public's interest in the affected resources:

> We do not dictate any particular allocation of water. Our objective is to resolve a legal conundrum in which two competing systems of thought—the public trust doctrine and the appropriative water rights system—existed independently of each other, espousing principles which seemingly suggested opposite results. We hope by integrating these two doctrines to clear away the legal barriers which have so far prevented either the Water Board or the courts from taking a new and objective look at the water resources of the Mono Basin. The human and environmental uses of Mono Lake—uses protected by the public trust doctrine—deserve to be taken into account. Such uses should not be destroyed because the state mistakenly thought itself powerless to protect them. 189 Cal.Rptr. at 369, 658 P.2d at 732.

See also United Plainsmen Ass'n v. North Dakota State Water Conservation Comm'n, 247 N.W.2d 457 (N.D.1976); Kootenai Envtl. Alliance, Inc. v. State Bd. of Land Comm'rs, 105 Idaho 622, 671 P.2d 1085 (1983). See generally, Dunning, the Public Trust Doctrine and Western Water Law: Discord or Harmony?, 30 Rocky Mtn.Min.L.Inst. 17 (1985); Johnson, Public Trust Protection for Stream Flows and Lake Levels, 14 U.C. D.L.Rev. 233 (1980).

The applicability of the public trust doctrine to the federal lands has been the subject of considerable scholarly debate and comparatively little judicial attention. The leading precedent for the use of the trust doctrine in the federal field is the following *Redwood Park* litigation, which dealt with compelling facts in the setting of one of the strongest conservation statutes in public land law, the National Park Service Organic Act, 16 U.S.C.A. § 1. The case involved logging on private lands adjacent to the Redwood National Park near Eureka, California. The public redwood groves were especially vulnerable because the park as originally created was comprised of many separate parcels; some were so narrow that these 300-foot high trees (coast redwoods are the tallest living things in the world) were said to be taller than the park units were wide. The trees are among the oldest living things in the world—some were alive at the time of Christ. Further, they provide valuable heartgrain redwood in enormous quantities and jobs for the chronically depressed economy on California's North Coast.

SIERRA CLUB v. DEPARTMENT OF INTERIOR

United States District Court, Northern District of California, 1974.
376 F.Supp. 90.

SWEIGERT, District Judge.

This is an action by plaintiff, Sierra Club, against the Department of the Interior, and officials of the Department, to obtain judgment of this court directing defendants to use certain of their powers to protect Redwood National Park from damage allegedly caused or threatened by certain logging operations on peripheral privately-owned lands.

The action is now before the court on defendants' motion [to dismiss.] * * *

* * *

We will proceed to consider the government contention that the Second Claim of the amended complaint fails to state facts upon which relief can be granted.

This Second Claim of the amended complaint alleges in substance and effect as follows:

That subsequent to the establishment of the Redwood National Park in 1968 plaintiff learned that logging operations on slopes surrounding and upstream from the park were seriously endangering the park's resources, and that these dangers were reported to defendants and were offered in testimony at United States Senate hearings in Washington, D.C., on May 10, 1971;

That on September 24, 1971, plaintiff formally petitioned the Secretary of the Interior to take immediate action pursuant to his authority under the Redwood National Park Act to prevent further harm to the park's resources, and that a task force was then created by the Department of the Interior to make intensive field investigations of the threatened and actual damage to the Redwood National Park and to prepare a report of its findings;

That defendants have taken no action to prevent damage to the park from the consequences of logging on lands surrounding or upstream from the park, except to request the voluntary cooperation of timber companies to reform their operations on minor portions upstream and upslope from the park; that the timber companies have not effectively cooperated with this request and that defendants manifest no intent to protect the park from further damage to the park's trees, soil, scenery and streams;

That past and present logging operations on privately-owned steep slopes on the periphery of the park leave the park vulnerable to high winds, landslides, mudslides and siltation in the streams which endangers tree roots and aquatic life.

Plaintiff, citing 16 U.S.C.A. § 1 (hereinafter referred to as the National Park System Act) and 16 U.S.C.A. § 79a et seq., particularly §§ 79b(a), 79c(c), 79c(d)) (thereinafter referred to as the Redwood National Park Act) contends that defendants have a judicially-enforceable duty to exercise certain powers granted by these provisions to prevent or to mitigate such actual or potential damage to the park and its redwoods as is alleged in the complaint.

* * *

The National Park System Act, 16 U.S.C.A. Sec. 1, provides for the creation of the National Park Service in the Department of the Interior which Service shall:

> promote and regulate the use of Federal areas known as national parks, monuments, and reservations * * * by such means and measures as conform to the fundamental purpose of said parks, monuments, and reservations, which purpose is to conserve the scenery and the natural and historic objects and the wild life therein and to provide for the enjoyment of the same in such manner and by such means as will leave them unimpaired for the enjoyment of future generations.

The responsibilities of the Secretary of the Interior concerning public lands have been stated in Knight v. United Land Association, 142 U.S. 161 (1891) as follows:

> The secretary [of the Department of the Interior] is the guardian of the people of United States over the public lands. The obligations of his oath of office oblige him to see that the law is carried out, and that none of the public domain is wasted or is disposed of to a party not entitled to it. 142 U.S. 161 at 181 (1891). See also, Utah Power & Light v. United States, 243 U.S. 389 at 409 (1916); Davis v. Morton, 469 F.2d 593 at 597 (10th Cir.1972).

In addition to these general fiduciary obligations of the Secretary of the Interior, the Secretary has been invested with certain specific powers and obligations in connection with the unique situation of the Redwood National Park.

The Redwood National Park was created on October 2, 1968 by the Redwood National Park Act, 16 U.S.C.A. Secs. 79a–79j,

> to preserve significant examples of the primeval coastal redwood (Sequoia sempervirens) forests and the streams and seashores with which they are associated for purposes of public inspiration, enjoyment, and scientific study * * *. 16 U.S.C.A. Sec. 79a.

Congress limited the park to an area of 58,000 acres; appropriated 92 million dollars to implement the Act, of which, according to the Second Claim of the Amended Complaint, 20 million dollars remain unspent; and conferred upon the Secretary specific powers expressly designed to prevent damage to the park by logging on peripheral areas.

Title 16 U.S.C.A. Sec. 79c(e) provides:

> In order to afford as full protection as is reasonably possible to the timber, soil, and streams within the boundaries of the park, the Secretary is authorized, by any of the means set out in subsection (a) and (c) of this section, to acquire interests in land

from, and to enter into contracts and cooperative agreements with, the owners of land on the periphery of the park and on watershed tributary to streams within the park designed to assure that the consequences of forestry management, timbering, land use, and soil conservation practices conducted thereon, or of the lack of such practices, will not adversely affect the timber, soil, and streams within the park as aforesaid.

The question presented is whether on the allegations of the amended complaint, considered in the light of these statutory provisions, this court can direct the Secretary to exercise the powers granted under 16 U.S.C.A. Secs. 79c(e), 79b(a), 79c(d).

Under the Administrative Procedure Act agency action becomes nonreviewable only upon a clear and convincing showing that Congress intended to preclude judicial review. Abbott Laboratories v. Gardner, 387 U.S. 136 at 141 (1967).

The mere fact that the statute is couched in terms of a grant of discretion to the agency does not necessarily indicate an intent to preclude judicial review of the exercise of such discretion; judicial nonreviewability must be determined by an analysis of the entire statutory scheme.

Good sense suggests that the existence, nature and extent of potentially damaging conditions on neighboring lands and the effect thereof on the park, and the need for action to prevent such damage are matters that rest, primarily at least, within the judgment of the Secretary. However, neither the terms nor the legislative history of the Redwood National Park Act are such as to preclude judicial review of the Secretary's action or inaction.

In Rockbridge v. Lincoln, 449 F.2d 567 (9th Cir.1971) our Circuit * * * held that, in view of the trust relationship of the Secretary toward the Indians * * * such discretion as was vested in the Secretary was not an unbridled discretion * * * and, therefore, a cause for judicial relief under the Administrative Procedural Act was stated * * *

* * *

In view of the analogous trust responsibility of the Secretary of the Interior with respect to public lands as stated in Knight v. United Land, supra, and the analogous legislative history indicating a specific set of objectives which the provisions of the Redwood National Park Act were designed to accomplish, we consider Rockbridge, supra, to be strongly persuasive to the point that a case for judicial relief has been made out by plaintiff.

* * *

We are of the opinion that the terms of the statute, especially § 79c(e), authorizing the Secretary "in order to afford as full protection as is reasonably possible to the timber, soil, and streams within the boundaries of the park"—"to acquire interests in land from, and to enter into contracts and cooperative agreements with, the owners of land on the periphery of the park and on the watersheds tributary to streams within the park"—impose a legal duty on the Secretary to utilize the specific powers given to him whenever reasonably necessary for the protection of the park and that any discretion vested in the Secretary concerning time, place and specifics of the exercise of such powers is subordinate to his paramount legal duty imposed, not only under his trust obligation but by the statute itself, to protect the park.

* * *

* * * Although the inquiry into the facts is to be searching and careful, the ultimate standard of review is a narrow one that stops short of substitution of the court's judgment for that of the Secretary.

* * *

Accordingly, defendants' motion to dismiss and defendants' motion for summary judgment should be, and hereby are, denied.

SIERRA CLUB v. DEPARTMENT OF INTERIOR
United States District Court, Northern District of California, 1975.
398 F.Supp. 284.

SWEIGERT, District Judge.

* * *

The Legislative Background:

The Redwood National Park, situated in the counties of Del Norte and Humboldt, Northern California, was created on October 2, 1968, by the Redwood National Park Act, 16 U.S.C.A. §§ 79a–79j (hereafter "the Act"). The purpose of the park, as set forth in the Act, is

> "to preserve significant examples of the primeval coastal red-wood (Sequoia semper-virens) forests and the streams and seashores with which they are associated for purposes of public inspiration, enjoyment, and scientific study * * *." 16 U.S. C.A. § 79a.

The Act authorized acquisition of not more than 58,000 acres of previously privately owned land for which the United States was to pay just compensation, 16 U.S.C.A. § 79c(b). It authorized $92,000,000 for this land acquisition, 16 U.S.C.A. § 79j; of that $92,000,000 only $72,000,000 has been actually appropriated thus far by the Congress; of that $72,000,000, $2,800,000 remains unspent.

As stated in this court's previous opinion the issue for decision is whether the Secretary, since the establishment of the Park, has taken reasonable steps to protect the resources of the Park and, if not, whether his failure to do so has been under the circumstances arbitrary, capricious, or an abuse of discretion. * * *

In the pending case the conduct of the Secretary must be considered in the light of a very unique statute—a statute which did more than establish a national park; it also expressly vested the Secretary with authority to take certain specifically stated steps designed to protect the Park from damage caused by logging operations on the surrounding privately owned lands.

As the legislative history shows, these specific provisions were put into the statute because the Park boundaries authorized by Congress represented a compromise and did not include certain lands within the Redwood Creek Watershed upslope and upstream from the sourthernmost portion of the Park. Out of its concern that continued logging operations on those privately owned lands could cause damage within the Park, the Congress expressly invested the Secretary with these specific powers to take administrative action designed to protect it.

These specific powers include:

(1) power to modify the boundaries of the Park with particular attention to minimizing siltation of the streams, damage to the timber and preservation of the scenery, 16 U.S.C.A. § 79b(a).

(2) power to acquire interests in land from and to enter into contracts and cooperative agreements with the owners of land on the periphery of the Park and on watersheds tributary to streams within the Park designed to assure that the consequences of forestry management, timbering, land use and soil conservation practices conducted thereon, or the lack of such practices, would not adversely affect the timber, soil and streams within the Park, 16 U.S.C.A. § 79c(e).

(3) power to acquire lands and interests in land bordering both sides of the highway near the town of Orick to a depth sufficient to maintain a corridor—a screen of trees between the highway and the land behind the screen and the activities conducted thereon, 16 U.S.C.A. § 79c(d).

As pointed out in this court's previous decision, there is, in addition to these specific powers, a general trust duty imposed upon the National Park Service, Department of the Interior, by the National Park System Act, 16 U.S.C.A. § 1 et seq., to conserve scenery and natural and historic objects and wildlife [in the National Parks, Monuments and reservations] and to provide for the enjoyment of the same in such manner and by such means as will leave them unimpaired for the enjoyment of future generations (see: Knight v. United Land Ass. 142 U.S. 161 [1891]).

The Evidence

The evidence in the pending case shows that, beginning in April of 1969, the Secretary has conducted a series of five consecutive studies of damage and threats of damage to the Park caused by the logging operations of certain timber companies on adjacent lands. These studies have resulted in many specific recommendations for steps to be taken by the Secretary, pursuant to his various powers set forth in the statute, to prevent or minimize such damage.

[The opinion discusses each of the five reports at length. The reports analyzed the factual setting; emphasized the destructive effects of nearby logging on the Park; and urged that the Park Service develop a master plan and otherwise take action to protect the Park from the logging. The following excerpt from one of the reports is illustrative.]

* * *

The Curry Task Force Report—1973

In February, 1973, the defendants released a document prepared by Dr. Richard Curry, an official within the Department of the Interior. The Curry Task Force Report * * * set forth in detail the damage and threats of damage to the Park resources posed by logging practices on the lands adjacent to the Park. * * * The Curry Task Force Report found, as did the earlier reports, that, while landslides, erosion, and consequent high sediment loads in Redwood Creek are naturally occurring phenomena within the Redwood Creek watershed, man's timber harvesting activities within the watershed accelerate and aggravate these natural processes. In this regard, the Curry Task Force Report specifically identified such timber harvesting practices as clearcutting, the use of bulldozers within unstable areas to yard logs, and the construction of layouts and road systems over steep and unstable terrain.

The Curry Task Force Report made five specific recommendations for actions to be taken by the Secretary:

"1. Since the greatest threat to the Park emanates from man-induced acceleration of natural erosion processes, it is imperative that present land use practices be revised. The Secretary must secure the cooperation of the companies * * * to use harvesting techniques that minimize the degree of ground surface and vegetation disruption and to perform maintenance management on the harvested land in an effort to reduce the rate of erosion in these areas.

"These actions might include but are not limited to:

"a. Cable logging or such other system that minimizes ground disruption.

"b. More sensitive placement of the road net so as to minimize land slippage.

"c. A high performance road maintenance system which would include an effective erosion control program. * * *

"d. Application of stabilization procedures in active slide areas.

"e. Minimize the burning of slash.

"f. Planting of areas where regeneration from seeding and/or sprouting may be difficult.

"2. The Secretary should seek by cooperative agreement with the companies at least a two-year cutting moratorium extending at least 75 feet from the bank of all second order and higher tributary streams that are upslope from the Corridor.

The purpose is to permit the accumulation of baseline data for these streams. At the end of the period, the companies would be permitted to continue with their operations as long as the integrity of the stream is maintained.

"3. The acquisition in fee of a management zone around the 'worm' portion of the Redwood Creek unit that would be contoured to deal with specific impact and terrain conditions. The buffer would average 800 feet in width or encompass approximately 1,650 acres. * * *"

* * *

The evidence shows, and the court finds, that to date the Secretary has not implemented any of the recommendations made by or on behalf of his own agency in the above mentioned studies except (1) to enter into so-called "cooperative agreements" with the timber companies who own and operate on the lands surrounding the Park and (2) to conduct further studies.

Defendants' Contentions

The Secretary contends that these cooperative agreements amount to reasonable compliance with the intent of the statute and with his trust duties, pointing out that the timber companies voluntarily abstained from logging operations within an 800–foot zone of the Park until 1973 when they resumed logging under the so-called cooperative agreements; that their operations since 1973 have conformed to these agreements and that the agreements have restrained the harvesting practices of the timber companies and have thus mitigated damage to the Park.

The Secretary further points out that he is presently conducting another study through the U.S. Geological Survey of the Redwood Creek watershed and that this study, headed by a Dr. Richard Janda, is expected to be completed by the fall of 1975, at which time the Secretary will be in a position to further consider the Park situation.

The Secretary also contends that his failure to thus far implement other recommendations made by his own agency has been reasonable because of lack of sufficient scientific data to justify some of the recommendations already received and because of lack of the funds that would be required for the adoption of others.

* * *

Plaintiff's Contentions

On the other hand, plaintiff Sierra Club contends that the Secretary has complied with neither the intent of the statute nor with his general fiduciary duty to protect the Park * * *.

Plaintiff contends and the Court finds that the so-called cooperative agreements with the three timber companies are in fact not contracts or cooperative agreements within the meaning of Section 79c(e) because only one has been signed by one of the timber companies, and none of them has been signed by the Secretary; that they are, therefore, not legally binding contracts enforceable against the timber operators; also that, even if the so-called cooperative agreements were enforceable, their language is so general and so full of qualifications as to render them practically meaningless and unenforceable for that reason as well; also, that in any event the so-called cooperative agreements do not purport to carry out any of the recommendations of the defendants' studies with the arguable exception of Recommendation Number One of the Curry Task Force Report and, indeed, are contrary to other specific recommendations.

* * *

The Court further finds that the cooperative agreements do not fully implement even Curry Task Force Recommendation Number One in that the agreements set up an arbitrary 800 foot area surrounding the corridor portion of the Park while the recommendations do not so limit the harvesting restrictions.

The Court also finds that, even assuming none of the above deficiencies existed, the restraints placed upon the companies by the so-called cooperative agreements are unreasonably inadequate to prevent or reasonably minimize damage to the resources of the Park resulting from timber harvesting operations; that there is substantial on-going damage presently occurring to the timber, soil, streams, and aesthetics within the Park downslope from and as a result of clearcutting within the so-called buffer zone, even as such clearcutting is done in conformity with the so-called cooperative agreements.

With respect to the defendants' contentions concerning unavailability of funds, the Court further finds that it is the Congress which must make the ultimate determination whether additional sums should be authorized or appropriated and also the ultimate determinations concerning the items to which such funds should be applied; that the Secretary has never yet gone to the Congress, through the executive or otherwise, either to request the appropriation of the balance of money authorized by the statute, or to obtain whatever additional sums of money may be necessary to implement the specific powers of the statute designed for the protection of the Park.[6]

Finally, the Court finds that in light of the emphasis in each of the Secretary's own studies that time is of the essence, the Secretary has taken (to the detriment of the Park) an unreasonably long period of time to negotiate the proposed cooperative agreements. * * *

* * *

The foregoing findings must be considered in the light of what might be called an implied recognition by the defendants of some degree of fault on their part. This recognition is evidenced by the fact that, prior to the time the Curry Report was released to the public (which was not until after and as a result of legal steps taken in this action by the Sierra Club under the Freedom of Information Act), the

---

6. The only step taken by the Secretary in this direction was to consult, not the Congress, but only the Executive Office of Management of the Budget (OMB) concerning the recommendation of the Curry Report that certain property be acquired in fee; the OMB evidently advised against such acquisition.

Department of Interior had intentionally removed from the Report the last two pages which contained the five recommendations for action to be taken by the Secretary of the Interior. The existence of these last two pages was thereafter discovered only in the course of subsequent discovery proceedings which were initiated by the Sierra Club in the instant action.

With all due respect for the narrow limits of judicial intervention in matters entrusted primarily to executive agencies, the Court concludes that, in light of the foregoing findings, the defendants unreasonably, arbitrarily and in abuse of discretion have failed, refused and neglected to take steps to exercise and perform duties imposed upon them by the National Park System Act, 16 U.S.C.A. § 1, and the Redwood National Park Act, 16 U.S.C.A. § 79a, and duties otherwise imposed upon them by law; and/or that defendants have unreasonably and unlawfully delayed taking such steps.

Therefore, pursuant to the Administrative Procedure Act, 5 U.S.C.A. §§ 701–706 (particularly at § 701(a), § 706(1) and § 706(2)(A)); the Mandamus Act, 28 U.S.C.A. § 1361; the National Park System Act, 16 U.S.C.A. § 1 et seq.; Redwood National Park Act, 16 U.S.C.A. § 79a et seq.; and other applicable law, it is hereby ordered:

That defendants Secretary of the Interior and Assistant Secretary for Fish, Wildlife and Parks, take reasonable steps within a reasonable time to exercise the powers vested in them by law (particularly 16 U.S.C.A. §§ 79c(e), 79c(d) and 79b(a)), and to perform the duties imposed upon them by law (particularly 16 U.S.C.A. § 1), in order to afford as full protection as is reasonably possible to the timber, soil and streams within the boundaries of the Redwood National Park from adverse consequences of timbering and land use practices on lands located in the periphery of the Park and on watershed tributaries to streams which flow into the Park; that such action shall include, if reasonably necessary, acquisition of interests in land and/or execution of contracts or cooperative agreements with the owners of land on the periphery or watershed, as authorized in 16 U.S.C.A. § 79c(e); that such action shall include, if reasonably necessary, modification of the boundaries of the Park, as authorized in 16 U.S.C.A. § 79b(a); and that such action shall include, if reasonably necessary, resort to the Congress for a determination whether further authorization and/or appropriation of funds will be made for the taking of the foregoing steps, and whether the powers and duties of defendants, as herein found, are to remain or should be modified.

Defendants are further ordered to file herein, and serve upon plaintiff, on or before December 15, 1975, (unless such period is further extended), a progress report upon their compliance with the foregoing order, or, in lieu of compliance, a report, showing cause why compliance has not been made, is not being or will not be made with the foregoing order.

The Court reserves power to make such further orders as may be found to be advisable or necessary in connection with the subject matter.

* * *

NOTES

1. The court here professes to apply a "narrow" standard of review. Is the remedy narrow? The Court assumed continuing jurisdiction over the case and ordered the National Park Service to take action to afford as full protection as is reasonably possible to preserve the resource; to act within a specified time period; to negotiate contracts and acquire land, if appropriate; to lobby in Congress for more acquisition funds; and to file a progress report with the court on a fixed date.

2. What was the crucial factor in this case—the public trust doctrine or the Freedom of Information Act, which allowed plaintiffs to build a strong record based on documents obtained from the Park Service?

3. Pursuant to the District Court's order, the Department of the Interior undertook a series of efforts without beneficial results. At that point, it became apparent that the Park Service was not the only federal agency with which the Sierra Club was at odds. On February 1, 1976, Interior requested the Office of Management and Budget, through which the Executive submits legislation to Congress, to seek additional statutory authority for the regulation of off-park timber operations; the OMB disapproved the request. On March 1, 1976, the Department requested voluntary compliance with timber harvesting guidelines; the timber companies rejected the guidelines. On the same date, the Department asked the Governor of California to review an earlier rejection by the State Board of Forestry of adoption of the same proposed guidelines; as of June 7, 1976, the Governor had not responded. In addition to these rebuffs, the Department determined that it lacked sufficient appropriations to embark on acquisitions beyond those already made.

In the third Redwoods decision, Sierra Club v. Department of the Interior, 424 F.Supp. 172 (N.D.Cal.1976), the district court found that the Department had made a good faith attempt to perform its statutory duties as ordered, that it was therefore "purged" of its previously-found failure to do so, and that "in order adequately to exercise its powers and perform its duties in a manner adequately to protect the Park, Interior * * * stands in need of new Congressional legislation and/or new Congressional appropriations."

Those appropriations were subsequently provided by Congress in the Redwood Park Expansion Act of 1978, Pub.L.No. 95–250, 92 Stat. 163 (1978), which authorized the purchase of an additional 48,000 acres for the Park in the amount of $349 million, the largest expenditure ever made for the National Park System. Among other things the 1978 Act provided economic benefits to certain forest industry workers who lost their jobs due to the decrease in timber harvesting. See, e.g., Hoehn v. Donovan, 711 F.2d 899 (9th Cir.1983); Patterson v. Donovan, 707 F.2d 1011 (9th Cir.1983).

CHARLES F. WILKINSON, THE PUBLIC TRUST DOCTRINE IN PUBLIC LAND LAW *

14 U.C.D.L.Rev. 269 (1980).

* * *

The federal public lands are at the outer reaches of the public trust doctrine. Analysis should fairly begin with a statement by the Supreme Court in *Illinois Central Railroad Co. v. Illinois*. The Court said that the doctrine, in its classic form, operates as a bar against the large-scale disposition of lands under navigable waterways. In dictum, the Court added that title to land under navigable waterways is "different from the title the United States holds in the public lands which are open to pre-emption and sale." That language amounts to a clear finding that the classic public trust doctrine does not operate on the inland public lands. Put another way, inland federal lands are not "trust resources" according to the classic formulation of the doctrine.

* * *

In addition to the lack of direct support in either common law or Indian law, there are a number of compelling policy reasons supporting the conclusion that the public trust doctrine, at least in its classic form, does not apply to the public lands. First, the history of public land policy denies the existence of any prohibition against disposition of federal lands. * * * No serious suggestion could be made that private title to some 1.4 billion acres is clouded due to the United States' inability to convey clear title. Second, public land law is a heavily statutory field. The legislative matrix is sufficiently comprehensive that doubts can fairly be raised as to whether there is room for a broad, common law doctrine to operate.

Another basis for objection arises from the diversity of the public lands. * * * For example, it is one thing to refer to the dominant-use National Park Service as a trustee; it is a far different matter to place traditional trust obligations on the BLM, which must reconcile the congressionally sanctioned multiple-use tug and pull among economic and non-economic uses. This range of geographic and legal diversity makes it difficult to apply a single, unitary doctrine to all of the public lands.

Finally, while there may be majesty aplenty on the public lands, there are many, even in these land-appreciative days, who would say that most of the public land holdings are common, even mundane.

* * *

In spite of these factors, there is an imposing and growing body of case law suggesting that the public trust doctrine applies to the public lands.[32] Many of these cases use trust language only in passing and

---

* Reprinted with permission of the University of California-Davis Law Review.

32. See Kleppe v. New Mexico, 426 U.S. 529, 539–40 (1976); Ivanhoe Irrigation

with little analytical content. Nevertheless, the teaching of existing law seems to be that public land law has borrowed important components from the public trust doctrine. Although the obligations of Congress and federal agencies are plainly different from the duties of states when they act as trustees of navigable waterways, public trust notions have charged and vitalized public land law, particularly in the modern era.

* * *

I. The Existence of the Trust

* * *

The modern statutes are premised on the high station that today's society accords to the economic and environmental values of the federal lands and resources. They are rigorous laws designed to protect the public's interest in the public's resources. The legislation requires that public lands and resources not be sold, except in limited and exceptional circumstances; that the public resources are to be nurtured and preserved; that the public is to play a measured but significant role in decision-making; and that the lands and resources are to be managed on a sustained-yield basis for future generations.

The whole of these laws is greater than the sum of its parts. The modern statutes set a tone, a context, a milieu. When read together they require a trustee's care. Thus we can expect courts today, like courts in earlier eras, to characterize Congress' modern legislative scheme as imposing a public trust on the public resources.

Dist. v. McCracken, 357 U.S. 275, 294–95 (1958); Alabama v. Texas, 347 U.S. 272, 273–74, 277 (1954) (per curiam); United States v. California, 332 U.S. 19, 40 (1947); United States v. City & County of San Francisco, 310 U.S. 16, 28–29 (1940); Utah Power & Light Co. v. United States, 243 U.S. 389, 409 (1917); Causey v. United States, 240 U.S. 399, 402 (1916); Light v. United States, 220 U.S. 523, 536–37 (1911); Camfield v. United States, 167 U.S. 518, 524 (1897); Knight v. United States Land Ass'n, 142 U.S. 161, 178, 181 (1891); United States v. Trinidad Coal & Coking Co., 137 U.S. 160, 170 (1890); United States v. Beebe, 127 U.S. 338, 342 (1888); Dred Scott v. Sandford, 60 U.S. (19 How.) 393, 448 (1856); Pollard v. Hagan, 44 U.S. (3 How.) 212, 221–22, 224 (1845); United States v. Hughes, 626 F.2d 619, 621 (9th Cir.1980); United States v. Curtis-Nevada Mines, Inc., 611 F.2d 1277, 1283–84 (9th Cir.1980); Ventura County v. Gulf Oil Corp., 601 F.2d 1080, 1083 (9th Cir.1979), aff'd, 100 S.Ct. 1593 (1980); Massachusetts v. Andrus, 594 F.2d 872, 890, 892 (1st Cir.1979); Edwards v. Carter, 580 F.2d 1055, 1067 n. 8 (D.C.Cir. 1978); United States v. Ruby Co., 588 F.2d 697, 704–05 (9th Cir.1978); West Virginia Div. of Izaak Walton League of America, Inc. v. Butz, 522 F.2d 945, 955 (4th Cir. 1975); Wilderness Soc'y v. Morton, 479 F.2d 842, 891 (D.C.Cir.) (en banc), cert. denied, 411 U.S. 917 (1973); Davis v. Morton, 469 F.2d 593, 597 (10th Cir.1972); Hannifin v. Morton, 444 F.2d 200, 202 (10th Cir. 1971); Beaver v. United States, 350 F.2d 4, 8 (9th Cir.1965), cert. denied, 383 U.S. 937 (1966); Pan Am. Petroleum Corp. v. Pierson, 284 F.2d 649, 655 (10th Cir.1960); United States v. West, 232 F.2d 694, 696–99 (9th Cir.1956); Forbes v. United States, 125 F.2d 404, 408 (9th Cir.1942); United States ex rel. Roughton v. Ickes, 101 F.2d 248, 252–53 (D.C.Cir.1938); In re Stuart Transp. Co., 495 F.Supp. 38, 39–40 (E.D.Va. 1980); Friends of Yosemite v. Frizzell, 420 F.Supp. 390, 393 (N.D.Cal.1976); Sierra Club v. Department of Interior, 398 F.Supp. 284, 287 (N.D.Cal.1975); Sierra Club v. Department of Interior, 376 F.Supp. 90, 93, 95–96 (N.D.Cal.1974); Stewart v. Penny, 238 F.Supp. 821, 827 (D.Nev. 1965); United States v. Blaylock, 159 F.Supp. 874, 877 (N.D.Cal.1958); United States v. Thompson, 41 F.Supp. 13, 15–16 (E.D.Wash.1941).

The fact that the public trust doctrine in public land law must rest on implication should surprise no one. The doctrine has always rested on implication. * * *

The shifting notions of trust responsibility reflect fundamental changes in legal perceptions of the government's role in public land law. As recently as the 1950's, the courts conceptualized the United States as a proprietor in regard to the public lands. The public lands were viewed as capital assets over which federal control could be asserted, much as if Congress and the land management agencies were private parties managing private affairs. This conceptualization of the government as a proprietor was the source of a range of doctrines with broad consequences. For example, public participation in rulemaking was not considered appropriate because public land management was an internal affair. Standing was narrowly construed to restrict public access to the courts. Sovereign immunity barred a considerable amount of litigation. The doctrine of "committed to agency discretion by law" was invoked to deny judicial review. When judicial review was available, it was sharply circumscribed by numerous decisions giving broad sway to agency discretion.

These developments, of course, have been almost completely reversed by recent statutes and judicial decisions. It is now established that the United States acts as a sovereign government—not just as a proprietor—in regard to the public lands. * * * It is the public to whom public lands managers are ultimately accountable.

These various trends merge in the longstanding tendency of the courts to describe the public lands as being held in trust. It is the product of a search of two centuries to articulate the government's duties and responsibilities. The trust concept has been properly invoked as the best available formulation of the central doctrinal forces in public land law—that increasingly tough strictures are required, and have been imposed, on land management officials; that land management is not a private business; that ultimate accountability is to the public; and that over time the public and Congress have come to place ever greater importance on the nation's public natural resources.

The trust notion, as a generic concept, is an appropriate description of the federal role in public land law. It is a common-sense description that has evolved in regard to the inland public lands just as it has developed in closely related subject areas. The more difficult issue * * * is determining the scope and content of the trust.

II. Scope and Content of the Trust

* * *

A. A Constraint on Congressional Action

One possible use of the public trust doctrine is as a limit on the powers of Congress, just as the classic doctrine has been found to restrict state legislatures. * * *

* * * [A] constitutionally based trust doctrine is probably not enforceable against Congress for several reasons. * * *

B. A Limitation on Federal Agencies

The public trust could also operate as a limitation on the discretion of administrative agencies. First, it might be used, as it has been in several states, to require express legislative authority when public resources are being unreasonably used by administrative agencies to promote private gain. Second, it would provide the basis for an ultimate "hard look" doctrine for reviewing administrative action. As such, it would be a doctrine advanced by environmentalists and by industry and would have no ideological content. The doctrine could be invoked by industry, for example, to emphasize the high standard of care incumbent on the Forest Service if it mishandled a timber sale, or on the BLM if it unreasonably delayed the processing of competitive bidding on a mineral lease.

Several of the major public lands cases in the last decade have used trust language to reach results sharply curtailing administrative discretion. The *Alaska Pipeline* case, the *Monongahela* case, the *Georges Bank* case, and the *Redwood National Park* cases are leading examples. In each of these cases, the trust language was used only as a backdrop; the *Redwood National Park* decisions could have been based on separate grounds, and in the other decisions the trust was mentioned only briefly. But the invocation of the trust concept served to set a general context for the litigation and provided a benchmark with which to measure the obligations of the administrative agencies.

C. A Rule of Construction

The construction of statutes against the background of a duty to the public would affect the interpretation of a number of statutes. For example, the question of impliedly reserved water rights has been largely resolved on National Forest lands, but the extent of protection afforded to wildlife and public recreational and aesthetic opportunities by other land-management systems has not been determined. * * * The answers to all of these questions would be affected if the courts construed the acts to effectuate Congress' intent to act as a trustee charged with the duty of protecting and preserving the public resources.

D. An Action-Forcing Mechanism

Another use of the public trust doctrine in regard to public lands is what might be called the action-forcing cases. The injunction in the *Redwood National Park* litigation, for example, went beyond prohibitory commands; the court also required the agency to take affirmative action to protect the park's resources. * * * The questions arise whether public land managers can be compelled to take affirmative action, including litigation, to protect federal lands, and whether the public trust doctrine can play a part in such determinations.

* * *

NOTES

1. Is there room for a judicially-created rule like the public trust doctrine in a heavily statutory field such as public land law? The *Redwood Park* litigation remains the most compelling application of the public trust doctrine in public land and resources law. Trust notions have been referred to in later cases but the doctrine does not seem to have been the sole basis for imposing strict judicial review in any of them. See, e.g., United States v. Curtis-Nevada Mines, Inc., 611 F.2d 1277 (9th Cir.1980), infra at page 463, and Commonwealth of Massachusetts v. Andrus, 594 F.2d 872 (1st Cir.1979).

2. The Sierra Club filed an action to require the United States to take action to protect federal reserved water rights in Utah and Nevada. Sierra Club v. Andrus, 487 F.Supp. 443 (D.D.C.1980), aff'd on other grounds sub nom. Sierra Club v. Watt, 659 F.2d 203 (D.C.Cir. 1981). Plaintiff argued that the trust duties of the National Park Service and the BLM required those agencies to take affirmative steps to safeguard their water resources. Judge Richey read the legislative history of the 1978 amendment to the Redwood Park Act as limiting the public trust doctrine:

> Plaintiff asserts that in addition to the statutory duties discussed above, defendants hold National Park and Bureau of Land Management resources in trust for the public and, therefore, are charged with duties and obligations of a trustee. To the extent that plaintiff's argument advances the proposition that defendants are charged with "trust" duties distinguishable from their statutory duties, the Court disagrees. Rather, the Court views the statutory duties previously discussed as comprising *all* the responsibilities which defendants must faithfully discharge.

> The legislative history of the 1978 amendment to 16 U.S. C.A. § 1a–1 makes clear that any distinction between "trust" and "statutory" responsibilities in the management of the National Park System is unfounded. Moreover, Congress specifically addressed the authority upon which plaintiff relies to support its "trust theory":

>> The committee has been concerned that litigation with regard to Redwood National Park and other areas of the system may have *blurred the responsibilities* articulated by the 1916 Act creating the National Park service * * *.

>> [T]he committee strongly endorses the Administration's proposed amendment to the Act of August 18, 1970, concerning the management of the National Park System *to refocus and insure the basis for decisionmaking concerning the system continues to be the criteria provided by 16 U.S.C.*

> *§ 1 * * *. This restatement of these highest principles of management is also intended to serve as the basis for any judicial resolution of competing private and public values and interest in * * * areas of the National Park System.*

Senate Report 95–528, supra, at 14, 7–8 (emphasis added). By asserting an explicit statutory standard "as the basis of any judicial resolution" of Park management issues, Congress eliminated "trust" notions in National Park System management. The Court also concludes that §§ 1701 and 1782(c) of title 43 United States Code embody the entire duty and responsibility to manage and protect Bureau of Land Management lands generally with which the Secretary is charged. (Emphasis in original).

What weight should be given to the Committee Report construing the terms of the 1916 National Park Service organic act? Does 16 U.S.C.A. § 1 itself create or embody a trust?

The trust was also rejected in water litigation in Sierra Club v. Block, 622 F.Supp. 842 (D.Colo.1985), appeal pending, infra page 397.

3. The author of a later article disagrees with the principal excerpt, concluding that "a court's use of the doctrine to regulate agency decisionmaking is * * * little more than a sham—a mask for the unauthorized substitution of judicial for administrative discretion." Jawetz, The Public Trust Totem in Public Land Law: Ineffective—and Undesirable—Judicial Intervention, 10 Ecology L.Q. 455, 457 (1982). Other commentary includes Note, Proprietary Duties of the Federal Government under the Public Land Trust, 75 Mich.L.Rev. 586 (1977); Lazarus, Changing Conceptions of Property and Sovereignty in Natural Resources: Questioning the Public Trust Doctrine, 71 Iowa L.Rev. 631 (1986).

4. Whatever the direction of the doctrine in the future, public trust implications for this field continue to be discovered in unexpected quarters, e.g., Twining v. New Jersey, 211 U.S. 78, 97 (1908) ("Thus among the rights and privileges of National citizenship recognized by this court are * * * the right to enter the public lands * * *.") Still further research has revealed that the origins of the public trust doctrine in public land law are old—very, very old:

> After his father's death Beowulf king of the Danes governed his stronghold and was for a long time famous among nations. Then the great Healfdene was born. Healfdene, a fierce old veteran, ruled the Danes all his life. To him four children in all were born—Heorogar, Hrothgar, Halga the Good, and a daughter who, we are told, became the consort of Onela, the Swedish king.
>
> Such success in arms and so great a fame attended Hrothgar that his kinsmen were eager to serve under him, and in this way the number of his young retainers increased until he had a formidable army. It came into his mind to command the

erection of a building that should be the greatest banqueting hall ever known, in which he could apportion to young and old everything that God had entrusted to him, with the exception of public lands and human life.

BEOWULF 28 (orig. ed. 8th cent.) (D. Wright trans., 1957).

D. AN INTRODUCTION TO PUBLIC LAND USE PLANNING: THE NATIONAL ENVIRONMENTAL POLICY ACT

It is not possible, nor would it be desirable, to attempt a detailed recitation of all quirks or problems in the procedures utilized by each federal land management agency. They are simply too many, too various, or too technical for investigation here. Further, many facets of agency procedures are apparent from the cases and materials throughout this book. This section instead concentrates on one common procedural element of public land management decisionmaking, the National Environmental Policy Act of 1969 (NEPA), 42 U.S.C.A. § 4321 et seq., as an introduction to public land use planning.

Detailed planning for public land use and resource allocation is a fairly recent phenomenon. Since the enactment of NEPA, Congress has mandated formal planning procedures for the Forest Service and the BLM; the judicial reception to the first round of formal planning efforts by those agencies is examined in chapter seven, § C(3), and chapter eight, § C(3). The National Park Service and the Fish and Wildlife Service have evolved internally their own planning processes. Some specific resource disposition statutes also ordain planning-type procedures. See, for example, the Outer Continental Shelf Lands Act as construed in Village of False Pass v. Clark, 733 F.2d 605 (9th Cir. 1984), infra at page 343. These editors contend that legal requirements for formal land use plans are likely to change federal land and resources law profoundly and for the better. See Wilkinson & Anderson, Land and Resource Planning in the National Forests, 64 Or.L.Rev. 1 (1985); Coggins & Evans, Multiple Use, Sustained Yield Planning on the Public Lands, 53 U.Colo.L.Rev. 229 (1981). Some of our colleagues agree on the profundity, but view modern planning as a combination of fiscal madness and rabid hypertechnicality, both born of the intrusiveness of the law. See, e.g., Behan, RPA/NFMA—Time to Punt, 79 J. of Forestry 802 (1981), supra at page 39.

The National Environmental Policy Act is the precursor and model for the more specific planning systems, and the land management agencies must observe NEPA procedures while promulgating land use plans. NEPA remains the most important procedural public land management statute because its application is not limited to formal planning. The law requires every federal agency to comply with it in all situations when major actions are contemplated; it forces the agency to put its reasons, reasoning, and conclusions into writing; and the citizens who disagree with the conclusions can seek judicial review of the action. The great majority of the cases in this book that were commenced after 1970 have been premised at least in part on NEPA.

Some claim that NEPA is merely another layer of bureaucratic red tape or a mechanism allowing willful zealots to delay worthy developments, while some ardent environmentalists express disappointment with NEPA's limitations and lack of substantive impact. All will agree, however, that the statute has been at the cutting edge of recent change in public land management.

The legislative history does little to illuminate the intended meaning and effect of the short and imprecise National Environmental Policy Act because few legislators had any idea of what they were doing. President Nixon proclaimed the statute the herald of a new environmental era while believing it to be nothing more than an innocuous statement of policy. It turned out to be a good deal more. In spite of a relatively hostile reception by the Supreme Court, NEPA has been ingrained into the fabric of administrative decisionmaking, and the Congress has repeatedly rejected efforts to repeal or significantly amend it.

NEPA has three main parts. Section 101 sets forth a series of ambiguous goals for the government and the Nation in terms of environmental quality. 42 U.S.C.A. § 4331. This section tends to be ignored by reviewing courts, which is odd because the second main part, section 102, begins with the command that "to the fullest extent possible * * * the policies, regulations and public laws of the United States shall be interpreted and administered in accordance with the policies set forth in this act." Id. § 4332(1). Section 102 also contains the "action-forcing" mechanism around which most controversy has swirled. The responsible official must prepare an environmental impact statement to accompany "every recommendation or report on proposals for legislation and other major federal actions significantly affecting the quality of the human environment." Id. § 4332(2)(C). The statement must include an evaluation of adverse environmental impacts and a discussion of alternative means, among other things. The third part of NEPA creates the President's Council on Environmental Quality.

NEPA requires that all federal administrators consider the consequences of their actions before acting. The law encourages but does not command them to act in a way consonant with the goal of a healthful and pleasing environment. The environmental impact statement (EIS) must be drafted, subjected to public comments, and reviewed by other agencies in connection with all major actions. Many federal agencies were for a long time less than eager to comply with it "to the fullest extent possible"; some land managers, political scientists, and economists still resent the "transaction costs" NEPA imposes. Agency resistance eventually gave way to resignation, however, after courts enforced the statutory requirements in thousands of NEPA lawsuits since 1970.

In NEPA litigation, environmental plaintiffs often must surmount a galaxy of procedural objections before the court will reach the statutory merits. But the host of administrative law doctrines—described in section B supra—now seldom constitute final barriers if plaintiff has been persistent and timely.

NEPA litigation ordinarily raises one of two questions: should the agency be forced to write a full EIS before undertaking the proposed action?; or, if an EIS has been prepared, is it adequate? The first problem turns on the answers to a series of subquestions derived from the trigger phrase, proposal for "major federal action significantly affecting the quality of the human environment." Only if the agency is not proposing a federal action, or if its action will not significantly affect the environment, can it escape the EIS requirement. See, e.g., Defenders of Wildlife v. Andrus, 627 F.2d 1238 (D.C.Cir.1983), infra at page 861; Cabinet Mountains Wilderness v. Peterson, 685 F.2d 678 (D.C.Cir.1893), infra at page 872. To determine whether the action will have a significant environmental effect, the agency must prepare a "mini-EIS," called an environmental assessment (EA) or environmental record (ER). If the conclusion is negative, the agency makes a finding of no significant impact (FONSI).

If the agency has promulgated an EIS, the procedural questions involve the preparation methodology and the contents of the impact statement when completed and reviewed. Was there an adequate time to comment? Were adverse opinions and comments included and discussed? Was a rigorous, interdisciplinary approach utilized? Was the final product that of the agency or merely a redraft of an interested private party's version? Were the environmental effects of the alternative discussed? Was the statement sufficiently detailed? The possibilities are boundless.

In spite of the many reported NEPA decisions, some questions inherent in its broad and cryptic commands remain unanswered. Commentary is voluminous. For general reference, see W. Rodgers, ENVIRONMENTAL LAW Ch. 7 (1977); F. Anderson, NEPA IN THE COURTS (1973); Liroff, NEPA Litigation in the 1970's: A Deluge or a Dribble, 21 Nat.Resources J. 315 (1981). The common law of NEPA continues to evolve, and the following cases begin to demonstrate its impact in federal land and resources law.

KLEPPE v. SIERRA CLUB

Supreme Court of the United States, 1976.
427 U.S. 390.

Mr. Justice POWELL delivered the opinion of the Court.

Section 102(2)(C) of the National Environmental Policy Act of 1969 (NEPA) requires that all federal agencies include a detailed statement of environmental consequences—known as an environmental impact statement—"in every recommendation or report on proposals for legislation and other major Federal actions significantly affecting the quality of the human environment." 42 U.S.C.A. § 4332(2)(C). The United

States Court of Appeals for the District of Columbia Circuit held that officials of the Department of the Interior (Department) and certain other federal agencies must take additional steps under this section, beyond those already taken, before allowing further development of federal coal reserves in a specific area of the country. For the reasons set forth, we reverse.

I

Respondents, several organizations concerned with the environment, brought this suit in July 1973 in the United States District Court for the District of Columbia. The defendants in the suit, petitioners here, were the officials of the Department and other federal agencies responsible for issuing coal leases, approving mining plans, granting rights-of-way, and taking the other actions necessary to enable private companies and public utilities to develop coal reserves on land owned or controlled by the Federal Government. Citing widespread interest in the reserves of a region identified as the "Northern Great Plains region," and an alleged threat from coal-related operations to their members' enjoyment of the region's environment, respondents claimed that the federal officials could not allow further development without preparing a "comprehensive environmental impact statement" under § 102(2)(C) on the entire region. They sought declaratory and injunctive relief.

The District Court, on the basis of extensive findings of fact and conclusions of law, held that the complaint stated no claim for relief and granted the petitioners' motions for summary judgment. Respondents appealed. Shortly after oral argument but before issuing an opinion on the merits, the Court of Appeals in January 1975 issued an injunction—over a dissent—against the Department's approval of four mining plans in the Powder River Coal Basin, which is one small but coal-rich section of the region that concerns respondents. 509 F.2d 533. An impact statement had been prepared on these plans, but it had not been before the District Court and was not before the Court of Appeals. In June 1975 the Court of Appeals ruled on the merits and, for reasons discussed below, reversed the District Court and remanded for further proceedings. 514 F.2d 856. The court continued its injunction in force.

*   *   * On January 12, 1976, we stayed the injunction and granted the petitions for certiorari. 423 U.S. 1047. We have been informed that shortly thereafter the Secretary of the Interior (Secretary) approved the four mining plans in the Powder River Coal Basin that had been stayed by the injunction.

II

The record and the opinions of the courts below contain extensive facts about coal development and the geographic area involved in this suit. The facts that we consider essential, however, can be stated briefly.

The Northern Great Plains region identified in respondents' complaint encompasses portions of four States—northeastern Wyoming, eastern Montana, western North Dakota, and western South Dakota. There is no dispute about its richness in coal, nor about the waxing interest in developing that coal, nor about the crucial role the federal petitioners will play due to the significant percentage of the coal to which they control access. The Department has initiated, in this decade, three studies in areas either inclusive of or included within this region. The North Central Power Study was addressed to the potential for coordinated development of electric power in an area encompassing all or part of 15 States in the North Central United States. It aborted in 1972 for lack of interest on the part of electric utilities. The Montana-Wyoming Aqueducts Study, intended to recommend the best use of water resources for coal development in southeastern Montana and northeastern Wyoming, was suspended in 1972 with the initiation of the third study, the Northern Great Plains Resources Program (NGPRP).

While the record does not reveal the degree of concern with environmental matters in the first two studies, it is clear that the NGPRP was devoted entirely to the environment. It was carried out by an interagency, federal-state task force with public participation, and was designed "to assess the potential social, economic and environmental impacts" from resource development in five States—Montana, Wyoming, South Dakota, North Dakota, and Nebraska. Its primary objective was "to provide an analytical and informational framework for policy and planning decisions at all levels of government" by formulating several "scenarios" showing the probable consequences for the area's environment and culture from the various possible techniques and levels of resource development. The final interim report of the NGPRP was issued August 1, 1975, shortly after the decision of the Court of Appeals in this case.

In addition, since 1973 the Department has engaged in a complete review of its coal-leasing program for the entire Nation. On February 17 of that year the Secretary announced the review and announced also that during study a "short-term leasing policy" would prevail, under which new leasing would be restricted to narrowly defined circumstances and even then allowed only when an environmental impact statement had been prepared if required under NEPA. The purpose of the program review was to study the environmental impact of the Department's entire range of coal-related activities and to develop a planning system to guide the national leasing program. The impact statement, known as the "Coal Programmatic EIS," went through several drafts before issuing in final form on September 19, 1975— shortly before the petitions for certiorari were filed in this case. The Coal Programmatic EIS proposed a new leasing program based on a complex planning system called the Energy Minerals Activity Recommendation System (EMARS), and assessed the prospective environmental impact of the new program as well as the alternatives to it. We have been informed by the parties to this litigation that the Secretary is in the process of implementing the new program.[8]

Against this factual background, we turn now to consider the issues raised by this case in the status in which it reached this Court.

III

The major issue remains the one with which the suit began: whether NEPA requires petitioners to prepare an environmental impact statement on the entire Northern Great Plains region. Petitioners, arguing the negative, rely squarely upon the facts of the case and the language of § 102(2)(C) of NEPA. We find their reliance well placed.

As noted in the first sentence of this opinion, § 102(2)(C) requires an impact statement "in every recommendation or report on proposals for legislation and other major Federal actions significantly affecting the quality of the human environment." Since no one has suggested that petitioners have proposed legislation on respondents' region, the controlling phrase in this section of the Act, for this case, is "major Federal actions." Respondents can prevail only if there has been a report or recommendation on a proposal for major federal action with respect to the Northern Great Plains region. Our statement of the relevant facts shows there has been none; instead, all proposals are for actions of either local or national scope.

The local actions are the decisions by the various petitioners to issue a lease, approve a mining plan, issue a right-of-way permit, or take other action to allow private activity at some point within the region identified by respondents. Several Courts of Appeals have held that an impact statement must be included in the report or recommendation on a proposal for such action if the private activity to be permitted is one "significantly affecting the quality of the human environment" within the meaning of § 102(2)(C). See, e.g., Scientists' Institute for Public Information, Inc. v. AEC, 481 F.2d 1079, 1088–1089 (1973); Davis v. Morton, 469 F.2d 593 (CA10 1972). The petitioners do not dispute this requirement in this case, and indeed have prepared impact statements on several proposed actions of this type in the Northern Great Plains during the course of this litigation. Similarly, the federal petitioners agreed at oral argument that § 102(2)(C) required the Coal Programmatic EIS that was prepared in tandem with the new national coal-leasing program and included as part of the final report on the proposal for adoption of that program. Their admission is well made, for the new leasing program is a coherent plan of national scope, and its adoption surely has significant environmental consequences.

---

8. The petitioners in No. 75–561 have included in their brief a press release by the Secretary announcing the new program, and a detailed description of the program. Pending full operation thereof, the short-term leasing policy remains in effect.

[See NRDC v. Hughes, infra at page 333.]

But there is no evidence in the record of an action or a proposal for an action of regional scope. The District Court, in fact, expressly found that there was no existing or proposed plan or program on the part of the Federal Government for the regional development of the area described in respondents' complaint. It found also that the three studies initiated by the Department in areas either included within or inclusive of respondents' region—that is, the Montana-Wyoming Aqueducts Study, the North Central Power Study, and the NGPRP—were not parts of any plan or program to develop or encourage development of the Northern Great Plains. That court found no evidence that the individual coal development projects undertaken or proposed by private industry and public utilities in that part of the country are integrated into a plan or otherwise interrelated. These findings were not disturbed by the Court of Appeals, and they remain fully supported by the record in this Court.

Quite apart from the fact that the statutory language requires an impact statement only in the event of a proposed action, respondents' desire for a regional environmental impact statement cannot be met for practical reasons. In the absence of a proposal for a regional plan of development, there is nothing that could be the subject of the analysis envisioned by the statute for an impact statement. Section 102(2)(C) requires that an impact statement contain, in essence, a detailed statement of the expected adverse environmental consequences of an action, the resource commitments involved in it, and the alternatives to it. Absent an overall plan for regional development, it is impossible to predict the level of coal-related activity that will occur in the region identified by respondents, and thus impossible to analyze the environmental consequences and the resource commitments involved in, and the alternatives to, such activity. A regional plan would define fairly precisely the scope and limits of the proposed development of the region. Where no such plan exists, any attempt to produce an impact statement would be little more than a study along the lines of the NGPRP, containing estimates of potential development and attendant environmental consequences. There would be no factual predicate for the production of an environmental impact statement of the type envisioned by NEPA.

IV

A

The Court of Appeals, in reversing the District Court, did not find that there was a regional plan or program for development of the Northern Great Plains region. It accepted all of the District Court's findings of fact, but concluded nevertheless that the petitioners "contemplated" a regional plan or program. The court thought that the North Central Power Study, the Montana-Wyoming Aqueducts Study, and the NGPRP all constituted "attempts to control development" by individual companies on a regional scale. It also concluded that the interim report of the NGPRP, then expected to be released at any time, would provide the petitioners with the information needed to formulate the regional plan they had been "contemplating." The Court therefore remanded with instructions to the petitioners to inform the District Court of their role in the further development of the region within 30 days after the NGPRP interim report issued; if they decided to control that development, an impact statement would be required.

We conclude that the Court of Appeals erred in both its factual assumptions and its interpretation of NEPA. We think the court was mistaken in concluding, on the record before it, that the petitioners were "contemplating" a regional development plan or program. It considered the several studies undertaken by the petitioners to represent attempts to control development on a regional scale. This conclusion was based on a finding by the District Court that those studies, as well as the new national coal-leasing policy, were "attempts to control development by individual companies in a manner consistent with the policies and procedures of the National Environmental Policy Act of 1969." But in context, that finding meant only that the named studies were efforts to gain background environmental information for subsequent application in the decisionmaking with respect to individual coal-related projects. This is the sense in which the District Court spoke of controlling development consistently with NEPA. Indeed, in the same paragraph containing the language relied upon by the Court of Appeals, the District Court expressly found that the studies were not part of a plan or program to develop or encourage development.

Moreover, at the time the Court of Appeals ruled there was no indication in the record that the NGPRP was aimed toward a regional plan or program, and subsequent events have shown that this was not its purpose. The interim report of the study, issued shortly after the Court of Appeals ruled, described the effects of several possible rates of coal development but stated in its preface that the alternatives "are for study and comparison only; they do not represent specific plans or proposals." All parties agreed in this Court that there still exists no proposal for a regional plan or program of development.

Even had the record justified a finding that a regional program was contemplated by the petitioners, the legal conclusion drawn by the Court of Appeals cannot be squared with the Act. The court recognized that the mere "contemplation" of certain action is not sufficient to require an impact statement. But it believed the statute nevertheless empowers a court to require the preparation of an impact statement to begin at some point prior to the formal recommendation or report on a proposal. * * *

* * *

The Court's reasoning and action find no support in the language or legislative history of NEPA. The statute clearly states when an impact statement is required, and mentions nothing about a balancing of factors. Rather, as we noted last Term, under the first sentence of § 102(2)(C) the moment at which an agency must have a final statement ready "is the time at which it makes a recommendation or report on a *proposal* for federal action." Aberdeen & Rockfish R. Co. v. SCRAP, 422 U.S. 289, 320 (1975) (*SCRAP II*) (emphasis in original). The procedural duty imposed upon agencies by this section is quite precise, and the role of the courts in enforcing that duty is similarly precise. A court has no authority to depart from the statutory language and, by a balancing of court-devised factors, determine a point during the germination process of a potential proposal at which an impact statement *should be prepared.* Such an assertion of judicial authority would leave the agencies uncertain as to their procedural duties under NEPA, would invite judicial involvement in the day-to-day decisionmaking process of the agencies, and would invite litigation. As the contemplation of a project and the accompanying study thereof do not necessarily result in a proposal for major federal action, it may be assumed that the balancing process devised by the Court of Appeals also would result in the preparation of a good many unnecessary impact statements.[15]

B

Assuming that the Court of Appeals' theory about "contemplation" of regional action would permit a court to require preproposal preparation of an impact statement, the court's injunction against the Secretary's approval of the four mining plans in the Powder River Basin nevertheless would have been error. The District Court had found that respondents would not have been entitled to an injunction against any individual projects even if their claim of the need for a regional impact statement had been valid, because they had shown no irreparable harm that would result absent such an injunction and the record disclosed that irreparable harm *would* result to the intervenors who sought to carry out their business ventures and to the public who depended upon their operations. The Court of Appeals made no finding as to the equities at the time it originally entered the injunction; when it continued the injunction following its decision on the merits, it stated only that the "harm" justifying an injunction "matured" whenever an impact statement is due and not filed. But on the Court of Appeals' own terms there was in fact no harm. First, the Court of Appeals itself held that no regional impact statement was due at that moment, and it was uncertain whether one ever would be due. Second, there had been filed a comprehensive impact statement on the proposed Powder River Basin mining plans themselves, and its adequacy had not been challenged either before the District Court or the Court of Appeals in this

---

15. This is not to say that § 102(2)(C) imposes no duties upon an agency prior to its making a report or recommendation on a proposal for action. The section states that prior to preparing the impact statement the responsible official "shall consult with and obtain the comments of any Federal agency which has jurisdiction by law or special expertise with respect to any environmental impact involved." Thus, the section contemplates a consideration of environmental factors by agencies during the evolution of a report or recommendation on a proposal. But the time at which a court enters the process is when the report or recommendation on the proposal is made, and someone protests either the absence or the adequacy of the final impact statement. This is the point at which an agency's action has reached sufficient maturity to assure that judicial intervention will not hazard unnecessary disruption.

case, or anywhere else.[16] Thus, in simple equitable terms there were no grounds for the injunction: the District Court's finding of irreparable injury to the intervenors and to the public still stood, and there were— on the Court of Appeals' own terms—no countervailing equities.

V

Our discussion thus far has been addressed primarily to the decision of the Court of Appeals. It remains, however, to consider the contention now urged by respondents. They have not attempted to support the Court of Appeals' decision. Instead, respondents renew an argument they appear to have made to the Court of Appeals, but which that court did not reach. Respondents insist that, even without a comprehensive federal plan for the development of the Northern Great Plains, a "regional" impact statement nevertheless is required on all coal-related projects in the region because they are intimately related.

There are two ways to view this contention. First, it amounts to an attack on the sufficiency of the impact statements already prepared by the petitioners on the coal-related projects that they have approved or stand ready to approve. As such, we cannot consider it in this proceeding, for the case was not brought as a challenge to a particular impact statement and there is no impact statement in the record. It also is possible to view the respondents' argument as an attack upon the decision of the petitioners not to prepare one comprehensive impact statement on all proposed projects in the region. This contention properly is before us, for the petitioners have made it clear they do not intend to prepare such a statement.

We begin by stating our general agreement with respondents' basic premise that § 102(2)(C) may require a comprehensive impact statement in certain situations where several proposed actions are pending at the same time. NEPA announced a national policy of environmental protection and placed a responsibility upon the Federal Government to further specific environmental goals by "all practicable means, consistent with other essential considerations of national policy." § 101(b), 42 U.S.C.A. § 4331(b). Section 102(2)(C) is one of the "action-forcing" provisions intended as a directive to "all agencies to assure consideration of the environmental impact of their actions in decision-making." Conference Report on NEPA, 115 Cong.Rec. 40416 (1969). By requiring an impact statement Congress intended to assure such consideration during the development of a proposal or—as in this case—during the formulation of a position on a proposal submitted by

16. Even had the Court of Appeals determined that a regional impact statement was due at that moment, it still would have erred in enjoining approval of the four mining plans unless it had made a finding that the impact statement covering them inadequately analyzed the environmental impacts of, and the alternatives to, their approval. So long as the statement covering them was adequate, there would have been no reason to enjoin their approval pending preparation of a broader regional statement; that broader statement, when prepared, simply would have taken into consideration the regional environmental effects of the four mining plans once they were in operation, in determining the permissibility of further coal-related operations in the region. See Part V, infra.

private parties. A comprehensive impact statement may be necessary in some cases for an agency to meet this duty. Thus, when several proposals for coal-related actions that will have cumulative or synergistic environmental impact upon a region are pending concurrently before an agency, their environmental consequences must be considered together. Only through comprehensive consideration of pending proposals can the agency evaluate different courses of action.[21]

Agreement to this extent with respondents' premise, however, does not require acceptance of their conclusion that all proposed coal-related actions in the Northern Great Plains region are so "related" as to require their analysis in a single comprehensive impact statement. Respondents informed us that the Secretary recently adopted an approach to impact statements on coal-related actions that provides:

> "A. As a general proposition, and as determined by the Secretary, when action is proposed involving coal development such as issuing several coal leases or approving mining plans in the same region, such actions will be covered by a single EIS rather than by multiple statements. In such cases, the region covered will be determined by basin boundaries, drainage areas, areas of common reclamation problems, administrative boundaries, areas of economic interdependence, and other relevant factors."

At another point, the document containing the Secretary's approach states that a "regional EIS" will be prepared "if a series of proposed actions with interrelated impacts are involved * * * unless a previous EIS has sufficiently analyzed the impacts of the proposed action(s)." Thus, the Department has decided to prepare comprehensive impact statements of the type contemplated by § 102(2)(C), although it has not deemed it appropriate to prepare such a statement on all proposed actions in the region identified by respondents.

Respondents conceded at oral argument that to prevail they must show that petitioners have acted arbitrarily in refusing to prepare one comprehensive statement on this entire region, and we agree. The determination of the region, if any, with respect to which a comprehensive statement is necessary requires the weighing of a number of relevant factors, including the extent of the interrelationship among proposed actions and practical considerations of feasibility. Resolving these issues requires a high level of technical expertise and is properly left to the informed discretion of the responsible federal agencies. Absent a showing of arbitrary action, we must assume that the agencies have exercised this discretion appropriately. Respondents have made no showing to the contrary.

21. Neither the statute nor its legislative history contemplates that a court should substitute its judgment for that of the agency as to the environmental consequences of its actions. See Scenic Hudson Preservation Conference v. FPC, 453 F.2d 463, 481 (CA2 1971), cert. denied, 407 U.S. 926 (1972). The only role for a court is to insure that the agency has taken a "hard look" at environmental consequences; it cannot "interject itself within the area of discretion of the executive as to the choice of the action to be taken." Natural Resources Defense Council v. Morton, 458 F.2d 827, 838 (1972).

Respondents' basic argument is that one comprehensive statement on the Northern Great Plains is required because all coal-related activity in that region is "programmatically," "geographically," and "environmentally" related. Both the alleged "programmatic" relationship and the alleged "geographic" relationship resolve, ultimately, into an argument that the region is proper for a comprehensive impact statement because the petitioners themselves have approached environmental study in this area on a regional basis. Respondents point primarily to the NGPRP, which they claim—and petitioners deny—focused on the region described in the complaint. The precise region of the NGPRP is unimportant, for its irrelevance to the delineation of an appropriate area for analysis in a comprehensive impact statement has been well stated by the Secretary:

> "Resource studies [like the NGPRP] are one of many analytical tools employed by the Department to inform itself as to general resource availability, resource need and general environmental considerations so that it can intelligently determine the scope of environmental analysis and review specific actions it may take. Simply put, resource studies are a prelude to informed agency planning, and provide the data base on which the Department may decide to take specific actions for which impact statements are prepared. The scope of environmental impact statements seldom coincide with that of a given resource study, since the statements evolve from specific proposals for federal action while the studies simply provide an educational backdrop." Affidavit of Oct. 28, 1975, App. 191.

As for the alleged "environmental" relationship, respondents contend that the coal-related projects "will produce a wide variety of cumulative environmental impacts" throughout the Northern Great Plains region. They described them as follows: Diminished availability of water, air and water pollution, increases in population and industrial densities, and perhaps even climatic changes. Cumulative environmental impacts are, indeed, what require a comprehensive impact statement. But determination of the extent and effect of these factors, and particularly identification of the geographic area within which they may occur, is a task assigned to the special competency of the appropriate agencies. Petitioners dispute respondents' contentions that the interrelationship of environmental impacts is region-wide and, as respondents' own submissions indicate, petitioners appear to have determined that the appropriate scope of comprehensive statements should be based on basins, drainage areas, and other factors. We cannot say that petitioners' choices are arbitrary. Even if environmental interrelationships could be shown conclusively to extend across basins and drainage areas, practical considerations of feasibility might well necessitate restricting the scope of comprehensive statements.

In sum, respondents' contention as to the relationships between all proposed coal-related projects in the Northern Great Plains region does not require that petitioners prepare one comprehensive impact statement covering all before proceeding to approve specific pending applications.[26] As we already have determined that there exists no proposal for regionwide action that could require a regional impact statement, the judgment of the Court of Appeals must be reversed, and the judgment of the District Court reinstated and affirmed. The case is remanded for proceedings consistent with this opinion.

So ordered.

Mr. Justice MARSHALL, with whom Mr. Justice BRENNAN joins, concurring in part and dissenting in part.

While I agree with much of the Court's opinion, I must dissent from Part IV, which holds that the federal courts may not remedy violations of the National Environmental Policy Act of 1969 (NEPA)—no matter how blatant—until it is too late for an adequate remedy to be formulated. As the Court today recognizes, NEPA contemplates agency consideration of environmental factors throughout the decisionmaking process. Since NEPA's enactment, however, litigation has been brought primarily at the end of that process—challenging agency decisions to act made without adequate environmental impact statements or without any statements at all. In such situations, the courts have had to content themselves with the largely unsatisfactory remedy of enjoining the proposed federal action and ordering the preparation of an adequate impact statement. This remedy is insufficient because, except by deterrence, it does nothing to further early consideration of environmental factors. And, as with all after-the-fact remedies, a remand for preparation of an impact statement after the basic decision to act has been made invites *post hoc* rationalizations, cf. Citizens to Preserve Overton Park v. Volpe, 401 U.S. 402, 419–420 (1971), rather than the candid and balanced environmental assessments envisioned by NEPA. Moreover, the remedy is wasteful of resources and time, causing fully developed plans for action to be laid aside while an impact statement is prepared.

* * *

NATURAL RESOURCES DEFENSE COUNCIL v. HUGHES

United States District Court, District of Columbia, 1977.
437 F.Supp. 981.

JOHN H. PRATT, District Judge.

Introduction

Plaintiffs in this action seek declaratory and injunctive relief to restrain defendants from further implementation of a new Federal Coal

---

26. Nor is it necessary that petitioners always complete a comprehensive impact statement on all proposed actions in an appropriate region before approving any of the projects. As petitioners have emphasized, and respondents have not disputed, approval of one lease or mining plan does not commit the Secretary to approval of any others; nor, apparently, do single approvals by the other petitioners commit them to subsequent approvals. Thus, an agency could approve one pending project that is fully covered by an impact statement, then take into consideration the environmental effects of that existing project when preparing the comprehensive statement on the cumulative impact of the remaining proposals.

Leasing Program, and from entering into any coal leases unless and until defendants comply with their statutory obligations under § 102 of the National Environmental Policy Act (NEPA), 42 U.S.C.A. § 4332.

* * *

B. *Coal Reserves.*

The United States contains an estimated 1.58 trillion tons of identified coal reserves approximately one half of which are located in the western United States. The federal government owns approximately 60% of the western coal resource. Most of the large coal resource in the eastern and midwestern United States is privately owned.

Federal coal has, however, played a minimal role in total U.S. production. In 1960 federal coal accounted for only 1.3% of the total coal mined. This mining share has increased only slightly to its current level approximating 3%.

C. *Federal Coal Leasing Policy Prior to 1973.*

The Department of the Interior has general authority to manage the public lands of the United States, and the responsibility to provide for the orderly development of the nation's mineral resources, including coal resources. Historically, and until 1970, the coal leasing policy of the federal defendants was reactive in nature, responding to lease requests on a case-by-case basis without regard to the total reserves under lease or the need for additional leasing, and without an assessment of the environmental impacts of leasing.[4]

In 1970, the Department of the Interior imposed a moratorium on coal leases and prospecting permits. This action resulted from a Bureau of Land Management coal lease study which discovered a sharp increase in the total federal acreage under lease and a consistent decline in coal production.

From 1945 to 1970, the number of acres of federal land leased for coal development *increased* from about 80,000 to approximately 778,000, almost a ten-fold increase. In the same period, annual coal production from these federal lands *declined* from about 10 million tons in 1945 to approximately 7.4 million tons in 1970. These leased areas contain an estimated 16 billion tons of coal reserves, 10.6 billion of which are mineable by strip mining. An additional 10 billion tons are potentially recoverable from federal acreage for which "preference right" applications for coal leases have been filed.[5] The additional ten

4. Prior to 1970 there were two ways for private parties to gain access to federal coal under the Mineral Leasing Act of 1920, 30 U.S.C.A. § 181 et seq. (1970). The first was by competitive bidding, in areas where coal was known to exist in workable quantities. If the existence or workability of coal was not known, however, the federal defendants could issue a prospecting permit authorizing exploration. If the permittee discovered coal in commercial quantities, he could apply for a "preference right" lease under 30 U.S.C.A. § 201(b). This section of the Act granting "preference right" leases has recently been repealed. Federal Coal Leasing Amendments Act of 1975, Pub.L.No. 94–377, § 4, 90 Stat. 1085 (1976).

5. The recent legislation which repealed the Interior Department's authority to grant "preference right" leases under 30 U.S.C.A. § 201(b), did so "subject to valid existing rights."

billion tons include quantities of coal which, due to the size of the lease unit, location, or transportation costs, may not be economically recoverable.

D. *Evolution of the Current Federal Coal Leasing Policy.*

In February 1973, the Secretary of the Interior announced a new coal leasing policy. The policy embodied short-term and long-term actions. The long-term policy consisted of the formulation of a planning system to determine the size, timing, and location of future coal leases, and the preparation of an environmental impact statement with respect to the entire federal coal leasing program.[6] The short-term action included a complete moratorium on the issuance of new prospecting permits, and a near-total moratorium on the issuance of new federal coal leases. Respecting the latter, new leases would be issued only to maintain existing mines or to supply reserves for production in the near future.

In October 1973, the Director of BLM established a schedule for the implementation of a new coal leasing system entitled Energy Minerals *Allocation* Recommendation System (EMARS).[8] The purpose of this new system was to allow the Interior Department to resume the issuance of federal coal leases by providing a mechanism for shifting to an environmentally acceptable coal leasing program.

In May 1974, approximately seven months after the announcement of the proposed leasing program, the *draft* programmatic environmental impact statement (DEIS) was filed by the Interior Department with the Council on Environmental Quality[9] (CEQ).

The release of the DEIS was followed by four months of public commentary during which five open hearings were held throughout the country. Approximately seven hundred pages of suggestions and criticism were received by the Department of the Interior. Among those

6. It is noteworthy that the programmatic impact statement prepared for the new coal leasing policy was the first of its kind undertaken by the Department. A programmatic statement is one which considers the aggregate effects of a broad federal policy. This is to be distinguished from a regional impact statement or a site-specific statement both of which are designed to assess the environmental impact of individual projects or project areas.

8. As described in the draft EIS, EMARS was basically a three-part system: (1) allocation, (2) tract selection, and (3) leasing. During the *allocation* process federal agencies related inventoried federal coal resources to projections of coal-derived energy needs. Total national energy needs were disaggregated into regional demands for coal derived BTU's. In the *tract selec-*

tion phase, federal coal leasing targets were then established in each region or area, flowing from the total national projections for coal based energy needs. The *leasing phase* was to begin with a detailed pre-planning of the coordinated mining and rehabilitation factors required for reclamation and subsequent surface resource management. This phase would conclude with (A) pre-sale evaluations, (B) lease sales, (C) post sale evaluation procedures, and (D) lease issuance.

9. A few days *prior* to the release of the DEIS, previous federal defendant Hughes, then Assistant Secretary for Program Development and Budget, wrote to the Under Secretary of the Interior Department that he (Hughes) had reluctantly released the DEIS despite the fact that it had "major weaknesses." * * *

comments were requests by the CEQ and the Environmental Protection Agency (EPA) that a new draft EIS be prepared.[10]

Other federal agencies were almost universally critical of the draft statement.[11]

In September 1975, the *final* programmatic EIS was released with some modifications. Prominent among the amendments were those which changed the Energy Minerals *Allocation* System to an Energy Minerals *Activity* System.

The primary distinction between the first and the second systems is that the *allocation* process emphasized interdepartmental *federal* identification of coal reserves to be considered for leasing, whereas the *activity* system relied almost entirely upon industry and public nominations for the ascertainment of reserve tracts ripe for development.

The Secretary of the Interior, on January 26, 1976, announced the implementation of the new coal leasing policy (the long-term plan) based upon, *inter alia*, adoption of the Energy Minerals *Activity* Recommendation System. The new policy expressly lifted the moratorium on new major federal coal leasing which had been in effect since late 1970. The Secretary announced, however, that the short-term policy would be retained until the new competitive coal leasing system was fully operational.

* * *

On May 7, 1976, the Secretary of the Interior issued new regulations which effectively exempted "preference right" lease applications from the short-term criteria. 43 C.F.R. § 3521.1 (1977). The effect of these regulations was to confine the Department's short-term criteria to competitive leasing; "preference right" leases could be and were issued without reference to the short-term criteria.

The Interior Department on June 1, 1976, issued a call for the nomination of specific federal coal leasing tracts as suitable or unsuitable for federal leasing. Also on that date, final regulations clarifying the procedures for the implementation of EMARS were issued.

10. The CEQ concluded in its September 6, 1974 letter to Secretary Morton, "You and your staff, the President, Congress, other agencies and the public need the best possible information on which to formulate intelligent policy decisions on a program of such importance to the nation. An adequate program environmental impact statement can, at least in part, serve this purpose. *Unfortunately, the informational and analytical deficiencies of the current draft EIS prevent it from doing so.* (Emphasis added). We believe, therefore, that a new draft environmental impact statement is necessary."

The EPA concurred * * *:

"In accordance with our procedure of rating environmental impact statements at the draft stage, we are rating this statement as category 3 (inadequate)."

11. For example, the Atomic Energy Commission, in its staff report on the DEIS, dated September 18, 1974, commented:

"Without discounting the considerable effort that was evidently expended to prepare this report, we suggest that it falls far short of its purpose, and that any future proposals to lease federal coal lands will be vulnerable to attack on environmental and conservationist grounds unless a more substantial case can be made."

The Bureau of Land Management, on August 9, 1976, issued a statement that, pursuant to the nominations process which ended July 31, 1976, coal companies and private individuals had identified 680 tracts in eight states as areas upon which they would bid if offered for federal coal lease.

The Secretary on July 25, 1977 adopted new short-term leasing standards to correct abuses in short-term leasing under previous criteria. These revised standards also would permit the issuance of any "preference right" lease, on an *ad hoc* basis, without limitation, and any competitive lease if,

(1) the lessee controls land which is contiguous to the land to be leased (there is no requirement that there be an existing mine in operation); and

(2) the amount of reserves to be leased does not exceed eight years as contracted for or expected levels of production; and

(3) no new major transportation facilities are to be constructed.

It is plaintiffs' basic contention that defendants' actions as outlined above have been pursued in the absence of an adequate final programmatic EIS and are therefore unlawful and invalid. We turn now to defendants' response on procedural as well as substantive grounds.

* * *

F. *The Defendants' Claim That The Controversy Is Non-Justiciable.*

Defendants next contend that plaintiffs' challenge to the sufficiency of the final programmatic EIS is non-justiciable unless and until the program which is discussed in the EIS is implemented by specific, concrete application. This requires no extended response.

The Supreme Court's observation in Kleppe v. Sierra Club, 427 U.S. 390 (1976), a case which involved the question whether a regional EIS was required at all rather than the issue of non-justiciability, is relevant to defendants' assertion:

"The time at which a court enters the process is when the report or recommendation on the proposal is made, and someone protests either the absence or the adequacy of the final impact statement. This is the point at which an agency's action has reached sufficient maturity to assure that judicial intervention will not hazard unnecessary disruption. With the issuance of the final programmatic EIS and the implementation of the new coal leasing policy, this claim that the actions of the defendant have not sufficiently matured is impossible to accept. The issues raised herein are ripe for decision." 427 U.S. at 406, n. 15.

The claim that the actions of defendants have not sufficiently matured is impossible to accept. The issues raised herein are clearly justiciable.

* * *

H. *Adequacy of Compliance With § 102 of NEPA.*

Defendants, on the merits, contend that the final programmatic EIS issued September 19, 1975, complies with the requirements of NEPA. We examine this contention in some detail, starting off with the language of the statutory provision.

* * *

This provision compels all federal agencies to satisfy its requirements absent clear and unavoidable conflict in statutory authority. Flint Ridge Dev. Co. v. Scenic Rivers Ass'n, 426 U.S. 776, 788 (1976). Section 102 duties are not inherently flexible. They must be complied with "to the fullest extent." Calvert Cliffs' Coordinating Committee, Inc. v. United States Atomic Energy Commission, 449 F.2d 1109, 1115 (1971). This is a "high standard * * * which must be rigorously enforced by the reviewing Courts." Id.

In performing its function of review, "[t]he Court's task is to determine whether the EIS was compiled with objective good faith and whether the resulting statement would permit a decisionmaker to fully consider and balance the environmental factors." Concerned About Trident et al. v. Rumsfeld et al., 555 F.2d 817, 827 (D.C.Cir.1976).

Our review is also subject to certain limitations. As the Supreme Court recently pointed out:

"Neither the statute nor its legislative history contemplates that a court should substitute its judgment for that of the agency as to the environmental consequences of its actions. (Citation omitted). The only role for a court is to insure that the agency has taken a 'hard look' at environmental consequences; it cannot 'interject itself within the area of discretion of the executive as to the choice of the action to be taken.' " Kleppe v. Sierra Club, supra, 427 U.S. at 410 n. 21.

The determination as to whether, when, and how to lease more federal coal remains largely within the Secretary's discretion. Our sole obligation in this action is to ascertain whether the final programmatic EIS filed herein has satisfied the statutory criteria of NEPA.

Although NEPA merely requires an agency to file a final impact statement, 42 U.S.C.A. § 102(2)(C), the CEQ has severed the process into two parts, requiring a Draft Environmental Impact Statement (DEIS) and a Final Environmental Impact Statement (EIS). Council on Environmental Quality Guidelines, 40 C.F.R. § 1500.7(a) (1975).

With regard to the DEIS, the Guidelines state:

Each environmental impact statement shall be prepared and circulated in draft form for comment in accordance with the provisions of these guidelines. *The draft statement must fulfill and satisfy to the fullest extent possible at the time the draft is prepared the requirements established for a final statement by section 102(2)(C).* (Emphasis added). 40 C.F.R. § 1500.7 (1975).

Although courts have construed the legal status of these regulations as advisory and not entitled to binding effect, Hiram Clarke Civic Club, Inc. v. Lynn, 476 F.2d 421, 424 (5th Cir.1973), it is important to note when considering their weight that the President delegated the authority to the CEQ to issue these guidelines as to the manner of agency compliance with section 102 of NEPA. Exec. Order No. 11514, 3 C.F.R. 1966–70 Comp.P. 902. Both the Department of the Interior and the BLM have promulgated regulations specifically governing the preparation of the draft statements.[15] In our view, neither the DEIS nor the Final Programmatic EIS complies with these regulations. As has been previously set forth the DEIS when released in May 1974 was the object of heavy criticism from various federal agencies, environmental groups, representatives of the coal industry, and even employees of the Interior Department (such as former Assistant Secretary Hughes).

The commentary critical of the DEIS was directed more recurrently toward, *inter alia,*

(a) the inadequacy of the Department's explanation of the EMARS program, and

(b) the paucity of alternatives to the proposed leasing policy (i.e., the Department's insufficient showing that the institution of a national coal leasing program was even necessary).

We believe these comments to be equally applicable to the Final EIS inasmuch as there have been no significant remedial changes in the above two areas nor in numerous other sections of the statements.

(a) The EMARS System.

The EMARS System, which is the "heart" of the new national coal leasing policy, is set out in only four of the Draft Programmatic's 700 pages.

In the Final Programmatic EIS, although the length of the EMARS explanation had increased to 11 pages, the original Energy Minerals *Allocation* Recommendation System was substantively changed to the Energy Minerals *Activity* Recommendation System without the proper explanation.[17]

This important amendment substituted a procedure of industry nominations, designed to provide BLM with data as to the location and quantity of coal to be leased, for the original allocation system in which federal agencies related inventoried Federal coal resources to national projections of coal-derived energy needs.[18] While it is outside the scope

---

15. The Department Manual, supra, ch. 2, § 9.B(1), 36 Fed.Reg. 19346 (1971), 43 C.F.R. § 516, mandates the draft statement to be "as complete as possible." The BLM manual requires, with greater specificity, that the draft statement be one "analyzing the best information available regarding the possible environmental impacts of an action and all reasonable alternatives." BLM Manual § 1792.05(D)(1), 37 Fed.Reg. 15016 (1972).

17. The Final Statement merely indicated "the description of the proposed EMARS process has been rewritten and expanded to reflect comments and suggestions received."

18. In its recent report to Congress on the final coal leasing proposal, the GAO made the following critical comment concerning the second EMARS system:

"Interior indicates that specifying exact demands on Federal Coal is impossi-

of our review to consider the respective merits of the two programs, we believe that this amendment constitutes a significant departure from the first EMARS system and, hence, a detailed comparative explanation would be required under NEPA. This was not provided. It is not difficult to conclude that neither the distinction between these two programs, nor the potential ramifications thereof, were adequately considered in the Final EIS. Nor was the public afforded an opportunity to comment upon this substantial modification.

This lack of detailed exploration in the Final Programmatic EIS contravenes (1) the purpose of NEPA as "an environmental full disclosure law," Monroe County Conservation Council v. Volpe, 472 F.2d 693, 697 (2d Cir.1972), and (2) the statutory requirement of inter-agency and public consultation prior to the release of a Final Impact Statement. 42 U.S.C.A. § 4332(C).

We hold the Final EIS to be inadequate with regard to the section concerning EMARS. To comply reasonably and in good faith with section 102 of NEPA, the Department of the Interior must expand its EMARS explanation through the issuance of a supplemental draft programmatic statement consistent with the Order attached hereto.

(b) Lack of alternatives to the present policy.

With regard to the alleged inadequate explication of alternatives, it is well settled that NEPA requires an exploration of all reasonable alternatives. Natural Resources Defense Council, Inc. v. Morton, 458 F.2d 827, 837 (1972). At the same time, the statute does not impose an obligation to consider every remote possibility. Natural Resources Defense Council, Inc. v. Callaway, 524 F.2d 79, 93 (2d Cir.1975). What is required is information sufficient to permit a reasoned choice of alternatives.

Two types of alternatives emerge in the factual context of this case and should be considered. The first is *whether* a new program should be undertaken at all. This is the alternative of "no action." The second is, if such a program is found to be necessary, *what type* of system should be utilized.

Absent from the Draft Programmatic EIS was any mention or consideration of the first alternative of "no action." This is the most significant alternative, since only an adequate explanation for its rejection can provide the new program with its very *raison d'etre*. The detailed consideration of "no action," and its thoughtful rejection by the Department, would have laid the groundwork for the consequent implementation of the new policy. Yet the Draft was silent on this point. Since this option was not included in the DEIS and since a second draft was not issued for comment, the public as well as governmental agencies were deprived of their statutory right to comment thereon.

ble beyond saying that greater amounts of coal are anticipated to come from federal lands. While exact long-term demands might not be measurable, we believe that Interior should have reasonable goals of how much to lease and when to lease, based on the best possible estimates of how much coal to expect from developing the leases." Such data is not provided in the Final EIS.

The Final Statement perfunctorily devoted a few paragraphs to the "no action" alternative. Apparently, the Department and the BLM believed this to be sufficient to fulfill their regulatory obligations which specifically require the consideration of the "no action" alternative. It appears, however, that the Department's treatment of this alternative is sufficient neither under the statute nor under the regulations.

Defendants' position in support of the program, i.e., that because federal coal production is rapidly increasing more federal coal must be leased, is countered by the plaintiffs' response that the argument ignores the magnitude of the amount of coal currently under lease. Plaintiffs cite the BLM coal reserve statistics which reveal that approximately 26 billion tons of potentially recoverable federal coal are presently under lease. At the estimated 1985 rate of federal coal production (320 million tons per annum) plaintiffs state that these outstanding leases would provide enough coal for the next 121 years.

As is noted previously, coal mined on federal lands constitutes only 3% of all coal mined in the United States. Even with a significant increase in production, the BLM figures reveal that the amount of federal coal currently under lease could satisfy such a demand for many decades. Therefore, an anticipated eighteen-month delay in the issuance of major new leases, caused by the issuance of the injunction sought by plaintiffs would in our judgment have no significant effect upon the availability of coal in the United States.

In light of these statistics, the threshold question as to *whether* the proposed policy is even *necessary* should have been addressed and considered in depth. The cursory treatment of the "no action" alternative provided in the Final EIS does not satisfy the statutory mandate of § 102(C) of NEPA. The Department did not take a "hard look" at this policy option during its decision making process.   *   *   *

While we have focused specifically upon two deficiencies, our criticism is not confined to those areas. Numerous other aspects of the Final EIS were the topic of agency and public criticism. These areas, such as lack of administrative alternatives to the program and the failure to relate the new program to coal already under lease, shall also be reconsidered by the Department in the supplemental Draft Statement.

To conclude, the environmental consequences of any national coal leasing program cannot be gainsaid and require no elaboration. The program under consideration was the result of a decision apparently made long before and apart from the preparation of the Draft EIS. Because of its inadequacy, both government agencies and the public were deprived of a meaningful opportunity to comment. The Final EIS suffers from similar inadequacies as well as the fact that its finality prevented comment even though the original EMARS, the core of the program, had been drastically changed. The undisputed facts show a clear violation of the letter and purpose of NEPA.

I. *The Appropriateness of Injunctive Relief.*

Defendants state that the issuance of an injunction prohibiting the continuation of the new coal leasing policy will substantially inhibit the development of long-range national energy planning. We can find no evidence in the record to support this allegation.

* * *

Defendants further argue that regardless of the outcome of the issue of the adequacy of the Final EIS, they may issue leases if a separate impact statement has been prepared for each proposed lease when required by NEPA. As an initial proposition in a different factual setting, this may be true. We are not concerned with individual leases but rather the formulation of a national coal leasing policy. If regional or site-specific EIS's are permitted to act as curative of programmatic deficiencies and as a substitute for a Final EIS, the policy of long-range environmental planning would be defeated.[22] Thus, the filing of separate site-specific EIS's are not a substitute for an adequate final programmatic EIS.

* * *

This Circuit has recently held that when an action is undertaken which violates NEPA, there is a presumption that injunctive relief should be granted against the continuation of the action until the agency complies with the statute. Realty Income Trust v. Eckerd, 564 F.2d 447 at 456 (D.C.Cir.1977). In this action the Interior Department has clearly violated NEPA by its release of an inadequate programmatic impact statement. The Final EIS was not prepared with objective good faith nor would it permit a decision-maker to fully consider and properly balance the environmental factors.

The irreparable injury to the environment which would be caused were the new national coal leasing policy to continue is clear. The plaintiffs have satisfied the requirements for injunctive relief.

* * *

NOTES

1. To some extent NEPA has been merged into somewhat more precise planning statutes, such as FLPMA and the National Forest Management Act of 1976, but it remains in force even as to such planning processes. Does *Kleppe* destroy in whole or part NEPA's clout as a planning mandate? If you were a bureaucrat wishing to rush a pet

---

22. Defendants also argue that "preference right" lease applications are to be considered on an "ad hoc" basis and hence outside the purview of the National Leasing Program. Therefore, defendants state that such leasing should not be subject to any court order relating to the National Leasing Program. We disagree. After careful review of the record we have determined that when the Final Programmatic EIS was released, "preference right" leases were consistently referred to as a part of the National Program. There is no evidence in the Final Statement or any facts offered by defendants which would lead us to conclude that the "preference right" applications were outside the ambit of the Program. For the purposes of this injunction and compliance with NEPA, "preference right" leasing will also be enjoined until the Programmatic EIS deficiencies are remedied.

project along, does *Kleppe* offer an avenue for escaping from NEPA paperwork?

2. In how many ways is *Hughes* inconsistent with *Kleppe*, a Supreme Court decision in the same area handed down just a few months earlier? Should an adequate site-specific EIS cure the deficiencies in a programmatic EIS? Would the Supreme Court have granted injunctive relief in the *Hughes* case?

3. In 1980, the Supreme Court made explicit a point implicit in *Kleppe* (at footnote 21): judicial review of NEPA decisions is limited to issues of procedural compliance because the substantive choice to proceed with the contested project is vested in the agency, not the courts. Strycker's Bay Neighborhood Council, Inc. v. Karlen, 444 U.S. 223, 227–28 (1980). The Supreme Court has taken the narrow view of every NEPA question it has chosen to decide. See, e.g., Weinberger v. Catholic Action of Hawaii, 454 U.S. 139 (1981); Baltimore Gas & Elec. Co. v. NRDC, 462 U.S. 87 (1983); Andrus v. Sierra Club, 442 U.S. 347 (1979). In spite of the Court's reluctance to allow the tail of environmental evaluation to wag the dog of normal government operations, NEPA remains a critical element in public land management. See Note: The National Environmental Policy Act in Public Land and Resources Law, infra at page 355.

4. For practical advice on ensuring that a required EIS will pass popular and judicial muster, see Friedman, The Environmental Impact Statement Process, 22 Practical Law. 47 (1976).

5. The parties later settled the *Hughes* litigation, much to the dismay of affected coal companies, and the settlement contributed to another five year delay in issuing new coal leases. Federal coal leasing is examined in more detail infra at chapter six, § B(3).

VILLAGE OF FALSE PASS v. CLARK
United States Court of Appeals, Ninth Circuit, 1984.
733 F.2d 605.

WALLACE, Circuit Judge:

The Village of False Pass, another village, one individual, and eight organizations (Village) appeal from a denial, in part, of summary judgment in their action for declaratory and injunctive relief against the Secretary of the Interior's (Secretary) proposed sale of oil leases in the St. George Basin of the Bering Sea. The Secretary and various intervenor oil companies cross-appeal the partial summary judgment and an injunction against them. The case involves an important marine environment, rare whales, large sums of money, a search for increasingly scarce energy resources, and three basic statutory schemes: the Outer Continental Shelf Lands Act, 43 U.S.C. § 1331 et seq. (OCSLA), the National Environmental Policy Act of 1969, 42 U.S.C. § 4321 et seq. (NEPA), and the Endangered Species Act of 1973, 16 U.S.C. § 1531 et seq. (ESA). * * *

I

The St. George Basin, located off the west coast of Alaska in the Bering Sea, is a rich and diverse marine area, home to many animals and "the gateway to virtually every marine mammal, fish, and bird species moving between the North Pacific and the Bering Sea." Village of False Pass v. Watt, 565 F.Supp. 1123, 1129 (D.Alaska 1983). It may also hold large oil and gas reserves, perhaps 1.12 billion barrels of extractable oil. Id. at 1139. Although the chances of discovering such commercial quantities of oil or gas are about 28% and 37% respectively, id. at 1130, the oil companies bidding on St. George Basin leases are willing to spend almost a half-billion dollars for the right to investigate those chances on the specific parcels of Lease Sale 70.

The planning for Lease Sale 70 began in 1979 when the Department of the Interior's Bureau of Land Management requested resource reports from various agencies about oil and gas leasing in the St. George Basin. In early 1980, the Secretary designated 479 parcels as Lease Sale 70, and by the fall of 1981 he had prepared a Draft Environmental Impact Statement for the sale. In the summer of 1982, the Secretary asked the National Marine Fisheries Service (Fisheries Service) to prepare a Final Biological Opinion about the effects of the proposed lease sale on fish and marine mammals. That December, the Secretary issued a Final Environmental Impact Statement (Final Statement) that included information from several agencies' impact studies, among them preliminary biological studies from the Fisheries Service. Although the Final Statement provided two sets of oil spill analyses, one for spills over 1,000 barrels and one for spills of 10,000 barrels or more, it did not provide an explicit worst case analysis for oil spills of 100,000 barrels.

On March 7, 1983, the Secretary signed a Final Notice of Sale for Lease Sale 70. * * *

Soon after the Final Notice issued, the Village sued to declare that the Secretary acted arbitrarily and that his decisions were based on inadequate information, and to enjoin the lease sale. It claimed, among other things, that the lease sale decision * * * violated NEPA because the Final Statement did not include a worst case analysis of "large" or "major" oil spills, and the impact of Lease Sale 70 on the resources of the St. George Basin, including whales. * * *

In his Order following summary judgment, the district judge enjoined execution of leases under the lease sale until the Secretary prepared either a worst case analysis or supplemental environmental impact analysis of the effects of seismic testing before the exploration stage on gray and right whales, reconsidered his Final Notice of Sale after that analysis, and included in the Final Notice or another order either the Fisheries Service's suggested reasonable and prudent exploration and drilling restrictions to protect the whales, or a justification of why such restrictions were unnecessary.

On appeal, the Village argues * * * the district court improperly refused, under NEPA, to require a worst case analysis at the lease sale stage of "the effects" of oil and gas activity on all species in the St. George Basin. Although it did not initially limit its argument to the need for a worst case analysis of a 100,000 barrel spill, in its briefs and at oral argument the Village acknowledged it seeks only worst case analyses of a "major oil spill" of 100,000 barrels or more. Cross-appealing, the Secretary and the intervenor oil companies argue that the district court erred under NEPA in requiring a worst case analysis, or supplemental environmental analysis, of impacts of seismic surveys preliminary to the exploration stage on gray and right whales. * * *

II

The Supreme Court recently explained the basic structure of OCSLA in Secretary of the Interior v. California, ___ U.S. ___, 104 S.Ct. 656 (1984). Three of the four statutory stages identified by the Court for developing an off-shore oil well concern us: lease sales, see 43 U.S.C. § 1337(a); exploration, see 43 U.S.C. § 1340(b); and development and production, see 43 U.S.C. § 1351(a). These stages are separate and distinct. As the Court stated, "by purchasing a lease, lessees acquire no right to do anything more. Under the plain language of OCSLA, the purchase of a lease entails no right to proceed with full exploration, development, or production * * * the lessee acquires only a priority in submitting plans to conduct those activities. If these plans, when ultimately submitted, are disapproved, no further exploration or development is permitted." Id.; see also id. at ___, 104 S.Ct. at 671. "Each stage involves separate regulatory review that may, but need not, conclude in the transfer to lease purchasers of rights to conduct additional activities on the OCS." Id. at ___, 104 S.Ct. at 669. Although the present case applied OCSLA in a different factual situation, there is no doubt that we are bound by the Court's analysis of OCSLA.

In prescribing this structure for oil and gas leasing, OCSLA makes no direct reference to ESA. * * *

OCSLA does make reference to NEPA, however. See 43 U.S.C. §§ 1331(p), 1344(b)(3), 1346(a) (by implication), 1351(e)–(h), (k). It specifically does not limit NEPA's basic application, see 43 U.S.C. § 1866; instead, the two statutory schemes are complementary. In sections 1346 and 1351, OCSLA requires preparation of a full environmental impact statement. At the lease sale stage, OCSLA implies this review must meet NEPA standards. See 43 U.S.C. § 1346(a)(1) ("The Secretary shall conduct a study * * * in order to establish information needed for assessment and management of environmental impacts * * *.") At the development and production stage, the implication is even clearer. See 43 U.S.C. § 1351(e)(1) ("At least once the Secretary shall declare the approval of a development and production plan in any area * * * to be a major federal action [and thus trigger NEPA].").

Under the three steps for specific off-shore oil and gas development, therefore, OCSLA appears to require the application of NEPA at both the lease sale and development and production stages. That does not foreclose its application also at the exploration stage. By NEPA's own terms, it applies to "every ＊ ＊ ＊ major Federal action [ ] ＊ ＊ ＊." 42 U.S.C. § 4332(2)(C). Thus, as the Secretary's regulations promulgated under OCSLA indicate, NEPA may apply of its own force to the exploration stage, too. See 30 C.F.R. § 250.34–4(a) (1982) ("Prior to approval of an *exploration* or development and production plan, ＊ ＊ ＊ the Director [of the Minerals Management Service] shall review the environmental impacts ＊ ＊ ＊ to determine ＊ ＊ ＊ whether approval ＊ ＊ ＊ constitutes a major Federal action ＊ ＊ ＊ requiring prepara- tion of an Environmental Impact Statement pursuant to [NEPA] ＊ ＊ ＊.") (emphasis added).

Thus, it is clear that OCSLA prescribes three distinct stages for offshore oil and gas activities: leasing, exploration, and development and production. ESA appears to apply equally to each stage of its own force and effect. Under OCSLA's general environmental provision, NEPA also applies to each stage of its own force and effect. OCSLA's specific references to NEPA at the leasing and development and pro- duction stages, however, provide additional impetus for its application. Those specific references also emphasize the discrete nature of each stage. Our analysis of this case, therefore, requires us to take into consideration the three separate stage approach of OCSLA.

III

[The court held that the Secretary did not violate the ESA.]

IV

In its NEPA argument, the Village claims the Secretary, by prepar- ing the Final Statement for Lease Sale 70 without including a worst case analysis, failed to observe the procedure required by law. The particular type of worst case analysis the Village seeks at the lease sale stage "is one in which a large spill of 100,000 bbl or greater is assumed to occur" under poor conditions, affects various sealife "including a substantial part of the gray and right whale populations," lingers in the environment, and causes "physiological impacts, about which there is uncertainty at present, [that] are assumed to be the worst." This argument essentially conflates two strands of analysis by the district court.

First, the district court concluded "that the leasing stage environ- mental impact statement need not include speculative or uncertain information concerning potential or anticipated environmental conse- quences affecting only exploration or production stages of an oil lease. The catastrophic spill envisioned by the plaintiffs is such an event." *Village of False Pass v. Watt*, 565 F.Supp. at 1148. Second, the district court went on to consider the need for particular worst case analyses of oil spill (of whatever size) ＊ ＊ ＊. As to the other impacts, the district judge held: "I cannot conclude that the missing oil spill information is essential to a reasoned choice among the alternatives at this time." Id.

at 1152. His underlying reasoning was that Lease Sale 70 proceeds in stages, oil spills occur only at stages after the lease sale stage, and additional environmental information about that impact will become available and should be considered at those subsequent stages. Therefore, he concluded, NEPA did not require worst case analyses at the lease sale stage. Id. at 1152–53.

We review the adequacy of the Final Statement under the "prepared in observance of the procedure required by law" standard of 5 U.S.C. § 706(2)(D): does the Final Statement contain "a reasonably thorough discussion of the significant aspects of the probable environmental consequences," and does its "form, content and preparation foster both informed decision-making and informed public participation," California v. Block, 690 F.2d at 761 (9th Cir.1977) [infra at page 1001.]

Once satisfied that the Secretary has taken this procedural and substantive "hard look" at environmental consequences in the Final Statement, our review is at an end. We now consider whether, under the Council on Environmental Quality regulations implementing NEPA, read in light of OCSLA, the Secretary's Final Statement satisfies this "hard look" standard of California v. Block without undertaking a worst case analysis of a 100,000 barrel oil spill.

A

The Council on Environmental Quality (CEQ), established under 42 U.S.C. § 4342, promulgates uniform, mandatory regulations for implementing the procedural provisions of NEPA. Recognizing that the universe of information about environmental impacts remains incomplete in many cases, the CEQ promulgated 40 C.F.R. § 1502.22 (1982). Under this regulation, an agency must prepare a worst case analysis in two instances:

> If (1) the information relevant to adverse impacts is *essential to a reasoned choice among alternatives* and is not known and the overall costs of obtaining it are exorbitant or (2) the information * * * is *important to the decision* and * * * (* * * the means for obtaining it are beyond the state of the art) the agency * * *. [if it proceeds] shall include a worst case analysis * * *.

The district court apparently found the incomplete information on the effects of oil spills was not "essential to a reasoned choice among alternatives." The district judge did not state his findings and reasoning why his worst case analysis should be based upon "essential to a reasoned choice" as distinguished from "important to the decision." We are initially confronted with the question of whether a remand is necessary to determine the basis of the standard adopted by the district court.

When confronted recently by a similar situation, we concluded that we could proceed with our disposition of the appeal. Because the missing information was "significant," we concluded it was unnecessary to distinguish between "essential" and "important" in that case. *Save Our Ecosystems v. Clark*, [747 F.2d 1240] (9th Cir.1984). While we have expressed some doubt as to the wisdom of the distinction in the regulation, id., district courts should attempt to apply its mandate. Therefore, we believe a district court reviewing a worst case analysis claim under NEPA should make clear the basis for its decision by choosing one of the two applicable CEQ standards, explaining the basis for that choice, and then applying the chosen standard.

As we concluded in Save Our Ecosystems v. Clark, however, in this particular case remand is not required. The parties agree that the "important to the decision" standard applies and apparently believe that if it does not justify a worst case analysis neither would the "essential to a reasoned choice" standard. They have briefed and argued the case applying the "important to the decision" test and we see no harm in our reviewing this appeal by that standard. This approach is similar to that used by the Fifth Circuit in Sierra Club v. Sigler, 695 F.2d 957, 973 (5th Cir.1983), where the court decided the missing information was beyond the state of the art and reviewed the case based on the "important" standard in spite of the district court's use of the "essential" test.

B

The Village would have a better argument for the importance of a worst case analysis at the lease sale stage of a 100,000 barrel oil spill if that were the only time the Secretary could review the potential environmental impacts of those leases and their possible exploration and development and production. As our earlier discussion of OCSLA's three stage process made clear, however, NEPA may require an environmental impact statement at each stage: leasing, exploration, and production and development. Furthermore, each stage remains separate. The completion of one stage does not entitle a lessee to begin the next. A failure to consider at the lease sale stage a worst case analysis of an oil spill of 100,000 barrels does not foreclose consideration of such an analysis at later stages, and does not foreclose disapproval of lessee activity at those stages based on that analysis. Unlike Sierra Club v. Sigler, 695 F.2d at 963, where the approval of construction permits for a tanker port—equivalent to approval of development and production plans for an oil lease—presented the last opportunity for the government to act responsibly on a worst case analysis of a major oil spill, Lease Sale 70 does not commit the chief resources of the participants or agency. Under these circumstances, we agree with the Fifth Circuit's statement that "the unavailability of information, even if it hinders NEPA's 'full disclosure' requirement, should not be permitted to halt all government action * * *. This is particularly true when information may become available at a later time and can still be used to influence the agency's decision." Id. at 970. Given the adequate analysis of an over 10,000 barrel oil spill already contained in the Final Statement, these factors alone might answer the question whether information about a 100,000 barrel spill was important at the lease sale stage.

The Village argues, however, that the relative difficulties in cancelling or suspending a lease, or disapproving an exploration or development and production plan after the lease sale stage, make the information from a 100,000 barrel worst case analysis important at this initial stage. Viewed out of context, some of the statutory terms for suspension or cancellation of a lease seem to specify conditions more specific than the discretion the Secretary might have to grant a lease. See, e.g., 43 U.S.C. § 1334(a)(1)(B) ("threat of serious, irreparable or immediate harm or damage to * * * the * * * environment" justifies suspension). These statutory terms are not exclusive, however. See 43 U.S.C. § 1334(a) (suspension regulations "shall include, but not be limited to," the statutory examples). The Secretary, in 30 C.F.R. § 250.12(a)(1)(iv) (1982), recaptures the full measure of his discretion under NEPA: "the Director [of the Minerals Management Service] may suspend * * * any * * * activity * * * for any * * * purpose necessary for the implementation of the National Environmental Policy Act." This correspondingly broadens the ability of the Secretary to continue a suspension. See 30 C.F.R. § 250.12(d)(3) (1982). It also relaxes the constraints on cancellation: after five continuous years of suspension the Secretary may cancel for environmental reasons. See 30 C.F.R. § 250.12(d)(5) (1982). The Secretary may also cancel anytime after the submitting of a development and production plan if the lessee breaches a conservation regulation or condition imposed by the Secretary. See, e.g., 30 C.F.R. § 250.12(f)(3) (1982). Of course, some restraints on cancellation remain. See, e.g., 30 C.F.R. § 250.12(d)(4) (1982). In the similar situation of plan disapprovals the Secretary retains even more discretion. Even if he has not prescribed regulations essentially prohibiting the objectionable features of the plan, cf. 43 U.S.C. § 1351(h)(1)(A) (allowing disapproval for failure to show compliance with regulations promulgated by the Secretary), he may disapprove the plan if he finds exceptional environmental circumstances. See, e.g., 43 U.S.C. § 1351(h)(1)(D). Furthermore, the Secretary has full discretion to order modification of the plan for consistency with "[e]nvironmental, safety, and health requirements," e.g., his discretion under NEPA, see 30 C.F.R. § 250.34–2(f), (g)(1)(v) (1982). The Secretary may cancel a lease for failure to comply with these plans over which he retains so large a discretion. See 43 U.S.C. § 1351(j). Such cancellation does not entitle the lessee to any compensation. Id.

We do not find these apparently minor alterations of the Secretary's discretion between the initial and subsequent stages sufficient, by themselves, to make missing information about a 100,000 barrel oil spill important at the lease sale stage. A 100,000 barrel spill could only occur at a later stage, and the Secretary has already made an adequate analysis of an over 10,000 barrel spill. The CEQ's tiering regulations recommend a broad "environmental impact statement on a specific action at an early stage (such as * * * site selection)" and then later analysis by supplement or subsequent statement when such tiering "helps the * * * agency to focus on the issues which are ripe for decision and exclude from consideration issues * * * not yet ripe." 40 C.F.R. § 1508.28(b) (1982). This indicates that minor changes in the Secretary's discretion because of a project's momentum do not bar consideration of environmental information in stages. The discrete stages of the OCSLA process suggest the same thing. Indeed, "the purchase of a lease entails no right to proceed with full exploration, development, or production." Secretary of the Interior v. California, ___ U.S. at ___, 104 S.Ct. at 670.

The Village asserts another objection, however: "the court assumed that EISs for exploration and development production would be forthcoming * * * this is far from certain." The Secretary has represented, however, that he "fully intends to prepare a production and development EIS for the St. George Basin in accordance with the mandate of 43 U.S.C. § 1351(e)(1)." The Village counters that even if the Secretary does prepare an impact statement for development and production, he need only prepare it for one site plan, and might choose one development and production site that would not require a worst case analysis of a 100,000 barrel oil spill, while another site might require this information. The statute states: "At least once the Secretary shall declare the approval of a development and production plan in any area * * *, to be a major Federal action," and thus trigger NEPA. 43 U.S.C. § 1351(e)(1). As the legislative history of OCSLA indicates, however, this mandatory NEPA study of a development and production plan "does not in any way limit the applicability of NEPA to later approval of later plans." H.R.Rep. No. 95–590, 95th Cong., 2d Sess. 166–67, *reprinted in* 1978 U.S.Code Cong. & Ad.News 1450, 1572. If a development and production plan is the type that would, if NEPA applied, ordinarily require a worst case analysis of a large oil spill, it is difficult to imagine that the approval of the plan would not be major federal action. Indeed, the intervenors would go further; they believe the approval of exploration plans also triggers NEPA. Furthermore, we have recently held that the CEQ's worst case regulation may apply to environmental assessments that do not require a full environmental impact statement under NEPA. See Southern Oregon Citizens Against Toxic Sprays, Inc. v. Clark, 720 F.2d 1475, 1480–81 (9th Cir.1983).

Thus, the Village's argument that later review is unlikely also fails. It cannot make the difference in information between the Secretary's adequate 10,000 barrel spill analysis and a hypothetical 100,000 barrel spill "important" to the lease sale decision. Further information about the probability and location of a 100,000 barrel spill will become available as lessees survey their tracts, or test them, or plan for production and development. The lease sale itself does not directly mandate further activity that would raise an oil spill problem, but it does require an overview of those future possibilities. The over 10,000 barrel analysis in the Final Statement provides that overview in the circumstances of this case. Discounting the marginal improvement of information covered in a 100,000 barrel worst case analysis by the current uncertainty at the lease sale stage of such a spill, the Secretary did not abuse his discretion in delaying further consideration of whether the missing information will become important until a later stage.

Other courts have followed the general principle that staged development encourages staged consideration of uncertain environmental factors. See, e.g., County of Suffolk v. Secretary of the Interior, 562 F.2d 1368, 1378 (2d Cir.1977) ("where a multistage project can be modified or changed in the future to minimize or eliminate environmental hazards disclosed as the result of information that will not be available until the future, and the Government reserves the power to make such a * * * change after the information is * * * incorporated in a further EIS, it cannot be said that deferment violates the 'rule of reason.' "), cert. denied, 434 U.S. 1064 (1978). * * * The Supreme Court has approved this general principle under OCSLA. Against this background, we find the Secretary did not abuse his discretion in considering information about a 100,000 barrel oil spill not important to his lease sale decision, given his adequate analysis of the impacts of an over 10,000 barrel spill on the entire St. George Basin environment and the improved information that will be available in later stages of the OCSLA process when, at least once, he will prepare another environmental impact statement under NEPA covering similar issues.

V

As the Court of Appeals for the District of Columbia observed several years ago, *"the lease sale itself is only a preliminary and relatively self-contained stage within an overall oil and gas development program which requires substantive approval and review prior to implementation of each of the major stages: leasing, exploring, and producing."* North Slope Borough v. Andrus, 642 F.2d 589, 593 (D.C.Cir.1980) (emphasis in original). The Supreme Court has recently reinforced this principle in Secretary of the Interior v. California, ___ U.S. ___, 104 S.Ct. 656, 78 L.Ed.2d 496 (1984). * * * Within the staged structure of OCSLA and on the facts of this case, we hold the Secretary took the required "hard look" under NEPA at environmental consequences of his lease sale decision in the Lease Sale 70 Final Statement, as supplemented by the Supplemental Statement, without including a worst case analysis of a 100,000 barrel oil spill. On the basis of the Secretary's apparent compliance with the terms of the district court's order to prepare a Supplemental Statement and reconsider his lease sale decision, we hold we need not reach the question whether NEPA required imposition of that order.

AFFIRMED.

CANBY, Circuit Judge, concurring in part and dissenting in part:

I concur in parts I, II and III of Judge Wallace's thoughtful and well-crafted opinion. I respectfully dissent from part IV, however, because I believe that a "worst case" analysis of a major oil spill is necessary at the lease sale stage under NEPA and its relevant implementing regulation, 40 C.F.R. § 1502.22 (1982).

The prime purpose of NEPA in requiring Environmental Impact Statements is to assure that federal decision-makers consider the environmental consequences of their major actions before the decision to act is made. See Kleppe v. Sierra Club, 427 U.S. 390, 409 (1976); Conference Report on NEPA, 115 Cong.Rec. 40416 (1969). Where some of the consequences are unknown, as they unquestionably are here, and are important to the decision, the Council on Environmental Quality has required that the worst possible consequences be assessed. 40 C.F.R. § 1502.22 (1982). The regulation is thus designed to assure what common sense would in any event dictate: that a decision-maker be given the opportunity to decide against taking action when the benefits to be gained, although substantial, are outweighed by the risk, although small, of a truly catastrophic environmental impact. The weighing and balancing of gains against risks is, of course, the province of the decision-maker. But the decision-maker must be informed of the extent of a possible catastrophe, a worst case, at a time when he or she is free to make an unfettered decision to refrain from an action because the slight risk of immense harm overshadows the potential benefits. I am satisfied that in the present case, that moment occurs no later than the lease sale stage, before sale and execution of any leases.

Prior to sale, the Secretary has absolute discretion to decline to lease an OCS tract. See 43 U.S.C. § 1344(a). He can therefore decline to lease on the ground that exploration or development will run a small but real risk of immense environmental harm. Once the Secretary leases a tract, however, he loses that freedom, and consequently commits himself to incur such a risk. The reasons why the Secretary loses his freedom upon sale of the leases are both legal and practical.

As a legal matter, the Secretary is allowed to cancel an existing lease for environmental reasons only if he determines that:

> (i) continued activity * * * *would probably cause* serious harm or damage to * * * [the] environment; (ii) the threat of harm or damage will not disappear or decrease to an acceptable extent within a reasonable period of time; and (iii) the advantages of cancellation outweigh the advantages of continuing such lease or permit in force.

43 U.S.C. § 1334(a)(2)(A) (emphasis added); 43 U.S.C. § 1351(h)(1)(D). The requirement of a determination that continued activity "would *probably* cause serious harm to the environment" is a forceful restriction on the Secretary's authority. At least under ordinary circumstances, it prohibits cancellation because of the possibility of a major oil spill; as we observed in Southern Oregon Citizens Against Toxic Sprays v. Clark, 720 F.2d 1475, 1479 (9th Cir.1983), a major oil spill is not a *probable* occurrence, but rather is "an event of low probability but catastrophic effects." The effect of the statute, therefore, is that sale of the leases ends the Secretary's right to call a total halt to exploration and development out of concern over remote environmental catastrophes.

The majority opinion views the restrictions on the Secretary's discretion after leasing as only "minor alterations," because the statute is not exclusive and the Secretary may by regulation expand his power to suspend or cancel leases. I cannot agree. It is true that the Secretary's power to *suspend* operations remains broad, but we have held that the power to suspend is exceeded when the suspension is so open-ended as to amount to a cancellation of a lease. Union Oil Co. of California v. Morton, 512 F.2d 743, 750–51 (9th Cir.1975). Suspension is therefore a temporary remedy and, being temporary, cannot eliminate the possibility of a major oil spill. Only cancellation can do that.

Perhaps the majority opinion is correct in stating that the Secretary by regulation could expand his powers of cancellation, but the proposition is by no means self-evident. In *Union Oil Co. of California,* 512 F.2d at 750, we held that the Secretary's statutory authority to "prescribe * * * such * * * regulations as he determines to be necessary and proper * * * for the conservation of the natural resources of the outer Continental Shelf," 43 U.S.C. § 1334(a), did not authorize him to issue a regulation effectively cancelling a lease. In 1978, three years after the decision in *Union Oil,* Congress amended OCSLA to expand the power of the Secretary to cancel a lease or disapprove exploration or development plans, but the House Report stated that "the Secretary is given authority to disapprove a plan, *but only for [the] specified reasons."* In any event, the Secretary has not regulated to expand his powers of cancellation; the present regulation tracks the language of 43 U.S.C. § 1334(a)(2)(A) and permits cancellation only when continued activity under the lease "would probably cause serious harm or damage * * * to the * * * environment." 30 C.F.R. § 250.12(d)(4)(i). The identical language appears in the statute and regulation requiring the Secretary to disapprove development plans because of exceptional environmental circumstances. 43 U.S.C. § 1351(h)(1)(D); 30 C.F.R. § 250.34–2(g)(2)(iii)(C) (1982). Our decision should be based on the constraints in existing regulations, which now bind the Secretary. See California v. Block, 690 F.2d 753, 762–63 (9th Cir.1982) (EIS required at first stage of multi-stage project where regulation commits agency to action at later stage).

Even if the majority is correct in concluding that the Secretary is not *legally* committed upon the sale of leases to a program of exploration and development, the Secretary is committed "as a practical matter." See California v. Block, 690 F.2d at 761. Once the leases are sold, immense amounts of money change hands, expensive exploration projects are undertaken, and the Department of Interior and various state agencies plan for the consequences of the lease program. As the First Circuit has stated, "[e]ach of these events represents a link in a chain of bureaucratic commitment that will become progressively harder to undo the longer it continues." Massachusetts v. Watt, 716 F.2d 946, 952 (1st Cir.1983). Moreover, cancellation of a lease may require the payment of very substantial compensation to the lessee. 43 U.S.C. § 1334(a)(2)(C). That possibility is bound to be a significant deterrent to cancellation. The combined impact of all of these factors renders the lease sale a practical commitment by the Secretary to a program of exploration and, if oil or gas is discovered, to production. It is therefore at the lease sale stage that the Secretary needs to know the worst environmental consequences that may result from that program.

* * *

I would therefore hold the unknown consequences of a major oil spill to be "important" to the lease sale decision within the meaning of 40 C.F.R. § 1502.22(b) (1982), and would require the EIS to include a worst case analysis of its consequences. Once the leases are sold, the risk of such a spill has been taken.

NOTES

1.   Offshore oil and gas leasing is addressed again in chapter six, § B(4). What function did NEPA serve in *Village of False Pass?* What good will it do the villagers to have the Department assess the effects of a massive oil spill? Is NEPA litigation by definition merely a delaying tactic? If so, is that necessarily bad?

2.   The worst case analysis regulation cited in the principal case was the subject of a number of rulings criticized by industry. See also, e.g., Save Our Ecosystems v. Clark, 747 F.2d 1240 (9th Cir. 1984), supra at page 634; National Wildlife Federation v. United States Forest Service, 592 F.Supp. 931 (D.Or.1984), appeal pending, supra at page 651. In 1986, the Council on Environmental Quality amended 40 C.F.R. § 1502.22 to eliminate the phrase "worst case analysis" and to include provisions relating to "reasonably foreseeable significant adverse impacts" supported by "credible scientific evidence." See 51 Fed.Reg. 15618 (April 25, 1986):

Section 1502.22.   Incomplete or unavailable information.

When an agency is evaluating reasonably foreseeable significant adverse effects on the human environment in an environmental impact statement and there is incomplete or unavailable information, the agency shall always make clear that such information is lacking.

(a) If the incomplete information relevant to reasonably foreseeable significant adverse impacts is essential to a reasoned choice among alternatives and the overall costs of obtaining it are not exorbitant, the agency shall include the information in the environmental impact statement.

(b) If the information relevant to reasonably foreseeable significant adverse impacts cannot be obtained because the overall costs of obtaining it are exorbitant or the means to obtain it are not known, the agency shall include within the environmental impact statement: (1) a statement that such information is incomplete or unavailable; (2) a statement of the relevance of the incomplete or unavailable information to evaluating reasonably foreseeable significant adverse impacts on the human environment; (3) a summary of existing credible scientific evidence which is relevant to evaluating the reasonably foreseeable significant adverse impacts on the human environment; and (4) the agency's evaluation of such impacts based upon theoretical approaches or research methods generally accepted in the scientific community. For the purposes of this section, "reasonably foreseeable" includes impacts which have catastrophic consequences, even if their probability of occurrence is low, provided that the analysis of the impacts is supported by credible scientific evidence, is not based on pure conjecture, and is within the rule of reason.

Which version is preferable as a matter of policy? The amended rule is expected to be attacked by environmental groups arguing, among other things, that the original version is compelled by Congress' intent in enacting NEPA so that the changes cannot be made administratively.

3. Promulgation of environmental impact statements has become a significant industry in itself, financially benefitting biologists, hydrologists, sociologists, consultants, the paper industry, and many others, especially lawyers. The process is time-consuming and expensive. Is it worth it? Can you answer that question without knowing what would have occurred without NEPA? Is NEPA just another example of proliferating paperwork and red tape that contributes to governmental inefficiency and frustration of citizens' legitimate aims? Or is it a necessary device to ensure that bureaucrats engage in a minimum of thought before taking irreversible actions that may be very unwise? Should the federal government be efficient? At least sufficiently so to see that its trains run on time?

NOTE: THE PLACE OF NEPA IN PUBLIC LAND AND RESOURCES LAW

The Supreme Court and other courts have stressed that NEPA is merely procedural; even if the EIS reveals that the proposed action could be disastrous environmentally, the statute imposes no obligation on the agency to act differently—or at least no obligation that a court will enforce. The decision in NRDC v. Hodel, 624 F.Supp. 1045 (D.Nev. 1986), infra at page 749, is a good example of a court strictly limiting its review of a facially bad agency choice of policy. Theoretically, the importance of NEPA as a component of public land and resources law should decline in inverse proportion to the growth of substantive statutory law governing public land management, agencies' increasing familiarity with NEPA requisites, and heightened congressional oversight of public land decisions (as evidenced in, e.g., Pacific Legal Found. v. Watt, 529 F.Supp. 982 (D.Mont.1981), supra at page 260.)

Many of the recent cases in this volume, however, attest to the fact that the National Environmental Policy Act remains a major focus of public land law and litigation. The discerning student will soon realize that the results in NEPA cases are strongly influenced by substantive factors in spite of Supreme Court admonitions. The relief granted in

NRDC v. Hughes, supra, for instance, is inexplicable except for the Department's seeming blind ardor for a resumption of coal leasing without any good articulated reason for doing so. In another pivotal NEPA opinion—one that revolutionized public rangeland management—the court clearly was influenced by the environmentally harmful effects of the BLM's usual management policy. NRDC v. Morton, 388 F.Supp. 829 (D.D.C.1974), infra at page 704.

Similar themes echo in the more sophisticated decisions handed down since 1980. In the area of mineral leasing, the opinion in Sierra Club v. Peterson, 717 F.2d 1409 (D.C.Cir.1983), infra at page 562, achieves by NEPA interpretation for onshore oil and gas leasing roughly the same result that Congress dictated for offshore leasing as seen in *Village of False Pass:* the possibility of phased environmental evaluation by reducing the lessee's interest from a property right to an exclusive procedural right. See also Sierra Club v. Hathaway, 579 F.2d 1162 (9th Cir.1978) (geothermal leasing). Timber harvesting too has felt the sting of a NEPA backlash. See National Wildlife Fed'n v. United States Forest Service, 592 F.Supp. 931 (D.Or.1984), infra at page 651, Thomas v. Peterson, 753 F.2d 754 (9th Cir.1985), infra at page 669. In public rangeland planning and management, the new era promised by NRDC v. Morton, cited above has not yet materialized. See NRDC v. Hodel, 624 F.Supp. 1045 (D.Nev.1986), infra at page 749. Wildlife law, however, was sharpened by the decision in Foundation for North American Wild Sheep v. United States, 681 F.2d 1172 (9th Cir.1982), infra at page 877, holding that the Forest Service could not approve a mining road without far more detailed consideration of the adverse effects on wildlife and mitigation measures to avoid such effects. Another NEPA decision of critical significance for the wilderness resource is California v. Block, 690 F.2d 753 (9th Cir.1982), infra at page 1001. NEPA was the mechanism in every one of these cases that required the agency to think more broadly and deeply about the consequences of its decision for other resources and values; that kind of thinking is the beginning and essence of public land use planning.

Public land use planning is now a prerequisite to public resource allocation. That the orientation of such planning is more environmental than economic is due primarily to the National Environmental Policy Act of 1969. Now well into the second half of its second decade, NEPA is alive, well, and thriving. The future promises more innovative applications of this facially innocuous but inherently revolutionary law.

Chapter Five

THE WATER RESOURCE

The water resource is the appropriate starting place for studying the federal public resources, for all other resource uses are dependent upon the availability of water. Mineral extraction and processing often require great quantities of water. In the form of geothermal steam or as hydropower, water is itself an energy resource. Western farmers rely on expansive irrigation systems—90% of all water in the eleven western states is used for irrigation—and ranchers need sufficient rain to regenerate forage. Little timber grows in arid areas, and in many places rivers remain principal highways for transporting logs to the mill. Wildlife needs water for survival and for habitat maintenance. Water is also a prime source of recreation opportunities and an essential part of ecosystems that society wishes preserved for future generations. Water is truly the lifeblood of the land.

Acquisition of water rights is principally a matter of state law, but the United States also has a limited role in water allocation. As a constitutional matter, valid federal water laws are supreme: the Property, Commerce, Treaty, and Supremacy Clauses give Congress ample authority to legislate on issues relating to water. The Supreme Court decides disputes between states involving interstate rivers, and Congress may allocate water among states by statute, as it did in the instance of the Colorado River. Land management agencies hold water rights. Moreover, largescale water resources development is mainly a creature of federal money if not federal law. Congress can also affect state water law when it acts to regulate navigation, to prevent floods, or to control water pollution.

Water policy on the public lands involves more than the distribution of water among competing users. Land management practices often determine the character of the streams and lakes within a watershed. Timber harvesting can cause stream blockages and erosion, and it sometimes affects water flow: the temperature and quantity of run-off may vary according to the timber harvesting pattern. Overgrazing has destroyed groundcover and caused soil compaction; rainfall, instead of being absorbed and cooled by spongy soils, runs off in sheets, carrying soil with it and carving out gulleys and arroyos. Mineral development can contribute to water pollution and soil erosion if not conducted properly. Moreover—even if the site of a timber cut, hardrock mine, or oil drilling operation is designed to reduce or eliminate impacts on water—development projects of all sorts usually require road systems, which often cause severe erosion. Land and resource planners therefore must give prime consideration to protection of watercourses if downstream consumptive users, wildlife, and recreationists are to have adequate supplies of clean, cool water.

This chapter does not attempt to duplicate a course in water law; it is limited to several aspects of water allocation that are intimately tied to the protection and development of the federal lands. Section A examines the law governing the acquisition of federal water rights on the public lands. This section introduces the dominant state system of prior appropriation that evolved under the aegis of federal law; it considers the authority of Congress to preempt state law and create federal reserved rights; and it investigates the ability of federal land management agencies to establish water rights and otherwise influence water use. Section B treats federal watershed management by analyzing some restraints on activities that affect riparian zones.

A. THE ACQUISITION OF WATER RIGHTS ON THE PUBLIC LANDS

1. THE ORIGINS OF WATER LAW ON THE PUBLIC LANDS

Water law defines legal rights to a limited, moving, and largely renewable resource. Geographic variations in the quantity of water available, competition among the many various uses, and differing political and social contexts have resulted in different state legal systems for allocation of water rights.

At English Common Law, the owner of land adjacent to a watercourse acquired water rights in the stream as part of the estate in real property. Each riparian owner was entitled to the "natural flow" of the stream, with the result that none could use the water for consumptive purposes other than "natural uses" such as household or stockwatering. Instream, nonconsumptive uses (e.g., for mills) were permitted since the natural flow would be preserved. The English Rule of riparian rights is valuable as a means of resource preservation but is unsuited to the demands of modern industry, commerce, and agriculture where water is relatively scarce.

The riparian doctrine, as modified to meet the needs of a society that had greater demands for water, was adopted in the eastern states and in some western states:

> The American rule of reasonable use differs in two major respects from the English rule of natural flow. First, in order to maintain an action, it is essential for the complainant to show that he would suffer actual damages if the defendant continued his use. Noninjurious use of the water does not give rise to a cause of action. However, noninjurious use also cannot ripen into a prescriptive right. Second, the use of water on nonriparian land is not "necessarily unprivileged." Instead, its legality is evaluated by criteria of reasonableness, defined as early as 1883 in *Red River Roller Mills v. Wright:*

> > In determining what is a reasonable use, regard must be had to the subject-matter of the use; the occasion and

> manner of its application; the object, extent, necessity, and duration of the use; the nature and size of the stream; the kind of business to which it is subservient; the importance and necessity of the use claimed by one party, and the extent of the injury to the other party; the state of improvement of the country in regard to mills and machinery, and the use of water as a propelling power; the general and established usages of the country in similar cases; and all the other and ever-varying circumstances of each particular case, bearing upon the question of the fitness and propriety of the use of the water under consideration.
>
> In the 85 years since then, not much that is helpful has been added to this general definition of so abstract a proposition as "reasonableness."

Hanks, The Law of Water in New Jersey, 22 Rutgers L.Rev. 621, 630 (1968). The "American rule" allows for more utilitarian use of water in that water users are permitted to consume a "reasonable" quantity of water, but other limiting rules were retained from the Common Law doctrine. An old and established use of water is a factor—but is not by itself controlling—in determining what is reasonable under the balancing test used to resolve competing riparian rights. Many riparian states have adopted the rule that water can be used only on riparian land in the watershed. A modern instance is Dimmock v. City of New London, 157 Conn. 9, 245 A.2d 569 (1968). For a discussion of the English and American riparian systems, see 7 R. Clark, WATER AND WATER RIGHTS, Ch. 31 (1976); Restatement, Second, Torts §§ 850–59 (1979).

A number of western states (California, Kansas, Nebraska, North Dakota, Oklahoma, Oregon, South Dakota, Texas, and Washington) adopted by case law the "California doctrine," which respects both riparian and appropriative rights. See generally W. Hutchins, WATER RIGHTS LAWS IN THE NINETEEN WESTERN STATES, Ch. 10 (1974). All of the other western states (except Hawaii) are pure "Colorado doctrine" states, recognizing only water rights established by prior appropriation. Even the "California doctrine" states have moved to the appropriation system by statute. The result is that for most purposes the prior appropriation doctrine now holds sway in all states west of the 100th Meridian.

The "pure" prior appropriation doctrine arose from customs prevalent in the early mining camps on the public lands and, later, on western farmlands that could not grow crops unless irrigation water was applied to them. The goal was always to reward, and provide stability to, water development for economic purposes in the water-scarce West. An appropriator—whether or not the owner of riparian land—obtained a vested property right superior to all later users if he actually diverted water out of the stream and put it to a beneficial use, a term that generally includes domestic uses and economic uses such as agriculture, mining, manufacturing, power generation, and stockwatering. "First in time, first in right" was the watchword, even if the first user took all of the water in the stream. Courts would not allow any balancing of equities or proration in years of shortage—the time-based system established a firm and ascertainable hierarchy. There was no "watershed limitation" because miners often needed to transport water many miles by elaborate systems of ditches and canals in order to mine at locations where no water existed. A leading case is Irwin v. Phillips, 5 Cal. 140 (1855), in which the California Supreme Court ratified the customs of the miners in the Gold Country.

State procedures for the determination of water rights are as deeply embedded as the substantive legal rules. Early on, states provided for general stream adjudications in which courts entered detailed decrees adjudging all rights, by priority, within entire watersheds. Later, most states established administrative agencies with procedures for issuing and recording permits that set out water rights with relative precision. Those priorities are enforced by water masters. Taking water out of priority is roughly equivalent to an act of war.

The traditional prior appropriation doctrine, which allocated water on a laissez-faire basis to the first consumptive user, has been modified in various respects. Some states now allow diversions only if they are in the "public interest." Several legislatures have departed from the time-honored requirement of a physical diversion out of a watercourse by empowering state agencies to set minimum stream flows for protection of fish, wildlife, recreation, and the aesthetic qualities of streams and lakes. Tarlock, Appropriation for Instream Flow Maintenance: A Progress Report on "New" Public Western Water Rights, 1978 Utah L.Rev. 211. States also have begun to impose conservation requirements on wasteful irrigation projects, thus making the saved water available for new uses. See Shupe, Waste in Western Water Law: A Blueprint for Change, 61 Or.L.Rev. 483 (1982). A few states have recently applied the public trust doctrine to protect instream values. Dunning, The Public Trust Doctrine and Western Water Law: Discord or Harmony?, 30 Rocky Mtn.Min.L.Inst. 17 (1985). These developments could lead to fundamental change. Wilkinson, Western Water Law in Transition, 56 U.Colo.L.Rev. 317 (1985); Thorson, Brown & Desmond, Forging Public Rights in Montana Waters, 6 Pub.Land L.Rev. 1 (1985). For most purposes, however, water allocation is still dominated by deeply-entrenched state laws that have distributed most western water on a first-come, first-served basis to users who have actually diverted water from a watercourse and applied it to specified beneficial uses.

The following excerpt from an award-winning law review article illustrates some practical problems of accommodating the prior appropriation system to new energy-related developments on the public lands.

**WILLIAM E. HOLLAND, MIXING OIL AND WATER: THE
EFFECT OF PREVAILING WATER LAW DOCTRINES
ON OIL SHALE DEVELOPMENT** *

52 Den. L.J. 657 (1975).

* * *

II. WATER SUPPLY AND WATER LAWS

A. *Natural Supply*

The primary sources of surface water in the oil shale areas are the
Green River in Wyoming, the Green and White Rivers in Utah, and the
White and Colorado Rivers in Colorado.   The average yearly runoff
from the White River basin over a period of 58 years (to 1968) was
458,000 acre-feet. [An acre-foot is about 325,000 gallons.] That from
the Colorado River main stem to Glenwood Springs, Colorado, is 2
million acre-feet.   Runoff from the Green River basin is 3.92 million
acre-feet at Green River, Utah.   There are also groundwater supplies,
but these are more difficult to measure and are largely uncatalogued.
However, in absolute terms it is clear that there is enough water for
almost unlimited oil shale development.   Natural limits on water
supply are not the problem.

B. *"The Law of the River"*

All of the streams in the oil shale region ultimately flow into the
Colorado River above Glen Canyon Dam.   They are thus subject to the
Colorado River Compact, which allocates the total flow of the Colorado
River among seven western states and Mexico.   The primary division is
that between the Upper Basin states, Colorado, Utah, Wyoming, and
New Mexico, and the Lower Basin states, Arizona, California, and
Nevada.   In 1922 the signers of the Compact assumed that a flow of 18
million acre-feet annually was available, and they allocated 7.5 million
acre-feet to each of the Basins.   The delivery of that amount to the
Lower Basin at Lee Ferry was made a binding commitment on the
Upper Basin states.   * * * But over the past 30 years, the actual flow
has been little over 13 million acre-feet per year, and about 14 million
per year for the 50 years since the Compact was formed.   The Upper
Basin states have recently agreed among themselves that they can
depend upon a residual amount of about 6.2 million acre-feet.   This
includes reservoir evaporation of 700,000 acre-feet, leaving a net supply
available for consumptive use of 5.5 million acre-feet.

* * *

The Upper Colorado River Basin Compact of 1948 gives Arizona
50,000 acre-feet annually from the Upper Basin water and divides the
residue on a percentage basis: Colorado, 51.75 percent; New Mexico,

11.25 percent; Utah, 23 percent; Wyoming, 14 percent. There is thus a separate limit in each state on the consumption of water, irrespective of consumption in the other states. Actual amounts available for consumption are approximately 2.8 million acre-feet in Colorado, 1.25 million acre-feet in Utah, and 0.77 million acre-feet in Wyoming.

C. *Appropriation*

The Colorado River Compacts are not the only limitations on supply in the oil shale areas. Prior users of both surface waters and groundwater are also protected by the laws. In all three oil shale states, water is the property, not of the land owner, but of the public. The states allocate water rights by the prior appropriation system, under which the application of water to a beneficial use gives the user a vested right to that amount of water, subject only to conflicting rights which existed earlier. There are three areas which are especially important to oil shale development: priority of rights; "diligence"; and transfers of rights.

1. Priority

Except as modified by statute, the elements necessary to establish an appropriation right in water are an intent to appropriate, actual diversion or capture of water, and application of the water to a beneficial use. Assuming that the appropriation goes forward diligently to completion, the date of the right is the date of the first act evidencing an intent to take water for a beneficial use. These doctrines have been modified by statutory filing systems which make most rights a matter of public record.

* * *

It is possible that in some cases unappropriated water exists where the records indicate there is none, for in all three states it is "beneficial use" which is the measure of the right, not the amount stated in an application, or given by decree, in Colorado. Thus, if application is made and a permit granted for diversion of 8 cfs [cubic feet per second], but only 4 cfs is ever put to use, the right is only to the use 4 cfs. Upon proof of these facts the "paperright" may be reduced to that amount, leaving 4 cfs available for use elsewhere, if it has not already been appropriated by a second user. * * *

Conversely, there are some rights, dating from the days before filing was required, that may not be of record. These unseen icebergs lurk in the path of any present-day appropriator who needs to know what supply he can count on.

* * *

2. "Diligence"

The filing of applications for water will not necessarily secure a water supply even if water remains unappropriated. Applications which are not diligently pursued will not give rise to a right to water. In the absence of statute "due diligence" is an issue of fact, and the meaning of the term in any given case is therefore determined through the judicial process.   *   *   *

In Colorado, since there is no filing requirement for rights in surface water and all rights are decreed in special court adjudications, diligence with respect to those rights is still a question for the courts.   *   *   *

Since the lead time needed to establish an oil shale production facility is at least 2 years, and since most associated municipal uses must develop over an even longer period, it is clear that groundwater supplies for oil shale cannot be reserved in advance in Colorado.   *   *   *

The statutory grants of discretion are not unlimited, and they should not be construed as granting power to extend time indefinitely as a means of reserving water, whether for oil shale development or any other use.   The original purpose behind the prior appropriation doctrine was to *prevent* reservation of water which could not be put to immediate use.   The Utah statute's reference to "diligence" indicates an intent to maintain the court-developed standard, which in one much-quoted case was said to consist of

> that constancy or steadiness of purpose or labor which is usual with men engaged in like enterprises, and who desire a speedy accomplishment of their designs,—such assiduity in the prosecution of the enterprise as will manifest to the world a *bona fide* intention to complete it within a reasonable time.

*   *   *

3. Transfer of Rights

Where unappropriated waters cannot be found, water may be acquired by acquisition of existing appropriation rights.   All appropriation states consider water rights at least in theory to be property and therefore saleable and transferable by other means.   Rights may be transferred in all three of the oil shale states, at least in some circumstances.   Most transfers may be expected to be by purchase.   *   *   *

The importance of water to the economy of arid states quickly led to its transfer being hedged about with legal and administrative precautions, so that under existing doctrines transfer is subject to a number of difficulties.   The major barriers are those involving protection of junior appropriators [and] seasonal rights.

a. *Protection of Junior Appropriators*

One hurdle which the states have erected in the path of a would-be purchaser in an attempt to protect other users is a requirement of administrative approval of certain transfers.   *   *   *

Alongside the administrative protections there exists a judicial doctrine that vested water rights must be protected in any transfer. The problem arises in the following manner.   Few uses of water consume all the water which is diverted. The unconsumed portion which returns to the stream is called "return flow." This flow is then subject to appropriation by other users. Thus, if an irrigator diverts 8 cfs, of which 4 cfs finds its way back to the stream, that 4 cfs will augment the flow downstream and can be diverted a second time. The downstream appropriator acquires a right to this 4 cfs, and his right must be protected. If the upstream irrigation right is sold to an industrial user, still with the same place of use, who diverts the same 8 cfs but consumes 7 cfs, the downstream user is damaged by the loss of 3 cfs to which he has a vested right.

* * *

In order to protect the junior appropriators in such situations, transfer of the senior right is prevented. Courts have ameliorated the limitation by allowing transfers of part of the right, to the extent that no other user would be harmed. The same result is directed by statute in Utah, where the state engineer is directed to approve changes in part, if that may be done without impairing vested rights. Thus in *Green v. Chaffee Ditch Co.*[109] an irrigator owned an adjudicated right to divert 16 cfs during the irrigation season. He sold this right to the City of Fort Collins for municipal use, and the city converted the right to a storage right. Upon protest by other users, the court found that the irrigator had never diverted more than 8 cfs, and furthermore that he diverted a maximum of 360 acre-feet per year for a use which was 25 percent efficient (75 percent return flow), with a resulting consumption of 95 acre-feet per year. The city, however, returned only 50 percent of its diversions to the stream. The city's right was therefore reduced to a maximum of 8 cfs rate of flow, and a total yearly flow of 19 acre-feet, to achieve a consumption of 95 acre-feet. This flow could be diverted and stored only during the period April 15 to October 15, the period in which the irrigation right could be used. The seller, then, was found to have owned only one-half of his paper right, and the purchaser was able to divert only one-half of that.

Purchase of existing rights for oil shale development is likely to involve both of the problems which the City of Fort Collins faced in *Chaffee Ditch.* The major problem is that most existing rights in the oil shale areas are for irrigation, a low-efficiency use with return flows of 75 to 90 percent. Oil shale production is a much more efficient use. Most estimates are that over 60 percent of total diversion will be consumed; and direct processing and upgrading uses will consume 90 percent of the water diverted to them. An oil shale processor with 90 percent efficiency buying rights from irrigators who had 10 percent efficiency would have to purchase rights to 90 cfs in order to divert only 10 cfs! (The irrigator would return 9 cfs and consume 1 out of every 10 diverted. But the oil shale processor will consume 9 and return only 1. Since he *must* return the full 9 cfs for every 1 he diverts, he must purchase 9 times the amount he actually requires and divert only 1 of the 9. The others he must send down the stream.) The only possible

109. 150 Colo. 91, 371 P.2d 775 (1962).

way to avert this difficulty is for the oil shale processor to purchase the right of every user who has appropriated any part of the return flow from the water rights he has purchased, except those uses which do not add up to more than his own direct return flow. This will probably significantly affect the price he must pay.

* * *

b. *Seasonal Rights and Storage*

Oil shale developers seeking to purchase existing rights will also face the other difficulty illustrated in *Chaffee Ditch:* many existing water rights are seasonal. Purchase of these rights gives the purchaser a right to divert water only during the period allowed under the original use.

Oil shale is not a seasonal industry. The high capital investment required would make it uneconomical to shut down production during periods of low water availability. Thus it would be necessary to follow the procedure of the City of Fort Collins in *Chaffee Ditch* and smooth out the supply by storing water during the irrigation season and using it during the remainder of the year. * * *

HAROLD A. RANQUIST, THE WINTERS DOCTRINE AND HOW IT GREW: FEDERAL RESERVATION OF RIGHTS TO THE USE OF WATER *
1975 B.Y.U.L.REV. 639.

* * *

The United States owned all western lands not privately held under previous sovereigns and possessed the power to dispose of these lands and the water, together or separately. By its acquiescence, the United States permitted those persons whose rights were recognized by the developing customs and rules to possess the public lands and waters and to divert those waters out of their watersheds and across the public lands to distant mining claims and irrigated tracts. The existence of federal authority to dispose of the water on one hand, and the actual disposition of that water under the growing doctrine of prior appropriation on the other, resulted in conflict between the first appropriator of water and the federal patentee who claimed an unencumbered title.

Shortly after the close of the Civil War, legislative proposals were made to have Congress withdraw the mines from the public domain of the West and either operate or sell them to obtain revenue to retire the Civil War debt. The opposition of western Senators and Congressmen resulted, however, in the enactment of legislation in 1866 which expressly confirmed both the rights of the miners and the rights of the appropriators of water. A current water rights treatise explains the effect of the 1866 Act:

* Reprinted with permission of the Brigham Young University Law Review and Harold A. Ranquist.

The Act of 1866 thus gave *formal* sanction of the Government to appropriations of water on public lands of the United States, whether made before or after passage of the act, and rights of way in connection therewith, provided that the appropriations conformed to principles established by customs of local communities, State or Territorial laws, and decisions of courts. The act contained no procedure by which such rights could be acquired from the United States while the lands remained part of the public domain. *What it did was to take cognizance of the customs and usages that had grown up on the public lands under State and Territorial sanction and to make compliance therewith essential to the enjoyment of the Federal grant.*

* * * The act merely recognized the obligation of the Government to respect private rights which had grown up under its tacit consent and approval. *Jennison v. Kirk,* 98 U.S. 453, 459 (1879). It proposed no new system, but sanctioned, regulated, and confirmed the system already established, to which the people were attached.

An 1870 amendment to the 1866 Act provided that all federal patents, homestead rights, or rights of preemption would be subject to any vested and accrued water rights or rights-of-way for ditches or reservoirs acquired or recognized under the Act of 1866. * * *

Seven years later, in 1877, Congress passed the Desert Land Act which

provided that water rights on tracts of desert land should depend upon bona fide prior appropriation; and that all surplus water over and above actual appropriation and necessary use, together with the water of all lakes, rivers, and other sources of water upon the public lands and not navigable, should be held free for appropriation by the public for irrigation, mining, and manufacturing purposes, subject to existing rights. * * *

The highest courts of the various states could not agree on whether the application of the 1877 Act was limited to arid and desert lands or included all lands. The question was finally settled by the United States Supreme Court in 1935 * * *.

* * *

* * * Because the states created and enforced comprehensive systems of water law, a pattern of reliance on state law developed and the role of federal law was ignored for many years. * * * The painful howls of protest from the states and from their water users were at least understandable. This response resulted in part from the failure to recognize the already established principle that the source of the authority to administer the use of water was the federal sovereign. It also demonstrated a failure to fully appreciate the concept of federal supremacy as applied to the fulfillment of the federal sovereign's objectives.

CALIFORNIA OREGON POWER CO. v. BEAVER PORTLAND CEMENT CO.

Supreme Court of the United States, 1935.
295 U.S. 142.

[California Oregon, the petitioner, purchased its land on the Rogue River in Oregon from a predecessor who had obtained a homestead patent in 1885. Neither had ever diverted any water. Beaver Portland possessed upstream land that was patented after 1885. Beaver Portland engaged in drilling and blasting operations that lessened the flow of the river and otherwise interfered with the power generation facilities that California Oregon sought to build.

California Oregon claimed that its senior federal patent carried with it riparian rights as a matter of federal law, thus guaranteeing it the natural flow of the stream. Beaver Portland argued that state law applied because the Desert Lands Act of 1877 put an end to any riparian rights that might attach to subsequent federal patents. The Oregon Supreme Court had held that no federal patents issued after 1877 carried riparian rights. In addition, an Oregon statute provided that no riparian right could be exercised after 1909 unless water had been diverted and put to a beneficial use. Beaver Portland thus argued that California Oregon could have no riparian rights under state law.

The Court first stated that the 1866 and 1870 federal legislation, referred to in the Ranquist article, validated prior appropriative rights and that subsequent patentees from the United States therefore took subject to pre-existing water rights vested by local law.]

*   *   *

If the acts of 1866 and 1870 did not constitute an entire abandonment of the common-law rule of running waters in so far as the public lands and subsequent grantees thereof were concerned, they foreshadowed the more positive declarations of the Desert Land Act of 1877, which it is contended did bring about that result. That act allows the entry and reclamation of desert lands within the states of California, Oregon, and Nevada (to which Colorado was later added), and the then territories of Washington, Idaho, Montana, Utah, Wyoming, Arizona, New Mexico, and Dakota, with a proviso to the effect that the right to the use of waters by the claimant shall depend upon *bona fide* prior appropriation, not to exceed the amount of waters actually appropriated and necessarily used for the purpose of irrigation and reclamation. Then follows the clause of the proviso with which we are here concerned:

> "* * * all surplus water over and above such actual appropriation and use, together with the water of all lakes, rivers and other sources of water supply upon the public lands and not navigable, shall remain and be held free for the appropriation and use of the public for irrigation, mining and manufacturing purposes subject to existing rights." [43 U.S. C.A. § 321].

* * * If this language is to be given its natural meaning, and we see no reason why it should not, it effected a severance of all waters upon the public domain, not theretofore appropriated, from the land itself. From that premise, it follows that a patent issued thereafter for lands in a desert-land state or territory, under any of the land laws of the United States, carried with it, of its own force, no common law right to the water flowing through or bordering upon the lands conveyed.

* * *

As the owner of the public domain, the government possessed the power to dispose of land and water thereon together, or to dispose of them separately. The fair construction of the provision now under review is that Congress intended to establish the rule that for the future the land should be patented separately; and that all non-navigable waters thereon should be reserved for the use of the public under the laws of the states and territories named. The words that the water of all sources of water supply upon the public lands and not navigable "shall remain and be held free for the appropriation and use of the public" are not susceptible of any other construction. The only exception made is that in favor of *existing* rights; and the only rule spoken of is that of *appropriation.* It is hard to see how a more definite intention to sever the land and water could be evinced. The terms of the statute, thus construed, must be read into every patent thereafter issued, with the same force as though expressly incorporated therein, with the result that the grantee will take the legal title to the land conveyed, and such title, and only such title, to the flowing waters thereon as shall be fixed or acknowledged by the customs, laws, and judicial decisions of the state of their location. If it be conceded that in the absence of federal legislation the state would be powerless to affect the riparian rights of the United States or its grantees, still, the authority of Congress to vest such power in the state, and that it has done so by the legislation to which we have referred, cannot be doubted.

* * *

Second. Nothing we have said is meant to suggest that the act, as we construe it, has the effect of curtailing the power of the states affected to legislate in respect of waters and water rights as they deem wise in the public interest. What we hold is that following the act of 1877, if not before, all non-navigable waters then a part of the public domain became *public juris,* subject to the plenary control of the designated states, including those since created out of the territories named, with the right in each to determine for itself to what extent the rule of appropriation or the common-law rule in respect of riparian rights should obtain. For since "Congress cannot enforce either rule upon any state," Kansas v. Colorado, 206 U.S. 46, 94, the full power of choice must remain with the state. The Desert Land Act does not bind or purport to bind the states to any policy. It simply recognizes and gives sanction, in so far as the United States and its future grantees are concerned, to the state and local doctrine of appropriation, and seeks to remove what otherwise might be an impediment to its full and success-ful operation.

* * *

[The decree in favor of Beaver Portland was affirmed.]

NOTES

1. The Court concluded that as of the passage of the Desert Lands Act in 1877, "if not before," state water law governed in determining what kind of water rights, if any, attached when federal patents were issued. Why did state water laws and local customs apply on the public lands well before 1877? Is the application of state water law on the public lands governed by the same principles as State ex rel. Cox v. Hibbard, 31 Or.App. 269, 570 P.2d 1190 (1977), supra at page 211 (state mining laws) and Omaechevarria v. Idaho, 246 U.S. 343 (1918), supra at page 153 (state grazing laws)?

2. Although construing the Desert Lands Act, the holding in *Beaver Portland* is not limited to Desert Lands Act patents; instead, the Court held that a general severance of estates in land and water was accomplished on all public lands in the listed desert land states. Should the language of the federal law have been construed to establish a federal rule of appropriation? The Court found that the effect of the Act was to leave water allocation to whatever system a state chose, in part because "Congress cannot enforce either rule upon any state." Is that correct? See generally F. Trelease, FEDERAL-STATE RELATIONS IN WATER LAW 138–147 (1971).

2. FEDERAL RESERVED RIGHTS

The doctrine of federal reserved water rights was first recognized in Winters v. United States, 207 U.S. 564 (1908). In *Winters,* the United States, as trustee for the Indian tribes occupying the Fort Belknap reservation in Montana, sought to enjoin upstream defendants on the Milk River from withdrawing water that was required for an irrigation project on the reservation. The defendants had appropriated water under Montana law after the reservation was established in 1888 but before 1898, when the Indian irrigation project was constructed. The Court held that the creation of the Fort Belknap reservation not only set aside land but also impliedly reserved a sufficient quantity of water to fulfill the purposes of the reservation. The priority date was the date of the reservation: "The power of the Government to reserve the waters and exempt them from appropriation under the state laws is not denied, and could not be. That the Government did reserve them we have decided * * *. This was done May 1, 1888 * * *."

Winters superimposed a judicially implied federal water right on a state system that based water rights on prior appropriation. Inchoate rights had been established without any diversion or application to a beneficial use—the hallmarks of prior appropriation law. See generally Collins, The Future Course of The *Winters* Doctrine, 56 U.Colo.L.Rev. 481 (1985). The following case presaged the expansion of *Winters* from an Indian law doctrine to one potentially applicable on all public lands.

It also illustrates the nature of Congress' preemptive power over water uses on the federal lands.

FEDERAL POWER COMM'N v. OREGON

Supreme Court of the United States, 1955.
349 U.S. 435.

Mr. Justice BURTON delivered the opinion of the Court.

As in First Iowa Coop. v. Federal Power Commission, 328 U.S. 152, this case illustrates the integration of the federal and state jurisdictions in licensing water power projects under the Federal Power Act. In the *First Iowa* case we sustained the authority of the Commission to license a power project to use navigable waters of the United States located in Iowa [contrary to Iowa law]. Here, without finding that the waters are navigable, the Commission has issued a comparable license for a power project to use waters on lands constituting reservations of the United States located in Oregon. The State of Oregon questions the authority of the Commission to do this and the adequacy of the provisions approved by the Commission for the conservation of anadromous fish. For the reasons hereafter stated, we sustain the Commission.

* * *

The Pelton Project is designed to include a concrete dam 205 feet high and a powerhouse containing three 36,000-kilowatt generators. It is to be built across the Deschutes River on reserved lands of the United States located below the junction of its Metolius and Crooked River tributaries.[4] The western terminus of the dam is to occupy lands, within the Warm Springs Indian Reservation, which have been reserved by the United States for power purposes since 1910 and 1913. The eastern terminus of the dam is to be on lands of the United States which, at least since 1909, have been withdrawn from entry under the public land laws and reserved for power purposes. * * *

* * *

Following extended hearings, the Commission's presiding examiner recommended the license. * * *

* * *

I. APPLICABILITY OF THE FEDERAL POWER ACT.

On its face, the Federal Power Act applies to this license as specifically as it did to the license in the *First Iowa* case. There the jurisdiction of the Commission turned almost entirely upon the naviga-

---

4. The Deschutes River is entirely within the State of Oregon. It drains the eastern slope of the Cascade Range and flows northward, across the lands of the United States here involved, to the Columbia River, which it meets about 15 miles above The Dalles. The Commission has made no findings as to its navigability or as to the relation between its flow and the navigability of other streams. Throughout its lower 130 miles, which include the project site, it flows in a narrow canyon with an average fall of 17.6 feet per mile and, apparently, it is generally recognized as incapable of sustaining navigation. Accordingly, throughout this litigation, the river has been treated by all concerned as not constituting "navigable waters" of the United States as defined in § 3(8) of the Federal Power Act, 16 U.S.C.A. § 796(8). We do not pass either upon that question or upon the relationship to interstate commerce of the proposed use of the waters of the river.

bility of the waters of the United States to which the license applied. Here the jurisdiction turns upon the ownership or control by the United States of the reserved lands on which the licensed project is to be located. The authority to issue licenses in relation to navigable waters of the United States springs from the Commerce Clause of the Constitution. The authority to do so in relation to public lands and reservations of the United States springs from the Property Clause.

*   *   *

In the instant case the project is to occupy lands which come within the term "reservations," as distinguished from "public lands." In the Federal Power Act, each has its established meaning. "Public lands" are lands subject to private appropriation and disposal under public land laws. "Reservations" are not so subject.[10] The title to the lands upon which the eastern terminus of the dam is to rest has been in the United States since the cession by Great Britain of the area now comprising the State of Oregon. Even if formerly they may have been open to private appropriation as "public lands," they were withdrawn from such availability before any vested interests conflicting with the Pelton Project were acquired. Title to the bed of the Deschutes River is also in the United States. Since the Indian Treaty of 1855, the lands within the Indian reservation, upon which the western end of the dam will rest, have been reserved for the use of the Indians. More recently they were reserved for power purposes and the Indians have given their consent to the project before us. Accordingly, there is no issue here as to whether or not the title to the tribal lands is in the United States.

There thus remains no question as to the constitutional and statutory authority of the Federal Power Commission to grant a valid license for a power project on reserved lands of the United States, provided that, as required by the Act, the use of the water does not conflict with vested rights of others. *   *   * Authorization of this project, therefore, is within the exclusive jurisdiction of the Federal Power Commission, unless that jurisdiction is modified by other federal legislation. See United States v. Rio Grande Irrigation Co., 174 U.S. 690, 703.

II. INAPPLICABILITY OF THE DESERT LAND ACT OF 1877 AND RELATED ACTS.

The State of Oregon argues that the Acts of July 26, 1866, July 9, 1870, and the Desert Land Act of 1877 constitute an express congressional delegation or conveyance to the State of the power to regulate

---

10. SEC. 3. The words defined in this section shall have the following meanings for purposes of this Act, to wit:

"(1) 'public lands' means such lands and interest in lands owned by the United States as are subject to private appropriation and disposal under public land laws. It shall not include 'reservations', as hereinafter defined;

"(2) 'reservations' means national forests, tribal lands embraced within Indian reservations, military reservations, and other lands and interests in lands owned by the United States, and withdrawn, reserved, or withheld from private appropriation and disposal under the public land laws; also lands and interest in lands acquired and held for any public purposes; but shall not include national monuments or national parks; *   *   *." 16 U.S.C.A. § 796(1) and (2).

the use of these waters. The argument is that these Acts preclude or restrict the scope of the jurisdiction, otherwise apparent on the face of the Federal Power Act, and require the consent of the State to a project such as the one before us.

The nature and effect of these Acts have been discussed previously by this Court. The purpose of the Acts of 1866 and 1870 was governmental recognition and sanction of possessory rights *on public lands* asserted under local laws and customs. Jennison v. Kirk, 98 U.S. 453. The Desert Land Act severed, for purposes of private acquisition, soil and water rights *on public lands,* and provided that such water rights were to be acquired in the manner provided by the law of the State of location. California Oregon Power Co. v. Beaver Portland Cement Co., 295 U.S. 142. See also, Nebraska v. Wyoming, 325 U.S. 589, 611–616.

It is not necessary for us, in the instant case, to pass upon the question whether this legislation constitutes the express delegation or conveyance of power that is claimed by the State, because these Acts are not applicable to the reserved lands and waters here involved. The Desert Land Act covers "sources of water supply upon the public lands * * *." The lands before us in this case are not "public lands" but "reservations." Even without that express restriction of the Desert Land Act to sources of water supply on public lands, these Acts would not apply to reserved lands. "It is a familiar principle of public land law that statutes providing generally for disposal of the public domain are inapplicable to lands which are not unqualifiedly subject to sale and disposition because they have been appropriated to some other purpose." United States v. O'Donnell, 303 U.S. 501, 510. The instant lands certainly "are not unqualifiedly subject to sale and disposition * * *." Accordingly, it is enough, for the instant case, to recognize that these Acts do not apply to this license, which relates only to the use of waters on reservations of the United States.

III. APPLICATION OF THE FEDERAL POWER ACT TO THIS PROJECT.

* * *

We conclude, therefore, that, on the facts here presented, the Federal Power Act is applicable in accordance with its terms, and that the Federal Power Commission has acted within its powers and its discretion in granting the license now before us.

The judgment of the Court of Appeals, accordingly, is

Reversed.

Mr. Justice DOUGLAS, dissenting.

* * *

Oregon's position has for its support two other decisions of this Court, both construing the Desert Land Act. The first of these is California Oregon Power Co. v. Cement Co. * * *

* * *

Those cases should control here. The Desert Land Act applies to "public lands"; and the Federal Power Act, 41 Stat. 1063, as amended, 16 U.S.C.A. § 791a et seq., grants the Commission authority to issue licenses for power development "upon any part of the public lands and reservations of the United States." § 4(e). The definition of those terms in the Act says nothing about water rights. And, as I have pointed out, it has been the long-term policy of Congress to separate western land from water rights.

* * *

The reason is that the rule adopted by the Court profoundly affects the economy of many States, ten of whom are here in protest. In the West, the United States owns a vast amount of land—in some States, over 50 percent of all the land. If by mere Executive action the federal lands may be reserved and all the water rights appurtenant to them returned to the United States, vast dislocations in the economies of the Western States may follow. * * * Certainly the United States could not appropriate the water rights in defiance of Oregon law, if it built the dam. It should have no greater authority when it makes a grant to a private power group.

NOTE

In FPC v. Oregon, the state's objections were based upon the dam's impact on anadromous fish, especially steelhead, which spawn in fresh-water streams, migrate out to the ocean, and then return to the original spawning grounds as adult fish. The objections of wildlife agencies in Washington State also fell to federal power in a protracted and bitter legal struggle. See Washington Dept. of Game v. FPC, 207 F.2d 391 (9th Cir.1953), cert. denied, 347 U.S. 936 (1954); City of Tacoma v. Taxpayers of Tacoma, 357 U.S. 320 (1958); City of Tacoma v. Taxpayers of Tacoma, 60 Wn.2d 66, 371 P.2d 938 (1962).

FPC v. Oregon upheld preemptive federal power to approve and license dam sites over state objections, but the case did not directly involve the acquisition of water rights. The full implications of the reserved rights doctrine were not apparent until over fifty years after *Winters,* when non-Indian federal reserved water rights were passed upon for the first time by the Supreme Court.

ARIZONA v. CALIFORNIA
Supreme Court of the United States, 1963.
373 U.S. 546.

[The Colorado River and its tributaries are a principal source of water for seven states in the arid Southwest. Arizona invoked the original jurisdiction of the Supreme Court by filing an action against the State of California for an allocation of the River's water. Although the basic controversy concerned the amount of water each state had a legal right to use, alleged federal reserved rights were also involved. The case was referred to a special master to take evidence and recommend a decree. The Court held, at 373 U.S. 595–601:]

In these proceedings, the United States has asserted claims to waters in the main river and in some of the tributaries for use on

Indian Reservations, National Forests, Recreational and Wildlife Areas and other government lands and works.

* * *

The Master ruled that the principle underlying the reservation of water rights for Indian Reservations was equally applicable to other federal establishments such as National Recreation Areas and National Forests. We agree with the conclusions of the Master that the United States intended to reserve water sufficient for the future requirements of the Lake Mead National Recreation Area, the Havasu Lake National Wildlife Refuge, the Imperial National Wildlife Refuge and the Gila National Forest.

We reject the claim of the United States that it is entitled to the use, without charge against its consumption, of any waters that would have been wasted but for salvage by the Government on its wildlife preserves. Whatever the intrinsic merits of this claim, it is inconsistent with the Act's command that consumptive use shall be measured by diversions less returns to the river.

Finally, we note our agreement with the Master that all uses of mainstream water within a State are to be charged against the State's apportionment, which of course includes uses by the United States.

NOTES

1. On Arizona v. California, see generally Meyers, The Colorado River, 19 Stan.L.Rev. 1 (1966).

2. Cappaert v. United States, 426 U.S. 128 (1976), involved construction of a 1952 Proclamation by President Truman under the Antiquities Act of 1906, 16 U.S.C.A. § 431, adding Devil's Hole to the Death Valley National Monument in Nevada. In 1968, the Cappaert ranch began pumping groundwater pursuant to a state permit. The groundwater depletion lowered the level of the hydrologically connected pool in adjacent Devil's Hole, thus endangering the existence of the rare Devil's Hole pupfish that lived only in the pool. The Court held that the 1952 Proclamation implicitly reserved sufficient water to preserve the habitat of the pupfish, that the 1968 rights of the Cappaerts were junior to the federal reservation, and that the Cappaerts could pump only as much water as would not imperil the pupfish. Chief Justice Burger explained:

This Court has long held that when the Federal Government withdraws its land from the public domain and reserves it for a federal purpose, the Government, by implication, reserves appurtenant water then unappropriated to the extent needed to accomplish the purpose of the reservation. In so doing the United States acquires a reserved right in unappropriated water which vests on the date of the reservation and is superior to the rights of future appropriators. Reservation of water rights is empowered by the Commerce Clause, Art. I, § 8, which permits federal regulation of navigable streams, and the Property Clause, Art. IV, § 3, which permits federal regulation of federal lands. The doctrine applies to Indian reservations and other federal enclaves, encompassing water rights in navigable and nonnavigable streams.

* * *

In determining whether there is a federally reserved water right implicit in a federal reservation of public land, the issue is whether the Government intended to reserve unappropriated and thus available water. Intent is inferred if the previously unappropriated waters are necessary to accomplish the purposes for which the reservation was created. * * *

* * *

The implied-reservation-of-water-rights-doctrine, however, reserves only that amount of water necessary to fulfill the purpose of the reservation, no more. * * *

3. The McCarran Amendment, 43 U.S.C.A. § 666(a), provides a limited waiver of sovereign immunity by the United States in water rights litigation in state courts:

Consent is given to join the United States as a defendant in any suit (1) for the adjudication of rights to the use of water of a river system or other source, or (2) for the administration of such rights, where it appears that the United States is the owner of or is in the process of acquiring water rights by appropriation under State law, by purchase, by exchange, or otherwise, and the United States is a necessary party to such suit. * * *

In United States v. District Court in and for Eagle County, 401 U.S. 520 (1971), the Court held that the "or otherwise" language meant that federal reserved rights are subject to adjudication in state court. The opinion noted that the McCarran Amendment extends only to general stream adjudications; thus the waiver of immunity applies only to comprehensive proceedings in which the state joins all potential water rights claimants in a watershed, not to actions that might be filed against the United States by individual water users. In subsequent cases, the Supreme Court held that the waiver in the McCarran Amendment also applies to adjudications of Indian reserved water rights. Colorado River Water Cons. Dist. v. United States, 424 U.S. 800 (1976); Arizona v. San Carlos Apache Tribe, 463 U.S. 545 (1983).

At the time of the opinion in *Eagle County,* Colorado was the only western state in which adjudication of water rights took place entirely in court. In 1979, Montana adopted a somewhat similar system. In most other western states, adjudications are first held in administrative agencies charged with enforcing the state water laws. See generally Stone, Montana Water Rights—A New Opportunity, 34 Mont.L.Rev. 57, 70–71 (1973). Whether the United States will be required under the McCarran Amendment (which waives sovereign immunity as to "any suit") to appear in state administrative proceedings in order to establish federal and Indian reserved rights is still unresolved.

4. The classic prior appropriation doctrine has little room for instream uses. Even under the recently-enacted state minimum streamflow laws, instream rights are junior and must give way to senior rights in years of low flows. On many streams, such junior priorities are nothing more than "paper rights," because virtually the entire flows have been appropriated by consumptive users. The following case reflected the Forest Service's attempts to obtain federal instream water rights with senior priority dates.

UNITED STATES v. NEW MEXICO
Supreme Court of the United States, 1978.
438 U.S. 696.

Mr. Justice REHNQUIST delivered the opinion of the Court.

The Rio Mimbres rises in the southwestern highlands of New Mexico and flows generally southward, finally disappearing in a desert sink just north of the Mexican border. The river originates in the upper reaches of the Gila National Forest, but during its course it winds more than 50 miles past privately owned lands and provides substantial water for both irrigation and mining. In 1970, a stream adjudication was begun by the State of New Mexico to determine the exact rights of each user to water from the Rio Mimbres. In this adjudication the United States claimed reserved water rights for use in the Gila National Forest.   *   *   *

I

The question posed in this case—what quantity of water, if any, the United States reserved out of the Rio Mimbres when it set aside the Gila National Forest in 1899—is a question of implied intent and not power.   *   *   * The Court has previously concluded that whatever powers the States acquired over their waters as a result of congressional Acts and admission into the Union, however, Congress did not intend thereby to relinquish its authority to reserve unappropriated water in the future for use on appurtenant lands withdrawn from the public domain for specific federal purposes.

Recognition of Congress' power to reserve water for land which is itself set apart from the public domain, however, does not answer the question of the amount of water which has been reserved or the purposes for which the water may be used. Substantial portions of the public domain *have* been withdrawn and reserved by the United States for use as Indian reservations, forest reserves, national parks, and national monuments. And water is frequently necessary to achieve the purposes for which these reservations are made. But Congress has seldom expressly reserved water for use on these withdrawn lands. If water were abundant, Congress' silence would pose no problem. In the arid parts of the West, however, claims to water for use on federal reservations inescapably vie with other public and private claims for the limited quantities to be found in the rivers and streams. This competition is compounded by the sheer quantity of reserved lands in the Western States, which lands form brightly colored swaths across the maps of these States.[3]

The Court has previously concluded that Congress, in giving the President the power to reserve portions of the federal domain for specific federal purposes, *impliedly* authorized him to reserve "appurtenant water then unappropriated *to the extent needed to accomplish the purpose of the reservation*." While many of the contours of what has come to be called the "implied-reservation-of-water doctrine" remain unspecified, the Court has repeatedly emphasized that Congress reserved "only that amount of water necessary to fulfill the purpose of the reservation, no more." Each time this Court has applied the "implied-reservation-of-water doctrine," it has carefully examined both the asserted water right and the specific purposes for which the land was reserved, and concluded that without the water the purposes of the reservation would be entirely defeated.

This careful examination is required both because the reservation is implied, rather than expressed, and because of the history of congressional intent in the field of federal-state jurisdiction with respect to allocation of water. Where Congress has expressly addressed the question of whether federal entities must abide by state water law, it has almost invariably deferred to the state law. Where water is necessary to fulfill the very purposes for which a federal reservation was created, it is reasonable to conclude, even in the face of Congress' express deference to state water law in other areas, that the United States intended to reserve the necessary water. Where water is only valuable for a secondary use of the reservation, however, there arises the contrary inference that Congress intended, consistent with its other views, that the United States would acquire water in the same manner as any other public or private appropriator.

*   *   *

The State District Court referred the issues in this case to a Special Master, who found that the United States was diverting 6.9 acre-feet per annum of water for domestic-residential use, 6.5 acre-feet for road-water use, 3.23 acre-feet for domestic-recreational use, and .10 acre-foot for "wildlife" purposes. The Special Master also found that specified amounts of water were being used in the Gila National Forest for stockwatering and that an "instream flow" of six cubic feet per second was being "used" for the purposes of fish preservation [under the implied reserved rights doctrine]. [The state courts held that no

3. The percentage of federally owned land (*excluding* Indian reservations and other trust properties) in the Western States ranges from 29.5% of the land in the State of Washington to 86.5% of the land in the State of Nevada, an average of about 46%. Of the land in the State of New Mexico, 33.6% is federally owned. Because federal reservations are normally found in the uplands of the Western States rather than the flatlands, the percentage of water flow originating in or flowing through the reservations is even more impressive. More than 60% of the average annual water yield in the 11 Western States is from federal reservations. The percentage of average annual water yield range from a low of 56% in the Columbia-North Pacific water-resource region to a high of 96% in the Upper Colorado region. In the Rio Grande water-resource region, where the Rio Mimbres lies, 77% of the average runoff originates on federal reservations.

instream flow had been reserved for "aesthetic, environmental, recreational, or 'fish' purposes." They also held that no water had been reserved for stockwatering.]

* * *

II

A

* * *

The United States contends that Congress intended to reserve minimum instream flows for aesthetic, recreational, and fish-preservation purposes. An examination of the limited purposes for which Congress authorized the creation of national forests, however, provides no support for this claim. In the mid and late 1800's, many of the forests on the public domain were ravaged and the fear arose that the forest lands might soon disappear, leaving the United States with a shortage both of timber and of watersheds with which to encourage stream flows while preventing floods. It was in answer to these fears that in 1891 Congress authorized the President to "set apart and reserve, in any State or Territory having public land bearing forests, in any part of the public lands wholly or in part covered with timber or undergrowth, whether of commercial value or not, as public reservations." Creative Act of March 3, 1891, § 24, 16 U.S.C.A. § 471 (repealed 1976).

The Creative Act of 1891 unfortunately did not solve the forest problems of the expanding Nation. To the dismay of the conservationists, the new national forests were not adequately attended and regulated; fires and indiscriminate timber cutting continued their toll. To the anguish of Western settlers, reservations were frequently made indiscriminately. President Cleveland, in particular, responded to pleas of conservationists for greater protective measures by reserving some 21 million acres of "generally settled" forest land on February 22, 1897. President Cleveland's action drew immediate and strong protest from Western Congressmen who felt that the "hasty and ill considered" reservation might prove disastrous to the settlers living on or near these lands.

Congress' answer to these continuing problems was three-fold. It suspended the President's Executive Order of February 22, 1897; it carefully defined the purposes for which national forests could in the future be reserved; and it provided a charter for forest management and economic uses within the forests. Organic Administration Act of June 4, 1897, 16 U.S.C.A. § 473 et seq. In particular, Congress provided:

> *No national forest shall be established, except to improve and protect the forest within the boundaries, or for the purpose of securing favorable conditions of water flows, and to furnish a continuous supply of timber for the use and necessities of citizens of the United States;* * * * *[16 U.S.C.A. § 475]* (emphasis added).

The legislative debates surrounding the Organic Administration Act of 1897 and its predecessor bills demonstrate that Congress intended national forests to be reserved for only two purposes—"[t]o conserve the water flows, and to furnish a continuous supply of timber for the people." [14] 30 Cong.Rec. 967 (1897) (Cong. McRae). See United States v. Grimaud, 220 U.S. 506, 515 (1911). National forests were not to be reserved for aesthetic, environmental, recreational, or wildlife-preservation purposes.

> "The objects for which the forest reservations should be made are the protection of the forest growth against destruction by fire and ax, and preservation of forest conditions upon which water conditions and water flow are dependent. The purpose, therefore, of this bill is to maintain favorable forest conditions, without excluding the use of these reservations for other purposes. They are not parks set aside for nonuse, but have been established for economic reasons." 30 Cong.Rec. 966 (1897) (Cong. McRae).

Administrative regulations at the turn of the century confirmed that national forests were to be reserved for only these two limited purposes.

Any doubt as to the relatively narrow purposes for which national forests were to be reserved is removed by comparing the broader

14. The Government notes that the Act forbids the establishment of national forests except *"to improve and protect the forest within the boundaries,* or for the purpose of securing favorable conditions of water flows, and to furnish a continuous supply of timber," and argues from this wording that "improvement" and "protection" of the forests form a third and separate purpose of the national forest system. A close examination of the language of the Act, however, reveals that Congress only intended national forests to be established for two purposes. Forests would be created only "to improve and protect the forest within the boundaries," or, *in other words,* "for the purpose of securing favorable conditions of water flows, and to furnish a continuous supply of timber."

This reading of the Act is confirmed by its legislative history. Nothing in the legislative history suggests that Congress intended national forests to be established for three purposes, one of which would be extremely broad. Indeed, it is inconceivable that a Congress which was primarily concerned with limiting the President's power to reserve the forest lands of the West would provide for the creation of forests merely "to improve and protect the forest within the boundaries"; forests would be reserved for their improvement and protection, but only to serve the purposes of timber protection and favorable water supply.

This construction is revealed by a predecessor bill to the 1897 Act which was introduced but not passed in the 54th Congress; the 1896 bill provided:

> "That the object for which public forest reservations shall be established under the provisions of the act approved March 3, 1891, shall be to protect and improve the forests *for the purpose* of securing a continuous supply of timber for the people and securing conditions favorable to water flow." H.R.119, 54th Cong., 1st Sess. (1896) (emphasis added).

Earlier bills, like the 1897 Act, were less clear and could be read as setting forth either two or three purposes. Explanations of the bills by their congressional sponsors, however, clearly revealed that national forests would be established for only two purposes. Compare, for example, H.R.119, 53d Cong., 1st Sess. (1893) ("[N]o public forest reservations shall be established except to improve and protect the forest within the reservation or for the purpose of securing favorable conditions of water flow and continuous supplies of timber to the people") with its sponsor's description of the bill, id., at 2375 (Cong. McRae) ("The bill authorizes the President to establish forest reservations, and to protect the forests 'for the purpose of securing favorable conditions of water flow and continuous supplies of timber to the people' ").

language Congress used to authorize the establishment of national parks. In 1916, Congress created the National Park Service and provided that the

> "fundamental purpose of the said parks, monuments, and reservations * * * is to conserve the scenery and the natural and historic objects and the wild life therein and to provide for the enjoyment of the same * * * unimpaired for the enjoyment of future generations." 16 U.S.C.A. § 1.

When it was Congress' intent to maintain minimum instream flows within the confines of a national forest, it expressly so directed, as it did in the case of the Lake Superior National Forest:

> "In order to preserve the shore lines, rapids, waterfalls, beaches and other natural features of the region in an unmodified state of nature, no further alteration of the natural water level of any lake or stream * * * shall be authorized." 16 U.S.C.A. § 577b.

National park legislation is not the only instructive comparison. In the Act of Mar. 10, 1934, 16 U.S.C.A. § 694, Congress authorized the establishment within individual national forests of fish and game sanctuaries, *but only with the consent of the state legislatures.* * * * If, as the dissent contends, * * * Congress in the Organic Administration Act of 1897 authorized the reservation of forests to "improve and protect" fish and wildlife, the 1934 Act would have been unnecessary. Nor is the dissent's position consistent with Congress' concern in 1934 that fish and wildlife preserves only be created "with the approval of the State legislatures."

As the dissent notes, in creating what would ultimately become Yosemite National Park, Congress in 1890 explicitly instructed the Secretary of the Interior to provide against the wanton destruction of fish and game inside the forest and against their taking "for the purposes of merchandise or profit." * * * By comparison, Congress in the 1897 Organic Act expressed no concern for the preservation of fish and wildlife within national forests generally. * * *

B

Not only is the Government's claim that Congress intended to reserve water for recreation and wildlife preservation inconsistent with Congress' failure to recognize these goals as purposes of the national forests, it would defeat the very purpose for which Congress did create the national forest system. * * * The water that would be "insured" by preservation of the forest was to "be used for domestic, mining, milling, or irrigation purposes, under the laws of the State wherein such national forests are situated, or under the laws of the United States and the rules and regulations established thereunder." Organic Administration Act of 1897, 16 U.S.C.A. § 481. As this provision and its legislative history evidence, Congress authorized the national forest system principally as a means of enhancing the quantity of water that would be available to the settlers of the arid West. The Government, however, would have us now believe that Congress intended to partially defeat this goal by reserving significant amounts of water for purposes quite inconsistent with this goal.

C

In 1960, Congress passed the Multiple-Use Sustained-Yield Act of 1960, 16 U.S.C.A. § 528 et seq., which provides:

> "It is the policy of Congress that the national forests are established and shall be administered for outdoor recreation, range, timber, watershed, and wildlife and fish purposes. The purposes of sections 528 to 531 of this title are declared to be supplemental to, but not in derogation of, the purposes for which the national forests were established as set forth in the [Organic Administration Act of 1897.]"

The Supreme Court of New Mexico concluded that this Act did not give rise to any reserved rights not previously authorized in the Organic Administration Act of 1897. "The Multiple-Use Sustained-Yield Act of 1960 does not have a retroactive effect nor can it broaden the purposes for which the Gila National Forest was established under the Organic Act of 1897." 90 N.M., at 413, 564 P.2d at 618. While we conclude that the Multiple-Use Sustained-Yield Act of 1960 was intended to broaden the purposes for which national forests had previously been administered, we agree that Congress did not intend to thereby expand the reserved rights of the United States.[21]

　＊　＊　＊ As discussed earlier, the "reserved rights doctrine" is a doctrine built on implication and is an exception to Congress' explicit deference to state water law in other areas. Without legislative history to the contrary, we are led to conclude that Congress did not intend in enacting the Multiple-Use Sustained-Yield Act of 1960 to reserve water for the *secondary* purposes there established.[22] A reservation of additional water could mean a substantial loss in the amount of water available for irrigation and domestic use, thereby defeating Congress' principal purpose of securing favorable conditions of water flow. Congress intended the national forests to be administered for broader purposes after 1960 but there is no indication that it believed the new

---

21. The United States does not argue that the Multiple-Use Sustained-Yield Act of 1960 reserved additional water for use on the national forests. Instead, the Government argues that the Act confirms that Congress *always* foresaw broad purposes for the national forests and authorized the Secretary of the Interior as early as 1897 to reserve water for recreational, aesthetic, and wildlife-preservation uses. As the legislative history of the 1960 Act, demonstrates, however, Congress believed that the 1897 Organic Administration Act only authorized the creation of national forests for two purposes—timber preservation and enhancement of water supply—and intended, through the 1960 Act, to *expand* the

purposes for which the national forests should be administered. See, e.g., H.R. Rep. No. 1551, 86th Cong., 2d Sess., 4 (1960).

Even if the 1960 Act expanded the reserved water rights of the United States, of course, the rights would be subordinate to any appropriation of water under state law dating to before 1960.

22. We intimate no view as to whether Congress, in the 1960 Act, authorized the subsequent reservation of national forests out of public lands to which a broader doctrine of reserved water rights might apply.

purposes to be so crucial as to require a reservation of additional water. By reaffirming the primacy of a favorable water flow, it indicated the opposite intent.

III

What we have said also answers the Government's contention that Congress intended to reserve water from the Rio Mimbres for stockwatering purposes. The United States issues permits to private cattle owners to graze their stock on the Gila National Forest and provides for stockwatering at various locations along the Rio Mimbres. The United States contends that, since Congress clearly foresaw stockwatering on national forests, reserved rights must be recognized for this purpose. The New Mexico courts disagreed and held that any stockwatering rights must be allocated under state law to individual stockwaterers. We agree.

While Congress intended the national forests to be put to a variety of uses, including stockwatering, not inconsistent with the two principal purposes of the forests, stockwatering was not itself a direct purpose of reserving the land.[23]   *   *   *

IV

Congress intended that water would be reserved only where necessary to preserve the timber or to secure favorable water flows for private and public uses under state law. This intent is revealed in the purposes for which the national forest system was created and Congress' principled deference to state water law in the Organic Administration Act of 1897 and other legislation. The decision of the Supreme Court of New Mexico is faithful to this congressional intent and is therefore

Affirmed.

Mr. Justice POWELL, with whom Mr. Justice BRENNAN, Mr. Justice WHITE, and Mr. Justice MARSHALL join, dissenting in part.

I agree with the Court that the implied-reservation doctrine should be applied with sensitivity to its impact upon those who have obtained water rights under state law and to Congress' general policy of defer-

---

23. As discussed earlier, the national forests were not to be "set aside for non-use," 30 Cong.Rec. 966 (1897) (Cong. McRae), but instead to be opened up for any economic use not inconsistent with the forests' primary purposes. Ibid. One use that Congress foresaw was "pasturage." Ibid. See also id., at 1006 (Cong. Ellis); id., at 1011 (Cong. De Vries). As this Court has previously recognized, however, grazing was merely one use to which the national forests could possibly be put and would not be permitted where it might interfere with the specific purposes of the national forests including the securing of favorable conditions of water flow. Under the 1891 and 1897 forest Acts, "any use of the reservation for grazing or other lawful purpose was required to be subject to the rules and regulations established by the Secretary of Agriculture. To pasture sheep and cattle on the reservation, at will and without restraint, might interfere seriously with the accomplishment of the purposes for which they were established. But a limited and regulated use for pasturage might not be inconsistent with the object sought to be attained by the statute." United States v. Grimaud, 220 U.S. 506, 515–516 (1911). See also Light v. United States, 220 U.S. 523 (1911).

ence to state water law. I also agree that the Organic Administration Act of 1897 cannot fairly be read as evidencing an intent to reserve water for recreational or stockwatering purposes in the national forests.[1]

I do not agree, however, that the forests which Congress intended to "improve and protect" are the still, silent, lifeless places envisioned by the Court. In my view, the forests consist of the birds, animals, and fish—the wildlife—that inhabit them, as well as the trees, flowers, shrubs, and grasses. I therefore would hold that the United States is entitled to so much water as is necessary to sustain the wildlife of the forests, as well as the plants. I also add a word concerning the impact of the Court's holding today on future claims by the United States that the reservation of particular national forests impliedly reserved instream flows.

I

* * * Although the language of the statute is not artful, a natural reading would attribute to Congress an intent to authorize the establishment of national forests for three purposes, not the two discerned by the Court. The New Mexico Supreme Court gave the statute its natural reading in this case when it wrote:

> "The Act limits the purposes for which national forests are authorized to: 1) improving and protecting the forest, 2) securing favorable conditions of water flows, and 3) furnishing a continuous supply of timber."

Congress has given the statute the same reading, stating that under the Organic Administration Act of 1897 national forests may be established for "the purposes of improving and protecting the forest or for securing favorable conditions of water flows, and to furnish a continuous supply of timber * * *."

> "[T]he Court not surprisingly attempts to keep this provision in the background, addressing it only * * * in a footnote," United States v.

---

1. I express no view as to the effect of the Multiple-Use Sustained-Yield Act of 1960, on the United States' reserved water rights in national forests that were established either before or after that Act's passage. Although the Court purports to hold that passage of the 1960 Act did not have the effect of reserving any additional water in then-existing forests, this portion of its opinion appears to be dicta. As the Court concedes, "The United States does not argue that the Multiple-Use Sustained-Yield Act of 1960 reserved additional water for use on the national forests." Likewise, the State argues only that "[n]o reserved rights for fish or wildlife can be implied in the Gila National Forest *prior to the enactment of the Multiple-Use Sustained-Yield Act of June 12, 1960.* * * *" Indeed, the State has gone so far as to suggest that passage of the 1960 Act may well have expanded the United States' reserved water rights in the national forests, presumably with a priority date for the additional reserved rights of 1960. Read in context, the New Mexico Supreme Court's statement that the 1960 Act "does not have a retroactive effect nor can it broaden the purposes for which the Gila National Forest was established under the Organic Act of 1897," appears to mean nothing more than that the 1960 Act did not give the United States additional reserved water rights *with a priority date of before 1960*—a proposition with which I think we all would agree. But there never has been a question in this case as to whether the 1960 Act gave rise to additional reserved water rights with a priority date of 1960 or later in the Gila National Forest.

Sotelo, 436 U.S. 268, 283 (1978) (REHNQUIST, J., dissenting), where it decides that the Act should be read as if it said national forests may "be created only 'to improve and protect the forest within the boundaries,' or, *in other words,* 'for the purpose of securing favorable conditions of water flows, and to furnish a continuous supply of timber.' " (emphasis in original). The Court then concludes that Congress did not mean to "improve and protect" any part of the forest except the usable timber and whatever other flora is necessary to maintain the watershed. This, however, is not what Congress said.

The Court believes that its "reading of the Act is confirmed by its legislative history." The matter is not so clear to me. From early times in English law, the forest has included the creatures that live there. J. Manwood, A Treatise and Discourse of the Laws of the Forrest 1–7 (1598); 1 W. Blackstone, Commentaries 289. Although the English forest laws themselves were not transplanted to the shores of the new continent, see generally Lund, Early American Wildlife Law, 51 N.Y.U.L.Rev. 703 (1976), the understanding that the forest includes its wildlife has remained in the American mind. In establishing the first forest reservations, the year before passage of the Organic Act of 1891, Congress exhibited this understanding by directing the Secretary of the Interior to "provide against the wanton destruction of the fish * * * and game found within said reservation, and against their capture or destruction, for the purposes of merchandise or profit." Act of Oct. 1, 1890, § 2, 26 Stat. 651.

* * *

One may agree with the Court that Congress did not, by enactment of the Organic Administration Act of 1897, intend to authorize the creation of national forests simply to serve as wildlife preserves. But it does not follow from this that Congress did not consider wildlife to be part of the forest that it wished to "improve and protect" for future generations. It is inconceivable that Congress envisioned the forests it sought to preserve as including only inanimate components such as the timber and flora. Insofar as the Court holds otherwise, the 55th Congress is maligned and the Nation is the poorer, and I dissent.[5]

II

Contrary to the Court's intimations, I see no inconsistency between holding that the United States impliedly reserved the right to instream flows, and what the Court views as the underlying purposes of the 1897 Act. The national forests can regulate the flow of water—which the Court views as "the very purpose for which Congress did create the

---

5. No doubt it will be said that the waterflow necessary to maintain the watershed including the forest will be sufficient for the wildlife. This well may be true in most national forests and most situations. But the Court's opinion, as I read it, recognizes no reserved authority in the Federal Government to protect wildlife itself as a part of the forest, and therefore if and when the need for increased waterflow for this purpose arises the Federal Government would be powerless to act. Indeed, upstream appropriators could be allowed to divert so much water that survival of forest wildlife—including even the fish and other life in the streams—would be endangered.

national forest system," only for the benefit of appropriators who are downstream from the reservation. The reservation of an instream flow is not a consumptive use; it does not subtract from the amount of water that is available to downstream appropriators. Reservation of an instream flow therefore would be perfectly consistent with the purposes of the 1897 Act as construed by the Court.[6]

I do not dwell on this point, however, for the Court's opinion cannot be read as holding that the United States never reserved instream flows when it set aside national forests under the 1897 Act. The State concedes, quite correctly on the Court's own theory, that even in this case "the United States is not barred from asserting that rights to minimum instream flows might be necessary for erosion control or fire protection on the basis of the recognized purposes of watershed management and the maintenance of timber." Thus, if the United States proves, in this case or others, that the reservation of instream flows is necessary to fulfill the purposes discerned by the Court, I find nothing in the Court's opinion that bars it from asserting this right.

NOTES

1. Did Justice Rehnquist rewrite the 1897 Organic Act? Would Congress as constituted in 1897 likely have intended the broad-based reservation of water prayed for in United States v. New Mexico? Are the terms of proclamations withdrawing national forests relevant to water reservation questions? What does "securing favorable conditions of water flows" mean? Does *New Mexico* make water rights more certain and stable? For discussion of the main case, see Fairfax & Tarlock, No Water For the Woods: A Critical Analysis of United States v. New Mexico, 15 Idaho L.Rev. 509 (1979), in which the authors dispute the majority's analysis of the legislative history of the 1897 Organic Act. Boles & Elliot, United States v. New Mexico and the Course of Federal Reserved Water Rights, 51 U.Colo.L.Rev. 209 (1980), and Trelease, Uneasy Federalism—State Water Laws and National Water Uses, 55 Wash.L.Rev. 751 (1980), conclude that the opinion provides needed security for rights obtained under state law; they note that the United States can obtain water rights through condemnation procedures if the national interest requires the establishment of instream flows on a particular stream.

2. After *New Mexico* was handed down, the Department of Interior released a comprehensive Solicitor's Opinion discussing the nature and extent of the federal water rights of the National Park Service, the Fish and Wildlife Service, the Bureau of Reclamation, and the Bureau of Land Management. The following excerpts are from the opinion, which remains a leading source of law. Other aspects of the opinion have been modified, see infra at page 405, but the analysis of federal reserved rights remain in force.

6. It is true that reservation of an instream flow might in some circumstances adversely affect appropriators upstream from the forest. There would be no inconsistency with the 1897 Act, however, for that Act manifestly was not intended to benefit upstream appropriators.

**FEDERAL WATER RIGHTS OF THE NATIONAL PARK
SERVICE, FISH AND WILDLIFE SERVICE, BUREAU
OF RECLAMATION, AND THE BUREAU OF
LAND MANAGEMENT**
88 Interior Decisions 553 (1979).

V. RESERVED WATER RIGHTS APPLICABLE TO AREAS ADMIN-
ISTERED BY THE NATIONAL PARK SERVICE

* * *

A. *National Parks*

* * *

This statement of fundamental purpose encompasses a variety of consumptive and non-consumptive reserved water rights necessary to conserve scenic, natural, historic and biotic elements and to provide for sustained public enjoyment thereof.

I conclude that the particular reserved water rights for national park areas encompassed under 16 U.S.C.A. § 1 include water required for:

1. *Scenic, natural and historic conservation uses,* such as: ecosystem maintenance (e.g., protecting forest growth and vegetative cover, watershed protection, soil and erosion control, lawn watering, fire protection), maintenance of water-related aesthetic conditions (e.g., minimum stream flows and lake levels), and maintenance of natural features (e.g., wilderness protection, geysers, waterfalls).

2. *Wildlife conservation uses,* such as: the protection, reproduction and management of migratory wildlife and birds (e.g., wildlife and bird watering, habitat maintenance, irrigation for hay and other food staples); and the protection, reproduction and management of fish and other aquatic life (e.g., minimum stream flows and lake levels).

3. *Sustained public enjoyment uses,* such as: visitor accommodation uses through NPS and concessioneer operations (e.g., campground uses and maintenance, hotel water and sewer uses), public facility uses (e.g., water fountains, sewage), visitor activities (e.g., visitor centers, park office, shop uses); and visitor enjoyment of the scenic, natural, historic and biotic park resources (e.g., trail maintenance, minimum stream flows and lake levels for waterborne public enjoyment and recreation, hay and watering of horses and mules used by park visitors).

4. *NPS personnel uses* to provide the above uses, such as domestic uses (ranger stations, NPS residences), NPS animal maintenance (e.g., hay and watering of NPS horses and mules).

* * *

B. *National Monuments*

* * *

1. *Pre-1916 National Monuments*

Between 1906 and 1916, the President acted several times to create national monuments [pursuant to the Antiquities Act of 1906, 16 U.S. C.A. §§ 431–33.] The proclamations establishing these early national monuments are brief, generally citing the statutory language, naming the landmarks, structures or other objects to be protected, stating that the "public good would be promoted" by the reservation, and giving a land description.

Clearly the proclamations intended to reserve such water as necessary to provide for the proper care and management of the stated landmarks, structures, or objects of historic or scientific interest, the *raison d'etre* for the reservation. It is less clear, however, whether the early proclamations also reserved water rights for the protection of other unstated elements of the national monuments (e.g., biological resources) and for their public enjoyment.

* * *

[T]he promotion of the public good is a primary purpose of the monument reservation and * * * it includes public enjoyment of both stated and unstated monument objectives. Moreover, * * * the 1916 National Park Service Organic Act, discussed below, merely confirmed the purposes for which national monuments have always been reserved. Finally, [a pre-1916] priority date for reserved water rights in conserving objects not expressly covered until the 1916 Act is supported by a "relation-back" theory in Arizona v. California, supra (Lake Mead National Recreation Area given priority dates of 1929 and 1930 when executive orders withdrew lands "pending determination as to the advisability of including such lands in a national monument," though no national monument was created and Lake Mead National Recreation Area purposes were not expressly stated until 1964). This "relation-back" theory is not inconsistent with the *New Mexico* Court's view of the effect of the 1960 Multiple Use-Sustained Yield Act on national forests, since that statute indicated that the additional purposes were supplemental and subsidiary to the 1897 Organic Act purposes, while the 1916 Act merely confirmed the "fundamental purpose" for which national monuments have always been reserved. Thus, I conclude that pre-1916 national monuments receive the reserved water rights discussed above in the national park context, carrying a priority date of the date of the establishing presidential proclamation.

2. *Effect of the 1916 National Park Service Organic Act*

With the passage of the 1916 National Park Service Organic Act, the purposes of national monuments were explicitly stated for the first time:

> [T]he fundamental purpose of said * * * monuments * * * is to conserve the scenery and the natural and historic objects and the wildlife therein and to provide for the enjoyment of the same in such manner and by such means as will leave

them unimpaired for the enjoyment of future generations. [16 U.S.C.A. § 1].

As previously developed in the national park context, this statement of "fundamental purpose" incorporates the reserved water rights described above which are necessary for scenic, natural, historic and biotic conservation, and sustained public enjoyment thereof.

* * *

VI. RESERVED WATER RIGHTS IN AREAS ADMINISTERED BY THE FISH AND WILDLIFE SERVICE

The Fish and Wildlife Service (FWS) administers a number of areas to which reserved water rights may properly be ascribed. Arizona v. California, supra, at 601. Most of these areas are now components of the National Wildlife Refuge System (hereinafter "NWRS"), which consists of:

> [A]ll lands, waters, and interests therein administered by the Secretary as wildlife refuges, areas for the protection and conservation of fish and wildlife that are threatened with extinction, wildlife ranges, game ranges, wildlife management areas, or waterfowl production areas * * *.

* * *

[The Opinion discusses differing language in various executive orders establishing wildlife refuges.]

It is clear that either style of executive order creates reserved water rights to the extent "reasonably necessary to fulfill the purposes of the Refuge," since the second style language comes from Havasu Lake National Wildlife Refuge given such water rights in Arizona v. California, supra. Though the Arizona Court did not focus on purposes for the reservation, but rather on demonstrable management needs in determining the quantity of reserved water rights, subsequent refinements of the reserved water right doctrine would appear to limit such needs to the extent needed for the specific purposes of maintaining "a refuge and breeding ground for migratory birds and other wildlife." Such reserved water rights include consumptive and non-consumptive water uses necessary for the conservation of migratory birds and other wildlife (e.g., watering needs, habitat protection, ecosystem food supply, fire protection, soil and erosion control) and attendant FWS personnel needs (e.g., refuge staff domestic needs). These reserved water rights carry the priority date of the establishing executive order.

In addition to refuges created by Executive action, several refuges have been created or explicitly authorized by statute, largely within national forest boundaries. See 16 U.S.C. §§ 671–697a (1976). These statutory refuges obtain reserved water rights in waters unappropriated as of the date of enactment necessary to fulfill stated refuge purposes.

* * *

VII. NATIONAL WILD AND SCENIC RIVERS SYSTEM

The Wild and Scenic Rivers Act, 16 U.S.C. §§ 1271–1287 (1976), contains an express, though negatively phrased, assertion of federal reserved water rights:

> *Designation* of any stream or portion thereof as a national wild, scenic or recreational river area *shall* not *be construed as a reservation of the waters of such streams for purposes* other than those specified in this chapter, or *in quantities* greater than *necessary to accomplish these purposes.*[99]

The legislative history of the Wild and Scenic Rivers Act emphasizes the congressional intent to reserve unappropriated waters necessary to fulfill the Act's purposes. In explaining the conference report on the Senate floor, Senator Gaylord Nelson, a principal sponsor and floor manager of the bill in the Senate, read the following sectional analysis:

> Enactment of the bill would reserve to the United States sufficient unappropriated water flowing through Federal lands involved to accomplish the purpose of the legislation. Specifically, only that amount of water will be reserved which is reasonably necessary for the preservation and protection of those features for which a particular river is designated in accordance with the bill.

Thus, the intent to reserve unappropriated waters at the time of river designation is clear and the remaining question is the scope of the reserved water right. The previously quoted excerpt suggests that the scope question is to be resolved by examining the purposes of the Act, limited by protecting those features which led to a particular river's designation. The purposes of the Act were to implement the policy section (see 16 U.S.C. § 1272 (1970)). The policy reads in pertinent part:

> It is hereby declared to be the policy of the United States that certain selected rivers of the Nation which, with their immediate environments, possess outstandingly remarkable scenic, recreational, geologic, fish and wildlife, historic, cultural, or other similar values, shall be preserved in free-flowing condition, and that they and their immediate environments shall be

---

99. 16 U.S.C. § 1284(c) (1970) (italics added). The preceding subsec., 16 U.S.C. § 1284(b), provides: "Nothing in this chapter shall constitute an express or implied claim or denial on the part of the Federal Government as to exemption from State water laws."

The meaning of this provision is difficult to discern, especially in light of Congress' express invocation of the reserved water rights doctrine in the next subsection. Even without considering sec. 1284(c), no consistent reading of this provision appears possible. Giving literal effect to the "no implied claim * * * as to exemption from State water laws" phrase, denies the literal effect of the "no express or implied * * * denial * * * as to exemption from State water laws" phrase, and vice versa. There is no clarifying legislative history. I therefore must conclude that the provision is a *non sequitor* roughly designed to preserve the *status quo* of federal-state relations in water law under "established principles of law," including the reserved water rights doctrine. 16 U.S.C. § 1284(b).

protected for the benefit and enjoyment of present and future generations. [16 U.S.C.A. § 1271].

It is my opinion that the extent of the water reserved is the amount of unappropriated waters necessary to protect the particular aesthetic, recreational, scientific, biotic and historic features ("values") which led to the river's inclusion as a component of the National Wild and Scenic Rivers System, and to provide public enjoyment of such values.

* * *

[I]t is clear that river designation does not automatically reserve the entire unappropriated flow of the river and an examination of the individual features which led to each component river's designation must be conducted to determine the extent of the reserved water right.

VIII. NATIONAL WILDERNESS PRESERVATION SYSTEM

* * *

Wilderness area designation is undertaken for the purpose of preserving and protecting wilderness in its natural condition without permanent improvements or human habitation, to fulfill public purposes of recreation, scenic, scientific, educational, conservation, and historic use. I conclude that formally designated wilderness areas receive reserved water rights necessary to accomplish these purposes.

* * *

UNITED STATES v. CITY AND COUNTY OF DENVER
Supreme Court of Colorado, 1982.
656 P.2d 1.

[These appeals involve federal reserved water rights in three Water Divisions of Western Colorado; at issue are asserted federal water rights in seven national forests, Rocky Mountain National Park, three national monuments, 1,500 public springs on BLM lands, and two mineral hot springs. The lengthy opinion is the only reported decision on many pertinent implied reserved federal water rights issues, only a few of which are excerpted below.]

ERICKSON, Justice.

* * *

* * * In seeking to invoke the reserved rights doctrine as a basis for its claimed water rights, the United States seeks to proceed outside Colorado's prior appropriation system for the adjudication of water rights. The integration of the competing legal theories into a common, rational, and comprehensive system of water distribution marks a reconciliation between two fundamental themes in the development of this State.

The first is the role of the United States as the sovereign and proprietor of the territory which became the State of Colorado in 1876.

* * *

* * *

The other fundamental theme of Colorado's development essential to the disposition of these appeals is this State's leading role in the development of the doctrine of prior appropriation which generally governs, in one form or another, the acquisition of water rights in the nineteen western states. An essential purpose of the systematic distribution of water under Colorado law is to secure an orderly and stable society. Because of our semiarid climate, an orderly and stable legal system for the right to use water has always been a paramount concern of the people of this State and, historically, the Colorado doctrine of prior appropriation grew and developed to meet the stark necessities of our environment.

*   *   *

A. *National Forests*

*   *   *

2. *Instream Flows in National Forests*

The federal government claims that it has a reserved water right for instream water flows necessary to fulfill national forest purposes. The water court found: (1) that the United States has no instream flow rights for recreational, scenic, and wildlife protection purposes; and (2) that since the United States did not claim any instream flow rights for the Organic Act of 1897 purposes of watershed and timber protection, the court could not award such water rights. We agree with the water court's determinations.

The United States Supreme Court expressly found in United States v. New Mexico that the Organic Act of 1897 does not provide for instream flows for recreational, wildlife, and scenic purposes. The water court decision is in accordance with that interpretation of federal law. The United States has also failed to demonstrate that the instream flow right it claims is necessary to fulfill the national forest purposes. The United States has shown sparse evidence to support its claim that instream flows serve the national forest purposes of watershed and timber protection.[35] It is more likely that Congress did not wish to enlarge the consumption of water arising on national forest lands by protecting minimum instream flows when it established the national forest system in 1897.

*   *   *

Nowhere has the United States shown that without instream flows the purposes of the national forests would be defeated. On the contrary, congressional policies to further the economic development of the West would be frustrated if we were now to hold that the many private

35. The United States claims that it proved instream flows were necessary for watershed protections. One government witness stated that: "If you * * * let the stream dry up you wouldn't be fulfilling the purposes of the watershed protection." The argument that instream flows are necessary for timber protection was supported by a claim that "trees growing next to the creek * * * are going to get more water." None of these statements sup- ports a claim that the purposes of the Organic Act of 1897 can be fulfilled only by maintaining an instream minimum flow; nor do they demonstrate any congressional intent to expand federal reserved rights. See also United States v. Alpine Land & Reservoir Co., 503 F.Supp. 877 (D.Nev. 1980) (the federal government did not show a need for instream flow rights for 1897 Act purposes).

appropriators in the national forests must relinquish their long-utilized water rights to downstream appropriators so that the federal government can maintain unneeded minimum stream flows. Many public and private appropriators—cities, industries, farmers, and ranchers—have depended on water diversions from national forest lands high in the Rocky Mountains. Minimum flow rights would upset these long-held expectations in favor of junior appropriators downstream and outside the national forest reservations. We therefore find that the United States does not have an instream flow claim for reserved water rights in the national forests.

[The Colorado Supreme Court then held that, because the reserved rights doctrine should be "narrowly construed," the Multiple Use, Sustained Yield Act did not reserve any water for federal purposes.]

B. *Dinosaur National Monument*

1. *Instream Flow Rights*

The United States claims that it has a reserved instream flow water right in the Yampa River for recreational boating within Dinosaur National Monument. It argues that recreational boating is a purpose for which national monuments are established and that an implied water right exists in an amount necessary to fulfill the purpose.

* * *

National monuments may be created by presidential proclamation to preserve public lands of outstanding historic or scientific interest. 16 U.S.C. § 431 (1976). In 1915, President Wilson established Dinosaur National Monument on an eighty acre tract of Utah land for the purpose of preserving an "extraordinary deposit of Dinosaurian and other gigantic reptilian remains." Presidential Proclamation of Oct. 4, 1915, 39 Stat. 1752 (1915). In 1938, the Monument was expanded into Colorado to include canyon lands formed by the Yampa River. The 1938 proclamation noted the presence of objects of historic and scientific interest in its reservation of 200,000 Colorado acres. Moreover, the proclamation placed the Monument under the "supervision, management, and control" of the National Park Service. Presidential Proclamation of July 14, 1938, 53 Stat. 2454 (1938). * * *

To ascertain if there is an implied reservation of waters for recreational boating, we must determine whether Congress intended to establish a recreational purpose when it established the Monument. The issue is particularly important in this context because of the enormous potential economic impact of minimum stream flows on vested and conditional Colorado water rights.[44] We do not believe that Congress intended to reserve water for recreational purposes under the legislation allowing for the creation of national monuments.

---

44. Dinosaur National Monument is located at the lowest reaches of the Yampa River in Colorado. To find a reserved right to instream flow that far downstream would have a significant impact on numerous upstream users. * * *

Dinosaur National Monument was originally established to preserve impressive prehistoric fossils. There is no question that the 1915 proclamation and the underlying legislation on which it is based, the American Antiquities Preservation Act of 1906, 16 U.S.C. §§ 431 et seq. (1976), were primarily concerned with scientific and historic purposes, not recreational purposes. *See, e.g.,* H.R.Rep. No. 11016, 59th Cong., 1st Sess. (1906) (national monuments have narrower purposes than national parks). The federal government argues, however, that the provisions in the 1938 proclamation, which place management of the Monument under the National Parks Service Act of 1916, carries with it an implied reservation of water for purposes recognized under the 1916 Act. Purposes under the 1916 Act include the conservation and enjoyment of scenic, natural, and historic objects. The United States' argument places "recreational purposes" (including instream flows for river rafting) under the rubric of "enjoyment of scenic, natural, and historic objects."

We cannot accept the federal government's assertion that the National Parks Service Act expands the purposes for which national monuments are granted reservations of water. Acceptance of this argument would mean that Congress has, sub silentio, eliminated all basic distinctions between national monuments and national parks. We are, in effect, asked to treat monuments as having the same recreational and aesthetic purposes as national parks. Our review of the statutory and legislative record convinces us that Congress intended national monuments to be more limited in scope and purpose than national parks.

* * *

[The Court distinguished *Cappaert,* supra at page 374.]

We believe that Dinosaur National Monument was established for the purpose of preserving outstanding objects of historic and scientific interest. Recreational boating is not a purpose for which the 1938 acreage was implicitly or explicitly reserved. The federal government therefore is not entitled to a reserved water right for minimum stream flows in the Yampa River through Dinosaur National Monument for recreational purposes.

The water court expressed a willingness to grant some stream flows for the purpose of preserving fish habitats of historic and scientific interest. It rested its conclusions on the language of 16 U.S.C. § 1 which states that conservation of "wildlife" is a purpose for which national monuments will be administered. As we have discussed above, the National Park Service Act should not be used as a basis for expanding the monument purposes which support a reservation of water. In our view, the relevant reservation document is the presidential proclamation of 1938, which enlarged Dinosaur National Monument to protect "objects of historic and scientific interest." 53 Stat. 2454 (1938). However, the water court was correct in ordering the master-referee to determine whether the 1938 proclamation intended to reserve water for fish habitats of endangered species of historic and scientific interest, and if so, to quantify the minimal amount of water necessary to fulfill that purpose. We therefore remand to the water court for further proceedings on the issue of fish habitats.

* * *

C. *Rocky Mountain National Park*

Rocky Mountain National Park was created from previously reserved national forest lands which were transferred to the Park in 1915 and again in 1930. The water court held that the priority date of any reserved water rights for Rocky Mountain National Park was the date on which the national forest lands were transferred to national park status. The United States argues that, for reservation purposes common to national forest lands and national park lands, the priority dates should be fixed by the dates of the initial national forest reservation. We agree that the earlier date is the proper benchmark.

* * * [T]o the extent that the purposes of the national forests and national parks overlap, the federal government has reserved water rights in the amount minimally necessary to effectuate the purposes of the national forest lands. See United States v. New Mexico, supra; Cappaert v. United States, supra. Reservation of water for other purposes, however, will have a priority date from the time the national park was established.

The water court has decreed various water rights in Rocky Mountain National Park with priority dates of 1915 and 1930. The water court must reexamine its decree and award the United States water rights sufficient to meet the purposes of watershed and timber resources protection with a priority date based on the date the transferred lands were reserved to the national forests.

* * *

[The Court ruled that the United States did have reserved rights in connection with reserved public springs and waterholes, but only to the extent that "water from public springs and waterholes is available for the purposes of human and animal consumption in the amount necessary to prevent monopolization of the water resources." The Court also ruled that the federal reservation of water from mineral hot springs did carry with it any right to use the water for geothermal power production.]

NOTES

1. On remand from the decision in United States v. Denver, the water judge held that the government did not reserve minimum stream flows for preservation of fish habitats in the Yampa River within Dinosaur National Monument:

> The Presidential Proclamation of 1915, with respect to the original reservation of lands contains the following recitation:

> > "Whereas * * * there is located an extraordinary deposit of Dinosaurian and other gigantic reptilian remains of

the Juratrias period, which are of great scientific interest and value, and it appears that the public interest would be promoted by reserving these deposits as a National Monument * * *." Presidential Proclamation of October 4, 1915.

In the letter of transmittal to * * * President [Franklin Roosevelt] accompanying the proposed Proclamation, then Secretary of the Interior Harold Ickes sets out the objects of prehistoric, historic, and scientific interest which it was thought would justify the reservation under the Antiquities Act. Reference is made to the dinosaur remains and the "spectacular canyons along the Green and Yampa Rivers where the dinosaurs roamed and obtained most of their food." Reference is also made to archaeological value of caves occupied by prehistoric cave dwellers, granaries, pottery, arrowheads, monos, pictographs and other artifacts "giving evidence of the occupation of the area by prehistoric man." * * *

From the face of these documents, it appears that the primary purpose of the reservation of Dinosaur National Monument was the preservation of those specifically mentioned objects or relics of prehistoric, historic, archaeological, geological and scientific interest. The Court has examined the Toll Report prepared and compiled in 1933 and presented to the Director of National Parks, Buildings and Reservations. In that Report, Toll makes reference to scenic, scientific, geologic, biological, historical, educational, recreational, and commercial possibilities of the area. In the biological section mention is made of mountain sheep, wild horses, beaver, sage brush, cottonwood trees, pinions and junipers. No mention is made of any fish as objects of biological or scientific interest. * * *

In all of the materials generated by the government in making the determination to enlarge the Monument, only passing almost anecdotal references are made to the existence of fish. Toll, in discussing "recreational possibilities" in his 1933 Report, states simply that "there are whitefish in the Yampa River." The other reference to whitefish (which arguably could have been a reference to squawfish) was a reported conversation between McMechen and his guide concerning recreational fishing.

The Court concludes that neither the Presidential Proclamation nor the relevant underlying documents contemporaneous with its issuance suggest that fishes or other wildlife were thought by the President to be of scientific, biological, or historic importance at the time the reservation was made.

* * *

In the Matter of the Application for Water Rights of the United States of America in Dinosaur National Monument, in Moffat County, Colora-

Coggins & Wilkinson—Fed.Land & Res.Law 2nd Ed. UCB—15

do, Case No. W. 18 (Dist.Ct., Water Div. No. 6, Colo., March 14, 1985), appeal pending.

Does this record support a purpose to reserve instream flows? Is the Solicitor's Opinion correct in finding, supra at page 386, that the purposes of national monuments, as units of the National Park System, should be determined by looking to the expansive purposes set out in 16 U.S.C.A. § 1?

2. The Forest Service Manual asserts that several water uses, not addressed in United States v. New Mexico, are encompassed within the two primary purposes of the 1897 Organic Act; these include domestic use at ranger stations and other facilities; fire protection; road construction; irrigation of tree nurseries; stockwatering and pasture irrigation for Forest Service stock; and domestic use by permittees. One consent decree in Colorado recognizes those uses, which (like the rights upheld by the Colorado Supreme Court in United States v. Denver) do not involve substantial quantities of water. Much more controversial is the Forest Service's claim for reserved rights for channel maintenance, i.e., a sufficient water flow each spring to flush debris out of stream channels. The agency asserts that such flows are required to transport sediment, maintain streambank stability, and afford adequate riparian vegetation so that streams in national forests will continue to serve their function of transporting water to downstream users. The argument, which, if accepted, would result in substantial instream flows in the spring, has been rejected twice on the ground that the evidence submitted did not support the claim. See United States v. Denver, supra, 656 P.2d at 22, n. 35. United States v. Alpine Land & Reservoir Co., 697 F.2d 851, 859 (9th Cir.1983), cert. denied, 464 U.S. 863 (1983). The agency has made the same argument in several pending cases, based on much more substantial records. If the Forest Service can establish that substantial flows are necessary to protect the channel and to avoid the adverse "watershed" consequences, does the purpose of channel maintenance come within the scope of the 1897 Organic Act as construed in United States v. New Mexico?

3. United States v. Denver remains the only state court decision ruling comprehensively on federal reserved rights. Although states have jurisdiction under the McCarran Amendment, general stream adjudications are so expensive that several states have chosen not to institute them, thus deferring resolution of federal claims. When general stream adjudications are commenced, they often take years, sometimes decades, to work their way to a conclusion. Colorado is an exception, because its elaborate water court system issues a new set of updated decrees every six months. As the following case illustrates, the McCarran Amendment does not eliminate all federal jurisdiction, even in Colorado.

SIERRA CLUB v. BLOCK

United States District Court, District of Colorado, 1985.
622 F.Supp. 842.

KANE, District Judge.

I. INTRODUCTION

* * *

Sierra Club contends that federal reserved water rights exist in each of the designated wilderness areas which federal defendants administer in Colorado, and that these reserved water rights are implied from the Wilderness Act, 16 U.S.C. §§ 1131 et seq. It is further asserted that federal defendants have failed to claim these reserved water rights in violation of their duties under 16 U.S.C. § 526, the Wilderness Act, and the "public trust doctrine". Finally, Sierra Club maintains that federal defendants' failure to carry out their statutory and trust obligations is arbitrary and capricious and unlawfully withholds agency action.

* * *

III. BACKGROUND

* * *

As the legislative history and the provisions of the Wilderness Act make abundantly clear, the primary motivation of Congress in establishing the wilderness preservation system was to "guarantee that these lands will be kept in their original untouched natural state."

* * *

In preserving the natural state of the wilderness areas, Congress prohibited or seriously limited most uses inconsistent with the protection of the wilderness, such as mining, timbercutting, road-building, and other commercial uses. See 16 U.S.C. § 1133(c) and (d). In this respect, wilderness areas differ greatly from the national forests, for example, where such uses are permitted.

In Colorado, there are presently 24 areas which were originally part of the national forests but have been designated as wilderness pursuant to the Wilderness Act. It is within these areas that Sierra Club contends federal reserved water rights exist.

IV. FEDERAL RESERVED WATER RIGHTS

* * *

In determining whether there is a federally reserved water right implicit in a federal reservation of public land, the threshold question necessarily is whether the government has in fact withdrawn the land from the public domain and reserved it for a public purpose. Once it has been determined that the government has withdrawn and reserved the land, the primary issue is whether the government intended to reserve unappropriated water.

* * *

Although often used interchangeably, the terms "withdraw" and "reserve" have different meanings. "Withdrawal" generally refers to the act of removing certain lands from the operation of federal mining, homestead or other disposal and use-related laws. "Reservation", on the other hand, as stated above, generally refers to the dedication of federal lands to a specific federal purpose. The reason these terms are used interchangeably is that, usually, a reservation includes a withdrawal.

In the instant case, each of the subject wilderness areas was created from previously reserved national forest lands in Colorado. Defendant-intervenors argue that, because the lands had already been withdrawn from the public domain and reserved for national forest purposes, subsequent wilderness designation did not constitute a "withdrawal from the public domain."

* * *

Although wilderness designation was not the *original* withdrawal from the public domain and reservation of the land in this case, it does not follow that wilderness areas were not withdrawn and reserved or that the implied-reservation-of-water doctrine is not applicable. On the contrary, application of the definitions of "withdrawal" and "reservation" to this case, as well as legislative history of the Wilderness Act, clearly demonstrate that the wilderness areas were in fact withdrawn and reserved.

* * *

The fact that the Wilderness Act withdrew the designated wilderness areas from disposal or use-related laws and that it established specific purposes for the wilderness areas amply demonstrates that Congress intended that these areas be "withdrawn" and "reserved". The use of the word "reservation" * * * by members of Congress, in referring to the wilderness areas, further evidences Congress' intent to "withdraw" and "reserve" the wilderness areas. Accordingly, I hold that a withdrawal and reservation of these lands has been made.

* * *

Defendant-intervenors' contention that the Wilderness Act is merely a land management statute is similarly without merit. Defendant-intervenors attempt to liken the Wilderness Act to land management statutes such as the Federal Land Policy and Management Act (FLPMA), the Multiple-Use Sustained-Yield Act of 1960 (MUSYA), the Taylor Grazing Act, and the Wild Free-Roaming Horses & Burros Act. Defendant-intervenors overlook the fact, however, that none of these land management statutes effect a withdrawal and reservation of lands as does the Wilderness Act. The legislative history of the Wilderness Act reveals that the creation of a national wilderness preservation system was foremost in the minds of the members of Congress. Any additional provisions regarding management of wilderness areas were only incidental to the withdrawal and reservation of lands under the Act: * * * Thus, an analogy to these land-management statutes is irrelevant in this case.

In sum, the Wilderness Act does effect a withdrawal and reservation of wilderness areas to which the implied-reservation-of-water doctrine applies. Wilderness designation creates an entirely new category of lands dedicated to preservation and conservation. Wilderness is not simply a land-management status. Rather, wilderness areas are federal reservations whose status, as concerns the implied-reservation-of-water doctrine, is equal to that of other federal reservations such as national forests, parks, and monuments.

Since the Wilderness Act does effect a withdrawal and reservation of wilderness areas, the question now is whether the government intended to reserve unappropriated water in those areas. As stated previously, central to this inquiry is a careful examination of both the asserted water right and the specific purposes for which the land was reserved.

The Wilderness Act contains several congressional statements of purpose for the National Wilderness Preservation System. Under 16 U.S.C. § 1131(a), wilderness areas are designated for the purpose of "preservation and protection in their natural condition, * * * to secure for the American people of present and future generations the benefits of an enduring resource of wilderness." * * *

These purposes were emphasized again and again during the hearings and debates on the Wilderness Act.

* * *

At first blush, it would appear that the purposes of conserving water flows and providing a continuous supply of timber conflict with the conservation and recreational purposes set forth in the Wilderness Act. Defendant-intervenors argue that these purposes do conflict and that the Wilderness Act, like the MUSYA in *New Mexico,* creates only secondary purposes to which no reserved water rights can attach. Defendant-intervenors' argument ignores, however, the legislative history of the Wilderness Act. Additionally, their reliance on *New Mexico* as dispositive of this issue is misplaced because *New Mexico* is distinguishable in several respects.

First, the legislative history establishes that Congress was indeed concerned with protecting the watersheds and preserving water flows for downstream irrigation and domestic use as well as preserving the character of the wilderness and providing for recreation:

> If we do not act now to conserve our vanishing wilderness, it will soon be lost forever. The wilderness not only is important to those who love the outdoor life and the sportsmen who hunt and fish there; it is equally needed for nature studies and general scientific inquiry, and for wise watershed and wildlife conservation.

110 Cong.Rec. 5942 (statement of Sen. Church) (emphasis added). It was further stated that

> one of the purposes of the proposed legislation is to prevent a further opening up of the area, which is what has occurred in

past years, so that the scenic and wilderness values, which are the predominant values, can be preserved, and so that the wildlife and the *watershed* can be preserved as well.

110 Cong.Rec. 5895 (statement of Sen. Church) (emphasis added).

Congress was aware of the need to protect the watersheds in these mostly high alpine wilderness areas and, clearly, it intended to carry over and maintain this important purpose in the Wilderness Act. This purpose does not, however, conflict with the other purposes of the Wilderness Act. On the contrary, preservation of wilderness areas in their natural state actually enhances water quality and quantity. By protecting the natural state of the watersheds, rather than destroying their potential yield by allowing commercial development or other similar intrusions, wilderness areas improve the availability, as well as the purity, of the water for downstream users. See S.R.Rep. No. 109, 88th Cong., 1st Sess. at 15 (1963) (wilderness areas "provide watershed protection and clear, pure water for users below them").

* * *

New Mexico is distinguishable from the instant case in several respects. First, as stated above, unlike the MUSYA, the Wilderness Act is not a land-management statute. Nor does the Act constitute an attempt to *add* to the primary purposes of existing reservations, such as the national forest, as the MUSYA did in *New Mexico.* Rather, the Wilderness Act is the *initial legislation* creating an *entirely new reservation* of federal lands.

Second, as discussed above, the conservation and recreation purposes of the Wilderness Act do not conflict with the purposes of conserving water flow.

* * *

Finally, unlike *New Mexico,* both the legislative history and the Wilderness Act itself are replete with statements expressing Congress' intent that each of the purposes of the Act are primary and "crucial."

* * *

In sum, it is clear that Congress intended each of the purposes specified in the Wilderness Act to be primary, rather than secondary, in nature. For this reason, in addition to those stated above, *New Mexico* is inapposite.

Moreover, contrary to defendant-intervenors' assertions, Congress intended to reserve previously unappropriated waters in the wilderness areas to the extent necessary to accomplish these purposes. It is beyond cavil that water is the lifeblood of the wilderness areas. Without water, the wilderness would become deserted wastelands. In other words, without access to the requisite water, the very purposes for which the Wilderness Act was established would be entirely defeated. Clearly, this result was not intended by Congress. * * * Thus, I now hold that federal reserved water rights do exist in previously unappropriated water in each of the Colorado wilderness areas designated as such pursuant to the Wilderness Act and managed by federal defendants.

Insofar as the purpose of conserving water flows was originally attached to creation of the national forests, the priority of reserved rights for that purpose dates back to the original forest reservation. Reserved rights for the remaining primary purposes of the Wilderness Act vest on the date of the individual reservations or designations as wilderness.

* * *

* * * Application of the law to the established facts in this case demonstrates that these reserved water rights exist and that Sierra Club is entitled to judgment on this issue. * * *

V. STANDARD OF REVIEW

* * *

Sierra Club maintains that the Wilderness Act creates a duty on the part of federal defendants to protect all wilderness resources; particularly, reserved water rights. It is asserted that federal defendants' failure to claim federal reserved water rights in Colorado wilderness areas violates this duty, is arbitrary and capricious, and constitutes unlawfully withheld agency action under § 706. * * *

Federal defendants also seek summary judgment on this issue. Federal defendants admit that they have declined to request the Attorney General to initiate litigation claiming reserved water rights in the wilderness areas. Federal defendants contend, however, that this inaction was not arbitrary and capricious, an abuse of discretion, or otherwise unlawful under § 706 for two reasons. First, federal defendants argue that the Wilderness Act imposes no express duty to assert reserved water rights in the wilderness areas. Second, they claim a rational basis for not claiming reserved water rights because the existence of these rights was uncertain up to the time of this lawsuit.

To begin with, the Wilderness Act unequivocally imposes certain duties on the part of agencies and officials administering the wilderness areas. Sections 1131(a) and 1133(b) require that the wilderness character of these areas be protected and preserved. Further, Congress stated that these areas shall be administered "for the use and enjoyment of the American people in such manner as will leave them unimpaired for future use and enjoyment as wilderness. * * *" 16 U.S.C. § 1131(a). Finally, § 1133(b) mandates that the "wilderness areas shall be devoted to the public purposes of recreational, scenic, scientific, educational, conservation, and historical use" and that the agencies charged with administering the wilderness areas shall administer the areas for these purposes.

These mandates evince Congress' intent to impose a duty on the administering agencies to protect and preserve all wilderness resources, including water. Thus, there is a general duty under the Wilderness Act to protect and preserve wilderness water resources. There is, however, no specific *statutory* duty to claim reserved water rights in the wilderness areas even though Congress impliedly reserved such rights in order to effectuate the purposes of the Act, as discussed above.

In the absence of a clear statutory directive, I cannot say that federal defendants unlawfully withheld agency action under § 706(1). That section applies where a federal agency refuses to act in disregard of its legal duty to act. Here, there simply is no specific legal duty on the part of federal defendants to claim reserved water rights in the wilderness areas in state adjudications.

Further, absent such an explicit legal duty, I am without power to order the Attorney General to instigate litigation to claim these rights. * * * As stated in Sierra Club v. Department of the Interior, 424 F.Supp. 172 (N.D.Cal.1976),

> decisions of the Congress and/or the Executive concerning further, future, additional legislation, funds or *litigation,* involve new policy-making which is the *exclusive function* of the Congress and the Executive under the doctrine of separation of powers.

* * *

Moreover, I cannot say that federal defendants' inaction in this case was arbitrary, capricious, or otherwise unlawful under § 706(2)(A). There has been considerable controversy on the issue of whether federal reserved water rights exist in the wilderness areas. * * * Given this controversy and federal defendants' contention that they did not claim the reserved water rights because of the "uncertainty" that these rights exist, I cannot say that their decision not to claim the reserved water rights was irrational or that there was a clear error of judgment.

I can say, however, that if federal defendants had carefully analyzed the legislative history of the Wilderness Act, Congress' intent to reserve water for the wilderness areas would have been apparent. I am dismayed by federal defendants' benign neglect of this issue of federal reserved water rights in the wilderness areas as well as their failure to take any kind of action to determine whether they existed. To the extent that this benign neglect may have fostered an improper understanding of the law, federal defendants have not acted with the degree of responsibility rightfully to be expected of them. Just as clearly as judges should not inject themselves into prerogatives of the Executive, that same Executive should not ignore or disregard the intent and policy established by Congress.

Nevertheless, I find that federal defendants' failure to assert reserved water rights in the wilderness areas does not violate the provisions of the APA.

* * *

I am still obligated, however, to insure federal defendants' compliance with statutory law. Specifically, I must determine whether federal defendants' failure to assert federal reserved water rights in the wilderness areas conflicts in any way with their general statutory duty to protect wilderness water resources.

As the briefs and the administrative record show, reserved water rights is only one of several tools available to federal defendants to meet their statutory duty to protect and preserve wilderness water resources. Despite Sierra Club's attempts to prove that assertion of reserved water rights is the *only* means by which to protect the water resources, I find that the briefs and the administrative record are simply inadequate to fully evaluate this issue. Thus, I shall remand to the agencies involved to reevaluate their alternatives in light of this decision that federal reserved water rights do exist in the wilderness areas.

Now that the issue of whether reserved water rights exist in these areas has been resolved, it is necessary to give federal defendants the opportunity to consider further the usefulness of these rights in complying with their statutory duty to protect wilderness water resources. These federal defendants are required to meet clear statutory obligations. How they meet this responsibility is a matter left to their discretion. Whether they must meet this responsibility is no longer subject to dispute. In remanding this action to the federal defendants, I order them to come forward with a memorandum explaining their analysis, final decision, and plan to comply with their statutory obligations regarding protection and preservation of wilderness water resources.

VI. PUBLIC TRUST DOCTRINE

Sierra Club asserts that in addition to the statutory duties discussed above, federal defendants hold the wilderness areas in trust for the public under the "public trust doctrine" and, therefore, are charged with the duties and obligations of a trustee, including the duty to claim reserved water rights for these areas. Federal defendants have moved to dismiss this claim, pursuant to Fed.R.Civ.P. 12(b)(6), on the ground that they have no trust responsibility for the wilderness areas under the "public trust doctrine".

* * *

Under the "public trust doctrine", which is a common law concept, "[a]ll the public lands of the nation are held in trust [by the government] for the people of the whole country." Light v. United States, 220 U.S. 523, 537, (1911). Consistent with the right to use the lands for public purposes, the government has a duty under this doctrine to protect and preserve the lands for the public's common heritage.

However, "it is not for the courts to say how that trust shall be administered. That is for Congress to determine." *Light,* 220 U.S. 523, 537. Where Congress has set out statutory directives, as in the instant case, for the management and protection of public lands, those statutory duties "compris[e] *all* the responsibilities which defendants must faithfully discharge." Sierra Club v. Andrus, 487 F.Supp. 443, 449 (D.D.C.1980) (emphasis in original). Further, resort to the "public trust doctrine" as an additional remedy in this case is unnecessary given the duties already imposed by the Wilderness Act. Additionally, even if I found that the "public trust doctrine" applied and that federal defendants violated a trust duty by not claiming federal reserved water rights in the Colorado wilderness areas, as discussed above, I could not grant the relief requested by Sierra Club and order federal defendants to initiate litigation to claim those rights. Accordingly, I grant federal defendants' motion to dismiss this claim for relief.

* * *

NOTES

1. Compare New Mexico v. Aamodt, 618 F.Supp. 993 (D.N.M.1985) (no federal reserved rights to divert water for snow making and domestic use at ski area within national forest).

2. What can the Forest Service do to protect wilderness water short of asserting reserved rights in judicial proceedings? One route is the denial or conditioning of access to federal lands under the right-of-way provisions of FLPMA, 43 U.S.C.A. §§ 1761–71, which impose a duty to protect the environment. See generally Wilkinson & Anderson, Land and Resource Planning in the National Forests, 64 Or.L.Rev. 1, 235–38 (1985), discussing the use of "FLPMA flows" to require protection of fish and wildlife in conjunction with proposed water diversion projects on federal lands.

3. In Sierra Club v. Watt, 659 F.2d 203 (D.C.Cir.1981), the court denied (possibly in dictum, as justiciability was questionable) that any reserved rights attach to BLM lands:

> Appellant's argument fails because the lands administered by the BLM—and thus affected by the Land Policy Act—*constitute the public domain.* Congress did not "withdraw land from the public domain" when it passed the Land Policy Act, it merely set forth "purposes, goals and authority for the use" of the public domain.[3] Thus, no water rights were reserved by the mere fact of the Act's passage. We are in substantial agreement with the argument submitted by the Government:

>> Under the controlling decisions of the Supreme Court, the distinction between reservations and unreserved public lands is fundamental. Reserved rights attach only to the former, and then only when water is necessary to fulfill the primary purpose of the reservation. No water is reserved for uses that are merely permissive upon a reservation. *A fortiori,* then, no reserved rights arise under [the Land Policy Act], for no reservation of land is effected.

> We are also persuaded that a specific provision of the Land Policy Act precludes the construction that the Act effects a reservation of water rights. One of the savings provisions of the Act provides:

3. Indeed, the Land Policy Act contains an express provision by which BLM lands can be withdrawn, 43 U.S.C. § 1714. The BLM lands appurtenant to the water courses in issue have apparently not been withdrawn pursuant to this provision. We do not now decide whether a withdrawal pursuant to § 1714 might result in federal reserved water rights. The presence of an express withdrawal procedure in the Land Policy Act substantially bolsters the view that the passage of that Act alone did not result in a reservation of water rights.

(g) Nothing in this Act shall be construed as limiting or restricting the power and authority of the United States or—

(1) as affecting in any way any law governing appropriation or use of, or Federal right to, water on public lands;

(2) *as expanding* or diminishing *Federal* or State jurisdiction, responsibility, interests, or *rights in water resources development or control * * *.*

43 U.S.C. § 1701 (note) (emphasis added). We interpret the italicized portions of the statute to mean that no federal water rights were reserved when Congress passed the Land Policy Act. * * *

* * *

All of the lands under BLM jurisdiction have been withdrawn for various reasons at various times. FLPMA states that the public lands will be retained permanently and are to be managed for multiple use and sustained yield to achieve the purposes outlined in § 1701. Is FLPMA a de facto reservation of the BLM lands? What more must Congress do to effect a reservation of the BLM lands? Given that the basic management criteria for both national forests and public lands are virtually identical, does it make any sense that one system has implied reserved water rights and the other does not?

4. What is the actual on-the-ground impact on other water users of reserved water rights established for wilderness areas? The date of the reservation, the quantity of water reserved, and the impact of the right on other water users must be determined. For example, the court in Sierra Club v. Block held that water rights in wilderness areas vest on designation as wilderness. The quantity of reserved water would seem to be very great—possibly the entire flow of water in the streams. But the real impact is likely to be minimal: most existing wilderness areas are at high elevations in unpopulated areas, and downstream users benefit from the creation of instream flows. In these terms, what conclusions can be reached concerning national parks, future wilderness areas declared on BLM lands, wild and scenic rivers, and national wildlife refuges? It is worth noting, for example, that many wetlands providing bird habitat were established relatively early in the 20th century for the primary purpose of wildlife protection, and that they often are located in low-lying areas below irrigated farmland using water from creeks feeding into the refuges.

3. CONGRESSIONALLY–DELEGATED CONTROL OVER WATER

Leaving aside water rights expressly or impliedly reserved by statute, can a land management agency appropriate unappropriated water (thus not disturbing any existing vested rights) if the kind of water right claimed by the United States is not recognized by state law? Must the federal government comply with all state filing requirements?

The 1979 Solicitor's Opinion, supra, written by then-Solicitor Leo Krulitz, concluded that the federal government is not bound by state definitions of diversion and beneficial use, and can exercise what the opinion termed "non-reserved rights": "Federal agencies [can make] some water uses that neither comply with state law nor can be justified under the reservation doctrine. The power of Federal agencies to make such uses cannot be denied under the Supremacy Clause, if the water has been taken through the exercise of constitutional power." 86 I.D. at 574–75. A similar conclusion was reached in Note, Federal Acquisition of Non-Reserved Water Rights After *New Mexico,* 31 Stan.L.Rev. 885 (1979). Another writer criticized the Solicitor's Opinion as "advocacy," arguing that the position on non-reserved rights is "flawed" and that the practical effects would be "disastrous." Comment, Federal Non-Reserved Water Rights, XV Land & Water L.Rev. 68 (1980).

The 1979 opinion generated a series of subsequent administrative statements on the subject. Krulitz' successor, Solicitor Clyde Martz, issued a supplemental opinion limiting the scope of federal non-reserved water rights as set out in the 1979 opinion. Martz recognized congressional authority to endow federal land agencies with authority to establish water rights outside of state law, but concluded that FLPMA accomplished no such delegation. 88 I.D. 253 (1981). The new Reagan Administration Interior Solicitor William Coldiron then issued yet another opinion, which disclaimed the existence of non-reserved rights altogether. 88 I.D. 1055 (1981). According to the Coldiron opinion, Congress granted the states exclusive sovereignty over the control of rights to use non-navigable waters when it admitted states into the Union. All rights must be acquired in accordance with state laws. The only exceptions are federal reserved rights and the navigation servitude. The western water establishment, never one to understate the evils of federal incursions into state water prerogatives, proclaimed that "the nightmare is over." See Shurts, FLPMA, Fish and Wildlife, and Federal Water Rights, 15 Envtl.L. 115 (1985).

The Department of Justice then issued its own opinion on federal non-reserved water rights. U.S. Dept. of Justice, Office of Legal Counsel, Federal "Non-Reserved" Water Rights (June 16, 1982). The Justice Department opinion, quoted in the following excerpt, treated the question as a matter of federal preemption and construction of the specific legislation that assertedly delegated the authority.

CHARLES F. WILKINSON & H. MICHAEL ANDERSON, LAND AND RESOURCE PLANNING IN THE NATIONAL FORESTS *
64 Or.L.Rev. 1 (1985).

The reserved rights doctrine is one method of federal control over water consumption on federal lands, including national forests. Congress, by reserving water, preempts water allocation under state law to

* Reprinted with the permission of the
Oregon Law Review.

the extent that a certain quantity of water is necessary to achieve the purposes of the reservation. A different approach is the congressional delegation of the authority to protect the purposes for which land is administered by federal agencies. Congress has the power both to control water use on the public lands without deferring to state law and to delegate such power to federal land management agencies. The inquiry is whether Congress in fact has made such a delegation as part of the organic authority of a particular agency.

* * *

The issue of whether federal land management agencies can set instream flows for nonconsumptive purposes such as recreation and wildlife preservation has generated considerable commentary in federal administrative opinions and in legal literature. Although the phrase "non-reserved" rights has been used to describe such administrative authority, the term is singularly unhelpful: by phrasing the concept in the negative, the term "non-reserved" rights lacks content. Most water rights are "non-reserved." Water rights established by the Supreme Court in equitable apportionment cases or by the Secretary of the Interior pursuant to the power of congressional apportionment are "non-reserved" rights, as are water rights established under state law.

The Forest Service's power to set instream flows is better described—and understood—simply as a congressional delegation of authority over water resources within the agency's jurisdiction. There is no connection with the reserved rights doctrine except that the ultimate source of authority is lodged in Congress.

It is useful to compare the reserved rights claimed by the federal government in *United States v. New Mexico* with the rights asserted under the Forest Service's delegated power. In *New Mexico,* the Forest Service argued for a far-flung system of minimum stream flows that would apply to every watercourse within all national forests. * * * [T]he Forest Service claimed a priority dating back to 1897, when the Organic Act was passed, or to the date that a forest was subsequently added to the system. * * *

* * *

In contrast, instream flows set pursuant to delegated administrative authority are conceptually different and the actual impacts are much more modest. Instream flows established by delegated authority are site-specific and prospective. The Forest Service, managing water much like any other resource pursuant to the agency's broad authority, would take action on a particular stream only when its planning process showed a need to protect that resource. If the stream flow were dangerously low, the agency would proceed according to administrative rules. It would give notice to the public, including the state water agency, that it is considering the establishment of a minimum instream flow of a specific quantity of water at specific times of the year for the particular stream. Importantly, the priority date would be the date of the public notice. The agency would take action only after public hearings. Thus, no existing rights would be affected by these prospective rights and all potential future users would be given notice.

Delegated administrative authority to set instream flows is a logical and essential aspect of the Forest Service's organic authority to manage its lands on a multiple-use basis. Several western states lack instream flow programs, while others are moving slowly to establish instream flows. The Forest Service, however, has an independent statutory mandate to manage the wildlife and recreation resources on all national forest lands.

The notion that Congress has delegated authority to the Forest Service to make site-specific, future-looking decisions follows from the case law. Although Congress has traditionally deferred to state water law, Congress also has delegated to the Forest Service expansive management authority over diverse activities under the 1897 Organic Act's mandate [in 16 U.S.C.A. § 551] to regulate "occupancy and use" in the national forests. As early as 1911, the Court recognized delegated administrative authority that allowed the Forest Service to override state fencing laws. Fencing laws, like state water laws, are deeply engrained in the West. Yet the agency's power to regulate was found in the "occupancy and use" directive. More recently, delegated administrative authority has permitted federal regulation of wildlife, a traditional prerogative of the states. Forest Service regulatory authority also was confirmed in the controversial domain of hardrock mining, another area with strong traditions of local control. Forest Service delegated authority over water resources is fortified by the highly specific provision in the 1897 Organic Act that "waters within the boundaries of national forests may be used * * * under the laws of the State or under the laws of the United States and the rules and regulations established thereunder." [1238]

Ultimately, the question is whether the congressionally defined management purposes for the national forests are broad enough to encompass the kinds of control over water discussed here. Whatever the law may be with regard to the Bureau of Land Management, it is certain that the Forest Service's organic statutes define a considerably broader scope of agency authority. The most extensive administrative opinion on the subject, issued in 1981 by the Department of Justice, acknowledged Congress's authority to preempt state law by delegating authority over water matters to federal agencies and recognized that the question boils down to the construction of each land management agency's statutory authorization:

> Federal water rights may be asserted without regard to state law [through] specific congressional directives that override inconsistent state law, and the establishment of primary purposes for the management of federal lands * * * that would be frustrated by the application of state law.

The issue is not free from uncertainty, but a principled analysis supports the conclusion that the Forest Service possesses delegated authority to set instream flows on designated watercourses.

* * *

1238. 16 U.S.C. § 481 (1982). * * *.

NOTES

1. Dean Trelease disagrees, at least as to BLM lands, acknowledging federal supremacy but arguing that Congress has intended to defer to state law and has delegated no such authority. He also suggests that judicial rulings to the contrary might well be overridden by westerners' public will: "I think it very likely that the federal non-reserved right to appropriate instream flows on the public domain without regard to state law will have a short life. But if I am wrong on the law of federalism and the Solicitor's arguments [in the 1979 decision] carry the day in court, other voices might carry the day in Congress." Trelease, Uneasy Federalism—State Water Laws and National Water Uses, 55 Wash.L.Rev. 751, 774 (1980).

2. No federal statute expressly delegates to any land management agency the authority to establish water rights unilaterally as a matter of federal law. On the other hand, the organic statutes of the principal agencies all require, in varying language, that the agencies protect fish and wildlife and encourage outdoor recreation. Given the traditional dominance of state control over water, does the BLM have delegated authority to set instream flows with a modern priority date? Does the Forest Service or the Park Service? Does the result change, for each of those agencies, when it is managing a wilderness area under the Wilderness Act? When it is managing a segment of a river under the Wild and Scenic Rivers Act?

3. The BLM is engaged in litigation involving yet another breed of federal water right. The agency applied to the Nevada State Engineer for a state permit granting it minimum instream flows in the tributaries feeding Blue Lakes, a series of high mountain lakes in northwestern Nevada, in order to protect fishing, swimming, and boating. Nevada state law does not recognize instream rights. To the surprise of most observers, the State Engineer granted the BLM a state permit, reasoning that the state could not limit the BLM's federal statutory duty to protect all multiple uses. In the Matter of Applications 36414, et al. (July 26, 1985). Nevada agricultural and grazing interests were not happy with the State Engineer's decision and have challenged the ruling in eight separate lawsuits in various Nevada state courts. Whither the Sagebrush Rebellion?

NOTE: FEDERAL WATER RESOURCES DEVELOPMENT

The federal government influences national water policy in numerous ways that do not necessarily involve public land law, but which often complicate resource decisions on the federal lands. Space and relevancy considerations prevent in-depth consideration of legal problems stemming from projects for reclamation, flood control, navigation, recreation, hydropower, and other purposes, but a summary to provide perspective is in order.

1. *Reclamation.* The nineteenth century homestead policy initially dovetailed with the twentieth century reclamation policy. The

biggest homesteading years in terms of patent issuance occurred after
the passage of the Reclamation Act of 1902. The face of the West has
been fundamentally reshaped by the large reclamation dams that
supply subsidized federal water to western irrigators, large and small.
See supra at page 128.

2. *Power Production and Flood Control.* The federal government
has been in charge of maintaining navigability since the beginning of
the Republic. The federal power over navigation is plenary and virtually unlimited. Gibbons v. Ogden, 22 U.S. (9 Wheat.) 1 (1824); 2
WATERS AND WATER RIGHTS 5–15 (R. Clark ed., 1967). The
narrow authority to prevent obstructions to navigation in the Rivers
and Harbors Act of 1899, 33 U.S.C.A. §§ 403–07, has grown into a large-
scale series of programs for water resources regulation and flood
control administered by several federal agencies.

Beginning in 1920, the federal government assumed control over
hydroelectric generation. Federal Power Act, 16 U.S.C.A. §§ 790 et
seq. The FPC, before it was absorbed into the Department of Energy,
both built its own facilities and licensed private developments. The
issue of federal power to do so, even in contravention of state law and
state desires, was decided in FPC v. Oregon, supra at page 370.

Courts have read the Federal Power Act broadly to deny or delay
projects. See Udall v. FPC, 387 U.S. 428 (1967). In Namekagon Hydro
Co. v. FPC, 216 F.2d 509 (7th Cir.1954), the court upheld the denial of a
license for a dam and hydroelectric project on the ground that 6½ miles
of a 22-mile stretch of a highly scenic river would be flooded. In Scenic
Hudson Preservation Conference v. FPC, 354 F.2d 608 (2d Cir.1965), the
court remanded a proceeding on a license for a pumped storage facility
because the FPC had not "probe[d] all feasible alternatives," which the
court found to be a requirement of Section 10(a) of the Federal Power
Act, 16 U.S.C.A. § 803(a): "The Commission's renewed proceedings
must include as a basic concern the preservation of natural beauty and
of national historic shrines, keeping in mind that, in our affluent
society, the cost of a project is only one of several factors to be
considered." But the licence issued in the end. Scenic Hudson Preservation Conference v. FPC, 453 F.2d 463 (2d Cir.1971), cert. denied, 407
U.S. 926 (1972). A hydroelectric project was allowed to proceed on the
New River in North Carolina even though the Secretary of Interior was
considering the area for inclusion in the Wild and Scenic Rivers
System. North Carolina v. FPC, 533 F.2d 702 (D.C.Cir.1976), vacated
and remanded, 429 U.S. 891 (1978).

In the Pacific Northwest, 31 dams, most of them federal, have been
constructed on the Columbia River and its major tributaries. The
primary purpose was to provide inexpensive hydroelectric power, but
these dams also supply irrigation water, control floods, and provide
recreation benefits. The development has been devastating to the
Columbia's bountiful natural salmon and steelhead runs. Young fish
migrating toward the sea have been ground up in turbine generators,
and adult fish returning upstream to spawn have been killed by

nitrogen supersaturation, the same phenomenon that causes the "bends" in deepsea divers. Even with fish ladders, the dams pose formidable obstacles to the migrating fish. Mitigation attempts of many kinds have been made, but even some considerable successes have done little to still the outcries of the commercial and sport fisheries, Indian tribes, state agencies, and environmental groups. See Wilkinson & Conner, The Law of the Pacific Salmon Fishery: Conservation and Allocation of a Transboundary Common Property Resource, 32 Kan.L.Rev. 17 (1983).

In 1980 Congress passed the Pacific Northwest Electric Power Planning and Conservation Act, 16 U.S.C.A. § 838–839h. The Act authorizes the Bonneville Power Administration (BPA) to reallocate limited supplies of federally produced hydropower generated by Columbia River dams and to acquire power resources from non-federal entities. The Act restricts BPA authority to expand generating capacity: resource acquisition will be governed by a regional power planning and conservation plan developed by a new interstate Regional Council. The Council, which is not a federal agency, is composed of two members each from Oregon, Washington, Idaho, and Montana.

The regional energy plan gives first priority to conservation measures, second to renewable resources, third to processes that use waste heat ("cogeneration"), and fourth to thermal power plants. In addition,

> even more unique than the priority the Act accords to conservation and renewable resources is its concern for revitalization of Columbia basin fish and wildlife that have been adversely affected by construction and operation of regional hydroelectric power projects. The Act directs the Regional Council to develop a comprehensive program to protect, mitigate and enhance fish and wildlife resources. This feature * * * belatedly eleva[tes] fish and wildlife considerations to equal status with the other purposes for which Columbia Basin Water projects are operated.

Blumm and Johnson, Promising a Process for Parity: The Pacific Northwest Electric Power Planning and Conservation Act and Anadromous Fish Protection, 11 Envtl.Law 497 (1981). See also Blumm, Fulfilling the Parity Promise: A Perspective on Scientific Proof, Economic Cost, and Indian Treaty Rights in the Approval of the Columbia Basin Fish and Wildlife Program, 13 Envtl.Law 103 (1982). The Act is the subject of Symposium, 13 Envtl.L. Nos. 3 & 4 (1983).

3. *Environmental Protection.* Under section 404 of the Clean Water Act, the Army Corps of Engineers must issue a permit for the discharge of dredged or fill materials into "navigable waters," defined in the Act as "the waters of the United States." See 33 U.S.C.A. §§ 1311, 1344, 1362. Corps regulations, which defined "waters" as including freshwater wetlands, were upheld in United States v. Riverside Bayview Homes, Inc., 106 S.Ct. 455 (1985). In considering permit applications, the Corps must consider effects of the proposed project on endangered species many miles downstream. Riverside Irrig. Dist. v.

Andrews, 758 F.2d 508 (10th Cir.1985). In addition to this comprehensive regulatory program, the Corps also has undertaken a massive water development agenda through dams and channel improvements. Flood control is the primary raison d'etre for Corps projects, see 33 U.S. C.A. § 701 et seq., although the agency also operates several large reclamation projects. Land acquired by the Corps for projects, of course, becomes public land and is administered primarily for recreation. Hundreds of water resources projects have been challenged in court, usually on NEPA grounds. See generally W. Rodgers, ENVIRONMENTAL LAW Ch. 7 (1977). In Trout Unlimited v. Morton, 509 F.2d 1276 (9th Cir.1974), the court held that the EIS on the Teton Dam, although far from perfect, was not so flawed as to justify judicial relief: thereafter the Teton Dam burst, killing several people and causing millions of dollars of property damage.

In times of water scarcity, allocation of water from federal dams can pose thorny issues. In County of Trinity v. Andrus, 438 F.Supp. 1368 (E.D.Cal.1977), for instance, the County sought to force the Bureau of Reclamation to release water downstream to preserve salmon and steelhead habitat instead of diverting it to irrigation uses. The court held that the statutory phrase, "the Secretary is authorized and directed to adopt appropriate measures to insure the preservation of fish and wildlife," allowed the Bureau to balance other factors against the fish habitat preservation, and refused any relief. This decision was handed down before TVA v. Hill, 437 U.S. 153 (1978), infra at page 785, construing a somewhat similar statutory command. Other cases involving allocation of reclamation water include EDF v. Andrus, 596 F.2d 848 (9th Cir.1979) (EIS required before allocation to nonirrigation users); City of Santa Clara v. Kleppe, 418 F.Supp. 1243 (N.D.Cal.1976).

Endangered Species Act constraints have halted several water developments, at least temporarily. TVA v. Hill, supra; Riverside Irrig. Dist. v. Andrews, supra; Carson-Truckee Water Conservancy Dist. v. Clark, 741 F.2d 257 (9th Cir.1984), cert. denied, 105 S.Ct. 1842 (1985) (Interior Department, in operating dam, may devote to endangered species protection all water not contracted for). See generally Tarlock, The Endangered Species Act and Western Water Rights, 20 Land & Water L.Rev. 3 (1985).

Other major developments in the state courts also highlight the sharply increased emphasis on the protection of nonconsumptive water uses. See supra at page 360. Of particular importance is National Audubon Society v. Superior Court, 33 Cal.3d 419, 189 Cal.Rptr. 346, 658 P.2d 709 (1983), supra at page 303, in which the court found that the public trust doctrine imposes limits on water diversions. Since federal water projects are subject to state law in a number of contexts, California v. United States, 438 U.S. 645 (1978), the *Mono Lake* decision could herald yet another limitation on the operation of such projects.

B. WATERSHED MANAGEMENT

NORTHWEST INDIAN CEMETERY PROTECTIVE ASSOCIATION v. PETERSON

United States Court of Appeals, Ninth Circuit, 1985.
764 F.2d 581.

CANBY, Circuit Judge:

These consolidated actions contest the plans of the United States Forest Service (Forest Service) to permit timber harvesting and to construct a road in the Blue Creek Unit of the Six Rivers National Forest in California. The Blue Creek Unit consists of 76,500 acres located in the Siskiyou Mountains. The Forest Service has inventoried approximately 31,500 of these acres as a roadless area. On its northern boundary, the Blue Creek Unit adjoins the Eightmile and Siskiyou inventoried roadless areas. Blue Creek, the stream after which the Unit was named, flows into the Klamath River and contains important spawning habitat for several anadromous fish species.

Contained within the Blue Creek Unit is a segment of land known as the "high country," which is considered sacred by Yurok, Karok, and Tolowa Indians who live in the surrounding region. Although the Indians use specific sites within the Blue Creek Unit for prayer and religious uses, the sacred area encompasses an entire region.

In 1972, the Forest Service began to prepare a multiple-use management plan and environmental impact statement (EIS) for the management of the Blue Creek and Eightmile Planning Units within the Six Rivers National Forest. In 1974 and 1975, the Forest Service circulated a draft, supplemental draft and final EIS which proposed various land use management plans for the Blue Creek Unit. In 1981, the "Blue Creek Unit Implementation Plan" (Management Plan) proposed to permit harvesting of 733 million board feet of Douglas fir from the Blue Creek Unit over an 80 year period.

In 1977, the Forest Service issued another draft EIS that proposed various alternative routes to complete construction of the last 6.02 miles (Chimney Rock Section) of a paved road from Gasquet, California to Orleans, California (G–O Road). In 1982, the final EIS was issued for the proposed construction of the Chimney Rock Section through the Blue Creek Unit.

Plaintiffs objected to both proposed projects and, after exhausting administrative remedies, filed these actions in the district court. * * * The complaints alleged that the Forest Service decisions to construct the Chimney Rock Section of road and to timber the Blue Creek Unit violated: (1) the first amendment of the United States Constitution; (2) the American Indian Freedom of Religion Act of 1978 (AIFRA), 42 U.S.C. § 1996; (3) the National Environmental Policy Act (NEPA), 42 U.S.C. § 4321 et seq., and the Wilderness Act, 16 U.S.C. § 1131 et seq.; (4) the Federal Water Pollution Control Act (FWPCA), 33 U.S.C. § 1251 et seq.; (5) water and fishing rights reserved to

American Indians on the Hoopa Valley Indian Reservation, and defendants' trust responsibility to protect those rights; (6) the Administrative Procedure Act (APA), 5 U.S.C. § 706; (7) the Multiple-Use Sustained-Yield Act, 16 U.S.C. §§ 528–531; and (8) the National Forest Management Act of 1976, 16 U.S.C. § 1600 et seq.

* * *

The district court * * * issued an injunction: (1) preventing construction of the G–O road and any timber harvesting or construction of logging roads in the high country; (2) preventing timber harvesting or construction of logging roads in the Blue Creek Roadless Area until an EIS was prepared evaluating its wilderness potential as part of adjoining roadless areas; and (3) enjoining timber harvesting and construction of logging roads anywhere in the Blue Creek Unit until an EIS was prepared specifying adequate measures to mitigate the impact of those activities on water quality and fish habitat in Blue Creek, and until studies were completed demonstrating that the proposed logging activities would not violate the FWPCA or reduce the supply of anadromous fish to the Hoopa Valley Indian Reservation. The government appeals.

ISSUES

On this appeal we address the following issues raised by the Forest Service:

(1) Whether the district court erred in enjoining road construction and timbering in the high country of the Blue Creek Unit on the ground that such activity would impermissibly burden the Indian plaintiffs' first amendment right to the free exercise of their religion;

(2) Whether the district court erred in holding that the EISs prepared for the road and land management plans failed adequately to discuss the effects on water quality of the proposed actions;

(3) Whether the district court erred in holding that the Forest Service's proposed actions would violate the Federal Water Pollution Control Act and state water quality standards.

DISCUSSION

I. *First Amendment*

[The court held that the Forest Service roading and logging proposal violated the Indians' free exercise rights and that the trial court's findings of fact with regard to the absence of a compelling governmental interest were not clearly erroneous.]

* * *

II. *Adequacy of the Environmental Impact Statements*

* * *

B. *Project Effects on Water Quality*

The district court found that the Chimney Rock draft and final EISs were inadequate because: (1) they failed sufficiently to disclose the impact of the road construction on water quality; (2) they failed to discuss the cumulative impact of the road construction and implementation of the Management Plan on water quality; and (3) they failed adequately to describe what measures would be taken to mitigate adverse impacts on water quality. In addition, the district court found that the draft, supplemental draft, and final EISs prepared for the Blue Creek Management Plan inadequately described measures to mitigate adverse impacts on water quality in Blue Creek.

The government does not take issue with the legal standards applied to the EISs by the district court. Rather, it contends that the Chimney Rock draft and final EISs do address erosion and sedimentation problems relative to road construction. It also argues that cumulative sedimentation effects on water quality and fishlife are disclosed in the 1975 Blue Creek EIS for both the Chimney Rock Section and the proposed Management Plan and that it was unnecessary to readdress them in the Chimney Rock EISs. Further, it claims that the EISs do identify specific mitigation measures.

1. *Impact of Road Construction on Water Quality*

The draft and final EISs prepared for the Chimney Rock Section do address erosion and sedimentation effects of road construction on Blue Creek. The EISs state that total increased sedimentation would raise the sedimentation yield in Blue Creek by 5.5 percent, resulting in only a "small decrease" in water quality. The EISs do not, however, address increased sedimentation contributed by road-caused landslides, because of the difficulty inherent in predicting such slope failures. Thus, the potential risks to water quality stemming from the uncertainty in predicting landslides are ignored in the discussion of sedimentation effects. These risks must be revealed if they appear substantial.

The district court found that landslide risks were substantial and that debris from landslides triggered by the road construction would result in as much as a 500% increase in sediment loads in Blue Creek. These findings are not clearly erroneous. The failure to disclose such risks in the EISs renders them inadequate.

2. *Cumulative Sedimentation Effects on Water Quality*

The district court was correct in finding that the Chimney Rock EISs do not address cumulative sedimentation effects on water quality arising from the proposed road and timber projects. Nor did the district court ignore the 1975 Blue Creek EIS, which the government contends does address cumulative effects.

The Blue Creek EIS does not adequately discuss cumulative effects because there the effects were judged as "average" increases in sediment over a period of years. State water quality standards, however, pertain to individual amounts of turbidity at a particular time and are not written in terms of averages over years. The discussion of cumulative effects in the Blue Creek EIS is therefore inadequate and likely underestimates the actual cumulative effects of both projects on water quality.

The district court's finding that the EISs do not contain an adequate discussion of the cumulative effects of both projects on water quality is consequently not clearly erroneous.

3. *Mitigation Measures*

The applicable regulations require that an EIS discuss "[m]eans to mitigate adverse environmental impacts" of the proposed action. 40 C.F.R. § 1502.16(h). The Chimney Rock and Blue Creek EISs discuss mitigation measures in part, but neither EIS analyzes the mitigation measures in detail or explains how effective the measures would be. A mere listing of mitigation measures is insufficient to qualify as the reasoned discussion required by NEPA. The district court's conclusion that the EISs are inadequate for this reason is sound.

III. FWPCA

The Federal Water Pollution Control Act requires each state to implement its own water quality standards with which federal agencies must comply. See 33 U.S.C. §§ 1313, 1323. The North Coast Regional Water Quality Control Board in California determines water quality standards for the Blue Creek area. See Water Quality Control Plan for Klamath River Basin 1–A (208 Plan). This 208 Plan provides that "[t]urbidity shall not be increased more than 20 percent above naturally occurring background levels." Further, it provides that "[t]he suspended sediment load and suspended discharge rate of surface waters shall not be altered in such a manner as to cause nuisance or adversely affect beneficial uses." The government challenges the district court's ruling that implementation of the Management Plan and construction of the Chimney Rock Section would violate FWPCA because either activity would increase turbidity and suspended sediment levels above the 20 percent ceiling level established by the 208 Plan.

The government first argues that the standards established in the 208 Plan are no longer applicable to the Forest Service. It contends that these standards were superseded by California's and EPA's acceptance of Forest Service Best Management Practices (BMPs). The government claims that these BMPs are the applicable water quality standards for the Forest Service.

The BMPs, however, are merely a means to achieve the appropriate state 208 Plan water quality standards. There is no indication in the 208 Plan or in the agreements between the Forest Service and the Water Quality Control Board that the BMPs were to be considered standards in and of themselves. Adherence to the BMPs does not automatically assure compliance. In fact, the federal statute contemplates that any activity conducted pursuant to a BMP can be terminated or modified if a change in that activity requires a stricter BMP. See

33 U.S.C. § 1288(b)(4)(B)(iv)(II). Of course, a stricter BMP would be required if, as here, the conducted activity resulted in a violation of state water quality standards.

The government's second argument is that even if the state 208 Plan standards are applicable, FWPCA requires only that state plans include "procedures and methods * * * to control [silviculturally related nonpoint source pollution] to the extent feasible." See 33 U.S.C. § 1288(b)(2)(F)(ii). It claims that the BMPs ensure that the contemplated activities will be conducted in a manner which will prevent pollution to the extent feasible. It argues that so long as the BMPs are utilized, there is no violation of the state water quality standards.

This argument is but a variation of the one before, and fails for the same reasons. Adherence to the BMPs does not automatically ensure that the applicable state standards are being met. The district court found that the state standards would be violated if the Forest Service projects were implemented as described in the EISs. This finding is not clearly erroneous.

* * *

V. *Conclusion*

We vacate those portions of the district court's order that enjoin defendants from harvesting timber or constructing logging roads until they have (1) prepared an EIS evaluating the wilderness potential of the Blue Creek Area together with the Eight-mile and Siskiyou Roadless Areas; and (2) completed studies demonstrating the proposed logging activities would not reduce the supply of anadromous fish in those portions of the Klamath River that flow through the Hoopa Valley Indian Reservation.

In all other respects the decree of the district court is affirmed.

NOTES

1. Forest Service logging activities causing erosion were also found violative of NEPA in National Wildlife Federation v. United States Forest Service, 592 F.Supp. 931 (D.Or.1984), appeal pending, *infra* at page 651. The litigation involved anadromous fish habitat in the Mapleton Ranger District in Oregon's Siuslaw National Forest. The district court held that NEPA requires site-specific environmental analysis for timber harvesting in the Mapleton Ranger District because the region's high concentration of high-risk and landslide-prone land varies significantly from the rest of the national forest. The court also ordered a "worst case analysis" in the EIS because the facts upon which the Forest Service must rely were uncertain.

2. Three aspects of the Clean Water Act (referred to as the FWPCA in *Northwest Indian Cemetery*), 33 U.S.C.A. §§ 1251–1376, bear on public land watershed management. See generally W. Rodgers, ENVIRONMENTAL LAW 354–61 (1977), 187–205 (1984 Supp.). First, section 402 (33 U.S.C.A. § 1342) requires a permit for the discharge of a

pollutant from a point source into the waters of the United States. Point sources include pipes, ditches, channels, tunnels, and conduits. Id. § 1362(14). Current regulations exclude most grazing and logging activities. 40 C.F.R. § 122.27(b) (1985). Point source permits are issued either by the Environmental Protection Agency or by the states, and federal agencies must comply with state requirements. 33 U.S.C.A. § 1323. Second, under section 404 (33 U.S.C.A. § 1344) the Army Corps of Engineers issues dredge and fill permits. See supra page 411.

Third, section 208 (33 U.S.C.A. § 1288), involved in *Northwest Indian Cemetery*, deals with nonpoint sources of pollution. The Act mandates states to prepare water quality management plans to combat nonpoint pollution, but planning is moving slowly in most instances. Logging and grazing operations are the principal sources of nonpoint pollution on federal lands. In many cases—although not, as the principal case shows, in California—the states have exercised their authority to regulate nonpoint pollution on the public lands sparingly; usually federal-state memoranda of understanding simply provide that the federal agencies will take responsibility for controlling nonpoint pollution within their jurisdictions. The Forest Service has additional obligations under the NFMA to protect riparian areas. 16 U.S.C.A. §§ 1604(a)(3)(E), 1604(a)(3)(F). See generally Wilkinson & Anderson, Land and Resource Planning in the National Forests, 64 Or.L.Rev. 1, 217–255 (1985), and the authorities cited there.

3. Leaving aside the technicalities of the Clean Water Act—which, mercifully, are beyond the scope of this book—what is the proper allocation of authority over water pollution on the public lands? Should the states have the right to assume primary authority, as they do on other land areas within their borders? Should authority be vested in either the state or federal agency in the first instance, with the other having power to impose more stringent standards? Is NEPA, as construed in *National Indian Cemetery*, a sufficient mechanism to insure that the federal land agencies will avoid water pollution from the operations they authorize? Should erosion on the public lands be treated as a water pollution matter or as a land management issue?

Chapter Six

THE MINERAL RESOURCE

Mining legally is the most preferred intensive economic use of the public lands. Marshall's 1848 discovery of gold in the California foothills prompted an immediate run on federal resources—not only on hardrock minerals but also on the water, timber, and land that were necessary to sustain mining operations. The availability of minerals from the public lands is often seen as the key to national mineral policy; public debates still rage over regulation of mining to prevent or diminish its adverse effects on other resources and amenities. In a few instances, such as the establishment of the Naval Petroleum Reserves, the federal government has retained control of mineral resources for its own use. In nearly all other cases, however, the focus of dispute is on the acquisition of private rights in minerals, and the government is not involved in their disposition thereafter.

Earlier chapters have highlighted general principles of federal lands and resources law that grew out of and still apply to federal mining law. As an historical matter, mining law started as state law (Hicks v. Bell, 3 Cal. 219 (1853), supra at page 192), which in turn derived from local custom (Morton v. Solombo Mining Co., 26 Cal. 527 (1864), supra at page 103), until the 1872 mining law absorbed it. For many years thereafter, the constant tension between the federal drive to develop mineral resources and the federal government's need to use them itself led to the great withdrawal controversies culminating in United States v. Midwest Oil Co., 236 U.S. 459 (1915), supra at page 147, and in the Mineral Leasing Act of 1920. The withdrawal problem continues, but the questions of preemption of state regulation (evidenced in, e.g., Gulf Oil Corp. v. Wyoming Oil and Gas Comm'n, 693 P.2d 227 (Wyo.1985), supra at page 221), have come to the fore. Also newly prominent are federal planning statutes, most notably NEPA, FLPMA, and NFMA. The Court in Kleppe v. Sierra Club, 427 U.S. 390 (1976), supra at page 323, cleared the way for resumption of federal coal leasing, but the decision in NRDC v. Hughes, 437 F.Supp. 981 (D.D.C.1977), supra at page 333, blocked it again. From those broad themes, this chapter moves to more detailed consideration of hardrock mining and mineral leasing.

The first section of this chapter deals with the General Mining Law of 1872. It is a political symbol as well as the legal means for obtaining public hardrock minerals: as the most prominent of the free disposition laws still on the books, it is seen as the embodiment of frontier free enterprise. Section B examines the separate and contrasting system, generally called mineral leasing, for the disposition of fuel minerals. Since 1920, federal statutes governing oil shale, coal, oil and gas, and geothermal energy have retained federal ownership and control of the land overlying those resources. The final section includes materials on federal reservations of minerals, both hardrock and leasable, in which the United States retained subsurface rights to minerals underlying lands now in private ownership.

A. HARDROCK MINERALS: THE GENERAL MINING LAW OF 1872

Except as otherwise provided, all valuable mineral deposits in lands belonging to the United States, both surveyed and unsurveyed, shall be free and open to exploration and purchase, and the lands in which they are found to occupation and purchase, by citizens of the United States and those who have declared their intention to become such, under regulations prescribed by law, and according to the local customs or rules of miners in the several mining districts, so far as the same are applicable and not inconsistent with the laws of the United States. 30 U.S.C.A. § 22.

In essence, the General Mining Law of 1872 declares that whoever discovers and develops a valuable mineral deposit may mine that deposit virtually free of charge and competition; the miner also has the right to receive a free patent to the land above the deposit. The mineral location system is based on self-initiation, and the miner needs no federal license or grant of permission to prospect and mine other than the words of the "Hardrock" Act. The 1872 Act effectively zoned nearly all of the public lands for hardrock mining.

Other considerations have gradually combined to obscure the statutory simplicity. The right accorded the discoverer has become less absolute as lands are withdrawn, access and development are conditioned, and ancient statutes reinterpreted. Repeal of the 1872 Act is advocated periodically, most recently by President Carter, but no such attempt has yet succeeded.

While *prospecting,* and before discovery, the miner is protected in his occupation of the land by the doctrine of *pedis possessio.* To obtain a patent to the land in which minerals are located, the miner must *discover* a *valuable mineral deposit, locate* the claim (at which time he has an *unpatented mining claim*), do *assessment work,* and then apply for a *patent.* Those elements of the location system are treated in the first six subsections. The seventh shows that the right to the minerals created by the 1872 Act is eroding even without repeal of the Act.

On hardrock mining generally, see the six-volume treatise produced by the Rocky Mountain Mineral Law Foundation, AMERICAN LAW OF MINING 2d (1984); MacDonnell, Public Policy for Hard-Rock Minerals Access on Federal Lands: A Legal-Economic Analysis, 71 Colo. School of Mines Q. 1 (1976). Professor John Leshy has completed an incisive treatment of mining law issues, to be published as THE MINING LAW OF 1872: A STUDY IN PERPETUAL MOTION (1986). The annual proceedings of the Rocky Mountain Mineral Law Institute, collected annually in separate volumes, generate a good percentage of the legal literature on hardrock mining.

1. LOCATABLE MINERALS

The invitation in 30 U.S.C.A. § 22, that "all valuable mineral deposits in lands belonging to the United States * * * shall be free and open to exploration and purchase" has been limited by Congress and the courts in several ways.

Numerous minerals are no longer covered by the 1872 General Mining Act. Coal had already been made subject to sale at public auction by the Coal Act of 1864, 13 Stat. 205, and the Coal Lands Act of 1873, 17 Stat. 607, controlled until coal was made a leasable mineral under the Mineral Leasing Act of 1920. The Acquired Lands Act of 1947, 30 U.S.C.A. §§ 351–59, provides that all minerals on acquired lands, which amount to about eight percent of all federal lands, are subject to lease, not location. The Materials Disposal Act of 1947, 30 U.S.C.A. §§ 601–02, as amended by the Common Varieties Act of 1955, 30 U.S.C.A. § 611, provides for sale of sand, stone, gravel, pumice, cinders, and other designated "common" minerals, unless the deposit "has some property giving it distinct and special value," id. § 601. The Geothermal Steam Act of 1970, 30 U.S.C.A. §§ 1001–25, makes federal geothermal resources leasable. Other special statutes are discussed in 1 AMERICAN LAW OF MINING 2d §§ 6.04–6.05 (1984).

Oil and gas have posed special problems. In 1897, Congress passed the Oil Placer Act, 29 Stat. 526, confirming the status of oil, gas, and oil shale as locatable minerals under the Hardrock Act. The executive withdrawals of millions of acres of federal lands from petroleum location led to the passage of the Mineral Leasing Act of 1920, 30 U.S.C.A. §§ 181 et seq., which removed several minerals from the scope of the General Mining Law. Other minerals as well have been placed in the "leasable" category by subsequent legislation and are discussed in section B below. But apart from the minerals specifically dealt with by Congress, and in light of the truism that everything that is not animal or vegetable is mineral, there remains the question of what is a mineral for purposes of the 1872 Act.

ANDRUS v. CHARLESTONE STONE PRODUCTS CO.
Supreme Court of the United States, 1978.
436 U.S. 604.

Mr. Justice MARSHALL delivered the opinion of the Court.

Under the basic federal mining statute, which derives from an 1872 law, "all valuable mineral deposits in lands belonging to the United States" are declared "free and open to exploration and purchase." 30 U.S.C.A. § 22. The question presented is whether water is a "valuable mineral" as those words are used in the mining law.

I

* * * The claim at issue in this case, known as Claim 22, is one of a group of 23 claims near Las Vegas, Nev., that were located in 1942. In 1962, after respondent had purchased these claims, it discovered water on Claim 22 by drilling a well thereon. This water was used to prepare for commercial sale the sand and gravel removed from some of the 23 claims.

* * *

[The Ninth Circuit held on its own motion that a valid claim had been made on Claim 22 because water is a valuable mineral under the 1872 Act. 553 F.2d 1209 (9th Cir.1977).]

II

We may assume for purposes of this decision that the Court of Appeals was correct in concluding that water is a "mineral," in the broadest sense of that word, and that it is "valuable." * * *

This Court long ago recognized that the word "mineral," when used in an Act of Congress, cannot be given its broadest definition. * * * As one court observed, if the term "mineral" in the statute were construed to encompass all substances that are conceivably mineral, "there would be justification for making mine locations on virtually every part of the earth's surface," since "a very high proportion of the substances of the earth are in that sense 'mineral.'" Rummell v. Bailey, 7 Utah 2d 137, 140, 320 P.2d 653, 655 (1958). See also Robert L. Beery, 25 I.B.L.A. 287, 294–296 (1976) (noting that "common dirt," while literally a mineral, cannot be considered locatable under the mining law) * * *.

The fact that water may be valuable or marketable similarly is not enough to support a mining claim's validity based on the presence of water. Many substances present on the land may be of value, and indeed it seems likely that land itself—especially land located just 15 miles from downtown Las Vegas—has, in the Court of Appeals' words, "an intrinsic value," id., at 1216. Yet the federal mining law surely was not intended to be a general real estate law; as one commentator has written, "the Congressional mandate did not sanction the disposal of federal lands under the mining laws for purposes unrelated to mining." 1 American Law of Mining, supra, § 1.18, at 56.

In order for a claim to be valid, the substance discovered must not only be a "valuable mineral" within the dictionary definition of those words, but must also be the type of valuable mineral that the 1872 Congress intended to make the basis of a valid claim.

III

* * *

Our opinions thus recognize that, although mining law and water law developed together in the West prior to 1866, with respect to federal lands Congress chose to subject only mining to comprehensive federal regulation. When it passed the 1866 and 1870 mining laws, Congress clearly intended to preserve "pre-existing [water] right[s]."

* * *

* * * [W]ithout benefit of briefing, the court below decided that "it would be incongruous * * * to hazard that Congress was not aware of the necessary glove of water for the hand of mining." Congress was indeed aware of this, so much aware that it expressly provided a water rights policy in the mining laws. But the policy adopted is a "passive" one, 2 Waters and Water Rights § 102.1, at 53 (R. Clark ed. 1967); Congress three times (in 1866, 1870, and 1872) affirmed the view that private water rights on federal lands were to be governed by state and local law and custom. It defies common sense to assume that Congress, when it adopted this policy, meant at the same time to establish a parallel federal system for acquiring private water rights, and that it did so *sub silentio* through laws designed to regulate mining. In light of the 1866 and 1870 provisions, the history out of which they arose, and the decisions construing them in the context of the 1872 law, the notion that water is a "valuable mineral" under that law is simply untenable.

IV

The conclusion that Congress did not intend water to be locatable under the federal mining law is reinforced by consideration of the practical consequences that could be expected to flow from a holding to the contrary.

A

Many problems would undoubtedly arise simply from the fact of having two overlapping systems for acquisition of private water rights. Under the appropriation doctrine prevailing in most of the Western States, the mere fact that a person controls land adjacent to a body of water means relatively little; instead, water rights belong to "[t]he first appropriator of water for a beneficial use," but only "to the extent of his actual use." * * *

With regard to minerals located under federal law, an entirely different theory prevails. The holder of a federal mining claim, by investing $100 annually in the claim, becomes entitled to possession of the land and may make any use, or no use, of the minerals involved. See 30 U.S.C.A. § 28. Once fee title by patent is obtained, even the $100 requirement is eliminated.

One can readily imagine the legal conflicts that might arise from these differing approaches if ordinary water were treated as a federally cognizable "mineral." A federal claimant could, for example, utilize all of the water extracted from a well like respondent's, without regard for the settled prior appropriation rights of another user of the same water. Or he might not use the water at all and yet prevent another from using it, thereby defeating the necessary Western policy in favor of "actual use" of scarce water resources. As one respected commentator has written, allowing water to be the basis of a valid mining claim "could revive long abandoned common law rules of ground water ownership and capture, and * * * could raise horrendous problems of priority and extralateral rights." We decline to effect so major an alteration in established legal relationships based on nothing more than an overly literal reading of a statute, without any regard for its context or history.

B

A final indication that water should not be held to be a locatable mineral derives from Congress' 1955 decision to remove "common varieties" of certain minerals from the coverage of the mining law. 30 U.S.C.A. § 611. This decision was made in large part because of "abuses under the general mining laws by * * * persons who locate[d] mining claims on public lands for purposes other than that of legitimate mining activity." * * * Apparently, locating a claim and obtaining a patent to federal land was so inexpensive that many "use[d] the guise of mining locations for nonmining purposes," including the establishment of "filling stations, curio shops, cafes, * * * residence[s] [and] summer camp[s]."

* * *

V

It has long been established that, when grants to federal land are at issue, any doubts "are resolved for the Government, not against it." United States v. Union Pacific R. Co., 353 U.S. 112, 116 (1957). *A fortiori,* the Government must prevail in a case such as this, when the relevant statutory provisions, their historical context, consistent administrative and judicial decisions, and the practical problems with a contrary holding all weigh in its favor. Accordingly, the judgment of the Court of Appeals is

Reversed.

NOTES

1. In what specific ways would the Ninth Circuit's opinion have revolutionized water law in the West?

2. For other examples of what is and is not a qualifying mineral, see United States v. Toole, 224 F.Supp. 440 (D.Mont.1963) (peat and organic soil); Dunluce Placer Mine, 30 L.D. 357 (1900) (stalagtites, stalagmites, and other "natural curiosities"); King v. Bradford, 31 L.D. 108 (1901) (brick clay); Holman v. Utah, 41 L.D. 314 (1912) (clay and limestone); Hughes v. Florida, 42 L.D. 401 (1913) (shell rock); Earl Douglass, 44 L.D. 325 (1915) (fossil remains of prehistoric animals); Opinion of the Solicitor, M–36625 (Aug. 28, 1961) (geothermal steam); United States v. Elkhorn Min. Co., 2 IBLA 383 (1971) (radon gas); United States v. Barngrover, 57 I.D. 533 (1941) ("silt" or drilling mud").

3. Compare United States v. Union Oil Co., 549 F.2d 1271 (9th Cir. 1977), infra at page 585, holding that geothermal energy, of which water is a main component, is a mineral for the purposes of the Stock-Raising Homestead Act of 1916.

4. Just as "all valuable minerals" are not available under the location system, so too is hardrock mining prohibited on some "lands belonging to the United States." Perhaps the most severe limitation on mining locations is withdrawals of the land from entry for all mining. Miners have often regretted their failure to consult the record systems in BLM state offices before expending their efforts. See Ritchie, Title Aspects of Mineral Development on Public Lands, 18 Rocky Mtn.Min.L. Inst. 471 (1973); Portland Gen. Elec. v. Kleppe, 441 F.Supp. 859 (D.Wyo. 1977), supra at page 243.

2. PROSPECTOR'S RIGHTS BEFORE DISCOVERY: PEDIS POSSESSIO

A miner does not achieve a valid unpatented claim until a valuable mineral deposit has been discovered and the physical steps of location have been completed. Prior to that time, courts have protected miners prospecting in good faith from claim jumpers, but the protection is conditioned.

HANSON v. CRAIG

United States Court of Appeals, Ninth Circuit, 1909.
170 F. 62.

ROSS, Circuit Judge. * * *

The plaintiffs in error, as well as the defendants in error, are eight in number, and made the location under which they respectively claim as an association claim of 160 acres of placer ground. The location of the defendants in error was prior in point of time, having been made on the 5th day of January, 1906; the ground then staked by them being 1,320 feet wide by a mile long, on Wildcat Creek, a tributary of Treasure Creek, in the Fairbanks mining district of Alaska. That claim was called the "Red Dog Association Claim." * * * [O]n the 12th of March, 1906, the defendants in error made arrangements to commence sinking a shaft upon the ground thus claimed in search of gold, and with that end in view it was arranged that the defendant in error Cale should go to Fairbanks, which was about 18 miles distant, to procure the necessary tools, blankets, and other supplies, and to return to the claim and commence work thereon on the 16th of March, 1906, and that in the meantime the defendant in error Carroll and one Hugh Dougherty as the representative of the defendant in error Alice Dougherty, should begin the sinking of a shaft on the claim, which they did on the 14th of March, 1906, continuing such work during the 14th and a part of the 15th of that month, during which time they sunk the hole to a depth of about six feet. It appears that in the evening of March 15th Carroll and Dougherty left the claim, taking with them their tools and other belongings, for the reason that Cale was expected to return from Fairbanks [on March 16th]. * * *

* * * Cale returned to within one mile of the Red Dog association claim on the 18th of March, with his tools and supplies, but, instead of going onto the ground and commencing work, stopped at the camp of the defendant in error Carroll, and from there went back to Fairbanks Creek, and did not return to the ground in dispute until the afternoon of the 21st of March, when [he struck gold.] * * *

This discovery of gold, however, was subsequent to the location which was made by the plaintiffs in error on the 16th day of March, 1906, of a claim called "Try Again Association Claim," which location included a part of the ground covered by the Red Dog association claim. The plaintiffs in error so marked the boundaries of the Try Again association claim as that they could be readily traced upon the ground, and commenced sinking a shaft upon that portion of it which overlapped the Red Dog association claim of the defendants in error, and continuously prosecuted their work until they made a discovery of gold thereon on the 15th day of April, 1906 * * *.

* * * [T]he real question for decision in this case is whether the defendants in error had such possession of the Red Dog association claim as precluded the plaintiffs in error from entering upon the ground and making their location of March 16, 1906 * * *. The exclusive right of possession is by section 2322 of the Revised Statutes conferred only on one who has made a valid location, one of the essentials of which is, as has been said, a discovery of mineral. Prior to that time all such mineral land is in law vacant and open to exploration and location * * *; for every miner upon the public domain is entitled to hold the place in which he may be working against all others having no better right. Zollars v. Evans (C.C.) 5 Fed. 172. The matter is, we think, well and tersely put by Costigan on Mining Law, p. 156, where he says:

> " 'Pedis possessio' means actual possession, and pending a discovery by anybody the actual possession of the prior arrival will be protected to the extent needed to give him room for work and to prevent probable breaches of the peace. But, while the pedis possessio is thus protected, it must yield to an actual location on a valid discovery made by one who has located peaceably, and neither clandestinely nor with fraudulent purposes."

* * *

* * * Applying the foregoing decisions to the present case, it is impossible to hold upon the record here that the defendants in error had such a possession * * * as precluded any other good-faith prospector from peaceably going within those boundaries and himself making a discovery and location.

* * *

NOTE

Pedis possessio rights can be transferred, e.g., United Western Minerals Co. v. Hannsen, 147 Colo. 272, 363 P.2d 677 (1961). A prospector diligently seeking discovery is protected from entry by another under the homesteading laws, e.g., Cosmos Exploration Co. v. Gray Eagle Oil Co., 112 F. 4 (9th Cir.1901). Can the United States cut timber or issue a grazing lease on an area subject to pedis possessio rights? What would be the effect on a prospector if the United States were to withdraw the area from mining prior to discovery? See United States v. Carlile, 67 I.D. 417 (1960) (no vested rights). See also Cole v. Ralph, 252 U.S. 286, 294–95 (1920) (holder of pedis possessio right is protected against private parties but "is treated as a licensee or tenant at will" as to the United States).

GEOMET EXPLORATION, LIMITED v. LUCKY MC URANIUM CORP.

Supreme Court of Arizona, 1979.
124 Ariz. 55, 601 P.2d 1339.
Cert. dismissed, 448 U.S. 917 (1980).

HAYS, Justice.

Geomet appealed from a decision granting exclusive possession of certain unpatented mining claims to Lucky Mc Uranium Corporation. The Court of Appeals affirmed, 124 Ariz. 60, 601 P.2d 1344 (App.1979).

*   *   *

By use of modern scintillation equipment in September of 1976, plaintiff/appellee, Lucky Mc Uranium Corporation, detected "anomalies" (discontinuities in geologic formations) indicative of possible uranium deposits in the Artillery Peak Mining District in Yuma County, land in the federal public domain. In November, 1976, Lucky proceeded to monument and post 200 claims (4,000 acres), drill a 10-foot hole on each claim, and record notices pursuant to A.R.S. §§ 27–202, 27–203 and 27–204.

Subsequently, defendant/appellant, Geomet, peaceably entered some of the areas claimed by Lucky and began drilling operations. Employees of Geomet were aware of Lucky's claims but considered them invalid because there had been no discovery of minerals in place and Lucky was not in actual occupancy of the areas Geomet entered.

Lucky instituted a possessory action seeking damages, exclusive possession and a permanent injunction against trespass by Geomet or its employees. There was insufficient evidence to establish a valid discovery, but the trial court found that Lucky was entitled to exclusive possession and a permanent injunction. *   *   *

Additionally, the court found that Geomet had entered the land in bad faith, knowing that Lucky was claiming it.

We must decide a single issue: Should the actual occupancy requirement of *pedis possessio* be discarded in favor of constructive possession to afford a potential locator protection of contiguous, unoccupied claims as against one who enters peaceably, openly, and remains in possession searching for minerals?

PEDIS POSSESSIO

Mineral deposits in the public domain of the United States are open to all citizens (or those who have expressed an intent to become citizens) who wish to occupy and explore them "under regulations prescribed by law, and according to the local customs or rules of miners in the several mining districts, so far as the same are applicable and not inconsistent with the laws of the United States." 30 U.S.C. § 22.

The doctrine of *pedis possessio* evolved from customs and usages of miners and has achieved statutory recognition in federal law as the "law of possession," 30 U.S.C. § 53:

> No possessory action between persons, in any court of the United States, for the recovery of any mining title, or for damages to any such title, shall be affected by the fact that the paramount title to the land in which such mines lie is in the United States; but each case shall be judged by the law of possession.

Regardless of compliance with statutory requisites such as monumenting and notice, one cannot perfect a location, under either federal or state law, without actual discovery of minerals in place. Best v. Humboldt Placer Mining Co., 371 U.S. 334 (1963). Until discovery, the law of possession determines who has the better right to possession.

* * *

If the first possessor should relax his occupancy or cease working toward discovery, and another enters peaceably, openly, and diligently searches for mineral, the first party forfeits the right to exclusive possession under the requirements of *pedis possessio.* Cole v. Ralph, 252 U.S. 286, 295 (1920); Davis v. Nelson, 329 F.2d 840 (9th Cir.1964).

* * *

Conceding that actual occupancy is necessary under *pedis possessio,* Lucky urges that the requirement be relaxed in deference to the time and expense that would be involved in actually occupying and drilling on each claim until discovery. Moreover, Lucky points out that the total area claimed—4,000 acres—is reasonable in size, similar in geological formation, and that an overall work program for the entire area had been developed. Under these circumstances, Lucky contends, actual drilling on some of the claims should suffice to afford protection as to all contiguous claims. Great reliance is placed on MacGuire v. Sturgis, 347 F.Supp. 580 (D.C.Wyo.1971), in which the federal court accepted arguments similar to those advanced here and extended protection on a group or area basis. Geomet counters that *MacGuire,* supra, is an aberration and contrary to three Wyoming Supreme Court cases upholding the requisite of actual occupancy.

To adopt the premise urged by Lucky eviscerates the actual occupancy requirement of *pedis possessio* and substitutes for it the theory of constructive possession even though there is no color of title. We are persuaded that the sounder approach is to maintain the doctrine intact.

* * *

We have canvassed the Western mining jurisdictions and found the requirement of actual occupancy to be the majority view. Davis v. Nelson, supra; United Western Minerals Co. v. Hannsen, 147 Colo. 272, 363 P.2d 677 (1961); Adams v. Benedict, 64 N.M. 234, 327 P.2d 308 (1958); McLemore v. Express Oil Co., 158 Cal. 559, 112 P. 59 (1910).

There are always inherent risks in prospecting. The development of *pedis possessio* from the customs of miners argues forcefully against the proposition that exclusive right to possession should encompass claims neither actually occupied nor being explored. We note that the doctrine does not protect on the basis of occupancy alone; the additional requirement of diligent search for minerals must also be satisfied. The reason for these dual elements—and for the policy of the United States in making public domain available for exploration and mining—is to encourage those prepared to demonstrate their sincerity and tenacity in the pursuit of valuable minerals. If one may, by complying with preliminary formalities of posting and recording notices, secure for himself the exclusive possession of a large area upon only a small portion of which he is actually working, then he may, at his leisure, explore the entire area and exclude all others who stand ready to peaceably and openly enter unoccupied sections for the purpose of discovering minerals. Such a premise is laden with extreme difficulties of determining over how large an area and for how long one might be permitted to exclude others.

We hold that *pedis possessio* protects only those claims actually occupied (provided also that work toward discovery is in progress) and does not extend to contiguous, unoccupied claims on a group or area basis.

* * *

Finally, Lucky asserts that Geomet cannot invoke *pedis possessio* because Geomet, knowing that Lucky claimed the area, entered in bad faith. Lucky relies principally on Bagg v. New Jersey Loan Co., supra, and Woolsey v. Lassen, 91 Ariz. 229, 371 P.2d 587 (1962). It is true that a potential locator must enter in good faith.

There is language in our decisions that appears to indicate that mere knowledge of a prior claim constitutes bad faith. Although we are sure that our holdings were sound in the cases Lucky cites, certain statements may have been an inadvertent oversimplification of the issue of good faith and we take this opportunity to clarify the point.

In general terms, good faith may be defined as honesty of purpose and absence of intent to defraud.

Both *Bagg* and *Woolsey,* supra, dealt with those who had discovered minerals in place and were in actual occupancy when others attempted to usurp their claims. These facts immediately distinguish them from the instant case, in which Lucky had neither made discovery nor was in actual occupancy of the areas Geomet entered.

While acting as agent to oversee claims of the Arizona Mining Company, Mr. Bagg attempted to locate claims for himself. An agent is duty-bound not to acquire a private interest antagonistic to that of his employer.

Woolsey concerned a claim against a previous locator who had already discovered mineral and was in actual possession under a lease from the state. Under the circumstances, the challenger simply could not prove a superior right to possession.

In summary, both cases differ significantly from this case in their factual framework and did not depend for their resolution solely upon the element of knowledge. We stand by our conclusions in those cases but wish to emphasize that mere knowledge of a previous claim, in and of itself, does not constitute bad faith.

Since Geomet's entry concededly was open and peaceable, we hold that the entry was in good faith.

* * *

We reverse the trial court, order that the injunction be quashed, and remanded for proceedings consistent with this opinion.

NOTES

1. Is *pedis possessio* the kind of open-ended doctrine that should expand its coverage to meet the needs of new technologies and changing times? Should courts adopt the more liberal rule of MacGuire v. Sturgis? To what extent is the Arizona Supreme Court bound by decisions of lower federal courts? Is *pedis possessio* a matter of federal or state law? How does one "occupy" 4000 acres? See generally Olson, New Frontiers in Pedis Possessio: MacGuire v. Sturgis, VII Land & Water L.Rev. 367 (1972).

2. The somewhat limited protection afforded miners while prospecting creates calls for reform:

> Even without a judicial or legislative broadening of pedis possessio to meet present circumstances, the current customs of the miners, or the mining industry, have a great deal of impact. The complete exploration necessary to make an actual discovery of such a mineral as uranium at great depth requires a rather extensive accumulation of capital, engineering, and technological experience and expertise, and a substantial organization. Once such a deposit is found, it requires even greater capital, engineering skill, and technological resources to develop and produce it, process it, and ultimately to market it. Unless a party is able to perform all of these functions himself, he is not likely to be in a position to fail to adhere to the current customs because at some stage of the sequence of location, exploration, discovery, production, processing, and marketing, he invariably will have to enter into an arrangement or accommodation with some other member of the industry who has elected to abide by those customs.

At the present time, all that a locator or operator can do to achieve pedis possessio is just the most that is feasible under the circumstances. * * * All possible efforts should be made to demonstrate the existence and ownership of the claims and the continuing work * * * on their behalf.

* * *

* * * Protection of possessory interests prior to discovery under * * * new circumstances is needed, but it probably is not afforded by the traditional application of pedis possessio. With the location of the claims and the existence of a proper plan for their exploration, the courts might liberalize the doctrine to grant that protection. However, the court decisions to date have not indicated the judiciary feels such a change would be proper. Therefore, operators at this time are in continuous jeopardy of loss of claims, but they really have little choice until the laws have been altered or broadened by legislation or judicial application.

Fiske, Pedis Possessio: Modern Use of an Old Concept, 15 Rocky Mtn. Min.L.Inst. 181, 215–16 (1969). See also Note, The General Mining Law and the Doctrine of *Pedis Possessio:* The Case for Congressional Action, 49 U.Chi.L.Rev. 1026 (1982).

As Leshy, supra, demonstrates, courts have long adjusted their interpretations of the General Mining Law to accommodate the practical needs of the mining industry. But even when the rules in the law books do not keep pace with mining technology, the industry can make pragmatic adjustments in the field to minimize conflict and get on with the business of making discoveries. See Marsh & King, Staking Mining Claims on Revoked Public Land Withdrawals: Issues and Alternative Strategies, 30 Rocky Mtn.Min.L.Inst. 9–1, 9–29 to 9–30 (1985):

Widely publicized mining claim staking rushes in areas of high mineral potential are usually closely monitored by local law enforcement agencies. Law enforcement personnel will prevent (and rightfully so) any affirmative efforts to exclude rival claimants except perhaps verbal and written admonitions to "stay off my claim." Experience has shown that such admonitions are totally ignored. Even in the absence of law enforcement agencies, an aura of conviviality rather than hostility seems to develop. Physical violence between rival claimants is eschewed, and would certainly be viewed with a jaundiced eye in the courts.

It is not only possible but almost universally the case that multiple rivals are "occupying" the same parcel of land while diligently (feverishly might be a more accurate description) seeking a discovery. Under these circumstances, it would seem that no such diligent occupant is entitled to any rights under the doctrine of *pedis possessio* as against another such diligent occupant, recognizing that both of them might gain *pedis possessio* rights as against a less enthusiastic participant.

As between two or more such diligent occupants, utilizing the traditional analytical framework, correlative rights should be determined on the basis of the first rival to couple the notice posting and discovery requirements in states where applicable law permits the locator a specified period within which to mark the boundaries of his claim and record a certificate of location.

* * *

3. DISCOVERY OF A VALUABLE MINERAL DEPOSIT

CASTLE v. WOMBLE
Opinion of the Secretary of the Interior, 1894.
19 L.D. 455.

[On July 2, 1889, Martin Womble filed in the local land office his application for a homestead patent based on preemption. The preemption statutes excluded from homesteading lands that are mineral in character. Walter Castle and other miners who had located the Empire Quartz opposed Womble's application. A local officer held that a valuable discovery had been made. The General Land Office affirmed, and Womble appealed to the Secretary.]

The law is emphatic in declaring that "no location of a mining claim shall be made until the discovery of the vein or lode within the limits of the claim located." (Revised Statutes, 2320.) And this Department said in the Cayuga Lode (S.L.D., 703), 5—"This is a prerequisite to the location, and, of course, entry of any mining claim. Without compliance with this essential requirement of the law no location will be recognized, no entry allowed." Has such discovery been made in this case?

In the case of Sullivan Iron Silver Mining Co. (143 U.S. 431), it was commonly believed that underlying all the country in the immediate vicinity of land in controversy was a horizontal vein or deposit, called a blanket vein, and that the patent issued was obtained with a view to thereafter develop such underlying vein. The supreme court, however, said, page 435, that this was mere speculation and belief, not based on any discoveries or tracings, and did not meet the requirements of the statute, citing Iron Silver Mining Co. v. Reynolds (124 U.S. 374).

In the last cited case the court, on page 384, says that the necessary knowledge of the existence of minerals may be obtained from the outcrop of the lode or vein, or from developments of a placer claim, previous to the application for patent, or perhaps in other ways; but hopes and beliefs cannot be accepted as the equivalent of such proper knowledge. In other words, it may be said that the requirement relating to discovery refers to present facts, and not to the probabilities of the future.

In this case the presence of mineral is not based upon probabilities, belief and speculation alone, but upon facts, which, in the judgment of the register and receiver and your office, show that with further work, a paying and valuable mine, so far as human foresight can determine, will be developed.

After a careful consideration of the subject, it is my opinion that where minerals have been found and the evidence is of such a character that a person of ordinary prudence would be justified in the further expenditure of his labor and means, with a reasonable prospect of success, in developing a valuable mine, the requirements of the statute have been met. To hold otherwise would tend to make of little avail, if not entirely nugatory, that provision of the law whereby "all valuable mineral deposits in lands belonging to the United States * * * are * * * declared to be free and open to exploration and purchase." For, if as soon as minerals are shown to exist, and at any time during exploration, before the returns become remunerative, the lands are to be subject to other disposition, few would be found willing to risk time and capital in the attempt to bring to light and make available the mineral wealth, which lies concealed in the bowels of the earth, as Congress obviously must have intended the explorers should have proper opportunity to do.

Entertaining these views, your judgment is affirmed.

UNITED STATES v. COLEMAN
Supreme Court of the United States, 1968.
390 U.S. 599.

Mr. Justice BLACK delivered the opinion of the Court.

In 1956 respondent Coleman applied to the Department of the Interior for a patent to certain public lands based on his entry onto and exploration of these lands and his discovery there of a variety of stone called quartzite, one of the most common of all solid materials. It was, and still is, respondent Coleman's contention that the quartzite deposits qualify as "valuable mineral deposits" under 30 U.S.C.A. § 22 and make the land "chiefly valuable for building stone" under 30 U.S.C.A. § 161.[2] The Secretary of the Interior held that to qualify as "valuable mineral deposits" under 30 U.S.C.A. § 22 it must be shown that the mineral can be "extracted, removed and marketed at a profit"—the so-called "marketability test." Based on the largely undisputed evidence in the record, the Secretary concluded that the deposits claimed by respondent Coleman did not meet that criterion. As to the alternative "chiefly valuable for building stone" claim, the Secretary held that respondent Coleman's quartzite deposits were a "common variet[y]" of stone within the meaning of 30 U.S.C.A. § 611, and thus they could not serve as the basis for a valid mining claim under the mining laws. The Secretary denied the patent application, but respondent Coleman remained on the land, forcing the Government to bring this present action in ejectment in the District Court against respondent Coleman

2. The 1872 Act, supra, was supplemented in 1892 by the passage of the Act of August 4, 1892, 27 Stat. 348, 30 U.S.C.A. § 161, which provides in § 1 in pertinent part: "That any person authorized to enter lands under the mining laws of the United States may enter lands that are chiefly valuable for building stone under the provisions of the law in relation to placer mineral claims * * *."

and his lessee, respondent McClennan. The respondents filed a counterclaim seeking to have the District Court direct the Secretary to issue a patent to them. The District Court, agreeing with the Secretary, rendered summary judgment for the Government. On appeal the Court of Appeals for the Ninth Circuit reversed, holding specifically that the test of profitable marketability was not a proper standard for determining whether a discovery of "valuable mineral deposits" under 30 U.S.C.A. § 22 had been made and that building stone could not be deemed a "common variet[y]" of stone under 30 U.S.C.A. § 611. We granted the Government's petition for certiorari because of the importance of the decision to the utilization of the public lands.

We cannot agree with the Court of Appeals and believe that the rulings of the Secretary of the Interior were proper. The Secretary's determination that the quartzite deposits did not qualify as valuable mineral deposits because the stone could not be marketed at a profit does no violence to the statute. Indeed, the marketability test is an admirable effort to identify with greater precision and objectivity the factors relevant to a determination that a mineral deposit is "valuable." It is a logical complement to the "prudent-man test" which the Secretary has been using to interpret the mining laws since 1894. Under this "prudent-man test" in order to qualify as "valuable mineral deposits," the discovered deposits must be of such a character that "a person of ordinary prudence would be justified in the further expenditure of his labor and means, with a reasonable prospect of success, in developing a valuable mine * * *." Castle v. Womble, 19 L.D. 455, 457 (1894). This Court has approved the prudent-man formulation and interpretation on numerous occasions. See, for example, Chrisman v. Miller, 197 U.S. 313, 322; Cameron v. United States, 252 U.S. 450, 459; Best v. Humboldt Placer Mining Co., 371 U.S. 334, 335–336. Under the mining laws Congress has made public lands available to people for the purpose of mining valuable mineral deposits and not for other purposes. The obvious intent was to reward and encourage the discovery of minerals that are valuable in an economic sense. Minerals which no prudent man will extract because there is no demand for them at a price higher than the cost of extraction and transportation are hardly economically valuable. Thus, profitability is an important consideration in applying the prudent-man test, and the marketability test which the Secretary has used here merely recognizes this fact.

The marketability test also has the advantage of throwing light on a claimant's intention, a matter which is inextricably bound together with valuableness. For evidence that a mineral deposit is not of economic value and cannot in all likelihood be operated at a profit may well suggest that a claimant seeks the land for other purposes. Indeed, as the Government points out, the facts of this case—the thousands of dollars and hours spent building a home on 720 acres in a highly scenic national forest located two hours from Los Angeles, the lack of an economically feasible market for the stone, and the immense quantities of identical stone found in the area outside the claims—might well be thought to raise a substantial question as to respondent Coleman's real intention.

Finally, we think that the Court of Appeals' objection to the marketability test on the ground that it involves the imposition of a different and more onerous standard on claims for minerals of widespread occurrence than for rarer minerals which have generally been dealt with under the prudent-man test is unwarranted. As we have pointed out above, the prudent-man test and the marketability test are not distinct standards, but are complementary in that the latter is a refinement of the former. While it is true that the marketability test is usually the critical factor in cases involving nonmetallic minerals of widespread occurrence, this is accounted for by the perfectly natural reason that precious metals which are in small supply and for which there is a great demand, sell at a price so high as to leave little room for doubt that they can be extracted and marketed at a profit.

We believe that the Secretary of the Interior was also correct in ruling that "[i]n view of the immense quantities of identical stone found in the area outside the claims, the stone must be considered a 'common variety' " and thus must fall within the exclusionary language of § 3 of the 1955 Act, 69 Stat. 368, 30 U.S.C.A. § 611, which declares that "[a] deposit of common varieties of * * * stone * * * shall not be deemed a valuable mineral deposit within the meaning of the mining laws * * *." Respondents rely on the earlier 1892 Act, 30 U.S.C.A. § 161, which makes the mining laws applicable to "lands that are chiefly valuable for building stone" and contend that the 1955 Act has no application to building stone, since, according to respondents, "[s]tone which is chiefly valuable as building stone is, by that very fact, not a common variety of stone." This was also the reasoning of the Court of Appeals. But this argument completely fails to take into account the reason why Congress felt compelled to pass the 1955 Act with its modification of the mining laws. The legislative history makes clear that this Act (30 U.S.C.A. § 611) was intended to remove common types of sand, gravel, and stone from the coverage of the mining laws, under which they served as a basis for claims to land patents, and to place the disposition of such materials under the Materials Act of 1947, 61 Stat. 681, 30 U.S.C.A. § 601, which provides for the sale of such materials without disposing of the land on which they are found.

* * *

For these reasons we hold that the United States is entitled to eject respondents from the land and that respondents' counterclaim for a patent must fail. The case is reversed and remanded to the Court of Appeals for the Ninth Circuit for further proceedings to carry out this decision.

NOTES

1. Does *Coleman* necessarily follow from Castle v. Womble? Is it "imprudent" to stake a claim to a low grade deposit that will increase in value as higher grade ores are depleted? Compare Andrus v. Shell

Oil Corp., 446 U.S. 657 (1980), infra at page 513. See also Hallenbeck v. Kleppe, 590 F.2d 852, 859 (10th Cir.1979); Foster v. Seaton, 271 F.2d 836, 838 (D.C.Cir.1959). On the development of the marketability test within the Department of Interior under Solicitor Frank J. Barry in the 1960's, see 1 AMERICAN LAW OF MINING § 4.81A (1978).

2. What factors are *not* relevant to "marketability" or "profitability"? Distance to mills or markets? Alternative capital investment opportunities? Is any profit sufficient, or should the locator have to demonstrate a rate of profit equivalent to that experienced by other industries? Do costs include the "incalculable" value of an endangered species? See Lundberg, infra at page 799. The BLM, the Forest Service, and the states have recently begun imposing some environmental constraints, including reclamation requirements, on mining operations on unpatented mining claims; must those costs be included in marketability? See United States v. Kosanke Sand Corp., 80 I.D. 538, 546 (1973) ("To the extent federal, state, or local law requires that anti-pollution devices or other environmental safeguards be installed and maintained * * * [such expenditures] may properly be considered * * * with the issue of marketability * * *."). See also In re Pacific Coast Molybdenum Co., 90 I.D. 352, 361 (1983). Cf. Kerr-McGee Corp. v. Hodel, 630 F.Supp. 621 (D.D.C.1986), infra at page 538.

3. If development of mineral resources is the goal, why should profitability enter the picture at all? Is it a guarantee of sorts that the deposit will in fact be developed? Or is it judicial lawmaking intended to modernize an anachronistic statute without benefit of congressional guidance?

4. The *Coleman* test has its supporters, e.g., Note, Marketability and the Mining Law: The Effect of United States v. Coleman, 10 Ariz.L. Rev. 391 (1968) (*Coleman* has "cleared away much semantic confusion, simplified a technical rule, and greatly diminished the area of future controversy"), and detractors, e.g., Reeves, The Law of Discovery Since Coleman, 21 Rocky Mtn.Min.L.Inst. 415, 416–17 (1976) ("either the Supreme Court did not understand the marketability rule or it did not understand the issues involved in the appeal").

5. The aftermath of *Coleman* was reported in the Los Angeles Times at B–1 (Feb. 16, 1970):

> A barren mountain hillside, soon to be planted with shrubbery and trees, is all that remains of Alfred Coleman's 14-year battle with the U.S. government. All, except his determination not to quit.
>
> A landmark Supreme Court decision in 1967 voided Coleman's 18 mining claims, located on 720 scenic acres overlooking Baldwin Lake near Big Bear.
>
> A federal court order followed in 1969, evicting the 73-year-old San Bernardino man from the property. But, it wasn't until two weeks ago that a bulldozer, leased by the U.S. Forest Service, razed Coleman's stone and wood cabin and the

outside equipment buildings. The rubble was burned as Coleman, unnoticed nearby, took photographs of the flaming debris.

* * *

The mining industry considers the decision contrary to and
an infringement of the mining laws.

And, Alfred Coleman sees the action as part of a bureaucratic morass that he says is leading to degeneration of government.

* * *

[Coleman's lawyer said last week:]

"Mr. Coleman has been badly handled—they had no right
to do any of these things. His house was located on a valid
millsite which has never been questioned.

"The forest service knew we were working on an agreement with the government and that Congressman Jerry Pettis
has a bill in committee for Coleman's relief. This is very high-
handed and unAmerican," Nilsson said.

6. The Department of Interior has developed a "ten-acre test"
governing patents for placer claims. Unlike lode claims, placer claims
must "conform as nearly as practicable with the United States system
of public-land surveys." 30 U.S.C.A. § 35. The smallest legal subdivision of public lands is 10 acres. 30 U.S.C.A. § 36. Reading the two
provisions together, Interior has concluded that a claimant must show
that each ten-acre tract in a placer claim is "mineral in character." A
discovery within the meaning of *Coleman* need not be proved on every
10-acre tract: if a "discovery" is made anywhere on the claim, then the
"mineral in character" requirement may be met on other tracts by
geological inference coupled with market availability. Miners' objections to the test were rejected in McCall v. Andrus, 628 F.2d 1185 (9th
Cir.1980), cert. denied, 450 U.S. 996 (1981).

7. Some cases have suggested that a higher standard for a valid
discovery may apply for national forest lands, as compared with BLM
lands. See, e.g., Converse v. Udall, 399 F.2d 616, 622 (9th Cir.1968),
cert. denied, 393 U.S. 1025 (1969) ("The prudent man test has long been
strictly applied against one who asserts discovery on national forest
lands, when the contest is between him and the government."). Conservation organizations raised the issue in In re Pacific Coast Molybdenum
Co., 90 I.D. 352, 361–63 (1983), involving Misty Fjords National Monument, set aside by ANILCA in 1980; the Act withdrew the area from
mining but recognized valid existing claims. In ruling on whether
certain claims within the Monument were valid, the Interior Board of
Land Appeals rejected the conservationists' argument:

Appellants also suggest that because of ANILCA the prudent man marketability test must be "strictly" applied. Thus,
they suggest "a stronger showing of marketability is required
for important recreation areas, such as Misty Fjords, than for
other public lands." It is true that a number of cases in the

past have indicated that a higher standard of proof is required for claims located in national forests than for other public lands. In actual practice, the Board has long since abandoned this position. We take this opportunity to expressly repudiate it.

The genesis of this rule in the Department lies in cases such as United States v. Dawson, 58 I.D. 670 (1944), and United States v. Langmade, 52 L.D. 700 (1929). All of these early cases, as well as the Federal court decisions on which they were based (United States v. Lillibridge, 4 F.Supp. 204 (S.D.Cal. 1932); United States v. Lavenson, 206 F. 755 (W.D.Wash.1913)), involved fact situations which called into question the *bona fides* of the mineral claimant. In *Dawson* and *Langmade* millsites and mining claims had been located on lands valuable for recreation sites and there were specific indications that the claims were a mere subterfuge to acquire title to these sites for purposes not associated with mining. *Lillibridge* involved the same problem, whereas *Lavenson* involved allegations that land valuable for water power was being acquired under the general mining laws. * * *

Subsequent decisions, however, ignored the clear basis of this rule and blindly applied the standard to all lands in national forests. Indeed, in United States v. Gray, A–28710 (Supp.) (May 7, 1964), the Deputy Solicitor attempted to premise the rule on a totally different basis. Thus, he stated that "[w]hile it is also clear that valid mining claims may be perfected within the limits of forest reservations, it is also clear that the validity of such mining claims is to be determined by a comparison of the relative value of the lands in question for forest or mineral purposes." No citation accompanied this statement, as the law did not support it. * * * Id. at 254. This holding was reaffirmed * * * in this Board's decision in United States v. Kosanke Sand Corp. (On Reconsideration), 80 I.D. 538, 547–48 (1973).

Having invoked the comparative value test in Gray, however, the Deputy Solicitor then proceeded to state that "I think it is reasonable, and entirely in accordance with prior Departmental and judicial decisions, to apply a higher standard and more rigid compliance with the requirements of the mining law where the claim is located within a National Forest." Thus was the standard separated from its moorings in considerations of bona fides.

As a conceptual matter, the theory that the situs of the land alters the nature of the test applied is untenable. Where the mining laws apply, they necessarily apply with equal force and effect, regardless of the characteristics of the land involved. The test of discovery is the same whether the land be unreserved public domain, land in a national forest, or even land in a national park.[11]

8. The Coleman test is applied less strictly when the contest is between rival claimants, and the government is not a party. The reasoning seems to be that, since no patent to federal lands is involved, such private disputes do not implicate the broader public concerns at stake when patents to public lands and minerals are at issue. See, e.g., Boscarino v. Gibson, __ Mont. __, 672 P.2d 1119, 1122–24 (1983). Do these considerations justify two separate lines of authority within the law of discovery? If so, should different standards apply in national forests as opposed to BLM lands? See Frizzell & Kunz, Primer on the Theory and Proof of Discovery of Valuable Mineral Deposits Under the 1872 Mining Law, 6 Pub.Land L.Rev. 103 (1985). See generally Haggard & Curry, Recent Developments in the Law of Discovery, 30 Rocky Mtn.Min.L.Inst. 8–1 (1984).

NOTE: URANIUM

Uranium is a metalliferous mineral subject to location under the 1872 General Mining Law. Obviously, however, it differs from "ordinary" minerals in several significant characteristics. Its radioactivity makes it easier to locate in some respects as well as more dangerous to extract, process, and use. Its use in nuclear generating plants is, of course, highly controversial, and such controversy extends backward to methods of processing. See, e.g., Comment, Ground and Surface Water In New Mexico: Are They Protected Against Uranium Mining and Milling?, 18 Nat.Res.J. 941 (1978).

Uranium sparked perhaps the last great American hardrock rush in the 1950's, with old-time prospectors, weekend explorers, and large mining companies all competing for discoveries in several regions of the West, most notably the Colorado Plateau. As with the California Gold Rush and succeeding strikes in the 19th century, enthusiasm was rampant, and brother literally fought brother for the new wealth. Illustrative is Smaller v. Leach, 136 Colo. 297, 316 P.2d 1030 (1957), cert. denied, 356 U.S. 936 (1958). Plaintiffs owned a scintillator, used for detecting radioactive mineralized deposits, and agreed among themselves to share any deposits located with its use. One of the plaintiffs, in company with defendants who had been informed of the agreement, did discover valuable deposits but defendants staked the claims for themselves. In the course of awarding plaintiffs the one-half interest in the claims they sought, the Colorado Supreme Court commented on history repeating itself in a new guise:

> As we view the record this case turns primarily upon the question as to whether on December 26, 1954, a valid and binding contract was entered into *(and the scope thereof)* be-

---

11. This discussion assumes the validity of the location. Thus, where land is closed to mineral entry, a subsequent discovery is irrelevant as the mining laws no longer apply so as to permit a discovery.

[Eds: Cf. Kerr-McGee Corp. v. Hodel, 630 F.Supp. 621 (D.D.C.1986), infra at page 538].

tween the parties relating to the ownership of locations for possible uranium claims to be located on or near Soapy Hill. Since Hiroshima was leveled in World War II the world has seen the rise of the atomic era. The active search for the wonder elements uranium and thorium has thrilled as well as disturbed mankind. It has already wrought wondrous economic changes in many sectors of our state as well as other parts of the west and has brought the hope and partial realization of medical relief, scientific advances and cheap power to the world along with the threat of destruction by atom and H bombs. It has in the instant case turned brother against brother in a bitter quest for riches by one and the hope of sustaining integrity as well as securing wealth in the other. Our mining laws were developed years ago, first out of customs and laws of the miners and their courts, later out of Acts of the Congress and the State Legislature. Since their adoption we have had the uranium rush which, because this mineral is not usually located like other minerals have been in the past, presents difficulties. True it is that lodes of primary uranium ores have been found and may be noted by outcrops as well as radio activity; yet many secondary ores of this metal have been created by deposits of thermal waters or other means spreading the element in not only cracks, fissures, faults and fossilized trees, but also along stream and river channels and in old lake beds where no outcrops may exist. One of the most successful ways of discovering uranium, therefore, has been by means of radio detecting instruments and other modern scientific means such as fluorescent lights, photographic film, electroscope tests and even surface growing plant life. The scintillator and Geiger Counter allowing gamma ray measurements have become as familiar in the west today as the gold pan and pick and shovel were in an earlier period. The old form of grubstake agreement whereby the man who had no time or aptitude for prospecting could furnish the burro, beans and bacon to another for a half share of any discoveries made, has its modern day version in the loaning to a friend, for the weekend, of one's scintillator or counter on shares of whatever is found. And, weekend instrument prospectors have made some of our largest and best discoveries. * * *

Modern technology in the form of geiger counters and scintillators has caused courts some difficulties in determining when discovery had occurred. In Globe Mining Co. v. Anderson, 73 Wyo. 17, 318 P.2d 373 (1957), an action to quiet title to lode mining claims, the Wyoming Supreme Court stated:

> [T]hus, there was no evidence of a sampling and assaying of a vein, lode, or rock in place in [various claims] and, therefore, no discovery on these claims—unless we recognize the readings of electrical instruments such as scintillation and Geiger counters as sufficient to support discovery. This we are

reluctant to do, since such counters while helpful in prospecting for uranium cannot be relied upon as the *only* test. 318
P.2d at 380.

The test was progressively relaxed thereafter. In Rummell v. Bailey, 7
Utah 2d 137, 320 P.2d 653 (1958), the Utah Supreme Court held that a
valid discovery could be based on radiometric detection plus geological
analysis of the immediate vicinity, particularly when there are known,
physically discovered deposits nearby. In Dallas v. Fitzsimmons, 137
Colo. 196, 323 P.2d 274 (1958), the Colorado Supreme Court held that
radiometric results, in combination with other evidence of assaying and
the type of rock in place, satisfy the definitional requirements of
discovery. In Berto v. Wilson, 74 Nev. 128, 324 P.2d 843 (1958), the
initial "discovery" was made by the U.S. Geological Survey in preparing anomaly maps from airborne surveys. The court validated the
claim of the first on-the-ground locator, commenting that while more
evidence of discovery might be required in a government contest, a
slight showing of scintillator readings sufficed as against a rival locator.
See also Western Standard Uranium Co. v. Thurston, 355 P.2d 377
(Wyo.1960). See generally 1 AMERICAN LAW OF MINING 2d
§ 35.14[2][a][iv] (1984).

Illustrative decisions on the validity of uranium claims in relation
to prior and subsequent withdrawals include Portland General Elec. Co.
v. Kleppe, 441 F.Supp. 859 (D.Wyo.1977), supra at page 243; Willcoxson
v. United States, 313 F.2d 884 (D.C.Cir.1963) (purported sale under
Isolated Tracts Act).

In the Uranium Mill Tailings Radiation Control Act of 1978, 42
U.S.C.A. §§ 7901–42, Congress imposed stricter regulation on uranium
processing operations and tailings disposal. See generally 5 AMERI-
CAN LAW OF MINING 2d at ch. 177 (1984).

4. LOCATION

The caveat in 30 U.S.C.A. § 23 ("no location of a mining claim shall
be made until the discovery of a vein or lode within the limits of the
claim located") seems to require that discovery must precede location.
The courts, however, have found that "the order of time in which these
acts occur is not essential" to the establishment of a valid unpatented
mining claim, e.g., Union Oil Co. v. Smith, 249 U.S. 337 (1919), thus
sanctioning the common practice of staking a claim before a discovery
is made. Strauss, Mining Claims on Public Lands, 1974 Utah L.Rev.
185, 189–90:

> In practice [even though a discovery has not been made] once a
> claim has been recorded any person wishing to interfere with it
> has the burden of going forward to show his superior right.
> Thus, should there be any private dispute over possession of
> the land, the fact that a claim has been recorded will require
> the adverse claimant to show that he has made a discovery, or
> in some other manner obtained a claim to title, before he can
> show that the first claimant has made no discovery. In a

dispute between the government and the locator, the government currently undertakes to show prima facie reason to believe that the claim is invalid, for example because no discovery has been made, before the locator is called upon to prove his claim. In practice, then, recordation gives the appearance of creating the right which the law indicates matures only upon actual discovery. Miners and prospectors generally believe that once they have recorded a claim they have acquired a property right in the government land thus located. Having marked his corners, pounded in his stake, and filed his forms at the county courthouse, the prospector believes that he has—and in practice is often treated as if he does have—an absolute possessory right to that land and its minerals.

The General Mining Law, 30 U.S.C.A. § 28, provides:

> The miners of each mining district may make regulations not in conflict with the laws of the United States, or with the laws of the State or Territory in which the district is situated, governing the location, manner of recording, amount of work necessary to hold possession of a mining claim, subject to the following requirements: The location must be distinctly marked on the ground so that its boundaries can be readily traced. All records of mining claims made after May 10, 1872, shall contain the name or names of the locators, the date of the location, and such a description of the claim or claims located by reference to some natural object or permanent monument as will identify the claim. * * *

Typically, state statutes require: (1) a valuable discovery; (2) prompt posting at or near the place of discovery to give notice; (3) development work to determine the character and extent of the deposit; (4) marking on the ground to establish the boundaries of the claim; and (5) recording of a notice or certificate, usually with the county clerk or recorder. See AMERICAN LAW OF MINING 2d at chs. 33, 35 (1984). State laws are compiled in Rocky Mountain Mineral Law Foundation, DIGEST OF MINING CLAIM LAWS (R. Pruitt ed., 1978). There is no limit on the number of claims that a person can locate. Once validly located, markers such as stakes need not be maintained in order to avoid a forfeiture of the claim. Dodge v. Wilkinson, 664 P.2d 157 (Alaska 1983).

ERHARDT v. BOARO

Supreme Court of the United States, 1885.
113 U.S. 527.

On the trial the plaintiff produced evidence tending to show that on the seventeenth of June, 1880, one Thomas Carroll, a citizen of the United States, while searching, on behalf of himself and the plaintiff, also a citizen, for valuable deposits of mineral, discovered, on vacant unoccupied land of the public domain of the United States, in the

Pioneer mining district mentioned, the outcrop of a vein or lode of quartz and other rock bearing gold and silver in valuable and paying quantities.

* * *

[Plaintiff posted a notice reading:]

"HAWK LODE.

"We, the undersigned, claim 1,500 feet on this mineral-bearing lode, vein, or deposit.

"*Dated June* 17, 1880.

JOEL B. ERHARDT, 4-5ths.

THOMAS CARROLL, 1-5th."

—That on the same day, at the point of his discovery, Carroll commenced excavating a discovery shaft, and sunk the same to the depth of about eighteen inches or two feet on the vein; that on the thirtieth of the month, in the temporary absence of himself and the plaintiff, the defendant Boaro, with knowledge of the rights and claims of the plaintiff and Carroll, entered upon and took possession of their excavation, removed and threw away or concealed the stake upon which their written notice was posted, and, at the point of Carroll's discovery of the vein or lode, erected a stake and posted thereon a discovery and location notice as follows:

"JOHNNY BULL LODE.

"We, the undersigned, claim 1,500 feet on this mineral-bearing vein or lode, running six hundred feet north-east and nine hundred feet south-west, and 150 feet on each side of the same, with all its dips and spurs, angles, and variations.

"*June* 30, 1880.

ANTHONY BOARO.

W.L. HULL."

The evidence also tended to show that Boaro and Hull entered upon the premises thus described, about July 21, 1880, and remained thereafter continuously in possession; that threats of violence to the plaintiff and Carroll, if they should enter upon the premises, or attempt to take possession of them, were communicated to Carroll as having been made by Boaro early in August following; that in consequence of such threats, and the possession held by Boaro, Carroll was prevented from resuming work upon and completing the discovery shaft, and from entering upon any other part of the lode or vein, and performing the acts of location required by law within the time limited.

* * *

FIELD, J. As seen by the statement of the case, the court below, in its charge, assumed that the notice on the stake, placed by Carroll at the point of his discovery, contained no specification or description of the ground claimed by the locators, because it did not designate the number of feet claimed on each side of that point, or in any direction from it. The court accordingly instructed the jury that the notice was deficient, and under it the locators could not claim any more than the very place in which the stake was planted, and that elsewhere on the same lode beyond the point of discovery any other citizen could make a valid location. In this instruction we think the court erred. The statute allows the discoverer of a lode or vein to locate a claim thereon to the extent of 1,500 feet. The written notice posted on the stake at the point of discovery of the lode or vein in controversy, designated by the locators as "Hawk Lode," declares that they claim 1,500 feet on the "lode, vein, or deposit." It thus informed all persons, subsequently seeking to excavate and open the lode or vein, that the locators claimed the whole extent along its course which the law permitted them to take. It is, indeed, indefinite in not stating the number of feet claimed on each side of the discovery point; and must, therefore, be limited to an equal number on each side; that is, to 750 feet on the course of the lode or vein in each direction from that point. To that extent, as a notice of discovery and original location, it is sufficient. Greater particularity of description of a location of a mining claim on a lode or vein could seldom be given until subsequent excavations have disclosed the course of the latter. These excavations are to be made within 60 days after the discovery. Then the location must be distinctly marked on the ground, so that its boundaries can be readily traced, and, within one month thereafter, that is, within three months from the discovery, a certificate of the location must be filed for record in the county in which the lode is situated, containing the designation of the lode, the names of the locators, the date of the location, the number of feet claimed on each side of the center of the discovery shaft, the general course of the lode, and such a description of the claim, by reference to some natural object or permanent monument, as will identify it with reasonable certainty. Rev.St. § 2324; Gen.Laws Colo. §§ 1813, 1814.

But during the intermediate period, from the discovery of the lode or vein and its excavation, a general designation of the claim by notice, posted on a stake placed at the point of discovery, such as was posted by Carroll, stating the date of the location, the extent of the ground claimed, the designation of the lode, and the names of the locators, will entitle them to such possession as will enable them to make the necessary excavations and prepare the proper certificate for record.

* * *

[Plaintiffs] did not lose their right to perfect their location, and perform the necessary work for that purpose, by the wrongful intrusion upon the premises, and by threats of violence if they should attempt to resume possession. As against the defendants, they were entitled to be reinstated into the possession of their claim. They could not be deprived of their inchoate rights by the tortious acts of others; nor could the intruders and trespassers initiate any rights which would defeat those of the prior discoverers.

The government of the United States has opened the public mineral lands to exploration for the precious metals, and, as a reward to the successful explorer, grants to him the right to extract and possess the mineral within certain prescribed limits.

*   *   *

*   *   * And whenever preliminary work is required to define and describe the claim located, the first discoverer must be protected in the possession of the claim until sufficient excavations and development can be made, so as to disclose whether a vein or deposit of such richness exists as to justify work to extract the metal. Otherwise, the whole purpose of allowing the free exploration of the public lands for the precious metals would in such cases be defeated, and force and violence in the struggle for possession, instead of previous discovery, would determine the rights of claimants.

*   *   *

It follows from what we have said that the judgment of the court below must be reversed, and the case remanded for a new trial; and it is so ordered.

NOTES

1. In Sanders v. Noble, 22 Mont. 110, 55 P. 1037 (1899), Sanders and others made a valuable discovery. They named the find the Never Sweat, posted notice at the point of discovery, and then left the vicinity for 30 days to fulfill another contract. While the Never Sweat operators were gone, Noble and others made a valuable discovery in the vicinity and located the Yukon, which partially overlapped the Never Sweat. Under a Montana statute, a claimant has 90 days after posting of notice to define the boundaries of the claim. The Court held for the owners of the Never Sweat:

> If the question which we have discussed were res integra, we should be disposed to take a view of the federal statute (section 2324) differing from the rule of Erhardt v. Boaro, supra, and to agree with the California and Oregon cases cited, which interpret the law as requiring an immediate marking of the location on the ground, so that the boundaries can be readily traced, or that a possession pedis be had until they can be so marked within a reasonable time. There is a great deal to be said in support of the argument that Congress never meant to allow the discoverer to stop his work, leave his claim, and postpone marking his boundaries for any period of time. The effect of the present construction is to give advantages to the discoverer beyond what the statute seems to fairly contemplate; and yet, if the right to postpone the marking of the boundaries for 90 days exists, there is no escape from the conclusion that the right to swing in good faith during that time goes with it. This is so because the reason for allowing the right to postpone is to definitely ascertain the strike, so that the discoverer may secure the benefit of his location

before marking. Therefore, where the discoverer gives, as he must under the state statute, the general course of his vein in his discovery notice, and, notwithstanding those courses, he can postpone marking the ground for 90 days thereafter, so that the boundaries of his claim may be traced, it should necessarily follow that, if the course given in the notice posted is not the true course of the lode as ascertained, he may swing his claim so as to include within his boundaries ground that was not embraced in the notice of discovery, provided it includes the true course of the vein claimed. This right to postpone thus gives a discoverer a circle to move his claim in until he marks its boundaries, the radius of the circle being ordinarily a distance equal to the longest distance claimed from the point of discovery. This, for a time, practically withdraws a large area from the public domain, and compels prospectors to abide the time when the discoverer of a vein may elect to mark his ground. We doubt if Congress ever intended such a consequence. The question, however, involves federal laws and statutes complementary of federal laws; so we feel bound by the interpretations of the United States courts, hence dismiss the subject with the foregoing observations of our own.

The application of what we have said necessarily leads to the conclusion that the defendants in this case had no right to embrace in the location of the Yukon any of the ground included within the boundaries of the Never Sweat as the plaintiffs defined said boundaries, within the period of 90 days after their discovery of the Never Sweat.

Is the Montana Supreme Court correct in finding that the case is controlled by Erhardt v. Boaro? Is the issue a matter of federal or state law?

2. The physical nature of the valuable deposit is important to the miner, for the Act specifies different criteria for the boundaries of lode and placer claims. A lode claim may not exceed 1500 feet in length or 300 feet on each side of the middle of the vein; the end lines of the claim must be parallel. 30 U.S.C.A. § 23. There is no requirement that lode claims conform to survey lines, and lode claims are often irregular in shape. Placer claims must conform "as near as practicable" to survey lines where the area has been surveyed, 30 U.S.C.A. § 35. Otherwise no provisions govern the shape of the exterior boundaries of placer claims. A single claimant cannot locate a placer claim of more than 20 acres, 30 U.S.C.A. § 35, but associations of persons may locate placer claims of 20 acres per person, not to exceed a claim of 160 acres for an association of eight or more people. 30 U.S.C.A. § 36. Misidentification of a lode as a placer, or vice versa, is a ground for invalidating the claim. Cole v. Ralph, 252 U.S. 286 (1920).

Classically, "lodes" or "veins" referred to lines or aggregations of mineral embedded in rock in place, while "placer" meant ground containing mineral deposits not in place, United States v. Ohio Oil Co., 240 F. 996 (D.Wyo.1916). The definition in practice is not always helpful. See Globe Mining Co. v. Anderson, 78 Wyo. 17, 318 P.2d 373 (1957) (widespread horizontal deposit containing scattered mineralized zones deemed a lode). Sherwood & Greer, Mining Law in a Nuclear Age: The Wyoming Example, III Land & Water L.Rev. 1, 26 (1968):

> Three principal factors determinative of the existence of a lode emerge from this considerable body of authorities: (1) the character of the surrounding country rock; (2) the form, trend or continuity of the orebody itself; and (3) the existence of a reasonable definition or boundary between the mineralized zone and the country rock. From one case to the next factors tend to recede or emerge individually as the facts warrant, making it difficult to assign to them an order of importance. But the foregoing illustrations make clear that courts have tended to concentrate on the mode of occurrence, rather than some intrinsic quality of a mineral deposit which might determine the manner in which it should be located.

3. Before 1976, recordation standards were governed only by state law, which require recording with the county clerk or recorder but which typically have no mechanism to determine whether a claim had been abandoned. Consequently, there were an estimated six to ten million inactive claims located on the public lands. Anderson, Federal Mineral Policy: The General Mining Law of 1872, 16 Nat.Res.J. 601, 603 (1976). Six years after the Public Land Law Review Commission recommended federal recordation, Congress in the 1976 FLPMA moved to implement the recommendation. All old claims as well as new locations must be recorded with the Bureau of Land Management, or they will "conclusively" be deemed abandoned. 43 U.S.C.A. § 1744(c). See infra at page 478.

5. THE UNPATENTED MINING CLAIM

Upon locating a valuable lode or placer claim, hardrock miners have "the exclusive right of possession and enjoyment of all the surface included within the lines of their locations." 30 U.S.C.A. § 26. United States v. Etcheverry, 230 F.2d 193, 195 (10th Cir.1956) describes this unique interest:

> The law is well settled by innumerable decisions that when a mining claim has been perfected under the law, it is in effect a grant from the United States of the exclusive right of possession to the same. It constitutes property to its fullest extent, and is real property subject to be sold, transferred, mortgaged, taxed, and inherited without infringing any right or title of the United States.

UNITED STATES v. RIZZINELLI
United States District Court, District of Idaho, 1910.
182 F. 675.

DIETRICH, District Judge. The defendants are charged with the maintenance of saloons upon mining claims within the limits of the Coeur d'Alene National Forest without a permit, and in violation of the rules and regulations of the Secretary of Agriculture. The claims were duly located, subsequent to the creation of the forest reserve, and they are possessory only, no application for patent ever having been made.

* * *

[T]he Secretary of Agriculture, * * * formulated an elaborate set of regulations, published in what is known as the "Use Book". The particular rules alleged to have been ignored by the defendants are as follows:

> "Reg. 6. Permits are necessary for all occupancy, uses, operations or enterprises of any kind within national forests, whether begun before or after the national forest was established, except: (a) Upon patented lands; (b) upon valid claims for purposes necessary to their actual development and consistent with their character; (c) upon rights of way amounting to easements for the purposes named in the grants; (d) prospecting for minerals, transient camping, hunting, fishing, and surveying for lawful projects."

> "Reg. 19. The following acts within national forests are hereby forbidden: * * * (c) Erecting or conducting telephone, telegraph, or power lines, hotels, stores, sawmills, power plants, or other structures, or manufacturing or business enterprises, or carrying on any kind of work, except as allowed by law and national forest regulations, and except upon patented lands or upon a valid claim for the actual development of such claim, consistent with the purposes for which it was initiated."

* * *

[The court found that the Forest Service had been validly delegated authority to adopt the regulations in the Use Book pursuant to the Forest Service Organic Act of 1897.]

The defendants here have the possessory title only. They have a distinct but qualified property right, and, even if we assume that their interest is vested, it is one which may be abandoned at any moment, or forfeited. The primary title, the paramount ownership, is in the government, and upon abandonment by the locator, or his failure to comply with the conditions upon which his continuing right of possession depends, the entire estate reverts to the government; all the time, it retains the title, with a valuable residuary and reversionary interest. This interest, whatever it may be, it has the right to protect and obviously the interest which it retains is the entire estate, less that which is granted by the terms of section 2322, providing that locators shall have "the exclusive right of possession and enjoyment of all the surface of their locations." * * * The inquiry is substantially limited to the meaning of the phrase "exclusive enjoyment," for, notwithstanding the existence of the Coeur d'Alene forest reserve, it is conceded that the defendants are entitled to the exclusive possession of their claim not only as against third persons, but as against the United States. * * * The government inserts, after the word "enjoyment," the phrase "for mining purposes," and the defendants the phrase "for all purposes." No other language is suggested, and, indeed, no middle ground appears to be possible; the "enjoyment" is either for mining purposes alone, or for all purposes without qualification or restriction. Under a familiar rule of statutory construction, the necessity of reading into the statute one or the other of these two phrases to make it complete, and its adaptability to either of them, of itself operates strongly to determine the question in favor of the government, for it is well settled that in public grants nothing passes except that which is clearly and specifically granted, and all doubts are to be resolved in favor of the government. But, independent of this rule, considerations pertinent to the construction of private grants and contracts clearly lead to the conclusion that the right of enjoyment which Congress intended to grant extends only to mining uses. The general purpose of the mineral laws is well understood; it was to encourage citizens to assume the hazards of searching for and extracting the valuable minerals deposited in our public lands. In form the grant is a mere gratuity; but, in considering the propriety of such legislation, it may well have been thought that by reason of the stimulus thus given to the production of mineral wealth, and rendering the same available for commerce and the arts, the public would indirectly receive a consideration commensurate with the value of the grant. In that view doubtless the legislation has for a generation been generally approved as embodying a wise public policy. But under what theory should the public gratuitously bestow upon the individual the right to devote mineral lands any more than any other public lands to valuable uses having no relation to mining, and for what reason should we read into the statute such a surprising and unexpressed legislative intent?

With much earnestness the consideration is urged that it has become more or less customary to erect valuable buildings upon lands embraced in mineral claims to be used for purposes having no necessary relation to mining operations, and that great hardship would ensue and important property rights would be confiscated if the locator's "enjoyment" of the surface be limited to uses incident to mining. But even if it be true, as suggested, that in many localities sites for dwelling houses and business structures could not be conveniently obtained except upon lands containing valuable mineral deposits and embraced in located claims, the fact is without significance and lends no support to the defendants' contention.

* * *

Holding, therefore, that the right of a locator of a mining claim to the "enjoyment" of the surface thereof is limited to uses incident to mining operations, no serious difficulty is encountered in reaching the further conclusion that forest reserve lands embraced in a mining claim continue to constitute a part of the reserve, notwithstanding the mineral location, subject, of course, to all the legal rights and privileges of the locator. The paramount ownership being in the government, and it also having a reversionary interest in the possessory right of the locator, clearly it has a valuable estate which it is entitled to protect against waste and unlawful use. It is scarcely necessary to say that it is the substantial property right of the government, and not the extent to which such right may be infringed in the present case, that challenges our consideration. The burden imposed upon the principal estate by the construction and maintenance of a little saloon building may be trivial, and the damage wholly unappreciable. But that is not to the point. If a worthless shrub may as a matter of legal right be destroyed in the location of a saloon, the entire claim may be stripped of its timber, however valuable, to give place for other saloons and other structures having no connection with the operation of the mine. To concede any such right at all is necessarily to concede a right without limit; there is no middle ground. It is therefore repeated that, subject to the locator's legitimate use for mining purposes, the government continues to be the owner of the land, and is interested in conserving its value and preventing injury and waste.

* * *

[The convictions for maintaining saloons on mining claims were affirmed.]

NOTES

1. Residences reasonably incident to mining are permissible. See, e.g., United States v. Langley, 587 F.Supp. 1258 (E.D.Cal.1984). Can the holder of an unpatented claim cut timber for sale to a third party? See Shiver v. United States, 159 U.S. 491 (1895). Can the claimant lease part of the claim for grazing? See United States v. Etcheverry, 230 F.2d 193 (10th Cir.1956). Can the holder cut timber for construction of a residence or graze stock for the miner's own domestic purposes? Cf. Teller v. United States, 113 F. 273, 282–84 (10th Cir.1901). The Surface Resources Act of 1955, 30 U.S.C.A. § 612, expressly imposed a "reasonably incident to mining" test. Do uses incident to mining include "a mobile home, several vehicles—both operable and inoperable—assorted animals including a bull, cows, chickens and several dogs, a sweat lodge, a chicken coop or enclosure, and a garden"? The court in Bales v. Ruch, 522 F.Supp. 150 (E.D.Cal.1981), held not. See generally Miller, Surface Rights Under the General Mining Law: Good Faith and Common Sense, 28 Rocky Mtn.Min.L.Inst. 761 (1983).

2. Extralateral rights attach to properly located unpatented mining claims, and allow the miner of a lode claim to follow a vein or lode beyond the sidelines of the claim. Extralateral rights were recognized by custom in the mining camps and are governed today by § 26 of the Mining Act:

> The locators of all mining locations made on any mineral vein, lode, or ledge, * * * shall have the exclusive right of possession and enjoyment of all the surface included within the lines of their locations, *and of all veins, lodes, and ledges throughout their entire depth,* the top or apex of which lies inside of such surface lines extended downward vertically, although such veins, lodes, or ledges may so far depart from a perpendicular in their course downward as to extend *outside the vertical side lines of such surface locations.* But their right of possession to such outside parts of such veins or ledges shall be confined to such portions thereof as lie between vertical planes drawn downward as above described, through the end lines of their locations, so continued in their own direction that

such planes will intersect such exterior parts of such veins or ledges. Nothing in this section shall authorize the locator or possessor of a vein or lode which extends in its downward course beyond the vertical lines of his claim to enter upon the surface of a claim owned or possessed by another. (Emphasis added.)

An example of extralateral rights can be seen from this illustration from Rocky Mountain Mineral Law Foundation, DIGEST OF MINING CLAIM LAWS 12 (R. Pruitt, ed., 1978):

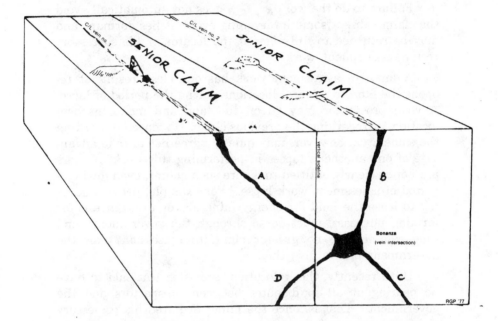

Figure 6—

"EXTRALATERAL RIGHTS ILLUSTRATED. Senior Claim, located along vein no. 1, may follow the dipping vein outside the sidelines projected vertically downward and mine parts A and C. Junior Claim, located along vein no. 2, may likewise follow the dipping vein outside the sidelines and mine parts B and D. The area of vein intersection, where rich orebodies usually form, belongs to the Senior Claim, even though it lies within the vertical boundaries of the Junior Claim."

One problem, of course, is that lode claims are not always neat rectangles. See Iron Silver Mining Co. v. Elgin Mining & Smelting Co., 118 U.S. 196, 199 (1886), which appends a diagram of several highly irregular claims. The Mining Law requires that "the end lines be parallel to each other;" while non-parallel end lines will not invalidate a claim, they will eliminate extralateral rights. On extralateral rights, see generally 2 AMERICAN LAW OF MINING 2d at ch. 37 (1984).

3. The mining district customs almost invariably required that a miner must continue to develop the mine after discovery was made. This assured maximum development of the resource, and provided

protection against those who tried to hold several valuable claims but work only a few of them. The General Mining Act codified this custom in the provision that an unpatented claim will be forfeited unless "not less than $100 worth of labor shall be performed or improvements be made during each year." 30 U.S.C.A. § 28. Most states require recording with the county clerk or recorder to establish that the work was done.

4. Strauss, Mining Claims on Public Lands: A Study of Interior Department Procedures, 1974 Utah L.Rev. 185, 191:

> Failure to do the work * * * does not automatically void the claim; absent some intervening event, it lies dormant and may be returned to full vigor if the locator or his successors resume assessment work.

> A lapse in assessment work has one clear result: it re-opens the land to mineral locations during the period of lapse. A rival prospector may go on the land and make his own location, disregarding the previous claim. Prospectors working the same area, however, may quietly agree not to take advantage of one another's lapses in performing this work. Others are not as clearly entitled to ignore such claims, even during a period of assessment work lapse. For example, persons desiring to lease the land for energy minerals, or to acquire it for farming purposes, must do so through the government; and they can acquire no greater claim to possession than the government has to give them.

> Until recently, the 'relocation' provision was said to have no bearing at all in disputes between prospectors and the government. That is, once the miner acquired his possessory right, subsequent failure to perform the annual assessment work was thought to give no right of recapture to the government or persons claiming through it; the claim persisted until it was affirmatively abandoned, and the failure to do assessment work did not prove abandonment. A recent Supreme Court decision [Hickel v. Oil Shale Corp., 400 U.S. 48 (1970), infra at page 509] has stated a less drastic rule, at least for those cases in which relocation of the land by competing miners has been prohibited by withdrawal of the land from the operation of the mining laws: a failure to comply substantially with the assessment work requirement after the withdrawal permits the government to defeat an otherwise valid claim. It remains unclear, however, whether the same reasoning applies to unworked claims on land which remains open to location. More importantly for present purposes, the government has never felt able simply to ignore apparently lapsed claims encumbering its lands, no matter how long the lapse. Following early court pronouncements that the property character of perfected mining claims requires notice and hearing before a claim may be found invalid, the government has consistently

felt required to search out all claimants and bring administrative proceedings to declare their claims invalid.

Forfeitures of unpatented claims are not favored by the law and must be shown by clear and convincing evidence. See, e.g., Justice Mining Co. v. Barclay, 82 F. 554 (D.Nev.1897); 2 AMERICAN LAW OF MINING 2d §§ 46.03–46.05 (1984). Historically, no filing was required with the federal government, but FLPMA, passed in 1976, requires annual filing of an affidavit of assessment work performed and provides that the failure to make such filing "shall be deemed conclusively to constitute an abandonment of the mining claim." 43 U.S.C.A. § 1744(c). This requirement went into effect immediately for claims located after the passage of FLPMA. Locators prior to October 21, 1976 were given three years to comply and then, like post–1976 locators, were required to file annually. Id. Is pre-FLPMA abandonment law dead? What rules apply to a dispute between two rival locators when the alleged abandonment occurred before FLPMA? The FLPMA recordation provisions are analyzed in United States v. Locke, 105 S.Ct. 1785 (1985), infra at page 478.

5. Obviously, great numbers of unpatented claims are not only a cloud on government title, but also create serious land management problems for public lands agencies. Must the BLM contest claims in an agency adjudication, and then face subsequent court proceedings, or may it under proper circumstances bypass its own administrative remedy and go directly to court? The question was litigated in response to modern ingenuity fully worthy of "The Great Barbeque" of the 19th century.

UNITED STATES v. ZWEIFEL

United States Court of Appeals, Tenth Circuit, 1975.
508 F.2d 1150, cert. denied sub nom. Roberts v. United States,
423 U.S. 1008 (1975).

LEWIS, Chief Judge.

Twenty-seven persons who, through Merle I. Zweifel, filed association mining claim certificates covering large tracts of public land in Wyoming, appeal from a judgment of the United States District Court for the District of Wyoming invalidating their claims and quieting title to the lands in the United States.

* * *

I

Zweifel advertised a claim-staking service and thereby induced the appellants and others to invest in his plan to stake association placer mining claims covering portions of the Green River Formation in Wyoming. Zweifel filed location certificates for several thousand such claims between 1965 and 1971. After filing the certificates, Zweifel communicated with firms holding coal prospecting permits or leases for the same lands; citing the Multiple Mineral Development Act, 30 U.S. C.A. § 526(e), he demanded survey and other information from those firms, and he requested that agreement be reached for the processing and extraction of locatable minerals commingled in the coal deposits.

On October 17, 1972, the United States brought suit against some 267 claimants, including the appellants, to invalidate claims that Zweifel purported to have located throughout nine counties of Wyoming. The government alleged that these claims constituted a cloud on its title to public lands. In a nonjury trial, the government's witnesses included six persons who, as geologists or mining engineers, had inspected some of the lands for which Zweifel had filed location certificates. They testified that they had observed no mineral discovery or production activity, nor any posts, stakes or location notices, on any of the Zweifel claims. An official of the Wyoming Tax Department testified of the absence of any record of mineral production for purposes of assessing state ad valorem taxes on production. * * * Finally, officials of the Bureau of Land Management testified that insofar as they had inspected Zweifel's claims they had observed no development or mining activity. A BLM inspector testified that it would have been impossible for Zweifel to locate, as his filed location certificates indicated, 2,000 mining claims in one day. The appellants presented no evidence; the court took notice, however, of interrogatories tending to show that Zweifel had represented to the appellants that he or his agents had performed necessary location and discovery work on the claims.

* * *

The court below held that the challenged Zweifel claims constituted a cloud on the title of the United States to public lands and that the government had proved prima facie that the claims were invalid on the following grounds. (1) The claims were not located in good faith for mining purposes. (2) The claimants made no discovery of mineral deposits locatable under federal mining law. (3) The claimants made no discovery of valuable mineral deposits. (4) The claims were not located in compliance with federal and state procedures with respect to the fixing of notice on and designating the boundaries of each claim.

* * *

The appellants' chief argument both at trial and on appeal is that the statutes giving the Secretary of the Interior plenary authority over the administration of public lands and the regulations authorizing the government to initiate administrative proceedings to invalidate mining claims create an exception to section 1345's jurisdictional grant to the district courts. Appellants thus contend that the Department of the Interior has exclusive original jurisdiction over actions commenced by the government for the sole purpose of invalidating unpatented mining claims. Appellants infer that the government has attempted to obscure the jurisdiction issue by styling its action to invalidate mining claims as one to quiet title. We begin by denying that the government acted improperly in this respect.

II

* * *

As the appellants observe, private claimants are prohibited from seeking federal court interference with proceedings to determine the validity of claims pending before the Department of the Interior. Once the Secretary has initiated an administrative contest, the jurisdiction of the courts is withdrawn as respects suits filed by *private* claimants either to halt the administrative proceedings or to substitute the court's determination of claim validity for that of the Interior Department. These authorities, however, do not foreclose the government's entering federal court to vindicate its title to public lands, United States v. Nogueira, 9 Cir., 403 F.2d 816. Nor do the statutes conferring upon the Secretary authority over the administration of public lands constitute, by their terms, an exception to federal court jurisdiction under 28 U.S. C.A. § 1345 [providing for jurisdiction in all civil actions commenced by the United States.] To read into these statutes an implied exception to the general grant of jurisdiction would, in cases like the present one, pointlessly defeat the policy of the mining laws to keep the public mineral lands open to qualified locators and thereby to encourage discovery of valuable deposits. See 30 U.S.C.A. § 22; United States v. Coleman, 390 U.S. 599. Were we to insist upon full administrative consideration of patently invalid claims, followed by court review of administrative action, we would needlessly prolong the period during which qualified locators would forbear from discovery work on the clouded lands.

We therefore hold that the United States may, at its election, proceed either in the administrative tribunal of the Department of the Interior or, under 28 U.S.C.A. § 1345, in the district court to clear title to public lands where the validity of unpatented mining claims is at issue.

* * *

Appellants' more compelling argument is that even if the district court had jurisdiction over the government's action, the court should nevertheless have deferred to the Department of the Interior for an administrative determination of the Zweifel placer claims' validity.
* * *

Certainly the Interior Department is charged with primary responsibility for determinations of the validity of mining claims. But we believe that the court below correctly refused to insist upon a prior administrative inquiry to the challenged Zweifel claims for two reasons.

First, the agency to which appellants would have the court turn was itself very much a part of this litigation, and the agency's position with respect to the claims was clear. * * *

Second, the conclusion of the court below that Zweifel did not locate appellants' claims in good faith for mining purposes did not involve a factual inquiry with respect to which courts, because of their relative inexperience in the area, must defer to the expertise of the

Interior Department. The issue of good faith in filing location certificates involves an inquiry into the intent of the locator. United States v. Nogueira, supra, 403 F.2d at 823. Courts, we submit, regularly decide such questions, and the district court in the present case was fully qualified to do so. * * *

III

Appellants acknowledge the established rule that in an action to contest mining claims the government bears the burden of establishing prima facie the invalidity of the claims, the burden then shifting to the claimant to prove that his claims are valid. United States v. Springer, 9 Cir., 491 F.2d 239; Foster v. Seaton, 106 U.S.App.D.C. 253, 271 F.2d 836. Appellants do not apparently dispute that the government established prima facie the invalidity of their claims. Rather they urge reexamination of the rule requiring only prima facie proof of invalidity in light of the general federal principle that the party who has pleaded the existence or nonexistence of a fact must bear the whole burden of proving the same.

In both *Foster* and *Springer* claimants sought court review of adverse rulings by the Interior Department. They argued that the rule requiring the government to make only a prima facie showing of claim invalidity in agency contests contravened provisions of the Administrative Procedure Act that require the proponent of a rule or order to bear the burden of proof, except as otherwise provided by statute. In response to this argument both courts reasoned as follows. The mining laws give a person the right to initiate a claim to public lands by means of the unilateral act of entry. After he complies with all the requirements of the law as to discovery, location, and assessment work, his entry may ripen into a claim against the United States. In a contest proceeding, therefore, the claimant rather than the government is the proponent of a ruling that he has complied with applicable mining laws. The government must go forward with sufficient evidence to establish prima facie the invalidity of contested claims, and the burden then shifts to the claimant to show by a preponderance of the evidence that his claim is valid. United States v. Springer, supra, 491 F.2d at 242; Foster v. Seaton, supra, 271 F.2d at 838.

We believe the same reasoning applies in the present quiet title action. "Were the rule otherwise, anyone could enter upon the public domain and ultimately obtain title unless the Government undertook the affirmative burden of proving that no valuable deposit existed." Foster v. Seaton, supra, 271 F.2d at 838. We agree with the cited authorities that Congress did not intend to place this burden on the Secretary of the Interior.

We have considered appellants' other assignments of error and believe them to be similarly without merit. The judgment of the court below is therefore affirmed.

NOTES

1. Would the result have been different if Zweifel's locations had been made in a national forest and the Forest Service, rather than the BLM, sought to file the quiet title action?

2. Merle Zweifel is just one of many to run bogus claim-staking services, but, as Professor Leshy explains in THE MINING LAW OF 1872: A STUDY IN PERPETUAL MOTION (1986), he was surely the most picaresque:

> Until [Zweifel's] flamboyance, greed, and disarming candor about the game he was playing attracted so much attention that he could no longer be tolerated, the "old Prospector," as he styled himself, filed several million mining claims on federal land all over the west. (He himself put the figure at 30 million acres, which included an unspecified amount of land claimed on the outer continental shelf.) When Congress authorized the Central Arizona Project, part of which required construction of an aqueduct from the Colorado River to Phoenix and Tucson, the old prospector was there, filing claims on 600,000 acres along the aqueduct route. When interest in oil shale development began to revive on Colorado's west slope after 1960, Zweifel surfaced with 465,000 acres of mining claims in the Piceance Basin. Acknowledging that he would never actively explore the land (because that would damage the scenery, he said) he exploited the Law's offer of free access to the federal lands with a vengeance. His "real goal in life," he was reported as saying, was to "discredit bureaucrats and their hypocritical ways," though he also admitted that fighting large companies "is an enjoyment I can't pass up," and that, finally, "I do have a lust for money."

Merle Zweifel has now passed on, but one of his colleagues sued the Secretary of Interior for damages resulting from the invalidation of large numbers of claims. Among several other things, the complaint requested damages of "$1,346,390,400.00 due to breach of contract" and "three hundred billion dollars in damages due to breach of fiduciary duty, bad faith and unfair dealing." Relief was denied. Roberts v. Clark, 615 F.Supp. 1554 (D.Colo.1985).

3. Although the attempts at under-the-table appropriation are seldom as blatant or baseless as Zweifel's, abuses of the mining laws have been common since their inception. See generally Sheridan, HARD ROCK MINING ON THE PUBLIC LAND (1977); Senzel, Revision of the Mining Law of 1872, Study for the Senate Comm. on Energy and Natural Resources, 95th Cong., 1st Sess. (1977) (Committee Print). In a study of 240 western mining claims, selected at random, the GAO found in 1974 that only one was being mined and only three had ever been mined. Comptroller General, Modernization of 1872 Mining Law Needed to Encourage Domestic Mineral Production, Protect the Environment, and Improve Public Land Management 8 (1974). Usually, as

in *Coleman,* the motivation is acquisition of the land for other than mineral purposes.   One famous example was United States Senator Ralph Cameron's attempt to locate a claim on the trailhead of the Bright Angel Trail into the Grand Canyon in order to charge access fees.   See Cameron v. United States, 252 U.S. 450 (1920).   BLM and Forest Service employees still must evict occasional "snowbirds" from their mineral claims on BLM lands near the outskirts of sunny resorts in the Southwest and continue the seemingly never-ending process of rooting out thousands of "miners" from prime recreation spots in back canyons from the Pacific Northwest to the Rocky Mountains.

6. THE PATENTED CLAIM

A holder of an unpatented claim may seek a fee patent pursuant to 30 U.S.C.A. § 29:

> A patent for any land claimed and located for valuable deposits may be obtained in the following manner: Any person, association, or corporation authorized to locate a claim * * * having claimed and located a piece of land for such purposes * * * may file in the proper land office an application for a patent. * * * The claimant at the time of filing his application, or at any time thereafter, within the sixty days of publication, shall file with the register a certificate of the United States supervisor of surveys that $500 worth of labor has been expended or improvements made upon the claim by himself or grantors. * * * If no adverse claim shall have been filed with the register of the proper land office at the expiration of the sixty days of publication, it shall be assumed that the applicant is entitled to a patent, upon the payment to the proper officer of $5 per acre, and that no adverse claim exists; and thereafter no objection from third parties to the issuance of a patent shall be heard, except it be shown that the applicant has failed to comply with the terms of this chapter.
> * * *

Placer claims are governed by the substantially similar provisions of 30 U.S.C.A. § 37, although the payment is $2.50 per acre and the ground need not be surveyed if the lines conform to subdivisions of a public survey.   Claimants may also obtain a five-acre, non-adjacent, nonmineral parcel for use as a millsite.   See 30 U.S.C.A. § 42.

A patent to a lode claim carries with it the same extralateral rights that attached to the unpatented lode claim.   The applicant for the patent has the burden of proof as the "proponent of an order" under the Administrative Procedure Act. 5 U.S.C.A. § 556(d).   Cf. Foster v. Seaton, 271 F.2d 836 (D.C.Cir.1959); United States v. Zweifel, supra. The *Coleman* test for value is applied as of the date of the application for patent (or the date of the contest to an unpatented claim), not the date that discovery was originally made.   Best v. Humboldt Placer Mining Co., 371 U.S. 334 (1963).   Thus, "even if at one time there was a valid mineral prospect on claimed land, changed economic conditions can destroy" the original discovery.   Bales v. Ruch, 522 F.Supp. 150, 153 (E.D.Cal.1981).

The patent ordinarily grants a fee simple.   Patents located in wilderness areas, however, include only the minerals, not the surface estate.   16 U.S.C.A. § 1133(d)(3).   Claims located after 1955 are subject to management of the surface resources by the United States while the claim is unpatented under the Surface Resources Act of 1955, 30 U.S. C.A. § 612(b), but that Act does not place any limitations on the fee character of the patent once it is issued.

With the end of the disposition era and the advent of the *Coleman* test, the Department of Interior has developed "a grudging and somewhat tightfisted approach toward claims under the mining laws." Strauss, Mining Claims on Public Lands: A Study of Interior Department Procedures, 1974 Utah L.Rev. 185, 187.   That point is made visually in Anderson, Federal Mineral Policy: The General Mining Law of 1872, 16 Nat.Res.J. 601, 604 (1976):

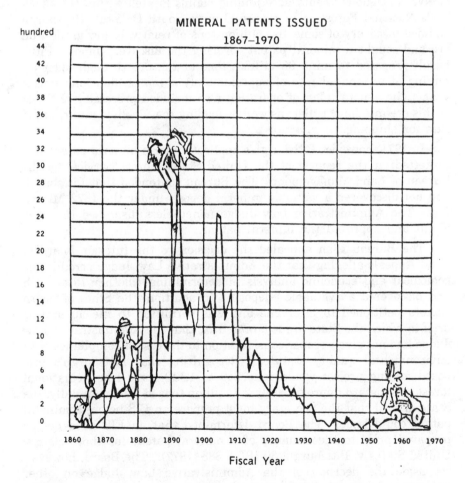

MINERAL PATENTS ISSUED
1867–1970

Fiscal Year

The highwater mark for the issuance of patents was 1892 when 3,242 patents were issued.   In all, approximately 64,000 patents, totaling 2.9 million acres have issued. See generally Current Mineral Laws of the United States, House Comm. on Interior and Insular Affairs, 94th Cong., 1st Sess. (Comm. Print No. 13) (1976).

What factors are relevant in advising a holder of an unpatented claim whether to go to patent?

STATE OF SOUTH DAKOTA v. ANDRUS
United States Court of Appeals, Eighth Circuit, 1980.
614 F.2d 1190, cert. denied, 449 U.S. 822 (1980).

HENLEY, Circuit Judge.

* * *

I

Pittsburgh [Pacific Company] filed an application under the General Mining Act of 1872, 30 U.S.C.A. § 21 et seq., for a mineral patent to twelve contiguous twenty acre mining claims located within the Black Hills National Forest in Lawrence County, South Dakota. Pittsburgh claimed discovery of some 160 million tons of relatively low grade iron ore and sought a mineral patent covering the discovery lands. Pittsburgh proposed to mine 96 million tons of the ore through open pit mining at an annual rate of approximately seven million long tons a year. The general plan of operation also included processing the best of this ore into hard pellets as well as loading these pellets into railroad cars for shipping.

In 1971, however, Pittsburgh's application for a mineral patent was contested, at the request of the United States Forest Service, by the Bureau of Land Management. The Bureau contended that Pittsburgh had not discovered a valuable mineral deposit under the 1872 Mining Act. The Administrative Law Judge nonetheless dismissed the complaint and approved the mineral patent.

The Bureau then appealed the decision to the Interior Board of Land Appeals alleging that the Administrative Law Judge erred in his geological and economic analysis in determining whether Pittsburgh had discovered a "valuable" deposit. In addition, the State of South Dakota petitioned to intervene and was permitted to file an amicus brief in which the State argued, inter alia, that the Administrative Law Judge had not given proper consideration to the cost of compliance with environmental quality statutes. Recognizing that Pittsburgh's proposed mining project would take 240 to 1,140 acres from a national forest and discard approximately 2.3 million tons of waste annually, the State argued that the Secretary must prepare an EIS before a mineral patent could issue. The Board determined that an EIS need not be prepared prior to the issuance of a mineral patent for these claims. United States v. Pittsburgh, 30 IBLA 388 (1977). The Board, however, set aside the decision of the Administrative Law Judge on other grounds and remanded the case for further hearings with respect to the expense of complying with environmental laws as well as any other issue which might arise.

Subsequently, the State filed an original action in federal district court seeking to compel preparation of an EIS prior to the issuance of a mineral patent naming as defendants the United States Department of the Interior and Pittsburgh. Both defendants moved to dismiss contending the issuance of a mineral patent is not a major federal action which requires an EIS, and Judge Bogue granted the motion. South Dakota v. Andrus, 462 F.Supp. 905 (D.S.D.1978).

II

The issue on this appeal is whether the United States Department of the Interior is required by § 102(2)(C) of the National Environmental Policy Act, 42 U.S.C.A. § 4332(C) to file an EIS prior to the issuance of a mineral patent.

Our starting point is, of course, the statutory language. Section 102(2)(C) provides in part that an EIS is required for "major Federal actions which significantly affect the quality of the human environment." Applied to this case, § 102(2)(C) mandates the filing of an EIS if (1) the issuance of a mineral patent is an "action" within the meaning of the provision, and (2) the alleged federal action is "major" in the sense that it significantly affects the quality of the human environment.

A

We turn first to the question whether the granting of a mineral patent constitutes an "action" within the meaning of NEPA. As the district court noted, it is well established that the issuance of a mineral patent is a ministerial act. Both the Supreme Court, in a series of decisions in the early part of this century, Wilbur v. United States ex rel. Krushnic, 280 U.S. 306, 318–19 (1929); Cameron v. United States, 252 U.S. 450, 454 (1920); Roberts v. United States, 176 U.S. 221, 231 (1900), and, more recently, the Interior Board of Land Appeals, United States v. Kosanke Sand Corp., 12 IBLA 282, 290–91 (1973); United States v. O'Leary, 63 ID 341 (1956), have so concluded.

Ministerial acts, however, have generally been held outside the ambit of NEPA's EIS requirement. Reasoning that the primary purpose of the impact statement is to aid agency decisionmaking, courts have indicated that nondiscretionary acts should be exempt from the requirement.

In light of these decisions, it is at least doubtful that the Secretary's nondiscretionary approval of a mineral patent constitutes an "action" under § 102(2)(C).

B

But even if a ministerial act may in some circumstances fall within § 102(2)(C), we still cannot say that the issuance of a mineral patent is a "major" federal action under the statute. This conclusion does not stem from the court's belief that an agency itself must propose to build a facility and directly affect the environment in order to constitute a "major" federal action within the meaning of NEPA. We fully recognize that NEPA's impact statement procedure has been held to apply where the federal government grants a lease, Cady v. Morton, 527 F.2d 786 (9th Cir.1975); Davis v. Morton, 469 F.2d 593 (10th Cir.1972); [or] issues a permit or license * * *.

In each of these cases, however, an agency took a "major" federal action because it enabled a private party to act so as to significantly affect the environment. Such enablements have consistently been held subject to NEPA. See National Forest Preservation v. Butz, 485 F.2d 408, 412 (9th Cir.1973), and authorities cited therein. But in the instant case, the granting of a mineral patent does not enable the private party, Pittsburgh, to do anything. Unlike the case where a lease, permit or license is required before the particular project can begin, the issuance of a mineral patent is not a precondition which enables a party to begin mining operations. 30 U.S.C.A. § 26.

* * *

In recent years the mining laws governing the locating of mineral claims have remained unchanged, 30 U.S.C.A. §§ 22, 26, and modern decisions have continued to allow locators of mining claims to extract minerals without a patent provided they have met the statutory prerequisites. See, e.g., Lombardo Turquoise Milling & Mining Co. v. Hemanes, 430 F.Supp. 429 (D.Nev.1977).

In light of the fact that a mineral patent in actuality is not a federal determination which enables the party to mine, we conclude in present context that the granting of such a patent is not a "major" federal action within the meaning of § 102(2)(C).[5]

III

In reaching this conclusion, we do not decide the question whether an EIS should be required at some point after the mineral patent has issued. While a federal agency need not prepare an EIS during the "germination process of a potential proposal," Kleppe v. Sierra Club, 427 U.S. 390, 401 n. 12, 406 (1976), this is not to say that at some later date an EIS will not be required. We note that Pittsburgh's proposed mining project is substantial and that if Pittsburgh decides to build the mine many actions may be necessary. For example, the claims at issue will presumedly need permits from the Forest Service for roads, water pipelines and railroad rights of way. 43 U.S.C.A. § 1761(a)(1) and (a)(6). Moreover, the company may possibly seek to make land exchanges with the Forest Service. We leave to another day the question whether an EIS would be required in connection with any one or more such actions.

5. Assuming that the issuance of a mineral patent is a major federal action significantly affecting the quality of the human environment, appellant argues that requiring the Secretary to prepare an EIS is not incompatible with the Secretary's duties under the General Mining Act of 1872. Although we believe that appellant's contention is questionable, cf. Natural Resources Defense Council, Inc. v. Berklund, 609 F.2d 553 (D.C.Cir.1979), in light of our conclusion that the issuance of a mineral patent is not a major federal action, we find it unnecessary to address this argument.

It is sufficient for the moment to conclude that in the present case an EIS need not be filed prior to the issuance of a mineral patent.

[Affirmed.]

NOTE

Does NEPA apply to the intermediate steps of pedis possessio, location, discovery, or unpatented claim?

7. INROADS ON THE RIGHT TO PROSPECT AND MINE

It was held early on and has been assumed for generations that the Mining Act creates an absolute right in the miner, first to prospect, thereafter to mine any valuable deposit discovered, and finally to get fee title to the mineral land. The right is said to override any attempted administrative restriction or other land use consideration. Cf. Haggard, Regulation of Mining Law Activities on Federal Lands, 21 Rocky Mtn.Min.L.Inst. 349 (1975). Under this absolute standard, mining is a dominant if not exclusive public land use, and no "balancing" of relative values and detriments of other uses is allowable. This interpretation, together with the many admitted abuses of the Act, have led to attempts to replace it with a leasing system similar to that governing oil and gas drilling on the federal lands. See section B(5) infra.

Others contend that the right to mine was never as absolute as miners have assumed. Looking to general statutes such as the Forest Service Organic Act of 1897, 16 U.S.C.A. §§ 478, 551, or to the language of the 1872 Act itself ("under regulations prescribed by law", 30 U.S. C.A. § 22), some have argued that federal land management agencies have a regulatory power which, if not broad enough for agencies to forbid prospecting or mining, at least allows them to impose conditions for mitigation of the damage done by exploring and mining operations.

The autonomy of the hardrock miner has been limited by a number of modern regulatory programs. This section examines the Surface Resources Act of 1955; administrative regulation, first undertaken by the Forest Service in 1974; the mining provisions in the Federal Land Policy and Management Act of 1976; and state attempts to oversee hardrock mining. It concludes with cases seeking to draw the line between regulation and taking.

UNITED STATES v. CURTIS–NEVADA MINES, INC.
United States Court of Appeals, Ninth Circuit, 1980.
611 F.2d 1277.

HUG, Circuit Judge:

This case concerns the right of the general public to use the surface of land upon which unpatented mining claims have been located, when that use does not interfere with mining activities. The principal issue is whether the owner of unpatented mining claims has the right to exclude members of the general public from such use of the surface of the land for recreational purposes or access to other public lands unless they have obtained a specific governmental permit or license for such use. To resolve this issue, we are called upon to construe the provisions of the Surface Resources and Multiple Use Act of 1955 ("Multiple Use Act") (codified at 30 U.S.C.A. §§ 611–612).

The United States brought this action to enjoin Curtis-Nevada Mines, Inc. and its president, Robert Curtis, from prohibiting members of the public from using the surface of appellees' unpatented mining claims for recreational purposes or for entrance to adjacent National Forest lands. Since 1970, appellees located approximately 203 mining claims on public lands administered by the Bureau of Land Management under the Department of the Interior and on lands within the Toiyabe National Forest administered by the Forest Service under the Department of Agriculture. These claims cover approximately 13 square miles; 21 of the claims are in Nevada and the remainder in California. This action arose after appellees prevented members of the public from entering their unpatented mining claims and barred access to several roads which crossed their claims. * * *

The District Court, ruling on cross motions for summary judgment, held that under section 4(b) of the Multiple Use Act, 30 U.S.C.A. § 612(b), the public is entitled to use the surface of unpatented mining claims for recreational purposes and for access to adjoining lands, but that this use and access is available only to those members of the public who hold specific recreation licenses or permits from a state or federal agency. United States v. Curtis-Nevada Mines, Inc., 415 F.Supp. 1373 (E.D.Cal.1976). The United States appeals from the portion of the judgment that allows access to the mining claims only to those persons having specific written licenses or permits from a state or federal agency. We reverse that portion of the judgment and affirm the remainder of the judgment.

I

Curtis states that he located and filed the 203 claims after stumbling upon an outcropping of valuable minerals while on a deer hunting trip. He states that, within this 13-mile area, he has located gold, platinum, copper, silver, tungsten, pitchblend, palladium, triduim, asmium, rhodium, ruthenium, scanduim, vanduim, ytterbuim, yttrium, europium, and "all the rare earths." These minerals he maintains have a value in the trillions. The mining activity of the appellees was very limited. At the time this litigation was instituted there was only one employee, who performed chiefly caretaking duties such as watching after equipment and preventing the public from entering the claims.

Hunters, hikers, campers and other persons who had customarily used the area for recreation were excluded by the appellees. Curtis posted "no trespassing" signs on the claims and constructed barricades on the Blackwell Canyon Road and the Rickey Canyon Road, which lead up into the mountains and provide access to the Toiyabe National

Forest. After receiving numerous complaints, the United States filed this action asserting the rights of the general public to the use of the surface of the mining claims. * * * The court denied the request of the United States that Curtis be enjoined from using guards or manned gates. The court held that Curtis can use gates or barricades if personnel are available to remove the barricades for persons requesting admittance with a proper permit.

II

Section 4(b) of the Multiple Use Act provides in pertinent part:

> Rights under any mining claim hereafter located under the mining laws of the United States shall be subject, prior to issuance of patent therefor, to the right of the United States to manage and dispose of the vegetative surface resources thereof and to manage other surface resources thereof (except mineral deposits subject to location under the mining laws of the United States). Any such mining claim shall also be subject, prior to issuance of patent therefor, to the right of the United States, its permittees, and licensees, to use so much of the surface thereof as may be necessary for such purposes or for access to adjacent land: *Provided, however,* That any use of the surface of any such mining claim by the United States, its permittees or licensees, shall be such as not to endanger or materially interfere with prospecting, mining or processing operations or uses reasonably incident thereto * * *.

30 U.S.C.A. § 612(b).

As noted by the district court, the meaning of "other surface resources" and of "permittees and licensees" is somewhat ambiguous. The principal issues in this case are whether recreational use is embodied within the meaning of "other surface resources" and whether the phrase "permittees and licensees" includes only those members of the public who have specific written permits or licenses. We agree with the district court that administrative interpretation of the language by the Solicitor's Office in the Department of Interior does not provide any clear direction in the construction of this section of the statute, 415 F.Supp. at 1378.

We look first to the legislative history of the Act. As this court has previously noted, Congress did not intend to change the basic principles of the mining laws when it enacted the Multiple Use Act. Converse v. Udall, 399 F.2d 616, 617 (9th Cir.1968), cert. denied, 393 U.S. 1025 (1969). The Multiple Use Act was corrective legislation, which attempted to clarify the law and to alleviate abuses that had occurred under the mining laws. H.R.Rep. No. 730, 84th Cong., 1st Sess. 7–8, reprinted in [1955] 2 U.S.Code Cong. & Admin.News, pp. 2474, 2480 (hereinafter House Report 730) * * *.

This concept of multiple use of surface resources of a mining claim was not intended, however, to interfere with the historical relationship between the possessor of a mining claim and the United States.

* * * "[T]he United States would be authorized to manage and dispose of surface resources, or to use the surface for access to adjacent lands, so long as and to the extent that these activities do not endanger or materially interfere with mining, or related operations or activities on the mining claim." Id. at 10, U.S.Code Cong. & Admin.News, p. 2483.

Under the general mining law enacted in 1872, individuals were encouraged to prospect, explore and develop the mineral resources of the public domain through an assurance of ultimate private ownership of the minerals and the lands so developed. * * *

* * *

* * * However, claimants could continue mining activities on the claims, without ever obtaining a patent. As a practical matter, mining claimants could remain in exclusive possession of the claim without ever proving a valid discovery or actually conducting mining operations. This led to abuses of the mining laws when mining claims were located with no real intent to prospect or mine but rather to gain possession of the surface resources. Furthermore, even persons who did have the legitimate intent to utilize the claim for the development of the mineral content at the time of the location often did not proceed to do so, and thus large areas of the public domain were withdrawn, and as a result these surface resources could not be utilized by the general public for other purposes.

It was to correct this deficiency in the mining law that Congress in 1955 enacted the Multiple Use Act. Some of the abuses and problems that the legislation was designed to correct are detailed in House Report 730:

> The mining laws are sometimes used to obtain claim or title to valuable timber actually located within the claim boundaries. Frequently, whether or not the locator so intends, such claims have the effect of blocking access-road development to adjacent tracts of merchantable Federal timber, or to generally increase costs of administration and management of adjacent lands. The fraudulent locator in national forests, in addition to obstructing orderly management and the competitive sale of timber, obtains for himself high-value, publicly owned, surface resources bearing no relationship to legitimate mining activity.

> Mining locations made under existing law may, and do, whether by accident or design, frequently block access: to water needed in grazing use of the national forests or other public lands; to valuable recreational areas; to agents of the Federal Government desiring to reach adjacent lands for purposes of managing wild-game habitat or improving fishing streams so as to thwart the public harvest and proper management of fish and game resources on the public lands generally, both on the located lands and on adjacent lands.

Under existing law, fishing and mining have sometimes been combined in another form of nonconforming use of the public lands: a group of fisherman-prospectors will locate a good stream, stake out successive mining claims flanking the stream, post their mining claims with "No trespassing" signs, and proceed to enjoy their own private fishing camp. So too, with hunter-prospectors, except that their blocked-out "mining claims" embrace wildlife habitats; posted, they constitute excellent hunting camps.

The effect of nonmining activity under color of existing mining law should be clear to all: a waste of valuable resources of the surface on lands embraced within claims which might satisfy the basic requirement of mineral discovery, but which were, in fact, made for a purpose other than mining; for lands adjacent to such locations, timber, water, forage, fish and wildlife, and recreational values wasted or destroyed because of increased cost of management, difficulty of administration, or inaccessibility; the activities of a relatively few pseudominers reflecting unfairly on the legitimate mining industry.

H.R.Rep. No. 730 at 6, U.S.Code Cong. & Admin.News, pp. 2478–79.

* * *

In the district court proceedings Curtis asserted that recreational uses are not encompassed within the meaning of "other surface resources" in § 612(b). However, as the district court properly held, the phrase "other surface resources" was clearly intended to include recreational uses. It is apparent from the previously quoted portions of House Report 730 at 6, as well as committee hearings cited by the district court, 415 F.Supp. at 1378, that recreation was one of the "other surface resources" to which 30 U.S.C.A. § 612(b) refers. This conclusion is further buttressed by the Bureau of Land Management regulations implementing the Multiple Use Act. It is therefore a surface resource that the United States has a right to manage and that the United States and its permittees and licensees have a right to use so long as the use does not "endanger or materially interfere with prospecting, mining or processing operations or uses reasonably incident thereto." 30 U.S.C.A. § 612(b).

The remaining question that the district court addressed concerns the identification of the "permittees and licensees" of the United States entitled to use the surface resources. The district court held that the "permittees and licensees" are only those who have specific written permits or licenses from any state or federal agency allowing those persons to engage in any form of recreation on public land. The court mentions hunting, fishing or camping permits as illustrative of the required permits. It is at this point that we disagree with the district court.

Historically the United States has managed the lands within the public domain as fee owner and trustee for the people of the United States. Light v. United States, 220 U.S. 523, 527 (1911); Camfield v.

United States, 167 U.S. 518, 524 (1897). Also, in the management of public lands, the United States has historically allowed the general public to use the public domain for recreation and other purposes, and often without a specific, formal permit. Such access has been described as an implied license.

Originally, grazing of livestock was such a use that was allowed without a formal permit. In Buford v. Houtz, 133 U.S. 320 (1890), the Supreme Court found an implied license to graze livestock on the public lands and acquiescence in the practice by the government as proprietor of the public lands * * *.

This principle of an implied license of the public to use lands within the public domain freely without a formal license was again reaffirmed by the court in Light v. United States [supra] * * *.

In McKee v. Gratz, 260 U.S. 127 (1922), the Court applied this concept of an implied license to include a license to use large tracts of uncultivated lands for recreational uses. Mr. Justice Holmes in the opinion of the Court stated:

> The strict rule of the English common law as to entry upon a close must be taken to be mitigated by common understanding with regard to the large expanses of unenclosed and uncultivated land in many parts at least of this country. Over these it is customary to wander, shoot and fish at will until the owner sees fit to prohibit it. A license may be implied from the habits of the country.

Id. at 136.

The historical principle that no formal permission, permit, or license is required for use of public lands for general recreational use or access to adjoining lands was formalized by the Forest Service with regard to National Forests in 1942 when it enacted a regulation which states in pertinent part:

> The temporary use or occupancy of national forest lands by individuals for camping, picnicking, hiking, fishing, hunting, riding, boating, parking of vehicles and similar purposes may be allowed without a special use permit; provided * * * that permits may be required for such uses when in the judgment of the Chief of the Forest Service the public interest or the protection of such lands requires the issuance of permits.

36 CFR § 251.1(a)(2) (1979).

A similar policy of holding public lands open for recreational use has been followed by the Bureau of Land Management in its administration of the 457 million acres of public lands not set aside for national forests, parks or other special uses.

These regulations confirm a traditional policy for the use of public lands allowing the public to use lands within the public domain for general recreational purposes without holding a written, formal permit, except as to activities which have been specifically regulated.

The Multiple Use Act was designed to open up the public domain to greater, more varied uses. To require that anyone desiring to use claimed lands for recreation must obtain a formal, written license would greatly restrict and inhibit the use of a major portion of the public domain.[7] It is doubtful that Congress would intend that such use be dependent upon a formal permit, because the federal agencies do not generally issue or require permits for recreational use of public lands. To require a formal written permit would either put the public in a position of having to obtain permits but having no place from which to obtain them, or it would require the government to institute procedures to issue permits, a process which the government argues is burdensome and unnecessary.

One of the clear purposes of the 1955 legislation was to prevent the withdrawal of surface resources from other public use merely by locating a mining claim. The inertia of the situation was previously with the mining claimant who retained exclusive possession of the surface of the claim until the location was invalidated by affirmative action. As to claims located after the 1955 legislation, however, the inertia works the other way. Essentially, the surface resources remain in the public domain for use as before with the exception that the mining claimant is entitled to use the surface resources for prospecting and mining purposes and that the other uses by the general public cannot materially interfere with the prospecting and mining operation. Thus, the vast acreage upon which mining claims have been located since 1955 or claims which, by operation of the statute, have become subject to the provisions of section 612(b), remain open for public use except for the restrictions imposed where actual mining or prospecting operations are taking place.[8]

* * *

Consequently, in light of the historical background of the use of the public domain for many purposes without express written permits or licenses we do not find in the legislative history of the 1955 act an intent to so limit the meaning of "permittees and licensees." Most assuredly, the B.L.M. or the Forest Service can require permits for public use of federal lands in their management of federal lands;

7. A report from the Department of Agriculture, to the House Committee on Interior and Insular Affairs concerning the proposed legislation stated that as of January 1, 1952 there were 84,000 unpatented claims, covering 2.2 million acres of national forest but only 2% of these mines were producing minerals in commercial quantities and probably no more than 40% could be considered valid. As of January 1, 1955 there were an estimated 166,000 claims covering 4 million acres. H.R.Rep. 730, 84th Cong., 1st Sess., reprinted in [1955] 2 U.S.Code Cong. & Admin.News, pp. 2474, 2492–93.

8. Section 5 of the Multiple Use Act, 30 U.S.C.A. § 613 provides an in rem proce-dure to identify which unpatented claims will be subject to the provisions of § 612. Briefly stated § 613 provides that the federal agency having responsibility for administering the surface resources may publish a notice requiring claimants to file within 150 days a verified statement concerning their mining claims. Failure to file the statement constitutes a waiver of any rights in the claims that are contrary to the limitations of § 612. The failure to file does not, however, affect the validity of the claim itself but only subjects the claim to the limitations of § 612. Thus, a claim located prior to 1955 may, by this procedure, become subject to the limitations of § 612.

however, they need not do so as a prerequisite to public use of surface resources of unpatented mining claims.

It should be noted that mining claimants have at least two remedies in the event that public use interferes with prospecting or mining activities. Section 612(b) provides that "any use of the surface * * * shall be such as not to endanger or materially interfere with prospecting, mining or processing operations or uses reasonably incident thereto." The mining claimant can protest to the managing federal agency about public use which results in material interference and, if unsatisfied, can bring suit to enjoin the activity. Secondly, a claimant with a valid claim can apply for a patent which, when granted, would convey fee title to the property.

In the present case, appellees have not presented any evidence that the public use of land included within their unpatented mining claim has "materially interfered" with any mining activity. Absent such evidence, section 612(b) applies in this case to afford the general public a right of free access to the land on which the mining claims have been located for recreational use of the surface resources and for access to adjoining property. Therefore, we reverse the portion of the judgment that requires specific written permits or licenses for entry onto the mining claims, and we remand this case to the district court for entry of an injunction consistent with the views expressed in this opinion.

NOTES

1. Does the reasoning in *Curtis-Nevada* apply to locations made before the effective date of the 1955 Act? To prospecting begun before 1955?

2. The court in *Curtis-Nevada* did not cite Leo Sheep v. United States, 440 U.S. 668 (1979), supra at page 112. Should it have?

3. Just exactly what does "manage the vegetative resources" mean, and what is the scope of the authority it confers? Does the 1955 Act have any impact on the kind of patent to be issued? Will the prudent claim holder now seek a patent more often?

4. The 1955 Act deals not just with public access and surface management, but also refers to "uses reasonably incident" to mining. Is there a similar limit on pre-1955 claims? See supra at page 450. See also, e.g., United States v. Langley, 587 F.Supp. 1258, 1262–63 (E.D. Cal.1984).

5. The Surface Resources Act has had impacts on other forms of recreational mining. See People v. Wilmarth, 132 Cal.App.3d 383, 183 Cal.Rptr. 176, 179 (1982), upholding a warrantless search:

> Vegetation consists of "plant life" (Webster's New Internat.Dict. (3d ed. 1971) p. 2537). Marijuana is a plant (Health & Saf.Code, § 11018). Entry by Agent Dimmick, a federal officer, on land the site of an unpatented mining claim to search for, remove or otherwise deal with illegally cultivated marijuana is squarely within the authority reserved by Con-

gress to the federal government to "manage and dispose of the vegetative surface resources" on such land. Arguably, illegally grown marijuana is not a "resource" within the meaning of the act; nevertheless, its discovery and removal is directly related to management of other vegetation indisputably within that classification.

NOTE: FOREST SERVICE MINING REGULATIONS

In the late 1960's and early 1970's, two conservation battles over mining—an ASARCO proposal to build an access road to a molybdenum claim deep in the White Cloud Mountains in Idaho and a dispute over development in the Stillwater Complex in the Custer and Gallatin National Forests in Montana—drew the Forest Service into the regulation of hardrock mining. Although authority for administering the 1872 Act is lodged in the BLM, the Forest Service moved against excessive mining practices under the Surface Resources Act of 1955. Forest Service authority to obtain judicial relief enjoining unreasonably destructive prospecting operations under the 1955 Act was upheld in United States v. Richardson, 599 F.2d 290 (9th Cir.1979), cert. denied, 444 U.S. 1014 (1980).

In the meantime, the agency promulgated regulations in 1974 under the aegis of its 1897 Organic Act. 36 C.F.R. Part 228 (1985). The regulations require all miners to conduct operations so as to minimize adverse environmental effects on the national forest surface resources. See Friends of the Earth, Inc. v. Butz, 406 F.Supp. 742 (D.Mont.1975), dismissed as moot, 576 F.2d 1377 (9th Cir.1978). A miner must file a notice of intent with the local district ranger before commencing any operation that might cause surface disturbance. If the district ranger determines that such operations will "likely cause significant disturbance of surface resources," the miner must then file a plan of operations. The ranger reviews and revises the submitted plan with the operator until both agree upon an acceptable plan. The regulations direct the ranger to make an initial response within 30 days if possible, and not later than 90 days. The final operating plan should include surface environmental protection and reclamation requirements, as well as a bond requirement to cover the costs of damage or unfinished reclamation. Pending final approval of the plan, the district ranger may allow work on such operations so long as it is conducted to minimize environmental impacts. The regulations also provide for access restrictions, operations in wilderness areas, periodic inspection by the Forest Service, and remedies for noncompliance with the regulations. See 36 C.F.R. §§ 228.1–.15 (1985).

The authority of the Forest Service to adopt the regulations was challenged from the outset on the basis that the regulations would infringe on hardrock miners' historic right to self-initiate mining operations on the Public Lands. Rep. John Melcher, Chairman of the House Subcommittee on Public Lands, wrote to Forest Service Chief John McGuire on June 20, 1974 concerning the proposed regulations:

Following publication of the proposed regulations, Subcommittee Members and many others in the House received a large volume of mail urging that steps be taken to stop their issuance. Much of the correspondence was from small miners and prospectors who attacked the regulations as being an infringement on their rights to prospect and mine on public domain National Forest lands. Many feared that the regulations would drive individual prospectors and the small mining companies out of the National Forests by imposing unreasonable restrictions and costs on their activities. * * *

* * *

The Subcommittee is strongly of the opinion that whatever authority may exist for such regulations lies in the 1897 Organic Act (16 U.S.C.A. §§ 478, 551) and not in the other acts cited in the proposed regulations. The Subcommittee also believes that the 1897 Act clearly cannot be used as authority to prohibit prospecting, mining and mineral processing in the National Forests. Certainly a proper balance must be struck between the legitimate needs of the miner to enter and use the National Forests for mining purposes on the one hand and the demands that they be protected from unnecessarily harmful effects resulting from mining activities on the other. Leaving aside the question of specific statutory authority, any regulations issued must rise or fall on the reasonableness test; that is, such regulations cannot extend further than to require those things which preserve and protect the National Forests from needless damage by prospectors and miners. In applying the reasonableness test, Forest Service administrators must keep constantly in mind that the miner has a statutory right, not a privilege, under the 1897 Act to go upon the open public domain lands in National Forests for mineral exploration and development purposes. Administrators may not unreasonably restrict the exercise of that right.

* * *

Mining industry attacks on the legality of the regulations—couched in terms of protecting surface resources rather than regulating mining—culminated in the following opinion.

UNITED STATES v. WEISS

United States Court of Appeals, Ninth Circuit, 1981.
642 F.2d 296.

J. BLAINE ANDERSON, Circuit Judge:

Appellants contend that the district court erred in granting summary judgment to the United States and in enjoining them from conducting any mining activity which could result in the disturbance of surface resources until they had complied with regulations under 36 CFR 252. We affirm the judgment of the district court.

BACKGROUND

The appellants are owners of unpatented placer mining claims located within the St. Joe National Forest in Idaho. They were informed by the Forest Service that regulations had been promulgated which required that they file an operating plan for their mining operations. While the appellants had been in contact with the Forest Service regarding their operations, they had not signed and filed a final plan of operations nor had they submitted a bond which the Forest Service required pursuant to the regulations.

The United States filed a complaint in district court to enjoin the appellants until an approved plan of operations had been filed, and a $2,000 bond was posted. Finding no genuine issue of material fact, the district court granted summary judgment to the United States and enjoined the appellants as requested.

The regulations in question are 36 CFR 252, which were promulgated by the Secretary of Agriculture on August 28, 1974. 36 CFR 252 sets forth rules and procedures which are intended to regulate the use of the surface of national forest land used in connection with mining operations authorized by the United States mining laws. 36 CFR § 252.1. The purpose of the regulations is "to minimize adverse environmental impacts on National Forest System surface resources" that can be caused by mining, while, at the same time, not interfering with the rights conferred by the mining laws. Id. Under the regulations, the Forest Service must be notified of any mining-related operation that is likely to cause a disturbance of surface resources. The initiation or continuation of such an operation is subject to the approval of the Forest Service.

Appellants' contention on appeal is that the regulations have not been promulgated pursuant to adequate statutory authority. They argue that the Organic Administration Act of 1897, 30 Stat. 35 and 36, 16 U.S.C. §§ 478 and 551, does not authorize the adoption of these regulations. Therefore, they argue that the regulations have no force and effect.

DISCUSSION

36 CFR 252 has been promulgated by the Secretary of Agriculture under the authority of the Organic Administration Act of June 4, 1897, specifically, 30 Stat. 35 and 36, 16 U.S.C. §§ 478 and 551. These provisions are part of the statutory scheme which covers the national forests and which confers administration of the national forests upon the Secretary of Agriculture.

Under §§ 478 and 551, the Secretary may make rules and regulations for the protection and preservation of the national forests, and persons entering upon national forest land must comply with those rules and regulations. The authority of the Secretary to regulate activity on national forest land pursuant to these sections has been upheld in a variety of non-mining instances. See United States v. Grimaud, 220 U.S. 506 (1910) (regulations concerning sheep grazing in national forests); McMichael v. United States, 355 F.2d 283 (9th Cir. 1965) (regulations prohibiting motorized vehicles in certain areas of national forest); Mountain States Telephone & Telegraph Co. v. United States, 499 F.2d 611 (1974) (regulations requiring special use permit and payment of fees for a microwave relay facility within a national forest); Sabin v. Butz, 515 F.2d 1061 (10th Cir.1975) (regulations setting up a permit system for ski operations and instructions on national forest land). That authority has also been sustained to prohibit non-mining activity upon unpatented mining claims. United States v. Rizzinelli, 182 F. 675 (D.Idaho 1910). However, the precise issue of whether these statutory provisions empower the Secretary to regulate mining operations on national forest land does not appear to have been decided before.[4] See United States v. Richardson, 599 F.2d 290, 293 (9th Cir.), cert. denied, 444 U.S. 1014 (1980).

We believe that the Act of 1897, 16 U.S.C. §§ 478 and 551, granted to the Secretary the power to adopt reasonable rules and regulations regarding mining operations within the national forests.

The national forests are to be open for entry "for all proper and lawful purposes, including that of prospecting, locating, and developing the mineral resources thereof." 16 U.S.C. § 478. However, "[s]uch persons must comply with the rules and regulations covering such national forests." Id. Thus it is clear that persons entering the national forests to prospect, locate, and develop mineral resources therein are subject to and must comply with the rules and regulations covering the national forests.

The Act of 1897, 30 Stat. 35, 16 U.S.C. § 551, as amended, grants authority to the Secretary to make "rules and regulations and [to] establish such service as will insure the objects of such reservations, namely, to regulate their occupancy and use and to preserve the forests thereon from destruction; * * *" The section specifically states that the Secretary shall make provision for the protection of the national forests against destruction by fire and depredation. Thus the Secretary has been given the authority to promulgate reasonable rules and regulations which will protect the national forests and which will help to carry out the purposes for which the national forests were created.

The regulations in question, 36 CFR 252, were designed to minimize adverse environmental impacts on the surface resources of the national forests. Such regulations were authorized by the Act of 1897.

The fact that these regulations have been promulgated many years after the enactment of their statutory authority does not destroy the Congressional authorization given. The failure of an executive agency to act does not forfeit or surrender governmental property or rights. United States v. California, 332 U.S. 19, 39–40 (1946); United States v. Southern Pacific Transp. Co., 543 F.2d 676, 697 (9th Cir.1976). In this

4. In recent Ninth Circuit cases concerning 36 CFR 252, its validity has been accepted without discussion. See United States v. Richardson, 599 F.2d at 292; United States v. Curtis-Nevada Mines, 415 F.Supp. 1373, 1379 (E.D.Cal.), affirmed in relevant part, 611 F.2d 1277 (9th Cir.1980); Ventura County v. Gulf Oil Corp., 601 F.2d 1080, 1084 (9th Cir.), aff'd, 445 U.S. 947 (1980).

situation, a mining claimant may not claim any sort of prescriptive right which would prevent the government from protecting its superior vested property rights.

In analyzing the issue before us, we are keenly aware of the important and competing interests involved. Mining has been accorded a special place in our laws relating to public lands. The basic mining law of 1872 encouraged the prospecting, exploring, and development of mineral resources on public lands. "The system envisaged by the mining laws was that the prospector could go out into the public domain, search for minerals and upon discovery establish a claim to land upon which the discovery was made." United States v. Curtis-Nevada Mines, Inc., 611 F.2d 1277, 1281 (9th Cir.1980). So long as they complied with the laws of the United States and applicable state and local laws, locators of mining locations were given "the exclusive right of possession and enjoyment of all the surface included within the lines of their location," along with the subsurface rights. 30 U.S.C. § 26.

On the other hand, our national forests have also been a fundamental part of the use of our public lands. National forests were established to improve and protect our forest land, to secure "favorable conditions of water flows, and to furnish a continuous supply of timber for the use and necessities of citizens of the United States; * * *" 16 U.S.C. § 475. The object of the Organic Administration Act of 1897 was "to maintain favorable forest conditions, without excluding the use of reservations for other purposes. They are not parks set aside for nonuse, but have been established for economic reasons. 30 Cong.Rec. 966 (1897) (Cong. McRae)." United States v. New Mexico, 438 U.S. 696, 708 (1978).

Moreover, while locators were accorded the right of possession and enjoyment of all the surface resources within their claim, the "primary title, the paramount ownership is in the government * * * it retains the title, with a valuable residuary and reversionary interest." United States v. Rizzinelli, et al., 182 F. at 681 (D.Idaho, 1910). "The paramount ownership being in the government, and it also having a reversionary interest in the possessory right of the locator, clearly it has a valuable estate which it is entitled to protect against waste and unlawful use." Id. at 684.

We believe that the important interests involved here were intended to and can coexist. The Secretary of Agriculture has been given the responsibility and the power to maintain and protect our national forests and the lands therein. While prospecting, locating, and developing of mineral resources in the national forests may not be prohibited nor so unreasonably circumscribed as to amount to a prohibition, the Secretary may adopt reasonable rules and regulations which do not impermissibly encroach upon the right to the use and enjoyment of placer claims for mining purposes.[5]

[Affirmed.]

5. We emphasize that the reasonableness of the regulations has not been put into issue. Although authority exists for the promulgation of regulations, those reg-

NOTES

1. In United States v. Goldfield Deep Mines Co. of Nevada, 644 F.2d 1307 (9th Cir.1981), cert. denied, 455 U.S. 907 (1982), defendant violated Forest Service regulations by failing to file an operating plan or to obtain proper authority to conduct business on national forest land. Goldfield was found liable for trespass; the United States received $17,560 in damages to enforce the judgment and cover the anticipated cost of restoring the area to its original condition.

2. In November, 1980, the BLM promulgated its mining regulations, which generally track the Forest Service procedures. See 43 C.F.R. Pt. 3800 (1985). In December, 1980, the Fish and Wildlife Service proposed regulations governing the impacts of mining within wildlife refuges; however, it never promulgated the rules. See 45 Fed. Reg. 86512 (1980). The BLM regulations are described in Martz, Love & Kaiser, Access to Mineral Interests by Right, Permit, Condemnation, or Purchase, 28 Rocky Mtn.Min.L.Inst. 1075, 1090–93 (1982).

3. FLPMA, 43 U.S.C.A. § 1732(b) provides that:

> * * * Except as provided in section 314, [43 U.S.C.A. § 1744, dealing with recordation of mining claims] section 603, [43 U.S.C.A. § 1782, dealing with the BLM Wilderness Study] and subsection (f) of section 601 of this Act [43 U.S.C.A. § 1781(f), dealing specially with the California Desert Conservation Area] and in the last sentence of this paragraph, no provision of this section or any other section of this Act shall in any way amend the Mining Law of 1872 or impair the rights of any locators or claims under that Act, including, but not limited to, rights of ingress and egress. In managing the public lands the Secretary *shall,* by regulation or otherwise, *take any action necessary to prevent unnecessary or undue degradation of the lands.* [emphasis supplied].

Does the BLM have general authority to regulate mining on unpatented claims? See Sherwood, Mining-Claim Recordation and Prospecting Under the Federal Land Policy and Management Act of 1976, 23 Rocky Mtn.Min.L.Inst. 1, 8–10 (1977):

> Section [1733(a)] of the Organic Act requires the Secretary of the Interior to "issue regulations necessary to implement the provisions of this Act with respect to the management, use, and protection of the public lands, including the property located thereon," and, under Section [1733(g)], "the use, occupancy, or development of any portion of the public lands contrary to any regulation of the Secretary or other responsible authority, or contrary to any order issued pursuant to any

ulations may, nevertheless, be struck down when they do not operate to accomplish the statutory purpose or where they encroach upon other statutory rights. Appellants have not attempted to comply with the regulations; therefore, those issues are not before us on this appeal. Compare, Agins v. City of Tiburon, 447 U.S. 255, 258–262 (1980).

such regulation, is unlawful and prohibited." Further, Section [1740] provides:

> The Secretary, with respect to the public lands, shall promulgate rules and regulations to carry out the purposes of this Act and of other laws applicable to the public lands, and the Secretary of Agriculture, with respect to lands within the National Forest System, shall promulgate rules and regulations to carry out the purposes of this Act.
>
> *   *   *

But Section [1732(b)] makes it clear, as we have seen, that none of these provisions of the Organic Act "in any way amend the Mining Law of 1872 or impair the rights of any locators or claims under that Act, including, but not limited to, rights of ingress and egress." At the very most, the Secretary has the power to promulgate rules and regulations *to carry out the purposes of laws applicable to the public lands*; if Congress had wanted to give the Secretary general authority to impair the rights of mining claims and mining-locators under the 1872 Act, it knew how to do so—witness the exceptions to the proviso already discussed. It did not do so, and the Secretary has therefore scratched around hopefully, looking for other congressional authority which might give the Department the power to impair the rights of locators and mining claims.

Incredibly, the Secretary has newly asserted authority to do whatever he pleases with respect to the 1872 Law under the provisions of Title 30, Section 22, of the United States Code, which he describes as the source of "the general regulatory authority of the Department under the mining law of 1872". That section of the 1872 Law provides that valuable mineral deposits on the public lands may be appropriated "under regulations prescribed by law, and according to the local customs or rules of miners in the several mining districts, so far as the same are applicable and not inconsistent with the laws of the United States."

The 1872 Law just quoted is not a grant of authority to the Secretary of the Interior to make law or to prescribe regulations. Even in that period Congress knew how to grant the authority to make regulations to officers of the Executive Branch; for example, see the Act of March 3, 1873, which provided:

> The Commissioner of the General Land-Office is authorized to issue all needful rules and regulations for carrying into effect the provisions of this and the four preceding sections.

No such grant of authority appears in Title 30, Section 22, and the only grant of authority to promulgate regulations in the 1872 Act is found in Title 30, Section 28, which grants that authority to "the miners of each mining district". Title 43,

Section 1201 of the United States Code, also relied upon by the Department, authorizes enforcement and carrying into execution, by appropriate regulations, of "every part of the provisions of this title not otherwise specifically provided for." But the power to enforce and carry the law into execution is not the power to amend the law or impair the rights of locators or claims. The Secretary has a good imagination, but no authority to issue regulations which add to the obligations of a locator or impair the rights accorded to a mining claim, except as specifically granted in the Organic Act.

See also Haggard, Regulation of Mining Law Activities on Federal Lands, 21 Rocky Mtn.Min.L.Inst. 349 (1975), concluding that before the passage of FLPMA, the BLM, like the Forest Service, had no authority to pass regulations in the style of the Forest Service's regulations.

4. FLPMA also provides, for the first time, that miners are required to file information about their claims with the BLM at certain intervals; failure to file constitutes conclusive evidence of abandonment. 43 U.S.C.A. § 1744. The constitutionality of the filing requirement was upheld in Western Mining Council v. Watt, 643 F.2d 618 (9th Cir.1981), cert. denied, 454 U.S. 1031 (1981), and Topaz Beryllium Co. v. United States, 649 F.2d 775 (10th Cir.1981). In the *Topaz Beryllium* case, Judge McKay commented for the court that "the challenged regulations do not constitute the regulatory horrible that appellants attempt to vivify." The FLPMA filing requirement later reached the Supreme Court.

UNITED STATES v. LOCKE

Supreme Court of the United States, 1985.
471 U.S. 84.

Justice MARSHALL delivered the opinion of the Court.

* * *

I

From the enactment of the general mining laws in the nineteenth century until 1976, those who sought to make their living by locating and developing minerals on federal lands were virtually unconstrained by the fetters of federal control. * * *

By the 1960s, it had become clear that this nineteenth century laissez faire regime had created virtual chaos with respect to the public lands. In 1975, it was estimated that more than six million unpatented mining claims existed on public lands other than the national forests; in addition, more than half the land in the National Forest System was thought to be covered by such claims. Many of these claims had been dormant for decades, and many were invalid for other reasons, but in the absence of a federal recording system, no simple way existed for determining which public lands were subject to mining locations, and whether those locations were valid or invalid. As a result, federal land managers had to proceed slowly and cautiously in taking any action affecting federal land lest the federal property rights of claimants be unlawfully disturbed. Each time the Bureau of Land Management (BLM) proposed a sale or other conveyance of federal land, a title search in the county recorder's office was necessary; if an outstanding mining claim was found, no matter how stale or apparently abandoned, formal administrative adjudication was required to determine the validity of the claim.

After more than a decade of studying this problem in the context of a broader inquiry into the proper management of the public lands in the modern era, Congress in 1976 enacted the Federal Land Policy and Management Act. Section 314 of the Act establishes a federal recording system that is designed both to rid federal lands of stale mining claims and to provide federal land managers with up-to-date information that allows them to make informed land management decisions.[2] For claims located before FLPMA's enactment, the federal recording system imposes two general requirements. First, the claims must initially be registered with the BLM by filing, within three years of FLPMA's enactment, a copy of the official record of the notice or certificate of location. Second, in the year of the initial recording, and "prior to December 31" of every year after that, the claimant must file with state officials and with BLM a notice of intention to hold the claim, an affidavit of assessment work performed on the claim, or a detailed reporting form. Section 314(c) of the Act provides that failure

---

2. The text of 43 U.S.C. § 1744 provides, in relevant part, as follows:

"Recordation of Mining Claims

"(a) Filing requirements

"The owner of an unpatented lode or placer mining claim located prior to October 21, 1976, shall, within the three-year period following October 21, 1976 and prior to December 31 of each year thereafter, file the instruments required by paragraphs (1) and (2) of this subsection. * * *

"(1) File for record in the office where the location notice or certificate is recorded either a notice of intention to hold the mining claim (including but not limited to such notices as are provided by law to be filed when there has been a suspension or deferment of annual assessment work), an affidavit of assessment work performed thereon, on a detailed report provided by section 28-1 of title 30, relating thereto.

"(2) File in the office of the Bureau designated by the Secretary a copy of the official record of the instrument filed or recorded pursuant to paragraph (1) of this subsection, including a description of the location of the mining claim sufficient to locate the claimed lands on the ground.

"(b) Additional filing requirements

"The owner of an unpatented lode or placer mining claim or mill or tunnel site located prior to October 21, 1976 shall,

within the three-year period following October 21, 1976, file in the office of the Bureau designated by the Secretary a copy of the official record of the notice of location or certificate of location, including a description of the location of the mining claim or mill or tunnel site sufficient to locate the claimed lands on the ground. The owner of an unpatented lode or placer mining claim or mill or tunnel site located after October 21, 1976 shall, within ninety days after the date of location of such claim, file in the office of the Bureau designated by the Secretary a copy of the official record of the notice of location or certificate of location, including a description of the location of the mining claim or mill or tunnel site sufficient to locate the claimed lands on the ground.

"(c) Failure to file as constituting abandonment; defective or untimely filing

"The failure to file such instruments as required by subsections (a) and (b) of this subsection shall be deemed conclusively to constitute an abandonment of the mining claim or mill or tunnel site by the owner; but it shall not be considered a failure to file if the instrument is defective or not timely filed for record under other Federal laws permitting filing or recording thereof, or if the instrument is filed for record by or on behalf of some but not all of the owners of the mining claim or mill or tunnel site."

to comply with either of these requirements "shall be deemed conclusively to constitute an abandonment of the mining claim * * * by the owner."

The second of these requirements—the annual filing obligation—has created the dispute underlying this appeal. Appellees, four individuals engaged "in the business of operating mining properties in Nevada," purchased in 1960 and 1966 ten unpatented mining claims on public lands near Ely, Nevada. These claims were major sources of gravel and building material: the claims are valued at several million dollars, and, in the 1979–1980 assessment year alone, appellees' gross income totalled more than one million dollars.[6] Throughout the period during which they owned the claims, appellees complied with annual state law filing and assessment work requirements. In addition, appellees satisfied FLPMA's initial recording requirement by properly filing with BLM a notice of location, thereby putting their claims on record for purposes of FLPMA.

At the end of 1980, however, appellees failed to meet on time their first annual obligation to file with the Federal Government. After allegedly receiving misleading information from a BLM employee,[7] appellees waited until December 31 to submit to BLM the annual notice of intent to hold or proof of assessment work performed required under section 314(a) of FLPMA, 43 U.S.C. § 1744(a). As noted above, that section requires these documents to be filed annually "prior to December 31." Had appellees checked, they further would have discovered that BLM regulations made quite clear that claimants were required to make the annual filings in the proper BLM office "on or before December 30 of each calendar year." 43 CFR § 3833.2–1(a) (1980) (current version at 43 CFR 3833.2–1(b)(1) (1984)). Thus, appellees' filing was one day too late.

This fact was brought painfully home to appellees when they received a letter from the BLM Nevada State Office informing them that their claims had been declared abandoned and void due to their tardy filing. In many cases, loss of a claim in this way would have minimal practical effect; the claimant could simply locate the same claim again and then rerecord it with BLM. In this case, however, relocation of appellees' claims, which were initially located by appellees' predecessors in 1952 and 1954, was prohibited by the Common Varieties Act of 1955, 30 U.S.C. § 611; that Act prospectively barred

6. From 1960 to 1980, total gross income from the claims exceeded four million dollars.

7. An affidavit submitted to the District Court by one of appellees' employees stated that BLM officials in Ely had told the employee that the filing could be made at the BLM Reno office "on or before December 31, 1980." The 1978 version of a BLM Question and Answer pamphlet erroneously stated that the annual filings had to be made "on or before December 31" of each year. Later versions have corrected this error to bring the pamphlet into accord with the BLM regulations that require the filings to be made "on or before December 30."

Justice STEVENS and Justice POWELL seek to make much of this pamphlet and of the uncontroverted evidence that appellees were told a December 31 filing would comply with the statute. However, at the time appellees filed in 1980, BLM regulations and the then-current pamphlets made clear that the filing was required "on or before December 30." * * *

location of the sort of minerals yielded by appellees' claims. Appellees' mineral deposits thus escheated to the Government.

After losing an administrative appeal, appellees filed the present action in the United States District Court for the District of Nevada. Their complaint alleged, *inter alia,* that § 314(c) effected an unconstitutional taking of their property without just compensation and denied them due process. On summary judgment, the District Court held that § 314(c) did indeed deprive appellees of the process to which they were constitutionally due. * * * Alternatively, the District Court held that the one-day late filing "substantially complied" with the Act and regulations.

* * *

III

A

Before the District Court, appellees asserted that the section 314(a) requirement of a filing "prior to December 31 of each year" should be construed to require a filing "on or before December 31." Thus, appellees argued, their December 31 filing had in fact complied with the statute, and the BLM had acted ultra vires in voiding their claims.

Although the District Court did not address this argument, the argument raises a question sufficiently legal in nature that we choose to address it even in the absence of lower court analysis. It is clear to us that the plain language of the statute simply cannot sustain the gloss appellees would put on it. As even appellees conceded at oral argument, § 314(a) "is a statement that Congress wanted it filed by December 30th. I think that is a clear statement * * *" While we will not allow a literal reading of a statute to produce a result "demonstrably at odds with the intentions of its drafters," with respect to filing deadlines a literal reading of Congress' words is generally the only proper reading of those words. To attempt to decide whether some date other than the one set out in the statute is the date actually "intended" by Congress is to set sail on an aimless journey, for the purpose of a filing deadline would be just as well served by nearly any date a court might choose as by the date Congress has in fact set out in the statute. "Actual purpose is sometimes unknown," and such is the case with filing deadlines; as might be expected, nothing in the legislative history suggests why Congress chose December 30 over December 31, or over September 1 (the end of the assessment year for mining claims, 30 U.S.C. § 28), as the last day on which the required filings could be made. But "[d]eadlines are inherently arbitrary," while fixed dates "are often essential to accomplish necessary results." Faced with the inherent arbitrariness of filing deadlines, we must, at least in a civil case, apply by its terms the date fixed by the statute.

Moreover, BLM regulations have made absolutely clear since the enactment of FLPMA that "prior to December 31" means what it says. As the current version of the filing regulations states:

"The owner of an unpatented mining claim located on Federal lands * * * shall have filed or caused to have been filed *on or before December 30* of each calendar year * * * evidence of annual assessment work performed during the previous assessment year or a notice of intention to hold the mining claim." 43 CFR § 3833.2–1(b)(1) (1984) (emphasis added).

Leading mining treatises similarly inform claimants that "[i]t is important to note that the filing of a notice of intention or evidence of assessment work must be done *prior* to December 31 of each year, i.e., on or before December 30." 2 American Law of Mining § 7.23D, p. 150.2 (Supp.1983) (emphasis in original). If appellees, who were businessmen involved in the running of a major mining operation for more than 20 years, had any questions about whether a December 31 filing complied with the statute, it was incumbent upon them, as it is upon other businessmen, to have checked the regulations or to have consulted an attorney for legal advice. Pursuit of either of these courses, rather than the submission of a last-minute filing, would surely have led appellees to the conclusion that December 30 was the last day on which they could file safely.

In so saying, we are not insensitive to the problems posed by congressional reliance on the words "prior to December 31." But the fact that Congress might have acted with greater clarity or foresight does not give courts a *carte blanche* to redraft statutes in an effort to achieve that which Congress is perceived to have failed to do. * * * Nor is the judiciary licensed to attempt to soften the clear import of Congress' chosen words whenever a court believes those words lead to a harsh result.

* * * When even after taking this step nothing in the legislative history remotely suggests a congressional intent contrary to Congress' chosen words, and neither appellees nor the dissenters have pointed to anything that so suggests, any further steps take the courts out of the realm of interpretation and place them in the domain of legislation. The phrase "prior to" may be clumsy, but its meaning is clear. Under these circumstances, we are obligated to apply the "prior to December 31" language by its terms.

* * *

B

Section 314(c) states that failure to comply with the filing requirements of §§ 314(a) and 314(b) "shall be deemed conclusively to constitute an abandonment of the mining claim." We must next consider whether this provision expresses a congressional intent to extinguish all claims for which filings have not been made, or only those claims for which filings have not been made *and* for which the claimants have a specific intent to abandon the claim. The District Court adopted the latter interpretation, and on that basis concluded that § 314(c) created a constitutionally impermissible irrebuttable presumption of abandonment. The District Court reasoned that, once Congress had chosen to make loss of a claim turn on the specific intent of the claimant, a prior hearing and findings on the claimant's intent were constitutionally required before the claim of a non-filing claimant could be extinguished.

In concluding that Congress was concerned with the specific intent of the claimant even when the claimant had failed to make the required filings, the District Court began from the fact that neither § 314(c) nor the Act itself defines the term "abandonment" as that term appears in § 314(c). The District Court then noted correctly that the common law of mining traditionally has drawn a distinction between "abandonment" of a claim, which occurs only upon a showing of the claimant's intent to relinquish the claim, and "forfeiture" of a claim, for which only non-compliance with the requirements of law must be shown. Given that Congress had not expressly stated in the statute any intent to depart from the term-of-art meaning of "abandonment" at common law, the District Court concluded that § 314(c) was intended to incorporate the traditional common-law distinction between abandonment and forfeiture. Thus, reasoned the District Court, Congress did not intend to cause a forfeiture of claims for which the required filings had not been made, but rather to focus on the claimant's actual intent. As a corollary, the District Court understood the failure to file to have been intended to be merely one piece of evidence in a factual inquiry into whether a claimant had a specific intent to abandon his property.

This construction of the statutory scheme cannot withstand analysis. While reference to common-law conceptions is often a helpful guide to interpreting openended or undefined statutory terms, this principle is a guide to legislative intent, not a talisman of it, and the principle is not to be applied in defiance of a statute's overriding purposes and logic. Although § 314(c) is couched in terms of a conclusive presumption of "abandonment," there can be little doubt that Congress intended § 314(c) to cause a forfeiture of all claims for which the filing requirements of §§ 314(a) and 314(b) had not been met.

To begin with, the Senate version of § 314(c) provided that any claim not properly recorded "shall be conclusively presumed to be abandoned and shall be void." * * * The [Conference Committee] Report stated: "Both the Senate bill and House amendments provided for recordation of mining claims and for *extinguishment* of abandoned claims." (emphasis added).

In addition, the District Court's construction fails to give effect to the "deemed conclusively" language of § 314(c). If the failure to file merely shifts the burden to the claimant to prove that he intends to keep the claim, nothing "conclusive" is achieved by § 314(c). The District Court sought to avoid this conclusion by holding that § 314(c) does extinguish automatically those claims for which *initial* recordings, as opposed to annual filings, have not been made; the District Court attempted to justify its distinction between initial recordings and annual filings on the ground that the dominant purpose of § 314(c) was to avoid forcing BLM to the "awesome task of searching every local title record" to establish initially a federal recording system. Once this purpose had been satisfied by an initial recording, the primary purposes of the "deemed conclusively" language, in the District Court's view, had been met. But the clear language of § 314(c) admits of no distinction between initial recordings and annual filings: failure to do either "shall be deemed conclusively to constitute an abandonment." And the District Court's analysis of the purposes of § 314(c) is also misguided, for the annual filing requirements serve a purpose similar to that of the initial recording requirement; millions of claims undoubtedly have now been recorded, and the presence of an annual filing obligation allows BLM to keep the system established in § 314 up to date on a yearly basis. To put the burden on BLM to keep this system current through its own inquiry into the status of recorded claims would lead to a situation similar to that which led Congress initially to make the federal recording system self-executing. The purposes of a self-executing recording system are implicated similarly, if somewhat less substantially, by the annual filing obligation as by the initial recording requirement, and the District Court was not empowered to thwart these purposes or the clear language of § 314(c) by concluding that § 314(c) was actually concerned with only initial recordings.

For these reasons, we find that Congress intended in § 314(c) to extinguish those claims for which timely filings were not made. Specific evidence of intent to abandon is simply made irrelevant by § 314(c); the failure to file on time, in and of itself, causes a claim to be lost.

C

A final statutory question must be resolved before we turn to the constitutional holding of the District Court. Relying primarily on Hickel v. Shale Oil Corp., 400 U.S. 48 (1970), [infra at page 509], the District Court held that, even if the statute required a filing on or before December 30, appellees had "substantially complied" by filing on December 31. We cannot accept this view of the statute.

The notion that a filing deadline can be complied with by filing sometime after the deadline falls due is, to say the least, a surprising notion, and it is a notion without limiting principle. If 1-day late filings are acceptable, 10-day late filings might be equally acceptable, and so on in a cascade of exceptions that would engulf the rule erected by the filing deadline; yet regardless of where the cutoff line is set, some individuals will always fall just on the other side of it. * * * A filing deadline cannot be complied with, substantially or otherwise, by filing late—even by one day.

Hickel v. Shale Oil Co., supra, does not support a contrary conclusion. *Hickel* suggested, although it did not hold, that failure to meet the annual assessment work requirements of the general mining laws, 30 U.S.C. § 28, which require that "not less than $100 worth of labor shall be performed or improvements made during each year," would not render a claim automatically void. Instead, if an individual complied substantially but not fully with the requirement, he might under some circumstances be able to retain possession of his claim.

These suggestions in *Hickel* do not afford a safe haven to mine owners who fail to meet their filing obligations under any federal mining law. Failure to comply fully with the physical requirement that a certain amount of work be performed each year is significantly different from the complete failure to file on time documents that federal law commands be filed. In addition, the general mining laws at issue in *Hickel* do not clearly provide that a claim will be lost for failure to meet the assessment work requirements. Thus, it was open to the Court to conclude in *Hickel* that Congress had intended to make the assessment work requirement merely an indicia of a claimant's specific intent to retain a claim. Full compliance with the assessment work requirements would establish conclusively an intent to keep the claim, but less than full compliance would not by force of law operate to deprive the claimant of his claim. Instead, less than full compliance would subject the mine owner to a case-by-case determination of whether he nonetheless intended to keep his claim.

In this case, the statute explicitly provides that failure to comply with the applicable filing requirements leads automatically to loss of the claim. Thus, Congress has made it unnecessary to ascertain whether the individual in fact intends to abandon the claim, and there is no room to inquire whether substantial compliance is indicative of the claimant's intent—intent is simply irrelevant if the required filings are not made. *Hickel*'s discussion of substantial compliance is therefore inapposite to the statutory scheme at issue here. As a result, *Hickel* gives miners no greater latitude with filing deadlines than have other individuals.[14]

IV

Much of the District Court's constitutional discussion necessarily falls with our conclusion that § 314(c) automatically deems forfeited those claims for which the required filings are not timely made. The

14. Since 1982, BLM regulations have provided that filings due on or before December 30 will be considered timely if postmarked on or before December 30 and received by BLM by the close of business on the following January 19th. 43 CFR 3833.0–5(m) (1983). Appellees and the dissenters attempt to transform this regulation into a blank check generally authorizing "substantial compliance" with the filing requirements. We disagree for two reasons. First, the regulation was not in effect when appellees filed in 1980; it therefore cannot now be relied on to validate a purported "substantial compliance" in 1980. Second, that an agency has decided to take account of holiday mail delays by treating as timely filed a document postmarked on the statutory filing date does not require the agency to accept all documents hand delivered any time before January 19th. The agency rationally could decide that either of the options in this sort of situation—requiring mailings to be received by the same date that hand deliveries must be made or requiring mailings to be postmarked by that date—is a sound way of administering the statute.

Justice STEVENS further suggests that BLM would have been well within its authority to promulgate regulations construing the statute to allow for December 31st filings. Assuming the correctness of this suggestion, the fact that two interpretations of a statute are equally reasonable suggests to us that the agency's interpretation is sufficiently reasonable as to be acceptable.

District Court's invalidation of the statute rested heavily on the view that § 314(c) creates an "irrebuttable presumption that mining claims are abandoned if the miner fails to timely file" the required documents—that the statute presumes a failure to file to signify a specific intent to abandon the claim. But, as we have just held, § 314(c) presumes nothing about a claimant's actual intent; the statute simply and conclusively deems such claims to be forfeited. As a forfeiture provision, § 314(c) is not subject to the individualized hearing requirement of such irrebuttable presumption cases as Vlandis v. Kline, 412 U.S. 441 (1973) or Cleveland Bd. of Education v. LaFleur, 414 U.S. 632 (1974), for there is nothing to suggest that, in enacting § 314(c), Congress was in any way concerned with whether a particular claimant's tardy filing or failure to file indicated an actual intent to abandon the claim.

There are suggestions in the District Court's opinion that, even understood as a forfeiture provision, § 314(c) might be unconstitutional. We therefore go on to consider whether automatic forfeiture of a claim for failure to make annual filings is constitutionally permissible. The framework for analysis of this question, in both its substantive and procedural dimensions, is set forth by our recent decision in Texaco, Inc. v. Short, 454 U.S. 516 (1982). There we upheld a state statute pursuant to which a severed mineral interest that had not been used for a period of 20 years automatically lapsed and reverted to the current surface owner of the property, unless the mineral owner filed a statement of claim in the county recorder's office within two years of the statute's passage.

A

Under *Texaco,* we must first address the question of affirmative legislative power: whether Congress is authorized to "provide that property rights of this character shall be extinguished if their owners do not take the affirmative action required by the" statute. Even with respect to vested property rights, a legislature generally has the power to impose new regulatory constraints on the way in which those rights are used, or to condition their continued retention on performance of certain affirmative duties. As long as the constraint or duty imposed is a reasonable restriction designed to further legitimate legislative objectives, the legislature acts within its powers in imposing such new constraints or duties. * * *

This power to qualify existing property rights is particularly broad with respect to the "character" of the property rights at issue here. Although owners of unpatented mining claims hold fully recognized possessory interests in their claims, we have recognized that these interests are a "unique form of property." The United States, as owner of the underlying fee title to the public domain, maintains broad powers over the terms and conditions upon which the public lands can be used, leased, and acquired. See, e.g., Kleppe v. New Mexico, 426 U.S. 529, 539 (1976).

"A mining location which has not gone to patent is of no higher quality and no more immune from attack and investigation [than] are unpatented claims under the homestead and kindred laws. If valid, it gives to the claimant certain exclusive possessory rights, and so do homestead and desert claims. But no right arises from an invalid claim of any kind. All must conform to the law under which they are initiated; otherwise they work an unlawful private appropriation in derogation of the rights of the public." Cameron v. United States, 252 U.S. 450, 460 (1920).

Claimants thus must take their mineral interests with the knowledge that the Government retains substantial regulatory power over those interests. * * *

Against this background, there can be no doubt that Congress could condition initial receipt of an unpatented mining claim upon an agreement to perform annual assessment work and make annual filings. That this requirement was applied to claims already located by the time FLPMA was enacted and thus applies to vested claims does not alter the analysis, for any "retroactive application of [FLPMA] is supported by a legitimate legislative purpose furthered by rational means. * * *" The purposes of applying FLPMA's filing provisions to claims located before the Act was passed—to rid federal lands of stale mining claims and to provide for centralized collection by federal land managers of comprehensive and up-to-date information on the status of recorded but unpatented mining claims—are clearly legitimate. In addition, § 314(c) is a reasonable, if severe, means of furthering these goals; sanctioning with loss of their claims those claimants who fail to file provides a powerful motivation to comply with the filing requirements, while automatic invalidation for noncompliance enables federal land managers to know with certainty and ease whether a claim is currently valid. Finally, the restriction attached to the continued retention of a mining claim imposes the most minimal of burdens on claimants; they must simply file a paper once a year indicating that the required assessment work has been performed or that they intend to hold the claim. Indeed, appellees could have fully protected their interests against the effect of the statute by taking the minimal additional step of patenting the claims. As a result, Congress was well within its affirmative powers in enacting the filing requirements, in imposing the penalty of extinguishment set forth in § 314(c), and in applying the requirements and sanction to claims located before FLPMA was passed.

B

We look next to the substantive effect of § 314(c) to determine whether Congress is nonetheless barred from enacting it because it works an impermissible intrusion on constitutionally protected rights. * * * Regulation of property rights does not "take" private property when an individual's reasonable, investment-backed expectations can continue to be realized as long as he complies with reasonable regulatory restrictions the legislature has imposed.

C

Finally, the Act provides appellees with all the process that is their constitutional due. In altering substantive rights through enactment of rules of general applicability, a legislature generally provides constitutionally adequate process simply by enacting the statute, publishing it, and, to the extent the statute regulates private conduct, affording those within the statute's reach a reasonable opportunity both to familiarize themselves with the general requirements imposed and to comply with those requirements. * * * The requirement of an annual filing thus was not so unlikely to come to the attention of those in the position of appellees as to render unconstitutional the notice provided by the 3-year grace period.

Despite the fact that FLPMA meets the three standards laid down in *Texaco* for the imposition of new regulatory restraints on existing property rights, the District Court seemed to believe that individualized notice of the filing deadlines was nonetheless constitutionally required. The District Court felt that such a requirement would not be "overly burdensome" to the Government and would be of great benefit to mining claimants. The District Court may well be right that such an individualized notice scheme would be a sound means of administering the Act. But in the regulation of private property rights, the Constitution offers the courts no warrant to inquire into whether some other scheme might be more rational or desirable than the one chosen by Congress; as long as the legislative scheme is *a* rational way of reaching Congress' objectives, the efficacy of alternative routes is for Congress alone to consider.

* * * Because we deal here with purely economic legislation, Congress was entitled to conclude that it was preferable to place a substantial portion of the burden on claimants to make the national recording system work. * * * The judgment below is reversed, and the case remanded for further proceedings consistent with this opinion.

It is so ordered.

Justice O'CONNOR, concurring.

I agree that the District Court erred in holding that § 314(c) of the Federal Land Policy and Management Act of 1976 (FLPMA) violates due process by creating an "irrebuttable presumption" of abandonment. * * *

* * *

The unusual facts alleged by appellees suggest that the BLM's actions might estop the Government from relying on § 314(c) to obliterate a property interest that has provided a family's livelihood for decades. The Court properly notes that the estoppel issue was not addressed by the District Court and will be open on remand. * * *

* * *

Justice POWELL, dissenting.

* * *

In the present case there is no claim that a yearly filing requirement is itself unreasonable. Rather, the claim arises from the fact that the language "prior to December 31" creates uncertainty as to when an otherwise reasonable filing period ends. Given the natural tendency to interpret this phrase as "by the end of the calendar year," rather than "on or before the next-to-the-last day of the calendar year," I believe this uncertainty violated the standard of certainty and definiteness that the Constitution requires. * * *

* * *

Justice STEVENS, with whom Justice BRENNAN joins, dissenting.

The Court's opinion is contrary to the intent of Congress, engages in unnecessary constitutional adjudication, and unjustly creates a trap for unwary property owners. First, the choice of the language "prior to December 31" when read in context in 43 U.S.C. § 1744(a) is, at least, ambiguous, and, at best, "the consequence of a legislative *accident,* perhaps caused by nothing more than the unfortunate fact that Congress is too busy to do all of its work as carefully as it should." In my view, Congress actually intended to authorize an annual filing at any time prior to the close of business on December 31st, that is, prior to the end of the calendar year to which the filing pertains. Second, even if Congress irrationally intended that the applicable deadline for a calendar year should end *one day before* the end of the calendar year that has been recognized since the amendment of the Julian calendar in 8 B.C., it is clear that appellees have substantially complied with the requirements of the statute, in large part because the Bureau of Land Management has issued interpreting regulations that recognize substantial compliance. Further, the Court today violates not only the long-followed principle that a court should "not pass on the constitutionality of an Act of Congress if a construction of the statute is fairly possible by which the question may be avoided," but also the principle that a court should "not decide a constitutional question if there is some other ground upon which to dispose of the case."

* * *

In my view, this unique factual matrix unequivocally contradicts the statutory presumption of an intent to abandon by reason of a late filing. In sum, this case presents an ambiguous statute, which, if strictly construed, will destroy valuable rights of appellees, property owners who have complied with all local and federal statutory filing requirements apart from a one-day "late" filing caused by the Bureau's own failure to mail a reminder notice necessary because of the statute's ambiguity and caused by the Bureau's information to appellees that the date on which the filing occurred would be acceptable. Further, long before the Bureau declared a technical "abandonment," it was in complete possession of all information necessary to assess the activity, locations, and ownership of appellees' mining claims and it possessed all information needed to carry out its statutory functions. Finally, the Bureau has not claimed that the filing is contrary to the congressional purposes behind the statute, that the filing affected the Bureau's land-use planning functions in any manner, or that it interfered "in any measurable way" with the Bureau's need to obtain information. A showing of substantial compliance necessitates a significant burden of proof; appellees, whose active mining claims will be destroyed contrary to Congress' intent, have convinced me that they have substantially complied with the statute.

I respectfully dissent.

NOTE

1. Does the BLM, in administering FLPMA, have the authority to adopt regulations allowing filings made on December 31? If so, is not the statute sufficiently ambiguous to allow for the construction argued for by these claimants? Leaving aside the estoppel issues to be dealt with on remand, do the Lockes have any remedies? Can Congress respond to their equitable arguments?

2. As a policy matter, is the forfeiture provision in section 1744 appropriate? In its most recent report, the BLM stated that it had recorded 1.7 million mining claims since 1976; 1.1 million claims are still active, and approximately 140,000 new claims are received each year. Bureau of Land Management, U.S. Dept. of the Interior, MANAGING THE NATION'S PUBLIC LANDS—FISCAL YEAR 1984, 20 (1985).

3. Chapter three presented a series of cases involving attempts by states to regulate mining on the public lands. *Ventura County* struck down local regulation of mineral leasing, supra at page 213, and *Brubaker,* supra at page 217, held invalid a county's effort to control hardrock mining. *Hibbard,* supra at page 211, upheld Oregon's application of its dredge and fill law to hardrock mining, while *Wyoming Oil and Gas Conservation Commission,* supra at page 221, allowed stringent state regulation of access to an oil and gas drilling site. The following case presents a more intricate variation on the same theme.

GRANITE ROCK COMPANY v. CALIFORNIA COASTAL COMMISSION

United States Court of Appeals, Ninth Circuit, 1985.
768 F.2d 1077, 106 S.Ct. 1489 (1986) (postponing question of jurisdiction until hearing of the case on the merits).

WALLACE, Circuit Judge:

*   *   *

I

Granite Rock is engaged in the business of mining chemical grade white limestone. Its mining operations involved in this appeal are located on an unpatented mining claim on land owned by the federal government in the Los Padres National Forest at Pico Blanco. Granite Rock acquired the mining claim at Pico Blanco in 1959 pursuant to the Act of May 10, 1872 (Mining Act). It began mining the claim in 1981 after the United States Forest Service (Forest Service) approved its five-year plan of operations, which it had submitted as required for significant mining activities pursuant to regulations implemented under the Act of June 4, 1897 (Organic Administration Act).

In 1983, the Coastal Commission advised Granite Rock that the California Coastal Act, Cal.Pub.Res.Code §§ 30000–30900 (West 1977 & Supp.1985) (Coastal Act), required the company to obtain a state permit to continue its mining operations. The California legislature passed the Coastal Act in 1976 pursuant to the state's inherent police powers, as a reenactment of a 1972 initiative, and as an implementation of the federal Coastal Zone Management Act, 16 U.S.C. §§ 1451–1464 (CZMA), which encourages state regulation of coastal zones. Granite Rock brought this action for declaratory and injunctive relief to prevent the Coastal Commission from enforcing the state permit requirement. Because there were no factual issues in dispute, Granite Rock brought a motion for summary judgment challenging the state's legal authority to require the permit.

The district court denied Granite Rock's motion for summary judgment and then dismissed the action. * * * Granite Rock appeals.

II

* * *

The Supreme Court recently articulated the test for federal preemption:

> [S]tate law can be preempted in either of two general ways. If Congress evidences an intent to occupy a given field, any state law falling within that field is preempted. If Congress has not entirely displaced state regulation over the matter in question, state law is still preempted to the extent it actually conflicts with federal law, that is, when it is impossible to comply with both state and federal law, or where the state law stands as an obstacle to the accomplishment of the full purposes and objectives of Congress.

Silkwood v. Kerr-McGee Corp., 464 U.S. 238 (1984).

* * *

A

The legislative intent is clear on whether the CZMA neutralizes other federal law which might preempt the state. The Conference Committee stated that "[t]he Conferees * * * adopted language which would make certain that there is no intent in this legislation to change Federal or state jurisdiction or rights in specified fields." This passage refers to section 307(e)(2) of the CZMA, 16 U.S.C. § 1456(e)(2), which states that "[n]othing in this chapter shall be construed * * * as superseding, modifying, or repealing existing laws applicable to the various Federal agencies."

Similarly, the Senate Report demonstrates Congress's intent not to restore state authority within the coastal zone if a federal act otherwise preempts it over a specific subject matter. In its statement of the CZMA's purpose, the Senate explained that the CZMA is merely a cooperative funding provision that "has as its main purpose the encouragement and assistance of States in preparing and implementing man- agement programs to preserve, protect, develop and whenever possible restore the resources of the coastal zone of the United States." The Senate indicated that the CZMA is designed to promote this purpose of "enhanc[ing] state authority," through the means of providing "Federal grants-in-aid to coastal states to develop coastal zone management programs [and] * * * grants to help coastal states implement these management programs once approved." 1972 U.S.Code Cong. & Ad. News at 4776. See also Secretary of the Interior v. California, 464 U.S. 312 (1984) (*Secretary of the Interior*). These grants were intended only to give coastal states an incentive "*to exercise their full authority* over the lands and waters in the coastal zone," 16 U.S.C. § 1451(h) (emphasis added), and not to restore authority that the states might previously have lost through federal preemption. * * *

Thus, even if we assume that the land in question falls within the coastal zone, the legislative history and certain provisions of the CZMA conclusively demonstrate that Congress intended the CZMA *not* to change the status quo with respect to the allocation of state and federal power over lands within the coastal zone. * * *

B

The purpose of the Mining Act is to encourage mining on federal lands. United States v. Weiss, 642 F.2d 296, 299 (9th Cir.1981) (*Weiss*). In 1970, Congress renewed its adherence to this policy, although it also declared its fidelity to the additional goal of lessening any adverse environmental impact from such mining. 30 U.S.C. § 21a. Then, in 1974, the Secretary of Agriculture promulgated regulations " 'to mini- mize adverse environmental impacts on National Forest System surface resources' that can be caused by mining, while, at the same time, not interfering with the rights conferred by the mining laws." *Weiss*, 642 F.2d at 297, *quoting* 36 C.F.R. § 252.1 (1975) (recodified at 36 C.F.R. § 228.1 (1984)). See generally 36 C.F.R. pt. 228 (1984). These regula- tions require miners to notify the Forest Service of any mining related operation that is likely to "cause disturbance of surface resources." Id. § 228.4(a). "The initiation or continuation of such an operation is subject to the approval of the Forest Service." *Weiss*, 642 F.2d at 297. See 36 C.F.R. §§ 228.4–.5 (1984).

Although a general federal purpose to encourage a particular activity does not automatically preempt state environmental regulation that incidentally discourages the activity, see, e.g., *Silkwood*, 104 S.Ct. at 626; Commonwealth Edison Co. v. Montana, 453 U.S. 609, 633 (1981), we disagree with the Coastal Commission's converse argument that a state regulation which prohibits mining unless the miner obtains a state permit automatically escapes preemption if issuance of the permit is conditioned only on reasonable requirements. In First Iowa Hydro-Electric Cooperative v. Federal Power Commission, 328 U.S. 152 (1946) (*First Iowa*), the Supreme Court held that the Federal Power Act, which establishes a federal permit system authorizing the construction of hydroelectric dams, preempted a state law that prohibited such activity unless the petitioner first obtained a state permit. The Court reasoned that

> [t]o require the petitioner to secure the actual grant to it of a state permit * * * as a condition precedent to securing a federal license for the same project under the Federal Power Act would vest in the Executive Council of Iowa a veto power over the federal project. Such a veto power easily could destroy the effectiveness of the Federal Act. It would subordinate to the control of the State the "comprehensive" planning which the Act provides shall depend upon the judgment of the Federal Power Commission or other representatives of the Federal Government.

* * * The Court [did not] make a prohibition/regulation distinction and inquire into the reasonableness of the state's conditions for issuing or denying the permit. The additional permit system was preempted simply because it would undermine the federal permit authority.

We applied the same reasoning in Ventura County v. Gulf Oil Corp., 601 F.2d 1080 (9th Cir.1979), *aff'd mem.*, 445 U.S. 947 (1980), to hold that the Mineral Lands Leasing Act of 1920, 30 U.S.C. §§ 181–263, preempted a county zoning ordinance that prohibited oil exploration and extraction activities on federal land unless a county permit was first obtained. We determined that there was an actual conflict between local and federal governments because "the Ventura authorities wish[ed] to regulate conduct which Congress has authorized." We reasoned that the Departments of Interior and Agriculture had already issued federal permits, and thus "Ventura cannot prohibit that use, either temporarily or permanently, in an attempt to substitute its judgment for that of Congress."

The Court has recognized that the *First Iowa* doctrine extends only to state permit mechanisms that actually intrude into the sphere of federal permit authority. * * *

In deciding whether the *First Iowa* doctrine applies in this case, we must determine whether federal law establishes authority in a federal agency to prohibit or permit mining in national forests conditioned on meeting environmental protection standards and, if so, whether the state permit authority exercised in this case intrudes into that sphere of authority. We conclude that Forest Service regulations mandate that the power to prohibit the initiation or continuation of mining in national forests for failure to abide by applicable environmental requirements lies with the Forest Service. 36 C.F.R. §§ 228.4–.5 (1984). We find unpersuasive the argument that the Mining Act and these regulations do no more than encourage mining subject to minimum federal environmental regulation, leaving the states free to condition the ability to mine on adhering to more stringent requirements. See, e.g., State ex rel. Andrus v. Click, 97 Idaho 791, 796, 554 P.2d 969, 974 (1976). On the other hand, we do not believe they go so far as to occupy the field of establishing environmental standards, striking a federally determined balance between encouraging mining and protecting the environment in national forests. The Forest Service regulations recognize that a state may enact environmental regulations in addition to those established by federal agencies. See 36 C.F.R. § 228.8 (1984); see also 16 U.S.C. § 551a. Moreover, a state may urge the Forest Service to withhold or revoke a federal mining permit from a miner who does not abide by all applicable state and federal standards. But an independent state permit system to enforce state environmental standards would undermine the Forest Service's own permit authority and thus is preempted.

Our conclusion is bolstered by the fact that even the Forest Service is limited in the amount of regulation it may impose as a condition of mining in national forests because of the federal policy to encourage mining on federal lands. See Weiss, 642 F.2d at 299; see also 30 U.S.C. § 21a; 36 C.F.R. § 228.5(a) (1984). To allow a second tier of permit authority to be exercised by the states would undermine the Forest Service's ability to keep the applicable environmental requirements within the range of reasonableness. See Weiss, 642 F.2d at 299; 36 C.F.R. § 228.5(a) (1984). Current federal law allows the states to establish environmental standards that the Forest Service will apply in exercising its permit authority. See id. § 228.8. But by reserving final permit authority in the Forest Service, see id. §§ 228.4–.5, it also affords the Forest Service the power necessary to promote the federal purpose of maintaining the reasonableness of the overall regulatory mix. See 30 U.S.C. § 21a; 36 C.F.R. § 228.5(a) (1984).

Our conclusion is not affected by the fact that the Forest Service staff stated in its environmental assessment of Granite Rock's plan of operation that "Granite Rock is responsible for obtaining any necessary permits which may be required by the California Coastal Commission." A routine staff statement cannot change the effect of the formally adopted regulations.

REVERSED.

NOTES

1. What provisions in the Forest Service regulations disallow this state regulation? Can Granite Rock be squared with Hibbard, supra at page 211? Does the opinion conclude that any state permit system for hardrock miners is preempted? Should the court have examined the implementation of the state system to determine whether it amounts to reasonable regulation or, on the other hand, a veto?

2. Inevitably, as the following cases illustrate, the more stringent controls over mining have raised questions whether takings have occurred.

FREESE v. UNITED STATES
United States Court of Claims, 1981.
639 F.2d 754.
Cert. denied, 454 U.S. 827 (1981).

KUNZIG, Judge:

* * * Plaintiff is the owner of five unpatented mining claims located on federal lands. In 1972, Congress incorporated these lands into the newly established Sawtooth National Recreation Area (Sawtooth). The law creating Sawtooth expressly terminated the ability of existing claimholders to proceed to patent upon claims located in the recreation area, i.e., to obtain fee title to the lands in which the claims are located. This case concerns the question whether Congress' action amounts to an unconstitutional taking by inverse condemnation. We hold for the Government. While plaintiff's opportunities have been somewhat narrowed, plaintiff has not suffered a deprivation of "private property" within the meaning of the fifth amendment.

* * * The owner of the mining claim "shall have the exclusive right of possession and enjoyment" of the claim. 30 U.S.C. § 26 (1976). Ownership of a mining claim does *not* confer fee title to the lands within which the claim is located. Fee title passes only upon the issuance of a patent therefor. See Best v. Humboldt Placer Mining Co., 371 U.S. 334, 336 (1963).

* * *

Between the years 1955 and 1970, plaintiff acquired five unpatented mining claims upon federal lands located in Idaho.[1] In 1972, Congress established the Sawtooth National Recreation Area, including within its boundaries the lands containing plaintiff's claims. 16 U.S.C. §§ 460aa–460aa–14 (1976) (Sawtooth Act). The Sawtooth Act expressly provides that, "Subject to valid existing rights, all Federal lands located in the recreation area are hereby withdrawn from all forms of location, entry, and patent under the mining laws of the United States." 16 U.S.C. § 460aa–9 (1976). The Act further provides that, "Patents shall not hereafter be issued for locations and claims heretofore made in the recreation area under the mining laws of the United States." 16 U.S.C. § 460aa–11 (1976). The impact of these provisions is that, while the right of possession and enjoyment attaching to valid claims existing upon the effective date of the Act is expressly recognized and preserved, the ability to obtain patents upon these claims is expressly denied. Plaintiff now contends that he has suffered an unconstitutional taking

1. The United States has the power under the mining laws to initiate a contest of the validity of unpatented mining locations. See United States v. Springer, 491 F.2d 239, 241 (9th Cir.), cert. denied, 419 U.S. 834 (1974). Heretofore, the Government has failed to initiate any such contest against plaintiff's claims. Solely for the purpose of disposing of the pending motions, the Government requests this court to assume *arguendo* the validity of plaintiff's claims.

by virtue of the denial of his ability to obtain patents upon the five unpatented mining claims which he held upon the effective date of the Act.[2] Plaintiff's contention has no merit. There is no maintainable legal theory in support of his view that he has suffered a deprivation of "private property" as that term is used in the fifth amendment.

* * *

It is a matter beyond dispute that federal mining claims are "private property" enjoying the protection of the fifth amendment. Judge Finesilver of the federal district court has nicely summarized the applicable concepts:

> A mining claim is an interest in land which cannot be unreasonably or unfairly dissolved at the whim of the Interior Department. Once there is a valid discovery and proper location, a mining claim, in the language of the Supreme Court, is "real property in the highest sense." Legal title to the land remains in the United States, but the claimant enjoys a valid, equitable, possessory title, subject to taxation, transferable by deed or devise, and otherwise possessing the incidents of real property.

Oil Shale Corp. v. Morton, 370 F.Supp. 108, 124 (D.Colo.1973). Had plaintiff suffered an uncompensated divestment of his federal mining claims, we would have a clear constitutional violation. See North American Transportation & Trading Co. v. United States, 53 Ct.Cl. 424 (1918), aff'd, 253 U.S. 330 (1920). The case before us, however, does not present such facts. Instead, all of plaintiff's "valid existing rights" in his mining claims are expressly recognized and preserved by the Sawtooth Act. His rights of use, enjoyment and disposition in his unpatented mining claims remain undiminished.

Plaintiff's argument rests upon the two following propositions: 1) that his right to the issuance of a patent upon each of his mining claims vested as soon as he completed the discovery and location of each claim, and 2) that, as a consequence, he has suffered an unconstitutional divestment of his vested rights through the denial of his ability to obtain patents upon his claims. Plaintiff is correct in his assumption that the divestment of a vested right to a patent is tantamount to divestment of the patent itself, i.e., a divestment of "property". See Benson Mining and Smelting Co. v. Alta Mining and Smelting Co., 145 U.S. 428, 431, 433 (1892). The flaw in plaintiff's argument, however, inheres in his view that he has a vested right to the issuance of patents. The law is well-settled that this vested right does not arise until there has been full compliance with the extensive procedures set forth in the federal mining laws for the obtaining of a patent. See Wyoming v. United States, 255 U.S. 489, 497 (1921); Benson Mining and Smelting Co. v. Alta Mining and Smelting Co., 145 U.S. 428, 433 (1892); Willcoxson v. United States, 313 F.2d 884, 888 (D.C.Cir.), cert. denied, 373 U.S.

---

2. For purposes of these cross-motions, plaintiff makes no contention that he has actually been hindered in any way in his ability to exploit his mining claims. His argument relates solely to the denial of his ability to obtain patents, i.e., fee title to the lands.

932 (1963); cf. Andrus v. Utah, 446 U.S. 500 (1980) (Taylor Grazing Act reserves discretion on the part of Interior Secretary to classify lands within a federal grazing district as proper for school indemnity selection). In this case, plaintiff had not yet taken the first step towards obtaining patents upon any of his mining claims when the Sawtooth Act intervened on August 22, 1972.

The case before us thus ultimately reduces to the question whether plaintiff has suffered an unconstitutional divestment solely by virtue of the fact that he no longer has the option *to apply for* patents upon his claims. Common sense dictates a negative response. At best, plaintiff has suffered a denial of the opportunity to obtain greater property than that which he owned upon the effective date of the Sawtooth Act. This cannot fairly be deemed the divestment of a property interest, save by the most overt bootstrapping.

* * * Defendant's motion for partial summary judgment is granted. Count I of plaintiff's petition is dismissed.

NOTES

1. Can *Freese* be squared with the reasoning in South Dakota v. Andrus, 614 F.2d 1190 (8th Cir.1980), supra at page 460, that issuance of a patent is only a "ministerial act"? Would the result have been different if Freese had filed an application for a patent but no action had been taken on the application?

2. After a patent application is denied and applicant has pursued all administrative remedies, what is the statutory period for judicial review? May the applicant allege a valid claim and seek judicial review by means of a counterclaim to an ejectment proceeding nine years after the final agency decision? See United States v. Webb, 655 F.2d 977 (9th Cir.1981) (no statute of limitations for judicial review of a decision by the Department of Interior Board of Land Appeals). See also United States v. Smith Christian Mining Enterprises, Inc., 537 F.Supp. 57 (D.Or.1981).

SKAW v. UNITED STATES
United States Court of Appeals, Federal Circuit, 1984.
740 F.2d 932.

COWEN, Senior Circuit Judge.

* * * [T]he United States Claims Court (Claims Court) * * * held that the appellants (plaintiffs) were not entitled to recover for a Fifth Amendment taking of their unpatented mining claims. We vacate the judgment of the Claims Court and remand the case to it.

I. *Factual Background and Prior Proceedings*

Plaintiffs, holders of unpatented mining claims situated in Shoshone County, Idaho, in the vicinity of the upper St. Joe River, from Spruce Tree Campground to Heller Creek, properly recorded them with the Bureau of Land Management, as required by the Federal Land

Policy and Management Act of 1976, 43 U.S.C. § 1744. The principal minerals claimed were garnet and gold. Plaintiffs never applied for a patent on any of the claims in issue.

In 1968, Congress established the national wild and scenic rivers system to preserve selected rivers with outstandingly remarkable values in a free-flowing condition, with the rivers and their immediate environments protected for the benefit and enjoyment of present and future generations. The Wild and Scenic Rivers Act of 1968 designated eight rivers as components of the system, and listed 27 rivers as potential additions to the system, including in section 5(a)(22): "Saint Joe, Idaho: The entire main stem."

Section 9 of the 1968 Act, 16 U.S.C. § 1280, provides:

(a) Nothing in this chapter shall affect the applicability of the United States mining and mineral leasing laws within components of the national wild and scenic rivers system except that—

* * *

(iii) subject to valid existing rights, the minerals in Federal lands which are part of the system and constitute the bed or bank or are situated within one-quarter mile of the bank of any river designated a wild river under this chapter *or any subsequent Act* are hereby withdrawn from all forms of appropriation under the mining laws and from operation of the mineral leasing laws including, in both cases, amendments thereto. [Emphasis added.]

* * *

On November 10, 1978, the Wild and Scenic Rivers Act was amended by section 708 of the National Parks and Recreation Act of 1978, 16 U.S.C. § 1274(a)(23). The amendment added the St. Joe River as a part of the national system, providing in pertinent part as follows:

Dredge or placer mining shall be prohibited within the banks or beds of the main stem of the Saint Joe and its tributary streams in their entirety above the confluence of the main stem with the North Fork of the river. * * * For the purposes of this river, there are authorized to be appropriated not more than $1,000,000 for the acquisition of lands or interest in lands. [Emphasis added.]

Id.

Since the mining claims are located within the St. Joe National Forest, plaintiffs are required to comply with Forest Service regulations promulgated for the protection and preservation of national forests. 36 C.F.R. § 228 (1983) (formerly 36 C.F.R. § 252). * * *

Plaintiffs' operating plan was filed with the Forest Service in 1976, but that agency withheld action on the plan for 2 years while it considered the need for an environmental impact statement. In 1978, action on the plan was again deferred pending the outcome of a mineral contest proposed to be filed in behalf of the Forest Service by the

Bureau of Land Management (BLM) of the Department of the Interior (Interior). So far as the record shows, no decision approving or rejecting the plan has ever been made by the Forest Service.

The present action was filed in the then Court of Claims on March 5, 1979, claiming just compensation in the amount of ten million dollars, and alleging that:

1. The mining claims at issue were validly owned and are leased in compliance with the mining laws of the United States.

2. The United States effected a legislative taking of the mining claims by the enactment of section 708 of the National Parks and Recreation Act of 1978.

3. Pursuant to that Act, the United States has prevented and prohibited the owners of the claims from exercising rights possessed under the Federal mining laws.

* * *

II. *The Validity of the Unpatented Mining Claims*
* * *

[The Interior Department found the claims invalid for, among other things, abandonment and a lack of discovery. The Claims Court agreed and held, alternatively, that no taking had occurred even if the claims were assumed to be valid. In this opinion, the Federal Circuit reversed and remanded for further proceedings on the validity of the claims. The opinion then turned to the taking issue, assuming *arguendo* that the claims were valid.]

III. *The Legislative Taking Issue*

We cannot agree with the following holding of the Claims Court that section 708 was not a legislative taking which deprived plaintiffs of the right to just compensation because:

> Congress made no provision for the vesting of specifically defined property in the United States as of a particular date, nor was provision made for judicial determination and payment of just compensation. Section 708 does not affirmatively direct the Secretary of the Interior to exercise the power of eminent domain.

2 Cl.Ct. at 802.

In the *Regional Rail Reorganization Act Cases,* 419 U.S. 102, 126–27 (1974), the Supreme Court made it clear that none of these elements is an essential ingredient of a legislative taking. There the Court stated:

> The general rule is that whether or not the United States so intended, "[i]f there is a taking, the claim is 'founded upon the Constitution' and within the jurisdiction of the Court of Claims to hear and determine." "[I]f the authorized action * * * does constitute a taking of property for which there must be just compensation under the Fifth Amendment, the Govern-

ment has impliedly promised to pay that compensation and has afforded a remedy for its recovery by a suit in the Court of Claims.

Moreover, there was no occasion for the Congress to provide for the vesting of the property in the United States, because it already held both legal and equitable title, subject only to plaintiffs' possessory rights.

In addition, the last sentence of section 708 indicates that Congress intended to pay compensation for any property interest taken because it provides:

> For the purposes of this river, there are authorized to be appropriated not more than $1,000,000 for the acquisition of lands or interest in lands.

16 U.S.C. § 1274(a)(23).

In the *Regional Rail Reorganization Act Cases,* the Supreme Court scrutinized the regulatory act before it to see if Congress had withdrawn the Tucker Act grant of jurisdiction to the Court of Claims. In the same way, we find that there is nothing in the language of section 708 indicating that Congress intended to withdraw the Tucker Act remedy for the recovery of just compensation. Also, we have not found nor have we been cited to anything in the legislative history which indicates such a Congressional intent.

Because it collides with a recent declaration by this court, we must also disagree with the conclusion of the Claims Court that there was no inverse condemnation of the plaintiffs' claims because there has been no physical invasion of plaintiffs' property. In Yuba Goldfields, Inc. v. United States, 723 F.2d 884, 887 (Fed.Cir.1983), a case involving somewhat similar facts, this court, speaking through Chief Judge Markey, stated:

> Neither physical invasion nor physical restraint constitutes a *sine qua non* of a constitutionally controlled taking.

We agree with the holding of the Claims Court that without doubt, the United States has the authority to regulate the use of the land on which the claims are located and that section 708 is a lawful exercise of the regulatory power of the government to protect and promote the general welfare. There remains, however, the difficult question whether such regulatory action has resulted in depriving plaintiffs of any economically viable use of the claims. Agins v. City of Tiburon, 447 U.S. 255, 260 (1980). Because of material factual disputes which the parties so designated and jointly submitted to the trial court, we hold that this crucial issue could not properly be resolved on summary judgment and that it cannot be decided by this court on the present record.

The analysis of whether a particular regulatory act constitutes a legislative taking remains one of the most troublesome line-drawing exercises in the judicial function, characterized by a few basic precepts and the admonition that each case turns on its own peculiar facts. In the field of land use regulation, the emphasis which Justice Holmes placed on the degree of value diminution suffered by the property owner has continued to be the central focus of modern case law on the subject. See Pennsylvania Coal Co. v. Mahon, 260 U.S. 393 (1922). However devised or articulated, the heart of the inquiry is whether the governmental action is so onerous as to constitute a Fifth Amendment taking. As the Claims Court correctly stated, permissible governmental regulatory action does not constitute a compensable taking merely because the result may diminish the value of the property or prevent its most beneficial use. Penn Central Transportation Co. v. New York City, 438 U.S. 104 (1978).

The Supreme Court recently stated that to determine whether a regulation amounts to a Fifth Amendment taking requires—

> essentially ad hoc, factual inquiries that have identified several factors—such as economic impact of the regulation, its interference with reasonable investment backed expectations, and the character of the governmental action * * *.

Kaiser Aetna v. United States, 444 U.S. 164, 175 (1979).

As we have stated above, this inquiry necessitates a remand of the case to the trial court for resolution of the following factual issues, which were listed in the joint submission of counsel for the parties to the Claims Court:

> a. Which of the claims, in whole or in part, fall within the definition of beds and banks as referred to in Public Law 95–625, Sec. 708?

> b. Can the Plaintiffs' alleged unpatented mining claims be mined by methods other than placer or dredge mining methods?

> c. If there was only a portion of the claims taken, can the remainder be mined or is there in effect a taking of the whole by taking of part?

IV. *The Idaho Statutes*

The Idaho Dredge and Placer Mining Protection Act, Idaho Code Title 47, ch. 13, which was enacted in 1955, requires operators of dredge or placer mining on lands and beds of streams in the state of Idaho to obtain a permit from the state agency. This requirement, as applied to operations on the federal public domain, was upheld by the Idaho Supreme Court. State ex rel. Andrus v. Click, 97 Idaho 791, 554 P.2d 969 (1976).

The conclusion of the Claims Court that there was no inverse condemnation of plaintiffs' mining claims was based in part upon its finding that the plaintiffs had no permit from the state of Idaho that was interfered with or barred by the enactment of section 708. * * *

The state of Idaho could not lawfully deny plaintiffs the right to mine. By complying with the state statute, plaintiffs could have obtained a permit to mine their claims until 1977, when the Idaho permit statute was amended by an act of the Idaho Legislature (Idaho Code section 47–1323), prohibiting dredge mining in any form on the St. Joe River or its tributaries. We assume that if plaintiffs had applied for a permit to conduct dredge mining (which plaintiffs say is the only feasible method of mining their claims) in 1977 or thereafter, the state would have denied the permit. Since the Claims Court rested its decision in part on the 1977 Act, we hold that plaintiffs' right to recover is not affected by that act, because, in so far as plaintiffs' claims are concerned, it was in conflict with and was preempted by previously enacted federal mining law. Act of May 1, 1872, codified as 30 U.S.C. §§ 21, et seq. Kleppe v. New Mexico, 426 U.S. 529, 543 (1976); Ventura County v. Gulf Oil Corporation, 601 F.2d 1080 (9th Cir.1979) aff'd 445 U.S. 947 (1980). Under the Act of May 1, 1872, plaintiffs had the property right to possess and mine to exhaustion the minerals located on their unpatented claims without payment of royalty. Since it prohibited dredge mining on federal land, compliance with the 1977 Act would have made it impossible for plaintiffs to exercise rights theretofore granted by the mining laws. The Idaho Supreme Court has recognized that federal legislation necessarily overrides such a conflicting state law. State ex rel. Andrus v. Click, 97 Idaho 791, 554 P.2d 969, 974 (1976) (dictum).

V. *The Forest Service Regulations*

The government asserts that plaintiffs are not entitled to recover because they had not satisfied a pre-condition of their right to mine their claims by obtaining Forest Service approval of their plan of operation as required by the regulations, 36 C.F.R. § 252. We are astonished at this contention because the record shows that plaintiffs' failure to obtain an approved plan of operation was due to the delaying actions of the Forest Service.

In accordance with the regulations, plaintiffs submitted a plan of operations to the Forest Service on April 26, 1976 (App. pp. 193–204). The Forest Service withheld action on the plan for 2 years while it considered whether an environmental impact statement was required.

* * *

The government admits that the Forest Service has never made a decision, either approving or disapproving plaintiffs' plan of operation.

As the Ninth Circuit aptly declared in a case involving the same regulations, there is nothing in the regulations which authorizes the Forest Service to prohibit plaintiffs' right to the possession and enjoyment of their claims, or to encroach impermissibly upon those rights by circumscribing their use in a manner that amounts to a prohibition. United States v. Weiss, 642 F.2d 296, 299 (1981).

For the reasons stated, the government's defense based on plaintiffs' lack of an approved plan of operations is flatly rejected.

VACATED AND REMANDED.

NOTES

1. Can a state close an area of public lands to mining because of environmental damage? Because of health effects? Can Congress do so? In either case, is there a taking? If the Forest Service acts in a timely fashion and rejects an operating plan on the ground that it provides inadequate protection for surface resources, has there been a taking? Does the issue turn on whether the Forest Service decision was arbitrary and capricious? Can *Skaw* be reconciled with *Freese?*

2. Numerous environmental statutes affect mineral development on unpatented claims, including most prominently the Clean Air Act, e.g., Connery, The Effects of the Clean Air Act Amendments of 1977 on Mining and Energy Developments and Operations, 24 Rocky Mtn.Min. L.Inst. 1 (1978); and the Clean Water Act, e.g., United States v. Earth Sciences, Inc., 599 F.2d 368 (10th Cir.1979) (gold leaching operation is a point source subject to regulation). See generally Hecox & Desautels, Federal Environmental Regulations Applicable to Exploration, Mining and Milling, 25 Rocky Mtn.Min.L.Inst. 9-1 (1979). Regulation by the states is increasing and is in some states stricter than federal requirements. Burling, Local Control of Mining Activities on Federal Lands, XXI Land & Water L.Rev. 33 (1986).

3. Proposals continue to be advanced for further reform of the Hardrock Act. Those measures, which involve the adoption of elements of the mineral leasing system, are considered after materials on the contrasting statutes providing for mineral leasing. See Section B(5), infra.

B. MINERAL LEASING

A leasing disposition system for some non-metalliferous minerals developed separately from the location system for hardrock minerals more because of history than geology. There was little need to reward discoverers of coal in the West, as it was abundant and non-competitive. And as *Midwest Oil,* supra at page 147, illustrated, the federal government realized by 1909 there was little sense in giving away oil reserves one day and buying them back for the Navy the next. Leasing instead of granting was not an innovation: it had been the practice with lead mines for several decades in the early 1800's. But the modern watershed is the Mineral Leasing Act of 1920, as amended, 30 U.S.C.A. §§ 181 et seq., which has been the model for the Outer Continental Shelf Lands Act of 1953, 43 U.S.C.A. §§ 1331–43, and the Geothermal Steam Act of 1970, 30 U.S.C.A. §§ 1001–25. Coal leasing requirements were tightened by the Federal Coal Leasing Amendments of 1975, 30 U.S.C.A. § 201 et seq., and all strip mining operations are now subject to the Surface Mining Control and Reclamation Act of 1977, 30 U.S. C.A. §§ 1201–1328.

The leasable minerals include the fossil fuel minerals (oil, gas, oil shale, coal, native asphalt, bituminous rock, and solid and semi-solid bitumin); the fertilizer and chemical minerals (phosphate, potash, sodium, and, in a few states, sulphur); minerals (principally oil and gas) on the outer continental shelf; geothermal resources; and all minerals, except the "common varieties," that are located on acquired lands, including hardrock minerals. Minor acts cover other situations. See 1 AMERICAN LAW OF MINING 2d § 20.05 (1984).

Many cases already encountered in this volume concerned mineral leasing. Some idea of the theoretical environmental protection mechanisms that have grown up around onshore oil and gas leasing can be garnered from County of Ventura v. Gulf Oil Corp., 601 F.2d 1080 (9th Cir.1979), aff'd, 445 U.S. 947 (1980), supra at page 213. That the states sometimes believe that those protections are insufficient is evident from such cases as Gulf Oil Corp. v. Wyoming Oil and Gas Cons. Comm'n, 693 P.2d 227 (Wyo.1985), supra at page 221. Overriding questions concerning the scope and validity of withdrawals and reservations are often answered in the context of federal mineral leasing. Udall v. Tallman, 380 U.S. 1 (1965), supra at page 288; Pacific Legal Found. v. Watt, 529 F.Supp. 982 (D.Mont.1981), supra at page 260; National Wildlife Fed'n v. Burford, 23 ERC 1609 (D.D.C.1985), supra at page 265. Two coal cases in chapter four, § C, illustrate in miniature the downfall of the federal coal leasing program in the 1970's. Kleppe v. Sierra Club, 427 U.S. 390 (1976), supra at page 323; NRDC v. Hughes, 437 F.Supp. 981 (D.D.C.1977), supra at page 333. Offshore oil and gas leasing was introduced by Village of False Pass v. Clark, 733 F.2d 605 (9th Cir.1984), supra at page 343. See also Commonwealth Edison Co. v. Montana, 453 U.S. 609 (1981), supra at page 230; Wilderness Soc. v. Morton, 479 F.2d 842 (D.C.Cir.1973), cert. denied, 411 U.S. 917 (1973), supra at page 294.

Development of domestic energy sources was one of the Nation's highest natural resource priorities in the 1970's, and might well be again. Most such development will take place on federal lands, and it will be governed by these leasing systems as modified by later legislative commands. Cries to "open up the federal lands" to oil and gas exploration constantly recur in American history, but onshore public lands have been relatively minor contributors to national oil and gas supplies; the primary exploration efforts have been concentrated on the offshore lands. In July, 1979, President Carter came down from the mountain with oil shale and coal tablets, calling for an accelerated "synfuels" (liquified and gassified shale oil and coal) development program. These resources are also found primarily on the public lands. The rapidly proliferating laws and regulations governing energy law in general are beyond the scope of this book. See W. Rodgers, ENERGY AND NATURAL RESOURCES LAW (2d ed., 1983); A. Aman, ENERGY AND NATURAL RESOURCE LAW (1983); D. Zillman & L. Lattman, ENERGY LAW (1983). This section is aimed at an understanding of the federal leasing systems by which federal energy resources are made available to private developers. After summarizing the main features of leasing, following subsections will take up legal problems of particular leasable minerals.

1.　AN OVERVIEW OF MINERAL LEASING SYSTEMS

It is difficult to generalize about all mineral leasing because the major acts materially differ and special provisions abound. But certain common features distinguish leasing from location systems:

1.　There is no right of self-initiation. Permission must be obtained from the federal government to prospect, develop, or produce leasable minerals.

2.　The United States receives an economic return in the form of royalties, rents, and bonus payments.

3.　Provisions can be and are included in leases to protect other competing resources and the environment.

4.　In many cases, the United States has discretion whether to accept any bid and whether to allow a lessee to explore for minerals or extract minerals found.

5.　The United States can force diligent development of the resource.

6.　In general, because the issuance of prospecting permits and competitive leases is discretionary, the United States has the power to control mineral development planning and to require lessees to conform operations to land-use goals.

One major feature of leasing systems historically is the distinction between areas where minerals are known to exist and areas of unknown potential. That distinction still makes a difference in onshore oil and gas and geothermal leasing. In known mineral areas, no exploration permits are necessary and development and production rights can be obtained only through competitive bidding. In the competitive bidding procedures, the BLM, at the request of a private party or on its own initiative, publishes a notice to offer specific lands for lease. Eligible parties (citizens and domestic corporations) may then submit bids in accordance with highly detailed requirements. The United States may reject all bids, the most common basis being the inadequacy of the bid. Examples of royalties are: $12\frac{1}{2}\%$ to 25% for oil and gas, depending upon the amount of production; since 1976, at least $12\frac{1}{2}\%$ for surface-mined coal; and 10 to 15% for geothermal steam. A bonus is also included in the bid, and leases are almost always issued to the qualified bidder with the highest bonus bid, since the royalty is usually fixed by the BLM in advance. "Considerable administrative effort is required to determine whether the highest qualified bid is adequate payment for the mineral resource, especially when the demand for the resource currently is low but may increase substantially in the future as a result of improvements in technology * * *." Office of Technology Assessment, MANAGEMENT OF FUEL AND NONFUEL MINERALS IN FEDERAL LAND 131 (R. Wright ed., 1979).

The location and extent of oil shale deposits are generally known. Prospecting is unnecessary, and all remaining federal oil shale leasing is now competitive. In 1975, Congress provided that all coal leasing would be by competitive bidding, "subject to existing rights" that may have been obtained earlier by noncompetitive lease or otherwise. See 30 U.S.C.A. § 201(b). The transition to an all-competitive system has been confusing. See § B(3) infra. Similarly, all offshore oil and gas leasing is by competitive bidding, although the form and contents of the bidding process can vary dramatically. See Watt v. Energy Action Ed. Found., 454 U.S. 151 (1981).

For onshore oil and gas leases in areas where those minerals are not known to exist, a dual system of noncompetitive leasing is utilized. Parcels that have never been subject to lease, in areas open to leasing, may be leased to the first qualified applicant if the Secretary decides to grant any leases. See Udall v. Tallman, 380 U.S. 1 (1965), supra at page 288. In the more common situation of re-leasing after earlier leases have expired, the BLM utilizes a "simultaneous drawing," or "lottery" system to award noncompetitive leases. After the BLM announces that an area is available for lease, anyone may submit an entry card; all cards submitted are deemed to be filed simultaneously. A drawing then determines who is entitled to the lease. The first applicant drawn wins the lottery if qualified and the entry card meets the technical requirements on payment of a nominal sum; otherwise, the lease goes to the next qualified applicant drawn. If the lease is in a "hot" area, an oil company may pay a substantial sum to purchase the lease, but the overall odds of profiting from the lottery are poor. Many applications are submitted by filing services.

With certain exceptions, noncompetitive leases return royalties at rates fixed by statute or regulation, and the miner pays no bonus. As a consequence, returns to the government from noncompetitive leases are significantly less than under the competitive system. See Sprague & Julian, An Analysis of the Impact of an All Competitive Leasing System on Onshore Oil and Gas Leasing Revenue, 10 Nat.Res.J. 515 (1970). That result is deemed partly justified in that miners in areas of unknown deposits must undergo the expense and uncertainty of exploration. In early 1980, the Department suspended all noncompetitive leasing of oil and gas on public lands because of widespread fraud: according to the BLM, "the noncompetitive leasing system * * * has been subjected to such thorough manipulation that the possibility of lawful, bona fide participants successfully obtaining a lease has, in many cases, been reduced to a very low level." 5 Public Land News 3 (March 6, 1980). Several months later, after an investigation and review of practices, the suspension was lifted. More fraud has since been uncovered and much more is alleged and suspected. Such fraud and the low return have convinced several federal legislators to introduce bills forbidding future noncompetitive oil and gas leasing.

Development and exploration rights are easier to obtain for geothermal and oil and gas developers working in areas where deposits are not known. No prospecting permit is required for these minerals; rather, noncompetitive leases covering rights to explore, develop, and produce are issued initially.

The mineral lease period varies according to the mineral. Coal leases entered into after the Coal Leasing Amendments of 1975 are to be for 20 years, 30 U.S.C.A. § 207(a), as are most leases of oil shale and hardrock minerals. Competitive oil and gas leases have primary terms of five years, and ten years are allowed in noncompetitive leases. In most cases, the lease can be automatically extended if minerals are being produced in commercial quantities—the functional equivalent of a discovery under the Hardrock Act.

The acreage limitations for mineral leases also vary according to the mineral. A 2,560-acre limit applies to noncompetitive oil and gas leases and geothermal leases, while oil shale leases may encompass 5,120 acres. Competitive oil and gas leases are limited to units of 640 acres. There are no limits on the number of individual coal leases, but they cannot be combined into a logical mining unit of more than 25,000 acres. The total acres that a lessee can maintain under all leases is also restricted. Leases must include provisions for rents and royalties, and they also require diligent development of the resource, with statutory and administrative requirements varying according to the resource. See generally Office of Technology Assessment, supra, at 130.

One way to protect other resources from mining of leasable land is to refuse to lease the land altogether, either by formally withdrawing it or by refusing to open it for leasing. See United States ex rel. McLennan v. Wilbur, 283 U.S. 414 (1931). See also the controversy over mineral leasing in wilderness areas, which remained open for leasing until December 31, 1983, infra at page 988. The Mineral Leasing Act of 1920 also gives the Secretary ample authority to include lease provisions to protect the environment. In fact, however, lease provisions and regulations dealing with soil erosion, air and water pollution, and restoration had long been cast in such broad terms that enforcement was difficult. That picture has changed dramatically in recent years, as many of the cases in this section illustrate. The Surface Mining Control and Reclamation Act of 1977 contains relatively strict reclamation requirements for coal mining, 30 U.S.C.A. §§ 1265(b), 1272, and requires protection of non-mineral resources and values "to the extent possible using the best technology currently available * * *." 30 U.S.C.A. § 1265(b)(24). The United States has authority to cancel the lease for violations. See generally Boesche v. Udall, 373 U.S. 472 (1963).

The foregoing summary was a description of all mineral leasing, but each leasable resource is unique legally as well as physically. Shale oil is a good starting point for consideration of individual leasing systems, because the effects of the location system still linger three generations after shale oil became leasable.

2. SHALE OIL

WILLIAM E. HOLLAND, MIXING OIL AND WATER: THE EFFECT OF PREVAILING WATER LAW DOCTRINES ON OIL SHALE DEVELOPMENT
52 Den.L.J. 657 (1975).

The largest single deposit of fossil energy known to exist in the world is the oil shale formation underlying 16,000 square miles of several basin areas in Colorado, Utah, and Wyoming. Known as the Green River Formation, this deposit was laid down in three lake beds in the Eocene Age. It ranges in thickness from a few hundred feet to about 7 thousand feet. Even excluding beds which contain less than 10 gallons of oil per ton of shale, the formation is estimated to contain more than 2 trillion barrels of oil.

* * *

The Green River Formation is by no means the only oil shale deposit in the United States. There are known deposits in 30 states totaling an estimated 72 trillion tons. Only the Green River Formation has present commercial significance, as the other deposits are much lower in grade and quality, generally assaying below 15 gallons per ton. However, there are Alaskan deposits of unknown extent but locally very rich, with up to 160 gallons per ton.

* * *

Even allowing for considerable error in the estimates, these figures dwarf proven petroleum reserves, and they dwarf present rates of consumption. In 1972 the United States consumed approximately 6 billion barrels of petroleum and about 22.6 billion cubic feet of natural gas, which is the energy equivalent of approximately 4.4 billion barrels of petroleum. Thus, if the oil in that part of the Green River Formation which contains more than 10 gallons per ton were totally recoverable, it would replace both petroleum and natural gas for nearly 200 years at 1972 levels of consumption.

* * *

The technological and economic barriers to shale oil production stem from the fact that the organic minerals in shale are not fugacious, as are petroleum and natural gas, but are bound to the rock itself. The organic matter in oil shales is called kerogen. It can be converted into oil and gas by heating the shale to about 900 degrees Fahrenheit in a process called retorting. This is accomplished by either of two basic methods: mining, either underground or open pit, followed by retorting of the mined shale; or in situ retorting by burning the shale beds in place and extracting and condensing the combustion products. The resulting shale oil is a black, highly viscous substance that is difficult to pour. To make it pipelineable, shale oil must be upgraded to remove wax-forming components; nitrogen and sulfur, in which it is rich, can be removed at the same time by conventional techniques. The result is a high grade synthetic crude oil, "syncrude," suitable for refining into products equivalent to those produced from petroleum.

The difficulty of separating the oil from the rock has held back oil shale production to the present time simply because known methods involved capital costs too great to allow competition with petroleum. The recent rise in petroleum prices, if permanent, could remove that barrier. * * *

HICKEL v. OIL SHALE CORP.
Supreme Court of the United States, 1970.
400 U.S. 48.

Mr. Justice DOUGLAS delivered the opinion of the Court.

This case involves six groups of claims to oil shale located in Colorado and asserted under the General Mining Act of 1872. Section 28 provides that until a patent issued "not less than $100 worth of labor shall be performed or improvements made during each year." And § 29 provides that a patent to the claim could issue on a showing that the claimant had expended $500 worth of labor or improvements on the claim. These claims are not patented and were canceled in the early 1930's on the ground that the amount of labor or improvements specified in § 28 had not been made "during each year."

Some of the claimants in this case applied for patents between 1955 and 1962. The General Land Office rejected the patent applications because the claims had been canceled. On appeal, the Secretary of the Interior, acting through the Solicitor, ruled that these cancellations were effective, later judicial determinations of the invalidity of the grounds for cancellation notwithstanding. [The District Court and Court of Appeals both held that the cancellations were void.] The case is here on petition for certiorari, which we granted to consider whether Wilbur v. Krushnic, 280 U.S. 306, and Ickes v. Virginia-Colorado Development Corp., 295 U.S. 639, had been correctly construed and applied to invalidate the Secretary's action in protection of the public domain.

Before we come to a consideration of the *Krushnic* and *Virginia-Colorado* cases it should be noted that in 1920, Congress by enacting § 21 of the Mineral Lands Leasing Act, 41 Stat. 445, 30 U.S.C.A. § 241(a), completely changed the national policy over the disposition of oil shale lands. Thereafter such lands were no longer open to location and acquisition of title but only to lease. But § 37 contained a Saving Clause which covered "valid claims existent on February 25, 1920, and thereafter maintained in compliance with the laws under which initiated, which claims may be perfected under such laws, including discovery." 30 U.S.C.A. § 193. Respondents contend that their claims fall within that exception.

Respondents assert that a like claim was recognized and approved in the *Krushnic* case. In that case, however, labor in the statutory amount had been performed, including the aggregate amount of $500. The only default was in the failure to perform labor for one year during the period. Mandamus for the issuance of a patent was directed, the Court saying:

"Prior to the passage of the Leasing Act, annual performance of labor was not necessary to preserve the possessory
right, with all the incidents of ownership * * *, as against
the United States, but only as against subsequent relocators.
So far as the government was concerned, failure to do assessment work for any year was without effect. Whenever $500
worth of labor in the aggregate had been performed, other
requirements aside, the owner became entitled to a patent,
even though in some years annual assessment labor had been
omitted." 280 U.S., at 317.

The Court further held that the claims were "maintained" within
the Saving Clause of the Leasing Act by a resumption of the assessment
work before a challenge of the claim by the United States had intervened.

Virginia-Colorado also involved claims on which labor had been
expended except for one year. It was alleged, however, that the
claimant had planned to resume the assessment work but for the
Secretary's adverse action and that the claims had not been abandoned.
The Court held that the claims had been "maintained" within the
meaning of the Saving Clause of the Leasing Act of 1920.

Those two cases reflect a judicial attitude of fair treatment for
claimants who have substantially completed the assessment work required by 30 U.S.C.A. § 28. There are, however, dicta both in *Virginia-
Colorado* and in *Krushnic* that the failure to do assessment work gives
the Government no ground for forfeiture but inures only to the benefit
of relocators.

Indeed 30 U.S.C.A. § 28 * * * provides that upon the failure to
do the assessment work, "the claim or mine upon which such failure
occurred shall be open to relocation in the same manner as if no
location of the same had ever been made," provided the assessment
work has not been "resumed" upon the claim "after failure and before
such location." It is therefore argued that so far as the 1872 Act is
concerned the failure to do the assessment work concerns not the
Government but only "rival or adverse claimants."

* * * [F]ailure to maintain a claim made it "subject to disposition only" by leasing by the United States. Hence if we assume,
arguendo, that failure to do assessment work as provided in the 1872
Act concerned at the time only the claimant and any subsequent
relocator, the United States, speaking through the Secretary of the
Interior, became a vitally interested party by reason of the 1920 Act.
* * *

It appears that shortly before 1920 oil shale claims were affected by
a speculative fever. Then came a period of calm. By the late forties
and continuing into the sixties speculators sought out the original
locators or their heirs, obtained quitclaim deeds from them, and thereupon eliminated all other record titleholders by performing assessment
work for one year. It appears that 94 of the 98 claims involved in the
present litigation were of that character. There is nothing reprehensi-

ble in the practice, if the procedure is one which Congress has approved. But the command of the 1872 Act is that assessment work of $100 be done "during each year" and the Saving Clause of § 37 of the 1920 Act requires that for lands to escape the leasing requirement the claims must be "maintained in compliance with the laws under which initiated."

The legislative history of the 1872 Act does not throw much light on the problem. * * * While the objective of the 1872 Act was to open the lands "to a beneficial use by some other party," once the original claimant defaulted, the defeasance inevitably accrued to the United States, owner of the fee. On that premise it would seem that the dicta in *Krushnic* and in *Virginia-Colorado* are not valid.

The history of the 1920 Act throws a little light on the problem.

* * *

The "perfection" of the claims "under such laws" thus seemingly meant compliance with "everything" under 30 U.S.C.A. § 28, which taken literally would mean assessment work of $100 "during each year."

If we were to hold to the contrary that enforcement of the assessment work of § 28 was solely at the private initiative of relocators, the "maintenance" provision of § 37 becomes largely illusory, because relocation of oil shale claims became impossible after the 1920 Act. * * * That meant that a claim could remain immune from challenge by anyone with or without any assessment work, in complete defiance of the 1872 Act.

The Court concluded in *Virginia-Colorado* that the lapse in assessment work was no basis for a charge of abandonment. We construe that statement to mean that on the facts of that case failure to do the assessment work was not sufficient to establish abandonment. But it was well established that the failure to do assessment work was evidence of abandonment. If, in fact, a claim had been abandoned, then the relocators were not the only ones interested. The United States had an interest in retrieving the lands. The policy of leasing oil shale lands under the 1920 Act gave the United States a keen interest in recapturing those which had not been "maintained" within the meaning of § 37 of that Act. We agree with the Court in *Krushnic* and *Virginia-Colorado* that every default in assessment work does not cause the claim to be lost. Defaults, however, might be the equivalent of abandonment; and we now hold that token assessment work, or assessment work that does not substantially satisfy the requirements of 30 U.S.C.A. § 28, is not adequate to "maintain" the claims within the meaning of § 37 of the Leasing Act.

Unlike the claims in *Krushnic* and *Virginia-Colorado*, the Land Commissioner's findings indicate that the present claims had not substantially met the conditions of § 28 respecting assessment work.

* * *

Respondents rely upon the response of the Department of the Interior to the *Virginia-Colorado* case in which the Secretary declared the contest in that case to be "void." He also declared that "other Departmental decisions in conflict with this decision are hereby over-ruled." Shale Oil Co., 55 I.D. 287, 290. This decision, they argue, nullified the previous contest proceedings in which their claims were voided. Moreover, they contend that this administrative rule of 35 years, upon which the Department itself has relied, may not now be retroactively changed. In addition, they claim that these contest deci-sions, if still valid, are subject to direct judicial review at this time, testing both substantive and procedural errors, such as lack of notice.

These contentions present questions not decided below. Therefore, on remand all issues relevant to the current validity of those contest proceedings will be open, including the availability of judicial review at this time. To the extent that they are found void, not controlling, or subject to review, all issues relevant to the invalidity of the claims will be open, including inadequate assessment work, abandonment, fraud, and the like. Likewise all issues concerning the time, amount, and nature of the assessment work will be open so that the claimants will have an opportunity to bring their claims within the narrow ambit of *Krushnic* and *Virginia-Colorado*, as we have construed and limited these opinions.

Reversed and remanded.

Mr. Justice HARLAN, Mr. Justice WHITE, and Mr. Justice MAR-SHALL took no part in the consideration or decision of this case.

The CHIEF JUSTICE and Mr. Justice STEWART dissent. They believe the Court of Appeals in this litigation correctly construed and applied this Court's decisions in *Krushnic* and *Virginia-Colorado*. Ac-cordingly, unless those decisions are to be overruled, they would affirm the judgment before us.

NOTES

1. What does it tell you about mining law that the validity of these claims was still being litigated 50 years after they were located (and that the litigation is far from over)? Should the holding in *Oil Shale Corp.* to the effect that the United States is a rival locator be extended to all mineral locations? Compare 43 U.S.C.A. § 1712(e)(3): "nothing in this section shall prevent a wholly owned Government corporation from acquiring and holding rights as a citizen under the Mining Law of 1872."

2. Sixteen years after the *TOSCO* decision, as the principal case is usually called, the question whether sufficient assessment work on such claims had in fact been performed had not been finally decided. See Tosco Corp. v. Hodel, 611 F.Supp. 1130 (D.Colo.1985), infra at page 522.

3. In the meantime, the Court had another occasion to consider the validity of ancient oil shale claims.

ANDRUS v. SHELL OIL CORP.

Supreme Court of the United States, 1980.
446 U.S. 657.

Mr. Chief Justice BURGER delivered the opinion of the Court.

* * *

The question presented is whether oil shale deposits located prior to the 1920 Act are "valuable mineral deposits" patentable under the savings clause of the Act.

I

The action involves two groups of oil shale claims located by claimants on public lands in Garfield County, Colo., prior to the enactment of the Mineral Leasing Act. * * *

In 1964, the Department issued administrative complaints alleging that the * * * claims were invalid. The complaints alleged, *inter alia,* that oil shale was not a "valuable mineral" prior to the enactment of the 1920 Mineral Leasing Act.

The complaints were consolidated and tried to a hearing examiner who in 1970 ruled the claims valid. The hearing examiner observed that under established case law the test for determining a "valuable mineral deposit" was whether the deposit was one justifying present expenditures with a reasonable prospect of developing a profitable mine. See United States v. Coleman, 390 U.S. 599 (1968); Castle v. Womble, 19 L.D. 455 (1894). He then reviewed the history of oil shale operations in this country and found that every attempted operation had failed to show profitable production. On the basis of this finding and other evidence showing commercial infeasibility, the hearing examiner reasoned that "[i]f this were a case of first impression," oil shale would fail the "valuable mineral deposit" test. However, he deemed himself bound by the Department's contrary decision in Freeman v. Summers, 52 L.D. 201 (1927). There, the Secretary had written:

"While at the present time there has been no considerable production of oil shales, due to the fact that abundant quantities of oil have been produced more cheaply from wells, *there is no possible doubt of its value and of the fact that it constitutes an enormously valuable resource for future use by the American people.* It is not necessary, in order to constitute a valid discovery under the general mining laws sufficient to support an application for patent, that the mineral *in its present situation* can be immediately disposed of at a profit." (Emphasis added.)

The hearing examiner ruled that Freeman v. Summers compelled the conclusion that oil shale is a valuable mineral subject to appropriation under the mining laws, and he upheld the * * * claims as valid and patentable.

The Board of Land Appeals reversed. Adopting the findings of the hearing examiner, the Board concluded that oil shale claims located prior to 1920 failed the test of value because at the time of location there did not appear "as a *present* fact * * * a reasonable prospect of success in developing an operating mine that would yield a reasonable profit." (Emphasis in original.) The Board recognized that this conclusion was at odds with prior departmental precedent, and particularly with Freeman v. Summers; but it rejected that precedent as inconsistent with the general mining law and therefore unsound. The Board then considered whether its newly enunciated interpretation should be given only prospective effect. It found that respondents' reliance on prior rulings was minimal and that the Department's responsibility as trustee of public lands required it to correct a plainly erroneous decision. Accordingly, it ruled that its new interpretation applied to the Mountain Boy and Shoup claims, and that those claims were invalid.

Respondents appealed the Board's ruling to the United States District Court for the District of Colorado. * * * [I]t reversed the Board's ruling and held that the claims at issue were valid.

The Court of Appeals for the Tenth Circuit affirmed. * * * We granted certiorari because of the importance of the question to the management of the public lands. We affirm.

II

The legislative history of the 1920 Mineral Leasing Act shows that Congress did not consider "present marketability" a prerequisite to the patentability of oil shale.[6] In the extensive hearings and debates that preceded the passage of the 1920 Act, there is no intimation that Congress contemplated such a requirement; indeed, the contrary appears. During the 1919 floor debates in the House of Representatives, an amendment was proposed which would have substituted the phrase "deposits in paying quantities" for "valuable mineral." That amendment, however, was promptly withdrawn after Mr. Sinott, the House floor manager, voiced his objection to the change:

> "Mr. SINOTT. That language was put in with a great deal of consideration and we would not like to change from "valuable" to "paying." *There is quite a distinction.* We are in line with the decisions of the courts as to what is a discovery, and I think that it would be a very dangerous matter to experiment with this language at this time." 58 Cong.Rec. 7537 (1919) (emphasis added).

An examination of the relevant decisions at the time underscores the point. Those decisions are clear in rejecting a requirement that a miner must "demonstrate[ ] that the vein * * * would pay all the expenses of removing, extracting, crushing, and reducing the ore, and

6. Congress was aware that there was then no commercially feasible method for extracting oil from oil shale. * * *

leave a profit to the owner," Book v. Justice Mining Co., 58 F. 106, 124 (D.C.Nev.1893), and in holding that "it is enough if the vein or deposit 'has a present *or prospective* commercial value.'" Madison v. Octave Oil Co., 154 Cal. 768, 99 P. 176, 178 (1908) (emphasis added).

To be sure, prior to the passage of the 1920 Act, there existed considerable uncertainty as to whether oil shale was patentable.[7] That uncertainty, however, related to whether oil shale was a "mineral" under the mining law, and not to its "value." ＊ ＊ ＊ In 1897, Congress enacted the Oil Placer Act authorizing entry under the mining laws to public lands "containing petroleum or other mineral oils." 29 Stat. 526 (1897). This legislation put to rest any doubt about oil as a mineral. But because oil shale, strictly speaking, contained kerogen and not oil, its status remained problematic.

That this was the nature of the uncertainty surrounding the patentability of oil shale claims is evident from remarks made throughout the hearings and debates on the 1920 Act. In the 1918 Hearings, Congressman Barnett, for example, explained:

> "Mr. BARNETT. ＊ ＊ ＊ If the Department should contend that shale lands come within the meaning of the term 'oil lands' they must perforce, by the same argument, admit that they are placer lands within the meaning of the act of 1897.
>
> "The Chairman. And patentable?
>
> "Mr. BARNETT. And patentable under that act."

The enactment of the 1920 Mineral Leasing Act put an end to these doubts. By withdrawing "oil shale ＊ ＊ ＊ in lands valuable for such minerals" from disposition under the general mining law, the Congress recognized—at least implicitly—that oil shale *had been* a locatable mineral. In effect, the 1920 Act did for oil shale what the 1897 Oil Placer Act had done for oil. And, as Congressman Barnett's ready answer demonstrates, once it was settled that oil shale was a mineral subject to location, and once a savings clause was in place preserving pre-existing claims, it was fully expected that such claims would be patentable. The fact that oil shale then had no commercial value simply was not perceived as an obstacle to that end.

III

Our conclusion that Congress in enacting the 1920 Mineral Leasing Act contemplated that pre-existing oil shale claims could satisfy the

---

7. Mr. John Fry, one of the Committee witnesses who represented the oil shale interest before Congress, was candid on that point:

"Mr. TAYLOR. There is a large amount of this shale land that has been located and is now held under the placer law. But none of it has yet gone to patent.

"The Chairman. Has one acre of this land withdrawn in Colorado been patented?

"Mr. FRY. No.

"The Chairman. So you do not know what the holding of the department will be?

"Mr. FRY. We do not."

discovery requirement of the mining law is confirmed by actions taken in subsequent years by the Interior Department and the Congress.[8]

A

On May 10, 1920, less than three months after the Mineral Leasing Act became law, the Interior Department issued "Instructions" to its General Land Office authorizing that office to begin adjudicating applications for patents for pre-1920 oil shale claims. The Instructions advised as follows:

> "Oil shale having been thus recognized by the Department and *by the Congress* as a *mineral* deposit and a source of petroleum * * * lands valuable on account thereof *must be held to have been subject to valid location and appropriation under the placer laws* to the same extent and subject to the same provisions and conditions as if valuable on account of oil and gas."
> 47 L.D. 548, 551 (1920) (emphasis added).

The first such patent was issued immediately thereafter. Five years later, the Department ruled that patentability was dependent upon the "character, extent, and mode of occurrence of the oil-shale deposits." Dennis v. State of Utah, 51 L.D. 229, 232 (1925). Present profitability was not mentioned as a relevant, let alone a critical, consideration.

In 1927, the Department decided Freeman v. Summers, 52 L.D. 201. The case arose out of a dispute between an oil shale claimant and an applicant for a homestead patent, and involved two distinct issues: (1) whether a finding of lean surface deposits warranted the geological inference that the claim contained rich "valuable" deposits below; and (2) whether present profitability was a prerequisite to patentability. Both issues were decided in favor of the oil-shale claimant: the geological inference was deemed sound and the fact that there was "no possible doubt * * * that [oil shale] constitutes an enormously valuable resource for future use by the American people" was ruled sufficient proof of "value."

For the next 33 years, *Freeman* was applied without deviation. It was said that its application ensured that "valid rights [would] be protected and permitted to be perfected." Dept. of Interior Ann.Rep. 30 (1927). In all, 523 patents for 2,326 claims covering 349,088 acres were issued under the *Freeman* rule. This administrative practice, begun immediately upon the passage of the 1920 Act, "has peculiar weight [because] it involves a contemporaneous construction of [the] statute by the men charged with the responsibility of setting its machinery in

---

8. This Court has observed that "the views of a subsequent Congress form a hazardous basis for inferring the intent of an earlier one. United States v. Price, 361 U.S. 304 (1960). This sound admonition has guided several of our recent decisions. See, e.g., TVA v. Hill, 437 U.S. 153, 189–193 (1978). Yet we cannot fail to note Chief Justice Marshall's dictum that "[w]here the mind labours to discover the design of the legislature, it seizes everything from which aid can be derived." United States v. Fisher, 2 Cranch 358, 386, 2 L.Ed. 304 (1805). In consequence, while arguments predicated upon subsequent congressional actions must be weighed with extreme care, they should not be rejected out of hand as a source that a court may consider in the search for legislative intent.

motion." It provides strong support for the conclusion that Congress did not intend to impose a present marketability requirement on oil shale claims.

B

In 1930 and 1931 Congressional Committees revisited the 1920 Mineral Leasing Act and re-examined the patentability of oil-shale claims. Congressional interest in the subject was sparked in large measure by a series of newspaper articles charging that oil-shale lands had been "improvidently, erroneously and unlawfully, if not corruptly, transferred to individuals and private corporations." 74 Cong.Rec. 1079 (1930) (S.Res. 379). The articles were based upon accusations levelled at the Interior Department by Ralph S. Kelly, then the General Land Office Division Inspector in Denver. Kelly's criticism centered on the Freeman v. Summers decision. Fearing another "Teapot Dome" scandal, the Senate authorized the Committee on Public Lands to "inquire into ✱ ✱ ✱ the alienation of oil shale lands."

The Senate Committee held seven days of hearings focusing almost exclusively on "th[e] so-called Freeman-Summers case." At the outset of the hearings, the Committee was advised by Assistant Secretary E.C. Finney that 124 oil shale patents had been issued covering 175,000 acres of land and that 63 more patent applications were pending. Finney's statement prompted this interchange:

"Senator PITTMAN: Well, were the shales in those patented lands of commercial value?

"Mr. FINNEY: If you mean by that whether they could have been mined and disposed of at a profit at the time of the patent, or now, the answer is no.

✱ ✱ ✱

"Senator PITTMAN: So the Government has disposed of 175,000 acres in patents on lands which in your opinion there was no valid claim to in the locator?

"Mr. FINNEY: No; that was not my opinion. I have not held in the world, that I know of, that you had to have an actual commercial discovery of any commodity that you could take out *and market at a profit*. On the contrary, the department has held that that is not the case. ✱ ✱ ✱ " (Emphasis added.)

✱ ✱ ✱

The Senate Committee did not produce a report. But one month after the hearings were completed, Senator Nye, the Chairman of the Committee, wrote the Secretary of Interior that he had "conferred with Senator Walsh and beg[ged] to advise that there is no reason why your Department should not proceed to final disposition of the pending applications for patents to oil shale lands in conformity with the law." The patenting of oil shale lands under the standards enunciated in *Freeman* was at once resumed.

At virtually the same time, the House of Representatives commenced its own investigation into problems relating to oil shale patents. The House Committee, however, focused primarily on the question of assessment work—whether an oil shale claimant was required to perform $100 dollars work per year or forfeit his claim—and not on discovery. But the impact of the *Freeman* rule was not lost on the Committee:

* * *

"Mr. SWING (interposing). I realize that [we are dealing with claims that are thought to be valid], and I understand the feeling of Congress, and I think generally the country, that in drawing the law we do not want to cut the ground from under the person who has initiated a right."

Congressman Swing's statement of the "feeling of Congress" comports with our reading of the 1920 statute and of congressional intent. To hold now that *Freeman* was wrongly decided would be wholly inconsistent with that intent. Moreover, it would require us to conclude that the Congress in 1930–1931 closed its eyes to a major perversion of the mining laws. We reject any such conclusion.

C

In 1956 Congress again turned its attention to the patentability of oil shale. That year it amended the mining laws by eliminating the requirement that locators must obtain and convey to the United States existing homestead surfaceland patents in order to qualify for a mining patent on minerals withdrawn under the 1920 Mineral Leasing Act. Where a surface owner refused to cooperate with the mining claimant and sell his estate, this requirement prevented the mining claimant from patenting his claim. In hearings on the amendment, it was emphasized that oil-shale claimants would be principal beneficiaries of the amendment.

* * *

The bill was enacted into law without floor debate. Were we to hold today that oil shale is a nonvaluable mineral we would virtually nullify this 1956 action of Congress.

IV

The position of the Government in this case is not without a certain irony. Its challenge to respondents' pre-1920 oil shale claims as "nonvaluable" comes at a time when the value of such claims has increased sharply as the Nation searches for alternative energy sources to meet its pressing needs. If the Government were to succeed in invalidating old claims and in leasing the lands at public auction, the Treasury, no doubt, would be substantially enriched. However, the history of the 1920 Mineral Leasing Act and developments subsequent to that Act persuade us that the Government cannot achieve that end by imposing a present marketability requirement on oil shale claims.[11] We conclude that the original position of the Department of Interior, enunciated in the 1920 Instructions and in Freeman v. Summers, is the correct view of the Mineral Leasing Act as it applies to the patentability of those claims.[12]

The judgment of the Court of Appeals is affirmed.

Affirmed.

Mr. Justice STEWART, with whom Mr. Justice BRENNAN and Mr. Justice MARSHALL join, dissenting.

*   *   *

A

There is not one shred of evidence that Congress enacted the savings clause of the Mineral Leasing Act with the purpose of exempting oil shale claims from the usual requirements of patentability. On its face, the 1920 version of the provision applied with identical effect to "coal, phosphate, sodium, oil, oil shale, and gas," and required that all outstanding valid claims to such minerals meet the existing standards of the mining law in order to be perfected.

* * * Descriptions by legislators of the savings clause drew no distinction between oil shale and other covered claims. * * * But it did not accord such claims any special legislative treatment.

Equally unambiguous are the Instructions which the Secretary of the Interior published three months after passage of the Act. These expressly stated that:

> "[L]ands valuable on account [of oil shale] must be held to have been subject to valid location and appropriation under the placer mining laws, *to the same extent and subject to the same provisions and conditions as if valuable on account of oil or gas.* Entries and applications for patent for oil shale placer claims will therefore, be adjudicated * * * in accordance *with the same legal provisions and with reference to the same*

11. This history indicates only that a present marketability standard does not apply to oil shale. It does not affect our conclusion in United States v. Coleman that for other minerals the Interior Department's profitability test is a permissible interpretation of the "valuable mineral" requirement.

12. The dissent overlooks the abundant evidence that Congress since 1920 has consistently viewed oil shale as a "valuable mineral" under the general mining law.

* * *

The dissent also overlooks that beginning in 1920 and continuing for four decades, the Interior Department treated oil shale as a "valuable mineral." In paying deference to the doctrine that a "contemporaneous [administrative] construction * * * is entitled to substantial weight," the dissent ignores this contemporaneous administrative practice. The best evidence of the 1920 standard of patentability is the 1920 Interior Department practice on the matter. The suggestion of the dissent that "future events [such] as market changes" were not meaningful data under the Castle v. Womble test, is inaccurate. As a leading treatise has observed "[t]he future value concept of Freeman v. Summers is nothing more than the 'reasonable prospect of success' of Castle v. Womble, and the reference to 'present facts' in Castle v. Womble, * * * relates to the existence of a vein or lode and not to its value." 1 American Law of Mining, § 4.76 at 697, n. 2.

requirements and limitations as are applicable to oil and gas placers."   47 L.D. 548, 551 (1920) (emphasis added).

Such a contemporaneous construction of the statute by the agency charged with its application is entitled to substantial weight.   See Udall v. Tallman, 380 U.S. 1, 16.

B

The savings clause of the Mineral Leasing Act thus directs that the validity of all claims brought thereunder—including those relating to oil shale—must be judged according to the general criteria of patentability that were established in the mining law as of 1920.   And I am convinced that nothing that Congress has done since 1920 can be read to have modified this mandate.

The Court points to congressional committee hearings that were held in 1931 on the Secretary's 1927 Freeman v. Summers decision, and notes that there resulted from this inquiry no legislative rejection of the Department's then prevailing generous treatment of oil shale claims.   But of far greater significance, in my opinion, is the fact that not a single remark by a Senator or Representative, let alone by a congressional committee, can be found approving the liberal standard enunciated in Freeman v. Summers, even though such a statement could not, in any event, have overridden the plain meaning of the savings clause of the Mineral Leasing Act.   See TVA v. Hill, 437 U.S. 153, 191–193.

The Court purports to find support for its position in legislation enacted by Congress in 1956.   But that legislation dealt with the totally unrelated problem of competing surface and mineral estates, and has nothing to do with the question at issue here.

The only reasonable inference that can be drawn from the events of 1931 and 1956 is that on those two occasions, as in 1920, Congress declined to assume that every pre-1920 oil shale claim would turn out to be unpatentable.   It seems to me wholly fallacious to interpret these indications of caution as a congressional intent to exempt oil shale claims from longstanding principles of patentability.

C

The respondents' patent applications were, I think, quite properly rejected at the administrative level for the simple reason that they failed to satisfy the requirements of the general mining law as of 1920.

* * *

Of controlling significance here is the fact that, by 1920, two refinements of this "prudent man test" had occurred.   First, it was clear that, although the patent applicant did not have to demonstrate that his mining efforts would definitely yield some profit, he at least had to show that they probably would.   Cataract Gold Mining Co., 43 L.D. 248, 254 (1914).   See Cole v. Ralph, 252 U.S. 286, 299 (1920); Cameron v. United States, supra, 252 U.S., at 459, United States v. Iron

Silver Min. Co., 128 U.S. 673, 684 (1884).[4] Second, this required showing of probable profitability had to rest primarily on presently demonstrable, not speculative fact. See Davis v. Wiebbold, 139 U.S. 507, 521–524 (1891); Castle v. Womble, supra ("the requirement relating to discovery refers to present facts, and not to the probabilities of the future."). Thus, the applicant could not satisfy the applicable standard by pointing to such highly uncertain future events as market changes or technological advances in an attempt to demonstrate a reasonable prospect of success.

*   *   *

NOTES

1. Did Freeman v. Summers accurately interpret the law of discovery? Compare United States v. Coleman, 390 U.S. 599 (1968), supra at page 433. Did the Court overrule *Coleman* or Castle v. Womble, at least in part? To what extent? Should the decision hinge on the meaning of the 1920 Act or the 1872 Act?

2. Assuming that Freeman v. Summers was erroneous, what is wrong with the IBLA changing its position in a subsequent adjudication? In a different context, the Court in Atchison, Topeka & Santa Fe Ry. Co. v. Wichita Bd. of Trade, 412 U.S. 800, 808 (1973), stated: "Whatever the ground for the departure from prior norms * * * it must be clearly set forth so that the reviewing court may understand the basis of the agency's action and so may judge the consistency of that action with the agency's mandate."

3. Is this an unexamined instance of estoppel against the government? Who relied on the erroneous interpretation? When? Does this decision prevent the Department from correcting mistakes in other old decisions? See Comment, Emergence of an Equitable Doctrine of Estoppel Against the Government—The Oil Shale Cases, 46 U.Colo.L. Rev. 433 (1975); Tosco Corp. v. Hodel, 611 F.Supp. 1130 (D.Colo.1985) (finding government estoppel as to oil shale claimants).

4. Did Congress really "approve" or "ratify" the Freeman v. Summers decision? In TVA v. Hill, 437 U.S. 153 (1978), infra at page 785, the Court gave little weight either to explicit approval by an appropriations committee or to an appropriations act. Should it matter that the 1931 investigation was by the Interior Committee? Are the statements of individual legislators in 1931 or 1956 concerning their interpretation of a law passed by an earlier Congress entitled to any weight or do they "represent only the personal views of these legislators"?

5. In EDF v. Andrus, 619 F.2d 1368 (10th Cir.1980), the court held that, despite technological changes in the interim, the 1973 impact

---

4. The authorities cited by the Court, do not support a contrary rule. They state that an applicant for a mineral patent need not establish with certainty that a paying mine exists or can be developed on his land, but they do not in any way reject the rule of Castle v. Womble, supra, that the applicant must show that there exists a "reasonable prospect of success" in his developing a profitable mine.

statement on oil shale leasing program did not have to be supplemented by another EIS six years later.

The most recent decision in the oil shale case is Tosco Corp. v. Hodel, 611 F.Supp. 1130 (D.Colo.1985). Judge Finesilver, in a 90-page opinion, concluded—among many other things—that the claimants had substantially complied with the annual assessment work requirement and that, in any event, the Interior Department was estopped by its assurance over a 30-year period that non-performance of assessment work would not bar the issuance of oil shale permits. The court also held that the claimant was entitled to a patent once substantial assessment work—defined as $500 worth—was completed. If the United States wins the appeal in this case, another decade or so of oil shale claim litigation is in prospect.

6. President Carter's synfuels program called for shale oil production of 400,000 barrels per day by 1990. See National Geographic, Special Report (February, 1981). But by 1986, oil prices had declined precipitously, the scandal- and incompetence-plagued federal Synfuels Corporation was virtually defunct, and Exxon Corporation had abruptly terminated its multi-billion dollar Colony Project in Western Colorado. It is highly unlikely that any appreciable quantities of shale oil will be produced by 1990—or by 2000. See generally Duncan, Oil Shale Mining Claims: Alternatives for Resolution of an Ancient Problem, 17 Land and Water L.Rev. 1 (1982); Fischer, The New Synthetic Fuels Program: Boomlet or Bust?, 16 Tulsa L.J. 357 (1981); Spence & Ruda, Synthetic Fuels—Policy and Regulation, 51 U.Colo.L.Rev. 465 (1980); Dempsey, Oil Shale and Water Quality: The Colorado Prospectus Under Federal, State, and International Law, 58 Den.L.J. 715 (1981); Laitos, The Effect of Water Law on the Development of Oil Shale, 58 Den.L.J. 751 (1981).

3. COAL (AND CHEMICAL MINERALS)

Federal coal leasing policy pursuant to the Mineral Leasing Act of 1920 prior to the early 1970s was described in these terms by Judge Pratt in Natural Resources Defense Council v. Hughes, 437 F.Supp. 981 (D.D.C.1977), supra at page 333.

> The United States contains an estimated 1.58 trillion tons of identified coal reserves approximately one half of which are located in the western United States. The federal government owns approximately 60% of the western coal resource. Most of the large coal resource in the eastern and midwestern United States is privately owned.

> Federal coal has, however, played a minimal role in total U.S. production. In 1960 federal coal accounted for only 1.3% of the total coal mined. This mining share has increased only slightly to its current level approximating 3%.

> * * *

> From 1945 to 1970, the number of acres of federal land leased for coal development increased from about 80,000 to

approximately 778,000, almost a ten-fold increase. In the same period, annual coal production from these federal lands declined from about 10 million tons in 1945 to approximately 7.4 million tons in 1970. These leased areas contain an estimated 16 billion tons of coal reserves, 10.6 billion of which are mineable by strip mining. An additional 10 billion tons are potentially recoverable from federal acreage for which "preference right" applications for coal leases have been filed. The additional ten billion tons include quantities of coal which, due to the size of the lease unit, location, or transportation costs, may not be economically recoverable.

See generally Fairfax & Andrews, Debate Within and Debate Without: NEPA and the Re-definition of the "Prudent Man" Rule, 19 Nat.Res.J. 505, 516 (1979). ("From these figures, the disturbing reality of the situation emerged: mining interests were renting thousands of federal acres but were delaying production.") Since 1970, the federal coal leasing program has been fundamentally reformed. In 1971, Secretary Morton imposed a moratorium on the issuance of new coal leases and, with minor exceptions, banned all new prospecting permits in 1973. The moratorium was upheld in Krueger v. Morton, 539 F.2d 235 (D.C. Cir.1976).

As the discussion in Kleppe v. Sierra Club, 427 U.S. 390 (1976), supra at page 323, indicated, the Interior Department had studied regional coal leasing policies on several occasions and was, at that time, undertaking a comprehensive review in order to set national long-term coal leasing policy. The EIS for the new policy released in 1975 was struck down in the 1977 case of NRDC v. Hughes, 437 F.Supp. 981 (D.D.C.1977), supra at page 333. The court in *Hughes* issued an injunction against virtually all new coal leasing, but the case was later settled and some preference right leasing activity was allowed to go ahead. The settlement is discussed in Krulitz, Management of Federal Coal Reserves, 24 Rocky Mtn.Min.L.Inst. 139, 143–150 (1978).

The Coal Leasing Amendments of 1975, Pub.L. 94–377, 90 Stat. 1083, which became effective on August 4, 1976, revised the coal provisions of the 1920 Act in several significant respects. See generally Krulitz, supra; Hustace, The New Federal Coal Leasing System, 10 Nat.Res.Law. 323 (1977). Some of the reasons for the Amendments were recited in House Comm. on Interior & Insular Affairs, Federal Coal Leasing Act Amendments Act of 1975, H.Rep. No. 94–681, 94th Cong., 1st Sess. (1975). They can be summarized as follows:

a. *Speculation.* Of the 533 leases issued, only 59 were in production; no diligence or operational requirements had ever been enforced against the remaining 474. Almost half the existing leases were preference right leases, gained at "virtually no cost." Lease brokers "—not coal producers or users—are the predominant holders of Federal coal prospecting permits."

b. *Concentration.* Of the 144 federal lessees, 15 control 66 percent of the acreage under lease because of the front-end money required for competitive bidding and because of the large allowable maximum acreages (46,000 acres per state).

c. *Fair Return.* Royalties to the government are low, and "72 percent of these 'competitive' sales had less than two bidders."

d. *Environmental Protection.* Very little control over environmental effects has been exercised because lease issuance has been on a "reaction basis" to industry proposals.

e. *Social and Economic Impacts* have not been adequately taken into account.

f. *Need for Information.* An independent assessment of the overall situation is desirable.

The 1975 Amendments also abolished prospecting permits and noncompetitive leases for coal, subject to "valid existing rights." In American Nuclear Corp. v. Andrus, 434 F.Supp. 1035 (D.Wyo.1977), the court found that an application for a coal prospecting permit did not qualify as a valid existing right:

> The only possible conclusion that can be reached, after reading of the cases * * * and the legislative history, is that no valid existing rights were created until at least a prospecting permit had been issued under the Mineral Leasing Act. An application for a coal prospecting permit is simply not the kind of valid existing right that was contemplated under Section 4 of the Federal Coal Leasing Amendments Act of 1975.

Much closer questions were presented, however, concerning the protection when applications for prospecting permits had been granted and the permitees had done everything necessary to qualify for a lease.

* * *

NATURAL RESOURCES DEFENSE COUNCIL v. BERKLUND

United States Court of Appeals, District of Columbia Circuit, 1979.
609 F.2d 553.

PER CURIAM: The Natural Resources Defense Council (NRDC) and the Environmental Defense Fund (EDF) brought this suit for a declaratory judgment empowering the Secretary of Interior (the Secretary) to reject coal mining lease applications on environmental grounds, even when an applicant has otherwise fulfilled the requirements for a lease under Section 2 of the Mineral Leasing Act of 1920 ("the Act").[1] Two power companies, Utah Power and Light Co. (Utah Power) and Chaco Energy Co. (Chaco), intervened to support the Department's position that the Secretary obtains no such discretion either under the Act or the National Environmental Policy Act (NEPA). The district

---

1. 30 U.S.C.A. § 201(b) (amended 1976). The 1976 amendments eliminated prospecting permits and attending lease applications. Hence this appeal is limited to some 183 lease applications submitted pri- or to 1976. [The lower court found:] "as of October 1974, in six western states, at least 496,000 acres containing some 12 billion tons of coal were subject to 183 preference right lease applications."

court agreed,[3] and on examination of the statutory framework and the effect of NEPA, we affirm.

I. BACKGROUND

* * *

Until the past decade, the Department routinely granted applications for prospecting permits where the existence of coal deposits was not yet known. A prospecting permittee could then apply for the so-called "preference right lease" which would be granted automatically upon a demonstration that the land contained commercial quantities of coal. The United States Geological Survey would advise the Department that commercial quantities existed if the applicant found coal that could be physically extracted at a profit. Thus, environmental considerations were absent from the decision to grant a prospecting permit and the decision to grant a lease to a permittee.

The Department introduced environmental considerations in its regulations of January 18, 1969. Accordingly, prospecting permits would be granted only after examination of the environmental effects; permittees would be granted leases only after environmental scrutiny and would be allowed to mine only after approval of a mining plan. Although the Department stopped issuing permits for coal exploration in 1973, the requirements continue to apply to lease applications by holders of outstanding prospecting permits.

In addition, outstanding applications are now subject to regulations passed in 1976 that redefine the statutory term, "commercial quantities," and in other ways alter the procedures for obtaining leases. The new regulations require permittees applying for leases to establish through detailed procedures the profitability of the proposed mining while accounting for the costs of complying with environmental requirements.[11] Where the applicant supports his claim with a reasonable factual basis responsive to the agency's recommended reclamation requirements, the lease shall be granted.

3. 448 F.Supp. at 933–937. Plaintiffs below raised two other issues that do not concern us here. First, they argued for the inclusion of environmental costs in the definition of "commercial quantities," the statutory term that sets the critical condition for granting a lease under section 2(b) of the Act. The agency resolved this issue by promulgating such a definition on May 7, 1976. See 43 C.F.R. §§ 3520.1–1 through 3521.1–5 (1978). See 458 F.Supp. at 928 n. 2. The appellants' satisfaction with this resolution is apparent in the transcript of the district court proceedings.

Plaintiffs below also claimed under § 102 of NEPA that the Secretary must prepare an environmental impact statement (EIS) on any proposed issuance of a coal lease under Section 201(b) where the

issuance would constitute major federal action significantly affecting the quality of the human environment. In oral argument before this court, the parties indicated total agreement with the Department's position that major coal leases having such an impact will be accompanied by an EIS, in accord with the district court's conclusion, see 458 F.Supp. at 937 n. 20, 939.

11. The new regulations require the permittee to show a reasonable expectation that his revenues will exceed development and operating costs. 43 C.F.R. § 3520.1–1(c) (1978). Operating costs include the cost of "complying with existing governmental regulations, reclamation and environmental standards, and proposed lease terms." 43 C.F.R. § 3521.1–1(c)(2)(vi) (1978).

II. THE MERITS

We find no reason to reject the district court's conclusion that the Secretary has no discretion to reject a coal lease application by a prospecting permittee who has otherwise fulfilled the requirements of § 201(b).

A. *The Coal Leasing Program*

The only condition that the permittee must meet to obtain a lease is to establish the presence of "commercial quantities" of coal.[14] The Act provides that a permittee meeting this condition "shall be entitled to a lease under this chapter for all or part of the land in his permit." [15] This language is unequivocal and clear, and compels our conclusion that the applicant who satisfies the condition is entitled to a lease.

Petitioners argue that the Secretary's general discretion under § 201(a) extends to lease applications under § 201(b). We approve of the district court's reasoning that the § 201(b) prospecting permit, and resulting lease application, constitute a separate, statutory program, not one of the "other methods" within the Secretary's discretion for issuing leases under § 201(a).

Finally, petitioners claim that the Secretary's discretion can be inferred from the term "preference right lease," assigned in the legislative history to leases under § 201(b). The meaning of the term is, in fact, ambiguous. Not used in the statute, nor defined in the House Report, the term has, however, been construed by the agency consistently for nearly 60 years to mean an automatic entitlement of a prospecting permittee who establishes the presence of commercial quantities of coal in the area covered by the permit. This interpretation has not been disturbed by Congress or the courts, and it influences our conclusion here.

The Department's regulations since 1969 have required it to scrutinize environmental effects in evaluating permit and lease applications, in stipulating lease terms, and in approving mining plans. These regulations considerably assist the Secretary's protection of public lands even though he cannot reject an entitled lease applicant out of hand. Thus, the definition of "commercial quantities" of coal itself accommodates the cost of protecting the environment, as do lease terms and mining plans under the Department's supervision. We are satisfied therefore, that the Department and the district court assured only narrow limits on the Secretary's authority to protect public lands are imposed by § 201(b).

B. *The Effect of NEPA*

Petitioners claim that NEPA gives the Secretary authority to reject lease applications by prospecting permittees. ∗ ∗ ∗ [T]he plain

14. 30 U.S.C.A. § 201(b) (amended 1976). The applicant also must be acting as permittee, that is, he must have found the coal within the permit area and during the permit period. Id.

15. Id.

meaning of the statute as well as undisturbed administrative practice for nearly 60 years leaves the Secretary no discretion to deny a § 201(b) lease to a qualified applicant.

We find that the Department in fact abided by NEPA's requirements "to the fullest extent possible" by introducing environmental analysis at crucial points in the leasing process, pending total revision of the leasing program. The agency requires a demonstration that the estimated revenues can reasonably be expected to exceed estimated costs. Those costs can include the costs of complying with lease terms demanding complete reclamation and safeguards against environmental harm. Even after a lease is granted the awardee may be precluded from harming the environment if the agency disapproves his mining plan. Petitioners claim that these measures fall short of NEPA's policies because they do not account for "societal costs" of environmental harm. We find, to the contrary, that these costs can be figured into the assessment of commercial quantities, covered in stringent lease provisions, or adopted as criteria for measuring proposed mining plans. If the Secretary fails to exercise his authority through such measures, then a challenge under NEPA may be appropriate. In the meantime, not even the policies of NEPA, which are of the utmost importance to the survival of our environment, can rewrite § 201(b) to undermine the property rights of prospecting permittee lease applicants. Congress evidently understood this, as it amended § 201 to eliminate obstacles to coordinated energy and environmental planning.

For the some 183 lease applications outstanding under the former version of the provision, the property rights anticipated by permittee applicants cannot be diminished. Where environmental damage from granting leases to entitled parties is certain, the Secretary is authorized to negotiate an exchange for other mineral leases of similar value. This interim measure will have to do, until all coal development can be conducted under the amended version of the Act.

For the foregoing reasons, the district court's judgment is affirmed as to the Secretary's discretion under § 201(b).

NOTES

1. How does the discretion of the Secretary differ in each of these situations: the issuance of preference right coal leases; the suspension of areas from competitive oil and gas leasing (see Udall v. Tallman, 380 U.S. 1 (1965), supra at page 288, and the issuance of patents to hardrock claimants (see South Dakota v. Andrus, 614 F.2d 1190 (8th Cir.1980), supra at page 460)?

2. Attorneys in the Solicitor's Office long were divided on several issues decided in NRDC v. Berklund; indeed, the controversy went beyond the Solicitor's Office and developed into a "department-wide donnybrook." Fairfax & Andrews, Debate Within and Debate Without: NEPA and the Redefinition of the "Prudent Man" Rule, 19 Nat.Res.J. 505, 506 (1979). On the question whether the 1920 Act allowed discretion in the issuance of preference right coal leases, some of those

lawyers relied on a dictum in Chapman v. Sheridan-Wyoming Coal Co., 338 U.S. 621, 628 (1950), that the Act does not "create a private contract right that would override [the Secretary's] continuing duty to be governed by the public interest in deciding to lease or withhold leases." They also relied on Section 102(1) of NEPA, 42 U.S.C.A. § 4332(1) ("the public laws * * * shall be interpreted and administered in accordance with [NEPA policies].")

UTAH INTERNATIONAL, INC. v. ANDRUS
United States District Court, District of Colorado, 1980.
488 F.Supp. 976.

KANE, District Judge.

* * * Plaintiff Utah International, Inc., seeks the issuance of a preference right coal lease for certain federal lands located in the Danforth Hills of northwestern Colorado where it began exploring for coal almost fifteen years ago. Because of the failure to issue such a lease upon a showing in 1970 that plaintiff had discovered coal in commercial quantities on these lands and the determination that plaintiff will have to meet certain new or additional requirements in order to obtain a lease, plaintiff has sued the Secretary of Interior, the Director of the Bureau of Land Management, and other federal land officials. Plaintiff seeks a declaratory judgment that a determination of the existence of coal in commercial quantities in the subject lands was made in 1970, that such determination vested in plaintiff a right to the issuance of a lease, and that such a lease should now issue; a declaratory judgment that policies and regulations promulgated after 1970 cannot be applied to require plaintiff to meet new or additional requirements in order to obtain a lease, or, if such policies and regulations would otherwise apply, then in the alternative that certain 1976 regulations are invalid as applied to plaintiff; and an order requiring the Secretary of the Interior and his authorized representatives to issue to plaintiff a preference right lease for the lands covered by Prospecting Permit No. C–0123475. The action is currently before the court on cross-motions for summary judgment.

[Plaintiff had a prospecting permit extended to January, 1969; before expiration, it applied for a preference right lease. Rejection of the lease application was reversed by the IBLA on the basis of a U.S. Geological Survey report concluding that the applicant had established the existence of commercial quantities of coal. The lease was not issued, however, and the moratorium intervened.]

* * *

9. On or about January 26, 1976, the Secretary of the Interior adopted a new federal coal leasing policy including a restatement of short-term criteria which must be met before preference right coal leases would issue and including a new proposed definition of the term 'coal in commercial quantities.'

10. On May 7, 1976, the Secretary of the Interior published (at 41 F.R. 18847) regulation 43 C.F.R. § 3520.1–1 which, among other things, defined 'commercial quantities of coal.'

11. On or about July 25, 1977, in the case of Natural Resources Defense Council v. Hughes [454 F.Supp. 148], the Department of the Interior, in a memorandum filed with the Court, changed its policy and indicated that preference right coal leases could be issued even where they do not conform to the short-term criteria so long as lease issuance would be in the 'public interest.'

12. On September 27, 1977, in the *Hughes* case, the United States District Court for the District of Columbia issued an order by which it enjoined officials of the Department of the Interior, pending the accomplishment of specified actions, from 'taking any steps whatsoever, directly or indirectly, to implement the new coal leasing program, including calling for nominations of tracts for federal coal leasing and issuing any coal leases, except when the proposed lease is required to maintain an existing mining operation at the present levels of production or is necessary to meet existing contracts and the extent of the proposed lease is not greater than is required to meet these two criteria for more than three years in the future.'[1]

13. On July 5, 1977, plaintiff filed documents required to support a claim of an 'initial showing' of 'commercial quantities of coal' under regulation 43 C.F.R. 3521.1–1(b) of May 7, 1976, at the same time expressly disclaiming any obligation to make the showing called for by the regulation.

14. To date no lease has been issued to plaintiff, nor has plaintiff's application been rejected.

The question presented is whether a decision by the Bureau of Land Management dated April 29, 1970, finding that plaintiff had discovered coal in commercial quantities in federal lands covered by Prospecting Permit No. C–0123475, vested in plaintiff a right to be issued a preference right coal lease, so that plaintiff cannot be required to meet new or additional requirements established after that decision.

* * *

II

A preliminary question is whether this matter is ripe for judicial decision. * * *

---

1. Without deciding what impact it might otherwise have had on this litigation, the final environmental impact statement for the new federal coal leasing program was issued on April 30, 1979, and the Secretary reached a final decision on the program on June 2, 1979. As represented by defendants, "[t]his secretarial decision was the last step in the process required by the court's order in *Hughes*, * * *, and the injunction expired on that date."

Second, defendants cite a number of cases that they say stand for the proposition that plaintiff must continue to exhaust the administrative process in order to show that it is entitled to a lease. [See Hunter v. Morton, 529 F.2d 645, 648–49 (10th Cir.1976); and Hannifin v. Morton, 444 F.2d 200 (10th Cir.).]

* * * [T]he critical difference between the cases cited and the case at bar—and a difference that defendants make too little of—is that in the former cases there was only the filing of an application which was in process at the time of some moratorium or change in policy, while in the instant case there had been an agency determination some substantial time before any such moratorium or change.[2] The difference is well-illustrated by comparing the situation in Utah International, Inc. v. Andrus, 488 F.Supp. 962 (D.Utah June 15, 1979) with the situation here. In *Utah International*, the United States Geological Survey had made a determination that plaintiff, regarding another prospecting permit, had discovered coal in commercial quantities, but there had been no decision by the Bureau of Land Management that Utah International was therefore entitled to a lease. The determination by the USGS was an important, even critical, input to the leasing decision process, but it was not itself a decision by the responsible agency. Here there was not only a USGS recommendation, but a formal agency adjudication by the Office of Appeals and Hearings, dated April 29, 1970, deciding that plaintiff had discovered coal in commercial quantities and remanding the file to the land office "for further appropriate action looking toward issuance of the preference right coal lease requested." The line drawn in the Utah district court's decision and this one is the line between pending applications that have been filed but not acted upon and applications that have been acted upon and decided. Such a line should be clear even to the myopic and give some sense of finality to the administrative process generally.

In sum, because of a final agency decision on the central question of this case, a finding that the cases cited by defendants are not applicable to the situation here, and a delay of ten years since the agency determination of April 29, 1970, I find that this action is cloyingly ripe for judicial decision.

III

* * *

Although the Secretary retained discretion in the granting of prospecting permits, until 1969 permits were issued routinely upon request where consistent with the law. Upon receipt of an application for a coal prospecting permit, the Bureau of Land Management (BLM) referred it to the United States

2. Defendants have repeatedly characterized the agency action in 1970 as nothing more than a finding by the Geological Survey that coal had been discovered in commercial quantities. That is not a correct characterization. Not only was there a Geological Survey recommendation, but a formal agency adjudication that commercial quantities of coal had been discovered, and a remand for further appropriate action.

Geological Survey (USGS), the agency responsible for making the geologic, economic and other technical judgment * * *. If the USGS determined that sufficient information was not available, it notified the BLM that issuance of a prospecting permit was appropriate. Environmental consequences of issuing these permits were not examined or considered.

> After the prospecting permit was issued, and if the permittee submitted an application for a preference right lease, the BLM again referred the lease application to USGS for a determination of whether the permittee had demonstrated that the land contained commercial quantities of coal. Determination of commercial quantities was based solely on whether the coal existed, its character and heat-giving quality, and whether it could be physically extracted at a profit without regard to environment impact or costs.[4] *Consistent with defendants' interpretation of § 201(b), if the USGS determined that commercial quantities of coal had been found, the lease was issued automatically to the applicant.* The lessee could then extract the federal coal deposits specified in the lease pursuant to applicable laws, regulations and stipulations in the lease itself.

458 F.Supp. at 929 (footnote omitted; emphasis added). Accord, Peabody Coal Co. v. Andrus, 477 F.Supp. at 121, 123; Natural Resources Defense Council v. Hughes, 437 F.Supp. at 983–84.[5]

* * *

It is clear, then, that the only prerequisite to the issuance of a preference right lease was an agency determination that the holder of a prospecting permit had discovered coal in commercial quantities. Once that determination was made by the BLM, generally on the basis of a USGS report, the Secretary had no discretion to deny the issuance of a lease. In the present case, the BLM had made this determination in April, 1970, under the then-existing definition of "commercial quantities" and according to long-established agency practice. Utah International's application for a preference right coal lease was no longer "pending" in the sense of awaiting a determination of its entitlement to a lease, and the government was not at liberty some three to six years later to revoke its earlier determination and apply some new and

---

4. The fundamental reform in the 1976 regulations was to change the definition of "coal in commercial quantities" from one focusing solely on the quality and workability of the discovered coal to one that, in addition, internalized the environmental costs of its extraction and subsequent reclamation. See 43 C.F.R., Parts 3520 and 3521 (1976).

5. In Peabody Coal Co. v. Andrus, 477 F.Supp. 120, 121 (D.Wyo.1979), the district court said:

Prior to the year 1972, permits to prospect for coal and extensions of these permits were granted pro forma almost without exception by the Department of Interior. Many of these prospecting permits ripened into preference right leases and it was the policy of the Interior Department to award such leases when commercial quantities of coal were discovered on the public lands.

It is now beyond cavil that a reasonable administrative construction given to a statute by an agency charged with its administration is entitled to substantial weight, especially when such construction was contemporaneous with the statute's enactment and expresses longstanding agency practice.

different policy, however more enlightened or obscured that new policy might be.

Defendants argue that the Secretary of the Interior retains broad, continuing authority to reconsider decisions concerning the public lands until such time that a grant or some other formal disposition is actually issued, citing a number of Supreme Court decisions dated near the turn of this century. See, e.g., Knight v. United States Land Association, 142 U.S. 161, 176–82 (1891). * * *

* * *

In a more recent case, Boesche v. Udall, 373 U.S. 472 (1963), the Supreme Court cited these earlier decisions and recognized the general authority of the Secretary:

> We think that the Secretary, under his general powers of management over the public lands, had authority to cancel this [oil and gas] lease administratively *for invalidity at its inception,* unless such authority was withdrawn by the Mineral Leasing Act. * * *
>
> * * *
>
> * * * Since the Secretary's connection with the land continues to subsist, he should have the power, in a proper case *to correct his own errors.*

373 U.S. at 476–78 (emphasis added). The Tenth Circuit has also recognized the proposition established by these cases. * * *

While it is established law that the Secretary of the Interior has supervisory authority over the disposition of the public lands, subject to pertinent provisions of administrative and substantive law, these cases do not apply to the situation here. The sort of continuing authority which they illustrate has to do with the Secretary's ability to deal with error or fraud in the administrative process, and not his ability to apply changes in policy determinations already made. * * * In the present case there is no allegation of error in the factual determination of 1970 or in the application of 1970 agency practice. Nor is there any allegation of fraud. Accordingly, the determination must stand.

The controversy here has not centered on legislative changes in federal coal leasing policy, as evidenced in the Federal Coal Leasing Amendments Act of 1975, but I note that the revision of § 201(b) was expressly "subject to valid existing rights." Section 4, Pub.L. 94–377, 90 Stat. 1085 (1976). The Senate Committee on Interior and Insular Affairs, in S.Rep. No. 94–296, 94th Cong., 1st Sess. 15 (1975), said:

> The Committee wishes to stress that the repeal of Subsection 2(b) [30 U.S.C. § 201(b)] is expressly "subject to valid existing rights" and thus is not intended to affect any valid prospecting permit outstanding at the time of enactment of the amendments. Any applications for preference right leases based on such permits could be adjudicated on their merits * * * if the requirements of Subsection 2(b) of the 1920 Act * * * were met.

The federal district court in Wyoming discussed this preservation of existing rights in American Nuclear Corp. v. Andrus, 434 F.Supp. 1035 (D.Wyo.1977), and held that "[a]n application for a coal prospecting permit is simply not the kind of valid existing right that was contemplated" by Congress. * * * [Here,] the Secretary had no discretion to deny Utah International a lease once Utah International had fulfilled the statutory requirements of the Mineral Leasing Act of 1920, as administered by defendants. By the express terms of the statute, Utah International had made the required showing of coal in commercial quantities, and was entitled to a lease. Accordingly, I hold that Utah International obtained a vested right in a preference right coal lease on the April 29, 1970 date of the BLM decision and that regulations promulgated subsequent to that date cannot be applied to preclude that right. Defendants have unlawfully withheld the issuance of plaintiff's lease and the decision to apply subsequent regulations to that lease is not legally tolerable.

IV

The holding above establishes the right of Utah International to obtain a lease based on the showing of coal in commercial quantities in 1970. It should be clear that this holding does not preclude the Secretary from endeavoring to protect the environment or excuse Utah International from compliance with applicable [state and federal] environmental laws. * * *

* * *

Finally, it is also clear that regulations promulgated by the Department of the Interior on January 19, 1969 are applicable to plaintiff's lease. These regulations require a technical examination prior to the issuance of a lease in order to formulate lease provisions, as well as approval of a mining plan prior to any actual mining operations. * * *

It is not within the judicial province to establish the actual terms of the lease to be issued plaintiff. That role lies with defendants. * * *

NOTES

1. The large volume of litigation generated by applications and permits outstanding at the commencement of the moratorium illustrates the relative advantages to lessees of preference right leases. Other decisions have forced the courts to draw very fine lines in determining whether the coal company or lease broker caught in the middle possessed a valid existing right. The *Utah International* decision from Utah, contrasted in the principal case, held that plaintiff had no right to have its lease application judged by pre-1976 standards when the Geological Survey determined the existence of commercial quantities but the BLM never officially adopted the Survey's findings. (The court noted, incidentally, that the "plain meaning of coal in 'commercial quantities' is precisely the same as the definition of 'valuable mineral deposits' upheld in *Coleman*.") Peterson v. Department of

the Interior, 510 F.Supp. 777 (D. Utah 1981), concerned a prospector whose application for an extension of his prospecting permit's term was held in abeyance for seven years and then denied. The court agreed with the IBLA that administrative delay cannot create a valid existing right and that the Secretary has statutory discretion to grant or deny such extensions. It went on to hold, however, that the Secretary did not have to deny the extension and that the plaintiff had a valid existing right to have his application considered as it "would have been, prior to the enactment of the FCLAA and the reformation of the coal leasing policy."

2.   Readjustment or renegotiation of old leases could be a crucial future issue. Section 7(a) of the Amendments specifies that coal leases issued after 1976 must provide for a royalty "of not less than 12½ per centum." Pre-1976 leases were subject to readjustment at the end of their 20 year terms. In Rosebud Coal Sales Co. v. Andrus, 667 F.2d 949 (10th Cir.1982), the BLM neglected to give notice of readjustment until more than two years after the 20 years passed; the court held that the attempted readjustment thereafter was invalid, but did not indicate whether the lease would continue under its old terms so long as it produced or whether the agency could later readjust the lease terms. In a subsequent case, the BLM gave timely notice of readjustment but still lost. The agency tried to impose a 12½% royalty on the lessee (a 1000% increase on the old royalty of 17½¢ per ton) in the belief that § 7(a) made 12½% the mandatory minimum. The court in FMC Wyoming Corp. v. Watt, 587 F.Supp. 1545 (D. Wyo.1984), ruled that § 7(a) was not intended to be "retroactive" and that the new rate was arbitrary and capricious in view of the burdens it would impose on the lessee.

NOTE: THE SURFACE MINING CONTROL AND RECLAMATION ACT

The Surface Mining Control and Reclamation Act of 1977 (SMCRA), 30 U.S.C.A. §§ 1201–1328, applies to all surface coal mining operations, not just those on public lands. See generally U.S. Dept. of Interior, Final Environmental Impact Statement: Federal Coal Management Program 1–17 (1979). Among other things, the lengthy Act sets environmental protection performance standards for mining operations and establishes requirements for reclamation. All strip-mined land must be reclaimed, and reclamation plans must be approved prior to the starting up of new mines. SMCRA also establishes a procedure to designate lands unsuitable for all or certain kinds of surface mining operations. The extensive permanent regulations adopted in 1979 are located at 30 C.F.R. Parts 700–707, 730–845 (1985). See generally Kite, The Surface Mining Control and Reclamation Act of 1977: An Overview of Reclamation Requirements and Implementation, XIII Land & Water L.Rev. 703 (1978); Harvey, Paradise Regained? Surface Mining Control and Reclamation Act of 1977, 15 Houston L.Rev. 1147 (1978); Swift, Implementation of SMCRA From a Coal Operator's Perspective, 25 Rocky Mtn.Min.L.Inst. 4–1 (1979).

SMCRA withstood constitutional challenges in two companion cases involving private lands. Hodel v. Virginia Surface Mining & Reclamation Association, Inc., 452 U.S. 264 (1981); Hodel v. Indiana, 452 U.S. 314 (1981). The Supreme Court upheld congressional Commerce Clause authority to regulate surface mining, finding that the Act did not usurp a state function in violation of the Tenth Amendment, and that the Act on its face did not effect a taking of property.

Utah International, Inc. v. Department of the Interior, below, is the only reported litigation involving SMCRA disputes on public lands; many courts in private lands cases from the eastern United States have interpreted SMCRA within the same period. Geographical and political differences account for this disparity. Western public land states had stringent state reclamation standards prior to SMCRA, and those states generally supported passage of the Act. Additionally, most coal production in the western United States occurs in the plains region where coal seams are relatively close to the surface. In contrast, underground mines are much more common in the East, and eastern operators are subjected to more Office of Surface Mining (OSM) inspections and enforcement actions than western operators. See generally Barry, The Surface Mining Control and Reclamation Act of 1977 and the Office of Surface Mining: Moving Targets or Immovable Objects?, 27A Rocky Mtn.Min.L.Inst. 169, 204 (1982).

Regulation of mining operations under the permanent phase of SMCRA can occur in a variety of ways. Surface coal mining on private lands within a state is controlled either by a state program approved by the Secretary of Interior, 30 U.S.C.A. § 1253, or by the federal program in instances where a state fails to submit an adequate surface coal mining program, id. § 1254. SMCRA also requires implementation of a federal program for control of all surface coal mining and reclamation operations on public lands. Id. § 1273(a). States with approved state programs may, however, enter into cooperative agreements with the Secretary of Interior providing for state regulation of surface coal mining operations on public lands within the state. Id. § 1273(c). The Secretary of Interior has approved the state programs of all major western coal producing states.

Implementation of SMCRA on the public lands has caused some confusion because of uncertainty over the roles of the Interior agencies (OSM, BLM, and USGS), the Forest Service, and state agencies. See Barry, supra, at 325–333. Currently, the OSM authorizes states with cooperative agreements to review and approve SMCRA mining permit applications; in states without cooperative agreements, OSM reviews and approves permit applications for surface coal mining on federal lands.

In November 1979, several environmental groups petitioned the Secretary of the Interior for a declaration that certain federal lands in Utah, the Alton Coal Fields, were unsuitable for surface mining under the Surface Mining Control and Reclamation Act, 30 U.S.C.A. § 1272. Secretary Andrus granted the petition in December, 1980, ruling that mining in the Alton Coal Fields, just southwest of Bryce Canyon National Park, would adversely affect important historic, cultural, scientific, aesthetic, and natural values of the Park. Suits were promptly filed by a variety of plaintiffs, including two companies that hold federal coal leases in the affected area. In one preliminary decision, the court denied the request of the new Interior Secretary to remand the decision to him for reconsideration. 13 Env't.Rep.—Current Devs. 1216 (1982). In December 1982, the court dismissed many of the coal company plaintiffs' claims. Considering the claim that plaintiffs were entitled to an adjudicatory decision, the court opined:

> * * * UII and NEICO emphasize the effect of the unsuitability designation on their "property interests" as the basis for requiring adversary process. * * *
>
> It is true that UII and NEICO own coal leases. However, they have not yet obtained permits to extract the coal covered by those leases. It is also not a foregone conclusion that mining permits would be granted. Furthermore, the unsuitability designation only forecloses surface coal mining and it does not preclude extraction of the coal by other means. The extent of procedural rights available for protection of a property interest is dependent upon legal arrangements which may qualify or define the scope of a party's legal interest in the property. The uncertainty concerning the nature of UII's and NEICO's claimed property interests requires that their motion for partial summary judgment be denied.
>
> * * *
>
> There can be little doubt in reading SMCRA and its legislative history that the focus of the petition designation process is land use planning. This involves the weighing of several competing policy and value considerations that affect several parties. Decisions of this nature are best arrived at through legislative rather than adjudicatory hearings. * * *
>
> * * *
>
> The factual determinations made by the Secretary related to matters of public policy and value choices: the effect of general phenomena upon the national park, the experience of park visitors, or upon the condition of public properties. This court is convinced that the Alton decision was a rulemaking proceeding for which additional procedural devices were not required under the Constitution. There is also nothing about these facts which is extremely compelling. Therefore, it was not an abuse of the Secretary's discretion to deny UII's and NEICO's request for adjudicatory proceedings.
>
> [The court held that "irreparable damage" is not required to determine unsuitability.]
>
> * * *

Utah International, Inc. v. Department of the Interior, 553 F.Supp. 872, 878–79, 880, 885 (D.Utah, 1982). Later, according to an attorney for the

Sierra Club, UIC dropped most of its claims, and intervenors reached a settlement with the federal defendants. The Alton Fields unsuitability designation stands, and the deposit will not be mined. The only remaining questions are whether UIC suffered a taking of its property, a claim pending in Interior, and whether intervenors are entitled to attorney's fees.

Since 1981, national coal strip-mining regulation has been in shambles. Secretary Watt's attempts to water down the statutory requirements generally failed in litigation, but his apparent aim to destroy the effectiveness of the OSM through budgetary and other changes appears to have succeeded as of 1986. See generally Hoch, Regulatory Revisions to the Surface Mining Control and Reclamation Act: An Exercise in Administrative Legislation, 31 Kan.L.Rev. 279, 288–303 (1983); Menzel, Redirecting the Implementation of a Law: The Reagan Administration and Coal Surface Mining Regulation, 43 Pub.Ad.Rev. 411 (1983).

NOTE: COAL LEASING AFTER THE MORATORIUM

Resumption of largescale coal leasing was a high priority of Secretary Watt, but the efforts of the Interior Department toward that goal met with little success between 1981 and 1986. The Fort Union sale was enjoined for the reasons explained in NWF v. Watt, 571 F.Supp. 1145 (D.D.C.1983), supra at page 261, and never took place. The Powder River Basin sale in 1982 sparked congressional inquiry, appointment of the Linowes Commission, and litigation—and, later, was indirectly responsible for Mr. Watt's forced resignation. The Western Natural Resource Litigation Digest § 5.25 (1985) summarizes the status of the lawsuits [Northern Cheyenne Indian Tribe v. Hodel and National Wildlife Federation v. Burford, 82–1094 & 82–116 BLG, D.Mont., filed Apr. 21, 1982] brought to enjoin the sale as of February, 1986:

> The largest offering of federal coal lease tracts ever held by the Bureau of Land Management (BLM) of the Department of Interior (DOI) took place in Cheyenne, Wyoming, in late April, 1982. 1.6 billion tons of federal coal from the Powder River Basin of Wyoming and Montana are involved. Six of the original tracts were eliminated from the sale reducing the coal sold by about 2.24 billion tons (35%). Surface owner consents were not filed with BLM for five of the tracts. (The 1977 Surface Mining Control and Reclamation Act prevents issuing of leases unless the resident owner of the surface estate consents to leasing.) The sixth tract was withdrawn because of discrepancies in estimated tonnage. These tracts may be offered later this year.

> The Northern Cheyenne's request for a temporary restraining order to block the lease sale was denied. However, the judge noted that prospective bidders would take their leases subject to the outcome of the litigation. The State of Wyoming joined with the Department in objecting to the delay in the lease offering.

* * *

05/29/84. The Linowes Commission criticized "serious errors in Judgment" in the 1982 sale. Review of the commission report may delay the Powder River Basin Federal Coal lease sales scheduled for October 1985.

05/29/85. In a 44-page decision U.S. District Judge James Battin ruled the 1982 Powder River coal sale void. The judge determined that the DOI's environmental impact statement failed to address potential social and economic effects on the Northern Cheyenne Indian Tribe. Although the Tribe's lawsuit was consolidated with a National Wildlife Federation suit in 1982, this ruling is only on the Tribe's suit. Judge Battin said he did not believe the suits brought by the Tribe and the environmental group contained the same issues. The NWF case is still before Judge Battin.

* * *

The Powder River Basin leases were sold for a few cents a ton. Senators claimed that the United States lost more than $100 million on the transaction (if it is upheld), and allegations of leaks from within the Department and of other forms of fraud were rife. Secretary Watt appointed the Linowes Commission to determine whether fair market value was received; the Commission Report was highly critical of current leasing practices. Commission, Fair Market Value Policy for Federal Coal Leasing (1984). It was to the Linowes Commission that Mr. Watt referred when he announced that he had appointed "a Black, a woman, a Jew, and a cripple." That remark cost Mr. Watt his job.

Since his departure, the Department's ardor to sell coal has abated considerably, although lip service is still paid to the idea. The soft coal market due to the relatively low demand for electricity, the large amounts of coal already under lease, and reduced leasing budgets all indicate that coal leasing probably will not be resumed before the end of this century in any sort of big way. If and when coal leasing resumes, hopeful companies may have to contend with another obstacle.

KERR–McGEE CORPORATION v. HODEL
United States District Court, District of Columbia, 1986.
630 F.Supp. 621.

BARRINGTON D. PARKER, District Judge:

In this consolidated proceeding, the Kerr-McGee Corporation and the Global Exploration and Development Corporation seek declaratory, injunctive, and mandatory relief compelling the Department of Interior and the Secretary of Interior to issue them preference rights mining leases for phosphate mining in the Osceola National Forest, located in the State of Florida. The Department of Agriculture and its Secretary are also named defendants. * * *

The matter is before the Court on cross motions for summary judgment. Plaintiffs contend that on January 10, 1983, the Secretary of Interior wrongfully denied their applications for phosphate leases thus depriving them of vested rights to engage in phosphate mining. In response to those allegations, the federal defendants and the intervenors contend that the applications were denied because the reclamation technologies relied upon and proferred by the plaintiffs were inadequate to ensure restoration of the mined portions of the Osceola Forest to the purposes for which they were acquired and the historical uses to which they had been put, as required by the Mineral Leasing Act for Acquired Lands, 30 U.S.C. §§ 351 et seq. (1982). Specifically, the Secretary found that plaintiffs had not discovered "valuable deposits" of phosphate as required under the Act, because the costs of reclamation would be prohibitively high.

* * *

BACKGROUND

A

The Osceola National Forest was established in 1931 by President Herbert Hoover pursuant to the Creative Act of 1891. The vast majority of the Forest was acquired under the authority of the Weeks Act of 1911. The primary purposes behind the acquisition and development were timber production, water shed protection, fish and wildlife protection, and preservation and maintenance of recreational opportunities. National Forest Preservation Comm'n., Sen.Doc. No. 44, 71st Cong., 2d Sess. 6 (1929). Osceola Forest consists of nearly 158 thousand acres located in North-Central Florida. Included within that acreage are cypress swamps, pine lands, unique hardwood wetlands, and upland hardwood forests. Highly diverse creek and river systems within the area serve as a source of high quality surface and ground water, and provides an important water shed for North-Central Florida. The Forest also provides a home for important varieties of fish and wildlife species and for a number of valued and certain limited and endangered species.

The authority for phosphate leasing on federal land and the limits on the Interior Secretary's ability to lease, depends upon whether the lands are classified as "public domain" or "acquired" lands. Public domain lands are lands that have never left the control of the United States. The Mineral Leasing Act authorizes the Secretary to lease phosphate deposits on those lands. Public domain lands comprise a very limited portion of the Osceola National Forest.

For acquired lands, lands that have been either granted or sold to the United States, the source of mineral leasing authority stems from the Mineral Leasing Act for Acquired Lands, 30 U.S.C. § 352. That section provides in relevant part:

> No mineral deposit covered by this section shall be leased except with the consent of the head of the executive department * * * having jurisdiction over the lands containing such deposit * * * and subject to such conditions as that official may prescribe to insure the adequate utilization of the

lands for the primary purposes for which they have been acquired or are being administered. * * *

* * *

During the mid-to-late 1960s, the plaintiffs applied to the Interior Department for permits to prospect for phosphate deposits on acquired lands. The permits were issued by the Department's Bureau of Land Management pursuant to the Mineral Leasing Act for Acquired Lands and were made expressly subject to all regulations, then existing or subsequently enacted, including Special Stipulations required by the Forest Service, Department of Agriculture. The Stipulations, designed to restore and protect the surface value of the land to be mined, were attached to and made a part of the permits.

Subsequently, between 1969–1972, the plaintiffs applied to Interior for preference right leases to mine phosphate on the lands embraced by their prospecting permits alleging discovery of "valuable deposits" within the meaning of section 211(b) of the Mineral Leasing Act. Thereafter, the United States Geological Survey certified that valuable deposits had been discovered and recommended that leases be issued. The certifications were based on quality and quantity standards that had been applied by the Interior Department for some time. In 1976, Kerr-McGee filed suit to compel the Interior Department to issue the leases.

B

The present litigation is the latest of several law suits filed in recent years, relating to phosphate mining in the Forest. * * *

In response to that litigation, the Department undertook in early 1972, the preparation of an environmental analysis and meanwhile, suspended all actions on pending lease applications. In June 1974 a Final Environmental Statement on Phosphate Leasing on the Osceola National Forest in Florida ("1974 Final Environmental Statement") [was issued]. The Statement analyzed the environmental impact of phosphate mining upon various aspects of the Osceola Forest, including the areas' water supply, wildlife, and other natural resources, and reviewed various measures proposed to lessen and mitigate adverse environmental effects.

* * *

C

* * *

The key to the issuance of a phosphate lease is governed by an interpretation of the phrase "valuable deposit of phosphate" within the meaning of the Mineral Leasing Act, 30 U.S.C. § 211(b). From 1960 and extending through 1970, the determination as to whether a phosphate prospecting permittee had discovered valuable deposits was undertaken by Interior officials on basis of physical characteristics, namely, the quality, quantity, thickness and extent of a deposit. This approach was used without regard for mining and marketing costs or other factors bearing upon the economic feasibility of mine development. During this period, there was no regulation, decision, opinion or instruction reflecting a departmental interpretation of the term as used in the Act, or purporting to recognize the propriety of the practice.

Over the period 1969–1972, both Kerr-McGee and Global filed applications with the Interior Department for leases to mine phosphate in Osceola claiming a discovery of valuable phosphate deposits. Following publication of the 1974 Final Environmental Statement, the Solicitor of the Interior opined in a memorandum of June 30, 1975, the meaning of the words "valuable deposits," as used in section 211(b) and other sections of the Mineral Leasing Act * * *:

> The use by the Congress of the identical term ["valuable deposits"] in the Mining Law of 1872, the 1917 Potassium Act, and the Mineral Leasing Act shows that it intended the test to be the same under all three statutes. The meaning commonly recognized for valuable deposit at that time was the prudent man test.

Shortly thereafter, in October 1975, additional studies showing the impact of phosphate leasing on hydrology and endangered species were directed by the Interior Secretary. At that point, all actions on pending phosphate lease applications in Osceola were suspended pending completion of the studies.

On May 7, 1976, shortly after the lawsuit, *Kerr-McGee v. Kleppe* was filed in this District Court, the Interior Department promulgated new regulations—41 Fed.Reg. 18847. This regulation [2] formally defined "valuable deposit" of phosphate, as used in the Mineral Leasing Act, as a deposit "of such a character and quantity that a prudent person would be justified in the further expenditure of his labor and means with a reasonable prospect of success in developing a valuable mine." The regulation also provided that a permittee must "show that there is a reasonable expectation that * * * revenues from the sale of the mineral will exceed * * * costs of developing the mine, and extracting, removing and marketing the mineral."

During the period 1978–1981, both plaintiffs submitted to the Bureau of Land Management the information required for an "initial showing" of lease entitlement under the 1976 regulations. Specifically, in compliance with the newly adopted regulations calling for a description of the proposed measures to be taken to reclaim the surface, the plaintiffs responded and indicated that they intended to utilize a form of sand/clay mix technology for surface reclamation of the mined area. Kerr-McGee indicated that it would utilize a so-called "sand-spray process" developed at Brewster Phosphates. On strength of those representations, the Bureau of Land Management advised Kerr-McGee and Global that their initial showings complied with the regulations.

2. The 1976 regulations, as later amended, are contained and codified at 43 C.F.R. Part 3520 (1982).

D

On February 4, 1982, the Forest Service of the Agriculture Department submitted to the Bureau of Land Management the final requirements to be attached to Kerr-McGee's and Global's lease applications. This was required of all applicants in order to proceed with the "final showings" as required under the new regulations. In turn, the Bureau was required to attach the stipulations to any lease which might be issued to phosphate lease applicants in Osceola Forest. The Forest Service then submitted a requirement to be attached to all leases. The requirement, Stipulation No. 4, specified that:

> The lessee shall, except for permanent lakes created by mining, reestablish watercourses, soil stability and productivity, approximate landforms and elevations, and wetland and upland of similar vegetative communities and species diversity in approximate proportions as those existing prior to mining. *The purpose of reclamation is to reestablish plant and aquatic communities with similar interspersion of community types, i.e., pine flatwoods, cypress swamps, creek swamps and lakes.* The soil medium shall be *reestablished* to support forest tree growth by: (a) providing a ratio of clay to sand in a mixture that will retain sufficient moisture and nutrients in the root zones of forest trees making up the vegetative community; (b) by returning overburden, including topsoil, over the clay and sand mixture. (emphasis added)

By August 1982, both Kerr-McGee and Global had submitted the required "final showings." In responding to the requirement that they provide information as to the estimated cost of complying "with applicable regulations, reclamation and environmental standards, and proposed lease terms," they submitted costs based upon their intended use of sand-clay mix reclamation processes.

While the 1974 Final Environmental Statement contained a general discussion of the importance of and the problems of reclamation, it did not present or discuss government reclamation standards or the possibility of meeting them. Indeed, it was pessimistic on the possibility of reclamation of native species following phosphate mining, particularly with reference to swamp hardwood plant communities. It noted that differences in climate and soil between Central and North Florida made projecting reclamation results from the former area to the Osceola difficult. The 1978 hydrology and endangered species reports which the Interior Secretary initiated in 1975 did not address the pertinent reclamation issues presented in the 1982 law suits filed before the Middle District of Florida federal court.

The 1979 Supplemental ES, described reclamation methods currently in use and in development, including the sand spray and other processes for creating a sand/clay mix fill. However, it expressed qualified optimism and doubt about the success of reclamation efforts based on the then present state of technological knowledge. It stated that observations of trial planting suggested that reclamation to wooded upland and wetland communities was "possible," and concluded that "the present primitive state-of-the-art of phosphate mine reclamation" precluded the evaluation of the potential impact of future mining and reclamation by extrapolating cited results. It also concluded that research was needed to provide techniques for reestablishing the plant species and vegetative community types then found. Otherwise, it reaffirmed the pessimism on revegetation of native species as was noted in the 1974 Final Environmental Statement.

In October 1981, a Forest Service team submitted an evaluation of the Brewster sand-spray process of reclamation focusing on the use of the sand/clay mix as a growth medium. At that point only 15 percent of the Brewster areas had been reclaimed. The evaluation reported that plant life in the Forest would be very difficult to reestablish and productivity levels would be low on land reclaimed by the observed process. It postulated that if a uniform (homogeneous) mix of sand tailings and clay slimes could be achieved, this would provide a "satisfactory base" for the Forest. However, the report specifically found that a homogeneous mix had not yet been achieved.

E

In September 1982 and in response to the lawsuits filed in the Florida federal courts, the Interior Secretary established an interagency task force to assess reclamation technology and to prepare a supplemental Environmental Assessment ("EA") on the environmental consequences of reclamation technologies. * * *

The interdepartmental team conducted a full review of available scientific literature on phosphate mining reclamation, particularly wetlands reclamation, undertook field trips to on-going reclamation project sites—including those then underway at a Brewster phosphate mine using the sand-spray process. * * *

An exhaustive review and study of the conventional and experimental methods of reclaiming lands mined for phosphate was undertaken and on January 7, 1983, the interdepartmental team published its report. The study concluded that no new technology had been developed since the 1979 Supplemental ES and that technology capabilities were insufficient to ensure a reasonable likelihood of the successful reclamation of mined areas consistent with the requirements established for mining in Osceola. As to the Brewster sand-spray process, the team found that it still had not achieved the homogeneous mix of sand and clay, a noted deficiency in the 1981 Forest Service Report, and that on [the] basis of available information, it was impossible to project to the Forest results from tests of sand/clay mix techniques.

The interdepartmental team report was then transmitted to the Interior Secretary with the recommendation that all pending lease applications in Osceola National be rejected. The Secretary assumed full jurisdiction over the matter and on January 10, 1983, issued his decision rejecting Kerr-McGee's and Global's lease applications. His decision was predicated on a determination that:

> * * * [A] mineral deposit discovered under a prospecting permit must be of "such a character and quantity that a prudent person would be justified in the further expenditure of his labor and means with a reasonable prospect of success in developing a valuable mine." The Forest Service, as prescribed by law, has established reclamation stipulations which were used in processing [plaintiffs'] preference right lease applications. The Department of the Interior has performed studies which indicate current technology is not capable of meeting the prescribed reclamation standards. The fact that no reclamation technology exists which can reclaim these lands precludes the possibility that this phosphate deposit could meet the valuable deposit test.
>
> * * *

Although Kerr-McGee and Global dispute the Environmental Assessment team's conclusion as to the feasibility of reclamation of Osceola lands following phosphate mining, they have not identified or referred to any significant and factual data which were not considered in the preparation of the 1983 Environmental Assessment report.

F

The plaintiffs charge that the 1983 decision of the Interior Secretary was impermissibly tainted by political considerations. While the record shows that there was intense lobbying and political activity exercised by parties both in support of as well as opposed to phosphate mining in the Osceola Forest, there is no hard credible evidence to support such a charge. Further, the sequence of events and developments prior to the Secretary's action do not support much less compel an inference that political considerations or factors unduly influenced his decision in any manner.

* * *

In the more than 12-year lapse of time when plaintiffs first filed their lease applications to January 1983, there were unresolved disputes about relevant and basic technical issues necessary to a final decision. Disputes were found within the units of the Departments of Interior and Agriculture, the agencies which had the responsibility of helping to decide the question as to whether phosphate strip mining could be consistent with the primary purposes behind the acquisition and development of the Forest, and equally important—whether technologies were developed and available which would allow restoration of the land. * * *

ANALYSIS

The Osceola National Forest is predominately acquired land and was purchased by the federal government for special purposes. As such, it is accorded a protective status. The primary purposes for which it is being administered by the Forest Service include timber production, water shed protection, recreation, and fish and wildlife. 16 U.S.C. § 528. The Weeks Act of 1911, under which the Forest was purchased, gave the Secretary of Agriculture authority to recommend lands for purchase "as in his judgment may be necessary to the regulation of the *flow of navigable streams* or for the *production of timber.* * * *" 43 Stat. 654 (1924) (emphasis added). * * *

The basic purposes of national forest lands are also found in the Organic Administration Act of 1897, through which Osceola National Forest was created. The Act provided that "no national forest shall be established, except to improve and protect the forest within the boundaries, or for the purpose of securing favorable conditions of water flows, and to furnish a continuous supply of timber. * * *" 16 U.S.C. § 475. The Supreme Court had occasion to consider the Organic Act and its legislative history in United States v. New Mexico, 438 U.S. 696 (1978). It concluded: "Congress intended national forests to be reserved for only two purposes—'[t]o conserve the water flows, and to furnish a continuous supply of timber for the people.'"

Nowhere in the substantial legislative history of the purposes of the national forests in general or the Osceola National Forest in particular, is there included a reference to mineral development or phosphate mining. Indeed, it appears that mineral development is incompatible with the primary purposes and uses of the forest and has a great potential of destroying the natural resources of the Forest. Strip mining, the technique used to secure the phosphates, is highly destructive of natural resources. In the process, the forest area to be mined is leveled, cleared of all vegetation and trees, and wetland areas are drained. The overburden has a depth of 20 to 60 feet. Electrical powered walking draglines, resembling giant scoops, strip the overburden and dig the mining cuts to remove the phosphate matrix averaging 8 to 10 feet thick from the earth. The mining cuts formed by these draglines average 150–200 feet wide and several thousand feet in length.

The acquired lands of the United States which are included in the Osceola Forest may be leased for mineral development only upon conditions imposed by the Mineral Leasing Act for Acquired Lands. * * * [L]eases may prescribe such conditions as "to ensure the adequate utilization of the lands for the primary purposes for which they have been acquired or are being administered. The determination of what conditions should be imposed if a mineral lease is issued is committed by law to the Secretary of Agriculture." 30 U.S.C. § 352.

Applicants such as Kerr-McGee and Global, to ensure their entitlement to phosphate leases, are required to demonstrate the discovery of "valuable deposits" of phosphates on the lands covered by their prospecting permits 30 U.S.C. § 211(b). The term "valuable deposits of phosphates" as used in 30 U.S.C. § 211(b) is found in 43 C.F.R. § 3520.1–1(c). See Utah International Inc. v. Andrus, 488 F.Supp. 962, 968–69 (D.Utah 1979).

In determining whether a prospecting permittee has discovered a "valuable deposit" of phosphate, the cost of compliance with lease terms is an important element which must be considered, and if the applicant lacks the technological capability to comply with prescribed lease terms, he cannot satisfy the test and is not entitled to a lease. Natural Resource Defense Council, Inc. v. Berklund, 458 F.Supp. 925, 936–37 (D.D.C.1978), aff'd, 609 F.2d 553 (D.C.Cir.1979). The restoration technologies necessary to ensure the adequate utilization of the Osceola Forest for its primary purposes did not exist in January 1983 or in 1984, and did not exist at any earlier time.   To demonstrate the discovery of "valuable deposits" of phosphates, Kerr-McGee and Global must comply with the terms and conditions imposed by the Forest Service and are required to show the economic and technological feasibility of reclaiming the lands covered by the lease applications.

Until February 1982, when the Forest Service submitted to the Bureau of Land Management the final stipulations to be attached to any leases which might be issued to phosphate lease applicants in the Forest, the Interior Secretary could not determine whether the plaintiffs had satisfied the "valuable deposit" test, and no lease entitlement was vested in the plaintiffs. The earlier practices of the Department of Interior in issuing phosphate preference right leases before 1970 did not alter or change the statutory requirements and did not establish a legal standard which the Interior Secretary was bound to recognize in determining plaintiffs' lease entitlement. Nor did the prior determination of the Geological Survey Service in 1969 and 1970, that Kerr-McGee had discovered valuable phosphate deposits on lands covered by its prospecting permits, vest any right to receive leases for which it made application. The same is true for any subsequent determination of the Geological Survey Service or any other departmental finding made between 1969 and 1983. None of those determinations precluded the Interior Secretary from subsequently finding that the requisite discovery had not been shown.

CONCLUSION

The January 10, 1983, decision of the Secretary of Interior was not arbitrary and capricious but, rather, was justified and supported by substantial and credible evidence. * * *

NOTES

1. Did the court decide that plaintiffs did not discover a valuable phosphate deposit or that they could not reclaim the land? Does it matter which is the basis for decision?

2. Does or should the holding affect the meaning of "commercial quantities," the discovery standard for coal?

3. Does designation of lands as a national forest place them in "special protective status"? Did this court turn United States v. New Mexico on its head?

4. OIL AND GAS

Oil and gas leasing under the 1920 Mineral Leasing Act got off to a rocky start.

MAMMOTH OIL CO. v. UNITED STATES
Supreme Court of the United States, 1927.
275 U.S. 13.

Mr. Justice BUTLER delivered the opinion of the Court.

This suit was brought by the United States against the petitioners in the District Court of Wyoming to secure the cancellation of an oil and gas lease made by the United States to the Mammoth Oil Company April 7, 1922, and to set aside a supplemental agreement made by the same parties February 9, 1923. An accounting and possession of the leased lands and general relief were also demanded. The complaint alleged that the lease and agreement were made without authority of law and in consummation of a conspiracy to defraud the United States. The District Court held that the transaction was authorized by the Act of June 4, 1920, found that there was no fraud, and dismissed the case. The Circuit Court of Appeals sustained that construction of the Act; but on an examination of the evidence, held that the lease and agreement were obtained by fraud and corruption, reversed the decree and directed the District Court to enter one canceling the lease and agreement as fraudulent, enjoining petitioners from further trespassing on the leased lands and providing for an accounting by the Mammoth Oil Company for all oil and other petroleum products taken under the lease and contract. 14 F.(2d) 705.

The lease covered 9,321 acres in Natrona County, Wyoming—commonly known as Teapot Dome—being Naval Reserve No. 3 created April 30, 1915, by an executive order of the President made pursuant to the Act of June 25, 1910, c. 421, 36 Stat. 847, as amended August 24, 1912, c. 369, 37 Stat. 497. The part of the Act of June 4, 1920 relied on to sustain the lease contains the following: "*Provided,* That the Secretary of the Navy is directed to take possession of all properties within the naval petroleum reserves * * * to conserve, develop, use, and operate the same in his discretion, directly or by contract, lease, or otherwise, and to use, store, exchange, or sell the oil and gas products thereof, and those from all royalty oil from lands in the naval reserves, for the benefit of the United States * * *".

March 5, 1921, Edwin Denby became Secretary of the Navy and Albert B. Fall, Secretary of the Interior. May 31, 1921, the President made an order purporting to commit the administration of all oil and gas bearing lands in the naval reserves to the Secretary of the Interior, subject to the supervision of the President. The lease and agreement were signed for the United States by Fall as Secretary of the Interior and by Denby as Secretary of the Navy. The evidence shows that the latter was fully informed as to the substance of the transaction, and it is not necessary here to consider the validity or effect of the executive order.

* * *

So far as concerns the power under the Act of June 4, 1920 to make them, the lease and agreement now before the court cannot be distinguished from those held to have been made without authority of law in Pan American Petroleum and Transport Company v. United States, 273 U.S. 456. And the United States is entitled to have them canceled.

Were the lease and supplemental agreement fraudulently made?

The decisions below are in conflict, and we have considered the evidence to determine whether it establishes the charge. The complaint states that the lease and agreement were made as the result of a conspiracy by Fall and H.F. Sinclair to defraud the United States; that Fall acted for the United States and Sinclair acted for the Mammoth Oil Company; that the negotiations were secret and the lease was made without competition; that responsible persons and corporations desiring to obtain leases were by Fall in collusion with Sinclair denied opportunity to become competitors of the Mammoth Company; that a company known as the Pioneer Oil Company asserted a mining claim to lands in the reserve; that the claim was worthless and known to be so by Fall; that he had Sinclair procure a quitclaim deed covering the valueless claim and, then, to make it impossible for others to compete with Sinclair's company, Fall made its transfer condition the granting of the lease; that Fall agreed with one Shaffer that Sinclair would cause a part of the leased lands to be set aside for the benefit of Shaffer, and required Sinclair, in order to get the lease for the Mammoth Company, to agree that Shaffer should have a sublease on some of the land; that before and after the making of the lease Fall kept the negotiations and execution secret from his associates, the Congress and the public. And, in general terms, the complaint charges that Fall and Sinclair conspired to defraud the Government by making the lease without authority and in violation of law and to favor and prefer the Mammoth Company over others.

As is usual in cases where conspiracy to defraud is involved, there is here no direct evidence of the corrupt arrangement. Neither of the alleged conspirators was called as a witness. The question is whether the disclosed circumstances prove the charge. * * *

* * *

[The Court examined the evidence of fraud at great length.]

The complaint did not allege bribery; and, in the view we take of the case, there is no occasion to consider and we do not determine whether Fall was bribed in respect of the lease or agreement. [He pretty clearly was bribed. Eds.] It was not necessary for the Government to show that it suffered or was liable to suffer loss or disadvantage as a result of the lease or that Fall gained by or was financially concerned in the transaction. It requires no discussion to make it plain that the facts and circumstances above referred to require a finding that pending the making of the lease and agreement Fall and Sinclair, contrary to the Government's policy for the conservation of oil reserves for the Navy and in disregard of law, conspired to procure for the Mammoth Company all the products of the reserve on the basis of exchange of royalty oil for construction work, fuel oil, etc.; that Fall so favored Sinclair and the making of the lease and agreement that it was not possible for him loyally or faithfully to serve the interests of the United States or impartially to consider the applications of others for leases in the reserve, and that the lease and agreement were made fraudulently by means of collusion and conspiracy between them.

* * *

* * * The lease and supplemental agreement were fraudulently made to circumvent the law and to defeat public policy. No equity arises in favor of the lessee or the other petitioners to prevent or condition the granting of the relief directed by the Circuit Court of Appeals. Petitioners are bound to restore title and possession of the reserve to the United States, and must abide the judgment of Congress as to the use or removal of the improvements or other relief claimed by them.

Decree affirmed.

Mr. Justice VAN DEVANTER and Mr. Justice STONE took no part in the consideration or decision of this case.

NOTES

1. One can deduce the clarity of the record by imagining how much evidence the 1926 Supreme Court would require to reverse a finding of a district judge on a heavily factual issue such as fraud. The Teapot Dome scandal in the Harding Administration is said to have retarded federal oil and gas leasing for a half century. See generally B. Noggle, TEAPOT DOME: OIL AND POLITICS IN THE 1920's (1962).

2. The Mineral Leasing Act allowed the Secretary to issue non-competitive leases in areas without known geological structures to the first qualified applicant to apply. When earlier leases in such areas terminated, the Secretary could withdraw such areas from leasing. See Wright v. Paine, 289 F.2d 766 (D.C.Cir.1961); Haley v. Seaton, 281 F.2d 620 (D.C.Cir.1960). See also Wilber v. United States, 46 F.2d 217 (D.C. Cir.1930), aff'd, 283 U.S. 414 (1931). Where the lands were not withdrawn, however, the new land rush was on.

THOR–WESTCLIFFE DEVELOPMENT, INC. v. UDALL
United States Court of Appeals, District of Columbia Circuit, 1963.
314 F.2d 257.

J. SKELLY WRIGHT, Circuit Judge.

Section 17 of the Mineral Leasing Act of 1920 provides that public lands "not within any known geological structure of a producing oil or gas field" shall be leased "to the person first making application" at not less than fifty cents per acre. In an effort to eliminate the chaos which sometimes resulted from competition among applicants to be literally the "person first making application" for leases having speculative value far in excess of leasing costs, the Secretary of the Interior promulgated a regulation providing for simultaneous filing and a public drawing in the event of multiple applications. Appellant attacks this regulation as unresponsive to the statutory command that the lease be given to the "person first making application." The District Court granted summary judgment in favor of the Secretary. We affirm.

Experience in the administration of the Act has demonstrated that land subject to leasing after expiration or cancellation of a prior lease often has significant speculative value [4] in spite of the fact that it is not actually "within any known geological structure of a producing oil or gas field." In order "to assure public notice and fuller public participation in the process of reissuing relinquished leases," [5] Regulation 192.43 provides for the posting of descriptions of such expired lease land in each Interior Department land office on the third Monday of each month, together with "a notice stating that the lands in such leases are subject to the simultaneous filings of lease offers from the time of such posting until 10:00 o'clock a.m. on the said fifth working day thereafter." If at 10:00 a.m. on the fifth day more than one offer has been received to lease the same acreage, the priorities are determined by lot.

Prior leases on the lands in suit expired by operation of law on June 30, 1961. Appellant filed its applications for leases on July 3, 1961, the next business day. On July 17, 1961, the lands were posted under the procedure described above and applications for leases were accepted until 10:00 a.m. on the "fifth working day thereafter." Appellant filed no applications during this interval. A drawing was held among those applications filed during this period and intervenor Boyle was the winner. Appellant's applications of July 3, 1961, were rejected as untimely. Having exhausted its remedies within the Department, appellant brought suit for a judgment declaring Regulation 192.43 invalid and granting the leases to it.

Appellant, ignoring Mr. Justice Frankfurter's famous dictum,[6] stands firmly on the literal language of the statute. It was the "person first making application" after the prior leases expired, it argues, and consequently the Secretary must comply with the statutory mandate. The Secretary relies upon the regulation, which he justifies as necessary to end the mad scrambles, breaches of the peace, damage to tract books, and corruption of land office employees as applicants compete to be the "person first making application." Appellant does not contest the existence of these problems with respect to cancellation or other premature termination of a lease, but asserts (1) that these problems do not exist where leases terminate by expiration, (2) that other methods

---

4. Geological information acquired during a prior lease as to the proximity of a known structure often greatly enhances the value of the property for mineral purposes.

5. Miller v. Udall, 307 F.2d 676, 677–678, n. 1 (1962).

6. "The notion that because the words of a statute are plain, its meaning is also plain, is merely pernicious oversimplification." United States v. Monia, 317 U.S. 424, 431 (dissenting opinion) (1943).

of meeting these problems are available, and (3) that in any event this regulation on its face conflicts with the statutory requirement and is therefore invalid.

The Secretary has full authority under the Act "to prescribe necessary and proper rules and regulations" to accomplish its purposes. Stripped to its essence, the question presented here simply is: does Regulation 192.43 comport with the Secretary's statutory authority? It is not for us, nor for appellant, to suggest a method for solving the problems which have arisen in the administration of the Mineral Leasing Act. Congress has consigned that function to the Secretary. Our inquiry ends when we determine whether or not the method adopted by the Secretary is "unreasonable and plainly inconsistent" with the statute, having in mind that regulations "constitute contemporaneous constructions by those charged with administration of these statutes which should not be overruled except for weighty reasons." Commissioner v. South Texas Co., 333 U.S. 496, 501 (1948).

* * * This, of course, does not mean that the Secretary is permitted to grant a lease to one other than "the person first making application." It does mean that the Secretary is to determine who that first person is. Hence the provision in the Act authorizing the promulgation of regulations. 30 U.S.C. § 189. It is likewise clear that the language "person first making application" is not so definite, particularly when prior experience with its application is considered, as to render an interpretative or implementing regulation inappropriate.

* * * We find, considering the language and purpose of the statute, as well as the experience of the Secretary in the implementation thereof, that the regulation is neither unreasonable nor inconsistent with the plain language of the Act.

* * *

It must be owned that the procedure outlined in Regulation 192.43, on superficial examination, bears little resemblance to the "person first making application" language of the statute. But Congress could hardly have supposed that granting $.50 per acre mineral leases can be accomplished as simply as the statutory language seems to indicate. The history of the administration of the statute furnishes compelling proof, familiar to the membership of Congress, that the human animal has not changed, that when you determine to give something away, you are going to draw a crowd. It is the Secretary's job to manage the crowd while complying with the requirement of the Act. Regulation 192.43 is the Secretary's effort in this direction. We cannot say that it is an impermissible implementation of the statutory purpose.

Affirmed.

Until recently, most litigation over federal onshore oil and gas leasing has been relatively sparse and technical. The student interested in the mechanical aspects of federal leasing is directed to the general treatises on oil and gas law, to the several casebooks on that subject, and particularly to the Rocky Mountain Mineral Law Foundation's THE LAW OF FEDERAL OIL AND GAS LEASES (1976). Recent cases raising picky questions of regulation interpretation and leasing procedure include Naartex Consulting Corp. v. Watt, 722 F.2d 779 (D.C.Cir. 1983), cert. denied, 467 U.S. 1210 (1984) (designation of filing service interest on lottery application); Lowey v. Watt, 684 F.2d 957 (D.C.Cir. 1982) (waiver of filing service interest); McDonald v. Watt, 653 F.2d 1035 (5th Cir.1981); Brick v. Andrus, 628 F.2d 213 (D.C.Cir.1980) (entry of name in specified order on entry card); Winkler v. Andrus, 494 F.Supp. 946 (D.Wyo.1980) (assignee of lease is not a bona fide purchaser). In Ahrens v. Andrus, 690 F.2d 805 (10th Cir.1982), the court voided a BLM award of leases by noncompetitive lottery based on a "trivial, supertechnical, and inconsequential" reason for invalidating first-drawn entry cards. The question whether the initially successful applicants were indispensible parties was left, more or less, in limbo.

Only in the past decade have cases with more general import for the public interest become common. The first concerns the distinction between lands that overlay known geological structures (KGSs) and those that do not. In Udall v. King, 308 F.2d 650 (D.C.Cir.1962), the court held that the Secretary could find that an area subject to a pending noncompetitive lease application was within a KGS and refuse to lease it except competitively. Compare Barash v. Seaton, 256 F.2d 714 (D.C.Cir.1958).

ARKLA EXPLORATION COMPANY v. TEXAS OIL & GAS CORP.

United States Court of Appeals, Eighth Circuit, 1984.
734 F.2d 347.

BOWMAN, Circuit Judge.

Under the Mineral Lands Leasing Act (MLA), 30 U.S.C. §§ 181–287, before government lands may be leased for oil or gas exploration without competitive bidding, the Secretary of the Interior (the Secretary) must determine that the lands are not within a "known geological structure of a producing oil or gas field" (KGS). Id. at § 226. At issue in this case is whether the Secretary made a proper KGS determination before granting valuable oil and gas exploration leases to Texas Oil and Gas Corporation (TXO) on a noncompetitive basis. The District Court for the Western District of Arkansas held that the Secretary's determination was improper and, therefore, that these leases were not validly issued. The Secretary and TXO appeal from that decision. For the reasons stated herein, we affirm the decision of the district court.

* * *

[Johnson, the BLM employee who reviewed the lease applications, determined that the lands sought were outside KGSs by applying a Department rule that a KGS would extend only a mile from a producing well; thus, a KGS could encompass only the nine sections immediately surrounding a well. The procedural history of the case was long and confused, and the administrative record was voluminous but unilluminating. The court set out this background, ruled against all of the procedural defenses asserted by TXO and the U.S., and went on to consider whether the KGS determination was supportable.]

Standard for Reviewing the KGS Determination

The Secretary's KGS determination may be set aside if it is arbitrary, capricious, or contrary to law or to the Secretary's regulations. 5 U.S.C. § 706(2)(A). * * * [The court found that, because of the complexity of the case, the district judge was correct to use supplementary evidence "to explain the record and to determine the adequacy of the procedure followed and the facts considered by the Secretary in reaching his decision."]

Validity of the KGS Determination

The Secretary and TXO argue that the lands in question were properly classified as non-KGS. But the Department, in making the KGS determination, did not consider pertinent geologic information that readily was available to it or actual competitive interest that had been shown in the Fort Chaffee area. Instead, the Department made its determination under an arbitrary one-mile stepout rule. These actions ignore Congressional intent in enacting the MLA and are inconsistent with that statute. * * *

The Department's treatment of the lease applications in this case brings to mind the legend of the tribesmen who sold Manhattan Island for a few trinkets and a small quantity of strong drink. * * *

The analogy is not perfect, however, because the Department in this case probably had far more insight into the value of what it was selling than did the Indians in their transaction with the Dutch. In spite of a wealth of information available to him, Johnson, an experienced geologist with special knowledge of the Fort Chaffee area, was constrained by the admonitions of his superiors to limit any KGS extension to not more than one mile beyond the section in which the well was located. Thus, he was not free to use the full range of his expertise in making KGS determinations. Instead, he used a method for KGS determinations that was specifically rejected by Congress in response to the protests of the oil industry—an arbitrary mileage system.

Prior to his cancellation of the leases, the Secretary ordered the USGS to conduct a review of the Tulsa USGS office's KGS determination. The result was the Girard report, which thus far has been the only official administrative review of the KGS determination for the TXO leases. The covering memorandum to the report from the Director of USGS makes the following statement with regard to USGS policy on KGS determinations in the Fort Chaffee area:

> The history of the oil and gas industry's desires with regard to KGS's is that the Geological Survey define them in a restricted fashion. Consistently, the industry has challenged the Survey as being too liberal in its interpretations, and consistently the courts have supported the existing interpretation. Therefore,

in the Fort Chaffee case, the Survey has found itself in a difficult situation. Any layman reviewing production in and around Fort Chaffee would conclude that the Fort Chaffee area is potentially productive. However, for our personnel to have defined the KGS's in any way other than the determination which was made, would have put the Survey and the Department in a position that was open to challenge in the courts.

This statement helps to explain the "criticism" received by Johnson for attempting to make KGS determinations beyond the one-mile stepout. The USGS feared court challenge, but the fear of being sued is no excuse for a failure to implement Congressional intent. The USGS, which by its own admission never has had a KGS determination reversed for being too broad, had every reason to believe that, if challenged, its proper judgment would be sustained. Instead, it bowed to industry pressure by using an arbitrary mileage standard, which surely never would be challenged as being over-inclusive, since the State of Arkansas used it as a minimum spacing unit for producing wells.

A. Congress and the MLA

* * * The broad purpose of the MLA was to provide incentives to explore new, unproven oil and gas areas through noncompetitive leasing, while assuring through competitive bidding adequate compensation to the government for leasing in producing areas.

A major controversy in the Congressional hearings arose over where the line should be drawn between competitive and noncompetitive lands. Review of the legislative history of the MLA reveals that several arbitrary mileage rules for identifying lands to be leased competitively were considered but that all were rejected. Oil industry spokespersons protested that these proposals did not comport with the geologic realities of oil fields. They argued that allowing competitive leasing only within known geological structures would truly reflect the way in which oil accumulates underground. Congress accepted that argument and the law as enacted provided that competitive leasing would be the rule for lands lying within "known geological structures of producing oil or gas fields." The legislative history of the Act shows that oil industry spokespersons represented and Congress understood that, for purposes of the MLA, the term KGS, though a broad term, basically meant domes and anticlines which contained producing wells. Given that meaning, a KGS could extend considerably less or considerably more than one mile from a given well, depending on the geology of the area. The legislative history makes it clear that when it enacted the MLA, Congress accepted the factual premise that no arbitrary mileage rule can, other than by sheer chance, define a KGS.

Concededly, KGS is a broad term, and the Secretary has authority to determine its meaning. Even so, this authority must operate within the confines of Congressional intent, not to mention common sense. These confines were exceeded when, based on a map nearly void of pertinent information other than one-mile sections around producing wells, the Secretary disposed of valuable public resources at fire sale prices. This was no substitute for the use of proper procedures to determine if the lands to be leased are within a KGS. That an arbitrary mileage rule was used by the Tulsa USGS office as the sole KGS determinant in itself clearly demonstrates that the KGS determination in this case was at odds with the express intent of Congress.

B. Geologic Information

A great deal of geologic information was available to the Tulsa USGS office, including National Gas Policy Act determinations, various relevant technical logs, annual reservoir pressure reports, subsurface structure maps, and cross sections of the Fort Chaffee area. * * *

The Secretary argues that Johnson was an experienced geologist and that his use of the one-mile rule was a result of his familiarity with the geology of Fort Chaffee acquired during his long tenure with the Tulsa office of the USGS. No one disputes Johnson's expertise as a geologist or his familiarity with the Fort Chaffee area. Johnson applied the one-mile rule in this case not because of geological expertise, but because he previously had received criticism from his superiors for attempting to deviate from the rule. If in fact Johnson had been allowed free rein to use his knowledge in interpreting all the available data, this case may never have arisen. In any event, for the Department to fix the boundaries of a "known *geological* structure" without first considering pertinent geologic information that readily was available to it is plainly inconsistent with the MLA. Equally inconsistent is the Secretary's decision to grant the TXO leases based upon such a KGS determination.

C. Competitive Interest

Perhaps even more serious than the Secretary's failure to make use of the available geologic data and expertise is his failure to consider actual competitive interest in the Fort Chaffee area shown by Arkla and other oil companies. Arkla had made numerous inquiries to BLM about obtaining leases on Fort Chaffee. Prior to the issuance of the leases in question, Arkla had bid on various drainage leases within Fort Chaffee. In one sale, Arkla's bids of $151.51 per acre on two sections within the Fort were rejected as too low. These sections were but one section away from the TXO lease area, which was leased for only $1 per acre. There also was other information available to USGS giving them notice of the considerable interest in the Fort Chaffee lands. In light of this, the use of an arbitrary mileage system ignores the Congressional intent to promote competitive leasing within known geological structures of producing oil and gas fields.

* * * Thus, the USGS's own study reveals that competitive interest and risk of exploration were not considered in making the Fort Chaffee KGS determinations. Because relative risk of exploration and exploration interest lie at the heart of the competitive/noncompetitive leasing dichotomy in the MLA, the failure of the USGS and the

Secretary to consider these factors renders the KGS determination unlawful.

The judgment of the district court is affirmed.

JOHN R. GIBSON, Circuit Judge, dissenting.

The court's opinion today has much appeal. It affirms the necessity for competitive bidding for the oil leases in question and will result in substantial income for Arkansas schools. See 30 U.S.C. §§ 191, 355. The court, however, paints with too broad a brush, substantially exceeding our proper narrow scope of review, and I must respectfully dissent.

I find it hard to conclude that the district court did anything other than conduct a de novo hearing and substitute its judgment for that of the Secretary. ＊ ＊ ＊

＊ ＊ ＊

While the court may feel that a poor job was done in the processing of these leases and that Johnson could have been more thorough, our task is simply to determine whether the actions of the Secretary, acting through Johnson, were arbitrary or capricious. If there is a rational basis for the actions, we do not set them aside. The rational basis exists. I would reverse the judgment of the district court.

NOTES

1. Should the KGS determination be solely "objective" (i.e., geological factors only) or "subjective" (degree of lessee interest) as well? Compare Fundingsland v. Colorado Ground Water Comm'n, 171 Colo. 487, 468 P.2d 835 (1970) (upholding the Groundwater Commission's "three-mile test" by which a radius of three miles was drawn around existing wells to determine whether new wells would cause interference; the test was admittedly arbitrary but was upheld as being within the agency's discretion).

2. The oil and gas industry reportedly is perturbed at the implications of including "competitive interest" among relevant KGS factors. Why would this be so? The Arkla leases spurred calls from Senator Bumpers, among others, to do away with all noncompetitive leasing.

3. In Angelina Holly Corp. v. Clark, 587 F.Supp. 1152 (D.D.C. 1984), the court upheld the Secretary's decision to deny plaintiff's lease applications after the Department extended the KGS area to include the application areas. The court also denied plaintiff's claim that it was inconsistent and discriminatory to award other noncompetitive leases in the same area.

COPPER VALLEY MACHINE WORKS, INC. v. ANDRUS
United States Court of Appeals, District of Columbia Circuit, 1981.
653 F.2d 595.

MacKINNON, Circuit Judge.

The principal issue in this appeal is whether a restriction in a drilling permit prohibiting summer drilling in the interest of conservation worked a "suspension of operations and production" that would extend the life of an oil and gas lease under section 39 of the Mineral Leasing Act of 1920, as amended, 30 U.S.C. § 209.

I. BACKGROUND

Effective February 1, 1966, the Secretary of Interior issued oil and gas lease A–063937 to run for an initial "period of ten years and so long thereafter as oil or gas is produced in paying quantities."

Near the end of the primary lease term, Copper Valley Machine Works, Inc. (Copper Valley), the designated operator of the lease, asked the Oil and Gas Supervisor of the United States Geological Survey about "extending the 10-year lease term by drilling across the expiration date." Subsequently Copper Valley filed for the Supervisor's consideration an application for a permit to drill. On January 30, 1976 the drilling permit application was approved,

> subject to conditions attached to the permit and conditions and requirements described below:
>
> *   *   *
>
> 10. The approved application and development plan provides for operation *during the winter season only,* as approved by the appropriate surface managing agency.

(emphasis added). This "winter season only" restriction was considered "necessary because the lease itself was issued without any stipulations for protection of the tundra/perma-frost environment during the months of summer thaw."

A. Subsequent History

The events that then led to this dispute are described in a memorandum from the Acting Director of the Geological Survey to the Secretary of Interior:

> The well was commenced on January 31, 1976 (the expiration date of the primary term), and reached a depth of 100 feet before having to shutdown for the 1976 summer season. Following the summer shutdown from May to November 1976, operations were recommenced on February 5, 1977, and after reaching a depth of 1,070 feet on March 20, 1977, electric logs were run in the well. After evaluating the electric logs and examining the samples, the Supervisor concluded that the operator had satisfied the "diligent drilling" requirements of 43 CFR 3107.2–3,[3] and recommended to BLM that the lease be extended to January 31, 1978.
>
> After the 1977 summer shutdown, the Supervisor advised the operator and the lessee that the lease would expire January 31,

---

3. 43 C.F.R. § 3107.2–3. *Period of extension.*

Any lease on which actual drilling operations, or for which under an approved cooperative or unit plan of development or operation, actual drilling operations were commenced prior to the end of its primary term and are being diligently prosecuted at that time, *shall be extended for 2 years* and so long thereafter as oil or gas is produced in paying quantities.

(Emphasis added.)

1978, absent a well physically and mechanically capable of production in paying quantities by that date.

On January 20, 1978, the operator wrote the Supervisor and requested that the lease be extended for twelve (12) months to compensate for the two periods of summer shutdown in 1976 and 1977. The Supervisor considered this letter to be *an application to the Secretary* for an extension of lease Anchorage 063937 pursuant to 43 CFR 3103.3–8 [4] [Emphasis added.]

Although acknowledging that Copper Valley had been "unable to conduct operations on a full-time basis since January of 1976 by the imposition of the requirement that operations would be permitted only during the winter months," the Acting Director recommended that no extension of the lease be granted or recognized.

On May 22, 1978, the Secretary of Interior followed the Acting Director's recommendation, ruling that

the lease is considered to have expired by operation of law as of midnight, January 31, 1978, absent the existence of a well on that date which had been determined by the Supervisor as capable of producing in paying quantities. The reasons for the denial [of extension] are that (1) the lessee accepted the imposed restriction that drilling could be conducted only during the winter season without complaint until 11 days preceding the lease expiration date and (2) the 2-year lease extension earned by drilling across the end of the primary term of January 31, 1976, afforded sufficient additional time, despite the restriction, in which to have completed a well that was physically capable of production in paying quantities.

* * *

B.   Decision of the District Court

On July 17, 1978, Copper Valley was advised of the Secretary's May 22nd action, and on August 18 sought a declaratory judgment * * * that the Secretary's refusal to permit another 12 months of operations was unlawful. Copper Valley relied on section 39 of the Mineral Leasing Act of 1920, as amended, which provides in part:

In the event the Secretary of Interior *in the interest of conservation,* shall direct * * * *the suspension of operations and production* under any lease granted under the terms of this

4.   43 C.F.R. § 3103.3–8 provides:

Suspension of operations and production.

(a) * * * As to oil and gas leases, no suspension of operations and production will be granted on any lease in the absence of a well capable of production on the leasehold, except where the Secretary directs a suspension in the interest of conservation. * * *

(b) The term of any lease will be extended by adding thereto any period of suspension of all operations and production during such term pursuant to any direction or assent of the Secretary.

(c) A suspension shall take effect as of the time specified in the direction or assent of the Secretary. Rental and minimum royalty payments will be suspended during any period of suspension of all operations and production directed or assented to by the Secretary, * * *

* * *

Act, any payment of acreage rental or of minimum royalty prescribed by such lease likewise shall be suspended during such period of suspension or operations and productions; *and the term of such lease shall be extended by adding any such suspension * * * thereto.*

30 U.S.C. § 209 (emphasis added).

On the parties' cross-motions for summary judgment, the district court ruled in favor of the Secretary. * * *

II. ANALYSIS

Copper Valley's principal contention on appeal is that the drilling permit's "winter season only" restriction, by preventing drilling operations for 6 summer months a year, worked a "suspension of operations and production" "in the interest of conservation" and therefore, under § 209, mandated an automatic extension of the lease for a period equal to the length of the suspension. The Government responds that the drilling restrictions did not create suspensions within the meaning of § 209.

A. "In the Interest of Conservation"

We note at the outset that there is no contention that the "winter season only" restriction was not ordered "in the interest of conservation." The parties agree that carrying on drilling operations during the summer months would have substantially damaged the permafrost character of the leasehold area. Preventing such damage is obviously in the interest of conservation if that term is to receive its ordinary meaning. While the prevention of environmental damage may not have been the "conservation" that Congress principally had in mind in 1933 when it passed § 209,[6] suspending operations to avoid environmental harm is definitely a suspension in the interest of conservation in the ordinary sense of the word. And there was no indication that Congress intended that "conservation" be given any interpretation other than its ordinary meaning.[8]

---

6. A congressional report accompanying the bill that became § 209 stated:

[I]t is * * * a matter of public knowledge that there has existed for some time past, and still exists, a condition of overproduction [of petroleum and natural gas]. This condition has resulted in the adoption by the Interior Department of an administrative policy of conservation of oil and gas.

H.R.Rep. No. 1737, 72nd Cong., 1st Sess. 3 (1932).

8. This conclusion is consistent with *Gulf Oil Corp. v. Morton*, 493 F.2d 141 (9th Cir.1974). The court in *Morton* interpreted § 5(a)(1) of the Outer Continental Shelf (OCS) Lands Act, 43 U.S.C. § 1334(a)(1), a provision similar to 30 U.S.C. § 209. Section 5(a)(1) authorizes the Secretary of Interior to provide, "in the interest of conservation," for the "suspension of operations or production." The court rejected the oil company's argument that "interest of conservation" is confined to conservation of oil and gas, id. at 145, and concluded the Secretary was empowered to suspend drilling operations to prevent undue harm to the marine environment.

* * *

B. "Suspension of Operations and Production"

1. The Secretary's "Surprise Theory"

The Secretary asserts that § 209 "was designed by Congress to cover only unanticipated interruptions of drilling." Under this view, whether a § 209 suspension has occurred depends on whether the "winter season only" restriction was a surprise to Copper Valley. It is in this context that the Secretary emphasizes that the lease gave "notice that drilling activities would be subject to restriction," that Copper Valley "did not protest against the restriction until two years after the permit was issued," and that Copper Valley "continued to pay rent during the thaw months without attempting to assert that the drilling permit condition was a surprise." We find it unnecessary to consider whether summary judgment was appropriate on the question whether Copper Valley could foresee the suspension of drilling, for we reject as unpersuasive the Secretary's attempt to narrow the scope of the plain terms of § 209.

As indicated in note 6 supra, § 209 was enacted in a period when the Secretary was suspending the drilling operations of oil and gas lessees in order to alleviate the problem of excess petroleum production. The congressional report explained that the bill

> relieve[s] lessees of coal and oil lands from the necessity of paying prescribed annual acreage rental, during periods when operations or production is suspended, in the interest of conservation, either by direction or assent of the Secretary of the Interior, and [provides] that the period of such suspension shall be added to the term of the lease.
>
> * * *

H.R.Rep. No. 1737, 72nd Cong., 1st Sess. 2–3 (1932).

Because some of the oil and gas lessees who benefitted from the lease extensions and rent moratoriums of § 209 might have been surprised by the petroleum glut and the Secretary's ensuing suspensions, the Government contends that the section, which by its terms applies to any Secretary-imposed "suspension of operations and production," actually applies only to those suspensions that are the product of unanticipated events. To state this contention is to suggest its refutation. The plain meaning of a statute cannot be overcome by speculation as to some unstated purpose. Nothing in the legislative history of § 209 suggests, much less establishes, the narrow interpretation the Secretary would have us adopt. * * * The Secretary's speculation, suspect on its own terms, has no support in the legislative history and cannot modify the statute's plain terms.

We thus find it irrelevant, insofar as extension of the lease is concerned, that Copper Valley paid rent without protest during the two year extension of the ten year primary term. By paying rent Copper Valley protected its rights by eliminating the basis for any contention by the Secretary that it was in default. Whether the lease was extended or not, rent would eventually be due for the full two year period. Now Copper Valley has fully satisfied its rent obligation through the extension period it will receive by virtue of the suspension.

The Secretary also contends that Copper Valley's interpretation of § 209 could double the term of all leases on Alaskan tundra, contrary to the congressional intent that the term of a non-producing non-competitive lease be limited to 10 years, with the possibility of a single 2-year extension. 30 U.S.C. § 226(e). Contrary to the Secretary, we perceive no conflict between Copper Valley's reading of § 209 and a sensible reading of § 226(e). Without undertaking to decide that issue, which is not before us, we note that § 226(e) gives the lessee a minimum number of years in which to develop the resources subject to his lease. Section 209, consistent with this policy, extends the life of the lease to the extent that the lessee is deprived of his full term by the Secretary's suspension of drilling operations in the interest of conservation. Far from undermining § 226(e), § 209 effectuates the policy it reflects. The law was intended to apply uniformly throughout the United States and give lessees in Alaska the same full term of enjoyment as lessees in the lower 48 states. If climatic conditions in Alaska cause the Secretary to order a suspension in the interest of conservation it is not to be considered as being any the less a suspension because the reason that prompted its imposition was foreseeable.

*   *   *

D. Disposition of the Case

In this case the Secretary, far from adequately explaining his departure from the precedent of *Texaco,* has completely ignored it. Affording different treatment to similar situations is the essence of arbitrary action. The Secretary also has arbitrarily ignored the language of § 209. Ordinarily this agency conduct would call for a remand for proper application of the appropriate legal standards, if the agency under the law could reasonably adhere to the result its challenged decision has reached. On the undisputed facts here, however, we conclude that no reasonable interpretation of § 209 can deny Copper Valley the extension it claims. Accordingly, the judgment of the district court granting summary judgment for the Secretary should be vacated and the district court in accordance with the foregoing opinion should grant the motion of Copper Valley for summary judgment in its favor.[12]

Judgment accordingly.

---

12. We cannot join the speculation that ordering a lease extension in this case will "create significant new land title difficulties in areas which have been subject to leasing, make new investment in oil exploration substantially more risky and expensive, and shortchange the United States as lessor, by conferring an unbargained-for windfall on the holders of existing leases." The Secretary has not acquainted us with these asserted problems. If conditions in Alaska require a special exception from § 209's plain meaning and policy then Congress is free to create one. In any event, were speculation within our province, we would venture that assuring oil and gas lessees, through lease extensions, the full exploration period that Congress has given them would *promote* new investment in oil exploration and benefit the United States. The United States is not shortchanged in the process; it is merely held to the lease terms specified in its statutory bargain.

JOHN H. PRATT, District Judge, concurring in the remand:

I concur in the remand, but for reasons different than the majority's.

Congress intended the term "conservation" in § 209 to refer to the conservation of mineral resources, and not to more general environmental protection measures which may restrict production. The history of the 1933 statute shows that the concept of mineral conservation was advanced repeatedly by the bill's sponsors and managers, and was agreed to by opponents. * * * The majority reads "conservation" in its modern sense, and inadequately weighs the special meaning of the term "conservation" intended by Congress.

The Interior Department, which had authored and advocated the 1933 and 1946 statutes, interpreted § 209 to apply only to mineral conservation. This example of contemporaneous construction by the responsible cabinet officer is strong evidence of the original meaning, especially where Congress reenacts the statute consistently with that construction. The Department acted consistently with this interpretation in subsequent administrative adjudication and rulemaking. * * *

I think a remand appropriate however, for the Secretary and his subordinates relied on legally irrelevant grounds to deny the extension. The District Court should return the case to the Secretary and require him to decide explicitly whether winter-only drilling restrictions are "suspensions" under § 209, and to state the policy and legal reasons for his choice among plausible interpretations of § 209.

There are sound practical and legal reasons for this approach. We know little more about Alaskan drilling than the fact that it is expensive and difficult. By pronouncing a rule at sharp variance with present practice in Alaska, we may create significant new land title difficulties in areas which have been subject to leasing, make new investment in oil exploration substantially more risky and expensive, and shortchange the United States as lessor, by conferring an unbargained-for windfall on the holders of existing leases. These are cogent reasons for seeking a careful exercise of the Secretary's expert judgment before deciding the interpretive issue presented here. Udall v. Tallman, 380 U.S. 1, 16–18 (1965). By pronouncing a flat rule before the Secretary has acted, we may significantly impede Alaskan oil development vital to meeting the Nation's current and future energy needs. I doubt Congress intended that result.

SIERRA CLUB v. PETERSON

United States Court of Appeals, District of Columbia Circuit, 1983.
717 F.2d 1409.

MacKINNON, Senior Circuit Judge:

* * *

I

The land originally involved in this dispute encompassed a 247,000 acre roadless area in the Targhee and Bridger-Teton National Forests of Idaho and Wyoming, known as the Palisades Further Planning Area. In its most recent Roadless Review and Evaluation, RARE II,[1] the Forest Service designated this entire area as a Further Planning Area and consequently, the land may be considered for all uses, including oil and gas exploration, as long as its potential wilderness quality is preserved.

In 1980, the Forest Service received applications for oil and gas leases in the Palisades Further Planning Area. After conducting an Environmental Assessment (EA), the Forest Service recommended granting the lease applications, but with various stipulations attached to the leases. Because the Forest Service determined that issuance of the leases with the recommended stipulations would not result in significant adverse impacts to the environment, it decided that, with respect to the *entire* area, no Environmental Impact Statement was required at the leasing stage.

The leasing program approved by the Forest Service divides the land within the Palisades Further Planning Area into two categories— "highly environmentally sensitive" [3] lands and non-highly environmentally sensitive lands. The stipulations attached to each lease are determined by the particular character of the land. All of the leases for the Palisades contain "standard" and "special" stipulations. These stipulations require the lessee to obtain approval from the Interior Department before undertaking any surface disturbing activity on the lease, but do not authorize the Department to *preclude* any activities which the lessee might propose. The Department can only impose conditions upon the lessee's use of the leased land.

In addition, a No Surface Occupancy Stipulation (NSO Stipulation) is attached to the leases for lands designated as "highly environmentally sensitive." This NSO Stipulation *precludes* surface occupancy unless and until such activity is specifically approved by the Forest Service.

For leases *without* a No Surface Occupancy Stipulation, the lessee must file an application for a permit to drill prior to initiating exploratory drilling activities. The application must contain a surface use and

---

1. Two Roadless Area Review and Evaluations (RARE I and II) were conducted by the Forest Service to evaluate undeveloped areas within National Forests in order to recommend appropriate areas to Congress for designation as part of the National Wilderness Preservation System. See Wilderness Act, 16 U.S.C. § 1131 et seq. (1976).

As a result of RARE II, areas studied by the Forest Service were classified as either Wilderness, Non-wilderness or Further Planning Areas. Further Planning Areas, such as the Palisades, are lands which re-

quire additional, more intensive study before the Forest Service can recommend Wilderness or Non-wilderness status to Congress. Until a decision is reached on the ultimate status of the land, its present character is to be maintained.

3. "Highly environmentally sensitive" areas * * * include lands necessary for the protection of threatened or endangered wildlife species; lands with slope gradients of more than 40%; lands with regionally unique plant or animal species; and lands with significant cultural resources.

operating plan which details the proposed operations including access roads, well site locations, and other planned facilities. On land leased without a No Surface Occupancy Stipulation the Department *cannot* deny the permit to drill; it can only impose "reasonable" conditions which are designed to mitigate the environmental impacts of the drilling operations.

II

Following an unsuccessful administrative challenge to the decision to issue all the leases in accord with the Forest Service's plan, the Sierra Club sought declaratory and injunctive relief * * *. The Sierra Club argued that leasing land within the Palisades without preparing an EIS violated NEPA. The federal defendants responded that because of the finding of "no significant impact" contained in the Environmental Assessment, it was not necessary to prepare an EIS.

The district court upheld the finding of "no significant impact" and the decision to lease without preparing an EIS. The court based its decision upon the conclusion that the lease stipulations were valid and that the government could thereby "preclude any development under the leases." The court granted the federal defendants' motion for summary judgment, stating that "[t]he stipulations included in the leases * * * will effectively insure that the environment will not be significantly affected until further analysis pursuant to NEPA."

The Sierra Club appeals only that portion of the district court's judgment which involves lands leased *without* a No Surface Occupancy Stipulation. The Sierra Club concedes that the Department retains the authority to preclude all surface disturbing activities on land leased with a NSO Stipulation until further site-specific environmental studies are made. By retaining this authority, the Department has insured that no significant environmental impacts can occur from the act of leasing lands subject to the NSO Stipulation.

Approximately 80% of the Palisades was designated as highly environmentally sensitive and, therefore, leased *with* the NSO Stipulation. Only the remainder, approximately 28,000 acres, is at issue in this appeal. As to this smaller area, the Sierra Club contends that the Department cannot *preclude* surface disturbing activities, including drilling, on lands leased without the NSO Stipulation. The Department has only retained, Sierra Club asserts, the authority to "condition" surface disturbing activities in an effort to "mitigate" any environmental harm which might result from the activities. Thus, *some* surface disturbing activities may result from the act of issuing leases without NSO Stipulations on lands within the 28,000 acres. Appellant asserts, therefore, that the finding of "no significant impact" and the decision not to prepare an EIS, insofar as land leased within this smaller area is concerned, was improper. Because on these leases the Secretary cannot *preclude* surface disturbing activity, including drilling, the Sierra Club argues that the decision to lease is itself the point of irreversible, irretrievable commitment of resources—the point at which NEPA mandates that an environmental impact statement be prepared. We agree.

III

* * *

An agency's finding of "no significant impact" and consequent decision not to prepare an EIS can only be overturned if the decision was arbitrary, capricious, or an abuse of discretion. Cabinet Mountains Wilderness v. Peterson, 685 F.2d 678, 681 (D.C.Cir.1982). Judicial review of an agency's finding of "no significant impact" is not, however, merely perfunctory as the court must insure that the agency took a "hard look" at the environmental consequences of its decision. Kleppe v. Sierra Club, 427 U.S. 390, 410 n. 21 (1976).

Cases in this circuit have employed a four-part test to scrutinize an agency's finding of "no significant impact." The court ascertains

(1) whether the agency took a "hard look" at the problem;

(2) whether the agency identified the relevant areas of environmental concern;

(3) as to the problems studied and identified, whether the agency made a convincing case that the impact was insignificant; and

(4) if there was an impact of true significance, whether the agency convincingly established that changes in the project sufficiently reduced it to a minimum.

Cabinet Mountains Wilderness, supra, 685 F.2d at 682. Applying the foregoing test to this agency decision, we are satisfied that the agency has taken the requisite "hard look" and has "identified the relevant areas of environmental concern." However, in our opinion, the finding that "no significant impact" will occur as a result of granting leases *without* an NSO Stipulation is not supportable on this record.

The finding of "no significant impact" is premised upon the conclusion that the lease stipulations will prevent any significant environmental impacts until a site-specific plan for exploration and development is submitted by the lessee. At that time, the federal appellees explain, an appropriate environmental analysis, either an Environmental Assessment or an EIS, will be prepared. In bifurcating its environmental analysis, however, the agency has taken a foreshortened view of the impacts which could result from the act of *leasing.* The agency has essentially assumed that leasing is a discrete transaction which will not result in any "physical or biological impacts." The Environmental Assessment concludes

that there will be no significant adverse effects on the human environment due to oil and gas lease issuance. Therefore, no environmental impact statement will be prepared. The determination was based upon consideration of the following factors * * * (a) few issued leases result in active exploration operations and still fewer result in discovery or production of oil or gas; (b) the act of issuing a lease involves no physical or biological impacts; (c) the cumulative environmental effect of lease issuance on an area-wide basis is very small; (d) effects of lease activities once permitted will be mitigated to protect areas of critical environmental concern by appropriate stipulations including no-surface occupancy; (e) if unacceptable environmental impacts cannot be corrected, activities will not be permitted; and (f) the action will not have a significant effect on the human environment.

The conclusion that no significant impact will occur is improperly based on a prophecy that exploration activity on these lands will be insignificant and generally fruitless.

While it may well be true that the majority of these leases will never reach the drilling stage and that the environmental impacts of exploration are dependent upon the nature of the activity, nevertheless NEPA requires that federal agencies determine at the outset whether their major actions can result in "significant" environmental impacts. Here, the Forest Service concluded that any impacts which might result from the act of leasing would either be insignificant or, if significant, could be mitigated by exercising the controls provided in the lease stipulations.

Even assuming, *arguendo,* that all lease stipulations are fully enforceable, once the land is leased the Department no longer has the authority to *preclude* surface disturbing activities even if the environmental impact of such activity is significant. The Department can only impose "mitigation" measures upon a lessee who pursues surface disturbing exploration and/or drilling activities. None of the stipulations expressly provides that the Department or the Forest Service can *prevent* a lessee from conducting surface disturbing activities.[7] Thus, with respect to the smaller area with which we are here concerned, the decision to allow surface disturbing activities has been made at the *leasing stage* and, under NEPA, this is the point at which the environmental impacts of such activities must be evaluated.

NEPA requires an agency to evaluate the environmental effects of its action at the point of commitment. The purpose of an EIS is to insure that the agency considers all possible courses of action and assesses the environmental consequences of each proposed action. The

---

7. * * * In response to the court's question as to whether the agency could refuse to approve a lessee's plan to build an access road (a surface disturbing activity) during exploration, counsel for the government stated:

There's a very fine line between preclusion and strict control. The agency has retained strict control. They have the authority. They have the right to put certain conditions on road building.

[The government has] never contended that we could preclude all exploration and all development in these non-highly sensitive areas.

Furthermore, counsel for the Sierra Club asserted without contradiction that the government could not *deny* an application for a permit to drill, but could only enforce the lease stipulations to control and/or mitigate any environmental damage which result from the drilling.

* * *

EIS is a decision-making tool intended to "insure that * * * environmental amenities and values may be given appropriate consideration in decisionmaking * * *." 42 U.S.C. § 4332(2)(B). Therefore, the appropriate time for preparing an EIS is *prior* to a decision, when the decisionmaker retains a maximum range of options. * * * On the facts of this case, that "critical time," insofar as lands leased without a NSO Stipulation are concerned, occurred at the point of leasing.

Notwithstanding the assurance that a later site-specific environmental analysis will be made, in issuing these leases the Department made an irrevocable commitment to allow *some* surface disturbing activities, including drilling and roadbuilding. While theoretically the proposed two-stage environmental analysis may be acceptable, in this situation the Department has not complied with NEPA because it has sanctioned activities which have the potential for disturbing the environment without fully assessing the possible environmental consequences.

The Department asserts that it cannot accurately evaluate the consequences of drilling and other surface disturbing activities until site-specific plans are submitted. If, however, the Department is in fact concerned that it cannot foresee and evaluate the environmental consequences of leasing without site-specific proposals, then it may delay preparation of an EIS provided that it reserves both the authority to *preclude* all activities pending submission of site-specific proposals and the authority to *prevent* proposed activities if the environmental consequences are unacceptable. If the Department chooses not to retain the authority to *preclude* all surface disturbing activities, then an EIS assessing the full environmental consequences of leasing must be prepared at the point of commitment—when the leases are issued. The Department can decide, in the first instance, by which route it will proceed.

* * *

Because we find that the Department did not comply with the requirements of the National Environmental Policy Act when it leased the 28,000 acres of non-highly environmentally sensitive lands within the Palisades, we reverse the judgment of the district court and remand the case for further proceedings not inconsistent with this opinion.

CONNER v. BURFORD
United States District Court, District of Montana, 1985.
605 F.Supp. 107, appeal pending.

HATFIELD, District Judge.

* * *

Plaintiffs ask the court to declare unlawful the decisions by the Chief of the Forest Service, the Director of the Bureau of Land Management and the Secretary of the Interior to deny plaintiffs' protests and appeals against the issuance of oil and gas leases in the Flathead and the Gallatin National Forests. Plaintiffs contend that defendants violated NEPA by failing to prepare and consider environmental impact statements ("EIS") prior to making decisions which will significantly affect the environments of the forests in question. Further, plaintiffs claim violations of the Endangered Species Act by defendants in failing to sufficiently consult with the United States Fish and Wildlife Service before taking such action. The court is asked to set aside the agency actions as being not in accordance with the above cited law. * * * Additionally, plaintiffs ask the court to enjoin the issuance of any more leases until the agencies comply with NEPA and ESA.

The federal defendants assert they complied with NEPA and ESA by conducting environmental assessments ("EA's"), obtaining biological opinions, and establishing variously applied stipulations, including a No Surface Occupancy Stipulation ("NSO"), in the leases which render the environmental impact and the danger to threatened and endangered species at the leasing stage insignificant. Defendants assert that subsequent analysis and decision-making, based on individual proposals for further activity on the leases, will continue to uphold the mandates of NEPA and ESA.

I. THE NATIONAL ENVIRONMENTAL POLICY ACT

The NEPA challenge requires the court to determine whether the federal defendants initiated a "major federal action significantly affecting the quality of the human environment. * * *" 42 U.S.C. § 4332(2)(C). If the defendants did initiate such an action, they are required to prepare and analyze an environmental impact statement before deciding what action should occur. The standard of review of the decision to forego an EIS at the leasing stage is that of reasonableness. Foundation for North American Wild Sheep v. U.S., 681 F.2d 1172 (9th Cir.1982). This court finds that the decision to forego an EIS was unreasonable. The EIS should serve to assist agencies in making decisions before any significant steps are taken which may damage the environment. * * *

In this case, the leasing stage is the first stage of a number of successive steps which clearly meet the "significant effect" criterion to trigger an EIS.

Leases without NSO stipulations have been set aside for lack of NEPA compliance because they fail to ensure that environmentally damaging activity can be precluded by the federal agency. Sierra Club v. Peterson, 717 F.2d 1409 (D.C.Cir.1983). This ruling clearly extends to leases which allow surface occupancy on any part of the leased acreage.

This court must therefore consider the reasonableness of leasing lands which have an NSO stipulation covering the entire area of the lease. To use the NSO stipulation as a mechanism to avoid an EIS when issuing numerous leases on potential wilderness areas circumvents the spirit of NEPA. Subsequent site-specific analysis, prompted by a proposal from a lessee of one tract, may result in a finding of no significant environmental impact. Obviously, a comprehensive analysis of cumulative impacts of several oil and gas development activities must be done before any single activity can proceed. Otherwise, a piecemeal invasion of the forests would occur, followed by the realization of a significant and irreversible impact.

The issuance of a lease with an NSO stipulation does not guarantee an EIS before any development would occur. In fact, NSO stipulations can be modified or removed without an EIS. This court is compelled to set aside the decisions of defendants to lease without preparation of an EIS. The idea of possible site specific assessments in the future does not comply with the objective of protecting the area for possible wilderness designation.

> *   *   * the promise of a site specific EIS in the future is meaningless if later analysis cannot consider wilderness preservation as an alternative to development.

California v. Block, 690 F.2d 753 at 762–763 (9th Cir.1982).

*   *   *

NOTES

1. Does the result in *Copper Valley* follow from the statute? Is there any real difference between conditions and suspensions? Is it relevant that no oil leasing on the delicate Alaskan tundra was even contemplated by Congress when it amended § 39 of the Mineral Leasing Act in 1932? Does the decision automatically extend all oil and gas leases in Alaska with similar conditions? How should the Department respond to future dilatory drillers?

2. Do the lease stipulations in Sierra Club v. Peterson extend the leases to the extent they prohibit operations during the primary lease term? Are the two decisions fundamentally at odds over the degree of property right awarded a lessee from the government? If *Conner* is followed, what does the lessee get and what discretion does the Department have?

3. *Gulf Oil,* discussed in *Copper Valley,* supra at note 8, has been distinguished in later cases, e.g., County of Suffolk v. Secretary of the Interior, 562 F.2d 1368 (2d Cir.1977). Is *Conner* contra to Sierra Club v. Peterson (or to Village of False Pass v. Clark, 733 F.2d 605 (9th Cir. 1984), supra at page 343)?

4. See generally Nelson, Oil and Gas Leasing on Forest Service Lands: A Question of NEPA Compliance, 3 Pub.Land L.Rev. 1 (1982); Pring, "Power to Spare": Conditioning Federal Resource Leases to Protect Social, Economic, and Environmental Values, 14 Nat. Resources Law. 305 (1981); Comment, The Interrelationships of the Mineral Leasing Act, the Wilderness Act, and the Endangered Species Act: A Conflict in Search of Resolution, 12 Envtl.L. 363 (1982); Axline, Private Rights to Public Oil and Gas, 19 Ida.L.Rev. 505 (1983).

5. Retroactive application of new BLM oil leasing regulations apparently depends on the validity of the old regulation. The court in Stewart Capital Corp. v. Andrus, 701 F.2d 846 (10th Cir.1983), overturned a BLM attempt to deny a lease on the basis of a new regulation;

the same court earlier had allowed a retroactive application of a new regulation when the regulation it replaced was void. Enfield v. Kleppe, 566 F.2d 1139 (10th Cir.1977). For cases dealing with extensions where no lease restrictions existed, see *Enfield,* supra; Peabody Coal Co. v. Andrus, 477 F.Supp. 120 (D.Wyo.1979) ("valid existing right" entitles applicant to an extension); California Portland Cement Co., 40 IBLA 339 (1979).

6. The character of the land sought to be leased may also cause the Department to condition or deny leases. As to lands within the National Wildlife Refuge System, see Udall v. Tallman, 380 U.S. 1 (1965), supra at page 288. See also Duesing v. Udall, 350 F.2d 748 (D.C. Cir.1965), cert. denied, 383 U.S. 912 (1966). Lease applications can be rejected when the land is being studied for inclusion in the Wild and Scenic Rivers System, Rosita Trujillo, 21 IBLA 289 (1975). Such rejections—or suspensions—act as partial withdrawals in fact if not in theory and can be accomplished without a formal public land order. Rowe v. United States, 464 F.Supp. 1060 (D. Alaska 1979). See also Burglin v. Morton, 527 F.2d 486, 488 (9th Cir.1976), upholding the Secretary's discretionary refusal to lease on the ground that the Mineral Leasing Act, 30 U.S.C.A. § 226(a), provides that oil and gas deposits "may" be leased. But see Mountain States Legal Found. v. Andrus, 499 F.Supp. 383 (D.Wyo.1980), supra at page 272.

NOTE: OIL AND GAS LEASING ON THE OFFSHORE LANDS

Many observers had long assumed that states owned the submerged lands beyond the tide lines. See Pollard v. Hagan, 44 U.S. (3 How.) 212 (1845), supra at page 72. In 1947, however, the Supreme Court ruled that the offshore lands were and always had been owned by the United States as an aspect of the national character of the federal government. United States v. California, 332 U.S. 19 (1947). In United States v. Maine, 420 U.S. 515 (1975), the Court confirmed that its ruling applied to all coastal states, including the original thirteen.

In the meantime, Congress in 1953 had ceded to the coastal states ownership of the seabed and resources in the three-mile belt seaward of the coast. Submerged Lands Act of 1953, 43 U.S.C.A. §§ 1301–15. A few months later, Congress asserted federal control, but not ownership, over the outer continental shelf and its resources beyond the three-mile limit. Outer Continental Shelf Lands Act of 1953 (OCSLA), as amended, 43 U.S.C.A. §§ 1331–43. A different kind of jurisdiction was asserted by the United States in the Fishery Conservation and Management Act of 1976 (FCMA), 16 U.S.C.A. §§ 1801–82: while not claiming ownership per se, Congress decreed that all living resources between three and 200 miles offshore, with a few exceptions, could be harvested or exploited only in accordance with a new federal-regional regulatory scheme. Congress has also cooperated with and financed states in imposing controls over developments in and around the tidal margins by means of the Coastal Zone Management Act (CZMA), 16 U.S.C.A.

§§ 1451–64. The Marine Sanctuaries Act (MSA), 16 U.S.C.A. §§ 1431–34, and other more limited and specialized legislation, such as the Marine Mammal Protection Act of 1972 (MMPA), 16 U.S.C.A. §§ 1361 et seq., and the Deepwater Port Act of 1974 (DPA), 33 U.S.C.A. §§ 1501 et seq., also aim at more protection of the coastal and marine environments.

The various forms of jurisdiction and sovereignty that the United States has asserted over offshore areas do not amount to a claim of fee ownership of the underlying lands nor to an assumption of complete, exclusive jurisdiction over the waters. See, for example, Treasure Salvors, Inc. v. The Unidentified Wrecked and Abandoned Sailing Vessel, believed to be the *Nuestra Senora de Atocha,* 569 F.2d 330 (5th Cir.1978), a contest between the government and treasure seekers who had located an ancient Spanish galleon off Florida. The United States claimed that both OCSLA and the 1906 Antiquities Act, 16 U.S.C.A. §§ 431–33, vested ownership of the sunken ship in it. The court held that, as the latter statute applied only to lands owned or controlled by the federal government, it did not support the government's claim because OCSLA asserted only jurisdiction, not ownership.

There is no coherent overall management system for the federal offshore lands. Navigation is subject to Coast Guard regulations, and obstructions to navigable capacity must be cleared by the Army Corps of Engineers. Offshore oil and gas can be leased by Interior's BLM in cooperation with the U.S. Geological Survey. Fisheries resources are largely within the ambit of the National Oceanic and Atmospheric Administration, currently located in the Department of Commerce, but inshore fisheries of the same fish plus other species are subject to regulation by the Fish and Wildlife Service. Most offshore regulation is also affected by international treaty obligations. See Montgomery, The Multiple Use Concept as the Basis for a New Outer Continental Shelf Legislative Policy, 62 Ky.L.J. 327 (1974) (advocating a uniform, multiple-use management approach). In United States v. Alexander, 602 F.2d 1228 (5th Cir.1979), the court held that the Secretary of the Interior lacked power under OSCLA to promulgate regulations for the conservation of resources such as coral which would apply to anyone other than oil and gas lessees.

Although oil and gas leasing on the outer continental shelf has been the focal point of controversy in recent years, deep-water off-shore drilling is a comparatively new phenomenon. Platforms had been constructed in shallow water off Santa Barbara as early as 1897, but it was not until mid-century that any platform was constructed out of sight of land. Since then, rapid technological advances have enabled drillers to prospect and produce in such hostile environments as the North Sea. But advanced technology inevitably produces new risks and unanticipated side effects: more difficult operations raise the possibility, even likelihood, of major blowouts and oil spills that will threaten ecologically fragile coastal areas and other offshore resources.

The Secretary of the Interior's belated efforts to impose more stringent regulation on drilling in the Santa Barbara Channel after the notorious blowout of 1969 can be traced in Gulf Oil Corp. v. Morton, 493 F.2d 141 (9th Cir.1973); Union Oil Co. v. Morton, 512 F.2d 743 (9th Cir. 1975); and Sun Oil Co. v. United States, 572 F.2d 786 (Ct.Cl.1978). See also California ex rel. Younger v. Morton, 404 F.Supp. 26 (C.D.Cal. 1975); Southern California Ass'n of Governments v. Kleppe, 413 F.Supp. 563 (D.D.C.1976). These cases in essence established that the Secretary could suspend operations in the interest of conservation, broadly defined, but only for a limited time, otherwise the lessee's interest would be "taken."

The Santa Barbara incident illustrated the lack of foresight on the part of leasing authorities, and it helped give birth to NEPA, which has since become the main ground of litigation for plaintiffs opposed to further lease sales. See, e.g., NRDC v. Morton, 458 F.2d 827 (D.C.Cir. 1972); County of Suffolk v. Secretary of the Interior, 562 F.2d 1368 (2d Cir.1977). Resource conflicts on the frontier of the public lands raise issues conceptually similar to those common on the onshore lands. The St. Georges Bank lease sale off Massachusetts posed the spectre of oil spills harming the fishery in the area, said to be one of the world's most productive. See Commonwealth of Massachusetts v. Andrus, 594 F.2d 872 (1st Cir.1979); Massachusetts v. Watt, 716 F.2d 946 (1st Cir.1983). Several lease sales allegedly threatened to harm endangered species of whales and other wildlife. See, e.g., North Slope Borough v. Andrus, 642 F.2d 589 (D.C.Cir.1980); Village of False Pass v. Clark, 733 F.2d 605 (9th Cir.1984), supra at page 343. A potential conflict between oil and gas drilling and subsistence hunting and fishing rights was the focus of conflict in Village of Gambell v. Hodel, 774 F.2d 1414 (9th Cir.1985). See generally P. Swan, OCEAN OIL AND GAS DRILLING (1979).

The leading OCSLA case is Secretary of the Interior v. California, 464 U.S. 312 (1984), discussed in False Pass, supra at page 343. It concerned a new twist on the age-old problem of state vs. federal law. The Supreme Court held that the contested lease sales did not "directly affect" California's coastal zone and thus, under the Coastal Zone Management Act, 16 U.S.C.A. §§ 1451–64, the Secretary did not have to find the lease sales "consistent" with California's coastal zone plan. As the False Pass court emphasized, however, the main message of Secretary is that the lessee does not purchase any rights to explore for or produce oil and gas; instead, the federal offshore oil and gas lessee obtains only the exclusive procedural right to seek further administrative permission to conduct developmental activities. These offshore oil and gas leasing developments have provided models for resolution of onshore mineral leasing disputes. See, e.g., Copper Valley Mach. Works, Inc. v. Andrus, 653 F.2d 595 (D.C.Cir.1981), supra at page 556; cf. Sierra Club v. Peterson, 717 F.2d 1409 (D.C.Cir.1983), supra at page 562.

The structure of the offshore oil and gas leasing program is also subject to judicial review. In Watt v. Energy Action Educational

Foundation, 454 U.S. 151 (1981), the Court upheld secretarial discretion to determine the form and requirements of systems for bidding on offshore leases. Secretary Watt, as one of his first acts in office, announced his intention to lease one billion acres, almost the entire outer continental shelf, during the next five years. This is more than twenty-five times the acreage leased during the preceding thirty years. Shortly thereafter, the District of Columbia Circuit Court of Appeals struck down and remanded the more modest program of accelerated leasing proposed by Secretary Andrus. California v. Watt, 668 F.2d 1290 (D.C.Cir.1981). News reports concerning the 1983 Environmental Protection Agency scandals—alleging that an EPA official suppressed a report on prospective environmental damage—were influential in another judge's decision to halt further Georges Bank leasing. See Conservation Law Found. v. Watt, 560 F.Supp. 561 (D.Mass.1983), aff'd, 716 F.2d 946 (1st Cir.1983). Congress too has impeded mineral development by imposing moratoria on leasing in certain areas. Politics, litigation, and the removal of Mr. Watt apparently will ensure that his ambitious leasing program will not be carried out in this century.

The literature on offshore oil and gas leasing—and on outer continental shelf activities generally—is burgeoning. See, e.g., Kirwan, Application of the Clean Air Act to Petroleum Operations on the Outer Continental Shelf, 13 Nat. Resources Law. 411 (1980); Deller, Federalism and Offshore Oil and Gas Leasing: Must Federal Tract Selections and Lease Stipulations be Consistent with State Coastal Zone Management Programs?, 14 U.C.D.L.Rev. 105 (1980); Martin, Deep-Sea Mining Between Convention and National Legislation, 10 Ocean.Dev. & Int'l L. 175 (1981); Schenke, The Marine Protection, Research, and Sanctuaries Act: The Conflict Between Marine Protection and Oil and Gas Development, 18 Hous.L.Rev. 987 (1981); Ball, Good Old American Permits: Madisonian Federalism on the Territorial Sea and Continental Shelf, 12 Envtl.L. 623 (1982); Kevin, The Legal Framework for Energy Development on the Outer Continental Shelf, 10 UCLA-Alaska L.Rev. 143 (1981).

5. GEOTHERMAL ENERGY

OWEN OLPIN & A. DAN TARLOCK, WATER THAT IS NOT WATER *
XIII Land & Water L.Rev. 391 (1978).

Geothermal energy is energy derived from heat beneath the earth's surface. Sub-surface temperatures are primarily controlled by the conductive flow of heat through solid rocks, the convective flow in circulating fluids, and by mass transfer in magma. "Where conduction is dominant, temperatures increase continuously with depth, but not at a constant gradient. The important interrelations are those between thermal gradient, heat flow, and thermal conductivity. * * *" At

* Reprinted by permission of LAND AND WATER LAW REVIEW, Owen Olpin and A. Dan Tarlock.

the present time we are unable to exploit commercially the heat produced by the thermal gradient. Instead, commercial interest centers on the exploitation of hydrothermal convective systems, geothermal anomalies. The Far West is an area of recent volcanism, high regional conductive heat flow and a relatively shallow mantle. As a result there are a number of "hot spots" where high silica varieties of volcanic rock at shallow levels below the crust can sustain high-temperature convection systems for a prolonged period of time.
* * *

According to the United States Geological Survey, there are three known vapor-dominated fields with commercial potential in the United States, but there are many potential liquid-dominated fields. The Geysers in Northern California is already in commercial production and is thought to have a potential of 1000–2000 megawatts. The other two potential steam fields are located in Yellowstone and Mount Lassen Volcanic National Parks. Geothermal leasing is prohibited in national parks so liquid-dominated systems will be the source of commercial geothermal production in the foreseeable future.
* * *

The federal government and thirteen Western states have some form of regulation of geothermal resources to promote their development. Prior to the passage of federal and state legislation there was great uncertainty as to the proper legal classification of geothermal resources, and it was argued that this uncertainty impeded their development. When the federal government and the states turned to the problem of encouraging and regulating geothermal development, most legislation followed either the mineral or water model, although some states classified geothermal resources as *sui generis* to no particular end. Most federal and state geothermal legislation was enacted between 1967 and 1975. * * *

The federal government and most of the states define geothermal resources but not in a manner designed to integrate them into the property rights regimes of other resources. Rather, geothermal resources have been defined almost exclusively for the purposes of assigning them to an existing regulatory regime to provide a definition of a leaseable resource. * * *
* * *

Because the object of state legislation has been to promote geothermal resource development, it is not surprising that many states elected, directly or indirectly, to treat geothermal resources as minerals. Mineral resources are generally owned by the state, the discoverer, or the overlying landowner, and the classification of geothermal resources as minerals has the advantage of assigning them to a regime where exclusive property rights are recognized. Water, on the other hand, is said to be the property of the state in the sense that the state, in its sovereign capacity, is trustee for the public. Private rights can be obtained but usually by a valid appropriation. If geothermal resources are classified as water, the overlying landowner would have no right to lease them if he had not perfected an appropriation. State "ownership" could be used by the state to assert an exclusive right to lease all non-federally-owned geothermal resources and to collect royalties from state lessees. There have been vigorous constituencies within each state to treat geothermal as water, so states sometimes have dual classifications embedded within their statutes even when the resource is formally defined as a mineral or at least not water.

* * *

The other competing definition of the resource is the federal definition [in 30 U.S.C.A. §§ 1001(a) and (b)] of the Geothermal Steam Act of 1970 * * *:

> Geothermal steam and associated geothermal resources means (i) all products of geothermal processes, embracing indigenous steam, hot water and hot brines; (ii) steam and other gases, hot water and hot brines resulting from water, gas, or other fluids artificially introduced into geothermal formations; (iii) heat or other associated energy found in geothermal formations; and (iv) any by-product derived from them.

* * *

> "Byproduct" means any minerals (exclusive of oil, hydrocarbon gas, and helium) which are found in solution or in association with geothermal steam and which have a value of less than 75 per centum of the value of the geothermal steam or are not, because of quantity, quality, or technical difficulties in extraction and production, of sufficient value to warrant extraction and production by themselves.

NOTES

1. The controversy over whether to classify the geothermal resource as a mineral or as water, or to adopt a sui generis approach, is complicated in that geothermal fluids also can be used for agricultural and domestic uses, for heat, or even for their dissolved mineral or gas content, or inherent chemical constituents. See Olpin, Tarlock & Austin, Geothermal Development and Western Water Law, 1979 Utah L.Rev. 773, 781–83. Those authors argue that the analogy to ground water is inappropriate and that overlying property owners should have the right to exploit the geothermal resource; there should be a rebuttable "presumption of noninterference" that geothermal deposits are separate from freshwater aquifers. They believe that such an approach will encourage development while also allowing holders of vested property rights in ground water to hold geothermal developers liable for interference if in fact the two resources are physically interconnected and damage occurs. But see Sato & Crocker, Property Rights to Geothermal Resources, 6 Ecology L.Q. 250 (1977). Cf. Werner, Geothermal Leasing, 54 Ore.L.Rev. 623 (1975).

In many ways, exploitation of the geothermal resource more resembles the development of hydroelectric generating facilities than mining or mineral leasing. The object is energy, not fuel or mineral extraction, and the medium is water convection, not particular substances.

The federal mode of allocation and regulation under the Geothermal Steam Act of 1970, 30 U.S.C.A. §§ 1101–26, however, proceeds in a fashion more similar to the system for leasable minerals than to that for hydroelectric licensing. Compare Udall v. FPC, 387 U.S. 428 (1967).

2. Interesting questions are bound to arise when the same land may be valuable for leasable or hardrock minerals as well as geothermal resources. As between conflicting claims to leasable and hardrock minerals, the Multiple Mineral Development Act of 1954, 30 U.S.C.A. §§ 521–31, established an uneasy compromise aimed at compatible dual development. See Osborne v. Hammit, 377 F.Supp. 977 (D.Nev.1964). Cf. Kanab Uranium Corp. v. Consolidated Uranium Mines, 229 F.2d 434 (10th Cir.1955). If a geothermal area has been the subject of a prior valid mineral claim or lease, the Geothermal Steam Act provides that qualified applicants can convert their claims, permits, and leases into geothermal leases. 30 U.S.C.A. § 1003(a). In Getty Oil Co. v. Andrus, 607 F.2d 253 (9th Cir.1979), a disappointed geothermal lease applicant lost its challenge to an award of a grandfathered placer mining lease on the same plot. The plaintiff in Crownite Corp. v. Watt, 752 F.2d 1500 (9th Cir.1985), also was denied a leasehold conversion, because it had not invested in geothermal investigations.

3. Geothermal resources may be hydrologically interconnected with other water systems. If groundwater or geothermal development off federal lands threatened to interfere with the federal geothermal resource, could the United States assert a reserved water right to the geothermal water? Three withdrawals might be read to establish federal reserved rights: a 1930 executive order withdrawing hot springs from development; a 1967 withdrawal from mining of all lands valuable for geothermal steam development; and the Geothermal Act of 1970. Olpin, Tarlock & Austin, supra, 1979 Utah L.Rev. at 808 n. 100. The Court in United States v. City and County of Denver, 656 P.2d 1 (Colo.1982), supra at page 390, held that reservation as a hot spring did not reserve the water for geothermal energy production.

Proposed geothermal development in a national forest adjacent to Yellowstone has been opposed by Park Service officials because of concern that geothermal wells would adversely affect Yellowstone's "fragile plumbing." Does the United States have a reserved right, with a priority date of 1872, when Yellowstone National Park was established? Compare Cappaert v. United States, 426 U.S. 128 (1976). Should federal geothermal lessees be able to claim federal reserved rights? Olpin, Tarlock & Austin, supra, at 807–10, argue that they should not and that the federal government should be required to condemn competing state water rights since favoring a lessee of federal lands over purely private rights is not essential to the purpose of the federal reservation. See United States v. New Mexico, 438 U.S. 696 (1978), supra at page 376.

4. The Geothermal Steam Act excludes from leasing national parks, recreation areas, and wildlife refuges, but it does not mention wilderness areas. 30 U.S.C.A. § 1014(c). The Wilderness Act preceded

the geothermal legislation and it is naturally silent on geothermal leasing. Whether such leasing is allowed in wilderness areas is not an idle inquiry: there are known geothermal resources in wilderness areas and developers have applied, unsuccessfully, for leases. The question of compatibility is examined in Comment, Geothermal Leasing in Wilderness Areas, 6 Envt'l L. 489 (1975).

5. There is more literature than litigation on acquisitions of geothermal rights on the public lands. See Sato & Crocker, Property Rights to Geothermal Resources, 6 Ecology L.Q. 250 (1977); Davis, Geothermal Resources for the Small Developer, 3 J.Contemp.L. 241 (1977); Root, Contents of a Geothermal Lease: Some Suggestions, 8 Nat.Res.Law. 659 (1976); Aidlin, Geothermal Resources—A Program to Accelerate Development and Use of a Promising Supplemental Energy Source, 7 Nat.Res.Law. 655 (1974); Bjorge, The Development of Geothermal Resources and the 1970 Geothermal Steam Act—Law in Search of Definition, 46 Colo.L.Rev. 1 (1974); Olpin, The Law of Geothermal Resources, 14 Rocky Mtn.Min.L.Inst. 123 (1968). The first issue of XIII Land & Water L.Rev. (1977) contains 15 articles on geothermal resource development. NEPA compliance was upheld in regard to geothermal leasing in Oregon's Alvord Desert in Sierra Club v. Hathaway, 579 F.2d 1162 (9th Cir.1978).

6. MINERAL LEASING: A MODEL FOR HARDROCK MINING REFORM?

Abolition or reform of the location system for hardrock minerals has long been advocated; most reformers urge the adoption of all or some of the elements of the leasing system to replace it. They argue that the location system provides no return to the federal government, does not allow for sufficient environmental regulation, is not subject to comprehensive planning, does not require development, does not eliminate stale claims, and does not discourage fraud. The offer of free minerals and free land are seen as unnecessary subsidies. It is, they claim, an outdated law that has seen its day. See generally J. Leshy, THE MINING LAW OF 1872: A STUDY IN PERPETUAL MOTION (1986); Anderson, Federal Mineral Policy: The General Mining Law of 1872, 16 Nat.Res.J. 601 (1976); and Hagenstein, Changing An Anachronism: Congress and the General Mining Law of 1872, 13 Nat.Res.J. 480 (1973). The arguments pro and con are collected in Senzel, Revision of the Mining Act of 1872, Study for the Senate Comm. on Energy and Nat. Res., 95th Cong., 1st Sess. (1977).

Advocates of the location system argue that the incentives in the 1872 Act are necessary to promote mineral production. Hardrock minerals typically are found in irregular occurrences of unknown extent; putting shackles on the right of self-initiation would discourage exploration. Furthermore, they contend, development and production are more complex and expensive than that required for leasable minerals; "due diligence" requirements are therefore inappropriate. A regulatory system and comprehensive bidding would work to the disadvantage of the small miner, the "bird dog" who often makes the discovery and then transfers the claim to a larger company. As a philosophical matter, it is said that the General Mining Law helped open the West and now stands as one of the Nation's last bastions of free enterprise. See generally Sherwood, Mining Law at the Crossroads, VI Land & Water L.Rev. 161 (1970); Hansen, Why a Location System for Hard Minerals?, 13 Rocky Mtn.Min.L.Inst. 1 (1967).

The Public Land Law Review Commission recommended that the public lands should stay open for self-initiated prospecting, but that an easily obtained permit should be required after preliminary exploration; the miner then would have to pay rent or royalties, and would receive a patent only to the minerals, not the surface. Public Land Review Commission, ONE–THIRD OF OUR NATION'S LAND 121–30 (1970). In 1977, President Carter proposed legislation, since abandoned, to adopt a leasing system. See H.R. 9292, 95th Cong., 1st Sess. (1977). A 1979 Comptroller General's Report took a middle ground, concluding that an all-leasing system would operate to the disadvantage of small miners and that administrative costs would be "exorbitant" in comparison with the return. Comptroller General, REPORT TO THE CONGRESS: MINING LAW REFORM AND BALANCED RESOURCE MANAGEMENT (1979).

What are the specific differences between the two systems? What elements of the leasing system, if any, should be applied to hardrock mineral exploration? Has the point been reached where a wholesale switch to the leasing system has been rendered unnecessary by reforms in the classic location system? Is it significant that there has been no public sentiment for a return to the location system for coal, oil, or gas?

C. FEDERAL RESERVED MINERAL RIGHTS

In addition to the minerals underlying the federal lands and the continental shelf, the United States also owns or controls the rights to minerals under another 60-odd million acres of private property. Land patents issued under a few federal disposition statutes reserved to the United States all or some mineral rights. As a result, on five percent of the land in the eleven western states and Alaska, the surface estate of the private land owners is servient to the federal subsurface mineral interests.

Federal reservations of minerals vary according to the statute in question and the provisions included in the patent issued by administrative officers. The railroad land grant statutes decreed that mineral lands could not be selected by the grantees; in lieu selection was allowed when minerals were known to exist under alternate sections proposed for selection. If, however, the selected land was later found to be mineral in character, the grant was not affected. Burke v. Southern Pac. Ry. Co., 234 U.S. 669 (1914). The first general reservation in favor of the United States was in the Coal Lands Act of 1909, 30 U.S.C.A. § 81, which required that coal would be reserved in subsequent agricultural patents. Then followed several mineral reservation acts including the Agricultural Entry Act of 1914, 30 U.S.C.A. §§ 121–23 (reservation of oil, gas, and other specified minerals) and the Stock-Raising Homestead Act of 1916, 43 U.S.C.A. §§ 291–301 (reservation of "coal and other minerals"). Over 32 million acres were patented under the 1916 Act. Some disposition acts allowed issuance of a patent without the mineral reservation if the land could be shown to be non-mineral in character; that kind of provision was of limited assistance to patentees because of the difficulty of proof. The Stock-Raising Homestead Act did not include such an option. Further, some statutes made varying provision for the posting of a bond for protection of permanent improvements if mineral entry were made, and for compensation for any damages to crops or grazing land. The courts, however, have not been generous to surface owners in awarding damages. See Kinney-Coastal Oil Co. v. Kieffer, 277 U.S. 488 (1928); Holbrook v. Continental Oil Co., 73 Wyo. 321, 278 P.2d 798 (1955); Stocker, Protection For Surface Owners of Federally Reserved Mineral Lands, 2 UCLA-Alas.L.Rev. 171 (1973). The individual statutes are discussed in Carpenter, Severed Minerals as a Deterrent to Land Development, 51 Den.L.J. 1 (1974).

Obviously, the inconsistent statutory pattern can create serious problems for farmers, ranchers, and even suburbanites in areas that were once farm or grazing land:

* * *

Pausing for a moment, one can envisage an entire residential subdivision on Stock-Raising Homestead Act lands. There are many such developments today, and more are being built. In come the prospectors, bearing not only their 1916 picks and shovels, but their modern day bulldozers and draglines. They may not harm the permanent improvements; that much is clear. And they must make restitution for damages to "crops." So they set to work in the lawn areas of the suburb, and perhaps also in the parks, greenbelts, and other "unimproved" areas. On at least one occasion such activity, or the threat of it, has prompted Congress to take the unusual step of specific legislation withdrawing the subject minerals from location and leasing.

Carpenter, supra, 51 Den.L.J. at 24–25. See also Brimmer, The Rancher's Subservient Surface Estate, V Land & Water L.Rev. 49, 50 (1970).

UNITED STATES v. UNION PACIFIC R.R. CO.
Supreme Court of the United States, 1957.
353 U.S. 112.

Mr. Justice DOUGLAS delivered the opinion of the Court.

This is an action brought in the District Court by the United States to enjoin the Union Pacific Railroad Company from drilling for oil and gas on "the right of way" granted it by § 2 of the Act of July 1, 1862, 12 Stat. 489, 491, for the construction of a railroad and telegraph line. The claim of the United States is that "the right of way" granted by the Act is not a grant that includes mineral rights. * * *

The "right of way" which was granted by § 2 of the Act was "for the construction of said railroad and telegraph line." As an aid to the construction of the railroad, "every alternate section of public land" on each side of the road was also granted. § 3. Section 3 further provided "That all mineral lands shall be excepted from the operation *of this act* * * *." (Italics added.)

* * *

It would also seem from the words of the Act that, whatever rights may have been included in "the right of way," mineral rights were excepted by reason of the proviso in § 3 excepting "mineral lands." The exception of "mineral lands," as applied to the right of way, may have been an inept way of reserving mineral rights. The right of way certainly could not be expected to take all the detours that might be necessary were it to avoid all lands containing minerals. But that the proviso applies to § 2 as well as to § 3 is plain. While the grant of "the right of way" is made by § 2 and the exception of "mineral lands" is contained in § 3, the exception extends not merely to § 3 but to the entire Act.

It is said that the exception in § 3 was in terms made applicable to the entire Act merely to leave no doubt that land grants to other railroads, contained in §§ 9, 13 and 14 of the Act, were not to include "mineral lands." But the exception in § 3 is not limited merely to a few enumerated sections any more than it is limited to § 3. The proviso makes sense if it is read to reserve all mineral rights under the right of way, as well as to reserve mineral lands in the alternate sections of public land granted in aid of the construction of the road. Indeed, we can see no other way to construe it if it is to apply, as it does, not merely to § 3, but to the entire Act, including § 2 which grants the right of way.

The reservation of the mineral resources of these public lands for the United States was in keeping with the policy of the times. The gold strike in California in 1848 made the entire country conscious of the potential riches underlying the western part of the public domain. The method of asserting federal control over mineral lands was not finally settled until the Act of July 26, 1866, 14 Stat. 251, prescribed the procedure by which mineral lands could be acquired. But meanwhile— from 1849 to 1866—the federal policy was clear. As the Court said in Ivanhoe Mining Co. v. Keystone Consolidated Mining Co., 102 U.S. 167, the federal policy during this interim period was to reserve mineral lands, not to grant them. The policy was found to be so "uniform" in this interim period that the Court, in construing an 1853 Act governing public lands in California, held that a grant to California did not include mineral lands, although they were not specifically excepted.

The case is much stronger here, for "mineral lands" are specifically reserved. It is, therefore, wholly in keeping with the federal policy that prevailed in 1862, when the present right of way was granted, to construe "mineral lands" to include mineral resources under the right of way. For it was the mineral riches in the public domain that

Congress sedulously sought to preserve until it formulated the special procedure by which all mineral resources were to be administered. In United States v. Sweet, 245 U.S. 563, Mr. Justice Van Devanter, our foremost expert on public land law, discussed this policy at length and cited in support of this federal policy the very Act we have under consideration in the present case. We would have to forget history and read legislation with a jaundiced eye to hold that when Congress granted only a right of way and reserved all "mineral lands" it nonetheless endowed the railroad with the untold riches underlying the right of way. Such a construction would run counter to the established rule that land grants are construed favorably to the Government, that nothing passes except what is conveyed in clear language, and that if there are doubts they are resolved for the Government, not against it. These are the reasons we construe "mineral lands" as used in § 3 of the Act to include mineral rights in the right of way granted by § 2.

The system which Congress set up to effectuate its policy of reserving mineral resources in the alternate sections of public land granted by § 3 was by way of an administrative determination, prior to issuance of a patent, of the mineral or nonmineral character of the lands. Patents were not issued to land administratively determined to constitute mineral lands. And, the administrative determination was final. Burke v. Southern Pacific R. Co., 234 U.S. 669. Such an administrative system was obviously inappropriate to the right of way granted by § 2. The land needed for the right of way was not acquired through the issuance of a patent, but by the filing of a map showing the definite location of the road, followed by its actual construction.

* * *

Because the administrative system, by which the exception of "mineral lands" was administered in relation to the lands granted by § 3, is inappropriate to the right of way granted by § 2, we are urged to conclude that the exception of "mineral lands" in § 3 was not intended to apply to § 2. But, construing the grant in § 2 favorably to the Government, as we must, we cannot conclude that Congress meant the policy it expressed, by excepting "mineral lands" in § 3, to be inapplicable to § 2 in the face of its admonition that the exception is applicable to the entire Act. Nor can we conclude that, because the administrative system, by which mineral resources in the grant of land under § 3 were reserved, was inappropriate to § 2, Congress did not intend appropriate measures to reserve minerals under the right of way granted by § 2. We cannot assume that the Thirty-seventh Congress was profligate in the face of its express purpose to reserve mineral lands.

To be sure, Congress later on designed a more precise and articulated system for the separation of subsoil rights from the other rights in the western lands. See, for example, the Act of March 3, 1909, 35 Stat. 844, 30 U.S.C.A. § 81. It would have been better draftsmanship, if, in referring to § 2, Congress had used the words "mineral rights" instead of "mineral lands." Yet it will not do for us to tell the Congress "We see what you were driving at but you did not use choice words to describe your purpose."

*   *   *

Great reliance is placed on Great Northern R. Co. v. United States, 315 U.S. 262, for the view that the grant of a right of way in the year 1862 was the grant of a fee interest. In that case we noted that a great shift in congressional policy occurred in 1871: that after that period only an easement for railroad purposes was granted, while prior thereto a right of way with alternate sections of public land along the right of way had been granted. In the latter connection we said, "When Congress made outright grants to a railroad of alternate sections of public lands along the right of way, there is little reason to suppose that it intended to give only an easement in the right of way granted in the same act." But we had no occasion to consider in the Great Northern case the grant of a right of way with the reservation of "mineral lands." The suggestion that a right of way may at times be more than an easement was made in an effort to distinguish the earlier "limited fee" cases. To complete the distinction, Mr. Justice Murphy with his usual discernment added, "None of the cases involved the problem of rights to subsurface oil and minerals."

The latter statement goes to the heart of the matter. There are no precedents which give the mineral rights to the owner of the right of way as against the United States. We would make a violent break with history if we construed the Act of 1862 to give such a bounty. We would, indeed, violate the language of the Act itself. To repeat, we cannot read "mineral lands" in § 3 as inapplicable to the right of way granted by § 2 and still be faithful to the standard which governs the construction of a statute that grants a part of the public domain to private interests.

*   *   *

Mr. Justice FRANKFURTER, whom Mr. Justice BURTON and Mr. Justice HARLAN join, dissenting.

*   *   *

In a line of decisions going back to St. Joseph & D.C. Railroad Co. v. Baldwin, 103 U.S. 426, this Court has consistently recognized that the Act of 1862 and its companion Acts gave to the railroads the entire present interest in the public lands allocated to them for a right of way.

*   *   *

*   *   *

This consistent course of construction is bound to give the impression that Congress was rather free-handed in its disposition of the public domain ninety years and more ago. And so it was. We said in Great Northern R. Co. v. United States, 315 U.S. 262, 273:

> "Beginning in 1850 Congress embarked on a policy of subsidizing railroad construction by lavish grants from the public domain. *   *   *"

During this period "there passed into the hands of western railroad promoters and builders a total of 158,293,000 acres, an area almost equaling that of the New England states, New York and Pennsylvania combined." * * *

This "lavish" congressional policy brought results, for in 1869 the much desired transcontinental route was completed. With realization of the goal, however, the mood of uncritical enthusiasm toward railroad enterprises began to veer. * * *

The General Right of Way Statute of 1875, 18 Stat. 482, 43 U.S.C.A. § 934 et seq., was significantly different from the Act of 1862 and its companions. It granted the railroads neither alternate sections of public land nor direct financial subsidy. * * *

Detailed study of the history of federal right of way legislation led us to conclude in the Great Northern case that a right of way granted by the 1875 Act was an easement and not a limited fee. From this it followed that the railroad had no right to the underlying minerals. Basic to the Court's characterization of the right of way as an easement was the recognition that "Since it [the General Right of Way Statute] was a product of the sharp change in Congressional policy with respect to railroad grants after 1871, it is improbable that Congress intended by it to grant more than a right of passage, let alone mineral riches." * * *

* * *

It is said that § 3's exception of "mineral lands" from its grant of alternate sections of public land may also have been an inept way of reserving the rights to the minerals underneath the right of way granted by § 2. This attributes to the 1862 Congress a desire to convey only the fee interest in the surface. Such attribution contradicts the scheme both of the Act itself and of subsequent public land legislation. The Act plainly contemplated, and was interpreted to provide, an administrative determination of the mineral character of the land granted by § 3 prior to the issuance of the patent. Land found to be "mineral" was not patented but was replaced by other land. If minerals were subsequently found on patented land, they were held to belong to the railroad, and not to the Government, Burke v. Southern Pacific R. Co., 234 U.S. 669, notwithstanding § 3's exception of "mineral lands." Since this exception did not reserve the right to minerals in land that passed under § 3 itself, it is difficult to understand how it could have reserved the right to minerals in land that passed as a right of way under § 2. The fact that the exception was made applicable to the entire Act may be explained without distorting § 2. Sections 9, 13 and 14 of the 1862 Act authorize construction of certain other railroads "upon the same terms and conditions in all respects as are provided in this act for the construction of the" Union Pacific. By amending § 3's proviso to cover the entire Act, Congress left no doubt that the exception of mineral lands also applied to the land grants made to those other railroads.

If Congress had reserved the right to the minerals underlying the thousands of miles of right of way granted by its transcontinental railroad legislation of 1862, 1864 and 1866, it might reasonably be expected that it would have manifested some consciousness of this reservation when, in the Act of July 26, 1866, 14 Stat. 251, it finally settled upon a general federal mineral policy. * * *

This failure of Congress to provide for disposition of the minerals lying beneath the right of way may not fairly be attributed to oversight. No congressional policy of reserving mineral rights from public land grants was in existence in the 1860's. Such a policy did not begin to evolve until the last decade of the nineteenth century, when Congress reserved the mineral rights to certain lands sold to cities for cemetery and park purposes, 26 Stat. 502, 43 U.S.C.A. § 729. And it received its first general application in the Act of March 3, 1909, 35 Stat. 844, 30 U.S.C.A. § 81, which permitted agricultural entrymen on public lands subsequently found to contain coal deposits to obtain patents to the land, with coal rights reserved to the United States. * * * In 1910 the Act was extended to provide for issuance of patents to lands that were known to contain coal at the time they were settled for agricultural purposes. 30 U.S.C.A. § 83 et seq. The Surface Patent Act of 1914, 30 U.S.C.A. § 121 et seq., applied the statutory policy with respect to coal to all withdrawn non-metallic mineral lands. This Act has been described as "perhaps the first serious attempt, not locally limited, to sever the surface title from the mineral title in disposing of the public domain." Morrison and De Soto, Oil and Gas Rights, 508. It was followed by the Stock-Raising Homestead Act of 1916, 43 U.S.C.A. § 291 et seq., which reserved all minerals to the United States while providing for the granting of surface patents. Significantly, in the comprehensive Mineral Leasing Act of 1920, Congress did what it had not done in 1866—it set forth a plan for the development of the minerals that the 1909–1916 Acts had reserved for the United States.

* * *

NOTES

1. It was often said of Justice Douglas that he was a better judge than historian.

2. Should the opinion in *Leo Sheep,* supra at page 112, have discussed the principal case?

3. As between a homestead and railroad right-of-way through it, which has the non-mineral subsurface estate? See Energy Transp. Systems, Inc. v. Union Pacific R.R. Co., 435 F.Supp. 313 (D.Wyo.1977), aff'd, 606 F.2d 934 (10th Cir.1979) (coal slurry pipeline; homestead wins).

4. If Burke v. Southern Pacific R. Co., discussed in the principal case, had been decided after *Union Pacific,* would it have come out the same way?

UNITED STATES v. UNION OIL CO. OF CALIFORNIA

United States Court of Appeals, Ninth Circuit, 1977.
549 F.2d 1271.
Cert. denied sub nom. Ottoboni v. United States, 435 U.S. 911 (1978).

BROWNING, Circuit Judge.

This is a quiet title action brought by the Attorney General of the United States pursuant to * * * the Geothermal Steam Act of 1970, 30 U.S.C.A. § 1020(b), to determine whether the mineral reservation in patents issued under the Stock-Raising Homestead Act of 1916, 43 U.S.C.A. § 291 et seq., reserved to the United States geothermal resources underlying the patented lands. The district court held that it did not. We reverse.

Various elements cooperate to produce geothermal power accessible for use on the surface of the earth. Magma or molten rock from the core of the earth intrudes into the earth's crust. The magma heats porous rock containing water. The water in turn is heated to temperatures as high as 500 degrees Fahrenheit. As the heated water rises to the surface through a natural vent, or well, it flashes into steam.

Geothermal steam is used to produce electricity by turning generators. In recommending passage of the Geothermal Steam Act of 1970, the Interior and Insular Affairs Committee of the House reported: "[G]eothermal power stands out as a potentially invaluable untapped natural resource. It becomes particularly attractive in this age of growing consciousness of environmental hazards and increasing awareness of the necessity to develop new resources to help meet the Nation's future energy requirements. The Nation's geothermal resources promise to be a relatively pollution-free source of energy, and their development should be encouraged." H.R.Rep. No. 91–1544, 91st Cong., 2d Sess., reprinted at 3 U.S.Code Cong. & Admin.News 5113, 5115 (1970).

Appellees are owners, or lessees of owners, of lands in an area known as "The Geysers" in Sonoma County, California. Beneath the lands are sources of geothermal steam. Appellees have developed or seek to develop wells to produce the steam for use in generating electricity. The lands were public lands, patented under the Stock-Raising Homestead Act. All patents issued under that Act are "subject to and contain a reservation to the United States of all the coal and other minerals in the lands so entered and patented, together with the right to prospect for, mine, and remove the same." Section 9 of Act, 43 U.S.C.A. § 299. The patents involved in this case contain a reservation utilizing the words of the statute. The question is whether the right to produce the geothermal steam passed to the patentees or was retained by the United States under this reservation.

There is no specific reference to geothermal steam and associated resources in the language of the Act or in its legislative history. The reason is evident. Although steam from underground sources was used to generate electricity at the Larderello Field in Italy as early as 1904, the commercial potential of this resource was not generally appreciated in this country for another half century. No geothermal power plants went into production in the United States until 1960. Congress was not aware of geothermal power when it enacted the Stock-Raising Homestead Act in 1916; it had no specific intention either to reserve geothermal resources or to pass title to them.

It does not necessarily follow that title to geothermal resources passes to homesteader-patentees under the Act. The Act reserves to the United States "all the coal and other minerals." All of the elements of a geothermal system—magma, porous rock strata, even water itself [5]—may be classified as "minerals." When Congress decided in 1970 to remove the issue from controversy as to future grants of public lands, it found it unnecessary to alter the language of existing statutory "mineral" reservations. It simply provided that such reservations "shall hereafter be deemed to embrace geothermal steam and associated geothermal resources." Geothermal Steam Act of 1970, 30 U.S.C.A. § 1024.[6] Thus, the words of the mineral reservation in the Stock-Raising Homestead Act clearly are capable of bearing a meaning that encompasses geothermal resources.

The substantial question is whether it would further Congress's purposes to interpret the words as carrying this meaning. * * *

* * *

[The opinion recounted movements in the early 20th century to conserve mineral resources. In 1909, Congress enacted the Coal Lands Act, 30 U.S.C.A. § 81, providing for a reservation of coal, followed by statutes reserving all minerals.]

We turn to the statutory language. The title of the Act—"The Stock-Raising Homestead Act"—reflects the nature of the intended grant. The Act applies only to areas designated by the Secretary of Interior as "stock-raising lands"; that is, "lands the surface of which is, in his opinion, chiefly valuable for grazing and raising forage crops, do not contain merchantable timber, are not susceptible of irrigation from any known source of water supply, and are of such character that six hundred and forty acres are reasonably required for the support of a

---

5. * * *

No one contends that water cannot be classified as mineral. Appellees argue only that the water should not be included in the term "minerals" in this statutory setting. This is basically a question of legislative intent, dealt with in detail later in the text. To the extent that the argument rests on the meaning of the word itself, however, the government is entitled to have the ambiguity resolved in its favor under "the established rule that land grants are construed favorably to the Government, that nothing passes except what is conveyed in clear language, and that if there are doubts they are resolved for the Government, not against it." United States v. Union Pac. R.R., 353 U.S. 112, 116 (1957).

Appellees argue that the term "minerals" is to be given the meaning it had in the mining industry at the time the Act was adopted, and that this understanding excluded water. This is a minority rule, United States v. Isbell Constr. Co., 78 Interior Dec. 385, 390–91 (1971), even as applied to permit conveyances. 1 American Law of Mining § 3.26, at 551–53 (1976).

6. Members of the Subcommittee on Mines and Mining of the House Committee on Interior and Insular Affairs went to some lengths to make it clear that whether the term "minerals" as used in prior legislation included geothermal resources was a question for the courts, on which the official position of the 89th Congress was one of neutrality. * * *

family. * * *" 43 U.S.C.A. § 292. The entryman is required to make improvements to increase the value of the entry "for stock-raising purposes." Id. § 293. On the other hand, "all entries made and patents issued" under the Act must "contain a reservation to the United States of all the coal and other minerals in the lands," and such deposits "shall be subject to disposal by the United States in accordance with the provisions of the coal and mineral land laws." Id. § 299. The subsurface estate is dominant; the interest of the homesteader is subject to the right of the owner of reserved mineral deposits to "reenter and occupy so much of the surface" as reasonably necessary to remove the minerals, on payment of damages to crops or improvements. Id.

The same themes are explicit in the reports of the House and Senate committees. * * *

* * *

Appellees argue that references in the Congressional Record to homesteaders' drilling wells and developing springs indicate that Congress intended title to underground water to pass to patentees under the Act. These references are not to the development of geothermal resources. As we have seen, commercial development of such resources was not contemplated in this country when the Stock-Raising Homestead Act was passed. Moreover, in context, the references are to the development of a source of fresh water for the use of livestock, not to the tapping of underground sources of energy for use in generating electricity.[18]

This review of the legislative history demonstrates that the purposes of the Act were to provide homesteaders with a portion of the public domain sufficient to enable them to support their families by raising livestock, and to reserve unrelated subsurface resources, particularly energy sources, for separate disposition. This is not to say that patentees under the Act were granted no more than a permit to graze livestock, as under the Taylor-Grazing Act, 43 U.S.C.A. §§ 315 et seq. To the contrary, a patentee under the Stock-Raising Homestead Act receives title to all rights in the land not reserved. It does mean, however, that the mineral reservation is to be read broadly in light of the agricultural purpose of the grant itself, and in light of Congress's equally clear purpose to retain subsurface resources, particularly sources of energy, for separate disposition and development in the public interest. Geothermal resources contribute nothing to the capacity of the surface estate to sustain livestock. They are depletable subsurface reservoirs of energy, akin to deposits of coal and oil, which it was the particular objective of the reservation clause to retain in public ownership. The purposes of the Act will be served by including

18. "A fair and reasonable [ruling] would hold the surface owner to be entitled only to fresh waters that reasonably serve and give value to his surface ownership. Salt water and geothermal steam and brines should be held the property of the mineral owner who owns such substances as oil, gas and coal, since the functions and values are more closely related. Geothermal steam is a source of energy just as fossil fuels such as oil, gas and coal are sources of energy." Olpin, The Law of Geothermal Resources, 14 Rocky Mountain Mineral Law Institute 123, 140–41 (1968).

geothermal resources in the statute's reservation of "all the coal and other minerals." Since the words employed are broad enough to encompass this result, the Act should be so interpreted.

* * *

Whether the United States is estopped from interfering with the rights of private lessees without compensating them for any losses they may sustain will be open on remand.

Reversed and remanded.

NOTES

1. The court says the "substantial question is whether it would further Congress's purposes to interpret the words as carrying this meaning." Would the *Leo Sheep* Court, supra at page 112, have defined the issue in that manner? Is not the more precise and accurate question whether Congress in 1916 intended to include geothermal resources within the category of "minerals" reserved? Is there any doubt what the answer to the latter question is?

2. Did the meaning of "mineral" change appreciably between 1872 and 1916? Compare Andrus v. Charlestone Stone Products, 436 U.S. 604 (1978), supra at page 421.

3. Private parties with reserved minerals under federal lands are in a less advantageous position than the federal lessees in *Union Oil*. The Surface Mining Control and Reclamation Act, 30 U.S.C.A. § 1272(e)(2) provides, with certain exceptions, that no coal mining which disturbs the surface "shall be permitted * * * on any federal lands within the boundaries of any national forest"—subject to "valid existing rights." In Ramex Mining Corp. v. Watt, 753 F.2d 521 (6th Cir. 1985), plaintiff first argued that the underlying mineral estate it had leased was not on federal lands because the mineral estate itself was private property; the court abruptly rejected that claim. The court also found that the area in question was a national forest, even though it had not been formally set aside as such, because all land purchased under the Weeks Act of 1911, 16 U.S.C.A. § 521, automatically became national forest land. Plaintiff's taking claim was deemed not ripe for decision.

4. The Stock-Raising and Homestead Act of 1916 authorized the use of the private surface estate by the United States to "occupy so much of the surface * * * as may be required for all purposes reasonably incident to the mining or removal of the [reserved] coal or other minerals." 43 U.S.C.A. § 299. The Geothermal Steam Act of 1970 allows federal "utilization" of the private surface estate over reserved geothermal resources. 30 U.S.C.A. § 1002. Did the United States also reserve a right to construct a geothermal power plant at the mining site without compensating the surface owner? In Occidental Geothermal, Inc. v. Simmons, 543 F.Supp. 870 (N.D.Cal.1982), the court found that patents issued under the 1916 Act included a reservation of geothermal plant siting rights. Analysis of the unique nature of the energy source revealed that "removal" and "utilization" are inextrica-

bly linked; when steam is transported long distances, it loses its heat and pressure. In contrast, other energy minerals, such as oil and coal, may be mined, removed, and subsequently utilized at remote sites.

WATT v. WESTERN NUCLEAR, INC.
Supreme Court of the United States, 1983.
462 U.S. 36.

Justice MARSHALL delivered the opinion of the Court.

The Stock-Raising Homestead Act of 1916, the last of the great homestead acts, provided for the settlement of homesteads on lands the surface of which was "chiefly valuable for grazing and raising crops" and "not susceptible of irrigation from any known source of water supply." 43 U.S.C. § 292. Congress reserved to the United States title to "all the coal and other minerals" in lands patented under the Act. 43 U.S.C. § 299. The question presented by this case is whether gravel found on lands patented under the Act is a mineral reserved to the United States.

I

* * *

On February 4, 1926, the United States conveyed a tract of land near Jeffrey City, Wyoming, to respondent's predecessor-in-interest. The land was conveyed by Patent No. 974013 issued pursuant to the SRHA. As required by the Act, the patent reserved to the United States "all the coal and other minerals" in the land.

In March 1975 respondent Western Nuclear, Inc. (Western Nuclear), acquired a fee interest in a portion of the land covered by the 1926 patent. Western Nuclear is a mining company that has been involved in the mining and milling of uranium ore in and around Jeffrey City since the early 1950's. In its commercial operations Western Nuclear uses gravel for such purposes as paving and surfacing roads and shoring the shaft of its uranium mine. In view of the expense of having gravel hauled in from other towns, the company decided that it would be economical to obtain a local source of the material, and it acquired the land in question so that it could extract gravel from an open pit on the premises.

After acquiring the land, respondent obtained * * * a [state] permit authorizing it to extract gravel from the pit located on the land. Respondent proceeded to remove some 43,000 cubic yards of gravel.
* * *

On November 3, 1975, the Wyoming State Office of the BLM served Western Nuclear with a notice that the extraction and removal of the gravel constituted a trespass against the United States[.] * * *
* * *

After a hearing, the BLM determined that Western Nuclear had committed an unintentional trespass. Using a royalty rate of 30¢ per cubic yard, the BLM ruled that Western Nuclear was liable to the United States for $13,000 in damages for the gravel removed from the site. [The IBLA affirmed. The District Court affirmed the administrative ruling.]

Respondent appealed to the Court of Appeals for the Tenth Circuit. That court reversed, holding that the gravel extracted by Western Nuclear did not constitute a mineral reserved to the United States under the SRHA. * * *

In view of the importance of the case to the administration of the more than 33 million acres of land patented under the SRHA, we granted certiorari. We now reverse.

II

As this Court observed in a case decided before the SRHA was enacted, the word "minerals" is "used in so many senses, dependent upon the context, that the ordinary definitions of the dictionary throw but little light upon its signification in a given case." Northern Pacific R. Co. v. Soderberg, 188 U.S. 526, 530 (1903). In the broad sense of the word, there is no doubt that gravel is a mineral, for it is plainly not animal or vegetable. But "the scientific division of all matter into the animal, vegetable or mineral kingdom would be absurd as applied to a grant of lands, since all lands belong to the mineral kingdom." While it may be necessary that a substance be inorganic to qualify as a mineral under the SRHA, it cannot be sufficient. If all lands were considered "minerals" under the SRHA, the owner of the surface estate would be left with nothing.

Although the word "minerals" in the SRHA therefore cannot be understood to include all inorganic substances, gravel would also be included under certain narrower definitions of the word. For example, if the term "minerals" were understood in "its ordinary and common meaning [as] a comprehensive term including every description of stone and rock deposit, whether containing metallic or non-metallic substances," gravel would be included. If, however, the word "minerals" were understood to include only inorganic substances having a definite chemical composition, gravel would not be included.

The various definitions of the term "minerals" serve only to exclude substances that are not minerals under any common definition of that word. Cf. United States v. Toole, 224 F.Supp. 440 (D.Mont.1963) (deposits of peat and peat moss, substances which are high in organic content, do not constitute mineral deposits for purposes of the general mining laws). For a substance to be a mineral reserved under the SRHA, it must not only be a mineral within one or more familiar definitions of that term, as is gravel, but also the type of mineral that Congress intended to reserve to the United States in lands patented under the SRHA. Cf. Andrus v. Charlestone Stone Products Co., 436 U.S. 604 (1978).[5]

5. The specific listing of coal in the reservation clause of the SRHA sheds no   light on what Congress meant by the term "minerals." * * *

The legal understanding of the term "minerals" prevailing in 1916 does not indicate whether Congress intended the mineral reservation in the SRHA to encompass gravel. On the one hand, in Northern Pacific R. Co. v. Soderberg, supra, this Court had quoted with approval a statement in an English case that "everything except the mere surface, which is used for agricultural purposes; anything beyond that which is useful for any purpose whatever, whether it is *gravel,* marble, fire clay, or the like, comes within the word 'mineral' when there is a reservation of the mines and minerals from a grant of land." 188 U.S., at 536 (emphasis added), quoting Midland Ry. v. Checkley, L.R. 4 Eq. 19, 25 (1867). * * *

On the other hand, in 1910 the Secretary of the Interior rejected an attempt to cancel a homestead entry made on land alleged to be chiefly valuable for the gravel and sand located thereon. Zimmerman v. Brunson, 39 Pub.Lands Dec. 310, overruled, Layman v. Ellis, 52 Pub. Lands Dec. 714 (1929). Zimmerman claimed that gravel and sand found on the property could be used for building purposes and that the property therefore constituted mineral land, not homestead land. In refusing to cancel Brunson's homestead entry, the Secretary explained that "deposits of sand and gravel occur with considerable frequency in the public domain." He concluded that land containing deposits of gravel and sand useful for building purposes was not mineral land beyond the reach of the homestead laws, except in cases in which the deposits "possess a peculiar property or characteristic giving them a special value."

Respondent errs in relying on *Zimmerman* as evidence that Congress could not have intended the term "minerals" to encompass gravel. Although the legal understanding of a word prevailing at the time it is included in a statute is a relevant factor to consider in determining the meaning that the legislature ascribed to the word, we do not see how any inference can be drawn that the 64th Congress understood the term "minerals" to exclude gravel. It is most unlikely that many members of Congress were aware of the ruling in *Zimmerman,* which was never tested in the courts and was not mentioned in the reports or debates on the SRHA. Even if Congress had been aware of *Zimmerman,* there would be no reason to conclude that it approved of the Secretary's ruling in that case rather than this Court's opinion in *Soderberg,* which adopted a broad definition of the term "mineral" and quoted with approval a statement that gravel is a mineral.

III

Although neither the dictionary nor the legal understanding of the term "minerals" that prevailed in 1916 sheds much light on the question before us, the purposes of the SRHA strongly support the Government's contention that the mineral reservation in the Act includes gravel. As explained below, Congress' underlying purpose in severing the surface estate from the mineral estate was to facilitate the concurrent development of both surface and subsurface resources.

While Congress expected that homesteaders would use the surface of SRHA lands for stockraising and raising crops, it sought to ensure that valuable subsurface resources would remain subject to disposition by the United States, under the general mining laws or otherwise, to persons interested in exploiting them. It did not wish to entrust the development of subsurface resources to ranchers and farmers. Since Congress could not have expected that stock-raising and raising crops would entail the extraction of gravel deposits from the land, the congressional purpose of facilitating the concurrent development of both surface and subsurface resources is best served by construing the mineral reservation to encompass gravel.

A

*   *   *

Congress' purpose in severing the surface estate from the mineral estate was to encourage the concurrent development of both the surface and subsurface of SRHA lands. The Act was designed to supply "a method for the *joint use* of the land by the entryman of the surface thereof and the person who shall acquire from the United States the right to prospect, enter, extract and remove all minerals that may underlie such lands." H.R.Rep. No. 35, 64th Cong., 1st Sess. 4, 18 (1916) (emphasis added). The Department of the Interior had advised Congress that the law would "induce the entry of lands in those mountainous regions where deposits of mineral are known to exist or are likely to be found," and that the mineral reservation was necessary because the issuance of "unconditional patents for these comparatively large entries under the homestead laws might withdraw immense areas from prospecting and mineral development."

To preserve incentives for the discovery and exploitation of minerals in SRHA lands, Congress reserved "all the coal and other minerals" *   *   *. Congress plainly contemplated that mineral deposits on SRHA lands would be subject to location under the mining laws, and the Department of the Interior has consistently permitted prospectors to make entries under the mining laws on SRHA lands.

B

Since Congress intended to facilitate development of both surface and subsurface resources, the determination of whether a particular substance is included in the surface estate or the mineral estate should be made in light of the use of the surface estate that Congress contemplated. As the Court of Appeals for the Ninth Circuit noted in United States v. Union Oil Co. of California, 549 F.2d 1271 (CA9) cert. denied, 434 U.S. 930 (1977), "[t]he agricultural purpose indicates the nature of the grant Congress intended to provide homesteaders via the Act."
*   *   *

*   *   *

Given Congress' understanding that the surface of SRHA lands would be used for ranching and farming, we interpret the mineral reservation in the Act to include substances that are mineral in character (i.e., that are inorganic), that can be removed from the soil, that can be used for commercial purposes, and that there is no reason to suppose were intended to be included in the surface estate. This interpretation of the mineral reservation best serves the congressional purpose of encouraging the concurrent development of both surface and subsurface resources, for ranching and farming do not ordinarily entail the extraction of mineral substances that can be taken from the soil and that have separate value.[14]

Whatever the precise scope of the mineral reservation may be, we are convinced that it includes gravel. * * * Insofar as the purposes of the SRHA are concerned, it is irrelevant that gravel is not metalliferous and does not have a definite chemical composition. What is significant is that gravel can be taken from the soil and used for commercial purposes.

* * *

IV

* * *

It is also highly pertinent that federal administrative and judicial decisions over the past half-century have consistently recognized that gravel deposits could be located under the general mining laws until common varieties of gravel were prospectively removed from the purview of those laws by the Surface Resources Act of 1955, 30 U.S.C. § 611. While this Court has never had occasion to decide the appropriate treatment of gravel under the mining laws, the Court did note in United States v. Coleman, 390 U.S. 599, 604 (1968), that gravel deposits had "served as a basis for claims to land patents" under the mining laws prior to the enactment of the Surface Resources Act of 1955.

The treatment of gravel as a mineral under the general mining laws suggests that gravel should be similarly treated under the SRHA, for Congress clearly contemplated that mineral deposits in SRHA lands would be subject to location under the mining laws, and the applicable regulations have consistently permitted such location. * * *

14. * * *

We note that this case does not raise the question whether the owner of the surface estate may use a reserved mineral to the extent necessary to carry out ranching and farming activities successfully. Although a literal reading of the SRHA would suggest that any use of a reserved mineral is a trespass against the United States, one of the overriding purposes of the Act was to permit settlers to establish and maintain successful homesteads. There is force to the argument that this purpose would be defeated if the owner of the surface estate

were unable to use reserved minerals even where such use was essential for stock-raising and raising crops.

* * *

In this case, however, respondent cannot rely on any right it may have to use reserved minerals to the extent necessary for ranching and farming purposes, since it plainly did not use the gravel it extracted for any such purpose. The gravel was used for commercial operations that were in no way connected with any ranching or farming activity.

V

Finally, the conclusion that gravel is a mineral reserved to the United States in lands patented under the SRHA is buttressed by "the established rule that land grants are construed favorably to the Government, that nothing passes except what is conveyed in clear language, and that if there are doubts they are resolved for the Government, not against it." United States v. Union Pacific R. Co., 353 U.S. 112, 116 (1957). In the present case this principle applies with particular force, because the legislative history of the SRHA reveals Congress' understanding that the mineral reservation would "limit the operation of this bill *strictly to the surface of the lands.*" H.R.Rep. No. 35, supra, at 18 (emphasis added). In view of the purposes of the SRHA and the treatment of gravel under other federal statutes concerning minerals, we would have to turn the principle of construction in favor of the sovereign on its head to conclude that gravel is not a mineral within the meaning of the Act.

VI

For the foregoing reasons, we hold that gravel is a mineral reserved to the United States in lands patented under the SRHA. Accordingly, the judgment of the Court of Appeals is

Reversed.

Justice POWELL, with whom Justice REHNQUIST, Justice STEVENS, and Justice O'CONNOR join, dissenting.

The Court's opinion may have a far-reaching effect on patentees of, and particularly successors in title to, the 33,000,000 acres of land patented under the Stock-Raising Homestead Act of 1916 (SRHA). * * * [T]he Court adopts a new definition of the statutory term: "[T]he Act [includes] substances that are mineral in character (i.e., that are inorganic), that can be removed from the soil, that can be used for commercial purposes, and that there is no reason to suppose were intended to be included in the surface estate."

This definition compounds, rather than clarifies, the ambiguity inherent in the term "minerals." It raises more questions than it answers. Under the Court's definition, it is arguable that all gravel falls within the mineral reservation. This goes beyond the Government's position that gravel *deposits* become reserved only when susceptible to commercial exploitation. And what about sand, clay, and peat? As I read the Court's opinion it could leave Western homesteaders with the dubious assurance that only the dirt itself could not be claimed by the Government. It is not easy to believe that Congress intended this result.

* * *

In 1916, when the SRHA was enacted, the Department of the Interior's rule for what it considered to be a "valuable mineral deposit" as those terms are used under the general mining laws was clear[.] [The opinion discussed several Interior Department interpretations.]

* * *

Thus, it was beyond question, when SRHA was adopted in 1916, that the Department had ruled consistently that gravel was not a mineral under the general mining laws. The legislative history is silent on exactly how Congress defined "mineral," but it is equally clear that the Department participated actively in drafting SRHA and in advising Congress. In light of this record, one must conclude the Congress intended the term "minerals" in the new statute to have the meaning so recently and consistently given it by the Department in construing and applying the general mining laws. As it was the agency authorized to implement the SRHA, its contemporaneous construction should be persuasive as to congressional intention. This Court previously had accorded this respect to the Department of Interior.

* * *

III

* * *

The first attempt by the Department of Interior to acquire ownership of gravel on SRHA lands did not occur until this case began in 1975. One would think it is now too late, after a half-century of inaction, for the Department to take action that raises serious questions as to the nature and extent of titles to lands granted under SRHA.[20] Owners of patented land are entitled to expect fairer treatment from their Government. In my view, the Department should be required to adhere to the clear intent of Congress at the time this legislation was adopted. I would affirm the judgment of the Court of Appeals.

Justice STEVENS, dissenting.

Whether gravel is a mineral within the meaning of the Stock-Raising Homestead Act of 1916 may be a matter of considerable importance in the semiarid lands of the West, but it is of much less importance to the rest of the Nation. For that reason, as well as those set forth at some length in my concurring opinion in Watt v. Alaska, 451 U.S. 259, 273 (1981), I believe the Court of Appeals should have been permitted to make the final decision upon the unique question of statutory construction presented by this case. Accordingly, while I join

---

20. The Department is in no position to adopt a new policy for land patents long granted. See Andrus v. Shell Oil Co., 446 U.S. 657 (1980). Its prior actions have caused the population generally, including respondent, to understand that gravel was not a reserved mineral. Cf. Western Nuclear, Inc. v. Andrus, 475 F.Supp. 654, 660 (Wyo.1979) ("Until [1975], it was the practice of the Wyoming Highway Department, construction companies, and the ranchers owning the surface estate to treat the gravel as part of the surface estate, the gravel being sold or used by the rancher with the approval of the [Bureau of Land Management]"). As Justice Rehnquist stated for the Court in Leo Sheep Co., supra:

"Generations of land patents have issued without any express reservation of the right now claimed by the Government. Nor has a similar right been asserted before. * * * This Court has traditionally recognized the special need for certainty and predictability where land titles are concerned, and we are unwilling to upset settled expectations. * * * "

Justice POWELL'S opinion explaining why the judgment of the Court of Appeals should be affirmed, I believe an even better disposition would have been simply to deny certiorari.

NOTES

1. Can gravel under a 1916 Act patent be used for ranching and farming purposes, as discussed in note 14 of the majority opinion? Would such an approach lead to multiplicitous litigation over various alleged ranching and farming purposes?

2. The Taylor Grazing Act authorized exchanges of lands to consolidate federal lands into manageable units, but the private party receives a patent of former public land reserving "all minerals to the United States." 43 U.S.C.A. § 315g(c) (repealed 1976). Should the Taylor Act be construed in the same manner as the Stock-Raising Homesteading Act? One author advances the proposition that it should not because the Taylor Act allows bilateral exchanges and is not an entry statute. Ames, The Expansion of Mineral Reservations in Federal Patents—The Taylor Grazing Act's Exchange Provisions, 6 J.Contemp.L. 93 (1979).

3. Congress in some instances has provided increased protection to surface owners. FLPMA allows future patents to be issued without reservations of minerals; it also permits present surface owners to apply for a complete patent, but they must pay fair market value for the minerals. In both cases, if mineral deposits are unknown, minerals will remain with the United States unless the BLM finds that the federal reservation "is interfering with or precluding appropriate non-mineral development of the land and that such development is a more beneficial use of the land than mineral development." 43 U.S.C.A. § 1719(b)(1). In SMCRA, Congress decided that the surface owner must give consent before the federal government can enter into a coal lease. 30 U.S.C.A. § 1304(c). The Solicitor's views of the surface owner consent provisions are set out in Krulitz, Management of Federal Coal Reserves, 24 Rocky Mtn.Min.L.Inst. 139, 179–85 (1978). On surface owner protection in lease provisions for other leasable minerals, see Office of Technology Assessment, MANAGEMENT OF FUEL AND NONFUEL MINERALS IN FEDERAL LAND 208–10 (R. Wright ed., 1979).

4. In practical terms, federal reserved mineral rights have caused less of a furor than might be expected. Private owners initially may not be pleased to find that their lands are subject to reservations, but most of them have received substantial prices from coal, oil, and other developers for selling out their interest. Such land acquisition costs are insignificant when valuable deposits are found.

The federal reservations include hardrock deposits as well, but prospectors do not do much digging around on farms, ranches, and backyards. This reason has to do in part with geography: valuable hardrock deposits are less likely to occur on the flat, low-lying agricultural and stock-raising land subject to the mineral reservations.

5.   United States v. Union Oil Co. (geothermal resources reserved) and United States v. Union Pacific R.R. Co. (oil and gas reserved) are two of the leading cases on the general subject of federal reserved rights.   Others are United States v. New Mexico, 438 U.S. 696 (1978), supra at page 376 (instream flow for recreation, wildlife, and aesthetic purposes held not reserved); and Leo Sheep v. United States, 440 U.S. 668 (1979), supra at page 112 (easement for public access for recreation purposes held not reserved).   Can those cases be reconciled?   Were the same or similar canons of construction applied in each case?   Is there a single rule that can, or should, be applied to all federal reserved rights cases?   Or is it preferable to approach the issue on an ad hoc basis, looking only at the specific statute in each case?   Would it be appropriate to utilize a single canon of construction to the effect that Congress is presumed to reserve such rights as are appropriate for the reasonable, long term protection and preservation of resources on the public lands?   Should wildlife, recreation, and preservation be considered as resources under such a formulation?   Compare United States v. Curtis-Nevada Mines, Inc., 611 F.2d 1277 (1980) supra at page 463 (Surface Resources Act of 1955 allows public access to unpatented claims located after 1955).   See generally Wilkinson, The Field of Public Land Law: Some Connecting Threads and Future Directions, 1 Pub.Land L.Rev. 1, 29–38 (1980).

Chapter Seven

THE TIMBER RESOURCE

More so than with any of the other "economic" resources, a regime of legal constraints on agency discretion is a newcomer to federal timber policy. The congressional directives were until recently thought plain by virtually everyone connected with federal timber management: the Forest Service was to harvest timber on the national forests in the manner that it thought best. In addition to a handful of minor timber management statutes, the major enactments were the Forest Reserves Amendment of 1891, 16 U.S.C.A. § 471 (repealed 1976), authorizing the President to set aside forest reserves; the Organic Act of 1897, 16 U.S.C.A. §§ 473–78, 479–82 (§ 476 repealed 1976), setting general guidelines for administering the forests; and the Multiple-Use, Sustained-Yield Act of 1960, 16 U.S.C.A. §§ 528–31. Each was deemed a grant of unfettered authority. Neither did the courts much intrude: Forest Service powers and discretion were routinely upheld in the few cases challenging them. E.g., Light v. United States, 220 U.S. 523 (1911), supra at page 137; Hi-Ridge Lumber Co. v. United States, 443 F.2d 452 (9th Cir.1971), infra at page 602. Timber litigation mostly was a miscellany of timber theft convictions and private contract disputes until 1970.

This historical autonomy was due in large part to the rich tradition in the Forest Service nurtured by Gifford Pinchot from the time he became the head of the Forestry Division in the Department of Agriculture in 1898. Though he originally had no trees to manage, Pinchot's brand of conservation and silviculture effectively became official federal policy in 1905 when the forest reserves were transferred from Interior to the Agriculture Department and the Forest Service was formally created to manage them. Even today, Pinchot's name is commonly invoked within the Forest Service and in congressional hearings.

The Forest Service unquestionably has gained its share of detractors since its early years, as annual harvests from the national forests increased during the New Deal and then shot up with the demands of the war effort and the post-World War II construction boom. The Service now concedes that it made serious professional and political misjudgments. Even so, most knowledgeable critics (from any direction) recognize that the agency's history and heritage have put it a cut above most federal bureaus. It has commonly been cited as a model of efficient, decentralized administration. Typical of mixed modern criticism are the comments of a writer for a Ralph Nader Task Force:

> Eyes drooping and fur falling out, Smokey the Bear spends his
> days lounging in the sun at the National Zoo in Washington,
> D.C. For twenty years, he and his Forest Service publicists

have alerted the American people to the wild beauty of the National Forests and to the need to protect them from human destruction. "Only *you* can prevent forest fires," Smokey warned, and visitors to the National Forests heeded his warning.

Smokey symbolized the Forest Service of old. In his day, forest rangers cared more about building new campsites, stocking remote lakes with fish, and preventing the public from burning down its wilderness playground than they did about filling ever larger timber harvesting quotas. Forest Service officials approached their jobs with a sometimes arrogant professionalism, but also with a love and respect for the forest. With flair and energy, they worked to achieve "the greatest good of the greatest number in the long run."

In the last ten years, the spirit of Smokey has dissolved in the logging hysteria that grips the Forest Service. Pressured by the timber industry to speed the cutting of highly scenic timberlands in the National Forests, the Forest Service has been substituting a new respect for the timber dollar for its old respect for the land. Smokey continues to warn against forest fire, but the Forest Service has lost most of its rapport with the public.

Fortunately, the spirit of Smokey lives on in the actions of many Forest Service officials. A walk through the agency's architecturally stark headquarters in Washington, D.C., quickly convinces you of the fact. The electric, unbureaucratic atmosphere of self-confident professionalism, imagination, and dedication is startling. What the Forest Service needs is not new foresters, but new direction.

D. Barney, THE LAST STAND xix (1974).

Legal standards—both legislative and judicial—are now very much a part of federal timber policy. Section A of this chapter looks at contract disputes between the Forest Service and timber companies. The second section analyzes forest practices under the rubric of multiple use, sustained yield, the traditional theory of timber management, concluding with the clearcutting controversy and its climax, the *Monongahela* decision in 1975. The final section deals with modern national forest law stemming from stricter judicial review, NEPA, and the forestry legislation of the 1970's, including the seminal National Forest Management Act of 1976.

For the history of the Forest Service and its practices, see H. Steen, THE UNITED STATES FOREST SERVICE: A HISTORY (1976); G. Robinson, THE FOREST SERVICE (1975); S. Dana & S. Fairfax, FOREST AND RANGE POLICY (2d ed. 1980); Huffman, A History of Forest Policy in the United States, 8 Envt'l L. 239 (1978); Wilkinson, The Forest Service: A Call for a Return to First Principles, 5 Pub.Land L.Rev. 1 (1984). National forest issues in the eastern United States are treated in W. Shands & R. Healy, THE LANDS NOBODY WANTED (1977).

A. TIMBER CONTRACTS

A significant part of the Forest Service's budget and resources is directed toward the administration of timber sales to private parties.

GLEN O. ROBINSON, THE FOREST SERVICE
61–75 (1975).

Presale Preparation. The sale action plan for the district contains an annual schedule of proposed timber sales based on the allocation of allowable cut among the districts and silvicultural or other management prescriptions. Consistent with general budget planning, the planned sales for the year will become part of the work program. If final appropriations allow, the sale may then be advertised. Before advertising, however, two major steps must be completed: first, a *multiple-use survey* is made (for most, but not all sales) and a report prepared. Second, the sale area's boundaries are defined and marked, the timber is "cruised" (i.e., surveyed for volume and quality) and appraised as to market value. This information is the basis for a *timber report and appraisal.*

* * *

The Sale. Once the timber sale report and appraisal are made, the sale is advertised for bids. A thirty-day, formal public advertisement must be given for all sales except those under $2,000 in appraised value (for which it is discretionary). The notice includes, among other things, the location and volume of timber, the appraised value, and the time and place when initial bids will be opened and subsequent oral bids, if any, will be received. More detailed information is contained in a sales prospectus which, together with the formal advertisement, is mailed to prospective bidders on the service's mailing list (those who have previously expressed interest in sales).

* * *

For advertised sales, the service employs two methods of bidding: sealed bid and oral auction following sealed bids. In the former, the sale is based on sealed bids only; in the latter, the sealed bids are followed by an oral auction among bidders who meet the appraised value. Choice of the particular method depends on local sale conditions. For eastern and southern forests, sealed bids are predominantly used. However, in the West, the service has favored oral auction because it enables local mills dependent on public timberlands to meet outside competition.

* * *

The Harvest. In implementing the prior plans governing the sale, the sale contract, of course, specifies the roads to be constructed, the area to be cut, and the type of cut as prescribed in the sale plan. The sale contract goes well beyond these general specifications, however, in prescribing the details of road design and construction, logging methods, and provision for removal of residues. The performance of these requirements by the operator is subject to inspection and general supervision by the service. Noncompliance is the basis for a fine, or for egregious malperformance, a declaration by the service of a breach of contract and suspension of operations. Occasionally such sanctions are required, but from all evidence not often enough to ensure reliably adequate performance. Some of the fault, of course, lies with the plans and design of the sale, the type of cut or the road design, and not with the execution by the operator. But even the best, most carefully designed road, harvest plan, or logging method cannot prevent careless execution by an operator. Since his short-term incentive induces him to cut the costs imposed by management constraints, a systematic supervision and rigorous enforcement of contract specifications is required and it has not been always forthcoming * * *

Cleanup and Reforestation. After a particular area has been cut, the unutilized residue or *slash* must be removed (or burned) and the site prepared for regeneration. * * * [C]urrent contracts call for removal of all utilizable timber, nonutilizable residue is provided for either by requiring removal by the contractor or a payment in lieu of removal.

* * *

Increasingly, the Forest Service has come to rely on artificial reforestation by seeding or planting. Cutover areas will regenerate naturally, over some period of time. This is true even of large clear-cut areas, though, of course, the larger the area, the less seed naturally available and the longer the period of time required for nature to seed the area. Other variables such as soil conditions, climate, and competing growth obviously affect the natural regeneration process. However, for large areas, natural regeneration is too indefinite in its results to be relied on for commercial management. * * * The additional cost of artificial regeneration is generally more than recouped by the earlier establishment of a new stand and its faster growth (though * * * this is not invariably the case).

NOTES

1. To prevent collusive bidding, Congress, in the NFMA of 1976, established a presumption that bidding would be by sealed bids "except where the Secretary provides otherwise by regulation." 16 U.S.C.A. § 472a(e). One study concluded that oral bidding brings higher prices, but that it cannot be proven to cause collusion. Johnson, Oral Auction Versus Sealed Bids: An Empirical Investigation, 19 Nat.Res.J. 315 (1979). Small companies in timber-dependent communities assert that, without oral auctions, they will lose contracts to larger companies due to the vagaries of a system based on a single blind bid. After the use of sealed bidding increased, section 472a(e) was rewritten in 1978, and oral bidding again preponderates.

2. One aspect of selling timber from the public lands that Robinson does not address is thievery. See Christensen, Hot Logs, Oregon Times 38 (August, 1978):

> HEY EVERYBODY, FUEL UP YOUR HUGHES CAYUSE, STICK A CLIP IN YOUR MACHINE GUN, LETS GO CUT SOME WOOD!

* * *

> Timber theft ranks hands-down as the biggest single money crime in Oregon. The F.B.I. estimates that as much as $43 million worth of timber is being stolen from federal forests in Oregon every year. If that figure is correct, it could mean that about one out of every 12 trees being harvested on Forest Service or BLM lands is going unpaid for. A loss equivalent to $20 for every man, woman and child in Oregon.

> And despite this, enforcement efforts are numerically laughable * * *. Don Purkerson, one of the handful of USFS law enforcement officers in Oregon, laments, "I've seen cedar trees with stumps near as wide as my office, cut down and pillaged. You see a big forest giant like that laying there on the ground with just maybe the best timber sawed out of its middle—just raped!—and it makes you damn near cry."

HI-RIDGE LUMBER CO. v. UNITED STATES
United States Court of Appeals, Ninth Circuit, 1971.
443 F.2d 452.

BARNES, Circuit Judge:

Appellant, Hi-Ridge Lumber Company (hereinafter Hi-Ridge), appeals from an entry by the district court of a summary judgment granted in favor of the United States and other defendants. * * *

This controversy arose from an auction sale held by the Forest Service on June 26, 1963, at which Hi-Ridge submitted the high bid. Appellant asserts that immediately upon the conclusion of the oral bidding, the representative of the Pacific Northwest Regional Forester who conducted the auction made an "informal" award of the contract to it.

Prior to the bidding, information was provided to prospective bidders which contained the terms of sale and contract requirements. The right to reject any and all bids was specifically reserved.

The affidavits reveal that after the oral bidding on a timber sale of this nature, the apparent high bidder is asked to fill out a confirmation bid form, which is sent to the Regional Forester's office. If the bid is approved, the Regional Forester or the Assistant Regional Forester to whom this authority has been delegated awards the sale by signing a memorandum to the Forest Supervisor, informing him that the sale is awarded to the successful bidder as of the date stated in the memorandum. The Supervisor then notifies the successful bidder by certified mail, and asks him to sign the necessary contract forms. After those forms are properly executed, the Regional Forester or his delegate signs the contract on behalf of the United States.

Soon after the bidding ended, a controversy arose as to the duty of the party awarded the contract to build roads. The advertised sample contract provided that 10.7 miles of road were to be constructed, of which 1.8 miles were outside and *north* of the sale area. Hi-Ridge took the position that its plan to haul the timber *south* to its plant rendered the 1.8 mile northern road segment unnecessary and therefore not required by the contract. Because of this, the contract award was withheld and discussed with higher Forest Service officials. The latter notified Hi-Ridge that the 1.8 mile road segment requirement could be deleted only if compensating road work were done, or the price was adjusted. When Hi-Ridge refused and adhered to its position, the matter was submitted to the Chief of the Forest Service with the recommendation that all bids be rejected and the sale readvertised.

In July of 1963, the Chief advised the Regional Forester that all bids were to be rejected and the timber again offered for sale. After Hi-Ridge was notified that all bids were rejected, it requested that the Chief of the Forest Service reconsider his decision. On June 8, 1964, the Chief reversed his decision that all bids were to be rejected, and concluded that the contract should be awarded to Hi-Ridge. In his new ruling, the Chief noted that in light of the previously unconsidered possibility of hauling the timber to the south instead of the north, the contract terms offered became somewhat ambiguous. Because of the risk that a reoffering might not result in a contract financially more favorable to the government, he believed that the appraisal oversight justified overriding in this case the policy that a purchaser would have to build substitute roads or agree to a price revision in lieu of building roads he would not use.

The Double Dee Lumber Company, second highest bidder at the auction, appealed to the Secretary of Agriculture according to the then applicable regulation. In December of 1965, the Secretary reversed the Chief of the Forest Service and decided that all bids must be rejected. His decision was based on a ruling by the Comptroller General that issuance of a road construction modification is improper in a case such as this.

The actions of the Forest Service officials in conducting the sale were taken under the provisions of 36 C.F.R. Section 221.10 which in relevant part provided as follows:

> "*Awards of Advertised Timber.* (a) Advertised timber will be awarded to the highest bidder upon satisfactory showing by him of ability to meet financial requirements and any other conditions of the sale offer unless:
>
> "(1) Determination is made to reject all bids.
>
> * * *
>
> "(c) If the highest bid is not accepted and the sale is still deemed desirable, all bids may be rejected and the timber readvertised; or, if the highest bidder cannot meet the require-

ments under which the timber was advertised or the withhold-ing of award to him is based on one or more of paragraphs 4, 5, and 6 above, award at the highest price bid may be offered to the next highest qualified bidders in order of their bids until the award is accepted by one or refused by all of the qualified bidders."

The manual of the Forest Service further provided in Section 2431.7 that pursuant to Section 221.10 "[a]ll bids may be rejected only when such rejection is in the interest of the United States."

A cursory reading of the regulations clearly reveals that their basic scheme calls for the exercise of discretion in carrying out government timber sales. We are called upon to determine whether a governmen-tal officer has acted within the delegated scope of discretion.

Before we may determine whether the Secretary's determination to reject all bids for the reasons stated was a permissible exercise of the discretion delegated to him, however, we must first consider the effect of Section 10 of the Administrative Procedure Act hereinafter ("Act"), 5 U.S.C.A. Section 701(a) on the availability of review by this Court. Section 10 provides that the Act applies to provide review "except to the extent that * * * (2) agency action is committed to agency discretion by law." Lacking specific legislative instruction as to the availability of judicial review, the court must balance the need for the speedy and efficient enforcement of Congressional programs and the growing demands on judicial resources against an individual's interest in having a claim adjudicated.

* * *

* * * The relevant provision, 16 U.S.C.A. § 476, readily pro-vides such an inference. At length, it delegates to the Secretary power to provide rules and regulations to govern such sales as well as explicitly authorizing him to exercise his discretion in many instances. Section 476 as an example of his broad discretion specifically provides that "In cases in which advertisement is had and no satisfactory bid is received, or in cases in which the bidder fails to complete the purchase, the timber may be sold, without further advertisement, at private sale, in the discretion of the Secretary of Agriculture, at not less than the appraised valuation, in quantities to suit purchasers".[a]

In determining reviewability we must also examine the regulations and investigate the nature and breadth of the discretion delegated to the Forest Service in the sale of timber. Under the regulations in effect, the Forest Service could "reject all bids with or without reason." S & S Logging Co. v. Barker, 366 F.2d 617 (9th Cir.1966). Although there were requirements which had to be met before a contract could be awarded to the next highest bidder, there were none attached to a decision to reject all bids. The caveat in the manual (which does not rise to the status of a regulation) that such a rejection must be made

---

a. [Ed.] Section 476 was repealed by the NFMA of 1976. Timber sales now are governed by 16 U.S.C.A. § 472a.

"only when in the interest of the United States" can be read to call for an informed managerial discretion. The only restriction upon the discretion to reject all bids is that this power should be invoked only in situations to benefit the government, rather than those private parties with whom its agents deal.

Our reading of the discretionary power relating to the rejection of all bids convinces us that several compelling reasons exist to justify nonreview because the decision is committed to agency discretion. First, the authority delegated is quite broad. While we assume that the regulations provide sufficient guidelines to review a decision to award the contract to one who was not the highest bidder, we have no standards before us by which we could review the rejection of all bids. The development of such criteria and factors to be weighed would be too onerous a burden upon this or any court. Secondly, the decision whether to award a specific contract in view of the government's need for revenue, management of timber and its road-building needs, is one which is necessarily based upon some expertise in the financial and ecological management of our natural resources. This Court has neither the technical expertise nor the intuitive knowledge gained from daily acquaintance with this subject to provide an informed review of executive decision-making. Thirdly, the timber sale activities of the Forest Service are in the nature of a continuing and comprehensive managerial function. The decision in question reflects managerial policies which may be important to the overall program of the agency. Although we may be able to understand the basic issue of whether compensating consideration is required in lieu of unnecessary road-work, it is likely that this policy is one of a complex group with which we are generally unfamiliar. Finally, our review of the facts assures us that the Forest Service appeals procedures provide a fair and expeditious forum in which dissatisfied participants in the bidding may lodge their protests and have them fully considered. What took place in this case confirms that view.

* * *

NOTES

1. Earlier cases had seemed to indicate that normal rules of construction would apply to Forest Service contract disputes. E.g., Bloedel Donovan Lumber Mills v. United States, 74 F.Supp. 470 (Ct.Cl. 1947). Does *Hi-Ridge* effectively give the Department of Agriculture the unilateral right to interpret its own contracts?

2. In S & S Logging Co. v. Barker, cited in *Hi-Ridge*, plaintiff brought suit against the local Forest Service officials for conspiracy to restrain trade after they had rejected its high bid. The court upheld summary dismissal of the action, and incidentally commented that the action was purely discretionary and thus unreviewable. 366 F.2d at 624 n. 6. But see Everett Plywood Corp. v. United States, 512 F.2d 1082 (Ct.Cl.1975) (successful breach of contract suit against the Forest Service for failure to extend time). Forest Service discretion to sell

fire-damaged timber on an unpatented mining claim was upheld in Bradley-Turner Mines, Inc. v. Branagh, 187 F.Supp. 665 (N.D.Cal.1960).

3. Compare the extent of judicial review in *Hi-Ridge* with that given to the actions of the Bureau of Land Management in Wilderness Society v. Morton, 479 F.2d 842 (D.C.Cir.1973), supra at page 294, and to the actions of the National Park Service in Sierra Club v. Dept. of Interior, 376 F.Supp. 90 (N.D.Cal.1974), supra at page 305. Should the standard of review applied to the actions of a public land management agency be different when the agency is accused of harming the public interest in the land than when the agency is accused of dealing unfairly with a private party? Should a court today find that the kind of decision in *Hi-Ridge* is committed to agency discretion? See supra page 279.

4. In Everett Plywood Corp. v. United States, 651 F.2d 723 (Ct.Cl. 1981), the court considered whether, under the doctrine of frustration, the government may cancel a timber contract without liability for damages. After the plaintiff had begun road construction into the specified contract areas, the Forest Service discovered that continued construction would result in extensive soil and watershed damage. An agreement was reached modifying the contract, but Everett reserved the right to seek damages under the original contract. Neither the contract nor agency regulations provided cancellation for environmental reasons. The trial judge found that, under the doctrine of frustration of purpose, the government had not breached the contract because the obligation had become incapable of being performed without rendering performance worthless to the government.

The Court of Claims held that because of the government's superior position in determining the provisions of the contract, and because the Forest Service was in a position to foresee adverse environmental consequences, the contract allocated the risk to the government: "There can therefore be no doubt that high reasons of public policy do not endow public officials with authority to repudiate contracts, though they may influence courts to refrain from interference by way of specific performance, etc., and from awarding damages that exceed a reasonable compensation for the lost contract rights." Id. at 728. In holding the government liable for damages for breach of the original contract, the court stated:

> The first impression one has is that the trial judge has seized on a contract doctrine evolved for quite unlike circumstances in order to further the high cause of environmentalism. It is a cause with numerous and devoted adherents, some of whom will not tolerate the balancing of environmental considerations against others perhaps equally high but of a different nature. Here the cause is deemed to override the normal obligations of a government contract, i.e., if the Secretary of Agriculture is acting on behalf of the environment he can make any contract of his Department null and void. The effort of the government which has stepped into the market

place and made contracts binding on others, to void them as applied to itself on behalf of some high public policy, is an old phenomenon in the law. The obligation of contracts clause is, of course, in the Constitution, but by its terms applies only to the states. Lynch v. United States, 292 U.S. 571, 579 (1934) holds, however, that the just compensation clause of the fifth amendment prohibits the repudiation in whole or part of U.S. Government contracts. * * *

* * *

Both of these views establish a rule that at minimum would excuse the government from performing in this case if (1) the recognition that continued performance of the contract would lead to environmental damage was a supervening event that should excuse performance, (2) the risk of the event was not borne by the government, and (3) the environmental damage would render the value of performance worthless to the government. The trial judge, following the approach suggested by Corbin ("Corbin view"), found that the recognition that continued logging would result in unacceptable damage to the soil, to the watershed, and to the regeneration of the forest was an event that should excuse performance; that although this risk was foreseeable, it was not borne by the government; and lastly that the NFS's purpose and motives in entering the contract were not commercial but instead were designed to accommodate public policy objectives in administering the national forests. Thus the trial judge considered the fact that environmental damage was foreseeable only to be probative and not dispositive. * * *

* * *

At the outset, we have already distinguished between the power of the government to terminate the contract and the extent of its liability for the exercise of that power. Clearly, the government ought not to have stood idly by and continued with the contract if unacceptable damage to the environment were foreseen. On the other hand, whether the government can terminate the contract and escape making compensation is another issue, the issue we are concerned with. * * *

* * *

Even if the government's knowledge that environmental damage could occur was not dispositive and only probative, given the facts of this case and the decisions of this court in the area of impracticability of performance, the risk of the occurrence of the event is on the government. * * * It was defendant, not plaintiff, who as owner of the tracts to be harvested would be presumed to be the party informed as to soil conditions and geologic structure that might indicate that logging would endanger the environment.

In the instant case, the ARM contract contained provisions covering rate redetermination for devalued timber, cost adjustment for physical change, liability for loss of timber, termination by purchaser for catastrophe, and termination for changed conditions. All of these provisions discuss various supervening events and the effect such events should have upon the contract. In cases of less than catastrophic physical change or damage to timber or the surrounding area, the purchaser is granted cost adjustments. In the event of a catastrophic event making performance impracticable, the purchaser is granted the option of terminating the contract. Additionally, the contract permitted a waiver by mutual agreement of those contract requirements that would no longer serve their purpose because of changed conditions. In view of these express provisions specifically granting relief to a purchaser from loss and catastrophe and the absence of any provision allowing the government similar relief from environmental damage, the contract as fairly read allocates to defendant the risk of being in breach if it must cancel because of the risk of environmental damage.

Given the Forest Service's ability to dictate terms, is there a situation in which a defense of "environmental frustration" might be successful?

5. During the 1970's, the federal timber bidding procedures worked to the benefit of timber companies: they purchased timber based on prices at the time of the bidding, but actual harvesting did not take place for several years (depending upon the duration of the timber contracts, 36 C.F.R. §§ 223.31–223.33 (1985)), when rising timber values were much higher. In the 1980's, however, the timber industry in the public lands states went into decline as the housing industry entered a deep recession. The timber sold in federal contracts for $300 per thousand board feet in 1980 brought less than $200 per thousand in 1982. The timber companies took the issue both to Congress and the courts.

NORTH SIDE LUMBER CO. v. BLOCK
United States Court of Appeals, Ninth Circuit, 1985.
753 F.2d 1482.

GOODWIN, Circuit Judge.

* * *

North Side, the class it represents, and plaintiffs-intervenors are timber companies that have contracts to cut and pay for timber in the national forests in Oregon and Washington. They brought this action against the Secretary of Agriculture and several of his subordinates, asking for a judgment declaring the contracts void and restraining the defendants from enforcing them. They did not seek money damages.

Because of a depressed market for lumber and logs, the timber companies can perform their contracts only at a loss. If they do not perform, they will be liable to the government for the difference between the contract price they agreed to pay for the timber and the price the same timber brings when the government resells it to new purchasers, plus interest. Either performance at a loss or default with payment of damages to the government will bankrupt at least some of the timber companies.

The district court preliminarily enjoined the Secretary from enforcing the contracts held by North Side and the class of 109 privately-held timber companies it represents. * * *

The timber companies make two claims for relief. The first, which we will refer to as the impracticability claim, asserts that contingencies unforeseen at the time the contracts were made render the contracts void under the contract law doctrines of commercial impracticability, frustration of purpose, and impossibility of performance. The second, which we will refer to as the statutory claim, asserts that enforcement of the contracts would violate 16 U.S.C. §§ 473–482 and the Multiple-Use Sustained-Yield Act of 1960, 16 U.S.C. §§ 528 et seq.

The timber companies contend that both claims fall within the district court's federal question jurisdiction, 28 U.S.C. § 1331. It is true that the claims arise under federal law as § 1331 requires. The statutory claim obviously involves federal statutes. The impracticability claim also arises under federal law because federal common law of contracts applies to contracts with the federal government.

But the analysis of jurisdiction cannot stop with § 1331, because the claims in this case are in essence against the federal government, and thus are barred by sovereign immunity unless the government has consented to suit. The timber companies contend that the Administrative Procedure Act, 5 U.S.C. § 702, waives the government's sovereign immunity to this action. Section 702 reads in part:

> An action in a court of the United States seeking relief other than money damages and stating a claim that an agency or an officer or employee thereof acted or failed to act in an official capacity or under color of legal authority shall not be dismissed nor relief therein be denied on the ground that it is against the United States or that the United States is an indispensable party.

The waiver of immunity is limited by the proviso of § 702 that

> Nothing herein * * * confers authority to grant relief if any other statute that grants consent to suit expressly or impliedly forbids the relief which is sought.

The Tucker Act, 28 U.S.C. §§ 1346 and 1491, is a "statute that grants consent to suit" on government contracts. We conclude that it impliedly forbids relief on the impracticability claim but not the statutory claim. It thus precludes a § 702 waiver of sovereign immunity on the impracticability claim. Moreover, on the impracticability claim, we have been able to identify from the record in this case no claim of an official action or failure to act within the meaning of 5 U.S.C. § 702. In the absence of such a claim, § 702 does not waive immunity.

The Tucker Act gives the United States Claims Court jurisdiction over "any claim against the United States founded * * * upon any express or implied contract with the United States," 28 U.S.C. § 1491(a) (1); it exercises this jurisdiction concurrently with the district courts for actions claiming less than $10,000. 28 U.S.C. § 1346(a)(2). The Act is more than just a grant of jurisdiction over government contract claims; it is also a limited waiver of sovereign immunity and a limitation on the remedies available in actions on government contracts. The Tucker Act has been construed as permitting the Claims Court to grant money damages against the government in contract actions but not injunctive or declaratory relief. [citing authority].

The impracticability claim * * * is subject to the Tucker Act's implied restrictions on relief. It is concerned solely with rights created within the contractual relationship and has nothing to do with duties arising independently of the contract. As such, the impracticability claim is "founded * * * upon [a] * * * contract with the United States" and is therefore within the Tucker Act and subject to its restrictions on relief. If we were to construe § 702 to waive sovereign immunity on the impracticability claim, Congress' intent not to allow post-award declaratory relief on government contracts would be frustrated. The district court does not have jurisdiction of the impracticability claim.

* * *

The district court has jurisdiction over the claim that enforcement of the contracts would violate 16 U.S.C. §§ 473–482 and the Multiple-Use Sustained-Yield Act of 1960, but does not have jurisdiction over the claim that the contracts are void for impracticability, frustration, or impossibility. Because the district court granted the injunction based on the impracticability claim and rejected the statutory claim, we vacate the judgment.

* * *

BOOCHEVER, Circuit Judge, dissenting.

* * *

NOTES

1. As a matter of policy, should Congress expressly provide for judicial relief in the *North Side* situation? In *Everett Plywood?* In *Hi-Ridge?*

2. After *North Side* was argued, Congress enacted the Federal Timber Contract Payment Modification Act of 1984, 16 U.S.C.A. § 618. The TCPMA relieved timber companies of some obligations. Under the Act, purchasers will be able to buy back up to 55% of their contracts at the original bid price, subject to a maximum of 200 million board feet. The buy-out charge is figured by formulas that depend on the financial structure of the timber contractor. In the Act, Congress also approved a five year extension on performance of pre-1982 contracts.

B. TRADITIONAL FOREST SERVICE MANAGEMENT

1. THE MULTIPLE–USE, SUSTAINED–YIELD ACT

Although the Forest Service Organic Act referred only to management for timber and water, 16 U.S.C.A. § 476, see United States v. New Mexico, 438 U.S. 696 (1978), supra at page 376, the Forest Service had in fact managed its lands on a multiple use basis from its inception. Aldo Leopold and Bob Marshall both labored from within to expand recreational opportunities in national forests. By the 1950's, the wilderness movement had begun to make its presence felt. The traditional users—timber operators, reclamation interests, and ranchers—all argued for greater allocation to their particular needs. The Forest Service went to Congress, delicately arguing both that new legislation was necessary to clarify the agency's mission and that it had possessed such broad authority all along. The result was the Multiple-Use, Sustained-Yield Act of 1960 (MUSY Act), 16 U.S.C.A. § 528–31, the key provisions of which assiduously listed the five multiple uses in alphabetical order:

It is the policy of the Congress that the national forests are established and shall be administered for outdoor recreation, range, timber, watershed, and wildlife and fish purposes. The purposes of this Act are declared to be supplemental to, but not in derogation of, the purposes for which the national forests were established as set forth in the Act of June 4, 1897 * * *.
16 U.S.C.A. § 528.

As used in this Act, the following terms shall have the following meanings:

(a) "Multiple use" means: The management of all the various renewable surface resources of the national forests so that they are utilized in the combination that will best meet the needs of the American people; making the most judicious use of the land for some or all these resources or related services over areas large enough to provide sufficient latitude for periodic adjustments in use to conform to changing needs and conditions; that some land will be used for less than all of the resources; and harmonious and coordinated management of the various resources, each with the other, without impairment of the productivity of the land, with consideration being given to the relative values of the various resources, and not necessarily the combination of uses that will give the greatest dollar return or the greatest unit output.

(b) "sustained yield of the several products and services" means the achievement and maintenance in perpetuity of a high-level annual or regular periodic output of the various renewable resources of the national forests without impairment of the productivity of the land. 16 U.S.C.A. § 531.

The Multiple Use Act has meant all things to all people. "Multiple use" is difficult if not impossible to define concretely: the usual formulations are so abstract that they cannot be applied with predictability, rationality, or uniformity to actual land management problems. A widely used definition of the multiple use concept, that it is "a practice in which a given land area functions in two or more compatible ways," merely illustrates its abstractness. For example, what is a "given land area"? If the area considered is an entire forest, then multiple use may be achieved by dividing the forest into sections and allocating a different use to each section. This, however, restricts the area in which a given activity may occur, and is to that extent considered undesirable. If, on the other hand, the "land area" is a relatively small plot, mutually exclusive uses such as timber harvesting and recreation could not occur simultaneously.

The Forest Service has treated this problem as if it is at least partially artificial because, no matter what use is made of the land, some other use will surely be compatible with it. Thus, clearcutting is deemed compatible with selected wildlife habitat enhancement (it increases forage for deer), and wildlife enhancement is compatible with recreation (although it does not necessarily follow that clearcutting is compatible with recreation).

The literature on the meaning and application of multiple use, sustained yield management has burgeoned without appreciably clarifying the concept as a legal standard. See Loesch, Multiple Uses of Public Lands—Accommodation or Choosing Between Conflicting Uses, 16 Rocky Mtn.Min.L.Inst. 1 (1971) (emphasizes the expertness of the administrator and the "flexibility" afforded by the system); Strand, Statutory Authority Governing Management of the National Forest System—Time for a Change?, 7 Nat.Res.L. 479 (1974) (accepts the principle but argues for better definition and stronger standards); Comment, Managing the Federal Lands: Replacing the Multiple Use System, 82 Yale L.J. 787 (1973) (calls for abolition). Particularly valuable for understanding the conceptual problems—if not the solutions—is the Symposium on Forest Policy at 8 Envt'l L. 239 (1978).

In 1968, the Forest Service sold 8.7 billion board feet of timber from the Tongass National Forest in Southeast Alaska to U.S. Plywood-Champion Papers, Inc. The transaction, calling for harvest over a period of 50 years, was the largest timber sale ever contracted by the Forest Service. The sale was attacked on several grounds, one of which was the MUSY Act. In Sierra Club v. Hardin, 325 F.Supp. 99 (D. Alaska 1971), the Court denied relief:

> Plaintiffs introduced substantial testimony as well as documentary evidence, much of it in the form of offers of proof, to show that the Tongass National Forest is being administered predominantly for timber production. While the material undoubtedly shows the overwhelming commitment of the Tongass National Forest to timber harvest objectives in preference to other multiple use values, Congress has given no indication as

to the weight to be assigned each value and it must be assumed that the decision as to the proper mix of uses within any particular area is left to the sound discretion and expertise of the Forest Service. Accordingly, evidence was admitted only for the purpose of showing that the Forest Service failed to give consideration [48] to any of the competing uses or that it took into consideration irrelevant matters which it should not have considered. Plaintiffs' parade of expert witnesses might have swayed the decision of the Forest Service or influenced the result in this case had it been properly presented at an administrative proceeding. Introduced as non-record evidence in this proceeding, however, it utterly fails to impeach the record provided by the Forest Service by showing that the administrative decision makers either lacked actual knowledge or failed to consider the myriad reports and studies available to them. The court must presume, therefore, that the Forest Service did give due consideration to the various values specified in the Multiple Use-Sustained Yield Act. Having investigated the framework in which the decision was made, the court is forbidden to go further and substitute its decision in a discretionary matter for that of the Secretary.[49]

As the court noted, the Tongass sale demonstrated an "overwhelming commitment * * * to timber harvest objective in preference to other multiple use values." Does the opinion demonstrate that the Multiple Use Act leaves the allocation of resources entirely to the unfettered discretion of the Forest Service? Could the Service legally decide to cut every tree in the Tongass National Forest? Could it decree that no trees at all will be cut? The decision was later remanded by the following unreported order.

48. The Act requires that the Forest Service give "due" consideration to the various competing uses. Plaintiffs argue that "due" could only mean "equal." This interpretation would seem to be precluded by the language of § 531, which clearly contemplates that some areas may be unsuited to utilization of all resources. "Due" is impossible to define and merely indicates that Congress intended the Forest Service to apply their expertise to the problem after consideration of all relevant values. In the absence of a more satisfactory or objective standard the court considered that evidence in the record of "some" consideration was sufficient to satisfy the Act absent a showing that no *actual* consideration was given to other uses.

Professor Reich comments on the breadth of the Multiple Use-Sustained Yield Act of 1960 in a paper entitled "Bureaucracy and the Forests" (copyright The Fund for the Republic, Inc., Center for the Study of Democratic Institutions at Santa Barbara, California), as follows:

"The standards Congress has used to delegate authority over the forests are so general, so sweeping, and so vague as to represent a turnover of virtually all responsibility. 'Multiple use' does establish that the forests cannot be used exclusively for one purpose, but beyond this it is little more than a phrase expressing the hope that all competing interests can somehow be satisfied and leaving the real decisions to others."

49. The Forest Service had at its disposal a number of highly technical studies covering a broad range of possible use alternatives. A great deal of expertise went into the composition of Multiple Use Plan for the Chatham Ranger District, which was referred to in drawing up the timber sale contract. The contract itself contains a number of provisions relating to environmental safeguards, including a provision allowing the Forest Service to exempt up to 800,000 acres within the sale area from cutting.

SIERRA CLUB v. BUTZ
United States Court of Appeals, Ninth Circuit, 1973.
3 E.L.R. 20292.

MERRILL, J.

Plaintiffs-appellants have moved this court to remand the cause to the District Court of the District of Alaska to enable the filing of a motion for new trial upon the ground of newly discovered evidence.

The evidence to which reference is made is a report by A. Starker Leopold and Reginald H. Barrett to U.S. Plywood-Champion Papers, Inc., respecting the manner in which the sales contract should be carried out, with due consideration given to social values other than the economic yield of pulp or lumber. It was the view of this team of experts that "the basic precepts on which the original timber sale contract were based are not today acceptable." It recommended "that the company explore with the Forest Service the possibility of revising the cutting plan to provide more adequate protection for the wide spectrum of ecologic values that is characteristic of Southeastern Alaska." Two alternative cutting plans were proposed, and the report recommended renegotiation of the contract to provide for reduced cutting.

The report thus primarily addresses itself to matters of administrative judgment: whether cutting plans should be modified and the contract renegotiated.

In our judgment, however, it may bear as well on one of the issues presented by this case: whether the contract violated the terms of the Multiple Use-Sustained Yield Act, 16 U.S.C.A. §§ 528–531. This issue was considered by the District Court in its opinion in this case, 325 F.Supp. 99, 122–124 (D.Alas.1971). The question it discussed was whether the Forest Service had given "due" consideration to the various purposes (other than timber) for which the national forests are to be administered under the Act. The court, at 325 F.Supp. 123 n. 48, discussed what should be regarded as "due" consideration under the Act and concluded that what was intended was that the Forest Service should "apply their expertise to the problem after consideration of all relevant values." It concluded that "some" consideration was sufficient. (For the purposes of this order we accept this interpretation, with the caution that "due consideration" to us requires that the values in question be informedly and rationally taken into balance. The requirement can hardly be satisfied by a showing of knowledge of the consequences and a decision to ignore them.)

* * *

In our judgment the report tendered upon this motion may be found to bear upon the stated issues: Whether the Forest Service in truth had knowledge of the ecological consequences of the contract and cutting plan to which it agreed; whether in reaching its decision it failed to consider the available material (the report appends a 10-page list of material cited in the report in existence at the time the contract was entered into); further, a relevant question may be whether consideration was given to alternatives (such as those recommended by the report), which, while giving prime consideration to timber values, would still afford protection to the other values to which due consideration must be given.

* * *

* * * The case is remanded to the District Court * * *.

NOTES

1. Even though the foregoing conclusory treatment is the most definitive interpretation of the multiple use standard located anywhere, it has no value as precedent in the Ninth Circuit because the opinion was not published. See Rule 21(c), Rules of the Ninth Circuit Court of Appeals.

2. In cautioning "that 'due consideration' to us requires that the values in question be informedly and rationally taken into balance," has the court propounded an enforcible standard? If so, is it substantive or procedural?

3. Other opinions construing the MUSY Act of 1960 include Dorothy Thomas Foundation, Inc. v. Hardin, 317 F.Supp. 1072 (W.D. N.C.1970) (narrow judicial review), and National Wildlife Federation v. United States Forest Service, 592 F.Supp. 931 (D.Or.1984), infra at page 651.

Does the MUSY Act allow for any significant judicial role? See Coggins, Of Succotash Syndromes and Vacuous Platitudes: The Meaning of "Multiple Use, Sustained Yield" for Public Land Management (Part I), 53 U.Colo.L.Rev. 229 (1982), who concludes:

> The multiple use, sustained yield statutes are not very good laws. They represent congressional buck-passing, and they allow bureaucratic lawmaking. They give managers a latitude that would be deemed undue in other more visible areas of the law. It is easy to see why courts assiduously avoid interpreting them and why the agencies persist in emphasizing the single resources that they can measure in dollars. And it is just as likely as not that things will continue in legal limbo. Unlike the 1976 Congress, the present Congress appears unwilling to look closely at public land management. The agencies, especially the BLM, seem unable to replace expediency with balanced, long-range planning. The courts may well continue their disinclination to say what the laws mean.

> Nevertheless, a close reading of those statutes demonstrates that they are not like Oakland: there is some *there* there. The multiple use laws contain a series of "shalls" and "shall nots" that ought to be binding on public land managers. They demand an equality of resource treatment, and they forbid practices that detract from the future productivity of the land. They demand thought and foresight, and they prohibit

economic optimization of single resources. The larger statutory context also requires a broader management viewpoint than
that heretofore evidenced. Most significantly, the multiple use
legislation requires, implicitly and explicitly, land use planning
that will govern and make predictable (and also "legal") subsequent individual resource allocations. * * *

If the courts decide to oversee multiple use management,
will any practical reforms follow? Yes. The massive commitment of an entire forest to one purpose, as in the *Tongass
National Forest* litigation would be per se illegal. * * *
Effective judicial review would also mean more protection for
users, less reliance on questionable economic theory, and more
conservatism in management practice. In defending their
actions, the agencies would have to confront their actual reasoning and bases for decision. Annual reinvention of the
wheel would not be required. Getting it round the first time
would be.

4. Multiple use "policy" is not always made in ivory towers,
especially in an agency as relatively decentralized as the Forest Service.
H. Kaufman, THE FOREST RANGER 78–80 (1967):

Every Ranger and former Ranger interviewed in the
course of this study has been involved in appeals cases of some
kind. It is accepted as one of the hardships of doing public
business in a democratic government and is not ordinarily
treated as a discredit, even if a field officer is eventually
overruled. Yet it is a bother, at best—a distraction from the
more "productive" labors of the members of the Forest Service,
a cause of additional paperwork, a generator of inspections and
inquiries from higher levels. And it is certainly true that, at
worst, a Ranger whose constituency is *constantly* restive and
rebellious is likely to stimulate some doubts about his judi-
ciousness and skill. So Rangers prefer to avoid them if they
can, and are often confronted with a delicate choice between
the annoyance and risk of continuous skirmishing with local
interests on the one hand, and conceding away elements of the
Forest Service program (perhaps to save the remainder) on the
other.

Sometimes they make concessions. When his forest supervisor wanted to spray herbicides on stands of commercially
undesirable species of trees (in order to destroy the valueless
trees and make way for more merchantable growth), one
Ranger persuaded him to delay the project indefinitely because
the Ranger anticipated the hunting and fishing clubs and other
associations of wildlife enthusiasts would raise a hue and cry
about the alleged injury to birds, small game, and fish. In
another case, a plan to require grazing permittees to put ear
tags on their cattle because the Ranger discovered they were
running more animals than their permits allowed was deferred

when the permittees organized resistance to the program. Another Ranger elected not to press for the termination of a special-use permit under which a small town within the boundaries of his district used national forest property for a town dump; although the dump was an eyesore and a potential fire hazard, he thought the town officials could muster enough support to defeat such a move. On one district, the Ranger was trying to eliminate grazing from some high-altitude, snow-covered, water storage areas, but only slowly and cautiously, so as to minimize the opposition this would provoke. On another, protests by nature lovers concerned about songbirds and game forced deferral of spraying designed to eliminate the highly destructive spruce budworm.

In every instance, to have pressed forward regardless of local sentiment unquestionably would have cost far more in the long run than was gained in the short run; tactically, the concessions were certainly sound. But these examples do indicate how local pressure can influence the behavior of field officers, slowing or modifying what actually happens on the ground as compared with what is mandated from central headquarters.

Thus, a needed step is not taken here, an undesirable permit is issued there, a measure is recommended in order to avoid trouble—and an agency-wide policy can be eroded. From the standpoint of this study, it does not matter whether acquiescence by field officers in the demands of local special interests results from the assimilation of Service personnel into the communities in which they live or from the overwhelming nature of the pressure brought to bear upon them; the erosive impact on policy is the same. Nor does it matter that no single action, as the illustrations demonstrate, is likely by itself to have much effect on policy; multiplied many times, over long periods, in large numbers of Ranger districts, the cumulative impact could be considerable. Unity does not demand uniformity, but it does require consistency and coordination. It is in this sense that "capture" of the men "on the firing line" is a challenge to the unity of the Forest Service, as it is to the unity of any large organization.

NOTE: THE RESOURCES PLANNING ACT OF 1974

The Forest Service long had been disadvantaged by the ups-and-downs of the annual congressional budgeting process. In the Forest and Rangeland Renewable Resources Planning Act of 1974 (RPA), as amended, 16 U.S.C.A. §§ 1601–13, Congress recognized that forest lands are capital assets and that the agency requires reliable estimates of future funding to plan for timber management practices such as reforestation. The RPA directs the Forest Service periodically to prepare three planning documents: (1) an Assessment describing the renewable resources of all the nation's forest and range lands (every ten years); (2) a Program, with a planning horizon of at least forty-five years, proposing long-range objectives and setting out the specific costs for all Forest Service activities (every five years); and (3) an Annual Report evaluating Forest Service activities in comparison with the objectives proposed in the Program. In addition, the RPA requires the President to submit two documents to Congress: (1) a Statement of Policy, which is based upon the Program and which can be modified by Congress, to be used in framing future budget requests for Forest Service activities (every five years); and (2) a Statement of Reasons, an explanation accompanying each annual proposed budget that does not request funds necessary to achieve the objectives of the Statement of Policy.

Despite optimistic expectations, the RPA has not fundamentally altered the Forest Service budget or budgetary politics in the White House or Congress. Budget proposals and appropriations almost immediately fell below the amounts recommended in the 1975 Program and the resulting 1976 Statement of Policy. When President Carter's proposed 1979 budget fell well short of the funding envisioned by the Statement of Policy (intended to guide future budget requests), the National Wildlife Federation sued, taking the position that the President's Statement of Reasons did not explain the shortfall to the extent required by the RPA. In particular, the Federation objected to low budget levels for programs such as recreation and reforestation. The Court of Appeals held that the action was properly dismissed:

> Sometimes the great public importance of an issue militates in favor of its prompt resolution. See Duke Power Co. v. Carolina Environmental Study Group, Inc., 438 U.S. 59, 95–96 (1978) (Rehnquist, J., concurring) & id. at 102–03 (Stevens, J., concurring) (contending that the majority ignored powerful jurisdictional and justiciability arguments because it thought it important to consider on the merits the constitutionality of the Price-Anderson Act's liability limitations for nuclear accidents). At other times, however, the public interest dictates that courts exercise restraint in passing upon crucial issues. We think such restraint is necessary where, as here, appellants ask us to intervene in wrangling over the federal budget and budget procedures. Such matters are the archetype of those best resolved through bargaining and accommodation between the legislative and executive branches. We are reluctant to afford discretionary relief when to do so would intrude on the responsibilities—including the shared responsibilities—of the coordinate branches.

National Wildlife Federation v. United States, 626 F.2d 917 (D.C.Cir. 1980); the opinion also includes a useful description of the RPA's provisions.

Although Congress and the Executive have not met the Forest Service's financial needs defined in the five-year Program, the RPA seems to have had some beneficial influence within the agency: the

Act's national planning process has probably caused the Forest Service to improve its long-range planning—in spite of Professor Behan's gloomy analysis, supra at page 39.   Nevertheless, the RPA is best understood as the last gasp of the era of unfettered Forest Service discretion.   The following material shows that, even before the RPA was enacted, events were moving quickly toward expanded judicial review and enactment of the National Forest Management Act of 1976 (NFMA).

2. THE WATERSHED: CLEARCUTTING, THE *MONON-GAHELA* DECISION, AND THE NATIONAL FOREST MANAGEMENT ACT

Federal timber policy was reshaped by the clearcutting controversy of the late 1960's and early 1970's, which irrevocably altered the perception of the Forest Service held by Congress, the courts, and the public.   The 1975 *Monongahela* decision, infra at page 623, brought Forest Service practices center stage.   A tangible and direct result was the National Forest Management Act of 1976.

Clearcutting means the complete removal of timber from an area, somewhat like shaving the land.   It is a well-established silvicultural practice and, if properly conducted in an appropriate region, is an economically more efficient method of providing a larger flow of timber from the national forests.   Many claim that it is an indispensible option if the present harvest level is to be maintained.

Clearcutting is one of the three varients of "even-aged management," a system aiming at a new forest in which all of the trees in a given area will be of roughly the same age.   The "seed tree" method of harvesting is similar to clearcutting except that a few large trees per acre are left to provide seed for natural regeneration.   "Shelterwood" or "shade tree" cutting leaves more trees per acre, usually to provide some filtered sunlight for the young trees.   Seed tree and shelterwood cutting both result in an even-aged forest because the veteran trees originally left standing are usually removed in an early second harvest. The "conversion period" is the period between the time when even-aged management in a given area begins and the time when harvesting of old-growth ends; at that point, the stand has been converted into a "managed forest."

Selective cutting, the other means of timber harvesting, differs from even-aged management in that it produces a diversified forest. Trees are removed individually or in small groups, and gradual harvesting continues over the entire rotation period.

Clearcutting often has economic advantages over selection harvesting.   Marking trees is largely eliminated; yarding costs are lower; road engineering and construction costs are diminished (logging roads often must be improved or reconstructed after the passage of several years); and administrative costs of preparing sales are lower.   Clearcutting also has some environmental advantages.   Even-aged management can be conducted with a less extensive road system, thus causing less soil erosion. Further, large trees are subject to windthrow, or blowdown; selection cutting lessens protection and leaves the remaining trees vulnerable to wind damage. In addition, some animals such as deer, black bear, and ruffed grouse thrive on the sunlight and browse created by clearcuts. In some cases, clearcutting may be necessary to prevent the spread of insects or disease. See generally CLEARCUTTING: A VIEW FROM THE TOP 126–48 (E. Horwitz, ed. 1974).

The more frequent justification for even-aged management is that some tree species in some climates cannot regenerate under a selection regime. The economically valuable Douglas fir, for example, is "shade-intolerant;" it cannot grow without direct sunlight. There are few young Douglas firs in old-growth forests. Without management, another species such as hemlock will become dominant; i.e., without clearcutting, no new Douglas fir forest will replace the old.

Clearcutting also has prominent environmental disadvantages. Beauty is subjective, but most agree that a clearcut area is an insult to the eye, an ugly practice that no amount of blending with the natural terrain can much change. The effects of clearcutting remain long after the harvest. Most people can easily perceive the differences between a second-growth managed forest and a varied, virgin stand. Many say it is the difference between a tree farm and a cathedral. Beyond that, some argue that it is wrong to "prefer" one "valuable" species rather than letting the stand progress naturally to a climax stage. See generally Tribe, Ways Not to Think About Plastic Trees: New Foundations for Environmental Law, 83 Yale L.J. 1315 (1974).

Even-age management has serious impacts on wildlife and soil conditions. Species of birds, insects, bats, and small animals live in the old trees. Some forms of nitrogen-fixing bacteria, which provide essential nutrients for the soil, live only in dead or down timber. Ultimately, the productivity of the soil in old growth forests depends on the generations of trees that have rotted back into the earth. No forester can be certain of the long-range result if the process stops: it will take hundreds of years to discover the answer.

Clearcutting also has serious effects on water resources. The erosion can turn a pure mountain stream chocolate at the time of the cut and lesser erosion can continue in later years. Water temperature and runoff are affected: with no cover, snow will melt earlier in the season, increasing the spring flow and leaving unnaturally low and warm water in the summer and fall. Buffer zones and conservative clearcutting schedules can alleviate, though not eliminate, some of these conditions. But clearcutting has by no means always been conservative, and there are overcut watersheds with wholly different temperature and flow conditions than existed in their pristine states.

After World War II, increased demand for timber brought more intensive management to the national forest system. Clearcutting was accelerated in forests where it was already an existing practice. In some forests it was employed for the first time and often heavy management expenditures caused the Forest Service's costs to exceed revenues from the sales. Local resentment grew, especially in areas near the Bitterroot National Forest in Montana and the Monongahela National Forest in West Virginia.

In 1969, Senator Lee Metcalf of Montana commissioned the School of Forestry at the University of Montana to study Forest Service practices in the Bitterroot. The resulting report was termed the "Bolle Report" after its principal author, Dr. Arnold Bolle.

A UNIVERSITY VIEW OF THE FOREST SERVICE
S.Doc. No. 91–115, 91st Cong., 2d Sess. 14–16 (1970).

* * *

THE PROBLEM

The problem arises from public dissatisfaction with the Bitterroot National Forest's overriding concern for sawtimber production. It is compounded by an apparent insensitivity to the related forest uses and to the local public's interest in environmental values.

In a federal agency which measures success primarily by the quantity of timber produced weekly, monthly and annually, the staff of the Bitterroot National Forest finds itself unable to change its course, to give anything but token recognition to related values, or to involve most of the local public in any way but as antagonists.

The heavy timber orientation is built in by legislative action and control, by executive direction and by budgetary restriction. It is further reinforced by the agency's own hiring and promotion policies and it is rationalized in the doctrines of its professional expertise.

This rigid system developed during the expanded effort to meet national housing needs during the post-war boom. It continues to exist in the face of a considerable change in our value system—a rising public concern with environmental quality. While the national demand for timber has abated considerably, the major emphasis on timber production continues.

The post-war production boom may have justified the single-minded emphasis on timber production. But the continued emphasis largely ignores the economics of regeneration; it ignores related forest values; it ignores local social concerns; and it is simply out of step with changes in our society since the post-war years. The needs of the post-war boom were met at considerable social as well as economic cost. While the rate and methods of cutting and regeneration can be defended on a purely technical basis, they are difficult to defend on either environmental or long-run economic grounds.

* * *

Many local people regard the timber production emphasis as an alien orientation, exploiting the local resource for non-local benefit. It is difficult for them to distinguish what they see from the older forest exploitation which we deplored in other regions. They feel left out of any policy formation or decision-making and so resort to protest as the only available means of being heard.

Many of the employees of the Forest Service are aware of the problems and are dissatisfied with the position of the agency. They recognize the agency is in trouble, but they find it impossible to change, or, at least, to change fast enough.

Multiple-use is stated as the guiding principle of the Forest Service. Given wide lip-service, it cannot be said to be operational on the Bitterroot National Forest at this time.

*   *   *

NOTE

In the East, clearcutting was being challenged contemporaneously. Many argued that it was especially inappropriate in that region because the clearing of mixed hardwood stands and replacement by pines destroyed the existing diversity of species. The West Virginia legislature adopted resolutions calling for a federal investigation into timber harvesting practices in the Monongahela National Forest. See, e.g., Wessling, Monongahela *   *   * From the Beginning, 82 Amer. Forests 28 (1976). Lengthy congressional hearings in the spring of 1972 culminated in a subcommittee report setting out broad rules for harvesting in general and clearcutting in particular. Report of Subcomm. on Public Lands, Senate Interior & Insular Affairs Comm., Clearcutting on Federal Timberlands, 92d Cong., 2d Sess. 8–9 (1972). These "Church guidelines," named after subcommittee chairman Sen. Frank Church of Idaho, were ultimately incorporated with some modifications into the NFMA of 1976, 16 U.S.C.A. §§ 1604(g)(3)(E), (F).

Many thought that the Forest Service had dug in its heels in defense of massive clearcutting. As pointed out in S. Dana & S. Fairfax, FOREST AND RANGE POLICY 227 (2d ed. 1980), it was not that simple:

> Contrary to widespread belief, the Forest Service was not, on the Monongahela or elsewhere, intransigent. At first, however, their response was defensive. In the Pinchot tradition, foresters have a calling as well as a profession. Many believed that they knew what was best for the forests and that they were doing quite well without public interference. They failed to recognize that land management decisions were frequently matters of value or preference rather than technique and that being a forester does not necessarily qualify one to decide what are appropriate goals for public land management. They got into trouble by failing to prepare the public adequately for a change in management regime; and then, under severe and unfamiliar attack in the 1960s, they responded with dismay and hostility.

> Belatedly, the agency did respond. Nationally and locally it began to reconsider the priorities of its land management program, giving fuller attention to public perceptions of forest

values. The Forest Service admitted error in cases where clear cutting had been improperly employed. On the Monongahela, a new multiple-use plan was drawn up, all the timber sales were withdrawn and redesigned, and clear cuts were limited in size and range. The agency accepted thirteen of the West Virginia Forest Management Practices Committee's fifteen recommendations, demurring only in the matter of eschewing clear cutting as a management option.

Unfortunately, by the time the Forest Service and the profession began to admit and correct mistakes and explain their practices more adequately and sensitively, clear cutting had become a national issue and the national mood was such that the critics refused to be mollified. ＊ ＊ ＊

WEST VIRGINIA DIV. OF THE IZAAK WALTON LEAGUE OF AMERICA, INC. v. BUTZ

United States Court of Appeals, Fourth Circuit, 1975.
522 F.2d 945.

FIELD, Circuit Judge:

Alleging that the Forest Service was entering into contracts for the sale of timber in the Monongahela National Forest of West Virginia the terms of which violated the Organic Act of 1897 (hereinafter "Organic Act"), the plaintiffs instituted this action seeking both declaratory and injunctive relief. Specifically, the plaintiffs challenged three proposed timber sales which in the aggregate covered the harvesting of 1077 acres. Under the sales contracts 649 acres were designated for selective cutting while the remaining 428 acres were to be harvested by clearcutting in units ranging in size from five to twenty-five acres. While the trees to be harvested by the selective method would be individually marked, the contracts provided that in the clearcut area all merchantable timber would be cut and none of the trees would be individually marked. The plaintiffs charged that the contracts with respect to the 428 acres violated the sales provision of the Act, 16 U.S. C.A. § 476, which reads in pertinent part as follows:

> "For the purpose of preserving the living and growing timber and promoting the younger growth on national forests, the Secretary of Agriculture, ＊ ＊ ＊ may cause to be designated and appraised so much of the dead, matured or large growth of trees found upon such national forests as may be compatible with the utilization of the forests thereon, and may sell the same ＊ ＊ ＊. ＊ ＊ ＊ Such timber, before being sold, shall be marked and designated, and shall be cut and removed under the supervision of some person appointed for that purpose by the Secretary of Agriculture ＊ ＊ ＊."

＊ ＊ ＊ [The parties stipulated] that the three contracts in question were representative of other contracts for the sale of timber in the Monongahela National Forest and that they involved the sale and cutting of trees, some of which were neither dead, physiologically matured nor large. It was further [agreed] that the Forest Service was selling timber pursuant to procedures under which each tree was not individually marked prior to cutting, although the boundaries of cutting areas were marked. * * * [T]he district court granted the plaintiffs' motion for summary judgment. In doing so, the court declared that the practice, regulations and contracts of the Forest Service which (1) permit the cutting of trees which are not dead, mature or large growth, (2) permit the cutting of trees which have not been individually marked and (3) allow timber which has been cut to remain at the site violate the provisions of the Organic Act. The court enjoined the Forest Service from contracting for or otherwise allowing the cutting of timber in the Monongahela National Forest in violation of the Organic Act. * * *

* * *

The Service takes the position that "large growth of trees" signifies a sizeable stand or grouping of trees, and that the district court erroneously converted this phrase into "large growth trees" which in effect requires that each individual tree be identified as "large". We think the district court correctly construed this statutory phrase. The stated purpose of "promoting the younger growth" clearly refers to the characteristics of the individual trees, and in our opinion the use of the phrase "large growth of trees" in the latter part of the same sentence likewise refers to the individual trees, the words "large growth" being used in contradistinction to the prior reference to "younger growth". To accept this contention that "large growth of trees" means a sizeable stand or group of trees would treat the words "dead and mature" as surplusage, and violate the "well known maxim of statutory construction that all words and provisions of statutes are intended to have meaning and are to be given effect, and words of a statute are not to be construed as surplusage". Wilderness Society v. Morton, [supra at page 294]. The interpretation urged by the defendants would lead to the absurd result that while in small areas of the forest the authority of the Secretary would be restricted, he would nevertheless be free to cut any trees he might desire from a sizeable stand or group of trees (defined by the Government as ten acres or more), regardless of whether the individual trees in such group or stand were small or large, young or old, immature or mature. In our opinion such a paradoxical result would be at odds with the purpose of the Organic Act as well as the plain language of the statute.

The Service further contends that in treating "mature" trees as only those which are physiologically mature, the court ignored other accepted silvicultural tests of maturity. Here again we agree with the district court that the language of the statute means physiological maturity rather than economic or management maturity. A tree is physiologically mature when because of age and condition its growth begins to taper off or it loses its health and vigor, and while age and size are indicators of physiological maturity, they are not exclusively so. From the economic viewpoint a tree is considered mature when it has the highest marketable value, and management maturity is defined as the state at which a tree or stand best fulfills the purpose for which it was maintained, e.g., produces the best supply of specified products. We think unquestionably that in using the word "mature" Congress was referring to physiological maturity. This appears to be the meaning of "mature" in forestry terminology today, and was the accepted meaning of the word at the time the Organic Act was passed by the Congress. * * * Since Congress used the word in its physiological sense at the time of the passage of the Organic Act, we know of no canon of statutory construction which would justify or require that its meaning be changed merely because during the intervening years the timber industry has developed the commercial concept of economic or management maturity. * * *

Turning to that part of Section 476 which requires that the timber "before being sold, shall be marked and designated", we find the statutory language to be simple and unambiguous. The term "marked" in the context of forestry is well defined and means "selection and indication by a blaze, paint * * * or marking hammer on the stem of trees to be felled or retained". "Designate", on the other hand, is a much broader term and merely means to "indicate". The two words are not synonymous or interchangeable and in using them conjunctively it is evident that Congress intended that the Forest Service designate the area from which the timber was to be sold and, additionally, placed upon the Service the obligation to mark each individual tree which was authorized to be cut. This plain reading of the statutory language is buttressed by reference to the statement of Gifford Pinchot, the first Chief of the Forest Service, in his 1898 Surveys of Forest Reserves:

> "In reserves where timber is sold it will be necessary to indicate unmistakably before the cutting what trees are to be cut and afterwards to ascertain that these trees, and these only, have been taken."

* * *

This emphasis placed on such selective marking by those who urged the passage of the Organic Act and were charged with the responsibility of its implementation is entitled to particular weight.

* * *

The Service urges that we follow the decision in Sierra Club v. Hardin, 325 F.Supp. 99 (D.C.D.Alas.1971), which involved the largest sale ever conducted by the Forest Service, covering an estimated 1,090,000 acres of timber land. The district court, observing that the "presale marking of individual trees would be so onerous that only isolated sales on small tracts could be made," concluded that since the contract contemplated "continued cooperation" between the Forest Service and the buyer compatible with the overall plan for utilization of the forest, it satisfied the purpose of Section 476. In reaching this cryptic conclusion the district court engaged in no analysis of either the clear statutory language or the legislative history, and in all candor we do not find its interpretation of the Organic Act persuasive.

While we base our decision primarily upon a literal reading of the statute we find convincing support for our conclusion in the background and legislative history of the Organic Act. * * *

*   *   *

This legislative history demonstrates that the primary concern of Congress in passing the Organic Act was the preservation of the national forests. While the Act as finally passed rejected the position of the extremists who wished to forbid all cutting in the forests, it specifically limited the authority of the Secretary in his selection of timber which could be sold. He could select the timber to be cut only from those trees which were dead, physiologically mature or large, and then only when such cutting would preserve the young and growing timber which remained. Following the addition of "large growth of trees" to the bill, the sponsors repeatedly made it clear that the Act would permit the sale only of the individual trees which met its specific requirements which, in the words of Senator Pettigrew, were "the large trees, the dying trees and trees that will grow no better in time * * *".

*   *   *

The appellants also rely upon the subsequent legislation, together with administrative interpretations and practices of the Forest Service, which they contend support their interpretation of the Organic Act. We find it unnecessary to comment upon any of the legislation with the exception of the Multiple-Use Sustained-Yield Act of 1960. * * * Appellants take the position that this language is a clear Congressional directive to the Secretary of Agriculture to apply modern principles of forestry management and * * * [a ratification of] the management practices which the Service had developed over the years.

In effect, appellants appear to argue that the Multiple-Use Act has by implication repealed the restrictive provisions of the Organic Act. In our opinion, however, this argument falls short of the mark on several grounds. First of all, it is at odds with the well established rule that repeal of a statute by implication is not favored. In addition to the foregoing principle, Section 1 of the Multiple-Use Act specifically recognizes the continued viability of the Organic Act in the following language:

"The purposes of this Act are declared to be supplemental to, but not in derogation of, the purposes for which the national forests were established as set forth in the Act of June 4, 1897 (16 U.S.C. § 475)."

Appellants' argument in this respect also elides the fact that in and out of Congress there has not been unanimous agreement with respect to the interpretation and application of the Multiple-Use Act. Over a decade after its passage controversy over its meaning and intent, as well as the management practices of the Forest Service, including even-aged management and clearcutting, has continued unabated. This division of opinion on the scope of the Multiple-Use Act, as well as the administrative conduct of the Forest Service, was pointed out in the 1972 Subcommittee Report on Clearcutting:

"It is obvious from the extensive testimony received by the Subcommittee * * * on proposed timber management legislation, that timber production has become a priority activity in Federal forest land management. Some construe this as out of step with the spirit and intent, if not the letter, of both the Multiple Use-Sustained Yield and the National Environmental Policy Act of 1969. * * *"

The language of the Multiple-Use Act is broad and ambiguous, and from our review of the material at hand we are satisfied that in enacting this legislation Congress did not intent to jettison or repeal the Organic Act of 1897. We are equally satisfied that this Act did not constitute a ratification of the relatively new policy of the Forest Service which applied the principles of even-aged management and clearcutting in all of the national forests.

It is apparent that the heart of this controversy is the change in the role of the Forest Service which has taken place over the past thirty years. For nearly half a century following its creation in 1905, the National Forest System provided only a fraction of the national timber supply with almost ninety-five per cent coming from privately owned forests. During this period the Forest Service regarded itself as a custodian and protector of the forests rather than a prime producer, and consistent with this role the Service faithfully carried out the provisions of the Organic Act with respect to selective timber cutting. In 1940, however, with private timber reserves badly depleted, World War II created an enormous demand for lumber and this was followed by the post-war building boom. As a result the posture of the Forest Service quickly changed from custodian to a production agency. It was in this new role that the Service initiated the policy of even-aged management in the national forests, first in the West and ultimately in the Eastern forests, including the Monongahela. The appellants urge that this change of policy was in the public interest and that the courts should not permit a literal reading of the 1897 Act to frustrate the modern science of silviculture and forest management presently practiced by the Forest Service to meet the nation's current timber demands. Economic exigencies, however, do not grant the courts a license to rewrite a statute no matter how desirable the purpose or result might be. * * *

We are not insensitive to the fact that our reading of the Organic Act will have serious and far-reaching consequences, and it may well be that this legislation enacted over seventy-five years ago is an anachronism which no longer serves the public interest. However, the appropriate forum to resolve this complex and controversial issue is not the courts but the Congress. * * *

Affirmed.

NOTES

1. As noted in *Monongahela,* a district judge in Alaska had earlier given short shrift to the arguments based on the 1897 Organic Act. The principal case was followed almost immediately by Zieske v. Butz, 406 F.Supp. 258 (D.Alaska 1975), agreeing with the *Monongahela* decision and enjoining clearcutting by Ketchikan Pulp Company under a Forest Service contract in Alaska. Several other cases then pending are summarized in the H.Rep. 94–1478, pt. 1, 94th Cong., 2d Sess. 14–17 (1976).

2. As to contemporary meanings attributed to statutory words, and the degree of literalness in interpreting them, compare United States v. Union Oil Co., 549 F.2d 1271 (9th Cir.1977), supra at page 585. As to repeal by implication, compare TVA v. Hill, 437 U.S. 153 (1978), infra at page 785, which holds that implied repeals are disfavored in the extreme.

NOTE: PASSAGE OF THE NATIONAL FOREST
MANAGEMENT ACT OF 1976

After the *Monongahela* decision, the forest products industry immediately turned to Congress for a repeal of the offending provision in the 1897 Organic Act. Environmentalists used the clearcutting issue as a lever to open a far ranging congressional debate on all forest management practices. Legislation introduced by Senator Jennings Randolph would have severely restricted forest service timber operations, while other bills supported by industry would have done little more than remove the strictures of the 1897 Act.

The National Forest Management Act of 1976, enacted 14 months after the *Monongahela* decision, was a compromise, but one so comprehensive as to amount to a new organic act for the Forest Service. The Act repealed the 1897 provision and is laced with qualifying language, but it addressed on-the-ground forestry issues with a specificity unthinkable in earlier times. The passage of the Act and its provisions are discussed in detail in D. LeMaster, DECADE OF CHANGE: THE REMAKING OF FOREST SERVICE AUTHORITY DURING THE 1970's (1984). See also Stoel, The National Forest Management Act, 8 Envt'l L. 549 (1978); Mulhurn, The National Forest Management Act of 1976: A Critical Examination, 7 B.C.Envt'l Aff.L.Rev. 99 (1979); Strong, The National Forest Management Act of 1976—What Impact on Federal Timber Management?, 13 Idaho L.Rev. 263 (1977); Haines, Monongahela and the National Forest Management Act of 1976, 7 Envt'l L. 345 (1977); Hall & Wasserstrom, The National Forest Management Act of 1976—Out of the Courts and Back to the Forests, 8 Envt'l L. 523 (1978). A good capsule account is in S. Dana & S. Fairfax, FOREST AND RANGE POLICY 327–41 (2d ed. 1980). The primary committee reports are Senate Agriculture and Forestry Comm., S.Rep. No. 94–893, 94th Cong., 2d Sess. (1976) and House Agriculture and Forestry Comm., H.Rep. No. 94–1378, 94th Cong., 2d Sess. (1976).

The NFMA has generated little litigation in its early years because most of its provisions set standards for plans to be developed for each national forest, a process that Congress contemplated would not be completed for roughly a decade. The NFMA implementing regulations were promulgated September 1979. The Act continues existing land management plans in effect until new ones are adopted. 16 U.S.C.A. § 1604(c). In the meantime, Congress intended the 1972 "Church Guidelines" for timber harvesting to be binding on the Forest Service during the hiatus between 1976 and adoption of NFMA plans. See National Wildlife Federation v. United States Forest Service, 592 F.Supp. 931 (D.Or.1984), appeal pending, infra at page 651; Texas Committee on Natural Resources v. Bergland, 573 F.2d 201 (5th Cir. 1978), cert. denied, 439 U.S. 966 (1978). NFMA planning, like the process mandated for the BLM by FLPMA, chapter seven, § C infra, is among the major agents for change in modern public land law. See § C(3) infra.

C. MODERN FOREST MANAGEMENT

1. FEDERAL TIMBER POLICY

The following table can be used as a basis for discussing the place of the national forests in American forest policy.

Area and Volume Statistics by Ownership Classes, 1982

| | | In billion board feet | | | | | |
| | | Total softwood sawtimber volume | | | Total hardwood sawtimber volume | | |
Ownership classes	Commercial area held million acres	Inventory	Growth	Removals	Inventory	Growth	Removals
National forests	88.7	1,009.3	11.0	11.6	49.2	1.7	.5
Other Public	47.0	235.2	4.7	4.9	50.9	2.1	.7
Forest industry	68.8	314.3	11.7	19.5	80.6	3.3	2.1
Other private	278.0	426.7	22.2	14.8	412.8	17.8	11.0
National Total	482.5	1,985.5	49.7	50.8	593.5	24.9	14.2

Source: Department of Agriculture, Forest Service, "An Analysis of the Timber Situation in the United States 1952–2030," (1982).

Commercial forest land traditionally has been defined as land capable of producing 20 cubic feet of timber per acre per year. The "other public" lands category in the table includes state, county, and municipal lands, and 4.7 million acres of BLM lands. Most of the issues raised here in regard to the Forest Service apply also to the smaller BLM holdings.

1. *Timber Inventory and Timber Types.* As the table shows, national forests account for about 18% of the Nation's commercial timber land, but that figure is misleading because it does not measure the amount of inventory, or volume of wood, on those acres. Although the inventory of hardwood timber on national forest lands is not a significant part of the nation's standing hardwood timber, the Forest Service presides over more than half of the nation's inventory of

softwood timber. Softwood timber, which is in greater demand than hardwood, is the primary source of construction lumber, and is thus essential to the housing industry.

2. *Old Growth Forests.* As the two columns on the left show, the forest industry owns 314 billion board feet of softwood timber on 68.8 million acres, or about 4622 board feet per acre. But, on national forest lands, the softwood inventory per acre is 2¼ times greater than on private industry lands: the inventory of 1,009 billion board feet of timber on 88.7 million acres averages out to 11,374 board feet per acre. The disparity is even greater for "other private" lands (miscellaneous private holdings of 20 acres or more) which hold an average of only 1,535 board feet per acre.

These disparities arise because most private lands have been cut over and no large old-growth trees remain. In many cases, private lands have been harvested by "cut and run" or "highgrading" practices, in which the best timber was cleared and no reforesting undertaken. In contrast, many of the federal lands have never been cut at all, leaving massive stands of old-growth timber intact. These valuable stands, especially in the national forests of the Pacific Northwest, include magnificent virgin fir, redwood, cedar, and pine forests. These trees are straight, large, normally accessible, and provide the highest quality lumber. Harvesting them is said to be the solution for meeting the Nation's growing demand for timber. On the other hand, such stands are unique ecological resources that cannot be replaced for generations, if ever.

In 1973, a blue-ribbon presidential commission concluded: "The central issue for meeting the wood needs for the 1970's and 1980's is: at what rate should the old growth inventory on the national forests be converted to well-managed new stands to meet both current and future timber needs." REPORT OF THE PRESIDENT'S ADVISORY PANEL ON TIMBER AND THE ENVIRONMENT 9 (1973). The panel urged departures from the conservative harvesting practices of the Forest Service and recommended that the timber harvest be accelerated.

3. *Intensive Management.* The second and third columns from the left on the table show that the annual growth rate for softwood industry lands is 3.7% (amounting to 11.7 billion board feet from an inventory of 314.3 board feet), while the growth rate for national forest lands is just 1%. Industry lands produce more growth because more intensive management practices are employed. High yield management is based on growing "thrifty, young trees," starting with the prompt planting of seedings, sometimes genetically improved. Years later, precommercial and commercial thinning cleans out some trees to provide more light and soil to those remaining; fertilizers and other enhancement methods are also commonly employed. A short "rotation" period (the time over which an area of forest is harvested) is used so that the intensive management cycle can be repeated. (When Weyerhauser Company called itself—correctly—"The Tree Growing

Company," a Sierra Club representative replied—correctly—"Yes. They grow small trees.")

The federal old-growth forests have low growth rates because they have attained an age when annual growth tapers off. Indeed, some old growth forests actually have a negative growth rate: the slow growth of the live trees does not equal the annual mortality rate of wood fiber through rot and disease. Environmental aesthetics and silviculture collide over whether and at what rate these ancient stands should be liquidated:

> It is also appropriate to emphasize that the legal profession has a similar kind of responsibility in its own canons of ethics as the members of the medical and forestry professions have with respect to the public health. This responsibility includes ensuring not only that laws are not permitted that allow forests to be wasted, but that the forests be adequately protected so that man may always enjoy all their qualities. One must question the views of many lawyers who believe that more old growth forests should be put into withdrawals or reserves by laws attempting to preserve them forever in their untouched state. Such a goal is patently ridiculous and indicates that law schools need to teach prospective members of the legal profession a few facts of life about the ecology of plants. All trees have a date certain with death, just like every person. Trees were placed here by higher laws than man's for serving the human race, and they must continue to do so through protection, management and renewal, the principal purposes of the forestry profession.

> When there are homeless people in the world, there is no more of a right to waste wood than there is a right to waste food when there are hungry people. Whether people like it or not, the old forest must make way for the new.

Hagenstein, The Old Forest Maketh Way for the New, 8 Envt'l L. 479, 494–95 (1978). For an argument that old growth is necessary for the stability of forest ecosystems as a whole, see Juday, Old Growth Forests: A Necessary Element of Multiple Use and Sustained Yield National Forest Management, 8 Envt'l L. 497 (1978).

4. *Rate of Removal.* Although old-growth removal is itself a subject of controversy, many industry critics believe that Forest Service harvesting schedules are too conservative on all lands. The rate at which the softwood inventory is removed annually can be obtained by dividing the fourth column on the table by the second column. How does the rate of removal on Forest Service lands compare with that on industry lands? The Forest Service's comparatively low rate of harvest is due to several factors, including the use of a long rotation period; for example, the rotation period for Douglas fir is 100 years in many national forests compared with periods of 60, 50 or even 40 years on intensively managed private Douglas fir forests. In addition, Forest

Service long-range projections sometimes build in conservative assumptions; for example, some computer analyses have assumed less than maximum returns from practices such as thinning and genetic improvement. Since the present harvest cannot exceed future growth potential, these conservative projections tend to keep annual removal lower than it otherwise might have been.

The use of economics as a means of making policy decisions is increasingly relied upon in modern forestry. The Forest Service currently uses computer modeling to make a number of management decisions, and there is every indication that trend will continue. Economists, however, do not agree on the proper application of economic theory to public timberlands. Compare Krutilla & Haigh, An Integrated Approach to National Forest Management, 8 Envt'l L. 373 (1978) with R. Stroup & J. Baden, NATURAL RESOURCES: BUREAUCRATIC MYTHS AND ENVIRONMENTAL MANAGEMENT (1983). See also FORESTS IN DEMAND: CONFLICTS AND SOLUTIONS (C. Hewitt & T. Hamilton eds., 1982); Behan, Political Popularity and Conceptual Nonsense: The Strange Case of Sustained Yield Forestry, 8 Envt'l L. 309 (1978); Irland, Economics of Wilderness Preservation, 7 Envt'l L. 51 (1976); Williams, Benefit-Cost Analysis in Natural Resources Decisionmaking: An Economic and Legal Overview, 11 Nat. Res.Law. 761 (1979).

5. *"Other Private" Forests.* The table also indicates that almost 60% of commercial forest land is located in non-industry private holdings. Most studies conclude that establishing improved management practices on those lands is one way to help meet market demands and lessen the pressure on federal lands in the future. Coordinating silvacultural practices on these small, widely-dispersed holdings, however, is no easy matter. See Towell, Managing Private Nonindustrial Forestlands: A Perennial Issue, 26 J. of Forest Hist. 192 (1982).

6. *Timber-Dependent Communities.* Twenty-two percent of federal commercial timberlands are located in the Great Lakes Area, New England, and the South. In those areas, and in many regions in the West, the economies of numerous small communities are partially or heavily dependent on jobs created by timber harvesting on federal lands. Accelerated cutting of old growth can result in a "fall down" when the last old growth is cut, severely harming local economies, because timber harvesting must cease or decrease when the large stands are gone. This has led to the Forest Service's policy of non-declining even flow, a conservative version of sustained yield management that requires a relatively level annual cut to avoid the lapse that would occur if old-growth timber is harvested on an accelerated basis. See infra at page 665.

7. *Wilderness.* The question of how much timber to remove entirely from harvest by placing the land in untouchable categories is, of course, subject to continuing debate.

8. *Timber Management Practices.* How to cut is as divisive an issue as whether to cut. Modern forestry tries to see that streams are

protected from fallen timber, that yarding (physically removing the cut timber from the logging site) is carried on with minimum erosion or damage to the remaining stand, that slash (residue such as limbs and stumps) is properly disposed of, and that restocking occurs promptly and efficiently. Many argue that such practices do not go far enough; clearcutting in particular continues to stir their ire. Another delicate issue is road building, which can cause as much or more erosion damage as timber harvesting.

9. *Below-Cost Sales.* For the national forest system as a whole, revenues far exceed costs. In 1981 and 1982, for example, the system was $712 million "in the black." Many of the profitable sales, however, take place in the Pacific Northwest, while sales in other regions, especially in the Rocky Mountains, are often below-cost—the government's costs of growing and selling trees exceed revenues from timber sales—due to low-quality commercial timber land. Roadbuilding is a large cost constituent, and roads can be used for nontimber purposes such as recreation and wildlife management; even when appropriate portions of road costs are allocated to nontimber benefits, however, many sales still fail to pay their way. In one survey, the General Accounting Office found that costs exceeded revenues in 27% of all sales in 1981 and in 42% of all sales in 1982. See General Accounting Office, Congress Needs Better Information on Forest Service's Below-Cost Timber Sales (GAO/RCD–84–96, 1984). The Forest Service is under fire from fiscal conservatives, who object to these subsidies, and environmentalists, who oppose the extensive road systems into roadless areas where many of the proposed below-cost sales will occur. Industry argues that below-cost sales are necessary to support local communities dependent on a continuing flow of timber from national forests. See infra at page 668.

10. *Miscellaneous Issues.* Other policy questions, which will be treated only tangentially here, include log exports to foreign countries, the application of economic theory, and bidding practices. An excellent work for the uninitiated is M. Clawson, FORESTS: FOR WHOM AND FOR WHAT? (1975).

The issues raised in this section will recur in the remaining materials on modern forest management.

2. THE NATIONAL ENVIRONMENTAL POLICY ACT

The NFMA has become a principal legal focus of national forest management, but other statutes still control some management aspects, and other issues affect the Service. In the 1970's and 1980's, the Forest Service administratively withheld tens of millions of roadless acres from timber production in order to study their suitability for wilderness designation. See infra chapter eleven, § B. Further, the National Environmental Policy Act requires the Forest Service to use its procedures for all major activities. NEPA also opened the courthouse doors to unsatisfied forest users to a degree equalled by no other statute. A NEPA case involving watershed management in a national forest has already been examined. Northwest Indian Cemetary Protective Assoc. v. Peterson, 764 F.2d 581 (9th Cir.1985), supra at page 413. Other such cases question Forest Service and BLM roadbuilding, widespread use of economic poisons, and other management activities.

SAVE OUR ECOSYSTEMS v. CLARK
United States Court of Appeals, Ninth Circuit, 1984.
747 F.2d 1240.

FLETCHER, Circuit Judge:

Plaintiffs in these consolidated cases challenge the spraying of herbicides on United States Forest Service (USFS) and Bureau of Land Management (BLM) lands. Both cases involve whether research on and disclosure of the potential carcinogenic, teratogenic and mutagenic effects of the herbicides is required under the National Environmental Policy Act of 1969.

The district court enjoined portions of both the BLM spraying program for the Eugene District of Oregon in *Save Our Ecosystems v. Clark* (SOS) and the USFS program for the State of Oregon in *Merrell v. Block* (Merrell). We affirm the district court's holdings in the two cases that the USFS and the BLM violated NEPA and the regulations of the Council on Environmental Quality (CEQ). However, we modify the injunctions to enjoin all spraying until the agencies comply with NEPA.

FACTUAL BACKGROUND

A. SOS v. Clark.

In 1978 the BLM prepared a programmatic environmental impact statement (PEIS) entitled "Vegetation Management With Herbicides: Western Oregon, 1978–1987." The statement discussed the environmental impacts of a ten-year program of herbicide spraying,[1] intended to destroy undergrowth thereby increasing the growth rate of conifers. The PEIS was to be supplemented annually by an environmental assessment (EA), upon which would be based the decision whether to spray in the succeeding year, and, if so, how the spraying would be done.

In 1979 an organization called Southern Oregon Citizens Against Toxic Sprays (*SOCATS*) filed suit to enjoin the BLM from spraying in the Medford District. In that case, Judge Frye enjoined the spraying because the BLM had failed to prepare a "worst case analysis" (WCA) under 40 C.F.R. § 1502.22 (1981). That decision was affirmed by this court. See Southern Oregon Citizens Against Toxic Sprays v. Clark, 720 F.2d 1475 (9th Cir.1983) (SOCATS).

In response to the district court decision in *SOCATS*, the BLM prepared a worst case analysis of its spraying program for the Eugene

---

1. The herbicides proposed for use by the BLM were 2,4–D, Silvex, Simazine, Atrazine, Diuron, Tordon, Dalapon, Banvel, Krenite, and Roundup. *FINAL* *EIS*, Summary. Silvex was later dropped from the program after EPA suspended its registration because it was contaminated with dioxin.

district. The plaintiffs in this case challenge its adequacy. Judge Belloni agreed with plaintiffs, but limited the injunction to prohibiting aerial spraying in a portion of the district and granted defendant's motion to stay the injunction pending appeal. We vacated the stay and reinstated the original injunction.

B. Merrell v. Block.

The *Merrell* case arises out of the USFS spraying program for its forests in Oregon, a program very similar to that of the BLM. In 1978 the Forest Service prepared a PEIS on "Vegetation Management With Herbicides" covering the Pacific Northwest Region.[2] The PEIS was to be supplemented annually by an EA. Soon after spraying commenced in 1979, numerous and serious health problems were reported in the Five Rivers Valley, including spontaneous abortions, birth defects in humans and animals, and various other illnesses. The EPA began an investigation into these problems, but the Forest Service declined requests by the county health department and board of commissioners to delay the spraying. The Forest Service conducted no research of its own into these problems and, in its 1981 EA, concluded that the continued use of the herbicides would have no significant impact on the human environment and declined to prepare an EIS.

In 1981 Paul Merrell, a resident of the Five Rivers area of the Suislaw National Forest, filed a suit seeking an injunction against further spraying in that national forest. * * *

As in *SOS,* Judge Belloni enjoined only a portion of the spraying program * * *

DISCUSSION

I. SOS v. Clark.

A. Worst Case Analysis.

1. NEPA Requires Analysis of Uncertain Risks.

CEQ regulations require an EIS to contain a "worst case analysis" when "the information relevant to adverse impacts is essential * * * and is not known and the overall costs of obtaining it are exorbitant or * * * the information * * * is important and the means to obtain it are not known. * * *" 40 C.F.R. § 1502.22 (1981).

* * *

On their face these regulations require an ordered process by an agency when it is proceeding in the face of uncertainty. First, the agency must determine whether the information is important or essential and whether it can be obtained. If it cannot be obtained or if the costs of obtaining it are exorbitant, the agency must do a worst case analysis weighing the need for the action against all possible adverse impacts. The agency must consider the range of worst possible effects

2. The PEIS was prepared after Judge Skopil enjoined the use of 2,3,4–T, and Silvex by the Forest Service because of dioxin contamination. See Citizens Against Toxic Sprays v. Bergland, 428 F.Supp. 908 (D.Or.1977).

and the likelihood of these effects occurring. It must also consider the costs of proceeding without the information.

The BLM acknowledges that the issue of *whether* a WCA is required has been determined by our decision in *SOCATS*, where we held that the BLM must prepare a worst case analysis bottomed on the assumption that its herbicides are not safe. We noted that scientific uncertainty existed regarding the carcinogenacity of the herbicides and that "[w]hen uncertainty exists, it must be exposed." This is not all that is required, however. Besides exposing the *fact* of uncertainty, because of that uncertainty, a spectrum of possible events must be considered.

* * *

The * * * mere fact that the possibility of an event occurring is remote or unlikely does not obviate the necessity to do a worst case analysis.[6]

Both the CEQ regulation and other NEPA cases contemplate analysis of a "spectrum of events." [7] With these requirements in mind, we examine the WCA prepared by the BLM in this case.

2. Adequacy of the WCA.

The WCA prepared by the BLM is brief and cursory, and proceeds from an entirely wrong assumption. The BLM admits that no level of exposure to the herbicides has been proven safe, but assumes in the WCA that "a point is reached at which it becomes clear that no human health effect will occur." Judge Belloni said, "Plainly, the worst result that can occur as a result of proceeding in the face of uncertainty as to whether a herbicide causes cancer is that it *does* cause cancer." We agree. We observed in *SOCATS* that, "The possibility that the safe level of dosage for herbicides is low or nonexistent creates a possibility of 'significant adverse effects on the human environment.' * * * This potential calls for a worst case analysis."

The BLM argues that the analysis plaintiffs say is necessary would be pure guesswork because no credible data exist to support the proposition that cancer can occur at any dose. This contention is specious in light of the evidence presented by plaintiffs' experts and the

---

[6.] For example, even one chance out of 10,000 that a catastrophic event (such as nuclear disaster) would occur is relevant information to a decisionmaker. Even if an event is unlikely, if responsible scientific critics present opposing points of view as to the possible environmental effects of a project, the agency has an obligation to respond to those views.

7. The "range of alternative" analysis required under NEPA is not unlike the WCA regulation that requires analysis of a spectrum of events. NEPA requires the consideration of a range of alternatives to the proposed action, including the no-action alternative. "The EIS discussion of alternatives must make clear the reasons for the agency's choice, address the environmental effects of the alternatives, compare them, explain how future options may be narrowed by present decisions, and respond to the recommendations of responsible critics." Rogers, *Environmental Law* 793–94 (1977) (footnotes omitted), and cases cited therein.

A worst case analysis could discuss, for example, a 1% chance of event X, a 10% chance of event Y and a 20% chance of event Z, while an EIS for leasing might discuss the effects of leasing 0, 10,000, and 50,000 acres.

holding of *SOCATS* that "[t]he agency may not omit the analysis only because it believes that the worst case is unlikely." 720 F.2d at 1479. The duty of an agency is to analyze the costs and environmental effects of the worst case and its costs and *then* to provide its assessment of the likelihood of the event occurring. The district court was correct in finding the WCA deficient.[9]

B. Public Comment Period for the WCA.

The BLM provided five days for public comment on the WCA before it made its final decision. It argues that the WCA was part of the EA and, accordingly, need be made available only at some time prior to the final decision.

* * *

* * * When an EA is the functional equivalent of an EIS, it is subject to the same procedures. Judge Belloni was correct in holding that the WCA was subject to the minimum 45-day comment period for draft EIS's contained in 40 C.F.R. § 1506.10(c) (1983).

II. Merrell v. Block.

A. NEPA Requires Research on the Environmental Effects of the USFS Program.

Judge Belloni found that "[w]hen USFS and BLM completed their EAR's [environmental assessment reports or EA's] they did not do any actual research on the health effects of using the listed herbicides in the area. Instead, they simply relied on research already completed by EPA when that agency registered the chemicals under FIFRA."

The Forest Service argues that Judge Belloni's decision requires it to do original research on the use of the herbicides and that such a requirement is beyond the scope of a court's authority under NEPA. Neither of these contentions is accurate.

Judge Belloni did not specify *what* the Forest Service must do, rather, he held that it could not rely solely on EPA registration under FIFRA.[12] The Forest Service could appropriately consider EPA's data on the herbicides in the specific context of the area in which it proposes to spray; it could require the chemical companies, such as amicus Monsanto, to provide the data and necessary research on their herbi-

---

9. More and more chemicals are added to our environment daily without adequate information about the long-range effects on health and environment. The EPA, in effect, acknowledges that data on the herbicides in this case are inadequate since the registration is conditional under an exception to the normal registration process.

* * *

12. Judge Belloni's decision is bolstered by recent disclosures of widespread fraud in the tests performed by independent testing laboratories. See, e.g., Smith, *Creative Penmanship in Animal Testing Prompts*

EPA Controls 198 Science 1227–29 (1977). As to 2,4–D, the EPA stated that

> a number of the currently available studies are inconclusive or scientifically invalid. Significant gaps were also found in the existing data base.
>
> In addition, no sound clinical studies are available to answer questions raised by accident reports and other reports of adverse effects. These problems make it impossible, at this time, to complete a comprehensive scientifically sound assessment of any potential hazards associated with the chemical.

cides for similar analysis; it could commission studies or undertake its own research or any combination of these options that would satisfy its obligations under NEPA to provide an adequate analysis of the effects of its spraying program in the targeted area.[13]

1. *Reliance on EPA Registration is Improper.*

The EPA registration process for herbicides under FIFRA is inadequate to address environmental concerns under NEPA, particularly where, as here, the registration is only conditional. Conditional registration is a recognition that less than complete data exists. FIFRA does not require or even contemplate the same examination that the Forest Service is required to undertake under NEPA. FIFRA registration is a cost-benefit analysis that no unreasonable risk exists "to man or the environment taking into account the economic, social and environmental costs and benefits of the use of any pesticide." 7 U.S.C. § 136(bb).

Reliance on EPA data is clearly improper under this court's holdings in Oregon Environmental Council v. Kunzman, 714 F.2d 901 (9th Cir.1983) and *SOCATS.* In *Kunzman* we held that the Forest Service's spraying of carbaryl over populated areas violated NEPA where the PEIS and EA failed to address adequately the health effects of "spraying on people living or working in or near the areas sprayed." * * *

* * * We followed this decision in *SOCATS*, stating that "[t]he BLM must assess independently the safety of the herbicides that it uses." *SOCATS*, at 1480.

2. *The Forest Service Must Do Research If No Adequate Data Exists.*

We recognized in *SOCATS* that an agency may be required to do independent research on the health effects of a herbicide. This is not a new requirement.

* * *

* * * Only if the costs are exorbitant or the means of obtaining the information is beyond the state of the art is the agency excused from compliance and allowed to perform a worst case analysis. 40 C.F.R. § 1502.22(b). The Forest Service presents no evidence and makes no argument that the costs are exorbitant or that research is impossible. Rather, it argues that it cannot be forced to do it. Section 1502.22 clearly contemplates original research if necessary.

Federal agencies routinely either do their own studies or commission studies of the particular area in which a proposed project is to be located. Almost every EIS contains some original research. And, almost every time an EIS is ruled inadequate by a court it is because more data or research is needed. * * * The Forest Service cannot

---

13. EPA's data is partial at best, and suspect at worst, because of the testing scandals. * * *

abdicate its responsibilities by relying on another agency. It must evaluate the impact of its own actions.

B. Preparation of a Joint EIS.

Plaintiffs argue that 40 C.F.R. § 1501.5(a) requires the preparation of a joint EIS by the EPA, BLM, and USFS. This argument is unpersuasive in this case. * * *

Although both the BLM and the Forest Service are engaged in forest spraying programs, the programs are in separate areas. The EPA's function is clearly distinct. We are unwilling to find that the district court erred in refusing to mandate a joint EIS. This is not to say that the agencies and the public might not be better served were a joint EIS prepared. The programs of the BLM and the Forest Service are similar. The geographic areas in some instances are close. The terrain and conditions in the BLM and forest service areas may be very similar. Neither agency can ignore the program by the other. To the extent the program of one affects the other or the effects of the programs are cumulative neither agency can avoid assessing the impact of its program on the other. Joint participation by the EPA as a resource, consultant and expert would indeed be beneficial.

III. Scope of the Injunctions.

* * *

We are puzzled by the limited scope of the injunctions in these cases. Judge Belloni limited the injunctions in both cases in two ways, by limiting the territorial scope of the injunctions and by restricting the injunctions to aerial spraying (allowing ground spraying to go forward).

Irreparable damage is presumed when an agency fails to evaluate thoroughly the environmental impact of a proposed action. See *Friends of the Earth Inc. v. Coleman*, 518 F.2d 323, 330 (9th Cir.1975). Only in a rare circumstance may a court refuse to issue an injunction when it finds a NEPA violation.[15] * * *

The "rare circumstance" arose in *American Motorcyclist Association v. Watt*, 714 F.2d 962 (9th Cir.1983) (AMA), where the court found more harm would result to the environment from granting the injunction than by refusing to grant it.[16] * * *

15. See Plater, Statutory Violations and Equitable Discretion, 70 Cal.L.Rev. 524, 575 (1982) ("It does not appear that any lower court, much less the Supreme Court, has ever found in a proceeding on the merits that federal actions violating NEPA could continue in opposition to the statutory mandates"). This is still true except for the unusual circumstances rule of *AMA*.

16. In *AMA* we held that a substantial likelihood existed that the BLM's Desert Conservation Plan violated NEPA, because of its inconsistencies with the County of Inyo's general plan, but refused to issue a preliminary injunction in face of attack by the motorcyclists because such conduct "would leave fragile desert resources vulnerable to permanent damage from increased recreational use." We were troubled by the challenge by the County of Inyo that the plan was inconsistent with the county's general plan, but found that the harm to the desert area outweighed the harm to the planning process. 714 F.2d at 966.

The refusal to issue the injunction in *AMA* was in order to *protect* the environment. * * *

We find no such justification here that would excuse a total ban on spraying. The district court should have enjoined the spraying programs of the BLM and USFS in their entirety until NEPA requirements were fulfilled.

* * *

NOTES

1. Does the opinion require an unreasonable amount of paperwork dealing with speculative and remote possibilities? Should government testing be consolidated in one agency, such as EPA, to avoid needless duplication? The regulation on worst case analyses cited in the principal case was amended in 1986. See supra at page 354.

2. Should trial judges be able to withhold injunctions for minor and technical violations of NEPA? See County of Del Norte v. United States, 732 F.2d 1462 (9th Cir.1984), infra at page 975; cf. Weinberger v. Romero-Barcelo, 456 U.S. 305 (1982). If such equitable discretion exists under NEPA, should it be exercised to deny injunctive relief here?

3. One court struck down a worst case analysis, prepared to analyze the effects of a spraying program to eradicate the gypsy moth, on the basis of the "readability" requirement of NEPA. See 40 C.F.R. §§ 1502.1, 1502.2(b) (1985):

> In the present case, the worst case analysis * * * is hypertechnical, complex and replete with lengthy equations and calculations. When asked to interpret a portion of the worst case analysis, defense witness Dr. Richard Wilson, Chairman of the Department of Physics at Harvard University, stated that he was unable to decipher the precise meaning of the passage, but given 15 minutes of study he could probably untangle the message. This testimony illustrates the complexity of this portion of the document.

Oregon Environmental Council v. Kunzman, 614 F.Supp. 657 (D.Or. 1985).

4. NEPA remains central to Forest Service land use planning even after the NFMA. E.g., Thomas v. Peterson, 753 F.2d 754 (9th Cir. 1985), infra at page 669 (failure to consider effects of logging road); Conner v. Burford, 605 F.Supp. 107 (D.Mont.1985), supra at page 567 (failure to consider effects of mineral leasing); Foundation for North American Wild Sheep v. United States, 681 F.2d 1172 (9th Cir.1982), infra at page 877 (EIS required for construction of mining road through area occupied by Desert Bighorn Sheep); Lee v. Bergland, 673 F.2d 1338 (9th Cir.1982) (programmatic EIS sufficient in denying plaintiff renewal of forest residence permit); Alabama v. United States Forest Service, 11 ELR 20779 (N.D.Ala.1981) (rerouting of hiking trail is not a "major federal action" requiring preparation of an environmental impact statement).

5. But there are limits to NEPA's scope and applicability:

NATIONAL WILDLIFE FEDERATION v. COSTON
United States Court of Appeals, Ninth Circuit, 1985.
773 F.2d 1513.

DUNIWAY, Circuit Judge:

The National Wildlife Federation and the Montana and Idaho Wildlife Federations appeal from the district court's order denying their motion for a preliminary injunction to halt road construction projects in the Northern Region of the Forest Service authorized by a regional Capital Investment Program. We affirm.

I. *Background.*

The Forest Service has responsibility for managing the National Forest System. 36 C.F.R. 200.3(b)(2) (1984). Each National Forest is managed by a Forest Supervisor. In addition, the National Forests have been organized into nine administrative regions, each directed by a Regional Forester.

The Forest Supervisor of each National Forest within Region I has responsibility for the land management activities in the Forest under his control. He decides whether or not to initiate and eventually approve or disapprove a road construction project in that Forest, except as an administrative appeal to the Regional Forester may dictate otherwise. These decisions are based on the National Environmental Policy Act of 1969, 42 U.S.C. §§ 4321 et seq., process, which includes documentation ranging from broad programmatic Environmental Impact Statements (EISs) to site specific project Environmental Analyses (EAs), and extensive public involvement opportunities. Once this process has been completed, the Regional Forester has the responsibility of assigning regional priorities for the allocation of limited funds to programs and projects which have been approved by each Forest Supervisor.

Tom Coston is Regional Forester for Region I, a region embracing thirteen National Forests in the states of Montana, Idaho, North Dakota, and South Dakota. In 1981, Coston implemented an amendment to the Forest Service Manual (FSM) which set out a regional Capital Investment Road and Bridge Program (CIP). (FSM 7710.33.) The CIP formalized existing procedures for determining how regional funds should be allocated for construction proposals approved by Region I Forest Supervisors.

The CIP amendment states:

Regional policy is to provide centralized program management for road and bridge construction, reconstruction, and betterment public works projects estimated to cost in excess of $25,000. [sic] The Regional Forester shall reserve and allocate funds for these projects to Forests based on Regional priority and availability of funds. * * *

The Regional objective is to manage public works construction funds effectively and maintain accountability for both quantity and quality in meeting Regional goals. Objective is to identify and keep current 5 years of capital investment projects which meet the following program objectives. The objectives are listed in order of Regional priority.

a. Provide new road and bridge access to commercial timber lands in RARE II and other unroaded areas released or available for development.

b. Provide adequate road and bridge access to harvest timber areas threatened or damaged by pests.

c. Construct new roads and bridges in areas not classified as unroaded to support the 5 year timber harvest program.

d. Repair pavement structures and bridges where analyses clearly show a need to protect investment or resolve safety and emergency problems. * * *

e. Construct/reconstruct roads, bridges and terminal facilities to meet the Region's timber harvest, other resource or environmental needs.

The amount of funds available for each category shall be determined annually by the Regional Forester, depending on the final budget advice and the needs identified by the Forest Supervisors.

(FSM 7710.33—1–2).

The CIP operates in the following manner: Forest Supervisors annually update data files for construction projects currently in the system and submit to the Regional Forester proposals for additional projects based on the five categories set out above. (FSM 7710.33—2). All such proposals are reviewed by a Regional office team consisting of representatives from Engineering; Timber Management; Recreation; Administrative Services; Planning, Programming; and Budgeting; and other staff as required. This team ranks each project by priority in each of the five categories after considering the following factors: forest priority; importance of project; previously committed cost-share or other written agreements; regional program objectives. (FSM 7710.33—3). Each project is only compared with the other projects in the same category and the same fiscal year. The review team submits its recommendations for priority ranking of the construction projects within each category for each of the five fiscal years to the Regional Forester.

The Regional Forester reviews these recommendations in conjunction with other budget considerations and submits a proposed budget to the Chief of the Forest Service which expresses construction needs in total miles, total cost and total resource production for the Region. Following Congress' adoption of the Forest Service's budget, the Chief allocates funds for road and bridge construction to the Regions. Upon receiving final budget advice from the Chief, the Regional Forester assigns a percentage of available funds to each of the five priority categories for the current fiscal year. He then advises the Forest

Supervisors of the final ranking of projects for the current fiscal year and the tentative ranking of projects for the following four fiscal years. (FSM 7710.33—2).

After the Regional Forester issues his list of priority rankings of proposed projects, any project may be abandoned or deferred for a variety of reasons including environmental concerns, schedule delays in complying with NEPA, and technical difficulties in design. Such decisions are made by the Forest Supervisor unless an administrative appeal is upheld. A high percentage of projects are dropped, deferred or modified during the course of the fiscal year. Before construction begins on any project, the Forest Supervisors must complete NEPA requirements. A project approved for funding through the CIP process is not actually funded until a Public Works Contract is awarded.

The majority of road construction projects in Region I, including those involving timber sale contracts, do not come under the CIP. In 1984, for example, an estimated 86 percent of roads constructed in Region I did not involve CIP funds.

In June, 1984, the wildlife federations brought this action against the United States Forest Service and Coston, alleging that the CIP violates the National Environmental Policy Act of 1969 (NEPA), 42 U.S.C. §§ 4321 et seq., the Endangered Species Act, 16 U.S.C. §§ 1531 et seq., and the Administrative Procedure Act (APA), 5 U.S.C. § 706(2) (d). They moved for a preliminary injunction restraining Coston from proceeding with CIP-authorized road construction projects and from accepting and awarding bids for new CIP projects. *They did not challenge the adequacy of EAs or EISs undertaken at the regional or site level, nor did they challenge the approval by Forest Supervisors of any of the individual construction projects which they sought to enjoin.* (Emphasis ours.) * * *

* * *

III. *The NEPA Claim.*

* * * The federations argue that the Forest Service violated NEPA by failing to prepare a programmatic EIS on the priorities and objectives of the CIP, and by failing to prepare an annual EIS on the decisions by the Regional Forester as to which roads may actually receive funds under the program.

It is clear that NEPA requires the preparation of an EIS not only in proposals for specific Forest Service projects, but also in proposals for large-scale, substantive Forest Service programs which significantly affect the environment. The federations argue that the CIP is such a program. They view CIP as a "concerted road building program" which permanently removes roadless areas from future consideration by Congress for inclusion into the National Wilderness Preservation System. See California v. Block, 9 Cir., 1982, 690 F.2d 753, 762–63. Moreover, they argue that road construction under the CIP destroys habitat and reduces big game populations as well as hunting and wilderness recreation opportunities. For these reasons, the federations conclude that NEPA requires that the Forest Service prepare an EIS with regard to the 1981 development and implementation of the CIP, as well as EISs with regard to the regional Forester's annual CIP funding decisions.

The heart of this case is a dispute as to the true nature of the CIP. Affidavits of Forest Service officials responsible for the implementation of the CIP state that the CIP is purely a budgeting and scheduling process and not a substantive program. Relying on Andrus v. Sierra Club, 1979, 442 U.S. 347, the Forest Service argues that the CIP does not represent a proposal for legislation or major federal action requiring the preparation of an EIS under NEPA Section 102(2)(C).

* * *

Like the appropriations requests in *Andrus,* the CIP does not "propose" federal actions but instead "fund[s] actions already proposed," and already subject to NEPA analysis. The wildlife federations' description of the CIP as a substantive road-building program is misleading. The CIP merely sets out procedures for the Regional Forester to review construction proposals submitted by the Forest Supervisors in order to establish regional priorities for the allocation of limited federal funds. As in *Andrus,* to require the Forest Service to prepare programmatic and annual EISs on the CIP would be to create "unnecessary redundancy."

Road construction and other land management activities of the Forest Service are conducted in compliance with NEPA requirements at various planning levels. The Forest Service prepares EISs to analyze its recommended five-year national resource program. EISs are prepared in connection with the development of the Forest Service's Regional Guides, which direct land management planning at the regional level. In addition, each Forest Supervisor prepares an EIS to accompany a comprehensive Forest-level Land and Resource Management Plan. 16 U.S.C. § 1604(g)(1); 36 C.F.R. 219.10(c)(1), (f), (g), (h) (1984). At the site level, environmental analyses are undertaken in conjunction with the planning of individual construction projects. In Region I, the Regional Forester will award no CIP funds for the construction of a specific road until the appropriate Forest Supervisor has completed all NEPA requirements with regard to that project.

* * *

IV. *The APA Claim.*

The federations allege that Coston violated Forest Service regulations in implementing the CIP in 1981. 36 C.F.R. § 216 et seq. (1983). These regulations required public disclosure and opportunity for public review and comment with respect to "the formulation of standards, criteria, and guidelines needed for Forest Service programs." 36 C.F.R. § 216.2 (1983). Under the APA, this court is to set aside agency action found to be arbitrary, capricious, an abuse of discretion, or otherwise not in accordance with law, 5 U.S.C. § 706(2)(A), or without observance of procedure required by law, 5 U.S.C. § 706(2)(D). The federations argue that the CIP is a "program" under 36 C.F.R. § 216.1(a) (1983), and therefore, Coston's failure to carry out the Forest Service public comment regulations with respect to the formulation of the CIP was arbitrary and capricious and without observance of procedure required by law.

Under the definition applicable in 1981, "'program' means land and resource activities, or combinations of them, conducted by the Forest Service. ＊ ＊ ＊" 36 C.F.R. § 216.1 (1983). (Part 216 was revised in April, 1984, and the definition was eliminated. 49 Fed.Reg. 16991–16994; 36 C.F.R. § 216 et seq. (1984).) This section noted that "[s]upport activities, such as personnel matters and procurement and service contracting, are generally not included under this definition of program." 36 C.F.R. § 216.1(a) (1983). The federations argue that the "aptly named" Capital Investment Program is a "program" under these regulations because "[c]ertainly the construction of many miles of roads is a land or resource activity." However, as we have seen, the CIP is not a substantive program for the proposal and construction of roads. It involves a "land and resource activity" only to the extent that it sets out procedures for the allocation of regional funds for such activity. The district court was not clearly erroneous in concluding that the federations failed to demonstrate sufficiently their chance of success on the merits of their APA claim.

AFFIRMED.

NOTE

1. Why is roadbuilding in roadless areas the first priority? Does or does not the CIP embody an important policy determination? Should that make a difference in NEPA analysis?

3. PLANNING

Lawsuits involving direct challenges to the level of timber harvesting are inordinately complex due to the quantity of data, the imprecision of projections of future timber growth, the necessity for numerous professional judgments on economic and silvicultural issues, and the intricacies of the computer, including the Forest Service's timber program, FORPLAN. Lawyers must develop legal arguments and marshall the evidence, but the work of foresters and economists is more likely to determine the outcome of litigation.

In broad terms, timber harvests for a national forest are calculated in this manner. First, planners determine what land is suitable for timber management. They must exclude, for example: land allocated to other uses, such as wilderness; noncommercial timberland, traditionally defined as land growing less than twenty cubic feet of wood per acre annually; and land not suitable for harvesting due to inaccessibility or to fragile slope or soil conditions. The land available for harvest is the suitable land base, or inventory. Second, the Forest Service must calculate the amount of timber that will be harvested from the inventory. The two primary factors used to calculate the sale quantity—or "the allowable cut"—are the volume of timber and the rotation period, i.e., the time over which a stand will be harvested before a second harvesting schedule can begin. If, for example, estimated volume is 500 million board feet (mmbf) and a conservative rotation period of 100 years is used, the annual allowable cut will be 5 mmbf. The volume and rotation period calculations both depend in part upon the estimated rate of growth in the future because harvesting must be conducted on a sustained yield basis; if optimistic projections for stand management (e.g., thinning, fertilization, reforestation, and use of genetically superior stocks) are used, the volume will be higher and so will be the resulting harvest level. Thus, if substantial stand improvement measures are assumed, and the volume is calculated at 750 mmbf, the annual cut can be set at 7.5 mmbf, still using the same rotation period of 100 years. Similarly, if a broad definition of suitability is used, more land will be included in the inventory so that the same rotation period will produce a higher cut. Further, if the rotation age is lowered, the allowable cut increases. Third, after the allowable cut is set, planners must determine harvesting methods (clearcutting or selective cutting; tractor, cable, balloon, or helicopter logging) and the process for regenerating the stand.

Many of the administrative appeals and court cases challenging the NFMA plans probably will be set in the milieu of calculating the allowable cut because it is the premise on which all subsequent management of national forests is based. Commercial timber is the most valuable commodity resource in the National Forest System. The operations of most Forest Service field offices are effectively organized around the allowable cut. In spite of increased emphasis on the wildlife, recreation, and preservation resources, the operative slogan of many forest rangers is still GOTAC ("get out the allowable cut").

The first opinion following arose before the NFMA provisions became effective, but it presaged the kinds of issues that will be contested under the 1976 Act. The second opinion also does not implicate the NMFA as directly as future cases will do—and its factual situation is by no means typical—but it too illustrates the ways in which planning processes promise to alter decisional equations.

AMERICAN TIMBER CO. v. BERGLAND

United States District Court, District of Montana, 1979.
473 F.Supp. 310.

RUSSELL E. SMITH, District Judge.

In this action plaintiffs challenge the validity of the Draft Environmental Impact Statement (DEIS) and Final Environmental Impact Statement (FEIS) issued by the Flathead National Forest.

The corporate plaintiffs all own and operate sawmills and related facilities which depend on the Flathead National Forest (Flathead Forest) for an adequate supply of timber to meet their operational needs. As a consequence they also have an interest in decisions affecting the general management of the forest. The corporate plaintiffs' mills employ together approximately 245 persons directly and additional workers indirectly through their logging subcontractors. The products of the mills are lumber and related wood products used primarily in home construction in Montana and throughout the United States.

* * *

In 1969, the Supervisor of the Flathead Forest issued a timber management plan for the years 1969 to 1979, setting forth, among other things, the rate and manner of timber harvest for the Flathead Forest, as well as various silvicultural practices for the forest. That plan, as adjusted for matters not material here, called for an annual allowable cut of 181.6 MM board feet using conventional logging techniques. The allocation of lands for commercial timber growing and harvesting had been made in a prior land management plan also issued by Flathead Forest personnel.

In April 1972, the new forest supervisor, original Defendant Edsel L. Corpe, issued a public brochure called "Fact Sheet" which proposed reducing the annual allowable cut from 181.6 MM board feet to 128.6 MM board feet. The fact sheet was followed in July 1973 by a "Draft Environmental Statement, Interim Revision, Flathead National Forest" which proposed to set the annual allowable cut (by then renamed "programmed harvest") at 110.4 MM board feet. The FEIS, issued May 30, 1974, established the annual allowable cut at 121.4 MM board feet.

The DEIS and FEIS proposed changes not only for the 1969 timber management plan, but also for the preceding land management plan. However, no separate land management plan or timber management plan was issued, the intent of the Forest Service personnel being that the FEIS would itself constitute the plan for modification of both the prior land use and timber management plans.

From what has been said it is obvious that the sort of planning represented by the timber management plan, the fact sheet, and the environmental impact statements is a continuing process in the Forest Service. The FEIS here is labeled "Interim Revision—Flathead National Forest Ten-Year Timber Management Plan," and the plan itself envisages revisions prior to the expiration of ten years.

The FEIS does state a policy which is designed to provide a continuous, sustained, even yield of timber, and at the same time accommodate the principles of multi-use management.

Two basic controversies are presented: one, what amount of timber may be cut annually; and, two, whether the plans for the management of the Flathead Forest provide for an adequate and timely removal of presently-mature timber. The timber industry wants the volume of what is now called the "programmed harvest" to be raised, and, along with the individual plaintiffs, it wants the mature timber removed in a timely manner to prevent loss because of age, disease, and fire. The court's function is not to decide these issues but to determine whether the Forest Service in deciding them complied with the requirements of the National Environmental Policy Act.

The reduction in the potential yield was a result of (1) a change in the stratification of the land base; (2) a change in the conversion period (i.e., as used in the FEIS, the time allowed for the removal of the old growth, mature timber, high and low risk); and (3) a change in the projected yield of the managed timber lands. These factors are discussed separately.

(1)

The most important factor accounting for 60% to 80% of the reduction in the potential yield was the change in the land stratification. In the DEIS and FEIS, the components of stratification (i.e., high area, marginal, special, standard, and deferred) are all defined in general terms. Illustratively, "high area" is defined as "[l]and areas of subalpine and alpine vegetation types. These are thin soil areas where trees are usually unmerchantable, slow growing, and difficult to regenerate. These areas often have high scenic values."

Prior to 1972, the high area zone had been determined. In 1972 the land stratification was changed, and an additional 194,568 acres were placed in the high area zone. Of this, 118,034 acres had previously been classified as commercial forest land. Since the high area zone was not to be logged, or at least logged only under very special conditions, this reduction in commercial forest land reduced the amount of harvestable timber. The high area zone is not described legally or by reference to geographic landmarks, and is shown in the DEIS and FEIS only as a figure in a land stratification table. Likewise, neither the 1972 fact statement nor the DEIS describe the methods of classification, but from responses to criticisms of the DEIS contained in the FEIS it appears that the district rangers, using their individual judgments as to the application of regional guidelines, made the classification, and from the record it appears that the results were shown by delineating the high area zones on maps. These maps do not form a part of the FEIS but are available in the offices of the Flathead Forest. Nowhere do the reasons why the judgments as to the classifications of the 118,034 acres made prior to 1972 differed from those made in the FEIS.

(2)

The 1969 plan fixed the conversion period [a] at 34 years and indicated that it could be lowered to 32 years.

The FEIS states:

> The conversion period for removal of old-growth sawtimber stands will be temporarily lengthened to 50 years rather than the 42-year period provided for in the existing timber management plan. This will provide additional recovery time between regeneration cuts in order to stabilize the hydrologic balance in

---

a. [Ed.] The time period over which an old-growth forest is completely harvested and converted into a managed, second-growth stand.

watersheds. As more specific hydrologic information is developed, drainage by drainage, the old-growth conversion period may be adjusted.

In the comments generated by criticisms, it was stated that the true conversion period for "all mature sawtimber (high and low risk) was changed from 39 years in the original plan to about 43 years in the revised plan." FEIS, p. 33.

The record reveals a conflict of opinion between the hydrologists employed by the Forest Service and those employed by the timber industry. If, however, the conflicts be resolved in favor of the Forest Service experts, as they must, still it is clear that the Forest Service hydrologists, in considering the conversion period, treated the forest as a unit. In fact the watersheds differ; some show signs of erosion; some do not; there is a more rapid regeneration in some water sheds than in others. The DEIS was criticized because, in the determination of the conversion period, there was a blanket rather than a separate watershed appraisal, and while this criticism is mentioned in the FEIS, it is not answered.

Further justifications for the change in the conversion period were stated in this language:

> Other factors in the decision to change the conversion period include aesthetics (this is a technical term meaning the Flathead would look like a wreck to many people if all its old-growth timber were cut in the next 34 years) and recognition that the taxpayers can't afford the cost of building roads that fast.

These justifications are completely conclusory. Whether the aesthetes were considering a spread between 34 and 50 years as the FEIS suggests, or a spread of 39 to 43 years as the comments suggest, cannot be known. But a difference in the time lag could make a great difference in the balance between the beauty sacrificed by a speedy removal and the beauty achieved by the lessening of the dangers from fire and blister rust. Apparently the balancing, if any, was done by others than Forest Service personnel, and in any event the basis upon which it was done is not clear.

What factors went into the conclusion that the "taxpayers can't afford the cost of building roads that fast" is not shown. Was the continuing inflation considered? Were the costs of roads providing for an early removal of high-risk timber compared with the savings from a reduced mortality? Further, since the cost of roads is a factor in determining the programmed annual harvest, it is not quite clear how it affects the determination of the potential yield.

(3)

The conclusion that the managed timber stands would not yield as much as had been projected in earlier plans is supported by a statement that the change is due to "improved information." What the information is is not shown.

*   *   *

I would not fault the DEIS or the FEIS for their treatment of the land base. It is true that the stratifications are fixed with little explanation, and it may well be that the stratifications were adopted from previous studies and not especially made for the DEIS here. Where, however, an agency is engaged in a continuing study, I think the results of previous work may be incorporated in a DEIS. Whether the work was done for a previous study or for the DEIS here, the land stratification represents the judgment of professional foresters applying definitions to particular land and reflecting that judgment in area maps. Certainly the process could be more elaborate and could employ studies analyzing the soil and relating the average temperature and snowfall to specific areas. But I think a professional forester is competent to express a judgment as to whether a given area has fragile soils, and more is not needed.

I do fault the FEIS for its treatment of conversion periods. It is conceded by all that mature trees are, as they age, increasingly subject to mortality by fire, insects, disease, and epiphytes. An essential part of any long-term forest management problem involves a consideration of the removal of mature high-risk timber. In 1969 the authors of the 1969–1979 management plan were extremely conscious of that problem and stated that the "key to the allowable cut * * * is to select a conversion period for cutting the mature high risk stands." It was then determined that 43% of the forested area was in the high-risk category; that there was an annual mortality rate of 18 MM board feet; and that a conversion period of 34 years was selected and it was suggested that under proper management a conversion period of 32 years might be proper. In view of the removal problem, the authors were concerned with reducing rather than increasing the conversion period. The authors of the 1974 FEIS lengthened the conversion period and initially justified it solely on hydrological grounds. The FEIS did not discuss the volumes of timber lost by reason of the increase in the conversion period. It did not discuss the reasons for treating the entire forest uniformly instead of relating conversion periods to differing watersheds. It did not discuss the reasons for postponing the restocking of 24,400 unstocked acres until the fourth decade and the effect that a prompt restocking might have on a conversion period. It did not discuss the potential losses resulting from the fact that a delay in regeneration caused by a delay in cutting reduces the potential growth of the forest. If, as the FEIS states, the annual programmed harvest, and hence the actual cutting, will be less than the potential yield, then the actual removal of the high-risk timber will take longer than the stated conversion period if the calculations are based on potential yield rather than on programmed harvest. This is not discussed.

It is possible that the problem presented by the high-risk timber is so close to the surface of a professional forester's mind that all of the questions posed here were considered and answered in the minds of the authors of the DEIS and FEIS, and it may be that all of the merits of a long conversion period were balanced against all of the demerits of such a period and that a balance was struck in favor of the longer period. But the paper work does not reveal what the concerns were or what balances were struck. Certainly the reader of the DEIS and FEIS is not made aware of the process by which the conclusions were reached. In light of that, I conclude that the FEIS was not proposed under the "procedures required by law," and I hold it to be invalid.

I am not sure just what difference this ruling makes. The limiting factor in presently-proposed sales seems to be the economic situation of the Forest Service and not the determination of potential yield. The issuance of any injunctive relief might be dependent upon what plans the Forest Service has in the offing. I will take evidence on the remedy if necessary.

NOTES

1. Can a court appropriately review Forest Service decisions on the land base suitable for inclusion in the inventory? On the rotation period? On the conversion period? Can a court require that an adequate record be prepared so that members of the public, and their experts, can make informed judgments?

2. Is it agency action or inaction when the Forest Service decides not to cut a certain amount of timber? Is that a fair characterization? Compare Defenders of Wildlife v. Andrus, 627 F.2d 1238 (D.C.Cir.1980), infra at page 861, holding that an agency decision not to prevent state action was inaction and thus exempt from NEPA.

3. What standard of review was applied in *American Timber?* The case was decided by a court within the Ninth Circuit; did its "in-depth" review exceed that of other Ninth Circuit cases such as Hi-Ridge Lumber Co. v. United States, 443 F.2d 452 (9th Cir.1971), supra at page 602?

NATIONAL WILDLIFE FEDERATION v. UNITED STATES FOREST SERVICE

United States District Court, District of Oregon, 1984.
592 F.Supp. 931, appeal pending.

AMENDED OPINION

SOLOMON, Senior District Judge:

National Wildlife Federation, Oregon Wildlife Federation, and Siuslaw Task Force (plaintiffs) filed this action to enjoin the United States Forest Service from conducting proposed timber sales in the Mapleton Ranger District of the Siuslaw National Forest. Joined in this action as defendant-intervenors are companies that purchase or log timber from the Mapleton District, road construction companies, and trade associations representing Oregon timber and logging interests.

Plaintiffs contend that the timber sales proposed by the Forest Service in its Mapleton Ranger District Seven Year Action Plan will violate: (1) the National Forest Management Act of 1976, 16 U.S.C. § 1600 et seq.; (2) the Multiple-Use Sustained-Yield Act of 1960, 16 U.S.C. §§ 528–531; (3) and the National Environmental Policy Act of 1969, 42 U.S.C. §§ 4321–4361.

Facts

The Mapleton Ranger District is one of five ranger districts in the Siuslaw National Forest. The Mapleton District consists of approximately 200,000 acres in the center of Oregon's coast range. The streams in the Mapleton District provide spawning and rearing habitats for many species of anadromous fish, including coho salmon, chinook salmon, sea-run cutthroat trout, and steelhead trout. The district also provides habitats for many species of nongame fish, such as sculpins, dace, and squawfish.

Heavy rainfall and steep slopes make the Mapleton District particularly susceptible to soil erosion. It has the highest concentration of landslide-prone landtypes in the Siuslaw National Forest. As early as 1963, Forest Service personnel noticed that timber harvesting damaged soil, watersheds, and fish habitats in the district. Throughout the 1960's, soil specialists warned that logging and road construction could seriously affect soil and watershed stability. In 1969, the Regional Forester placed a moratorium on timber harvesting in the part of the Mapleton District between the Smith and Umpqua Rivers. This moratorium was to remain in place until a study determined if logging was compatible with soil and water resource protection. The study was inconclusive because of poor design, personnel problems, and equipment breakdown. In 1980, the Forest Service lifted the moratorium.

Since 1965, Forest Service personnel repeatedly recommended a land suitability analysis to identify critical areas in the district. In 1974, a forest-wide study of land types was performed which identified some of these critical areas, but it did not classify any area as non-harvestable. In the 1970's some attempts were made to alleviate the impact of logging on the fragile Mapleton District slopes. Most changes were designed to avert the damage caused by road construction. The Forest Service also adopted some new harvesting techniques[5] and implemented stream buffer zones that leave trees standing along stream banks.

In 1975, a severe storm hit the Mapleton District. A Forest Service survey of 70 percent of the district showed 245 landslides. Of these slides, 9 percent were natural events, 14 percent were road related, and 77 percent were in clearcut units apparently unrelated to roads or landings. In this survey, clearcut slides scoured 8.98 miles of streams,

---

5. Yarding techniques were changed from high-lead and tractor removal to skyline and helicopter removal of felled trees. The Forest Service also started using an interdisciplinary team to evaluate each proposed timber sale. The team is made up of several resource specialists including a soil scientist and fish biologist.

road-related slides scoured 4.95 miles of streams, and natural slides scoured 3.35 miles of streams.

Later landslide surveys show similar results. In 1978, a Forest Service survey of ninety-nine slides shows that seventy-five were clear-cut-related. These clearcut slides accounted for 60 percent of the landslide volume and more than three miles of scoured streams. A 1982 Forest Service aerial photo survey showed fifty road-related and seventy-nine clearcut-related landslides. These slides scoured 14.29 miles of streams.

Erosion and landslides are natural phenomena in the Mapleton District. But, road building and timber harvesting have dramatically increased the rate of landslide erosion. The present Forest Service management techniques have eliminated some, but not all, of the practices responsible for the increased landslide erosion.[6] Unless all such practices are eliminated, the accelerated landslide erosion will cause major long-term damage to soil, water, and fishery resources.

Because intact vegetation reduces the potential for soil failure, the Forest Service tries to leave fragile or landslide-prone areas uncut. These uncut areas are known as vegetative leave areas. The Forest Service places these leave areas in the most landslide-prone areas. In particular, leave areas are situated in steep headwall[7] areas and along the banks of streams. It is uncertain whether leave areas, as used by the Forest Service in the Mapleton District, prevent landslides. There is insufficient statistical evidence to evaluate them. Only twelve headwall leave areas have been put in place in the Mapleton District. Of these, only five were successful, five were partially successful, and two were unsuccessful. These two experienced slides. The five partially successful areas were those where low to moderate risk headwalls were protected while adjacent unstable headwalls were left unprotected. The Forest Service has not perfected its prediction rate on either location or size of their leave areas.

The Forest Service employees who were surveyed in 1979, using a technique called the Delphi Method, predicted that 52 percent of the vegetative leave areas will survive. In 1981, they predicted a 32 percent survival rate for 5-acre leave areas and a 23 percent survival rate for 2.5-acre leave areas. Leave areas in the Mapleton District average 3 acres.

The Forest Service also uses "some protection" leave areas. "Some protection" leave areas are those which have only uncut understory and brush vegetation. The effectiveness of these partial leave areas has not been documented.

The most severe effects of landslides occur when large volumes of sediment and debris enter a stream channel and create a debris torrent.

6. For example, the Forest Service changed road construction techniques from sidecast to end-haul removal of debris. This change has lessened the amount of landslide activity caused by new roads. Sidecast roads accounted for most of the road-related slides that occurred in 1979 and a substantial part of the district's 646 miles of roads are sidecast roads.

7. Headwalls are the steep upper-slope areas close to the top of a ridge.

This mixture of soil, organic debris, sediment, and rocks can scour a stream channel to bedrock, damage streambank vegetation, and undercut adjacent slopes. Debris torrents can also reduce fish productivity by removing not only spawning gravel, but also rearing grounds, and organic debris. Landslides reduce the water quality and can also cause debris jams which block the passage of migrating fish. Debris torrents in clearcuts travel almost twice as far as debris torrents in undisturbed watersheds.

Forest Service models designed to assess the impact of timber management indicate that management activities have reduced fish habitat quality and quantity by 43 percent. An earlier model used in the 1979 Timber Resource Plan EIS reveals the potential productivity of fish habitat has been reduced by 28 percent for the Siuslaw National Forest and 50 percent for the Mapleton District. The Forest Service can rehabilitate some damage, like log jams, but its rehabilitation efforts for more complex damage have been only partially successful.

The experts disagree on the effect of timber management in the Mapleton District for its anadromous fish populations. Nevertheless, there is ample evidence that Forest Service management activity has damaged fish habitats in the Mapleton District. There is also evidence of a correlation between fish population and fresh water fish habitat.

In February, 1979, the Forest Service adopted a Timber Resource Plan (TR Plan) for the Siuslaw National Forest. The TR Plan sets out timber harvest levels and Forest Service objectives for the entire Siuslaw National Forest for a ten-year period.

The Forest Service prepared and filed an environmental impact statement for the TR Plan. One of the plaintiffs, the Siuslaw Task Force, participated in an early draft of the TR Plan. It did not appeal the adoption of the TR Plan by the Forest Service. The Environmental Impact Statement does not discuss alternative land allocations for the Siuslaw Forest but only different levels of timber harvests. The statement does not address the impact of timber harvesting specifically on the Mapleton District.

The Timber Resources Plan indicates that a separate Mapleton District land use plan will be prepared. Of the five ranger districts in the Siuslaw National Forest, only the Mapleton District does not have an environmental impact statement for a separate unit plan. The Forest Service makes detailed, site-specific plans for individual timber sales and prepares an environmental assessment for each sale. These individual assessments neither assess nor consider the cumulative impacts of all the proposed timber sales or the impact of nearby timber harvests which are not conducted by the Forest Service.

In December, 1982, the Forest Service issued a Seven Year Action Plan for the Mapleton District which contains the general location, the approximate lengths of proposed roads, and the approximate volume of timber to be removed from each timber sale. The Seven Year Action Plan implements the harvest level contained in the 1979 TR Plan. Each year a new seven year plan is adopted which deletes the proposed timber sales actually sold and which adds new sales for the seventh year.[11] The current Seven Year Action Plan proposes to harvest, primarily by clearcutting, approximately 100 million board feet a year.

In January, 1983, plaintiffs administratively appealed the Seven Year Action Plan. In February, 1983, the Siuslaw National Forest supervisor notified plaintiffs that the Seven Year Action Plan was not a decision document, and, therefore, could not be reviewed administratively. The Regional Forester upheld this ruling. Plaintiffs have also appealed many of the individual timber sales in the Seven Year Action Plan. The Forest Service has rejected all of them.

Contentions of the Parties

Plaintiffs contend that the Forest Service (1) violated either the Church Clearcutting Guidelines or the National Forest Management Act; (2) violated the Multiple Use Sustained Yield Act by clearcutting, which impaired the productivity of the land; and (3) did not comply with the National Environmental Policy Act (NEPA). Plaintiffs seek injunctive relief for these violations.

Defendant Forest Service contends (1) the Church Clearcutting Guidelines are not enforceable, or, if enforceable, they have not been violated; (2) the National Forest Management Act is inapplicable; (3) the Multiple-Use Sustained-Yield Act is not subject to judicial review because Congress has committed decisions under the Act to Forest Service discretion; (4) the Seven Year Action Plan does not require an environmental impact statement because it is not a proposal for major federal action; (5) the 1979 Environmental Impact Statement and individual environmental assessments satisfy NEPA requirements; and (6) violations of NEPA should not automatically result in an injunction, but instead, the court should balance the hardships.

* * *

Discussion

A. *Church Clearcutting Guidelines*

In March, 1972, the Senate Subcommittee on Public Lands published a set of guidelines for clearcutting on public lands. *Clearcutting on Federal Timberlands, Senate Committee on Interior and Insular Affairs* (March, 1972) (Church Guidelines). The Church Guidelines were a response to growing public concern over timber harvest operations on federal forest lands.

The Church Guidelines prohibit clearcutting on federal lands where "[s]oil, slope or other watershed conditions are fragile and subject to major injury." The members of the Church subcommittee were particularly concerned about landslides, soil erosion, and the destruction of streams and fish habitat. The subcommittee recom-

---

11. The Seven Year Action Plan is in effect a rolling schedule that is changed and updated every year.

mended against cutting fragile areas with steep slopes that could not be harvested without major watershed injury.

The Forest Service argues that the Church Guidelines are only recommendations and therefore are not judicially enforceable.[13] This was true until the National Forest Management Act (NFMA) of 1976 was passed. Two alternatives were proposed in the debate on the interim management of the forests pending adoption of the land-use plans which the NFMA required. The Senate version required the Forest Service to develop interim standards and to apply existing Forest Service regulations which incorporate the Church Guidelines. The House version required the Forest Service to incorporate the NFMA standards into its regulations "as soon as practicable." The Conference Committee adopted the House's language with the proviso that "[t]he conferees agree that 'the Church Guidelines' on clearcutting shall continue to be followed by the Forest Service pending incorporation into all unit plans of the management standards added [by the NFMA]."

* * * In my view, the Church Guidelines are the outer boundary of the Forest Service's discretion and are judicially enforceable.

Past timber harvests have inflicted serious damage on the fisheries in the Mapleton District. The Forest Service concedes this, but asserts that improved harvesting techniques and mitigation measures will prevent similar damage from the timber sales proposed in the Seven Year Action Plan. At first glance, the Forest Service appears to comply with the restrictions in the Church Guidelines. The Forest Service requires that an interdisciplinary team, consisting of resource experts (e.g., soil scientists, fishery biologists) prepare and evaluate each timber sale. If the interdisciplinary team determines that an area cannot be harvested without major injury, then the area is not harvested. An essential part of this determination, that no serious damage will result from the timber sales, rests on the assumption that Forest Service mitigation measures are effective. There is insufficient evidence to conclude that these timber sales will or will not result in major injury to fisheries. Because of this factual uncertainty and because the Forest Service has adopted new harvesting techniques and mitigation measures, I reject plaintiffs' contention that the Church Guidelines alone are a sufficient ground on which to enjoin the Seven Year Action Plan.

The Church Guidelines direct that only where it is essential for the care and production of trees (silviculture) in the region may the Forest Service engage in clearcutting. Plaintiffs have not shown that

---

13. The Forest Service and defendant-intervenors also argue that the National Forest Management Act has replaced the Church Guidelines. At the same time, they argue the clearcutting restrictions in the NFMA are not binding because the Siuslaw National Forest has not adopted a land-use plan under the NFMA. This contention, that because of timing they fall through the cracks, is tantamount to saying the Forest Service's actions are unreviewable during this period. The Forest Service is probably correct that the NFMA does not apply until a NFMA plan is adopted for the Siuslaw National Forest, but Congress did not leave a void when it enacted the NFMA. The Church Guidelines still apply.

clearcutting on the Mapleton District is not silviculturally essential. They only argue that the Forest Service failed to make a formal finding to that effect. Since December, 1982, the Forest Service has corrected this technical defect. It has evaluated the available silvicultural methods for every timber sale and has concluded that clearcutting is essential. The Forest Service has not violated this particular Church Guideline. The Forest Service has special expertise in this area, and its determination of what is silviculturally essential is entitled to great weight.

*   *   *

C. *National Environmental Policy Act*

*   *   *

The Forest Service and defendant-intervenors argue (1) that the Seven Year Action Plan is not a proposal for major federal action and, therefore, does not require an environmental impact statement; and (2) even if an environmental analysis is required, the Environmental Impact Statement in the 1979 TR Plan and the individual environmental assessments satisfy NEPA's requirements.

(1) *Does the Seven Year Action Plan require an Environmental Impact Statement?*

The Forest Service argues that the Seven Year Action Plan is not a major federal action but only a flexible planning schedule. *   *   * Here the Forest Service has selected seventy-five timber sales and decided their locations, road construction requirements, and approximate board foot harvest levels. Some sales have been consummated and environmental assessments have been performed on more than half of the remaining proposed sales. Except for one sale that was deferred, none of the environmental assessments concluded that a timber sale should not be harvested. The Forest Service's long-range marketing program, like the programs in *Port of Astoria* and *Environmental Defense Fund,* constitutes a proposal under NEPA.

*   *   * Here, the Mapleton District's Seven Year Action Plan proposes to cut approximately 100 million board feet of timber a year and to construct (or reconstruct) 176.4 miles of road. It is a proposal for major federal action which will significantly affect the human environment. I hold that the Forest Service acted unreasonably when it failed to prepare an environmental impact statement for this proposal.

(2) *Do the existing environmental documents for the Mapleton District satisfy NEPA?*

The Forest Service contends that the 1979 Environmental Impact Statement for the Timber Resources Plan and the environmental assessments accompanying each timber sale together satisfy NEPA.

(a) *Timber Resource Plan Environmental Impact Statement.*

The TR Plan describes a ten-year timber cutting program for the Siuslaw National Forest. The Environmental Impact Statement accompanying this forest-wide proposal is a "programmatic environmental impact statement." It averages the impact of the TR Plan's proposed harvest levels over the entire Siuslaw National Forest. It does not specifically discuss the Mapleton District.

The TR Plan determines the harvest levels for all of the Siuslaw National Forest. The Environmental Impact Statement considers the impact of these harvest levels. A separate environmental analysis was not done on the Mapleton District. The Forest Service contends that a separate analysis is not necessary because the impact of the Seven Year Action Plan had already been considered in the TR Plan. In support of this contention, the Forest Service relies on Ventling v. Bergland, 479 F.Supp. 174 (D.S.D.), aff'd. mem., 615 F.2d 1365 (8th Cir.1979). In *Ventling,* the court held that the Forest Service was not required to prepare a site-specific environmental impact statement on four timber sales. The court found that NEPA was satisfied because there was a comprehensive programmatic environmental impact statement and the sale area was indistinguishable from the rest of the forest. The court emphasized the homogeneity of the Black Hills National Forest. It noted that plaintiffs had not identified any characteristics of the proposed timber sales which varied significantly from the conditions examined in the programmatic environmental impact statement.

Unlike the forest in *Ventling,* the Mapleton District varies significantly from the rest of the Siuslaw National Forest. The Mapleton District has the greatest concentration of high-risk and landslide-prone land in the Siuslaw National Forest. The impact of harvesting on these lands will therefore be much greater than the average for the entire forest. The TR Plan Environmental Impact Statement sets forth the average reduction of fish habitat for the entire forest. The greatest reductions in fish habitat have occurred in the Mapleton District which is in the southern portion of the forest. The Environmental Impact Statement does not contain separate figures for the Mapleton District. Unlike *Ventling,* the Siuslaw National Forest is not "homogeneous."

The Forest Service did not intend for the TR Plan's Environmental Impact Statement to satisfy its NEPA obligations for the Mapleton District. The TR Plan decided how much timber would be harvested in the Siuslaw National Forest for a ten-year period. The TR Plan specifically provided for a separate unit management plan and also an environmental impact statement on the Mapleton District. The Forest Service prepared plans and environmental impact statements for each ranger district in the Siuslaw National Forest except the Mapleton District. In my view, the TR Plan's Environmental Impact Statement does not provide the specific environmental analysis on the Mapleton District Seven Year Action Plan that is required by NEPA.

(b) *Individual Timber Environmental Assessments.*

The Forest Service intends to prepare an environmental assessment for each timber sale in the Seven Year Action Plan. The purpose of an environmental assessment is to "[b]riefly provide sufficient evidence and analysis for determining whether to prepare an environmental impact statement or a finding of no significant impact." 40 C.F.R. § 1508.9(a)(1). These are site-specific analyses, and they concentrate on the specific issues presented in each timber sale. They supplement the analysis in the programmatic environmental impact statement. 40 C.F.R. § 1502.20. The Forest Service argues that these environmental assessments, in conjunction with the TR Plan's Environmental Impact Statement, are enough to satisfy NEPA. I disagree.

The Forest Service can comply with NEPA by preparing a programmatic environmental impact statement and site-specific environmental assessments. Oregon Environmental Council v. Kunzman, 714 F.2d 901, 905 (9th Cir.1983). Nevertheless, this court must review "the sufficiency of the environmental analysis as a whole." Southern Oregon Citizens Against Toxic Sprays, Inc. v. Clark, 720 F.2d 1475 at 1480 (1983) (*SOCATS*). The environmental assessments together with the TR Plan's Environmental Impact Statement must provide the information necessary for " 'the decision-maker to consider the environmental factors and to make a reasoned decision.' " *SOCATS* at 5682; see also Oregon Environmental Council, 714 F.2d at 904–05.

An examination of the environmental assessments on timber sales in the Seven Year Action Plan reveals two flaws in the environmental analysis. First, there are no Forest Service documents which consider the cumulative impact of the timber sales or of the other harvests in the Mapleton district. Second, there are no Forest Service documents which discuss the uncertainty of leave areas as a mitigation technique.[20]

i. Cumulative Effects

NEPA's comprehensive approach to environmental decision-making is designed to recognize and evaluate the long-term and cumulative effects of small and both related and unrelated actions. Council on Environmental Quality regulations require that the scope of an environmental impact statement include cumulative impacts. 40 C.F.R. § 1508.25. Cumulative impact is defined as:

> the impact on the environment which results from the incremental impact of the action when added to other past, present, and reasonably foreseeable future actions regardless of what agency (Federal or non-Federal) or person undertakes such other actions. Cumulative impacts can result from individually minor but collectively significant actions taking place over a period of time.

40 C.F.R. § 1508.7

In Natural Resources Defense Council, Inc. v. Callaway, 524 F.2d 79 (2d Cir.1975), the court held that an environmental impact statement for a Navy dumping proposal was inadequate under NEPA when

---

20. Plaintiffs also assert that the environmental assessments are invalid because the Forest Service does not have a no-action alternative. Out of the thirty-five environmental assessments performed, only one was not approved and that one was only deferred. I do not reach this issue.

it failed to discuss other dumping and dredging projects in the same area. It rejected the Navy's argument that many of the other projects had not been finally approved or that those projects were unrelated to the Navy's proposal. The court found that the other projects were more than mere speculation, that they were planned for the same geographical area, involved dredging and disposal of spoil, and presented similar pollution problems. The court therefore required the environmental impact statement to consider all of the projects in the area.

The watersheds in the Mapleton District will have the impact of (1) seventy-five timber sales from the Seven Year Action Plan; (2) timber sales on adjoining Bureau of Land Management land; and (3) timber harvests on private lands. These harvests are planned for the same geographical area, involve extensive clearcutting, and present similar threats to fish habitats. Although the Forest Service cannot control harvesting activities on adjacent non-Forest Service lands, clearcutting on these lands will have an impact on the fish habitat, and this other harvesting activity must be considered.

The Forest Service has not assessed the cumulative impact of all harvesting in and around the Mapleton District. The individual timber sale environmental assessments do not reveal that impact, and the TR Plan's Environmental Impact Statement is too general to address the specific problems in the Mapleton District. CEQ regulations and the reasoning in *Callaway* require that the Forest Service analyze the cumulative impacts in order to comply with NEPA. The Forest Service has failed to make that analysis.

ii. Worst Case Analysis

The CEQ regulations require a "worst case analysis" when an agency is faced with incomplete or unavailable information. 40 C.F.R. § 1502.22. This regulation codifies prior case law, and it is binding on all federal agencies. [*Eds.* This regulation was amended in 1986. See supra at page 354.]

The "worst case analysis" regulation sets out an ordered process which an agency must follow when the facts on which the agency relies are uncertain. The agency must first determine if the information is important or essential. Then it must decide whether the information can be obtained. If not, or if it can only be obtained at great cost, then the agency must do a worst case analysis. The agency must consider the range of worst possible effects and the likelihood of their occurrence. It must also consider the cost of proceeding without the information. Save Our Ecosystems v. Clark, 747 F.2d 1240, 1244–45 (9th Cir.1984) (SOS).

The effectiveness of leave areas in preventing landslides is at the heart of the Forest Service's case. The Forest Service admits that its practices damaged fish habitats in the past, but it asserts that leave areas and other mitigation techniques will prevent similar damage in the future. There is little evidence to support this assertion. Only twelve headwall leave areas have been set aside in the Mapleton

District. Of these, only five have been successful in preventing land-slides. The only other evidence of leave area effectiveness consists of the Delphi survey results and the unsupported predictions of the Forest Service personnel. The Forest Service does not discuss the uncertainty of leave-area effectiveness. It does not question the effectiveness of leave areas in calculating impact on fish habitat; it merely assumes it to be approximately 100 percent.[26]

Landslides damage fish habitats, but it is uncertain whether leave areas used by the Forest Service will effectively prevent landslides. Without accurate evidence of the effectiveness of leave areas as mitigation techniques, the Forest Service must prepare a worst case analysis. *SOS,* at 1245, *SOCATS,* at 1479–80.

The Forest Service has not made a worst case analysis. It did not make such an analysis in its TR Plan Environmental Impact Statement nor in subsequent environmental assessments. *SOCATS,* at 1480. It must do it now.

* * *

E. *Injunctive Relief*

The Forest Service and defendant-intervenors contend that before the proposed timber sales may be enjoined, the court must balance the equities. The Ninth Circuit Court of Appeals has recently ruled that this balancing is not necessary. *SOS,* at 1250. When an agency fails to comply with NEPA, irreparable damage is presumed, and absent un-usual (or rare) circumstances,[28] an injunction should issue. *SOS,* at 1250. There are no unusual circumstances here.

It is ordered that an injunction shall issue enjoining the Forest Service from offering for sale any timber in the Mapleton District Seven Year Action Plan until it complies with the National Environ-mental Policy Act as set forth in this opinion or until further order of the court.

NOTE

Was clearcutting in the Mapleton District "silvaculturally essen-tial"? To what extent are the Church Guidelines enforceable? What is the relationship between NEPA and NFMA planning?

26. The Forest Service starts with a 100 percent efficiency rate and adjusts it down according to the professional judgment of the interdisciplinary team. This adjust-ment is not significant. The average as-sumed efficiency is 99.9 percent.

28. An example of an unusual circum-stance is presented in defendant-interven-ors' primary case, American Motorcyclist Association v. Watt, 714 F.2d 962 (9th Cir. 1983). In *Watt,* the court refused to issue the injunction in order to protect the envi-ronment. Issuing the injunction would have harmed the environment, in contra-diction to the purpose of NEPA.

CHARLES F. WILKINSON & H. MICHAEL ANDERSON,
LAND AND RESOURCE PLANNING IN
THE NATIONAL FORESTS *
64 Or.L.Rev. 1 (1985).

For many reasons, planning on the public lands is inevitably imprecise. The plans must cover large areas of land and there is usually uncertainty over location of some resources, especially minerals and wildlife. Valuation of some resources, such as recreation and preservation, is difficult. Barriers to development, such as fragile soil conditions, may not be apparent until the implementation stage of the plan. Changing demands for various resources and the occurrence of natural phenomena such as insect infestation, droughts, and forest fires, add to the difficulty. For these and other reasons, planning on the federal lands has properly been called "an inexact art."

* * *

The Forest Service planning statutes * * * require planning on several tiers, although the national forests are the basic functional unit at which plans are made and carried out. The Forest and Rangeland Renewable Resources Planning Act of 1974 (RPA) requires several procedures at the national level * * *. Long-range plans, called Regional Guides, are also made by each of nine Forest Service regions for activities within each region.

At the national forest level, land management plans (alluded to in the RPA but elaborated upon in the NFMA) guide activities for ten to fifteen years and make projections for up to fifty years. These individual forest plans are the engines that drive the management process. Finally, the forest plans are implemented, usually at the ranger district or national forest level, by permits, contracts, and other instruments; examples are timber contracts, camping permits, grazing leases, rights-of-way, and special land use permits. Mineral leases for national forest lands are issued by the Department of the Interior, but the Forest Service is heavily involved in the planning process and the Department of the Interior usually follows its recommendations. Similarly, under the General Mining Law of 1872, the Department of the Interior adjudicates issues relating to mining claims and patents, but the Forest Service has independent regulatory authority over hardrock mining; even on issues solely within the jurisdiction of the Department of the Interior, the views of the Forest Service are given great weight.

* * *

By 1976 the mood of Congress had shifted dramatically in the wake of the clearcutting controversy. Upon introducing his bill, Humphrey observed that the MUSY Act had not succeeded and that a "fundamental reform" was needed. Humphrey stated: "We have had 15 years since the 1960 Multiple Use and Sustained Yield Act was passed. Much has happened, and as we look at what has transpired, the need

* Reprinted with permission of the Oregon Law Review.

for improvement is evident." He identified the central problem as the predominance of timber production over protection of other resources. Humphrey declared:

> The days have ended when the forest may be viewed only as trees and trees viewed only as timber. The soil and the water, the grasses and the shrubs, the fish and the wildlife, and the beauty that is the forest must become integral parts of resource managers' thinking and actions.

During the Senate hearings Humphrey observed that the Forest Service's record had brought into question the extent to which the agency could be trusted to guard and manage public resources. He proposed that the NFMA legislation be shaped to prevent the Forest Service from "turning the national forests into tree production programs which override other values."

Senator Randolph and other members of Congress shared Humphrey's views. * * *

* * *

The NFMA will require courts to scrutinize forest plans, and activities based on those plans, on both procedural and substantive grounds. The 1976 Act contains several substantive guidelines that are markedly more specific than the broad multiple-use language [of the MUSY Act], although less absolute than the Organic Act provision in *Monongahela.* In addition, the NFMA requires forest plans to be developed in accordance with NEPA's procedural requirements. The Forest Service has correctly stated the controlling law in advising its planners that reviewing courts are likely to conduct a "searching inquiry" into the procedural adequacy of forest plans and to require "full, fair, and bona fide compliance" with the NFMA. Once the plans become final and are determined to be valid, they themselves become law. Much like zoning requirements or administrative regulations, the plans are controlling and judicially enforceable until properly revised.

* * *

NOTE: NFMA TIMBER PLANNING

This note examines the NFMA provisions relating to the three central elements of timber planning: determining the suitable land base; calculating the allowable cut; and deciding upon the appropriate methods for harvesting and regenerating the timber. For additional analysis of the issues raised here, see generally Wilkinson & Anderson, supra.

1. *Physical Suitability.* Because of the events leading up to the NFMA, Congress gave special attention to the kinds of lands on which timber may be harvested. Impacts on watersheds were considered critical. The "physical suitability" provision, 16 U.S.C.A. § 1604(g)(3)(E), requires that the regulations and the forest plans shall:

> insure that timber will be harvested from National Forest System lands only where—

(i) soil, slope, or other watershed conditions will not be irreversibly damaged;

(ii) there is assurance that such lands can be adequately restocked within five years after harvest; [and]

(iii) protection is provided for streams, streambanks, shorelines, lakes, wetlands, and other bodies of water from detrimental changes in water temperatures, blockages of water courses, and deposits of sediment, where harvests are likely to seriously and adversely affect water conditions or fish habitat

*   *   *

Land that does not meet these standards must be classified as unsuitable and excluded from the inventory. The provision presumably extends to logging road construction, a major cause of erosion.

Does this provision provide a basis for searching judicial review? Is it significant that each criterion must be met separately? The Knutson-Vandenberg Act of 1930, 16 U.S.C.A. §§ 576a–c, allows the Forest Service to require deposits from timber operators to cover reforestation costs. That program has been less than entirely successful: a backlog of millions of acres has not been restocked and, although the NFMA authorized an expenditure of $200 million per year to eliminate the backlog, appropriations have not been forthcoming. Could a lack of funds for restocking be used to challenge timber sales under the above-quoted section?

2. *Economic Suitability.* The "economic suitability," or "marginal lands," provision, 16 U.S.C.A. § 1604(k), requires that planners "shall identify lands within the management area which are not suited for timber production, considering physical, economic, and other pertinent factors to the extent feasible, as determined by the Secretary" and shall be excluded from the inventory, except for "salvage sales or sales necessitated to protect other multiple-use values," such as big game habitat. See the material on below-cost sales, infra at page 668.

3. *Diversity.* The timber inventory is also limited by section 1604(g)(3)(B), which requires that Forest Service land management plans shall "provide for diversity of plant and animal communities based on the suitability and capability of the specific land area in order to meet overall multiple-use objectives, and within the multiple-use objectives of a land management plan adopted pursuant to this section, provide, where appropriate, to the degree practicable, for steps to be taken to preserve the diversity of tree species similar to that existing in the region controlled by the plan. *   *   * " The NFMA was passed in the context of the *Monongahela* dispute, where the Service, by replacing mixed, hardwood forests with pine stands, had reduced the diversity of tree species. The Act does not define diversity but the regulations define it as "the distribution and abundance of different plant and animal communities and species within the area covered by a land and resource management plan." 36 C.F.R. § 219.3 (1985). To preserve diversity of species, the Forest Service has designated "indicator spe-

cies" that serve as proxies for large numbers of species; in other words, rather than inventorying all species—which would be impossible— planners attempt to assure suitable habitat for the indicator species. Especially controversial has been the designation of the northern spotted owl, which uses old-growth Douglas fir as a preferred habitat, as an indicator species in the Pacific Northwest. The timber industry has argued that proposed forest plans may remove too much valuable timber land from the inventories in order to protect the spotted owl; environmentalists believe that more land should be set aside. Can the courts be expected to review such issues?

4. *Rotation Age and Culmination of Mean Annual Increment (CMAI).* After the suitable inventory is established, the harvesting schedule must be set. Section 1604(m) prohibits cutting unless "stands of trees * * * generally have reached the culmination of mean annual increment of growth," with narrow exceptions. Is this a recodification of the *Monongahela* rule that harvesting can occur only at biological maturity, not at the earlier point of economic maturity, recast for "stands" instead of individual trees? One writer assumes so, stating that the section "sets out a specific, enforcible maturity objective. * * * [C]ritics of Forest Service practices * * * now have a standard by which a court can judge the propriety of the sale." Mulhern, supra, 7 B.C.Envt'l Aff.L.Rev. at 114. The application of the statute will be complicated by the state of the forestry art: for instance, the "rotation age for ponderosa pine on site class 120 varies from 39 to 107 years, depending on the unit of measurement employed and the utilization standards assumed." S. Dana & S. Fairfax, FOREST AND RANGE POLICY 331 (2d ed. 1980).

5. *Nondeclining Even Flow (NDEF).* In the long term, one of the most telling effects of the NFMA could come from the practice of NDEF on the national forests. It, too, places limits on the harvesting schedule.

"Sustained yield" timber management is almost bereft of meaning as a management standard. Economic analysis of sustained yield formulations leads one around in a circle, according to Behan, Political Popularity and Conceptual Nonsense: The Strange Case of Sustained Yield Forestry, 8 Envt'l L. 309 (1978). Suppose a national forest has a managed, second-growth timber inventory of 100 million board feet, that the annual growth is 1 million board feet, and that the rotation cycle is 100 years. Sustained yield in its broadest sense means only that the forest be managed so that timber can be produced in perpetuity. Thus if all 100 million board feet were cut in 1980 and the ground were replanted, then the sustained yield "requirement" would be met because the stand would regenerate and 100 million board feet would again be available for harvest in 2080. At that point, there could be another wholesale cut, and so on. The example is the extreme, but the same reasoning applies to a schedule of 50 million board feet twice a century, 10 million board feet every 10 years, and other variations.

NDEF is the most conservative variant of sustained-yield management. As adopted by the Forest Service in 1973, the policy requires that the same level of harvest be maintained *annually in perpetuity* (with only slight deviations). The annual cut on an NDEF regime is easy to compute for the postulated forest: since annual growth is one million board feet and the rotation period is 100 years, the amount that can be removed annually forever is one million board feet per year. In practice, minor variations are allowed to react to market conditions or to meet other needs.

Instead of the managed, second-growth forest just described, assume a forest with a similar capacity for growth—the soil conditions, slopes, moisture, and exposure to sunlight are similar—except that it is a virgin, old-growth forest. In the old-growth forest, the timber inventory, because of the giant "overmature" trees, will be much greater and may approach, say, 500 million board feet on the same number of acres as the managed forest. Management of the old-growth stands in national forests in some areas of the Rocky Mountains and Pacific Northwest is at the cutting edge of controversy between industry and environmentalists.

If NDEF is not required in this hypothetical old growth forest, and a conservative "conversion period" of 100 years is used to achieve a managed forest, then an accelerated harvest of 5 million board annually can be employed. Then, in 2080, when the conversion period is completed and the old-growth is liquidated, the harvest must fall down to an average of 1 million board feet each year.

If NDEF is employed, the annual harvest of the old-growth stand cannot exceed the amount that can be produced annually in perpetuity. Potential annual yield is only about 1 million. This conservative, level harvesting schedule means no fall-down in later years to disrupt local communities. It also means that old-growth forests will be liquidated much more slowly and, in some cases, the numbers are such that there will always be a considerable amount of old growth in the forest. The computer modeling methods by which the formulae, economic projections, exceptions, and silvicultural assumptions are factored into the calculations are complex, and the method is less than an exact science, but application of NDEF will result in significantly reduced present harvests of old-growth stands. On NDEF, see M. Clawson, FORESTS; FOR WHOM AND FOR WHAT? 80–81 (1975); S. Dana & S. Fairfax, FOREST AND RANGE POLICY 331–34 (2d ed. 1980); Symposium, Western Wildlands (Winter, 1983); Symposium, Harvest Scheduling and the NFMA, 75 J. Forestry 699 (1977); Symposium, 8 Envt'l L. 239 (1978).

The relevant provision in the NFMA is 16 U.S.C.A. § 1611:

(a) The Secretary of Agriculture shall limit the sale of timber from each national forest to a quantity equal to or less than a quantity which can be removed from such forest annually in perpetuity on a sustained-yield basis: *Provided,* That, in order to meet overall multiple-use objectives, the Secretary may establish an allowable sale quantity for any decade which departs from the projected long-term average sale quantity that would otherwise be established: *Provided further,* That any such planned departure must be consistent with the multiple-use management objectives of the land management plan. Plans for variations in the allowable sale quantity must be made with public participation as required by section 1604(d) of this title. In addition, within any decade, the Secretary may sell a quantity in excess of the annual allowable sale quantity established pursuant to this section in the case of any national forest so long as the average sale quantities of timber from such national forest over the decade covered by the plan do not exceed such quantity limitation. In those cases where a forest has less than two hundred thousand acres of commercial forest land, the Secretary may use two or more forests for purposes of determining the sustained yield.

(b) Nothing in subsection (a) of this section shall prohibit the Secretary from salvage or sanitation harvesting of timber stands which are substantially damaged by fire, windthrow, or other catastrophe, or which are in imminent danger from insect or disease attack. The Secretary may either substitute such timber for timber that would otherwise be sold under the plan or, if not feasible, sell such timber over and above the plan volume.

Is this NDEF? How many exceptions are there? Do they swallow the rule set out before the first proviso? At one point, President Carter proposed a departure for the 1980's; the stated purpose was that more lumber on the market would reduce housing costs and, accordingly, inflation. Is such a reason likely to survive challenge in court?

6. *Clearcutting.* As to harvesting practices, Congress rejected a proposal that all clearcuts on national forest lands would be limited to 25 acres. Existing contracts were ratified, and 16 U.S.C.A. § 1604(g)(3) (F) provides that the regulations adopted by the Forest Service shall:

insure that [even-aged management shall be used] only where—

(i) for clearcutting, it is determined to be the optimum method, and for other such cuts it is determined to be appropriate, to meet the objectives and requirements of the relevant land management plan;

(ii) the interdisciplinary review as determined by the Secretary has been completed and the potential environmental, biological, esthetic, engineering, and economic impacts on each advertised sale area have been assessed, as well as the consistency of the sale with the multiple use of the general area;

(iii) cut blocks, patches, or strips are shaped and blended to the extent practicable with the natural terrain;

(iv) there are established according to geographic areas, forest types, or other suitable classifications the maximum size limits for areas to be cut in one harvest operation, including provision to exceed the established limits after appropriate public notice and review by the responsible Forest Service officer one level above the Forest Service officer who normally would approve the harvest proposal: *Provided,* That such limits shall not apply to the size of areas harvested as a result of natural catastrophic conditions such as fire, insect and disease attack, or windstorm; and

(v) such cuts are carried out in a manner consistent with the protection of soil, watershed, fish, wildlife, recreation, and esthetic resources, and the regeneration of the timber resource.

Does this provision allow intensive judicial scrutiny? Clearcuts must also comply with the provisions governing harvesting on all suitable lands. See § 1604(g)(3)(E), quoted supra at page 663.

7. *Below-Cost Sales.* The NFMA provides in section 1604(k) that the following process be followed to eliminate marginal lands from the inventory and includes a terse directive concerning economic suitability:

In developing land management plans pursuant to this [Act], the Secretary shall identify lands within the management area which are not suited for timber production, considering physical, economic, and other pertinent factors to the extent feasible, as determined by the Secretary, and shall assure that, except for salvage sales or sales necessitated to protect other multiple-use values, no timber harvesting shall occur on such lands for a period of 10 years. Lands once identified as unsuitable for timber production shall continue to be treated for reforestation purposes, particularly with regard to the protection of other multiple-use values. The Secretary shall review his decision to classify these lands as not suited for timber production at least every 10 years and shall return these lands to timber production whenever he determines that conditions have changed so that they have become suitable for timber production.

In addition, section 1604(*l*) directs the Forest Service to establish a process for comparing costs and receipts for timber sales and to report annually to Congress on below-cost sales—but sets no substantive standards.

During the NFMA hearings, eminent economist Dr. Marion Clawson and others objected to uneconomical sales. Below-cost sales had been one of several issues raised earlier by the influential Bolle Report concerning harvesting on the Bitterroot National Forest. The Senate bill included a reasonably strict cost-benefit analysis, the House version did not directly deal with the issue, and the Conference Committee arrived at the present section 1604(k). Later, the Committee of Scientists, a collection of leading experts designated by Congress to propose

NFMA rules to the Forest Service, concluded that below-cost sales must be limited by some "rules of reason." See generally D. LeMaster, DECADE OF CHANGE: THE REMAKING OF FOREST SERVICE STATUTORY AUTHORITY DURING THE 1970's, at 77 (1984). The Forest Service has continued making below-cost sales in areas of marginally productive timber. No judicial opinion has yet construed the economic suitability provision of the NFMA, but the following decision is plainly relevant. In it, the court examined a provision from the RPA of 1974 (which the court incorrectly labelled as being derived from the NFMA) concerning uneconomical roads.

THOMAS v. PETERSON
United States Court of Appeals, Ninth Circuit, 1985.
753 F.2d 754.

SNEED, Circuit Judge:

* * *

Plaintiffs—landowners, ranchers, outfitters, miners, hunters, fishermen, recreational users, and conservation and recreation organizations—challenge actions of the United States Forest Service in planning and approving a timber road in the Jersey Jack area of the Nezperce National Forest in Idaho. * * *

* * *

[Other portions of this opinion are reprinted infra at page 800.]

The National Forest Management Act Claim

The plaintiffs next allege, based on their own study and on a cost-benefit analysis prepared by the Forest Service, that the value of the timber to which the proposed road will provide access is less than the cost of the road. They claim that the construction of the road is therefore forbidden by the National Forest Management Act (NFMA), 16 U.S.C. §§ 1600–1614, which states that "Congress declares that the installation of a proper system of transportation to service the National Forest System, as is provided for in sections 532 to 538 of this title, shall be carried forward in time to meet anticipated needs on an economical and environmentally sound basis." 16 U.S.C. § 1608(a). The plaintiffs argue that a timber road is not economical within the meaning of the statute if its cost exceeds the value of the timber it accesses.

We disagree. The quoted section is worded as a declaration rather than a specific prescription. The statute does not define "economical." The sections to which the quoted section refers contain more specific requirements about forest road financing. See 16 U.S.C. §§ 535, 537, 538. None of those sections requires that the value of the accessed timber exceed the cost of the road. We must assume that if Congress wanted to include such a specific requirement it would have done so.

Plaintiffs rely on 16 U.S.C. § 535, which authorizes three methods of financing National Forest roads: (1) appropriated funds; (2) requirements on purchasers of National Forest timber and other products; (3)

cooperative financing with other public agencies and with private
agencies or persons. That section also provides that

> where roads of a higher standard than that needed in the
> harvesting and removal of the timber and other products
> covered by the particular sale are to be constructed, the pur-
> chaser of the national forest timber shall *not* be required to
> bear that part of the costs necessary to meet such higher
> standard.

16 U.S.C. § 535 (emphasis added). From this negative command, plaintiffs infer an underlying affirmative mandate that purchasers of timber
shall be required to bear the entire cost of roads that are *not* built to
higher standards than necessary for timber harvest and removal. The
inference is unjustified. The authorization of the use of appropriated
funds for road construction suggests that some roads may be built
whose cost is not borne entirely by timber purchasers. Congress could
reasonably have intended that the purchasers of timber might or might
not be required to bear the cost of construction of any particular road,
but that in no case should a purchaser be required to bear more than
the cost of a road meeting the minimum standards for timber harvest
and removal.

Plaintiffs also point to 16 U.S.C. § 472a(i), which is concerned with
road construction for access to timber purchased by enterprises qualifying as "small business concerns" under the Small Business Act, 15
U.S.C. §§ 631 et seq. That section gives such small businesses the right
to elect to have the Forest Service build roads for them under circumstances where ordinary purchasers would be required to build roads
themselves.[5] Subsection 472a(i)(2) requires that when a small business
makes such an election, "the price subsequently paid for the timber
shall include all of the estimated cost of the road." Plaintiffs argue
that this section requires small businesses to bear the cost of timber
roads, and that Congress could not have intended that large businesses
should bear less of a burden than small businesses.

The flaw in plaintiffs' argument is that section 472(a)(i)(2) is not a
general requirement that small business purchasers of timber bear the
costs of roads under all circumstances. It is only a requirement that
such purchasers bear the costs under circumstances where larger
purchasers are required to construct the roads themselves. It does not
exclude the possibility that the Forest Service may construct some
roads for which the purchaser, large or small, does not bear the entire
cost.

Plaintiffs also cite Forest Service regulations, Congressional committee reports, Congressional testimony, unenacted bills, and Forest
Service practices, all of which evince a concern for economically efficient management of the National Forests, for avoiding costs not
justified by benefits, for obtaining fair market value in the sale of

---

5. Construction of a road by a purchaser of National Forest timber is known as
"purchaser credit" construction. The cost
of the road is deducted from the price that
the purchaser pays for the timber.

National Forest resources, and for recovery of the costs of National Forest roads and other management expenses. These sources merely counsel economic prudence. They do not evidence a statutory requirement that timber roads be built only when the proceeds of the timber sales will defray construction costs.

The Forest Service interprets "economical" to permit consideration of benefits other than timber access, such as motorized recreation, firewood gathering, and access to the area by local residents. An agency's interpretation of the statute that it is charged with administering is entitled to substantial deference, see Udall v. Tallman, 380 U.S. 1, 16 (1965), and will be upheld unless unreasonable, see id. at 18. Here it is clearly reasonable.

We therefore affirm the holding of the district court that the NFMA does not require that the cost of a National Forest timber road be exceeded by the value of the timber that it accesses.

*   *   *

NOTES

1. The court's confusion over the source of the "economical" roads provision is due to the fact that the NFMA was styled as an amendment to the RPA, but the combined provisions are often referred to as the NFMA. The RPA had virtually no legislative history on the issue of economics. The NFMA does. See supra at page 668. Should § 1604(k) be construed differently in light of the thrust of the NFMA legislative history or is the language of the NFMA still so general that courts will defer in the manner of the Ninth Circuit in the principal case? Is the Committee of Scientists correct in believing that the agency is limited by "rules of reason"? Could some sales be so uneconomical that the courts would step in? Is the agency's documentation relevant?

2. The Agriculture Department recently ruled on the issue of adequate documentation in administrative appeals from the forest plan for the San Juan National Forest in Colorado and the combined plan for the Grand Mesa, Uncompahgre, and Gunnison (GMUG) National Forests, also in Colorado. Among other things, environmental appellants pointed to provisions in the NFMA regulations requiring forest supervisors to analyze prospective timber costs and receipts in considerable detail. According to the regulations, however, such economic analysis need only be "considered" in developing forest plan alternatives, which are to maximize "net public benefits." 36 C.F.R. § 219.14(b), (c) (1985). The comprehensive opinion, issued by Deputy Assistant Secretary Douglas W. MacCleery, on August 6, 1985, remanded the plans to the forest supervisors for further documentation and explanation:

> A particularly strong obligation is imposed on the Forest Service to explain the economic, social and environmental tradeoffs which are likely to occur when resource objectives or responses to expressed public issues are proposed which would

reduce economic efficiency (reduce present net value). Both the anticipated costs and the *benefits* of such resource objectives should be evaluated and explained so that decisionmakers and the public can readily understand the implications of decisions that would have an adverse impact on economic efficiency.

* * *

The selected alternatives for both the San Juan and the GMUG forest plans authorize modest increases in timber sales over volumes that have recently been offered on those forests. For the San Juan, timber sale levels have averaged about 26 million board feet (MMBF) annually in recent years. However, for the 23 years from 1960 through 1982, the average annual sale level was 50 MMBF. The selected alternative on the San Juan would provide for a 38 MMBF average annual allowable sale quantity during the period of the plan. For the GMUG, which in recent years has offered for sale an average of about 29 MMBF per year, the selected alternative provides an upper limit for the average annual allowable sale quantity of 35 MMBF during the period of the plan.

* * *

For both forest plans, the estimated costs associated with every alternative examined substantially exceed projected revenues for the entire planning horizon. * * * The benchmark analyses indicate that at current costs and prices, the timber sale level that is economically efficient if timber values and costs alone are considered is 7–9 MMBF per year on the San Juan and 4–9 MMBF per year on the GMUG.

The timber and associated road programs on both the San Juan and the GMUG account for the bulk of both costs and revenues, yet non-timber benefits account for the bulk of the benefits that make up [present net value]. These facts should lead to exploration of the question of whether it is possible to achieve the non-timber benefits more cost effectively through a management program of a different nature than presently proposed. The primary rationale cited in the planning documents to support the selected alternative seems to be that a healthy forest is necessary to achieve a high level of non-timber and amenity objectives; that vegetation management designed to achieve a forest having a more even distribution of age classes is necessary to provide a healthy forest; and that a timber sale program is the most appropriate way to accomplish such vegetation management. In view of the large net cost of vegetation management accomplished through the timber program, each of these assumptions needs to be explored and fully rationalized and documented.

The following are examples of questions that should be addressed: Is the timber program as currently proposed actually the most cost effective way to achieve the non-timber multiple

use objectives of the plan? To what extent can timber program costs be cut and/or revenues be enhanced while still
providing an appropriate level of non-timber multiple use
objectives? Are there other ways to accomplish vegetation
management more cost effectively than through a timber program as currently proposed? The Forest Service has been
exploring the use of prescribed fire for this purpose in Colorado. Does this technology, used in conjunction with timber
sales where economically efficient, hold promise to reduce the
cost of vegetation management?

Other questions that should also be explored include: Are the
non-timber multiple use benefits to be achieved through the
timber program really needed? Do projections of demand for
these non-timber objectives support the need for the Federal
expenditures required to achieve them? What are the high-
level non-timber and amenity benefits that would be lost and
who would be affected by the change and in what ways?

*   *   *

Since there is no indication in the planning documents that
increases in timber sales will be made only if there is an
increase in demand and prices for timber, an explanation is
needed as to why increasing the dependency of local community mill capacity and jobs which could result from an increase
in sales of National Forest timber with revenues exceeding
costs will contribute to greater national or local welfare—
especially since increased dependency upon submarginal timber sales would seem to result in potentially greater community instability due to uncertainties over continuation of a relatively high level of Federal funding to support a timber
program with costs greater than revenues. The [record of
decision] should address this question.

In summary, the [records of decision] for the San Juan forest
plan and the GMUG forest plan do not adequately explain why
the selected alternative provides the greatest net public benefits. Alternatives with lower levels of harvest are shown to
meet environmental requirements and appear to have the
same or similar present value of benefits for range, developed
recreation, other recreation, wilderness, wildlife and water, but
without the less favorable costs and revenue characteristics of
the selected alternative.

*   *   *

3. Should a court reach the same result as the Agriculture Department on facts similar to the Colorado appeals, or are these matters
that the judiciary should leave to agency discretion? Are the economically efficient levels of timber sales on these forests so far below the
levels proposed in the plans that these below-cost sales should be struck
down on substantive grounds as violating section 1604(k)?

4. As a policy matter, should Congress prohibit all below-cost sales? Should exceptions be made for timber-dependent communities? Should sales in such areas be phased out?

Chapter Eight

THE RANGE RESOURCE

One main impetus of the Sagebrush Rebellion was western resentment at federal regulation of livestock grazing. Although often overshadowed by energy and minerals problems, the determination of how many head of cattle or sheep will be allowed to graze the public lands remains a volatile resource allocation issue in the 1980's. Grazing is allowed in some wildlife refuges, and, for preexisting uses, in some wilderness areas, but the main focus of this chapter is BLM grazing regulation. The Bureau administers more than 170 million acres outside of Alaska for domestic livestock grazing. Emphasis on BLM range management does not mean that grazing is an unimportant resource use on other land systems; cattle and sheep use roughly 100 million acres in the national forests, for instance.

Multiple use has replaced dominant grazing use as the theoretical guiding management criterion. More people—such as motorcyclists, hikers, rockhounds, and wild burro enthusiasts—wish to see the public lands used in more ways, or not used at all. The depletion of the range is blamed on the ranchers as well as on the BLM. And Congress in the past decade has decreed that things have to change. Polarization remains common in range politics, as it has been for a century. Heated rhetoric nearly always dominates rational debate on preferred directions of public rangeland management. The following two excerpts, one from a cattlemen's association spokesman and the other from an outspoken gadfly, illustrate the diversity of views. Michieli, Response to "Role of Land Treatments on Public and Private Lands," in DEVELOPING STRATEGIES FOR RANGELAND MANAGEMENT 1421 (1984) concluded:

> Improved profitability of cattle enterprises is a pressing need. The nation's cattlemen have a major interest in the present national economic efforts underway.
>
> As part of the economic pressures, the nation's cattlemen desire to be better understood as they use and manage the rangelands, both public and private. In addition to cattle production, they are interested, as conservationists, in fish and wildlife, improved water quality, erosion control, and aesthetics. The cattlemen often do not get credit for the contributions they make to such benefits which accrue to the general public. The cost-benefit ratio of public range management programs considers only the animal production value. The non-livestock values—the side benefits, if you will—are not accounted for in the cost-benefit analysis of public range management programs. This is so even though these programs include requirements and restrictions intended to enhance nonlivestock bene-

fits and these requirements and restrictions impose extra costs on the livestock users as well as on the government itself.

The current cost-benefit ratio of public range management programs, therefore, exaggerates the cost of *livestock* management and/or undervalues the public benefits of such expenditures.

*   *   *

*   *   * [T]he grazing of rangelands can have positive influences on the vegetative and soil resources, rather than all negative impacts in uncontrolled situations, which are occurring less today. Some positive impacts of grazing * * * include:

- Grazed plants are often more productive than those ungrazed.

- Grazing reduces excessive accumulation of dead vegetation and mulch that may inhibit new growth.

- Grazing tramples seed into the ground.

There are many examples that rangelands properly used can maintain or improve the plant communities. There are also examples which show that prolonged nonuse can result in range deterioration as surely as overuse will. I believe that today we now all realize there are many ways to improve rangelands other than reduction in cattle numbers.

The rangelands of this nation, public and private, are a valuable national resource. They must receive the appropriate consideration by the users of such resource, including the general public. As one of the prime users, the nation's cattlemen are hopeful that their story will be heard and fully considered.

In Abbey, Even the Bad Guys Wear White Hats, HARPER'S, Jan. 1986, at 51, the writer takes a different philosophical tack:

There are some Western cattlemen who are nothing more than welfare parasites. They've been getting a free ride on the public lands for over a century, and I think it's time we phased it out. I'm in favor of putting the public lands livestock grazers out of business.

First of all, we don't need the public lands beef industry. Even beef lovers don't need it. According to most government reports (Bureau of Land Management, Forest Service), only about 2 percent of our beef, our red meat, comes from the eleven Western states. * * * More than twice as many beef cattle are raised in the state of Georgia than in the sagebrush empire of Nevada. And for a very good reason: back East, you can support a cow on maybe half an acre. Out here, it takes anywhere from twenty-five to fifty acres. In the red rock country of Utah, the rule of thumb is one section—a square mile—per cow.

Since such a small percentage of the cows are produced on public lands in the West, eliminating that industry should not raise supermarket beef prices very much. Furthermore, we'd save money in the taxes we now pay for various subsidies to these public lands cattlemen. Subsidies for things like "range improvement"—tree chaining, sagebrush clearing, mesquite poisoning, disease control, predator trapping, fencing, wells, stock ponds, roads. Then there are the salaries of those who work for government agencies like the BLM and the Forest Service. You could probably also count in a big part of the salaries of the overpaid professors engaged in range-management research at the Western land-grant colleges.

Moreover, the cattle have done, and are doing, intolerable damage to our public lands—our national forests, state lands, BLM-administered lands, wildlife preserves, even some of our national parks and monuments. * * *

Overgrazing is much too weak a term. Most of the public lands in the West, and especially in the Southwest, are what you might call "cowburnt." Almost anywhere and everywhere you go in the American West you find hordes of these ugly, clumsy, stupid, bawling, stinking, fly-covered, shit-smeared, disease-spreading brutes. They are a pest and a plague. They pollute our springs and streams and rivers. They infest our canyons, valleys, meadows, and forests. They graze off the native bluestem and grama and bunch grasses, leaving behind jungles of prickly pear. They trample down the native forbs and shrubs and cactus. They spread the exotic cheat grass, the Russian thistle, and the crested wheat grass. *Weeds.*

Even when the cattle are not physically present, you'll see the dung and the flies and the mud and the dust and the general destruction. If you don't see it, you'll smell it. The whole American West stinks of cattle. Along every flowing stream, around every seep and spring and water hole and well, you'll find acres and acres of what range-management specialists call "sacrifice areas"—another understatement. These are places denuded of forage, except for some cactus or a little tumbleweed or maybe a few mutilated trees like mesquite, juniper, or hackberry.

Considering the magnitude of the resource, the philosophical tenets of the main range users, and the difficulty of allocation, it is perhaps surprising that there has been relatively little litigation or legislation since passage of the Taylor Act. The more fundamental range allocation problems are just now reaching the courts. This chapter examines public rangeland management in each of its three main historical stages: before regulation commenced with the Taylor Grazing Act of 1934; the Taylor Act era from 1934 to 1976; and the decade since passage of the FLPMA.

A. THE COMMON LAW OF PUBLIC LAND GRAZING

Until passage of the Taylor Grazing Act, ranchers could argue with considerable precedent and persuasiveness that they had a "right" to run their herds on the public lands. Congress had never legislated otherwise, state law encouraged full and free use of the federal lands, and the United States Supreme Court had noted that congressional acquiescence in local practices conferred a sort of expectation or license to graze that prevailed until federal legislation decreed otherwise. Free grazing brought ranchers west, and they built their operations around it. A "base ranch" of 160, 320, or 640 acres would be homesteaded, typically on bottom land on or near a creek, and water rights would be established for stockwatering and subsistence farming. Other sections of land often were later added to the "deeded" ranch. But in many sectors of the West a spread cannot be profitable unless it encompasses several thousand acres. Some early settlers therefore selected their fee lands based on the availability of the public grazing land: for many ranchers, their public grazing acres exceed their fee lands several times over. As free grazing was replaced by permits and fees, the economics of ranching operations were altered dramatically. Some spreads would be jeopardized if nearby public lands were put to some other use. For these and other reasons, ranchers frequently believe that their permits or leases confer permanent, alienable, and inheritable property interests that cannot or should not be diminished by administrative action.

The judiciary recognized the ranchers' implied right of access to the public domain. In Buford v. Houtz, 133 U.S. 320 (1890), cattlemen owned 350,000 acres interspersed in an area of 921,000 acres, the rest of which was public land. They sought to enjoin sheepherders from trespassing on their lands to reach the public lands. In holding that plaintiffs' bill failed for want of equity because the relief sought would allow plaintiffs to monopolize grazing on the public lands, the Court commented:

> We are of opinion that there is an implied license, growing out of the custom of nearly a hundred years, that the public lands of the United States, especially those in which the native grasses are adapted to the growth and fattening of domestic animals, shall be free to the people who seek to use them where they are left open and unenclosed, and no act of government forbids this use. For many years past a very large proportion of the beef which has been used by the people of the United States is the meat of cattle thus raised upon the public lands without charge, without let or hindrance or obstruction. The government of the United States, in all its branches, has known of this use, has never forbidden it, nor taken any steps to arrest it. No doubt it may be safely stated that this has been done with the consent of all branches of the government,

and, as we shall attempt to show, with its direct encouragement.

* * *

The value of this privilege grew as the population increased, and it became a custom for persons to make a business or pursuit of gathering herds of cattle or sheep, and raising them and fattening them for market upon these unenclosed lands of the government of the United States. Of course the instances became numerous in which persons purchasing land from the United States put only a small part of it in cultivation, and permitted the balance to remain unenclosed and in no way separated from the lands owned by the United States. All the neighbors who had settled near one of these prairies or on it, and all the people who had cattle that they wished to graze upon the public lands, permitted them to run at large over the whole region, fattening upon the public lands of the United States, and upon the unenclosed lands of the private individual, without let or hindrance. The owner of a piece of land, who had built a house or enclosed twenty or forty acres of it, had the benefit of this universal custom, as well as the party who owned no land. Everybody used the open unenclosed country, which produced nutritious grasses, as a public common on which their horses, cattle, hogs and sheep could run and graze.

Abuses of and conflicts under the implied license were rampant, however, and judicial efforts to curb appropriation of the public lands for exclusive private use were largely unavailing. See Scott, The Range Cattle Industry: Its Effect on Western Land Law, 28 Mont.L.Rev. 155 (1967).

Grazing on the public domain has been a classic example of the "tragedy of the commons." As no controls or costs were imposed, it was in each rancher's best economic interest to run as many head as possible on the "free" range before somebody else did. The inevitable consequence was severe overgrazing and degradation of the forage-producing capacity of the land. See Cox, Deterioration of Southern Arizona's Grasslands: Effects of New Federal Legislation Concerning Public Grazing Lands, 20 Ariz.L.Rev. 697 (1979). State regulation on the public domain before 1934 was the only means of control available, but state law was more concerned with defining and encouraging private grazing rights than with regulation of their use for protection of the resource. Compare Omaechevarria v. Idaho, 246 U.S. 343 (1918), supra at page 153; Scott, supra. The failure or lack of state law to protect the range, coupled with drought conditions, led to the passage of the Taylor Grazing Act of 1934. See E. Peffer, THE CLOSING OF THE PUBLIC DOMAIN (1951).

The public domain was divided by the creation of national forest reserves in the 1890's and 1900's; grazing in national forests thus came under some primitive regulation (see Light v. United States, 220 U.S.

523 (1911), supra at page 137) while grazing on the unreserved lands remained free and unregulated. At least partly because of such regulation, national forest lands were far more productive by the mid-1930's than the public domain lands. See Box, The American Rangelands: Their Condition and Policy Implications for Management, in RANGELAND POLICIES FOR THE FUTURE 16 (1979). The Grazing Service was created in 1936 to implement the Taylor Act and was merged with the General Land Office in 1946 to form the BLM.

B. THE TAYLOR GRAZING ACT

The lands now entrusted to the BLM were never very productive as a general matter, being mostly arid or semi-arid, rocky, and high. Those same factors make them even more vulnerable to overuse and render restoration that much more difficult. By 1934, many areas had become virtual deserts, streams were fouled, "bad" plant species such as mesquite and sagebrush were gaining dominance, erosion was depleting the sparse topsoil, and the native grasses were declining in vigor and prevalence. Regulation pursuant to the Taylor Act has assisted in stemming the decline in the condition of the public lands, and, together with the efforts of individual ranchers, has promoted instances of local improvements. The great majority of lands under BLM jurisdiction, however, remain in "fair" or "poor" condition, meaning that they are producing less than half of their potential useful vegetation. See NRDC, Inc. v. Morton, 388 F.Supp. 829 (D.D.C.1974), infra at page 704.

Forest Service authority over grazing was inferable from the general management authority of the 1897 Organic Act. Light v. United States, 220 U.S. 523 (1911), supra at page 137. The Taylor Act, however is grazing legislation, aimed as much at helping the livestock industry as improving public land conditions. Still, it is not the sort of "Magna Carta" that miners have in the 1872 Mining Law, nor does the rancher's interest rise to the status of a property interest akin to the oil driller's leasehold or a timber operator's contract.

The Taylor Act imposed a new regimen explicitly favoring adjacent landowners and ending the tradition of free uncontrolled use by any grazer. See E. Peffer, supra at page 156. Because of the ranchers' perceived proprietary interest in the public domain grazing areas and because of the political weakness of the BLM, the Act also resulted in a system of semi-self-government. The holders of federal permits, through Stockmen's Advisory Boards and less formal means, largely controlled the administration of grazing districts for decades. It has been alleged that the BLM district officers until recently have acted more as agents for the ranching industry than as regulators of it. See Comment, Managing Federal Lands: Replacing the Multiple Use System, 82 Yale L.Rev. 787 (1973). Some ranchers remember first-hand the open and bureaucracy-free grazing commons and feel cheated by what they see as unjustifiable government interference into private affairs. The BLM has noted the pervasiveness of what it terms "ranch fundamentalism," an attitude described as rugged individualism opposed to all regulation. Only about 22,000 individuals and other ranching entities hold federal grazing permits and leases from the BLM, but they generally have been successful in opposing administrative actions aimed at reducing the value of or otherwise regulating their interest.

In short, many ranchers still believe that their existing permits to graze so many head are entitled to higher priority than any other resource use or consideration. Their ranching structure is built upon federal land availability, and they largely have been successful in defending that structure. Whether the belief has a legal basis and whether the status quo can continue substantially intact are main themes of this chapter. This section examines the nature of the rancher's interest, grazing fees, and instances of attempted regulation under the Taylor Act.

1. THE PRIVATE INTEREST IN THE PUBLIC LANDS

Determining the nature and quantum of private rights in public lands and resources is a somewhat problematic inquiry because of differences in the mechanisms by which the Congress has allocated those lands and resources. Mining claims, oil and gas leases, and timber contracts all give their holders a property interest in those resources, at least to a certain extent. Permits to graze, granted under the Taylor Act, differ substantially in the type and degree of property interest conferred upon the holder. The court in an early Taylor Act case, Red Canyon Sheep Company v. Ickes, 98 F.2d 308 (D.C.Cir.1938), grappled with that question in the context of a proposed land exchange with an owner of patented land within a national forest. The inholder would have received the grazing land on which Red Canyon, the appellant, held a federal grazing permit. The opinion analyzed the prerogatives of ranchers who had been granted such permits.

> Has a court of equity jurisdiction to protect the claimed rights of the appellants? This question requires first an analysis of the Taylor Grazing Act and a determination of the nature of the appellants' rights thereunder. * * *
>
>   * * *
>
> We note that under [43 U.S.C.A. §§ 315a, 315b, and 315f of] the Taylor Grazing Act the Congress has vested discretion in the Secretary of the Interior to create grazing districts, to establish and modify the boundaries thereof, and from time to time to reclassify the lands therein for other purposes. And Section 3 of the Act does not expressly speak of *rights* to permits; it uses the terms *authorized* and *entitled*. Nevertheless, looking at the Act in the light of its purpose and of its provisions as a whole, we think that the Congress intended that under it livestock owners, who, with their flocks, have been for a substantial period of time *bona fide* occupants of certain parts of the public domain, and who are able to make the most economic and beneficial use thereof because of their

ownership of lands, water rights, and other necessary facilities, and who can thus bring themselves within a preferred class under the regulations by which the Secretary is authorized to implement in more detail the general policy of the Act, are entitled to grazing permits not exceeding ten years in duration, should the Secretary create a grazing district including that portion of the range which such livestock owners have been occupying. By this we do not mean to rule upon the question whether the Secretary may be required, by grazers who have been using a particular portion of the public domain, to establish a grazing district upon the lands so used. Conceivably under the Act the Secretary might in his discretion conclude that such lands were more valuable for homesteading or other public purposes than for grazing. But we do conclude that if the Secretary determines to set up a grazing district including lands upon which grazing has been going on, then those who have been grazing their livestock upon these lands and who bring themselves within a preferred class set up by the statute and regulations, are entitled as of right to permits as against others who do not possess the same facilities for economic and beneficial use of the range. Therefore in view of the allegations of the bill that the appellants have such adjacent land holdings, water rights, and other facilities as to bring them within a preferred class under the regulations, we are of the view that the interim licenses which have been temporarily issued to them must, under the Act, ripen into permits, provided that Grazing District No. 4, which has been set up so as to include the lands upon which the appellants have been running their sheep, continues to exist and to include such lands.

* * *

* * *

* * * We recognize that the rights under the Taylor Grazing Act do not fall within the conventional category of vested rights in property. Yet, whether they be called rights, privileges, or bare licenses, or by whatever name, while they exist they are something of real value to the possessors and something which have their source in an enactment of the Congress. The jurisdiction of equity is flexible and should not be confined to rigid categories so that the granting of an injunction will depend upon nomenclature rather than upon substance.

* * *

We rule that the valuable nature of the privilege to graze which arises in a licensee whose license will in the ordinary course of administration of the Taylor Grazing Act ripen into a permit, makes that privilege a proper subject of equitable protection against an illegal act. To hold that the appellants' rights are not of sufficient dignity to be entitled to equitable protection would be inconsistent with the cases discussing other analogous subjects of equitable protection and with the purposes of the Act itself.

* * *

LaRUE v. UDALL
United States Court of Appeals, District of Columbia Circuit, 1963.
324 F.2d 428.

WILBUR K. MILLER, Circuit Judge.

The appellants operate a cattle ranch located within the boundaries of Carson City Grazing District No. 3, Nevada. They own in fee about 1,600 acres in five non-contiguous tracts, and are licensed to graze their cattle on approximately 10,000 acres of public land. Due to the railroad grants of the Nineteenth Century, the area is made up of both publicly and privately owned tracts in a checkerboard pattern.

Appellee North American Aviation, Inc., is a large corporation engaged in the development and manufacture of rocket engines and rocket power plants and in research in that field. Having progressed to the point where it needed a very large body of land in an isolated area for the development of its program, North American acquired title to a considerable portion of the privately owned lands in the portion of Carson City Grazing District No. 3 heretofore utilized by the appellants. In order to complete its project, North American needed to acquire the large acreage of public lands under grazing license to the appellants.

In exchange for this portion of Carson City Grazing District No. 3, which has an appraised value of $86,400, North American offered the United States more than 20,000 acres lying within the boundaries of Winnemucca Grazing District No. 2, Nevada, which has an appraised value of $90,100. This land is a substantial distance from the land North American desired to obtain.

The appellants protested that the exclusion of their cattle from the area sought by North American would seriously curtail, if not destroy, their ranching operation, as the lands owned by them in fee will not sustain it; and they asserted that § 8(b) of the Taylor Grazing Act which authorizes the Secretary of the Interior in some circumstances to make such exchanges does not authorize the exchange proposed by North American. * * *

Thereupon, the appellants complained to the United States District Court for the District of Columbia, challenging the legality of the exchange so approved. The District Court having affirmed the Secretary's decision, the appellants brought this appeal.

They contend that § 8(b) of the Taylor Grazing Act does not authorize the Secretary of the Interior to issue a patent for public grazing land to a private organization for industrial use, even for national defense purposes, especially when his act in so doing will terminate a grazing license and destroy a ranching operation. Their principal argument is that § 8(b) authorizes the exchange of publicly owned grazing lands for privately owned lands only when the public interests in grazing on the public range and in conservation will be benefited thereby. That North American will not use the lands for grazing or conservation purposes is not disputed.

The term "public interests" in § 8(b) is not defined by that section, nor is it limited or restricted in any way. If Congress had intended to restrict the meaning of those words in the manner urged by the appellants, we think it would have said so. Such a qualification could easily have been inserted in the statute. It seems to us that the Secretary correctly construed § 8(b) when he said in his opinion:

> " * * * [T]he benefit to the public interests, which is the criterion of the statute, need not be related exclusively to conservation of Federal grazing resources nor need it be shown that a proposed exchange will promote range management. * * * [T]he Taylor Grazing Act is a multiple purpose act and while its chief immediate purpose was to stop injury to the public domain by unregulated grazing and to promote the stabilization of the livestock industry, section 1 of the act authorizes the Secretary of the Interior to establish grazing districts in order to promote the highest use of the public domain 'pending its final disposal.' * * *

> "Thus nothing in the other sections of the act suggest that private interests may not acquire public land being used for grazing purposes to the detriment of those licensed to use the land."

> * * *

Even under appellants' restricted view of the meaning of the statutory words "public interests," it is clearly the Secretary's duty, in considering a proposed exchange, to consider its net result: to compare the advantages which the offered land would bring to conservation and the grazing industry with any disadvantage to those interests which might result to them from the withdrawal of the selected lands from a grazing district. This the Secretary seems to have done, as he held "that acquisition of the offered lands would block out holdings of public lands and would facilitate the administration and management of the area for grazing purposes." Thus appellee Udall gave another reason for approving the exchange in addition to his interpretation of § 8(b). We think he was right in both respects.

Appellants also assert that their grazing unit has been and is pledged as security for *bona fide* loans, and that therefore the Secretary may not terminate their grazing permit. As a basis for the assertion they rely upon the language we have italicized in the following portion of § 3 of the Taylor Grazing Act (43 U.S.C.A. § 315b): " * * * *no permittee complying with the rules and regulations laid down by the Secretary of the Interior shall be denied the renewal of such permit, if such denial will impair the value of the grazing unit of the permittee, when such unit is pledged as security for any bona fide loan.* * * * "

Their contention is that if the Secretary may not refuse to renew a permit when the permittee's grazing unit is pledged as security for a *bona fide* loan, "he can hardly bring about the same result indirectly by terminating a permit prior to the expiration of the term * * *." As the context shows, the provision relied upon by the appellants is one of the factors to be considered by the Secretary in establishing preferences between conflicting applications for permits on the federal range. By no means should it be construed as providing that, by maintaining a lien on his grazing unit, a permittee may also create and maintain a vested interest therein which will prevent the United States from exchanging it under § 8(b).

Another point on appeal is thus stated by the appellants:

> "Appellee Udall acted unlawfully and deprived appellants of due process (a) by denying a full and fair hearing in derogation both of the provisions of the Taylor Grazing Act and the Fifth Amendment; (b) by denying access to the full record on which appellee Udall's decision was based; and (c) by denying appellants the protection afforded by the Administrative Procedure Act."

As appellants were heard at length on their protest against the proposed exchange, it is apparent their real complaint is that no formal evidentiary hearing was held. We find nothing in the Taylor Grazing Act which requires a hearing on such a protest. * * *

* * *

Appellants' reliance on the Fifth Amendment disregards the provision of § 3 of the Act (43 U.S.C.A. § 315b) that

> " * * * So far as consistent with the purposes and provisions of this chapter, grazing privileges recognized and acknowledged shall be adequately safeguarded, but the creation of a grazing district or the issuance of a permit pursuant to the provisions of this chapter shall not create any right, title, interest, or estate in or to the lands."

The command of Congress that grazing privileges shall be adequately safeguarded "so far as consistent with the purposes and provisions of this chapter" does not mean that a grazing permit is to prevent the Government's exercise of the right of exchange, which is "one of the provisions of this chapter."

* * *

We have carefully considered all the other contentions made by the appellants, but do not find in them any reason for disturbing the Secretary's decision. As we said in Safarik v. Udall:

> "It is obvious that the Secretary of the Interior, in carrying out his functions in the administration and management of the public lands, must be accorded a wide area of discretion and it is a well-recognized rule that administrative action taken by him will not be disturbed by a court unless it is clearly wrong."

Instead of being clearly wrong, the Secretary's action seems to us to have been quite correct. The District Court's judgment upholding his decision will be affirmed.

It is so ordered.

BAZELON, Circuit Judge (concurring).

Under § 8(b) of the Taylor Grazing Act, 43 U.S.C.A. § 315g(b), any landowner may propose to exchange his land ["offered" lands] for federal land of equal value located within a grazing district ["selected" lands]; and the Secretary of the Interior may approve the exchange if "public interests will be benefited thereby." In this case, because the Secretary viewed the Taylor Act as a "multiple purpose" statute, he construed the term "public interests" as a broad reference to the general public interest, rather than being limited to grazing interests. In approving the exchange, the Secretary relied heavily on his finding that the exchange would benefit the general public interest, but he also found that the exchange would benefit grazing interests. This court holds that the exchange may be approved on either ground. I think approval can rest only on a finding of benefit to grazing interests.

* * *

The legislative history of the Act shows that in authorizing the Secretary to convey public lands to private individuals as part of an exchange, § 8(b) was intended not as a new source of power to alienate federal lands, but simply to promote consolidation of the grazing districts. As such, I think that the determination that "public interests will be benefited [by an exchange]" includes only public interests in furtherance of the grazing and range stabilization policies which are the subject of the Act. * * *

* * *

The decrease in grazing since 1934, together with the growing importance of Western commercial and industrial development, may indicate that the Taylor Act's emphasis on grazing is outdated. But Congress has not said so, nor has Congress relaxed its concern with land conservation and retention of federal ownership. If changed circumstances require a view of "public interests" under § 8(b) that goes beyond grazing interests, Congress—not the Secretary—must say so.

NOTES

1. What precisely is the legal definition of the interest that a rancher has in a grazing permit? A protectable privilege? A license subject to administrative curtailment "in the public interest"? Compare United States v. Cox, 190 F.2d 293, 296 (10th Cir.1951), cert. denied, 342 U.S. 867 (1951): "Although the permits are available to the ranchers, they are not an interest protected by the Fifth Amendment against the taking by the Government who granted them with the understanding that they could be withdrawn at any time without the payment of compensation."

2. The Taylor Act is but one of many that delegated to an administrator the power to decide a question on the basis of the "public interest." Is this more accurately characterized as "efficient administration" or "congressional cop-out"? Could Congress have foreseen in

1934 a future conflict between a grazing lessee and intercontinental ballistic missiles? Is that question relevant?

3. Is the Taylor Act a grazing statute, multiple use legislation, or something else?

4. Land exchanges are now governed by section 206 of FLPMA, 43 U.S.C.A. § 1716. See supra at page 273.

5. FLMPA contains several provisions concerning grazing permits. The major section is 43 U.S.C.A. § 1752, which should be read in its entirety, although most of its provisions will be considered in this section. Section 1752(h) provides that "[n]othing in this Act shall be construed as modifying in any way law existing on October 21, 1976, with respect to the creation of right, title, interest or estate in or to the public lands or lands National Forests by issuance of grazing permits and leases."

6. In Barton v. United States, 468 F.Supp. 962 (D.Utah 1979), plaintiffs sued for damages under the Federal Torts Claim Act, 28 U.S.C.A. §§ 2671–80, 1346(b), alleging inter alia that a land exchange between the United States and Utah, whereby the state lands that plaintiff grazed were transferred to the BLM, was a negligent act injuring them in that the BLM could now refuse them the grazing privileges previously granted by the State. The court held that the exchange was a discretionary act exempt from tort recovery pursuant to 28 U.S.C.A. § 2680(a). Compare Powell v. United States, 233 F.2d 851 (10th Cir.1956) (mining claim operator cannot recover damages for wrongfully authorized grazing on claim); Oman v. United States, 179 F.2d 738 (10th Cir.1949) (action may lie when BLM wrongfully abets "lease-jumping"); Chournos v. United States, 193 F.2d 321 (10th Cir. 1952) (but no action for animal trespass). The FTCA is also treated infra at chapter 10, § B.

UNITED STATES v. FULLER

Supreme Court of the United States, 1973.
409 U.S. 488.

Mr. Justice REHNQUIST delivered the opinion of the Court.

Respondents operated a large-scale "cow-calf" ranch near the confluence of the Big Sandy and Bill Williams Rivers in western Arizona. Their activities were conducted on lands consisting of 1,280 acres that they owned in fee simple (fee lands), 12,027 acres leased from the State of Arizona, and 31,461 acres of federal domain held under Taylor Grazing Act permits issued in accordance with § 3 of the Act, 48 Stat. 1270, as amended, 43 U.S.C.A. § 315b. The Taylor Grazing Act authorizes the Secretary of the Interior to issue permits to livestock owners for grazing their stock on Federal Government lands. These permits are revocable by the Government. The Act provides, moreover, that its provisions "shall not create any right, title, interest, or estate in or to the lands." Ibid.

The United States, petitioner here, condemned 920 acres of respondents' fee lands. At the trial in the District Court for the purpose of fixing just compensation for the lands taken, the parties disagreed as to whether the jury might consider value accruing to the fee lands as a result of their actual or potential use in combination with the Taylor Grazing Act "permit" lands. The Government contended that such element of incremental value to the fee lands could neither be taken into consideration by the appraisers who testified for the parties nor considered by the jury. Respondents conceded that their permit lands could not themselves be assigned any value in view of the quoted provisions of the Taylor Grazing Act. They contended, however, that if on the open market the value of their fee lands was enhanced because of their actual or potential use in conjunction with permit lands, that element of value of the fee lands could be testified to by appraisers and considered by the jury. The District Court substantially adopted respondents' position, first in a pretrial order and then in its charge to the jury over appropriate objection by the Government.

* * *

Our prior decisions have variously defined the "just compensation" that the Fifth Amendment requires to be made when the Government exercises its power of eminent domain. The owner is entitled to fair market value, United States v. Miller, 317 U.S. 369, 374 (1943), but that term is "not an absolute standard nor an exclusive method of valuation." * * *

The record shows that several appraiser witnesses for respondents testified that they included as an element of the value that they ascribed to respondents' fee lands the availability of respondents' Taylor Grazing Act permit lands to be used in conjunction with the fee lands. Under the District Court's charge to the jury, the jury was entitled to consider this element of value testified to by the appraisers. This Court has held that generally the highest and best use of a parcel may be found to be a use in conjunction with other parcels, and that any increment of value resulting from such combination may be taken into consideration in valuing the parcel taken. Olson v. United States, 292 U.S. 246, 256 (1934). The question presented by this case is whether there is an exception to that general rule where the parcels to be aggregated with the land taken are themselves owned by the condemnor and used by the condemnee only under revocable permit from the condemnor.

To say that this element of value would be considered by a potential buyer on the open market, and is therefore a component of "fair market value," is not the end of the inquiry. In United States v. Miller, supra, this Court held that the increment of fair market value represented by knowledge of the Government's plan to construct the project for which the land was taken was not included within the constitutional definition of "just compensation." * * *

* * * A long line of cases decided by this Court dealing with the Government's navigational servitude with respect to navigable waters evidences a continuing refusal to include, as an element of value in compensating for fast lands that are taken, any benefits conferred by access to such benefits as a potential portsite or a potential hydro-electric site. United States v. Twin City Power Co., 350 U.S. 222 (1956); United States v. Commodore Park, 324 U.S. 386 (1945).

These cases go far toward establishing the general principle that the Government as condemnor may not be required to compensate a condemnee for elements of value that the Government has created, or that it might have destroyed under the exercise of governmental authority other than the power of eminent domain. If * * * the Government need not pay for value that it could have acquired by exercise of a servitude arising under the commerce power, it would seem *a fortiori* that it need not compensate for value that it could remove by revocation of a permit for the use of lands that it owned outright.

We do not suggest that such a general principle can be pushed to its ultimate logical conclusion. In United States v. Miller, supra, the Court held that "just compensation" did include the increment of value resulting from the completed project to neighboring lands originally outside the project limits, but later brought within them. * * *

"Courts have had to adopt working rules in order to do substantial justice in eminent domain proceedings." United States v. Miller, supra, at 375. Seeking as best we may to extrapolate from these prior decisions such a "working rule," we believe that there is a significant difference between the value added to property by a completed public works project, for which the Government must pay, and the value added to fee lands by a revocable permit authorizing the use of neighboring lands that the Government owns. The Government may not demand that a jury be arbitrarily precluded from considering as an element of value the proximity of a parcel to a post office building, simply because the Government at one time built the post office. But here respondents rely on no mere proximity to a public building or to public lands dedicated to, and open to, the public at large. Their theory of valuation aggregates their parcel with land owned by the Government to form a privately controlled unit from which the public would be excluded. If * * * a person may not do this with respect to property interests subject to the Government's navigational servitude, he surely may not do it with respect to property owned outright by the Government. * * * We hold that the Fifth Amendment does not require the Government to pay for that element of value based on the use of respondents' fee lands in combination with the Government's permit lands.

* * * The provisions of the Taylor Grazing Act quoted supra make clear the congressional intent that no compensable property right be created in the permit lands themselves as a result of the issuance of the permit. Given that intent, it would be unusual, we think, for Congress to have turned around and authorized compensation for the value added to fee lands by their potential use in connection with

permit lands. We find no such authorization in the applicable congressional enactments.

Reversed.

Mr. Justice POWELL, with whom Mr. Justice DOUGLAS, Mr. Justice BRENNAN, and Mr. Justice MARSHALL join, dissenting.

I dissent from a decision which, in my view, dilutes the meaning of the just compensation required by the Fifth Amendment when property is condemned by the Government. * * *

* * *

The opinion of the Court recognizes that the just compensation required by the Fifth Amendment when the Government exercises its power of eminent domain is ordinarily the market value of the property taken. United States v. Miller, 317 U.S. 369, 374 (1943). It is commonplace, in determining market value—whether in condemnation or in private transactions—to consider such elements of value as derive from the *location* of the land. But today the Court enunciates an exception to these recognized principles where the value of the land to be condemned may be enhanced by its location in relation to Government-owned property. * * *

* * *

The Government's role here is not an ambiguous one—it is simply a condemnor of private land which happens to adjoin public land. If the Government need not pay location value in this case, what are the limits upon the principle today announced? Will the Government be relieved from paying location value whenever it condemns private property adjacent to or favorably located with respect to Government property? Does the principle apply, for example, to the taking of a gasoline station at an interchange of a federal highway, or to the taking of a farm which in private hands could continue to be irrigated with water from a federal reservoir? * * *

* * *

NOTES

1. Fuller lost about three-fourths of the base ranch and was not allowed to recover for the value that the permit lands might have added to the base ranch. If Fuller had purchased the base ranch after 1934, what would the sale price have been based on? According to Phillip Foss' leading study, "grazing permits are ordinarily capitalized into the value of the ranch so that if permits are stabilized a ranch buyer actually pays for both the private and public lands contained in the ranch unit." P. Foss, POLITICS AND GRASS 197 (1960).

2. Comment, U.S. v. Fuller—Eminent Domain—Taylor Grazing Permits As An Element Of Compensation For Condemned Land, 1973 Utah L.Rev. 75, 85–86:

> The Court has extended, by analogy, the no-compensation rule of navigation servitude to the condemnation of base lands which support public grazing permits, and thereby adversely has affected a critical meat-producing industry. The only way

to avoid this undesirable result is through legislation; suggestions for change already exist. Professor Reich has suggested that in the United States public permits and licenses constitute a "new property" interest and that some elements of due process and equal protection should be extended to the holders of these interests. He feels that:

> If revocation [of this type of interest] is necessary not by reason of the fault of the individual holder but by reason of overriding demands of public policy, perhaps payment of just compensation would be appropriate. The individual should not bear the entire loss for a remedy primarily intended to benefit the community.

The Public Land Law Review Commission has made [a] recommendation specifically concerning Taylor Grazing Permits. In its *Report to the President and to the Congress*, the Commission recommends that permits should be issued for a fixed statutory term and that compensation should be made for permits revoked before they expire. The Commission also felt that:

> The statutory and administrative practices of the Government have contributed to the concept of "permit value," whether or not the permit has the attributes of a property right. Loss of the permit prior to its expiration, therefore, should be compensated for, and the compensation standard should take into consideration the value of the base property with and without the permit.

Even if these recommendations become statutory, the situation presented by the instant case would be affected only indirectly because compensation would be provided for only the revocation of the permits themselves and not for the value the permits add to condemned fee land. The recommendations would, however, elevate the permit to something more than a mere revocable license and thereby strengthen the case for compensation which takes into account the value base lands are enhanced by unrevoked grazing permits. Ideally, the statutory changes should include some provision dealing specifically with the problem of condemned base land and unrevoked permits.

The author of Note, Use of Fair Market Value as a Measure of Compensation in Condemnation Proceedings, 87 Harv.L.Rev. 189, 195 (1973), concluded that "*Fuller* presents a persuasive case for denial of compensation because the permit system constituted a government subsidy."

3. FLPMA, 43 U.S.C.A. § 1752(a), provides for some degree of stability, setting ten years as the usual lease term. A shorter term is allowed if the land is pending disposal, if it will be put to some other public purpose within ten years, or if it is "in the best interest of sound land management to specify a shorter term." Id. § 1752(b).

4. 43 U.S.C.A. § 1752(g):

Whenever a permit or lease for grazing domestic livestock is canceled in whole or in part, in order to devote the lands covered by the permit or lease to another public purpose, including disposal, the permittee or lessee shall receive from the United States a reasonable compensation for the adjusted value, to be determined by the Secretary concerned, of his interest in authorized permanent improvements placed or constructed by the permittee or lessee on lands covered by such permit or lease, but not to exceed the fair market value of the terminated portion of the permittee's or lessee's interest therein. Except in cases of emergency, no permit or lease shall be canceled under this subsection without two years' prior notification.

Does this change the rule in *Fuller?*

5. Permittee ranchers were in the vanguard of the Sagebrush Rebellion, partly as a protest to reductions in permitted numbers of grazing animals. For different reasons, a small but hardy band of western economists supports the ranchers' claims for federal divestiture and privatization, arguing that "economic efficiency" would thereby be promoted. G. Libecap, LOCKING UP THE RANGE 102 (1981), concludes:

* * * Assigning title to existing [BLM grazing] permittees is the least costly way of granting private property rights. Title can be subsequently traded at low cost to others (including conservation and wildlife groups). Limited areas of great amenity value, where exclusion is for some reason difficult, can be retained under state or federal control. However, most of the 174 million acres administered by the Bureau of Land Management are not affected by those strict conditions and are amenable to private ownership. Recognizing existing uses of the range in assigning title is consistent with U.S. and state policies which have historically recognized prior appropriation claims for water, farmland, and hard-rock minerals.

Well-defined private rights capture individual incentive and initiative for using rangeland efficiently. Further, they insure response by profit-maximizing land owners to changing market demands for range use. Finally, they allow the U.S. to avoid socially costly scientific management programs advocated by the BLM. Private property rights are the necessary conditions for restoring and maintaining the productive value of a land area larger than New England and the Mid-Atlantic states combined which has been much maligned and fought over for one hundred years.

See also Baden & Stroup, Political Economy Perspectives on the Sagebrush Rebellion, 3 Pub.Land L.Rev. 103, 116 (1982).

2. GRAZING FEES

The price for leasing public rangeland traditionally has been lower than the going rate for comparable lands in private ownership. The Forest Service first charged a nominal fee for grazing on national forests in 1906. Not until 1931 was a new formula employed; fees then increased slowly but steadily up to $0.56 per animal-unit-month (AUM) by 1968, still well below market levels. (An AUM is the amount of forage eaten by one cow or five sheep or goats grazing for one month or about 750–800 pounds of grass.)

The BLM historically has charged even less than the Forest Service: its initial fee of $0.05 per AUM was in effect until 1946, and had risen to only $0.33 by 1968. The Supreme Court rejected a challenge to the initial BLM grazing fee in Brooks v. Dewar, 313 U.S. 354 (1941). In 1955, another lawsuit seeking to invalidate the fee structure was dismissed on technical grounds. The Secretaries of Agriculture and Interior conducted a joint fee study, called the Western Livestock Grazing Survey in 1966; the new study concluded that the fee for both systems should be increased to $1.23 per AUM over ten years. The first increase, to $0.44, was upheld in Pankey Land & Cattle Company v. Hardin, 427 F.2d 43 (10th Cir.1970).

In 1970, the Public Land Law Review Commission recommended that "fair market value" should be the standard for both agencies, while recognizing that on-the-ground conditions might be such that federal fees would remain somewhat below the rate for private lands. See Hart & Guyton, A Review of the Recommendations of PLLRC Directly Affecting Users of the Public Grazing Lands, 6 Land & Water L.Rev. 57 (1970). FLPMA, which included a policy statement that the United States should "receive fair market value of the use of the public lands and their resources unless otherwise provided for by statute," 43 U.S.C.A. § 1701(a)(9), then mandated a grazing fee study by both agencies and put a one-year freeze on grazing fees pending the outcome of the report. 43 U.S.C.A. § 1751(a). The report, which is a useful research source, was timely filed and it too concluded that the fee system should collect fair market value. See Secretary of Interior & Secretary of Agriculture, Study of Fees for Livestock Grazing on Federal Lands (1977).

In the Public Rangelands Improvement Act of 1978, 43 U.S.C.A. § 1905(a), Congress adopted this formula:

> For the grazing years 1979 through 1985, the Secretaries of Agriculture and Interior shall charge the fee for domestic livestock grazing on the public rangelands which Congress finds represents the economic value of the use of the land to the user, and under which Congress finds fair market value for public grazing equals the $1.23 base established by the 1966 Western Livestock Grazing Survey multiplied by the result of the Forage Value Index (computed annually from data supplied by the Economic Research Service) added to the Com-

bined Index (Beef Cattle Price Index minus the Price Paid Index) and divided by 100: *Provided,* That the annual increase or decrease in such fee for any given year shall be limited to not more than plus or minus 25 per centum of the previous year's fee.

The formula, which was opposed by the Administration, operated to keep fees substantially below fair market value during the seven years in which it was in effect. See S.Rep. No. 95–1237, 95th Cong., 2d Sess. 20–21, 58–59 (1978).

By 1985, grazing fees had dropped below $1.40 per AUM, compared to a west-wide fair market value of between $6–15 per AUM for equivalent grazing on private lands. As of January, 1986, Congress had not agreed on a new fee formula, and the Administration was threatening to impose higher grazing fees as a deficit reduction measure.

One of these editors has criticized many aspects of public rangeland management, including the subsidized fee. The evil in the latter, he argues, is that the subsidy is capitalized into the purchase price and mortgage value of the base ranch, leading the subsidy recipients to resist fiercely any cuts in their permitted AUMs, even when the reductions would ultimately redound to the ranchers' economic benefit. See Coggins & Lindeberg-Johnson, The Law of Public Rangeland Management II: The Commons and the Taylor Act, 13 Envtl.L. 1, 74–75 (1982). Other articles in the Public Rangeland Law series are at 12 Envtl.L. 535 (1982); 13 Envtl.L. 295 (1982); 14 Envtl.L. 1 (1983); and 14 Envtl.L. 497 (1984).

3. TAYLOR ACT REGULATION

PHILLIP FOSS, POLITICS AND GRASS
198–200 (1960).

The principal decision-makers of the federal grazing activity include the advisory board members, leaders of the stockmen's associations, a small number of congressmen, and some members of the federal grazing bureaucracy.

The advisory board system was initiated by the first director of grazing, F.R. Carpenter. Carpenter needed a mass of knowledge about local conditions in order to establish and operate the grazing districts. Probably no other system could have furnished this information so quickly. Some local representation or participation may also have been necessary to sell the program to the users. The advisory boards quickly assumed or were given more than an advisory role. They were most influential in drafting a code of rules and regulations; with some exceptions, they determined the allocation of permits; they supervised the expenditure of range improvement funds; they were probably the real decision-makers in setting grazing fees; they were influential in the selection and tenure of personnel; and they have played an active role in routine managerial decisions.

In theory, the boards carry out an advisory function only. In actuality, they formulate the broad policy, make the rules which spell out that policy and superintend the execution of these rules and policies.

District advisory boards are elected by the permittees in secret elections. Two members of each district board are elected to a state advisory board and each state advisory board, in turn, selects two of its members to the National Advisory Board Council. Voting participation by the permittees is very low and the rate of turnover on the boards is very slow. While the advisory board system may appear to be "democratized administration" or "home rule on the range," there are indications that it may be the formalization and legal recognition of the upper strata of a rural caste system.

The leaders of the stockmen's associations are especially powerful in the legislatures of the range states, in the advisory boards, and in the United States Senate. * * *

* * *

The administrators of the federal grazing activity are, of course, participants in the formulation of policy. In some instances administrators have been in general agreement with their stockmen clientele group and have acted as the spokesmen and chief lobbyists for their clientele. When administrators have acted contrary to the objectives of the stockmen they have ordinarily been unsuccessful and occasionally have been subjected to rather severe punitive sanctions.

The decision-makers described above comprise a governmental subsystem which has specialized objectives and which, in many ways, functions as a private, commercial organization. This subsystem might be called a special private government as opposed to a general public government. The special private government attaches to itself most of the trappings and authority of the general public government and very likely the public assumes that it is in fact an integral part of the general public government.

McNEIL v. SEATON

United States Court of Appeals, District of Columbia Circuit, 1960.
281 F.2d 931.

DANAHER, Circuit Judge.

This case involves appellant's claim that he has wrongfully been denied rights accruing to him under the Taylor Grazing Act and the Federal Range Code. * * *

* * *

The Secretary established Montana Grazing District No. 1 on July 11, 1935, as by section 1 of the Act he was authorized to do after notice and hearing. He issued the Federal Range Code pursuant to section 2 of the Act which "seeks to provide the most beneficial use of the public range and *to protect grazing rights* in the districts it creates. Chournos v. United States, 193 F.2d 321." (Emphasis added.) The Act in section 3 provided that * * *. Preference shall be given in the issuance of grazing permits to those within or near a district who are landowners engaged in the livestock business, bona fide occupants or settlers, or owners of water or water rights, as may be necessary to permit the proper use of lands, water or water rights owned, occupied, or leased by them * * *." This appellant qualified for the "preference" specified in the Act, for he had been continuously engaged in the livestock business in the area in question since 1925 and was so engaged over the five years prior to the date the Act was passed.

* * *

It is clear that a permittee *as against the United States* may acquire no "right, title, interest, or estate in or *to the lands*" (emphasis added) as section 3 provides, and the Government for its own use may without payment of compensation withdraw the permit privilege. Otherwise, consistently with the purposes and provisions of the Act, "grazing privileges recognized and acknowledged shall be adequately safeguarded." It would seem beyond peradventure that when the Secretary in 1935 created Montana Grazing District No. 1 which included lands upon which this appellant then was grazing, he and others similarly situated "who have been grazing their livestock upon these lands and who bring themselves within a preferred class set up by the statute and regulations, are entitled as of right to permits as against others who do not possess the same facilities for economic and beneficial use of the range."

What particular *number* of stock a preference applicant might be entitled to graze must depend upon circumstances, having in mind the orderly use of the public lands, the possibility of overgrazing, the forage capacity of the base property, available water and other factors pertinent to such a complicated administrative problem. Subject to such considerations and others specified in the Code, the extent of the appellant's grazing privileges was to be determined.

Thus stood appellant's status as of April 9, 1936, when the Secretary, pursuant to section 2 of the Act, entered into a cooperative agreement by which he licensed the South Phillips Cooperative State Grazing District to administer the Federal range lands in Montana District No. 1. Twenty years later, on June 19, 1956, through his delegated representative, he promulgated a Special Rule for part of Montana District No. 1. * * *

Affected particularly were lands involved in this controversy. The Special Rule revised or supplied definitions of terms basic to the administration both of the Act and the Range Code. To illustrate, the Secretary changed the "priority period" from the 5-year period immediately preceding June 28, 1934, to a 5-year period "immediately preceding January 1, 1953"; use of the Federal range as part of an established livestock operation was required "during each year of such priority period in connection with such Federal range." Base lands were to be considered as "dependent by use" (Class 1) "only where and to the extent that during each year of such priority period licenses for use of the Federal range in connection therewith were issued under the rules and regulations of the Montana Cooperative State Grazing Districts." Grazing privileges to be granted under the Special Rule were not to exceed the lesser of the amounts to be determined pursuant to the amended definitions. We need not detail other differences, the particulars of which may be noted by comparison of the referenced provisions. It is enough for our purposes to note that the status of this appellant as a preference applicant was no longer that which had been accorded to him by the Act and the Range Code prior to the Special Rule. Moreover, newcomers to livestock operations in the area during the amended priority period, 1948–1952, were to be given grazing privileges as to base lands "dependent by use" to the extent that they had been licensed during "such priority period" under the administration of the State Cooperatives.[23]

Appellant insists that not only has he not been accorded the rights to which he had become entitled as a matter of law, but that grazing privileges which should rightfully be his have been awarded to others who cannot qualify.   *   *   *

*   *   *

Appellant prays that we order the Secretary to issue a Class One permit for the grazing of 282 animal units and a Class Two permit to graze 157 animal units on the Federal range. We have no such authority.

He has asked that the Special Rule "be vacated, annulled and set aside" as void and of no effect. We decline to do so except as applied to him and in respects we shall mention. The Special Rule otherwise may be entirely proper as to parties not before us, or as to its general applicability respecting situations not shown on this record. We express no opinion on such aspects.

We say this much: this appellant clearly was entitled to "preference" under the Act and the Range Code, as we have shown. The word in the context here used is to be taken in its ordinary sense. Its meaning is plain.   *   *   *

So here. "Preference *shall be given*" to those like appellant who come within the Act. This appellant not only was engaged in stockraising when the Act was passed, but he qualified under the Range Code as and when first promulgated. He was entitled to rely upon the preference Congress had given him: to use the public range as dedicated to a special purpose in aid of Congressional policy. We deem his rights—whatever their exact nature—to have been "protected against tortious invasion" and to have been "founded on a statute which confers a privilege." Accordingly this appellant was entitled to invest his time, effort and capital and to develop his stockraising business, all subject, of course, to similar preferences to be accorded in the affected area to

---

23.   *   *   * The Government in its brief tells us that "The award of privileges for 1953 was an attempt by the Bureau to allow privileges in accord with the Taylor Grazing Act and the Federal Range Code without unduly upsetting recognized range operations." The brief does not explain how permits issued by the cooperative during a period of mismanagement become criteria with respect to the issuance of permits for the year 1953 and succeeding years.

others comparably situated. We see no basis upon which, by a special rule adopted more than twenty years after appellant had embarked upon his venture, he may lawfully be deprived of his statutory privilege.

To the extent that the Special Rule is repugnant to the Act and to the Range Code prior to 1956, if and as applied *to this appellant* to deprive him of his rights and to award others grazing privileges in derogation of appellant's preference status, it is void. We expect that if appellant should again apply for a grazing permit, his application will be processed in a manner not inconsistent with this opinion, but otherwise within the provisions of the Range Code.

*   *   *

Reversed.

Mr. Justice BURTON, concurring in part and dissenting in part: Insofar as the opinion of the Court sustains the validity of the special rule, I concur. I would go further and affirm the judgment of the District Court dismissing the complaint.

The authority of the Secretary of the Interior to make rules and regulations consistent with the Taylor Grazing Act is amply established in §§ 2 and 3 of the Act. 43 U.S.C.A. §§ 315a and 315b. The Federal Range Code promulgated by the Secretary is an exercise of that authority. It expressly provides for the adoption of special rules for grazing districts where local conditions make them necessary "in order better to achieve an administration consistent with the purpose of the act * * *." 43 CFR, 1959 Cum.Pocket Supp., § 161.16.

The special rule now before us was adopted in complete conformity with the procedure prescribed in the Code. It applies only to specifically described lands, including those in use by appellant, and it changes the basic period, by which it measures the prior use of lands, from the five-year period immediately preceding June 28, 1934 to the five-year period immediately preceding January 1, 1953. This procedure provides a way to dispose of the many different kinds of problems the Range Code was established to solve. The rule does not deprive appellant of any vested right, nor is it beyond the scope of the Secretary's rule-making power. It merely provides, in the interest of all concerned, a reasonable regulation of individual rights to the use of public land.

Neither the record nor the majority opinion provides an adequate basis for appellant's claim that the Range Code, by establishing the 1929–1934 priority period, has established in effect a permanent right to use the public range exempt from any modification of those rights even by the rule-making authority by which they were established. The Taylor Grazing Act did not purport to establish a specific and inflexible test as the basis for the preference. Rather, it was a starting point announcing a congressional policy as to the use of the federal range, and delegating authority to the Secretary to make and modify general or special rules for carrying out that policy. If the expectations of appellant were thus aroused, they were aroused not by the statute, but by the Range Code's amendable definition of "dependency by use" in terms of a specific priority period.

The present record does not establish the precise amount of appellant's preference under the special rule and we cannot properly consider the application of the special rule to appellant until he has been assigned a preference under it and grazing privileges are allotted or denied to him by virtue of it. The record does not show that the application to him of the special rule will result in sufficient prejudice to him to qualify him to attack it.

NOTES

1. Did the court transform a "privilege," something which by statute is not an interest in property, into a vested right? Is a change in figuring the base preference period the same thing as the exchange contemplated in *Red Canyon?*

2. On remand, McNeil's rights under the old preference were determined to be for 143 animal units, while he would have been entitled to 232 under the Special Rule. His attempt to overturn that determination in Montana was barred by the indispensible party rule. 199 F.Supp. 671 (D.Mont.1961). In the end, McNeil's initial victory was Pyrrhic, as the BLM's more restrictive allocation was affirmed. McNeil v. Udall, 340 F.2d 801 (D.C.Cir.1964). The cases arising from BLM efforts to implement and enforce the Taylor Act are concisely collected in Kingery, The Public Grazing Lands, 43 Denver L.J. 329 (1966).

3. Priority renewal of grazing leases is handled this way in FLPMA, 43 U.S.C.A. § 1752(c):

> So long as (1) the lands for which the permit or lease is issued remain available for domestic livestock grazing in accordance with land use plans prepared pursuant to section 1712 of this title or section 1604 of Title 16, (2) the permittee or lessee is in compliance with the rules and regulations issued and the terms and conditions in the permit or lease specified by the Secretary concerned, and (3) the permittee or lessee accepts the terms and conditions to be included by the Secretary concerned in the new permit or lease, the holder of the expiring permit or lease shall be given first priority for receipt of the new permit or lease.

Does this provision provide substantial protection to a rancher seeking renewal? A rancher-lawyer offers this insight into priority renewals:

> Priority renewal does have advantages. A permittee becomes intimately familiar with the range. In most districts, the high turnover of federal graziers does not permit them to get to know the range nearly as well. Only long use can teach an operator where the thicket is that hides the stubborn bull late in the fall. The seasonal pattern of drying up of the range and waterholes must be known to fully utilize the range resource. If the first areas to dry are not used early in the season, they

will be wasted. The rancher who expects to use the same range for many years in the future will be careful not to hurt the resource. The range cattle themselves get to learn the range. An old range cow can find hidden waterholes and meadows that a new cow would not. And with the first snows of fall, the old cows will lead the herd back to the home ranch.

Marc Valens, FEDERAL GRAZING LANDS: OLD HISTORY, NEW DIRECTIONS (1978) (unpublished manuscript).

DIAMOND RING RANCH, INC. v. MORTON
United States Court of Appeals, Tenth Circuit, 1976.
531 F.2d 1397.

WILLIAM E. DOYLE, Circuit Judge.

* * *

[Diamond Ring is a large ranch with a BLM permit to graze thousands of acres of public lands. In 1971, the ranch, without BLM knowledge or permission, aerially sprayed public as well as its private lands with a herbicide to kill sagebrush. Sagebrush defoliation allows more grass to grow but reduces food and habitat for some wildlife species, including antelope. The hearing examiner found that the spraying of the public land was intentional and willful, but put Diamond Ring on probation instead of suspending the grazing permit. On administrative appeal, the IBLA suspended the permit for two years. The district court reversed, holding that the offense was innocent and that the Taylor Act authorizes only fines, not suspensions or cancellations of the permit.]

The district court's holding that the Secretary was powerless to suspend or revoke a license as a sanction for violation of the Secretary's regulations and that the Secretary is limited to imposition of a monetary fine of $500 or less gives rise to the important issue in this case, for the view of the district court that Section 2 of the Act excludes the power to revoke grazing licenses would seriously undermine the entire body of law with respect to management of public lands.

First, Section 2 of the Act, 43 U.S.C.A. Sec. 315a, gives the Secretary of the Interior broad power to administer those public lands included within the "grazing districts" the Act authorizes him to establish. The section says that the Secretary

> shall make provision for the protection, administration, regulation, and improvement of such grazing districts * * * and he shall make such rules and regulations and establish such service, enter into such cooperative agreements, and do any and all things necessary to accomplish the purposes of this chapter and to insure the objects of such grazing districts, namely, to regulate their occupancy and use, to preserve the land and its resources from destruction or unnecessary injury, to provide for the orderly use, improvement, and development of the range * * *

The Act goes on to say that

> any willful violation of the provisions of this chapter or of such rules and regulations thereunder after actual notice thereof shall be punishable by a fine of not more than $500.

Superficial reading of Section 2, supra, might well give the impression that the Act confers on the Secretary great regulatory authority and responsibility but little enforcement power. Such a conclusion is an absurdity since a ranch of the magnitude of the Diamond Ring could pay the $500 fine frequently as part of the cost of its operations—a cost of doing business, like parking tickets on delivery trucks. If such a view were adopted, the Secretary would lose virtually all regulatory control. We do not suggest that we would ignore the legislative will if we were convinced that such an "absurdity" had emerged from the give and take of the legislative process in the way strong language is sometimes undercut by subsequent limitation.

Second, careful review of the legislative history of the Taylor Grazing Act dispels this possibility. * * *

* * *

Third, Congress on a number of occasions has amended the Taylor Grazing Act (in 1947, 61 Stat. 790; in 1948, 62 Stat. 533; in 1954, 68 Stat. 151) and presumably has been aware of the Secretary's interpretation, but has in no way disturbed the Secretary's power to revoke or suspend a license. * * * Therefore, it is reasonable to regard this congressional activity as approving the regulatory scheme the Secretary has established, and as suggesting agreement with the Secretary's assertion of the power to revoke or suspend a license for violation of a regulation.

The courts considering the existence of power to suspend in other contexts have recognized that it does repose in the Secretary. We have treated this as a question of first impression only because it has not been heretofore decided in the context of an actual revocation such as is present here. Nevertheless, every court that has taken up the problem has assumed that the Secretary had power to revoke licenses. True, these pronouncements have arisen in the context of condemnation proceedings where the question has been whether the enhancement of the value of privately owned land brought about by grazing licenses ought to be considered in fixing just compensation. See, e.g., United States v. Fuller, 409 U.S. 488 (1973); United States v. Cox, 190 F.2d 293 (10th Cir.), cert. denied, 342 U.S. 867 (1951); United States v. Jaramillo, 190 F.2d 300 (10th Cir.1951). Thus, in holding that the licensee under the Taylor Grazing Act does not enjoy any interest in the land but merely a revocable license, the holdings are persuasive in the case at bar. Indeed, the Supreme Court of the United States in United States v. Fuller, supra, recognized the proposition that the Secretary of the Interior acting under the Taylor Grazing Act has authority to issue permits and to revoke them. * * *

* * *

Next we consider whether the Secretary's modification of the penalty was improper exercise of discretion. The trial court in findings 35 and 36 said:

The penalty imposed by the Interior Board of Land Appeals is unduly harsh and oppressive, constitutes an abuse of discretion and an arbitrary and capricious act by the Interior Board of Land Appeals not supported by the evidence or by any rational basis.

The penalty imposed by the decision of the Interior Board of Land Appeals is disproportionate to any violation charged against Diamond Ring Ranch in the Violation and Hearing Notice, and is arbitrary, capricious and an abuse of discretion.

At bar we believe that the court was justified in disapproving the modification of the sanction by the review board. The board was concerned for the most part with upholding the power of the Secretary to cancel or suspend the license under the Grazing Act, and in our view it went quite far in imposing the penalty it selected in order to uphold the principle and emphasize its importance. After all, it was not shown that there was any real harm to the land or to the public. The Hearing Examiner considered the recommendation of the Bureau of Land Management that the permit or license be suspended and considered this under the circumstances "to be inordinately disproportionate to the gravity of the violation committed." The Examiner went on to say that "neither the Government nor the public suffered tangible harm from Respondent's act. This is not to say, however, that such unauthorized acts can be condoned or that Respondent should escape scot-free for an intentional violation of the regulations. The public land involved is under the management of the BLM and that agency alone has the authority to decide if, when, where and how sagebrush should be controlled." The Examiner then went on to impose a sanction which denied to the Ranch all grazing privileges in the Horse Heaven Pasture for a period of three years commencing March 1, 1973. He then ordered that there be a suspension of the sanction until such time as a verified showing is made by the BLM that a similar violation has occurred.

In the light of the Examiner's findings of fact and in view of the further consideration that the reports reveal a surprising dearth of prior prosecutions along this line, it is our view that the Hearing Examiner's approach was reasonable and much more in keeping with the underlying facts than was that of the Interior Board of Land Appeals. In our view the cause should be remanded to the district court with directions to that court to enter judgment directing the Secretary to adopt the findings and order of the Hearing Examiner and to vacate that of the Board of Land Appeals.

NOTES

1. Is there any significance in the fact that this was a case of first impression even though it arose 40 years after enactment of the Taylor Act?

2. The court noted that "there does not appear to be much indication that the particular spraying was seriously detrimental to the public land." How does this square with the Bureau of Land Management's contention that 2, 4–D eradicates sagebrush that provides the food and habitat needs for wildlife?

3. Section 1752(a) of the Federal Land Policy and Management Act of 1976 provides the Secretaries of Interior and Agriculture express authority to cancel, suspend, or modify a grazing permit or lease for any violation of a grazing regulation or of any terms contained in a permit or lease. Note that the provision for two years' notice of cancellation applies only to cancellations necessitated by dedication of the leased land to another public purpose, not to action taken under section 1752(a). See section 1752(g), quoted supra at page 692.

C. MODERN PUBLIC RANGE MANAGEMENT

As the foregoing materials indicate, BLM control over private grazing operations on public lands has been less than ironclad. In spite of episodic efforts to improve range conditions on a broad scale, such as those reflected in McNeil v. Seaton, 281 F.2d 931 (D.C.Cir.1960), supra, little in the way of drastic restrictions on grazing has been achieved. The Taylor Act has survived the statutory upheaval of the 1970's, but other statutes have ushered in a new, painful era of public range management, the ultimate effects of which are not yet apparent.

While many statutes promise to affect range management in one way or another, this section concentrates on three recent laws that have already been used to interfere with the traditional dominance of cows and sheep. The National Environmental Policy Act of 1969 has had more of an impact on grazing than on most other public land uses. The 1974 NEPA case that follows is probably the true beginning point of a new and considerably more rigorous body of federal range law. The Federal Land Policy and Management Act of 1976, as amended and supplemented by the Public Rangelands Improvement Act of 1978, has invested the BLM with new authority, duties, and constraints. FLPMA also imposes sweeping if ill-defined land use planning responsibilities. The Wild Free-Roaming Horses and Burros Act of 1971 has afforded an uncertain degree of protection to competitors for the scarce western forage. The reader is encouraged to speculate on what the developments recounted below may bode for legal governance of public rangeland management in the future.

1. THE NATIONAL ENVIRONMENTAL POLICY ACT

NATURAL RESOURCES DEFENSE COUNCIL, INC. v. MORTON

United States District Court, District of Columbia, 1974.
388 F.Supp. 829, aff'd per curiam, 527 F.2d 1386 (D.C.Cir.1976), cert. denied,
427 U.S. 913 (1976).

FLANNERY, District Judge.

This matter is before the court on cross-motions for summary judgment by plaintiffs, federal defendants and defendants-intervenors. It presents important issues concerning the applicability of the National Environmental Policy Act (NEPA), 42 U.S.C.A. § 4321 et seq., to the livestock grazing permit program of the Bureau of Land Management, United States Department of Interior. * * *

The Bureau of Land Management Permit Program

The Bureau of Land Management (BLM) is charged with managing and protecting over 171 million acres of public or national resource lands located in 11 western states. These lands not only contain valuable environmental and recreational resources, but also provide grazing for an estimated 14 percent of all livestock in the United States during some parts of their lives. Livestock operators hold approximately 24,000 BLM licenses, permits, and leases to graze their stock on 150 million of the 171 million acres administered by the Bureau. The issuance and regulation of these licenses constitutes one of the main activities of the BLM. It also carries on activities such as vegetation control and the construction of fences and watering facilities designed to improve grazing and protect the land, and works closely with other federal agencies in such areas as watershed maintenance and soil conservation.

The Bureau's management of the public lands is carried out at three levels or stages of intensity. About 7 million acres are, and will continue to be, managed in a merely custodial fashion due primarily to their scattered and isolated locations. Approximately 108 million acres are administered in a fashion the BLM describes as "the best management attainable within the limits of manpower and funding." It is, however, the goal of the BLM to bring 133 of the 171 million acres of public lands under the third category of management—intensive management—by the year 2000. Currently, however, only 25 million acres (18 percent) are under intensive management.

The 52 BLM grazing districts are the agency's basic management component. The procedures which these districts follow for administering an area under intensive management are rather involved. Each district is divided into planning units and a unit resource analysis (URA) containing a detailed inventory of resources is prepared for each one. After public comment, a land use plan called a management framework plan (MFP) containing a set of "goals, objectives, and constraints" is prepared for each planning unit. Once the MFP is completed, more specialized plans known as program activity plans are prepared for each type of resource-related activity, such as timbering, recreation and grazing, in the unit. An activity plan is designed to lay out in detail how the particular activity will comport with the objectives and constraints of the management plan for that particular unit. The program activity plan for grazing is called an allotment management plan (AMP). A planning unit may contain a number of grazing allotments. It is estimated that the program, continued under present trends, will result in the implementation of 8,230 AMP's (total projected need) by the year 2000. Approximately 1,015 AMP's were implemented prior to July 1973 and another 200 were pending at that time. Before any AMP or other activity plan is implemented it is first determined whether an environmental impact statement is required for the plan. It is against the background that the court must examine the BLM's compliance with NEPA.

The National Environmental Policy Act

*   *   *

The BLM has prepared a draft programmatic EIS for its entire livestock grazing program. See Bureau of Land Management, Draft Environmental Impact Statement, Livestock Grazing Management on National Resources Land (March 1974). The BLM contends that this statement will provide an overview of the cumulative impact of the grazing program and will serve as the foundation for subsequent environmental analyses and for supplemental impact statements which may be prepared for smaller land areas or on an individual basis for specific grazing management actions. The BLM does not indicate, however, under what circumstances it will be necessary to prepare supplemental statements.

Plaintiffs contend that the BLM has failed to comply with the provisions of sub-paragraph (C) of section 102(2) of NEPA in that it has issued and renewed grazing permits in each year from 1970 to the present, and proposes to continue doing so, without preparing an EIS dealing with the actual environmental impact of such actions. Plaintiffs argue that the overall programmatic EIS for grazing does not suffice since it fails to consider the individualized, "on the ground" effects on local environments. They ask that the court declare the actions of the BLM to be violations of NEPA and seek an order establishing a cut-off date for the preparation of appropriate EIS statements. It should be noted that plaintiffs do not seek to enjoin the present issuance of licenses nor do they ask that impact statements be prepared for every license or permit. They ask rather that detailed individual statements be prepared on an appropriate district or geographic level to assess the actual impact of the issuance of federal grazing permits on local environments.

The Taylor Grazing Act

The responses of the federal defendants and the defendants-intervenors differ significantly. Defendants-intervenors argue that NEPA does not require impact statements with regard to the licensing of public lands for grazing since the Taylor Grazing Act, 43 U.S.C.A. § 315 et seq., which established the licensing program is an operative and effective method of protecting the environment of the public lands, and to superimpose NEPA on the Taylor Act would substantially interfere with the enforcement of the latter. Defendants-intervenors further argue that the BLM's rules, regulations and administrative procedures protect the environment and should apparently be considered the functional equivalent of an impact statement. * * * This exemption clearly does not extend to the Taylor Grazing Act. An analogy of the Taylor Act to NEPA is invalid since the Taylor Act is not purely an environmental act, but was designed both to stop injury to the public domain by unregulated grazing and to promote stabilization of the livestock industry. * * * To call the Taylor Grazing Act purely environmental is to ignore its language and its history.

NEPA and the Grazing Program

Defendants-intervenors also contend that NEPA does not apply to the BLM licensing program since the program will not significantly affect the quality of the human environment and does not constitute major federal action. However, the statutory phrase "actions significantly affecting the quality of the environment" is intentionally broad, "reflecting the Act's attempt to promote an across-the-board adjustment in federal agency decision making so as to make the quality of the environment a concern of every federal agency." * * * Grazing clearly may have a severe impact on local environments. Moreover, in some states the BLM administers a huge proportion of the state's acreage. In Nevada, for example, 86 percent of the total area of the state is administered by the BLM and the record illustrates the damage that has occurred there from overgrazing and improper land management. The court is therefore persuaded that the grazing permit program produces significant impacts on individual locales. And when the cumulative impact of the entire program is considered it is difficult to understand how defendants-intervenors can claim either that the impact of the program is not significant or that the federal action involved is not major.

Federal defendants, unlike defendants-intervenors, concede that NEPA applies to the BLM grazing program but argue first that plaintiff's suit is premature and should await issuance of the final programmatic impact statement, and second that the Bureau is not in violation of the Act since the programmatic impact statement sufficiently complies with the intent of NEPA.

Exhaustion of Administrative Remedies

Federal defendants urge that plaintiffs' suit is not timely since under the doctrine of exhaustion of administrative remedies the BLM should have an opportunity to prepare an EIS which it believes satisfies NEPA's requirements before plaintiffs may seek court action. * * * Plaintiffs instead contend that the proposed statement, even if an excellent programmatic EIS, is insufficient standing alone. They argue that they need not await a final version of the impact statement since it is not review of the specifics of the final agency programmatic statement which they seek, but a declaration that a programmatic statement does not comply with the law. The court is in agreement with this analysis of the complaint.

* * * This court might be less willing to consider the plaintiffs' claims if the BLM had demonstrated more diligence in pursuing its own role. The Bureau did not determine to prepare a programmatic EIS on the grazing program until June, 1972, two and one-half years after the effective date of the Act. A preliminary draft was not then issued until March 1973, with a second draft in October 1973. In March 1974 the final draft was prepared and the federal defendants represented to the court that the final EIS was expected to be issued in the summer of 1974. Although the court would naturally prefer to await the filing of the final statement, it is clear that the BLM has delayed beyond reason. * * * Even in the unlikely event that significant alterations were made in the final statement, the agency has shown no willingness to alter the statement's format as a strictly programmatic assessment. Thus the eventual EIS will not be geographically individualized and its ultimate adoption will have no effect on plaintiffs' current suit.

One other factor has persuaded the court to reach the merits of this claim. Over the past four years the BLM has shown relatively slow progress in implementing a thorough management planning system which would assist in protecting the environment. As noted above, the BLM estimated that 8,320 AMP's are needed. Only 1,015 plans were implemented through fiscal year 1973, and completion of all AMP's is not estimated until the year 2000. Thus, in a substantial and practical sense there is a serious threat of injury to the public lands which lends urgency to plaintiffs' claims. While the court should always be reluctant to rule on issues before full and final agency determination, to wait until the filing of the final programmatic EIS would be a useless act and would thwart Congressional intent, reducing NEPA to a mere "paper tiger." Having considered the above, it appears to the court that there are no appropriate agency procedures which plaintiffs should be required to exhaust and that the situation dictates a decision by this court on the merits of the claim.

BLM's Programmatic Impact Statement

* * *

* * * In section 102 Congress authorizes and directs preparation of detailed impact statements "to the fullest extent possible." This language has been consistently construed to require compliance with NEPA unless such compliance would give rise to a violation of other statutory authority under which the agency is proceeding. * * * No such direct conflict between NEPA and the Taylor Grazing Act exists. The Taylor Act is not purely environmental since it is aimed at promoting the highest use of the public lands; NEPA seeks to protect the environment. *Compare* 43 U.S.C.A. § 315 *with* 42 U.S.C.A. § 4321. These two purposes, as pointed out above, are not the same, but are not in such conflict that a rigorous application of NEPA would give rise to violations of the Taylor Act.

* * * Plaintiffs do not ask that impact statements be filed for every license or permit issued or renewed by the BLM. Nor do they seek an immediate injunction of the licensing program which could admittedly have a most deleterious effect on the entire livestock industry. While the permit program might be jeopardized at some future time, livestock operators would not be affected at this time by a finding that the programmatic EIS prepared by the BLM was legally insufficient.

* * * In the BLM grazing license program the primary decision-maker is generally the individual district manager, with his staff, who approves license applications. While the programmatic EIS drafted by the BLM provides general policy guidelines as to relevant environmental factors, it in no way insures that the decision-maker considers all of the specific and particular consequences of his actions, or the alternatives available to him. The proposed EIS does not provide the detailed analysis of local geographic conditions necessary for the decision-maker to determine what course of action is appropriate under the circumstances.

Additionally, the programmatic EIS does not allow those who are not part of the decision-making process to adequately evaluate and balance the factors on their own. While NEPA does not require public hearings, it does provide a formalized procedure for such citizen input. In the present case the public will have the opportunity to comment only on the programmatic impact statement. Undoubtedly national organizations, such as plaintiff NRDC, will provide comments and engage in the review process. However, when it comes to the actual implementation of the licensing permit program at the local level, there will be no opportunity for particularized input by state and local citizens.[16] Even though the actual permits may be made public, that provides only information from the government to the citizens and does

---

16. The only real opportunity for local comment appears to be after the preparation of the unit resource analysis.

not allow information to flow from the citizens to the government.[17]

* * *

   * * * While the BLM has certain licensing requirements, they relate mainly to the timing and duration of the allowable grazing period and the number of animals involved.[18] The court has examined the Federal Range Code, 43 C.F.R. § 4110.0–2 et seq. (1973), portions of the BLM Manual, and sample licenses and finds them insufficient to fulfill the purpose defined for an impact statement. They do not adequately assess [19] the individual district or area situations so as to provide the local decision-maker with the data necessary to analyze the alternatives open to him and their consequences. A program statement may be very helpful in assessing recurring policy issues and insuring consideration of the cumulative impact that numerous decisions might have on the environment, but that does not mean that it will suffice to fulfill the NEPA mandate. The court is convinced that the BLM programmatic statement alone, unrelated to individual geographic conditions, does not permit the "finely tuned and 'systematic' balancing analysis" mandated by NEPA. See Calvert Cliffs' Coordinating Committee v. AEC, supra, 449 F.2d at 1113.

   While the BLM may decide in the future to prepare specific impact statements on new activities, for the present grazing will continue on millions of acres without adequate individualized assessment of the impact of such grazing on local environments, and extensive environmental damage is possible. Indeed, the plaintiffs note that the BLM Budget Justification for fiscal year 1973 estimated that only 16 percent of the BLM managed grazing land was in good or excellent condition while 84 percent was in fair, poor or bad condition. In addition, plaintiffs present evidence from both private and governmental sources demonstrating that serious deterioration of BLM lands is taking or has taken place. In its first annual report, the Council on Environmental Quality reported that overgrazing had dramatically affected the public lands.

   "Much of this land, particularly the vast public domain, remains in desperate condition, as wind, rain, and drought have swept over them and eroded their exposed soils. Although the effects of overgrazing in rich pastures or prairie farmland can be quickly corrected, the process is often irreversible on the

17. There has been some recognition by the BLM that this type of input is desirable, as witnessed by the expansion of the Grazing Advisory Boards from merely livestock operators to include some environmental representatives.

18. Permits and leases for terms, generally 10 years, are made only after an AMP is agreed to between BLM and the grazer. The AMP is therefore a part of the term permit. In areas for which no AMP has been prepared only annual licenses are issued.

19. Indeed the BLM itself, in its report concerning public lands in Nevada, indicates that the MFP's should be more specific in their recommendations and get away from "motherhood statements." The report also notes that many Nevada AMP's are ineffective and did not have sufficient studies made on them. This is not to say, however, that a thorough and adequate AMP, in conjunction with a programmatic statement might not meet the NEPA requirements. However, AMP's exist for only a portion of the millions of acres supervised by the BLM.

limited soils and arid climate of much of the public lands."
CEQ, Environmental Quality 182 (1970).

Unfortunately this situation has not been rectified since that date. A recent Bureau of Land Management report entitled Effects of Livestock Grazing on Wildlife, Watershed, Recreation and Other Resource Values in Nevada (April 1974) documents the serious damage being wrought on the environment. The report, compiled by a team of BLM resource managers, states flatly that wildlife habitat is being destroyed. "Uncontrolled, unregulated or unplanned livestock use is occurring in approximately 85 percent of the State and damage to wildlife habitat can be expressed only as extreme destruction." Id. at 13. Overgrazing by livestock has caused invasion of sagebrush and rabbitbrush on meadows and has decreased the amount of meadow habitat available for wildlife survival by at least 50 percent. The reduced meadow area has caused a decline in both game and non-game population. Id. at 26. In addition, there are 883 miles of streams with deteriorating and declining wildlife habitat, thus making it apparent, according to the report, that grazing systems do not protect and enhance wildlife values. Id. at 14, 29.[22]

While Congress has determined that public lands should be put to the best use possible, it has also demonstrated a strong interest in protecting the environment. In the present case over 100 million acres of public land are being leased for grazing although apparently no thorough analysis has been made of the specific impact of such activity. The court is, therefore, of the opinion that major federal actions having significant effects on the environment are being taken without full NEPA compliance, even though that Act has been in effect almost five years.

The court is aware that, like many agencies, the BLM has been given large scale tasks to be accomplished with limited manpower. That does not mean, however, that the agency may ignore or pay mere lip service to the NEPA requirements. * * *

For the above reasons the court will grant relief to the plaintiffs by entering a judgment declaring that the programmatic environmental impact statement prepared by the BLM, standing alone, is not sufficient to comply with the NEPA requirements. As noted above, plaintiffs have not sought an impact statement for each permit. The crucial point is that the specific environmental effects of the permits issued, and to be issued, in each district be assessed. It will be initially within the BLM's discretion to determine whether to make this specific assessment in a separate impact statement for each district, or several impact statements for each district, or one impact statement for several districts or portions thereof, or indeed by other means. So long as the actual environmental effects of particular permits or groups of permits in specific areas are assessed, questions of format are to be left to

---

22. Whether the original deterioration occurred before or during BLM management is irrelevant since the crucial questions are whether it can be allowed to continue and whether it will be exacerbated by continued grazing.

defendants. The court will maintain jurisdiction in order to facilitate future review of the methods chosen by the BLM, and a time period for agency formulation of procedures will be set by subsequent order on recommendation of the parties. An appropriate Judgment accompanies this Memorandum Opinion.

* * *

NOTES

1. In NRDC v. Morton, the court held that NEPA required the BLM to prepare environmental impact statements on the effects of present and proposed grazing on specific areas of the public lands. The BLM, citing lack of time, money, and manpower, failed to meet the court-imposed schedule. When the BLM filed its third notice of proposed deviation from the schedule, NRDC opposed the request and asked the court to order BLM to adhere to the existing schedule, with some modifications. In NRDC v. Andrus, 448 F.Supp. 802 (D.D.C.1978), the court ordered the BLM to follow a revised schedule that granted the agency some relief from the current schedule by granting additional time. Citing the continuing deterioration of the public rangelands, the court refused BLM's proposed deviation from the schedule which would delay for a substantial period of time completion of EIS's for the majority of the rangelands. The new revised schedule calls for completion of all statements by 1988.

2. Compliance with NRDC v. Morton promised to reverse traditional grazing management. Pursuant to the court's order, albeit tardily, the BLM began the process of preparing 212 (later reduced to 144) environmental impact statements at a cost estimated to be in excess of 100 million dollars. The environmental evaluations have revealed what many have known: the public lands generally are in poor condition compared to their historic potential; one clear cause for this condition is overgrazing; and improvement in range condition depends largely upon reducing the number of grazing animals and limiting the areas available for grazing. To the extent that allotment management plans are based on the information compiled in the impact statements, many—perhaps most—ranchers may be forced to accept reductions—some severe—in AUMs under permit. If the range responds to lower use and further improvements (such as water developments and eradication of undesirable plants), the rancher eventually will be able to utilize far more forage than is currently available. The shortrun effects, however, particularly on marginal operations, could be severe if not fatal.

3. If NRDC or another plaintiff should bring a lawsuit challenging the issuance of individual permits or leases on the ground that an EIS had not been completed, or was inadequate, would it succeed? Compare Kleppe v. Sierra Club, 427 U.S. 390 (1976), supra at page 323; NRDC v. Hodel, 624 F.Supp. 1045 (D.Nev.1986), infra at page 749.

4. In the Public Rangelands Improvement Act of 1978, 92 Stat. 1803, Congress amended FLPMA to provide that a lease period of less

than ten years may not be established for individual leases on the "sole basis" that land use plans or "court ordered environmental statements" have not been completed.   43 U.S.C.A. § 1752(b)(3).

5. Some indication of the depth of feeling engendered and the nature of the issues posed can be gleaned from the following excerpts from the East Roswell (New Mexico) Grazing Environmental Statement (1979) (ES). In essence, after determining that available forage production was far less than authorized grazing (the methodology for such determination being hotly but not factually disputed), the BLM opted in the ES for a program of temporary grazing reductions coupled with widespread herbicide applications to destroy competing plant species such as mesquite and creosote bush which had invaded the area. The invasion had been caused largely by overgrazing and the competing species in turn caused a decline in grass production. The BLM preferred option was summarized in the East Roswell ES thus:

> Livestock grazing would continue to be authorized on all 184 of the ES area's existing allotments (approximately 1,590,000 acres of public land). * * *

> The ES area's lands are presently classified as being suitable for grazing by cattle, sheep, goats, and/or horses. This classification would remain unchanged. The present grazing use of the public lands is primarily by cattle with some use authorized for domestic horses. Change from this present kind of use is not anticipated. * * *

> All allotments in the area are classified as being suitable for grazing yearlong and are presently authorized for such use. This classification and authorization would remain unchanged.

> There are approximately 175,167 AUMs (67,439 tons) of forage being produced on the ES area's public lands at the present time (this represents less than one half of the ES area's total vegetative production). The amount of forage being produced was determined by the 1977–78 range survey. * * *

> Of these 175,167 AUMs of forage, approximately 168,111 would initially be allocated to livestock use * * *. This allocation to livestock would be a reduction of approximately 65,774 AUMs from the present licensed use (233,885 AUMs).

> Allocations to livestock and big game would be expected to change as forage production changes. See Graph 1–1 for a display of the anticipated allocation of the forage production over a period of time. Monitoring would begin with implementation and changes in allocation would be made as forage increases. It is anticipated that, by the year 2000, adequate forage would be produced to provide for an allocation of approximately 367,389 AUMs to livestock. This would be an increase of approximately 199,278 AUMs over the initial allocation. * * *

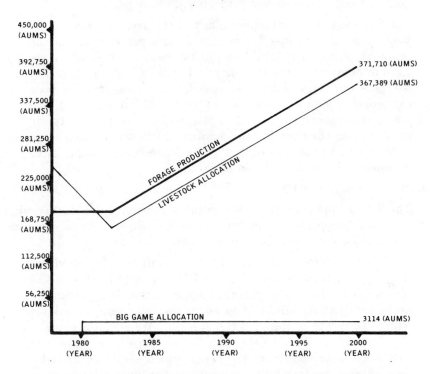

Graph 1-1
Allocation of Forage Over a 20 Year Time Period
With the Proposed Action

Approximately 2,893 AUMs of forage would be initially allocated to meet the needs of big game animals. Allocations for wildlife would change in proportion to changes in big game populations, based on the amount of forage required to meet their needs (projected increases in big game populations within the next 20 years would result in a requirement for approximately 3,114 AUMs by the year 2000, an increase of 221 AUMs). * * * Forage and vegetative production which are surplus to big game grazing requirements would be available for use as additional cover for other wildlife species, watershed protection, and enhancement of esthetic values.

* * *

East Roswell ES at 1–3 to 1–6.

As one might expect, the responses to the BLM proposal, even though not yet translated into actual specific reductions through the Allotment Management Plan process, aroused considerable reaction. The rancher whose letter is quoted below reflected the attitudes of many others; their comments were appended to the ES.

> I have gone through the East Roswell Grazing Environment Statement, and as a rancher I have to say it looks like the BLM is trying to put the rancher on the endangered species list! * * * This impact statement if passed in this form will do to part of the ranchers in this area what droughts, low cattle prices, hail and many other disasters have not been able

to do, that is to put them out of ranching completely! These are men with an average age above 50 years. What are they going to do? Who is going to give them a job?

The BLM says the economic impact of the area will be negligible. How can you lose 1.5 million dollars per year out of the economy of Southeastern New Mexico and not feel it? I am tired of hearing people say the rancher is raping the land that we take our very existence, and for the most part a poor existence! I plan to spend the rest of my life on my ranch, so I am sure not going to rape it! I plan to leave this ranch to my children some day but in the meantime I will try to teach them to love it and take care of it as their dearest possession. Most ranchers I know hold these same ideas.

East Roswell ES at 9–60.

The Sierra Club representative, perhaps sensing that a doom-crying response was inappropriate in the circumstances, was more sanguine about the BLM environmental evaluation:

I have reviewed the East Roswell Draft Grazing Environmental Impact Statement for the Rio Grande Chapter of the Sierra Club. The data presented indicate that it is absolutely necessary that AUMs be reduced in the near-term to a level which the forage of the land can sustain. We strongly support that proposal. To do otherwise is to knowingly allow the continued deterioration of the range which would be in violation of your responsibility to manage the public lands on a sustained yield, multiple use basis. To do otherwise would allow the continued deterioration of the land to the point where grazing would be impossible, wildlife habitat would be all but destroyed, and soil erosion and water pollution from silt would be intolerable.

* * *

In conclusion, we commend the BLM for a basically well-developed draft EIS. We urge modifications in the planned action to reduce the destruction of wildlife habitat and we caution against the proposed extent of herbicides use without sufficient experience to anticipate secondary effects of such massive alteration of ecosystems in a very short period of time (8 years).

East Roswell ES at 9–146 to 9–147.

And, of course, the politicians weighed in with their assessments and concerns. Stated New Mexico Congressman Runnels:

The environmental impact of your proposed study is subject to considerable debate, both pro and con, but the economic impact of the BLM project can be described in one word, "disaster".

Recognizing that the Roswell BLM office has previously taken the position that cattle and other forms of livestock are foreign to the natural environment of these public lands of Eastern New Mexico, it appears that some within BLM have made the decision to eliminate this unwanted (apparently in the eyes of BLM) domestic livestock by making it economically unfeasible for any rancher to continue such operations on BLM lands.

I recognize also that the above suggestion will be rejected, but all the concern displayed about the role of antelope and now the lesser prairie chicken in recent months can only lead one to believe that perhaps the Roswell Daily Record was correct in suggesting that perhaps the ranchers are confronted either with a conspired effort to force them off public lands or are victims of colossal, unflinching stupidity.

I don't know how many lesser prairie chickens you've eaten in recent months, but most of us place a greater need on an adequate beef and lamb supply at the super market. The BLM proposal once again smacks of the all too popular image which the average citizen has of the federal government, that being that too many in the federal government think they always have the answer as to what's best for the average citizen. They seem to forget who is working for whom.

* * *

By BLM's own figures this proposal would mean a loss of 27 percent of the present livestock sales in the area and net returns to the ranchers would decrease by 61 percent. I wonder if the BLM employees would be as excited about a proposal that we reduce their levels by 27 percent and cut the salaries of those remaining by 61 percent during the same time span we expect the local ranchers to sit by while BLM implements this grandiose plan.

* * *

East Roswell ES at 9–28 to 9–30. The Bureau responded:

The facts which have been presented in this document indicate that an over-statement of forage production, perpetuated over many years, has been made. This purported production, in many cases, has never been used, perhaps because ranchers recognize that it is an over-statement. This recognition is reflected by the licensed use that has been made through the years. However, overuse on many acres of rangeland in the ES area is evident and the alignment of stocking rates with the forage production in these cases is a recognition of fact, rather than being a theoretical loss of livestock production. Unless these rangelands are restored to a productive level which approaches their potential, this loss will not be recovered, but would remain at the reduced level. A 40 percent loss in the area's production of beef would not occur. In fact, this loss would even be less than 28 percent for two reasons: 1. ranchers may have actually sold down because of dry conditions, and 2. much of the beef production comes from farms and ranches which do not have public lands. * * *

East Roswell ES at 9–29.

6. Nelson, The New Range Wars: Environmentalists versus Cattlemen for the Public Rangelands, Office of Policy Analysis, Interior Department 116–17 (draft, 1980), commented:

Preparation of grazing EISs has in fact turned out to be very expensive. A BLM study of nine of the first EISs to be completed found that $5.7 million had been spent in direct preparation costs—an average of $630,000 per EIS. However, the direct preparation costs were only a fraction of the total EIS costs; for example, they did not include most of the inventories and land use planning required to lay the groundwork for writing the EIS. The same BLM study estimated that the direct preparation costs of the EIS were only about 10% of the total costs associated with completion of each grazing EIS. On this basis, the nine EISs could have cost as much as $50 million, or more than $5 million per statement. Seven million acres were covered by these grazing EISs, so the total cost per acre may well have been around $7 or $8 per acre.

There exists a limited market in grazing rights to public land in which one rancher may sell his rights to another rancher. In this market the rights to public land grazing might typically sell for anywhere from $30 to as much as $100 per AUM. Since the average AUM on BLM land requires about 12 acres, even using the highest purchase price of $100 an AUM, permanent grazing rights probably would be worth no more than $8 per acre. Hence, for the first nine grazing EISs, it appears that, if costs are completely accounted for, the total costs involved in grazing EISs approach the total value of the forage to ranchers for livestock grazing. To put the matter another way, if the government had instead used the EIS money to buy out grazing rights to public land, it might well have been able to buy out most of the grazing rights in the EIS areas for no more than the costs to prepare the EIS.

The costs of the first generation of EISs are likely higher than later ones and BLM's estimates of indirect or supporting costs for EISs may well be too high. But there is a strong case that the expenditures on grazing EISs far exceed what could be justified on any economically rational basis.

2. FEDERAL LAND POLICY AND MANAGEMENT ACT

Although the BLM had long asserted that it was a "multiple use" agency, see LaRue v. Udall, 324 F.2d 428 (1963), supra at page 683, and although it had temporary multiple use authority under the Classification and Multiple Use Act of 1964, 43 U.S.C.A. §§ 1411–18 (expired 1970), Congress did not give the BLM permanent authority to manage its lands for multiple use and sustained yield until 1976. 43 U.S.C.A. § 1732. Provisions directly applicable to range management have been quoted or paraphrased in prior notes in this chapter. In essence, Congress found in enacting FLPMA and PRIA that the rangelands are in bad condition, are deteriorating, and are to be improved. At the same time, Congress in those Acts showed its solicitude for present public land users by retaining preferences, requiring consideration of hardships, financing range improvements, and providing for individual and institutional advice from and consultation with ranchers. The BLM must thus tread a sensitive tightrope in determining forage allocation and in otherwise regulating public land use.

Neither consistent policy nor constancy of purpose have characterized BLM range regulation over the years. In the late 1970's, the Bureau made a conscious effort to develop administrative professionalism and long range policies premised on the need to improve range condition as a requisite to improved productivity of all renewable resources. The culmination of that effort was the issuance in 1979 of the BLM's public review draft of "Managing the Public Rangelands." In that document, the agency undertook its most detailed look at ecological damage to range resources and unveiled a general improvement program with specific goals for resource productivity gains. Neither the program nor the program objectives, however, were adopted as official policy. The advent of a new Administration in 1981 brought with it a new set of policies that did not emphasize improvement in range condition. Some manifestations of the earlier approach of reducing AUMs are evident in the following cases.

PERKINS v. BERGLAND
United States Court of Appeals, Ninth Circuit, 1979.
608 F.2d 803.

GOODWIN, Circuit Judge:

Two brothers, who grazed cattle on public land, sued the Department of Agriculture to challenge a reduction in their grazing permits. They appeal a summary judgment for the government.

Thomas and David Perkins hold permits entitling each of them to graze cattle within the Prescott National Forest. The permits are issued by the United States Forest Service, an arm of the Department of Agriculture, as authorized by 16 U.S.C.A. § 580*l*. In 1972, the Forest Supervisor, on recommendation of the local District Ranger, reduced Thomas's permit from 517 to 250 head of cattle (subsequently corrected to 266). The following year, the Supervisor similarly reduced David's permit from 158 to 50 head (later corrected to 58).

The agency based the reduction decisions on its finding that the public land involved had been damaged by overgrazing. The decisions were finally upheld by the Secretary of Agriculture in 1977. After exhausting administrative remedies, Thomas and David brought separate actions in district court, seeking judicial review and an injunction against enforcement of the reductions. The cases were consolidated in district court, and are considered together on appeal.

I

The district court correctly rejected the Perkins' first line of attack: that the reductions were so drastic as to constitute revocations of their grazing permits. The Perkins brothers argued that revocation requires application of the criteria found in the regulation governing revocation and suspension, 36 C.F.R. § 231.6 (1977).[1] The Forest Service admittedly did not apply those criteria here. However, the district court held, and we agree, that the permits were not in fact suspended or revoked.

The Forest Service reduced the allowable use of the lands for reasons unrelated to the punitive purpose of 36 C.F.R. § 231.6. That regulation allows revocation only in the case of misconduct by a grazing permittee, and in no way relates to allotment reductions necessitated by changed conditions of the range resulting from causes other than permittee misconduct. However drastic an effect on their livelihood the reductions here may have had, the permits were not revoked. Thus, the district court was right in rejecting the revocation theory.

II

The Perkins brothers argued, in the alternative, that the Secretary's decisions, if not "revocations", were nonetheless subject to judicial review. The government responded, and the district court agreed, that further review was unavailable because the decisions were "committed to agency discretion by law." 5 U.S.C.A. § 701(a)(2). This conclusion is challenged on two grounds: (1) the reduction decisions are not so committed; or (2), if so committed, the decisions are nevertheless subject to limited judicial review for clear arbitrariness, irrationality, or abuse of discretion.

Both sides purport to rely on the "law to apply" test established in Citizens to Preserve Overton Park v. Volpe, 401 U.S. 402 (1971), for determining when judicial review is precluded under section 701(a)(2). The Secretary also relies on a series of post-*Overton Park* cases in this circuit to support the district court's determination that the reduction decisions are immune from review. Neither party, however, appears to have called to the trial court's attention the new legislation enacted during the time this controversy was pending before the agency. Thus, the trial court never passed upon the effect of [FLPMA], a comprehensive public lands statute which now governs the reviewability issue.

FLPMA empowers the Secretaries of the Interior and Agriculture, each of whom grants grazing privileges on public lands within departmental jurisdictions, to incorporate in grazing permits and leases "such

---

1. * * * [Permits may be revoked or suspended if:]

"(c) The permittee violates or does not comply with, Federal laws or regulations or State laws relating to protection of air, water, soil and vegetation, fish and wildlife, and other environmental values when exercising the grazing use authorized by the permit."

terms and conditions as [the Secretary] deems appropriate for management of the * * * lands." 43 U.S.C.A. § 1752(e). The same section further provides that the Secretary must specify in the agreement "the numbers of animals to be grazed * * * and that * * * [the Secretary] may reexamine the condition of the range at any time and, if he finds on reexamination that the condition of the range requires adjustment in the amount or other aspect of grazing use, that the permittee or lessee shall adjust his use to the extent the Secretary concerned deems necessary."

If we were confronted with the quoted language alone, we would have to consider the government's argument that the Secretary's discretion is so broad in determining grazing capacity—necessarily exercised in accord with expert judgments—as to preclude all judicial review under *Overton Park.* Elsewhere, however, FLPMA explicitly provides that "it is the policy of the United States that * * * judicial review of public land adjudication decisions be provided by law." 43 U.S.C.A. § 1701(a)(6). This declaration of policy at the outset of FLPMA removes any doubt Congress might otherwise have allowed to obscure the reviewability of grazing reduction decisions made subsequent to the law's enactment. Since 1976, the Secretary's decision is reviewable.

III

The remaining issue thus requires us to define the scope of review appropriate to the Secretary's decisions here.

Appellants assert for the first time in this court that certain sections of the Multiple-Use Sustained-Yield Act of 1960 (MUSYA), 16 U.S.C.A. §§ 528 et seq., supply standards which a court can apply on judicial review to the highly technical assessment of the proper carrying capacity of grazing land. These statutory expressions give the appellants scant support. It must be presumed, at least initially, that those so-called standards were properly considered by the agency. These sections of MUSYA (16 U.S.C.A. §§ 528, 529, 531) contain the most general clauses and phrases. For example, the agency is "directed" in section 529 to administer the national forests "for multiple use and sustained yield of the several products and services obtained therefrom," with "due consideration [to] be given to the relative values of the various resources in particular areas." This language, partially defined in section 531 in such terms as "that [which] will best meet the needs of the American people" and "making the most judicious use of the land", can hardly be considered concrete limits upon agency discretion. Rather, it is language which "breathe[s] discretion at every pore." Strickland v. Morton, 519 F.2d 467, 469 (9th Cir.1975). What appellants really seem to be saying when they rely on the multiple-use legislation is that they do not agree with the Secretary on how best to administer the forest land on which their cattle graze. While this disagreement is understandable, the courts are not at liberty to break the tie by choosing one theory of range management as superior to another.

Thus, we conclude that only very narrow review is appropriate here. The district court should ascertain whether the agency's factual findings as to range conditions and carrying capacity are arbitrary and capricious. 5 U.S.C.A. § 706(2)(A). If not, the matter ends there. In making that inquiry, the court may consider the Perkins brothers' contention that the methods utilized by the Forest Service in determining capacity were irrational.[12] But their charge that the agency decision was "unrelated to reality" sheds no light on the subject. We find nothing in the statutes authorizing courts to choose between battling experts on the definition of "reality". Consequently, the trial court must refrain from entering that fray if it turns out that the appellants' position would require a choice between experts.

The judgment is vacated and the case is remanded to the district court for the very limited factual review available under the "arbitrary and capricious" standard.

Neither party is to recover costs in this court.

HINSDALE LIVESTOCK CO. v. UNITED STATES
United States District Court, District of Montana, 1980.
501 F.Supp. 773.

BATTIN, Chief Judge.

[Plaintiff Hinsdale held a BLM grazing permit which authorized grazing through November 30, 1980. In late August, 1980, the BLM told plaintiff to remove its cattle from the allotment because drought conditions then prevailing created an emergency in which the range would suffer severe damage if grazing continued. Plaintiff was notified that it must remove the cattle by September 10, and that it had 30 days to appeal. It instead brought this lawsuit.]

* * *

19. The data relied on by the defendant in reaching its decision that plaintiffs' cattle must be immediately removed from the public lands in order to prevent severe damage to the range land resource was based primarily on various written materials which defendant and authorized agent Terrence E. Wilson could not specify and on other principles that defendant Terrence E. Wilson testified to the effect that further grazing on the range resource in a year of drought is harmful to the range resource and makes it more difficult for the resource to recover from a year of drought.

20. These reasons do not create an emergency such as was asserted by the defendant in its letters of eviction to plaintiff; the Court finds this on the basis of expert testimony. These experts are August Hormay, on behalf of the plaintiff, and Dr. Donald Ryerson, on behalf of the defendants. Both witnesses testified that continued grazing of

---

12. To prove that the agency employed "irrational" methods for calculating carrying capacity, a contesting party must show that there is virtually no evidence in the record to support the agency's methodology in gathering and evaluating the data.

the range resource throughout the balance of plaintiffs' permit seasons this year does not in any way create an emergency to the range land resource.

* * *

23.   The Court is of the opinion that plaintiffs would suffer severe and irreparable damage and harm if they were forced from the public lands before the expiration of their permit periods for 1980.

* * *

26.   Plaintiffs have a good likelihood of success on the merits of an administrative appeal of the defendant's decision that their cattle must be evicted for the balance of the permit season.

27.   The Court is of the opinion that the actions of the defendant as set forth above are arbitrary and capricious in that the decisions were not based on scientific evidence, nor based on any input from plaintiffs involved.   The defendants' expert witness, Dr. Donald Ryerson, testified that all of the plaintiffs have been ranching their entire adult lives, were raised ranching, and that they have had extensive experience in conducting ranching operations on lands that include the public domain.   * * *

28.   These ranchers have experienced many droughts in the areas that are the subject of this lawsuit.   Evidence presented at hearing revealed they know how to judge the conditions of the range resource and have acted appropriately in managing their herds in accordance with the conditions of the range resources.

29.   The opinion of plaintiffs is that the range resources will not be severely damaged if the reduced number of livestock they now have on the range resources are allowed to remain there the balance of this permit season.

The Court adopts the opinion of Gus Hormay and these ranchers with respect to the condition of the range resource.   Testimony has revealed that drought conditions never create an emergency with respect to the range resource, contrary to the opinion of defendant Bureau of Land Management.   The appeal right granted plaintiffs was largely without meaning in that had the defendant prevailed, the plaintiffs would have been in trespass with their cattle subject to impoundment some 20 days before their time to appeal even ran.

30.   The plaintiffs were deprived of any notion of due process of law with respect to the defendant's decision affecting the allotments plaintiffs lease.   Significant portions of plaintiffs' privately owned and controlled land intermingle with the federal lands.   Plaintiffs did not have an opportunity to participate in the decision to evict the livestock from the allotments plaintiffs lease.   Tours the defendant conducted in conjunction with the plaintiffs were made subsequent to the Bureau's decision that evictions would be made.

* * *

32.   The Court finds the defendant is in violation of the contract entered into with plaintiff Hinsdale Livestock Company.

The allotment management plan provides for a rest rotation graz-ing system with two of seven pastures rested or unused each year.

Plaintiffs have made substantial investments related to the allot-ment plan covered by the seven pastures in the form of many miles of fence and construction of reservoirs.

The allotment plan, on page 23, states:

There is flexibility in management with this type of system. The rest pasture may be used in the event of * * * drought * * * but grazing will return to normal sequence immediate-ly following the deviation. This flexibility is necessary in adjusting to short term climate and vegetative changes * * *.

33. The Court is of the opinion that the defendant is in violation of this agreement in that it is now denying plaintiff Hinsdale Livestock Company the opportunity to utilize the rest pastures in this year of proven drought.

* * *

CONCLUSIONS OF LAW

1. Each of the above-stated Findings of Fact is hereby restated as a Conclusion of Law.

* * *

4. Plaintiffs were deprived of due process of law by defendants' actions in evicting plaintiffs from the allotments in question, said allotments intermingling federal lands with private lands of plaintiffs.

5. Defendants have denied plaintiffs any meaningful opportunity for administrative appeal of the decision by the defendant evicting plaintiffs from the allotments in question during the balance of the grazing season for 1980.

6. The immediate effect of the defendant's decision to evict plain-tiffs from the allotments in question for the balance of the 1980 grazing season is contrary to the policy of Congress expressed in 43 U.S.C. 1701(a)(6) which provides that it is the policy of the United States that judicial review of public land adjudication decisions be provided by law.

7. Plaintiffs will suffer irreparable harm if a preliminary injunc-tion does not issue. Such an injunction should issue enjoining defen-dants from evicting plaintiffs from the allotments in question pending plaintiffs' pursuit of administrative remedies.

8. The evidence and testimony reveals there is no emergency condition on the range resource in question that requires the immedi-ate removal of the livestock. The Court finds that the defendants will not be harmed by the issuance of a preliminary injunction enjoining defendant from implementing its decision to immediately evict plain-tiffs' livestock from the range resource. Therefore,

IT IS ORDERED that a preliminary injunction be and the same hereby is, granted restraining enforcement of the defendant's orders evicting plaintiffs' livestock from the allotments * * *.

IT IS FURTHER ORDERED that said preliminary injunction will remain in force and effect until such time as plaintiffs have been given the opportunity to exhaust their administrative remedies.

NOTES

1. *Perkins* holds that a court may review a permit reduction, but only to see whether the agency's findings were arbitrary or its methods irrational. What realistic chance of reversal do future plaintiffs have? What criteria are to be applied?

2. What standard of review did the *Hinsdale* court follow? Which statutes did the court construe? Were the agency's methods for calculating carrying capacity irrational? See also Valdez v. Applegate, 616 F.2d 570 (10th Cir.1980).

3. Compare the uses made by the two courts of FLPMA, 43 U.S. C.A. § 1752(e): "The Secretary concerned shall also specify [in the permit] the number of animals to be grazed and the seasons of use and that he may reexamine the condition of the range at any time and, if he finds on reexamination that the condition of the range requires adjustment in the amount or other aspect of grazing use, that the permittee or lessee shall adjust his use to the extent the Secretary concerned deems necessary. Such readjustment shall be put into full force and effect on the date specified by the Secretary concerned."

4. Had the recommendations in the BLM grazing district EISs prepared pursuant to the order in NRDC v. Morton, 388 F.Supp. 829 (D.D.C.1974), supra at page 704, been carried out, many more grazing reduction lawsuits likely would have been filed in protest. In 1981, however, Secretary Watt in effect placed a moratorium on grazing reductions, ostensibly for the reason that the studies showing the need for reductions were scientifically invalid. See NRDC v. Hodel, 624 F.Supp. 1045 (D.Nev.1986), infra at page 749, and Dahl v. Clark, 600 F.Supp. 585 (D.Nev.1984), infra at page 775. As a comparison of the basic approaches utilized by the *Perkins* and *Hinsdale* courts may illustrate, the results of future grazing reduction suits were not necessarily foreordained, in spite of the statutory wording.

NATURAL RESOURCES DEFENSE COUNCIL, INC. v. HODEL

United States District Court, E.D. California, 1985.
618 F.Supp. 848.

RAMIREZ, District Judge.

* * *

INTRODUCTION

The case before the Court is complex and involves issues of national importance and first impression. The regulations under attack are amendments to existing Department of Interior regulations with one common characteristic. Each pertains to the management of domestic livestock grazing on lands owned by the federal government and under the management jurisdiction of the BLM. Plaintiffs maintain in this action that defendants' rules and actions violate dozens of sections of several comprehensive federal statutes. * * *

* * *

One issue which has dominated all others in the instant litigation is plaintiffs' challenge to the Secretary's so-called "Cooperative Management Agreements" (CMAs) by which defendants have permitted selected ranchers to graze livestock on the public lands in the manner that those ranchers deem appropriate.[4] * * *

* * *

II. LEGISLATIVE AND HISTORICAL BACKGROUND

* * *

The history of grazing policy and politics in the west and in Washington, D.C., has been the story of competing interests, changing values, and, unfortunately, deteriorating resources. In order that the issues in this lawsuit may be more fully comprehended, a brief look at the development of this policy is essential.

A. The Public Domain

From the mid-nineteenth century until 1934, when Congress first enacted comprehensive legislation regulating rangeland management, the key battles over the public lands were between ranchers, who sought to monopolize the range for their own uses, and "homesteaders, nomadic herders," and a few government officials, who struggled to "keep the public lands open and available to all comers." The frontier attitudes of western ranchers made the western cattle industry firmly opposed to legal regulation. Nevertheless, many ranchers during this period employed sophisticated legal strategies for maintaining their monopoly over the use of public lands.

* * *

B. The Taylor Grazing Act of 1934

* * *

While the Secretary was given wide discretion and existing users were given generous preferences, Congress nevertheless, for the first time in the Taylor Act, directed the *Secretary,* and not the ranchers, to rule the range. In no uncertain terms Congress provided that the *extent* of livestock grazing (i.e., numbers of animals per acre) and the *timing* of livestock grazing (i.e., seasons of use) were to be *specified* by the Secretary. Thus, in deference to the recognized injury to the rangelands caused by the largely unregulated exploitation of public lands, and in the apparent hope that regulation would help stabilize the western livestock industry, Congress in the Taylor Act, essentially closed the public domain.

4. On August 21, 1984, defendants and plaintiffs stipulated that no additional CMAs would be executed until the instant litigation had been decided on the merits. Thus, there has been no need to decide plaintiffs' motion for preliminary injunction.

The process of carving up the land into grazing districts was swift, "hasty," and dominated by the stock industry itself. By the 1970's it was the view of many experts that the BLM had failed to achieve one of the principal goals of the Taylor Act, namely to improve range conditions or at a minimum to "stop injury to the public grazing lands by preventing overgrazing and soil deterioration." [11]

In 1975, the BLM reported to the Senate Committee on Appropriations that only about 19% of the acres under its control were "improving," while 65% were "static," and 16% were admittedly "declining." These estimates, as depressing as they were, apparently *understated* the static and declining condition of the already ravaged public lands according to subsequent reports issued by the BLM and the United States Accounting Office.

* * *

C. *Federal Land Policy & Management Act*

The Federal Land Policy & Management Act of 1976, 43 U.S.C. § 1701, et seq. (hereinafter FLPMA), was a comprehensive statement of the public policy of the United States, declaring that public lands be systematically inventoried and subjected to a land use planning process

* * *

* * *

FLPMA did *not* repeal the essential provisions of the Taylor Act, but rather *added* a new management structure within which the Secretary was to operate.

The Act contains an implicit denunciation of past practices of the BLM in managing public grazing lands:

> Congress finds that a substantial amount of the Federal range lands is deteriorating in quality, and that installation of additional range improvements could arrest much of the continuing deterioration and could lead to substantial betterment of forage conditions with resulting benefits to wildlife, watershed protection, and livestock production.

43 U.S.C. § 1751(b). FLPMA's principal management requirement is that the Secretary *"shall"* manage the public rangelands for "multiple use and sustained yield." 43 U.S.C. § 1732(a).[15] Moreover, the Act directs that land use plans be developed and that the public lands shall

---

11. * * * In 1977, the Comptroller General of the United States reported to Congress on the condition of the public rangelands and concluded bluntly:

The Nation's public rangelands have been deteriorating for years and, for the most part, are not improving. These vast lands need to be protected through better management by the Bureau of Land Management.

Deterioration can be attributed principally to poorly managed grazing by livestock—horses, cattle, sheep, and goats.

Livestock have been permitted to graze on public rangelands year after year without adequate regard to the detrimental effect on range vegetation.

* * *

15. "Sustained yield" is defined in FLPMA as "the achievement and maintenance in perpetuity of a high-level annual or regular periodic output of the various renewable resources consistent with multiple use." 43 U.S.C. § 1702(h).

* * *

be managed "in accordance with the land use plans" when they are available. Id.

1. Permit Issuance Requirements. The provisions of FLPMA which raise the principal disputes in this lawsuit, however, are the very specific requirements for permits and leases contained in 43 U.S.C. § 1752.[16] Since, as will be explained, these issues turn on the express language of Congress, a complete treatment of the permit and lease provisions is essential.

Under FLPMA the typical permit or lease (hereinafter the Court's reference to "permits" shall include within the meaning of that term "permits and leases") is intended to be for a duration of ten years except under specified conditions not relevant herein. Each permit may include such "terms and conditions" deemed appropriate by the Secretary so long as those terms and conditions are "consistent with the governing law." 43 U.S.C. § 1752(a). The terms and conditions in permits shall, however, include, but not be limited to, "the authority" of the Secretary "to cancel, suspend or modify" the permit "in whole or in part" pursuant to the terms and conditions in the permit, or to "cancel or suspend" the permit for violations by the permittee of grazing regulations or permit requirements. Id. Assuming that during the term of the permit the land has been used for livestock grazing, and that the permittee has complied with all permit requirements, and has accepted any new conditions of the Secretary, the holder of an expiring permit "shall be given first priority" for permit renewal at the end of ten years. 43 U.S.C. § 1752(c).

Under FLPMA, however, the Secretary is not given carte blanche authority to issue ten-year permits containing whatever terms and conditions are deemed appropriate. The statute is remarkably clear and specific in its requirement that *all* permits conform to one of two prescribed methods of issuance. 43 U.S.C. § 1752(d), (e). Furthermore, as noted, Congress directed that among the terms and conditions to be included in each permit shall be an express retention of authority by the Secretary to cancel, suspend, or modify the permit under specified circumstances. 43 U.S.C. § 1752(a).

2. Allotment Management Plans. The first of FLPMA's only two permissible methods of permit issuance is outlined in § 1752(d) and entails the incorporation into some permits of so-called Allotment Management Plans (hereinafter "AMPs"). AMPs have been described by Professor Coggins as "the penultimate step in the multiple use planning process" and as "basically land use plans tailored to specific grazing permits."[18] Congress has defined an AMP as being a document

---

16. In order to avoid confusion, the Court throughout this opinion refers to FLPMA of 1976 when it discusses provisions contained in 43 U.S.C. § 1701, et seq. The reader should note, however, that certain provisions of FLPMA were *amended* by the Public Rangelands Improvement Act of 1978, particularly by Sections 7 and 8 of that Act. Several of those 1978 amendments are reflected in the current version of 43 U.S.C. § 1701, et seq., and particularly in § 1752 discussed at length herein. The Court's reference is always to the *amended* version.

18. Coggins, The Law of Public Rangeland Management IV: FLPMA, PRIA, and

which "*prescribes* the manner in, and extent to, which livestock operations will be conducted. * * * " 43 U.S.C. § 1702(k)(1).[19] On the other hand, AMPs need only *describe* "the type, location, ownership, and general specifications for * * * range improvements" on grazing allotments, 43 U.S.C. § 1702(k)(2), and may include other appropriate terms and conditions the Secretary wishes to insert. 43 U.S.C. § 1702(k)(3). If the Secretary chooses to incorporate an AMP into a permit, § 1752(d) requires that the AMP be "tailored to the specific range condition of the area" and mandates that the Secretary review each AMP on a periodic basis to determine whether the AMP has been effective in improving range conditions in the area.

The Secretary is empowered to revise or terminate AMPs but only following "consultation, cooperation, and coordination" with the parties involved. 43 U.S.C. § 1752(d). In fact, the dominant import of subsection (d) is that the final *prescription* of grazing practices contained in any AMP must be the result of "careful and considered consultation, cooperation, and coordination with the lessees, permittees, and landowners involved." Id. The decision whether to incorporate an AMP into a permit is wholly within the discretionary judgment of the Secretary.

3. Permits Without AMPs. The statute, however, provides only a single alternative in the event the Secretary has *not* completed an AMP. In such cases, the Secretary need not proceed by way of consultation with permittees, but may simply issue permits which themselves prescribe appropriate livestock management practices. 43 U.S.C. § 1752(e). This short-cut method of prescribing grazing practices requires the Secretary to "incorporate in grazing permits and leases such terms and conditions as [the Secretary] deems appropriate" but also requires that the Secretary "shall specify" in each permit: (1) "the number of animals to be grazed" by the permittee; (2) "the seasons of use" for livestock grazing; and (3) a provision that the Secretary "may reexamine the condition of the range *at any time*" and, if necessary, "readjust" the livestock grazing prescription for the allotment. Id. (emphasis supplied).

the Multiple Use Mandate, 14 Envtl.L. 1, 24 (1983) (hereinafter cited as *Coggins IV*).

19. In language of particular importance to this lawsuit, allotment management plans are defined in FLPMA as follows:

(k) *An "allotment management plan"* means a document prepared in consultation with the lessees or permittees involved, which applies to livestock operations on the public lands or on lands within National Forests in the eleven contiguous Western States and which:

(1) *prescribes the manner in, and extent to, which livestock operations will be conducted* in order to meet the multiple-use, sustained-yield, economic and other

needs and objectives as determined for the lands by the Secretary concerned; and

(2) describes the type, location, ownership, and general specifications for the range improvements to be installed and maintained on the lands to meet the livestock grazing and other objectives of land management; and

(3) contains such other provisions relating to livestock grazing and other objectives found by the Secretary concerned to be consistent with the provisions of this Act and other applicable law.

43 U.S.C. § 1702(k) (emphasis supplied).

From the plain language of the statute there is no question in this Court's view that the AMP and no-AMP methods of permit issuance, provided for in § 1752(d) and (e) are the *only* permissible methods: § 1752(e) provides that the required permit conditions respecting "numbers of animals," "seasons of use," and "reexamination" and "readjustment," shall be incorporated into permits "in all cases" where an AMP is not so incorporated.

But even where an AMP *is* incorporated, the Secretary nevertheless must *prescribe* the manner in and extent to which livestock practices are conducted on grazing allotments. 43 U.S.C. § 1702(k)(1). Moreover, *all* permits, including those containing AMPs, must contain provisions by which the Secretary expressly retains authority to cancel, suspend, or modify permit terms and conditions. 43 U.S.C. § 1752(a), (d), and (e).

Thus, as a practical matter, the only significant difference between the two permissible methods for issuing livestock grazing permits under FLPMA are two: (1) permits containing AMPs must involve careful and considered consultation, cooperation, and coordination with permittees; and (2) the prescription of livestock practices in a permit containing an AMP must be tailored to the specific conditions of the range on the allotment, whereas the permit without an AMP may apparently reflect general or universal livestock management standards.

In sum, Congress by enactment of FLPMA, did not weaken but rather strengthened the mandate it handed the Secretary in 1934 to rule the range. By FLPMA's provisions requiring the Secretary to issue permits prescribing grazing practices and expressly retaining authority to cancel, suspend or modify, Congress gave specific meaning to its general instructions to the Secretary, to wit: "The Secretary *shall* manage the public lands. * * *" 43 U.S.C. § 1732(a) (emphasis supplied).

D. The Public Rangeland Improvement Act

The Public Rangelands Improvement Act of 1978, 43 U.S.C. § 1901, et seq. (hereinafter PRIA), clarified and refined the essential Congressional message to the Secretary, namely, that the public lands be managed with more attention paid to range *improvement.* Congress made several findings which shed light on the purposes of the various statutes pertaining to public management of grazing lands. "[V]ast segments of the public rangelands" were found to be "producing less than their potential" for the multiple uses for which those lands were being managed. 43 U.S.C. § 1901(a)(1). For this reason, Congress found that these vast areas were in "an unsatisfactory condition." Id. Congress recognized the need for additional funding to resurrect the damaged lands, 43 U.S.C. § 1901(a)(2), and noted [a broad variety of] unsatisfactory conditions. * * * Congress found that such devastating potential impact might be avoided through "intensive" maintenance, management, and improvement programs, 43 U.S.C. § 1901(a) (4), and established and reaffirmed the national policy and commitment to inventorying public lands, and to managing the public lands "so that they become as productive as feasible for all rangeland values." 43 U.S.C. § 1901(b)(1), (2). PRIA expressly reenacted the Taylor Act and FLPMA.

III. COOPERATIVE MANAGEMENT AGREEMENTS

A. *The Regulation and Program*

1. *Promulgation.* The regulation establishing the Cooperative Management Agreement (CMA) program authorizes the BLM to enter into special permit arrangements with selected ranchers who have demonstrated "exemplary rangeland management practices." 43 C.F.R. § 4120.1(a). "Exemplary practices" are not defined in the regulation, rather, the choice of ranchers is apparently within the discretion of BLM officials.

The expressed purpose of the CMA program is to allow these ranchers the heretofore *verboten* opportunity to "manage livestock grazing on the allotment as they determine appropriate." 48 Fed.Reg. at 21823–24 (proposed 43 C.F.R. § 4120.1). The BLM is bound by the terms of a CMA for ten years. All CMAs must be "consistent with, and incorporate by reference" existing land use plans and the "terms of the authorization[s]" issued to the cooperative permittee. 43 C.F.R. § 4120.1(a).[23] The rule envisions periodic evaluations and provides for cancellation or modification only in the event of unauthorized transfers, violation of whatever terms and conditions the Secretary inserts in the CMA, or violation of regulations unrelated to overgrazing.

2. *Implementation.* The scope of the CMA regulation is illuminated by the manner in which the BLM has implemented the program. On June 20, 1984, the Bureau issued the "BLM Manual Handbook H–4120–1", Document No. 182 (hereinafter "Handbook") which included procedural direction and standards for CMAs. Also, twenty-seven individual CMAs were entered into by the BLM prior to the filing of this lawsuit.

The Handbook defines a CMA as a "formal, written agreement between the BLM and a permittee * * * that recognizes the cooperator as the steward of the allotment" and which must "be consistent with, and incorporate by reference" relevant provisions of existing land use plans. The Handbook makes plain that CMAs are neither AMPs *nor* permits containing prescriptions for numbers of animals or seasons of use. In fact, defendants instruct BLM officers in the Handbook, that in the event an AMP is in existence when the CMA is executed:

> [t]he CMA *may* incorporate the objectives of the AMP, but *must* provide the permittee * * * with *special recognition* and an opportunity to exercise *additional* management flexibility.

Thus, the CMA *supersedes* existing authorizations.

---

23. What defendants intended by the term "authorizations" is facially mysterious.

The Handbook also clarifies how defendants have managed to reward favored permittees with "secure tenure." The instructions indicate that CMA permittees shall not be subject to evaluation before "the end of the first 5 years" at which time a "joint evaluation" will take place. The permittee is automatically entitled to a CMA renewal (transforming it into a fifteen-year contract) if the mutual examination reveals that the agreement's objectives are being met. If the objectives have *not* been realized after five years, the permittee is nevertheless entitled to an additional five years within which to comply. The BLM, therefore, forfeits any remedy for the rancher's failure to meet objectives except that of denying renewal of the CMA after ten years of noncompliance. This is secure tenure indeed.[26]

A review of the CMAs which have been drafted and executed by defendants, confirms that the Secretary's expressed purposes for the CMA program (secure rancher tenure and self-management) have been implemented. Example agreements cited by *both* plaintiffs' and defendants' counsel indicate that CMAs need not contain specific performance standards such as numbers of animals or seasons of use. See Spring Cove CMA, (August, 1984, Shoshone, Idaho District, BLM); *McMullin Bros. CMA,* (August, 1983, Miles City, Montana District, BLM). These agreements list no terms or conditions whatsoever which prescribe the manner in or extent to which livestock grazing shall be managed on these allotments. The permits which accompany these agreements are brief documents containing no grazing specifications. The agreements do contain, however, the BLM's promise of non-interference and secure tenure as outlined in the Handbook.

In short, the CMA program was intended to and did create and authorize a *new* regulatory form not contained in the Taylor Grazing Act, FLPMA, or PRIA.

B. The Administrative Procedures Act

Plaintiffs have contended that the CMA program was adopted in violation of basic public participation requirements of the Administrative Procedures Act (APA), 5 U.S.C. § 553. Although plaintiffs made reference in their briefs to four procedural arguments, the Court will herein address only two:[29] (1) that defendants' notice of proposed rulemaking was insufficient to alert the public to the issues relevant to the CMA program; and (2) that the statement accompanying the final rulemaking did not adequately explain the basis and purpose of the program nor respond adequately to public comments.

26. While defendants have ostensibly reserved authority to cancel, suspend, or modify CMAs for violations of the terms and conditions of the CMA, the only performance standards included in the CMA agreements are termed "objectives" rather than terms or conditions. Terms and conditions are purposefully vague. Thus, it is apparently impossible for a permittee to risk mid-term interruption of a CMA by mere overgrazing.

29. It shall be unnecessary to decide whether (1) defendants unlawfully implemented the CMA program *before* publishing the proposed or final rule in the *Federal Register;* or (2) whether "the Handbook," outlining the program's specific operation, should have been published in the *Federal Register* or otherwise subjected to notice and comment procedures.

* * *

1. Notice of Proposed Rulemaking.

* * *

Plaintiffs contend that the notice of the proposed CMA regulation failed to reveal the agency's reasoning sufficiently to permit a meaningful exchange of views with the public.

* * *

* * * A robust debate, albeit an unfruitful one for plaintiffs, occurred as a result of the proposed rulemaking. The essential elements of the new program were adequately outlined to fairly apprise the public of what BLM was about to do.

2. Statement of Basis and Purpose. The Court now turns to plaintiffs' stronger procedural argument. Under the APA, defendants were required to consider the issues raised in the public comments and to incorporate into the final rulemaking "a concise general statement of [the rule's] basis and purpose." 5 U.S.C. § 553(c).

* * *

Defendants, on February 21, 1984, published the final rule and a response to the comments received. Defendants acknowledged that many of the comments "expressed the view that as written [the CMA rule] provided insufficient authority and control" to the BLM, 49 Fed. Reg. 6444, and that some comments had criticized existing CMAs as having withstood "insufficient public review." Id. Defendants further conceded that some of the comments challenged the Secretary's statutory authority for promulgation of the CMA regulation. Id. Plaintiffs argue that although defendants acknowledged the negative comments, there was a total failure to *respond* to them and a failure to justify the final rule in light of the comments received. The record indicates, however, that defendants declined to rebut many of the public comments because, as stated in its response, the agency was *convinced* by the comments that "the proposed regulations should be modified to more clearly indicate the objectives and approach of the cooperative management agreement within the general framework of multiple use management." Id. In fact, defendants *modified* the proposed rule in an effort to accommodate many of the commentators' most urgent warnings.[31]

The Supreme Court has cautioned that an agency's failure to respond to specific comments is fatal to agency action only insofar as it demonstrates that a decision to act was not "based on a consideration of the relevant factors." Citizens to Preserve Overton Park, Inc. v. Volpe, 401 U.S. 402, 416, 136 (1971). * * *

* * *

Nevertheless, under the present facts, the question is a close one. On balance, however, defendants' statement of basis and purpose, when taken *in conjunction* with the notice of proposed rulemaking and particularly when considered in light of the revisions in the final rule made by defendants in direct response to public comments, demon-

---

31. On the other hand, plaintiffs are perfectly correct that several comments were neither acted upon nor specifically refuted. * * *

strates that defendants considered the significant issues relevant to promulgation of the CMA rule. * * *

Consequently, on this record, the Court declines to find that defendants failed to consider and respond to the relevant comments submitted in opposition to the proposed CMA regulation.

Thus, the Court will address plaintiffs' substantive statutory arguments.

C. Experimental Stewardship

Defense counsel's chief argument to uphold the CMA Program is premised on a clever interpretation of the Experimental Stewardship Program (ESP), contained in PRIA of 1978. 43 U.S.C. § 1908. Congress by enacting ESP directed the Secretary to select areas of the rangelands of representative conditions, trends, and forages and in concentrating on these areas to "explore innovative grazing management policies and systems which might provide incentives to improve range conditions." Id. The incentive projects were to be experimental and ready for Congressional review by December of 1985 when the Secretary was directed to report the "results" of the program.

The government has maintained that even if the CMA program cannot be upheld under the Taylor Act and FLPMA, it is nevertheless fully justified by ESP. For the reasons stated herein, the Court finds this argument unsound.

This Court would ordinarily defer to the Secretary's judgment on matters such as the applicability of a particular program to a concededly generous delegation of experimental authority. However, it is blatantly obvious from the record that the Secretary did not in fact rely upon ESP when he promulgated the regulation authorizing the CMA program. Not only is there no record of the Secretary ever relying on ESP for such authority, evidence in the record establishes that BLM has already completed its experimental stewardship projects. * * *

The apparent truth is that the CMA program was never intended as a stewardship experiment. The Court must therefore view counsel's ESP argument as a *post hoc* rationalization for the CMA program and, as such, deserving of none of the customary deference accorded agency interpretations.

* * *

It is also manifest from the language of section 1908 that the CMA program simply does not meet the description of the projects ESP was intended to encourage. The CMA program is *not* an experiment, but is a permanent system of permit issuance aimed at a group of favored permittees. * * *

Faced with such overwhelming evidence that ESP was never intended by Congress to open up exceptions to the permit issuance requirements in FLPMA, defense counsel argued at the hearing on this motion that the Secretary's ability to experiment under ESP "is bounded only by imagination." For this proposition, counsel relied exclusively upon scholarly comments of Professor Coggins, who described ESP in one of his articles in sweeping language:

> The Experimental Stewardship Program offers the BLM an opportunity to break out of an historical rut of range management counterproductivity. The agency is required to try new approaches, and the Act holds out carrots for cooperating ranchers. *The ability of the BLM to experiment is bounded only by imagination and available funding.*

Coggins IV, supra note 18, at 128 (emphasis supplied). Putting aside for present the lack of precedential value in a law review article, Professor Coggins was surely *not* to be understood to be opining that the Secretary's ability to experiment was not also bounded by existing law.[37] At any rate, it is the ruling of this Court that any experimentation with new permit issuance procedures *is* bounded by existing law, as well as by the Secretary's imagination, and the ESP does not create an exception to the FLPMA permit requirements. Therefore, in order to uphold the CMA regulation, this Court must be satisfied that the Secretary is authorized under the Taylor Act and FLPMA to enter into cooperative management agreements with selected ranchers.

D. Violations of Federal Grazing Statutes

Plaintiffs' principal contention is that the CMA regulation, as finally promulgated and implemented by the Secretary and the BLM, is a naked violation of defendants' affirmative duties under the Taylor Grazing Act, FLPMA, and PRIA. The Court agrees. The CMA program disregards defendants' duty to prescribe the manner in and extent to which livestock practices will be conducted on public lands. The program also overlooks defendants' duty of expressly reserving, in all permits, sufficient authority to revise or cancel livestock grazing authorizations when necessary.

1. Duty to Prescribe Practices. The CMA program authorizes a permanent system of preferential permit issuance. Since 1934, defendants have been authorized to issue such permits but have also been required "from time to time" to "specify" the "numbers of livestock" permittees may graze on the lands and the "seasons of use" for such livestock grazing purposes. 43 U.S.C. § 315b. By enacting FLPMA in 1976, Congress clarified this duty by obligating defendants to conform to one of two prescribed methods of permit issuance. 43 U.S.C. § 1752(d)–(e). Defendants may, after cooperation and consultation with ranchers, tailor a specific grazing prescription to each allotment by incorporating an AMP into each permit. Id., at § 1752(d). Defendants may, instead, choose to forego incorporation of an AMP, and, in such

---

37. A later article by Professor Coggins corrects any such misreading of his earlier statement about ESP. Coggins lambasts the proposed regulations at issue in this lawsuit. He argues that the "overall impulse in the regulations" is to "return grazing management to near-total rancher con- trol" and that, in his view, such experimentations "have little or no warrant in the statutes." Coggins, The Law of Public Rangeland Management V: Prescriptions for Reform, 14 Envtl.L. 497, 499 n. 8 (1984).

case, specify in the *permit itself* the prescription of numbers of livestock and seasons of use. Id., at § 1752(d). While these choices provide defendants with an extraordinary degree of flexibility and discretion, there is no question that defendants' choices under FLPMA are limited to these two. Because a CMA agreement represents a third choice, and one which violates the spirit and letter of the grazing statutes, the program is unlawful.

The original purpose of the CMA program was to allow selected permittees the opportunity to "manage livestock grazing on [their] allotment[s] as *they* determine appropriate." 48 Fed.Reg. at 21823 (proposed 43 C.F.R. § 4120.1) (emphasis supplied). Thus, any defense of the program begins on the shakiest of legs since the dominant message and command of defendants' Congressional mandate is that *defendants* shall prescribe the extent to which livestock grazing shall be conducted on the public lands. The apparent goal and inevitable result of the CMA program is to allow ranchers, for a term of at least ten years, to rule the range as they see fit with little or no governmental interference. * * * Some or all of these knowledgeable permittees may even be *inclined* to limit their livestock grazing to levels which will guarantee the vitality of such values, even at the expense of their own private ranching interests. Had Congress left a gap in its regulatory scheme which allowed defendants to decide whether individual ranchers should be entrusted with such decisions, this Court would be in no position to second guess the *wisdom* of the CMA program. However, Congress, in directing that the Secretary prescribe the extent of livestock practices on each allotment, precluded such entrustment, apparently because after years of rancher dominance of range decisions, it found substantial evidence of rangeland deterioration.

According to defendants' own Handbook Manual, CMAs *may* incorporate the objectives of an existing AMP, but *must* provide the permittee with special management flexibility. "Handbook," § .1(.11)(E), p. 2. Thus, any AMP which might be in existence when the CMA is signed retains no independent significance. The CMA itself need not be specially tailored to the allotment, and need not prescribe the extent to which livestock practices are conducted on the allotment. Thus, a decision by defendants to enter into a CMA with a permittee is plainly a decision by the Secretary and the BLM that an AMP need *not* be incorporated into the permit. 43 U.S.C. § 1752(e). Defendants are entitled to make such a determination, but Congress has instructed them that *"in all cases"* where an AMP is not incorporated, they "shall" specify in the permit "the numbers of animals to be grazed and the seasons of use * * *" Id. Defendants' assertion that the CMA regulation is valid because it requires specification of "performance standards" is without merit. The statute requires specification of numbers and seasons, not generalized standards or responsibilities. CMAs, by definition and in practice, fail to comply with this Congressional mandate.

The CMA program would be without statutory support even if, as defendants argue, CMA permits were governed by § 1752(d) pertaining to AMPS rather than by § 1752(e). As plaintiffs point out, although the statute leaves the details of a particular AMP to the discretion of the Secretary, "[a]n AMP is more, not less, detailed than a permit or lease." Congress, by defining AMPs as documents which "prescribe" [40] the extent to which livestock grazing may be conducted on public allotments, intended to reaffirm defendants' duty under the Taylor Grazing Act to specify numbers and seasons in each permit, whether issued pursuant to subsection (d) or subsection (e). Thus, even if CMAs were a species of AMP, or required wholesale incorporation of AMPs (which would obviously defeat the purpose of the program) defendants would nevertheless be required to specifically limit the extent to which livestock grazing may be conducted on each allotment.

2. Duty to Reserve Revision and Cancellation Authority. Defendants are also required to incorporate into each permit an express revocation or suspension clause, 43 U.S.C. § 1732(c), and must retain constant authority to "cancel, suspend, or modify" each permit "in whole or in part" for violations of permit or regulatory requirements. 43 U.S.C. § 1752(a). In permits without AMPs, such as those incorporating CMAs, defendants are required to specify in each permit that they "may reexamine the condition of the range at *any time*" and order whatever adjustments they deem appropriate. 43 U.S.C. § 1752(e) (emphasis supplied). Even permits incorporating AMPs must reserve authority for defendants to "revise or terminate such plans or develop new plans from time to time" after consultation with ranchers. 43 U.S.C. § 1752(d).

The CMA regulation and program falls far short of the standard set by Congress in FLPMA. While the rule, as promulgated, contains vague references to the BLM's authority to periodically evaluate the range, 43 C.F.R. § 4120.1(c), and to cancel or modify agreements under certain circumstances, § 4120.1(d), § 4170.1–4, the details of defendants' authority are left to the BLM's determination, and the BLM has determined to abdicate its authority in favor of secure rancher tenure.

* * *

Thus, for ten years, assuming only that the BLM complies with its CMA agreements and that certain rancher covenants which are unrelated to the condition of the public lands are fulfilled, CMA permittees are guaranteed secure tenure. This is not partial or substantial compliance with the permit issuance requirements of the grazing statutes—it is simple *non*compliance. The statutes cannot be reasonably interpreted to allow defendants to tie their own hands with respect to their authority to modify, adjust, suspend, or cancel permits. Nor is there

---

40. *Webster's Third New International Dictionary* 1792 (unabridged 1976) defines the word "prescribe" as meaning "to lay down a rule." Defendants apparently believe that Congress may just as well have meant "describe" when it used the word "prescribe." It has been noted that "[t]he Alice-in-Wonderland view that something means whatever one chooses it to mean makes for enjoyable reading, but bad law." *Autogiro Co. of America v. United States,* 384 F.2d 391, 397 (1967).

any statutory provision creating exceptions for "exemplary" ranchers or those grazing livestock on public lands which, in defendants' view, require no improvement. Permittees must be kept under a sufficiently real threat of cancellation or modification in order to adequately protect the public lands from overgrazing or other forms of mismanagement. Any other interpretation of Congressional intent is inconsistent with the dominant purposes expressed in the Taylor Grazing Act, FLPMA, and PRIA. See section II, supra. It is for Congress and not defendants to amend the grazing statutes. In the meantime, it is the public policy of the United States that the Secretary and the BLM, not the ranchers, shall retain final control and decisionmaking authority over livestock grazing practices on the public lands.

E.   Violation of the National Environmental Protection Act

Plaintiffs alternatively contend, and the Court agrees, that defendants have violated the National Environmental Policy Act (NEPA), 42 U.S.C. § 4332, by failing to prepare an Environmental Impact Statement (EIS) prior to implementing the CMA program. * * *

* * *

The EA acknowledges that serious environmental consequences might result from program abuse, but expresses the view that such abuse is "highly unlikely." The potential impacts, therefore, are nowhere described and there is no attempt whatever to quantify the degree of potential harm so that it may be weighed and balanced against the perceived risk of such harm coming to pass. In short, defendants simply did not take a hard look at the potential degrading environmental impacts which they conceded might result from program abuse.

* * *

Plaintiffs have raised substantial concerns through argument and indications to a voluminous administrative record that the free rein allowed permittees under the CMA program presents a risk of abuses of privilege reminiscent of times past. Thus, promulgation of the CMA rule is a major federal action which may have a significant impact upon the quality of the human environment. Defendants' EA, and particularly its failure to address "crucial factors, consideration of which was essential to a truly informed decision" renders its determination of no significant impact plainly unreasonable.

IV.   AMENDMENTS TO GRAZING REGULATIONS
* * *

[The court also invalidated new BLM regulations that diluted Allotment Management Plans and land use plans, deleted operator penalty provisions, and allowed supplemental feeding without BLM authorization because the agency had not followed APA and NEPA procedures in promulgating them. The court also held that plaintiffs' challenge to the BLM's new, restrictive definition of "affected interest" for purposes of public participation was not ripe for decision on the substantive merits. The part of the opinion dealing with land use plans is reproduced infra at page 747.]

V. CONCLUSION

The problems facing defendants in managing the public lands are gigantic. While the Court has noted that livestock grazing policy and politics have often involved conflicting interests butting heads on the western range, it is obvious that no such simplistic analysis tells the whole story. It is true that private business and ranching values are sometimes in basic conflict with environmental quality and other societal values. But nothing in this opinion should be construed as a finding by this Court that defendants have consciously compromised one set of values in favor of another. Rather, the assumption throughout has been that defendants and plaintiffs merely possess opposing views as to the best way to strike a proper balance between competing interests.

Moreover, the Court recognizes that Congress has left most grazing management judgments to the discretion of defendants. Therefore, the Court has only interposed a third viewpoint in those instances where Congress has already spoken clearly on the subject over which defendants and plaintiffs debate.

*   *   *

NOTES

1. The Justice Department decided not to appeal the decision in the principal case. Are there any grounds on which an appeal might have been successful? After this decision, what options remain for the BLM if it persists in trying to give permittee ranchers more discretion and responsibility for range condition?

2. What other implications does this decision hold for public rangeland management? Does it afford a legal basis for environmental challenges to individual AMPs and grazing permits? Does it require the Secretary to reduce permitted AUMs on an allotment if the challenger can show that permitted grazing exceeds the carrying capacity of the land? Does the Secretary have a duty to halt grazing on lands classified as "poor" or "fair" condition?

3. The principal case, in a portion reproduced below, also held— on procedural grounds—that the BLM regulations at issue unlawfully diluted land use planning requirements imposed by FLPMA. As the following section illustrates, preparation of land use plans for the public lands, in conjunction with environmental impact statements, promises to become one of the most important elements of the entire management process, with serious implications for all rangeland users, especially permittee ranchers.

3. LAND USE PLANNING ON THE BLM PUBLIC LANDS

COGGINS, THE LAW OF PUBLIC RANGELAND
MANAGEMENT IV: FLPMA, PRIA, AND
THE MULTIPLE USE MANDATE
14 Envtl.L. 1 (1983).

Very little that could be dignified with the label of "planning" for resource use took place on the public lands in the first thirty or forty years of range management under the Taylor Grazing Act of 1934. The BLM often down-played or ignored nonlivestock and nonmineral values. The agency paid some lip service to wildlife and recreation (usually hunting), but initiated few significant management changes in those directions, except the segregation of some areas for wildlife. Watershed, environmental quality, and other less tangible objectives did not figure heavily in the management equation.

The BLM has never taken inventory of all the resources under its control in any systematic, comprehensive fashion. The agency has persisted in overestimating forage to appease its rancher constituency. BLM efforts to reduce grazing pressures to levels within the land's carrying capacity, begun with the best intentions in the 1950's and 1960's, almost uniformly came to nought when the users applied political pressure. The BLM leadership's sporadic attempts at decentralization have ensured a lack of consistent policy in the field. BLM efforts to emulate the Forest Service have foundered due to politics and a lack of either money or intestinal fortitude.

The BLM's inability to plan is not entirely its own fault. Part of the failure to create and implement a rational land use system can be blamed on the longtime refusal of Congress to give the agency either organic planning authority or adequate funding. The evolution of the statutory authority of the BLM parallels that of the Forest Service, which evolved a decade or so earlier. Except for vestiges of public domain disposition and oversight of mineral claims and leases, the BLM's only statutory management mandate until 1976 was the Taylor Grazing Act of 1934. The Taylor Act contemplated neither multiple use, sustained yield management nor formal land use planning, except in a primitive fashion. But the Taylor Act did supply the first element of planning, previously lacking, by giving the agency some control over grazing use. Congress ignored the BLM when it enacted the Multiple-Use, Sustained-Yield Act of 1960 (MUSY Act) and the Wilderness Act of 1964. The Classification and Multiple Use Act (CMUA) of 1964 gave the agency temporary authority to manage and plan for multiple use and sustained yield.

The BLM began formal planning in 1969, the last year the CMUA was in effect. Preliminary BLM planning efforts were superseded in 1974 by NEPA and much of the agency's subsequent planning had been done in the impact statement context. Congressional dissatisfaction with BLM management finally led to FLPMA, which requires an intensive, but imprecise planning process. PRIA supplements and reenforces the FLPMA planning provisions and gives range management some substantive direction. Although the BLM is now actively engaged in formal planning under those laws, the agency has neither surmounted its former problems nor settled on a rational planning process. BLM preconceptions, frequent changes of policy direction, and lack of central coordination have all contributed to continuing difficulties in this area.

* * *

The BLM planning regulations lack the cohesiveness and direction necessary for satisfactory implementation of multiple use planning. The content required in the plans is sketchy, and the connection between policy guidance and the preparation of plans is hazy. Furthermore, the BLM planning regulations fail to define standards for plan preparation. The most glaring omission is that the regulations fail to indicate the extent to which planning actions bind the course of later land management.

Full implementation of FLPMA's planning requirements will necessitate vast bureaucratic resources and produce mountains of paperwork. The effort can be justified only by the magnitude of the problem Congress confronted. Had the BLM managed to satisfy all present and prospective public land users—including those whose preferred use is preservation—Congress would not have thought FLPMA necessary. The whole point of the statute, and of cognate legislation, is the need to deal with resource scarcity. Demand for public resources— typically at low or zero prices—far outstrips available supply. Resource allocation by pricing alone is inappropriate for the nation's natural heritage. Congress could have determined who gets what from the public lands, but it did not. Instead, FLPMA institutes a complicated, overlapping procedure to ensure that the ultimate decisionmakers actually think about all the relevant interests and considerations. The BLM is now much more accountable to Congress and to its own planning documents. The agency has only itself to blame for the widely lamented "loss of flexibility."

AMERICAN MOTORCYCLIST ASSOCIATION v. WATT

United States District Court, Central District of California, 1981.
534 F.Supp. 923, aff'd, 714 F.2d 962 (9th Cir.1983).

TASHIMA, District Judge.

Plaintiffs in all but one of these [five] consolidated actions, American Motorcyclist Association and Sports Committee, District 37, A.M.A., Inc. (collectively "AMA"), County of Inyo and National Outdoor Coalition ("NOC"), have each moved for a preliminary injunction restraining defendants, the Secretary of the Interior ("Secretary"), the Director of the Bureau of Land Management ("BLM"), Department of the Interior, and the California State Director of BLM, from implementing the California Desert Conservation Area Plan (the "Plan"), which was prepared by the BLM pursuant to Section 601 of the Federal Land Policy and Management Act of 1976 ("FLPMA"), 43 U.S.C. § 1781. Section 601 requires the Secretary to inventory the resources in the California Desert Conservation Area ("CDCA") and prepare a comprehensive land use management plan for the area. The CDCA and the Plan cover the more than 12 million acres of desert land in the State of California which are owned by the United States and administered by the BLM.

* * *

BACKGROUND

The CDCA Plan

The Plan is a long-range comprehensive plan for the management, use, development and protection of the over 12 million acres of land owned by the United States and administered by the BLM in the CDCA. Section 601 of FLPMA directs the Secretary to prepare and implement a plan which "take[s] into account the principles of multiple use and sustained yield in providing for resource use and development, including, but not limited to the maintenance of environmental quality, rights-of-way, and mineral development." 43 U.S.C. § 1781(d). The Plan was developed to provide general, regional guidance for management of the CDCA over a 20-year period. BLM, Final Environmental Impact Statement and Proposed Plan VII (1980) ("Final EIS"). It is designed to consider issues and resolve basic conflicts on a large scale in order to aid future decision-makers and "will be at the top of a hierarchy and provide the framework for subsequent plans for specific resources and uses, development of site specific programs or project action." Id. at E–2.

The following "planning components" are utilized in the Plan. Broad regional resource uses are addressed by a system of four multiple use classes: Controlled (Class C), which is designed to protect and preserve areas having wilderness characteristics described in the Wilderness Act, 16 U.S.C. § 1131 et seq., and which serves as a preliminary recommendation by the Secretary that the areas are suitable for wilderness designation by Congress; Limited (Class L), which protects sensitive natural scenic, ecological and cultural resources, but provides for low intensity multiple use; Moderate (Class M), designed to provide for a wide variety of use, yet mitigate damage to the most sensitive uses; and Intensive (Class I), which emphasizes development oriented use of lands and resources to meet consumptive needs, yet provides for some protection of resources. Plan at 13.

All land use actions and resource management activities within a multiple use class must meet the guidelines for that class.[4] The Plan

4. The guidelines are arranged in the Plan (at 14) according to the following list:

1. Agriculture
2. Air Quality
3. Water Quality
4. Cultural and Paleontological Resources
5. Native American Values
6. Electrical Generation Facilities
7. Transmission Facilities

contains a chart which sets out how each of the guidelines will affect uses in each class. For example, in accordance with the agricultural guidelines, agricultural uses, excluding livestock grazing, are not allowed in areas designated as Class C or Class L, but may be allowed on suitable lands within Class M and Class I.

A multiple use class may incorporate a number of types and levels of use consistent with the multiple use guidelines. Where such uses conflict, the conflicts—the major issues of the Plan—are addressed in twelve Plan Elements.[5] Each of the Plan Elements is subdivided into three areas of interest and responsibility: goals for the element, actions proposed for the element and implementation of the Plan as it affects the element. In each of the Plan Elements an attempt is made to identify existing or possible conflicts between varying uses and to provide the manager faced with resolution of these conflicts with a framework for making decisions relating to specific land uses.

The Plan also designates 75 Areas of Critical Environmental Concern ("ACEC"), pursuant to Section 103(a) of FLPMA, which defines an ACEC as an area "within the public lands where special management attention is required * * * to protect and prevent irreparable damage to important historic, cultural, or scenic values, fish and wildlife resources, or other natural systems and processes, or to protect life and safety from natural hazards." 43 U.S.C. § 1702(a).

Management prescriptions for each area proposed for ACEC designation have been or will be developed by the BLM. These prescriptions are "site specific" and include both actions which the BLM has authority to carry out and recommendations of action which the BLM has no direct authority to implement, such as cooperative agreements with other agencies and mineral withdrawals. Plan at 123. For example, ACEC # 4, the Saline Valley in Inyo County, has been so designated because it is a wildlife habitat. The management prescriptions developed include cooperative management with the California Department of Fish and Game, acquisition of non-BLM lands through exchange and purchase, reduction of the burro populations, limitation of vehicles to approved routes, designation of camping areas and closing the Saline Dunes to vehicle entry.

8. Communication Sites

9. Fire Management

10. Vegetation

11. Land Tenure Adjustment

12. Livestock Grazing

13. Mineral Exploration and Development

14. Motorized-Vehicle Access/Transportation

15. Recreation

16. Waste Disposal

17. Wildlife Species and Habitat

18. Wetland/Riparian Areas

19. Wild Horses and Burros

5. These twelve Plan Elements are:

Cultural Resources

Native American Values

Wildlife

Vegetation

Wilderness

Wild Horses and Burros

Livestock Grazing

Recreation

Motorized-Vehicle Access

Geology-Energy-Minerals

Energy Production and Utility Corridors

Land Tenure Adjustment Plan at 21.

Finally, the Plan identifies "Other Support Requirements," including special soil, air quality, and water resource programs, a trespass prevention program and a cadastral survey of the CDCA.

The Final Environmental Impact Statement

* * *

The Planning Process

The Plan and Final EIS were in preparation for over three years. The Secretary appointed the CDCA or Desert Advisory Committee ("DAC") in early 1977 as required by FLPMA, 43 U.S.C. § 1781(g). The DAC, which included members of the public with expertise in the various areas critical to the Plan, held numerous meetings and public seminars from 1977 to November, 1980. During that period, a number of techniques were utilized by the BLM to gain public input on the CDCA planning effort, including "feedback meetings" with interested groups, public hearings, three opinion polls and meetings and briefings with federal, state and local government entities. In December 1979, a "Draft Preview" was published to inform the public of the scope, content and background of the Draft Plan and EIS in preparation for public comment. The Draft Plan and EIS were published and released for public comment in February, 1980. During the comment period further public meetings and briefings were held. A proposed Plan and a Final EIS were published in October, 1980 and circulated for additional public comment. The Plan became effective on December 17, 1980, when former Assistant Secretary Martin approved a marked-up version of the Final Plan. Former Secretary Andrus subsequently concurred in the Plan. Since that time, the BLM has taken steps to implement the Plan within the constraints imposed by time and budgetary limitations. A final version of the Plan was published in April, 1981.

DISCUSSION

* * *

[The court held that plaintiffs had standing to challenge the plan but not the EIS.]

* * *

III. *The BLM's Procedural Violations*

Plaintiffs allege numerous violations by defendants of FLPMA, NEPA and the BLM planning regulations, which they claim invalidate the Plan. * * *

(a) *Procedures Required by FLPMA and the BLM Planning Regulations*

FLPMA requires that the Plan be prepared "in accordance with section 1712 of this title." 43 U.S.C. § 1781(d). Section 1712 applies to all public lands, 43 U.S.C. § 1712(a), and requires that:

> "The Secretary shall allow an opportunity for public involvement and by regulation shall establish procedures, including public hearings where appropriate, to give Federal, State, and

local governments and the public adequate notice and opportunity to comment upon and participate in the formulation of plans and programs relating to the management of the public lands."

43 U.S.C. § 1712(f).

* * *

I conclude that the BLM planning regulations were applicable to the CDCA planning process and that the BLM was bound to adhere to the procedures established by its own regulations. Defendants' argument that these regulations do not apply to the CDCA or to the Plan, is unpersuasive. First, there is no official interpretive or policy statement of the agency supporting this interpretation; it is asserted only in the declaration and deposition of a subordinate agency official. Second, although a federal agency's interpretation of a statute or regulation is entitled to great deference by reviewing courts, this rule applies only if the agency interpretation is reasonable and not clearly outside the agency's statutory authority. Here, even assuming that Ruch's testimony should be accorded the dignity of official agency interpretation, his interpretation is unreasonable since the statute, 43 U.S.C. § 1781(d), clearly requires the Secretary to comply with Section 1712 in the preparation and implementation of the Plan. In turn, Section 1712(f) delegates to the Secretary the authority to establish procedures to give federal, state and local governments and the public adequate notice and opportunity to comment upon and participate in the formulation of plans and programs relating to the management of public lands. Finally, the language of the regulations promulgated under the Secretary's § 1712(f) authority itself suggests that the regulations are applicable to the Plan. 43 C.F.R. § 1601.0–7 states: "[t]hese regulations apply to all BLM administered public lands." "Public lands" is defined as "any land or interest in land owned by the United States and administered by the Secretary of the Interior through the Bureau of Land Management." 43 C.F.R. § 1601.0–5(j). In short, defendants' claim that the BLM planning regulations were not meant to apply to the CDCA planning process because the Plan was somehow different from the usual land use plan is plainly unreasonable because this interpretation is in conflict with the statute, 43 U.S.C. §§ 1781(d) & 1712(f), and the language of the regulations themselves.

* * *

(b) *Violations of FLPMA and the BLM Planning Regulations*

I find on the record as a whole that there is a strong likelihood that plaintiffs will be able to prove at trial that, in several material respects, the BLM failed to follow its own planning regulations and that such failure resulted in the agency's violation of § 202(c)(9) & (f) of FLPMA. 43 U.S.C. § 1712(c)(9) & (f).

43 C.F.R. § 1601.5–7 requires that in preparing the Plan, the BLM evaluate the alternative courses of action developed in the planning process (and their effects according to planning criteria) and "develop a preferred alternative * * * [which] shall be incorporated into the

draft plan and draft environmental impact statement." No "preferred alternative" was designated in the Draft Plan and EIS published in February, 1980. This omission deprived state and local agencies and the public of the opportunity to focus their comments on the alternative which the agency was likely to recommend to the Secretary, at the draft stage before a final BLM decision had been made.

43 C.F.R. § 1601.3(i) requires that "ninety days * * * be provided for review of the draft plan, and draft environmental impact statement." Although defendants claim that the full 90 days were available, several of the appendices which were an integral part of the Plan were not available until well into the review period. By failing to make the appendices available at the outset, defendants made it impossible for state and local governments, the public, and special interest groups, such as AMA and NOC, to review and comment upon all of the changes which the Plan would effect and the data upon which these actions were based.

The BLM's failure to follow its own planning regulations by not designating a preferred alternative at the draft stage and by not allowing the full 90 days to review all of the integral draft plan documents prejudiced plaintiffs' ability to comment upon and participate in the formulation of the Plan as required by FLPMA, 43 U.S.C. § 1712(f).

Plaintiff Inyo County also claims that the BLM has violated § 202(c)(9) of FLPMA, 43 U.S.C. § 1712(c)(9), and 43 C.F.R. § 1601.4, which provide for the coordination of BLM resource management plans with the management plans of state and local governments. BLM State Directors and District Managers are required to keep apprised of state and local plans, to assure that consideration is given to them and to assist in resolving inconsistencies between BLM plans and such plans to the extent practical. Defendants claim to have taken state and local land use plans into account in developing the Plan and to have resolved inconsistencies to the extent required by § 1601.4. However, the failure of defendants to comply with 43 C.F.R. § 1601.4–2(c) & (d) makes it impossible for the Court to determine whether the BLM has complied with the mandate of 43 C.F.R. § 1601.4 and 43 U.S.C. § 1712(c)(9). Subsections 2(c) and (d) allow state and local agencies to notify the BLM of specific inconsistencies between their plans and BLM resource management plans and require that the plan document reflect how these inconsistencies were addressed and, if possible, resolved. Since this procedure was not followed in that defendants have not presented adequate evidence of their response to Inyo County's list of inconsistencies, I conclude that it is likely that Inyo County will be able to prove violations of 43 U.S.C. § 1712(c)(9) and 43 C.F.R. § 1601.4 at trial.

Finally, plaintiffs point out that the Decision Document (signed into law by former Assistant Secretary Martin on December 17, 1980) contained a number of material changes from the Final Plan and EIS which was circulated for comment, which changes were never subjected to the scrutiny of the DAC or published for examination and comment

by state and local governments and the general public.[13] The failure of
the BLM to allow any public and governmental participation relative to
these changes, which amount to significant actions in their own right,
appears to amount to a further violation of 43 U.S.C. §§ 1712(c)(9) & (f)
and 1781(d), and the BLM planning regulations.

*   *   *

IV. *Equitable Considerations*

It is not enough that plaintiffs have demonstrated likelihood of
success on the merits; they must also demonstrate that the equities of
the case require injunctive relief before trial, i.e., that they will suffer
irreparable harm absent issuance of a preliminary injunction, that the
balance of hardships tips in their favor and, since this is an environmental case where the public interest is implicated, that preliminary
injunctive relief would benefit the public in general.

On the record before the Court, I find that none of the plaintiffs
has made a sufficient showing of the equitable elements to justify the
issuance of a preliminary injunction restraining the implementation of
the Plan pending trial. In making this determination and in weighing
the public interest, I am mindful of Congress' concern that the CDCA is
"seriously threatened by air pollution, inadequate Federal management
authority, and pressures of increased use, particularly recreational use,
which are certain to intensify because of the rapidly growing population of southern California." 43 U.S.C. § 1781(a)(3). Accordingly, I
conclude that the public interest in maintaining the Plan and in
protecting the CDCA outweighs any possible harm to plaintiffs.

The only real showing of irreparable harm by plaintiffs NOC and
AMA is that their members will be deprived of some recreational
opportunities until trial. This deprivation is attributable to the reduction in the amount of vehicle use allowed under the Plan from that
permitted under the ICMP, which governed vehicle access prior to the
time that the Plan went into effect. AMA also claims that it will suffer
irreparable injury because the Plan precludes holding competitive
events outside of the three race routes established in the Plan. * * *
On the other hand, I find that there is a danger of harm to the CDCA
from the types of activities which these plaintiffs intend to pursue and
that the restrictions on access imposed by the Plan will serve to protect
fragile desert resources from the pressures of increased motorized
vehicle use. Plaintiffs AMA and NOC have failed to prove either that
their inconvenience pending trial outweighs the threat of harm to the

---

13. Such changes include:

(1) Designation of all Class "L" lands
as "sensitive areas" of public concern
requiring, without prior determination
by a BLM officer, a 60-day comment period, prior to approval of any application
for a plan of operations.

(2) The designation of a portion of the
CDCA as the "East Mojave National
Scenic Area."

(3) The inclusion of three race routes
which had never been developed as part
of any of the plan alternatives up to that
point.

(4) Increasing the ACEC's from 73 to
75 and the areas preliminarily recommended as suitable for wilderness designation from 43 to 45.

desert from more intensive recreational use or that it would be in the public interest to enjoin the operation of the Plan as it impacts their interests.

County of Inyo has presented a somewhat stronger case that it will suffer irreparable harm if the Plan is not preliminarily enjoined, in that its general planning duties have been hampered by the Plan, which imposes a number of restrictions in conflict with Inyo's Master Plan for adjacent private lands. Like the other plaintiffs, however, I find that the harm which Inyo will suffer as a result of the Plan's disruption of its planning activities is not sufficient to outweigh the harm to the CDCA and the public interest if implementation of the Plan is enjoined. It should also be noted that while the County's planning efforts may be impaired by uncertainty regarding the legal validity of the Plan, issuance of a preliminary injunction would do little to redress that injury, since the Plan's validity will remain uncertain until judgment has been entered on the merits in this action.

* * *

NOTES

1. In affirming the principal case, the Ninth Circuit Court of Appeals noted that the denial of standing to Inyo County on its NEPA claims "is in serious doubt." 714 F.2d at 965. The Court of Appeals nevertheless ruled that the public interest in protecting the fragile ecology of the CDCA outweighed possible NEPA violations insofar as the grant of an injunction pending trial was concerned. Citing Weinberger v. Romero-Barcelo, 456 U.S. 305 (1982) the court said that "the public interest is a factor which courts must consider in any injunctive action in which the public interest is affected."

2. If plaintiff prevails after a full trial on the merits, what remedy should the court grant? How likely is it that a new plan would differ substantially from the old? If the old plan is invalidated, what criteria will govern land use in the interim until a new plan is promulgated? To what extent can courts effectively review substantive plan provisions? Is observance of procedure more important in planning than in making management decisions?

3. Subsequent litigation growing out of the CDCA plan as it affects off-road vehicle use in the area is discussed in chapter nine, § D.

4. The variety and extent of user demand for the BLM lands has increased dramatically in recent years. The emergence of conflicting user interests has accentuated the need for more refined and comprehensive management by the Bureau of Land Management. In developing and revising land use plans for use of BLM public lands, the Secretary of the Interior is directed to:

(1) use and observe the principles of multiple use and sustained yield set forth in this and other applicable law;

(2) use a systematic interdisciplinary approach to achieve integrated consideration of physical, biological, economic, and other sciences;

(3) give priority to the designation and protection of areas of critical environmental concern;

(4) rely, to the extent it is available, on the inventory of the public lands, their resources, and other values;

(5) consider present and potential uses of the public lands;

(6) consider the relative scarcity of the values involved and the availability of alternative means (including recycling) and sites for realization of those values;

(7) weigh long-term benefits to the public against short-term benefits; * * *

43 U.S.C.A. § 1712(c). Is a land management agency better served by these rather opaque criteria or by the more precise planning requirements of the National Forest Management Act?

NATURAL RESOURCES DEFENSE COUNCIL, INC. v. HODEL

United States District Court, E.D. California, 1985.
618 F.Supp. 848.

[The main part of this opinion is reproduced at page 723 supra.]

* * *

B. *Dilution of Land Use Plans*

The grazing statutes are unequivocal in their endorsement of the land use planning process as the basis and guide for all future livestock management decisions. See 43 U.S.C. § 1711(a) (defendants must conduct an inventory of all public land resources); id. § 1712 (defendants must prepare land use plans for all public land regions); id. § 1732 (defendants are *bound* by land use plans and shall manage the public lands "in accordance" with same); id. § 1901(b)(2) (defendants' duty to manage the public lands "in accordance with management objectives and the land use planning process" was affirmed in PRIA). The legislature's emphasis on the importance of land use planning caused the leading commentator to observe that Congress "intended planning to be the centerpiece of future rangeland management" and "binding on all subsequent multiple use decisions." [50]

Reflecting this mandate, the former regulations *required* BLM officers to modify, suspend, or cancel all permits which were inconsistent with governing land use plans. These sections were deleted in 1984. The *new* section provides:

> Following careful and considered consultation, cooperation and coordination with the lessees, permittees, and other affected interests, the authorized officer *may modify* the terms and conditions of the permit or lease *if monitoring data show that*

---

50. *Coggins IV,* supra, note 18 at 15.

present grazing use is not meeting the land use plan or manage-
ment objectives.

43 C.F.R. § 4130.6–3 (1984) (emphasis supplied). Thus, under the revised regulations there is no reference whatsoever to the Secretary's authority to *cancel* or *suspend* permits which are inconsistent with land use plans. Moreover, permits apparently may not even be *modified* under the new regulation unless monitoring data establishes the inconsistency. Finally, and most fundamentally, the new regulation omitted the mandatory "shall" and replaced it with the discretionary "may" reversing defendants' policy of maintaining substantial consistency between plans and permits.

Because the Court agrees that the new policy was no-where explained or justified in the publication of the final rulemaking, it is unnecessary to resolve the questions of Congressional intent raised by plaintiffs.

Defendants received several highly critical comments on the change in the role of land use planning. The BLM's California Director, fearing the proposed regulation was contrary to law, pointed out that the elimination of provisions allowing cancellation of permits "strongly implies that no grazing permits * * * will be cancelled prior to their expiration" except for specific violations of regulations or permit conditions. See also Comments of N.R.D.C., Inc., August 10, 1983 at 24–25, Document No. 20 (defendants were warned that the revision might conflict with applicable law insofar as land use plans would no longer modify current practice or control future grazing decisions).

Most significantly, defendants' attention was directed during notice and comment to their own contrary legal position enunciated only a year before this proposal came to light. In 1982, defendants *rejected* a similar proposal to replace the word "shall" with the word "may" (while leaving in the regulation full authority to cancel or suspend inconsistent permits) on the ground that where changes in grazing permits "are required by land use planning, *the Bureau's authority is non-discretionary.*" 47 Fed.Reg. 41702, 41706 (1982) (emphasis supplied). Defendants were, therefore, aware that the new regulation was a radical departure from past practice. Defendants had shifted from an unwillingness to even make the obligation to modify, suspend, or cancel permits optional, to the about-face posture of proposing a far more sweeping dilution of the role of land use planning.

Despite the sweep of the new proposal, the level of criticism received, and the 180-degree policy turn, defendants limited their statement of basis and purpose to the following paragraph:

> A number of comments were received recommending retention
> of § 4120.2–1(c) which was proposed for deletion. Comments
> recommended retention to make it clear that under law, per-
> mits and leases are subject to land use plans and can be
> cancelled or modified. In the final rulemaking, § 4130.6–3 was
> added to provide for modification of permits and leases to meet
> the objectives of a land use plan allotment.

49 Fed.Reg. 6444 (February 21, 1984). If defendants' policy direction took a 180-degree turn, this statement provided 360-degrees of circular reasoning and no degree of explanation or justification. Absent from the statement is any response to objections to the elimination of authority to cancel or suspend permits when required by land use planning. Defendants' thinking regarding the wisdom of a discretionary rather than mandatory duty to maintain consistency between plans and permits is omitted. There is not a word spent explaining the need for monitoring data before action may be taken. Finally, there is evasion of *the fact*, not to mention explanation of the fact, that before promulgating this regulation defendants had perceived such a modification to be illegal.

Plaintiffs are entitled, therefore, to summary judgment on their APA claim regarding defendants' regulatory dilution of the role of land use plans in grazing administration. See 5 U.S.C. § 553(c).

* * *

NATIONAL WILDLIFE FEDERATION v. BURFORD
United States District Court, District of Columbia, 1985.
23 ERC 1609.

[The opinion is reproduced supra at page 265.]

NOTES

1. FLPMA § 1732(a) directs the BLM to manage "in accordance with" land use plans, and 16 U.S.C.A. § 1604(i) requires Forest Service management decisions to be "consistent with" land use plans. Should any distinction be drawn from the difference in wording?

2. Had the agency in *Hodel* been able to explain why it changed the regulations as it did, how should the court rule on the substantive challenges to them?

3. The court stated that "defendants are *bound* by land use plans" (original emphasis). Assuming that this statement is generally accepted, what implications does it hold for public rangeland management?

4. FLPMA § 1712 allows the agency to revise land use plans. Does NEPA apply to such modifications? If so, will an EA suffice? In Sierra Club v. Clark, 774 F.2d 1406 (9th Cir.1985), the BLM prepared an EIS on a plan modification to allow a motorcycle race.

5. The following case shows that in some areas of range regulation, it is still business as usual.

NATURAL RESOURCES DEFENSE COUNCIL, INC. v.
HODEL
United States District Court, District of Nevada, 1986.
624 F.Supp. 1045, appeal pending.

BURNS, J.

This is a complex case of first impression, brought by environmental organizations seeking to overturn certain decisions made by the

Bureau of Land Management (BLM) relating to livestock grazing on public lands in the Reno, Nevada area. The plaintiffs challenge the BLM's land use plan as being in conflict with Congressional statutory mandates, and as being arbitrary and capricious as a matter of administrative law. They also raise a variety of challenges to BLM's environmental impact statement which purports to evaluate its proposed plan in comparison to other alternatives.

* * *

The BLM lands are divided for grazing purposes into districts, and subdivided into planning areas, such as the "Reno Planning Area" which is the subject of this action. The Reno Planning Area encompasses an overall area of just over 5 million acres, about 700,000 of which are under BLM supervision. The planning areas are further divided into grazing allotments, for which the BLM issues grazing permits or licenses.

* * *

Pursuant to the decision in NRDC v. Morton [388 F.Supp. 829 (D.D.C.1974), supra at page 704] and [FLPMA and PRIA] the BLM undertook steps in the late 1970s to lay the groundwork for a comprehensive grazing management plan and EIS for the Reno area. The agency began gathering inventory data, listing the available resources in portions of the planning area. Agency specialists then began preparation of the Management Framework Plan (MFP), which is accomplished in three stages pursuant to agency regulations. At the first stage, or MFP I, individual planning recommendations were compiled and explained or justified based on substantive law or agency policies. At the next stage, MFP II, the agency attempted to identify and analyze resource conflicts between the various recommendations or uses. The MFP thus acts as a preliminary land use plan, striking some sort of balance among the competing pressures on the resources available. The MFP II for the Reno Planning Area was completed in mid-1981.

The MFP II then served as the "proposed action" with three other alternatives in terms of their environmental, economic, and social consequences. The plaintiffs herein took advantage of the opportunity to comment on the DEIS, and pointed out numerous perceived shortcomings. After purportedly considering these objections and considering the alternatives outlined, the BLM issued a Final Environmental Impact Statement (FEIS) which essentially incorporated the DEIS, and summarized the alternatives and predictions in tables. * * * The "proposed action" was then adopted as the MFP III, or final land use plan for grazing in the Reno planning area on December 21, 1982.

* * *

ANALYSIS

I. Violations of NEPA

 A. MFP Decision Preceded EIS Process

* * *

[P]laintiffs argue, in effect, that the BLM had decided that it liked the MFP III approach before it completed the NEPA/EIS process. In an ideal world, perhaps, agencies should refrain from any sort of policy decision until all environmental consequences have been fully analyzed. And perhaps the BLM can be validly criticized for operating in such a fashion in this case. But such policy-making criticisms do not rise to the level of NEPA violations, and none of the cases cited by plaintiffs so hold. I respectfully decline to indulge in the sort of administrative mind-reading that would be required under the theory advocated by plaintiffs in this section of their argument.

B. EIS Fails to Analyze Specific Proposals or Alternatives

* * *

The MFP II first categorized each of the approximately 55 grazing allotments in the Reno Area into one of three categories, based on an evaluation of each allotment's resources, potential, trend, and other factors outlined in Appendix K to the DEIS. The three categories are *Maintenance* ("M"), *Improvement* ("I"), and *Custodial* ("C"). Although the criteria are quite detailed, the basic features of the categories are as follows. In "M" allotments, the BLM feels that ecological conditions are adequate or improving, that present management policies are satisfactory, and no drastic changes are required over the status quo. In "I" allotments, the ecological condition is fair to poor, with a downward trend, there is the potential for improvement based on economically feasible measures, and present practices are not adequate to meet long term objectives. In "C" allotments, conditions are viewed as stable, but potential for improved productivity is limited, and there is little likelihood of cost-effective improvement.

The central feature of the MFP (which is the "proposed action" in the EIS) is to focus BLM efforts on the "I" category allotments. The plan calls for initially maintaining existing grazing levels for a period of about 5 years, and addressing problems on the "I" allotments through range improvements, grazing systems, and consultation with affected parties. This consultation and joint decision-making process is called Coordinated Resource Management and Planning, or CRMP in BLM jargon. The MFP also calls for further monitoring of the allotments so that adjustments in grazing levels, if necessary, can be undertaken at a later date. In the long term (beyond 5 years) the BLM plans to reduce grazing in the Reno Area by 30% (for livestock) and 20% overall (including all grazing species).

* * *

1. A Proper Grazing EIS Must Allocate Forage on Each Allotment

The general thrust of this argument is that the EIS must contain specific information as to each grazing allotment in the Reno planning area. Plaintiffs complain that the proposed action does not really describe specific, on-the-ground actions to be taken, but merely categorizes the allotments, and proposes that the BLM's main efforts will be focused on the "I" allotments. * * *

When fully considered, plaintiffs' argument here emerges as really a complaint against the vagueness of the MFP itself, and not so much as an indictment of the EIS under NEPA principles. It is true that the proposed action does not promise any specific measures will be taken by any particular dates. As described in the DEIS, the BLM intends to "continue to monitor", begin CRMP, propose possible adjustments in livestock levels, implement Allotment Management Plans (AMPS), and to implement grazing systems. All of these actions are, to some extent, hypothetical. The DEIS clearly explains the assumptions, including the assumption that the BLM will have the funding to carry out the specific actions eventually required under the MFP. Nevertheless, because the scope of the EIS is determined by the scope of the proposed action, it is unreasonable to expect the EIS to analyze possible actions in greater detail than is possible given the tentative nature of the MFP itself.

* * * Plaintiffs are really seeking an EIS for each allotment. A document addressing the ecological and other impacts for each set of permutations of stocking levels would be a completely unmanageable undertaking. * * *

* * *

2. *Range of Alternatives Addressed is Inadequate*

Plaintiffs [argue] that the four alternatives presented in the EIS do not constitute a wide enough range of alternatives. Plaintiffs observe that, in the short run, three of the alternatives studied are identical in the amount of forage allocated to livestock. Only one alternative, the so-called "resource protection alternative", calls for any reduction in livestock grazing within the first five years. And even under that alternative, only the "I" allotments would be affected; grazing levels would remain the same on "M" and "C" allotments.

* * *

Plaintiffs rely heavily on comparisons drawn between the facts of this case and California v. Block [690 F.2d 753 (9th Cir.1982), infra at page 1001.] * * * In that case a number of alternatives for classification of wilderness areas were discussed, but the overall range of *results* under the various alternatives was narrow: only 34% of the total area was allocated to wilderness under the most liberal of the alternatives. Plaintiffs attempt to analogize this case to *California v. Block* both in terms of the number of alternatives discussed, and in terms of the range of results discussed. (The most liberal alternative in this case contemplates only a 30% reduction in total forage consumption in the short term.) I find these arguments unpersuasive.

The scope of the program in *California v. Block* was enormous in its consequences compared with the proposed action in this case. The program in *California v. Block* involved classification of some 62 million acres of roadless land for wilderness or other purposes, including decisions that could potentially be irreversible if development were allowed to proceed on erstwhile roadless areas. In this case the BLM proposed only a very modest departure from the status quo, as de-

scribed earlier in this opinion. The land mass involved here is only
about 1% of the amount of acreage at issue in *Block*. The MFP calls
for ongoing adjustments in grazing levels through the CRMP process, to
prevent damage as conditions warrant. Plaintiffs are correct in observing that three of the alternatives studied call for the same level of
livestock use in the short run. They also correctly note that there is a
"spread" of only about 30 percent in forage consumption among all
alternatives. Nevertheless, I do not view these features as fatal under
a "rule of reason" standard, given the nature of the proposed action in
this case.

* * *

* * * NEPA should not be read as to require alternatives even
more extreme both in terms of monetary losses and job losses. Further,
as the allowable amount of grazing is decreased, the value of the
permits are also decreased, thus further reducing the funds available to
the BLM to pay for the necessary physical range improvements, which
are essential parts of all alternatives analyzed (except the No Action
alternative.) * * *

* * *

Plaintiffs finally argue, in this section of their motion, that the
BLM was under an obligation to at least consider an alternative that
attempts to redress the overall poor quality of the rangeland in the
planning area. They point out that under all alternatives nearly half
of the Reno area will remain in poor condition, and that "there will be
continued overuse of unprotected riparian habitat by livestock and/or
wild horses causing a decline in vegetation quality." * * *

* * * The "resource protection" alternative may not go as far as
plaintiff would wish in remedying range conditions, but it is not
reasonable to expect *any* feasible program to return all portions of the
Reno area to their prehistoric native condition. Moreover, the fact that
much of the area is expected to remain in "poor" condition does not
have any implications for the type of management. The "poor" label
refers only to the condition of the land relative to its "climax" ecological state, which is only a hypothetical and theoretical condition for
most of the public land under BLM supervision.

The fact that lands may be in a state below that of their aboriginal
pristine condition is content neutral for policy purposes. The important characteristic is whether the lands are producing at or near their
capacity, under multiple-use/sustained yield principles, as required by
FLPMA and PRIA. See 43 U.S.C. §§ 1712(c), 1903(b). This includes
productivity for livestock uses, which inherently involves a retreat from
the land's native condition or ecological climax state. Thus the arguments raised by plaintiffs in this regard, while factually correct, do not
represent NEPA violations. "Poor" ecological condition, as that term
is used by the BLM, does not necessarily mean that management
decisions or reasonable alternatives thereto have not accommodated the
competing pressures on public lands, or that insufficient attention is
being paid to environmental values.

3. EIS Should Have Considered a No-Grazing Alternative

Plaintiffs here argue that the BLM's internal policies, as well as CEQ regulations, required the BLM to include in the EIS an alternative analyzing the effects of a complete ban on livestock grazing within the Reno area. I find this argument lacks merit.

This argument must be evaluated against the historical background of the Reno planning area, and against the regulations and case authorities that discuss the scope of alternatives that must be included for an EIS to be valid. First, it is an indisputable fact that livestock grazing has been going on in the Reno planning area, on public lands, for more than a century. For better or worse, production of forage for livestock use is at least an important priority in the overall resource picture of this area. Second, the mandate of Congress in PRIA was that livestock use was to continue as an important use of public lands; they should be managed to maximize productivity for livestock and other specified uses. 43 U.S.C. § 1903. Third, NEPA does not require examination of alternatives that are so speculative, contrary to law, or economically catastrophic as to be beyond the realm of feasibility. The complete abandonment of grazing in the Reno planning area is practically unthinkable as a policy choice; it would involve monetary losses to the ranching community alone of nearly 4 million dollars and 290 jobs, not to mention unquantifiable social impacts. Of course, compared with the economy of the Reno area as a whole, ranching plays only a negligible role. Nevertheless, eliminating all grazing would have extreme impacts on this small community. A "no grazing" policy is simply not a "reasonable alternative" for this particular area.

* * *

Plaintiffs point to various informal agency memoranda and policy statements in their memorandum (PP. 37–38) indicating that the BLM would normally include a "no grazing" alternative in EISs. However, these promises are not enacted as agency regulations and the Bureau is legally free to change its mind, depending on how the political "wind blows" in Nevada and in the nation as a whole. See Dahl v. Clark, 600 F.Supp. 585 at 590 (D.Nev.1984).

* * *

4. Failure to Include Estimates of Carrying Capacity in EIS

Here again plaintiffs attack a lack of specificity in the EIS, this time concerning the absence of site-specific estimates of grazing capacity. Plaintiffs first observe that grazing permits are required to specify "the kind and number of livestock, the period(s) of use, the allotment(s) to be used, and the amount of use, in animal unit months, that can be made. * * *" 43 C.F.R. § 4120.2–1(a) (1982). * * *

The "proposed action" (as well as the "no action" and "maximization of livestock") alternatives each propose to continue previous levels of authorized livestock use. Although the gross figure is not broken down by allotments, it is necessarily true that the figure (43,973 AUMs) represents the BLM's estimated grazing capacity for the entire Reno area. This is true because it represents the total of all of the allotments' authorized livestock use, none of which may individually exceed capacity under current regulations. Because existing regulations assure that authorized grazing will not exceed carrying capacity, none of the alternatives analyzed will result in the "vegetative destruction and overall resource deterioration" that plaintiffs fear. Although the BLM will have to use site-specific data in adjusting livestock levels through the CRMP process under the MFP, it does not necessarily follow that such data must be analyzed in the EIS, in precisely the same detail. Again, the specificity of the EIS is governed by the proposed action; the EIS is not an administrative blueprint designed to allow the public to second-guess every possible future decision that the agency may have to make.

5. *EIS Does Not Adequately Describe the Proposed Action*

* * *

It is true that the DEIS does not explicitly detail the BLM's underlying reasoning, or forthrightly explain at any one place why the proposed action is felt to be superior to the other alternatives. This is perhaps confusing to the casual reader, who might observe that the proposed action is possibly more expensive than the "resource protection" alternative, results in less livestock grazing in the long run, and less overall improvement in ecological condition. Nevertheless, after a thorough and painstaking review of the EIS the reader understands that there are so many different tradeoffs and permutations of tradeoffs involved that no single explanation could fully justify every aspect of the MFP. The reader is left only with the impression that the BLM took its best cut at addressing the areas that it felt were in the most immediate need. It is also clear that subjective factors came into play, including the BLM's obvious desire to maintain for ranchers, what it describes (romantically perhaps) as a "preferred lifestyle." I believe that the DEIS adequately conveys to anyone who reads it in depth the reasons for (and the tradeoffs behind) the proposed action.[6]

I. *The MFP Allows Continued Resource Deterioration, Contrary to Statute*

* * *

A. *BLM Has Failed to Curtail Overgrazing*

Plaintiffs first correctly point to the legislative histories of the Taylor Grazing Act, FLPMA, and PRIA, to demonstrate Congress' general concern about overgrazing by livestock, and to indicate that

---

6. The "in depth" reading mentioned here may involve some reading "between the lines" of the DEIS. Why the agency would propose a course of action that can, with little effort, be seriously criticized as being more expensive, resulting in less long-run environmental improvement, and even less grazing in the long run can only be the source of speculation to the outsider. Certainly one obvious explanation is that the BLM performed an administrative policy pirouette under the baton of Secretary Watt around 1981, essentially deciding to postpone any grazing reductions indefinitely. See Dahl v. Clark, 600 F.Supp. 585, 589 (D.Nev.1984), discussed in more detail infra.

reductions in livestock levels were one of the methods mentioned by Congress to prevent further deterioration of rangelands. Plaintiffs then cite portions of the record, including the DEIS, which indicate that there has been overuse of some portions of the Reno area by livestock. The conclusion plaintiffs say should then follow is that BLM has violated the law, and that the relatively modest improvements predicted from the MFP are insufficient to comply with the statutory mandates.

The facts established by the enormous record in this case do show that there has been overgrazing in the Reno area, but that in only four allotments could it be *conclusively* determined that the overgrazing was due to livestock use. On eight allotments the overuse could have resulted from a combination of livestock, deer, and wild horses; on the three remaining allotments there was no livestock grazing whatsoever. Thus, overgrazing due to livestock was not endemic to the entire Reno area.

A second important point to note in this context is that even where overgrazing is found to exist, the remedy is not necessarily the immediate removal of livestock. I give due weight to the proposition put forth by defendants' experts that other methods, such as vegetation manipulation and seeding, fencing, water development, or other range improvements or grazing systems may serve to address problems of selective overgrazing without a mandatory reduction in livestock use. (See Heady and Spang affidavits *passim*.) While reductions in AUMS for livestock may be one accepted method of addressing range deterioration, as recognized by Congress (see 43 U.S.C. § 1903(b)), it is not the only method.

A third important point here concerns the quality of data available to the BLM for making livestock management decisions. * * * [T]he BLM reached the decision that in order to defend its actions against attack from ranching interests it would need a solid data base upon which to ground livestock reduction orders. * * * As explained by defendants' experts, in order for the BLM to be certain of the proper livestock carrying capacity of a given allotment the agency must have: (1) actual use data (what kinds of animals grazed where and for how long), (2) how much vegetation has been consumed (utilization data), and (3) the overall effect of the specified grazing (trend). (See Spang Affidavit p. 11). The BLM said it lacked the first type of data for much of the Reno area and felt (at least after 1981) that in its absence it should refrain from immediate changes in livestock numbers, and concentrate its efforts on other techniques of range management.

Plaintiffs claim that the BLM is allowing overgrazing to continue. In reality, however, their complaint is with the *methods* selected by the BLM to allocate the resources within its control. Rather than immediate reductions in livestock numbers, the BLM chose to install range improvements and grazing systems on the areas ("I" allotments) that the BLM says are in need of the greatest attention. Moreover, the MFP does call for a significant reduction in livestock numbers, although this is to take place over a longer period of time than plaintiffs insist on. Finally, the MFP is predicted to bring about an overall improvement in the rated quality of many of the allotments. In sum, it is not entirely certain that the BLM has allowed continued overgrazing or deterioration of resources, in violation of statutory mandates.

B. PRIA Claims: Rangeland Improvement

The converse argument is also put forward by plaintiffs in this section of their case, namely that the BLM is violating the affirmative mandates of PRIA by failing to assure the *improvement* of the public rangelands. As noted immediately above, however, the MFP does result in limited improvements in overall ecological and forage conditions in the Reno area. Plaintiffs characterize the BLM's management as "do nothing", but in reality it appears that the real argument is that the BLM does not do what plaintiffs want, namely redress range conditions through immediate reduction or elimination of livestock grazing.

It must be noted that it is yet too early for a court to evaluate a claim that the BLM has not complied with its own plan, or that it has not taken the steps promised in the MFP. * * *

Plaintiffs argue that FLPMA and PRIA provide "standards" against which the court can determine whether the MFP is "arbitrary, capricious or contrary to law." The declarations of policy and goals in 43 U.S.C. §§ 1701(a), 1732, 1901, 1903 and ancillary provisions contain only broad expressions of concern and desire for improvement. They are general clauses and phrases which "can hardly be considered concrete limits upon agency discretion. Rather, it is language which 'breathes discretion at every pore.'" Perkins v. Bergland, 608 F.2d at 806. Although I might privately agree with plaintiffs that a more aggressive approach to range improvement would be environmentally preferable, or might even be closer to what Congress had in mind, the Ninth Circuit has made it plain that "the courts are not at liberty to break the tie choosing one theory of range management as superior to another." Perkins v. Bergland, 608 F.2d at 807. The modest plans adopted by the BLM for dealing with range conditions in the Reno area are not "irrational" and thus cannot be disturbed by the court.

III. The MFP's Failure to Allocate Forage Violates FLPMA and PRIA

The real question posed in this section of the case is what are BLM land use plans supposed to look like? That is, what kind of detail must the MFP contain to qualify as a legitimate land use plan required by Congress? FLPMA and PRIA refer to the importance of land use planning in several places. See 43 U.S.C. §§ 1701(a)(2), 1712, 1732(a), 1901(b). But nowhere in the statutes did Congress describe in detail what sort of information must be included in a land use plan.

* * *

* * * It is therefore a reasonable assumption that Congress intended the BLM to continue its practice of setting grazing capacity at

the permit-decision stage, and that land use planning (as required by 43 U.S.C. § 1712) deal with broader issues. These broader issues might include long-term resource conflicts, long-term range trends, planning of range improvements, and concentrating the BLM's limited resources on certain key areas.

This is the type of planning adopted by the BLM in this case. Clearly, the agency will continue to set grazing capacity on an on-going basis when it issues or renews grazing permits or licenses. A land use plan need not encompass every localized decision that must be made in the foreseeable future. Indeed, the legislative history indicates that Congress recognized "land use planning as dynamic and subject to change with changing conditions and values."

The present BLM regulations cited by plaintiffs do not compel a contrary interpretation. * * * BLM district managers * * * know that after the first five years they must begin reducing livestock AUMs to meet the 30,618 level they have set as a long term goal, and that total consumption must not exceed 59,344 AUMs for all species. If they fail to take these long term limits into account in issuing grazing permits after the first five years of the plan then they may be liable to an enforcement action by plaintiffs, or others with a similarly deep concern for the environment.

* * * FLPMA and PRIA demand no more. The type of "planning" envisioned by plaintiffs, wherein the plan would effectively contain allotment management plans for each unit in the Reno area, allocating forage to each consumer species for each of the next ten years or more, is not a plan. It is an administrative straight-jacket which eliminates the room for any flexibility to meet changing conditions. In the absence of more directive legislation, or mandate from my appellate superiors, I will not command such a requirement. * * *

IV. Failure to Utilize Available Resource Data

* * *

Defendant's * * * affidavits * * * are persuasive in refuting the notion that there is such a thing as an *a priori* "carrying capacity" or grazing capacity for any one piece of land. Consider a hypothetical allotment which could support 100 head of cattle in one year, and not show signs of downward trend. However, in the following year, depending on only one variable such as climate the same allotment could perhaps support only 80 head. Cf. Hinsdale Livestock Co. v. United States, 501 F.Supp. 773, 777 (D.Mont.1980). Conversely, with the addition of certain range improvements that would improve dispersal of the livestock on the allotment, the same parcel could in the following year perhaps support 120 head without signs of deterioration. Each of these permutations could be further affected by other variables such as usage by wild horses, or mule deer, precipitation or temperature patterns, seeding, encroachment of inferior types of forage, changes in seasons of use, and so on. Unrealistic, then, is plaintiffs' theory that there is a fixed and immutable level of acceptable livestock use that can be administratively determined for years into the future.

* * *

Although the BLM had trend data for most of the area, such data alone is not useful for setting livestock grazing levels because a declining trend can be due to a wide number of factors, only one of which is overuse by livestock. * * *

Because of these and other difficulties, the BLM decided to revamp its methodology of setting grazing levels, based primarily on continued monitoring over longer periods of time, and not based on one-point-in-time studies such as [the Soil and Vegetation Inventory Method]. A new monitoring system for Nevada was developed by a joint task force and was adopted in 1981. It is a coincidence that this change in methodology took place around the time that Mr. Watt became Secretary of the Interior, and the ultimate result of the decision was the continuation of existing grazing levels in the Reno area. But there is no direct evidence in this record that the change in methodology was primarily prompted by a political decision to postpone any adjustments in allocation that would adversely affect ranching interests.

* * *

* * * If it were possible to glean more precise standards from the statutes or regulations, against which these policy decisions could be measured, then I might be more able to discern a pattern of illegal or arbitrary conduct, and to fashion appropriate relief. That is not the case before me. * * * The administrative record in this case does at least contain plausible support for defendants' position that existing monitoring data for the Reno area was not reliable for purposes of setting fixed grazing levels. While the BLM probably *could* have made defensible livestock adjustments where their data showed overutilization, poor range condition, and downward trend, this court cannot say it was "irrational" for them to refrain from doing so without the sort of monitoring data they desired. At this point, judicial inquiry is at an end.

* * *

CONCLUSION

* * *

After considerable thought and deliberation, I have come to the conclusion that the role plaintiffs would have me play in this controversy is an unworkable one. Plaintiffs are understandably upset at what they view to be a lopsided and ecologically insensitive pattern of management of public lands at the hands of the BLM, a subject explored at length by many commentators. Congress attempted to remedy this situation through FLPMA, PRIA and other acts, but it has done so with only the broadest sorts of discretionary language, which does not provide helpful standards by which a court can readily adjudicate agency compliance.

Boiled down and stripped of legalese[8] this is a case in which plaintiffs ask me to become—and defendants urge me not to become—

---

8. This litigation has brought forth a confounding number of acronyms such as FLPMA, PRIA, SVIM, URA, AMP, and CRMP (pronounced either "cramp,"

the rangemaster for about 700,000 acres of federal lands in western Nevada. For some reason, over the past 15 years or so, I and many of my Article III colleagues have become or have been implored to become forestmasters (Miller v. Mallery, 410 F.Supp. 1283 (D.Or.1976)), roadmasters (Ventling v. Bergland, 479 F.Supp. 174 (D.S.D.1979)), schoolmasters (Anderson v. Central Point School District, 554 F.Supp. 600 (D.Or.1982)), fishmasters (Washington Trollers Association v. Kreps, 466 F.Supp. 309 (W.D.Wash.1979)), prisonmasters, (Capps v. Atiych, 495 F.Supp. 802 (D.Or.1980), 559 F.Supp. 894 (D.Or.1982), watermasters (Sierra Club v. Andrus, 610 F.2d 581 (9th Cir.1979)), and the like. This trend has not escaped the notice and criticism of academic commentators.

That criticism has been based upon observations which include lack of training and expertise, lack of time, lack of staff assistance, and similar conditions. At bottom, however, the primary reason for the large scale intrusion of the judiciary into the governance of our society has been an inability or unwillingness of the first two branches of our governments—both state and federal—to fashion solutions for significant societal, environmental, and economic problems in America. Frankly, I see little likelihood that the legislative and executive branches will take the statutory (and occasional constitutional) steps which would at least slow, if not reverse, this trend. Fortunately, for reasons set out in this opinion which (to me) are legally correct, I am able to resist the invitation to become western Nevada's rangemaster.

* * *

NOTES

1. Read 43 U.S.C.A. §§ 1752 and 1903 in the Statutory Supplement. Assuming that some of the range deterioration adverted to by Judge Burns is demonstrably caused by livestock overgrazing, do plaintiffs have available good substantive arguments? If this decision is affirmed, is there any point to BLM planning? What is it?

2. Is the "no-grazing" alternative really "unthinkable"? Does it depend on whether you focus on local economic effects, which could be substantial, or on national economic effects, which likely would be close to zero? Again assuming proof of overgrazing, who should bear the brunt of correcting the situation? Are effects from overgrazing—such as erosion—on lands and waters outside the grazing district relevant in judicial review of the plan?

3. Judge Burns purports to apply a "rule of reason" in his NEPA analysis. Is this rule anything more than a statement of an individual judge's opinion or bias? Even if you answer in the affirmative, is there any realistic alternative judicial approach?

4. The court obviously was very reluctant to assume the task of monitoring BLM planning and management, citing, inter alia, the *Washington Trollers* case. In Washington v. Washington State Com-

"crimp," or "crump") and MFP (which I assure the reader is unpronounceable.)

mercial Passenger Fishing Vessel Ass'n, 443 U.S. 658 (1979), the Supreme Court agreed that, under the circumstances of the State's obdurate refusal to implement and comply with the law, the trial court was justified in assuming the role of "fishmaster" for Puget Sound to protect Indian fishing rights. Should the court's decision whether or not to become a "rangemaster" depend on whether the agency is implementing and complying with the law? On the seriousness of the abuses? On the complexity of the situation?

4. THE WILD, FREE–ROAMING HORSES AND BURROS ACT OF 1971

Wild horses and burros are not wildlife. Instead, they are feral, meaning that they are descended from the domesticated animals that escaped from the Spaniards long ago or from ranchers recently. Many westerners have long considered them pests that should be killed for dog food. In an unreported 1968 lawsuit to protect the remnants of the once vast herds of horses, a judge was bemused over attempting to "define Constitutional due process for a herd of mustangs." M. Bean, THE EVOLUTION OF NATIONAL WILDLIFE LAW 168–69 (1977). The judge could not do so, but Congress did.

Passage of the Wild Free-Roaming Horses and Burros Act of 1971 (WF–RHBA), 16 U.S.C.A. §§ 1331–40, was spurred by the efforts of thousands of school children appalled at the indiscriminate slaughter, and the Act is widely condemned as the product of mindless emotionalism. To the extent the Act was intended to increase populations of the feral ungulates, it is perhaps unique among wildlife statutes because it has been an unqualified, rapid success. Aside from Kleppe v. New Mexico, 426 U.S. 529 (1976), supra at page 194, upholding the Act as it applied to federal lands, the implementation of the WF–RHBA and litigation under it have been concerned with coping with alleged surpluses. All in all, it has not been a pretty story.

AMERICAN HORSE PROTECTION ASS'N, INC. v. FRIZZELL

United States District Court, District of Nevada, 1975.
403 F.Supp. 1206.

ROGER D. FOLEY, Chief Judge.

Plaintiff filed this action on July 23, 1975, in the United States District Court for the District of Columbia, seeking declaratory and injunctive relief against the various federal defendants concerning a proposed Bureau of Land Management (BLM) round up of wild horses in Stone Cabin Valley, Nevada. On July 24, 1975, the district court in the District of Columbia granted defendants' motion for a change of venue and ordered that the action be moved to the United States District Court for the District of Nevada.

* * *

FACTS

The Stone Cabin Valley contains about 385,000 acres of land (encompassing an area of approximately 600 square miles) and is located in central Nevada, about 25 miles east of Tonopah, Nevada. About 99% of the land is National Resource Land, within an established BLM grazing district; the remaining 1% is under private ownership. The land may be characterized as predominantly desert, with vegetation consisting of big sagebrush, black sagebrush, saltbrush, greasewood, and playa. At the higher elevations along the mountain ranges which border the Valley, vegetation consisting of pinion-juniper woodland is present.

Several desert land entry farms have been located in the Valley, but only one is active. Three cattle operations use the grazing unit, with about 2400 head consuming about 15,400 Animal Unit Months (AUMs) per year. A 1959 range survey showed production of vegetation in the Valley at 19,782 AUMs per year. Of these, 2,011 AUMs were reserved for wildlife and 17,771 AUMs for livestock. Since licensed livestock grazing use is 15,400 AUMs, about 2,300 AUMs remain uncommitted or available for wild horses.

Estimates of the number of wild horses in Stone Cabin Valley range from a figure of 200–300 (provided by plaintiff based on an aerial count conducted in June, 1975) to BLM estimates of 1000–1200 (based on statistically-computed estimates, using an 18% per year rate of increase). * * * This Court finds that the estimates of Dr. Kitchen and those of the BLM support a population of wild horses ranging from 900–1200 currently in Stone Cabin Valley.

Almost all of the material presented to this Court indicates that there is a serious overgrazing problem in the Stone Cabin Valley. * * * The primary dispute regarding range condition, then, is over how the deterioration has been caused, and not over the fact that the range is in poor condition.

Faced with the problem of a deteriorating range in Stone Cabin Valley, BLM officials in Nevada began exploring ways to preserve the range. In the fall of 1974, these officials settled on a proposal to remove approximately 400 wild horses deemed to be in excess of the 1971 population. On January 10, 1974, BLM's proposal to gather wild horses was submitted in final form * * *. On May 30, 1975, BLM Director Curt Berklund authorized the gathering and removal of about 400 excess wild free-roaming horses from the Stone Cabin Valley. * * *

BLM officials in Nevada prepared an Environmental Analysis Record (EAR) on the proposed round up as an interim program of range protection.[2] This report was signed on May 15, 1975, concluding that

---

2. The defendants do not contend, and this Court does not find, that the EAR meets the requirements of an environmen- tal impact statement under the National Environmental Policy Act (NEPA), 42 U.S. C.A. § 4332(2)(C).

* * * none of the alternative proposals discussed in this analysis constitute a major federal action significantly affecting the quality of the human environment and that an environmental impact statement will not be required for any alternative selected.

Five alternative actions were considered: (1) No action; (2) Delay action until the Tonopah Management Framework Plan (MFP) is revised (the revision is expected to be completed sometime in fiscal year 1977); (3) Remove 400 wild horses from Stone Cabin Valley; (4) Remove cattle by a number sufficient to reduce grazing demand to the 1971 level; and (5) Remove equal numbers of horses and livestock to reach the 1971 level of grazing demand. At the time the EAR was signed, the BLM officials in Nevada had already submitted their proposal to implement alternative (3) to BLM officials in Washington; the wild horse round up was awaiting approval by defendant Mr. Berklund, which came on May 30, 1975.

* * *

The round up began as scheduled. BLM has argued that the round up must proceed now before the cold and wet winter begins, since the method being used is not effective during such weather.[4] BLM estimates that the round up of 400 horses will take approximately six to eight weeks to complete. Since its beginning on September 10, more than 100 horses have been captured, according to BLM sources.

* * *

Violations of the Wild Horses' Act. Plaintiff argues that the BLM is violating its duties to manage and protect wild horses under the Wild Horses' Act, 16 U.S.C.A. § 1331 et seq. Defendants argue that wide discretion has been given to the Secretaries of Interior and Agriculture in managing wild horse populations, and that, under 5 U.S.C.A. § 701(a)(2), the round up is action committed by law to agency discretion and beyond judicial review. * * *

Defendant refers to 16 U.S.C.A. § 1333(b) (Section 3(b) of the Wild Horses' Act) as giving the Secretary the discretion to conduct this round up. This section reads:

(b) Where an area is found to be overpopulated, the Secretary, after consulting with the Advisory Board, may order old, sick, or lame animals to be destroyed in the most humane manner possible, and *he may cause additional excess wild free-roaming horses and burros to be captured and removed for private maintenance* under humane conditions and care. (emphasis added)

The regulations reinforce this grant of discretion to the Secretary:

4. The method being used is termed "water trapping". A corral is constructed which encircles a watering hole used by the horses. A man hiding in a blind nearby closes the corral gate whenever horses enter to use the water hole. The trapped horses are then transported to a holding corral, where medical tests and administrative tasks are performed. The horses are kept for a period of three or four weeks in the holding corral, pending the test results. * * *

(a) The authorized officer may relocate wild free-roaming horses and burros on public lands when he determines such action is necessary to: (1) Relieve overgrazed areas, * * * or (4) achieve other purposes deemed to be in the interest of proper resource and herd management * * * 43 C.F.R. § 4712.3–2(a). * * *

That the Wild Horses' Act gives a great deal of discretion to the Secretary is clear from the legislative history of the Act:

It should be pointed out that the Secretaries of Interior and Agriculture are given a high degree of discretionary authority for the purposes of protection, management, and control of wild free-roaming horses and burros on the public lands. The Act provides the administrative tools for protection of the animals from depredation by man. This is the paramount responsibility with which the Secretaries are charged under the terms of the statute. 1971 U.S.Code Cong. & Admin.News, p. 2160.

Thus, defendants' contention is well-founded that BLM and its authorized officers have discretion to order and conduct a round up in Stone Cabin Valley. But the Court feels that the grant of discretion in the Wild Horses' Act is not so broad so that there is no law to apply in this case. The BLM does have discretion in determining whether an area is overpopulated, whether to reduce the population by removing excess wild horses, and whether to place those excess wild horses on public lands or in the custody of private individuals. The Secretary even has discretion to destroy wild horses when "in his judgment such action is necessary to preserve and maintain the habitat in a suitable condition for continued use." 16 U.S.C.A. § 1333(c). But apart from those discretionary powers, the Secretary must proceed with his decisions "under humane conditions and care" and "in the most humane manner possible." Clearly, the Secretary does not have discretion to choose an inhumane manner of capturing and distributing excess wild horses. Section 1333(a) of Title 16 provides a further mandatory duty: "The Secretary is * * * directed to protect and manage wild free-roaming horses and burros as components of the public lands." Therefore, despite the broad discretion given to the Secretary, the Wild Horses' Act does contain some law to apply: is the Stone Cabin Valley round up a violation of the Secretary's duty to protect wild horses? Is this round up being conducted under humane conditions and care and in the most humane manner possible? The Court finds that the discretionary function exception to judicial review under the APA does not apply here; since judicial review under the APA is available, 5 U.S.C.A. § 706 provides the standard of review to be applied to this BLM action.

As discussed above, the applicable standard of review for the claimed violations of the Wild Horses' Act is whether BLM's actions are arbitrary, capricious, an abuse of discretion, or otherwise not in accordance with law. 5 U.S.C.A. § 706(2)(A). Defendants are clearly within the scope of their authority under the provisions of 16 U.S.C.A. § 1333 quoted above. On the affidavits and other matter submitted by both parties, this Court cannot conclude that the BLM round up decision is arbitrary and capricious.

The facts show that a seriously overgrazed range cannot continue to supply all of the needs for food placed on it by the various users: cattle, wild horses, and other wildlife. Wise range management techniques dictate that a given area must be restricted in use to those numbers that can be supported adequately and still allow the range to replenish its vegetation. The eventual result of an overused range is the complete destruction of that range, with so little vegetation that none of the users can survive on it. Consistent with the Secretary's duty to protect the wild horses, then, is management of the range in a manner designed to protect the habitat of the wild horses. Stone Cabin Valley is endangered because of overgrazing; BLM's decision to remove less than one-half of the wild horses in the Valley to reduce grazing pressures is arguably in the best interests of the remaining wild horses. This Court cannot say that the decision was arbitrary or capricious or in violation of BLM's duty to protect wild horses.

In a similar manner, BLM's decision to use the water trap method to capture the wild horses cannot be deemed arbitrary or capricious or in violation of BLM's duty to conduct round ups in the most humane manner possible. As discussed above, defendant Berklund's affidavit claims that a round up by helicopter is the most humane manner, but this method is not possible, in view of 18 U.S.C.A. § 47. [Eds: But see later-enacted 16 U.S.C.A. § 1378.] BLM has tried to accommodate various groups interested in the humane treatment of these horses; barbed wire is not being used, nor is the tranquilizer Sucostran. BLM has solicited the assistance of Wild Horse Annie's organization, WHOA!, and the National Wild Horse Association, and comments and suggestions from plaintiff have been considered by BLM officials. The Court finds that the round up is being conducted in the most humane manner possible, and that there is no violation of defendants' duties in this regard under the Wild Horses' Act. Plaintiff has not shown that this round up or any aspect of it constitutes a clear violation of the Wild Horses' Act which would enable this Court to conclude that plaintiff is likely to prevail on the merits of this contention.

Violations of NEPA. Plaintiff alleges that defendants should have filed an environmental impact statement (EIS) prior to making the decision to round up 400 wild horses in Stone Cabin Valley. * * * The problem in this case is that there is no procedure required by law for BLM's decision not to file an EIS, against which its decision can be measured.

* * * Since this Court finds that this round up of 400 horses in Stone Cabin Valley at this time will not have a *significant* effect on the Stone Cabin environment, an EIS was not required here; the Court does not decide whether the round up fits any of the other § 4332(2)(C) elements.

The BLM's Environmental Analysis Record (EAR) identifies several components of the Stone Cabin Valley ecosystem, including aquatic and terrestrial plant life, animal life (including horses, livestock, and wildlife), and the landscape character. Removing the wild horses will also involve other elements of the Stone Cabin environment, including air quality, water supply, land use compatibility, and various human interests such as cultural, historical, educational, and scientific values.

The Court has determined that removing 400 wild horses from Stone Cabin Valley at this time will not have a significant effect on any of the elements of the environment mentioned above. The removal of the horses will temporarily stabilize the vegetation in the Valley. The remaining horses, cattle, and other wildlife will have a slightly easier time finding adequate food. The air quality, water supply, and land use compatibility will be slightly improved. Since about 600 horses will remain in the Valley, the human cultural, historical, educational, and scientific interests will be preserved. * * * This may have been a different case had plaintiff been able to satisfy the Court that the proposed round up would extinguish the wild horse population in Stone Cabin Valley.

The overall effect of this round up will be to stabilize the range temporarily; the effect on the Stone Cabin environment, if any, will be a slight improvement in the quality of the range. This will have a positive effect on the other elements of the area, including the remaining wild horses.[10] * * *

* * *

Allegations of abuse of discretion. In analyzing plaintiff's contentions regarding arbitrary and capricious BLM action, apart from the alleged violations of the Wild Horses' Act discussed above, two major aspects of the BLM action are alleged to be arbitrary and capricious: (1) the decision that the land was overgrazed; and (2) the decision to resolve the overgrazing by rounding up wild horses, rather than removing cattle from the range.

The primary thrust of plaintiff's argument regarding the first aspect is that observations of the Stone Cabin Valley in June and July, 1975, show that the range is in good condition and not overgrazed. Plaintiff's expert, Dr. Kitchen, however, acknowledges that the range is

---

10. This Court is not saying that the BLM is free to round up wild horses whenever a particular range has an overgrazing problem. Nor is the Court saying that every time the removal of wild horses will have a limited, slightly positive effect on the environment of the range, the BLM can proceed to remove a certain number of those horses. BLM officials admit that more round-ups of wild horses may be necessary in the future. This Court decides only that the Stone Cabin Valley round up currently underway may continue as an interim measure to preserve the range until the EIS required by Judge Flannery is filed in 1977. This Court presumes that future round ups will be undertaken only after the data contained in the 1977 EIS has been evaluated and all other alternative actions have been considered, as required by NEPA. In other words, this opinion should not be read as giving the BLM a blank check to order the removal of wild horses without filing an impact statement whenever it determines that a range is overgrazed. In this case, this Court has determined that the removal of 400 horses from Stone Cabin Valley at this time will not have a significant effect on the quality of the human environment in that Valley.

in poor condition now as compared to fifty years ago, arguing that at this point, another year or two of grazing by the existing wild horses, cattle, and other wildlife will not have a substantial effect on the range. Defendants' experts argue that the range may look good to a layman after a favorable spring of precipitation, but that the overall condition remains extremely poor. Defendants' experts feel that immediate action is necessary to preserve the range. On the basis of these expert opinions that the range is in poor condition, this Court cannot say that the BLM decision that the range was overgrazed and that some remedial action was necessary was arbitrary, capricious, or an abuse of BLM discretion.

Plaintiff's contention that the decision to solve the overgrazing problem by removing wild horses was arbitrary is based on the assertion that wild horses were given a higher priority on the public lands than other grazers under the Wild Horses' Act. The only statutory or regulatory support for this assertion is at 43 C.F.R. § 4712.1-4: "Closures to livestock grazing":

> The authorized officer may close public lands to use by all or a particular class of domestic livestock where he finds it necessary to allocate all available forage to, or to satisfy other biological requirements of, wild free-roaming horses or burros.

>   *   *   *

The Court does not read this regulation as giving wild horses an exalted status on the public range. The regulation would seem to apply to a situation where wild horses and burros were in danger of extinction; the remedy of restricting a public range for the sole use of one element of the ecosystem would seem to be a last-resort type of measure.

To so restrict the public range to one user would also violate the BLM's statutory mandate to administer the public lands under its control in accordance with the principles of multiple use and sustained yield of the several products and services obtainable on those lands. See 43 U.S.C.A. §§ 1411–1418. The regulations of the Wild Horses' Act expressly refer to the policies of this Act (the Classification and Multiple Use Act) as applying to wild horses. 43 C.F.R. § 4710.0–6.

This Court feels that the sounder view is that neither wild horses nor cattle possess any higher status than the other on the public lands. The regulations under the Classification and Multiple Use Act provide:

> *No overall priority is assigned* [by the Act] or by the Secretary *to any specific use.* The Secretary or his delegate will authorize under applicable authority, that use or combination of uses which will best achieve the objectives of multiple use, taking into consideration all pertinent factors, including, but not limited to, ecology, existing uses, and the relative values of the various resources in particular areas. 43 C.F.R. § 1725.3–1. (emphasis added)

>   *   *   *

From these statutes and regulations, it appears that the public lands should be administered under the multiple use-sustained yield concept; management decisions should not be made after giving a priority to a particular user, but only after taking into account all of the various elements of the ecosystem involved.

Under the multiple use-sustained yield concept, then, the BLM had various alternatives available to them to alleviate the overgrazing on Stone Cabin Valley. The Wild Horses' Act gives the Secretary authority to remedy overgrazing by removing wild horses. 16 U.S.C.A. § 1333(b); 43 C.F.R. §§ 4712.3–2(a), 4712.3–2(b). Under the Taylor Grazing Act, 43 U.S.C.A. §§ 315–315o–1, the Secretary has the authority to restrict livestock grazing on overgrazed land within established grazing districts such as Stone Cabin Valley. 43 C.F.R. § 4115.2–1(d)(5); 43 C.F.R. § 4125.1–1(i)(8). The decision to remove some of the wild horses is not so contrary to the statutory authority, or so out of line with the principles of multiple use and sustained yield, that this Court can find it to be arbitrary or capricious. Had the BLM decided to remove 400 cattle from the Valley, this Court would probably reach the same conclusion: that decision would not be arbitrary or capricious, requiring this Court to set it aside.[12]

* * *

CONCLUSION

Plaintiff has not shown a sufficient likelihood of success on the merits of this action to justify the issuance of a preliminary injunction. Therefore, the round up of 400 wild horses in Stone Cabin Valley may continue, and the BLM may implement its planned distribution of captured wild horses to private individual applicants. Plaintiff's motion for a preliminary injunction is denied. * * *

NOTES

1. Should it have been significant that the Classification and Multiple Use Act, relied upon the principal case, had expired several years before the case arose?

2. What precisely was the purpose of the roundup, if not significantly to affect the quality of the environment?

3. Does the roundup regulation quoted follow from the Wild Horses statute? What is the difference between a "paramount responsibility" to protect the "animals from depredations by man" and an "exalted status" for the animals? Does the BLM have any obligation independent of the WF–RHBA to protect and preserve wild horses on the public lands?

4. In the Public Rangelands Improvement Act of 1978, Congress amended the WF–RHBA, 16 U.S.C.A. §§ 1332, 1333, and 1378, to guide and facilitate roundups of excess horses and burros.

5. Compare American Horse Protection Association, Inc. v. Kleppe, 6 E.L.R. 20802 (D.D.C. Sept. 9, 1976) (Challis Roundup), a case

12. The Court notes that the cattle ranchers using the Stone Cabin Valley have voluntarily agreed to reduce the numbers of cattle using the range. This agreement is designed to lessen the pressures on the range vegetation by the same factor as the removal of 400 wild horses.

very similar on its facts. The court held that an EIS was required, and found, inter alia, that one of the alternatives to wild horse capture which must be considered by the BLM is decreasing the amount of livestock grazing on the BLM ranges to increase the available forage for wild horses. The court in the *Challis* case also controverted every major holding in the *Stone Cabin Valley* case:

> 2.   The mandate of § 3(a) of the Wild Free-Roaming Horses and Burros Act of 1971, 16 U.S.C.A. § 1331(a), that "[a]ll management activities *shall* be at the minimal feasible level * * * *" requires at a minimum that before any roundup or other significant management activity is undertaken, careful and detailed consideration must be given to *all* alternative courses of action that would have a less severe impact on the wild horse population, and such careful and detailed consideration of alternatives was not shown to have been employed by the defendants here.

> 3.   The alternative of restricting livestock grazing on the critical winter range areas is such an alternative as described in Conclusion 2, supra, and would permit more horses to remain in the Challis Region and would thus result in a lower level of management activity.

> 4.   This alternative of restricting livestock grazing on the winter range areas is viable and should have been considered by the defendants, particularly in light of the mandate of the Wild Horse Act.

> 5.   The failure to give this alternative the full and careful consideration required by the Act renders the proposed roundup plan "arbitrary, capricious, an abuse of discretion, [and] otherwise not in accordance with" the clear mandate of the Act to keep all management activities at the minimum feasible level. 5 U.S.C. § 706(2)(A).

> 6.   The defendants' determination that the Challis Region is "overpopulated" and thus requires removal of some 130–260 wild horses was based on inadequate data. Moreover, the court finds that no reliable up-to-date population inventories were conducted and that the formula for projecting present herd size on the basis of the 1975 inventory utilized a reproduction ratio which is unsupported by, and in direct contradiction to, the credible evidence presented to the court. Accordingly, the determination of the number of horses to be removed in the roundup plan was arbitrary and capricious, and the decision to proceed with the roundup on the basis of this inadequate data base was and is an abuse of discretion by the defendants.

> 7.   The defendants' failure to give adequate consideration in either the Challis Wild Horse Management Plan or in the Environmental Analysis Record to other less drastic means of population control also renders the proposed roundup arbitra-

ry, capricious, an abuse of discretion, and contrary to the mandate of the Wild Free-Roaming Horses and Burros Act of 1971.

8. The decision by defendants not to have professional veterinary assistance on-site at all times during the roundup and the failure of defendants to develop contingency plans for veterinary assistance in case of unforeseen circumstances during the roundup renders the proposed roundup plan arbitrary.

In a later opinion in the same litigation, the appellate court held that the 1978 amendments allowed the BLM to take action without in-depth consideration of some alternatives required by the district court. AHPA v. Watt, 694 F.2d 1310 (D.C.Cir.1982). See generally Buckley & Buckley, Straying Wild Horses and the Range Landowner: The Search for Peaceful Coexistence, 4 Pub.Land L.Rev. 29 (1983).

6. In the Howe Massacre litigation, AHPA v. Dept. of the Interior, 551 F.2d 432 (D.C.Cir.1977), Idaho ranchers had conducted their own roundup, resulting in the death or mutilation of many of the animals. The court held that such lawlessness could not be validated by a state official's sham declaration that all of the horses were privately owned: the final decision on ownership, the court ruled, is vested in the federal agency. Compare Sheridan v. Andrus, 465 F.Supp. 662 (D.Colo.1979).

7. In the Palamino Valley Roundup case, AHPA v. Andrus, 460 F.Supp. 880 (D.Nev.1978), rev'd, 608 F.2d 811 (9th Cir.1979), the Nevada District Court again upheld a massive series of roundups in six Nevada grazing districts. The BLM planned to remove 3500 to 7000 horses annually. Conditions at the first roundup were at best atrocious, and the holding corral area was said to resemble an equine Buchenwald. The court admonished defendants that "such wholesale slaughter of animals (especially horses) is considered by many to be degrading to the human spirit and inappropriate conduct for a civilized human being." Nevertheless, relying on the *Stone Cabin Valley* decision, supra, the court viewed the roundups as authorized and justified: "inferentially, the population [of herds] at around the 1971 level should be maintained [under the act]." 460 F.Supp. at 885. Relying on NRDC v. Morton, 388 F.Supp. 829 (1974), supra at page 704, the court further opined that questions of NEPA compliance had been confided to the District of Columbia court. The Court of Appeals reversed and remanded, holding that the NEPA question was not usurped.

MOUNTAIN STATES LEGAL FOUNDATION v. CLARK

United States Court of Appeals, Tenth Circuit, 1984.
740 F.2d 792, order vacated, 765 F.2d 1468 (1985).

SETH, Chief Judge.

The complaint of plaintiffs, who are owners of grazing lands, brought this action against the Secretary of Interior and the United States for the unconstitutional taking, without condemnation proceedings, of forage on their private lands. This taking, it is alleged, resulted from the failure by the defendants to manage herds of wild horses contrary and in violation of the Wild Free-Roaming Horses and Burros Act, 16 U.S.C. § 1331 et seq. Mandamus is sought to require defendants to remove the horses from plaintiffs' lands. Also substantial damages were sought against the Secretary of Interior and other officials for willfully preventing the proper management of the horses under the Act to the damage of plaintiffs.

This case concerns grazing in the southwestern part of Wyoming known as the checkerboard. * * * In the area in question, which is about 115 miles long and 40 miles wide, the Rock Springs Grazing Association composed of a group of ranchers owns or leases the private lands. The area, of course, generally follows the railroad. The land is described as high desert, the forage is very limited, the area is sensitive to overuse, and there are few if any fences to mark property lines. The Grazing Association has been in business since 1909 and has used the area with seasonal variations during that time. The depositions indicate that with the limited forage and the need to use different portions of the area during different seasons a large acreage is required to support a horse or cow.

* * *

There apparently has been no attempt in recent years, and certainly not since 1971, by the ranchers to manage the herds of horses. It appears that a large percentage of the horses in the area are unclaimed. Since the Government has assumed control of the horses their numbers have increased greatly. The horses compete for forage with wild animals and with livestock on the entire range.

* * *

* * * The plaintiffs allege that the control and management of the horses is exclusively in the Government (and the Secretary agrees); that this control is complete; that the Government by the express provisions of the Act must remove horses from private lands when requested; that many such requests have been made by plaintiffs but the horses continued to consume the forage on plaintiffs' lands and thereby a taking of their property resulted. The plaintiffs sought a writ of mandamus to have the horses removed from their property, prayed for nominal damages for the consumption of forage, and for substantial damages against the Secretary for failure to administer the Wild Horse Act and thereby causing damage to plaintiffs.

The trial court issued the writ of mandamus and ordered all wild horses removed from the Association's land within one year and a reduction in the wild horse population on the public lands within two years. The trial court eventually dismissed the claim against the BLM director and granted the Government's cross-motion for summary judgment on the unconstitutional taking claim. The plaintiffs relinquished their claim for attorneys' fees and costs. The plaintiffs appeal the dismissal of their claim against the BLM director and the court's order denying nominal damages against the Government.

The horses generally, and especially those with identifiable characteristics of particular breeds, cannot be classified as "wild animals" in an attempt to compare them or the Act to other statutes relating to wild birds and wild animals. The horses do not have to be "wild animals" to come within the Act, but other requirements must be met. In the checkerboard area, the parties have assumed that the horses in question come within the definition in the Wild Horse Act.

Since the Government has assumed jurisdiction over the horses under the Act it has thereby taken the exclusive and complete control of the horses and also the duty to manage them. As to control, the Act and Regulations permit no one else to move the horses no matter where they are. No one else can manage the horses. Landowners cannot move them from their land. If the horses stray from public lands onto private lands the owners must request the Government to remove the horses if they want them off their land.

It is this complete and exclusive control which makes the Act unique. It cannot be compared, as we have stated, with statutes which relate to wild animals or birds. The drafters of the Act so made the control exclusive in the Government and complete with both the affirmative and negative provisions (with criminal penalties). The implications of the complete and sole control must be examined and applied to the legal relationship of the parties. This degree of control can become the significant factor in an examination of the liability of the Government.

The control feature is reinforced by an affirmative express management duty on Interior. The Act thus presumes (and the agency apparently acknowledges) that the management responsibility can and must be carried out. This is the physical management of the horses as to range use, water, location at seasons, and numbers. Thus it is mandated that the horses can be moved to places they should use for good range management and that their numbers be kept within proper limits.

The Act further presumes that Interior can and will control and manage the horses by including an explicit duty on Interior to remove the horses from private land when requested to do so. The agency has assumed this duty and an ability to so act.

The plaintiffs allege that the Secretary has not managed the horse herds as required in the Act, has not controlled them or their numbers, and also it has not removed horses from their private lands when requested to do so. See Roaring Springs Associates v. Andrus, 471 F.Supp. 522 (D.Nev.1978). * * * All concerned acknowledged the increase in numbers was causing problems. The Secretary in his Answer herein said:

> "Admit that an increase in wild horse population has resulted in an over-population and an excessive demand on the public range."

The requests to remove the horses were not met despite the statutory duty of Interior. This inaction knowingly permitted the horses to consume forage on plaintiffs' private land according to the pleadings and affidavits. This is alleged by plaintiffs as a taking of their forage crop—a taking of their *private personal property*. Substantial damages resulting from the taking of the forage is described but only nominal damages are prayed for.

* * *

It is only by reason of the checkerboarded ownership of the lands that horse control and management could become a factor or issue on the taking of plaintiffs' property. The BLM horse management practices for the District, insofar as it covers the checkerboard, is and was as applicable to private lands as it was to public lands. The Act was so drafted that the BLM was the only one who could *in any way* manage or control the impact of the increased number of horses using everybody's land. The affidavits describe the range damage caused by the increase in the number of horses and their seasonal management. This overuse was asserted to include consumption of the forage crops of plaintiffs and thereby it was alleged that a taking of private property had taken place.

The taking allegations are also based on the refusal of the BLM to remove the horses from plaintiffs' land. This may or may not be distinct from asserted failure to manage under the Act.

The allegations as to a taking do not refer or rely on a single event or occurrence but to a continued course of action during the year for a period of years. Personal property is within the constitutional protection as to "taking".

The issuance of the writ of mandamus did not become an issue on this appeal and no position is taken as to it.

The denial of damages against the Secretary is affirmed. The judgment of the trial court is reversed as to the issue of the taking of forage for a factual determination whether such forage was taken by the continued failure to manage the horses and by permitting their continued use of private lands by the increased number of horses and burros since 1971.

IT IS SO ORDERED.

McKAY, Circuit Judge, concurring in part and dissenting in part:

However innocuous it may at first appear, the court's opinion represents a radical departure from established constitutional precedent with sweeping implications for the enforcement of all environmental regulatory statutes.

* * *

In structure and purpose, the Wild Free-Roaming Horses and Burros Act is essentially identical to the Protection of Bald and Golden Eagles Act. 16 U.S.C. §§ 668–668(d) (1982). The Bald and Golden Eagles Act prohibits possession, commerce, killing or other activities with reference to the bald and golden eagle, whether dead or alive, their eggs and nests, with both criminal and civil penalties for violation. The Act is absolute in its terms except that there is a provision for obtaining a permit from the Secretary of Interior to destroy or

remove eagles that are destroying lifestock or agricultural crops. Id.
§ 668(a). This ameliorative provision is essentially identical to the
ameliorative provision of the Wild Free-Roaming Horses and Burros
Act. 16 U.S.C. § 1334 (1982). ＊ ＊ ＊

There are numerous other similar statutes and regulations particularly relating to endangered species, 16 U.S.C. §§ 1531–1543 (1982),
some of which notoriously do damage to domesticated livestock and
agricultural crops.

＊ ＊ ＊

It is important to set forth the detailed parallels in other government statutes and regulations in order to understand what is at stake
in this case. Notwithstanding the court's implied suggestion to the
contrary, the horses and burros regulated under this Act are legally
wild in the same sense that any other "wild" animal is wild. The Act
declares them to be so.

It is conceded that the basic stock of wild horses and burros were
on the checkerboard lands before the ranchers in this action obtained
these lands. The fact that they were once domesticated and that the
herds have been supplemented by other animals which were once
domesticated is totally irrelevant. There is no authority whatever for
suggesting that Congress cannot declare free roaming, unclaimed animals to be "wild." The beginning point for an analysis of the issues in
this case is the fact that the Act is a scheme designed to regulate wild
animals just as all the other acts regulate animals, birds, and insects
not owned by someone. Thus, to sustain this attack on the Wild Horses
and Burros Act (at least so far as it is based on the notion of fifth
amendment taking) is to fundamentally undermine all of the environmental protection schemes which Congress and state legislatures in
their wisdom may undertake to enact.

＊ ＊ ＊

Plaintiffs in this case have not even argued, much less put on proof
that they have been deprived of all beneficial use of their land. In
analyzing these cases challenging regulatory schemes under a claim of
fifth amendment rights, neither this court, the Supreme Court, nor any
other court has ever divided the property owners' interest into sections
such as mouths full of forage (individual lambs, individual trees), or
high rise buildings as opposed to vastly less profitable low density
development. Indeed, in Miller v. Schoene, 276 U.S. 272 (1928), the
Supreme Court rejected a taking without just compensation attack on a
regulatory scheme even though the state of Virginia through its own
personal agents went on the property owner's land to cut down and
remove trees to benefit apple orchard owners at the direct expense of
red cedar owners. That case is a much stronger case than the present
one for finding a taking because in Miller the government's scheme was
designed to protect apple trees on the lands of private land owners, not
the broad direct national interest as in this case.

＊ ＊ ＊

The opinion of the court is even more troublesome because it is impossible to determine from the court's opinion precisely what constitutes the taking under this sweeping new notion of the fifth amendment or at what point one begins to measure the taking. As the court itself has said of its opinion, "The allegations as to a taking do not refer or rely on a single event or occurrence but to a continued course of action during the year for a period of years." It apparently does refer to forage because of the court's citation to personal property as falling within the protection of the fifth amendment. Indeed, as presently structured, the court's opinion gives the trial court an imponderable task. On remand there are no damages to assess except nominal ones.

* * *

The court's opinion does not give us or the trial court the guidance necessary to determine whether the taking consists of all forage consumed by all wild horses on private land from the moment they enter the private land in the checkerboard area; all forage consumed and damage caused from the moment that there is a request for removal of horses from private lands; all forage consumed by some number of horses in excess of some undetermined reasonable number; the forage taken by all horses grazing on private lands in excess of the numbers which were there in 1971; forage consumed under one of the foregoing categories but only after a lapse of reasonable time after notice to the Secretary to remove a particular number of horses; or some other imponderable assessment for which the trial court is given inadequate theoretical guidance.

* * *

NOTES

1. The opinion in the principal case was withdrawn and a rehearing en banc granted by the Tenth Circuit on March 29, 1985. How should the full Tenth Circuit rule?

2. If the majority opinion prevails on rehearing, are all of the federal wildlife statutes in jeopardy? Will federal budgetary stress exacerbate the potential problem?

3. Compare American Farm Bureau Fed'n v. Block, 14 ELR 20763 (D.S.D., March 12, 1984). The plaintiffs alleged that the failure of the federal government to control populations of black-tailed prairie dogs on the Buffalo Gap National Grasslands, the Badlands National Park, and the Pine Ridge Indian Reservation allowed the proliferating prairie dogs to damage adjacent properties. The court held that plaintiffs could not recover under the Federal Torts Claims Act because they had not followed the requisite procedures and that no inverse condemnation occurred because the government did not own the animals.

4. The opinion in Dahl v. Clark, 600 F.Supp. 585 (D.Nev.1984), offers interesting insights into political realities and unrealities in public land management. Plaintiff ranchers sued to force the BLM to reduce the wild horse population in the area of their grazing allotments to 1971 levels. They claimed that rapidly increasing horse populations

(62 to 655 head in 13 years, they alleged) were harming range condition. In the course of his decision, Judge Reed made these observations:

> Defendants respond that they do not have an obligation under the law or regulations to reduce the wild horse population to 1971 levels. Defendants argue that the laws require them to remove wild horses only if actual ongoing substantial damage to the range is occurring because of an excess number of wild horses using it. Further, defendants argue that pursuant to his authority in 1981, Secretary of the Interior James Watt rejected prior BLM study methods and the conclusions reached from them as inaccurate, and directed the BLM officials in the field to maintain numbers of livestock and wild horses on the public lands at 1981 levels and to commence use of new monitoring studies as to range utilization. Secretary Watt believed the new study methods utilized more modern scientific methods.[1] * * *
>
> * * *
>
> In this case defendants' evidence indicates that using this outdated information the BLM adopted a range survey approach, an inventory procedure, in order to estimate the carrying capacities of the ranges for the purposes of preparation of the EISs. The results of EISs based on the range survey approach were alarming in many cases mandating drastic reductions in both livestock and wild horse use of the affected ranges. For example, in the Jersey Valley Allotments the applicable EIS would have required reduction of cattle use by 50–55% and reduction of wild horses to nothing in some areas.
>
> It was at that time in 1981 that the directive came forth from Secretary Watt renouncing all the previous studies and requiring BLM to start afresh, using as a starting place the existing numbers of wild horses and livestock in each range area and to commence use of new scientific approaches to determine range carrying capacities. Defendants' Exhibit O, Letter from James Watt. The levels of then existing wild horse and livestock populations were to be continued and the animals were to continue to use their respective then existing ranges. Population levels were made subject to adjustment on the basis of intensive monitoring studies that were to continue. The effect of Secretary Watt's 1981 instructions was to reverse what appear to be the BLM's longtime orientation from one of looking for downward trends in range conditions to one of looking for upward trends or at least static range conditions. Until Secretary Watt's directive, the studies of the BLM and their management consistently found range conditions poor and on a downward trend calling for reduction in livestock

---

1. Although the reason for Secretary Watt's directive is not clear, it appears to the Court that it most likely resulted from the fact that the previous studies indicated that use of the public domain by livestock and by wild horses would have to be drastically reduced due to damage to the range caused by overutilization.

numbers and removal of wild horses. Since the time Secretary Watt's letter was issued, the BLM has been making the opposite findings and recommendations. One has to admire the steadfast loyalty of the BLM officials in following the dictates of their superiors in the Department of Interior, no matter which way the wind blows at a particular time.

In this case, the BLM contends that all the data available to it in 1981 was outdated and unscientific. The evidence presented at trial, however, does not bear this out. It appears that the BLM had been conscientiously and efficiently studying the ranges on a continuing basis prior to and during the 1970s and early 1980s. Many of these studies (including those made on the subject allotments) were made on bases in conformity with the scientific approaches called for by Secretary Watt in his 1981 letter, rather than on the basis of the criticized "one point in time" observations. Such range investigations were frequent and continuous and cannot by any means be entirely discounted or discarded as inaccurate.

* * *

While Secretary Watt specifically rejected one point in time observation studies as being inaccurate, the thrust of his 1981 directive is to reject all pre-1981 studies apparently because of his conclusion that then current numbers of animals should be maintained. The Watt directive places BLM in the position in this case of having to attack its previous studies, conclusions, decisions, and to some extent its own expert personnel. Previous BLM studies had indicated a downward trend in range condition and the necessity of reduction of numbers. Previous BLM studies included not only one point in time studies but studies which required repeated observations such as photo trend plots. Many of the pre-1981 studies appear to meet the criteria which are now supposed to be met to achieve accurate and reliable results. Despite Secretary Watt's rejection of them, the BLM nonetheless relies upon these pre–1981 studies in its Exhibit G in attempting to show that the trend of the allotments is not downward and that the forage utilization is not excessive.

* * *

It doesn't appear, therefore, that so far as these three allotments are concerned, the Secretary of the Interior is carrying out his mandate under the Wild Horse Act, as amended. The decision to maintain 1981 numbers has not been made after determining the optimum number of horses to be maintained on the area. It is simply an arbitrary decision to maintain 1981 numbers. While the BLM has attempted to support Secretary Watt's decision as best it could, the preponderance of the evidence is that the decision to maintain 1981 wild horse population levels is not based upon any evidence, analysis or studies but simply on the decision Secretary Watt made in order to avoid reductions in livestock and wild horse populations in 1981.   * * *

The court found the 1981 decision by Secretary Watt unsupportable and arbitrary, but refused to grant the requested relief because it could not find in the WF–RHBA any requirement that horse populations must be limited to 1971 levels.

Chapter Nine

THE WILDLIFE RESOURCE

The public attitude toward wildlife as a resource has shifted from that of putting food on the table to one of recreational, scientific, and aesthetic interest, and wildlife management and protection gradually has become a legal matter. This century has seen the evolution of wildlife law from a set of relatively narrow state hunting and fishing rules to a more comprehensive, frequently interjurisdictional scheme of broader dimensions and perspectives. Wildlife law and wildlife management now emphasize habitat quality maintenance and enhancement, a trend accentuated by the rapid development of federal law in the area. See generally M. Bean, THE EVOLUTION OF NATIONAL WILDLIFE LAW (2d ed. 1983). In spite of the growth of federal law, however, wildlife management remains primarily a function performed by state agencies.

For most of the nineteenth century, the few rudimentary state wildlife statutes were ineffective for lack of wardens or other enforcement mechanisms. State fish and game agencies were then founded whose primary mission was at first the protection of the resource by curbing the more pernicious abuses. See Lund, Early American Wildlife Law, 51 N.Y.U.L.Rev. 703 (1976). The constitutional basis for pervasive state regulation was confirmed in Geer v. Connecticut, 161 U.S. 519 (1896), holding that a state could forbid the export of game taken within its borders without contravening the Commerce Clause of the Constitution, and indicating that wildlife was owned as property by the state in trust for the people. *Geer* was often cited for the proposition that states had by virtue of their ownership a sole management prerogative, a right excluding federal interference or participation even on reserved federal lands. The asserted prerogative was important not only for reasons of "states' rights" or sovereignty, but also because hunting and fishing license fees generate considerable state revenues.

Public land policy has always been prominent in wildlife management efforts. Starting in 1903, the federal government created a lands category devoted primarily to wildlife. One Congressman called President Theodore Roosevelt's proposal to create federal game refuges "the fad of game preservation run stark raving mad." When the bill died, Roosevelt took matters into his own hands. He asked, "Is there any law that will prevent me from declaring Pelican Island a Federal Bird Reservation?" When told that the island was federal property, he responded, "very well, I so declare it." With his Pelican Island Bird Refuge Proclamation of March 14, 1903, a national program for protecting wildlife habitat was born. Within two years, Congress became involved, first through delegation of authority to the president and later by the statutory establishment of specific refuges. Congress in

1966 consolidated the various wildlife and game areas into the National Wildlife Refuge System. In an even larger sense, the reservation of national forests and parks beginning in the late 19th century has proved crucial to national wildlife policy because such lands provide large, relatively undisturbed regions of prime wildlife habitat.

Federal wildlife law began to evolve, albeit unevenly, in other contexts around the turn of the century. Congress legislated for wildlife conservation in the territories, and in 1900, it ventured into general wildlife regulation. The Lacey Act, 16 U.S.C.A. §§ 701, 3371–78, and 18 U.S.C.A. § 42, forbade transportation or sale in interstate commerce of animals taken illegally in the state of origin, essentially backstopping state conservation efforts. The Migratory Bird Treaty Act of 1918 (MBTA), 16 U.S.C.A. §§ 703–11, directly interfered with and preempted state law. Under the MBTA, the Department of the Interior acts as a super game agency, managing migratory bird populations by establishing hunting seasons and bag limits and regulating methods of taking.

Otherwise, from 1918 until the mid-1960's, Congress concerned itself with wildlife regulation only to the extent of establishing a few grants-in-aid programs for state agencies, imposing minimal wildlife habitat planning requirements for federal water resource projects, authorizing the destruction of predator and pest species, and enacting legislation to protect the bald eagle. The Bald Eagle Act of 1940, 16 U.S.C.A. §§ 668–668d, imposes a flat ban on the killing or molesting of bald and golden eagles except with federal permission. Permits are available for meeting the religious needs of Indians and for the protection of domestic livestock against the depredations of golden eagles. From 1940 to 1971, the only new federal wildlife laws of any import were the Fish and Wildlife Coordination Act of 1958, 16 U.S.C.A. §§ 661–667e, and the Anadromous Fish Conservation Act of 1965, 16 U.S.C.A. §§ 757a–757f. The former commands federal agencies to ensure that "wildlife conservation" receives "equal consideration" and coordination with "other features of water-resource development programs" and requires reports to Congress on plans for mitigation of wildlife habitat losses due to federal projects. The 1965 Act did not seem to afford migrating salmon any real protection, but the Supreme Court held that its provisions supported a decision to reverse the grant of an FPC license to construct a dam. Udall v. FPC, 387 U.S. 428 (1967). Primitive versions of an Endangered Species Act were enacted in 1966 and 1969. NEPA, enacted in 1969, strongly influences many wildlife-related issues.

In retrospect, the Wild and Free-Roaming Horses and Burros Act of 1971 (WF–RHBA), 16 U.S.C.A. §§ 1331–40—the law upheld in Kleppe v. New Mexico, 426 U.S. 529 (1976), supra at page 194—was a watershed, the beginning of more activist congressional posture toward wildlife regulation. The Marine Mammal Protection Act of 1972 (MMPA) 16 U.S.C.A. §§ 1361–62, 1371–84, 1401–07, declared a moratorium on all taking of or commerce in all marine mammals, with a few exceptions for special situations, such as incidental taking of porpoises by tuna fishermen. The MMPA was followed in 1973 by the radically amended Endangered Species Act (ESA), 16 U.S.C.A. §§ 1531–43, called by some the most stringent wildlife law ever enacted by any country. The Act applies only to species of fauna and flora officially listed as endangered or threatened, but the species so designated are legally sheltered from virtually all human acts that could tend to diminish their stock. All federal agencies are enjoined to refrain from any action that jeopardizes the continued existence of listed species or harms their critical habitat. All persons are absolutely forbidden to kill, pursue, or harass such species on or off federal lands. The 1973 Endangered Species Act has become an important limitation on federal land management agency discretion; a section of this chapter is devoted to cases arising under it. Since 1973, Congress has enacted the Sikes Act Extension of 1974, 16 U.S.C.A. §§ 667a–670f, the Fishery Conservation and Management Act of 1976, 16 U.S.C.A. §§ 1801–82, and the Fish and Wildlife Conservation Act of 1980, 16 U.S.C.A. §§ 2901–11, and has amended the older wildlife laws.

The resulting mosaic of federal wildlife statutes remains fragmented and somewhat confused. Federal law applies only in certain specific situations having to do with selected federally-protected species. In most other cases, state law governs on the federal lands. At the same time, NEPA, the NFMA, and the FLPMA control management decisions that impinge on wildlife habitat.

States resisted the growth of federal wildlife law, but to no avail. *Geer* had not held that the federal government was powerless. See Coggins, Wildlife and the Constitution: The Walls Come Tumbling Down, 55 Wash.L.Rev. 295 (1980). The Supreme Court eroded the state ownership doctrine over the years (e.g., Missouri v. Holland, 252 U.S. 416 (1920)) until it overruled *Geer* in Hughes v. Oklahoma, 441 U.S. 322 (1979). In public land law, courts in a series of cases upheld wildlife management actions taken by federal agencies in defiance of state law. E.g., New Mexico State Game Commission v. Udall, 410 F.2d 1197 (10th Cir.1969), cert. denied, 396 U.S. 961 (1969). That series culminated with Kleppe v. New Mexico, 426 U.S. 529 (1976), supra at page 194, affirming the power of Congress to legislate for wildlife welfare. Kindred lower court opinions support federal authority to regulate wildlife off public lands under the Property Clause so long as there is some nexus with federal land management. E.g., United States v. Brown, 552 F.2d 817 (8th Cir.1977).

The expansive reach of federal power is illustrated by Palila v. Hawaii Dept. of Land and Natural Resources, 471 F.Supp. 985 (D.Hawaii 1979), aff'd, 639 F.2d 495 (9th Cir.1981). Private plaintiffs showed that the State's maintenance of feral sheep and goats in state forests for the benefit of sport hunters contributed to the destruction of habitat required by an endangered species of nonmigratory bird. The court upheld the application of the Endangered Species Act under the Commerce and Treaty Clauses in these circumstances, and ordered the

State to eliminate the "game" species. In dictum, the court intimated that the federal government could assert a property interest in the endangered species superior to that of the state. Compare Mountain States Legal Foundation v. Clark, 740 F.2d 792 (10th Cir.1984), vacated, 765 F.2d 1468 (10th Cir. 1985), supra at page 770.

Congress unquestionably has power over the taking of wildlife on the public lands, but the converse premise in *Kleppe*—that state law is in force until preempted—more accurately reflects on-the-ground wildlife management reality. The states remain the principal arbiters of hunting, fishing, and trapping, even on the public lands. Fish and game departments, joined by organizations of hunters, fiercely protect traditional state prerogatives. Federal authority over the taking of wildlife has been exercised sparingly.

In spite of state dominance over hunting and fishing, federal wildlife law has numerous implications for federal land managers. In some cases, particularly those involving migratory birds or endangered species, they must enforce federal proscriptions against hunting and fishing. Perhaps more importantly, the field of wildlife management now works from the premise of Aldo Leopold that healthy wildlife populations are most effectively achieved by assuring prime habitat; thus, the best wildlife management is in essence good land management. See A. Leopold, GAME MANAGEMENT (1933). The federal land agencies, of course, possess broad authority over developments affecting habitat on the public lands. As in most areas of natural resources management, divergent viewpoints on wildlife management philosophy are common. In Favre, Wildlife Rights: The Ever-Widening Circle, 9 Envt'l L. 241 (1979), for instance, the author makes a case for according wildlife species certain legal rights:

> Arguably, a major stumbling block to recognizing wildlife rights is the problem of how humans can presume to know animals' best interests when animals cannot communicate with humans. With the possible exception of the most intelligent animals, it may be questionable whether humans can ever truly know what a particular animal or species desires or needs. However, the presumption that certain interests are so fundamental that all humans should be accorded legal rights to protect these interests, whether or not they individually ask for them, should be extended to wildlife. As humans have both a self-interest and a moral obligation to recognize the rights of other human beings, they have an equivalent interest and obligation to recognize the interests of wildlife since the stability and integrity of the ecosystem is at stake. Moreover, the moral burden demanding this recognition is particularly great when human activities cause serious intrusions upon the interests of the wildlife community. Given the reasonable presumption that humans should recognize the fundamental interests of wildlife, important questions remain: What are wildlife's interests? What rights should wildlife be accorded?

After these rights are granted, how will conflicts between human rights and wildlife rights be resolved?

* * *

In the first area of conflict, where a particular species cannot coexist with humans, the only realistic solution is to set aside the acreage necessary to support their survival. Much of the critical land already is owned by the United States. Moreover, the federal government and some states have shown a willingness to set aside large tracts of land for the benefit of wildlife. Yellowstone National Park was the first example of a substantial amount of land preserved in its natural state. Many private organizations are also working toward the goal of preserving land in its natural state. For example, the Nature Conservancy recently completed a transaction that will preserve twenty-six square miles of land in the Santa Rosa Mountains of southern California for the benefit of the desert bighorn sheep. In 1977, the same organization acquired an option on 6,029 acres of land which are part of the critical habitat of the endangered Mississippi sandhill crane.

On the other end of the spectrum, Schectman, The "Bambi Syndrome": How NEPA's Public Participation in Wildlife Management is Hurting the Environment, 8 Envt'l L. 611 (1978), concludes:

* * * Non-native burros and native deer have increased in important scenic areas to the point where severe impacts are occurring to flora, fauna, and soil. Proper wildlife management requires reduction, and as a practical matter this can only be accomplished by shooting. * * * But attempts to reduce the herds have been delayed by NEPA actions and lengthy public involvement procedures. * * *

A common complaint was that the "Bambi Syndrome" subverted the involvement process. The public was concerned with individual animals and not their ecosystem as a whole, and seemed to respond more to emotional media presentations than technical assessments prepared by the managers. Skepticism towards the managers and emotionalism created by Walt Disney-like misconceptions of wildlife jeopardized the information function. The sentimental value of individual wildlife to the public became clear, but the decision-makers obtained few valuable comments or feasible alternatives; many suggested alternatives ranged from the emotional to the fanciful to the irrational. While the information function was partially served, managers felt that the public was often not interested in staff assessments and that the public input was simply not valuable enough to deserve a great deal of effort. In no case did the public suggest a feasible alternative that the staff had not previously considered. The public's "Bambi Syndrome" was simply incompatible with sound resource management.

* * *

If NEPA-caused delays continue, the wildlife manager will have two choices. He or she can comply with NEPA by holding ritualistic hearings, writing costly and unneeded impact statements, and collecting public input which contains little new information and does not contribute to the decision. Overdoing public input in this manner will assure compliance, but will be time-consuming and necessarily delay action. On the other hand, the manager can simply go out in the field and take action. From the actions and sentiments expressed by managers in this study, it is clear that the latter course may soon become the preferred alternative.

This chapter deals with the two main facets of wildlife management, regulation of direct killing of species and regulation of land and resource development that directly affects wildlife habitat. Section A concentrates on endangered and threatened species. The second section takes up managerial priorities within the National Wildlife Refuge System. Section C examines wildlife controversies in the national forests and on the BLM public lands.

For research assistance, the interested student may consult Coggins & Smith, The Emerging Law of Wildlife: A Narrative Bibliography, 6 Envt'l L. 583 (1975); Coggins & Patti, The Emerging Law of Wildlife II: A Narrative Bibliography of Federal Wildlife Law, 4 Harv.Envt'l L.Rev. 164 (1980); Coggins & Ward, The Law of Wildlife Management on the Federal Public Lands, 60 Or.L.Rev. 59 (1981). For factual background on wildlife management, see WILDLIFE AND AMERICA (H. Brokaw, ed. 1978). The only work approaching the status of "treatise" is M. Bean, THE EVOLUTION OF NATIONAL WILDLIFE LAW (2d ed. 1983); see also T. Lund, AMERICAN WILDLIFE LAW (1980).

A. ENDANGERED SPECIES PROTECTION

The Endangered Species Act of 1973, 16 U.S.C.A. §§ 1531–43, even as amended in 1978, Pub.L. No. 95–632, 92 Stat. 3751, is a formidable constraint on a wide variety of public land uses in certain situations. In general, the Act commands all agencies to "conserve" listed species, and "conservation" is defined very broadly. 16 U.S.C.A. § 1531(5). Section 9, 16 U.S.C.A. § 1538, prohibits "taking" by anyone, and that too is broadly defined. The big kicker has been section 7, 16 U.S.C.A. § 1536. Early cases provided inconsistent interpretations. Compare Sierra Club v. Froehlke, 534 F.2d 1289 (8th Cir.1976), with National Wildlife Federation v. Coleman, 529 F.2d 359 (5th Cir.1976), cert. denied, 429 U.S. 979 (1976). Then the Supreme Court rendered one of the leading decisions in natural resources law.

TENNESSEE VALLEY AUTHORITY v. HILL
Supreme Court of the United States, 1978.
437 U.S. 153.

Mr. Chief Justice BURGER delivered the opinion of the Court.

The questions presented in this case are (a) whether the Endangered Species Act of 1973 requires a court to enjoin the operation of a virtually completed federal dam—which had been authorized prior to 1973—when, pursuant to authority vested in him by Congress, the Secretary of the Interior has determined that operation of the dam would eradicate an endangered species; and (b) whether continued congressional appropriations for the dam after 1973 constituted an implied repeal of the Endangered Species Act, at least as to the particular dam.

I

The Little Tennessee River originates in the mountains of northern Georgia and flows through the national forest lands of North Carolina into Tennessee, where it converges with the Big Tennessee River near Knoxville. The lower 33 miles of the Little Tennessee takes the river's clear, free-flowing waters through an area of great natural beauty. Among other environmental amenities, this stretch of river is said to contain abundant trout. Considerable historical importance attaches to the areas immediately adjacent to this portion of the Little Tennessee's banks. * * *

In this area of the Little Tennessee River the Tennessee Valley Authority, a wholly owned public corporation of the United States, began constructing the Tellico Dam and Reservoir Project in 1967, shortly after Congress appropriated initial funds for its development. Tellico is a multipurpose regional development project designed principally to stimulate shoreline development, generate sufficient electric current to heat 20,000 homes, and provide flatwater recreation and flood control, as well as improve economic conditions in "an area characterized by underutilization of human resources and outmigration of young people." Of particular relevance to this case is one aspect of the project, a dam which TVA determined to place on the Little Tennessee, a short distance from where the river's waters meet with the Big Tennessee. When fully operational, the dam would impound water covering some 16,500 acres—much of which represents valuable and productive farmland—thereby converting the river's shallow, fast-flowing waters into a deep reservoir over 30 miles in length.

The Tellico Dam has never opened, however, despite the fact that construction has been virtually completed and the dam is essentially ready for operation. Although Congress has appropriated monies for Tellico every year since 1967 progress was delayed, and ultimately stopped, by a tangle of lawsuits and administrative proceedings. * * *

A few months prior to the District Court's decision dissolving the NEPA injunction, a discovery was made in the waters of the Little Tennessee which would profoundly affect the Tellico Project. Exploring the area around Coytee Springs, which is about seven miles from the mouth of the river, a University of Tennessee ichthyologist, Dr. David A. Etnier, found a previously unknown species of perch, the snail darter, or *Percina (Imostoma) tanasi.* This three-inch, tannish-colored fish, whose numbers are estimated to be in the range of 10,000 to 15,000, would soon engage the attention of environmentalists, the TVA, the Department of the Interior, the Congress of the United States, and ultimately the federal courts, as a new and additional basis to halt construction of the dam.

Until recently the finding of a new species of animal life would hardly generate a cause célèbre. This is particularly so in the case of darters, of which there are approximately 130 known species, 8 to 10 of these having been identified only in the last five years. The moving force behind the snail darter's sudden fame came some four months after its discovery, when the Congress passed the Endangered Species Act of 1973. This legislation, among other things, authorizes the Secretary of the Interior to declare species of animal life "endangered" and to identify the "critical habitat" of these creatures. When a species or its habitat is so listed, the following portion of the Act—relevant here—becomes effective:

> "The Secretary [of the Interior] shall review other programs administered by him and utilize such programs in furtherance of the purposes of this chapter. All other Federal departments and agencies shall, in consultation with and with the assistance of the Secretary, utilize their authorities in furtherance of the purposes of this chapter by carrying out programs for the conservation of endangered species and threatened species listed pursuant to section 1533 of this title and *by taking such action necessary to insure that actions authorized, funded, or carried out by them do not jeopardize the continued existence of such endangered species and threatened species or result in the destruction or modification of habitat of such species* which is determined by the Secretary, after consultation as appropriate with the affected States, to be critical."
> 16 U.S.C.A. § 1536 (emphasis added).

[In 1975, the Interior Secretary listed the snail darter as endangered, declared the area to be inundated as "critical habitat, and announced that impoundment of the river "would result in total destruction of the snail darter's habitat." The TVA insisted that transplantation of the fish to another river was the only remedy.]

Meanwhile, Congress had also become involved in the fate of the snail darter. Appearing before a Subcommittee of the House Committee on Appropriations in April 1975—some seven months before the snail darter was listed as endangered—TVA representatives described the discovery of the fish and the relevance of the Endangered Species

Act to the Tellico Project. At that time TVA presented a position which it would advance in successive forums thereafter, namely, that the Act did not prohibit the completion of a project authorized, funded, and substantially constructed before the act was passed. TVA also described its efforts to transplant the snail darter, but contended that the dam should be finished regardless of the experiment's success. Thereafter, the House Committee on Appropriations, in its June 20, 1975, Report, stated the following in the course of recommending that an additional $29 million be appropriated for Tellico:

"The *Committee* directs that the project, for which an environmental impact statement has been completed and provided the Committee, should be completed as promptly as possible * * *." H.R.Rep. No. 94–319, p. 76 (1975). (Emphasis added.)

Congress then approved the TVA general budget, which contained funds for continued construction of the Tellico Project. In December 1975, one month after the snail darter was declared an endangered species, the President signed the bill into law.

[The district court refused relief, but the court of appeals entered a permanent injunction against closure of the dam until Congress decided otherwise.]

* * *

Following the issuance of the permanent injunction, members of TVA's Board of Directors appeared before Subcommittees of the House and Senate Appropriations Committees to testify in support of continued appropriations for Tellico. The Subcommittees were apprised of all aspects of Tellico's status, including the Court of Appeals' decision. TVA reported that the dam stood "ready for the gates to be closed and the reservoir filled," and requested funds for completion of certain ancillary parts of the project, such as public use areas, roads, and bridges. As to the snail darter itself, TVA commented optimistically on its transplantation efforts, expressing the opinion that the relocated fish were "doing well and ha[d] reproduced."

Both Appropriations Committees subsequently recommended the full amount requested for completion of the Tellico Project. In its June 2, 1977, Report, the House Appropriations Committee stated:

"It is *the Committee's view* that the Endangered Species Act was not intended to halt projects such as these in their advanced stage of completion, and [the Committee] strongly recommends that these projects not be stopped because of misuse of the Act." H.R.Rep. No. 95–379, p. 104. (Emphasis added.)

As a solution to the problem, the House Committee advised that TVA should cooperate with the Department of the Interior "to relocate the endangered species to another suitable habitat so as to permit the project to proceed as rapidly as possible." Toward this end, the Committee recommended a special appropriation of $2 million to facilitate relocation of the snail darter and other endangered species which threatened to delay or stop TVA projects. Much the same occurred on the Senate side, with its Appropriations Committee recommending both the amount requested to complete Tellico and the special appropriation for transplantation of endangered species. Reporting to the Senate on these measures, the Appropriations Committee took a particularly strong stand on the snail darter issue:

> "This *committee has not viewed* the Endangered Species Act as preventing the completion and use of these projects which were well under way at the time the affected species were listed as endangered. If the act has such an effect, which is contrary to *the Committee's understanding* of the intent of Congress in enacting the Endangered Species Act, funds should be appropriated to allow these projects to be completed and their benefits realized in the public interest, the Endangered Species Act notwithstanding." S.Rep. No. 95–301, p. 99 (1977). (Emphasis added.)

TVA's budget, including funds for completion of Tellico and relocation of the snail darter, passed both Houses of Congress and was signed into law on August 7, 1977.

* * *

II

We begin with the premise that operation of the Tellico Dam will either eradicate the known population of snail darters or destroy their critical habitat. [But see note 3, infra at page 798.] Petitioner does not now seriously dispute this fact. In any event, under * * * 16 U.S. C.A. § 1533(a)(1) the Secretary of the Interior is vested with exclusive authority to determine whether a species such as the snail darter is "endangered" or "threatened" and to ascertain the factors which have led to such a precarious existence. By § 4(d) Congress has authorized— indeed commanded—the Secretary to "issue such regulations as he deems necessary and advisable to provide for the conservation of such species." 16 U.S.C.A. § 1533(d). As we have seen, the Secretary promulgated regulations which declared the snail darter an endangered species whose critical habitat would be destroyed by creation of the Tellico Reservoir. Doubtless petitioner would prefer not to have these regulations on the books, but there is no suggestion that the Secretary exceeded his authority or abused his discretion in issuing the regulations. Indeed, no judicial review of the Secretary's determinations has ever been sought and hence the validity of his actions are not open to review in this Court.

Starting from the above premise, two questions are presented: (a) would TVA be in violation of the Act if it completed and operated the Tellico Dam as planned? (b) if TVA's actions would offend the Act, is an injunction the appropriate remedy for the violation? For the reasons stated hereinafter, we hold that both questions must be answered in the affirmative.

(A)

It may seem curious to some that the survival of a relatively small number of three-inch fish among all the countless millions of species extant would require the permanent halting of a virtually completed dam for which Congress has expended more than $100 million. The paradox is not minimized by the fact that Congress continued to appropriate large sums of public money for the project, even after congressional Appropriations Committees were apprised of its apparent impact upon the survival of the snail darter. We conclude, however, that the explicit provisions of the Endangered Species Act require precisely that result.

One would be hard pressed to find a statutory provision whose terms were any plainer than those in § 7 of the Endangered Species Act. Its very words affirmatively command all federal agencies "to *insure* that actions *authorized, funded,* or *carried out* by them do not *jeopardize* the continued existence" of an endangered species or "*result* in the destruction or modification of habitat of such species * * *." 16 U.S.C.A. § 1536. (Emphasis added.) This language admits of no exception. Nonetheless, petitioner urges, as do the dissenters, that the Act cannot reasonably be interpreted as applying to a federal project which was well under way when Congress passed the Endangered Species Act of 1973. To sustain that position, however, we would be forced to ignore the ordinary meaning of plain language. It has not been shown, for example, how TVA can close the gates of the Tellico Dam without "carrying out" an action that has been "authorized" and "funded" by a federal agency. Nor can we understand how such action will "*insure*" that the snail darter's habitat is not disrupted.[18] Accepting the Secretary's determinations, as we must, it is clear that TVA's proposed operation of the dam will have precisely the opposite effect, namely the *eradication* of an endangered species.

Concededly, this view of the Act will produce results requiring the sacrifice of the anticipated benefits of the project and of many millions of dollars in public funds. But examination of the language, history, and structure of the legislation under review here indicates beyond

---

18. In dissent, Mr. Justice Powell argues that the meaning of "actions" in § 7 is "far from 'plain,'" and that "it seems evident that the 'actions' referred to are not all actions that an agency can ever take, but rather actions that the agency is *deciding whether* to authorize, to fund, or to carry out." Aside from this bare assertion, however, no explanation is given to support the proffered interpretation. This recalls Lewis Carroll's classic advice on construction of language:

"When *I* use a word," Humpty Dumpty said, in rather a scornful tone, "it means just what *I* choose it to mean— neither more nor less." Through the

Looking Glass, in The Complete Works of Lewis Carroll 196 (1939).

Aside from being unexplicated, the dissent's reading of § 7 is flawed on several counts. First, under its view, the words "or carry out" in § 7 would be superfluous since all prospective actions of an agency remain to be "authorized" or "funded." Second, the dissent's position logically means that an agency would be obligated to comply with § 7 only when a project is in the planning stage. But if Congress had meant to so limit the Act, it surely would have used words to that effect, as it did in the National Environmental Policy Act, 42 U.S.C.A. §§ 4332(2)(A), (C).

doubt that Congress intended endangered species to be afforded the highest of priorities.

* * *

Despite the fact that the 1966 and 1969 legislation represented "the most comprehensive of its type to be enacted by any nation" up to that time, Congress was soon persuaded that a more expansive approach was needed if the newly declared national policy of preserving endangered species was to be realized. By 1973, when Congress held hearings on what would later become the Endangered Species Act of 1973, it was informed that species were still being lost at the rate of about one per year, 1973 House Hearings 306 (statement of Stephen R. Seater, for Defenders of Wildlife), and "the pace of disappearance of species" appeared to be "accelerating." * * * That Congress did not view these developments lightly was stressed by one commentator:

> "The dominant theme pervading all Congressional discussion of the proposed [Endangered Species Act of 1973] was the overriding need *to devote whatever effort and resources were necessary* to avoid further diminution of national and worldwide wildlife resources. Much of the testimony at the hearings and much debate was devoted to the biological problem of extinction. Senators and Congressmen uniformly deplored the irreplaceable loss to aesthetics, science, ecology, and the national heritage should more species disappear." Coggins, Conserving Wildlife Resources: An Overview of the Endangered Species Act of 1973, 51 N.D.L.Rev. 315, 321 (1975). (Emphasis added.)

The legislative proceedings in 1973 are, in fact, replete with expressions of concern over the risk that might lie in the loss of *any* endangered species. Typifying these sentiments is the Report of the House Committee on Merchant Marine and Fisheries on H.R. 37, a bill which contained the essential features of the subsequently enacted Act of 1973; in explaining the need for the legislation, the Report stated:

> "As we homogenize the habitats in which these plants and animals evolved, and as we increase the pressure for products that they are in a position to supply (usually unwillingly) we threaten their—and our own—genetic heritage.
>
> "*The value of this genetic heritage is, quite literally, incalculable.*"

* * *

As the examples cited here demonstrate, Congress was concerned about the *unknown* uses that endangered species might have and about the *unforeseeable* place such creatures may have in the chain of life on this planet.

In shaping legislation to deal with the problem thus presented, Congress started from the finding that "[t]he two major causes of extinction are hunting and destruction of natural habitat." S.Rep. No. 93, 307, p. 2 (1973). Of these twin threats, Congress was informed that the greatest was destruction of natural habitats * * *.

As it was finally passed, the Endangered Species Act of 1973 represented the most comprehensive legislation for the preservation of endangered species ever enacted by any nation. Its stated purposes were "to provide a means whereby the ecosystems upon which endangered species and threatened species depend may be conserved," and "to provide a program for the conservation of such * * * species * * *." 16 U.S.C.A. § 1531(b). In furtherance of these goals, Congress expressly stated in § 2(c) that "all Federal departments and agencies *shall* seek *to conserve endangered species* and threatened species * * *." 16 U.S.C.A. § 1531(c). (Emphasis added.) Lest there be any ambiguity as to the meaning of this statutory directive, the Act specifically defined "conserve" as meaning "to use and the use of *all methods and procedures which are necessary* to bring *any endangered species* or threatened species to the point at which the measures provided pursuant to this chapter are no longer necessary." § 1532(2). (Emphasis added.) Aside from § 7, other provisions indicated the seriousness with which Congress viewed this issue * * *.

Section 7 of the Act, which of course is relied upon by respondents in this case, provides a particularly good gauge of congressional intent. As we have seen, this provision had its genesis in the Endangered Species Act of 1966, but that legislation qualified the obligation of federal agencies by stating that they should seek to preserve endangered species only "*insofar as is practicable and consistent with the*[*ir*] *primary purposes* * * *." Likewise, every bill introduced in 1973 contained a qualification similar to that found in the earlier statutes.
* * *

What is very significant in this sequence is that the final version of the 1973 Act carefully omitted all of the reservations described above.
* * *

* * * The Conference Report, H.R.Conf.Rep. No. 93–740 (1973), basically adopted the Senate bill, S. 1983; but the conferees rejected the Senate version of § 7 and adopted the stringent, mandatory language in H.R. 37. While the Conference Report made no specific reference to this choice of provisions, the House manager of the bill, Representative Dingell, provided an interpretation of what the Conference bill would require, making it clear that the mandatory provisions of § 7 were not casually or inadvertently included: * * *

> "Another example * * * [has] to do with the continental population of grizzly bears which may or may not be endangered, but which is surely threatened. * * * Once this bill is enacted, the appropriate Secretary, whether of Interior, Agriculture or whatever, *will have to take action* to see that this situation is not permitted to worsen, and that these bears are not driven to extinction. The purposes of the bill included the conservation of the species and of the ecosystems upon which they depend, and *every agency of government is committed* to see that those purposes are carried out. * * * [T]he agencies of Government can no longer plead that they can do

nothing about it. *They can, and they must. The law is clear."* 119 Cong.Rec. 42913 (1973). (Emphasis added.)

It is against this legislative background that we must measure TVA's claim that the Act was not intended to stop operation of a project which, like Tellico Dam, was near completion when an endangered species was discovered in its path. While there is no discussion in the legislative history of precisely this problem, the totality of congressional action makes it abundantly clear that the result we reach today is wholly in accord with both the words of the statute and the intent of Congress. The plain intent of Congress in enacting this statute was to halt and reverse the trend toward species extinction, whatever the cost. This is reflected not only in the stated policies of the Act, but in literally every section of the statute. All persons, including federal agencies, are specifically instructed not to "take" endangered species, meaning that no one is "to harass, harm,[30] pursue, hunt, shoot, wound, kill, trap, capture, or collect" such life forms. 16 U.S.C.A. §§ 1532(14), 1538(a)(1)(B). Agencies in particular are directed by §§ 2(c) and 3(2) of the Act to "use * * * *all methods* and procedures which are necessary" to preserve endangered species. 16 U.S. C.A. §§ 1531(c), 1532(2) (emphasis added). In addition, the legislative history undergirding § 7 reveals an explicit congressional decision to require agencies to afford first priority to the declared national policy of saving endangered species. The pointed omission of the type of qualifying language previously included in endangered species legislation reveals a conscious decision by Congress to give endangered species priority over the "primary missions" of federal agencies.

* * *

Furthermore, it is clear Congress foresaw that § 7 would, on occasion, require agencies to alter ongoing projects in order to fulfill the goals of the Act.[32] * * * A similar example is provided by the House Committee Report:

"Under the authority of [§ 7], the Director of the Park Service would be required *to conform the practices of his agency* to the need for protecting the rapidly dwindling stock of grizzly bears within Yellowstone Park. These bears, which may be endan-

30. We do not understand how TVA intends to operate Tellico Dam without "harming" the snail darter. The Secretary of the Interior has defined the term "harm" to mean "an act or omission which actually injures or kills wildlife, including acts which annoy it to such an extent as to significantly disrupt essential behavioral patterns, which include, but are not limited to, breeding, feeding or sheltering; *significant environmental modification or degradation which has such effects is included within the meaning of 'harm.'"* 50 CFR § 17.3 (1976) (emphasis added); see S.Rep. No. 93–307, p. 7 (1973).

32. Mr. Justice Powell characterizes the result reached here as giving "retroac-

tive" effect to the Endangered Species Act of 1973. We cannot accept that contention. Our holding merely gives effect to the plain words of the statute, namely, that § 7 affects all projects which remain to be authorized, funded, or carried out. Indeed, under the Act there could be no "retroactive" application since, by definition, any *prior* action of a federal agency which *would* have come under the scope of the Act must have already *resulted* in the destruction of an endangered species or its critical habitat. In that circumstance the species would have already been extirpated or its habitat destroyed; the Act would then have no subject matter to which it might apply.

gered, and are undeniably threatened, should at least be protected by supplying them with carcasses from excess elk within the park, *by curtailing the destruction of habitat by clearcutting National Forests surrounding the Park,* and by preventing hunting until their numbers have recovered sufficiently to withstand these pressures." H.R.Rep. No. 93–412, p. 14 (1973). (Emphasis added.)

One might dispute the applicability of these examples to the Tellico Dam by saying that in this case the burden on the public through the loss of millions of unrecoverable dollars would greatly outweigh the loss of the snail darter. But neither the Endangered Species Act nor Art. III of the Constitution provides federal courts with authority to make such fine utilitarian calculations. On the contrary, the plain language of the Act, buttressed by its legislative history, shows clearly that Congress viewed the value of endangered species as "incalculable." Quite obviously, it would be difficult for a court to balance the loss of a sum certain—even $100 million—against a congressionally declared "incalculable" value, even assuming we had the power to engage in such a weighing process, which we emphatically do not.

In passing the Endangered Species Act of 1973, Congress was also aware of certain instances in which exceptions to the statute's broad sweep would be necessary. Thus, § 10, 16 U.S.C.A. § 1539, creates a number of limited "hardship exemptions," none of which would even remotely apply to the Tellico Project. In fact, there are no exemptions in the Endangered Species Act for federal agencies, meaning that under the maxim *expressio unius est exclusio alterius* we must presume that these were the only "hardship cases" Congress intended to exempt. Cf. National Railroad Passenger Corp. v. National Assn. of Railroad Passengers, 414 U.S. 453, 458 (1974).[34]

Notwithstanding Congress' expression of intent in 1973, we are urged to find that the continuing appropriations for Tellico Dam constitute an implied repeal of the 1973 Act, at least insofar as it applies to the Tellico Project. In support of this view, TVA points to the statements found in various House and Senate Appropriations Committees' Reports; as described in Part I, supra, those Reports

---

34. Mr. Justice Powell's dissent relies on cases decided under the National Environmental Policy Act to support its position that the 1973 Act should only apply to prospective actions of an agency. The NEPA decisions, however, are completely inapposite. First, the two statutes serve different purposes. NEPA essentially imposes a procedural requirement on agencies, requiring them to engage in an extensive *inquiry* as to the effect of federal actions on the environment; by way of contrast, the Act is substantive in effect, designed to *prevent* the loss of any endangered species, regardless of the cost. Thus, it would make sense to hold NEPA inapplicable at some point in the life of a project, because the agency would no longer have a meaningful opportunity to *weigh* the benefits of the project versus the detrimental effects on the environment. Section 7, on the other hand, compels agencies not only to *consider* the effect of their projects on endangered species, but to take such actions as are necessary to *insure* that species are not extirpated as a result of federal activities. Second, even the NEPA cases have generally required agencies to file environmental impact statements when the remaining governmental action would be environmentally "significant." Under § 7, the loss of *any* endangered species has been determined by Congress to be environmentally "significant."

generally reflected the attitude of the *Committees* either that the Act did not apply to Tellico or that the dam should be completed regardless of the provisions of the Act. Since we are unwilling to assume that these latter Committee statements constituted advice to ignore the provisions of a duly enacted law, we assume that these Committees believed that the Act simply was not applicable in this situation. But even under this interpretation of the Committees' actions, we are unable to conclude that the Act has been in any respect amended or repealed.

There is nothing in the appropriations measures, as passed, which states that the Tellico Project was to be completed irrespective of the requirements of the Endangered Species Act. These appropriations, in fact, represented relatively minor components of the lump-sum amounts for the *entire* TVA budget. To find a repeal of the Endangered Species Act under these circumstances would surely do violence to the "'cardinal rule * * * that repeals by implication are not favored.'" Morton v. Mancari, 417 U.S. 535, 549 (1974) * * *. In practical terms, this "cardinal rule" means that "[i]n the absence of some affirmative showing of an intention to repeal, the only permissible justification for a repeal by implication is when the earlier and later statutes are irreconcilable." *Mancari,* supra, at 550.

The doctrine disfavoring repeals by implication "applies with full vigor when * * * the subsequent legislation is an *appropriations measure.*" * * * We recognize that both substantive enactments and appropriations measures are "Acts of Congress," but the latter have the limited and specific purpose of providing funds for authorized programs. When voting on appropriations measures, legislators are entitled to operate under the assumption that the funds will be devoted to purposes which are lawful and not for any purpose forbidden. Without such an assurance, every appropriations measure would be pregnant with prospects of altering substantive legislation, repealing by implication any prior statute which might prohibit the expenditure. Not only would this lead to the absurd result of requiring Members to review exhaustively the background of every authorization before voting on an appropriation, but it would flout the very rules the Congress carefully adopted to avoid this need. House Rule XXI(2), for instance, specifically provides:

> "No appropriation shall be reported in any general appropriation bill, or be in order as an amendment thereto, for any expenditure not previously authorized by law, unless in continuation of appropriations for such public works as are already in progress. *Nor shall any provision in any such bill or amendment thereto changing existing law be in order.*" (Emphasis added.)

See also Standing Rules of the Senate, Rule 16.4. Thus, to sustain petitioner's position, we would be obliged to assume that Congress meant to repeal pro tanto § 7 of the Act by means of a procedure expressly prohibited under the rules of Congress.

* * *

(B)

Having determined that there is an irreconcilable conflict between operation of the Tellico Dam and the explicit provisions of § 7 of the Endangered Species Act, we must now consider what remedy, if any, is appropriate. It is correct, of course, that a federal judge sitting as a chancellor is not mechanically obligated to grant an injunction for every violation of law. * * *

But these principles take a court only so far. Our system of government is, after all, a tripartite one, with each branch having certain defined functions delegated to it by the Constitution. While "[i]t is emphatically the province and duty of the judicial department to say what the law is," Marbury v. Madison, 1 Cranch 137, 177 (1803), it is equally—and emphatically—the exclusive province of the Congress not only to formulate legislative policies and mandate programs and projects, but also to establish their relative priority for the Nation. Once Congress, exercising its delegated powers, has decided the order of priorities in a given area, it is for the Executive to administer the laws and for the courts to enforce them when enforcement is sought.

Here we are urged to view the Endangered Species Act "reasonably," and hence shape a remedy "that accords with some modicum of common sense and the public weal." But is that our function? We have no expert knowledge on the subject of endangered species, much less do we have a mandate from the people to strike a balance of equities on the side of the Tellico Dam. Congress has spoken in the plainest of words, making it abundantly clear that the balance has been struck in favor of affording endangered species the highest of priorities, thereby adopting a policy which it described as "institutionalized caution."

Our individual appraisal of the wisdom or unwisdom of a particular course consciously selected by the Congress is to be put aside in the process of interpreting a statute. Once the meaning of an enactment is discerned and its constitutionality determined, the judicial process comes to an end. * * *

We agree with the Court of Appeals that in our constitutional system the commitment to the separation of powers is too fundamental for us to pre-empt congressional action by judicially decreeing what accords with "common sense and the public weal." Our Constitution vests such responsibilities in the political branches.

Affirmed.

Mr. Justice POWELL, with whom Mr. Justice BLACKMUN joins, dissenting.

The Court today holds that § 7 of the Endangered Species Act requires a federal court, for the purpose of protecting an endangered species or its habitat, to enjoin permanently the operation of any federal project, whether completed or substantially completed. This decision casts a long shadow over the operation of even the most important projects, serving vital needs of society and national defense, whenever it is determined that continued operation would threaten extinction of an endangered species or its habitat. This result is said to be required by the "plain intent of Congress" as well as by the language of the statute.

In my view § 7 cannot reasonably be interpreted as applying to a project that is completed or substantially completed when its threat to an endangered species is discovered. Nor can I believe that Congress could have intended this Act to produce the "absurd result"—in the words of the District Court—of this case. If it were clear from the language of the Act and its legislative history that Congress intended to authorize this result, this Court would be compelled to enforce it. It is not our province to rectify policy or political judgments by the Legislative Branch, however egregiously they may disserve the public interest. But where the statutory language and legislative history, as in this case, need not be construed to reach such a result, I view it as the duty of this Court to adopt a permissible construction that accords with some modicum of common sense and the public weal.

* * *

II

Today the Court, like the Court of Appeals below, adopts a reading of § 7 of the Act that gives it a retroactive effect and disregards 12 years of consistently expressed congressional intent to complete the Tellico Project. With all due respect, I view this result as an extreme example of a literalist construction, not required by the language of the Act and adopted without regard to its manifest purpose. Moreover, it ignores established canons of statutory construction.

A

The starting point in statutory construction is, of course, the language of § 7 itself. I agree that it can be viewed as a textbook example of fuzzy language, which can be read according to the "eye of the beholder." The critical words direct all federal agencies to take "such action [as may be] necessary to insure that actions authorized, funded, or carried out by them do not jeopardize the continued existence of * * * endangered species * * * or result in the destruction or modification of [a critical] habitat of such species * * *." Respondents—as did the Sixth Circuit—read these words as sweepingly as possible to include all "actions" that any federal agency ever may take with respect to any federal project, whether completed or not.

The Court today embraces this sweeping construction. Under the Court's reasoning, the Act covers every existing federal installation, including great hydroelectric projects and reservoirs, every river and harbor project, and every national defense installation—however essential to the Nation's economic health and safety. The "actions" that an agency would be prohibited from "carrying out" would include the continued operation of such projects or any change necessary to preserve their continued usefulness. The only precondition, according to respondents, to thus destroying the usefulness of even the most important federal project in our country would be a finding by the Secretary of the Interior that a continuation of the project would threaten the survival or critical habitat of a newly discovered species of water spider or amoeba.[13]

* * *

III

I have little doubt that Congress will amend the Endangered Species Act to prevent the grave consequences made possible by today's decision. Few, if any, Members of that body will wish to defend an interpretation of the Act that requires the waste of at least $53 million, and denies the people of the Tennessee Valley area the benefits of the reservoir that Congress intended to confer. There will be little sentiment to leave this dam standing before an empty reservoir, serving no purpose other than a conversation piece for incredulous tourists.

But more far reaching than the adverse effect on the people of this economically depressed area is the continuing threat to the operation of every federal project, no matter how important to the Nation. If Congress acts expeditiously, as may be anticipated, the Court's decision probably will have no lasting adverse consequences. But I had not thought it to be the province of this Court to force Congress into otherwise unnecessary action by interpreting a statute to produce a result no one intended.

Mr. Justice REHNQUIST, dissenting. * * *

NOTES

1. Does the holding or the Act go as far as Mr. Justice Powell asserts? If so, is that good, bad, or indifferent?

2. At least 74 species that reside in the public land states of the West are officially listed as endangered or threatened. 50 CFR § 17.11 (1985). These include 15 mammals, from the grizzly bear to the black-footed ferret to the Salt Marsh Harvest mouse; 18 birds, from the California condor to the light-footed clapper rail; eight reptile species; 26 fish; one crustacean, and six insects. That list does not include endangered or threatened plants, which also qualify. New species

---

13. Under the Court's interpretation, the prospects for such disasters are breathtaking indeed, since there are hundreds of thousands of candidates for the endangered list:

" 'The act covers every animal and plant species, subspecies, and population in the world needing protection. There are approximately 1.4 million full species of animals and 600,000 full species of plants in the world. Various authorities calculate as many as 10% of them—some 200,000—may need to be listed as Endangered or Threatened. When one counts in subspecies, not to mention individual populations, the total could increase to three to five times that number.' " * * *

(such as the grizzly bear in 1977) are being added all the time. One third of those 74 species are found primarily in California, but some strange creatures are known to reside in other Western states. Perhaps few have heard of the Columbian white-tailed deer, the San Joaquin kit fox, the Attwater's greater prairie chicken, the Santa Cruz long-toed salamander, the Pahranaget Bonytail, the Pahrump Killifish, or the unarmored three spine stickleback, but the remaining few of those little devils are under Uncle Sam's own wing just as much as the more glamorous species. And these are only the species on the federal list: states are free to make their own lists, and quite a few have done so.

Is there any public land project or management choice that is not potentially affected by the *Snail Darter* holding if there is (even the possibility of) an endangered species member in the vicinity? Clearcutting and peregrine falcons, power lines and bald eagles, or mine waste leaching and Pahrump Killifish are examples of potential applications. See generally Coggins & Russell, Beyond Shooting Snail Darters in Pork Barrels: Endangered Species and Land Use in America, 70 Geo. L.J. 1433 (1982); Lundberg, Birds, Bunnies, and the Furbish Lousewort—Wildlife and Mining on the Public Lands, 24 Rocky Mtn.Min.L. Inst. 93 (1978).

3. In October, 1978, the last minute deluge of legislation included lengthy amendments to the Endangered Species Act, passed in reaction to the *Snail Darter* decision. While many weakening provisos were inserted in several sections, the language of section 7 curiously was left untouched. Instead, Congress added new provisions to it creating a new cabinet-level committee to resolve otherwise irreconcilable conflicts between listed species and federal projects. Judicial review under the APA is allowed, but the action must be filed within 90 days. 16 U.S.C.A. § 1536(n). See generally Stromberg, The Endangered Species Act Amendments of 1978: A Step Backwards?, 7 Envt'l Aff. 33 (1979); Goplerud, The Endangered Species Act: Does it Jeopardize the Continued Existence of Species?, 1979 Ariz.L.Rev. 487. Variously termed the "God Committee" or the "Extinction Committee," the new ad hoc body in January, 1979 surprised the world and infuriated some members of Congress by ruling that the continued existence of the snail darter did indeed outweigh the completion and closing of the Tellico Dam, which was, in any event, difficult to justify on economic grounds. In a related action, the Committee also accepted a settlement of the Greyrocks/ Whooping Crane Habitat litigation, Nebraska v. REA, 12 ERC 1156 (D.Neb.1978), by which the builders of the water project were to provide an additional $13 million for habitat protection. Congress finally exempted Tellico from the ESA in September 1979, and the dam's gates were closed. As it turned out, however, so many snail darter populations were later discovered at other locations that the little fish eventually was removed from the list of endangered species. The comment by Zygmunt Plater, attorney for the plaintiffs in *TVA v. Hill*, is a fitting epitaph to this landmark litigation: "It's the only fish story I know where the fish gets smaller and smaller."

4. How many duties of how many types are created by section 7? Are there any limits to its application? Designation of critical habitat is one, of course, but many millions of acres have been proposed as critical habitat for the grizzly bear, and who can say how many acres will or should be protected for the bald eagle?

Undefined in the original Act, "critical habitat" now means "the specific areas within the geographical area occupied by the species, at the time it is listed in accordance with the provisions of Section 4 of this Act, on which are found those physical or biological features (I) essential to the conservation of the species and (II) which may require special management considerations or protection"; and geographical areas outside those occupied by the species which are essential for its conservation. 16 U.S.C.A. § 1532(5)(A). What effect could this definition have on public land management or use?

5. Note also the Supreme Court's dictum regarding "taking" at footnote 30 of the opinion. Does section 9 of the Endangered Species Act, 16 U.S.C.A. § 1538, pose an even greater threat to new *and existing* projects than § 7? Compare Note: Taking Wildlife by Accident, infra at page 850.

6. The number of potential endangered species cited in note 13 of Justice Powell's dissent is probably conservative. Depending on whether the counter is a "splitter" or a "lumper," there may be upwards of five million species in the world and an incalculable number of subspecies and populations. See N. Myers, THE SINKING ARK (1979).

CONSTANCE K. LUNDBERG, BIRDS, BUNNIES, AND THE FURBISH LOUSEWORT—WILDLIFE AND MINING ON THE PUBLIC LANDS *
24 Rocky Mtn.Min.L.Inst. 93 (1978).

* * * Some ministerial actions of agencies must be outside the scope of section 7. Although the NEPA interpretations of "action" have been rejected by the Supreme Court, Department of Interior interpretations of the scope of Interior's discretionary authority under NEPA may still have validity in interpreting the Department's obligations under the Endangered Species Act.

One such interpretation is that given by the Department of Interior Board of Land Appeals in United States v. Kosanke Sand Corporation. Two issues in *Kosanke* are relevant in determining the extent to which the Endangered Species Act may impact upon mining. The first is whether the issuance of a patent under the General Mining Act of 1872 requires an environmental impact statement. The second issue is whether environmental constraints on an unpatented mining claim may alter marketability and thus be a relevant issue in whether or not the patent should issue. The IBLA held that the issuance of a patent is a nondiscretionary action of the Department of Interior and thus the environmental impact statement requirement of § 102(2)(c) is inapplicable to patent determinations. * * * If the Department has no discretion in approving a patent, section 7 should be inapplicable. The Department of Interior cannot withhold issuance of a patent simply because of the presence of an endangered species or the critical habitat of an endangered species on the land covered by the patent application.

The presence of an endangered animal on the land may result in a determination that the application fails to meet the marketability test of United States v. Coleman. If the regional biologist has issued an opinion that mining on the claim will result in a taking of an endangered animal then there may not be a valuable mineral deposit because the applicant would be prohibited by section 9 of the Endangered Species Act from developing the claim. The Board in *Kosanke* directed further hearings on a number of issues including whether water was available to develop the claims and whether the additional costs imposed by pollution control standards under applicable federal, state, and local laws would render the claim unprofitable. Consideration of whether the presence of an endangered species will prevent mining activity is closely parallel to these two factors.

The application of the Endangered Species Act in relation to other mining laws may produce a result different from that under the General Mining Law. * * * Because the value of an endangered species exceeds anything to which a value can be assigned, any land which is critical habitat for an endangered species cannot be chiefly valuable for another purpose. The granting of oil, gas, and mineral leases is recognized as a discretionary act to which NEPA applies. Presumably the mandates of section 7 will also be applicable to minerals leasing.

THOMAS v. PETERSON
United States Court of Appeals, Ninth Circuit, 1985.
753 F.2d 754.

[Another part of this opinion is reproduced supra at page 669].

SNEED, Circuit Judge:

Plaintiffs sought to enjoin construction of a timber road in a former National Forest roadless area. The District Court granted summary judgment in favor of defendant R. Max Peterson, Chief of the Forest Service, and plaintiffs appealed. We affirm in part, reverse in part, and remand for further proceedings consistent with this opinion.

We conclude that:

* * *

(3) The Endangered Species Act (ESA) requires the Forest Service to prepare a biological assessment to determine whether the road and the timber sales that the road is designed to facilitate are likely to affect the endangered Rocky Mountain Gray Wolf, and construction of the road should be enjoined pending compliance with the ESA.

I

Statement of the Case

This is another environmental case pitting groups concerned with preserving a specific undeveloped area against an agency of the United States attempting to obey the commands given it by a Congress which is mindful of both environmentalists and those who seek to develop the nation's resources. Our task is to discern as best we can what Congress intended to be done under the facts before us.

Plaintiffs—landowners, ranchers, outfitters, miners, hunters, fishermen, recreational users, and conservation and recreation organizations—challenge actions of the United States Forest Service in planning and approving a timber road in the Jersey Jack area of the Nezperce National Forest in Idaho. The area is adjacent to the Salmon River, a congressionally-designated Wild and Scenic River, and is bounded on the west by the designated Gospel Hump Wilderness and on the east by the River of No Return Wilderness. The area lies in a "recovery corridor" identified by the U.S. Fish & Wildlife Service for the Rocky Mountain Gray Wolf, an endangered species.

* * *

After the passage of the Central Idaho Wilderness Act, the Forest Service, in keeping with its earlier expressed intention, proceeded to plan timber development in the Jersey Jack area. In November, 1980, the Forest Service solicited public comments and held a public hearing on a proposed gravel road that would provide access to timber to be sold. The Forest Service prepared an environmental assessment (EA), see 40 C.F.R. § 1508.9 (1984), to determine whether an EIS would be required for the road. Based on the EA, the Forest Service concluded that no EIS was required, and issued a Finding of No Significant Impact (FONSI), see 40 C.F.R. § 1508.13. The FONSI and the notice of the Forest Supervisor's decision to go ahead with the road were issued in a single document on February 9, 1981. The decision notice stated that "no known threatened or endangered plant or animal species have been found" within the area, but the EA contained no discussion of endangered species.

* * *

IV

The Endangered Species Act Claim

The plaintiffs' third claim concerns the Forest Service's alleged failure to comply with the Endangered Species Act (ESA) in considering the effects of the road and timber sales on the endangered Rocky Mountain Gray Wolf.

The ESA contains both substantive and procedural provisions. Substantively, the Act prohibits the taking or importation of endangered species, see 16 U.S.C. § 1538, and requires federal agencies to ensure that their actions are not "likely to jeopardize the continued existence of any endangered species or threatened species or result in the destruction or adverse modification" of critical habitat of such species, see 16 U.S.C. § 1536(a)(2).

The Act prescribes a three-step process to ensure compliance with its substantive provisions by federal agencies. Each of the first two steps serves a screening function to determine if the successive steps are required. The steps are:

(1) An agency proposing to take an action must inquire of the Fish & Wildlife Service (F & WS) whether any threatened or endangered species "may be present" in the area of the proposed action. See 16 U.S.C. § 1536(c)(1).

(2) If the answer is affirmative, the agency must prepare a "biological assessment" to determine whether such species "is likely to be affected" by the action. Id. The biological assessment may be part of an environmental impact statement or environmental assessment. Id.

(3) If the assessment determines that a threatened or endangered species "is likely to be affected," the agency must formally consult with the F & WS. Id. § 1536(a)(2). The formal consultation results in a "biological opinion" issued by the F & WS. See id. § 1536(b). If the biological opinion concludes that the proposed action would jeopardize the species or destroy or adversely modify critical habitat, see id. § 1536(a)(2), then the action may not go forward unless the F & WS can suggest an alternative that avoids such jeopardization, destruction, or adverse modification. Id. § 1536(b)(3)(A). If the opinion concludes that the action will not violate the Act, the F & WS may still require measures to minimize its impact. Id. § 1536(b)(4)(ii)–(iii).

Plaintiffs first allege that, with respect to the Jersey Jack road, the Forest Service did not undertake step (1), a formal request to the F & WS. The district court found that to be the case, but concluded that the procedural violation was insignificant because the Forest Service was already aware that wolves may be present in the area. The court therefore refused to enjoin the construction of the road. Plaintiffs insist, based on TVA v. Hill, 437 U.S. 153 (1978), that an injunction is mandatory once any ESA violation is found. Defendants respond, citing Village of False Pass v. Clark, 733 F.2d 605 (9th Cir.1984), that *TVA* applies only to substantive violations of the ESA, and that a court has discretion to deny an injunction when it finds a procedural violation to be *de minimis*.

We need not reach this issue. The Forest Service's failure goes beyond the technical violation cited by the district court, and is not *de minimis*.

Once an agency is aware that an endangered species may be present in the area of its proposed action, the ESA requires it to prepare a biological assessment to determine whether the proposed action "is likely to affect" the species and therefore requires formal consultation with the F & WS. The Forest Service did not prepare such an assessment prior to its decision to build the Jersey Jack road.

Without a biological assessment, it cannot be determined whether the proposed project will result in a violation of the ESA's substantive provisions. A failure to prepare a biological assessment for a project in an area in which it has been determined that an endangered species may be present cannot be considered a *de minimis* violation of the ESA.

The district court found that the Forest Service had "undertaken sufficient study and action to further the purposes of the ESA." Its finding was based on affidavits submitted by the Forest Service for the litigation.[7] These do not constitute a substitute for the preparation of the biological assessment required by the ESA.

Given a substantial procedural violation of the ESA in connection with a federal project, the remedy must be an injunction of the project pending compliance with the ESA. * * * A failure to prepare a biological assessment is comparable to a failure to prepare an environmental impact statement.

* * *

The district court, citing Palila v. Hawaii Dept. of Land and Natural Resources, 639 F.2d 495 (9th Cir.1981), held that "[a] party asserting a violation of the Endangered Species Act has the burden of showing the proposed action would have some prohibited effect on an endangered species or its critical habitat," and found that the plaintiffs in this case had not met that burden. This is a misapplication of *Palila.* That case concerned the ESA's prohibition of the "taking" of an endangered species, 16 U.S.C. § 1538(a)(1)(B), not the ESA's procedural requirements. Quite naturally, the court in *Palila* found that a plaintiff, in order to establish a violation of the "taking" provision, must show that such a "taking" has occurred. See 639 F.2d at 497. The holding does not apply to violations of the ESA's procedural requirements. A plaintiffs' burden in establishing a procedural violation is to show that the circumstances triggering the procedural requirement exist, and that the required procedures have not been followed. The plaintiffs in this case have clearly met that burden.

The Forest Service would require the district court, absent proof by the plaintiffs to the contrary, to make a finding that the Jersey Jack road is not likely to effect the Rocky Mountain Gray Wolf, and that therefore any failure to comply with ESA procedures is harmless. This is not a finding appropriate to the district court at the present time. Congress has assigned to the agencies and to the Fish & Wildlife Service the responsibility for evaluation of the impact of agency actions on endangered species, and has prescribed procedures for such evaluation. Only by following the procedures can proper evaluations be made. It is not the responsibility of the plaintiffs to prove, nor the

7. The district court relied on the Forest Service's assertion that it had worked in "close cooperation" with the F & WS, but that assertion is undermined by letters in the record from the F & WS indicating that the Forest Service had not consulted with the F & WS on the impact of the road and the timber sales on the gray wolf, and that the F & WS felt that the Forest Service was not giving the wolf adequate consideration.

function of the courts to judge, the effect of a proposed action on an endangered species when proper procedures have not been followed.

We therefore hold that the district court erred in declining to enjoin construction of the Jersey Jack road pending compliance with the ESA.

Finally, one additional development must be considered. The Forest Service's brief states that now a "biological evaluation" has been completed. The Service's memorandum opposing an injunction pending appeal states that the evaluation was completed on April 15, 1984, i.e., after oral argument in district court but before the court issued its decision. The brief claims that the evaluation concluded that wolves will not be affected if certain mitigation measures are taken. The Forest Service, however, has submitted the evaluation neither to this court nor to the district court, and the plaintiffs state in their brief that the Service has refused to show the evaluation to them. Obviously, therefore, this evaluation cannot serve as a basis for holding that the Forest Service has complied with the ESA. Should the Forest Service wish to enter its biological evaluation into the record, it will be for the district court to determine whether that evaluation is sufficient to satisfy the ESA's requirement of a biological assessment, and whether its preparation after the approval of the road can bring the Forest Service into compliance with the ESA. For this purpose, and for the purpose of fashioning an appropriate remedy for the Service's failure to comply with NEPA, we remand this case to the district court for proceedings consistent with this opinion.

AFFIRMED IN PART, REVERSED IN PART, AND REMANDED.

NOTES

1. The *Thomas* holding was foreshadowed in Lachenmeier, The Endangered Species Act of 1973: Preservation or Pandemonium, 5 Envtl.L. 29 (1974).

2. There was no proof that wolves actually inhabited the Jersey Jack area—only that there "may" have been wolves there. Should sightings of the species in the affected area be required before an injunction issues?

3. "In most managed forests, wildlife habitat is a byproduct of timber management. As demands have grown for increased production of wood fiber, recreation, and livestock, as well as for increased allocation of wilderness, it has become increasingly obvious that such cliches as 'good timber management is good wildlife management' will no longer suffice." J.W. Thomas, WILDLIFE HABITATS IN MANAGED FORESTS 11 (1979).

4. What human activities are compatible with the presence of wolves?

"Predator control" in the United States has a long and frequently ignominious history. Bounties on wolves, coyotes, eagles, and so forth have been common since the early seventeenth century and are only slowly disappearing today. A national "predators' rights" bill has been introduced periodically but never enacted. Other cases in this volume address, at least tangentially, the control, management, and protection of predatory species. The *Cabinet Mountains* case, infra at page 872, concerns mineral development that could adversely affect grizzly bear habitat. The *Alaska Wolf* litigation, infra at page 861, raises the question whether the Interior Secretary has a duty to protect this fierce but nonendangered predator. A similar long running saga surrounds the future of the Eastern Timber Wolf in Minnesota.

In the first reported decision, Fund for Animals v. Andrus, 11 E.R.C. 2189 (D.Minn.1978), plaintiffs challenged the government's program of trapping wolves in the vicinity of depredations.

The pertinent regulations provided that gray wolves could only be taken by authorized government personnel and only if the target wolf was "committing significant depredations on lawfully present domestic animals." Because illegal killing of wolves was common, the FWS recommended that the wolf population be kept down to avoid conflicts with humans. The FWS Director then issued a "special exception" to the regulation which allowed agents to trap wolves in the vicinity of Mr. Brzoznowski's farm if they posed an "imminent threat." The FWS began an "indiscriminate" wolf trapping program up to five miles from the farm. The court ruled the exception invalid. Excerpts from the opinion follow.

The Eastern Timber Wolf is a rather large animal, reaching 50 to 100 pounds in adulthood, and formerly roamed throughout the eastern portion of the United States from northern Minnesota to the northern tip of Florida, and throughout southeastern Canada. The present population in the United States consists of between 1,000 and 1,200 animals in northern Minnesota, approximately 40 on Isle Royale, and 6 to 10 in the upper peninsula of Michigan. The Eastern Timber Wolf, or gray wolf as it is commonly known, lives in a rather structured society consisting of a family pack, ordinarily comprised of 2 to 8 members, but in exceptional cases numbering over twice that size. Each pack exists and controls a geographic territory of 50 to 120 square miles in which it is autonomous. Each such territory is surrounded by a narrow buffer zone into which, and through which, other packs or lone wolves travel and hunt. Each pack is led by a dominant male and female pair which are usually the only wolves in the pack which procreate. An average litter is about five pups per year, under favorable breeding conditions. The general prey of the gray wolf is deer, moose, and beaver. However, they can become acclimated to taking domestic animals, especially when other feed is short, and have, historically, been the subject of persecution and slaughter by farmers and ranchers located on wolf range. Through 1965, when records were maintained, approximately 240 wolves were killed in Minnesota annually. A comparable number are probably still taken, legally or illegally. * * *

* * *

In February 1977, one Julius Brzoznowski, a farmer in northern Minnesota, commenced an action in this Court against the Secretary of the Interior and the United States of America based upon alleged loss of cattle to predator wolves. (Civil 5–77–19) This case is presently pending. [Brzoznowski apparently lost two cows to wolves; 17 confirmed instances were reported in all Minnesota in 1975–78. In that period, the FWS trapped more than 150 wolves, many of which were pups.] * * *

The plaintiffs seek an order of this Court directing the Secretary of Agriculture to provide living space to all gray wolves which are lawfully trapped in northern Minnesota. The evidence establishes that all other suitable areas in the State of Minnesota already contain the maximum wolf population which they are capable of supporting. There is no indication that any surplus wolves would be welcome elsewhere in the coterminous United States, Alaska, or Hawaii. Maintaining the captured wolves in captivity is financially, biologically, and practically inadvisable. The mandate of the Endangered Species Act does not include the impossible. * * *

* * * At first glance, the proposition that killing wolves is consistent with conserving the species appears difficult to accept. However, this is precisely the fact of the matter. * * *

SIERRA CLUB v. CLARK
United States Court of Appeals, Eighth Circuit, 1985.
755 F.2d 608.

JOHN R. GIBSON, Circuit Judge.

The chief issue before us is whether the Secretary of the Interior is authorized by the Endangered Species Act of 1973, 16 U.S.C. §§ 1531–1543 (1982), to issue regulations permitting the sport trapping of the Eastern Timber Wolf. Also in question are the legality of certain additional regulations expanding the predation control program of the wolf in northern Minnesota and the propriety of attorneys' fees awarded the Sierra Club. The district court concluded that public hunting of a threatened species such as the Eastern Timber Wolf is prohibited by the Act except in the extraordinary case where population pressures within the animal's ecosystem cannot otherwise be relieved. As the government had made no such showing, a motion for summary judgment that the sport trapping regulations violate the Endangered Species Act was granted. The district court also concluded that the additional regulations expanding the predation control program of the wolf were illegal, as they were made without explanation. It awarded the Sierra Club $55,369.45 under the attorney fee provision of the Endangered Species Act. We affirm the judgment of the district court as to the sport trapping of the wolf, reverse and remand as to the predation control regulations, and affirm the attorneys' fee award.

The case was submitted by stipulation, so the facts are not in controversy. There are approximately 1,000 to 1,200 Eastern Timber Wolves, commonly called gray wolves, in northern Minnesota. This population has remained stable since 1976, despite illegal kills estimated at as much as 25% of the population. There is no information that indicates that the wolf population has exceeded its carrying capacity or that population pressures exist that cannot be relieved other than by a sport season.

Minnesota's gray wolf population was originally listed as "endangered" under the Act.[2] However, after the Eastern Timber Wolf Recovery Team, a body of experts created pursuant to the Act and charged with the development of plans for the conservation and survival of the gray wolf, recommended that "depredation control" be used where wolves were killing domestic animals, in 1978 the Fish and Wildlife Service reclassified the gray wolf as "threatened"[3] in Minnesota and allowed trapping of depredating wolves. The implementing regulations were litigated in Fund for Animals v. Andrus, 11 Env't.Rep. Cas. (BNA) 2189 (D.Minn.1978). The district court enjoined the Fish and Wildlife Service from trapping wolves unless such action was necessary and was directed to the removal of specific wolves reasonably believed to have committed significant depredation upon livestock. The court later amended its order to restrict trapping to within one-quarter mile of the place where the predation occurred.

Several times following the litigation in *Fund for Animals,* the Minnesota Department of Natural Resources (DNR) requested that the Fish and Wildlife Service transfer control of the wolf to it and allow a public sport season. These requests were rejected both because of the failure of the requests to conform to the order in *Fund for Animals,* and because of the Service's position that the Endangered Species Act prohibits public sport trapping of threatened species unless there exists an extraordinary case where population pressures within a given ecosystem cannot be otherwise relieved.

In July 1982, however, the Service published proposed regulations granting the DNR's request for public sport trapping of the wolf. Comments were accepted, and public hearings were held in August 1982. On August 10, 1983, regulations were promulgated allowing public trapping of wolves with certain restrictions.[4] The regulations

---

2. An "endangered species" is defined as "any species which is in danger of extinction throughout all or a significant portion of its range." 16 U.S.C. § 1532(6).

3. A "threatened species" is "any species which is likely to become an endan-

gered species within the foreseeable future." 16 U.S.C. § 1532(20).

4. The regulations provide:

The Minnesota Department of Natural Resources may permit persons to take a gray wolf in zones 3, 4, and 5, as deline-

also modify the existing livestock predation control program: wolves may be taken within one-half mile of the farm where predation occurred; taking is not limited to individual predator wolves; there is no express requirement that wolves be taken in a humane manner.[5]

* * *

I

The Secretary argues that in denying him discretion to allow public sport trapping of the wolf the district court has destroyed the distinction made in the Act between endangered and threatened species. The Secretary claims that while Congress imposed in 16 U.S.C. § 1538(a)(1) a set of mandatory prohibitions regarding *endangered* species, including the taking of such species, it sought to protect *threatened* species by providing that "the Secretary shall issue such regulations as he deems necessary and advisable to provide for the conservation of such species," further clarifying and particularizing the directive by providing that "the Secretary may by regulation prohibit * * * any act prohibited under section 1538(a)(1)." 16 U.S.C. § 1533(d). Thus, argues the Secretary, Congress granted him discretion to determine whether to impose section 1538(a)(1) prohibitions, including the prohibition on taking, for a threatened species.

The extent of the Secretary's discretion, however, is limited by the requirement that the regulations he is to issue must provide for the *conservation* of threatened species. The term is defined in 16 U.S.C. § 1532(3):

> The terms "conserve", "conserving", and "conservation" mean to use and the use of all methods and procedures which are necessary to bring any endangered species or threatened species to the point at which the measures provided pursuant to this chapter are no longer necessary. Such methods and procedures include, but are not limited to, all activities associ-

ated in paragraph (d)(1) of this section: *Provided* that

(1) Such taking shall be permitted not more than 5 miles inside the boundary of zone 3, in areas of recurring wolf depredation on lawfully present domestic animals; and the extent of such taking shall be adjusted periodically to maintain an average population density of not less than 1 wolf per 10 square miles (the Minnesota Department of Natural Resources shall determine population density on the basis of generally accepted wildlife census techniques);

(2) In zone 4, such taking shall be permitted primarily in areas of recurring depredation, and the extent of such taking shall be adjusted periodically to maintain an average population density in the zone of not less than 1 wolf per 50 square miles (the Minnesota Department of Natural Resources shall determine

population density on the basis of generally accepted census techniques); and

(3) During the first year after the effective date of these regulations, not more than 50 gray wolves may be taken by the public in zone 4.

50 C.F.R. § 17.40(d)(2)(i)(C) (1983).

5. The regulations provide:

> Designated employees or agents of the Service or the Minnesota Department of Natural Resources may take a gray wolf without a permit in Minnesota, in zones 2, 3, 4, and 5, as delineated in paragraph (d)(1) of this section, in response to depredations by a gray wolf on lawfully present domestic animals: *Provided,* that such taking must occur within one-half mile of the place where such depredation occurred.

50 C.F.R. § 17.40(d)(2)(i)(B)(4) (1983).

ated with scientific resources management such as research, census, law enforcement, habitat acquisition and maintenance, propagation, live trapping, and transplantation, and, *in the extraordinary case where population pressures within a given ecosystem cannot be otherwise relieved, may include regulated taking.* (Emphasis added.)

In interpreting these provisions, our starting point must be the plain language of the statute. Further, we bear in mind that statutory definitions of words used elsewhere in the same statute furnish such authoritative evidence of legislative intent and meaning that they are usually given controlling effect. "Such internal legislative construction is of the highest value and prevails over * * * other extrinsic aids." 1A C. Sands, *Statutes and Statutory Construction* § 27.02, at 310 (4th ed. 1972). Here the plain language of the statute, including its definitional provisions, compels us to agree with the district court "that before the taking of a threatened animal can occur, a determination must be made that population pressures within the animal's ecosystem cannot otherwise be relieved." 577 F.Supp. at 787. Otherwise, such taking would not constitute an act of conservation under the Act and would fall without the scope of authority granted to the Secretary.

In reaching this conclusion, we are mindful that the Endangered Species Act is a law of limited scope whose provisions must be read together. * * * The provision under examination, section 1533(d), looks in two directions in the Act: first, as we have already observed, toward the definition of "conservation" in section 1532(3); second, by specific reference, toward section 1538(a)(1). If we turn to section 1538, we find that it prohibits, among other acts, the taking of any endangered species. Once again, we must turn to section 1532(19) for a statutory definition of taking. Further, we note that the terms "endangered species" and "threatened species" are also defined in section 1532(6) and (20) respectively. Thus, as we trace out the meaning of the provisions of section 1533(d), it becomes abundantly clear that the interrelationship of the various sections of the Act is crucial to the task of proper discernment. Congress declared as its policy in the Act "that all Federal departments and agencies shall seek to *conserve* endangered species and threatened species." 16 U.S.C. § 1531(c)(1) (emphasis added). This underscores the significance of the term "conservation" which appears so frequently in the Act. To fail to use Congress' definition of this key term would be to refuse to give effect to a crucial part of the enacted statutory law. See 1A C. Sands, supra, at 310.

* * *

The argument that the district court has eliminated the distinction between the two categories of threatened and endangered species is without merit. The district court made clear that two levels of protection would remain under its interpretation of the statute:

Section 1538(a)(1) strictly forbids the taking of an endangered animal under *any* circumstances. Only with regard to a threatened species may the Secretary exercise his discretion by ordering the taking of an animal. This discretion, however, is limited by that language found in the Act—only in the extraordinary case where population pressures within the ecosystem cannot otherwise be relieved can the Secretary permit the regulated taking of a threatened species.

577 F.Supp. at 788 (emphasis in original).

The Secretary argues that this interpretation is incorrect and instead that the proper scheme is one in which "endangered species can be taken under strictly controlled circumstances only when their numbers exceed the carrying capacity of their ecosystems" while "threatened species can be taken pursuant to regulatory measures which address the problems contributing to the species' decline." He bases this scheme solely on the definition of "conservation" in section 1532(3). In that definition the methods and procedures of conservation, including regulated taking where population pressures within an ecosystem cannot otherwise be relieved, are stated to be applicable to *both* endangered species and threatened species. The Secretary, retreating from the thrust of his earlier argument, argues that the section 1532(3) definition allows the taking of endangered species and should prevail over the prohibitions of section 1538(a)(1). Thus, while both the district court and the Secretary find two levels of protection in the Act, the Secretary argues that the 1532(3) definition affords him a discretionary base that the district court has ignored.

Once again, however, the Secretary has ignored the interrelations of the Act. Section 1533(d), when read in conjunction with the definition of "conservation" in section 1532, limits the Secretary's discretion as to threatened species. Section 1538(a)(1), when read in conjunction with the definition of "taking" in section 1532, further limits the Secretary's discretion as to endangered species. The definition of "conservation" in section 1532 does not nullify the provision of section 1538 that prohibits taking an endangered species, for the term "conservation" does not appear in section 1538. The Secretary simply ignores the language of the Act and the statutory definitions that Congress adopted to give it force. When we read sections 1533 and 1538 in light of their statutorily defined terms and in conjunction with each other, we find they clearly support the district court's interpretation of the two levels of protection provided.

* * * We conclude that the statute on its face limits the discretion of the Secretary to allow public sport hunting of threatened species.

II

The Secretary argues at length that legislative history reveals a congressional intent to give the Secretary discretion to allow taking of threatened species. We must interpret the statute in light of the purposes Congress sought to serve, and legislative history may play an important part in discerning these purposes. However, contrary to the

Secretary's position, we find that the legislative history supports our interpretation of the Act.

* * *

III

The district court also considered the changes the regulations made in the livestock predation control program:

> In addition to the regulations allowing a sport season, * * * the Secretary has sought to expand the current livestock predation control program beyond its present limits. The area in which the wolves may be trapped has gone from one-quarter mile, as previously ordered, to within one-half mile of the farm where the depredation occurred. More than that, there would no longer be a requirement that the trapper determine with reasonable cause the identity of the predating wolf or wolves. In addition, there would not be a requirement that the wolf or wolves be taken in a humane manner. These changes in the law are made without explanation. Certainly this court would encourage any changes in the predation control program that would help the government trapper along with taking as few wolves as possible. These new regulations, however, are not justified on that basis. This court has no choice but to conclude that these new regulations only go toward expanding the unnecessary taking of wolves, rather than being designed in accordance to the previous rulings of this court. Accordingly, these regulations concerning the predation control program are also determined to be illegal under the Endangered Species Act.

577 F.Supp. at 790.

In its promulgation of the regulations, the Fish and Wildlife Service stated that the distance limitation had been expanded to one-half mile because "topography occasionally eliminates the possibility of effective trapping." Regulations Governing the Gray Wolf in Minnesota, 48 Fed.Reg. 36,256, 36,258 (1983). It further stated it would allow the killing of any wolf caught within the one-half mile distance since farmer outrage over the release of a trapped wolf "cannot serve the cause of wolf conservation" and since "[a]lthough immature animals may themselves be unable to kill livestock, their existence and their need for food probably are major reasons for the occurrence of depredation, and they probably are learning to commit depredations." Id. Finally, while the regulations authorize the use of steel traps, the Service stated that "the steel trap when properly used is an effective and humane method of taking wolves." Id. at 36,263.

The Secretary argues on appeal that these statements were explanations, that finding an explanation inadequate is not identical to finding it nonexistent, and that "for all practical purposes, no analysis was conducted by the district court of whether the Service decision was reasonably based and reached after consideration of all relevant factors." The Sierra Club argues in reply that brief conclusory assertions do not rise to the level of explanations, that the expression of a need to take wolf pups did not explain the general taking of wolves permitted near farms where predation occurs, and that the elimination of the "humane manner" requirement was not specifically explained.

The parties agree that an agency must provide explanations when its rulemaking reflects significant changes in policy. As the regulations were promulgated under the informal rulemaking procedures of section 553 of the Administrative Procedures Act, the standard of review is whether the action was "arbitrary, capricious, an abuse of discretion, or otherwise not in accordance with law." 5 U.S.C. § 706(2) (A) (1982). The rescission or modification of rules is subject to this standard, and "an agency changing its course by rescinding a rule is obligated to supply a reasoned analysis for the change beyond that which may be required when an agency does not act in the first instance." Motor Vehicle Manufacturers Association v. State Farm Mutual Automobile Insurance Co., 463 U.S. 29 (1983).

We can find no indication in the district court's opinion that this standard was applied. There is a vast difference between a failure to explain and a failure to explain adequately. The argument that brief assertions do not rise to level of explanations is, essentially, an argument of *adequacy,* requiring an explicit test of such assertions. Similarly, once statements purporting to explain particular rules are made, the question becomes the *extent* to which they actually do so. The presence of the statements means that the necessary condition of their existence has been met. The next task of the reviewing court is to address the sufficiency of these statements under the "arbitrary and capricious" standard. Accordingly, we reverse the district court's conclusions as to the regulations involving predation control and remand for further consideration in light of our discussion above.

IV

The remaining issue is the propriety of the fees awarded Sierra Club's counsel by the district court. The district court made the following findings as to lodestar figures and other costs:

	Hourly Rate	Hours	Total
Attorneys:			
Brian O'Neill	$115	221	$25,415.00
Amy Bromberg	60	124	7,440.00
Other costs:			
Legal Assistants			213.75
Disbursements and Expenses			5,244.20
Student Interns	10	720	7,200.00
			$45,512.95

A 30% upward adjustment was then applied to the lodestar figures for the two attorneys, making the total fees and expenses awarded $55,369.45.

The Endangered Species Act provides that in suits brought by private parties to enforce the terms of the Act, the court may award the costs of litigation (including reasonable attorney and expert witness fees) to any party when the court determines such an award is appropriate. 16 U.S.C. § 1540(g)(4). In Ruckelshaus v. Sierra Club, 462 U.S. 680 (1983), the Supreme Court interpreted an identical provision in the Clean Air Act as allowing fees only when the petitioner achieves "some success on the merits" of its claims. Here the Sierra Club clearly has achieved such success. While we are reversing and remanding for further consideration of the predation control regulations, both parties treated this question as a relatively minor issue (for example, in his main brief the Secretary devoted but two of the eighteen pages of his argument to the issue). The Sierra Club has otherwise prevailed and is eligible for the award.

The Secretary argues, however, that the upward adjustment is not justified. The district court found that the multiplier of 30% was appropriate "due to both the contingent nature of the success attained by plaintiffs, and the public importance of that success." It further found that the issue was a "novel one" and a "difficult one which could not have been easily predicted." Id. at 8. The court found these extraordinary circumstances and the importance of the case to the management of all threatened species justified the enhancement.

* * *

We affirm the judgment of the district court as to the illegality of the regulations permitting sport trapping of the gray wolf, reverse and remand for further consideration of the expanded predation control regulations, and affirm the award of attorneys' fees.

ROSS, Circuit Judge, dissenting.

I respectfully dissent. The Secretary's authority to utilize regulated taking of threatened species as a method of conservation is *not limited* to the "extraordinary case where population pressures cannot be otherwise relieved." 16 U.S.C. § 1532(3) (1982). Instead, the Secretary's authority in this respect is limited only by the necessity that, if regulated taking is to be utilized, it must further the effort to bring threatened species "to the point at which the measures provided pursuant to * * * [the Endangered Species Act] * * * are no longer necessary." Id.

As applied to this case, the Secretary's authority to utilize regulated taking of timber wolves is limited only by the requirement that such method aid the effort of bringing the wolves to the point at which they can survive and propagate without the need of the protections of the Endangered Species Act. The fact that timber wolves do not exceed the population limits of its ecosystem is not determinative. Since the district court failed to make a finding that the sport trapping regulation at issue either furthered, or did not further, the effort to conserve the timber wolf, I would remand the case for a finding on this issue.

* * *

My conclusion in this case is buttressed by the following example: Several members of a pack of wolves became afflicted with a disease which is highly contagious between members of the species and which leaves visible signs of its presence. The Secretary seeks to utilize a regulated taking of the diseased animals to prevent the spread of the disease. However, a regulated taking of diseased animals which might infect an entire threatened species is not expressly set forth as a method of conservation in section 1532(3). Nor would such a circumstance constitute a "case where population pressures cannot be otherwise relieved." Yet, an appropriately defined regulated taking would clearly constitute a useful method of conservation in such a case. The majority's approach, however, would foreclose the use of regulated taking in such a case.

* * *

In sum, I would remand the case for a determination as to whether the Secretary's regulations further a conservation purpose. If it were established that this purpose could be furthered by letting the public kill wolves for sport and sell the pelts, then this method would not be foreclosed by the Endangered Species Act. In fact, the Endangered Species Act might actually require that this method be used. The majority's approach is overbroad and thus detrimental to possible future beneficial uses of regulated taking as a method of conservation. Accordingly, I must dissent.

I would also reduce substantially or eliminate the attorneys fees awarded by the district court. Even if the trial court was completely affirmed the 30 percent additur was clearly wrong.

NOTES

1. Is this the best or most efficient way of handling the predation problem? Consider the thousands of hours put in by biologists, administrators, witnesses, lawyers, and courts toward resolving this emotional imbroglio. Would it be better as well as cheaper just to pay for the few dozen cows that were killed by wolves?

2. Refer again to the wild horse roundup cases. Do they present the same question as *Minnesota Wolf Kill* litigation? Is that question primarily political? How do these cases cut against the notion that wildlife management is a science? As to the administrative response to the initial order, compare *Ruby Lake Refuge II,* infra at page 836.

3. Chief Justice Burger observed in *TVA v. Hill* that the worth of a species is incalculable, at least for a court. Is this necessarily so? Should it be so? What precisely is the value to society of the continued existence of a species? Should it matter if the species is a bald eagle or grey wolf on the one hand, or a slug, plant, bat, or snail darter on the other?

4. The use, often indiscriminate, of various poisons to kill animals that prey on domestic livestock or fowl or that annoy people has long been controversial.   In 1972, President Nixon by Executive Order banned the use of most such poisons on the public lands and the EPA cancelled the registration of the worst offender, Compound 1080, because it caused the deaths of thousands of "nontarget" wildlife species. In January 1982, President Reagan revoked that Executive order, 47 Fed.Reg. 4223 (1982), and it appeared that the war on the wild coyote would rapidly escalate.   The EPA subsequently decided to allow the use of 1080, but only in the form of sheep collars (coyotes tend to go for the sheep's throat) or of fairly tightly controlled single lethal dose baits. The new rules were upheld against challenges from both environmentalists and ranchers in National Cattlemen's Ass'n v. United States EPA, 773 F.2d 268 (10th Cir.1985).   See generally Coggins & Evans, Predators' Rights and American Wildlife Law, 24 Ariz.L.Rev. 821 (1983).

5. In the principal case, the award of attorneys fees to plaintiff was based on a provision in the Endangered Species Act.   When the governing statute does not contain such a provision, environmental plaintiffs have been able to recover costs and attorneys fees pursuant to the Equal Access to Justice Act, 28 U.S.C.A. § 2412, "unless the court finds that the position of the United States was substantially justified or that special circumstances make an award unjust."   Id. § 2412(d)(1) (A).   In spite of those limitations, the possibility of recovering attorneys fees could be the catalyst for a renewed explosion of public land and natural resources litigation.

B. THE NATIONAL WILDLIFE REFUGE SYSTEM

MICHAEL J. BEAN, THE EVOLUTION OF NATIONAL WILDLIFE LAW
126–34 (1977).

The National Wildlife Refuge System is the only extensive system of federally owned lands managed chiefly for the conservation of wildlife.   Its origins can be traced to the turn of the century, when the first federal wildlife refuges were established by Presidential proclamation.   Soon thereafter, Congress also became directly involved in the creation of wildlife refuges, first by authorizing the President in 1905 and 1906 to designate areas within Wichita National Forest and Grand Canyon National Forest, respectively, as wildlife ranges, and then by itself establishing a National Bison Range in Montana in 1908.

The stimulus for establishing a systematic program of refuge acquisition was provided by the Migratory Bird Treaty Act [of 1918].   The failure of that Act to authorize the acquisition of migratory bird habitat came to be recognized as a serious shortcoming.   To provide the needed acquisition authority, the Migratory Bird Conservation Act was passed in 1929. * * * As originally enacted, the Conservation Act provided that all refuges acquired pursuant to its authority be operated as "inviolate sanctuaries." By amendments in 1949 and 1958, however, the Secretary was authorized to permit public hunting, first on not more than twenty-five percent, and then forty percent, of the total area of any such refuge, if "compatible with the major purposes for which such areas were established." One final noteworthy feature of the Conservation Act is that it, unlike most other statutes authorizing federal acquisition of land, requires that the Secretary first obtain the consent of the state in which the lands to be acquired are located before acquisition can be carried out.

Enactment of the Migratory Bird Hunting Stamp Act in 1934 assured a steady source of funding for refuge acquisition under the Conservation Act, but in a way that almost assured the development of a refuge system keyed principally to the production of migratory waterfowl. * * *

* * * [M]ention should be made of the Department of Agriculture's Water Bank Program for Wetlands Preservation, carried out under authority of the Water Bank Act of 1970 [16 U.S.C.A. §§ 1301–11]. Under that program, the Secretary of Agriculture may enter into ten-year renewable agreements with private landowners and operators in important migratory waterfowl nesting and breeding areas. In return for payment of an agreed upon annual fee, the participating landowner or operator agrees "not to drain, burn, fill, or otherwise destroy the wetland character" of areas included in the program, or "to use such areas for agricultural purposes." If a private party violates the agreement and his violation "is of such a nature as to warrant termination of the agreement", he must forfeit all rights to receive future payments and refund past payments under the agreement. The total payments which the Secretary is authorized to make in any one year under the program may not exceed $10 million. Thus, the Water Bank Program offers a significant alternative to outright acquisition for the protection of migratory bird habitat.

* * *

Until 1966, there was no single law governing the administration of the many federal wildlife refuges. * * * A measure of rationalization was introduced into this system by passage of the "National Wildlife Refuge System Administration Act of 1966." That Act consolidated these various units [with different designations] into a single "National Wildlife Refuge System." Beyond that fact of consolidation, however, the Act did little to spell out standards to guide the administration of the System. Basically, it (1) placed restrictions on the transfer, exchange or other disposal of lands within the system, (2) clarified the Secretary's authority to accept donations of money to be used for land acquisition, and (3) most importantly, authorized the Secretary, under regulations, to "permit the use of any area within the System for any purpose, including but not limited to hunting, fishing, public recreation and accommodations, and access whenever he determines that such uses are compatible with the major purposes for which such areas were established" [16 U.S.C.A. § 668dd(d)(1)]. This authorization of "compatible" uses thus made clear that the national wildlife refuges were not necessarily to be managed as "single-use" lands, but more properly as "dominant use" lands.

The 1966 Act did not affect two earlier statutes relating to the management of wildlife refuges.   *   *   *   [The Refuge Recreation Act of 1962, 16 U.S.C.A. §§ 460k to k–4 and The Refuge Revenue Sharing Act of 1964, 16 U.S.C.A. § 715s.]

*   *   *

The three statutes just described constitute the basic authority within which the National Wildlife Refuge System operates. In recent years, a number of varied controversies have arisen regarding various aspects of the administration of that system. These controversies have concerned such issues as the Secretary's authority to permit or prohibit particular uses under the compatibility standard, his authority to transfer lands from the system, the application of the National Environmental Policy Act to decisions affecting the refuges, and, most fundamentally, which government agency has ultimate responsibility for their management.

The consolidation of so many disparate units effectuated by the National Wildlife Refuge System Administration Act could not, by itself, change the fact that some of those units were established for purposes somewhat different from those for which others were established. In particular, the System included some units which were expressly established both for the protection of wildlife *and* for grazing of domestic livestock. Reflecting that duality of purpose, certain of these units, known as "game ranges", were jointly administered until 1975 by the Fish and Wildlife Service and BLM. In that year, however, the Secretary of the Interior directed that sole management of three such game ranges be vested in BLM. The prospect that the Fish and Wildlife Service, whose paramount mission is wildlife conservation, would be divested of its authority in favor of the multiple use oriented BLM so alarmed wildlife proponents that a lawsuit to reverse the Secretary's action was filed almost as proposed legislation to achieve the same end was introduced.

Both the litigative and legislative efforts were successful. In Wilderness Society v. Hathaway [Civ. No. 75–1004 (D.D.C., Jan. 26, 1976)], the District Court for the District of Columbia enjoined the transfer on the ground that "the Secretary is required to exercise his discretion and authority with respect to the administration of game ranges and wildlife refuges through the Fish and Wildlife Service." One month later, that result was confirmed by the passage of an amendment to the National Wildlife Refuge System Administration Act specifically directing that all units of the System be administered through the Fish and Wildlife Service, and that all units then within the System remain so except under certain limited conditions.

*   *   *

Despite the express recognition in the Refuge Administration Act that up to forty percent of the area of any refuge acquired pursuant to the Migratory Bird Conservation Act may be opened to migratory bird hunting, several cases have challenged hunting generally or certain types of hunting as being incompatible with the major purposes for which such refuges were established. To date, no such efforts have met with success.

* * *

* * * Recent passage of "organic acts" or their equivalents for BLM and Forest Service management of the National Resource Lands and the National Forest System, respectively, invites the question whether similar "organic" authority is needed for Fish and Wildlife Service administration of the Refuge System. In fact, such legislation was introduced by Congressman Dingell at the time of the game range transfer controversy. It would have declared as a statement of policy that the various units of the System should be "managed to retain or restore the natural and primeval status of the environment, assuring the survival in a natural state of each indigenous plant and animal species." This statement of management policy would mark a significant departure from the "featured species" concept that has characterized the management of some units of the System.[56] Other aspects of the bill would have introduced equally novel ideas into the Refuge System. Among these were provisions designating certain coastal Alaskan areas as "marine and estuarine" sanctuaries, whose boundaries would extend three, or in some cases five miles out to sea, thus holding out the potential of melding together the Refuge System and the "marine sanctuary" system of the Marine Protection, Research and Sanctuaries Act. While the Dingell bill was not enacted, it represents the most comprehensive attempt thus far to give detailed legislative direction to the management of the Refuge System. As such, it will probably serve as the starting point for future such efforts.

SCHWENKE v. SECRETARY OF THE INTERIOR

United States Court of Appeals, Ninth Circuit, 1983.
720 F.2d 571.

NORRIS, Circuit Judge.

This case involves a series of executive orders and statutes dealing with livestock grazing and wildlife preservation on the Charles M. Russell National Wildlife Range (Russell Range or Range), an area of approximately 823,456 acres in northeastern Montana owned by the United States. We are called upon first to decide the relative priorities of wildlife and livestock in access to the natural forage resources of the

---

56. The 1968 Leopold Report * * * made the same call for ecosystem management of wildlife refuges in the following words:

Each refuge, though part of a network, should be viewed as an independent microcosm with many biological features and values of its own, all of which should be appreciated and if possible sustained in some harmonious combination. This overview of the refuge as an oasis for wildlife in general has not been especially evident in the management of the National Wildlife Refuges to date.

Range. Second, we must decide whether livestock grazing on the Russell Range is to be administered under the Taylor Grazing Act or the National Wildlife Refuge System Administration Act (Wildlife Refuge Act).

I

Plaintiffs are ranchers holding permits for grazing on the Russell Range. They brought this action against the Secretary of the Interior and officials of the Department of the Interior's Fish and Wildlife Service seeking a declaratory judgment that livestock grazing on the Russell Range should be administered under the Taylor Grazing Act, rather than the Wildlife Refuge Act, as a use entitled to equal status with wildlife preservation, and that the Fish and Wildlife Service had unlawfully subordinated livestock grazing on the Russell Range to wildlife protection.

The district court granted partial summary judgment in favor of the ranchers, holding that livestock grazing and wildlife conservation are of coequal priority and that grazing is to be administered under the Taylor Grazing Act. On appeal, the Secretary argues that the land constituting the Russell Range was set aside by the government in 1936 primarily for wildlife preservation and that livestock grazing was to be only an incidental use. Alternatively, the Secretary argues that if the government ever intended to accord livestock grazing and wildlife protection equal status, Congress changed that priority scheme by legislation passed in 1976. Finally, the Secretary contends that legislation passed by Congress in 1976 mandates that grazing on the Russell Range be administered under the Wildlife Refuge Act, not the Taylor Grazing Act.

II

The first important legislation dealing with livestock grazing in the Western States was the Taylor Grazing Act. * * * Shortly after passage of the Act, several grazing districts were created under the Taylor Grazing Act, including districts on the land that later became the Russell Range.[2]

2. These grazing districts were established on lands withdrawn from settlement and sale by Executive Order No. 6910 (Nov. 26, 1934). That order, signed in 1934, withdrew all unappropriated public land in several Western States from settlement and sale pending determination of "the most useful purpose to which such land may be put in consideration of the provisions of the [Grazing] Act * * * and for conservation and development of natural resources." The district court held that the order withdrew the Russell Range for grazing purposes under the Taylor Grazing Act. Because it could find no evidence that this withdrawal has been revoked, the district court held that grazing and wildlife had equal priority on the Range and the Russell Range must still be administered under the Taylor Grazing Act. The Secretary argues, and the ranchers seem to concede, that the district court erred on this point. The district court decision ignores Executive Order No. 7274 (Jan. 14, 1936), signed by President Roosevelt in 1936. That order amended E.O. 6910 to exclude "from the operation thereof all lands which are now, or may hereafter be, included within grazing districts duly established pursuant to the provisions of the TGA so long as such lands remain a part of any such grazing district." This order, both parties agree, revoked E.O. 6910 as to the Russell Range. Thus

In 1936, two years after passage of the Taylor Grazing Act, President Roosevelt issued Executive Order No. 7509, 3 C.F.R. 227 (1936). That order contained several important provisions. First, it created the Fort Peck Game Range on the land that is now the Charles M. Russell Range and ordered that the Range was to be "withdrawn from settlement, location, sale or entry and reserved and set apart for the conservation and development of natural wildlife resources and for the protection and improvement of public grazing land and natural forage resources."

Second, E.O. 7509 directed that conservation and development of wildlife on the Range were to be under the joint jurisdiction of the Secretary of the Interior and the Secretary of Agriculture and that grazing and natural forage resources on the Range were to be under the sole jurisdiction of the Secretary of the Interior.[3]

Third, the order specifically provided for a wildlife use. Since it is this part of E.O. 7509 that is at the heart of the present controversy, we set it out in full:

> [T]he natural forage resources [on the Range] shall be first utilized for the purpose of sustaining in a healthy condition a maximum of four hundred thousand (400,000) sharptail grouse, and one thousand five hundred (1,500) antelope, the primary species, and such nonpredatory secondary species in such numbers as may be necessary to maintain a balanced wildlife population, but in no case shall the consumption of forage by the combined population of the wildlife species be allowed to increase the burden of the range dedicated to the primary species.

Id. at 228

Finally, the order provided that "all the forage resources within this range or preserve shall be available, except as herein otherwise provided with respect to wildlife, for domestic livestock" under rules and regulations promulgated by the Secretary of the Interior under the authority of the Taylor Grazing Act.

E.O. 7509 can be read in several ways. It is possible, as the Secretary argues, to read the order as establishing an absolute priority for wildlife over livestock. E.O. 7509 specifically provides that "the natural forage resources [of the Russell Range] shall be *first* utilized" for the purpose of maintaining primary and nonpredatory secondary species of wildlife in such numbers as necessary to maintain a balanced wildlife population. While forage resources within the Range are

any withdrawal of the Russell Range lands effected by E.O. 6910 was no longer valid. The dispute in this case thus centers not on the meaning of E.O. 6910, but instead on the meaning of E.O. 7509, which followed it.

3. In 1936, when E.O. 7509 was issued, the Bureau of Land Management was a part of the Department of the Interior while the Fish and Wildlife Service was a part of the Department of Agriculture. It was not until three years later, in 1939, that Fish and Wildlife Service was moved to the Department of the Interior and the Secretary of the Interior thereby became responsible for administration of the entire Range.

available for livestock grazing, they are available "*except* as * * * otherwise provided [in the order] with respect to wildlife." The "first utilized" language applies to (1) primary species; (2) secondary species; and (3) a balanced wildlife population. It is not unreasonable to argue that the numbers set out in the order establish priority among types of wildlife and that the first utilized language, referring as it does to both "primary" and "secondary species," establishes an absolute priority for wildlife over livestock.

It is also possible to read E.O. 7509, as do the ranchers, as making no distinction between wildlife and livestock in terms of access to the resources of the Range. The preamble to E.O. 7509 provides that the Range is withdrawn from settlement and sale "for the conservation and development of natural wildlife resources and for the protection and improvement of public grazing lands and natural forage resources." Id. at 227. This passage, at least, does not distinguish between wildlife and livestock. Moreover, it is undisputed that from 1936 until 1976, the Bureau of Land Management and the Fish and Wildlife Service administered the Russell Range on the premise that wildlife and livestock had equal priority in access to the resources of the Range.

Neither the ranchers' nor the Secretary's position, however, is ultimately convincing. The ranchers' position—that grazing and wildlife preservation enjoy equal status on the Range—altogether ignores the language commanding that the resources of the Range shall be "first utilized" for the support of certain types of wildlife. The argument of the Secretary—that wildlife has absolute priority on the Range—ignores forty years of administration of the Range by the Fish and Wildlife Service and the Bureau of Land Management.[4] It also ignores the language of the order itself. E.O. 7509 refers to a "*maximum*" of 400,000 sharptail grouse and 1500 antelope. Had an absolute wildlife priority been intended, it is hard to see why such limits were established. Moreover, the last portion of E.O. 7509 provides that land

> acquired and to be acquired by the United States for the use of the Department of Agriculture for the conservation of migratory birds and other wildlife, shall be and remain under the exclusive administration of the Secretary of Agriculture and may be utilized for public grazing purposes only to such extent as may be determined by the said Secretary to be compatible with the utilization of said lands for the purposes for which they were acquired as aforesaid under regulations prescribed by him.

Id. at 228. This language clearly established an absolute priority for wildlife on any lands that may be acquired by the Department of

---

4. The ranchers argue that this historical practice should be dispositive in our interpretation of E.O. 7509. While lengthy historical practice can be a significant aid in interpreting unclear legislative or executive pronouncements, *see* Bryant v. Yellen, 447 U.S. 352 (1980); Andrus v. Shell Oil Co., 446 U.S. 657 (1980), it is useful only in interpreting language that is facially unclear. In the case of E.O. 7509, we cannot ignore the order's explicit language establishing a limited priority for wildlife on the Russell Range, even if the Bureau of Land Management and the Fish and Wildlife Service chose to do so for a number of years.

Agriculture for conservation of birds and wildlife. If such a priority had been intended on the entire Range, we would expect similarly explicit language to have been employed. Finally, if an absolute priority for wildlife had been intended on the entire Range there would have been no need then to carve out a priority for wildlife on particular parts of the Range.

We therefore reject both of these extreme positions. We instead are persuaded by an intermediate position that seems to us to represent a fairer reading of E.O. 7509 than that advanced by either the ranchers or the Secretary. We believe E.O. 7509 establishes a limited priority for wildlife beyond which grazing and wildlife preservation have equal status. It is clear that some priority for wildlife was intended. E.O. 7509 specifically provides that the resources of the Range shall be "first utilized" to support the primary and secondary species. It is equally clear, however, that that priority was limited. The order provides that the Range shall be first utilized for wildlife up to a maximum of 400,000 sharptail grouse, 1500 antelope, and that number of secondary species necessary to maintain a balanced wildlife population. We thus hold that E.O. 7509 established a priority in access to the forage resources of the Range for, in numbers within the Secretary's discretion, a maximum of 400,000 sharptail grouse, 1500 antelope, and that number of secondary species reasonably necessary to maintain a balanced wildlife population. Beyond those limits, wildlife and livestock have equal priority in access to the forage resources of the Range.

We do not believe the Secretary would vigorously dispute our reading of E.O. 7509. Fundamentally, our reading is that of the Secretary tempered by the numerical limits on priority for wildlife set out explicitly in the order. The Secretary does, however, argue that E.O. 7509, regardless of how it is read, is irrelevant to the priority scheme that must currently be employed on the Range because legislation passed by Congress in 1976 revoked E.O. 7509 and set forth a new priority scheme for access to the forage resources of the Range. It is to that argument that we now turn.

III

On October 15, 1966, Congress enacted the National Wildlife Refuge System Administration Act, (codified as amended at 16 U.S.C. §§ 668dd–668ee (1976)), establishing the National Wildlife Refuge System. Then, in 1976 Congress enacted the Wildlife Refuge Act Amendments, Pub.L. 94–223, 90 Stat. 199 (codified at 16 U.S.C. § 668dd (1976)). That legislation provided that

> [f]or the purpose of consolidating the authorities relating to the various categories of areas that are administered by the Secretary of the Interior for the conservation of fish and wildlife, * * * all lands, waters, and interests therein administered by the Secretary as wildlife refuges, * * * wildlife ranges, game ranges, wildlife management areas, or waterfowl production areas are hereby designated as the 'National Wildlife

Refuge System' (referred to herein as the 'System'), which shall
be ＊　＊　＊ administered by the Secretary through the United
States Fish and Wildlife Service.

The legislation thus transferred control of the Russell Range from
the Bureau of Land Management and the Fish and Wildlife Service
jointly to the Fish and Wildlife Service alone. The Secretary argues
that P.L. 94–223 was passed to assure that wildlife would have absolute
priority in access to the forage resources of the Range and that the
priority scheme it mandated superseded any scheme that may have
been effected by E.O. 7509. Pursuant to this interpretation of the 1976
Amendments, on May 3, 1978 the Secretary issued Public Land Order
5635, 43 Fed.Reg. 19046 (1978), which transferred control of the Russell
Range to the Fish and Wildlife Service, decreed that the Range was to
be administered under the Wildlife Refuge Act, and declared that E.O.
7509 had been modified to the extent necessary to conform to these two
orders.

The district court declared P.L.O. 5635 invalid. It held that the
1976 Amendments neither revoked the priority scheme set out in E.O.
7509 nor changed the statute under which the Range was to be
administered. The district court held further that the only effect P.L.
94–223 had in regard to the Russell Range was to transfer administrative responsibility for the Range to the Fish and Wildlife Service. On
appeal, the Secretary argues that we should reverse the district court
and hold P.L.O. 5635 a valid exercise of his power.

The district court based its holding on the fact that the language of
P.L. 94–223 did not explicitly revoke E.O. 7509 with respect to access to
the forage resources of the Range. It refused to consider the legislative
history of P.L. 94–223, relying on the "plain meaning" doctrine of
statutory construction. The court reasoned that because P.L. 94–223
was not "ambiguous"—because its meaning was plain—there was no
need to resort to legislative history. This, we believe, was error.

First, the district court misapplied the plain meaning rule. As
stated by the Supreme Court less than two years ago, "the plain-
meaning rule is 'rather an axiom of experience than a rule of law, and
does not preclude consideration of persuasive evidence if it exists.' "
Watt v. Alaska, 451 U.S. 259 (1981) (quoting Boston Sand Co. v. United
States, 278 U.S. 41, 48 (1928)).

＊　＊　＊

Second, the meaning of P.L. 94–223 is not altogether clear. It is
true that the language of the statute only transfers control of the
Range to the Fish and Wildlife Service and does not mention the
relative priorities of livestock and wildlife in access to the forage
resources of the Range. However, the primary mission of the Fish and
Wildlife Service is wildlife preservation. Fish and Wildlife Act of 1956,
§ 2, 16 U.S.C. § 742a (1976). It is certainly possible to argue that when
Congress transferred administrative responsibility for the Range to the
Fish and Wildlife Service it had in mind the primary mission of the
agency and intended to change the relative priority between livestock

and wildlife on the Range. In short, P.L. 94–223 is sufficiently ambiguous to justify resort to its legislative history.

When we consider the legislative history of P.L. 94–223, it is clear that both legislators and members of the Department of the Interior instrumental in the passage of P.L. 94–223 believed that wildlife either already had or would, after passage of the 1976 Amendments, have priority on the Range. The Assistant Secretary of the Interior noted during the hearings on the Amendments that "[the] BLM will continue to manage the areas for the dominant use of wildlife." One Congressman stated that the ranges under discussion "have been set aside primarily to protect the resident wildlife and their habitat * * *. All acknowledge that the law requires that fish and wildlife be first priority on these three ranges." 121 Cong.Rec. 36,597 (1975). The Senate Floor Manager of the bill explained that

> [t]he Executive Order which created the game ranges specified that grazing would be permitted only when compatible with wildlife needs.
>
> * * *
>
> [The Fish and Wildlife Service intention is] to permit continuation of grazing on the game ranges where it does not interfere with the wildlife for which the areas were created.
>
> * * *
>
> What the bill does, simply is to say to the Fish and Wildlife Service "You administer this for the preservation of the wildlife and to the extent that it is compatible therewith, continue to issue grazing permits or whatever reasonable use there is of public lands."
>
> * * *
>
> [I]t is the legislative intent, so far as this bill is concerned, that the Fish and Wildlife Service will continue to manage these ranges to be utilized to whatever extent possible for other uses besides preservation of the fish and wildlife, so long as it does not impinge upon it and make it impossible to preserve those values.

122 Cong.Rec. 2294–2295 (1976).

Were we to consider only the statute, read in light of its legislative history, we would rule that P.L. 94–223 commands that wildlife have priority in access to the forage resources of the Range and that the Range is to be administered under the Wildlife Refuge Act. We cannot consider the statute alone, however, for in determining its effect we must not only determine the meaning of P.L. 94–223 but must also determine whether the statute effectively revoked the contrary commands of E.O. 7509.

It is the law of our circuit that revocation or modification of an existing withdrawal should be express to be effective. See United States v. Consolidated Mines and Smelting Co., Ltd., 455 F.2d 432, 445–46 (9th Cir.1971). Repeal of a statute or order by implication is not favored. Watt v. Alaska, 451 U.S. 259, 267 (1981). We believe, given this rule, the priority scheme established by E.O. 7509 has not been revoked. Nowhere in the 1976 Amendments is anything said about priority in access to the forage resources of the Range. There is simply no mention of livestock, grazing, or E.O. 7509. Furthermore, the legislative history on this point is more indicative of confusion regarding the existing priority scheme than of an intent to change priorities. Many legislators seemed to think E.O. 7509 had established an absolute wildlife priority. Such confusion is not sufficient to revoke E.O. 7509. We thus hold that P.L. 94–223 did not revoke the priority scheme for access to the resources of the Range established by E.O. 7509.

IV

The Secretary contends also that P.L. 94–223 mandates that any grazing activity on the Russell Range be administered under the Wildlife Refuge Act rather than the Taylor Grazing Act, under which the Range was previously administered. The district court, however, held that P.L. 94–223 did not change the statute under which the Range is to be administered. We agree with the Secretary.

While the language of P.L. 94–223 does not explicitly change administration of the Range from the Taylor Grazing Act to the Wildlife Refuge Act, when the statute is read in conjunction with its legislative history the intention to change Range management to the Wildlife Refuge Act is clear. The Wildlife Refuge Act is the statute under which the Fish and Wildlife Service manages the National Wildlife Refuge System. It defies reason to suggest that Congress merely liked the personnel of the Fish and Wildlife Service more than those of the Bureau of Land Management. Congress clearly wanted the Russell Range administered by the Fish and Wildlife Service because of its underlying mission to protect wildlife. The Wildlife Refuge Act is an integral part of that mission and, we believe, was part of the change Congress intended in transferring administrative responsibility for the Russell Range from the Bureau of Land Management to the Fish and Wildlife Service.

Moreover, the legislative history of the 1976 Amendments indicates that at least some leading legislators believed that transfer of management from the Bureau of Land Management to the Fish and Wildlife Service changed the statute under which the Range was to be administered from the Taylor Grazing Act to the Wildlife Refuge Act. Senator Moss noted:

> On behalf of the Committee on Commerce I would like to assure the Senator from Montana that sole administration of the Kofa, Russell, and Sheldon Game Ranges by the Fish and Wildlife Service will not result in the instantaneous termination of existing grazing privileges on these areas. Rather, it is the committee's understanding that the Service will continue to honor valid existing grazing permits that were issued by BLM under the Taylor Grazing Act. When these permits expire, the Service will then reexamine them to determine if

continued grazing is compatible with wildlife needs. Grazing will be permitted to the extent compatible and will be administered by the Service pursuant to the National Wildlife Refuge Administration Act. I might note that the Service is currently administering over 1 million acres of refuge lands in 31 States for grazing purposes.

122 Cong.Rec. 2294 (1976).

We thus hold that, while P.L. 94–223 did not change the relative priorities of wildlife and livestock on the Charles M. Russell National Wildlife Range, it did change the statute under which the Range is to be administered from the Taylor Grazing Act to the National Wildlife Refuge System Administration Act.

V

The judgment of the district court is VACATED to the extent that it is inconsistent with this opinion. The cause is remanded for entry of declaratory judgment that (1) wildlife has priority in access to the forage resources of the Range up to the limits specified in E.O. 7509; (2) beyond those limits, wildlife and livestock have equal priority in access to the resources of the Range; and (3) the Range is to be administered under the Wildlife Refuge Act.

REMANDED.

NOTES

1. How could the legislative history have been clearer as to the intended effect of the law? Is there anything in the quoted legislative history indicating that grazing has any sort of equality with wildlife? As between an executive order and an act of Congress, which should take priority? Does your answer encompass public land orders? On interpretation of executive orders, see NWF v. Morton, 393 F.Supp. 1286 (D.D.C.1975), infra at page 927. After the Schwenke decision, what guidance does a manager have in resolving resource conflicts?

2. Litigation over management of national wildlife refuges apparently had been nonexistent until the mid-1970's. In Coupland v. Morton, 5 ELR 20504 (E.D.Va.), aff'd, 526 F.2d 588 (4th Cir.1975), the Fish and Wildlife Service severely restricted access to adjacent private land along a beach in the Back Bay refuge because the increasing traffic was adversely affecting the refuge. Plaintiffs demanded reopening, claiming that the FWS could not take such an action without filing an adequate environmental impact statement, among other things. The court denied relief. Later, however, political pressure forced the FWS to relax the access rules. See M. Bean, THE EVOLUTION OF NATIONAL WILDLIFE LAW 138 (1977).

3. Semantics has long been a severe problem with wildlife professionals: they often speak of "wildlife management," frequently preceded by "the science of," but no one has satisfactorily defined it. While its practitioners and apologists maintain that it is a body of generally

accepted principles derived from extensive research, their treatments suggest that modern practices of wildlife management are merely the residue of decades of one damn mistake after another. See generally J. Trefethan, AN AMERICAN CRUSADE FOR WILDLIFE (1975); D. Allen, OUR WILDLIFE LEGACY (rev. ed. 1962). "Multiple use management" suffers from the same semantic deficiencies; like obscenity, many profess to know it when they see it, but cannot put it into words.

The Alaska National Interest Lands Conservation Act, 16 U.S.C.A. § 3142(c) directs the Secretary of the Interior to conduct a study of the Arctic National Wildlife Refuge as a basis for mineral exploration guidelines. The Secretary's transfer of authority to conduct the study from the FWS to the U.S. Geological Survey was challenged in Trustees for Alaska v. Watt, 524 F.Supp. 1303 (D.Alaska 1981), aff'd, 690 F.2d 1279 (9th Cir.1982). In the course of his opinion invalidating the transfer, Judge Von Der Heydt considered the meaning of wildlife "administration" and "management:"

> The statutory language of the Refuge Act shows that the National Wildlife Refuge System must be administered by the Secretary of Interior through FWS. 16 U.S.C. § 688dd(a)(1) (1976). * * *
>
> Since the Arctic National Wildlife Refuge must be "administered" by FWS, the question before the court is whether the § 3142(d), (e) and (h) ANILCA functions assigned to USGS involve administration of the Refuge. If the functions involve administration, the delegation is beyond the Secretary's statutory authority and invalid.
>
> A.   *Wildlife Administration Defined*
>
> Congress did not define what it meant by "administered" in the Refuge Act. The words of the statute coupled with the legislative history, however, demonstrate that Congress simply meant "administered" to have its common meaning. "Administer," according to WEBSTER'S THIRD NEW INTERNATIONAL DICTIONARY (1976) means: "to manage the affairs of * * *." In the Refuge System Legislative History, the Senate report states "the U.S. Fish and Wildlife Service has responsibility for *management* in all areas of the refuge system." This leads to the conclusion that Congress intended FWS to "manage" the refuge system.
>
> "Manage," according to Webster means "to control and direct." Manage is a lesser included term of administer. Accordingly, in administering the Arctic National Wildlife Refuge, Congress intended FWS to control and direct the affairs of the Refuge.
>
> It remains to be determined, however, what FWS must do to comply with Congress's mandate that it administer or manage the Refuge. As two commentator's have recently expressed, "[t]here is no good definition of 'wildlife management,'

and there is little agreement on what wildlife managers should do." G. Coggins and M. Ward, The Law of Wildlife Management on The Federal Public Lands, 60 Ore.L.Rev. 59, 59 (1981). Nevertheless, these commentators point out that wildlife management is concerned with the effect of human activities on wildlife, and the wildlife manager's job is to control human beings and institutions in order to protect the wildlife population. The commentators conclude that: "Wildlife management is necessarily a means of regulating human access to a renewable natural resource in order to preserve it for future generations."

Although neither ANILCA nor the Wildlife Refuge Administration Act specifically address what wildlife administration entails, the legislative histories of both acts lead to the conclusion that wildlife management covers protection of wildlife and control of human access to the wildlife refuges. In addressing the management responsibilities of FWS the legislative history of ANILCA reasons: "[W]hile it is important to focus attention on the major species of each refuge, it is equally important that the Fish and Wildlife Service manage these units to conserve the entire spectrum of plant and animal life found on the refuge." ANILCA Report, *reprinted in* [1980] U.S.Code Cong. & Ad.News at 5118. The legislative history of the Wildlife Refuge Administration Act incorporates a wildlife management report which addresses control of human access to wildlife refuges for mineral exploration. The report concludes that access for mineral exploration must be controlled by FWS.

From a review of the legislative histories of ANILCA and the Wildlife Refuge Administration Act; relevant statements of commentators on the management issue; and the definitions of "administer" and "management;" the court concludes that in administering the Arctic National Wildlife Refuge, FWS is required to control and direct the Refuge by regulating human access in order to conserve the entire spectrum of wildlife found in the Refuge.

The national wildlife refuges do not offer "refuge" in one commonly accepted meaning of the word: hunting, fishing, and trapping have become normal activities on refuge lands, and other economically oriented practices, from haying to mineral leasing, also occur. Further, like the parks, some refuges are threatened with degradation from human overuse, particularly recreational use.

A Task Force of private individuals was appointed in 1977 to study and recommend changes in refuge management. The Task Force Report, issued in January 1978, was controversial in several respects, notably in calling for less human use and in advocating the limitation of hunting to situations where it could be shown that hunting would benefit wildlife populations. National Wildlife Refuge Study Task Force, RECOMMENDATIONS ON THE MANAGEMENT OF THE NATIONAL WILDLIFE REFUGE SYSTEM (1978). The Director of the Fish and Wildlife Service replied, Greenwalt, COMMENTS ON NWRS STUDY TASK FORCE RECOMMENDATIONS (1978), and Assistant Secretary of Interior Herbst then, on the basis of those two documents, issued FINAL RECOMMENDATIONS ON THE MANAGEMENT OF THE NWRS in April, 1979.

Neither administrator found fault with the Task Force's recommended revised mission statement:

> The special mission of the National Wildlife Refuge System is to provide, preserve, restore and manage a national network of lands and waters sufficient in size, diversity and location to meet society's needs for areas where the widest possible spectrum of benefits associated with wildlife and wildlands is enhanced and made available.

More specific recommendations, however, provoked lengthy replies and objections. For instance, in response to this Task Force recommendation:

> Grazing, timber harvesting and agricultural practices may be abusive and should be used only when necessary for proper management of wildlife resources, keeping in mind the desirability of maintaining natural ecosystems,

Director Greenwalt objected:

> that these practices can be useful tools in wildlife management and should be employed as such when warranted. * * * I feel strongly there is a growing concern—not necessarily reflected by the Task Force or its report—that this recommendation will be interpreted to mean that if the management practice (grazing, timbering or agriculture, etc.) is not truly beneficial—as opposed to neutral or not harmful—then it should not be used. I do not feel that is an acceptable nuance or interpretation and I cannot recommend to you any position that would tend to remove this degree of flexibility in rational and scientific management of the lands of the National Wildlife Refuge System.

Similarly, when the Task Force recommended that:

> Permission for exploration of extraction of oil and gas on refuges, when the Federal Government owns the subsurface rights, should be a prerogative of Congress, and legislation to establish this approach should be sought. Exploration and extraction of hardrock and all other minerals and steam should be banned,

the Assistant Director could not concur:

> As regards hardrock minerals, and geothermal steam, I agree * * * that such operations should be prohibited on refuges, except in those instances where there are valid existing rights.

While I feel that administrative procedures for affecting such a prohibition have been effective and responsibly exercised, I am directing the Service to study the advantages of having Congress legislate a complete ban on mining and mineral leasing, other than oil and gas, on refuges. * * *

With regard to oil and gas development on refuges, I believe that the Secretary's regulations which prohibit development except under very specific conditions have well served the purpose for which they were designed, the protection of refuge resource values. I agree with the Director that this process is sufficiently rigorous and subject to public scrutiny to assure that no hazard to fish or wildlife or their habitats is likely to result.

Because of recent lawsuits in which plaintiffs assert "the test of beneficiality [is] an absolute one," and because it would prevent public enjoyment of refuge lands, Mr. Greenwalt was very negative toward a key recommendation:

> Refuges are for wildlife and utilization by people should at no time be detrimental to wildlife resources, and to the extent possible should be beneficial.

Mr. Herbst "concurred" with the Task Force in this fashion:

> Refuges are established for the protection and enhancement of indigenous wildlife and their habitat; use by people should be compatible with that fundamental purpose; public use should be in strict conformance with applicable Federal statutes and the limitations required for the well-being of the resources and the habitat of the refuge in question.

The most provocative part of the Report was an omission: the Task Force neglected to state that sport hunting is a legitimate recreational use, and it called for biological justification of any management practice intended to produce "excessive numbers" for the hunters to harvest. Carefully straddling the fence, the Assistant Secretary accepted the recommendation "in principle."

> My concurrence is with the understanding that the policies of the Fish and Wildlife Service should continue to be based upon the notion that public hunting, fishing and trapping are appropriate uses of refuge lands so long as they are consistent with the NWRS' objectives to preserve, protect and enhance fish and wildlife resources and their habitat. There is no inconsistency between wisely administered hunting and fishing programs and the continued existence of Fish and Wildlife Resources.

DEFENDERS OF WILDLIFE v. ANDRUS

(Ruby Lake Refuge I)
United States District Court, District of Columbia, 1978.
11 E.R.C. 2098.

PRATT, D.J.,

FINDINGS OF FACT AND CONCLUSIONS OF LAW

The complaint in this action was filed June 29, 1978, seeking a declaratory judgment that special regulations of the United States Fish and Wildlife Service permitting recreational boating within the Ruby Lake National Wildlife Refuge [the "Refuge"] violate the Refuge Recreation Act of 1962 (16 U.S.C.A. § 460k) [the "Refuge Recreation Act"]. The complaint also seeks a preliminary and permanent injunction against opening the Refuge to use by motorboats and requests that the Court retain continuing jurisdiction of the action. * * *

* * *

Findings of Fact

I. *Ruby Lake National Wildlife Refuge.*

1.1 On July 2, 1938, by Executive Order No. 7923, President Franklin Roosevelt "reserved and set apart" the Refuge "as a refuge and breeding ground for migratory birds and other wildlife," in order to effectuate further the purposes of the Migratory Bird Conservation Act. The area so reserved and set apart, which was then denominated the Ruby Lake Migratory Waterfowl Refuge, comprised all lands and waters within a described area of approximately 37,640 acres in Elko and White Pine Counties, Nevada. 3 Fed.Reg. 1639 (July 7, 1938).

1.2 Section 5 of the Migratory Bird Conservation Act, 15 U.S.C.A. § 715d, authorizes the United States to purchase, rent or otherwise reserve areas "for use as inviolate sanctuaries for migratory birds * * *." Section 6 of this Act, 16 U.S.C.A. § 715e, requires that easements and reservations retained by any grantor from whom the United States received title "shall be subject to rules and regulations prescribed by the Secretary of [Interior] for the occupation, use, operation, protection and administration of the areas as inviolate sanctuaries for migratory birds * * *."

1.3 The primary purpose for which the Refuge was established is for use as a refuge, breeding ground and inviolate sanctuary for migratory birds.

* * *

1.6 The Refuge consists of 25,150 acres of wetlands and 12,468 acres of surrounding uplands. The wetlands portion of the Refuge consist of the 7,000-acre South Sump, which is the primary waterfowl nesting area, and the North and East Sumps, which are all maintained by a complex and intricate flowage of waters throughout the marsh basin. The average depth of water in the South Sump is approximately four feet, and in the North and East Sumps considerably less.

1.7   The management objectives of the Refuge are (1) to preserve, restore and enhance in their natural eco-systems all species of animals and plants that are endangered or threatened with becoming endangered on lands of the National Wildlife Refuge System; (2) to perpetuate the migratory bird resource for the benefit of people—to manage the refuge for an annual production of 5,000 canvasbacks and 5,000 redheads; (3) to preserve natural diversity and abundance of mammals and non-migratory birds on refuge land; and (4) to provide understanding and appreciation of fish and wildlife ecology and man's role in his environment, and to provide visitors with high quality, safe, wholesome, and enjoyable recreation which is fully compatible and consistent with, and which in no way harms or interferes with the area's primary purpose as a refuge and breeding ground for migratory birds and other wildlife.

1.8   All national wildlife refuges are maintained for the primary purpose of preserving, protecting and enhancing wildlife and other natural resources and of developing a national program of wildlife and ecological conservation and rehabilitation. These refuges are established for the restoration, preservation, development and management of wildlife and wildlands habitat; for the protection and preservation of endangered or threatened species and their habitat; and for the management of wildlife and wildlands to obtain the maximum benefits from these resources. 50 C.F.R. § 25.11(b).

II.   *The Refuge Supports Canvasback and Redhead Ducks and a Diverse Population of Other Migratory Birds and Wildlife.*

2.1   The Refuge provides one of the most important habitats and nesting areas for over-water nesting waterfowl in the United States. The Refuge is particularly valuable to the canvasback and redhead duck, which use the area in approximately equal numbers for nesting and broodrearing during the spring, summer and early fall.

2.2   Continental populations of both the redhead and the canvasback duck are low and both species have suffered throughout their respective ranges from encroachment and habitat loss. In 1972, the annual winter waterfowl inventory conducted by the United States Fish and Wildlife Service showed an all time low of 179,000 canvasbacks. The redhead has faced intensive drainage programs in the prairie-parkland region of central North America, the major breeding area of this species. A more comprehensive program oriented towards habitat protection is necessary to conserve and protect these species.

2.3   The canvasback duck and the redhead duck have been listed as "migratory birds," as defined by Section 11 of the Migratory Bird Conservation Act, 16 U.S.C.A. § 715j, and are protected by the Migratory Bird Treaty Act, 16 U.S.C.A. §§ 703 to 711, and by the Convention for the Protection of Migratory Birds, August 16, 1916, United States-Great Britain (on behalf of Canada), 39 Stat. 1702, T.S. No. 628; the

Convention for the Protection of Migratory Birds and Game Mammals, February 7, 1936, United States-Mexico, 50 Stat. 1311, T.S. No. 912; and the Convention for the Protection of Migratory Birds and Birds in Danger of Extinction and Their Environment, March 4, 1972, United States-Japan, 25 U.S.T. 3329, T.I.A.S. No. 7990. 50 C.F.R. §§ 10.12 and 10.13; 42 Fed.Reg. 59358–62 (Nov. 16, 1977).

2.4　In addition to the canvasback and redhead duck, numerous species of waterfowl and other birds using the Refuge have been so designated as "migratory birds," including the prairie falcon, the peregrine falcon, the bald eagle, the golden eagle, the trumpeter swan, the white-faced ibis, the snowy egret, the great blue heron, the black-crowned night heron, the ruddy duck, the ringed-necked duck, the sandhill crane, the Canada goose, the coot and the cinnamon teal.

Conclusions of Law

III.　*The Ruby Lake Special Regulations are Invalid in That They do not Include Appropriate Findings Necessary to Their Promulgation.*

3.1　On April 21, 1978, the Secretary of Interior promulgated the Ruby Lake Special Regulations, 50 C.F.R. § 25.34, 43 Fed.Reg. 16981–83 (April 21, 1978) (hereinafter referred to as "regulations").

3.2　These regulations permit year-round boating in an area designated as Zone 1 in the South Sump by boats without motors or boats with electric motors.

3.3　Beginning on July 1 on the east side and July 15 on the west side of an area designated as Zone 2 of the South Sump, and extending until December 31, boats without motors, boats with electric motors and boats with internal combustion motors of unlimited horsepower are permitted. No boat may exceed 20 miles per hour in any area or 5 miles per hour in areas so designated by the Refuge Manager.

3.4　Beginning on July 1 and extending until December 31, water-skiing is permitted on a designated area from 10 a.m. to 5 p.m. daily.

3.5　Beginning on August 1 and extending until December 31, boats without motors, boats with electric motors and boats with internal combustion motors of unlimited horsepower are permitted in an area designated as Zone 3 of the South Sump. No boat may exceed 20 miles per hour in any area or 5 miles per hour in areas so designated.

3.6　The Refuge Recreation Act of 1962 (16 U.S.C.A. § 460K) governs the Secretary's authority to permit recreation within the Ruby Lake National Wildlife Refuge and all other areas within the National Wildlife Refuge System, national fish hatcheries and other conservation areas administered by the Secretary for fish and wildlife purposes. The Refuge Recreation Act provides in pertinent part that:

> "In recognition of mounting public demands for recreational opportunities on areas within the National Wildlife Refuge System, *　*　* the Secretary of the Interior is authorized, as an appropriate incidental or secondary use, to administer such

areas or parts thereof for public recreation when in his judgment public recreation can be an appropriate incidental or
secondary use: Provided, That such public recreation use shall
be permitted only to the extent that is practicable and not
inconsistent with other previously authorized Federal operations or with the primary objectives for which each particular
area is established: * * * And provided further, That none
of the aforesaid refuges, hatcheries, game ranges, and other
conservation areas shall be used during any fiscal year for
those forms of recreation that are not directly related to the
primary purposes and functions of the individual area *until the
Secretary shall have determined—*

(a) *that such recreational use will not interfere with the
primary purposes for which the areas were established,* and

(b) that funds are available for the development, operation, and maintenance of these permitted forms of recreation. This section shall not be construed to repeal or
amend previous enactments relating to particular areas."

3.7　In supporting enactment, Congressman Dingell stated on the
floor of the House:

"The Secretary must make certain findings before he
throws these areas open to public use; the bill requires him to
find, for example, that there is sufficient money available to
administer and protect these areas, and *he must find that the
utilization for recreational use will not be harmful to the basic
purpose of the refuges.*" 108 Cong.Rec. 5548 (April 2, 1962)
(Emphasis added).

3.8　In determining to permit recreational use of a National Wildlife Refuge, the burden of proof is necessarily on the Secretary to
demonstrate that such use is incidental to, compatible with, and does
not interfere with the primary purpose of the refuge as "an inviolate
sanctuary for migratory birds."

3.9　The regulations violate the statutory standard because the
Secretary failed to make the determination required by the statute that
the permitted recreational use would not interfere with the Refuge's
primary purpose as an "inviolate sanctuary for migratory birds."

3.10　The Refuge Recreation Act does not permit the Secretary to
weigh or balance economic, political or recreational interests against
the primary purpose of the Refuge.

3.11　When Congress has sought to authorize the weighing or
balancing of competing interests it has done so explicitly.

3.12　Neither poor administration of the Refuge in the past, nor
prior interferences with its primary purposes, nor past recreational
uses, nor deterioration of its wildlife resource since its establishment,
nor administrative custom or tradition alters the statutory standard.
The Refuge Recreation Act permits recreational use only when it will
not interfere with the primary purpose for which the Refuge "was

established." The prior operation of the Refuge in a manner inconsistent with that purpose does not change the base point for applying the statute's standard. Past recreational use is irrelevant to the statutory standard except insofar as deterioration of the wildlife resource from prior recreational use serves to increase the need to protect, enhance and preserve the resource. Past recreational abuses may indeed require the Secretary to curtail recreational use to an even greater degree than mandated by the Refuge Recreation Act, in order to restore and rehabilitate the area promptly as required by the Secretary's existing regulations. 50 C.F.R. § 25.11(b).

IV. *This Court Will Not Supply Findings to Support the Regulations on Behalf of the Secretary.*

*   *   *

4.4 In adopting these regulations the Assistant Secretary balanced economic, political and recreational interests against the primary wildlife purpose of the refuge and reached a compromise.

4.5 The compromise reached by the Assistant Secretary in adopting these regulations was not supported by certain members of his staff. The former Refuge Manager, an expert in wildlife biology and management, testified in opposition to the regulation. The Deputy Associate Director for Wildlife refused to surname the regulations because in his opinion the regulations were not in the best interest of the Refuge and the resources for which it was established.

An Order consistent with the foregoing Findings of Fact and Conclusions of Law has been entered this day.

ORDER

In accordance with the Findings of Fact and Conclusions of Law issued this day, it is hereby

ORDERED;

1. The Ruby Lake Special Regulations (43 Fed.Reg. 16981) are declared unlawful.

2. Defendant Secretary of the Interior is hereby permanently enjoined from acting pursuant to the above cited regulations.

3. The Secretary shall, within five (5) days of the date of this Order, promulgate regulations which permit secondary uses of Ruby Lake only insofar as such usages are not inconsistent with the primary purpose for which the refuge was established.

4. In accordance with his statutory obligation, 16 U.S.C.A. § 460K, the Secretary shall take all appropriate and necessary steps to enforce the resulting regulations.

5. This action is dismissed.

NOTES

1. Five days after *Ruby Lake Refuge I,* the Secretary issued new regulations that differed from the old ones only in setting speed limits for powerboats. On August 18, 1978, the court threw out the new version and ordered yet another round of rulemaking. In the second decision, Judge Pratt made more detailed findings concerning the deleterious effects of powerboating on aquatic vegetation and wildfowl propagation. He concluded:

19. If the regulations are permitted to continue in effect they will immediately and irreparably damage plaintiff's interests and the wildlife resources of the Refuge. The use of powerboats of unlimited horsepower on the Refuge (including for waterskiing) will directly and immediately harm the wildlife resources of the Refuge (i) by reducing submergent aquatic vegetation which is the principal food source for migratory waterfowl; (ii) by reducing macroinvertebrate populations which are the principal food sources for ducklings (Id.); (iii) by breaking up broods, by separating ducklings from their hen, by forcing broods out of brooding areas, and thereby reducing brood size; and (iv) by reducing the reproductive success of late nesting and re-nesting hens.

20. Late nesting and re-nesting extends through September 1 of each season and occurs with sufficient frequency to be significant to the immediate and long-term productivity of the Refuge.

21(a). The level of boating use permitted by these regulations is not incidental to or compatible with, and will interfere with the primary purpose of the Refuge.

(b). The suggestion that horsepower limitations would not be appropriate, and would not aid the primary purpose of the Refuge, is completely contrary to all reason and the facts of the record.

(c). The proposed speed limitations to be used in conjunction with horsepower are so obviously unenforceable that to rely on a speed limitation, even as high as twenty miles an hour, is unrealistic because of its very unenforceability.

Conclusions of Law

22. The regulations violate the statutory standard of the Refuge Recreation Act because the degree and manner of boating use which they would permit is not incidental or secondary use, is inconsistent, and would interfere with the Refuge's primary purpose.

23. The regulations violate the statutory standard of the Refuge Recreation Act because the degree and manner of

boating use which they would permit is not practicable because of their unenforceability.

24. The Secretary's determination that the level of boating permitted by the regulations does not interfere with the Refuge's primary purpose is arbitrary and capricious.

25. Based on the record in this action, the use of boats with unlimited horsepower in the South Sump of the Refuge is inconsistent and interferes with its primary purpose as a refuge and breeding ground for migratory birds and wildlife.

Defenders of Wildlife v. Andrus, 455 F.Supp. 446 (D.D.C.1978) (*Ruby Lake Refuge II*).

2. The Task Force Report and Director Greenwalt's response were written some months before the *Ruby Lake Refuge* decisions were handed down. What bearing does Judge Pratt's opinion have on the future direction of national wildlife refuge management? Is any economic use not "secondary"? Is either the existence or extent of the conflict between primary and secondary uses a legal question? Does the opinion have application in other areas of public land law? Could the same result have been reached by invocation of the public trust doctrine?

3. Perhaps the most significant aspect of wildlife management in general and refuge management in particular is an omission: until the 1970's, no one challenged such decisions in reported litigation. Courts have since shown great deference to the assumed expertise of wildlife managers, e.g., Fund for Animals v. Frizzell, 530 F.2d 982 (D.C.Cir. 1975). As the *Ruby Lake Refuge* opinions indicate, however, that deference is eroding in the face of more determined attacks based on more explicit congressional mandates.

4. Plaintiffs in Humane Society v. Clark, No. 84–3630 (D.D.C., filed Nov. 29, 1984), seek an order halting hunting in numerous national wildlife refuges on the grounds that the FWS has opened the refuges to hunting without adequate evaluations of the impact of such hunting on the wildlife populations and that the FWS has abandoned annual review of the regulations governing such hunting. Plaintiffs' lengthy motion for summary judgment was pending in early 1986. Assuming that hunting is a recreational use within the meaning of the Refuge Recreation Act construed in *Ruby Lake,* supra, what arguments should plaintiffs make? What are their chances of success?

NATIONAL AUDUBON SOCIETY v. CLARK
United States District Court, District of Alaska, 1984.
21 E.R.C. 2069.

Before James M. Fitzgerald, District Judge.

On August 10, 1983, Deputy Under-Secretary of the Interior, William P. Horn, acting on behalf of then Secretary of the Interior James G. Watt (the Secretary), entered into a land exchange agreement with representatives of three Alaska Native Corporations. The three corporations, Cook Inlet Region, Inc. (CIRI), Calista Corp., and Sea Lion Corp., are referred to collectively as the CIRI Group. The Secretary transferred to the Natives a portion of St. Matthew Island, a wilderness area in the Alaska Maritime National Wildlife Refuge, in exchange for various land interests in the Kenai and Yukon Delta National Wildlife Refuges. The driving force behind the land exchange was to enable the CIRI Group to lease the St. Matthew Island parcel to private companies for construction and operation of support facilities for oil exploration and potential oil development in the Navarin Basin in the Bering Sea.

In making the exchange, the Secretary relied upon authorization granted in § 1302(h) [43 U.S.C.A. § 3192(h)] of the Alaska National Interest Lands Conservation Act (ANILCA). The conveyance is for fifty years, or so long as commercial oil production activities occur in the Navarin Basin.

Provisions were included in the land exchange agreement for an interim period of cooperative management between the CIRI Group and the Secretary. The agreement included additional conditions obligating the CIRI Group to comply with federal law, and, in certain instances, to obtain necessary permits from government agencies prior to land development. In addition, the agreement imposed restrictions on land use, and included stipulations to mitigate environmental impacts as well as to ensure restoration upon eventual reversion of the land to the federal government.

On the same day the exchange agreement was executed, the National Audubon Society and other environmental groups, joined by the Bering Sea Fishermen's Association, filed a complaint in this court in case no. A 83–425 (the exchange case) for declaratory and injunctive relief. The defendants named in the suit include the Secretary of the Interior and the CIRI Group. The relief now requested by the plaintiffs is a declaration that the exchange agreement is unlawful and void, and an injunction preventing the defendants from carrying out the terms of the agreement and prohibiting the defendants from in any way conducting any activity on St. Matthew Island under the terms of the agreement. * * *

* * * After an extensive examination of the record, I now conclude that Audubon has established that the Secretary, in executing the land exchange agreement, abused the discretion entrusted to him by law.

I. BACKGROUND

A. ANILCA and ANCSA

Several provisions of the Alaska National Interest Lands Conservation Act (ANILCA) and the Alaska Native Claims Settlement Act (ANCSA) are brought into the issues of this litigation. Congress enacted ANILCA in 1980. This Act designated approximately 105 million acres of federal land in Alaska for protection of its resource values through permanent federal ownership and management. The Alaska Maritime National Wildlife Refuge, within which St. Matthew

Island lies, was among the lands designated for environmental protection under ANILCA.

Congress enacted ANCSA in 1971 to effectuate a comprehensive settlement of all Native claims based on subsistence use and occupancy of land in Alaska. ANILCA expressly incorporated several provisions of ANCSA into its own statutory framework.

B.   St. Matthew Island

St. Matthew Island was established as a Wildlife Refuge in 1909. It was designated a wilderness area in the National Wilderness Preservation System on October 23, 1970. With its designation, Congress declared its intention that St. Matthew Island remain in its pristine form. Many factors contribute to the island's value as a wilderness area, including its isolation, remoteness, distance from shipping lanes and aircraft routes, rugged and varied terrain, and unique bird and mammal populations. Aside from minor evidence of past human presence on the island, St. Matthew remains essentially natural in appearance.

C.   Planned Oil Exploration and Development Activities

The draft environmental impact statement prepared in connection with plans for federal oil and gas leases in the Navarin Basin outlines three scenarios for transportation of oil and gas from the lease area: (1) pipeline to St. Matthew Island, the primary scenario, (2) pipeline to St. Paul Island, the alternative scenario, and (3) offshore loading. The offshore loading scenario includes locating marine-and air-support facilities on St. Matthew Island. Of the three scenarios, two involve development of St. Matthew Island.

Under the primary scenario, St. Matthew Island would play a role during both Phase I, the exploration phase, and Phase II, the development and the production phase. During Phase I, primary marine and air-logistics support would operate out of existing facilities in Dutch Harbor/Unalaska and Cold Bay. St. Matthew Island would serve as a forward base for limited air support.

During Phase II, both marine-and air-support facilities would be located on St. Matthew Island. Crude oil would be piped to a major storage, loading, and processing terminal on the island, and then transferred to shuttle tankers for shipment to a remote storage and trans-shipment terminal on the Alaska Peninsula. Gas resources, if developed, would be piped to facilities on St. Matthew Island, liquified, and transported direct to market by tankers.

II.   THE SECRETARY'S DECISION APPROVING THE LAND EXCHANGE

The exchange provision in § 1302(h) of ANILCA imposes two requirements before a land exchange may be approved. First, the Secretary must determine that the exchange will result in "acquiring lands for the purposes of [ANILCA]." Second, the exchange must further the "public interest" if the lands exchanged are of unequal value.

There are two principal documents in the record which explain the considerations and the rationale upon which the Secretary rested his decision to proceed with the challenged land exchange. These include (1) the Department of the Interior Record of Decision, and (2) the Public Interest Determination for the Proposed Acquisition of Inholdings in Kenai and Yukon Delta National Wildlife Refuges by Exchange for Lands on St. Matthew Island, Alaska.

According to these documents, the Secretary concluded that both requirements were met by the terms of the St. Matthew exchange. Concerning the first requirement, the Secretary's Determination concludes that ANILCA's purposes would be furthered in several important respects: (1) the interests obtained in the Kenai and Yukon Delta National Wildlife Refuge areas would "be consistent with and further the purposes of the refuges to which they are added"; (2) these acquisitions would "consolidate significant recreational lands and wildlife habitat lying within units of the National Wildlife Refuge System and National Wilderness Preservation System into permanent federal ownership"; (3) wildlife management benefits would result from this consolidation of conservation system units;[21] (4) protection of prime waterfowl habitat would be increased; (5) Native selection conveyance expenses would be reduced; and (6) the possibility of inconsistent land use by Natives within CSUs would be reduced.

Concerning the second requirement, the Secretary's Determination concludes that the St. Matthew Island exchange would also further the public interest. The Secretary offered seven major reasons for his conclusion:

(1) The exchange advances longterm CSU and general wildlife conservation and management objectives by (a) preventing the creation of over 100 Native inholdings within CSUs without permanent loss of a single CSU acre, (b) providing federal management and public enjoyment benefits which comport with congressional intent that CSU inholdings be eliminated primarily through land exchanges, and (c) improving the protection provided by § 22(g) of ANCSA [43 U.S.C.A. § 1621(g)] through the nondevelopment easement and permanent federal management on CSU lands.

(2) The exchange as a whole also advances the public interest in CSU objectives during the short term because the United States will (a) secure land interests in over three times the CSU acreage it will be conveying, (b) obtain clear title to and interest in more biologically and recreationally significant lands in terms of wildlife habitat quality than would be temporarily conveyed out of federal ownership, and (c) secure greater environmental protection by reason of the nondevelopment easement acquired in one of the most important waterfowl nesting habitats at Kokechik Bay, more than outweighing the temporary wildlife disruption authorized on St. Matthew Island.

21. Referred to as "CSU's."

(3) The exchange is in the public interest in terms of advancing the objectives of public enjoyment of CSUs because the United States would acquire acreage in the Kenai NWR which is heavily used by the public, while only temporarily disposing of land on St. Matthew Island lacking recreational potential.

(4) The level of protection of wildlife refuge values afforded by the St. Matthew Island land use stipulations and applicable laws and regulations also helps assure that the public interest in maintaining essential wildlife and coastal zone values is preserved in the exchange. The stipulations permit The Fish and Wildlife Service to review operations plans and to seek judicial review if development would damage wildlife resources.

(5) The interim management constraints provide immediate CSU management for all interests transferred or relinquished by the CIRI Group, even if the CIRI Group later exercises its option to rescind the exchange.

(6) Additionally, the CIRI's Group's intended use of the strategically located St. Matthew Island realty for a staging area for Navarin Basin energy development offers substantial environmental, human safety and economic public interest benefits because (a) the island's close location to the Navarin Basin provides critical time advantages in responding to environmental dangers and human safety emergencies when compared to other potential staging areas, and (b) the increased economic efficiency in offshore energy exploration and development allowed by St. Matthew Island's use may result in higher bidding revenues received on the lease sale and additional domestic oil and gas production.

(7) Finally, the exchange also would be favorable from other relevant public interest perspectives outside the conservation areas, including the fact that it promotes the expeditious settlement of the Alaska Native Land Claims and eliminates costs associated with federal conveyancing and management of unconsolidated parcels.

* * *

V. REVIEWABILITY OF THE SECRETARY'S PUBLIC INTEREST DETERMINATION

The CIRI Group, in its papers filed in connection with the summary judgment motions, argues that the Secretary's public interest determination is not subject to judicial review. The CIRI Group contends that it has been held in the Ninth Circuit, under statutes virtually identical to ANILCA § 1302(h), that public interest determinations regarding land exchanges are "committed to agency discretion by law" and are not judicially reviewable under the Administrative Procedure Act.

* * *

I conclude that the public interest determination and the decisions of the Secretary are in this case reviewable. I conclude as well that the arbitrary and capricious standard is appropriate to review the Secretary's determination as Judge Wright suggested as appropriate in *Keating.*

VI. REVIEW OF THE SECRETARY'S PUBLIC INTEREST DETER-MINATION

In authorizing the Secretary to make land exchanges of unequal value when in the "public interest," Congress did not impart what factors it intended the Secretary to consider in analyzing whether such an exchange is in the public interest. In his Public Interest Determination for the St. Matthew exchange, the Secretary identified what he considered to be the factors to be analyzed. The Secretary viewed this standard broadly, considering possible benefits to the nation's economic vitality and oil production capabilities as well as to its wilderness values.

* * *

I conclude the Secretary's broad view of the public interest in the context of land exchanges is a reasonable and permissible construction of ANILCA § 1302(h)'s statutory language. "Public interest" exchanges under ANILCA are exceptions to the general congressional requirement that the Secretary only enter into exchanges of equal monetary value. It therefore was reasonable for the Secretary to conclude that Congress intended that he take non-monetary benefits into account in determining whether the overall public interest would be furthered by a given exchange.[74]

* * *

In broad terms, the Secretary has stated that his Public Interest Determination is based on "a qualitative comparison of the temporary short-term loss of approximately 4,110 acres of wildlife and wilderness habitat on St. Matthew Island with the permanent addition of over 14,000 acres of wildlife habitat to the NWR System." And thereafter the Secretary summarizes the seven major reasons upon which he rests his determination.

I conclude that the broad discretion given the Secretary under § 1302(h) authorizes him to identify those interests which are to be considered in arriving at what is in the public interest. It is by now also well established that the court may not attempt to substitute its judgment for that of the Secretary. Rather, review of the Secretary's determination must focus on whether the decision rests on an adequate record and was reached after consideration of all relevant facts.

* * *

74. Although I believe the Secretary's construction of § 1302(h)'s "public interest" language is a reasonable one, I have found the Court's earlier statements in NAACP v. FPC, 425 U.S. 662 (1976), to require the Secretary to take special note of the purposes of ANILCA in making his public interest analysis. In that case, the Court stated that "[t]his Court's cases have consistently held that the use of the words 'public interest' in a regulatory statute is not a broad license to promote the general welfare. Rather, the words take meaning from the purposes of the regulatory legislation." Id. at 669. * * *

A. Prospective Benefits to Wildlife Conservation and Public Recreation

The Secretary declared in his document of decision that the Administrative Record demonstrated that the St. Matthew land exchange would clearly result in a "net benefit" to national wildlife and conservation values. He stated that a primary reason for his approval of this exchange was the remoteness of the possibility of danger to St. Matthew's environmental resources and the temporary quality of any potential environmental disruption. Conversely, he found that the prospective environmental and recreational benefits that the government would acquire in the Kenai and Yukon Delta NWRs would advance wildlife conservation values in both the short and long terms. Additionally, he concluded that the CIRI Group's proposed use of St. Matthew for an oil support base would be compatible with the purposes of the Alaska Maritime NWR, as required by ANCSA § 22(g).

1. Analysis of Land Interests Conveyed to the United States

The Kokechik Bay Nondevelopment Easement

In terms of acreage, the largest acquisition by the Secretary in the exchange amounts to approximately 8000 surface acres of waterfowl nesting habitat within the Yukon Delta NWR. Recognizing the importance of this nesting region in Alaska, Congress declared a primary purpose of the Yukon Delta NWR to be "to conserve fish and wildlife populations and habitats in their natural diversity including, but not limited to, shorebirds, seabirds, whistling swans, emperor, white-fronted and Canada geese, black brant and other migratory birds."

The site of the nondevelopment easement is in Kokechik Bay and the land is owned by Sea Lion Corp. The nondevelopment easement conveyed by Sea Lion Corp. to the Secretary under the exchange provided for the following rights:

> (a) the right of GRANTEE, in perpetuity, to prevent and prohibit GRANTOR, its successors and assigns, from developing *docking facilities, roads, canals, airstrips, utilities, transmissions lines, pipelines, tank facilities, structures not used for subsistence purposes, or excavations* or other topographical changes: *Provided,* that development on the Real Estate may be permitted with the prior written consent of the Secretary of the Interior or his designee.

> * * *

> (c) GRANTOR's covenant running with the land not to permit, authorize, or consent to the use of the Real Estate for purposes of exploration, development, or extraction of the subsurface estate underlying the Real Estate (where such power of permission, authorization or consent is necessary under law for subsurface use), unless such exploration, development, or extraction is expressly agreed to by GRANTEE.

> * * *

The lands subject to the nondevelopment easement contain excellent waterfowl nesting and brood rearing habitat. The most dense nesting concentrations of emperor geese are found in this area. In addition, the Kokechik Bay region is the breeding ground for half the world's population of black brant. Cackling Canada geese also breed chiefly in the areas surrounding the Kokechik Bay.

There can be absolutely no doubt that the lands subject to the nondevelopment easement are important to conservation and management objectives in protecting the black brant and the Cackling Canada and emperor geese. My inquiry does not stop here, however. The Secretary's determination that the St. Matthew exchange is in the national interest rests in substantial part upon his conclusion that the nondevelopment easement acquired in Kokechik Bay added significant environmental protections in this region.

My review of the environmental protections already in place prior to the St. Matthew exchange has revealed that the lands subject to the nondevelopment easement are for the most part located within the Yukon Delta NWR. As such, they are governed by the requirements of § 22(g) of ANCSA. This provision provides, in pertinent part, that:

> Notwithstanding any other provision of this chapter, *every patent* issued by the Secretary pursuant to this chapter—which covers lands lying within the boundaries of a National Wildlife Refuge on December 18, 1971—*shall contain a provision that such lands remain subject to the laws and regulations governing use and development of such Refuge.*

When the Secretary conveyed these lands to the CIRI Group, he imposed covenants, pursuant to § 22(g)'s requirements, that subjected almost all of the lands to the laws and regulations of the National Wildlife Refuge System. The laws and regulations governing use and development of wildlife refuges provide that only activities which are "compatible" with the major purposes for which a particular refuge was established may be permitted by the Secretary. Although compatibility is not expressly defined in either the National Wildlife Refuge System Administration Act or ANILCA, implementing regulations for the administration of § 22(g) covenants state that compatibility means that proposed uses must not "*materially impair* the values for which the refuge was established."

My reading of the language of § 22(g), which the Secretary properly inserted into the Kokechik Bay conveyances to the CIRI Group, suggests to me that these lands were already protected from incompatible uses even without the nondevelopment easement obtained by the Secretary. To this extent, I agree with Audubon's claim that the protections acquired under the easement were largely "redundant" of the environmental safeguards obtained through the § 22(g) covenants.

In this connection, the Secretary in his Public Interest Determination suggests that the nondevelopment easement on CSU lands (Kokechik Bay) will provide secure protection "against the vagaries of section 22(g) of the Alaska Native Claims Settlement Act, and eliminate the risk that the lands transferred and relinquished by the CIRI Group would be developed in a manner inconsistent with CSU objectives. The Final Ascertainment Report discloses that the primary federal statute governing the management of national wildlife refuge resources is the National Wildlife Refuge System Administration Act of 1966. Section 4(d) of the Act authorized the Director of the Fish and Wildlife Service to permit a wide array of development activities within national wild-life refuges provided that such activities are found to be compatible with the purposes for which a given wildlife refuge was established. In applying the test for compatibility, the proposed activity must be judged and its anticipated impacts assessed against the purposes for which a given refuge was established. Section 22(g) of ANCSA retains this "compatibility test" for lands selected by and conveyed to Natives within nation wildlife refuges in Alaska. The Kokechik Bay lands were included in the Yukon Delta NWR established in 1980.

The nondevelopment easement prohibits Sea Lion Corporation from constructing docking facilities, roads, canals, airstrips, utilities, transmission lines, pipelines, tank facilities, and other structures not used for subsistence purposes, or excavating or making other topo-graphic changes. Given the purpose for which the Yukon Delta NWR was established, there would seem to be considerable doubt as to whether docking facilities, roads, canals, airstrips, utilities, pipelines and the like would be compatible uses of the Kokechik Bay lands. Apart from that, the easement lands are located along the southern shore of Kokechik Bay within a flat band of low tundra up to three miles wide which extend from the water's edge to an undulating line of bluffs. At least one-half of this area is water in the form of tidal sloughs, ponds, and lakes. The primary human impact in the Kokechik Bay lowlands has always been egg collecting and spring hunting by Alaskan Natives. That is, the Kokechik Bay lowlands are very impor-tant for subsistence uses by Native peoples. Certainly the sort of development precluded by the nondevelopment easement, if not so precluded, would have to be considered under §§ 801(4) and 802(1) of ANILCA [43 U.S.C.A. §§ 3111(4), 3112(1)] for the possible impacts the construction and activity would have on subsistence users.

Finally, there is nothing that I have discovered in the Final Ascertainment Report that suggests the existence of any probable or potential threat of the kind of development prohibited by the nondevelopment easement obtained by the United States under the exchange. To the extent this matter is considered at all, the Ascertain-ment Report acknowledges that while the compatibility test of § 22(g) could be expected to preclude several types of development activities on the Kokechik lands, a number of other types of development activities could probably be found to be compatible if carefully managed. In sum, there is nothing in the Ascertainment Report that suggests that the likelihood of future construction or operation of docking facilities, roads, canals, airstrips, utilities, transmission lines, pipelines, and tank facilities at Kokechik Bay. Nor is there anything in the DEIS or any other source that I am aware of that suggests the construction of such facilities is now either contemplated or projected.

Thus it would be hard to find a more striking comparison between the potential or probable use of Kokechik Bay lowlands with the proposed use of CIRI's inholdings on St. Matthew Island. On St. Matthew Island construction of the type of facilities that would be barred by the nondevelopment easement in the Kokechik Bay lowlands is both certain and immediate.

* * *

In sum, I have concluded that contrary to the Secretary's statement in his Public Interest Determination, the nondevelopment easement obtained under the exchange adds little to the environmental protections already in place for Kokechik Bay. Hence, the Secretary's conclusion that the acquisition of the nondevelopment easement significantly advances long term CSU and general wildlife conservation and management objectives is not borne out when the land status and legal restrictions otherwise applicable are examined.

* * *

[The court held that the Nanivak Island relinquishments also did not further wildlife conservation, but that the Kenai Peninsula interests exchange was reasonable in light of available information.]

B. Potential Dangers to St. Matthew Island's Wilderness Values

In concluding that relinquishing lands on St. Matthew Island to the CIRI Group for use as an oil support facility was in the public interest, the Secretary assumed that there was little possibility of long term environmental danger to the island's unique wilderness values. Being mindful of the narrow confines of the standard of review in this case, I nevertheless have found this determination fails to consider the relevant facts in the Secretary's own administrative record. My review of the record has also led me to conclude that the Secretary's determination that the placement of an oil support facility within the Alaska Maritime NWR would be compatible with this refuge's strict environmental objectives was a clear error of judgment.

The Alaska Maritime NWR was created for the express purpose of "conserv[ing] fish and wildlife populations and habitats in their natural diversity." Congress considered protection of St. Matthew Island's environmental resources to be so important that it designated the island as a national wilderness area within a wildlife refuge, granting St. Matthew the highest order of federal environmental protection.

* * *

* * * Section 22(g) of ANCSA, in conjunction with § 304(b) of ANILCA, permits the Secretary to allow only those activities in natural wildlife refuges which are "compatible" with the major purposes for which a particular refuge was established.

* * *

I conclude that on the face of the underlying record the Secretary's assumption that the CIRI Group's intended use of St. Matthew as an oil base was compatible with the purposes of the Alaska Maritime NWR is a clear error of judgment. Indeed, contrary to the Secretary's repeated descriptions of the potential environmental damage to St. Matthew's unique wilderness values as "temporary" and "remote," the administrative record reveals there is a substantial risk of significant short and long term injury to the island's wilderness qualities. Such prospective environmental degradation would conflict with the express goal of the Alaska Maritime NWR to conserve the abundant wildlife populations and habitats of this refuge in their "natural diversity."

* * *

The most ominous potential environmental destruction that might accompany development of St. Matthew will affect wildlife, however. By FWS estimates, hundreds of thousands of seabirds nest in colonies on or immediately adjacent to the lands conveyed to the CIRI Group. FWS found that at least "13% of the *minimum estimate* for nesting seabirds on the island," may be adversely affected by development on St. Matthew. FWS warned that much or all of the population of murres and kittiwakes on the island, which constitute a major component of the area's entire bird population, may be endangered by CIRI Group development, for "any added disturbance could be critical to [their] survival." Most alarmingly, FWS has estimated that the project will adversely affect nearly half a million nesting seabirds for a period of 80 to 100 years.

Of particular concern, the FWS report and the DEIS point to the frequent air traffic that will feed the support facility as especially dangerous to St. Matthew's seabird nesting colonies. Near flying aircraft inhibit breeding and initiate panic flights, potentially causing entire colonies to take to the air, knocking eggs and chicks into the ocean or leaving them vulnerable to predators. Continued disruption may cause reproduction failure, and, "in the worse case, colonies may be totally abandoned."

* * *

In addition to a potential for serious long-term degradation to the seabird population of St. Matthew, the DEIS reveals that any major oil spill near the island is likely to cause substantial harm to the many whales that inhabit the island's waters. And by the FWS's own estimates, a major oil spill near the island is probable if pipelines eventually are used to transport oil to St. Matthew.

Although all of these facts appear on the face of the administrative record, the Secretary paid scant heed. Rather, he suggests in his Public Interest Determination that the St. Matthew Island stipulations for restoration and reconveyance assure that the land will be restored and returned to the National Wildlife and Wilderness System when use of the land as a support base for oil exploration or development comes to an end. He refers to the lands as "temporarily conveyed use of federal ownership" and to the "temporary wildlife disruption authorized on St. Matthew Island" under the land use stipulations. The Secretary reasons that the exchange is in the public interest in terms of advancing the objectives of public enjoyment of CSUs. This is said to be so since the public may have use of the Tustamena Lake campgrounds and the area at the confluence of the Russian River-Kenai River for camping, fishing, hiking, and nature observations. This is achieved while only "temporarily" disposing of isolated St. Matthew Island land which has virtually no recreational potential whatsoever.

The word "temporary" standing alone has little meaning. It largely depends for its context upon the frame of reference in which it appears. The exchange provides by its terms that the conveyance to the CIRI Group is for 50 years, or if oil and gas have been produced in the Navarin Basin and the land has been used in connection therewith, then so long as may be necessary for completion of production. What is important are the consequences upon wildlife and wilderness habitats by the activity associated with the use of the land, and not whether that use may be characterized as "temporary." The Secretary has in fact avoided consideration of the many relevant facts appearing in the Final Ascertainment Report detailing the environmental impacts upon wildlife and wilderness resources in the Alaska Maritime NWR which will be brought about by the proposed use of the land on St. Matthew Island. In sum, the Secretary in making his qualitative comparison of the "temporary" short-term loss of 4,110 acres of wildlife and wilderness habitats on St. Matthew Island has failed to consider most of the facts disclosed in the Final Ascertainment Report bearing on use of the land for a supply base.

* * *

It is correct that the stipulations are useful to minimize harm to the wildlife and wilderness habitat on St. Matthew Island, but the stipulations cannot otherwise justify the Secretary's Public Interest Determination. That is, the Secretary cannot avoid consideration of potential environmental impacts upon wildlife or wilderness habitats within the refuge resulting from construction and operation of the support base by merely suggesting that the stipulations will serve to mitigate the extent of the injury.

* * *

The record thus demonstrates that, contrary to the Secretary's findings, overall national wildlife conservation and management objectives will not be advanced either in the short or long terms under the exchange. Nor can speculative increases in protection of public access to rivers in the Kenai peninsula for recreational purposes significantly mitigate the sure and certain conflict with the conservation purposes of the Alaska Maritime NWR.

* * *

VII. CONCLUSION

I conclude that the Secretary's Public Interest Determination for the St. Matthew Island exchange suffers from serious errors of judgment and misapplication of law which have led to a clear error of judgment.

My review of the underlying record has convinced me that the Secretary, by failing to consider the protections otherwise provided by law and by failing to consider relevant facts appearing of record, seriously overestimated the benefits to CSU and general wildlife conservation and management objectives advanced by this exchange. Additionally, by characterizing the effects on St. Matthew Island as temporary and by erroneously assuming that the land use stipulations would provide sufficient protection to wildlife and wilderness habitats, the Secretary failed to adequately consider the likely negative effects on St. Matthew Island. Finally, the Secretary's determination under ANCSA § 22(g) that a support base located within the Alaska Maritime NWR would be compatible with the environmental protection purposes of this refuge is contrary to the underlying record. The Secretary's Public Interest Determination thus constitutes a clear error of judgment.

I conclude that the St. Matthew Island land exchange is invalid. I also conclude that Audubon's application for a preliminary injunction in case no. A 84–402 civil (the NEPA case) must be granted. My conclusion that the exchange is invalid demonstrates Audubon's "strong likelihood of success on the merits," and that an injunction would serve the public interest. Audubon has documented the irreparable injury that would occur on St. Matthew should development be permitted. Thus the requirements for granting injunctive relief are satisfied. Audubon is entitled to a preliminary injunction to prohibit any construction or other use of heavy equipment on St. Matthew Island.

* * *

NOTES

1. To these editors' knowledge, the opinion in the St. Matthew Island exchange case is the only instance in which a court has closely dissected the meaning of "public interest" in a public land lawsuit, even though the public land statutes are full of that and similar guidelines. Judicial concern with the public interest, however, goes back a long time, cf. United States v. Midwest Oil Co., 236 U.S. 459 (1915), supra at page 147 and is manifested often in other ways. See, e.g., NWF v. Burford, 23 E.R.C. 1609 (D.D.C.1985), supra at page 265 (public interest in injunctive relief). Does the court in the principal case allow the Secretary latitude appropriate to such a broad standard? Are the factors listed by the parties and the court the only factors relevant to the public interest? How does the conception of the role of the judiciary here compare with that in NRDC v. Hodel, 624 F.Supp. 1045 (D.Nev.1986), supra at page 749? Which approach is proper in complex public lands litigation?

2. Questions of the validity and extent of land withdrawals and reservations have broad implications for the wildlife resource. In Sagebrush Rebellion, Inc. v. Watt, 14 ELR 20679 (D.Idaho 1984), the court upheld Secretary Andrus' withdrawal of one half million acres of BLM land into the Snake River Birds of Prey Area (after the election of President Reagan). Secretary Andrus submitted the withdrawal to Congress in accordance with § 204 of FLPMA; the court did not

question the constitutionality of that procedure. Compare Pacific Legal Found. v. Watt, 529 F.Supp. 982 (D.Mont.1981), supra at page 260. In an earlier phase of the *Sagebrush Rebellion* case, the Ninth Circuit had allowed the Audubon Society to intervene on several grounds, including the following:

> In addition to having [avian] expertise apart from that of the Secretary, the intervenor offers a perspective which differs materially from that of the present parties to this litigation. Secretary Andrus is no longer Secretary of the Interior. His successor, Secretary Watt, was previously head of the Mountain States Legal Foundation, the organization which is representing the plaintiff Sagebrush Rebellion in this action. These facts support intervention and also give rise to the appellant's sobriquet for the case as "*Watt v. Watt.*"

Sagebrush Rebellion, Inc. v. Watt, 713 F.2d 525, 528 (9th Cir.1983).

NOTE: "TAKING" PROTECTED SPECIES BY ACCIDENT

Many private natural resources operations on federal lands may be in peril of criminal prosecution if their activities result in the death of protected species.

The Migratory Bird Treaty Act of 1918, 16 U.S.C.A. §§ 703–11, forbids the killing of migratory birds "by any means in any manner," id. § 703, unless in accordance with federal regulations, id. § 704. Long considered a hunting law, the MBTA as recently interpreted is an additional substantive limitation on some uses of the public lands. Courts in three unreported cases between 1973 and 1975 found oil companies guilty of criminal offenses under the Act for maintaining oil sludge pits in which birds died. In United States v. Corbin Farm Service, 444 F.Supp. 510 (E.D.Cal.1978), aff'd in part, 578 F.2d 259 (9th Cir.1978), the court declared that the negligent spraying of a toxic pesticide, causing the death of perhaps 1000 widgeons (anas americana), constituted a punishable "public welfare" offense, although the court found that only one offense could be charged if only one course of conduct was involved. That holding was taken a large step further in United States v. FMC Corp., 572 F.2d 902 (2d Cir.1978): the court affirmed an 18 count conviction of a corporation that had accidentally released toxic substances into a lagoon frequented by migratory waterfowl on an "ultra-hazardous activity" tort theory. Those cases arose from activities on private lands, but the holdings necessarily apply to private operations on public lands as well.

As the number of ways in which human activities can cause the death of birds is virtually limitless, so too is the potential extent of criminal liability should the Justice Department decide to prosecute. Clearcutting, acid mine leaching, and uninsulated power poles are just a few examples that readily come to mind, in addition to intentional use of economic poisons. The criminal penalties for violation of the MBTA (up to $500 per violation) are mild compared to those authorized under more recent statutes such as the Endangered Species Act of 1973 (up to $20,000 per violation). The FWS has defined "harm," a form of "taking" under the latter Act, to include:

> an act or omission which actually injures or kills wildlife, including acts which annoy it to such an extent as to significantly disrupt essential behavioral patterns * * * significant environmental modification or degradation which has such effects is included within the meaning of "harm". 50 C.F.R. § 17.3 (1977).

The FWS "taking" regulation, which was later amended in ways not pertinent here, prompted this speculation:

> If it is a valid interpretation, the impact of the ESA on land use will be enhanced beyond monetary liability and beyond the notorious section 7 limitations on federal activity. Almost any natural resource operation is in peril if the Justice Department decides to prosecute, for "environmental modification" is a normal incident to any large-scale project. Incidental destruction of a prairie dog town could eliminate the food supply of the endangered black-footed ferret. A quarry could "significantly disrupt" a grizzly bear. Various species of rare fish could be adversely affected by nearly any stream change even though the diverter or discharger had no knowledge that such fish existed. Endangered birds could be killed in oil pits or toxic lagoons just as other bird species have been. In each case, if the result is foreseeable, heavy fines or worse could follow. If the government or private organizations foresaw even this attenuated harm, the project itself, on either public or private property, might possibly be halted. It must be emphasized that these legal obstacles have not yet occurred nor been upheld in practice, but the theoretical basis for them, and the organizations and individuals willing to assert them, are present.

Coggins & Patti, The Resurrection and Expansion of the Migratory Bird Treaty Act, 50 Colo.L.Rev. 165, 195 (1979).

The "taking by accident" problem has resurfaced dramatically at the Kesterson National Wildlife Refuge in central California. The Refuge features the Kesterson Reservoir and is an important stopover and breeding ground for migratory birds, including several endangered species. Because of a failure to complete a drain into San Francisco Bay, the Reservoir is the terminus for water draining from the Westlands Water District, a part of the massive Central Valley Reclamation Project. That irrigation drainage water carries dangerous concentrations of selenium, a highly toxic element, among other substances leached from the soil in the irrigation process.

Selenium has proved deadly to waterfowl at Kesterson:

> Since 1919 federal scientists have been aware that farming the west side of the San Joaquin Valley would result in toxic contamination. Yet the issue received scant bureaucratic at-

tention until the spring of 1983 when biologists with the U.S. Fish and Wildlife Service checked 350 nests of coots, grebes, and other ducks at Kesterson and discovered the refuge had become an avian death trap. Says Harry Ohlendorf, a federal biologist who led the nesting survey, "We were looking into eggs and seeing things we'd never seen before."

Scientists found hatchlings and embryos without eyes, feet, or wings. Many were missing all or parts of their beaks. In some chicks, brains had pushed through the skulls. In birds the natural deformity rate is 1 percent. In Kesterson, the deformity rate in some species was 42 percent. The breeding failures were without precedent in the nation's 90-million-acre refuge system.

Adult birds suffered as well. Each day dozens of bloated carcasses were found floating in the refuge's tea-colored waters. And crayfish, snakes, muskrats, and raccoons that once flourished here had vanished. In short, the Kesterson Refuge had become a place that killed the animals it was supposed to protect.

Schneider, Crisis At Kesterson, The Amicus Journal, Fall, 1985, at 22, 24–25.

After allegations that the Bureau of Reclamation was dragging its feet and covering up the damage, and amidst a growing number of lawsuits, on March 15, 1985, Secretary of the Interior Hodel announced that continued operation of the Refuge for irrigation wastewater storage was in violation of the Migratory Bird Treaty Act. He first ordered that drainage into the Refuge cease, the effect of which was to have the Bureau cut off reclamation water to 50 or so San Joaquin Valley farming operations in this highly productive agricultural area. A few weeks later, a compromise was reached allowing water deliveries for another year. Virtually no one is fully satisfied by the existing state of affairs: at least a half dozen lawsuits have been filed, most of which seek some form of cleanup (the State of California declared Kesterson a hazardous waste site) or permanent closure of the drain into Kesterson. See Kosloff, Tragedy at Kesterson Reservoir: Death of a Wildlife Refuge Illustrates Failings of Water Law, 15 ELR 10386 (1985). As usual, the future is uncertain. The ultimate outcome of the Kesterson situation, however, seems certain to illuminate and sharpen many issues revolving around the relationships of wildlife refuges, wildlife law, and adjacent economic activities.

C. WILDLIFE CONSERVATION AND MANAGEMENT ON FOREST SERVICE AND BLM LANDS

Grizzly bears don't vote, and coyotes don't contribute to political campaigns; and all wildlife species are notoriously unresponsive to legal dictate. It is not odd, therefore, that wildlife welfare on the public lands long was ignored by legislatures except to the extent of delegating all management responsibility to the informed discretion of professional managers and biologists. Hunters vote, pay the freight for fish and game agencies, and are politically powerful; consequently, wildlife regulation historically has been hunting and fishing regulation aimed at the satisfaction of participants in those sports. The recognition of declines in habitat quantity and quality has led to renewed legislative interest and to a new wildlife management approach on federal lands exclusive of the National Wildlife Refuge System.

Contrary to the majority opinion in United States v. New Mexico, supra at page 376, the Forest Service from its inception has regarded wildlife as one of the major forest resources to be managed and protected like timber or watershed resources. This understanding was formalized in the 1960 Multiple-Use Sustained-Yield Act, declaring that fish and wildlife is one of the five resources to which "due consideration shall be given." 16 U.S.C.A. §§ 528–29. The authority of the BLM under FLPMA is comparable.

The law governing hunting and fishing on the public lands consists mostly of variant bodies of state administrative rules that govern who can shoot or angle for what species at which times. Typically, a state agency will, for each game species, set seasons, define bag limits, and prescribe the methods of taking. State wildlife agencies are financed by license fees and taxes paid directly and indirectly by sportsmen. State regulations tend to favor encouragement of the sport to the asserted detriment of "non-game" species and other values. Stocking and artificial propagation of fish and wildlife, for instance, are almost exclusively undertaken for the benefit of game species.

This section investigates regulation of hunting and wildlife management on BLM and Forest Service lands. *Baldwin,* following, deals with elk hunting, mostly in the national forests, and analyzes some of the guarantees and constraints of the United States Constitution in regard to hunting. The *Alaska Wolf* litigation implicates the seldom-asserted agency power to control killing, an issue that may well become increasingly important in the future for the BLM and the Forest Service. Subsequent cases indicate the variance in judicial approaches to situations where wildlife management and developmental interests collide.

BALDWIN v. MONTANA FISH & GAME COMM'N

United States Supreme Court, 1978.
436 U.S. 371.

Mr. Justice BLACKMUN delivered the opinion of the Court.

This case presents issues, under the Privileges and Immunities Clause of the Constitution's Art. IV, § 2, and the Equal Protection Clause of the Fourteenth Amendment, as to the constitutional validity of disparities, as between residents and nonresidents, in a State's hunting license system.

* * *

[Plaintiff Baldwin is a Montana outfitter and hunting guide. Other plaintiffs are Minnesota residents.]

II

The relevant facts are not in any real controversy and many of them are agreed:

A. For the 1975 hunting season, a Montana resident could purchase a license solely for elk for $4. The nonresident, however, in order to hunt elk, was required to purchase a combination license at a cost of $151; this entitled him to take one elk and two deer.

For the 1976 season, the Montana resident could purchase a license solely for elk for $9. The nonresident, in order to hunt elk was required to purchase a combination license at a cost of $225; this entitled him to take one elk, one deer, one black bear, and game birds, and to fish with hook and line. A resident was not required to buy any combination of licenses, but if he did, the cost to him of all the privileges granted by the nonresident combination license was $30. The nonresident thus paid 7½ times as much as the resident, and if the nonresident wished to hunt only elk, he paid 25 times as much as the resident.

* * *

Montana maintains significant populations of big game, including elk, deer, and antelope. Its elk population is one of the largest in the United States. Elk is prized by big game hunters who come from near and far to pursue the animal for sport.[9] The quest for big game has grown in popularity. During the 10-year period from 1960 to 1970 licenses issued by Montana increased by approximately 67% for residents and by approximately 530% for non-residents.[10]

Owing to its successful management programs for elk, the State has not been compelled to limit the overall number of hunters by means of drawings or lotteries as have other States with harvestable elk populations. Elk is not hunted commercially in Montana. Nonresident hunters seek the animal for its trophy value; the trophy is the distinctive set of antlers. The interest of resident hunters more often may be in the meat. Elk are now found in the mountainous regions of

9. It has been said that Montana is the State most frequently visited by nonresident hunters.

For the license year 1974–1975, Montana licensed hunters from each of the other 49 States, the District of Columbia, Puerto Rico, and 11 foreign countries. Approximately 43,500 nonresident hunting licenses for deer and elk were issued during that year. The District Court found that elk hunting is recreational in nature and, "except for a few residents who live in exactly the right place," expensive. There was testimony that for a typical seven-day elk hunt a nonresident spends approximately $1,250 *exclusive* of outfitter's fee and the

hunting license. Thus, while the nonresident combination license fee is not insubstantial, it appears to be a lesser part of the overall expense of the elk hunt.

10. The number of nonresident big game combination licenses is now restricted to 17,000 in any one license year. Mont.Rev.Codes Ann. § 26–202.1(16)(f) (Supp.1977). This limitation was imposed by 1975 Mont.Laws, ch. 546, § 1, effective May 1, 1976.

The number of nonresident hunters has not yet reached the 17,000 limit. There are no similar numerical limitations on resident elk or deer licenses.

western Montana and are generally not encountered in the eastern two-thirds of the State where the plains prevail. During the summer the animal moves to higher elevations and lands that are largely federally owned. In the late fall it moves down to lower privately owned lands that provide the winter habitat necessary to its survival. During the critical midwinter period elk are often supported by ranchers.

Elk management is expensive. In regions of the State with significant elk population, more personnel time of the Fish and Game Commission is spent on elk than on any other species of big game.

Montana has more than 400 outfitters who equip and guide hunting parties. These outfitters are regulated and licensed by the State and provide services to hunters and fishermen. It is estimated that as many as half the nonresidents who hunt elk in western Montana utilize outfitters. Three outfitter-witnesses testified that virtually all their clients were nonresidents.

The State has a force of 70 game wardens. Each warden district covers approximately 2100 square miles. To assist wardens in law enforcement, Montana has an "equal responsibility" statute. Mont. Rev.Codes Ann. § 26–906 (Supp.1977). This law makes outfitters and guides equally responsible for unreported game law violations committed by persons in their hunting parties. The outfitter thus, in a sense, is a surrogate warden and serves to bolster the State's warden force.

III

In the District Court the majority observed that the elk once was a plains animal but now roams the mountains of central and western Montana. About 75% of the elk taken are killed on federal land. The animal's preservation depends upon conservation. The majority noted that the appellants conceded that Montana constitutionally may charge nonresidents more for hunting privileges than residents. * * *

* * *

[The three-judge district court upheld the licensing system.]

IV

Privileges and immunities. Appellants strongly urge here that the Montana licensing scheme for the hunting of elk violates the Privileges and Immunities Clause [15] of Art. IV, § 2, of our Constitution. That Clause is not one the contours of which have been precisely shaped by the process and wear of constant litigation and judicial interpretation over the years since 1789. * * *

* * *

* * * Some distinctions between residents and nonresidents merely reflect the fact that this is a Nation composed of individual States, and are permitted; other distinctions are prohibited because they hinder the formation, the purpose, or the development of a single

---

15. "The Citizens of each State shall be entitled to all Privileges and Immunities of Citizens in the several States."

union of those States. Only with respect to those "privileges" and "immunities" bearing upon the vitality of the Nation as a single entity must the State treat all citizens, resident and nonresident, equally. Here we must decide into which category falls a distinction with respect to access to recreational big game hunting.

* * *

In more recent years, however, the Court has recognized that the States' interest in regulating and controlling those things they claim to "own," including wildlife, is by no means absolute. States may not compel the confinement of the benefits of their resources, even their wildlife, to their own people whenever such hoarding and confinement impedes interstate commerce. * * * And a State's interest in its wildlife and other resources must yield when, without reason, it interferes with a nonresident's right to pursue a livelihood in a State other than his own, a right that is protected by the Privileges and Immunities Clause. Toomer v. Witsell, 334 U.S. 385 (1948). See Takahashi v. Fish & Game Comm'n, 334 U.S. 410 (1948).

* * * The fact that the State's control over wildlife is not exclusive and absolute in the face of federal regulation and certain federally protected interests does not compel the conclusion that it is meaningless in their absence.

We need look no further than decisions of this Court to know that this is so. It is true that in Toomer v. Witsell the Court in 1948 struck down a South Carolina statute requiring nonresidents of the State to pay a license fee of $2,500 for each commercial shrimp boat, and residents to pay a fee of only $25, and did so on the ground that the statute violated the Privileges and Immunities Clause. Less than three years, however, after the decision in Toomer, so heavily relied upon by appellants here, the Court dismissed for the want of a substantial federal question an appeal from a decision of the Supreme Court of South Dakota holding that the *total* exclusion from that State of nonresident hunters of migratory waterfowl was justified by that State's assertion of a special interest in wildlife that qualified as a substantial reason for the discrimination. State v. Kemp, 73 S.D. 458, 44 N.W.2d 214 (1950), dis'd, 340 U.S. 923 (1951). In that case South Dakota had proved that there was real danger that the flyways, breeding grounds, and nursery for ducks and geese would be subject to excessive hunting and possible destruction by nonresident hunters lured to the State by an abundance of pheasants.

* * *

Does the distinction made by Montana between residents and nonresidents in establishing access to elk hunting threaten a basic right in a way that offends the Privileges and Immunities Clause? Merely to ask the question seems to provide the answer. We repeat much of what already has been said above: Elk hunting by nonresidents in Montana is a recreation and a sport. In itself—wholly apart from license fees—it is costly and obviously available only to the wealthy nonresident or to the one so taken with the sport that he sacrifices other values in order to indulge in it and to enjoy what it offers. It is not a means to the nonresident's livelihood. The mastery of the animal and the trophy are the ends that are sought; appellants are not totally excluded from these. The elk supply, which has been entrusted to the care of the State by the people of Montana, is finite and must be carefully tended in order to be preserved.

Appellants' interest in sharing this limited resource on more equal terms with Montana residents simply does not fall within the purview of the Privileges and Immunities Clause. Equality in access to Montana elk is not basic to the maintenance or well-being of the Union. Appellants do not—and cannot—contend that they are deprived of a means of a livelihood by the system or of access to any part of the State to which they may seek to travel. We do not decide the full range of activities that are sufficiently basic to the livelihood of the Nation that the States may not interfere with a nonresident's participation therein without similarly interfering with a resident's participation. Whatever rights or activities may be "fundamental" under the Privileges and Immunities Clause, we are persuaded, and hold, that elk hunting by nonresidents in Montana is not one of them.

V

Equal protection. Appellants urge, too, that distinctions drawn between residents and nonresidents are not permissible under the Equal Protection Clause of the Fourteenth Amendment when used to allocate access to recreational hunting. Appellees argue that the State constitutionally should be able to charge nonresidents, who are not subject to the State's general taxing power, more than it charges its residents, who are subject to that power and who already have contributed to the programs that make elk hunting possible. Appellees also urge that Montana, as a State, has made sacrifices in its economic development, and therefore in its tax base, in order to preserve the elk and other wildlife within the State and that this, too, must be counted, along with actual tax revenues spent, when computing the fair share to be paid by nonresidents. We need not commit ourselves to any particular method of computing the cost to the State of maintaining an environment in which elk can survive in order to find the State's efforts rational, and not invidious, and therefore not violative of the Equal Protection Clause.

* * *

* * * The legislative choice was an economic means not unreasonably related to the preservation of a finite resource and a substantial regulatory interest of the State. It serves to limit the number of hunter days in the Montana elk country. There is, to be sure, a contrasting cost feature favorable to the resident, and, perhaps, the details and the figures might have been more precisely fixed and more closely related to basic costs to the State. But, as has been noted, appellants concede that a differential in cost between residents and nonresidents is not in itself invidious or unconstitutional. And "a statutory classification impinging upon no fundamental interest

* * * need not be drawn so as to fit with precision the legitimate purposes animating it. * * * That [Montana] might have furthered its underlying purpose more artfully, more directly, or more completely, does not warrant a conclusion that the method it chose is unconstitutional." Hughes v. Alexandria Scrap Corp., 426 U.S. 794, 813 (1976).[23]

* * *

The judgment of the District Court is affirmed.

It is so ordered.

* * *

Mr. Justice BRENNAN, with whom Mr. Justice WHITE and Mr. Justice MARSHALL join, dissenting.

Far more troublesome than the Court's narrow holding—elk hunting in Montana is not a privilege or immunity entitled to protection under Art. IV, § 2, cl. 1, of the Constitution—is the rationale of the holding that Montana's elk hunting licensing scheme passes constitutional muster. The Court concludes that because elk hunting is not a "basic and essential activit[y], interference with which would frustrate the purposes of the formation of the Union," the Privileges and Immunities Clause * * * does not prevent Montana from irrationally, wantonly, and even invidiously discriminating against nonresidents seeking to enjoy natural treasures she alone among the 50 States possesses. I cannot agree that the Privileges and Immunities Clause is so impotent a guaranty that such discrimination remains wholly beyond the purview of that provision.

* * *

NOTES

1. The following year the Court held that an Oklahoma statute that prohibited the export of "natural" minnows from the State was an unconstitutional burden on interstate commerce. Hughes v. Oklahoma, 441 U.S. 322 (1979). Should a Commerce Clause objection to the Montana system have been raised in *Baldwin?*

2. During the same term, the Court decided Hicklin v. Orbeck, 437 U.S. 518 (1978), striking down on Privileges and Immunities grounds the "Alaska hire" law, giving hiring preference to Alaska residents for jobs, including those on the Alaska Pipeline, resulting from oil and gas leases to which the state was a party. Though not finding the task easy, Professor Tribe distinguished the cases on the ground that Montana elk "would not exist but for the voluntary undertaking by the citizens of Montana to preserve these animals.

---

23. The appellants point to the facts that federal land in Montana provides a significant contribution to the elk habitat, and that substantial apportionments to the State flow from the Wild Life Restoration Act of Sept. 2, 1937, 50 Stat. 917, as amended, 16 U.S.C.A. §§ 669–669i. We fail to see how these federal aspects transform a recreational pursuit into a fundamental right protected by the Privileges and Immunities Clause, or how they impose a barrier to resident-nonresident differentials. Congress knows how to impose such a condition on its largess when it wishes to do so. See 16 U.S.C.A. § 669. See also Pub.L. 94–422, 90 Stat. 1314, adding § 6(f)(8) to the Land and Water Conservation Fund Act of 1965.

* * * *Baldwin* is thus another decision evincing a special judicial solicitude for efforts by the states to protect the environmental and other needs of their citizens." L. Tribe, AMERICAN CONSTITUTION-AL LAW 38–40 (1979 Supp.)

3. While the non-resident's interest in hunting elk is something less than fundamental to the well-being of the Union, just where does it or should it rank in the hierarchy of property or protectible interests? Could a state outlaw hunting altogether? Could the federal government? Compare the interest of the out-of-state hunter in *Baldwin* with the interest of the grazing permittee in United States v. Fuller, 409 U.S. 488 (1973), supra at page 687.

4. Federal law—especially the Endangered Species Act—restricts hunting opportunities in other ways. In the Sunrise Hunting Case, Defenders of Wildlife v. Andrus, 428 F.Supp. 167 (D.D.C.1977), the court held that FWS regulations permitting waterfowl hunting from before sunrise until sunset were arbitrary. The court reasoned that the ESA imposes an affirmative duty that prohibits the agency from allowing hunting at times when there is a substantial chance that hunters can misidentify birds and mistakenly shoot an endangered bird. Cf. Connor v. Andrus, 453 F.Supp. 1037 (W.D.Tex.1978). Litigation in the longrunning dispute over the use of lead vs. steel shot has resulted in holdings favoring steel shot. National Rifle Ass'n v. Kleppe, 425 F.Supp. 1101 (D.D.C.1976), aff'd mem., 571 F.2d 674 (D.C.Cir.1978) (FWS regulations banning lead shot in certain areas upheld); NWF v. Hodel, 23 ERC 1089 (E.D.Cal.1985) (court ordered ban on lead shot in 22 counties where lead poisoning of bald eagles is threatened). The NWF filed suit in February 1986 to force a nationwide ban on the use of lead shot.

5. Hunting and fishing in or near units of the National Park System has sparked considerable recent litigation, and more is in prospect. In general, hunting is forbidden in National Parks—which is why Alaskans successfully sought to have several resource areas in Alaska designated as preserves instead of parks in the Alaska National Interest Lands Conservation Act. In Voyageurs Nat'l Park Ass'n v. Arnett, 609 F.Supp. 532 (D.Minn.1985), the court ruled that the State could not allow wildlife trapping on park land ceded back to the State pursuant to the Boundary Revision Act, 16 U.S.C.A. § 160a–1(b)(1)(E). [Is there any excuse for such statutory numbering?] Plaintiffs in National Rifle Ass'n v. Potter, 628 F.Supp. 903 (D.D.C.1986), failed in their attempt to overturn a regulation that restricted hunting and trapping in the National Park System to areas where it was mandated by federal law. Similarly, a regulation ending commercial fishing in Everglades National Park was sustained in Organized Fishermen of Florida v. Hodel, 775 F.2d 1544 (11th Cir.1985). Litigation is pending over Montana's buffalo hunt: the State issued licenses in December 1985 to kill buffalo that stray from Yellowstone National Park out of fear that the semi-wild animals might infect domestic cattle with brucellosis.

The extent of managerial discretion in federal agencies to avoid compliance with state law varies considerably by system, even after passage of FLPMA and NFMA in 1976. The National Park Service is largely unaffected by state law in managing national parks by virtue of its preservation mandate in 16 U.S.C.A. § 1, the enclave status of many parks, and the longstanding prohibition against hunting in the parks. New Mexico State Game Comm'n v. Udall, 410 F.2d 1197 (10th Cir. 1969), cert. denied, 396 U.S. 961 (1970). But its authority is somewhat more circumscribed on national monuments and other miscellaneous lands categories under its jurisdiction. See, e.g., The Cape Hatteras National Seashore Act, 16 U.S.C.A. § 459a–1.

In administering the National Wildlife Refuge System, the Fish and Wildlife Service is enjoined to follow state law to the uncertain extent of this language in 16 U.S.C.A. § 668dd(c):

The regulations permitting hunting and fishing of resident fish and wildlife within the System shall be *to the extent practicable, consistent with* state fish and wildlife laws and regulations. The provisions of this Act shall not be construed as affecting the authority, jurisdiction, or responsibility of the several States to manage, control, or regulate fish and resident wildlife under State law or regulations in any area within the System. (Emphasis added.)

The Forest Service also attempts to comply with state wildlife law. Authority to manage wildlife is implicit in the Multiple-Use Act, 16 U.S.C.A. §§ 528–31, directing the Secretary to administer the national forests for multiple use, including wildlife, but section 528 also disclaims any intent to affect "the jurisdiction or responsibilities of the several States with respect to wildlife and fish on the national forests." In Hunt v. United States, 278 U.S. 96 (1928), the Court summarily rejected Arizona's claim that the Secretary of Agriculture could not kill excess deer in violation of state law on the Kaibab National Forest and Game Reserve.

The Forest Service and the BLM now are both subject to the mandate of FLPMA § 302(b), 43 U.S.C.A. § 1732(b) (quoted in the following principal case). The judicial construction of the provision has been inconsistent. The vehicle for interpretation has been the annual proposal by the Alaska Department of Fish and Game to kill a large number of wolves in certain areas, including BLM lands, in order to increase depleted caribou or moose populations. The annual plan has been followed by annual litigation commenced by the Defenders of Wildlife. The first several decisions were inconclusive. Defenders of Wildlife v. Kleppe, C.A. No. 76–0283 (D.D.C.1976); Defenders of Wildlife v. Alaska Dept. of Fish and Game, C.A. No. A76–13 (D.Alaska 1976). Then in April 1977, Judge Gasch ruled that FLPMA empowered the Secretary to halt the assertedly destructive program, and that the Secretary's failure to do so was a major federal action triggering the need for an environmental impact statement. See Defenders of Wildlife v. Andrus, 9 ERC 2111 (D.D.C.1977) (Alaska Wolf III):

[T]he Act must be construed to mean that the Secretary does have the authority to close the federal lands to the instant wolf kill. By providing that the states' responsibility was not diminished by the Act, Congress intended to preserve to the states their traditional control over sport hunting and fishing seasons and the licensing of such hunting and fishing. However, by authorizing the Secretary to close the federal lands to hunting for public safety, administration and law enforcement reasons, Congress intended to vest defendants with some authority over the use of federal lands for hunting. The administration of the public lands includes their administration for multiple-use purposes, such as wildlife preservation, so that the Secretary can prevent, under certain circumstances, hunting on federal lands when a multiple use such as wildlife is seriously threatened. The court will not at this time delineate the exact parameters of the Secretary's authority to close federal lands to non-sport, state licensed hunting. The court determines only that the Secretary has the authority to prevent persons from coming on federal lands to hunt wildlife for purposes other than sport or subsistence where, as plaintiffs have shown to be true in the instant case, such hunting presents a serious threat to the existence of a form of wildlife on these lands, at least until BLM has the opportunity to assess and consider the impact of the proposed hunt and seek the cooperation of the state game officials.

While the resulting injunction against the wolf hunt was being appealed, the State of Alaska (not a party to the suit) sued in the District of Alaska for a judgment declaring that the federal agency was powerless to halt the hunt, and even if the power existed, no impact statement was required in the circumstances. Defenders of Wildlife intervened. The Alaska District Court held that there was federal authority but no necessity for an EIS. In the interest of comity, however, the court declined to order a resumption of the hunt. On appeal of that decision, the Secretary "conceded" that he had power, but game officials from eleven states as amicus curiae argued that he did not. The Ninth Circuit affirmed in February 1979, holding that NEPA did not apply whether or not the Secretary had power under FLPMA—which it declined to decide. Alaska v. Andrus, 591 F.2d 537 (9th Cir.1979). There matters rested for a year until the decision in the fifth Alaska Wolf Kill case.

DEFENDERS OF WILDLIFE v. ANDRUS

United States Court of Appeals, District of Columbia, 1980.
627 F.2d 1238.

McGOWAN, Circuit Judge: This is an appeal from an order of the District Court granting a preliminary injunction against the Secretary of the Interior. It raises the question of whether, under the circumstances of this case, the National Environmental Policy Act obligates the Secretary to prepare and circulate an environmental impact statement when he does not act to prevent the State of Alaska from conducting, as part of a wildlife-management program, a wolf hunt on certain federal land. Because the Secretary's conduct here does not constitute a "major Federal action" within the meaning of the Act, we hold that the Secretary is not so obligated, and we reverse.

I

The Background of this Action

On February 16, 1979, the Alaska Department of Fish and Game (ADFG) announced a program whose aim was to kill from aircraft 170 wolves (approximately sixty percent of the wolf population) in an area of 35,000 square miles in the interior part of the state. Many, perhaps most, of the wolves were to be killed on federal lands for which the Department of the Interior is responsible. On February 23, counsel for one of the appellees, Natural Resources Defense Counsel, Inc., asked the Department to prepare an environmental impact statement for Alaska's program before allowing it to begin. The Department, however, did not exercise whatever authority it may have to stop the program and did not prepare an impact statement. On March 12, appellees— organizations and individuals interested in the preservation of the environment in general and of wildlife in particular—filed a complaint asking for declaratory and injunctive relief against appellants—the Secretary and two other officials of the Department of the Interior.

The complaint predicted that, although the wolf hunt was proposed in order to increase the number of moose in the region by decreasing the numbers of their major predator, it would in fact weaken the moose herds by ending a "culling process [which] is natural selection in action, and [which] assures survival of the fittest moose * * *" and would devastate the wolf packs even beyond the ADFG's estimates. This interference with these two major species, the complaint continued, would disrupt the ecology of the entire area.

The complaint asserted that [FLPMA] authorizes the Secretary of the Interior to prevent the killing of wildlife on federal lands and requires him to evaluate whether he must intervene if he is fully to serve the environmental concerns of the Act. The complaint claimed as one of its "Violations of Law" that appellants failed to make that evaluation. The other violation of law the complaint alleged is that appellants had, but failed to meet, an obligation under [NEPA] to prepare an environmental impact statement before deciding not to prevent Alaska from killing wolves on Federal land.

On March 13, 1979, the United States District Court for the District of Columbia issued a temporary restraining order which enjoined appellants to "take all steps necessary to halt the aerial killing of wolves by agents of the State of Alaska" on the relevant federal lands. Although Alaska has apparently continued to kill wolves on its own lands, it has discontinued doing so on federal lands.

* * *

* * *   The District Court believed it was "confronted with a simple question: Does NEPA require the Secretary of the Interior to prepare an EIS prior to permitting an extensive wolf kill to take place on federal lands?"   The District Court reasoned that FLPMA requires the Secretary to "*manage* and *plan* the use of federal lands" and that "[c]learly, an environmental assessment of the wolf elimination program must be part of the decision-making process."   The District Court therefore issued a preliminary injunction which required appellants "to prevent any such killing of wolves pending preparation of an environmental impact statement on the potential effects of the wolf control program."

II

Earlier Related Cases

This is not the first time a federal court has been asked to order the Secretary of the Interior to keep Alaska from killing wolves on federal land.   * * *   Defenders of Wildlife v. Andrus, 9 ERC 2111 (Feb. 14, 1977).   * * *

* * *

After that injunction issued, the Secretary ordered the Governor of Alaska, by telegram, not to kill wolves on the relevant federal land. Alaska complied, but brought an action in the District Court for Alaska.   * * *   [The court recounted the various court decisions on the Alaska wolf kill proposals.]

* * *

Meanwhile, the Secretary had appealed from Judge Gasch's grant of a preliminary injunction.   Defenders of Wildlife v. Andrus, C.A. No. 77–1611.   On March 16, 1979, after the Ninth Circuit had handed down its decision, we vacated the injunction and directed that the complaint be dismissed "for want of equity."   In an unpublished memorandum accompanying our order, we said that "[s]ound principles of comity dictate that this court should not undertake an independent examination of the issues resolved by the Ninth Circuit ruling."   We also noted that recent developments in the case had infected it with a staleness which made the grant of equitable relief, always a matter within the court's discretion, inappropriate.

* * *

IV

The Secretary's Obligations Under NEPA

* * *

A

Having laid out the statutory background of this action, we turn to the specific issue we must resolve.   Does NEPA require that the Secretary prepare and circulate an environmental impact statement in the circumstances of this case?

Our discussion of that question must center around the fact that, while the plain language of the statute calls for an impact statement when there is "major Federal action," here it is the Secretary's *inaction* which is complained of. Appellees, as we understand them, respond that (1) the environmental consequences of action may be greater than the consequences of action, and (2) the purpose of the statute is to ensure that environmentally informed decisions are made, not simply that the environmental consequences of all federal programs are considered. We acknowledge the truth of the first response, but we do not understand it to change the language of the statute.

As to the second response, we agree that a purpose of the statute is to ensure that environmentally informed decisions are made. Nevertheless, as it is written, NEPA only refers to decisions which the agency anticipates will lead to actions. This common-sense reading of the statute is confirmed by the statutory directive that the impact statement is to be part of a "recommendation or report" on a "proposal" for action. That is, only when an agency reaches the point in its deliberations when it is ready to propose a course of action need it be ready to produce an impact statement. As the Supreme Court said in *Andrus v. Sierra Club,* "Of course an EIS need not be promulgated unless an agency's planning ripens into a 'recommendation or report on proposals for legislation [or] other major Federal actions significantly affecting the quality of the human environment.'" 442 U.S. 347, 350 n. 2 (1979). Logically, then, if the agency decides not to act, and thus not to present a proposal to act, the agency never reaches a point at which it need prepare an impact statement.

* * *

None of this is to say that agencies may, by manipulating the time at which they actually develop recommendations or reports on proposals, seek to avoid or perniciously to delay preparing an impact statement. It is simply to confirm that Congress did not expect agencies to prepare statements if there is to be no action.

B

Appellees argue that, by not inhibiting an action of a private party or a state or local government, the federal government makes that action its own within the meaning of NEPA. However, in no published opinion of which we have been made aware has a court held that there is "federal action" where an agency has done nothing more than fail to prevent the other party's action from occurring. Even here courts have not abandoned the requirement that it must be a specifically *federal* action which triggers the preparation of an impact statement. To borrow from the language of the criminal law of conspiracy, we may say that federal "approval" of another party's action does not make that action federal unless the federal government undertakes some "overt act" in furtherance of that other party's project. Thus, when the Supreme Court discussed two circuit court decisions which held that private actions permitted by the federal government might necessitate the preparation of an impact statement, the Court's examples of federal "permission" were such concrete acts as decisions "to issue a lease, approve a mining plan, issue a right-of-way permit, or *take other action to allow private activity* * * *." Kleppe v. Sierra Club, 427 U.S. 390, 399 (1976) (emphasis added).

* * *

C

Our somewhat exact reading of section 102(2)(C) [of NEPA] and our insistence on an "overt act" may seem literal and formalistic. But our approach is not only consonant with, but is commanded by, the principles and spirit of NEPA. This court has had occasion before to rule on requests that environmental impact statements be required beyond the bounds of the possible. In Sierra Club v. Andrus, 581 F.2d 895 (1978), we were asked to require Department of the Interior to prepare statements to accompany appropriation requests for all programs having significant environmental consequences. We declined to do so except "when the request for budget approval and appropriations is one that ushers in a considered programmatic course following a programmatic review." Id. at 903. What we said then bears repeating in some detail now:

> Plaintiffs' logic-based contention * * * leads logically to the conclusion that an EIS would have to accompany every budget request for the annual operation of an environmental-conservation program, or indeed of an agency whose activities may have significant environmental impact. The principle of *reductio ad absurdum* is part of the landscape of logic. Plaintiffs have not suggested a limiting principle to their logic.

* * *

> * * * There is a danger of overburdening NEPA by spreading its mandate too widely. The environmental analysis required by NEPA is governed by the rule of reason, as we have held in determining the scope of realistic alternatives to the proposed action and the intensity of the required analysis. A rule requiring preparation of an EIS on the annual budget request for virtually every ongoing program would trivialize NEPA * * *.

* * *

On appeal, in a unanimous opinion, the Supreme Court not only cited approvingly from the first two paragraphs quoted above; it carried our reasoning a step further by reversing that portion of our decision which said that appropriation requests do need to be accompanied by impact statements in the special circumstances we specified. Andrus v. Sierra Club, 442 U.S. 347 (1979).

NEPA would be impaired in the manner of which we warned in Sierra Club v. Andrus were we now to decide for appellees. No agency could meet its NEPA obligations if it had to prepare an environmental impact statement every time the agency had power to act but did not do so. Nor does it suffice to say that an agency's burden would be kept to a reasonable level by the fact that no impact statement is needed when the inaction could have no significant environmental results, for we have held that an agency which decides not to issue an impact statement must provide a written explanation of its reasons for that decision. This requirement is necessary to ensure that the agency's decision is well-considered and to provide a basis for the judicial review of the agency's decision. It would be an imaginative and vigorous agency indeed which could identify and prepare all the statements and explanations appellees' reading of NEPA would have the statute demand.

* * *

We have said, and we still believe, that "[c]onsiderations of administrative difficulty, delay or economic cost will not suffice to strip the section of its fundamental importance." Calvert Cliffs' Coordinating Committee v. Atomic Energy Commission, 449 F.2d 1109, 1115 (1971). But the obligation appellees would have us impose goes beyond the difficult and well into the impossible. Neither NEPA's language, nor the precedent interpreting it, nor the public policy behind it, requires us to reach that result.

V

The Relationship of NEPA and FLPMA

The District Court and appellees believe that the above analysis of the Secretary's duty under NEPA is insufficient. They reason that FLPMA imposes such supervisory duties on the Secretary that every failure to prohibit a state wildlife program which is carried out on Federal land and which may have significant environmental consequences must be accounted for with an impact statement. The District Court decided

> that the Secretary has a nondiscretionary duty to plan for and manage federal land and resources. In view of this responsibility, the Secretary must prohibit any major actions significantly affecting the human environment from occurring on federal lands until an environmental impact statement has been prepared and circulated. Accordingly, until an EIS has been prepared, the Secretary must take appropriate action to prevent aerial wolf killing on federal lands by the State of Alaska and its agents.

FLPMA * * * was enacted "to provide the first comprehensive, statutory statement of purposes, goals, and authority for the use and management of about 448 million acres of federally-owned lands administered by the Secretary of the Interior through the Bureau of Land Management." S.Rep. No. 94–583, 94th Cong., 1st Sess. 24 (1975). As such, it certainly imposes on the Secretary a general duty "to plan for and manage federal land and resources." However, the District Court's reasoning seems to us to upset an allocation of functions Congress carefully and explicitly made in FLPMA, for Congress there assigned the states the primary responsibility for the management of wildlife programs within their boundaries.

It is unquestioned that "the States have broad trustee and police powers over wild animals within their jurisdictions," Kleppe v. New Mexico, 426 U.S. 529, 545 (1976). Neither is it questioned that * * * Congress may, if it wishes, pre-empt state management of wildlife on federal lands [pursuant to the Property Clause]. Despite its ability to take control into its own hands, Congress has traditionally allotted the authority to manage wildlife to the states. For instance, in the Multiple Use-Sustained Yield Act of 1960, Congress declared:

> It is the policy of the Congress that the national forests are established and shall be administered for outdoor recreation, range, timber, watershed, and wildlife and fish purposes. * * * Nothing herein shall be construed as affecting the jurisdiction or responsibilities of the several States with respect to wildlife and fish on the national forests. * * *

16 U.S.C.A. § 528.

Even in writing specifically "environmental" legislation, Congress has adhered to that allocation. Thus, Congress stated in the National Wildlife Refuge System Administration Act,

> The Provisions of this Act shall not be construed as affecting the authority, jurisdiction, or responsibility of the several States to manage, control, or regulate fish and resident wildlife under State law or regulations in any area within the System.

16 U.S.C.A. § 668dd(c). Similarly, the Wild and Scenic Rivers Act provides that

> [n]othing in this chapter shall affect the jurisdiction or responsibilities of the States with respect to fish and wildlife.

16 U.S.C.A. § 1284(a).[7]

7. When Congress has wished to change this traditional allocation of tasks, it has done so self-consciously and precisely, as the Endangered Species Act of 1973, 16 U.S.C.A. § 1531 et seq., demonstrates. The House Committee responsible for the bill carefully noted that coherent national and international policies were needed adequately to protect endangered species. H.Rep. No. 93–412, 93d Cong., 2d Sess. 7 (1973). In the Act itself, Congress specifically provided:

Any State law or regulation which applies with respect to the importation or exportation of, or interstate or foreign commerce in, endangered species or threatened species is void to the extent that it may effectively (1) permit what is prohibited by this chapter or by any regulation which implements this chapter, or (2) prohibit what is authorized pursuant to an exemption or permit provided for in this chapter or in any regulation

which implements this chapter. This chapter shall not otherwise be construed to void any State law or regulation which is intended to conserve migratory, resident, or introduced fish or wildlife, or to permit or prohibit sale of such fish or wildlife.

16 U.S.C.A. § 1535(f). Even in this Act, however, the House Committee report continued the comments quoted above by reaffirming the importance of state management of wildlife:

[T]he states are far better equipped to handle the problems of day-to-day management and enforcement of laws and regulations for the protection of endangered species than is the Federal government. It is true, and indeed desirable, that there are more fish and game enforcement agents in the state system than there are in the Federal government.

Far from attempting to alter the traditional division of authority over wildlife management, FLPMA broadly and explicitly reaffirms it. Section 302(b) of FLPMA begins by directing that the Secretary shall regulate "the use, occupancy, and development of the public lands." After a proviso relating to the use of lands by federal agencies, section 302(b) continues:

Provided further, That *nothing in this* Act shall be construed as authorizing the Secretary concerned to require Federal permits to hunt and fish on public lands or on lands in the National Forest System and adjacent waters *or as enlarging or diminishing the responsibility and authority of the States for management of fish and resident wildlife.* However, the Secretary concerned *may* designate areas of public land and of lands in the National Forest System where, and establish periods when, no hunting or fishing will be permitted for reasons of public safety, administration, or compliance with provisions of applicable law. Except in emergencies, any regulations of the Secretary concerned relating to hunting and fishing pursuant to this section shall be put into effect only after consultation with the appropriate State fish and game department.

43 U.S.C.A. § 1732(b) (emphasis added.)[8]

H.Rep. No. 93–412, 93d Cong., 1st Sess. 7 (1973).

8. A glance at the legislative history confirms what is plain enough on the face of the statute—Congress intended that the primary responsibility for wildlife management would lie with the states. The Committee report on the House version of the bill explained that the bill

provides that hunting and fishing will be permitted in accordance with Federal and State laws and that no Federal permits for hunting or fishing are authorized by this section. It permits the Secretaries to close areas to hunting and fishing for reasons of public safety. The Secretaries are expected to use the authority granted by the bill to close areas only if essential to the public safety, and then only for the shortest periods needed to accomplish this purpose. Protection of the public safety includes prevention and avoidance of hazards to persons, animals, and property.

H.Rep. No. 94–1163, 94th Cong., 2d Sess. 6 (1976). The Conference Report makes the point even more clearly.

The conferees authorize the two Bureaus to ban hunting and fishing for reasons of public safety, administration, and compliance with applicable law. The word "administration" authorizes exclusion of hunting and fishing from an area in order to maintain supervision. It does not authorize exclusions simply because

hunting and fishing would interfere with resource-management goals.

H.Rep. No. 94–1724, 94th Cong., 2d Sess. 60 (1976).

We should note that the Conference Report probably overstates its case. Senator Metcalf, Chairman of the Conference Committee, explained that "in attempting to define the term 'administration,' the statement of managers confuses the issue and could be wrongly interpreted to prevent the Secretary from protecting the public lands." 122 Cong.Rec. S17668 (daily ed. Oct. 1, 1976). Likewise, in the House, Representative Melcher, Chairman of the Subcommittee of the House Interior Committee which handled the bill, engaged in a discussion with Representative Seiberling which suggested that "administration" is not to be quite so restrictively defined, as the following excerpt indicates:

MR. SEIBERLING. Therefore, I take it that the gentleman would agree that the BLM and the Forest Service could close lands under their jurisdiction to hunting and fishing for reasons related to the management of the wildlife habitat?

MR. MELCHER. Yes, I would agree to that, but we do expect to cooperate in all instances possible with the State Fish and Game Commissions to allow those authorities to set hunting seasons and to set requirements for hunting and fishing.

The first quoted sentence of section 302(b) self-evidently places the "responsibility and authority" for state wildlife management precisely where Congress has traditionally placed it—in the hands of the states. The second quoted sentence of the section arguably permits ("may"), but certainly does not require ("shall"), the Secretary to supersede a state program,[9] and even when he does so, it must be after consulting state authorities. We are simply unable to read this cautious and limited permission to intervene in an area of state responsibility and authority as imposing such supervisory duties on the Secretary that each state action he fails to prevent becomes a "Federal action." A state wildlife-management agency which must seek federal approval for each program it initiates can hardly be said to have "responsibility and authority" for its own affairs.

Appellees remind us that FLPMA directs the Secretary to "manage the public lands under principles of multiple use and sustained yield," 43 U.S.C.A. § 1732(a), and that

> "multiple use" means * * * a combination of balanced and diverse resource uses that takes into account the long-term needs of future generations for renewable and nonrenewable resources, including, but not limited to, recreation, range, timber, minerals, watershed, wildlife and fish, and natural scenic, scientific and historical values. * * *

43 U.S.C.A. § 1702(c). Appellees also remind us that, pursuant to his authority under FLPMA, 43 U.S.C.A. § 1714(e), the Secretary has ordered that some of the lands on which wolves are to be killed

> are withdrawn from settlement, sale, location, entry or selection under the operation of the public land laws, including but not limited to the mining laws * * * and are reserved and appropriated for the public purpose of preserving, protecting, and maintaining the resource values of said lands which would otherwise be lost. * * *

43 Fed.Reg. 59756 (December 21, 1978).

Nevertheless, the statutory provisions of which appellees remind us are all part of FLPMA. Section 302(b) of that Act expressly commands that "nothing in this Act" enlarges or diminishes the state's responsibility for managing wildlife. We are therefore unable to conclude that appellees' citations to FLPMA should alter our understanding of the Secretary's obligation to prepare an environmental impact statement

122 Cong.Rec. H12009 (daily ed. Sept. 30, 1976).

9. Several parties in these "wolf hunt" cases have urged that the Secretary has no such power. At one point, the Secretary himself was among these, though he later withdrew that contention. The State of Alaska brought Alaska v. Andrus to establish that proposition, and in this court's first Defenders of Wildlife v. Andrus, the International Association of Fish and Wildlife Agencies filed a brief *amicus* to the same effect. See Part II, supra. Some of the legislative history which gives force to the argument of these parties is cited in note 8 supra.

when he declines to exercise the power which FLPMA arguably gives him to preempt state wildlife-management programs.[10]

* * *

NOTES

1. Does the Secretary have authority under FLPMA to halt the wolf kill? Is the statute itself dispositive?

2. The court's remark that the Conference Report on FLPMA "probably overstates the case" as to the intended meaning of § 1732(b) in footnote 8 of the opinion is itself an understatement. The district court in the third *Alaska Wolf* lawsuit, supra at page 860, noted that the remarks of Senator Metcalf and Rep. Melcher, principal sponsors of the bill, were far more restrictive concerning state authority:

* * *

Mr. Metcalf. The language of the statement of the managers could be interpreted as so narrowing the definition of "administration" that the agency would be unable to close an area to hunting even where a number of species is drastically reduced. Carried further this language could be interpreted to mean that an area which was used for habitat research could not be closed to hunting or fishing "simply because hunting and fishing would interfere with resource management goals."

In this legislation for the first time we are giving BLM basic statutory authority to manage the public lands on a multiple-use basis. Two of those uses are hunting and fishing, but they should not take precedence over all other uses. Further, it makes no sense to give an agency authority and then to tie its hands.

When this matter was discussed by the conferees, the right—indeed the responsibility—of BLM and the Forest Service to manage wildlife habitat was agreed to by all. I believe the language in the statement of managers could be interpreted differently and thus does not accurately reflect the conferees' agreement on this issue.

* * *

Mr. Melcher. Yes. The intent of the bill and the intent of the conference report is to assure that wildlife habitat management, and wildlife itself, are included in the management on our Federal lands.

We do not, however, intend to interfere with the States' prerogatives in setting the seasons for hunting of wildlife and

10. It is possible to read appellees' complaint as alleging that the Secretary has violated duties under FLPMA quite apart from FLPMA's effect on his obligation to prepare an environmental impact statement. However, we do not understand the District Court to have done more than instruct the Secretary to halt the killing of wolves until he has prepared an environmental impact statement. Therefore, although our discussion of FLPMA has necessarily touched on the limited nature of the Secretary's obligations under the Act, we do not otherwise reach the question of whether he has violated it.

wildfowl. On that score the Federal agencies go back to what has been left as State prerogatives, but the general management of wildlife habitat is expected, and also is a Federal responsibility.

3. The court reads the phrase "nothing in this Act shall be construed * * * as enlarging or diminishing the responsibility and authority of the States for management of fish and resident wildlife" as giving states "responsibility and authority for state wildlife management." Is that necessarily correct? Does it depend on the extent of prior jurisdictional relationships? Is a program to increase moose or caribou populations by exterminating their predators more accurately characterized as hunting and fishing regulation or as general management of wildlife habitat?

4. Why did the court discuss FLPMA at all? Did the court hold that the Secretary had no duty under FLPMA or just that he had no mandatory duty in these circumstances? Should it have been argued that the Secretary's failure to halt the wolf kill was a breach of his basic duty to protect the resources on the public lands and was thus arbitrary and capricious? Would the result have been the same if Alaska proposed to shoot every wolf in the State or every caribou on the BLM lands?

5. Is the line between action and inaction as precise as the Court seems to assume? In Aberdeen & Rockfish Ry. Co. v. SCRAP, 422 U.S. 289, 318–19 (1975), the Court termed "clearly correct" the conclusion that the ICC's failure to suspend proposed rates subject to a general revenue proceeding was a major federal action. Is the refusal to grant permission to a private party action or inaction? Was the order in the Grazing EIS case, NRDC v. Morton, supra at page 704, directed at anything other than agency inaction? Can an agency propose to do nothing? Compare Bunch v. Hodel, 793 F.2d 129 (6th Cir. 1986) (distinguishing the principal case and concluding that drawdown of lake by state, which had leased lake to United States Fish and Wildlife Service, amounted to federal action.)

6. Aside from history, what justification is there for state wildlife management jurisdiction on federal lands? The need for local decisions to control local resources? Enforcement personnel? See Gottshalk, The State-Federal Partnership in Wildlife Conservation, in WILDLIFE IN AMERICA 290 (H. Brokaw, ed., 1978).

In addition to the regulation of hunting and fishing, wildlife management must provide for sound habitat protection. Watershed management has been explored in chapter five, § B. Timber and range practices impacting on wildlife populations have been treated in chapters seven and eight. NFMA and FLPMA planning will bear heavily on wildlife, but those cases have not yet reached the courts. The following two opinions, however, demonstrate the application of NEPA when wildlife habitat is threatened by resource development.

CABINET MOUNTAINS WILDERNESS v. PETERSON

United States Court of Appeals, District of Columbia Circuit, 1982.
685 F.2d 678.

ROBB, Senior Circuit Judge:

In this action in the District Court the plaintiffs challenged the decision of the United States Forest Service to approve a plan of operations for exploratory mineral drilling in the Cabinet Mountains Wilderness Area in Northwestern Montana. The plaintiffs alleged the Forest Service action violated the Endangered Species Act (ESA), and the National Environmental Policy Act (NEPA). ASARCO, Inc. intervened as a defendant to protect its interest as the drilling permittee. On cross-motions for summary judgment the District Court upheld the Forest Service's decision. Cabinet Mountains Wilderness v. Peterson, 510 F.Supp. 1186 (D.D.C.1981). The plaintiffs appeal. We affirm the judgment of the District Court.

The Cabinet Mountains Wilderness Area consists of approximately 94,272 acres and is part of the Cabinet-Yaak ecosystem, one of only six ecosystems in the continental United States that supports populations of grizzly bears. The bears are listed as a threatened species under the ESA. See 50 C.F.R. § 17.11(h) (1981). Although it is estimated that only about a dozen grizzly bears may inhabit a portion of the Cabinet Mountains area where drilling will take place, the area has been recognized as having a high potential for grizzly bear management.

ASARCO holds a claim block consisting of 149 unpatented mining claims totalling 2,980 acres, most of them located in the Cabinet Mountains Wilderness Area. In 1979 ASARCO submitted a proposal to conduct preliminary exploratory drilling. The Forest Service began an extensive review of the proposal, including an environmental assessment, biological evaluation, and biological opinion. The Forest Service approved the proposal and ASARCO drilled four holes between July and November of that year. On February 4, 1980 ASARCO submitted a proposal for the continuation of the 1979 exploration program to be conducted during 1980–1983. For 1980, 36 drill holes on 22 sites in the Chicago Peak area of the Wilderness were proposed with a similar level of activity expected to take place in each of the three succeeding years. The purpose of the drilling program is to assess the extent of copper and silver deposits in the area. * * *

In May 1980 the Forest Service completed a final environmental assessment which incorporated the recommendations made by the FWS in its biological opinion. In addition the Forest Service recommended measures designed to mitigate the adverse effects on the Wilderness Area with particular regard to the grizzly bears, including a prohibition on overnight camping by ASARCO personnel except in emergency situations, daily and seasonal restrictions on helicopter flights to avoid disturbing the grizzlies during important denning and feeding periods, restrictions on helicopter usage to specified flight corridors, reclamation of drilling sites, seasonal restrictions on drilling activity in specified areas of the Wilderness, and monitoring of ASARCO's operations by Forest Service personnel.   The plan devised by the FWS was expressly adopted by the Forest Service.

On June 17, 1980 the Kootenai National Forest Supervisor, William E. Morden, issued a "Decision Notice and Finding of No Significant Impact" which approved the ASARCO plan subject to the modifications contained in the environmental assessment and the complete compensation plan described in the FWS's biological opinion.   Morden concluded that the impacts of the proposed activity had been adequately assessed and appropriate measures initiated to ensure that "[t]he continued existence of the grizzly bear is not threatened nor is its critical habitat adversely modified."   Because the environmental assessment found there would be no significant impacts from the proposal as modified, Morden stated that an environmental impact statement (EIS) was unnecessary.   Approval was expressly limited to the proposed exploratory drilling activities; further activities such as developmental exploration or mineral extraction would require a comprehensive examination of environmental effects.

* * *

Two issues are presented for review: first, whether the agency erred by failing to prepare an EIS, second, whether the agency's decision to permit the drilling program violated the ESA.

Appellants contend that the Forest Service violated NEPA by failing to prepare an EIS.   * * *

Both the Forest Service and the FWS concluded that the ASARCO proposal could have an adverse impact upon the grizzly bears, particularly when other concurrent activities in the Cabinet Mountains area were taken into account.   Numerous specific recommendations were made to avoid this impact and mitigation measures to protect the grizzly bears were imposed upon the proposal.   As we have said these measures were designed to "completely compensate" both the adverse effects of the ASARCO proposal and the cumulative effects of other activities on the bears and their habitat.   In light of the imposition of these measures, the Forest Service concluded that implementation of the ASARCO proposal would not result in "any significant effects upon the quality of the human environment."   Therefore an EIS was found to be unnecessary.

This court has established four criteria for reviewing an agency's decision to forego preparation of an EIS: (1) whether the agency took a "hard look" at the problem;   (2) whether the agency identified the relevant areas of environmental concern;   (3) as to the problems studied and identified, whether the agency made a convincing case that the impact was insignificant;   and (4) if there was impact of true significance, whether the agency convincingly established that changes in the project sufficiently reduced it to a minimum.   Maryland-National Capital Park and Planning Comm'n v. United States Postal Service, 487 F.2d 1029, 1040 (1973).   The fourth criterion permits consideration of any mitigation measures that the agency imposed on the proposal.   As this court noted, "changes in the project are not legally adequate to avoid an impact statement *unless they permit a determination that such impact as remains, after the change, is not 'significant.'* " Id. (emphasis supplied) Other courts have also permitted the effect of mitigation measures to be considered in determining whether preparation of an EIS is necessary. Logic also supports this result. NEPA's EIS requirement is governed by the rule of reason, and an EIS must be prepared only when significant environmental impacts will occur as a result of the proposed action. If, however, the proposal is modified prior to implementation by adding specific mitigation measures which completely compensate for any possible adverse environmental impacts stemming from the original proposal, the statutory threshold of significant environmental effects is not crossed and an EIS is not required. To require an EIS in such circumstances would trivialize NEPA and would "diminish its utility in providing useful environmental analysis for major federal actions that truly affect the environment."

[The court found a contrary CEQ interpretation unpersuasive.]

Because the mitigation measures were properly taken into consideration by the agency, we have no difficulty in concluding that the Forest Service's decision that an EIS was unnecessary was not arbitrary or capricious. The record indicates that the Forest Service carefully considered the ASARCO proposal, was well informed on the problems presented, identified the relevant areas of environmental concern, and weighed the likely impacts.

When ASARCO submitted its four-year drilling proposal the agency prepared an environmental assessment, copies were circulated for comment, and public meetings were held. An extensive biological evaluation was conducted which concluded the proposed drilling could potentially affect the grizzly bears in two ways: habitat modification and increased human-bear interactions, including direct encounters and reductions in secure habitat due to human disturbances. The evaluation also pointed out that the cumulative effects of the proposal and other concurrent activities might be significantly greater than the effects of the drilling proposal considered by itself. As to habitat modification, the evaluation concluded the adverse effect would be insignificant. The total area involved in the drilling was estimated to be less than one-half acre and even this estimate was considered high because the drill sites could be reclaimed. The more serious threat was posed by the loss of secure habitat due to increased human activities in the area, particularly the disturbance of important denning and feeding sites. Timber sales and recreational activities were specifically referred to. To reduce such potential adverse effects to a minimum, fourteen recommendations were made, including completion of project activities by October 31 of each year, restrictions of helicopter flights to specified corridors, measures to reduce helicopter noise, seasonal restrictions on the use of helicopters in particular areas, prohibition of project activities in the Copper Gulch area after July 31 in order to protect potentially important late summer and early fall food sources, daily restrictions on helicopter flights during important feeding periods, monitoring of the project by a biological technician, closure of various roads to protect the bears during feeding periods and to enhance their security, prohibiting the carrying of firearms by ASARCO personnel, prohibiting overnight camping by project personnel except in emergency situations, and daily removal of food wrappers, containers and excess food.

The Forest Service also initiated formal consultation with the FWS. In its biological opinion the FWS expressed concern over the cumulative effects of human activities in the area and agreed that displacement of the bears from secure habitats was the most serious impact of the proposal. Although the FWS concluded that the drilling program was likely to jeopardize the bears, it set forth a number of measures which were designed to avoid this result. To reduce adverse effects to a minimum the FWS stated that restrictions set forth in the biological evaluation prepared by the Forest Service must be strictly adhered to. Because the Chicago Peak area is a potentially important denning area, the FWS recommended that September 30, rather than October 31, should be the annual termination date for drilling activities. In assessing the cumulative effects of activities in the area, the FWS used a 10-mile travel radius for the bears to determine which other activities were relevant. This estimated travel radius was based on several expert studies of grizzly bears' home range. Using this method the FWS determined that certain timber sales and roads were relevant in addressing the problem of cumulative effects. Therefore, in addition to modifying ASARCO's period of operations, the FWS recommended rescheduling or eliminating certain timber sales and implementing specified road closures to provide a more secure habitat for the bears. According to the FWS, this course of action would "completely compensate in specific ways the cumulative adverse effects of the proposed project and other ongoing and proposed Forest Service activities" and would "avoid jeopardizing the continued existence of the grizzly bear". The Forest Service's final environmental assessment incorporated the recommendations made in the biological evaluation and biological opinion and expressly adopted the complete compensation plan devised by the FWS.

Appellants have not demonstrated any deficiencies in the agency's decision making process. They allege that the agency did not address the issue of cumulative impacts, that the effectiveness of the mitigation measures is not factually supported, and that the measures are too vague to be enforced. All these contentions are without merit. As we have noted, the Forest Service carefully considered the cumulative effects of activities in the Cabinet Mountains area. This led to curtailment of timber sales and the closing of several roads. As to the factual basis of the agency's decision, the Forest Service and the FWS conducted a comprehensive evaluation of the proposal. Wildlife biologists were consulted and expert studies were referred to. For each identified area of concern, one or more measures were implemented to mitigate potential adverse environmental effects.

* * *

Finally, we perceive no difficulty in reading the project modifications as requiring compliance by ASARCO. The Forest Service approved the proposal subject to the restrictions and mitigation measures which had been devised during the review process. Failure to abide by the modifications would be contrary to terms of the approval. If necessary, the agency can redress any violations by revoking or suspending its permission to conduct the drilling program.

We conclude that the agency's decision not to prepare an EIS was reasonable and adequately supported. Courts cannot substitute their judgment for that of an agency if the agency's decision was "fully informed and well considered." Vermont Yankee Nuclear Power Corp. v. NRDC, 435 U.S. 519, 558 (1978). Thus, the decision as to whether an EIS should be prepared is left to the agency's informed discretion. See Kleppe v. Sierra Club, 427 U.S. 390, 412 (1976). Here the agency conducted a thorough analysis of the proposed action and imposed specific measures to address the relevant areas of environmental concern. The agency concluded the proposal as modified would not cause any significant environmental impacts. Appellants have not identified any deficiencies in the agency's decision. For us to overturn it under these circumstances would require an unjustifiable intrusion into the administrative process. We refuse to intrude.

For similar reasons we find that the Forest Service's decision to approve ASARCO's drilling project did not violate the ESA. Appellants however contend the District Court erred by refusing to conduct *de novo* review of the Forest Service's action, and by finding instead that the arbitrary and capricious standard was appropriate. 510 F.Supp. at 1189. They argue that Congress mandated *de novo* review under the ESA by including a provision for citizen suits and that the congressional intent to protect endangered species of plants and animals further supports this view. Appellants also attempt to analogize this situation to other statutes under which *de novo* review has been found to be required. We find these arguments unpersuasive.

* * *

Our conclusion is consistent with prior decisions of this court and other courts. Although we have not previously ruled on the question of the applicable standard of review under the ESA, we recently decided a case arising under the Act in accordance with the arbitrary and capricious standard. In North Slope Borough v. Andrus, 642 F.2d 589 (1980), we reviewed action of the Secretary of the Interior pertaining to an endangered species of whales and concluded:

> There is ample evidence that the Secretary was meaningfully alerted to the biological consideration attaching to Bowhead whales in the Beaufort Sea. The Secretary could reasonably conclude that the lease sale did not endanger the whales. For these reasons, the substantive prescription of section 7(a)(2) to preserve endangered life has been honored.

Id. at 609.　*　*　*

* * *

Applying the arbitrary and capricious standard to the circumstances of this case, we hold that the Forest Service's action was reasonable and supported by the record. The ESA requires federal agencies to ensure that any actions taken by them are "not likely to jeopardize the continued existence of any endangered or threatened species." 16 U.S.C. § 1536(a)(2) (Supp. IV 1980). Sufficient evidence exists to support the Forest Service's decision that the ASARCO proposal, as modified, will not endanger the Cabinet Mountains grizzly bear population. Our conclusion is based on the same factors which led us to conclude that the agency's decision regarding the EIS was not arbitrary or capricious. The agency imposed modifications on the ASARCO proposal to mitigate the perceived potential threats to the grizzly bears and adopted a compensation plan designed to offset the adverse effects of the drilling operations. Taking into consideration the imposition of these measures, the Forest Service reasonably concluded that the project would not jeopardize the continued existence of the grizzly bears.

We emphasize that our review of the agency's action is limited to the approval of the four-year exploratory drilling proposal. Similarly, the Forest Service and the FWS expressly limited their findings to the drilling program presented by ASARCO, which is minor in scope and temporary in nature. Any future proposals by ASARCO to conduct drilling activities in the Cabinet Mountains area will require further scrutiny under NEPA and the ESA.

* * *

FOUNDATION FOR NORTH AMERICAN WILD SHEEP v. UNITED STATES

United States Court of Appeals, Ninth Circuit, 1982.
681 F.2d 1172.

ELY, Circuit Judge:

Appellant Foundation for North American Wild Sheep brought this action, premised on National Environmental Policy Act, challenging appellee United States Forest Service's decision not to prepare an Environmental Impact Statement [EIS] prior to granting a special use permit to Curtis Tungsten, Inc. [Curtis] allowing the reconstruction and use of Road 2N06. The District Court granted the Service's motion for summary judgment, holding, *inter alia,* that the Service had taken a "hard look" at the problem and reasonably concluded that no EIS was required. We have jurisdiction pursuant to 28 U.S.C. § 1291. Because we conclude that the Service's decision not to prepare an EIS was unreasonable, we reverse and remand for further administrative proceedings.

I. FACTUAL BACKGROUND

Curtis owns and operates a tungsten mine located in the San Gabriel Mountains in the Angeles National Forest. Access to this mining operation may be had only by way of either of two roads: Road

2N06, also known as the Coldwater Canyon Truck Trail, and Road 2N09. Both roads pass through federally controlled forest land in the Angeles National Forest.

Originally constructed in 1933 by miners who used the road to haul gold ore from the San Gabriel Mountains, Road 2N06 traverses the upper reaches of Cattle and Coldwater Canyons. In 1938, heavy flooding occurred in the area, destroying the mine from which the gold ore had been extracted, and curtailing mining operations in the area. From 1938 until 1969, Road 2N06 was used regularly by private landowners, the Forest Service, and the general public. In 1969, however, heavy flooding once again occurred, causing extensive damage to Road 2N06 and rendering it impassable. The road remained closed until 1980 when Curtis repaired it sufficiently to permit vehicular traffic.

Road 2N09 was constructed on the floor of the Canyon and contains numerous stream crossings. Consequently, it is subject to frequent and severe flooding, especially during the rainy winter months. From 1969 until the reconstruction of Road 2N06 in 1980, Road 2N09 provided the sole means of access to the Curtis mining claim.

On September 27, 1978, Curtis applied for a special use permit to reopen and use Road 2N06. According to Curtis, Road 2N09 crosses more than twenty streams and is therefore frequently impassable due to flooding. Curtis further stated that the "down time" [7] caused by this flooding precluded the economical operation of his tungsten mine. Road 2N06, according to Curtis, crosses no streams and therefore provides a more reliable means of access to his mining claim. Accordingly, Curtis proposed to clear Road 2N06 of vegetation, widen it to twelve feet where necessary, and repair washed-out areas. This proposal sparked the controversy which resulted in the present appeal.

Upon hearing of the proposal to reopen Road 2N06, numerous environmentalists responded with vigorous protests. Road 2N06 passes directly through the area occupied by one of the few remaining herds of Desert Bighorn Sheep (*Ovis Canadensis Nelsoni*). These sheep, indigenous to the mountains of the Western United States, are purportedly extremely sensitive to environmental change. In the late nineteenth century, the sheep population was estimated to be approximately 1,500,000. Current estimates indicate that less than 40,000 remain in the mountainous regions of the United States. Because of the steadily diminishing Bighorn population, California law has long treated the sheep as a "protected" species of wildlife and prohibited all hunting for sport of the animal. Under federal law, the Bighorn is classified as a "sensitive" species entitled to special management protection.

The population of the herd directly at issue here is estimated at between 400 and 700 animals. This herd is unique in that it is one of the very few herds of Bighorn currently experiencing an increase in

---

7. Curtis initially estimated that Road 2N09 was impassable for 1.14 months per year. This estimate was consistently revised upward as time progressed.

population.[11] The Foundation contends that reopening Road 2N06 would reverse this trend and result in the eventual destruction of this herd. The Foundation premises this contention on the critical nature of the areas through which Road 2N06 passes to the continued viability of the Bighorn herd.

Road 2N06 passes directly through the area used by the Bighorn herd for the "lambing" and rearing of its young. The Bighorn requires a unique ecosystem for these functions and any disturbance of that ecosystem may be potentially catastrophic to the survival of the herd. Road 2N06 also passes near a "mineral lick" used by the Bighorn herd. The exact composition and function of this "lick" is not precisely known but it is believed that the "lick" provides both a nutrient, probably sodium, necessary for Bighorn survival and a forum for intraspecies interaction necessary for the well-being and productivity of the herd. The reopening of Road 2N06 also presents the possibility of habitat encroachment of a more general nature. According to the Foundation, the Bighorn sheep are peculiarly subject to stress-related diseases resulting from interaction with other species.

In response to these and other concerns, the Service drafted an Environmental Assessment [EA].[15] The EA considered four alternative courses of action. Alternative A provided for the unlimited, year-round use of both Road 2N06 and Road 2N09. Alternative B provided for the use of Road 2N06 for nine months and for the closure of Road 2N06 during the three-month period during which the sheep utilize the area for the "lambing" and rearing of their young. Alternative B further provided for the use of Road 2N09 during the time Road 2N06 was closed. Alternative C provided for the year-round use of Road 2N06 and prohibited use of Road 2N09. Alternative D was the "no project" alternative and prohibited the reopening of Road 2N06. Under Alternative D, access to the Curtis mining claim was to be had exclusively by way of Road 2N09.[17] The Service evaluated the alternatives under various criteria, and concluded that Alternative B should be implemented. The Service further concluded that, because Alternative B adequately mitigated the potential harm to the sheep, the action would have no significant effect on the quality of the human environment and therefore no EIS was required.

* * *

II. ANALYSIS
* * *

* * * Our review of the administrative record in the present case leads us ineluctably to the conclusion that the Service's determination

---

11. Despite the increasing population, the survival rate of Bighorn lambs was characterized as "poor" in the Environmental Assessment * * *

15. The Service initially prepared a Draft EA. The Draft was circulated and numerous comments received. The Service then made minor revisions in the Draft and reissued it as the Final EA. For the most part, the Final EA did not respond in other than a conclusory fashion to the comments previously received.

17. Alternative D was the choice recommended by the vast majority of the responses to the Draft EA.

that no EIS was required was, in fact, unreasonable. Accordingly, we reverse.

As noted above, NEPA requires the preparation of an EIS for all major federal actions significantly affecting the quality of the human environment. There is no dispute that the issuance of a permit to reopen and use Road 2N06 constitutes a major federal action within the meaning of NEPA. Accordingly, the proper resolution of this appeal turns solely upon the reasonableness of the Service's conclusion that issuance of the permit was not an action significantly affecting the quality of the human environment.

* * *

In accordance with its internal operating procedures, the Service prepared an EA regarding Curtis's application for a special use permit to reopen Road 2N06. The purpose of this EA was to determine whether an EIS was required, to facilitate preparation of an EIS if necessary, and to aid the Service in complying with NEPA if no EIS was required.[27] 40 C.F.R. § 1508.9; 7 C.F.R. § 3100.20. The EA purported to consider the impact on the Bighorn sheep resulting from the reopening of Road 2N06, considered the various alternatives set forth above, and concluded that no EIS was required. Our review of the EA, along with its appendices, leads us to conclude that the Service failed to take the requisite "hard look" at the environmental consequences of its action and that its conclusion that reopening Road 2N06 would have no significant effect on the human environment was unreasonable.

The EA at issue here failed to address certain crucial factors, consideration of which was essential to a truly informed decision whether or not to prepare an EIS.[29] Perhaps the most glaring shortcoming of the EA is its failure to include any estimate of the expected amount of truck traffic on Road 2N06 from the Curtis mine. We fail to see how the effect of reopening Road 2N06 can be evaluated intelligently without some consideration of the amount of traffic likely to flow along the road. Moreover, the EA lists as one of its assumptions that no unauthorized vehicular traffic will occur on Road 2N06 should it be reopened. No effort was made to quantify the amount of unauthorized traffic nor was the effect on the Bighorn of this traffic evaluated. The omission of any meaningful consideration of such fundamental factors precludes the type of informed decision-making mandated by NEPA.

The EA similarly fails to address certain other issues raised by correspondence received by the Service in response to its initial draft of the NEPA.[31] Road 2N06 passes close to a "mineral lick" used by the Bighorn. The California Department of Fish and Game, in a letter to

27. The EA itself listed as its only objective a determination of the appropriate route of access to the mining claims located in Cattle Canyon.

29. We do not suggest that the EA must conform to all the requirements of an EIS. We merely assess whether the EA, offered by the Service as the prime statement of reasons for its decision not to prepare an

EIS, is sufficient to establish the reasonableness of that decision.

31. Responses critical of the Draft EA were received from biologists, zoologists, the California Department of Natural Resources, and the California Department of Fish and Game. It is interesting that the Service relied heavily upon a study conducted by James DeForge for its estimates

the Forest Service, raised serious questions regarding the effect of traffic on Road 2N06 upon the sheep's use of this "lick." According to the Department of Fish and Game, reopening Road 2N06 would lead to abandonment of the "lick" and impair "the year-round social activity at the lick [that] is critical in maintaining the high level of productivity of the local herd." The Service failed to address either the effect of traffic upon the sheep's use of the "lick" or the effect of the loss of the mineral lick upon the sheep's continued viability. The EA further contained no discussion of whether there were other mineral licks available for use by the sheep.

Other significant questions raised by respondents to the initial draft of the EA were similarly ignored or, at best, shunted aside with mere conclusory statements. Substantial questions regarding the sheep's susceptibility to stress-related diseases were raised by numerous responses to the draft EA. One response indicated that stress caused by traffic on Road 2N06 could increase sheep mortality by reducing the sheep's resistance to disease, could inhibit reproduction, and could result in increased aberrant behavior among the young sheep. Rather than directly addressing this issue, the Service relied heavily upon instances where the sheep have indicated some tolerance of man's intrusion upon their habitat. Yet, with one exception discussed below, the circumstances surrounding these examples of the sheep's tolerance of man appear totally dissimilar to the potential intrusion at issue here. The sightings relied upon by the Service were made by hikers, sympathetic to the sheep, who apparently endeavored to induce as little apprehension in the sheep as possible. The EA provides no foundation for the inference that a valid comparison may be drawn between the sheep's reaction to hikers and their reaction to large, noisy ten-wheel ore trucks. If such a comparison legitimately may be drawn, the EA should so indicate. Moreover, the EA fails to provide any indication that the Service fully considered the potentially differing reactions of the sheep depending upon whether man's intrusion was occasional or relatively constant. We note, however, that the two reports regarding the Bighorn contained in Appendix J of the EA do not deal with the regular, long-term intrusion of man into the Bighorn habitat. Rather, they deal with the Bighorn's response to isolated and sporadic contacts with man. We are therefore left to speculate whether the Bighorn's supposed tolerance would continue if man were a regular visitor. Yet the very purpose of NEPA's requirement that an EIS be prepared for all actions that may significantly affect the environment is to obviate the need for such speculation by insuring that available data is gathered and analyzed prior to the implementation of the proposed action.

* * *

The Service vigorously asserts that the mitigation measures incorporated into the chosen alternative (Alternative *B*) reduce the potential impact upon the Bighorn to insignificant levels. We cannot agree.

of the population of the herd at issue here yet dismissed without comment Mr. DeForge's contention that the reopening of Road 2N06 would be very harmful to the sheep.

Alternative *B* contains certain measures designed to minimize the adverse impact of Road 2N06 upon the continued well-being of the sheep. First, Alternative *B* provides for the closure of Road 2N06 from April 1 until June 30 in order to avoid undue disturbance of the sheep during the "lambing" season. Second, Alternative *B* requires the maintenance of a secure, locked gate and a 24-hour guard at the entrance to Road 2N06. Third, a monitoring system is to be undertaken and Road 2N06 is to be closed in the event of a forty percent reduction in the use of the area by the sheep. Finally, the Service contends that the area can be repopulated with Bighorn sheep from other areas if necessary. The efficacy of these mitigation measures was severely attacked by numerous responses to the original draft of the EA.

Based upon our review of the record, we are convinced that, despite the above-referenced mitigation measures, the reopening of Road 2N06 is a major federal action that "may significantly degrade some human environmental factor." We are also convinced that the Service's conclusion to the contrary was plainly unreasonable.

We first address the Service's contention that the closure of Road 2N06 during the three-month "lambing" season will be adequate to mitigate the impact of the road upon the sheep. The Bighorn require a finely tuned ecological balance for their "lambing" and rearing functions and, according to Appendix J of the EA, "[a]ny disturbance of these [lambing] areas would be a catastrophe to the sheep as the ecosystems needed for lambing are extremely limited in this area."

Thus, it appears that the continued use of the lambing area through which Road 2N06 passes is essential to the continued productivity of the herd at issue here. Respondents to the draft EA strongly attacked the Service's assumption that the sheep would return to the area to perform their most sensitive function after that area had been invaded by man for nine months. The Service provided no basis for its assumption in the EA. Evaluation of the reasonableness of this assumption is doubly difficult because of the Service's failure to provide data regarding the quantity of traffic expected to flow through the area. The absence of this crucial information renders a decision regarding the sheep's reaction to the traffic on Road 2N06 necessarily uninformed. Without some sort of informed idea of how the sheep will react to Road 2N06 while it is open, it is impossible to determine whether they will return to the area to "lamb" once the road has been closed. Certainly substantial questions are raised whether the closure of Road 2N06 for three months will serve to mitigate the potential harm to the sheep. Where such substantial questions are raised, an EIS must be prepared.

We also find the provision for a locked gate and a guard at the entrance to Road 2N06 insufficient to reduce the environmental impact of the proposed reopening of the road to less than significant levels. Initially, it is noteworthy that one of the assumptions expressly set forth in the EA is that increased unauthorized traffic on Road 2N06 will result from the reopening of the road regardless of the precautions taken to prevent such traffic. Thus the efficacy of this measure is, under the Service's own assumptions, doubtful. Further this mitigation provision will only affect the quantum of harm resulting from unauthorized traffic. Consequently, it is manifestly insufficient to mitigate the harm to the sheep emanating from the authorized use of Road 2N06 by Curtis ore trucks and is inadequate to remedy the flaws contained in the Service's analysis of that harm.

We also find the monitoring and repopulation provisions contained in Alternative *B* insufficient to support a reasonable conclusion that the reopening of Road 2N06 will have no significant impact upon the quality of the human environment. NEPA expresses a Congressional determination that procrastination on environmental concerns is no longer acceptable. Yet the provision requiring closure of Road 2N06 in the event of a forty percent reduction in the use of the area by the sheep is just this type of procrastination. It represents an agency decision to act now and deal with the environmental consequences later. Such conduct is plainly inconsistent with the broad mandate of NEPA. Moreover, the provision implicitly treats a forty percent reduction in the sheep's use of the area surrounding Road 2N06 as insignificant. No support for such a conclusion is found in the record.

Reliance on the repopulation scheme as a basis for the conclusion that the reopening of Road 2N06 will have no significant impact on the quality of the environment ignores the requirement, found in the regulations of both the Council on Environmental Quality and the Service itself, that "the significance of an action must be analyzed in several contexts such as society as a whole * * *, the affected region, the affected interests and the locality." 40 C.F.R. § 1508.27; Forest Service Manual, Ch. 1950, § 38. In order for repopulation of the herd at issue here to be required, there must necessarily be an initial reduction in the population of the herd as well as a corresponding reduction in the sheep population as a whole. This overall population reduction was ignored by the Service. * * * Moreover, the transplant of sheep from another area to the area at issue here would necessarily result in a reduction in sheep population in the area from which the transplanted sheep were removed. This factor was also ignored by the Service.

An examination of the pertinent Forest Service regulations supports our conclusion that the Service was unreasonable in failing to prepare an EIS. * * *

III. CONCLUSION

We are mindful that it is not the province of this Court to substitute its judgment for that of the Service. Yet it must also be remembered that "[t]he spirit of the [NEPA] would die aborning if the facile, ex parte decision that the project was minor or did not significantly affect the environment were too well shielded from impartial review." Save Our Ten Acres v. Kreger, 472 F.2d 463, 466 (5th Cir. 1973).

In the present case, the Service failed to comply with its own regulations and, furthermore, failed to consider numerous issues obviously relevant to a determination of the likely effect of reopening Road 2N06 on the environment. Under these circumstances, we conclude that the Service's determination that no EIS was required was plainly unreasonable. Accordingly, the judgment of the District Court is reversed and the case is remanded for further proceedings not inconsistent with this Opinion.

Reversed.

NOTES

1. Can *Cabinet Mountains Wilderness* be squared with *Foundation for North American Sheep?* The grizzly is officially listed as threatened while the bighorn is not listed as either endangered or threatened. Does the species' status support an argument that both cases were wrongly decided? Was the decision in *North American Sheep* procedural or substantive? In *Cabinet Mountains Wilderness,* did either the Forest Service or the court "insure" that the grizzly bear population will not be substantially harmed?

2. In Gee v. Boyd, 105 S.Ct. 2123 (1985), three justices dissented from denial of certiorari on the ground that the Court should address the scope of review in NEPA cases, citing *North American Sheep,* among others, for the proposition that "[t]he lower courts have long been in dissarray on what standard of review to apply to an agency's decision not to undertake an EIS."

3. The Fish and Wildlife Conservation Act of 1980, 16 U.S.C.A. §§ 2901–11, popularly called the Nongame Act, sets in motion a process whereby states are encouraged to develop plans for conservation of species formerly neglected by state fish and game agencies with federal financial assistance.

4. In some situations, the public lands support wildlife taken by subsistence hunters and fishers. Special Indian hunting rights have been upheld in a few instances where tribes reserved hunting or fishing rights on off-reservation lands during treaty negotiations. See State v. Coffee, 97 Idaho 556 P.2d 1185 (1976) ("open and unclaimed" public lands). See also Kimball v. Callahan, 493 F.2d 564 (9th Cir.1974) (Klamath hunting rights on Winema National Forest). Subsistence rights have been codified in ANILCA, due to the large number of rural residents, Native and non-Native, who rely on the subsistence take of big game and salmon. See 43 U.S.C.A. §§ 3111–26. ANILCA establishes a preference for subsistence uses, id. § 3114, and requires federal agencies to evaluate the effects on subsistence when considering leases, permits, or other forms of development. Id. § 3120(a). In People of the Village of Gambell v. Hodel, 774 F.2d 1414 (9th Cir.1985), cert. granted, the court enjoined oil exploration on the outer continental shelf because the Secretary failed to evaluate the effects of the leases on subsistence uses by Alaskan Natives. See also, e.g., Kunaknana v. Clark, 742 F.2d

1145 (9th Cir.1984); Madison v. Alaska Dept. of Fish & Game, 696 P.2d 168 (Alaska 1985). As pressures on Alaskan herds and runs mount, it is not unlikely that the subsistence preference in ANILCA may lead to state-federal jurisdictional collisions reminiscent of the *Alaska Wolf Kill* cases.

Chapter Ten

THE RECREATION RESOURCE

The single greatest demand on the public lands in terms of total user-days is from persons seeking recreational opportunities. The burgeoning American penchant for recreation comes in varying forms, from motorized equipment to improved facilities to big game hunting to quiet contemplation of nature. It is exercised with varying degrees of intensity, and can create land management problems. Recreation is a resource like the more conventional ones: Congress has recognized that recreation is a valid and sometimes preferred land use and has encouraged and subsidized it on numerous occasions. Recreation is one of the major "multiple uses" to be provided for by the Forest Service and the BLM. The Fish and Wildlife Service is also enjoined to allow recreational use on refuges when it is compatible with wildlife purposes. Congress has charged the National Park Service "to conserve the scenery and the natural and historic objects and the wildlife [in parks] and to provide for the enjoyment of the same in such manner and by such means as will leave them unimpaired for future generations." National Park Act of 1916, 16 U.S.C.A. § 1. Unlike most federal lands systems, however, the National Park System includes many areas with specific statutory management guidelines or authority, and the specific limitations will override the general command. The tension in the quoted NPS mandate between recreation ("enjoyment") and preservation ("unimpaired") is reflected elsewhere in the statutes as well: by 16 U.S.C.A. §§ 1a–2, 1b, the Park Service is instructed both to "promote" and to "regulate" national park use.

Like other resources, intensive recreation can degrade the natural environment and pose conflicts with other resource uses. Access to hunting can be barred by mining claims; ski area proposals are fought by hikers, hunters, and bird-watchers; motorcyclists are despised by many but can find no other open country; increased sight-seeing visitations overwhelm the public use areas of Yellowstone; and so forth. As a general rule, the more mechanized or technologically advanced the form of recreation, the more potential for conflict and destruction it poses. Off-road vehicles, for example, are more dangerous to ecological stability than hikers or joggers, hunters make more of an impact than birdwatchers, and hotels cause more serious changes than tents. Quantity, too, is important: a horde of hikers will leave the terrain in worse condition than a single jeep. In one of the few worthwhile footnotes in legal literature, Professor Ralph Johnson captured the essence of the dilemma:

"Motorbikes are a particular bane in the wilderness. But, it is said, many people like to ride motorbikes on mountain trails. This led me to invite a number of friends to fill in the blank in

886

the following sentence: Because people like to ride motorbikes on mountain trails they should be allowed to do so, is like saying that because they like to _____ on mountain trails they should be allowed to do so. Unfortunately, none of the entries were printable."

Johnson, Recreation, Fish, Wildlife and the Public Land Law Review Commission, 6 Land & Water L.Rev. 283, 289 n. 18 (1970).

Substantial economic interests are at stake in recreation management decisions. The recreation industry includes resort operators, concessionaires, and manufacturers of motor homes, boats, off-road vehicles, skiing equipment, and other sporting goods. All of them have an interest in promoting intensive recreation. In addition, many small communities near the public lands are economically dependent on tourism.

More and more often, conflicts between recreation and other values or resources are being resolved in courts. Recreation is not ordinarily perceived as a "legal" matter, and until recently there have been relatively few litigated conflicts in which some recreational interest alone was central. Even so, the perceptive reader will have noticed that many cases in this volume involve the recreation resource. In Leo Sheep Co. v. United States, 440 U.S. 668 (1979), supra at page 112, the access rights at issue were intended for the benefit of fishermen. Fundamental questions of federal power and private rights have been litigated in the context of hunter access, as in United States v. Curtis-Nevada Mines, Inc., 611 F.2d 1277 (9th Cir.1980), supra at page 463. In United States v. Coleman, 390 U.S. 599 (1968), supra at page 433, the motivation of the locator may well have been more to build a vacation home than to exploit the mineral deposit. Perhaps the *Ruby Lake Refuge* case, supra at page 831, best illustrates the problems and conflicts inherent in intensive recreational use and the fundamental management difficulties in allocating scarce resources, a recurring theme throughout.

Recreation and American culture are intimately related. Preferred forms of recreation are influenced by available leisure time, prosperity, technology, and prevailing social mores. As recreation influences culture, so too does culture (and philosophy and morality) influence recreational policy—sometimes in bizarre fashion. For instance, in September 1982 it was reported that the Department of the Interior intended to ban nudity on a beach in Assateague National Seashore. The Republican Study Committee described this initiative as "yet another move to protect the environment." In April 1983 Secretary Watt disclosed that rock groups, prominently including the Beach Boys, were to be banned from performing in the annual July 4th celebration in a Washington, D.C. federal park, to be replaced by Las Vegas singer Wayne Newton. Mr. Watt said that rock concerts were "attracting the wrong element," but Presidential assistant Michael Deaver retorted: "the Beach Boys are an American institution. Anyone who thinks they play hard rock thinks Mantovani plays jazz."

After a Presidential scolding, the Secretary rescinded the ban the following day.

This chapter examines four federal recreational policy topics. The first section briefly treats federal acquisition of interests in land for recreational purposes. Section B considers recreational facilities on the public lands, including commercial developments such as ski areas. The third section describes the basis of federal liability under the Federal Tort Claims Act for mishaps to recreational licensees. Section D analyzes the implied license of access to federal lands for recreation and emerging restrictions on that license, focusing on allowable use by off-road vehicles.

A. ACQUISITION OF RECREATIONAL LANDS: THE LAND AND WATER CONSERVATION FUND

The Land and Water Conservation Fund, 16 U.S.C.A. §§ 460*l*–4 to 460*l*–11, is a keystone of federal recreational policy. The Fund is financed by special taxes and earmarked receipts (particularly from offshore oil and gas leasing). Over the last decade, authorized but not necessarily appropriated spending from the Fund has been $900 million annually. Since its inception in 1965, LWCF moneys have enabled federal agencies to purchase over 2.8 million acres for new recreational areas and enlargement of existing national parks, refuges, and forests. LWCF grants to states have bought an additional two million acres for state recreational land systems.

Calling the acquisitions financed by the LWCF "the so-called park-a-month program" and "park barrel politics," Secretary Watt in 1981 declared a moratorium on further land acquisition by either state or federal governments. He denied that the Administration had a "hit list" for deauthorizing parks (a rumor fed by his disparaging comments about urban parks), and suggested that Congress take a new tack:

> Does Congress believe we should take care of that which we have or does it believe we should grab for more lands to take off the tax rolls? That is a simple statement of the issue, but I am satisfied it cannot do both simultaneously and our recommendation is we take care of what we have because that's being a good steward and a good conservationist.

The LWCF controversy abated somewhat when Secretary Clark lifted the moratorium on spending, but actual spending since has not approached authorized or appropriated levels. On the legality of Secretary Watt's moratorium, cf. Dabney v. Reagan, 542 F.Supp. 756 (S.D. N.Y.1982); Glicksman & Coggins, Federal Recreational Land Policy: The Rise and Decline of the Land and Water Conservation Fund, 9 Colum.J.Envtl.L. 125 (1984). See generally Sax, Buying Scenery: Land Acquisitions for the National Park Service, 1980 Duke L.J. 709.

FRIENDS OF SHAWANGUNKS, INC. v. CLARK

United States Court of Appeals, Second Circuit, 1985.
754 F.2d 446.

OAKES, Circuit Judge.

This case presents the novel question whether amendment of a conservation easement acquired in part with federal funds under the Land and Water Conservation Fund Act of 1965 so as to permit expansion of a golf course with limited access constitutes a conversion "to other than public outdoor recreation uses" under section 6(f)(3) of the Act, 16 U.S.C. § 460*l*–8(f)(3).[1] The Secretary of the Interior, acting through the National Park Service's Acting Regional Director, determined that a section 6(f)(3) conversion would not occur. * * *

* * *

The Shawangunk Range, located in Ulster County, New York, is noted for spectacular rock formations, sheer cliffs, windswept ledges with pine barrens, fast-flowing mountain streams and scenic waterfalls, as well as a series of five mountain lakes, the "Sky Lakes." Of these, Lake Minnewaska is one, with extremely steep banks and many magnificent cliffs rising as high as 150 feet along its northern and eastern shores. Lake Minnewaska is situated approximately in the center on a general north-south line of 22,000 acres of permanent open space extending for some sixteen miles along the crest of the Shawangunks. Large tracts of land within the overall area are owned, maintained, and made available to the public for hiking and other limited recreational activities by, among others, the Village of Ellenville, the Palisades Interstate Park Commission (PIPC), the Mohonk Preserve, Inc., Mohonk Mountain Houses, Inc., and the Nature Conservancy.

In 1971, the State of New York purchased about 7,000 acres of land bordering Lake Minnewaska to the south and west for the formation of Minnewaska State Park. The park is under the jurisdiction and management of the PIPC, an interstate park commission formed by compact between the State of New York and the State of New Jersey.

In 1977, the PIPC added 1,609 acres of land to the park and purchased an approximately 239-acre conservation easement over Lake Minnewaska itself and certain land adjacent to it, all with the help of 50% federal matching funds from the Land and Water Conservation Fund. See 16 U.S.C. § 460*l*–8. The lands encumbered by the easement contain inter alia the lake itself, a nonoperating nine-hole golf course, a golf course pro shop, the water supply system for an adjacent resort building, and wooded land.

---

1. Section 6(f)(3) provides:

No property acquired or developed with assistance under this section shall, without the approval of the Secretary, be converted to other than public outdoor recreation uses. The Secretary shall approve such conversion only if he finds it to be in accord with the then existing comprehensive statewide outdoor recreation plan and only upon such conditions as he deems necessary to assure the substitution of other recreation properties of at least equal fair market value and of reasonably equivalent usefulness and location.

According to its terms, the easement is "for the purpose of, but not solely limited to, the conservation and preservation of unique and scenic areas; for the environmental and ecological protection of Lake Minnewaska and its watershed; and to prevent development and use in a manner inconsistent with the present use and operation of lands now owned and to be conveyed [to the PIPC] and to be part of Minnewaska State Park." It provides that the fee owner "shall not develop or erect new facilities within the described area; alter the landscape or terrain; or cut trees" but may

> operate, maintain and reconstruct existing facilities within the easement area, including, but not limited to buildings, roads, utilities and golf courses; provided that (a) Any reconstruction shall be in the same location and utilized for the same purpose as that which existed on the date hereof and that such reconstructed facilities shall be no larger in area than the facility being replaced.

In a limited exception to the prohibition against expanded or new construction, the PIPC agreed to the construction or reconstruction of several specific facilities, including "[t]he existing golf course pro shop and a golf course maintenance building" as well as "[a]n access road and parking lot for golf course patrons."

The Marriott Corporation, a national hotel and resort developer, acquired an option in 1980 to purchase approximately 590 acres, including the water and lands encumbered by the 239-acre easement. Marriott proposes to develop a resort facility, complete with a 400-room resort hotel and conference center, 300 condominium units, restaurants, ski facilities, and an expanded, professional grade 18-hole golf course. Eight golf course holes and related facilities, apparently with golf-cart roadways, would be constructed on property subject to the easement.

* * *

Despite the Friends' arguments, the PIPC resolved on July 20, 1981, to amend the conservation easement to allow the Marriott Corporation to expand the golf course as proposed, drill wells within the easement area, increase the use of water from Lake Minnewaska, and utilize acreage encumbered by the easement for purposes of computing total average density of residential development. In consideration, Marriott agreed to extend the area covered by the easement, permit public access to footpaths through the easement area and adjacent lands owned by Marriott, maintain the lake level above an elevation of 1,646 feet, limit development on its other adjoining property, and open the golf course to the public twenty-five percent of the time. On October 20, 1981, defendant Don H. Castleberry, as Acting Regional Director of the Mid-Atlantic Region of the National Park Service, issued a letter to the Deputy Commissioner and Counsel of the New York State Office of Parks and Recreation officially notifying the PIPC that the contemplated amendment of the conservation easement did not constitute a section 6(f)(3) conversion and therefore did not require any federal authorization. This lawsuit followed.

* * * [T]he district court denied the Friends' motion for summary judgment and granted the federal defendants' and Marriott's motion for summary judgment, holding that the amendment did not constitute a conversion. The court reasoned that because the public had no access to the lands encumbered by the easement these lands "presently are not intended for outdoor, public, recreational use" within the meaning of the Land and Water Conservation Fund Act of 1965. Hence,

> [w]hatever limited public access is contemplated by the terms of the proposed amendment to that easement, therefore, must be viewed as nothing less than a bonus to the public, and not as a diminution in, or conversion of, the availability of public, outdoor, recreation facilities.

* * *

DISCUSSION

We agree with the Friends that the district court wrongly decided that the easement lands presently are "not intended for outdoor, public, or recreational use." Rather, in light of the policies of the Department of the Interior and the purposes of the statute, we interpret section 6(f) (3) "public outdoor recreation uses" broadly, to encompass uses not involving the public's actual physical presence on the property. After all, Webster's Third New International Dictionary (1971) defines "recreation" as "refreshment of the strength and spirits after toil," id. at 1899; surely by exposing scenic vistas and serving as a buffer zone between Minnewaska State Park and developed areas, the easement area provides such refreshment.

* * *

* * * Here the Department of the Interior apparently agrees with the Friends that the term "public outdoor recreation uses" should be construed to include conservation easements such as the one at issue. Thus, the Department's Bureau of Outdoor Recreation Manual (Dec. 14, 1973) (hereinafter cited as Manual) indicates the Department's own broad construction of the Act, pointing out that acquisitions eligible for federal assistance as "lands and waters for public outdoor recreation," include "[n]atural areas and preserves and outstanding scenic areas where the objective is to preserve the scenic or natural values, including areas of physical or biological importance and wildlife areas." Outdoor recreation activities are defined to include "sightseeing" and "nature study." The Department thus recognizes as present recreation uses the very uses that the original conservation easement protects and we are unable to find that such an interpretation is either unreasonable or contrary to Congress's intent.

True, a mere surface view of the Act itself seems to show that Congress intended primarily to increase opportunities for active physical recreation. The statement of purposes, for example, envisions "individual active participation in [outdoor] recreation." 16 U.S.C.

§ 460*l*–4. Concededly, much of the Act deals with admission and special recreation use fees, see id. §§ 460*l*–5a, –6a, –6b, again contemplating actual physical entry. However, both the legislative history and the Act itself reveal Congress's broader concerns.

The Senate Report prominently mentions the need to improve "the physical *and spiritual* health and vitality of the American people." S.Rep. No. 1364, 88th Cong., 2d Sess. 4 (1964), *reprinted in* 1964 U.S. Code Cong. & Ad.News 3633, 3636 (emphasis added). Similarly, when President Kennedy first transmitted to Congress the draft legislation on which the Act is based, his accompanying letter referred specifically to the preservation of "irreplaceable lands of natural beauty and unique recreation value" and to "the enhancement of spiritual, cultural, and physical values resulting from the preservation of these resources."

It is after all a "conservation" fund act. Conservation may include, though it is by no means necessarily limited to, the protection of a present resource in its natural state. Indeed, the Act's stated purposes include "preserving" the "quality" of outdoor recreation resources. 16 U.S.C. § 460*l*–4. The focus on preservation reappears in section 460*l*–9(a)(1), which authorizes allocation of funds for federal acquisitions both to protect endangered and threatened species and also, by reference to section 460k–1, to protect "natural resources."

Thus, contrary to the district court's holding, the easement area presently *is* used for "public outdoor recreation uses," as that term of art was conceived by Congress and has been interpreted by the Interior Department. Having made this determination, we are next faced with the question whether the amendment at issue here constitutes a "conversion" of that easement to other than outdoor, public, recreation uses within the meaning of section 6(f)(3). Though the nature of a conservation easement makes the application of the concept of conversion somewhat elusive, we conclude that the proposed amendment does constitute such a conversion. The property acquired by PIPC through its purchase of the easement was the right to prevent further development of the land underlying the easement. By the proposed amendment, Marriott, the holder of the fee, would be permitted to engage in precisely such development, changing both the character of the land and the population having access to it. By the amendment, in effect, PIPC would convey away its right to prevent any change in the character of the land subject to the easement. The view that such a change constitutes a "conversion" is supported by the Department of the Interior's own practice. * * * It is plain that there is a conversion from public enjoyment of an unspoiled area to private golfing.

What is the consequence of this determination? The Secretary, in the words of section 6(f)(3), must determine that the conversion is "in accord with the then existing comprehensive statewide outdoor recreation plan" and grant his approval "only upon such conditions as he deems necessary to assure the substitution of other recreation properties of at least equal fair market value and of reasonably equivalent usefulness and location." These findings may seem simple, but they nevertheless must be made. * * *

* * *

Here we hold that the amended easement constitutes a conversion to "other than public outdoor recreation uses," 16 U.S.C. § 460*l*–8(f)(3), requiring the Secretary's approval. However, we would require approval by the Secretary in this case even if the Marriott Corporation planned to build a completely public outdoor recreation facility, because such a plan would be inconsistent with the original easement's prohibition of new facilities. Our reasoning runs as follows. The Act requires the Secretary to approve all "planning, acquisition, or development projects" before allocating federal funds. Id. § 460*l*–8(f)(1). It envisions that these "projects" will affect the future of the area acquired, preserving outdoor recreation opportunities for "present and future generations." Id. § 460*l*–4. Consistent with Congress's concern for lasting recreation opportunities, the Secretary approved federal funding for the Minnewaska easement in part because of the plans for the easement area's future—specific constraints on development and guarantees of environmental protection. Consequently, any future change that contravenes these plans retroactively calls into question the basis for the original federal funding. Such a change necessarily requires the Secretary's approval, whether or not the change falls within the Act's definition of a "conversion." Otherwise, the Secretary's initial approval of a "project" extending into the future would be meaningless. Once again, it would not be enough for the Secretary to find that federal approval is unnecessary; while the statutory criteria for approval would not apply to a change from one public use to another, positive approval is still required.

We recognize with Marriott the rather cumbersome process involving a considerable amount of time and effort that undertaking this development has entailed. * * * Unfortunately, or fortunately perhaps, the courts do not control the process, let alone establish it. When one undertakes to develop for private purposes a project involving the use of lands encumbered by a government interest, one's expectations are, or should be, that a certain amount of process and expense will be involved; presumably the anticipated rewards offset the cost and hassle, though surely the ultimate consumer will pay the cost of the benefit the process achieves, or there will be a hole in the developer's pocket. A court is left with the thought that one challenge of the years ahead is to cut down the process, thus lowering the cost, even while preserving the benefit. Meanwhile, the court's duty remains to follow the law as written and intended.

* * *

Judgment reversed; cause remanded. The district court should enter judgment prohibiting amendment of the easement without an appropriate determination by the Secretary as to the effect of conversion.

NOTES

1. Was the court correct in equating "preservation" with "recreation"? How do you define recreation? Are there any realistic limits to such a definition? Is this litigation a tempest in a teapot? Is the federal approval of the conversion the same as the NEPA process for considering a federal project?

2. The PLLRC in 1970 recommended that the federal role in recreation be limited to lands of "national significance." Congress has not implemented that PLLRC recommendation, but instead has encouraged many forms of recreation on the public lands in a variety of ways. In the Land and Water Conservation Fund Act, for instance, Congress decreed that the land management agencies may charge only nominal or zero fees for recreational access to federal lands. Should "fair market value" user fees be imposed? Why should recreation be subsidized? Should the federal government purchase recreation lands without national significance or special values as "sacrifice areas"?

3. Congress has created several federal lands categories primarily to serve recreational needs. The National Trails System Act, 16 U.S. C.A. §§ 1241–49, begins with the statement:

> In order to provide for the ever-increasing outdoor recreation needs of an expanding population and in order to promote public access to, travel within, and enjoyment and appreciation of the open-air, outdoor areas of the Nation, trails should be established (i) primarily, near urban areas of the Nation, and (ii) secondarily, within established scenic areas more remotely located. Id. § 1241(a).

By contrast, the stated purpose of the Wild and Scenic Rivers Act, 16 U.S.C.A. §§ 1271–87, is much narrower, directed primarily at preservation of free-flowing rivers. National Recreation Areas appear to fall somewhere in the middle. E.g., Lake Mead National Recreation Area Act, 16 U.S.C.A. § 460n–3:

> (a) Lake Mead National Recreation Area shall be administered by the Secretary of the Interior for general purposes of public recreation, benefit, and use, and in a manner that will preserve, develop, and enhance, so far as practicable, the recreation potential, and in a manner that will preserve the scenic, historic, scientific, and other important features of the area, consistently with applicable reservations and limitations relating to such area and with other authorized uses of the lands and properties within such area.

> (b) * * * the Secretary may provide for the following activities, subject to such limitations, conditions, or regulations as he may prescribe, and to such extent as will not be inconsistent with either the recreational use or the primary use of that portion of the area heretofore withdrawn for reclamation purposes:

        (1) General recreation use, such as bathing, boating, camping, and picnicking;

        (2) Grazing;

        (3) Mineral leasing;

        (4) Vacation cabin site use, in accordance with existing policies of the Department of the Interior relating to such use, or as such policies may be revised hereafter by the Secretary.

A more recent creation is the "gateway" park, whereby excess, scattered federal parcels in an area are lumped together as an urban recreation area. E.g., Golden Gate National Recreation Area Act, 16 U.S.C.A. §§ 460bb to 460bb–5. See NRDC v. Marsh, 586 F.Supp. 1387 (E.D.N.Y.1983).

J. WILLIAM FUTRELL, PARKS TO THE PEOPLE: NEW DIRECTIONS FOR THE NATIONAL PARK SYSTEM.*
25 Emory Law J. 255 (1976).

The National Park Service made a major effort to redress the urban outdoor recreation deficit, shifting its emphasis from traditional western parks such as Yosemite and Yellowstone to a proposed system of new urban parks. In 1970, Secretary of the Interior Walter Hickel stated:

Our existing national parks are unique, strikingly beautiful, and absolutely necessary elements of nation wide systems * * * but they are located in areas remote from the less affluent members of our society. Many of our people cannot get to the parks; therefore we must get parks to the people.

Hickel proposed the creation of a series of National Recreation Areas (NRAs) based on relatively pristine natural landscapes near America's largest cities. * * *

          * * *

The human needs for urban open space have not slackened despite budget shortfalls and escalating land costs. * * *

          * * *

The extent of current needs is indicated by BOR's 1970 estimate that a commitment of $6.3 billion over a five-year period to develop urban parks was a minimum figure necessary to maintain the continued livability of American cities.[41] In fact, BOR further estimated that at least $25 billion above existing expenditures would be required to

* Copyright © 1976 by the Emory Law Journal. Reprinted by permission of the Emory Law Journal of the Emory University School of Law.

41. The BOR report, entitled The Recreation Imperative: The Nationwide Outdoor Recreation Plan, was submitted for publication in July 1970, but was suppressed at the order of the Nixon Administration. In September 1974, the Senate Interior Committee published it as a special committee document. Senate Comm. on Interior and Insular Affairs, 93rd Cong., 2d Sess., The Recreation Imperative 298 (Comm.Print 1974).

provide urban areas in 1975 with the same amount of outdoor recreation space that was available in 1965.   *   *   *

*   *   *

The Service is pressed to maintain its current level of operations. Although visitation to national parks has tripled since 1960 and other responsibilities have increased with the addition of new areas, funding has remained almost constant. While in 1960 there was one employee for every 27,000 visitors, in 1972 the ratio had risen to one for every 44,000 visitors. The new urban NRAs have siphoned men and money from the older and more remote parks.   *   *   *

Park Service leaders, concerned though they may be by shortfalls in funding, increased visitor pressures, and land use problems, base their reservations concerning additional urban parks on philosophical grounds as well. They see the basic mission of the Park Service as the preservation of parks for future generations and view the movement to create new kinds of parks such as urban National Recreation Areas as a distortion of that primary preservation mission. Critics have suggested that the Park Service's best future course would be to re-emphasize its original mission of preservation and de-emphasize recreation. They aver that the ultimate purpose for which the parks were created has spiritual overtones and that the creation of urban parks erodes standards and weakens the National Park System by emphasizing recreation over preservation. Indeed, these proponents of purity recommend that the Park Service drop from the System those areas in which the prime emphasis is on recreational use, leaving such areas to management by state and local governments or by private enterprise. They fear that if the Park System continues to include these recreational areas, the distinction between what is of truly national significance and that which is merely a local amenity will increasingly be blurred, that the public image of the national parks will steadily tend toward mediocrity, and the strong preservation standards currently in effect in the System will be eroded.

B. RECREATIONAL FACILITIES

Conflicts often arise between those desiring solitary, active, noncommercial activities and those preferring more civilized, sedentary forms of entertainment. See, e.g., E. Abbey, DESERT SOLITAIRE (1972) (somewhat of a cult book). For some, just the existence of the federal lands is sufficient; they are content to enter on their own legs, carrying their basic requirements on their backs. They are a minority, perhaps a small minority. Most visitors desire more in the way of creature comforts and the means to let them pursue their more intensive interests. Boaters require ramps, casual visitors desire centers where someone explains the land's attractions, skiers need lifts (and, it seems, fern bars), motorcyclists need gasoline, and most want soft beds and good food. The land management agencies often contract with private concessionaires to provide such services when consistent with federal policy.

FRIENDS OF YOSEMITE v. FRIZZELL

United States District Court, Northern District of California, 1976.
420 F.Supp. 390.

RENFREW, District Judge.

* * *

* * * Defendants are various federal government officials connected with the administration of Yosemite and three corporations, Music Corporation of America, Inc., and its wholly owned subsidiaries, Yosemite Park and Curry Company and Music Corporation of America, Recreation. Yosemite Park and Curry Company holds an exclusive franchise from the National Park Service for the operation of tourist accommodations and services in Yosemite.

Plaintiffs object to * * * the firing of three of the plaintiffs from employment in Yosemite, and the mounting of what plaintiffs allege to be a publicity campaign promoting the use of the park by business and associational conventions. Plaintiffs contend that the publicity campaign constitute[s] a "breach of trust" by the National Park Service and violate[s] an "administrative ruling" within the meaning of the Administrative Procedure Act. * * *

I. BREACH OF TRUST

Plaintiffs contend that the federal defendants' actions violate the duties imposed upon the Secretary of the Interior by the National Park Service Act, 16 U.S.C.A. §§ 1, 1a–1, 20 et seq., and thereby constitute a "breach of trust." * * *

Plaintiffs rely upon Sierra Club v. Department of Interior, 376 F.Supp. 90 (N.D.Cal.1974), 398 F.Supp. 284 (N.D.Cal.1975) [supra at page 305], for the proposition that a breach of this fiduciary duty gives rise to a private cause of action. * * *

It is unnecessary to decide whether a private right of action would exist for a breach of trust under the facts of this case, because there is no evidence that any one connected with either the Department of the Interior or the National Park Service violated any legal duty. They have taken no actions that are not authorized by statute, nor have they failed to protect Yosemite in violation of any statutory duty. * * * Promotion of tourist travel to the park is clearly contemplated by 16 U.S.C.A. §§ 18, 18a–18d, 20a, and 20b. In fact, plaintiffs admit that "[t]here is no question that the National Park Service has the authority and power to carry out construction, organize Master Plans, and authorize commercial advertising." * * *

Plaintiffs' breach of trust contention really amounts to no more than an assertion that the federal defendants are wrong in their conclusion that the projects in question are not major federal actions significantly affecting the quality of the human environment. Plaintiffs have not alleged any facts which indicate bad faith or suggest that the Government has acted "unreasonably, arbitrarily [or] in abuse of discretion." See Sierra Club v. Department of Interior, supra, 398

F.Supp. at 293. Even assuming that the federal defendants erred in their decision not to issue an Environmental Impact Statement ("EIS"), it would not prove a breach of trust, but at most it would be a possible violation of NEPA.

* * *

Plaintiffs allege that the corporate defendants have mounted a publicity campaign designed to bring more tourists—including conventioneers—to Yosemite, and that the resulting increase in park use will have serious environmental effects. The question before the Court is whether an EIS should have been filed because the publicity campaign was a major federal action significantly affecting the quality of the human environment.

Defendants point out that the publicity in question is not a "federal action" at all—that the corporate defendants were responsible for any advertising that took place, and that the publicity was not subject to formal review or authorization by the Park Service. The corporate defendants do not normally submit advertising copy to the Park Service for approval, although they do present "unique, controversial, or otherwise unusual" copy to the office of Leslie P. Arnberger, Superintendent of Yosemite National Park, on an informal basis.

* * *

The advertising in this case can hardly be called a partnership venture between the corporate and federal defendants. The facts here seem much closer to those in Friends of Earth, Inc. v. Coleman, 518 F.2d 323 (9 Cir.1975), where the Court of Appeals for this circuit held that the Federal Aviation Administration did not need to file an EIS concerning the expansion of the San Francisco Airport, even though the agency had approved the plans and was supplying funds for part of the project. Characterizing the plaintiff's contention that an EIS must be prepared for state-funded parts of the airport expansion as "let[ting] the tail wag the dog," the court set out the following test for determining when another party's action becomes a "federal action":

> "Determination of whether federal and state projects are sufficiently interrelated to constitute a single 'federal action' for NEPA purposes will generally require a careful analysis of all facts and circumstances surrounding the relationship. At some point, the nexus will become so close, and the projects so intertwined, that they will require joint NEPA evaluation." 518 F.2d at 329.

The undisputed facts of the instant case show that such a nexus does not exist with regard to the corporate defendants' advertising. * * *

* * *

NOTES

1. Is the court's treatment of the advertising claim dispositive? Judge Renfrew states that "Promotion of tourist travel to the park is clearly contemplated by 16 U.S.C.A. §§ 18, 18a–18d, 20a, and 20b * * *. [T]he National Park Service has the power to * * * autho-

rize commercial advertising." Sections 18–18d refer only to the Secretary of Commerce and do not refer to parks. Sections 20a and 20b authorize the Park Service to select and assist private concessionaires, but do not mention advertising and are qualified by section 20, requiring "carefully controlled safeguards against unregulated and indiscriminate use, so that the heavy visitation will not unduly impair these [preservation] values." Should the Park Service advertise? Should it allow its concessionaires to do so?

2. In National Parks & Conservation Ass'n v. Kleppe, 547 F.2d 673, 676 (D.C.Cir.1976), the court observed that "[c]oncession activity in the national parks is a thriving business which is becoming increasingly dominated by large corporate concessioners. The relationship between the Park Service and the park concessioners is long-standing and has been fostered in large measure by various financial incentives aimed at maintaining the quality and continuity of goods and services available to park visitors." Park Service concession policies are severely criticized in Mantell, Preservation and Use: Concessions in the National Parks, 8 Ecology L.Q. 1 (1979), who concludes:

> The Concessions Policy Act of 1965, outdated when written, has provided concessioners with too much protection. It has helped entrench concessioners in the parks and has enabled them to wield an unjustifiable degree of influence over management policy and to obscure the purpose of the parks. In order to stimulate investment and create more services, the Act's design was to assure the concessioners a profit. As a result, those services with a low cost, but high return ratio, such as souvenir stores, snack bars, and liquor stores are particularly favored.

> The Park Service has been entangled in a statutory web of promoting and encouraging use of concessions. Park preservation and the concept of the park experience providing a contrast which reinvigorates have been virtually forgotten, giving way initially to the political necessity of creating park use, then acceding to concessioner pressure and, finally, to "user" desires.

> The parks should not be made to conform to the desires of vacationers. There is a need in America's recreation scheme for the experience national parks were originally designed to offer. National parks can provide the casual recreationist a nature experience in one of the nation's prime scenic areas and guarantee a similar opportunity to future generations.

3. In Glacier Park Foundation v. Watt, 663 F.2d 882 (9th Cir. 1981), a disappointed applicant for a concessions contract in Glacier National Park sued to invalidate the longterm contract granted to the successful bidder. The National Park Service had initially rejected both bids, but it negotiated further and then entered into agreement with the incumbent rival. The court held that plaintiff had no private right of action under the Concessions Act, 16 U.S.C.A. § 20d, but could

obtain review under the Administrative Procedure Act. The Park Service argued that it had not "finally" rejected the successful applicant, but the court found that a rejection is a rejection, and the Service must, according to its regulations, resolicit proposals. Compare Fort Sumter Tours, Inc. v. Andrus, 564 F.2d 1119 (4th Cir.1979). See also Free Enterprise Canoe Renters Ass'n v. Watt, 549 F.Supp. 252 (E.D.Mo. 1982).

———

The following case dealt with one of the most publicized disputes in the early years of the modern environmental era, the proposal by Walt Disney Productions for development of Mineral King.

SIERRA CLUB v. HICKEL
United States Court of Appeals, Ninth Circuit, 1970.
433 F.2d 24, aff'd, 405 U.S. 727 (1972).

TRASK, Circuit Judge:

This is an appeal from an order of the district court granting a preliminary injunction. * * *

The relief sought was a declaratory judgment and preliminary and permanent injunctions enjoining issuance of the permits required for implementation of a plan proposed by Walt Disney Productions, Inc., for a large scale commercial-recreational development in and near Mineral King Valley in the Sequoia National Game Refuge located within Sequoia National Forest in California. * * *

* * *

* * * [O]n October 10, 1966, a special use permit for planning was issued to Disney for a term of three years in order to enable Disney to make the necessary studies to prepare a master plan for the project which would meet with Forest Service approval. The plan was duly submitted and approved by the Forest Service on January 21, 1969, and is the plan that is the subject of this litigation.

In connection with the plan, the Department of the Interior has proposed to permit the State of California to construct a new access road to Mineral King Valley. The new highway would be 20.4 miles long, of which 6.5 miles would cross Bureau of Land Management (Department of Interior) land, 9.2 miles would cross Sequoia National Park (Department of Interior) land, 1.8 miles would cross Sequoia National Forest (Department of Agriculture) land, and the remaining 2.9 miles would cross various parcels of private property. It would approximately parallel the existing Mineral King roadway which appears on the map to be a tortuous road now described as substandard. In connection with the project, the Secretary of the Interior also agreed to grant a right of way for electrical transmission lines through the park.

In announcing the master plan and its approval, the Forest Service stated:

"Our goal is to provide a needed public service so that the scenic, aesthetic, and recreational resources of Mineral King can be enjoyed by the American people as part of their heritage. At the same time, we intend to work with the Disney organization to assure that the development can be accomplished without substantial impairment or permanent undesirable ecological impact. We are confident that these twin challenges have been faced in a creative and artistic fashion."

The initial description of the facilities proposed stated that accommodations would be provided for 1,505 overnight guests plus day visitors. A sub-level automobile reception center would be provided outside of the main Mineral King Valley with a cog-assist railway to transport people to the main village. No visitor automobiles would be allowed in Mineral King Valley proper. The announcement of the Forest Service continued:

"While the Mineral King area is certain to become increasingly popular, its ultimate development will be guided by aesthetic and ecological limitations, rather than market potential. The Disney master plan has been designed with this consideration uppermost."

On the merits, the Sierra Club contends that the Secretary of Agriculture who has the responsibility under Congress for management of the national forests has exceeded his authority and has acted illegally as well as arbitrarily and capriciously in approving the master plan proposed by Disney. It urges that the Secretary of Agriculture's proposal to issue a term permit for an eighty acre parcel for a term of thirty years for construction of improvements such as hotels, pools and parking lots, and to issue a revocable permit for additional acreage upon which such improvements as ski lifts, trails, and sewage treatment facilities would be built, would constitute illegal action in excess of authority. Second, the Sierra Club asserts that the action of the Secretary of the Interior in his proposal to permit the State of California to construct a road across Sequoia National Park for a distance of 9.2 miles to replace an existing road across the park would be illegal. Finally, the club asserts that no authority exists for the Secretary of the Interior to issue a permit for the construction of a transmission line across the park lands as a part of the master plan.

Encompassing all is the vehement argument of Sierra that the necessary result of the development proposal is the "permanent destruction of natural values" and the "irreparable harm to the public interest." These, it is asserted, are "irreversible effects of administrative lawlessness."

* * *

* * * With respect to the national forests, Congress has authorized the Secretary of Agriculture "to regulate their occupancy and use." Organic Administration Act, 16 U.S.C.A. § 551. With respect to national parks, Congress has authorized the Secretary of the Interior "to promote and regulate the use" of such parks, to "grant privileges,

leases, and permits for the use of land" in the parks, and to cooperate with the Secretary of Agriculture in administering contiguous national forests. Organic Act of the National Park Service, 16 U.S.C.A. § 1 et seq.

The Secretaries purport to act pursuant to these basic sources of authority, together with supplemental legislative support.

* * *

The proposal of Disney and the action taken by the Secretary is to permit a land use of forest lands by the issuance of two types of permits. The first type is a term permit for an aggregate of eighty acres with a maximum term of thirty years. The second is called a "revocable permit", meaning the Secretary imposes no limitation on time or acreage.

The district court has concluded that Congress has never expressly authorized revocable permits and that the only authority to issue them is under the general power to regulate the forests and under a 1928 Attorney General's opinion. Upon such a tenuous base, the broad application which is proposed here becomes questionable to the lower court. We find the Secretary's authority rests upon much firmer ground.

Originally the management of the lands reserved for national forests was under the supervision of the Secretary of the Interior. In 1905 these powers were transferred to the Secretary of Agriculture, and he was given authority to make rules and regulations to preserve the forests from destruction. As early as May 31, 1905, the Secretary of Agriculture was advised by the Attorney General that he had the authority to issue revocable permits.

This permit authority under the Secretary's general regulatory power was upheld by the Supreme Court in United States v. Grimaud, 220 U.S. 506 (1911). At the time of the amendment of 16 U.S.C.A. § 497 in 1956 to authorize the issuance of term permits for eighty acres for thirty years, the House Report commented on the practice of the Secretary to issue revocable permits under his general regulatory powers, saying:

> "The Department of Agriculture now has adequate authority to issue revocable permits for all purposes under the act of June 4, 1897 (16 U.S.C. 551)." House Report No. 2792, U.S. Code Cong. & Ad.News, 3635 (1956).

The court below has understandably relied upon the authority of the opinion of the Attorney General to the Secretary of War, 35 Op. Att'y.Gen. 485 (1928). That opinion is the basis for the court's discussion of the necessity that a revocable permit be terminable "at will" and that therefore *this* permit is not properly issued. We have found no such limitation apart from this Attorney General's opinion. The same erroneous premise results in the district court's concern about the removability of any improvements placed upon the land covered by the revocable permit. It is at the bottom of the district court's conclusion that a combination of a term permit and a revocable permit may be an impermissible and unlawful exercise of administrative authority. Beginning from a correct premise that the revocable permit is an approved device for forest management under Congressional mandate from the Attorney General, the Supreme Court and the Congress, we believe an entirely different conclusion would have been reached. The fact that the record discloses that there are now a total of at least eighty-four recreational developments on national forest lands in which there is such a combination of the term permit and the revocable permit is convincing proof of their legality. Many of these developments are ski developments making use of the maximum acres of the term permit plus revocable permits for additional acreage in amounts in some cases in excess of 6,000 acres. It seems apparent, as was obvious to both Senate and House Committees, that the eighty-acre long-term permit was a necessity to obtain proper financing for substantial permanent improvements, while developments of less magnitude and permanency, such as trails, slopes, and corrals, could be placed upon lands held under revocable permits. We find no indication in those reports that ski lifts are limited to the term permits. The planned development in the instant case discloses that most major improvements are to be located upon lands held under the eighty-acre term permits while lifts and trails will be installed "throughout about 13,000 acres." [16] Evidence of great concern for the ecology of the area and the preservation and conservation of natural beauty and environmental features appears throughout the planning reports * * *. We find little or no likelihood of success in opposing the proposed development upon the ground that there would be an illegal use of term and revocable permits.

A. Permit for Highway

The district court next discusses the proposal of the Secretary of Interior to issue a permit to the State of California to construct a segment of roadway through the national park. * * * The proposed road follows the alignment of the old road to some extent and substantially parallels it in others. The record shows a great deal of concern in its planning for preservation of aesthetic and ecological values. The defendant Superintendent of the National Park concerned has stated under oath that the construction will be engineered

> " * * * so that there will be a minimum impact on the
> national park values. The alignment of the road will be
> carefully selected to protect the Sequoia trees, natural areas,
> existing drainage ways, and the over-all ecology of the area."

No question is raised as to the wide discretion given to the Secretary of the Interior in managing national parks to construct and improve roads and trails therein. See 16 U.S.C.A. § 8. We know of no law and find little logic in a contention that a twisting, substandard, inadequate road through 9.2 miles of the park is legal but that an improved all weather

---

16. The gross acreage of Sequoia National Forest is 1,178,767 acres, which does not include areas within Sequoia National Park or King's Canyon National Park.

two lane highway along a new but approximately parallel alignment is illegal. No authorities have been cited in support of such a position. We cannot find in the appellee's contentions concerning this proposed road any degree of substantiality.

B. *Permit for Transmission Line*

Although not alleged in the complaint, appellee has questioned in its brief and the district court has alluded to the proposal of the Secretary of the Interior to grant permission for a right of way for a power line to provide electrical power for uses in connection with the project. Again, with deference, we fail to find this a substantial issue upon which to base the grant of a preliminary injunction. It seems unlikely that the appellee could prevail as to such a contention. Under 16 U.S.C.A. § 5 authority is clearly provided to the Department of the Interior in its management of parks to grant permits and easements for rights of way for "electrical poles and lines for the transmission and distribution of electrical power." * * *

* * *

The appellee has not shown with any degree of certainty that it will or can succeed. Neither has it shown that it, or its members or anyone else will suffer irreparable injury. This is not a case "clearly warranting" the grant of a preliminary injunction. The nation's natural resources are not the property of any particular group. One of the basic social ills of today is that we have too many people living too close together. It appears that the friction thus created is becoming increasingly abrasive. The satisfaction of the basic necessities of such a population creates environmental problems which are not within the expertise of this court. We cannot say, however, that the Secretary of Agriculture and the Secretary of the Interior have made an arbitrary and capricious judgment in determining to make available a vast area of incomparable beauty to more people rather than to have it remain inaccessible except to a rugged few.

* * *

NOTES

1. The United States Supreme Court reviewed only the question whether the Sierra Club had standing to bring this lawsuit. In affirming the Ninth Circuit, the Court actually broadened standing by stating in dictum that an organization could represent its members, and injury in fact existed if any member "used" the area allegedly to be despoiled. Sierra Club v. Morton, 405 U.S. 727 (1972). On remand, the District Court found that the Sierra Club had standing and allowed it to add new claims, including the contention that an environmental impact statement was required. The Forest Service acceded, and the process of compiling the information and writing the statement took several years. See Commentary, Mineral King Goes Downhill, 5 Ecology L.Q. 555 (1976). The project and the lawsuit were both later dropped.

2.   Ironically (and embarrassingly to some of its members), the Sierra Club had originally suggested the site it subsequently and successfully fought. See J. Sax, MOUNTAINS WITHOUT HANDRAILS 69–71 (1981).

3.   As the opinion suggests, many other recreational developments (including many of the Nation's major ski areas) were established under arrangements similar to those proposed for Mineral King. Is Sierra Club v. Hickel distinguishable from Wilderness Society v. Morton, 479 F.2d 842 (D.C.Cir.1973), supra at page 294, involving the Alaska Pipeline? F. Grad, 3 TREATISE ON ENVIRONMENTAL LAW 12–113 –114 (1978):

> The policy issue which has never been answered is whether the so-called revocable permit granted for a large tract in the context of a comprehensive and intensive development of the 80-acre tract under long-term lease is truly intended to be a revocable permit, though it may be so designated. The question which naturally occurs is whether a permit of this kind for the large tract is not intended to be coextensive with the longterm permit for the more intensive facility.

WILSON v. BLOCK

United States Court of Appeals, District of Columbia Circuit, 1983.
708 F.2d 735.

LUMBARD, Senior Circuit Judge:

These appeals challenge the grant of summary judgment by the District Court for the District of Columbia which affirmed the decisions of the Forest Service and the Department of Agriculture to permit private interests to expand and develop the government-owned Snow Bowl ski area on the San Francisco Peaks in the Coconino National Forest just north of Flagstaff, Arizona. * * *

* * *

The San Francisco Peaks are within the Coconino National Forest and are managed by the Forest Service. A 777 acre portion of the Peaks, known as the "Snow Bowl," has been used for downhill skiing since 1937 when the Forest Service build a road and ski lodge. The lodge was destroyed by fire in 1952 and was replaced in 1956. Ski lifts were built at the Snow Bowl in 1958 and 1962. Since 1962 the facilities have changed very little.

In April 1977 the Forest Service transferred the permit to operate the Snow Bowl skiing facilities from Summit Properties, Inc. to the Northland Recreation Company. In July 1977 Northland submitted to the Forest Service a "master plan" for the future development of the Snow Bowl, which contemplated the construction of additional parking and ski slopes, new lodge facilities, and ski lifts. * * *

* * *

On February 27, 1979 the Forest Supervisor of the Coconino National Forest issued his decision to permit moderate development of the Snow Bowl under a "Preferred Alternative," which in fact was not one of the six alternatives previously identified. The Preferred Alternative envisions the clearing of 50 acres of forest for new ski runs, instead of the 120 acres requested by Northland. The Preferred Alternative also authorizes construction of a new day lodge, improvement of restroom facilities, reconstruction of existing chair lifts, construction of three new lifts, and the paving and widening of the Snow Bowl road.

At the request of various persons, including certain of the plaintiffs, the Regional Forester on February 7, 1980 overruled the Forest Supervisor and ordered maintenance of the status quo. The Chief Forester on December 31, 1980 reversed the Regional Forester and reinstated the Forest Supervisor's approval of the Preferred Alternative.

* * *

The plaintiffs [Hopi and Navajo Indians asserting that San Francisco Peaks is one of their sacred areas] alleged that expansion of the Snow Bowl facilities would violate the Indians' First Amendment right to the free exercise of religion, the American Indian Religious Freedom Act, the fiduciary duties owed the Indians by the government, the Endangered Species Act, two statutes regulating private use of national forest land (16 U.S.C. §§ 497, 551), the National Historic Preservation Act, the Multiple-Use Sustained Yield Act, the Wilderness Act, the National Environmental Policy Act, and the Administrative Procedure Act.

* * *

[The court agreed with the district court that those claims were without merit.]

7. *Land Use Permits.*

In 1977 the Forest Service issued two permits to Northland for use of the Snow Bowl permit area, which on May 18, 1982 were amended to reflect the development approved under the Preferred Alternative. One of the amended permits, covering 24 acres, is a term permit valid until May 1, 1997. The Forest Service granted this permit under the Act of March 4, 1915, as amended, 16 U.S.C. § 497 (1976), which provides:

> The Secretary of Agriculture is authorized, under such regulations as he may make and upon such terms and conditions as he may deem proper, (a) to permit the use and occupancy of suitable areas of land within the national forests, not exceeding eighty acres and for periods not exceeding thirty years, for the purpose of constructing or maintaining hotels, resorts, and any other structures or facilities necessary or desirable for recreation, public convenience, or safety; * * *

Northland will build the ski lodge and all other permanent facilities upon the land covered by the term permit. The other permit, an annual or revocable permit covering the remaining 753 acres of the permit area, was issued by the Forest Service under the authority of the Act of June 4, 1897, as amended, 16 U.S.C. § 551 (1976), which authorizes the Secretary of Agriculture to "make such rules and regulations * * * as will insure the objects of such reservations, namely, to regulate their occupancy and use and to preserve the forests thereon from destruction." The land covered by the revocable permit will be used only for ski slopes.

The plaintiffs challenge the validity of the "dual permit" system employed by the Forest Service. They contend that 16 U.S.C. § 497, which authorizes permit areas no larger than 80 acres, constitutes the sole authority under which the Secretary may grant permits for the private recreational development of national forest lands. They accordingly claim that the Forest Service exceeded its authority in issuing a revocable permit under 16 U.S.C. § 551 and in granting permits covering 777 acres to a single developer. We agree with Judge Richey that § 497 does not limit the Secretary's authority under § 551 and that Congress has sanctioned the use of dual permits.

In 1905 Congress transferred the management of the national forests from the Secretary of the Interior to the Secretary of Agriculture. Act Feb. 1, 1905, c. 288, § 1, 33 Stat. 628. As early as May 31, 1905 the Attorney General informed the Secretary of Agriculture that the Act of 1897, as amended, authorized him to grant revocable permits for the private, commercial use of national forest land. 25 Op.Atty. Gen. 470 (1905). The Secretary of Agriculture thereafter routinely granted revocable permits for many purposes, including summer houses and camping grounds, under the 1897 Act. In 1911 the Supreme Court upheld the authority of the Secretary to grant revocable grazing permits under the Act. United States v. Grimaud, 220 U.S. 506 (1911).

In 1915 Congress enacted legislation, now § 497, which, in contrast to the Act of 1897, expressly authorized the Secretary of Agriculture to grant private permits to national forest land. The 1915 Act authorized the Secretary to grant term permits to areas not larger than five acres for periods not exceeding 30 years. The plaintiffs claim that the 1915 Congress intended to repeal whatever permit authority the Secretary possessed under the 1897 Act. The plaintiffs' argument has no support in the legislative history, which instead suggests that Congress acted not to repeal the Secretary's existing powers, but to enable him, for the first time, to grant long-term permits. The Congress recognized that the permanent structures necessary for recreational use of the national forests would not be built unless private parties could obtain secure tenure. * * * Significantly, the Congress had before it a letter from the Secretary of Agriculture which discussed the Secretary's practice of granting revocable permits under the 1897 Act. The letter stated:

> There is at the present time some hesitancy on the part of persons who want to use national-forest land upon which to construct summer residences, hotels, stores, and other structures involving a large expenditure, because of *the indefinite tenure of the permits to them which the present law provides for.* At the present time, however, *there are several thousand such permits in use,* upon which structures have been erected.

> In justice to those who desire to construct more substantial improvements, it is believed that the present law should be amended to give persons a better right than the *revocable permit now authorized.*

(emphasis supplied). We must therefore presume that when Congress acted in 1915 it had knowledge of the Secretary's practice under the 1897 Act. Accordingly, the absence in the Act and in the legislative history of any language expressly repudiating the Secretary's practice is strong evidence that Congress did not intend the 1915 Act to affect the Secretary's power to issue revocable permits. Certainly the plaintiffs have shown no reason to depart from the settled rule disfavoring repeal by implication.

We conclude, therefore, that the 1915 Act neither limited the Secretary's power to issue revocable permits to areas larger than five acres nor prohibited him from issuing revocable and term permits simultaneously. Our conclusion is reinforced by Congress' awareness of, but failure to repudiate, the continuing practice of the Forest Service after 1915 to issue revocable permits under the 1897 Act. The Forest Service, following the 1915 Act, believed that the purposes of the Act could not be achieved unless it had authority to issue term permits to areas larger than five acres. Congress in the 1930's and 1940's considered several bills that would have expanded the Forest Service's authority to grant term permits, but enacted none of them. These bills are nonetheless significant because the reports they generated gave Congress clear notice that the Forest Service was continuing to issue revocable permits for recreational uses, and further, was issuing dual permits. * * * Similarly, in connection with H.R. 1809 (80th Cong., 1st Sess. (1948)), the Acting Secretary of Agriculture sent the Chairman of the Committee on Agriculture a letter, which stated:

> Of course, the large majority of * * * permitted uses [in the national forests] are of relatively short duration or entail only small capital investments. In such circumstances *the type of terminable permit, renewable from year to year, which this Department is authorized to issue without limitation as to character of use or area,* is adequate.

In 1956 Congress finally amended the 1915 Act to grant the Secretary broader power to issue term permits. The amendment increased the acreage limitation in § 497 from five acres to 80 because effective recreational development of the national forests had been stymied by the five-acre limitation on term permits. *See* H.R.Rep. No. 2792, 84th Cong., 2d Sess., reprinted in 1956 U.S.Code Cong. & Ad.News 3634. The committee reports, far from repudiating the Secretary's practice of issuing revocable permits, expressly approved the practice:

> The Department of Agriculture now has adequate authority to issue revocable permits for *all* purposes under the act of June 4, 1897 (16 U.S.C. § 551). Its authority to issue term permits * * * would be broadened by S. 2216(.)

Congress has not amended either § 497 or § 551 in relevant part since 1956.

We conclude, then, that the Secretary has consistently interpreted the Act of 1915 as *not* limiting his authority to issue revocable permits under the Act of 1897; that Congress has for decades had knowledge of the Secretary's interpretation, but has never objected; and that on the one occasion when Congress did comment on the Secretary's interpretation and practice, in 1956, it expressed approval. Under these circumstances the Secretary's authority to issue revocable permits under § 551, whether or not exercised in connection with dual permits, cannot be doubted.   *   *   *

*   *   *

In Sierra Club v. Hickel, 433 F.2d 24, 35 (9th Cir.1970), affd. on other grounds sub nom. Sierra Club v. Morton, 405 U.S. 727 (1972), the Ninth Circuit approved the practice of issuing dual permits to ski resort operators.   *   *   * The Forest Service has continued, following the decision in *Sierra Club,* to grant dual permits to ski resort operators. There are presently about 200 ski developments in the national forests and most of them employ dual permits.

The case of Wilderness Society v. Morton, 479 F.2d 842 (D.C.Cir.) (en banc), cert. denied, 411 U.S. 917 (1973), cited by the plaintiffs, does not support their argument. In *Wilderness Society,* the plaintiffs challenged the issuance of rights-of-way and special land use permits by the Secretary of the Interior to a consortium of oil companies for the construction of the Alaska pipeline. The permits covered land greater in width than the express limitation contained in § 28 of the Mineral Leasing Act of 1920, 30 U.S.C. § 185. This court found that § 28 constituted the Secretary's sole authority to issue permits for the use of federal land for oil pipelines, and held that the Secretary had exceeded his authority in failing to adhere to the width limitations. The plaintiffs also contended that the permits issued by the Secretary violated § 497. The court found it unnecessary to decide that claim, and declined to comment on the Ninth Circuit's decision in *Sierra Club.* The court did, however, note that § 497 had "no provision comparable to that in Section 28 of the Mineral Leasing Act expressly stating that no rights-of-way for the uses in question shall be granted except under the provisions, conditions and limitations of the statute." 479 F.2d at 870. That distinction between the language of § 497 and of § 28, together with the legislative history recounted above, indicate clearly enough that § 497, unlike § 28, cannot be read as an exclusive grant of authority as to the uses in question.

Finally, the plaintiffs claim that even if the Secretary had authority under §§ 497 and 551 to issue dual permits to Northland, the 753-acre permit issued under § 551 is invalid because not actually revocable. We see no merit in this claim. The Forest Service's continuing power to revoke the § 551 permit is apparent from the permit's terms, which state that the permit will terminate on May 1, 1997 unless previously terminated "upon breach of any of the conditions herein *or at the discretion of the regional forester or the Chief, Forest Service."* (emphasis supplied). The plaintiffs argue that the permit is not truly revocable because the Forest Service's own regulations require a rational basis for the revocation of such permits, see 36 C.F.R. § 251.60(b) (1982), and subject revocations to administrative review. 36 C.F.R. § 211.19 (1982). The plaintiffs have not, however, cited any authority holding that a permit, to be "revocable," must be revocable at the mere arbitrary will of the issuing authority, and we decline to read such a requirement into the authorizing statute. The plaintiffs also argue that the permit is not revocable because the Forest Service is unlikely to revoke it before the term permit expires. The short answer is that the Forest Service has power to revoke.

* * *

NOTES

1.   Apparently, no court has ever struck down the Forest Service's exercise of its authority to restrict "occupancy and use" under the 1897 Organic Act. See generally United States v. Weiss, 642 F.2d 296 (9th Cir.1981), supra at page 472; Great American Houseboat Co. v. United States, 780 F.2d 741 (9th Cir. 1986) (authority to ban use of timeshare houseboats on Shasta Lake because timeshare device would lead to overcrowding of lake). Should the "occupancy and use" authority be construed as broadly when the Forest Service effectively is transferring a permanent interest in the land to a private party? Would the result be the same if the situation involved such a transfer of Park Service or BLM lands?

2.   The Forest Service has extensive dealing with concessionaires. The agency's policy is to give permits to individual ski instructors or ski schools only with the consent of the basic permittee; operators of winter sports areas in effect are granted an exclusive right to control instruction. An admittedly qualified ski instructor and three of his students sued the Forest Service to establish the instructor's right to teach at Aspen Mountain, Aspen Highlands, Buttermilk, and Snowmass, all located primarily on lands in the White River National Forest in Colorado. The operators of the four ski areas had not consented. The Tenth Circuit held that the manual provision did not violate the First Amendment and that it was within the Forest Service's authority. Sabin v. Butz, 515 F.2d 1061 (10th Cir.1975). In a later opinion, the court found that the practice did not constitute an antitrust violation. Sabin v. Berglund, 585 F.2d 955 (10th Cir.1978). This rationale for the manual provisions was offered in the first opinion:

> In essence the reasons given by the Forest Service for its position were that the area permittees were required to spend money and effort to develop the area and were in exchange given the exclusive right to carry on the associated businesses; that neither the Government nor the permittees could adequately serve the public if the activities were splintered into

many permits; that the exclusive permittee takes care of various public facilities which do not generate sales to bear their costs; and that the single permittee system allows the Government to be sure the public is properly served.

515 F.2d at 1068. See also Aspen Skiing Co. v. Aspen Highlands Skiing Corp., 105 S.Ct. 2847 (1985) (multi-area ski ticket arrangement is unlawful monopolization); Heath v. Aspen Skiing Corp., 325 F.Supp. 223 (D.Colo.1971).

3. Forest Service discretion cuts both ways. The Forest Service also has broad authority to revoke special land use permits for resort facilities. Ness Inv. Corp. v. United States Department of Agriculture, Forest Service, 512 F.2d 706 (9th Cir.1975).

4. In United States v. Hells Canyon Guide Service, 660 F.2d 735 (9th Cir.1981), the court affirmed a permanent injunction against a guide who persisted in operating jet and float boats in Hells Canyon National Recreational Area without obtaining a permit from the Forest Service. The Hells Canyon National Recreation Area Act, 16 U.S.C.A. § 460gg–7, empowered the Secretary to promulgate protective regulations, but the permit system was instead premised on the authority of the Forest Service Organic Act and the Wild and Scenic Rivers Act. Appellant argued that the permit system for Hells Canyon was invalid because the Forest Service had not promulgated regulations under the Hells Canyon Act. The court disagreed:

> The regulation of the use and occupancy of national parks, forests and waterways is a matter of great national importance. The strong national policy regarding the conservation of this country's natural resources dictates that we must view this legislation from a broad rather than a narrow perspective. When a statute is part of an organic whole, the statute should be viewed in context with the whole of which it is a part.
>
> 16 U.S.C. § 551 gives the Secretary of Agriculture the authority to regulate the use and occupancy of the national forests. This authority is assimilated into 16 U.S.C. § 1281(d), giving the Secretary the authority to regulate the use and occupancy of components of the Wild and Scenic Rivers System. The portion of the Snake River involved in this dispute is a component of this System. 16 U.S.C. § 1274(a)(12). Section 1281(a) of the Wild and Scenic Rivers System Act illustrates the recurring motivation of Congress by giving the Secretary a clear instruction regarding the administration of his regulatory power:
>
> > "[P]rimary emphasis shall be given to protecting [the component's] esthetic, scenic, historic, archeologic, and scientific features."
>
> This emphasis on *protection* permeates these regulatory schemes, and Hells Canyon is no exception. 16 U.S.C. § 460gg(a).

Appellants' argument would necessarily run contrary to the well expressed intention of Congress to protect the Hells Canyon National Recreation Area, as well as national forests, parks and waterways in general. It would require the Secretary to take an additional, in fact, a redundant, affirmative step before he would be able to take *any* action to protect an area placed under his direct supervision.

LAKE BERRYESSA TENANTS' COUNCIL v. UNITED STATES

United States Court of Appeals, Ninth Circuit, 1978.
588 F.2d 267.

PER CURIAM:

This class action was brought by the Lake Berryessa Tenants' Council against the United States, the Department of the Interior, the Bureau of Reclamation, and Robert A. Wier. The appellants challenge the government's action in ordering the removal of all privately-owned docks and certain houseboats from Lake Berryessa. * * *

FACTUAL BACKGROUND

Since the 1950's the United States has owned Lake Berryessa and the surrounding shoreline as part of the United States Department of the Interior, Bureau of Reclamation, Solano Project. The lake was formed in 1957 when Monticello Dam was completed.

In 1958 the Bureau of Reclamation entered into a management agreement with Napa County of the State of California whereby Napa County would administer and develop recreational facilities at the lake. The agreement was rewritten in 1962, and pursuant to its terms, Napa County was to develop the lake in accordance with the Public Use Plan prepared by the National Park Service in 1959. Napa County allowed seven concessionaires to develop resorts on the lake. The agreements between Napa County and the resort owners were all made subject to the management agreement between Napa County and the United States. Provisions were included in the management agreements and each of the concession agreements that the various concession agreements would remain effective if Napa County and the United States were to terminate the management agreement.

In 1974, Congress passed the Reclamation Development Act which authorized the Secretary of the Interior to develop, operate, and maintain recreational facilities at the lake. It further empowered the Secretary to administer the lake and surrounding land to provide for (in his opinion) the best public recreational use and enjoyment.

Napa County withdrew from its management role at the lake on July 1, 1975. The Bureau of Reclamation, with Robert A. Wier as recreation manager at the lake, assumed the management function for the United States.

The Bureau of Reclamation issued Operational Policy 1 which restricted the use of houseboats on Lake Berryessa. This was followed by Operational Policy 2 whereby the Bureau ordered the removal of all privately-owned floating structures (docks, berths, swim floats, and so forth) from Lake Berryessa which were not owned by the seven resort owners. It was these policy directives which form the basis of this action.

UNCONSTITUTIONAL TAKING

The district court found that there was no unconstitutional taking involved in the government's order requiring removal of the private, non-resort-owned floating structures from the lake. The appellants have shown no legally cognizable right or interest in the maintenance of their personal property on the federally-owned lake which might give rise to their claim of a "taking" by the government. No law authorized the installation of the private structures, nor did the management agreements between the United States and Napa County, or Napa County and the resort owners. Appellants cite no authority in support of their claim. * * *

* * * The United States Government owns all of the land and the water at Berryessa. The docks and houseboats have been allowed there only at the sufferance of the United States. The fact that the government has now requested removal does not create a cause of action for an unconstitutional taking in the dock and houseboat owners. They are not being deprived of any property for they can remove any personal property in which they have an interest.

* * * In the present case, the appellants show no colorable interest or estate in public lands. There was no "taking" by the government which would afford any relief to the appellants.

ESTOPPEL

Appellants argue that the government should be estopped from making them remove their docks and houseboats from Lake Berryessa. The only action shown by the appellants which resembles a representation by government officials was that Napa County officials had issued building permits to some of the dock owners. There is no showing of affirmative representations by any government official that a reasonable man would believe gave him either a right or an interest in regard to the installation of a dock, houseboat or any other floating structure. This makes the present case distinguishable from United States v. Wharton, 514 F.2d 406 (9th Cir.1975). * * *

* * *

The judgment of the district court is affirmed.

NOTES

1. Compare Ness Inv. Corp. v. United States, 595 F.2d 585 (Ct.Cl. 1979). Is *Lake Berryessa* "merely" a private property rights case? Were the expectations of the dock owners legitimate? Is the action here even more drastic than in Perkins v. Bergland, 608 F.2d 803 (9th Cir.1979), supra at page 717, or in United States v. Fuller, 409 U.S. 488 (1973), supra at page 687? Is plaintiff's property interest no more than

that of the sport hunters in Baldwin v. Montana Fish & Game Comm'n, 436 U.S. 371 (1978), supra at page 853? Would this have been a appropriate case to recognize "passive" estoppel against the United States?

2. From 1958 to 1975, was Napa County a federal agency or the agent of a federal agency? Does it make a difference to the outcome? Could it in other circumstances?

3. Like private developers, the United States often has problems with its contractors. Is there anything to prevent the federal agency from itself building a ski area, a resort, or dock facilities? What are the objections to such a course? Should the federal agency prefer a few large developers or operators to more numerous and unruly small individuals in permitting recreational facilities?

4. The 1915 Act construed in Wilson v. Block, supra, also authorized long-term permits to build summer homes in the national forests, a policy that is now being phased out. See 16 U.S.C.A. § 497. In Paulina Lake Historic Cabin Owners Ass'n v. United States Department of Agriculture, Forest Service, 577 F.Supp. 1188 (D.Or.1983), plaintiffs sought an injunction preventing the Forest Service from interfering with their use of cabins and lodges they had built on Forest Service lands pursuant to a special use permit first issued in 1939. The case climaxed a 20 year effort by the agency to terminate the permit. Plaintiffs claimed a further grace period when the buildings were placed on the National Register of Historic Places pursuant to the National Historic Sites Act, 16 U.S.C.A. §§ 460–470t. The court ruled that the NHSA does not provide a shield against transfer of title of the cabins to the United States pursuant to the terms of the permit. The court did award plaintiffs attorneys fees for work done getting the site placed on the Register.

5. In Bostic v. United States, 753 F.2d 1292 (4th Cir.1985), the court upheld the disqualification of improvements on plaintiffs' recreational properties for federal flood insurance under the Coastal Barrier Resources Act, 16 U.S.C.A. § 3501 et seq. The Act was passed in part because of the efforts of Secretary Watt to convince Congress that the fragile outer banks needed additional protection from intensive recreational development. The court found the Act rationally justified because: "Withdrawing such federal largess also lessens the incentive to build on a coastal barrier subject to flood damage, thereby minimizing the loss of human life."

C. FEDERAL LIABILITY FOR RECREATIONAL MISHAPS

Mountain climbing, motorcycle racing, and white water rafting pose obvious risks; camping in an area inhabited by grizzly bears can make even the stout-hearted nervous; and simple swimming in unknown swimming holes or driving on primitive backcountry roads can be dangerous activities. People, especially those less experienced at such pursuits, have sustained serious personal injuries when the recreational activity went awry. Not infrequently, such injured persons seek to hold the United States liable for their injuries.

The only legal basis for tort damage recovery against the federal sovereign is the Federal Tort Claims Act, 28 U.S.C.A. §§ 1291, 1346, 1402, 2401, 2402, 2411, 2412, 2671–80 (FTCA). The FTCA allows recovery for "personal injury or death caused by the negligent or wrongful act or omission of any employee of the Government while acting within the scope of his office or employment, under circumstances where the United States, if a private person, would be liable to the claimant in accordance with the law of the place where the act or omission occurred." Id. § 1346(b). Federal liability does not extend to performance of discretionary functions. The leading case is Dalehite v. United States, 346 U.S. 15 (1953). See generally Comment, Protecting Visitors to National Recreation Areas Under the Federal Tort Claims Act, 84 Colum.L.Rev. 1792 (1984).

Federal liability is thus dependent to an extent on state tort law, which raises a variety of interpretive problems. One is the extent to which the United States can be treated the same as a private party when it functions for public recreational benefit. Another concerns the application and integration of state recreational use statutes that severely limit private landowner liability. The cases following illustrate some—but certainly not all—of the interjurisdictional difficulties.

OTTESON v. UNITED STATES

United States Court of Appeals, Tenth Circuit, 1980.
622 F.2d 516.

SEYMOUR, Circuit Judge.

* * *

The tragic accident giving rise to this litigation occurred in San Juan National Forest in Colorado. The decedent Stacey Otteson was a passenger in a jeep returning from a pleasure trip. After traveling down a narrow dirt logging access road which reaches a dead end several miles beyond the point of the accident, the jeep was forced to return due to impassable snow and ice. On the way back, the jeep slid on an ice patch and rolled down an embankment. Stacey and the driver were killed, and two other passengers received minor injuries.

The estate of Stacey Otteson brought a wrongful death action against the United States under the Federal Tort Claims Act, 28 U.S.C. §§ 1346(b) and 2671 et seq. It alleged that Stacey's death resulted from the government's negligent failure to maintain the road free from ice, to warn of hazards on the road, or to close it when it became unsafe. The government moved for summary judgment, contending it is immune from liability under the Tort Claims Act on two grounds: 1) it was performing a "discretionary function" in the design and maintenance of the road; and 2) a private individual would not be liable under the facts of the case and the law of the forum state. The trial court found the second contention dispositive and granted the government's motion. We affirm.

*   *   *

The trial judge concluded that a private landowner is not liable for negligence to persons coming onto the land for recreational purposes under Colorado's "sightseer statute".[1] Therefore, he found as a matter of law *   *   * that the government had not waived its immunity from liability in accordance with the Tort Claims Act.

On appeal, plaintiff contends that the sightseer statute should not have been applied to bar its claim because the government is not in the same position as the private parties to whom the statute applies. The purpose of the statute is to encourage private landowners to open their land to the public for recreational purposes. However, plaintiff asserts that the government has an independent duty to maintain the national forests as public recreational areas. Therefore, plaintiff argues that the government has a corresponding duty to maintain the roads in the national forests for recreational use. Plaintiff would have us equate this duty with that which a political subdivision has to maintain public roads.

Plaintiff's argument misconceives the purposes of the national forests, as set forth in the National Forests Acts, 16 U.S.C. §§ 471a et seq. The recent Supreme Court case of United States v. New Mexico, 438 U.S. 696 (1978), contains a thorough discussion of the legislative history and purposes of the national forest system. The Court there held that the Acts establishing the national forests had "only two purposes—'[t]o conserve the water flows and to furnish a continuous supply of timber for the people'. *   *   * National forests were not to be reserved for aesthetic, environmental, recreational, or wildlife-preservation purposes." Id. at 707, 708. While the Court noted that the Multiple-Use Sustained-Yield Act of 1960 broadened the purposes for which national forests are maintained to include recreation, the Court made clear that recreation was a secondary and supplemental purpose, and that a national forest could not be established for recreation alone. 438 U.S. at 713–715.

Bearing in mind the primary purposes for which national forests have been established, we now consider plaintiff's argument that the Forest Service has a duty to maintain roads in the national forests

---

.1. Sections 33–41–101 et seq. of the Colorado Revised Statutes (1973) provide that:

"33–41–101. Legislative declaration. The purpose of this article is to encourage owners of land within rural areas to make land and water areas available for recreational purposes by limiting their liability toward persons entering thereon for such purposes.

*   *   *

"33–41–103. Limitation on landowner's liability. (1) Subject to the provision of section 33–41–105, an owner of land who either directly or indirectly invites

or permits, without charge, any person to use such property for recreational purposes does not thereby:

(a) Extend any assurance that the premises are safe for any purpose;

(b) Confer upon such person the legal status of any invitee or licensee to whom a duty of care is owed;

(c) Assume responsibility or incur liability for any injury to person or property or for the death of any person caused by an act or omission of such person."

under the same standard imposed on a political subdivision. While it is true that Congress has stated recreation to be one of the uses for the national forest road system,[4] the legislation and relevant regulations read as a whole clearly indicate that the roads are intended primarily to facilitate the harvesting, removal and management of timber. See 16 U.S.C. § 535 and 36 C.F.R. § 212.12 (1979). Although these provisions authorize the construction of roads of a higher standard than that needed for the harvesting and removal of timber, they do not require it. The road on which this accident occurred was constructed and maintained for logging.[5] We do not believe Congress intended to impose on the Forest Service the same standard of maintenance with respect to all logging roads that a political subdivision has regarding public thoroughfares. Therefore, we reject plaintiff's argument that the government should be treated as a political subdivision rather than a private landowner for purposes of the Tort Claims Act.

* * *

Plaintiff's argument that the government should not be treated as a private party under the Colorado sightseer statute because it is somehow obligated to keep the national forests open to the public is unpersuasive. The Forest Service regulations allow each Forest Supervisor, among others, to close or restrict the use of forest areas and roads.[6] If liability were imposed upon the government in cases such as this one, the Forest Service might well choose to close the forests to public use rather than bear the heavy burden of maintaining logging roads as public thoroughfares. This result is precisely what the Colorado sightseer statute was enacted to prevent. Thus, we hold that the government is entitled to the protection of the Colorado sightseer statute and is therefore only liable "[f]or willful or malicious failure to guard or warn against a known dangerous condition * * *." Colo. Rev.Stat. § 33–41–104(a) (1973).

* * *

* * * Accordingly, the trial court judgment is affirmed.

NOTES

1. Is the court's reasoning consistent with the historical policy of keeping national forest lands open for recreation? Was the United States serving as a proprietor or as a sovereign in constructing and maintaining this road? The NFMA requires that land use plans adopted by the Forest Service shall "insure consideration of the economic and environmental aspects of various systems of renewable resource management, including the related systems of silviculture and protection of forest resources, to provide for outdoor recreation (includ-

---

4. Title 16 U.S.C. § 532 (1970) * * *.

5. We need not decide what liability, if any, would be incurred by the Forest Service with respect to roads built to a standard higher than that required for logging. Thus this case is distinguishable from Miller v. United States, 597 F.2d 614 (7th Cir.

1979), cited by plaintiff. In *Miller*, the area in which the accident occurred was maintained by the government and included bathroom facilities and a boat dock.

6. See 36 C.F.R. §§ 261.50, 261.53, and 261.54 (1979).

ing wilderness), range, timber, watershed, wildlife, and fish." 16 U.S.
C.A. § 1604(g)(3)(A). Should this NFMA provision change the result in
Otteson? One FLPMA policy statement directs the BLM to manage "in
a manner that will protect the quality of scientific, scenic, historical,
ecological, environmental, air and atmospheric, water resource, and
archeological values; that, where appropriate, will preserve and protect
certain public lands in their natural condition; that will provide food
and habitat for fish and wildlife and domestic animals; and that will
provide for outdoor recreation and human occupancy and use." 43 U.S.
C.A. § 1701(a)(8). What should be the result if a similar accident were
to occur on BLM lands?

    2. Compare Bilderback v. United States, 558 F.Supp. 903 (D.Or.
1982). Rocky, a Forest Service pack horse, got loose; while wandering
on the road, Rocky was struck by plaintiffs' automobile, injuring them
(and killing Rocky). The United States contended that it had no duty
to keep its animals off the highways because Oregon allows livestock to
roam at large without trespass liability. The court rejected that
argument, holding instead that federal law preempted that aspect of
state law on the federal range. Then, finding in both analogous state
law and federal law a duty to prevent animals from wandering where
they ought not to be, the court adjudged the government negligent and
awarded damages.

DUCEY v. UNITED STATES

United States Court of Appeals, Ninth Circuit, 1983.
713 F.2d 504.

FLETCHER, Circuit Judge:

    Plaintiffs appeal from the district court's judgment for the defen-
dant United States in three consolidated wrongful death actions
brought pursuant to the Federal Tort Claims Act (FTCA). We have
jurisdiction under 28 U.S.C. § 1291 (1976). We reverse in part and
affirm in part.

FACTS

    The spouses of the three plaintiffs in these consolidated cases (the
"Users") were killed in a flash flood in the Lake Mead National
Recreational Area (LMNRA) in Nevada on September 14, 1974. The
Users had been camping at and boating from a recreational site on the
banks of the Colorado River in Eldorado Canyon. The National Park
Service (NPS), the agency that operated the LMNRA, provided a ranger
station, boat launching ramp, and comfort stations at the site. In the
same area Eldorado Canyon Resorts, Inc. (ECR), a concessioner of the
NPS, maintained and operated a cafe-store, boat slips, automobile
fueling and boat service facilities, rental cabins, and trailer spaces.

    The parties stipulated that on the day of the flood, each of the
Users was present "in the canyon that day for recreational purposes."
None of the Users had paid a fee directly to the NPS or to the United
States either to gain entrance to or to engage in recreational activities

on the public lands in the LMNRA or to use the NPS-provided facilities. Two of the Users had paid rental fees to ECR for use of a boat slip, one User had rented a trailer space, and all three Users had recently bought various goods at the ECR cafe-store.

Pursuant to the terms of the concession agreement between ECR and the NPS, ECR was obligated to remit to the United States 1¾% of its gross annual receipts from sales at the cafe-store and from boat slip and trailer space rentals and to fulfill certain other maintenance and caretaking responsibilities. However, ECR in fact made no payment to the NPS for the calendar year 1974.

Following the flood, the surviving spouses of the Users brought suit against the United States in district court for damages allegedly caused by a breach of duty of NPS and ECR employees to warn of or guard against the flood.

ANALYSIS

* * *

I. *Tort Liability of United States for Negligence of NPS Employees.*

The trial court applying the law of the place (Nevada), found the Government immune from tort liability under the Nevada recreational use statute, Nev.Rev.Stat. 41.510 (1973).[3] Plaintiffs challenge this holding, asserting that immunity under the recreational use statute does not obtain here. The government contends that, even if the ruling below were incorrect, the government is not liable because the government's conduct falls within the discretionary function exemption from tort liability contained in the FTCA.

A. *Immunity Under Recreational Use Statute.*

Apart from the generally applicable Nevada rules governing tort liability, the Nevada recreational use statute provides immunity for a landowner whose property is used for recreational purposes, subject,

---

3. Nev.Rev.Stat. § 41.510 (1973) states in pertinent part:

1. An owner, lessee or occupant of premises owes no duty to keep the premises safe for entry or use by others for hunting, fishing, trapping, camping, hiking, sightseeing, or for any other recreational purposes, or to give warning of any hazardous condition, activity or use of any structure on such premises to persons entering for such purposes, except as provided in subsection 3 of this section.

2. When an owner, lessee or occupant of premises gives permission to another to hunt, fish, trap, camp, hike, sightsee, or to participate in other recreational activities, upon such premises:

(a) He does not thereby extend any assurance that the premises are safe for such purpose, constitute the person to

whom permission is granted an invitee to whom a duty of care is owed, or assume responsibility for or incur liability for any injury to person or property caused by any act of persons to whom permission is granted, except as provided in subsection 3 of this section.

* * *

3. This section does not limit the liability which would otherwise exist for:

(a) Willful or malicious failure to guard, or to warn against, a dangerous condition, use, structure or activity.

(b) Injury suffered in any case where permission to hunt, fish, trap, camp, hike, sightsee, or to participate in other recreational activities, was granted for a consideration other than the consideration, if any, paid to the landowner by the state or any subdivision thereof. * * *

however, to several exceptions. In holding for the defendant, the trial court found that section 41.510(1), the immunity section, is applicable to the facts of this case and that neither of two possible exceptions contained in section 41.510(3) change the result. In particular, the district court found the consideration exception to the Nevada recreational use statute, subsection 41.510(3)(b), inapplicable on the ground that the various forms of "consideration" allegedly tendered by the Users—money for store purchases, moorage fees, and trailer space rental fees—were tendered not to the United States but to ECR and that "[m]oney paid to the concessioner is not payment to the Government."

Plaintiffs challenge this holding on the ground that the consideration exception is applicable on the facts of this case. The Government contends that the district court's conclusion should be upheld for two reasons: (1) since the Users made no direct payments for permission to enter, no "consideration" in the sense of subsection 41.510(3)(b) was tendered; and (2) even if such "consideration" in the sense of subsection 41.510(3)(b) was tendered, it was not tendered to the United States. We reject both of the Government's contentions and conclude that the exception is applicable here.

1. *Lack of Transfer of "Consideration."*

The Government argues first that even if the Government itself had operated the Eldorado Canyon facility none of the various forms of consideration ECR received are the sort of "consideration" in return for "permission to participate in recreational activities" required under subsection 41.510(3)(b). Like any other visitors to Eldorado Canyon, the Users paid no direct fee to enter the Canyon, to boat on the Colorado, or to hike, fish, sightsee, or participate in any other recreational activity in the Canyon. The only consideration tendered was for the purchase of products or for the use of the artificial amenities of trailer spaces and boat slips. The Government insists that subsection 41.510(3)(b) is applicable only where a fee is specifically charged for permission to enter. We do not read the exception so narrowly.

* * *

First, the language of the consideration exception itself suggests a broad reading of section 41.510(3)(b). The exception is worded not in narrow terms of "fee" or "charge," but rather in the far more encompassing terms, "for a consideration." "Consideration" is a term of art, a word with a well-understood meaning in the law, embracing any "right, interest, profit or benefit." *Black's Law Dictionary* 277 (rev. 5th ed. 1979). Used in a statute, it should be accorded that meaning. The statutory exception, then, is itself literally applicable to situations well beyond those involving a strict charging of a "fee" for "permission" to recreate.

* * *

The policy underlying the adoption of a consideration exception to the Nevada recreational use statute is to retain tort liability in actions involving recreational use of land where the use of the land for recreational purposes is granted not gratuitously but in return for an economic benefit. Since the potential for profit alone is thought sufficient to encourage those owners who wish to make commercial use of their recreational lands to open them to the public, the further stimulus of tort immunity is both unnecessary and improper. Furthermore, where a landowner derives an economic benefit from allowing others to use his land for recreational purposes, the landowner is in a position to post warnings, supervise activities, and otherwise seek to prevent injuries. Such a landowner also has the ability to purchase liability insurance or to self-insure, thereby spreading the cost of accidents over all users of the land.

* * *

Our conclusion is consistent with decisions of this and other courts, construing the consideration exceptions of the recreational use statutes of other states. In Graves v. United States Coast Guard, 692 F.2d 71, 73 (9th Cir.1982) (per curiam), we held that the California recreational use statute did not immunize the United States from liability for injuries arising out of the use of a riverside cabana, even though the only alleged "consideration" was the payment of a fee to private entrepreneurs for the privilege of camping near the river. We held that since the use of the cabana and access to the river were implied benefits received as a consequence of the payment of consideration to the campground operators, the camping fee was *consideration* in return not merely for "permission to camp" but also "to gain access to the river" and "to use waterside facilities" within the meaning of the consideration exception to the California recreational use statute. Id.

As in the cases discussed, the Users did not pay an entrance or permission fee or charge to participate in recreational activities in Eldorado Canyon. But, just as in the other cases, similar amenities were offered by the concessioners, and all but one of the Users had rented boat slips or trailer spaces and all had regularly purchased goods from the cafe-store.[11] Moreover, all were concededly participating in recreational activities in Eldorado Canyon, and not elsewhere, at the time of the flood. We conclude that if the United States itself had operated the Eldorado Canyon facility the rentals and purchases by the Users would constitute "consideration" in return for permission to recreate in Eldorado Canyon within the meaning of the consideration exception to the Nevada statute.[12]

11. Each of the Users actually rented a trailer space or boat slip or made purchases at the cafe-store in conjunction with his participation in recreational activities in Eldorado Canyon on September 14, 1974. * * *

12. Jones v. United States, 693 F.2d 1299 (9th Cir.1982) (inner tube rental fee not "fee" under Washington statute), and Smith v. United States, 383 F.Supp. 1076, 1080 (D.Wyo.1974) (vehicular fee to enter park not "charge" under Wyoming stat-

ute), aff'd on other grounds, 546 F.2d 872 (10th Cir.1976), are inapposite here. The statutory "consideration" language at issue in those cases was much more narrowly drafted than that contained in the Nevada statute. See Jones, 693 F.2d at 1301 (no immunity where "charging a fee of any kind" takes place); Smith, 383 F.Supp. at 1080 (no immunity where "charge" paid by those "who enter or go on the land"). Furthermore, neither *Smith* nor *Jones* considered the possibility that actual or potential economic benefits that accrue to the com-

2. *Lack of Payment of Consideration to United States.*

The Government contends that, even if moorage and trailer fees and cafe-store purchases constitute "consideration" in the sense of 41.510(3)(b), the exception does not apply since ECR, and not the United States, operated the cafe-store and rental facilities. The Government argues that since ECR had no power to deny permission to the Users to recreate in Eldorado Canyon and since the Users paid ECR and not the United States for all rentals and purchases, the consideration is not in return for permission to recreate as required by subsection 41.510(3)(b). We reject that argument.

Subsection 41.510(3)(b) does not specify to whom consideration must be tendered. We think it a fair reading of the provision, however, that consideration must be tendered directly or indirectly to a person who has the power to grant or deny permission to participate in recreational activities. Since the concession agreement did not give ECR the power to deny permission to recreate in Eldorado Canyon, the exception is applicable only if consideration was tendered, directly or indirectly, to the United States in return for permission to recreate in Eldorado Canyon. We conclude that this condition is met in this case.

Before entering its concession agreement with ECR, the United States certainly was free to deny permission to recreate in Eldorado Canyon. See Jones v. United States, 693 F.2d 1299, 1302–03 (9th Cir. 1982). Thereafter, however, it was not. The concession agreement required the concessioner to provide and maintain facilities, to offer services, and to pay to the government a fixed percentage of all revenues from operations. Implicit in the agreement was a commitment on the government's part that users would be allowed to enter the area to use the concession facilities. Under these circumstances, we conclude that the consideration tendered here by the Users to ECR was in return for permission to participate in recreational activities in Eldorado Canyon in the sense of subsection 41.510(3)(b).

In so holding, we break no new ground. While we recognize that the case law pertaining to the recreational use statutes of other jurisdictions must be viewed cautiously because of variations from statute to statute, we see our interpretation of subsection 41.510(3)(b) to be in keeping with this court's construction of similar consideration exception clauses in the recreational use statutes of other states.

* * *

Similarly, in Thompson v. United States, 592 F.2d 1104 (9th Cir. 1979), we denied immunity to the government. An injured motorcycle rider had paid a fee to a racing association in return for permission to participate in a motorcycle race. The racing association had previously paid a fee to the Bureau of Land Management for the right to hold a race on government land. Even though the injured rider had not himself paid a fee to the United States for permission to enter United

mercial operations of the government or its lessees in federal parks might constitute a "fee" or "charge" for permission to enter   the parks under the Washington or Wyoming statutes.

* * *

States land, we nonetheless held that, under the totality of the circumstances, the rider had tendered "consideration" in return for "permission to enter for [vehicular riding] purposes" within the meaning of the consideration exception to the California recreational use statute.

* * *

By holding the consideration exception applicable on the facts of this case, we do not imply that the exception applies to a broader geographic area than that over which the concessionaire has the explicit or implicit power to grant or deny permission to recreate.[15] All three of the Users were killed while in Eldorado Canyon, well within the geographical boundaries of ECR's concession facility.

B. *Discretionary Function or Duty Exemption to § 1346(b).*

The Government contends that, even if it derives no immunity from the Nevada recreational use statute, it is nonetheless immune under the discretionary function exemption of the FTCA. * * * The government asserts that the allegedly negligent acts and omissions of NPS employees upon which plaintiffs' claims are based constitute the exercise of a "discretionary" function or duty on the part of a federal employee in the sense of section 2680(a).

Whether an act or omission is a discretionary activity in the sense of section 2680(a) turns on whether the act or omission occurred on the "planning" level of governmental activity or on the "operational" level. In addition to examining the level at which the act or omission took place, our court has also considered "the ability of the judiciary to evaluate the act or omission and whether judicial evaluation would impair the effective administration of the government." While the government's decision to encourage recreation at Eldorado Canyon is the exercise of a discretionary function, the government's duty to warn of or guard against hazards resulting from that decision may nonetheless be actionable. The judgment and decision-making involved in day-to-day management of a recreational area are not the sort of decision-making contemplated by the exemption. See Thompson v. United States, 592 F.2d 1104, 1111 (9th Cir.1979).

The trial judge made no findings on the applicability of the discretionary function exemption. On remand, the trial court must examine the alleged acts of commission and omission alleged (among them, the failure to post signs warning of the possibility of a flood, the failure to remove or repair an earthen dam at one end of the canyon, and the failure to institute flood evacuation procedures) to determine whether, on the facts of this case, they fall within or without the discretionary function exemption.

* * *

15. The government, unlike private landowners, has vast areas of public lands, much of it open to the public for one use or another. Where application of the consideration exception is based on consideration in the form of purchases or rentals from a government concessioner, the exception applies only to that particular area to which the government must grant access for recreation because of its commitments to the concessioner.

II. *Tort Liability of United States for Negligence of ECR or Its Employees.*

The government argues that the negligence of ECR or its employees, as the negligence of "agents" of the United States, may not be imputed to the United States to form the basis of tort liability under section 1346(b). We agree.

The United States is not liable under the FTCA for the negligence of its independent contractors. * * *

* * *

The trial court did not err in finding that ECR was an independent contractor. ECR was required by the concession agreement to submit price lists for federal approval, to "maintain and operate" the facilities "to such extent and in such manner as the Secretary may deem satisfactory," to pay a fixed percentage of revenues to the United States, and to comply with numerous other contractual provisions. Many of these contractual provisions find their origin, however, in various rules and regulations which were issued by the Department of the Interior for "standard" concession agreements. As such, they are the sort of regulation-mandated contractual restrictions * * * that are designed to secure federal objectives and that, despite their restrictive effect on the activities of the contracting party, do not convert an independent entrepreneur into an "agent" of the federal government.

* * *

CONCLUSION

The district court erred in its determination that the consideration exception to the immunity provided by the Nevada recreational statute, Nev.Rev.Stat. § 41.510, did not apply to remove the shield of the statute from the United States for the alleged negligence of its employees. The district court's finding that ECR was an independent contractor whose negligence cannot be imputed to the United States was not error.

Material factual issues remain to be tried as to (1) whether the United States is entitled to the benefit of the discretionary function exemption of the FTCA; and (2) if not, whether the United States was negligent.

We AFFIRM in part, REVERSE in part, and REMAND for proceedings consistent with this opinion.

* * *

WILLIAM P. GRAY, District Judge, dissenting:

I agree with the district court that the Government was entitled to immunity under the Nevada Recreational Use Statute and therefore would affirm the judgment rendered by the trial court.

We start with the proposition that a person is welcome to make use of the wilderness areas of the United States, but that he does so at his own risk with respect to the hazards of the terrain and the elements. If the Government, or another owner, were to be exposed to liability if it fails to warn each such user of any potential danger from flooding or fire or avalanche, such areas doubtless would be placed off limits, to the great disadvantage of people that enjoy using them.

The burden of loss for the unfortunate deaths here concerned must lie where it falls, unless there is a valid reason to place it elsewhere. The Nevada statute attempts to recognize this problem and establish a reasonable balance of considerations: An owner of land that is willing to permit others the use of it for recreational purposes is freed from liability unless he requires a "consideration" for "permission * * * to participate in * * * recreational activities." I read the statute to mean quite clearly that the owner is exempt from liability unless he charges a *fee* for granting permission to participate in these recreational activities. Thus, I think that the attempt in the opinion to impose liability upon the owner in the event *any* transaction for consideration takes place while a person is on the property imposes a burden that is not intended by the statute. I cannot believe that the fact that the decedents may have bought coffee or a candy bar or paid a fee for a place to park a trailer should be allowed to negative the fact that they were given free access to the area.

In light of the foregoing, I am obliged respectfully to note my dissent.

NOTES

1. The Nevada statute does not exclude liability for injuries "where permission to hunt, fish, trap, camp, hike, sightsee, or to participate in other recreational activities was granted for a consideration." Note 3, supra. Did the United States charge for any of these activities? Did the United States allow use of its lands "gratuitously"? When plaintiffs bought candy bars at the cafe-store, what were they paying for? (Incidentally, what do you think of the deal ECR got from the Park Service?)

2. Before the advent of state recreational use statutes, federal liability for recreational accidents was more common. In Claypool v. United States, 98 F.Supp. 702 (S.D.Cal.1951), plaintiff was attacked by a grizzly while asleep in his tent in Yellowstone. Liability was found because the Park Service had notice of the danger from a prior incident. The court in Smith v. United States, 117 F.Supp. 525 (N.D. Cal.1953), found the Forest Service liable for failing to remove a rotten limb which fell on plaintiff. In Ashley v. United States, 215 F.Supp. 39 (D.Neb.1963), aff'd, 326 F.2d 499 (8th Cir.1964), however, a plaintiff whose arm was lacerated by a bear while he slept in his car was denied recovery. The court held that the NPS was not negligent for having failed to dispose of the bear earlier and that bear management was a discretionary function. It also rejected the contention that the NPS should have warned plaintiff to keep his car windows rolled up at all times. Similarly, the court in Harmon v. United States, 532 F.2d 669 (9th Cir.1975) exonerated the government from responsibility for the drowning of plaintiffs' decedents on a white water rafting trip in Idaho,

holding that because the danger was obvious and known, the decedents were contributorily negligent. See also Smith v. United States, 546 F.2d 872 (10th Cir.1976) (tourist fell into a superheated thermal pool in Yellowstone).

3. On the interpretation of various state recreational use statutes, see Jones v. United States, 693 F.2d 1299 (9th Cir.1982) (young girl injured in a snow sliding accident in Olympic National Park); Phillips v. United States, 590 F.2d 297 (9th Cir.1979) (hiker fell down a mountain); Thompson v. United States, 592 F.2d 1104 (9th Cir.1979) (motorcyclist injured in a race). Recovery was denied in each instance. But see Mandel v. United States, 719 F.2d 963 (8th Cir.1983) (camp counselor struck his head on a rock while diving into a pool; court remanded dismissal to determine whether omissions of government were wanton or willful); Miller v. United States, 597 F.2d 614 (7th Cir.1979) (plaintiff dove off a dock in a national wildlife refuge into three feet of water and became a quadriplegic; the court upheld a million dollar judgment on the ground that the Illinois statute exonerating owners of recreational land only applied to lands used on a casual basis for recreation and not to developed facilities).

4. Should Congress enact standards defining federal liability for recreational accidents on the public lands? What standards would be appropriate?

D. EMERGING LIMITS ON THE IMPLIED RECREATIONAL LICENSE

Americans have a right to visit publicly-owned lands for recreational purposes, but the right is merely a license, revocable at the will of Congress or at the informed discretion of an authorized land management agency. The upsurge in recreational use has spurred the development of new kinds of controls on intensive recreation, including rationing of recreational experiences, to save the most popular areas from overuse.

Federal efforts to limit access are unpopular inside as well as outside of land management agencies. At this stage of development, restrictions on the recreational license are still regarded as the last resort. Congress has seldom addressed this volatile issue. Consequently, few lawsuits have been brought to resolve conflicts between restrictive policies and the traditional right of free access. The major exception is off-road vehicles (ORVs).

Off-road vehicles pose a prominent danger to some public lands, but regulating them is especially troublesome. As Jim Ruch, former BLM State Director for California, has said: "You can't understand true multiple-use management until you've stood on the top of a sand dune with the members of the Desert Lily Society coming up one side and, coming up the other, the Barstow Bombers." Enforcement of any regulatory system will be difficult because of the nature of the activity and the extreme shortage of agency personnel in heavily used areas.

To date, however, philosophies and politics have been at such cross-currents that formulation of a coherent scheme of regulation is only now beginning to emerge.

NATIONAL WILDLIFE FEDERATION v. MORTON

United States District Court, District of Columbia, 1975.
393 F.Supp. 1286.

WILLIAM B. JONES, District Judge.

* * *

I. BACKGROUND

On February 8, 1972, the President, noting that the widespread and rapidly increasing use of off-road vehicles "—often for legitimate purposes but also in frequent conflict with wise land and resource management practices, environmental values, and other types of recreational activity—has demonstrated the need for a unified Federal policy toward the of such vehicles on the public land," issued Executive Order 11644. 3 C.F.R. p. 332 (1974). The Order directs various "agency heads" (defined to include the Secretary of Interior) to create an administrative framework within which designation of the "specific areas and trails on public lands on which the use of off-road vehicles may be permitted, and areas in which the use of off-road vehicles may not be permitted" would be made, and to set a date by which such designations shall be completed. The Order sets forth various environmental criteria to be employed in determining designations and further requires each agency head to ensure adequate opportunity for public participation both in the promulgation of the regulations and in the actual designation of areas and trails.

On April 15, 1974, land designation regulations were issued for public lands under the administration of BLM. 39 Fed.Reg. 13612 (April 15, 1974). These regulations not only prescribed the procedure and criteria to be employed in designating areas and trails; they went one step further, declaring that all public lands not restricted or closed to ORV use "remain open to off-road vehicle use and are hereby designated as open use areas and trails * * *." 43 C.F.R. § 6292.2(a) (1974).

Plaintiff alleges that these regulations fail to meet the requirements of Executive Order 11644 in the following respects:

(a) The regulations designate all BLM administered land (with the exception of those few areas previously closed or restricted) as open to off-road vehicle use without regard to the criteria for evaluating these lands prescribed by Executive Order 11644;

(b) The regulations fail to provide for public participation in the designation of BLM administered lands as required by Executive Order 11644;

(c) The regulations fail to set a date for completing the designation of BLM administered lands under the criteria of Executive Order 11644;

(d) The regulations fail to require that all BLM administered lands be evaluated for suitability for off-road vehicle use under the Executive Order's criteria;

(e) The regulations fail to adopt the specific criteria for evaluating BLM administered lands prescribed by Executive Order 11644.

* * *

III. DEFENDANTS' REGULATIONS FAIL TO COMPLY WITH THE REQUIREMENTS OF EXECUTIVE ORDER 11644

Section 3(a) of Executive Order 11644, requires the development and issuance of regulations and administrative instructions which "provide for administrative designation of the *specific* areas and trails on public lands on which the use of off-road vehicles may be permitted, and areas in which the use of off-road vehicles may not be permitted" (emphasis added). "Those regulations shall direct that the designation of such areas and trails will be based upon the protection of the resources of the public lands, promotion of the safety of all users of those lands, and minimization of conflicts among the various uses of those lands." The regulations "shall further require" that the designations "shall be in accordance with" three additional criteria which require the minimization of: damage to land resources, harassment of wildlife and disruption of wildlife habitats, and conflicts between ORV use and other existing or proposed recreational uses in contiguous areas. Finally, "areas and trails shall not be located" in specially-protected areas unless "the respective agency head determines that [ORV] use in such locations will not adversely affect their natural, aesthetic, or scenic values."

By its regulations, BLM not only details the mechanism by which designation is to be effected; it goes much further, designating as officially open to ORV use all land not otherwise restricted or closed. This blanket designation was done without regard to any of the criteria mandated by the Executive Order. While it might be argued that the various criteria will be employed in making subsequent "restricted" or "closed" designations, the Order manifestly contemplates evaluation of the land not only for purposes of restricting ORV use but also for designation of areas "on which the use of off-road vehicles may be permitted." Moreover, the Order speaks of designating "specific areas and trails on public lands" for use or non-use of ORV's. Here, BLM has engaged in wholesale designation unrelated to any specific tract of land.

Defendants justify this action on the ground that it "maintains the status quo while specific designations are made." In the first place, this assertion ignores the fact that, status quo or not, the Executive Order requires that *all* designations be based upon the criteria set forth therein and the criteria are to be applied to designations of both use and non-use of ORV's. In addition, designation as "open" does not truly maintain the status quo. As plaintiff notes, this designation, being an official governmental act, changes the character of the land use policy, tilting it in favor of ORV use. Future designations will not be made in the context of applying the required criteria to decide whether specific areas and trails should be opened or closed to ORV use. Instead, authorized officers will be required to employ the criteria in determining whether a specific area or trail's existing "open" status should be *changed* to "closed" or "restricted." This distinction creates a subtle, but nevertheless real, inertial presumption in favor of ORV use.

Instead of evaluating with regard to the environmental criteria mandated by Executive Order 11644 specific areas and trails to determine whether the use of ORV's should be permitted, BLM has engaged in a wholesale, blanket designation of "open" lands. By doing so, it has violated the express requirements of Executive Order 11644.

* * *

[The court then held that public participation opportunities had been inadequate and that the BLM regulations did not insure that "all" public lands would be evaluated and designated.]

Section 3(a) of Executive Order 11644 further requires that the following criteria be employed in making designations:

> Those regulations shall direct that the designation of such areas and trails will be based upon the protection of the resources of the public lands, promotion of the safety of all users of those lands, and minimization of conflicts among the various uses of those lands. The regulations shall further require that the designation of such areas and trails shall be in accordance with the following—

> (1) Areas and trails shall be located to minimize damage to soil, watershed, vegetation, or other resources of the public lands.

> (2) Areas and trails shall be located to minimize harassment of wildlife or significant disruption of wildlife habitats.

> (3) Areas and trails shall be located to minimize conflicts between off-road vehicle use and other existing or proposed recreational uses of the same or neighboring public lands, and to ensure the compatibility of such uses with existing conditions in populated areas, taking into account noise and other factors.

> (4) Areas and trails shall not be located in officially designated Wilderness Areas or Primitive Areas. Areas and trails shall be located in areas of the National Park system, Natural Areas, or National Wildlife Refuges and Game Ranges only if the respective agency head determines that off-road vehicle use

in such locations will not adversely affect their natural, aesthetic, or scenic values.

BLM's regulations set forth the following criteria:

Designations of restricted and closed areas and trails will be based on the following:

(a) The ability of the land and its resources to withstand and sustain off-road vehicle use impacts.

(b) Consideration of the scenic qualities of the land, and its cultural, ecological, and environmental values.

(c) The need for public use areas for recreation use.

(d) Consideration of off-road vehicle use impacts on other lands, use, and resources.

(e) The potential hazards to public health and safety, other than the normal risks involved in off-road vehicle use.

(f) The existing or potential quality and quantity of recreational experiences available.

(g) Consideration of the need to minimize harassment of wildlife or significant disruption of wildlife habitat.

(h) The furtherance of the purposes and policy of the National Environmental Policy Act of 1969.

A cursory reading of the language of the two excerpts set forth above suggests that BLM has significantly diluted the standards emphatically set forth in Executive Order 11644. A close comparison of the two sets of criteria confirms this impression. For example, where the Executive Order directs that "[a]reas and trails shall be located to minimize damage to soil, watershed, vegetation or other resources of the public lands," the BLM regulations state that designation will be based on "[t]he ability of the land to withstand and sustain off-road vehicle impacts" and "[c]onsideration of the scenic qualities of the land, and its cultural, ecological and environmental values." The Executive Order directs that "[a]reas and trails shall be located to minimize harassment of wildlife or significant disruption of wildlife habitats," while BLM requires only "[c]onsideration of the need to minimize harassment of wildlife or significant disruption of wildlife habitat."

In addition to diluting the criteria detailed in the Executive Order, BLM has added a substantive criteria [11] found nowhere in the Order, much less prescribed as a criterion. The Order does not direct that "in addition to" or "among other" criteria the following will be employed. Instead, it states that designation "will be based upon" and "shall be in accordance with" the delineated standards.

BLM seeks to justify its action on the basis that "the criteria of the Executive Order are applied in a system which considers all uses or potential uses of the public lands and the conflicts between them,

11. "The need for public use areas for recreation use." 43 C.F.R. § 6292.3(c) (1974).

including uses not specifically dealt with in the Executive Order such as grazing, mining, etc." Planning system or not, the Executive Order sets forth in unambiguous and mandatory language the criteria that are to be employed in the designation of areas and trails for use or non-use of ORV's. Defendants have not adhered to them in their regulations.

The Court thus concludes that defendants' regulations fail to comply with numerous requirements of Executive Order 11644. * * *

* * *

NOTES

1. Under what authority did President Nixon issue Executive Order 11644? Could the President have banned ORVs from the public lands? Is there a management power in the President, created by congressional acquiescence akin to the withdrawal power found in *Midwest Oil,* supra at page 147? Is there an independent and inherent executive public land management authority (the question left open in *Midwest Oil*)?

2. Neither the decision nor the underlying Executive Order was dispositive. See Sheridan, infra; Rosenberg, Regulation of Off-Road Vehicles, 5 Envt'l Aff. 175 (1976).

D. SHERIDAN, OFF–ROAD VEHICLES ON PUBLIC LAND
8–19 (1979)

From the standpoint of public land management, the initially important characteristic of the motorcycle, 4 x 4, and snowmobile boom was that it struck without warning. Recreational planners and economists who specialize in the use of natural resources for recreation did not anticipate the phenomenon; nor did they fully grasp its far-ranging significance once it was underway. * * *

In other words, the public land managers were ill prepared for the onslaught. This was particularly unfortunate because over half of all the off-road motorcycle, 4 x 4, and dune buggy driving in the nation takes place on federal land. Indeed, over half occurs on land managed by one federal agency—the Bureau of Land Management (BLM).

* * *

ORV BENEFITS

Motorized recreation gives pleasure to millions of Americans. That is its greatest benefit. There are also certain economic benefits derived from ORV and snowmobile recreation. For the most part, these benefits accrue to the people and firms who make the equipment and those who sell them. In addition, communities in areas which attract riders enjoy a certain influx of dollars. For example, gas stations, restaurants, and motels in communities such as Gorman, California, or Webb, New York, benefit from money spent by people who visit those areas for motorized recreation. The overall economic benefits of this recreation have never been determined. * * *

*   *   *

In regard to recreation today, our society's principal concern is utilitarian: the greatest good for the greatest number. And as John Rawls has made clear, much more is involved in the application of this principle than crude arithmetic. Society must be concerned, for example, with the allocation of scarce resources, in terms of both efficiency and fairness. A major utilitarian concern with ORV recreation is the destruction of natural resources caused by these vehicles. Another is the infringement of other people's rights to recreate. Another is the alternatives available to ORV users. *   *   *

ENVIRONMENTAL COSTS

ORVs have damaged every kind of ecosystem found in the United States: sand dunes covered with American beach grass on Cape Cod; pine and cyprus woodlands in Florida; hardwood forests in Indiana; prairie grasslands in Montana; chaparral and sagebrush hills in Arizona; alpine meadows in Colorado; conifer forests in Washington; arctic tundra in Alaska. In some cases, the wounds will heal naturally; in others they will not, at least for millennia.

*   *   *

CONFLICTS WITH OTHER USERS

Reports from public land managers in nine western states indicate that conflict occurs, upon occasion, between commercial users of the land, such as ranchers, and ORV recreationalists. The conflict with grazing, in fact, seems to be more common than with logging or mining. For example, New Mexico BLM director Arthur W. Zimmerman notes that complaints from ranchers have been received concerning trespass, cut fences, broken gates, polluted livestock water, new jeep roads, noise, gully erosion caused by hill climbs, and interference with their livestock operations. The less frequent complaints received from loggers and miners usually concern vandalism of their equipment and property by ORVers.

The most serious conflict arises between ORV operators and nonmotorized picnickers or campers, hikers, backpackers, sightseers, and so on—or between ORVers and persons using the land for educational purposes—students, teachers, researchers.

Nonmotorized recreationists do not enjoy their encounters with motorcycles, dune buggies, and four-wheel drive vehicles, numerous studies have shown. The ORV operator, on the other hand, is often quite tolerant, even oblivious of the person on foot or horseback.

ORVs, in other words, impair other people's enjoyment or understanding of the outdoors on public land. In terms of public policy, this is a problem equal in importance to ORV damage of the environment.

*   *   *

* * * [A]s a BLM Environmental Impact Statement noted: "Silence is a resource. These sounds which man typically associates with the pristine natural environments are perceived by the senses as solitude. The solitude of the desert is one of its * * * valuable resources." Substitute the word forest or prairie or mountain or meadow for desert and the truth of this statement still stands. The noise of an ORV punctures that solitude. Hikers and campers, for example, do not trek miles into the wilds to hear a chorus of internal combustion engines, however polite the drivers, however well-tuned their engines, although certainly a good muffler and a courteous driver make the experience less unpleasant than it would be. Direct encounters with ORV machines simply are not compatible with the quality of outdoor experience being sought by a majority of Americans.

* * *

* * *

BLM'S RESPONSE

The process of designating areas or trails open or closed to ORV use is a laborious undertaking for an agency such as the BLM, which administers 474 million acres of public land. The task is compounded by the fact that almost no control over ORV uses was exercised prior to Executive Order 11644, and hence behavior patterns of millions of ORV recreationists had already become established. In addition, BLM has fewer men and women per acre than the other land management agencies.

* * *

[The author describes the events leading up to and the decision in National Wildlife Federation v. Morton, supra.]

The final Environmental Impact Statement, prepared by Interior's Heritage Conservation and Recreation Service, on this plan was released to the public on April 21, 1978—more than 5 years after Executive Order 11644 and almost 1 year after a new Executive Order, 11989, was issued on the subject.

A key element in implementing Executive Order 11644 is designating which lands are suitable for ORV use and which are not. The California Desert ORV Plan, issued on November 1, 1973, is the first attempt by the BLM to apply the designation process. The plan provides scant protection for the area's natural and cultural resources but abundant opportunities for ORV recreation.

It designates 3 percent of the National Resource Lands as "closed" to ORVs, 6 percent as "open," and the remainder as "restricted," which means that ORV drivers are supposed to stay on existing roads and trails.

The major flaw in this scheme is that it does not take into account BLM's lack of presence in the field. A person can drive all day in the desert on a motorcycle or in a four-wheel drive vehicle and never see a BLM sign or enforcement officer. Indeed, the BLM has only slightly more than a dozen rangers to patrol 12 million acres of land. * * *

[Sheridan also discusses the somewhat more sophisticated Forest Service response to the ORV problem.]

AMERICAN MOTORCYCLIST ASSOCIATION v. WATT

United States District Court, Central District of California, 1982.
543 F.Supp. 789.

TASHIMA, District Judge.

This matter is before the Court on cross-motions for partial summary judgment by plaintiffs and certain of the defendants in one of the above-captioned cases: California Native Plant Society v. Watt, No. CV 81–489 AWT. *California Native Plant,* like each of these consolidated cases, calls into question the validity of the California Desert Conservation Area Plan (the "Plan"), which was prepared by the Bureau of Land Management ("BLM") pursuant to Section 601 of the Federal Land Policy and Management Act of 1976 ("FLPMA"), 43 U.S.C. § 1781. The Plan, and the procedure by which it was developed, were discussed extensively by this Court in an earlier opinion. American Motorcyclist Ass'n v. Watt, 534 F.Supp. 923 (C.D.Cal.1981) [supra at page 739]. In the interest of brevity, that discussion will not be repeated here.

The primary issue raised in the present motions relates to the "Motorized-Vehicle Access" element (the "MVA element") of the Plan. That element sets forth, among other things, restrictions on motorized vehicle use in those portions of the California Desert Conservation Area ("CDCA") designated by the Plan as "Class L" areas. In particular, the MVA element specifies that motorized vehicles will be allowed only on "approved routes of travel" in Class L areas, and sets forth specific criteria by which such routes are to be selected.

Plaintiffs seek a declaration that these route selection criteria for Class L areas are inconsistent with the provisions of 43 C.F.R. § 8342.1, a BLM regulation promulgated pursuant to the authority of FLPMA and certain other statutes,[4] and with Exec. Order No. 11,644 ("E.O. 11,644"), 3 C.F.R. § 332 (1974), as amended by Exec. Order No. 11,989 ("E.O. 11,989"), 3 C.F.R. § 120 (1978). Plaintiffs further request that the Court enjoin federal defendants (James G. Watt, Secretary of the Interior, and various officials of the BLM) from approving routes of travel using the criteria contained in the Plan, and ask for a writ of mandate compelling those defendants to revise the Plan so as to make it consistent with applicable executive orders and regulations.

* * *

* * * In essence, both 43 C.F.R. § 8342.1 and E.O. 11,644 require that routes for off-road vehicles ("ORVs") be selected so as to minimize adverse environmental effects. As will be elaborated below, I conclude

---

4. 43 C.F.R. § 8342.1 purports to be issued under FLPMA, 43 U.S.C. § 1701 et seq.; the Taylor Grazing Act, 43 U.S.C. § 315(a); the Endangered Species Act, 16 U.S.C. § 1531 et seq.; the Wild and Scenic Rivers Act of 1973, 16 U.S.C. § 1281(c); the Act of September 15, 1960 (the "Sikes Act"), as amended, 16 U.S.C. § 670 et seq.; the Land and Water Conservation Fund Act, 16 U.S.C. § 460 1–6a; the National Trails System Act, 16 U.S.C. § 1241 et seq.; and E.O. 11,644, 3 C.F.R. § 332 (1974), as amended by E.O. 11,989, 3 C.F.R. § 120 (1978).

that the criteria in the Plan are inconsistent with 43 C.F.R. § 8342.1, in that they allow for route approval without minimization of adverse environmental impacts. Under these circumstances, it is unnecessary to determine whether the provisions of E.O. 11,644 would also justify granting the relief sought by plaintiffs.

DISCUSSION

* * *

II. RIPENESS

Federal defendants contend that this case does not present a justiciable controversy because the route approval criteria contained in the Plan have not yet been applied. This contention must be rejected for two reasons.

First, plaintiffs have shown that on February 8, 1982, the Barstow office of the BLM approved a route of travel for a 400-vehicle "hare and hound" motorcycle race, to be run on February 14, 1982. Pursuant to the Recreation element of the Plan, approval of one-time competitive off-road vehicle events is subject, insofar as Class L areas are involved, to compliance with the permanent route selection criteria challenged in this case. Furthermore, it appears from the Environmental Assessment prepared by the BLM for use in considering the application for a race permit and from the Decision Record and Rationale issued by the BLM, that the agency did not apply the route approval criteria in the Plan in a manner consistent with 43 C.F.R. § 8342.1. Instead of ensuring "minimization" of environmental impacts as is required by § 8342.1, the BLM appears to have demanded only avoidance of "considerable adverse effects." The "considerable adverse effects" standard might have been taken either from E.O. 11,989, 3 C.F.R. § 120 (1978), or from 43 C.F.R. § 8341.2 (as distinguished from § 8342.1), both of which require that an ORV route be *closed* if "considerable adverse effects" are shown. This closure standard cannot properly be applied to initial route *approval*. Thus, it appears that the BLM is already applying the route selection criteria challenged in this action and that it is doing so in a manner inconsistent with 43 C.F.R. § 8342.1. Plaintiffs have, therefore, established that a present controversy exists which makes this case ripe for review.

Second, even if plaintiffs had not shown an instance of actual application of the challenged route selection criteria, this case satisfies the standards governing the availability of judicial review for newly promulgated administrative rules which are not yet being enforced or applied. * * * The issue they raise is legal in nature, and relates to agency rules which were promulgated in a relatively formal manner and with which compliance is expected;[9] thus, it is fit for judicial

---

9. The Plan states, at p. 11:

"This general plan is at the top of a heirarchy and it provides the framework for subsequent plans for specific resources and uses, and for development of site-specific programs or project actions, and it is responsive to specific land-use requests * * *."

Furthermore, in introducing the approval criteria challenged in the present action,

decision.   Since potentially irreparable environmental harm is threatened by application of these criteria, it would impose substantial
hardship on plaintiffs and would disserve the public interest [10] to
postpone review until after use of a given route has begun.   Similarly,
it would impose a substantial burden on both parties to require plaintiffs to challenge each permanent or one-time competitive event route
approval as it is granted by the BLM.   The Plan criteria are intended
for general application, and bind the discretion of BLM officials in
making route selections.   Accordingly, I conclude that the issue raised
by plaintiffs regarding these criteria is ripe for judicial review.

*   *   *

IV.   VALIDITY OF ROUTE SELECTION CRITERIA

*   *   *

In April of 1974, the BLM issued regulations intended to implement E.O. 11,644.   See 39 Fed.Reg. 13,612–15 (April 15, 1974).   *   *   *

The 1974 regulations were promptly challenged in federal court,
and were declared invalid in National Wildlife Fed'n v. Morton, 393
F.Supp. 1286 (D.D.C.1975).   *   *   *

In response to *National Wildlife,* the BLM eventually promulgated
regulations, pursuant to the authority of FLPMA as well as a number
of other statutes, which set forth route designation criteria nearly
identical to those set forth in E.O. 11,644.   See 43 Fed.Reg. 40,734
(September 12, 1978).[14]   Those regulations provide as follows:

> "The authorized officer shall designate all public lands as
> either open, limited, or closed to off-road vehicles.   All designa-
> tions shall be based on the protection of the resources of the
> public lands, the promotion of the safety of all the users of the
> public lands, and the *minimization of conflicts* among various
> uses of the public lands; and in accordance with the following
> criteria:

> "(a) Areas and trails shall be located to *minimize damage*
> to soil, watershed, vegetation, air, or other resources of the
> public lands, and to prevent impairment of wilderness suitabil-
> ity.

> "(b) Areas and trails shall be located to *minimize harass-
> ment* of wildlife or significant disruption of wildlife habitats.

the Plan states, at p. 91, that: "Decisions
on approval of vehicle routes for Class L
will be based on an analysis of each situation, using the following decision criteria."
[Emphasis added].

10.   The public interest would be dis-
served both by the potential for irreparable
damage to desert resources, and by the
substantial expense likely to be incurred if
the BLM proceeds with an elaborate route
approval process using criteria which are
later found to be invalid.

14.   The regulations took into account
the amendments to E.O. 11,644 effected by
E.O. 11,989, 3 C.F.R. 120 (1978).   See 43
C.F.R. § 8341.2.   E.O. 11,989, among other
things, amended E.O. 11,644 so as to require *closure* of ORV areas and trails
whenever an agency finds that ORV use
will cause or is causing "considerable adverse effects."   This closure standard is to
be distinguished from the initial *designation* criteria set forth in E.O. 11,644 and
mirrored in 43 C.F.R. § 8342.1.

Special attention will be given to protect endangered or threatened species and their habitats.

"(c) Areas and trails shall be located to *minimize conflicts between* off-road vehicle use and other existing or proposed recreational uses of the same or neighboring public lands, and to ensure the compatibility of such uses with existing conditions in populated areas, taking into account noise and other factors.

"(d) Areas and trails shall not be located in officially designated wilderness areas or primitive areas. Areas and trails shall be located in natural areas only if the authorized officer determines that off-road vehicle use in such locations will not adversely affect their natural, esthetic, scenic, or other values for which such areas are established."

43 CFR § 8342.1 (emphasis added).

The essence of plaintiffs' claim is that the route approval criteria for Class L areas found in the Plan are inconsistent with the above-quoted regulations, and with E.O. 11,644. The challenged criteria, which are contained in the MVA element of the Plan, are set forth in the following language:

* * *

"In Multiple-Use Class L areas, vehicle access is limited to only those routes 'approved' and marked as vehicle access routes. Routes not 'approved' for vehicle access in most instances will be obliterated, barricaded, signed, or shown 'closed' on maps. 'Approved' routes will be signed or otherwise marked or mapped so that those routes of travel which are clearly open will be readily identifiable.

"Route Designation Factors—Multiple-Use Class L

"Decisions on approval of vehicle routes for Class L *will be based* on an analysis of each situation, using the following decision criteria:

"(1) Is the route new or existing?

"(2) Does the route provide access for resource use or enjoyment?

"(3) Are there alternate access opportunities?

"(4) *Does the route cause considerable adverse impacts?*

"(5) Are there alternate access routes which do not cause considerable adverse impacts?"

Plan at 91 (emphasis added).

The route designation criteria, as shown above, are presented in such a manner so as to appear to be the exclusive standard pursuant to which route designation decisions are to be made. Concededly, the criteria are phrased in a neutral, interrogative form, such that they do not explicitly require that a route be approved if certain conditions are satisfied. At the same time, however, the criteria do not explicitly *prohibit* route designation in any defined situation. Thus, the Plan criteria would permit agency officials to make route designations without the minimization of environmental impacts and conflicts between uses expressly required by 43 C.F.R. § 8342.1. Furthermore, the criteria, even though neutrally phrased, will very likely lead BLM officials responsible for implementing the Plan to conclude that routes should be approved absent a finding of "considerable adverse impacts." The "considerable adverse impacts" standard is qualitatively different than the minimization criteria mandated by § 8342.1 and in practice is almost certain to skew route designation decision-making in favor of ORV use.

Defendants argue that various references in the Plan to E.O. 11,644, E.O. 11,989, and certain BLM regulations make it clear that the BLM does not intend to, or was not authorized to, apply the route selection criteria in a manner inconsistent with 43 C.F.R. § 8342.1. However, viewed in the context in which they appear, these references are not sufficient to counteract the impression, created in the presentation of the route designation criteria quoted above, that those criteria are to be the exclusive bases for route approval decisions. No mention of the executive orders or applicable BLM regulations is made in the text surrounding the criteria in the Plan. Furthermore, the Court has seen no language anywhere in the Plan which would alert a reader that the criteria presented in the Plan are inconsistent with 43 C.F.R. § 8342.1 or the executive orders. (If anything, the impression is given that the criteria faithfully implement these pre-existing directives.) Accordingly, I conclude that the Plan, viewed as a whole, is very likely to result in a route selection process which does not comply in significant respects with the express standards set forth in 43 C.F.R. § 8342.1.

V. SCOPE OF RELIEF

Although plaintiffs have requested a writ of mandate compelling federal defendants to revise the Plan so as to make it consistent with E.O. 11,644 and 43 C.F.R. § 8342.1, the Court concludes that declaratory and injunctive relief alone will be sufficient to adequately protect the interests of both plaintiffs and the public.

Accordingly, for the reasons stated above, the Court will enter judgment declaring that the route selection criteria for Class L areas contained in the Plan are inconsistent with 43 C.F.R. § 8342.1 and, therefore, invalid. The Court further will enjoin federal defendants from approving any route of travel in Class L areas, on either a one-time or permanent basis, without complying with the selection criteria set forth in 43 C.F.R. § 8342.1.

SIERRA CLUB v. CLARK
United States Court of Appeals, Ninth Circuit, 1985.
756 F.2d 686.

POOLE, Circuit Judge:

Plaintiffs Sierra Club, Desert Protective Council and California Native Plant Society ("Sierra Club") filed this action seeking judicial

review under the Administrative Procedure Act, 5 U.S.C. § 706(1), of
the failure of defendants Secretary of the Interior, Director of the
Bureau of Land Management ("BLM"), and California State Director of
BLM ("Secretary") to close Dove Springs Canyon to off road vehicle
("ORV") use. Sierra Club appeals from the district court's denial of
their motion for summary judgment, and the grant of the Secretary's
cross-motion for summary judgment. We affirm.

FACTS

Dove Springs Canyon is located in the California Desert Conservation Area ("Desert Area"), established in 1976, 43 U.S.C. § 1781, under
the Federal Land Policy Management Act ("the Act"), 43 U.S.C. § 1701
et seq. The Desert Area covers approximately 25 million acres in
southeastern California, approximately 12.1 million of which are administered by the BLM. Dove Springs Canyon is comprised of approximately 5500 acres; 3000 acres are designated "open" for unrestricted
use of ORVs.

Dove Springs Canyon possesses abundant and diverse flora and
fauna. Over 250 species of plants, 24 species of reptiles, and 30 species
of birds are found there. It also offers good habitat for the Mojave
ground squirrel, the desert kit fox, and the burrowing owl. Because the
rich and varied biota is unusual for an area of such low elevation in the
Mojave Desert, the Canyon was once frequented by birdwatchers and
naturalists, as well as hikers and fossil hunters.

Recreational ORV usage of Dove Springs Canyon began in 1965
and became progressively heavier in the ensuing years. By 1971, the
Canyon was being used intensively by ORV enthusiasts. It became
especially popular because the site's diverse terrain, coupled with
relatively easy access, provides outstanding hill-climbing opportunities.
By 1979, up to 200 vehicles used the Canyon on a typical weekend; over
500 vehicles used it on a holiday weekend. In 1973, the BLM adopted
its Interim Critical Management Program for Recreational Vehicle Use
on the California Desert ("Interim Program") which designated Dove
Springs Canyon as an ORV Open Area, permitting recreational vehicle
travel in the area without restriction.

Extensive ORV usage has been accompanied by severe environmental damage in the form of major surface erosion, soil compaction, and
heavy loss of vegetation. The visual aesthetics have markedly declined.
The character of the Canyon has been so severely altered that the
Canyon is now used almost exclusively for ORV activities.

In July of 1980 Sierra Club petitioned the Secretary of the Interior
to close Dove Springs Canyon to ORV use under the authority of
Executive Order No. 11644, as amended by Executive Order No. 11989,
and 43 C.F.R. § 8341.2 because of "substantial adverse effects" on the
vegetation, soil and wildlife in the Canyon. The Secretary responded
that the matter would be addressed in the California Desert Conservation Plan and Final Environmental Impact Statement ("the Final
Plan").

The Final Plan approved by the Secretary in December 1980 maintained unrestricted ORV use in Dove Springs of 3000 of the 5500 acres. Sierra Club filed this action on January 6, 1981, alleging that the Secretary's failure to close Dove Springs violated Executive Order No. 11644, as amended by Executive Order No. 11989, and 43 C.F.R. § 8341.2; 43 U.S.C. § 1732(b), which requires the Secretary to prevent "unnecessary or undue degradation of the lands;" and 43 U.S.C. §§ 1781(b) and (d), which require the Secretary to maintain and conserve resources of the Desert Area under principles of "multiple use and sustained yield." Sierra Club sought declaratory relief and a writ of mandate compelling closure.

On cross-motions for summary judgment the district court ruled in favor of the Secretary.

DISTRICT COURT RULING

The district court characterized Sierra Club's complaint as a challenge only to the "initial" designation of the Canyon under the 1980 Final Plan. The court said that Sierra Club had not alleged that ORV use has caused considerable adverse effects since the Plan's adoption, and although the complaint alleged that the failure to close the Canyon was in violation of the Executive Orders and the Regulation, the factual predicate for this claim antedated the adoption of the Plan. The court ruled that "[w]hatever may have been the merits of plaintiff's claim prior to the Plan's adoption, [the] controversy was mooted by the Secretary's and BLM's exercise of discretion under [the Act] to make the designation in the Plan. ∗ ∗ ∗ "

The court declined to rule whether the Regulation and the Executive Orders apply to the Plan where it is alleged that ORV use has caused considerable adverse effects since the Plan's adoption. It also ruled separately that there was no abuse of discretion by the agency in designating the Canyon for ORV use under the broad mandate of the Act, 43 U.S.C. § 1732(b) (unnecessary and undue degradation standard).

∗ ∗ ∗

ANALYSIS

The district court ruled that the plaintiffs' complaint was an attack upon the Canyon's initial designation as an "ORV freeplay area" in the Final Plan, and refused to address plaintiffs' contention that the Executive Orders and the Regulation required closure of the area after the Final Plan was adopted. Paragraphs 24 and 25 of plaintiffs' complaint do challenge the designation as violating 43 U.S.C. § 1732(b) and 43 U.S.C. § 1781(b) and (d). Paragraph 23, however, clearly alleges that defendants' failure to close Dove Springs Canyon to all ORV activity violates Executive Order No. 11989 and 43 C.F.R. § 8341.2. Moreover, Paragraphs 9, 10, 13 and 18 allege that ORV use will continue to cause adverse effects in Dove Springs Canyon in the future. Thus, plaintiffs properly raised this issue in their pleadings and the trial court erred in refusing to address it.

The district court also ruled that the Secretary's and BLM's exercise of discretion under the Act in designating the Canyon as open mooted the plaintiffs' claim. The plaintiffs in the district court and on appeal contend, however, that the closure standard contained in the Executive Orders and the Regulation applies independently of the designation process. The plain meaning of the provisions supports their view.

The Regulation provides:

> Notwithstanding the consultation provisions of § 8342.2(a), where the authorized officer determines that off-road vehicles are causing or will cause considerable adverse effects * * * the authorized officer shall immediately close the areas or trails affected. * * * Such closures will not prevent designation * * *, but these lands shall not be opened to the type(s) of off-road vehicle to which it was closed unless the authorized officer determines that the adverse effects have been eliminated and measures implemented to prevent recurrence.

43 C.F.R. § 8341.2(a). This provision creates a separate duty to close without regard to the designation process; it does not automatically become inoperative once the Secretary exercises his discretion to designate the land.

The district court erred in its analysis and conclusion that the Secretary's designation mooted the Sierra Club's claims. Nevertheless, we do not reverse the district court on account of this error because we must affirm if the record fairly presents any basis for affirmance. * * * Because we have decided that the closure standard of the Executive Orders and the Regulation applies independently of the designation of the land as open under the Act, the issue before us is whether the damage to Dove Springs Canyon amounts to "considerable adverse effects" which require the Canyon's closure. The parties agree that there is no genuine issue as to the extent of the damage to the Canyon, and therefore resolution of this issue depends upon whether the Secretary's interpretation of this phrase or that of the Sierra Club is to control.

* * *

The Secretary interprets "considerable adverse effect" to require determining what is "considerable" in the context of the Desert Area as a whole, not merely on a parcel-by-parcel basis. The Secretary contends such a broad interpretation is necessary and is consistent with 43 U.S.C. § 1781(a)(4) which expresses a congressional judgment that ORV use is to be permitted "where appropriate."

Sierra Club argues against the Secretary's interpretation. Sierra Club contends that the interpretation of the Executive Orders set forth by the Council on Environmental Quality (CEQ) in its August 1, 1977 memorandum is entitled to great deference, and that the CEQ's interpretation requires the closure of the Canyon. This argument fails on two grounds.

First, the CEQ's interpretation of the Executive Order does not directly conflict with the Secretary's interpretation of the regulation. While it states that "the term 'considerable' should be liberally construed to provide the broadest possible protection reasonably required by this standard," it does not purport to decide whether the term "considerable adverse effects" should be analyzed in the context of the entire Desert Area, or on a site-specific basis. Moreover, the memorandum acknowledges that the responsibility for closing particular areas rests with "responsible federal officials in the field" "[b]ased on their practical experience in the management of the public lands, and their first-hand knowledge of conditions 'on-the-ground.'"

Second, the authority of the CEQ is to maintain a continuing review of the implementation of the Executive Order. Executive Order No. 11644, § 8(b). The authority of the Secretary, on the other hand, is to promulgate regulations to provide for "administrative designation of the specific areas and trails on public lands on which the use of off-road vehicles may be permitted, and areas in which the use of off-road vehicles may not be permitted." Id. at § 3(a). Discretion rests with the Secretary, therefore, to determine whether and to what extent specific areas should be closed to ORV use. Thus, it is the Secretary's interpretation which is entitled to our deference.

Sierra Club argues that even if the CEQ's interpretation of the closure standard is not controlling, the Secretary's interpretation should not be adopted because it is unreasonable. Sierra Club insists that the sacrifice of any area to permanent resource damage is not justified under the multiple use management mandate of 43 U.S.C. § 1702(c) that requires multiple use "without permanent impairment of the productivity of the land and the quality of the environment." In further support of its position Sierra Club adverts to the requirement in the Act that the Secretary prevent "unnecessary and undue degradation" of the public lands, 43 U.S.C. § 1732(b). In addition, Sierra Club contends, when Congress established the Desert Area it intended the Secretary to fashion a multiple use and sustained yield management plan "to conserve [the California desert] resources for future generations, and to provide present and future use and enjoyment, particularly outdoor recreational uses, including the use, where appropriate, of off-road recreational vehicles." 43 U.S.C. § 1781(a)(4). Sierra Club argues that it is unreasonable for the Secretary to find ORV use "appropriate" when that use violates principles of sustained yield, substantially impairs productivity of renewable resources and is inconsistent with maintenance of environmental quality.

We can appreciate the earnestness and force of Sierra Club's position, and if we could write on a clean slate, would prefer a view which would disallow the virtual sacrifice of a priceless natural area in order to accommodate a special recreational activity. But we are not free to ignore the mandate which Congress wrote into the Act. Sierra Club's interpretation of the regulation would inevitably result in the total prohibition of ORV use because it is doubtful that any discrete area could withstand unrestricted ORV use without considerable adverse effects. However appealing might be such a resolution of the environmental dilemma, Congress has found that ORV use, damaging as it may be, is to be provided "where appropriate." It left determination of appropriateness largely up to the Secretary in an area of sharp conflict. If there is to be a change it must come by way of Congressional reconsideration. The Secretary's interpretation that this legislative determination calls for accommodation of ORV usage in the administrative plan, we must conclude, is not unreasonable and we are constrained to let it stand.

The court must review agency action to determine if it complies with the Secretary's interpretation of the Regulation. In Perkins v. Bergland, 608 F.2d 803 (9th Cir.1979), we held that the scope of review of an agency's factual findings is very narrow where the Secretary has been vested with substantial discretion, as in the administration of public land. * * * We noted that the various goals of "multiple use," "sustained yield," and how "best [to] meet the needs of the American people," vested in the Secretary discretion to determine optimum means of administering forest and range land. We concluded that the agency's factual findings as to range conditions and carrying capacity would be overturned only if arbitrary and capricious.

Under the California Desert Conservation Area Plan, approximately 4 percent (485,000 acres) of the total acreage is now open to unrestricted ORV use. Dove Springs itself constitutes only 0.025 percent of BLM administered lands in the Desert Area. Although all parties recognize that the environmental impact of ORV use at Dove Springs is severe, the Secretary's determination that these effects were not "considerable" in the context of the Desert Area as a whole is not arbitrary, capricious, or an abuse of the broad discretion committed to him by an obliging Congress.

* * *

NOTES

1. Precisely what accounts for the difference in results between the two principal cases? Did the ORV criteria or the law change between *AMA II* and the *Dove Canyon* decision?

2. *Dove Canyon* was followed in Sierra Club v. Clark, 774 F.2d 1406 (9th Cir.1985). In considering whether a Barstow to Las Vegas motorcycle race (with "thousands" of participants) would have ecological impacts "sufficiently egregious to violate the BLM's [interim wilderness study management guidelines] on nonimpairment," the court agreed that the test must be the effect of the race on the entire study area, not just the race route. Acknowledging the negative impacts, but finding justification from the fact that allowing the race might ameliorate illegal races, the court concluded that the race authorization "is a proper exercise of the BLM's discretion in providing for combined use of the desert."

3. See also Conservation Law Foundation of New England v. Clark, 590 F.Supp. 1467 (D.Mass.1984) (ORV management plan for Cape Cod National Seashore); California Ass'n of 4WD Clubs, Inc. v. Andrus, 672 F.2d 921 (9th Cir.1982) [text of order at 12 ELR 20457] (upholding permanent closure of two ORV corridors in the Imperial Sand Dunes).

WILDERNESS PUBLIC RIGHTS FUND v. KLEPPE

United States Court of Appeals, Ninth Circuit, 1979.
608 F.2d 1250, cert. denied, 446 U.S. 982 (1980).

MERRILL, Circuit Judge:

These cases involve the manner in which use of the Colorado River for rafting and boating is apportioned between concessioners approved by the National Park Service and noncommercial users. Permits from the National Park Service are required for river use and the dispute here concerns the apportionment made in granting permits.

In December, 1972, the Secretary of the Interior found that the boating and rafting use of the Colorado River in the Grand Canyon National Park had experienced such an increase that it posed a threat to the ecology of the river. A study was initiated for the purpose of ascertaining river capacity and it was decided that until completion of the study use of the river should be frozen at the 1972 level. Accordingly, river use was limited to 96,600 user days per year (a user day being one day spent on the river by one person). This total use was apportioned between two user groups in the ratio of actual 1972 use by each group: 89,000 user days or 92 percent of the total use was allotted to commercial concessioners of the Park Service who, for a fee, make guided trips through the canyon; 7,600 user days or 8 percent of the total was allotted to noncommercial users who apply for permits as private groups. Noncommercial users for the most part are experienced in river running and furnish their own equipment and supplies. Expenses are shared, as is the performance of the necessary duties involved. Permits for river use and the apportionment thereof have remained frozen at the 1972 level.

Appellants are, or represent, noncommercial river runners who, on various grounds, challenge the apportionment between commercial and noncommercial users. They assert that they, or those they represent, have applied for permits from the Park Service which were denied, the Service instead having granted permits to persons who used them for commercial purposes. In January, 1975, a member of Wilderness Public Rights Fund petitioned the Secretary for a change in the allocation system for the issuance of permits. The request was denied.

* * * The Wilderness Public Rights Fund action was brought in the Northern District of California in June, 1976. As relief it sought an injunction staying the issuance of permits for river use to commercial permittees and concessioners "until such time as it can be determined to what extent commercial services are necessary and appropriate." It sought a declaration that noncommercial users are entitled to priority over commercial users.

The Eiseman action was brought in the District of Arizona in March, 1977. It was more modest in its claims and in the relief sought. It did not seek priority for the noncommercial users over the commercial users. It sought equal access to the river and an order directing the Secretary and the Service to implement a plan providing equal access.

In both cases summary judgment in favor of appellees was granted and these appeals followed.

A number of statutes and regulations bear on the issues of these actions. 16 U.S.C.A. § 1 creates the National Park Service (hereinafter NPS) in the Department of the Interior and directs it to "promote and regulate the use of the Federal areas known as national parks, monuments and reservations * * * by such means and measures as conform to the fundamental purpose of said parks, monuments and reservations * * *." That purpose is stated to be "to conserve the scenery and the natural and historic objects and the wild life therein and to provide for the enjoyment of the same in such manner and by such means as will leave them unimpaired for the enjoyment of future generations."

16 U.S.C.A. § 3 provides in part:

"The Secretary of the Interior shall make and publish such rules and regulations as he may deem necessary or proper for the use and management of the parks, monuments, and reservations under the jurisdiction of the National Park Service * * *. He may also grant privileges, leases, and permits for the use of land for the accommodation of visitors in the various parks, monuments or other reservations [herein provided for] but for periods not exceeding thirty years; and no natural curiosities, wonders, or objects of interest shall be leased, rented, or granted to anyone on such terms as to interfere with free access to them by the public * * *."

Pursuant to this authority the Secretary has promulgated 36 C.F.R. § 7.4(h)(3) as follows:

"(3) No person shall conduct, lead, or guide a river trip unless such person possesses a permit issued by the Superintendent, Grand Canyon National Park. The National Park Service reserves the right to limit the number of such permits issued, or the number of persons travelling on trips authorized by such permits when, in the opinion of the National Park Service, such limitations are necessary in the interest of public safety or protection of the ecological and environmental values of the area."

The Concessions Policy Act, 16 U.S.C.A. § 20 provides in part:

"It is the policy of the Congress that such development [concessions] shall be limited to those that are necessary and appropriate for public use and enjoyment of the national park area in which they are located * * *."

Appellants first attack the failure of the NPS to follow the dictates of the Administrative Procedure Act. They contend that the allocation of user days between commercial and noncommercial users amounted to rule making and that no hearings were held where the noncommercial users could present their views, contrary to the requirements of the Administrative Procedure Act.

That Act, 5 U.S.C.A. § 553(a)(2), excepts from the rule-making procedures "a matter relating * * * to public property, loans, grants, benefits or contracts." The government contends that this exempts the action of the Secretary in freezing the 1972 river use and apportioning that use between the commercial and noncommercial users. We agree.

Appellants contend that allocation between commercial and noncommercial use of the river is not an acceptable method of accomplishing a limitation of river use. They propose that anyone wishing to run the river should apply for a permit, leaving to him, if his application be granted, the choice between joining a guided party or a noncommercial party; that permits then be granted by lottery or on a first-come-first-served basis. They assert that the record establishes that such a method is feasible. They contend that there is no justification for allocating between commercial and noncommercial use, and that to do so amounts to arbitrary action; that it denies them "free access" to the river contrary to 16 U.S.C.A. § 3 and permits development by concession to a degree in excess of that allowed by the Concessions Policy Act. We disagree.

The Secretary of the Interior, acting through the NPS, has the wide ranging responsibility of managing the national parks. 16 U.S.C.A. § 3. Pursuant to this authority, the NPS regulates use of the Colorado River through the permit requirement described in 36 C.F.R. § 7.4(h)(3), supra. In issuing permits, the Service has recognized that those who make recreational use of the river fall into two classes: those who have the skills and equipment to run the river without professional guidance and those who do not. The Service recognizes its obligation to protect the interests of both classes of users. It can hardly be faulted for doing so. If the overall use of the river must, for the river's protection, be limited, and if the rights of all are to be recognized, then the "free access" of any user must be limited to the extent necessary to accommodate the access rights of others. We must confine our review of the permit system to the question whether the NPS has acted within its authority and whether the action taken is arbitrary. Allocation of the limited use between the two groups is one method of assuring that the rights of each are recognized and, if fairly done pursuant to appropriate standards, is a reasonable method and cannot be said to be arbitrary. It is well within the area of administrative discretion granted to the NPS.

Throughout these proceedings Wilderness Public Rights Fund has persisted in viewing the dispute as one between the recreational users of the river and the commercial operators, whose use is for profit. It asserts that by giving a firm allocation to the commercial operators to the disadvantage of those who wish to run the river on their own the Service is commercializing the park. The Fund ignores the fact that the commercial operators, as concessioners of the Service, undertake a public function to provide services that the NPS deems desirable for those visiting the area. 16 U.S.C.A. § 20a. The basic face-off is not between the commercial operators and the noncommercial users, but between those who can make the run without professional assistance and those who cannot.

While the Concessions Policy Act, 16 U.S.C.A. § 20, supra, expresses the congressional intent that the granting of concessions shall be limited to "those that are necessary and appropriate for public use and enjoyment" of the park involved, the authority for the granting of concessions is given to the Secretary by 16 U.S.C.A. § 3, and there is no showing here of arbitrary action or abuse of that authority.

Appellants also complain that noncommercial applicants receive unfair and unequal treatment at the hands of the Service. They must apply to the Service for permits and thus must plan their trips well in advance. Deadlines must be met. The names of all in the proposed party (with signatures) must be set forth. Those who make the trip under guide may deal directly with the concessioners and make arrangements at the last minute. This comports with the NPS' right to regulate river trips in the interests of safety. 36 C.F.R. § 7.4(h)(3). We find nothing unreasonable in thus assuring, as matter of safety, that those who make the trip on their own without concessioners' supervision have undertaken the necessary preparation and possess the necessary skill to participate in the activities involved.

We conclude that allocation between the two classes of recreational users is not per se an arbitrary method of recognizing and accommodating the interests of the two classes. The question remaining is whether allocation has been fairly made pursuant to appropriate standards.

* * *

Appellants challenge the method used by the Park Service in determining allocation between the classes of users for the reason that it is founded on 1972 data. It is asserted that since that year there has been a substantial increase in the demand for use by noncommercial users, and that to freeze allocation of use on the basis of seven-year-old data in the face of rapid change is arbitrary and unreasonable.

We are informed, however, that the study initiated by the National Park Service has now been completed and that the interim basis for allocation between the two classes of users—freezing at the 1972 level—is being abandoned. A proposed management plan for the river and a draft environmental impact statement have been completed and published. The allocation departs from the 1972 level of 92 percent user days for commercial operators and 8 percent user days for noncommercial river runners. Under the plan, 70 percent of the user days will be allocated for commercial trips and 30 percent for noncommercial trips. The period assigned for comment has expired and it is anticipated that a final plan will be forthcoming in a matter of weeks.

This renders moot challenges to the specifics of the interim management plan, now about to be superseded by a final plan. The basis for the claim of arbitrariness—that the freezing of use and allocation of use at the 1972 levels is, in 1979, unreasonable—falls from the case.

Judgment affirmed.

NOTES

1. The court did not rule on the split of 92% for commercial uses and 8% for non-commercial. The subject matter of the administrative decision is the kind that courts have generally left to the agencies. But is this specific allocation so extreme that a court should require an especially strong administrative record and a compelling explanation in support of the decision?

2. Where in 16 U.S.C.A. §§ 1 or 3 does the Park Service find authority either to limit the number of ..aft trips or to allocate them between commercial and non-commercial users? Do the new regulations constitute a grant of "natural curiosities on such terms as to interfere with free access * * * by the public" (expressly forbidden by 16 U.S.C.A. § 3)?

3. Isn't "historical use" precisely the evil confronted in the allocation scheme? If so, how can it be a "rational basis" for the resulting allocation? Is there a better basis for allocation? At least in areas of unique or scarce scenic or aesthetic resources, is some sort of rationing system inevitable?

4. The individual river runners are not the only parties dissatisfied with Park Service policy concerning the Grand Canyon rafting. In August 1979 the Professional River Outfitters Association sent a letter, excerpted below, to their clients, (together with a card reading: "If you have no place to float, tie two environmentalists together and jump on their backs."):

YOUR CHANCES FOR A GRAND CANYON RIVER TRIP ARE JUST ABOUT TO BE *CHOPPED IN HALF*

The latest River Management Plan for Grand Canyon would *instantly cut by about 5,000 people* the number who can run the river each summer, and require those who were left to go on longer, more expensive trips (up to 18 days) in small rowboats.

Goodbye to the family river trip vacation. Goodbye to the one-week river trip—if the National Park Service gets this Plan rammed through.

Think about it. The river is the *only* path that goes all the way through the park. The Park Service is supposed to (1) protect it (2) help us enjoy it. Our taxes pay salaries to the same Park Service bureaucrats who are trying to shut us off the river. All they can say is they want everyone to have "a wilderness river running experience". Obviously, *they* presume to decide what that will be, and you're going to get *that* or *nothing at all*.

* * *

THE VACATION YOU SAVE MAY BE YOUR OWN

5.   Compare People ex rel. Younger v. County of El Dorado, 96 Cal. App.3d 403, 157 Cal.Rptr. 815 (1979).   Due to rapidly increasing usage for whitewater rafting and resulting noise, litter, and "unsanitary conditions," the County closed its portion of the south fork of the American River to all uses except swimming.   The appellate court struck down the closure ordinance as unreasonable and because "it denies the constitutional right of the public to use of and access to a navigable stream."   See generally Abrams, Governmental Expansion of Recreational Water Use Opportunities, 59 Or.L.Rev. 159 (1980).

6.   Could the Park Service ban all motorized trips?   All Colorado River trips, commercial or noncommercial?   If such a course were adopted, who would bear what burden of persuasion in a suit brought to lift the ban?   Does the Park Service have a legal obligation to meet recreational demand as best it can?   See also Great American Houseboat Co. v. United States, 780 F.2d 741 (9th Cir.1986) (upholding Forest Service regulation that banned the use of timeshare houseboats on Shasta Lake in Northern California because such ownership was analogous to rentals, and therefore a commercial use, and because the timeshare device would lead to overcrowding on the lake).

7.   For a different "recreational" use of the federal lands, see United States v. Beam, 686 F.2d 252 (5th Cir.1982); the court reversed the conviction of the Grand Dragon of the Texas Ku Klux Klan for conducting military maneuvers on national forest land without a permit.   The court found the agency regulation requiring a written permit for "public meetings, assemblies and special events" not applicable because the KKK activities were not open to the public.

JOSEPH L. SAX, FASHIONING A RECREATION POLICY FOR OUR NATIONAL PARKLANDS: THE PHILOSOPHY OF CHOICE AND THE CHOICE OF PHILOSOPHY *
12 Creighton L.R. 973 (1979).

A few years ago the National Park Service put forward a proposal for one of the less well-known areas that it manages.   It recommended the construction of an aerial tramway to the top of Guadalupe Peak in Guadalupe Mountains National Park, the highest point of elevation in Texas.   The plan seemed harmless enough.   Guadalupe Peak is a place of considerable scenic merit, the park receives very few visitors, and it is located on the much-travelled road from El Paso to Carlsbad Caverns. Yet the tramway proposal elicited a surprisingly substantial and vehement opposition, and the Park Service soon shelved the plan.

The more one thinks about the Guadalupe incident, the more puzzling it becomes. For in one form or another it is repeated almost daily in the management of the public recreation lands. Should we permit the construction of a ski resort in a relatively pristine mountain valley? Should motor boats be permitted on the Colorado River in Grand Canyon? Should hotels be removed from the parks, or should they remain but without such facilities as swimming pools and tennis courts? These are all only particular instances of a general question that is a great deal more puzzling than it at first seems: What recreational policy ought we to want for the National Parks?

It is customary to believe that controversies of the sort just mentioned revolve around disputes over protection of the parks' natural resources, but a moment's reflection makes clear that environmental or scientific principles are rarely decisive. Every human use impairs the natural setting to some extent and whether a tramway impairs it "too much" is a question of policy, not of science. As with the question whether to build a road, to allow the noise of motorboats and snowmobiles, or even to establish a hiking trail, the issue we are really deciding is what kind of recreation we want to facilitate, and how much intrusion upon the untrammeled ecosystem we are prepared to tolerate for that purpose.

To be sure, some uses are far less disruptive than others, but to say that we want to minimize damage is to restate the problem rather than to solve it. Five hundred visitors a year on the river in Grand Canyon would put a great deal less pressure on the canyon ecosystem than 5,000 or the 15,000 whom we now permit to use it, and there is a great range of opinion on the point at which development, or use, becomes a spoiling factor. Some people don't want motors on wild river trips because they drown out the bird-song; others defend such trips as their only reasonable means of access to the place and find a good deal in the experience even at the expense of some quietude.

Just as these questions cannot be resolved as matters of science, neither can they be decided by economics. Should the Guadalupe Peak tramway have been built in response to public demand? The Park Service estimated that with the tramway, visitations to the Park would have increased from about 60,000 to some 500,000 persons per year. Demand is simply a measure of how people are willing to spend their time and money. No doubt many more people would be prepared to ride up Guadalupe Peak than can, or will, walk it. But just as clearly, there are many people who would patronize gambling casinos, race tracks, elegant restaurants or high rise condominia if we were willing to build them in the parks. There is demand, perfectly legitimate it may be assumed, for all these activities. Yet, at least so far, we have been unwilling to meet that demand in the parks.

Another common view is that parks should be reserved for activities that require the special resources parklands uniquely contain, or that cannot be provided by private enterprise. That position seems to explain why we have traditionally resisted building swimming pools, golf courses and tennis courts in the parks, but it does not adequately respond to the individual who aspires to play tennis in the grand setting of Yosemite Valley rather than to hike there. Nor does it explain whether those who like the solitude and silence of the parks should be preferred to those who find pleasure in a motorized, people-filled tramway or safari down the river. To assert that solitude is the essence of the park experience is to state a preference, not a fact. Each of these experiences is unique in its way, and unavailable in the private market.

Nor, finally, can we avoid the problem by asserting that government should simply hold parklands available and permit each of us to decide for ourselves how to enjoy them. This is another way of describing a policy of variety or diversity. But such a policy can only avoid preferences on the assumption of unlimited abundance. If there were many Yosemite Valleys, we could provide the Yosemite experience as everyone, in his own way, chose it. Of course there are not *many* Yosemites; and though the parks are varied enough to accommodate much diversity, someone—and not each visitor for him or herself— must decide what will happen in the one Yosemite Valley, and the one Grand Canyon, that we do have. It is at these special kinds of places that conflict is at its most intense.

Management decisions must perforce be made, and those decisions themselves imprint an agenda on the landscape. * * * To a significant extent, management decisions effectively determine who the visitors will be, what they will do, and in what numbers, by choices that *must* be made, one way or the other.

To say that none of these management theories is decisive is not to suggest any of them is irrelevant. It is only to say that before we can think usefully about how much natural impairment we should tolerate, or where we want to draw the line in meeting demand, we need to decide what we are trying to achieve by having a public recreation policy.

If it were evident to everyone that the National Parks should be used simply to accommodate a portion of the enormous quantity of leisure time that Americans have to spend, a proposal to build a tramway that could increase recreational opportunities nearly ten-fold with a rather modest impact on the land would not have produced anything like the vigorous outcry it actually elicited. Nor would the familiar controversies over motorized recreation, ski resorts and commercial facilities in the parks have anything like the intensity that is now so evident. Beneath the multitude of specific disputes is a much deeper battle over the question whether park policy should reflect a preference for certain kinds of recreational experiences.

Chapter Eleven

THE PRESERVATION RESOURCE

It may seem incongruous to categorize preservation as a resource. Limited use or non-use of a land area, however, has all of the elements of exclusivity that characterize the more traditional resources. A pristine ecosystem is a finite entity that is nonrenewable, at least for generations, if its wilderness qualities are destroyed. While the "outputs" or values of preservation are less susceptible of measurement in economic terms, it is certainly not the least in terms of the value or worth attached to it by contemporary society.

The preservation resource escapes easy definition. To many, it connotes leaving well enough alone; they emphasize the need to protect natural ecosystems from human manipulation and to shield historic artifacts and buildings of particular value from profit-seekers and wrecking balls. To others, the concept is a means by which elitists lock up other resources, putting them off-limits to productive use. No prosaic definition will do. For these purposes, the description in the Wilderness Act is the appropriate starting point: wilderness is "an area where the earth and its community of life are untrammeled by man, where man himself is a visitor who does not remain." 16 U.S.C.A. § 1131(c).

Legally, preservation is accomplished by a setting aside, or, in public land terms, a withdrawal and reservation. The urge to preserve tangible things and areas of historic significance preceded the desire to set aside tracts of scenic, aesthetic, or ecological value. Famous battlegrounds, for instance, have always been of great popular interest. Compare, e.g., United States v. Gettysburg Electric Railway, 160 U.S. 668, (1896), supra at page 135. Yellowstone National Park was the first significant reservation for scenic purposes, but it was to be a "pleasuring ground" rather than a strict preserve. And in fact Yellowstone and the 37 other national parks have been festooned with lodges, shops, sanitary facilities, roads, and other amenities that many claim are antithetical to a "true wilderness experience." Nevertheless, the National Park System still encompasses some of the most spectacularly pristine country in the Nation; large amounts of land within the park system have been formally declared as wilderness and much of the remainder is managed primarily for maintenance of an essentially wilderness character.

Preservation of national parks and monuments involves protection from people. In the first section following, the questions revolve around the authority of Park Service managers to preserve the historic and archeological treasures of their lands and to combat external threats to the scenic and ecological integrity of Park System units. Section B sketches some highlights of river preservation, a matter of intense popular concern since before Mr. Justice Holmes noted that our rivers are treasures, not mere amenities. The final section in this chapter examines the designation and management of official wilderness areas created pursuant to the mandate of the Wilderness Act of 1964, 16 U.S.C.A. §§ 1131–36. It established the growing National Wilderness Preservation System, now the pinnacle of the movement for official preservation of natural systems and wonders in the United States and, indeed, in the world. "While the American conception of wilderness has almost always been a compound of attraction and repulsion, the relative strengths of these attitudes, both in single minds and in the national opinion, have not remained constant. Appreciation * * * [has grown] from an esoteric and eccentric notion into a broad public sentiment capable of influencing national policy and securing statutory protection for wild country." R. Nash, WILDERNESS AND THE AMERICAN MIND (3rd ed. 1982).

This chapter is limited to wilderness, rivers, monuments, and parks, but the move toward preservation also encompasses such diverse public lands as wildlife study areas, old-growth forests, and urban parks. The quickening of the trend toward preservation raises fundamental societal questions. Is the protection of natural resources undertaken at the expense of more crucial economic needs, or does preservation constitute, in effect, wise multiple use management of those resources? Should preservation be pursued for ecological reasons alone, or should it be promised on anthropocentric considerations, since wilderness can be, in the words of the late Supreme Court Justice William O. Douglas, "one pledge to freedom"? See also J. Sax, MOUNTAINS WITHOUT HANDRAILS (1981), supra at page 44. These broader philosophical issues have influenced past policy and are likely to be integral to future decisions concerning which resources should be preserved and how they should be managed once they are preserved.

A. PARKS AND MONUMENTS PRESERVATION

1. HISTORICAL ARTIFACTS

America's historical and archeological sites, many on public lands, constitute a resource deemed nationally important. In 1906, Congress enacted the Antiquities Act, 16 U.S.C.A. §§ 431–33. The first section authorized the withdrawal and reservation of lands containing objects or values of historic, scientific, or scenic significance as national monuments. See, e.g., Alaska v. Carter, 462 F.Supp. 1155 (D.Alaska 1978), supra at page 251. The second section was intended to halt commercial exploitation of cultural and historic objects on the public lands. See Collins & Green, A Proposal to Modernize the American Antiquities Act, 202 Science 1055 (Dec.1978):

> * * * Since the 1890's there had been great public interest in the art and history of the Indians of the southwestern United States, and this interest had created a great demand for authentic prehistoric artifacts. As a result, ruins

and cliff dwellings, such as Casa Grande, Mesa Verde, and Chaco Canyon, were indiscriminately excavated and vandalized. There were no state and federal laws that provided for the protection of prehistoric sites, and there were few professional archaelogists. Thus, the need for protective legislation was particularly acute when the Antiquities Act was passed in 1906.

The act, which was codified in section 433, title 16 of the U.S. Code, prohibited the appropriating, excavating, injuring, or destroying of any "historic or prehistoric ruin or monument" or "object of antiquity" found on government-owned or -controlled land, without the permission of the secretary of the department of the government having jurisdiction over the land. * * *

Enforcement problems hobbled the effectiveness of the Antiquities Act. The possibility of a maximum fine of $500 was not much more than a cost of doing business for violators taking artifacts often worth thousands of dollars. Further, the 1906 Act imposed penalties only on appropriators, not on dealers or other purchasers. Worse yet, although the Tenth Circuit upheld the constitutionality of the statute in United States v. Smyer, 596 F.2d 939 (10th Cir.1979), the Ninth Circuit—the other major circuit in terms of artifact finds on federal and Indian lands—struck down the Act's definition of "object of antiquity" as unconstitutionally vague. See United States v. Diaz, 499 F.2d 113 (9th Cir.1974).

Many of the enforcement difficulties experienced under the 1906 Antiquities Act were ameliorated by passage of the Archaeological Resources Protection Act of 1979 (ARPA), 16 U.S.C.A. §§ 470aa–470ll. In general, Congress ordained that no one may excavate, remove, or damage archaelogical resources on public or Indian lands without a permit. ARPA also prohibits trafficking in illegally acquired artifacts. The Act and its background are analyzed in Northey, The Archaeological Resources Protection Act of 1979: Protecting Prehistory for the Future, 6 Harv.Envtl.L.Rev. 61 (1982), and Rosenberg, Federal Protection for Archaeological Resources, 22 Ariz.L.Rev. 701 (1980). See generally Symposium, Legal Protection of America's Archaeological Heritage, 22 Ariz.L.Rev. 675 (1980). Northey, supra, concluded:

ARPA offers greater protection for archaeological resources on public lands than did prior federal law. ARPA's definition of "archaeological resource" includes a wide range of artifactual, contextual, and environmental information and can expand as archaeologists begin to use new types of information. ARPA's enforcement provisions give federal land managers the tools necessary to curtail commercial looting of archaeological sites and trading in illegally obtained archaeological resources.

In addition to providing increased protection, ARPA clarifies federal policy concerning the development of archaeological resources and establishes, in conjunction with other federal laws, a comprehensive program for the management of the remaining archaelogical resources on public lands and Indian lands. ARPA give the federal land managers considerable discretion to deny permits if development is inconsistent with land management plans or if conservation is more appropriate. ARPA leaves the resolution of conflicts with natural resource development to other federal laws; implicitly, ARPA says that the public interest in such cases requires preservation only of "archaeologically significant" resources. ARPA also contains the first statutory recognition of Indian religious and cultural interests in archaeological resources and offers them a greater role in archaeological resource management, particularly on Indian lands.

* * *

Congress' desire to protect treasure hunters and recreational users of public lands from unreasonable civil or criminal penalties has also resulted in several significant exceptions to ARPA. For example, the exemption provided to collectors of arrowheads found on the ground surface unduly restricts the Act's protection. There is no reason to give collectors of arrowheads greater protection than persons who destroy other resources, such as shell mounds, that are less clearly of archaeological interest. * * *

Congress did not want to subject mineral resource development, reclamation, and other multiple uses of public lands and Indian lands to additional permit requirements and therefore exempted these activities from ARPA. This exemption ultimately reduces the protection of both "insignificant" and significant archaeological resources. Congress could accomplish its objective by providing that these activities are conducted in compliance with a constructive ARPA permit as long as they are conducted in compliance with other federal laws. This would allow the federal land managers to use ARPA's criminal or civil penalty provisions to protect archaeological resources from destruction by developers.

* * *

Archaeological resources are valuable, vanishing, and nonrenewable. ARPA is a significant step toward halting unnecessary destruction of these resources and ensuring their rational development. The effort must not end here, however. Congress should amend the Act to eliminate unnecessary loopholes. The federal agencies should carefully draft regulations to provide the comprehensive protection for archaeological resources which Congress intended. The federal land managers should comply with the permit provisions of the Act and the regulations, give adequate consideration in the permit process to the interests of Native Americans and other concerned parties, and require conservation where appropriate.

Environmentalists and other citizens can, of course, contribute by reporting any illegal removal, damage, or destruction of archaeological resources on public lands and Indian lands. With such efforts, archaeological resources can be preserved for both the present and the future.

As to the legality of trade in wildlife artifacts, see Andrus v. Allard, 444 U.S. 51 (1979); United States v. Richards, 583 F.2d 491 (10th Cir. 1978); Delbay Pharmaceuticals, Inc. v. Department of Commerce, 409 F.Supp. 637 (D.D.C.1976).

By the Historic Sites Act of 1935, 16 U.S.C.A. §§ 461–70t, the Secretary of Interior was given the responsibility to implement "a national policy to preserve for public use historic sites, buildings, and objects of national significance for the inspiration and benefit of the people of the United States." Id. § 461. The Act requires salvage operations, at a minimum, whenever qualifying historical and archaeological resources are threatened by federal dams or by any alteration of the terrain caused as a result of any federal construction project or federally licensed activity or program. Id. § 469. Sections 469a–1 and 469a–2 extend the survey-evaluation-recovery program to all federal activities but impose few substantive constraints. See Barnidge v. United States, 101 F.2d 295 (8th Cir.1939) (Act confers right of condemnation); Aluli v. Brown, 437 F.Supp. 602 (D.Hawaii 1977); cf. Paulina Lake Historic Cabin Owners Ass'n. v. United States Department of Agriculture Forest Service, 577 F.Supp. 1188 (D.Or.1983).

2. EXTERNAL THREATS

In chapter ten, some internal threats to the "naturalness" of parks and monuments were considered, notably the plethora of human facilities at Yosemite and the overabundance of rafters in Grand Canyon. Control of human numbers, and limits on facilities for their convenience, are both means of keeping the Park Service's preservation mandate by avoiding overuse. Compare Wood, Pinchot and Mather, supra at page 141. The Park Service has adequate authority to deal with such internal problems, although its political base for doing so is frequently in question. In 1953, Bernard De Voto caustically described a situation many would claim still exists. De Voto, Let's Close the National Parks, Harper's 49, 51–52 (Oct., 1953):

So are the parks and national monuments themselves [beginning to erode away]. The deterioration of roads and plant that began with the war years, when proper maintenance was impossible, has been accelerated by the enormous increase in visitors, by the shrinkage of staffs, and by miserly appropriations that have prevented both repair and expansion of facilities. The [Park] Service is like a favorite figure of American legendry, the widow who scrapes and patches and ekes out, who by desperate expedients succeeds in bringing up her children to be a credit to our culture. (The boys work the graveyard shift in the mills; the girls' underwear is made of flour sacking.) Its general efficiency, the astonishingly good condition of its areas, its success at improvising and patching up is just short of miraculous. But it stops there, short of the necessary miracle. Congress did not provide money to rehabilitate the parks at the end of the war, it has not provided money to meet the enormously increased demand. So much of the priceless heritage which the Service must safeguard for the United States is beginning to go to hell.

*   *   *

The crisis is now in sight. Homeopathic measures will no longer suffice; thirty cents here and a dollar-seventy-five there will no longer keep the national park system in operation. I estimate that an appropriation of two hundred and fifty million dollars, backed by another one to provide the enlarged staff of experts required to expend it properly in no more than five years, would restore the parks to what they were in 1940 and provide proper facilities and equipment to take care of the crowds and problems of 1953. After that we could take action on behalf of the expanding future—and save from destruction the most majestic scenery in the United States, and the most important field areas of archeology, history, and biological science.

No such sums will be appropriated. Therefore only one course seems possible. The national park system must be temporarily reduced to a size for which Congress is willing to pay. Let us, as a beginning, close Yellowstone, Yosemite, Rocky Mountain, and Grand Canyon National Parks—close and seal them, assign the Army to patrol them, and so hold them secure till they can be reopened. They have the largest staffs in the system but neither those staffs nor the budgets allotted them are large enough to maintain the areas at a proper level of safety, attractiveness, comfort, or efficiency. They are unable to do the job in full and so it had better not be attempted at all. If these staffs—and their respective budgets—were distributed among other areas, perhaps the Service could meet the demands now put on it. If not, additional areas could be temporarily closed and sealed, held in trust for a more enlightened future—say Zion, Big Bend, Great Smoky, Shenandoah, Everglades, and Gettysburg. Meanwhile letters from constituents unable to visit Old Faithful, Half Dome, the Great White Throne, and Bright Angel Trail would bring a nationally disgraceful situation to the really serious attention of the Congress which is responsible for it.

Compare Futrell, Parks to the People, supra at page 895. An equally serious threat to the natural, historic, and aesthetic values of the parks and monuments may be private and public activities conducted outside park boundaries. The following case involved a challenge to the effects of one of the major water impoundments in the West.

FRIENDS OF THE EARTH v. ARMSTRONG
United States Court of Appeals, Tenth Circuit, 1973.
485 F.2d 1.
Cert. denied, 414 U.S. 1171 (1974).

SETH, Circuit Judge.

* * * The plaintiffs seek to have * * * [the Secretary of Interior] take such action as may be necessary to prevent the water being impounded in Lake Powell from spreading into any part of Rainbow Bridge National Monument.

* * *

The trial court, 360 F.Supp. 165 entered a judgment and decree granting plaintiffs' motion for summary judgment. This decree ordered the defendant officials to take action to have the waters from Lake Powell withdrawn from within the boundaries of Rainbow Bridge National Monument, and to prevent in the future such encroachment.

* * *

This case reaches us on the issue of whether or not the trial court was correct in holding that certain provisions of the Colorado River Storage Project Act of 1956 (43 U.S.C.A. § 620), and especially sections 1 and 3 thereof prohibit any water from Lake Powell entering any part of the Rainbow Bridge National Monument.

The record shows that the water enters the Monument when the water level in Lake Powell reaches 3,606 feet above mean sea level. The plaintiffs did not assert a claim based upon the possibility of physical damage to the Rainbow Bridge itself, but relied upon the statutory provisions in the Colorado River Storage Project Act.

We must conclude that the trial court was in error, and the case must be reversed.

Rainbow Bridge National Monument:

This Monument was created by Presidential Proclamation in 1910, and is a square tract of 160 acres in the southernmost portion of Utah between the Colorado River Canyon and the Arizona state line. The Monument has been visited by few people in past years because of its isolated location. It is a very important Monument and contains a unique work of nature. Rainbow Bridge itself is an impressive natural sandstone arch of great size extending across the inner gorge or cut of Bridge Creek within a larger canyon. Within and under the span, the inner gorge of Bridge Creek is seventy to seventy-five feet deep and extends below the lower base or abutment of the arch. It has steep, rocky, shelving, sandstone sides. Bridge Creek is an intermittent stream which flows into Lake Powell, the reservoir created by Glen Canyon Dam.

* * *

As the level of Lake Powell rises, the water, of course, backs up the side canyons including that of Bridge Creek. When the water level in the Lake reaches 3,606 feet above mean sea level, the reservoir water has moved up the bed of Bridge Creek to a point at the outer boundary of the 160-acre tract of land comprising Rainbow Bridge National Monument. At any higher level the water enters the Monument within the creek bed at the bottom of the deep Bridge Canyon. When the water level of Lake Powell reaches the level of 3,700 feet above sea level, which is the maximum design capacity for Glen Canyon Dam, the reservoir water will be standing in the inner gorge of the creek under the Rainbow Bridge Arch. At this level the water will there have a depth of about forty-eight feet, but will not rise enough to get out of the gorge or to reach the base of the Rainbow Bridge Arch since this point is some twenty-five feet above that level. The water, however, would then be well within the boundaries of the Monument although confined in the inner gorge of the creek.

As indicated, the water level is subject to frequent and wide variations. This results in an unsightly deposition of sediments and debris, as well as a conspicuous staining of the rocks at the various water levels all through the reservoir area.

The waters from Lake Powell first entered the outer boundaries of the Monument in May 1971, and withdrew as the Lake level dropped but again entered one or more times.

Glen Canyon Dam:

This Dam is on the Colorado River near the Arizona-Utah boundary and was built in the period 1957 to 1964. The Dam has a maximum design capacity at 3,700 feet above sea level.

* * *

The power facilities at the Dam are designed to generate a large amount of electricity to provide additional power to the Southwest, and to the Pacific Coast. * * *

* * *

The Statutes:

With the basic division of the Colorado River water agreed upon [among the Upper Basin and Lower Basin states], the planned development of the Colorado River Basin proceeded. In 1956 Congress passed the comprehensive Colorado River Storage Act (43 U.S.C.A. § 620 et seq.). * * * The Act authorized the Secretary of the Interior to construct and operate the initial units of the storage project consisting of Curecanti, Flaming Gorge, Navajo Dam, and Glen Canyon.

* * *

As part of the Storage Act, Congress included the two following provisions which are in issue here. The record shows this was done in response to the objections made by some conservation groups. Thus Congress in the Storage Act (43 U.S.C.A. § 620) included a proviso in section 1:

> "That as part of the Glen Canyon Unit the Secretary of the Interior shall take adequate protective measures to preclude impairment of the Rainbow Bridge National Monument."

* * *

* * * As construction of Glen Canyon Project proceeded, Congress passed annually the appropriation acts for construction of Glen Canyon Dam itself. These will be hereinafter considered, and are of great significance to the issues raised.

In 1968 Congress passed the Colorado River Basin Project Act (43 U.S.C.A. § 1501 et seq.). This was to further carry out the Colorado River water development. This Act is significant here because it was considered after Glen Canyon Dam was completed. In the Colorado River Basin Project Act at 43 U.S.C.A. § 1521(a), provision having been made for construction of the Central Arizona Project in the Lower Basin, it was provided that the full capacity of the aqueduct supplying water to this project could not be used unless Lake Powell was full or releases are made from Lake Powell to prevent the reservoir from exceeding the elevation of 3,700 feet or when water is released pursuant to other provisions of the Act.

* * *

From the above description of the legislation, it is apparent that Lake Powell is an important element or link in the Colorado River water and power development. It cannot be considered alone as all the existing projects in the Upper Basin, and the planned ones, are interrelated and interdependent. The projects have different purposes and functions, but are dependent on Lake Powell to provide basic storage necessary to fulfill the delivery requirements to the downstream states and Mexico, especially in dry years. * * * This interrelation created by the comprehensive plan for development is rather delicate and can be disturbed if the capacity of by far the largest storage or regulating unit is reduced significantly. The total development plan was given extensive consideration by water experts and by Congress.

* * *

Action by Congress Following The Storage Act:

The provisions contained in the Colorado River Storage Act (43 U.S.C.A. § 620 et seq.) quoted above which direct the Secretary to take protective measures as to Rainbow Bridge National Monument could not be a more specific reference. It is clearly and solely directed to the extension of Lake Powell water into the Monument. * * * With the inclusion of this provision, with additions to section 3, and with the elimination of the Echo Park Project, the conservation groups, or some of them, apparently withdrew their objections to the Act.

[Section 3 of the Storage Act] reads:

> "It is the intention of Congress that no dam or reservoir constructed under the authorization of this Act shall be within any national park or monument."

This reference is general and all-inclusive as contrasted to the section 1 reference to Rainbow Bridge National Monument. This is a clear and direct expression of the intent of Congress, but is made in the absence of any direct prohibition or affirmative directive. This is again in contrast with section 1; however, we do not consider this factor to be of particular significance, and will assume the section 3 language to be a direct prohibition directed to the appropriate officials.

* * * It was apparent, and it was discussed, that water would be in the Monument at the designed level [of 3700 feet above sea level]. Thus it was obvious from the start that water would be backed up into the Monument if nothing further were done. Of course, the record shows that nothing further was done, and the water has so entered the outer boundaries of the Monument.

The action taken by Congress after passage of the Storage Act demonstrates a repeal of sections 1 and 3 thereof. The record shows that in 1960, in reference to the 1961 Public Works Appropriation Bill, House Report No. 1634 (86th Cong.2d Sess.), the budget estimate for Glen Canyon Unit was reduced by $3,500,000. The House Committee Report stated in part:

> "Glen Canyon Unit—An appropriation of $23,535,000 is recommended, a reduction of $3,500,000 in the budget estimate of $27,035,000. * * * *The geological examination report on the problem indicates clearly that there will be no structural damage to Rainbow Bridge by the reservoir waters beneath it.* The Committee sees no purpose in undertaking an additional expenditure in the vicinity of $20,000,000, in order to build the complicated structures necessary to provide the protection contemplated." (Emphasis added).

The $3,500,000 was the request by the Commissioner to begin the protective works for the Monument.

The Senate Committee, on the same Appropriation Act, reached the same conclusion (S.Report No. 1763, 86th Cong.2d Sess.).

* * *

The matter was again considered during the hearings and in the reports for the 1962 Public Works Appropriation Act (see 87th Cong. 1st Sess., House Report No. 1125, and Senate Report No. 1097). Requested funds for protective works were again disallowed. The Senate Report No. 1097 explained why—that no damage would result and the costs were too great.

In the 1962 Appropriation Act, this proviso was inserted:

> "Provided, That no part of the funds herein appropriated shall be available for construction or operation of facilities to prevent waters of Lake Powell from entering any National Monument."

Thus the funds specifically requested for protective works by the Commissioner were again disallowed, and of greater significance, the express prohibition as to use of funds was thus added. At hearings again the matter was fully considered.

* * *

* * * [A]ll subsequent Appropriation Acts for public works to 1973 carry the same prohibition quoted above. Thus the proviso appeared in some twelve separate Acts, and was considered and enacted during virtually all stages of construction of Glen Canyon Dam and thereafter.

* * *

The record thus demonstrates affirmatively that Congress evaluated the consequences of water encroachment into Rainbow Bridge National Monument, and the difficulty, unsightliness of the protective dam, pumps, and tunnel, and the costs, and made a choice. The resultant specific prohibition as to the use of funds for protective works in the face of the inevitable water advance in the streambed under the Bridge has overridden the expression of intent in section 3 of the Storage Act as to Rainbow Bridge, and has overridden the specific reference to Rainbow Bridge in section 1 thereof. This indicates that Congress reached the decision not to modify the planned operation of the Glen Canyon Dam nor to authorize protective works to be built.

* * *

The Authorities:

* * *

Appropriation acts are just as effective a way to legislate as are ordinary bills relating to a particular subject. An appropriation act may be used to suspend or to modify prior Acts of Congress. * * * This is thus not really a situation of repeal by implication as in Posadas v. National City Bank, 296 U.S. 497, but more a reversal of a previous position after considering it fully in the public hearings and after the members apparently came to the conclusion that the protective works would be more detrimental than the presence of water in the Monument. The committee reports indicate it was concluded there would be no physical damage to the Rainbow Bridge itself. This "repeal," if it should be called that, thus was straightforward, direct, and after hearings on the subject.

* * *

The plaintiffs argue that the Dam and the Lake should be operated by the Bureau of Reclamation at a reduced level, and the Lake not be filled at any time above the 3,606 foot level. This is basically what the trial court directed. * * *

The data in the record shows that at a level of 3,700 feet above sea level the *total* storage is about 27,000,000 acre feet and with an *active* capacity somewhat less. With the water level at 3,606 feet, the *total* storage is 14,749,000 acre feet with active storage again at a lesser figure. The affidavits in the record show that this large reduction in storage will substantially reduce the amount of water available to each of the Upper Basin states, and will impair the operation of many facilities already constructed and perhaps prevent use of some entirely. It will also make many more in the planning stage impracticable. This results not only from the lack of water storage to meet downriver obligations, but also from the resulting decline in power revenues.

* * *

[Vacated and Remanded.]

McWILLIAMS, Circuit Judge (concurring in part and dissenting in part).

* * *

WILLIAM E. DOYLE, Circuit Judge, (concurring).

* * *

It is to be emphasized that Rainbow Bridge is not in peril, and we will cross that bridge if and when that problem arises. Plaintiffs do not contend that the Bridge will even get wet. Their objection is to the presence of water in Bridge Creek which is in the gorge in the center of the Monument area—far from the Bridge. We are not unsympathetic to their concern because the water makes the area more accessible and interferes with full aesthetic enjoyment of the Monument area. That fact does not, of course, empower us to grant the relief. We must follow the law.

LEWIS, Chief Judge, with whom HILL, Circuit Judge, joins, dissenting:

* * * To reach this result the majority must and does hold that sections 1 and 3 of the Colorado River Storage Act of 1956 (43 U.S.C.A. § 620, et seq., Public Law 485, 84 Cong.2d Sess.) have been repealed by implication or so modified as to be impotent under the express wording of the statutes as they still exist in the law. But however viewed I consider the action of the majority to be a deep trespass upon the prerogatives of Congress and a clear and dangerous violation of the doctrine of separation of powers.

* * *

In simple summation the court has done that which the Congress has many times refused to do and has, to all practical effect, enacted legislation which is actually pending before Congress for its consideration. Such judicial action is unprecedented and while the decision may be heralded by some as a good pragmatic solution to a difficult and controversial problem this is not a judicial prerogative. Current events in other unrelated fields indicate that more problems are created than solved by a softening of the basic concept of a firm and strict application of the doctrine of separation of powers.

I would affirm.

NOTES

1. Did the Tenth Circuit hold that an act of Congress was repealed because of subsequent congressional inaction? If so, the holding is probably unique. How does the court's premise that an act of Congress may be suspended or modified by a subsequent appropriations act square with the Supreme Court's recent reliance, in TVA v. Hill, 437 U.S. 153 (1978), supra at page 785, on the rule against repeal by implication, especially when the alleged repeal rests on an appropriations act? Is the appropriations record here so extensive and specific that a court ought to depart from the normal rule against repeals in appropriations measures?

2. The Tenth Circuit devoted much attention in its recitation of facts to the role of Lake Powell in power development of the Colorado River. Was the court weighing the value of Rainbow Bridge in its original and undisturbed setting against the value of Lake Powell filled to capacity? Is it inappropriate, as asserted by the dissent, for a court to undertake such balancing? Had Congress already done so when it included sections 1 and 3 in the Storage Act? See Comment, Friends of the Earth v. Armstrong—Water Under the Bridge, 1973 Utah L.Rev. 808. The "legislative remand" that would have resulted from affirmance was considered in J. Sax, DEFENDING THE ENVIRONMENT 175–93 (1970).

3. As to the court's finding (or judicial notice?) that "all of the existing projects in the Upper Basin * * * are interrelated and interdependent," compare Sierra Club v. Stamm, 507 F.2d 788 (10th Cir.1974), where the same court upheld a finding that an aqueduct and collection system possessed independent utility and could be treated in an environmental impact statement separate from the larger water project of which it was an integral component.

4. The Park Service was not a party in *Rainbow Bridge,* although in other cases it has requested the Justice Department to bring suit to protect Park Service lands. In Cappaert v. United States, 426 U.S. 128 (1976), for instance, the United States successfully sued private parties who were pumping groundwater to the detriment of a rare fish in Devil's Hole National Monument. Sometimes, however, there is disagreement among federal agencies. In a few resource cases, the Justice Department has represented one agency but has advised the court of the views of the dissenting agency by means of a "split brief." In *Rainbow Bridge,* the "client" of the Justice Department was the Bureau of Reclamation. Should the Park Service, if it disagreed with the flooding of the Monument, have requested the Secretary of Interior and Justice to file a split brief setting out the Park Service's views? Is the Secretary a "public trustee" of Rainbow Bridge?

5. The Tenth Circuit held the Secretary of the Interior's duty to prevent waters from entering the monument had been suspended by congressional inaction, but, in a part of the opinion not reproduced above, the court still directed the trial court to retain jurisdiction for ten years in case waters did threaten structural damage to the arch. Is the remedy consistent with the holding? Is the Secretary any longer under a legal obligation to protect the arch at all?

6. The Rainbow Bridge case involved conflicting federal programs and priorities. Even more serious external threats to park preservation arise from private activities on adjacent lands. The Park Service traditionally had entertained doubts about the constitutional power of the federal government to regulate lands near and within the parks, see Sax, Helpless Giants: The National Parks and the Regulation of Private Lands, 75 Mich.L.Rev. 239 (1976), but most of those issues have been laid to rest by Kleppe v. New Mexico, 426 U.S. 529 (1976), supra at page 194, and Minnesota v. Block, 660 F.2d 1240 (9th Cir.1981), supra at

page 203. Whether the Park Service has delegated authority to abate the increasing instances of threats from private development, however, remains unresolved.

ROBERT B. KEITER, ON PROTECTING THE NATIONAL PARKS FROM THE EXTERNAL THREATS DILEMMA *
XX Land & Water L.Rev. 355 (1985).

The 1980 report to Congress entitled the *State of the Parks* identified myriad "threats" that endangered the natural and cultural resources of the parks. While the report covered both internal and external threats to park resources, over fifty percent of the threats were traced to sources located outside of the parks. * * *

In the face of these threats, the national parks are not entirely defenseless. * * * The Organic Act provides the Park Service with the legal authority to deal with problems internal to the parks, such as overcrowding, resource destruction, and vehicle use. The Act apparently also imposes the legal responsibility on the Park Service to protect the parks from threatening external activities.

The Park Service, however, is generally unable to regulate or to control effectively activities or developments originating on federal, state or private lands located outside park boundaries. The Park Service cannot claim jurisdiction over these adjacent lands since they are not part of the parks. Nevertheless, the Park Service cannot ignore developments outside the parks in view of the threat posed to park resources and the preservation mandate of the Organic Act. Although park officials can rely upon existing federal and state environmental control legislation to challenge external activities or to influence the decision-making processes of coordinate federal agencies and local governments, these statutes often fail to protect park resources meaningfully. Most of them only establish general standards governing environmental quality and land use decisions without regard for the unique status of the national parks. Moreover, much of the federal legislation only applies when external threats originate on public lands; it has no application when these threats are traced to activities on private lands.

In several respects the present external threats problem mirrors the age-old debate over preserving versus utilizing public and private lands. Having created the national parks largely to preserve and protect the nation's unique natural resources from early settlement and exploitation, Congress now faces the issue of whether to protect the parks from developments on adjacent lands which could cause significant damage to park resources. Congress has already committed itself to the national parks by creating and expanding the park system, and there are indications that it is inclined to honor this commitment. The House of Representatives has twice passed a "Parks Protection Act" by

* Reprinted with permission of the Land
& Water Law Review.

a wide margin,[6] but the Senate has been less favorably disposed to the legislation. The question necessarily arises then as to the best approach to protect the national parks from external threats.

* * *

By the mid-twentieth century, with increased population growth and expanded resource and energy demands, it was inevitable that the parks would begin to feel the pressure of incompatible external activities. At about the same time that visitor use of parks surged dramatically, the Park Service also began experiencing added problems traceable to human activity outside park boundaries. Early external threats which attracted national attention included upstream logging activities on lands adjacent to Redwood National Park and the construction and operation of large coal-fired power plants near several southwestern parks. The more recent energy crises have slowed visitor pressures on the parks, but ironically the energy crises have also been responsible for even more external pressures. For example, the search for coal, oil and gas reserves has led to exploratory seismic and drilling activities on the borders of Glacier National Park and a proposed open pit mine next to Bryce Canyon National Park. Plans have also been prepared to develop geothermal energy sources on the border of Yellowstone National Park, and the lands immediately adjacent to Canyonlands National Park are being considered as a site for the long term storage of nuclear waste materials.

* * *

* * * The studies reveal that park managers are widely concerned about non-park activities which threaten air and water quality, wildlife and fish resources, and the general aesthetic quality of the parklands. The surveys also indicate that the parks are most usually threatened by adjacent activities such as: residential, commercial, industrial, and road development; logging, mining, and agriculture; energy extraction and production; and recreation. Both reports conclude that existing laws do not adequately protect park resources against continued degradation from external threats.

* * *

The number of reported threats ranged from zero in some of the smaller Park Service units to sixty-four in the Chattahoochee River National Recreation Area, a recently established unit located near Atlanta. Park administrators reported a systemwide average of 13.6 threats per park. Among the large national parks exceeding 30,000 acres in size, an average of 24.5 threats per park were reported. Significantly, the twelve national parks which constitute the United States component of the International Biosphere Reserves program— natural areas dedicated to long term ecosystem protection and monitoring—reported an average exceeding thirty-six threats per park. As noted in the Report, this constitutes almost three times the average number of threats faced by park units and should be cause for some

6. H.R. 2379, 98th Cong., 1st Sess. (1983); H.R. 5162, 97th Cong., 2d Sess. (1982). * * *

concern. Since the unique status of the Biosphere Reserves generally means that they are more closely monitored than other park units, the threat assessment in these parks is a more accurate reflection of present realities than the assessments obtained from other park units.

* * *

* * * [T]he Report reveals that America's largest national parks—"the crown jewels" of the system—face substantial problems which were largely undreamed of a generation ago. Among these parks, the Report ranks Glacier National Park as the most threatened park. * * *

* * * *

Since the external threats problem is endemic to the entire national park system, one approach Congress can follow is to devise a comprehensive solution that could be implemented systemwide. In the past Congress has adopted this strategy in responding to the parks' concessions problems and the threat of mining in the parks. The proposed Parks Protection Act similarly seeks to implement a systemwide solution to the external threats problem.

The external threats problem, however, may defy such a comprehensive approach. The national parks are amazingly diverse, and the nature and degree of external threats vary widely from park to park. The large, wilderness-like parks with ecosystems substantially intact generally face problems similar to those experienced by Glacier National Park. While external developments on nearby public and private lands threaten specific park resources, the cumulative effect of these activities severely threatens these parks' ecosystems. On the other hand, the smaller, non-wilderness parks, such as the national monuments and historic sites, are much less likely to be defined by ecosystem characteristics, and their concern usually is with controlling external activities that threaten to degrade the park's particular attractions. Congress can reasonably take some account of these and other notable differences among the parks in framing a response to the external threats problem. * * *

* * *

[T]he proposed Parks Protection Act adopted three basic approaches to the "threats" problem. It established a comprehensive parks management program which required park officials to study, document and report on park resources and threats to them. It created a federal agency review program that mandated Interior Department review of federal agency actions that might threaten park resources, and the bill required park officials to work cooperatively with federal, state and local officials responsible for managing lands surrounding the national parks.

* * *

There also is another approach to the external threats problem that would substantially protect selected parks, and that might be adopted alone or in conjunction with one of the proposed statutory schemes. Under this approach Congress should create a national resource area land management program to administer federal lands located adjacent to designated national parks and encompassed within the park's ecosystem boundaries. This would protect selected parks against incompatible activities traceable to these federal lands. Congress also should combine the national resource area approach with meaningful federal spending limitations keyed to insuring consistency in federal policy respecting the encompassed state and private lands. In particular, Congress should condition grants to the states under the Land and Water Conservation Fund Act upon a state's willingness to establish land-use policies protective of national park resources. Although this approach does not present a plausible systemwide solution for the parks' problems, it provides meaningful protection once Congress has been persuaded to act, and it does so without administrative restructuring or drastic displacement of state prerogatives.

* * *

NOTES

1. Does the Park Service already have sufficient authority under the National Park Service Organic Act of 1916, 16 ·U.S.C.A. § 1, to regulate inholdings? To regulate activities on adjacent lands? Compare the Forest Service's regulatory power under its 1897 Organic Act, 16 U.S.C.A. § 551. As a matter of policy, how broad should the Park Service's authority be? What should a Parks Protection Act provide?

2. In a controversy involving the construction of a sight-seeing tower overlooking the Gettysburg Battlefield, the Park Service was advised that it had no legal authority to prevent construction on private land. It instead negotiated an agreement with the private entrepreneur by which the tower would be located on a different tract of private property where it would supposedly have less adverse scenic impact on the battlefield. The Commonwealth of Pennsylvania then sued to block construction of the tower, relying on a provision of the state constitution establishing a public right to "the preservation of the natural, scenic, historic, and esthetic values of the environment." The Court denied injunctive relief for failure to show that the 307-foot tower would injure such values. Commonwealth v. National Gettysburg Battlefield Tower, Inc., 454 Pa. 193, 311 A.2d 588 (1973).

3. Another such conflict involved the construction of a nuclear plant on utility-owned land abutting the Indiana Dunes National Lakeshore; the plant location was opposed by the State of Illinois, the City of Gary, Indiana, and private organizations. The Seventh Circuit rejected plaintiffs' argument that the Atomic Energy Commission lacked jurisdiction to approve a site encroaching on national lakeshore administered by Interior. Porter County Chapter of Izaak Walton League of America, Inc. v. AEC, 515 F.2d 513 (7th Cir.1975). The Court did set aside AEC issuance of a construction permit on other grounds, but was subsequently reversed by the Supreme Court. Northern Indiana Public Serv. Co. v. Porter County Chapter of Izaak Walton League of America, Inc., 423 U.S. 12 (1975).

The Department of Interior did not appear in the *Indiana Dunes* litigation but it did take several steps to protect the facility. First, though it did not intervene in the AEC proceedings, it did testify on possible impacts to the Lakeshore. Second, when water seepage from ash ponds at the coal-fired plant was found to effect the Lakeshore, a mitigation agreement was negotiated with the company. Finally, when construction at the nuclear plant was found to cause dewatering within the Lakeshore, the Park Service urged the NRC to act and mitigation was ordered by the NRC.

4. There have been other attempts, not always successful, to eliminate "aesthetic nuisance" adjacent to units of the Park System. See, e.g., United States v. Arlington County, 487 F.Supp. 137 (E.D.Va. 1979) (Arlington Tower). Cf. New Jersey Builders Ass'n v. Dept. of Envt'l Protection, 13 ERC 1541 (N.J.Super.Ct.App.Div.1979) (Pine Barrens). See also Shepard, The Scope of Congress' Constitutional Power Under the Property Clause: Regulating Non-Federal Property to Further the Purposes of National Parks and Wilderness Areas, 11 B.C. Envtl.Aff. 479 (1984); Note, Protecting National Parks from Developments Beyond Their Borders, 132 U.Pa.L.Rev. 1189 (1984).

B. RIVER PRESERVATION

Over the course of time, the primary value of rivers has been perceived differently by Congress. For many decades the touchstone was navigability; from the beginning, the federal government has asserted a strong interest in maintaining the navigable capacity of waterways in order to assist the commerce of the Nation. Gibbons v. Ogden, 22 U.S. (9 Wheat.) 1 (1824). As advancing settlement reached the arid and semiarid areas of the West, a national emphasis on use of rivers for irrigation grew, culminating in the Reclamation Act of 1902. 43 U.S.C.A. §§ 371–76. Within a few years, the potential of rivers for hydroelectric power generation was recognized, leading to the Federal Power Act of 1920. 16 U.S.C.A. § 791 et seq. A third impetus for river development by means of dams, diversions, dredging, and channelization was flood control. 33 U.S.C.A. § 701 et seq. Since the 1930's, the Army Corps of Engineers has reworked the map of the eastern United States and the Bureau of Reclamation has done the same in the West. The national system of dams and diversions in the aggregate dwarf the Interstate Highway System as the engineering marvel of this hemisphere.

But water resource developments have costs as well as benefits, and many costs were not reflected in the traditional cost/benefit ratios used to justify more dams and storage projects. One of the first major political conservation battles in this century was fought over whether a river in Yosemite National Park should be dammed to provide a water supply for San Francisco. Some of the Hetch Hetchy story is recounted in Wood, supra at page 141. Later, many others came to believe that the sacrifice of the natural values of free-flowing rivers was ultimately counterproductive. In the 1960's and 1970's, the questions whether particular river segments were better suited to productive uses or to be preserved in free-flowing conditions reached emotional peaks in many areas of the United States. Private citizens in nearly all states have resorted to litigation to stop particular projects to which they objected.

Even before river litigation reached the flood stage, it was recognized that rearguard delaying actions had little ultimate favorable effect on river preservation. They were too little, too late. Instead, a system of prior protection was necessary whereby rational judgments on which river segments were worthy of preservation could be made before the crises were reached. In 1960, the National Park Service recommended to the Senate Select Committee on National Water Resources that some remaining free-flowing streams be preserved. The need for such preservation was documented in a 1962 Outdoor Recreation Review Commission Report, later endorsed by President Johnson. The concept of a river-based, parklike reservation reached initial fruition when Congress created in 1964 the Ozark National Scenic Riverways, 16 U.S.C.A. §§ 460m to 460m–7, under which the Current and Jack's Fork Rivers in Missouri became "National Rivers." The Buffalo River in Arkansas was also made a national river (sort of a ribbon national park administered by NPS) in 1972. See Buffalo National River Act, 16 U.S.C.A. §§ 460m–8 to 460m–14.

In 1968, Congress acted to create a nationwide system of rivers, protected in various degrees by classification, in the Wild and Scenic Rivers Act (WRSA), 16 U.S.C.A. §§ 1271–87.

SALLY K. FAIRFAX, BARBARA T. ANDREWS & ANDREW P. BUCHSBAUM, FEDERALISM AND THE WILD AND SCENIC RIVERS ACT: NOW YOU SEE IT, NOW YOU DON'T *
59 Wash.L.Rev. 417 (1984).

The WSRA was essentially a reform measure. It was specifically designed to blend with not always compatible missions of established agencies while remedying inadequacies in long-established state and federal approaches to land and water management programs. As with any entrant into a crowded policy arena, the Wild and Scenic Rivers Act was a compromise, sculpted to blend new interests with old. The final wording is ambiguous at precisely the points where advocates seek clarity. As a result, it is extremely difficult to identify "the" federal position on wild and scenic rivers specifically, or on water more generally.

* * *

In passing a national WSRA, Congress was responding to three major concerns. The first was the apparent inadequacy of state systems for preserving and protecting rivers, especially in the West. More Western States have historically followed the water rights doctrine of prior appropriation which evolved to encourage private development of

---

* Reprinted with permission of the Washington Law Review.

water. Traditionally, water left in place was not a "beneficial use" of water and, hence, was not protected under state law. Even though several state legislatures have moved to include instream uses within their appropriation systems, states still have the reputation of being poor guardians of these uses. A major goal of WSRA was to enhance both state and federal attention to protection of instream values.

Congress' second concern was to control federal water development. Section I of the Act declares that

> the established national policy of dam and other construction at appropriate sections of the rivers of the United States needs to be complemented by a policy that would preserve other selected rivers or sections thereof in their free-flowing condition to protect the water quality of such rivers and to fulfill other vital national conservation purposes.

The federal presence in developing water, spread among numerous agencies, was piecemeal and poorly integrated, yet powerful. As the country's "environmental consciousness" evolved, it became highly controversial. In passing WSRA, Congress sought balance in the federal program.

A third congressional goal behind WSRA was to increase congressional control over the federal land management agencies. In the 1960's and 1970's, "Congress took unprecedented steps in giving the land managing agencies specific directions for managing designated areas of the public lands" for environmental purposes. The WSRA was part of this trend toward specialized, environmentally protective legislation. It affected the activities of the National Park Service, the Bureau of the Land Management, the Fish and Wildlife Service, and the United States Forest Service. Whether these agencies were preservation or multiple-use entities made little difference; Congress intended to control federal agency activities affecting land along designated wild and scenic river corridors.

* * *

B. *Basic Provisions of the National Wild and Scenic Rivers Act*

The WSRA is a special-purpose statute designed to preserve "selected rivers," along with their "immediate environments," that possess one or more "outstandingly remarkable scenic, recreational, geologic, fish and wildlife, historic, cultural, or other similar values." [52] The rivers are to be protected for their "free-flowing" characteristics, which specifically include water quality.[53] These values are imprecise, frequently sounding more hortatory than implementable.

The Act is more concrete in defining classifications of rivers, methods of including them in the system, and responsibilities for federal and state agencies involved in the intricate management process. Pristine *wild* rivers,[54] relatively undisturbed *scenic* rivers,[55] or

---

52. 16 U.S.C. § 1271 (1982).   **54.** Id. § 1273(b)(1).

53. Id.   **55.** Id. § 1273(b)(2).

developed *recreational* rivers [56] may be included in the federal system. Congress also established a phased approach to river inclusion: in addition to *included,* fully protected rivers, it identified *potential additions* and administrative study rivers in order to protect rivers under consideration. Rivers may become included in one of two ways: by congressional action,[62] or by request from a state governor to the Secretary of the Interior.[63]   *   *   *

*   *   *

The potential for   *   *   * conflict is enhanced by the fact that Congress has been very unclear regarding management criteria. The WSRA requires the administering agency to protect each included river and enhance the values which caused it to be included in the national system. One might suppose that the degree of protection afforded a river would be based on the river's classification. However, one would be wrong: the Act specifies protections based on river classification *only* with regard to mining.[70] With this one exception, classification is not clearly linked either to designation or to management.[71]

The WSRA is much clearer when it moves from land management to agency programs affecting instream flow. This occurred partly because of the direct impact of streamflow manipulation on the "free flowing" qualities of protected streams, and partly because of the Act's specific prohibitions against federal water development activities. Section 7(a) of the Act forbids the Federal Energy Regulatory Commission (FERC) from licensing any project "on or directly affecting" any included river.[72] All other federal agencies are forbidden from undertaking or assisting any water resources project "that would have a direct and adverse effect on the values for which such river was established." [73]

*   *   *

NOTES

1. What is the relationship of the federal reserved water rights doctrine to rivers designated wild or scenic under the Act? Congress' declaration of purposes for the act is broad, including protection of "scenic, recreational, geologic, fish and wildlife, historic, cultural, or other similar values   *   *   *" and preservation of a "free-flowing condition." 16 U.S.C.A. § 1271. While Section 1284(b) states that "nothing

56. Id. § 1273(b)(3).

62. 16 U.S.C. § 1273(a), (c) (1982).

63. Id. § 1273(a)(ii).

70. Subject to valid existing rights, *wild* rivers are protected from any further mining or mineral-leasing activity within one-quarter mile of their banks. 16 U.S.C. § 1280(a)(iii) (1982). In *scenic* and *recreational* rivers, mining activity can proceed, but it may be regulated by the managing agency and will result in federal title being granted only to the mineral resources and such surface resources as are reasonably necessary for conducting mining operations. Id. § 1280(a)(i), (ii).

71. Surface coal mining cannot occur in any included rivers regardless of classification, but this prohibition is part of the Surface Mining Control and Reclamation Act of 1977, 30 U.S.C. §§ 1201–1328 (Supp. V 1981), and not WSRA.

72. 16 U.S.C. § 1278(a) (1982).

73. Id. The "adversity" requirement may not have much practical effect since any project that benefits a river in some respects can almost always be found to conflict with other values. The possible exception would be recreational rivers on which some instream development may have already occurred.

in this chapter shall constitute an express or implied claim or denial on the part of the Federal Government as to exemption from State water laws," Section 1284(c) provides that:

> Designation of any stream or portion thereof as a national wild, scenic or recreational river area shall not be construed as a reservation of the waters of such streams for purposes other than those specified in this chapter, or in quantities greater than necessary to accomplish these purposes.

Does this provision, along with the "free-flowing condition" language, amount to an assertion of a reserved minimum stream flow for the "purposes" of the Act? If the Act does reserve water rights, what is the quantity of water withdrawn from private appropriation? What priority date would attach to such a reserved right, if it does exist? Would it run from the date of statutory inclusion in the system, or from the original withdrawal from entry of public land along the river? See the 1979 Solicitor's Opinion on reserved water rights, supra at page 386. What of those rivers designated for potential inclusion in the System? Section 1278(b) restricts federal construction projects on potential additions, but there is no specific provision as to private appropriation via state water law during the study period. See generally Tarlock & Tippy, The Wild and Scenic Rivers Act of 1968, 55 Corn.L.Rev. 707 (1970); Goodell, Waterway Preservation: The Wild and Scenic Rivers Act of 1968, 7 B.C.Env.Aff.L.Rev. 43 (1978).

2. In 1982, the Reagan administration adopted guidelines for wild and scenic river management. 47 Fed.Reg. 39, 454 (1982). See Fairfax, Andrews & Buchsbaum, supra, 59 Wash.L.Rev. at 450:

> The Reagan guidelines rejected the Carter Administration's effort to redefine "wild" rivers to include areas where minor dams and other inconspicuous or "historical" or "cultural" structures existed. Moreover, the new guidelines follow the 1970 regulations by relying on the language of the Act to define river management criteria. Specific water quality standards, mining prohibitions, restrictions on dams, and controls on federal appropriation of land and water included in the Carter team draft were eliminated in the final version. The Carter language also allowed "selective timber harvest" in scenic river areas, while the final allows "timber harvest." Although the regulations are ostensibly a joint product of the Departments of Agriculture and the Interior, it would be a serious error to assume that the guidelines presage a uniform federal approach to the program. The provisions are suggestive rather than binding, and offer ample room for exercise of discretion by diverse agencies operating under significantly different mandates.

3. What of agency activities that occur outside the river corridor, such as a sediment-producing clearcut in the same watershed? The Forest Service has taken the position, on at least one occasion, that the Act does not require that areas outside the boundaries of a designated

river corridor be managed under the same standards as applicable to lands inside the boundaries. Decision of the Chief, Appeal of Elk Summit Land Use Plan (Dec. 29, 1976). Section 1283(a) of the Act was amended in 1978 to provide that an agency having jurisdiction over "any lands which include, border upon, or are adjacent to" any river included or proposed to be included in the system "shall take such action respecting management policies, regulations, contacts, plans, affecting such lands * * * as may be necessary to protect such rivers in accordance with the purposes of this chapter." Prior to amendment, section 1283(a) required only that an agency "review" such activities. Does the new language effectively extend the duty of mitigation to activities of other federal agencies on land removed from a river that may ultimately have impact on the river?

4. The 1968 Act allows the United States to acquire scenic easements, but the easements may not "affect, without the owner's consent, any regular use exercised prior to the acquisition of the easement." In condemnation proceedings, a district court held that the Interior Department was entitled to obtain an easement prohibiting logging, since one previous harvest, in 1958, was not a "regular" use; the defendants did, however, establish the regular use of a "salmon board"—a temporary fishing platform—and the court ruled that the defendant was entitled to continue the use. United States v. Hanten, 500 F.Supp. 188 (D.Or.1980). See also United States v. 55.0 Acres of Land, 524 F.Supp. 320 (W.D.Mo.1981) (ruling on various regular uses); Kiernat v. Chisago County, 564 F.Supp. 1089 (D.Minn.1983) (purchase of scenic easement does not limit more stringent land zoning by county).

5. The designation of wild and scenic rivers has been contentious on occasion. In June, 1980, Governor Brown of California requested Interior Secretary Andrus to designate five river segments in Northern California as wild or scenic. An expedited EIS process ensued. Counties in California and Oregon obtained preliminary orders enjoining the river designations, but the Ninth Circuit vacated the orders because no final agency action had occurred. The Ninth Circuit ruling came down on January 19, 1981, the last full day of the Carter Administration. Secretary Andrus had been optimistic enough to anticipate the decision: when President Carter had sent a routine memo to all cabinet officers requesting their resignations as of 5:00 p.m. on January 19th, Andrus asked permission not to submit his resignation and Carter agreed. The Secretary was attending a reception at the White House on the evening of January 19th when an aide phoned to say that the injunction had been lifted. Andrus returned to his office to sign the North Coast river proclamations, his last official act in office, thus sparking the following litigation.

COUNTY OF DEL NORTE v. UNITED STATES

United States Court of Appeals, Ninth Circuit, 1984.
732 F.2d 1462.

SCHROEDER, Circuit Judge.

This is a challenge to the Secretary of the Interior's designation of parts of five northern California rivers as components of the national wild and scenic river system under the Wild and Scenic Rivers Act. Plaintiffs include several California counties and entities that represent timber and water interests. The district court entered summary judgment in favor of the plaintiffs, holding that the designation was defective because of procedural irregularities. The government appeals.

Secretary of the Interior Cecil Andrus designated the rivers in January, 1981, during the waning hours of the Carter administration. As required by the National Environmental Policy Act, the designation followed completion of an Environmental Impact Statement (EIS). It is apparent from the record that the State of California, which originally proposed the designation, and the Heritage Conservation and Recreation Service (HCRS), the Department of the Interior division which processed the application,[1] favored expeditious completion of all NEPA requirements so that action could be taken on the proposal before the Carter administration left office. It is equally apparent that those opposing designation, including the plaintiffs in this case, wished to delay final consideration by the Secretary until the new President took office.

The principal issue before us is whether the designation is invalid because the HCRS failed to follow two EIS timing regulations, 40 C.F.R. §§ 1506.9 and 1506.10.

* * *

Resolution of the legal issue requires an understanding of the relationship between two of the regulations promulgated by the Council on Environmental Quality (CEQ) to ensure substantial compliance with the policies set forth in NEPA. The first regulation, 40 C.F.R. § 1506.9 (1983), requires that EISs be filed with EPA. It also provides that an EIS should not be filed with EPA before it is transmitted to commenting agencies and made available to the public. The second regulation, 40 C.F.R. § 1506.10 (1983), requires published notice in the Federal Register of the filing of an EIS that has been "filed [with EPA] during the preceding week." 40 C.F.R. § 1506.10(a). It provides that no decision on the proposed action may be made until at least 30 days after Federal Register publication. 40 C.F.R. § 1506.10(b)(2).

* * *

The sequence can be better visualized by use of the following time line:

1. The functions of the HCRS are now performed by the National Park Service. 46 Fed.Reg. 34,329 (1981).

July 18, 1980: Governor of California proposes inclusion of rivers in the wild and scenic river system.

September 16, 1980: Draft EIS filed with EPA.

November 5, 1980: Presidential election.

November 14, 1980: Some plaintiffs obtain temporary restraining order, extending comment period on the draft EIS.

December 1, 1980: Temporary restraining order dissolved for lack of jurisdiction.

December 5, 1980: Comment period on draft EIS is closed.

Friday, December 12, 1980: HCRS official files final EIS and signs form verifying that distribution has been completed. Copies of the final EIS are available at agency offices in San Francisco and Washington, D.C.

Monday, December 15, 1980: Distribution of final EIS by mail is completed.

Wednesday, December 17, 1980: Final EIS is available in quantity to the public. Plaintiffs' counsel obtain copies. Federal Register publishes notice that the final EIS has been filed with EPA.

January 19, 1981: Secretary of the Interior makes the designation.

The time line illustrates several important facts. First, the agency followed all timing requirements for preparation of the EIS itself. In fact, the comment period on the draft EIS lasted substantially longer than the minimum 45 days required by 40 C.F.R. § 1506.10(c). Second, the notice in the Federal Register, which signified filing with EPA, availability to the public, and circulation to commenting agencies of the EIS, did so accurately when it appeared on December 17. Finally, when the Secretary designated the rivers on January 19, more than the required 30 days following publication had passed. 40 C.F.R. § 1506.10(b)(2).

The irregularity in filing the notice before circulation therefore had no effect whatsoever on the plaintiffs' opportunity to review the EIS after publication of the notice; nor did it affect the opportunity of the interested agencies and members of the public to review the statement for 30 days following publication. The "premature" publication about which the plaintiffs complain is significant only because delay of a week in publication would have prevented the matter from being decided by Secretary Andrus rather than by his successor. It was, however, in large part the actions of these plaintiffs, in obtaining a temporary restraining order in November, 1980, that made the "prematurity" significant. The order delayed approval of the EIS for seventeen days before the district court dissolved it for lack of jurisdiction.

These facts are important to bear in mind in evaluating plaintiffs' claim that the designation should be set aside because of the deviation from the sequence of distribution and filing called for in the CEQ regulations. The regulations in question are part of a series issued under the authority of NEPA to establish orderly procedures for administration of the Act. Section 1500.1, which sets forth the purpose of the regulations, emphasizes that the procedures "must insure that environmental information is available to public officials and citizens before decisions are made and before actions are taken." 40 C.F.R. § 1500.1(b).

Section 1500.3 of the regulations states that compliance with them should not be subject to judicial review until after final action on the proposal, and that the Council intended that "any trivial violation of these regulations not give rise to any independent cause of action." 40 C.F.R. § 1500.3.

* * *

The regulations themselves thus contain an implicit admonition not to use claims of technical violations as tactics for delaying agency action. Any violation which in the end requires the agency action to be set aside must have borne some relationship to the decision making process itself.

The question in this case then becomes whether the violation of the regulations, by publishing notice in the Federal Register on the day circulation of the EIS was complete rather than during the following week, is "trivial." The purpose of 40 C.F.R. §§ 1506.9 and 1506.10 is to ensure that all pertinent information is available on proposed action for a period of 30 days before final action is taken, and that interested parties have notice of that availability. * * * The provision for publication the week following distribution and filing of the EIS is no more than a precautionary measure to ensure the desired result.

Here, although the HCRS failed to take the precaution, the result was achieved in any event. All distribution requirements had been met by the time of publication: the required 30 days did elapse; the EIS materials were available and accompanied the EIS through the final review process during the 30-day period. The integrity of the decision making process within the government and the public's opportunity to comment in accordance with all legal requirements were not compromised in any way.

Although this is a case of first impression under these regulations, the trivial error provision is analogous to the general rule that insubstantial errors in an administrative proceeding that prejudice no one do not require administrative decisions to be set aside. * * *

Plaintiffs argued strenuously before the district court that the Secretary in making the designation had failed to consider language from a California Superior Court opinion in a suit by many of these same plaintiffs to enjoin the California Governor from applying for federal designation of the rivers. County of Del Norte v. Brown, No. 292019 (Cal.Super.Ct. Sacramento Cty. 1980) (memorandum decision). The state court held that it had no power to prevent the application for wild and scenic river status under federal law. The court admonished, however, that in deciding on the designation the Secretary must take into account the state court's conclusion that the rivers could not be "permanently administered" under the California Wild and Scenic

Rivers Act, Cal.Pub.Res.Code § 5093.50–5093.69 (Cum.Supp.1984). The state's ability to "permanently administer" the rivers under state law is a requirement for the federal designation at issue here. 16 U.S.C. § 1273(a)(ii). The district court found that the admonition had not been drawn to the Secretary's attention and remanded to the agency * * *.

Full review of the record reveals, however, that the decision was both paraphrased in a memorandum to the Secretary and attached in full as an addendum to that memorandum. The Secretarial Issue Document noted the state court opinion, but concluded that sufficient other state law protections existed to satisfy the permanent administration requirement under the federal act. The record thus belies the contention that the state court opinion was not considered. In the absence of clear evidence to the contrary, courts presume that public officers properly discharge their duties, including reading memoranda addressed to them.

* * *

The judgment of the district court is reversed and the matter is remanded for entry of judgment in favor of the defendants.

NOTES

1. What protection is provided to rivers that are designated as potential additions to the System? Agencies are required by Section 1278(c) to inform the Secretary of Interior or Agriculture of "any proceedings, studies, or other activities within their jurisdiction" which affect or may affect a river listed as a potential addition to the System. Section 1278(b) sets forth restrictions on water resources projects similar to those for rivers already included in the system, effective for three years after the congressional designation of a river as a potential addition or for the duration of any longer study period provided the particular act of designation. In North Carolina v. FPC, 533 F.2d 702 (D.C.Cir.1976), vacated, 429 U.S. 891 (1976), the State opposed an FPC grant of a construction license for a hydroelectric project on the New River, claiming that the FPC was prohibited from doing so while the State's recommendation that the river be included in the National Wild and Scenic River System was before the Secretary of Interior for consideration. The District of Columbia Circuit affirmed the FPC action, holding that the restrictions of Section 1278(b) are triggered only upon actual designation by Congress. Congress subsequently amended Section 1278 to provide: "Any license heretofore or hereafter issued by the Federal Power Commission affecting the New River of North Carolina shall continue to be effective only for that portion of the River which is not included in the National Wild and Scenic Rivers System pursuant to Section 2 of this Act. * * *" Pub.L. No. 94–407, 90 Stat. 1238 (Sept. 11, 1976). Section 2 was concurrently amended to include the segment of the river submitted for inclusion by the State. Does this retroactive revocation of an FPC license by Congress amount to a taking?

2. See generally Tippy, Preservation Values in River Basin Planning, 8 Nat.Res.J. 259 (1968); Tarlock, Preservation of Scenic Rivers, 55 Ky.L.J. 745 (1967); Note, Conflict Over the New River and the Test Case for Wild and Scenic Rivers Act, 9 N.C.Cen.L.J. 192 (1978).

C. WILDERNESS PRESERVATION

1. THE EVOLUTION OF OFFICIAL WILDERNESS

America pioneered an international preservation movement when it established Yellowstone National Park in 1872; there are now over 1000 parks in 100 countries. Nash, The American Invention of National Parks, 22 Am.Quart. 726 (1970). The concept of preservation was taken a step further when, first by administrative fiat in 1924 and then by legislative action in 1964, the United States became the first nation to set aside areas in their pristine state as wilderness. In a world where natural places are becoming ever scarcer, future generations may count the preservation of wild lands as one of America's great contributions to civilization.

The subject of wilderness is treated in Professor Roderick Nash's comprehensive work, R. Nash, WILDERNESS AND THE AMERICAN MIND (3rd ed. 1982). A definition of wilderness is advanced in a remarkable Forest Service book that encompasses philosophical, historical, legal, economic, and management issues, J. Hendee, G. Stankey, & R. Lucas, WILDERNESS MANAGEMENT 9 (1978):

> What is wilderness? This is the crucial question for both allocation and management—the issue to which all allocation and management decisions must be related. At one extreme, wilderness can be defined in a narrow legal perspective as an area possessing qualities outlined in Section 2(c) of the Wilderness Act. At the other extreme, it is whatever people think it is; potentially, the entire universe, the *terra incognita* of people's minds. We can call these two extreme definitions legal wilderness and sociological wilderness.
>
> There is little possibility of deriving a universally accepted definition of sociological wilderness because perceptions of wilderness vary widely. For some urbanites with scant knowledge of, or experience in, the natural environment, wilderness might be perceived in any undeveloped wildland, uncut forest, or woodlot.
>
> On the other hand, legal wilderness as defined by the Wilderness Act of 1964 (Sec. 2c) is much more precise. "A wilderness, in contrast with those areas where man and his own works dominate the landscape, is hereby recognized as an area where the earth and its community of life are untrammeled by man, where man himself is a visitor who does not remain." This legal definition places wilderness on the "untrammeled" pole of the environmental modification continuum. Furthermore, the concept of legal wilderness in the Act is

sanctioned by the tradition of this particular kind of land use in America and rests on ideas espoused decades ago.

For example, Aldo Leopold envisioned wilderness as "a continuous stretch of country preserved in its natural state, open to lawful hunting and fishing, big enough to absorb a 2 weeks' pack trip, and kept devoid of roads, artificial trails, cottages, or other works of man." Robert Marshall offered a similar definition:

> * * * I * * * shall use the word *wilderness* to denote a region which contains no permanent inhabitants, possesses no possibility of conveyance by any mechanical means and is sufficiently spacious that a person in crossing it must have the experience of sleeping out. The dominant attributes of such an area are: First, that it requires any one who exists in it to depend exclusively on his own effort for survival; and second, that it preserves as nearly as possible the primitive environment. This means that all roads, power transportation and settlements are barred. But trails and temporary shelters, which were common long before the advent of the white race, are entirely permissible.

* * *

Some of the reasons for preserving wilderness were catalogued by Michael McCloskey, former Executive Director of the Sierra Club:

MICHAEL McCLOSKEY, THE WILDERNESS ACT OF 1964: ITS BACKGROUND AND MEANING *
45 Ore.L.Rev. 288 (1966).

What attitudes in America's cultural history produced national leadership that was finally able to persuade its citizens to value wilderness? The inquiry is an important prelude to understanding why the Wilderness Act was passed and what is expected of it.

An agglomeration of accumulating attitudes toward nature explains why today's leaders value wilderness and how they perceive it. Little in America's European intellectual heritage, however, stressed the value of nature in unsullied form.

* * *

* * * From the time of the earliest settlements, there is a thread of interest in wild nature which continues throughout America's intellectual history and finally flourishes in the twentieth century. The thread's early strands were formed in response to historical situations and political and religious values. The later strands assert values which are a contemporary rationale for having wilderness.

Early Valuations. One. Though the wilderness of a new continent was a challenge to those who explored it and settled it, from the

---

* Reprinted by permission. Copyright © 1966 by the University of Oregon.

beginning some valued that setting. The wilderness held a fascination for them on which they built their reputations. This attitude is reflected in the chronicles of exploration and settlement and in the accounts of early travelers. Moreover, wilderness was a gauge of capacity to triumph over adversity, and it was a setting for self-discovery. Wilderness allowed the frontier trappers and mountain men to build their legends. Even later transitory visitors, like Theodore Roosevelt, could use their experience in the West to build legends.

Two. The powerful presence of nature in the wilderness of a new continent also served as an aid to religion and as a setting for religious experience. Puritan preachers such as Jonathan Edwards used the omnipresent plan of nature as evidence of the planning of the God of his revealed religion. Deists, such as Thomas Jefferson, could look to nature's plan as the chief support of the cosmological proof of God's existence.

* * *

Three. Wilderness has also been viewed as a setting for political reform. It was the environment of Rousseau's "noble savage"—for untainted children of nature, and presumably a pre-condition of the good society.

* * *

Four. For those not interested in reforming society or who had been alienated by it, wilderness served as a refuge or sanctuary.

* * *

Five. Beginning with George Perkins Marsh in the latter part of the nineteenth century, a literary tradition began of describing threats to nature. Alarms were sounded about depletion of natural resources and massive wastage. In the writings of John Muir and others, the need to protect wild country was stressed.

* * *

Contemporary Valuations. Six. Today, as a result of the foregoing history, wilderness is regarded as a cultural heritage. In his association with the wilderness he spent three centuries taming, the American grew accustomed to being close to nature. Now that he has tamed so much of it, he misses it. Clearing the wilderness was a hardening experience that promoted self-reliance and self-respect. Wilderness has become a symbol imbedded in our national consciousness—a nostalgia for a lost opportunity. The wilderness that remains is a reassuring referrent for a symbolic idea that is valued in itself. Actual contact with wilderness today is primarily valued as an aesthetic experience.

* * *

With wilderness users tending to come from higher educational levels than other outdoor recreationists, a certain elitism surrounds discussions of this encounter. * * *

But the elitism may reflect primarily the greater ability of educated wilderness users to articulate their reactions to experience with wilderness, rather than lack of capacity to have such an experience on the part of less educated users.

*   *   *

Seven. In addition to being a setting for an aesthetic experience, wilderness is now regarded as an important setting for scientific research in the biological sciences. * * * Finally, the complex ecosystems that develop in undisturbed areas support a genetic diversity that maximizes the possibilities of the evolutionary process. Wilderness, in effect, becomes a "gene bank" that evolution can draw upon to offset man's influence in narrowing the number of species on the planet.

*   *   *

Eight. For some, maintenance of wilderness is evidence of serious intent to meet newly conceived ethical obligations. Moving beyond a mere humanistic "reverence for life," Aldo Leopold and others have advocated a new "land ethic" which substitutes a biocentric view of nature for the traditional anthropocentric view. Modern biological knowledge, they feel, should instill an "ecological conscience" in man that will cause him to live in harmony with the other living things of the earth. In response to that conscience, man should exercise self-restraint in the extent to which he disturbs the rest of nature.

Nine. Wilderness today is valued, particularly, as an opportunity for an educational experience. It provides the setting in which to learn the cultural, scientific, and ethical values associated with untrammeled nature.

*   *   *

Ten. Highly urbanized wilderness users value wilderness for therapeutic reasons. Writers like Sigurd Olson have reminded Americans that exertion in wilderness can be a tonic for regaining vigor and serve as an aid to physical recuperation.

*   *   *

Eleven. Finally, wilderness is regarded as the optimum setting for many sport forms of highest quality. These are sports such as mountain climbing, fly fishing, trophy hunting, cross-country backpacking, ski mountaineering, cave exploration, and amateur nature study. All require uncommon natural settings that cannot be duplicated by man.

———

Resource development is generally prohibited in wilderness areas; for that reason, timber companies, miners, power companies, and ranchers frequently oppose official wilderness, sometimes bitterly. Their objections are directed not only at the designation of wilderness per se, but also at studies by federal agencies of great blocs of lands for possible inclusion in the wilderness system. During those often lengthy study periods, the land is "locked up" to avoid destruction of its wilderness characteristics. Professor Robinson argues that the economic ramifications of these choices cannot be ignored solely on the rationale that the economic resources will be preserved for future generations:

GLEN O. ROBINSON, WILDERNESS:
THE LAST FRONTIER
59 Minn.L.Rev. Fig. 1 (1974).

*   *   *

It is sometimes argued that the protected resources are not really sacrificed: since they are preserved for the future, they should be considered more an investment than a current cost. Quite apart from the dubious assumption that preservation status is one which can be easily reversed when demand for the resource arises, the notion that nothing is lost in foregoing present consumption is simple nonsense. This assertion does not imply that the future value of the resource should not be considered; that, of course, is taken care of by capital budgeting techniques that are a part of any efficient management. The future economic value of the resource is part of the benefit-cost analysis of resource investment and use. In such an analysis, the period of investment ("preservation") of, say, a timber stand will obviously vary, depending on such factors as expected future yield and the interest (or discount) rate, which reflects the opportunity cost of capital tied up in the investment. But whatever that period would be, it would not correspond to the indefinite preservation of the resource. This is apparent even on the most restrictive assumptions. Suppose, for example, that the economic management objective were to maximize the *physical* annual productivity of a timber stand. Such an objective might lead to a relatively long period of investment—up to perhaps 120 years for Douglas fir timber—but it could not lead to an indefinite preservation. Allowing the stand to go uncut (or unburned) beyond the period of maximum incremental growth would yield diminishing physical productivity. If one introduces more refined notions of capital budgeting, the period of investment becomes even shorter. Thus, if one seeks not maximum *physical* yield but rather maximum *economic* yield, the age of the stand might be a fraction of the 120-year period mentioned above. Depending on the discount rate, the maximum economic yield of a stand may occur at periods as short as 30 to 60 years.

I am not suggesting that these maximization criteria should in all cases govern. I cite them simply to demonstrate the foolishness of the assumption that preservation can be justified as an economic investment for the future. Not only does preservation not correspond to economic criteria for efficient investment—that is, for efficient allocation of resources over time—but it also is directly antithetical to such a purpose. It is not just that preservation exceeds the period appropriate for efficient utilization of resources; it also leads to a deterioration in the economic resource as the forest matures into old age. Though conservationists are constantly, and correctly, reminding us that a forest left in a natural state can and does renew itself, no one would argue that the *economic* productivity of an unmanaged forest is equal to that of a well-managed one. Whether or not the wilderness benefit exceeds the sacrifice in economic productivity (capital value) has still to be resolved; the point here is merely that capital value *is* sacrificed.

———

On wilderness and economics, see also Walsh, Loomis, & Gillman, Valuing Option, Existence and Bequest Demands for Wilderness, Land Economics 14 (Feb. 1984); Bigelow, Selection of Wilderness Areas: An Economic Framework of Decision-Making, 11 Land Use and Env.L.Rev. 329 (1980); Sagoff, On Preserving the Natural Environment, 84 Yale L.J. 205 (1974).

Institutional wilderness began in 1924 when Aldo Leopold of the Forest Service succeeded in convincing the agency to set aside as wilderness 700,000 acres in the Gila National Forest in New Mexico. Leopold's writings, including A SAND COUNTY ALMANAC (1949), formed an important part of the philosophical basis for later wilderness proposals. By the mid-1930's 63 areas had been established but—true to the Forest Service's tradition of decentralized administration—considerable discretion was left to the field officials, who in some cases had allowed logging, grazing, and road building. Bob Marshall, a vigorous outdoorsman and founder of the Wilderness Society, became chief of the Forest Service's Division of Recreation in 1937. Among his many contributions to the wilderness movement during his two years in office were the so-called U Regulations, tightening the restrictions on uses in wilderness areas.

McMICHAEL v. UNITED STATES
United States Court of Appeals, Ninth Circuit, 1965.
355 F.2d 283.

MERRILL, Circuit Judge:

On July 9, 1963, appellants drove their motorcycles over twenty miles of trails within the Idaho Primitive Area of the Boise National Forest. They admit seeing a sign at the entrance to the primitive area stating that motorized vehicles were prohibited. Appellants were convicted of a misdemeanor and fined $100 each under 16 U.S.C.A. § 551 for violation of regulations prohibiting the operation of motorized vehicles within that portion of the national forests designated by the Secretary as "primitive areas." Upon this appeal they challenge the validity of those regulations.

The Idaho primitive area was established in 1931 pursuant to regulation in order:

"To conserve the primitive conditions of environment, habitation, subsistence and transportation for the enjoyment of those who cherish these early traditions and history of this country and desire to preserve in some degree the traits, qualities and characteristics upon which this Nation was founded.

To make it possible for people to detach themselves, at least temporarily, from the strain and turmoil of modern existence, and to revert to simple types of existence in conditions of relatively unmodified nature.

To afford unique opportunities for physical, mental and spiritual recreation and regeneration." (Idaho Primitive Area Report, March 17, 1931).

Appellants' position is that regulations establishing primitive, wilderness and wild areas and providing limitations upon the use to be made of such areas are not authorized by section 551. That section, they point out, directs the Secretary of Agriculture to "make provisions for the protection against destruction by fire and depredations upon [established] public forests"; and authorizes the Secretary to "make such rules and regulations and establish such service as will insure the objects of such reservations." They contend that while such regulations may relate to "occupancy and use," still, their purpose must be to "preserve the forests thereon from destruction." In support of their reading of section 551, appellants point to 16 U.S.C.A. § 475, enacted June 4, 1897, which provides in part:

"* * * No national forest shall be established, except to improve and protect the forest within the boundaries, or for the purpose of securing favorable conditions of water flows, and to furnish a continuous supply of timber for the use and necessities of citizens of the United States * * *."

The consistent administrative interpretation of section 551, however, has been that while recreational considerations alone will not support the establishment of a national forest, they are appropriate subjects for regulation. Congress has tacitly shown its approval of this interpretation by appropriating the sums required for its effectuation. Further Congress has expressly manifested its approval by actually adopting and furthering administrative policy in two enactments.

1. The Multiple-Use Sustained-Yield Act of 1960 * * * constitutes a recognition of past administrative construction * * *. [The Senate Report stated:]

"The authority to administer recreation and wildlife habitat resources of the national forest has been recognized in numerous appropriation acts and comes from the authority contained in the *Act of June 4, 1897,* to regulate the 'occupancy and use' of the national forest."

2. The Wilderness Act of September 3, 1964 is further indication that the Congressional policy supports the regulations in question.

* * *

NOTES

1. Compare this case to United States v. New Mexico, 438 U.S. 696 (1978), supra at page 376, as to the "purposes" for which national forests were established. Are the two views compatible? Note *McMi-*

chael's reliance on the Multiple Use, Sustained Yield Act. Can a 1960 statute serve as justification for administrative actions taken in 1930 and 1939? Since the Forest Service possessed delegated authority to establish this primitive area, did the administrative action designation impliedly reserve water rights to fulfill the purposes of the primitive area? For an earlier case upholding administrative authority to establish roadless areas for recreational purposes, see United States v. Perko, 108 F.Supp. 315 (D.Minn.1952), aff'd, 204 F.2d 446 (8th Cir.1953), cert. denied, 346 U.S. 832 (1953).

2. In 1969, before Congress directed official BLM wilderness studies, the BLM also began establishing "primitive" areas. See Foster, Bureau of Land Management Primitive Areas—Are They Counterfeit Wilderness?, 16 Nat.Res.J. 621 (1976).

2. THE WILDERNESS ACT OF 1964

Wilderness received little attention during World War II but the movement revived in the late 1940's and early 1950's, spearheaded by Howard Zahniser, Executive Director of the Wilderness Society. In 1956 Senator Hubert Humphrey introduced the first wilderness bill, which was stronger than the Act passed eight years later. Wilderness legislation was spurred by events proving the central thesis of Zahniser and other advocates: that congressional designation was essential because administrative wilderness could be administratively revoked at any time. In Utah, the proposed Echo Park Dam would have flooded a prime gorge. In Oregon, the old-growth French Pete Valley was returned to general forest designation for potential logging. In New Mexico, the Gila Wilderness itself was partially opened. Other intrusions on wilderness areas drew regional and national attention.

As Professor Nash explained:

> The concept of a wilderness system marked an innovation in the history of the American preservation movement. It expressed, in the first place, a determination to take the offensive. Previous friends of the wilderness had been largely concerned with defending it against various forms of development. But the post-Echo Park mood was confident, encouraging a bold, positive gesture. Second, the system meant support of wilderness in general rather than of a particular wild region. As a result, debate focused on the theoretical value of wilderness in the abstract, not on a local economic situation. Finally, a national wilderness preservation system [created by congressional, rather than administrative, action] would give an unprecedented degree of protection to wild country. R. Nash, WILDERNESS AND THE AMERICAN MIND 222 (3d ed. 1982).

The Forest Service opposed wilderness bills, arguing that statutory wilderness was contrary to multiple use, sustained yield management. Mollified by passage of the Multiple–Use, Sustained–Yield Act of 1960, which codified the agency's multiple use authority and included a provision that "the establishment and maintenance of areas of wilderness are consistent with the purposes * * * [of this Act]," 16 U.S.C.A. § 529, Forest Service opposition abated. An even more serious threat to wilderness legislation was the opposition of Congressman Wayne Aspinall of Colorado, Chairman of the Interior Committee, who refused to let any wilderness legislation out of committee until conservationists agreed to support his pet proposal, the creation of the Public Land Law Review Commission. But after concessions were made to miners, ranchers, and other economic interests in amendments, the Wilderness Act—still one of the most idealistic pieces of federal legislation ever enacted—became law on September 3, 1964.

The Forest Service previously had designated 54 areas as "wilderness," "wild," or "canoe." The Wilderness Act, 16 U.S.C.A. §§ 1131–36, made them the initial units in the National Wilderness Preservation System. 16 U.S.C.A. § 1132(a). These "instant wilderness areas" totalled 9.1 million acres. The Act also required the Forest Service to study an additional 5.4 million acres of designated "primitive areas" and to report to the President within 10 years on their suitability as wilderness. In turn, the President was to report his findings on the primitive areas to Congress. 16 U.S.C.A. § 1132(b). In the Department of Interior, ten-year studies for wilderness suitability were also required on all roadless areas in the National Refuge System and on all roadless areas of more than 5000 acres in the National Park System. 16 U.S. C.A. § 1132(c).

To quell longstanding interagency rivalries, the Act provided that any area included in the wilderness system would continue to be operated by the same agency that administered it before wilderness designation. 16 U.S.C.A. § 1131(b). To prove that neither conservationists nor Congress had yet learned all of the lessons of history, the Act ignored 62% of the public lands—the 470 million acres held by the BLM.

The definition of wilderness in 16 U.S.C.A. § 1131(c) reads precious little like an ordinary federal statute:

> A wilderness, in contrast with those areas where man and his own works dominate the landscape, is hereby recognized as an area where the earth and its community of life are untrammeled by man, where man himself is a visitor who does not remain. An area of wilderness is further defined to mean in this chapter an area of undeveloped Federal land retaining its primeval character and influence, without permanent improvements or human habitation, which is protected and managed so as to preserve its natural conditions and which (1) generally appears to have been affected primarily by the forces of nature, with the imprint of man's work substantially unnoticeable; (2) has outstanding opportunities for solitude or a primitive and unconfined type of recreation; (3) has at least five thousand acres of land or is of sufficient size as to make practicable its preservation and use in an unimpaired condition; and (4) may

also contain ecological, geological, or other features of scientific, educational, scenic, or historical value.

The first sentence of the section defines wilderness in an ideal sense. It
is similar to the definition offered by David Brower, happily mixing
metaphors, that wilderness is an area "where the hand of man has
never set foot." VOICES FOR THE WILDERNESS xi (W. Schwartz ed.
1969). The remainder of the section defines wilderness for legal purposes, and it is replete with qualifying phrases that depart from the
ideal. The definition remains important since subsequent additions to
the system must be within the spirit of the definition.

The crunch comes in sections 1133(c) and (d), however, for they
reflect the compromises that were made to protect many existing uses
and to allow for limited commercial use and resource development in
wilderness areas.

NOTE: SECTION 1133 AND CONFLICTING USES IN WILDERNESS

1. *Mining.* The Wilderness Act, 16 U.S.C.A. § 1133(d):

(2) Nothing in this chapter shall prevent within national
forest wilderness areas any activity, including prospecting, for
the purpose of gathering information about mineral or other
resources, if such activity is carried on in a manner compatible
with the preservation of the wilderness environment. * * *

(3) Notwithstanding any other provisions of this chapter,
until midnight December 31, 1983, the United States mining
laws and all laws pertaining to mineral leasing shall, to the
same extent as applicable prior to September 3, 1964 extend to
those national forest lands designated by this chapter as 'wilderness areas'; subject, however, to such reasonable regulations governing ingress and egress as may be prescribed by the
Secretary of Agriculture consistent with the use of the land for
mineral location and development and exploration, drilling,
and production, and use of land for transmission lines, water-
lines, telephone lines, or facilities necessary in exploring, drilling, producing, mining, and processing operations, including
where essential the use of mechanized ground or air equipment
and restoration as near as practicable of the surface of the land
disturbed in performing prospecting, location, and, in oil and
gas leasing, discovery work, exploration, drilling, and production, as soon as they have served their purpose. Mining
locations lying within the boundaries of said wilderness areas
shall be held and used solely for mining or processing operations and uses reasonably incident thereto; [and] hereafter,
subject to valid existing rights, all patents issued under the
mining laws of the United States affecting national forest
lands designated by this chapter as wilderness areas shall
convey title to the mineral deposits within the claim, together
with the right to cut and use so much of the mature timber

therefrom as may be needed in the extraction, removal, and beneficiation of the mineral deposits, if needed timber is not otherwise reasonably available, and if the timber is cut under sound principles of forest management as defined by the national forest rules and regulations, but each such patent shall reserve to the United States all title in or to the surface of the lands and products thereof, and no use of the surface of the claim or the resources therefrom not reasonably required for carrying on mining or prospecting shall be allowed except as otherwise expressly provided in this chapter * * *.

Section 1133(d)(3) also provides that wilderness lands would be withdrawn from the hardrock mining and mineral leasing laws on January 1, 1984.

Does this section affect claims properly located before the passage of the Act? Does the section restrict use of the surface even more than the Surface Resources Act of 1955, supra at page 463? Do the restrictions on the issuance of patents amount to a taking under the analysis in Freese v. United States, 639 F.2d 754 (Ct.Cl.1981), supra at page 495, for a miner with a valid pre-1964 claim?

While the January 1, 1984 withdrawal date has been incorporated into most statutes adding land to the system, there have been some exceptions. For example, Congress withdrew the Boundary Water Canoe Area Wilderness in 1978 from mining and the Sawtooth and Hell's Canyon Wilderness Areas in Idaho in 1982. On the other hand, Congress has provided that withdrawal of the Gospel Hump Wilderness in Idaho will not occur until January 1, 1988. Finally, a "special management zone" in The River of No Return Wilderness will remain open to locations for cobalt indefinitely. On mining in wilderness areas, see Matthews, Haak, & Toffenetti, Mining and Wilderness: Incompatible Uses or Justifiable Compromise?, Environment at 12 (April 1985); Martin, The Interrelationships of the Mineral Lands Leasing Act, the Wilderness Act, and the Endangered Species Act: A Conflict in Search of Resolution, 12 Envt'l Law 363 (1982); Watson, Mineral and Oil and Gas Development in Wilderness Areas and Other Specially Managed Federal Lands in the United States, 29 Rocky Mtn. Min.L.Inst. 37 (1983); Short, Wilderness Policies and Mineral Potential on the Public Lands, 26 Rocky Mtn.Min.L.Inst. 39 (1980).

Perhaps surprisingly, there is little hardrock mining in wilderness areas. See J. Hendee, G. Stankey & R. Lucas, WILDERNESS MANAGEMENT 284–85 (1978):

* * * Mining claims are numerous—just how numerous is hard to determine because, until recently, there was no requirement to notify the Forest Service when claims were filed on National Forest land. Claims were recorded in the county courthouse, along with many others on other lands. In 1960, the Forest Service estimated there were over 7,000 claims in wilderness and primitive areas larger than 100,000 acres (Outdoor Recreation Resources Review Commission

1962).   However, in 1974, there was no mineral extraction from any National Forest wilderness or primitive area.   Permits for prospecting in wilderness areas are required now, but only 10 were in effect in 1974.   *   *   *

See also Toffenetti, Valid Mining Rights and Wilderness Areas, 20 Land & Water L.Rev. 31 n. 1 (1985) (estimating as many as 10,000 potential claims in wilderness areas but little extraction).   This may be due to strict Forest Service mining regulations for wilderness areas.   36 C.F.R. § 228 (1985).   The Solicitor, noting the limited extent of mining activities in wilderness areas, has surmised that "possible causes include poor mineral prospects, stringent regulation of proposed mineral operations, and the reluctance of the mining industry to risk adverse public reaction by opening major mining operations in wilderness areas."   86 I.D. 89, 110 n. 50 (Feb. 13, 1979).

Secretary Watt in 1981 announced plans to issue mineral leases in several wilderness areas, but then ordered an emergency withdrawal of those areas at the request of the House Interior Committee.   See Pacific Legal Foundation v. Watt, 529 F.Supp. 982 (D.Mont.1981), discussed supra at page 260.   When he later revoked the withdrawal, Congress used the appropriations process to ban expenditure of federal funds for processing leases in wilderness areas and wilderness study areas through September 30, 1983, the end of the fiscal year.   This left a three-month "window" from September 30 through December 31, 1983, when all wilderness lands were to be withdrawn from mineral leasing pursuant to the Wilderness Act.   In late 1982, Secretary Watt declared that he would issue no new oil and gas leases in wilderness or wilderness study areas.   A large number of wilderness study areas, as opposed to statutory wilderness areas, however, are already subject to pending leases.   See generally 8 Pub.Land News No. 1, at 1–2 (Jan. 6, 1983).

2.   *Motorized Equipment and Vehicles.*   Section 1133(c) is a general prohibition:

> Except as specifically provided for in this chapter, and subject to existing private rights, there shall be no commercial enterprise and no permanent road within any wilderness area designated by this chapter and, except as necessary to meet minimum requirements for the administration of the area for the purpose of this chapter (including measures required in emergencies involving the health and safety of persons within the area), there shall be no temporary road, no use of motor vehicles, motorized equipment or motorboats, no landing of aircraft, no other form of mechanical transport, and no structure or installation within any such area.

The provision, which protects "existing private rights," is then qualified in several respects by section 1133(d).   The operation of aircraft and motorboats that "have already become established may be permitted to continue" subject to administrative restrictions.   16 U.S. C.A. § 1131(d)(1).   In United States v. Gregg, 290 F.Supp. 706 (W.D.

Wash.1968), a pilot was fined for landing an airplane in a wilderness area contrary to Forest Service regulations setting rigid conditions on the use of aircraft and other motorized vehicles. The defendant had an "established use" before 1964 and argued that the administrative prohibition violated the Act. Finding that the continuation of such established uses is discretionary with the Forest Service, since section 1133(d)(1) provides that they "may" continue, the court read the section strictly and upheld the conviction. The policy continues. 36 C.F.R. § 293.6 (1985).

The agencies managing wilderness have some discretion to use motorized equipment for the "purpose" of the Act, including rescue missions, section 1133(c), and for controlling fire, insects, and disease, section 1133(d)(1). Nevertheless, in Sierra Club v. Block, 614 F.Supp. 488 (D.D.C.1985), the court enjoined the Department of Agriculture's effort to control the infestation of the southern pine beetle to protect habitat of the endangered red cockaded woodpecker in several southern wilderness areas. The court based its opinion on the Department's failure to prepare an EIS on the effects of the use of motorized equipment and the cutting of trees. But in Sierra Club v. Block, 614 F.Supp. 134 (E.D.Tex.1985), on essentially the same facts, the court allowed the cutting of softwood essential to the control operations even though no EIS had been prepared. The Forest Service uses chain saws and other equipment to clear trails and construct some rough bridges; it fights some but not all fires; and it uses motorized equipment for rescue operations. For Forest Service policy on these issues and on other primitive improvements, see A Colloquy Between Congressman Weaver and Assistant Secretary Cutler, 75 J. Forestry 392 (1977).

3. *Grazing.* Under 16 U.S.C.A. § 1133(d)(4), "the grazing of livestock, where established prior to September 3, 1964, shall be permitted to continue subject to such reasonable regulations as are deemed necessary." Does this provision, unlike the discretionary language used for aircraft and motorboats, create a right where none existed before?

> * * * Traditionally, under the law grazing permits are held not as a matter of right but merely as a matter of privilege, with the administering agency having the right to discontinue permits on their expiration. Does this provision establish any statutory rights in existing permittees? The fact that the continuance of grazing is made subject to reasonable regulation by the secretary implies there was no intent to establish definite rights. Indeed, if there had been any intent to change the basic law on this point, there would have been considerable debate. There was none. Under the "reasonable regulations" that the Forest Service has prepared for its manual, continuance of grazing will be contingent on being consistent with wilderness values and maintenance of soil values. What the draftsmen of this section probably intended, then, was merely to make it clear that the existence of the Wilderness Act *per se* would not preclude continuance of grazing. The Forest Service

would still have the authority to decide whether grazing on a given site was desirable and at what levels of stocking.

McCloskey, The Wilderness Act of 1964: Its Background and Meaning, 45 Ore.L.Rev. 288, 311–12 (1966). In the Colorado Wilderness Act of 1980, Congress directed that, for all wilderness areas, existing grazing uses may continue, but reductions in grazing intensity may be made through agency planning processes to improve poor range conditions. Reductions may not be made, however, solely because the area in which grazing is permitted has been designated as wilderness. See 94 Stat. 3271 (1980).

4. *Logging.* The Act does not expressly refer to timber harvesting, but the legislative history, the general provisions of the act, and the ban on roads and motorized equipment all make it clear that commercial logging is a prohibited activity. Several courts have enjoined timber harvests on the grounds that the areas were being considered for wilderness designation and that wilderness suitability would be destroyed by logging. See, e.g., California v. Block, 690 F.2d 753 (9th Cir.1982), infra at page 1001. What are the circumstances in which limited logging can occur in accordance with the exceptions already discussed?

The only case involving logging in a designated wilderness area is Minnesota Public Interest Research Group v. Butz, 541 F.2d 1292 (8th Cir.1976), which allowed logging under former section 1133(d)(5), dealing specifically with the Boundary Waters Canoe Area. Advocates and opponents of logging, motorboating, snowmobiling, and mining brought the BWCA issue to a sometimes violent head. See, e.g., Johnson, Passionate Suitors for a Wild Paradise, Sports Illustrated 50 (Oct. 10, 1977). In 1978 Congress designated the 1,075,500-acre Boundary Water Canoe Area Wilderness, consisting of the BWCA plus additions to it. The Act repealed former section 1133(d)(5), and section 6 provided for the termination of all timber contracts within one year after passage. Among other things, section 6 also directs the Secretary to "expedite the intensification of resource management including emphasis on softwood timber production and hardwood utilization on the national forest lands in Minnesota outside the wilderness to offset" the reduction in harvest from the wilderness. The BWCAW Act is highly specific and includes many compromise provisions as to the use of motorboats and snowmobiles in specified areas. Section 11 of the 1978 Amendment established a mouthful entitled the Boundary Waters Canoe Area Mining Protection Area, an adjacent buffer zone of 222,000 acres where mining is prohibited so that adverse impacts from mining will not infringe on the wilderness area. See generally Minnesota v. Block, 660 F.2d 1240 (8th Cir. 1981), supra at page 205; Gaetke, The Boundary Waters Canoe Area Wilderness Act of 1978: Regulating Non-Federal Property Under the Property Clause, 60 Or.L.Rev. 157 (1981).

5. *Water Resources.* Under 16 U.S.C.A. § 1133(d)(4), the President has discretion to authorize the development of reservoirs, power projects, and supporting facilities including roads. The authority has apparently never been exercised.

Does the Act provide for reserved water rights by implication? Section 1133(d)(6) states only that "nothing in this chapter shall constitute an express or implied claim or denial on the part of the Federal Government as to exemption from state water laws." The Solicitor, looking to the purposes of the Act, has concluded that there was a reservation of water. See Solicitor's opinion, supra at page 386. See also Sierra Club v. Block, 622 F.Supp. 842 (D.Colo.1985), appeal pending, supra at page 397. Should the Wilderness Act be construed strictly, liberally, or neutrally on such an issue? If there was a reservation, is the priority date when the wilderness was established administratively or when the area was designated wilderness by Congress?

6. *Commercial Services.* Section 1133(d)(5) [former § 1133(d)(6)] modifies § 1133(c) and allows some commercial services, primarily those provided by guides, packers, and river-runners.

7. *Hunting and Fishing.* Section 1133(d)(7) provides that "nothing in this Chapter shall be construed as affecting the jurisdiction or responsibilities of the several States with respect to wildlife and fish in the national forests;" thus hunting and fishing are generally allowed in wilderness areas. Does the Forest Service have authority to set seasons or bag limits? To order closures of specified areas?

8. *Wilderness Management.* Unfortunately, wilderness areas cannot simply be left alone after designation. To remain pristine, an area subject to human use requires human regulation or management. Demand for the "wilderness experience" is growing, but the carrying capacity of many areas is exceeded by the influx of people. Rationing has been imposed in some areas, and is being considered for others. Philosophical questions of purity become concrete when officials are faced with fires, insect attacks, rescue operations, trail maintenance, hunting, sanitation, and mule trains. Activities on adjacent lands also pose management problems. See J. Hendee, G. Stankey, & R. Lucas, WILDERNESS MANAGEMENT 137–46 (1978); R. Nash, WILDERNESS AND THE AMERICAN MIND 316–41 (3rd ed. 1982).

The stereotype of wilderness users is of a class composed of the young, wealthy, leisured, and predominantly urban. In fact, several studies show that wilderness visitors tend to be slightly younger than average but that all age classes are fairly well represented; users are only moderately above-average in income, and as much rural as urban. Characteristics of wilderness users are skewed in only one respect: they tend to be relatively well educated. Thus "the stereotype is largely a myth * * * and should be discarded once and for all." J. Hendee, et al., supra, at 304–06.

3. EXPANDING THE WILDERNESS SYSTEM

Institutional wilderness has been established, or is being studied, in several different ways. It is important to keep them separate, for the legal consequences can differ.

There have been two kinds of administrative wilderness, the lands set aside by the Forest Service and the "primitive areas" established by the BLM. In addition to its creation of "instant wilderness," the Wilderness Act set in motion three separate ten-year studies of lands for wilderness suitability: the Forest Service lands labelled as primitive areas; all roadless areas in the National Wildlife System; and all National Park Service roadless areas of more than 5000 acres. 16 U.S. C.A. § 1133.

Since 1964, the wilderness designation process has moved apace on several fronts. In 1967, the Forest Service—in a momentous step—voluntarily began a comprehensive wilderness study process beyond the requirements of the Act. Under the Roadless Area Review Evaluation (RARE I), all Forest Service roadless areas were to be evaluated for their wilderness potential, although the Act mandated review only for those lands designated as primitive areas. After litigation over RARE I, and with the advent of a new administration in 1977, the Forest Service began RARE II, a more detailed roadless area review with an expanded inventory, totalling 62 million acres. In 1976, FLPMA required a study of all BLM roadless areas for wilderness potential. The law governing both of those study processes will be treated in this section.

Congress has enacted dozens of statutes to expand the system created by the 1964 Act. Statutory coverage has varied: some laws have dealt with individual wilderness areas; others have resolved wilderness designations on a statewide basis; and one, the Eastern Wilderness Act of 1975, designated wilderness for an entire region. The Alaska National Interest Lands Conservation Act of 1980, 16 U.S. C.A. §§ 3101–3233, was easily the largest such bill. ANILCA designated 56.4 million acres in Alaska as wilderness, nearly two-thirds of the entire system. All wilderness areas are listed in the Historical Note after 16 U.S.C.A. § 1132.

The National Wilderness Preservation System in 1986 includes 462 units totalling more than 88 million acres:

Agency	Units	Acres
Forest Service	341	32,086,580
Park Service	38	36,754,980
U.S. Fish & Wildlife Service	60	19,377,033
BLM	23	368,739
	462	88,587,332

Source: Barbara Maxfield, Public Affairs Specialist, U.S.Dept. of Interior (Feb. 1986).

Each area is governed generally by the provisions in the 1964 Act, but in some cases specific legislation will control.

The Wilderness Preservation System continues to grow, but the designation process differs among the federal land management systems.

a. THE NATIONAL FOREST SYSTEM

PARKER v. UNITED STATES

United States Court of Appeals, Tenth Circuit, 1971.
448 F.2d 793.
Cert. denied, 405 U.S. 989 (1972).

LEWIS, Chief Judge.

This appeal is taken by the United States, the Secretary of Agriculture, certain named subordinate federal officials, an intervenor, and Kaibab Industries, a lumber company, from a judgment of the District Court for the District of Colorado, 309 F.Supp. 593, enjoining the federal appellants and their contractor, Kaibab, from performing a contract of sale and harvest of designated timber located on public lands in the state of Colorado. The subject lands adjoin but are not contained within the bounds of a designated primitive or wilderness area and thus the case presents issues of first impression requiring interpretation of the Wilderness Act of September 3, 1964, 78 Stat. 890 and particularly section 3(b) of the Act, 16 U.S.C.A. § 1132(b) which provides:

> The Secretary of Agriculture shall, within ten years after September 3, 1964, review, as to its suitability or nonsuitability for preservation as wilderness, each area in the national forests classified on September 3, 1964 by the Secretary of Agriculture or the Chief of the Forest Service as "primitive" and report his findings to the President. The President shall advise the United States Senate and House of Representatives of his recommendations with respect to the designation as "wilderness" or other reclassification of each area on which review has been completed, together with maps and a definition of boundaries. * * * *Nothing herein contained shall limit the President in proposing, as part of his recommendations to Congress, the alteration of existing boundaries of primitive areas or recommending the addition of any contiguous area of national forest lands predominantly of wilderness value.* Notwithstanding any other provisions of this chapter, the Secretary of Agriculture may complete his review and delete such area as may be necessary, but not to exceed seven thousand acres, from the southern tip of the Gore Range-Eagles Nest Primitive Area, Colorado, if the Secretary determines that such action is in the public interest. (Emphasis added.)

The judgment of the district court has multiple effects:

(1) It determines as a fact that the timber contract pertains to an area, the East Meadow Creek Area of White River National Forest, that is predominantly of wilderness value and contiguous to the Gore Range-Eagles Nest Primitive Area; (2) it enjoins the sale and harvest of timber in the East Meadow Creek Area of White River National Forest until a determination is made by the President and Congress regarding

the area's inclusion in a wilderness area to be created from the Gore Range-Eagles Nest Primitive Area and suitable contiguous lands; (3) it requires that the East Meadow Creek Area, because of its wilderness character and contiguousness to the Gore Range-Eagles Nest Primitive Area, be included in the wilderness study report of the Secretary of Agriculture to the President and Congress. * * * Appellants * * * characteriz[e] the injunction as an unauthorized interference with a discretionary management function authorized by Congress and stemming from an unconsented suit against the United States. * * *

* * *

We have no difficulty in recognizing the general purpose of the Wilderness Act. It is simply a congressional acknowledgment of the necessity of preserving one factor of our natural environment from the progressive, destructive and hasty inroads of man, usually commercial in nature, and the enactment of a "proceed slowly" order until it can be determined wherein the balance between proper multiple uses of the wilderness lies and the most desirable and highest use established for the present and future. A concerned Congress, reflecting the wishes of a concerned public, did by statutory definition choose terminology that would seem to indicate its ultimate mandate.

* * *

Having initially established by definition that a wilderness cannot remain a wilderness if man invades and remains, the Act made at least three further provisions pertinent to our case. It designated the Gore Range-Eagles Nest Primitive Area, and other comparable areas, a preserved wilderness subject to some exceptions not here involved. It required the Secretary of Agriculture, through 16 U.S.C.A. § 1132(b), to review and report as findings to the President, and within a time certain, the suitability or nonsuitability of all such areas for preservation as wilderness within the national forests. In turn, the President was directed to advise the Congress of his recommendations on the subject *but*, as earlier emphasized in our citation of this section, the President was not to be bound by the action of the Secretary or findings of the Secretary and could recommend that the designated primitive areas be enlarged by the addition of contiguous areas predominantly of wilderness value.

Appellants do not attack the finding of the trial court, as such, that the East Meadow Creek Area is of wilderness value. And, indeed, the finding is supported by the record considered under any standard of appellate review. See 309 F.Supp. 593, 601. But of course such finding has no significance unless there is "law to apply," in that 16 U.S.C.A. § 1132(b) clearly means that the President and Congress shall have a meaningful opportunity to add contiguous areas predominantly of wilderness value to existing primitive areas for final wilderness designation. The lumber industry appellants do attack the trial court's designation of the contract lands as "contiguous" to the preserved wilderness area by pointing out that the Forest Service, after listening to various protests concerning the original contract contemplated with Kaibab, reduced the number of board feet in the proposed contract and in so doing preserved a bumper area between East Meadow Creek and the Gore Range-Eagles Nest Primitive Area. We are not impressed with this contention. The preservation of a "bumper" area does not probe the basic question presented, merely serves to lessen the impact of the agency action, and does not justify such action if otherwise prohibited. We reject this contention as dispositive of our issue.

Because this case is one of first impression, all appellants very properly set out the legislative history of the Wilderness Act as an argumentative premise that the Act was not intended to constitute a drastic cutback in the discretionary management judgment of the concerned administrative agencies and that the Act was intended to supplement and not supplant the Multiple Use-Sustained Yield Act of 1960. * * * [W]e accept the legislative history of the Act as indicating its terms should not be interpreted as a general curtailment of agency discretion in the normal day-by-day administration of the national forests, parks or other public lands. But we find nothing in the Wilderness Act as written or in its legislative history in formulation that would support an ambiguity in word or intent dictating an error in the interpretation of section 1132(b) as made by the trial court.

It is, of course, a cardinal rule of statutory construction that effect should be given to every provision of a statute. Should we, in the case at bar, concede to federal appellants the discretionary right to destroy the wilderness value of the subject area, one contiguous to a designated wilderness, we would render meaningless the clear intent of Congress expressed in 16 U.S.C.A. § 1132(b) that both the President and the Congress shall have a meaningful opportunity to add contiguous areas predominantly of wilderness value to existing primitive areas for final wilderness designation. This statutory limitation on agency discretion is, of course, a narrow one dictated by necessity as contained in the definition of wilderness and by the specifics of the statutory words creating the limitation.

The third and final aspect of the trial court's injunction affirmatively requires the federal appellants to include its study of the East Meadow Creek Area in its report to the President and Congress. Justification for this requirement is found in the regulations of the Forest Service itself.

The Forest Service, rather than include its detailed regulations in the Code of Federal Regulations, maintains the Forest Service Manual (FSM). The section of the regulations which is most helpful in the construction of 16 U.S.C.A. § 1132(b) is FSM § 2321(1):

> Each Primitive Area (so classified as of September 3, 1964) *and contiguous lands which seem to have significant wilderness resources* will be studied to determine whether to recommend that all or part should be included in the National Wilderness Preservation System. (Emphasis added.)

Following FSM § 2321(1) are lengthy and detailed directives describing the manner in which studies are to be made, listing the factors to be considered in making recommendations, giving instructions for conducting public hearings, and recognizing that the duty of the Forest Service is to study and recommend and that the President and Congress are to make the final determinations. The regulations contain not just one, but many references to the study of contiguous areas of significant wilderness value. It seems clear from the Forest Service's regulations that its construction of the Wilderness Act is in full accord with the decision of the court below. Indeed, the testimony and exhibits offered at trial show that the Forest Service has scrupulously adhered to the regulations and the statutory scheme in other wilderness reviews and recommendations. A review of the exhibits offered at trial shows numerous recommendations for addition of contiguous areas to the primitive areas for final wilderness classification.

The trial court, having determined as a fact that the East Meadow Creek Area had predominantly wilderness value which should be preserved for consideration at the executive and congressional level, was completely justified in directing inclusion of a study of the area in the mandated report to the President. This requirement in no way directs or limits the Secretary in his full discretionary right to make such recommendation to the President as he may deem proper.

We conclude, as did the trial court, that 16 U.S.C.A. § 1132(b) sets out "law to apply" under the facts of the case at bar and hold that consequently this action and the judgment neither constitute an unauthorized suit against the United States nor an unjustified judicial interference with the management powers of federal appellants.

* * *

The judgment is affirmed.

NOTES

1. The Tenth Circuit derived its duty to enjoin the timber contract from the "purposes" rather than the "language" of the Wilderness Act, did it not? Does this judicial methodology square with Kleppe v. Sierra Club, 427 U.S. 390 (1976), supra at page 323, in which the Court read NEPA literally and applied it narrowly? Are the purposes of the Wilderness Act such that it should be construed expansively in favor of wilderness designation and protection?

2. The *Parker* litigation also involved an early dispute over "purity". At the trial level, though not on appeal, the Forest Service argued that the East Meadow Creek area was not of wilderness character because of one access road and a "bug" road; the latter had been built 20 years earlier to fight infestation by the bark beetle, but was grown over and substantially unnoticeable. Otherwise, the area was "wild" in that it was "inhabited by animals, * * * thickly wooded, secluded, and unspoiled." 309 F.Supp. at 595–96. The court rejected the Forest Service's argument and held that the area possessed sufficient wilderness characteristics. Id. at 600–01. The "purist" controversy continued in several other primitive areas:

> * * * The Forest Service stresses such words as "untrammeled", and "retaining its primeval character" to construe the

statutory definition narrowly and restrict potential Wilderness status to areas which have *never* been significantly affected by man. How this works out in practice is illustrated by the Roadless Area Review Program. Out of 1,448 areas inventoried, 235 were selected for further study of their wilderness potential. Of these units, only three were in the eastern half of the United States. The Forest Service reasoned:

> Of the 187 million acres within the National Forest System, 87 percent are located in the western United States while 13 percent are in the East. Much of the eastern area, acquired after the initial establishment of the forest reserves from public domain, was formerly logged over or developed in other ways. Throughout the East, from north to south, the impacts of industry and relatively high population levels have drastically altered the original ecosystems of pioneer days.

> Critics of the Forest Service, including some of the 31 Senators who sponsored the Eastern Wilderness Areas bill, argue that the Service is imposing too narrow a construction on the language of the Act, a construction Congress did not intend when it passed the measure. They argue that the Act was intended to apply to areas which may have been subject to exploitation in the past, but which have been subsequently restored by natural processes to a pristine-like condition. * * * This dispute, which obviously involves far more than semantics, is still unresolved.

Haight, The Wilderness Act: Ten Years After, 3 Envt'l Aff. 275, 288 (1974). The Forest Service generally adopted a more liberal view of wilderness for study purposes in the late 1970's, but "purity" is a live question in eastern wilderness questions and in the BLM wilderness study under FLPMA.

3. Though the greater part of the public lands lies west of the Mississippi, people in the East, South, and Midwest can readily point to areas in those regions that are both public and primitive. Recognizing this, and finding that areas in "the more populous eastern half of the United States are increasingly threatened by the pressures of a growing and more mobile population, [and] large-scale industrial and economic growth," Congress in 1975 designated as wilderness 15 national forest areas totaling 206,988 acres in Alabama, Arkansas, Florida, Georgia, Kentucky, North Carolina, New Hampshire, South Carolina, Tennessee, Virginia, Vermont, West Virginia, and Wisconsin. Pub.L. No. 93–622, 88 Stat. 2096. Seventeen eastern study areas were also designated.

4. The Forest Service primitive area study mandated by the Wilderness Act, and litigated in *Parker,* ended within the 10-year deadline. The Service recommended to the President that most of the primitive areas be classified as wilderness; Congress then finally designated most of the areas. J. Hendee, G. Stankey, & R. Lucas, WILDERNESS MANAGEMENT 94–99 (1978).

5. The Wilderness Act made no mention of *de facto* wilderness—those wild lands in the National Forest System not already classified as wilderness or primitive areas—but the Forest Service instituted the Roadless Area Review Evaluation (RARE I) in 1967 to complement the congressionally mandated study of primitive areas. Forest supervisers were directed to prepare inventories of all roadless areas either more than 5000 acres or adjacent to a wilderness or primitive area. The inventory process moved slowly and was sharply criticized by the Council on Environmental Quality and environmentalists. D. Barney, THE LAST STAND 99–101 (1974).

The RARE I inventory was released in 1972; it included 1449 areas totalling 56 million acres—an area larger than the State of Idaho. Only 18% of these lands were commercial timber land, and much of that was of low commercial value. Still, RARE I lands represented a significant part of the Forest Service timber base. Reasoning that many of the inventoried lands did not have wilderness value, the Forest Service offered timber contracts on some of them. The Sierra Club promptly filed suit. A preliminary injunction was issued, prohibiting any cutting on RARE lands until an EIS was completed. Sierra Club v. Butz, 3 ELR 20071 (N.D.Cal.1972). The plaintiffs had sought only prospective relief and the injunction did not apply to contracts entered into before July 1, 1972. The Forest Service settled Sierra Club v. Butz, which was dismissed without prejudice, by agreeing in late 1972 to let no new timber contracts on RARE I lands until the completion of EISs. Then, in Wyoming Outdoor Coordinating Council v. Butz, 484 F.2d 1244 (10th Cir.1973), the court enjoined existing timber contracts in roadless areas because the Forest Service had not prepared EISs:

> Our case must be decided under the exacting standards of [NEPA, 42 U.S.C.A. § 4332(2)(C).] While we accept the findings that the harvest of timber would have no adverse effect on the livelihood of the elk, that the area did not contain a pristine forest, that it was traversed by numerous jeep roads, and the other evidentiary findings, nevertheless the undisputed facts remaining present a compelling case invoking the protective procedures of NEPA. As noted there will be 46 clearcut areas with removal of all timber from them, involving some 15.7 million board feet of timber. The clearcuts will cover 670 acres, dispersed through a gross sale area of 10,700 acres. The area is one traversed only by the jeep roads and is basically undeveloped. It is described in the findings as an area now "uninhabited except for various species of wildlife, four outfitter camps, and a number of elk * * *" located in the setting of the Teton National Forest.

> * * *

> * * * Without deciding whether there would be irreparable injury to any of the wildlife or permanent destruction of the forests by performance of the contracts, we feel there is an overriding public interest in preservation of the undeveloped character of the area recognized by the statute. This public

interest in preserving the character of the environment is one that the plaintiffs may seek to protect by obtaining equitable relief. The clearcutting of the timber planned obviously will have a significant effect on the environment for many years. Thus the threat of environmental injury without compliance with the statute's procedures justifies equitable relief.

The final EIS on RARE I lands was released in October, 1973, dropping most roadless areas from the inventory and designating 274 areas totalling 12.3 million acres for detailed study for wilderness suitability. On RARE I, see J. Hendee, G. Stankey, & R. Lucas, WILDERNESS MANAGEMENT 99–105 (1978); M. Clawson, FORESTS: FOR WHOM AND FOR WHAT? 64–68 (1975); Milton, National Forest Roadless and Undeveloped Areas: Develop or Preserve? 51 Land Economics 139 (1975).

The RARE I study lagged after the 1973 EIS. In 1977, the Forest Service essentially began the process anew by developing a new roadless area inventory and a new study process, which became RARE II. The new inventory included 2918 units (more than twice as many as RARE I) totalling slightly more than 62 million acres—one-third of all land within the national forest system. Studies were then undertaken to determine which areas should be declared non-wilderness and which should receive still further study.

CALIFORNIA v. BLOCK
United States Court of Appeals, Ninth Circuit, 1982.
690 F.2d 753.

TANG, Circuit Judge:

This appeal is from a summary judgment and injunction entered against the Forest Service for failing to comply with the National Environmental Policy Act, 42 U.S.C. §§ 4331–4332 (1976), in preparing an environmental impact statement ("EIS") on a Forest Service decision to allocate National Forest System land among three management categories. Four principal issues are raised. Did the district court err in holding that:

(1) the Final EIS did not contain an adequate discussion of the site-specific environmental consequences of the allocations?

(2) the Final EIS did not consider an adequate range of alternatives?

(3) the Forest Service did not give the public an adequate opportunity to comment on the proposed allocations?

(4) the National Forest Management Act, 16 U.S.C. § 1604 (1976), did not exempt the disputed allocations from review under the National Environmental Policy Act?

We affirm in part and reverse in part.

FACTS

This litigation concerns how the Forest Service intends to manage 62 million acres of the National Forest System. The National Forest

System contains approximately 190 million acres, and includes 154 National Forests and 19 National Grasslands. The Forest Service is charged additionally with administering a large portion of the National Wilderness Preservation System ("NWPS"), which currently includes more than 19 million acres. The latter system was created by Congress in 1964 to provide statutory protection for areas that are relatively untouched by humankind. 16 U.S.C. § 1131 (1976). Under the mandate of the enabling legislation, the Secretary of Agriculture is directed to recommend to Congress "primitive" areas that should be added to the Wilderness System. Id. at § 1132. Other legislation also obliges the Secretary to manage National Forest land to foster "multiple-use" of the system's resources, including recreation, lumbering, mining, grazing and commercial fishing.

* * *

In 1977, the Forest Service made a second attempt to evaluate programmatically the roadless areas in the National Forest System. This project, named RARE II, inventoried all roadless areas within the National Forest System and allocated each area to one of three planning categories: Wilderness, Further Planning and Nonwilderness. Areas designated as Wilderness were to be recommended to Congress for inclusion in the NWPS. A Further Planning designation meant that an area would be protected pending completion of unit management plans which would consider whether to recommend the area for inclusion in the NWPS. No controversy surrounds the Wilderness or Further Planning designations. The parties here dispute what a Nonwilderness designation means.

A draft EIS on the RARE II project was released to the public on June 15, 1978. The document consisted of a national planning description and twenty state and geographic area supplements. It identified ten alternative allocation methods which resulted in different allocations between the three planning categories, but did not tentatively endorse any of the alternatives as a Proposed Action. Each alternative reflected a different combination of decisional criteria. The criteria included Forest Service resource planning goals, wilderness attributes, public accessibility to wilderness areas, public comment and the economic effects of Wilderness classification.

Public comment was solicited concerning the decisional criteria, the allocations that resulted from the alternatives, and possible alternative approaches not considered in the draft. The draft EIS prompted over 264,000 comments.

The Final EIS was filed on January 4, 1979. It identified for the first time the Forest Service's Proposed Action and called for allocating 15 million acres of RARE II lands to Wilderness, 10.8 million acres to Further Planning, and 36 million acres to Nonwilderness. See Forest Service, U.S. Dep't of Agriculture, RARE II Final Environmental Impact Statement, Roadless Area Review and Evaluation 37 (1979) [hereinafter cited as "RARE II Final EIS"]. The Proposed Action was not one of the alternatives considered in the draft EIS, but represented an amalgam of all the decisional criteria considered in the draft EIS alternatives. The percentage allocation produced by the Proposed Action was within the range of percentage allocations produced by the draft EIS alternatives, but was not roughly identical to any one set of allocation percentages considered in the earlier alternatives.

The Final EIS, unlike the earlier draft, was circulated only to Congress and to affected federal and state agencies. Its recommendations were sent to the President on May 2, 1979, who approved them after making some minor changes in the allocations. The wilderness recommendations were subsequently transmitted to Congress.

On July 25, 1979, the State of California brought action in federal district court against the Secretary of Agriculture and the Forest Service, alleging violations of the National Environmental Policy Act ("NEPA"), 42 U.S.C. §§ 4331–4332 (1976), the Multiple-Use Sustained-Yield Act ("MUSY"), 16 U.S.C. § 528 (1976), and the National Forest Management Act ("NFMA"), 16 U.S.C. § 1604 (1976). * * *

California specifically challenged the Forest Service decision to designate forty-seven RARE II areas in California as Nonwilderness. On January 8, 1980, the district court granted California's motion for summary judgment. Without reaching the MUSY and NFMA claims, the court held that the RARE II Final EIS was inadequate to support the Nonwilderness designations of the disputed areas and therefore violated NEPA. It ruled that the Final EIS was deficient in three respects: (1) the EIS did not contain sufficient site-specific data to support the Nonwilderness designations; (2) the EIS did not consider an adequate range of alternatives; and (3) the Forest Service did not give the public an adequate opportunity to comment on the RARE II program.

Pursuant to these holdings, the district court enjoined the Forest Service from taking any action that might change the wilderness character of the disputed areas in California until it filed an EIS that satisfied NEPA's requirements and considered the impact of the decision upon the wilderness characteristics of these areas. The court excepted from its order activities that had been previously analyzed in an EIS apart from the RARE II Final EIS. The court also enjoined the Forest Service from relying upon the RARE II Final EIS in preparing forest plans pursuant to the NFMA.

* * *

DISCUSSION

I. *Did the RARE II Final EIS adequately examine the site-specific impact of the Proposed Action?*

The district court concluded that the RARE II Final EIS failed to consider adequately the site-specific impact of the RARE II decision. Specifically, the district court cited the following deficiencies:

— The EIS does not comprehensively describe any of the RARE II areas, limiting its evaluation per area to two pages of summary

index numbers that do not identify the areas' unique characteristics (e.g., landmarks, rare and endangered species);

— No attempt is made to assess the wilderness value of each area
(e.g., tourism, sales of wilderness oriented recreational equipment, conservation of wildlife and flora populations, soil conservation and stability, watershed protection, clean air and
water);

— The EIS does not discuss the impact of Nonwilderness designations upon each area's wilderness characteristics and values
(e.g., primary and secondary impacts, methods of mitigation,
and environmental damage);

— The EIS does not consider the effect of development on future
opportunities for wilderness classification (i.e., the effect upon
the benchmark characteristics identified in the Wilderness
Act);

— The EIS does not attempt to balance economic benefits of
Nonwilderness designation for an area against the consequent
environmental loss.

California v. Bergland, 483 F.Supp. 465, 483–87 (E.D.Cal.1980).

The Forest Service complains that the degree of detail required by
the district court is unwarranted, given the tentative nature of the
RARE II decision and the national scope of its impact. The central
contention is that a programmatic EIS describing the first step in a
multi-step national project need not contain the type of detailed site-
specific information normally contained in an EIS prepared for a more
narrowly focused project such as a dam or a federal mineral lease.

The detail that NEPA requires in an EIS depends upon the nature
and scope of the proposed action. * * * The critical inquiry in
considering the adequacy of an EIS prepared for a large scale, multi-
step project is not whether the project's site-specific impact should be
evaluated in detail, but when such detailed evaluation should occur.

NEPA requires that the evaluation of a project's environmental
consequences take place at an early stage in the project's planning
process. This requirement is tempered, though, by the statutory command that we focus upon a proposal's parameters as the agency defines
them. The requirement is further tempered by the preference to defer
detailed analysis until a concrete development proposal crystallizes the
dimensions of a project's probable environmental consequences. When
a programmatic EIS has already been prepared, we have held that site-
specific impacts need not be fully evaluated until a "critical decision"
has been made to act on site development. This threshold is reached
when, as a practical matter, the agency proposes to make an "irreversible and irretrievable commitment of the availability of resources" to a
project at a particular site.

The fundamental issue presented here is whether a "critical decision" has been made with respect to site development. The starting
point in our analysis is "to describe accurately the 'federal action' being

taken." The district court concluded that the RARE II decision contained two parts: (1) the Forest Services' recommendation to Congress that the Wilderness designated areas be included in the NWPS; and (2) in designing and implementing forest management plans during the next ten to fifteen years, the mandate that the Forest Service will not consider the wilderness *uses* or *features* of areas designated as Nonwilderness. All parties agree that RARE II encompasses the first component. They disagree whether RARE II encompasses the second.

The Forest Service argues that the district court erred in concluding that Nonwilderness designation is tantamount to a decision to permit development. It emphasizes that the RARE II process is only the first step in a multi-stage planning process to allocate roadless areas to competing social uses. At this step, the Service contends, a RARE II Nonwilderness designation means only that the areas will not be considered for inclusion in the NWPS during the first generation of forest management plans under the NFMA, a period lasting between ten to fifteen years. In the meantime the Forest Service will entertain specific development proposals concerning these areas, but will prepare separate EIS's if federal action is contemplated and will consider wilderness values in devising forest plans for these areas. Given the limited impact of the Nonwilderness designation, the Forest Service urges that it is permissible to limit the scope of the EIS to a generalized discussion of the designations' overall impact.

California argues, and the district court agreed, that the Forest Service unfairly minimizes the consequences of the Nonwilderness designation. California and the district court decision focus upon the following Forest Service regulation pertaining to Nonwilderness designated areas:

> Lands reviewed for Wilderness designation under the review and evaluation of roadless areas conducted by the Secretary of Agriculture but not designated as wilderness or designated for further planning and lands whose designation as primitive areas has been terminated will be managed for uses other than wilderness in accordance with this subpart. No such area will be considered for designation as wilderness until a revision of the forest plan under § 219.11(f) ＊ ＊ ＊.

36 C.F.R. § 219.12(e) (1981).

California and the district court decision interpret this regulation to mean that the Forest Service will not consider a Nonwilderness area's *wilderness features* for *any* purpose during the area's forest plan life. Thus, while an EIS on specific development proposals will consider substantial pollution effects, California argues that the Forest Service will be precluded from considering the desirability of utilizing the proposed site as a wilderness area, and will not consider wilderness features (e.g., solitude, primitive character and wilderness recreation) in assessing the environmental consequences. They conclude that if the wilderness features and values of each Nonwilderness area are ever to be individually evaluated, they must be evaluated now.

On balance, we conclude that California's description of the effect of Nonwilderness designation is more accurate and therefore affirm the district court. We agree with the Forest Service that the *last* sentence in the above quoted regulation only restricts the Forest Service from considering Nonwilderness areas for Wilderness designation, and does not explicitly forbid the Forest Service from considering Nonwilderness areas' wilderness features or values in devising forest plans. The sentence that *precedes* this clause, however, explicitly mandates that Nonwilderness areas "will be managed for uses other than wilderness." This command is not subject to any ambiguity. At least during the first generation of forest plans, Nonwilderness designated areas will be managed for purposes other than wilderness preservation. This command is repeated in the text of the Final EIS itself, which indicates that "[a]reas allocated to nonwilderness *will* become available on April 15, 1979, for multiple resource use activities *other than wilderness.*"

Future decisions concerning these areas will be constrained by this choice. While the regulations technically permit consideration of wilderness values and features in forest planning, such consideration is pointless in the absence of the discretion to manage a Nonwilderness area in a manner consistent with wilderness preservation. Similarly, the promise of site-specific EIS's in the future is meaningless if later analysis cannot consider wilderness preservation as an alternative to development. The "critical decision" to commit these areas for nonwilderness uses, at least for the next ten to fifteen years, is "irreversible and irretrievable." The site-specific impact of this decisive allocative decision must therefore be carefully scrutinized now and not when specific development proposals are made.

The deficiencies noted by the district court are precisely the omissions the Forest Service will need to correct in order to comply fully with NEPA. The prescribed content of the EIS is delineated in the Council of Environmental Quality ("CEQ") Guidelines in effect at the time of the EIS's issuance, which the Forest Service has incorporated into its own planning guidelines, and to which we grant "substantial deference" as the authoritative guide for NEPA's interpretation. Andrus v. Sierra Club, 442 U.S. 347, 358 (1979).

First, these guidelines require that the proposing agency "describe the environment of the area affected as it exists prior to a proposed action." 40 C.F.R. § 1500.8(a)(1) (1977) (superceded 1978). The Final EIS reflects only a feeble attempt to comply with this requirement. For each area in the RARE II inventory, the EIS contains a two page computer print-out which lists: (1) the location and acreage of the area; (2) its classification as one of forty basic landform types; (3) its Bailey-Kuchler classification as to ecosystem type; (4) the number of wilderness-associated wildlife species in the area; and (5) a competitive numerical rating score of each area's wilderness attributes. What this description fails to do is identify the distinguishing wilderness characteristics of each area. The indices utilized are simply too generalized. The Bailey-Kuchler classifications, for example, do not identify ecosystems less than 50,000 acres, yet many of the areas are smaller than this limit and contain a variety of different habitats. Similarly, while the EIS lists wildlife numbers, it reveals nothing concerning wildlife types and quantity, or whether rare and endangered wildlife species exist in a particular area.

The Wilderness Attribute Rating System ("WARS") score is even less informative. The WARS score utilized four distinct factors identified in the Wilderness Act (naturalness, apparent naturalness, opportunity for solitude, and opportunity for a primitive recreation experience) and assigned a numerical rating to each area from one to seven, depending on the degree of naturalness or opportunity exhibited. The four factors rated were combined to give a potential WARS score from four to twenty-eight for each area, and then the area score was competitively ranked against the WARS scores assigned to all other roadless areas. Thus, the only information the Final EIS reveals concerning the wilderness attributes of each area is a single number. Instead of identifying the unique wilderness attributes of each area, it treats wilderness characteristics as essentially fungible, and lumps them together for competitive ranking against other areas which may or may not be similar.

Second, the CEQ Guidelines require "agencies to assess the positive and negative effects of the proposed action as it affects both the national and international environment," id. at § 1500.8(a)(3)(i), and to discuss "[a]ny irreversible and irretrievable commitments involved in the proposed action should it be implemented." Id. at § 1500.8(d)(7). This inquiry requires an agency to assess the wilderness value of each area and to evaluate the impact of Nonwilderness designations upon each area's wilderness characteristics and value. We agree with the district court that the RARE II Final EIS is deficient in both respects. While the value of wilderness is discussed in broad terms, no attempt is made to assess the intrinsic worth of the wilderness features of any particular area, nor to forecast the value lost under various developmental regimes.

Third, the CEQ Guidelines require an EIS to discuss "[s]econdary or indirect * * * consequences for the environment." Id. at § 1500.8(a)(3)(ii), and to discuss specifically "the extent to which the action irreversibly curtails the range of potential uses of the environment," id. at § 1500.8(a)(7). As noted by the district court, the RARE II Final EIS fails to comply with this requirement because it does not consider the effect of Nonwilderness classification upon future opportunities for wilderness classification. Under Forest Service regulations, Nonwilderness areas may be reconsidered for Wilderness System inclusion in devising the second generation of forest plans ten to fifteen years hence. In the interim, however, these areas will be managed for uses other than wilderness. The foreclosing of the wilderness management option requires a careful assessment of how this new management strategy will affect each area's benchmark characteristics as identified in the Wilderness Act.

Fourth, the CEQ Guidelines require an agency to indicate "what other interests and considerations of Federal policy are thought to offset the adverse environmental effects of the proposed action." Id. at § 1500.8(a)(8). While the EIS carefully identifies the economic benefit attributable to development in each area, no effort is made to weigh this benefit against the wilderness loss each area will suffer from development. This evaluation need not be in the form of a formal cost benefit analysis, but it should reflect that the Forest Service has compared for each area the potential benefits of Nonwilderness management against the potential adverse environmental consequences.

The Forest Service argues that most of the above-mentioned deficiencies are rectified if the worksheets prepared by the Forest Supervisors to compute the score for the WARS are considered part of the RARE II Final EIS. A typical WARS worksheet consists of approximately twelve pages of site-specific data regarding a single inventoried area. First, for the reasons given by the district court, we question whether the worksheets contain the type of site-specific analyses required by NEPA. Second, in any event we conclude that the worksheets cannot be fairly considered as part of the RARE II Final EIS. It is settled in this circuit that any supporting data or studies expressly relied upon in an EIS must be "available and accessible" to the public. The WARS worksheets, however, are scattered all over the country in various Regional Foresters' offices, dooming any practical attempt to review comprehensively the worksheets. Given this inaccessibility, the worksheets may not be considered in determining the RARE II Final EIS's adequacy.

We concede that conducting a detailed site-specific analysis of the RARE II decision will be no simple task and will be laden with empirical uncertainty. The scope of the undertaking here, however, was the Forest Service's choice and not the courts'. NEPA contains no exemptions for projects of national scope. Having decided to allocate simultaneously millions of acres of land to nonwilderness use, the Forest Service may not rely upon forecasting difficulties or the task's magnitude to excuse the absence of a reasonably thorough site-specific analysis of the decision's environmental consequences.

II. *Did the RARE II Final EIS consider a reasonable range of alternatives?*

The Final EIS lists eleven alternatives, of which three—"all Wilderness", "no Wilderness" and "no action"—were included as points of reference rather than as seriously considered alternatives. * * * Each alternative reflects a different combination of the following decisional criteria: (1) resource outputs assigned to each area by the Forest Service; (2) guidelines from the Multiple-Use Sustained-Yield Act, 16 U.S.C. § 528–531 (1976); (3) visitor accessibility; (4) landform features; (5) wildlife features; (6) ecosystems; and (7) Wilderness Attribute Rating System rating. * * * The alternative ultimately selected by the Forest Service, the Proposed Action, utilizes elements of all the decisional criteria. * * * None of the eight alternatives seriously considered by the Forest Service designates more than thirty-three percent of the roadless acreage to Wilderness, and none designates less than thirty-seven percent of that acreage to Nonwilderness. More than one-half of the roadless acreage is allocated to Nonwilderness in six of the eight alternatives.

The district court held that the RARE II Final EIS failed to consider an adequate range of alternatives. The court ruled that the EIS should have considered at least three other alternatives:

— Expanding the number of classifications beyond the broad categories Wilderness, Nonwilderness and Future Planning. Other classifications might include limited or conditioned development, areas suitable for geographical use restrictions, and areas particularly susceptible to successfully mitigating environmental damage caused by development;

— Increasing production on federally owned land that is currently open to development;

— Allocating to Wilderness a share of the RARE II acreage at an intermediate percentage between 34% and 100%.

The Forest Service challenges the district court's ruling on three overlapping grounds: (1) California has not met its burden of proof in establishing that the three alternatives suggested by the district court are "potentially viable" alternatives at this stage of planning; (2) the district court ignored the Forest Service's use of the Further Planning category when the court criticized the Final EIS for not further refining its classifications; and (3) it would be premature to consider the three alternatives suggested by the district court, given the limited scope of the RARE II decision. The connecting theme in all three contentions is that the RARE II decision is too tentative and preliminary in character to warrant consideration of these alternatives at this planning stage.

* * * As with the standard employed to evaluate the detail that NEPA requires in discussing a decision's environmental consequences, the touchstone for our inquiry is whether an EIS's selection and discussion of alternatives fosters informed decision-making and informed public participation.

Following these standards, we conclude that the Forest Service was reasonable in not considering the first alternative suggested by the district court. We therefore reverse the district court's ruling that the Forest Service must consider this alternative. The focal point of our inquiry must be the underlying environmental policy, and whether the agency's proposed action comports with that policy. The policy problem RARE II seeks to confront is how to allocate a scarce resource—wilderness—between the two competing and mutually exclusive demands of wilderness use and development. * * *

The first alternative suggested by the district court is not responsive to these policy concerns. The conditional use categories suggested by the district court all contemplate some type of development or nonwilderness use. The policy question which RARE II seeks to answer, however, is how much land should be opened to *any* type of development or nonwilderness use. Consideration of conditional use categories does not aid the agency in reaching an informed decision.

We conclude that the second alternative is essential to making a "reasoned choice," however. We therefore affirm the district court's ruling that the Forest Service must consider this alternative. The policy at hand demands a trade-off between wilderness use and development. This trade-off, however, cannot be intelligently made without examining whether it can be softened or eliminated by increasing resource extraction and use from already developed areas. The economic value of nonwilderness use is a function of its scarcity. Benefits accrue from opening virgin land to nonwilderness use, but the benefits' worth depend upon their relative availability elsewhere, and the comparative environmental costs of focusing development in these other areas.

The RARE II Final EIS fails to make such an inquiry. The effect is profound. All eight of the alternatives seriously considered by the Forest Service assume that at least thirty-seven percent of the RARE II areas should be developed. No justification is given for this fundamental premise or the trade-off it reflects. In the absence of an alternative that looks to already developed areas for future resource extraction and use, the RARE II decisional process ends its inquiry at the beginning. Although the RARE II Final EIS poses the question whether development should occur at all, it uncritically assumes that a substantial portion of the RARE II areas should be developed and considers only those alternatives with that end result.

As for the third alternative, we also agree with and affirm the district court's ruling that NEPA requires the Forest Service to consider an alternative that allocates more than a third of the RARE II acreage to Wilderness. Whether the RARE II decision is viewed as a decision to develop or merely as the first step in a protracted planning process, it is puzzling why the Forest Service did not seriously consider an alternative that allocated more than a third of the RARE II acreage to Wilderness. All of the RARE II acreage, by definition, met the minimum criteria for inclusion in the NWPS. Nonetheless, without any explanation the final EIS seriously considered only those alternatives that allocate more acreage to Nonwilderness than to Wilderness. Moreover, with the sole exception of Alternative I, Nonwilderness acreage allocations exceed Wilderness allocations by a substantial margin, ranging from five-to-two for Alternative D, to nineteen-to-one for Alternative E. While nothing in NEPA prohibits the Forest Service from ultimately implementing a proposal that allocates more acreage to Nonwilderness than to Wilderness, it is troubling that the Forest Service saw fit to consider from the outset only those alternatives leading to that end result.

In response, the Forest Service urges that we should not focus upon the final acreage allocations resulting from each alternative, but upon the diversity of decisional criteria utilized in formulating the alternatives. The agency contends that it is the different mixes of decisional criteria, rather than the ultimate acreage allocations, which matters for NEPA review of alternatives.

We disagree. First, as noted by the district court, nothing intrinsic in the decisional criteria requires not considering an alternative that allocates more than thirty-three percent of the RARE II lands to Wilderness. Instead, what appears to have been instrumental in skewing the alternatives away from Wilderness were the numerical values assigned to the decisional criteria in each of the alternatives.

Second, little explanation is given to justify the numerical values given these variables. The Final EIS, for instance, offers no explanation of how resource output levels were assigned to each area. The EIS states that the levels "may appear to have been arbitrarily selected but, in fact, represent a realistic establishment of acceptable resource trade-offs to provide various alternative approaches." The Final EIS, however, does not explain what the tradeoffs were or why they were considered acceptable or realistic. Rather than utilizing the Final EIS as an instrument for airing the issue of resource demand, the Forest Service instead shrouded the issue from public scrutiny behind the claim of administrative expertise.

The Final EIS's consideration of wilderness attributes appears similarly arbitrary. Five alternatives, including the Proposed Action, utilize a predetermined WARS score percentile cut-off to determine area allocation. Compare Alternative C (target group designated Nonwilderness unless WARS score in top 10 percentile for region, then designated Further Planning); Alternative D (initial target group includes all areas with WARS score in top 40 percentile); Alternative F (areas with a WARS score in top 30 percentile allocated to Further Planning if not otherwise allocated to Wilderness); Alternative I (initial target group includes all areas with WARS score in top 50 percentile); and Proposed Action (Step #5 adjustment allocates areas in Further Planning category with a WARS score in top 30 percentile to Wilderness category; areas in Nonwilderness category with a WARS score in top 5 percentile allocated to Further Planning category).

The required cut-off score fluctuates substantially between alternatives. Yet, the Final EIS does not explain how the cut-offs were initially assigned or why they change radically between alternatives. Although NEPA does not require the Forest Service to select any particular cut-off, we conclude that the Forest Service's statutory responsibility to explain its decision requires it to justify the cut-offs it considered.

Third, as the district court noted, the Forest Service's argument is defective in emphasizing decisional inputs and criteria over the actual results generated by those inputs and criteria. Although it is worthwhile to consider a broad range of variables in constructing policy alternatives, the procedure becomes meaningless if the variables are assigned numerical values such that only a limited range of outcomes result. This occurred here. In the absence of any reasonable explanation justifying the assignment of numerical values to the decisional criteria that the Forest Service selected, we conclude it was unreasonable for the Forest Service to overlook the obvious alternative of allocating more than a third of the RARE II acreage to a Wilderness designation.

III. *Did the Forest Service provide sufficient opportunity for public comment on RARE II and respond adequately to the comments?*

A. *Was NEPA violated by not soliciting further public comment on the Proposed Action?*

The district court held that the Forest Service violated NEPA by not circulating for public comment a supplemental draft EIS describing the Proposed Action. * * *

* * *

* * * [W]e conclude that the Proposed Action differed sufficiently from the alternatives canvassed in the draft EIS to warrant the circulation for public comment of a draft supplement describing the Proposed Action. First, the Proposed Action's allocation between the three designated categories differed substantially from the allocation percentages generated by the alternatives considered in the draft EIS, seriously diluting the relevance of public comment on the draft EIS alternatives. Second, although the decisional criteria employed in the Proposed Action were used earlier in one or more of the alternatives contained in the draft EIS, none of the draft EIS alternatives utilized all or most of the decisional criteria found in the Proposed Action. The Proposed Action amalgamated so many different analytical techniques that the final method of allocation could not be fairly anticipated by reviewing the draft EIS alternatives. Third, public comment on the draft EIS focused on the final acreage allocations rather than the decisional criteria, lessening the importance of the similarity between the criteria used in the draft EIS alternatives and the criteria used in the Proposed Action. Thus, circulation of a draft supplement for public comment was in order.

B. *Did the Forest Service adequately respond to site-specific comments?*

The Forest Service requested public comment on the site designations listed in the draft EIS. In response, the Forest Service received 85,258 letters, 76,831 petitions, and 101,549 response forms. In response to these comments, the Forest Service tabulated the number of comments, listed the number of responses (per RARE II area) that recommended either Wilderness, Nonwilderness or Further Planning, and incorporated these lists into Step #1 of the Proposed Action. Comments detailing reasons for designating a particular area in a classification were forwarded to the Regional Forester as part of Step 2 of the Proposed Action.

The district court held that this procedure violated CEQ Guidelines found in 40 C.F.R. 1500.10(a) (1977) (superceded 1978). * * *

[The court affirmed this ruling.]

* * *

IV. *Does section 1604(c) of the National Forest Management Act exempt the RARE II areas from compliance with NEPA?*

In an argument not joined in by the other appellants, Webco Lumber Company argues that the district court erred in holding that NEPA applies to decisions to implement land management plans existing prior to October 22, 1976, the effective date of the National Forest Management Act ("NFMA"), 16 U.S.C. § 1604 (1976). We agree with the district court and affirm.

NFMA provides standards and guidelines which the Forest Service must follow in developing land and resource management plans for units of the National Forest System. Section 1604 directs the Forest Service to develop and implement plans for each unit by 1985. In the interim, § 1604(c) provides: "[u]ntil such time as a unit of the National Forest System is managed under plans developed in accordance with this subchapter, the management of such unit may continue under existing land and resource management plans." Webco argues that this language validates development under any management plan extant prior to NFMA's effective date, whether or not the project was authorized in accord with NEPA. Webco in particular argues that timber harvesting in three national forests—the Klamath, Six-Rivers and Shasta-Trinity—is not subject to further NEPA review because timber management plans existed for these three national forests prior to NFMA's effective date.

Webco's contention is ill-considered. NEPA must be complied with to "the fullest extent possible" unless there is a "clear and unavoidable conflict in statutory authority." Flint Ridge Dev. Co. v. Scenic Rivers Ass'n, 426 U.S. 776, 788 (1976). No such conflict exists here because nothing in NFMA specifically prohibits compliance with NEPA. The Senate Report concerning the NFMA specifically states that NFMA "does not alter the responsibilities of the Forest Service to comply with [NEPA] or the guidelines of the Council of Environmental Quality."

* * *

The only section in NFMA that specifically mentions NEPA states that the NFMA regulations shall "specify procedures to insure that land management plans are prepared in accordance with the National Environmental Policy Act * * *." 16 U.S.C. § 1604(g)(1) (1976). The Senate Report explains that this provision "is neither intended to enlarge nor diminish the Forest Service's responsibilities under the [National Environmental Policy] Act." S.Rep. No. 94–893, 94th Cong., 2d Sess. 14.

Section 1604(g)(1) and NFMA's legislative history clearly indicate that Congress did not intend to exempt any national forest plan from NEPA review. Section 1604(c) does authorize continued management under plans predating NFMA, but the section does not speak to whether NEPA's requirements can be disregarded. All the section appears to mean is that management plans predating NFMA are not automatically invalidated by NFMA's enactment. The legislative history which Webco cites is consonant with this limited aim.

* * *

Affirmed in part, Reversed in part, and Remanded.

[Appendix omitted].

NOTES

1. As of 1967, the 36 million national forest acres declared by the Forest Service in the principal case to be nonwilderness had no special preservation designation and were general forest lands, subject to multiple use management. Then came RARE I, RARE II, and ratification of the original classification—they were not suitable as wilderness. In all of this, where is the "proposal for action" to trigger NEPA?

2. In light of the magnitude of the task, is a site specific NEPA statement a realistic requirement? Does not Kleppe v. Sierra Club, 427 U.S. 390 (1976), supra at page 323, leave that determination to the Forest Service?

3. Why the continuing emphasis on crossing every "t" and dotting every "i" so that Congress will receive the information that it "must have" to act on the Forest Service proposals? Recall that RARE II is not a congressionally mandated study. Is Congress incapable of ordering further information on specific roadless areas if and when it deems it necessary?

4. Did the injunction itself cover the inventoried roadless areas in all national forests?

5. One can hope that note 22 of the lower court opinion, 483 F.Supp. at 486 n. 22, discussing the lack of specificity in the Forest Service's comments on individual roadless areas, will not be lost in the shuffle of appellate review:

> The comments are of a brief, and very general nature. For example, one comment under the "opportunity for solitude" attribute merely stated "good topographical variation." The type of land features or vegetation present in this area is undisclosed. Major features of an area are reduced to highly generalized description such as "mountain" or "river." One can hypothesize how the Grand Canyon might be rated: "Canyon with river, little vegetation."

6. The Forest Service responded administratively to the Ninth Circuit decision in California v. Block. In February, 1983, former Assistant Secretary John Crowell announced plans to scrap RARE II and start over with a new program dubbed "RARE III." Under RARE III, the Forest Service proposed to reevaluate the original roadless areas in NFMA plans for each national forest. Areas outside of California previously recommended by RARE II as "non-wilderness" would be open to multiple use management while their wilderness potential was being studied. Areas recommended as "wilderness" and

"further planning" by RARE II would be subject only to those uses allowed in wilderness areas. In essence, RARE III would effectuate RARE II proposals while further wilderness studies are being carried out. 8 Public Land News, No. 3, pages 1–3 (Feb. 3, 1983). Mr. Crowell later defended his action:

> When I announced my Feb. 1 decision, I candidly admitted one element of it was vulnerable to legal attack. That element was the decision to carry out already planned and on-going timber sale and road construction activities on a very small number of acres in the roadless areas that had not been recommended for wilderness by RARE II. * * * [O]n-going activities in the roadless areas could be stopped by legal action instituted by almost anyone who so desired simply by asserting the appeals court's decision as precedent.

> Why did I decide to let such activities proceed? It was on the chance that the Forest Service could continue those activities with only small disruption from occasional, carefully targeted lawsuits.

Portland Oregonian, Mar. 22, 1983, at B–7. Could a decision to allow timber harvesting in these roadless areas survive judicial scrutiny?

A Forest Service rule promulgated in September 1983 requires evaluation of all lands in forest plans for suitability for wilderness designation; "other essentially roadless areas may be subject to evaluation at the discretion of the Forest Supervisor." 36 C.F.R. § 219.17 (1985).

7. In 1984, Congress reacted to California v. Block in dramatic fashion, passing 19 wilderness bills that added 8.6 million acres to the NWPS. Congress enacted individual state bills for Arizona (1 million acres), Arkansas, California (3.2 million acres), Florida, Georgia, Mississippi, New Hampshire, New Mexico, North Carolina, Oregon (850,000 acres), Pennsylvania, Tennessee, Texas, Utah (750,000 acres), Vermont, Virginia, Washington (1 million acres), Wisconsin, and Wyoming (883,000 acres). Congress failed to reach agreement on bills for Colorado, Idaho, Montana, and several states with smaller amounts of potential wilderness. Each individual state Act placed the newly-designated lands under the umbrella provisions of the Wilderness Act of 1964, but most of the statewide statutes carry specific provisions reflecting compromises regarding the state in question or individual areas within states.

8. One continuing point of contention has been over "release" of RARE II (or, now, RARE III) lands not designated as wilderness by congressional statewide acts. Industry has argued that such lands should be permanently released to non-wilderness uses. Typically, release language in recent wilderness bills states that "the Department of Agriculture shall not be required to review the wilderness option prior to the revisions of the [NFMA] plans." E.g., Pub.L. No. 98–328, 98 Stat. 272 (1984) (Oregon Wilderness Act). In most instances, therefore, a national forest that completes its forest plan in 1986 will not

evaluate its roadless areas for wilderness suitability until at least 1996. See, also, e.g., the Georgia Wilderness Act, Pub.L. No. 98–514, 98 Stat. 2416 (1984) ("without passing on the question of the legal and factual sufficiency of the RARE II [EIS] * * * with respect to * * * [national forest] lands in states other than Georgia, such [EIS] shall not be subject to judicial review with respect to [national forest] lands in the State of Georgia."). Such release language does not apply to areas designated for further planning in some statewide acts. On released roadless areas, see City of Tenakee Springs v. Block, 778 F.2d 1402 (9th Cir.1985) (failure to comply with NEPA in proposal for road construction). On further planning areas, see Sierra Club v. Peterson, 717 F.2d 1409 (D.C.Cir.1983), supra at page 562 (failure to comply with NEPA in mineral lease issuance).

MONTANA WILDERNESS ASSOCIATION v. UNITED STATES FOREST SERVICE

United States Court of Appeals, Ninth Circuit, 1981.
655 F.2d 951.
Cert. denied, 455 U.S. 989 (1982).

NORRIS, Circuit Judge:

Environmentalists and a neighboring property owner seek to block construction by Burlington Northern of roads over parts of the Gallatin National Forest. They appeal from a partial summary judgment in the district court granting Burlington Northern a right of access to its totally enclosed timberlands. * * *

I.

Defendant-Appellee Burlington Northern, Inc. owns timberland located within the Gallatin National Forest southwest of Bozeman, Montana. This land was originally acquired by its predecessor, the Northern Pacific Railroad, under the Northern Pacific Land Grant Act of 1864. The Act granted odd-numbered square sections of land to the railroad, which, with the even-number sections retained by the United States, formed a checkerboard pattern.

To harvest its timber, Burlington Northern in 1979 acquired a permit from defendant-appellee United States Forest Service, allowing it to construct an access road across national forest land. The proposed roads would cross the Buck Creek and Yellow Mules drainages, which are protected by the Montana Wilderness Study Act of 1977, Pub.L. 95–150, 91 Stat. 1243, as potential wilderness areas. The proposed logging and road-building will arguably disqualify the areas as wilderness under the Act.

The plaintiffs, Montana Wilderness Association, The Wilderness Society, and Nine Quarter Circle Ranch, having contested the granting of the permit, filed suit after it was granted, seeking declaratory and injunctive relief. * * *

* * *

II.

The sole issue on appeal is whether Burlington Northern has a right of access across federal land to its inholdings of timberland.[2] Appellees contend that the recently enacted Alaska National Interest Lands Conservation Act (Alaska Lands Act) establishes an independent basis for affirming the judgment of the district court. They argue that § 1323(a) of the Act requires that the Secretary of Agriculture provide access to Burlington Northern for its enclosed land.

Section 1323 is a part of the administrative provisions, Title XIII, of the Alaska Lands Act. Appellees argue that it is the only section of the Act which applies to the entire country; appellants argue that, like the rest of the Act, it applies only to Alaska. Section 1323 reads as follows:

> Sec. 1323. (a) Notwithstanding any other provision of law, and subject to such terms and conditions as the Secretary of Agriculture may prescribe, the Secretary shall provide such access to nonfederally owned land within the boundaries of the National Forest System as the Secretary deems adequate to secure to the owner the reasonable use and enjoyment thereof: *Provided,* That such owner comply with rules and regulations applicable to ingress and egress to or from the National Forest System.

> (b) Notwithstanding any other provision of law, and subject to such terms and conditions as the Secretary of the Interior may prescribe, the Secretary shall provide such access to nonfederally owned land surrounded by public lands managed by the Secretary under the Federal Land Policy and Management Act of 1976 (43 U.S.C. 1701–82) as the Secretary deems adequate to secure to the owner the responsible use and enjoyment thereof: *Provided,* That such owner comply with rules and regulations applicable to access across public lands.

This section provides for access to nonfederally-owned lands surrounded by certain kinds of federal lands. Subsection (b) deals with access to nonfederal lands "surrounded by public lands managed by the Secretary [of the Interior]." Section 102(3) of the Act defines "public lands" as certain lands "situated in Alaska." Subsection (b), therefore, is arguably limited by its terms to Alaska, though we do not find it necessary to settle that issue here. Our consideration of the scope of § 1323(a) proceeds under the assumption that § 1323(b) is limited to Alaska.

Subsection (a) deals with access to nonfederally-owned lands "within the boundaries of the National Forest System." The term "National Forest System" is not specifically defined in the Act.

[2.] If Burlington Northern does not have an enforceable right of access, the protected status of the federal land may remove the Secretary of Agriculture's usual discretion to grant access over Forest Service land. Section 3(a), Montana Wilderness Study Act, Pub.L. 95–150, 91 Stat. 1243 (1977). Burlington Northern's remedy would be the eventual exchange of its inholdings for other federal land of comparable value. 16 U.S.C. § 1134(a); H.R.Rep. No. 95–620, 95th Cong., 1st Sess. 6 (1977).

The question before the court is whether the term "National Forest System" as used in § 1323(a) is to be interpreted as being limited to national forests in Alaska or as including the entire United States. We note at the outset that the bare language of § 1323(a) does not, when considered by itself, limit the provision of access to Alaskan land. We must look, however, to the context of the section to determine its meaning.

Elsewhere in the Act, Congress used the term "National Forest System" in a context which refers to and deals with national forests in Alaska. Title V of the Act is entitled "National Forest System." Section 501(a) states: "The following units of the National Forest System are hereby expanded * * *." It is not unreasonable to read Section 1323(a) as referring to the "National Forest System" in the context in which it is used in Title V of the Act, rather than to all national forests in the United States.

* * *

That interpretation is supported by a review of the entire Act which discloses no other provision having nation-wide application. We therefore conclude that the language of the Act provides tentative support for the view that § 1323(a) applies only to national forests in Alaska. * * *

The legislative history concerning § 1323 is surprisingly sparse. The report of the Senate committee which drafted the section is ambiguous. At times when the Senate could have been expected to comment on its intention to make a major change in current law, it did not. * * *

The appellees, however, have uncovered subsequent legislative history that, given the closeness of the issue, is decisive. Three weeks after Congress passed the Alaska Lands Act, a House-Senate Conference Committee considering the Colorado Wilderness Act interpreted § 1323 of the Alaska Lands Act as applying nation-wide:

> Section 7 of the Senate amendment contains a provision pertaining to access to non-Federally owned lands within national forest wilderness areas in Colorado. The House bill has no such provision.

> *The conferees agreed to delete the section because similar language has already passed Congress in Section 1323 of the Alaska National Interest Lands Conservation Act.*

H.R.Rep. No. 1521, 96th Cong., 2d Sess., 126 Cong.Rec. H11687 (daily ed. Dec. 3, 1980) (emphasis supplied).

This action was explained to both Houses during discussion of the Conference Report. Both houses then passed the Colorado Wilderness bill as it was reported by the Conference Committee.

Although a subsequent conference report is not entitled to the great weight given subsequent legislation, it is still entitled to significant weight, particularly where it is clear that the conferees had carefully considered the issue. The conferees, including Representatives Udall and Sieberling and Senator Melcher, had an intimate knowledge of the Alaska Lands Act. Moreover, the Conference Committee's interpretation of § 1323 was the basis for their decision to leave out an access provision passed by one house. In these circumstances, the Conference Committee's interpretation is very persuasive. We conclude that it tips the balance decidedly in favor of the broader interpretation of § 1323.[12] We therefore hold that Burlington Northern has an assured right of access to its land pursuant to the nationwide grant of access in § 1323.

* * *

NOTES

1. Would the same result obtain if the Buck Creek and Yellow Mules drainages had been designated as wilderness under the 1964 Act?

2. Note that *Montana Wilderness* does not implicate the difficult problems caused by the *Leo Sheep* ruling, supra at page 112. Congress can still say whether private parties do or do not have access rights over the public lands, but Congress cannot now say that it reserved an easement for access in 1862. As a matter of policy, is it preferable to encourage development of inholdings or buy them out? The principal case is discussed in Comment, Wilderness Values and Access Rights: Troubling Statutory Construction Brings the Alaska Lands Act Into Play, 54 U.Colo.L.Rev. 593 (1983).

b. THE NATIONAL PARK AND WILDLIFE REFUGE SYSTEMS

JOHN C. HENDEE, GEORGE H. STANKEY & ROBERT L. LUCAS, WILDERNESS MANAGEMENT
106–07, 121–23 (1978).

Soon after passage of the Act, Interior estimated that 22.5 million acres of National Park System land and 24.1 million acres of Fish and Wildlife Service holdings were subject to becoming study areas—which increased as new units were added to the National Park and Wildlife Refuge Systems. The National Park Service eventually identified for

---

12. We recognize a facial problem or tension between 1323(a) and a portion of § 5(a) of the Wilderness Act, 16 U.S.C. § 1134(a). We need not decide in this case whether it is repeal by implication. In passing, we note only that it is arguable that the two can stand together. § 1134(a) deals specifically with right of access "[i]n any case where State-owned or privately-owned land is completely surrounded by national forest lands *within areas designated by this chapter as wilderness* * * *." (emphasis added). § 1323(a), on the other hand, deals with " * * * access to nonfederally owned land within the boundaries of the National Forest System

* * * " § 1134(a) is addressed specifically to an area designated as "wilderness," while § 1323(a) is addressed to National Forest System lands in general. In cases involving wilderness areas, the Secretary has the option of exchanging land of equal value so that the wilderness area may be preserved. Thus, § 1134(a) could be construed to apply in the specific case of a wilderness area, and § 1323(a) could be construed to apply in all other cases.

Whether or not they are in fact irreconcilable we leave to another case when the issue is squarely presented for review.

review 63 units covering over 28 million acres while Fish and Wildlife Service identified 113 units and 29 million acres (U.S. Congress 1973).

The reviews themselves were very slow in reaching Congress. Only one area, the Great Swamp National Wildlife Refuge in New Jersey, was submitted and classified during the first 5 years of the Act. The first National Park Service areas, Craters of the Moon National Monument in Idaho (43,000 acres) and Petrified Forest National Park in Arizona (50,000 acres), were not added to the NWPS until 8 years after passage of the Act. However, by 1974, the end of the 10-year period, the Park Service had completed review and submitted wilderness proposals on 56 areas. Wilderness studies of NPS units added after the Act's passage were deferred for later study (13 areas as of 1975).

The absence of an explicit allocation procedure explains much of the delay and difficulty encountered by the National Park Service and Fish and Wildlife Service. Traditionally, the Park Service had zoned roadless and undeveloped tracts in the individual Park's Master Plans. For example, much of Yellowstone's 2.2 million acres is *de facto* wilderness which had been zoned roadless by the Park Service in Yellowstone's Master Plan. The problem the Department faced in meeting the obligations of the Wilderness Act was much the same as that faced by the Forest Service in the Roadless Area Review—determining specific boundaries for wilderness study.

In June 1972, Assistant Secretary of the Interior for Fish and Wildlife and Parks, Nathaniel Reed, issued a memo to the Directors of the National Park Service and the Fish and Wildlife Service defining criteria to be followed in determining an area's suitability for wilderness designation. In particular, the memo specified conditions that were sufficient or insufficient to exclude an area from wilderness designation. Among those conditions were the following:

1. Areas should not be excluded from wilderness designation solely because established or proposed management practices require the use of tools, equipment, or structures, if these practices are necessary for the health and safety of wilderness travelers, or the protection of the wilderness area.

2. Areas that otherwise qualify for wilderness will not be excluded because they contain unimproved roads created by vehicles repeatedly traveling over the same course, structures, installations, or utility lines, which can be and would be removed upon designation as wilderness.

3. Areas which presently qualify for wilderness designation but which will be needed at some future date for specific purposes consistent with the purpose for which the National Park or National Wildlife Refuge was originally created, and fully described in an approved conceptual plan, should not be proposed for wilderness designation.

These and other guidelines emerged as the basic allocation principles governing Department of the Interior recommendations. However, Interior officials and conservationists continue to disagree over official guidelines. For instance, the Wilderness Society argues that Interior's classification guidelines confuse the stringent management criteria in Section 4 of the Wilderness Act with the flexible entry criteria in Section 2. As a result, they argue, Interior officials interpret wilderness classification as a decision to cease virtually all management activity unless specific authorization is given in the wilderness legislation for an area. Based upon this interpretation, wilderness designation would be rejected in many areas because it would end management activities needed to accomplish objectives of the legislation originally establishing the Park or Refuge. The Wilderness Society suggests that a management activity need meet only a minimum necessity test (administrators need demonstrate only that a management activity is the minimum necessary for proper administration of the area both for the purposes for which the Park or Refuge was originally established and as wilderness). If the activity meets this test, it does not constitute a sufficient reason to disqualify an area for classification as wilderness.

Currently, the National Park Service manages 36,754,980 acres in 37 designated wilderness areas. Over 32 million of these acres were established in the Alaska National Interest Lands Conservation Act. Three areas in Alaska—Gates of the Arctic Wilderness (over 7 million acres); Noatak Wilderness (5.8 million acres); and Wrangell-Saint Elias Wilderness (8.7 million acres)—together comprise well over one-half of all National Park wilderness acres. In 1984, in its spurt of wilderness designations, Congress carved out two large wilderness areas in Yosemite National Park (676,000 acres) and Sequoia and Kings Canyon National Parks (736,980 acres). The Park Service has also recommended to Congress that it include another 8.77 million acres of parkland in the NWPS.

As of February 1986, the Fish and Wildlife Service administered over 19.3 million acres in 60 areas within the NWPS. The "average" size is about 300,000 acres, but the average is deceiving. In 1980, ANILCA added over 18.5 million acres in just 13 areas to the National Wildlife Refuge System. The Arctic Wildlife Refuge Wilderness (8 million acres) alone accounts for well over one-third of all the wilderness acres managed by FWS. The FWS currently has no areas under study for wilderness designation.

Preservation of the wilderness resource requires protection of the quality of its air as well as preservation of land and the living things on it. The Clean Air Act Amendments of 1977, 42 U.S.C.A. § 7401 et seq., restrict construction of major emitting facilities that will cause significant deterioration of air quality in areas zoned as "Class I." Class I areas include all national wilderness areas over 5,000 acres and all national parks over 6,000 acres. The 1977 amendments also require EPA regulation of air pollution which impairs visibility over Class I areas. See Connery, The Effects of the Clean Air Act Amendments of 1977 on Mining and Energy Developments and Operations, 24 Rocky

Mtn.Min.L.Inst. 1 (1978); Postel, Air Pollution, Acid Rain, and the Future of Forests, American Forests 25 (July, 1984).

c. BUREAU OF LAND MANAGEMENT LANDS

Congress commanded wilderness review of BLM lands in section 603 of FLPMA, 43 U.S.C.A. § 1782. A report by the Secretary on areas already designated as "natural" or "primitive" was to be sent to the President by July 1, 1980. Within fifteen years, the BLM must inventory and study all other roadless areas of more than 5000 acres and report the results to the President, who then is to report to Congress on each recommendation within two years after receipt.

The BLM process promises to be at least as difficult as RARE I and II. There is more land but fewer employees to review it. In addition, on BLM roadless areas there will be considerably more competing uses in the form of hardrock mining, mineral leasing, and grazing. A significant amount of commercial use is assured since the inventory will include many areas that are reached by jeep trails, but these do not seem to qualify as roads. This "purity" issue is resolved because legislative history defines "roadless" broadly: "A way maintained solely by the passage of vehicles does not constitute a road." Ferguson, Forest Service and BLM Wilderness Review Programs and Their Effect on Mining Law Activities, 24 Rocky Mtn.Min.L.Inst. 717, 744 (1978).

The initial BLM roadless area inventory, excluding primitive and natural areas, included about 174 million acres. Incredibly, by 1980 the BLM had determined that approximately 150 million acres of the original inventory lack wilderness characteristics, and these areas have been released from further study.

Although the BLM administers just 23 wilderness areas totalling 368,739 acres as of 1986, the agency is still studying nearly 25 million acres in 900 roadless areas for their wilderness potential. The BLM review is comprehensively analyzed in Leshy, Wilderness and its Discontents—Wilderness Review Comes to the Public Lands, 1981 Ariz.St. L.J. 361.

STATE OF UTAH v. ANDRUS
United States District Court, District of Utah, 1979.
486 F.Supp. 995.

ALDON J. ANDERSON, Chief Judge.

This is a case of first impression involving important questions concerning the administration and use of public lands. Plaintiff, the United States, filed suit on May 25, 1979, seeking a temporary restraining order to prevent Cotter Corporation (hereinafter Cotter) from engaging in "any construction, road building, leveling land, or destroying primitive, scenic and wildlife characteristics" on certain federal land. The court granted the order.

The State of Utah moved to intervene as a party defendant. It was unopposed and the motion was granted by the court. * * *

* * *

FACTS

This case involves access to mining claims located on both federal and state land. The state land is surrounded by land in federal ownership and land access to section 36 is possible only by crossing federal property. The state land was granted to Utah by the United States under the Utah Enabling Act (Act of July 16, 1894, 28 Stat. 107). The major portion of the land in territorial Utah, at the time of statehood, was in federal ownership. In order to provide a tax base for the new state, the federal government granted to Utah certain sections of land in each township—specifically, sections 2, 16, 32 and 36. But this grant was not unconditional nor was it a unilateral gift. In order to receive the grant, Utah, like other states, was required to use the proceeds of the granted lands for a permanent state school trust fund. Utah met all the conditions of the federal grant and, upon statehood, received the sections of land.

As a result of the state school land grants, the pattern of property ownership in much of Utah represents a checkerboard, with sections of school trust land interspersed within federal land. Since nearly two-thirds of Utah's land is in federal ownership, and since this land frequently surrounds state school sections, the question of access rights and activity on state school and federal land is of utmost importance to both Utah and the United States. In most situations, neither sovereign can take any action with regard to its land holding without impacting the other's land.

On October 21, 1976, the United States Congress passed the Federal Land Policy and Management Act (FLPMA) intended to provide, in part, a new statutory base for the Bureau of Land Management's (BLM) administration of the lands within its jurisdiction. Only a few are pertinent here. Under section 201(a) [43 U.S.C.A. § 1711(a)], the BLM is directed to conduct an inventory of all BLM managed lands and their resource and other values. Under § 603(a) [43 U.S.C.A. § 1782(a)], BLM is directed to examine all roadless areas of 5000 acres or more which have been identified during the inventory process as having wilderness characteristics. Based on this review BLM is to recommend to the President whether or not each such area should be preserved as wilderness according to the provisions of the Wilderness Act (16 U.S.C.A. § 1131 et seq.). During this period of review BLM is to manage the lands so as to prevent impairment of wilderness characteristics and unnecessary and undue degradation of the environment. (Section 603(c), 43 U.S.C.A. § 1782(c)). It was against this historical and statutory backdrop that Cotter located its mining claims and began building a road to gain access to those claims.

Cotter Corporation is a uranium mining and exploration company wholly owned by Commonwealth Edison, a public utility serving Northern Illinois. Between January and June, 1976, Cotter acquired additional federal claims and the state mineral lease on section 36. The federal claims were located pursuant to the Mining Law of 1872 (30 U.S.C.A. § 22 et seq.).

During that last six months of 1977, Cotter conducted drilling operations on federal land to the north and to the south of the lands at issue here. These operations indicated a "trend" of uranium ore between the two drilling points. Subsequent drilling operations confirmed the trend. In order to conduct these operations, Cotter constructed access roads, but did not notify BLM of the construction activity. In June, 1978, Cotter began to construct a road across the lands in question here in order to further its exploratory drilling.

In the meantime, BLM proceeded with the inventory and wilderness area examination required by FLPMA. During the review, BLM identified a portion of roadless unit UT–05–236 as being appropriate for designation as a Wilderness Study Area (WSA). The proposed study unit includes the lands in question here. In April, 1979, BLM published the proposed area in the Federal Register and has received public comment on the proposal. As yet BLM has not finally decided to designate the area a formal WSA. The court is informed that in all likelihood the area will be so designated.

When BLM became aware of Cotter's road building activity in June, 1978, it contacted Cotter personnel and advised them of BLM's interest in the area and requested that the road building activity be brought to a halt. Cotter agreed to this request and ceased all construction activity for approximately one year. On May 24, 1979, Cotter notified BLM of its intention to begin construction of a road to gain access to section 36. BLM then instituted this proceeding.

OPINION

At stake here are three very important and conflicting interests. The state of Utah has a clear interest in protecting its rights under the grant of school trust lands and in being able to use those lands so as to maximize the funds available for the public schools. Cotter, of course, has an interest in developing its claims in the most economical way possible. Finally, the United States has an interest in preserving for future generations the opportunity to experience the solitude and peace that only an undisturbed natural setting can provide. As noted herein, these public interests conflict. This is reflected in the more narrow questions of statutory interpretation and reconciliation posed for decision. In order to resolve the issues and effect a balance of interests, it is important to examine such interest and its statutory base.

I. State School Trust Land

As previously explained, the state school land grants were not unilateral gifts made by the United States Congress. Rather, they were in the nature of a bilateral compact entered into between two sovereigns. In return for receiving the federal lands Utah disclaimed all interest in the remainder of the public domain, agreed to forever hold federal lands immune from taxation, and agreed to hold the granted lands, or the proceeds therefrom, in trust as a common school fund. Thus, the land grants involved here were in the nature of a contract, with a bargained-for consideration exchanged between the two governments. See Utah v. Kleppe, 586 F.2d 756, 758 (10th Cir.1978), cert. granted 442 U.S. 928 (1979) [eds.: Rev'd, supra at page 62].

Recognition of the special nature of the school land grants is important both in determining the Congressional intent behind the grant and in understanding judicial treatment of similar grants. Generally, land grants by the federal government are construed strictly, and nothing is held to pass to the grantee except that which is specifically delineated in the instrument of conveyance. E.g., United States v. Union Pacific Railroad Co., 353 U.S. 112, 116 (1957). But the legislation dealing with school trust land has always been liberally construed. Wyoming v. United States, 255 U.S. 489, 508 (1921); Utah v. Kleppe, supra at 761. Further, it is clear that one of Congress' primary purposes in enacting the legislation was to place the new states on an "equal footing" with the original thirteen colonies and to enable the state to "produce a fund, accumulated by sale and use of the trust lands, with which the State could support the [common schools]". Lassen v. Arizona Highway Dept., 385 U.S. 458, 463 (1967).

Given the rule of liberal construction and the Congressional intent of enabling the state to use the school lands as a means of generating revenue, the court must conclude that Congress intended that Utah (or its lessees) have access to the school lands. Unless a right of access is inferred, the very purpose of the school trust lands would fail. Without access the state could not develop the trust lands in any fashion and they would become economically worthless. This Congress did not intend.

Further, traditional property law concepts support Utah's claimed right of access. Under the common law it was assumed that a grantor intended to include in the conveyance whatever was necessary for the use and enjoyment of the land in question. Mackie v. United States, 194 F.Supp. 306, 308 (D.Minn.1961). When a grantor conveys only a portion of his land, and the land received by the grantee is surrounded by what the grantor has retained, it is generally held that the grantee has an easement of access, either by implication or necessity, across the grantor's land. E.g., United States v. Dunn, 478 F.2d 443, 444 & n. 2 (9th Cir.1973). Although this common law presumption might not ordinarily apply in the context of a federal land grant, the liberal rules of construction applied to school trust land allow for the consideration of this common law principle and justify its application here.[11]

Therefore, the court holds that the state of Utah and Cotter Corporation, as Utah's lessee, do have the right to cross federal land to

11. The case of Leo Sheep Co. v. United States, 440 U.S. 668 (1979) is not apposite. In that case the United States Supreme Court held that the government had not reserved an access easement in a particu-lar land grant because the government had the power to condemn the land in question. The defendants in this case have no such power.

reach section 36, which is a portion of the school trust lands. The extent and nature of that right, however, remain to be determined. In order to reach that decision the court must examine the character and extent of BLM's authority under the Federal Land Policy and Management Act.

II. Federal Land Policy and Management Act

FLPMA represents an attempt on the part of Congress to balance a variety of competing interests, including those enumerated above. To some extent, the statute appears to be internally inconsistent, reflecting different concerns of environmentalists, miners, and ranchers. For example, in section 102 [43 U.S.C.A. § 1701(a)(8)] outlining the Congressional declaration of policy, the statute declares it to be the policy of the United States to manage the public lands

> in a manner that will protect the quality of scientific, scenic, historical, ecological, environmental, air and atmospheric, water resource, and archeological values; * * * that will provide food and habitat for fish and wildlife and domestic animals, and that will provide for outdoor recreation and human occupancy and use * * *

The same section declares national policy to be the management of public lands in a manner

> [that] recognizes the Nation's need for domestic sources of minerals, food, timber and fiber from the public lands including implementation of [the Mining and Minerals Policy Act of 1970] section 21a of Title 30 as it pertains to the public lands. [Sec. (12)]

On their face these two provisions appear contradictory. Indeed, it is difficult to imagine how an agency is both to encourage mining or logging and preserve land in its natural condition. It is only when the statute is viewed in a dynamic rather than a static context, and is viewed as applying to *all* public lands, that the conflict can be resolved. If all the competing demands reflected in FLPMA were focused on one particular piece of public land, in many instances only one set of demands could be satisfied. A parcel of land cannot both be preserved in its natural character and mined. Thus, it would be impossible for BLM to carry out the purposes of the Act if each particular management decision were evaluated separately. It is only by looking at the overall use of the public lands that one can accurately assess whether or not BLM is carrying out the broad purposes of the statute. If one's view is expanded to the complex entirety of land management decisions, then the statute is not necessarily internally inconsistent. Some lands can be preserved, while others, more appropriately, can be mined. BLM is not required to fully implement section 21a of Title 30 each time it makes a decision under FLPMA. Consequently, BLM is not obliged to, and indeed cannot, reflect all the purposes of FLPMA in each management action.

Cotter contends that BLM must take all potential values into account when it designates an area as a WSA. The statute, however, envisions a dynamic *process,* not a static one-time-only decision. FLPMA is addressed in part to solving the problem of the lack of a comprehensive plan for the use, preservation and disposal of public lands. The purpose of the inventory and the wilderness review is to enable BLM to ascertain the character of the lands within its jurisdiction, and the best use to which particular portions of land can be put— given such things as wilderness characteristics, mineral values, and the nation's needs for recreation, energy, etc. BLM is entitled to address this problem one step at a time.

BLM is not required to immediately balance the mineral values against the wilderness values of a particular piece of land prior to designating the land a WSA. BLM may, consistent with FLPMA, look first at potential wilderness characteristics and then proceed to study the area for all its potential uses prior to formulating its final recommendations to the Executive.

A. BLM's Authority Under FLPMA

Under section 603(c) [43 U.S.C.A. § 1782(c)], BLM is required, during the period of wilderness review, to manage the public land

> in a manner so as *not to impair the suitability of such areas for preservation as wilderness, subject,* however, to the continuation of *existing mining * * * uses * * * in the manner and degree* in which the same *was being conducted* on October 21, 1976: *Provided,* That, in managing the public lands [BLM] shall by regulation or otherwise *take any action required to prevent unnecessary or undue degradation* of the lands and their resources or to afford environmental protection.

(Emphasis added in part.)

Cotter argues that this language authorizes only one management standard: preventing undue or unnecessary degradation of the environment. It is Cotter's position that the use of the word "impair" "merely gives direction to the existing authority of [BLM] to manage with a view toward environmental protection."

The United States, on the other hand, argues that under section 603(c) there are two management standards: one that applies to uses of the land existing on October 21, 1976, and one that applies to uses coming into existence after that date. Under this interpretation, existing uses are to be regulated only to the degree required to prevent unnecessary and undue degradation. New uses, however, may be (indeed, must be) regulated to the extent necessary to prevent impairment of wilderness characteristics. Obviously, the latter standard is more strict.

The Solicitor of the Department of Interior has issued on opinion dated September 5, 1978, (hereinafter referred to as "Solicitor's Opinion") which interprets the effect of section 603(c). Under this interpretation, section 603(c) does indeed mandate two standards, the first of which governs regulation of uses not in existence on October 21, 1976, and the second of which governs uses existing on that date. Generally, the interpretation of a statute by those charged with its execution is entitled to great deference. E.g., Udall v. Tallman, 380 U.S. 1, 16 (1965). The court can find no reason not to give such deference in this case.

Further, the Solicitor's interpretation finds support in the Act's legislative history. In the Report [H.Rep. No. 94–1163, 94th Cong.2d Sess. 17 (1976), U.S.Code Cong. & Admin.News 1976, p. 6175] accompanying the House version of what was to become FLPMA, the language of section 603(c) was described as follows:

> While tracts are under review, they are to be managed in a manner to preserve their wilderness character, *subject to continuation of existing grazing and mineral uses and appropriation under the mining laws.* The Secretary *will continue* to have authority to prevent unnecessary and undue degradation of the lands, including installation of minimum improvements, such as wildlife habitat and livestock control improvements, where needed for the protection or maintenance of the lands and their resources * * *. (Emphasis added.)

It appears to the court that the above passage indicates that the authority to manage lands so as to prevent impairment of wilderness characteristics was meant to be a new addition to the Secretary's continuing authority to regulate all uses so as to prevent undue degradation. Other parts of the legislative history confirm this view.

* * *

* * * It appears that the Senate and the House were concerned about devising a way to protect both existing uses and wilderness values present on tracts not subject to existing uses. As interpreted by the Solicitor, section 603(c) reflects that concern. The Secretary's authority to preserve wilderness is subject to existing uses which may not be arbitrarily terminated, nor regulated solely with a view to preserving wilderness characteristics. But the Secretary may continue to regulate such uses in order to prevent unnecessary or undue degradation. On the other hand, activity on lands with potential wilderness value which are not subject to existing uses may be regulated more stringently so as to preserve wilderness characteristics. The Solicitor's interpretation is consistent with the Act's legislative history and reflects the full measure of Congressional intent in the adoption of 603(c). Cotter's interpretation reflects only one of Congress' concerns, i.e., protection of existing uses.

Finally, the Solicitor's interpretation is supported by the language and structure of the statute itself. The word "impair" would prevent many activities that would not be prevented by the language of "unnecessary or undue degradation." For example, commercial timber harvesting, if conducted carefully, would not result in unnecessary or undue degradation of the environment. But the same activity might well impair wilderness characteristics as those are defined in 16 U.S.

C.A. § 1131. Compare Parker v. United States, 309 F.Supp. 593 (D.Colo.1970), aff'd, 448 F.2d 793 (10th Cir.1971), cert. den. sub nom., Kaibab Industries v. Parker, 405 U.S. 989 (1972), with Minnesota Public Interest Research Group v. Butz, 541 F.2d 1292 (8th Cir.1976). Further, if Congress had not intended to mandate two standards, it would merely have indicated that the Secretary was to continue to manage all lands so as to prevent unnecessary degradation. If one takes the position that this is what Congress intended, then the language of impairment must be mere surplusage. Statutory rules of construction are against such a finding.[14] Wilderness Society v. Morton, 479 F.2d 842, 856 (D.C.Cir.1973), cert. den., 411 U.S. 917 (1978).

Moreover, legislative history confirms that the language of impairment was not surplusage. * * *

Therefore, the court holds that under the terms of FLPMA the BLM has the authority to manage public lands so as to prevent impairment of wilderness characteristics, unless those lands are subject to an existing use. In the latter case BLM may regulate so as to prevent unnecessary or undue degradation of the environment.

B. Cotter's Rights Under FLPMA

Given that there are two standards by which BLM can manage the public lands, it remains to be determined what standards apply to Cotter's activity. Cotter argues that its activity falls within the existing use provision of 603(c). The main thrust of Cotter's argument is as follows:

(1) under the Mining Law of 1872, Cotter has a right of access to its unpatented claims;

(2) Cotter, as Utah's lessee, also has a right of access to state school land;

(3) these rights, even though not exercised prior to October, 1976, constitute existing uses under FLPMA.

Section 603(c) mandates that existing uses may continue in the "same manner and degree" as being conducted on October 21, 1976. Unless the statute is referring to activity that was actually taking place on that date, there is no way to give meaningful context to the "manner and degree" language. In order to determine whether or not a given

---

14. There is further indication within FLPMA itself that the Congress intended two management standards. Section 302(b) provides:

Except as provided in 1744, 1781(f) and 1782 [section 603] of this title *and in the last sentence of this paragraph,* no provision * * * shall in any way amend the Mining Law of 1872 * * *.

The last sentence of 302(b) is as follows:

In managing the public lands the Secretary shall, by regulation or otherwise, take any action necessary to prevent un-

necessary or undue degradation of the lands.

If the standard of undue degradation were not separate and distinct from the impairment standard contained in section 603(c), there would have been no need to include both the last sentence and reference to section 603(c) in section 302(b). By making distinct reference to both standards in 302(b), Congress indicated its intent to formulate two different approaches to management of the public lands.

operation is being conducted in the same manner and degree as it was formerly being conducted, there must be *some* former activity against which the extent of the present operation can be measured. Presumably, when the statute refers to existing uses being carried out in the same manner and degree it is referring to *actual* uses, not merely a statutory right to use.

Cotter next points to section 302(b) as an indication that its rights of access cannot be denied under FLPMA. Cotter's emphasis in quoting 302(b) is, however, selective. Section 302(b) provides in pertinent part:

> *Except as provided in* 1744, 1781(f) and *1782* [*section 603*] of this title and in the last sentence of this paragraph no provision of this section or any other section of this Act shall in any way amend the Mining Law of 1872 or impair the rights of any locators of claims under that Act, including, but not limited to, rights of ingress and egress. (Emphasis added.)

Cotter emphasizes only the latter portion of this section and from this argues that no provision of FLPMA can be taken to amend the Mining Law of 1872. On its face, however, this section makes clear that section 603 *does* amend the Mining Law of 1872. Rights under that law, including rights of ingress and egress, can be impaired by virtue of section 603. Moreover, the Mining Law itself makes clear that rights of access to mining claims are not absolute. Such rights are subject to regulation under 30 U.S.C.A. § 22.

* * *

It is clear that the Congress intended to provide a balanced solution to the problem of land management during the inventory process. While Congress did not intend the use of public lands to be frozen pending the outcome of the inventory process, neither did it want future uses to be foreclosed by the impact of present activity. Further, the Congress recognized that it might not be possible to both allow present uses and prevent foreclosure of certain other future uses.

This is consistent with the decision in Parker v. United States, supra. In that case, involving the Wilderness Act, the court held that the Department of Agriculture could not take any action that would foreclose Congressional consideration of an area's potential for wilderness designation. In this case, if BLM could not prevent activity that would permanently impair wilderness characteristics, then those characteristics could be destroyed before either BLM or the Congress had the chance to evaluate an area's potential uses. This Congress did not intend.

Therefore, the court holds that (1) BLM may regulate activity on federal land so as to prevent impairment of potential wilderness characteristics; (2) the authority to so regulate is subject to uses actually existing on October 21, 1976; (3) section 603 does amend the Mining Law of 1872 and subjects rights thereunder to BLM's authority to regulate so as to prevent wilderness impairment; (4) section 201 does not mandate that BLM allow all potential uses to take place on a particular portion of land regardless of wilderness characteristics.

BLM's authority is, however, limited to preventing *permanent* impairment of potential wilderness values. Although it is not explicitly provided for in FLPMA, it is consistent with Congress' attempt to balance competing interests and with the Wilderness Act which provides the legislative backdrop for section 603 to find that if a given activity will have only a temporary effect on wilderness characteristics and will not foreclose potential wilderness designation then that activity should be allowed to proceed.

The definition of wilderness provided for in the Wilderness Act (16 U.S.C.A. § 1131[c]) and incorporated by reference into FLPMA in section 603(a) contemplates that some human activity can take place in wilderness areas as long as the area "*generally* appears to have been affected *primarily* by the forces of nature, with the imprint of man's work *substantially* unnoticeable * * *."

Further, the draft statement of BLM's Interim Management Policy and Guidelines for Wilderness Study Areas (January 12, 1979, at 9) recognizes that temporary activities, the negative impacts of which could be substantially reversed through appropriate reclamation procedures, would not impair wilderness characteristics under the terms of 603(c).

There has been a great deal of argument in this case over whether or not the effects of Cotter's proposed road and drilling operations can be successfully reclaimed. Unfortunately the factual matters inherent in such an argument have not been sufficiently addressed. At the July 12 hearing on the motion for permanent injunction, Cotter proffered, for the first time, its reclamation plan. BLM has not had the opportunity to review the plan nor to make a comparison of the costs and feasibility of reclamation of a land access route over the cost and effect of other forms of access.

In view of the court's findings and conclusions of law, the BLM must be given the opportunity to review and respond to Cotter's reclamation plan. BLM has no formal regulations for review of proposed activity within potential WSA. But BLM is authorized under FLPMA to manage the public lands "by regulation or otherwise * * *." See sections 302(b) and 603(c). Thus, the agency's authority is not dependent on the issuance of formal regulations. Further, in a lawsuit involving issues of the magnitude and importance as those involved here, it is imperative that all parties have the opportunity to respond to critical factual issues. Moreover, the question of the adequacy of a reclamation plan is precisely the kind of question to which the expertise of an administrative agency is most relevant. The court is ill-equipped at this stage of the litigation to make a factual determination on the complex question of the comparative costs and feasibility of reclamation efforts over other forms of access. Thus, the court orders that BLM must be given the opportunity to expeditiously review Cotter's reclamation plan with a view to determining whether or not the impact of the proposed road will be temporary or permanent and with a view toward comparing the cost and feasibility of reclamation with the cost and feasibility of alternative forms of access.

If BLM should decide that the effects of the road will, indeed, be permanent, then the parties (and probably this court) may be required to confront this and other disputed issues. In the interest, however, of giving this judgment finality for the purposes of appeal and for purposes of the parties' own planning, the court chooses not to keep jurisdiction over the lawsuit. The court is aware that should BLM delay reviewing the reclamation plan or make a decision contrary to Cotter's interest, that the parties may need to institute a new lawsuit in order to obtain a final resolution of their dispute. In that event, the court will give the new lawsuit the highest priority and will handle the matter as expeditiously as possible. However, in light of the possibility that further litigation will be necessary, and in light of the fact that throughout the litigation BLM has assumed that the effects of the road would be permanent and thus has put the questions of regulation of access to federal and state land at issue, the court will address the questions remaining in the lawsuit.

III. FLPMA and the State School Lands

The state must be allowed access to the state school trust lands so that those lands can be developed in a manner that will provide funds for the common schools. Further, because it was the intent of Congress to provide these lands to the state so that the state could use them to raise revenue, Lassen v. Arizona Highway Dept., supra, the access rights of the state cannot be so restricted as to destroy the lands' economic value. That is, the state must be allowed access which is not so narrowly restrictive as to render the lands incapable of their full economic development.

* * *

Thus, the court finds that (1) BLM can regulate the method and route of access to state school trust lands; (2) this regulation may be done with a view toward preventing impairment of wilderness characteristics (assuming no existing use); (3) the regulation may not, however, prevent the state or its lessee from gaining access to its land, nor may it be so prohibitively restrictive as to render the land incapable of full economic development.

IV. FLPMA and Access Rights Over Federal Land

Section 701(h) [codified at 43 U.S.C.A. § 1701 note (Supp.1979)] of FLPMA provides:

All actions by the Secretary concerned under this Act shall be subject to valid existing rights.

The Solicitor has interpreted this section to mean that valid existing rights cannot be taken pursuant to section 603. The court agrees with this interpretation. The court has also found, however, that Cotter's right of access to both its federal and state claims can be regulated.

The parties have stipulated that "Cotter's proposed road appears to be the only feasible and least environmentally disruptive *land access* for Cotter to its targeted drilling sites *and* for entry into state section 36 * * *." Thus, in this case, regulation to prevent wilderness impairment could result in total prohibition of land access. BLM has contended that helicopter access is available, feasible and acceptable to the agency. Cotter contends that such access would be prohibitively expensive and would not result in any substantial saving of the environment. This issue was not, however, the subject of live testimony with full cross-examination. The court is not, therefore, provided with sufficient information on which to base a ruling. To further complicate the case, it is not clear that the entire proposed road is necessary for Cotter to gain access to section 36. This is important because different criteria may be applied to judge the propriety of regulation of state, as opposed to federal, access rights. It may be that requiring helicopter access to section 36 would be sufficiently expensive so as to render minerals on that section incapable of economic development. Therefore, requiring such access and denying land access would violate the intent of the school trust grant. It may be, however, that requiring such access to federal claims would not be so expensive as to constitute a taking under 701(h). If the entire road is not necessary to gain access to section 36, then it could be that substantial parts of it could be prohibited, while other parts could not. Unfortunately, on the record as it now stands, this matter is far from clear.

Finally, the record contains very little factual information relevant to the taking issue. The court recognizes that a government can regulate without engaging in a taking. The court also recognizes, however, that when regulation reaches the point of seriously impinging on "investment-backed expectations," it can constitute a taking. Pennsylvania Coal Co. v. Mahon, 260 U.S. 393 (1922); Goldblatt v. Hempstead, 364 U.S. 590 (1962). Given its current information, the court feels that there is a substantial question of a taking in this case if access to federal claims are indefinitely prohibited or if alternative access is unreasonably expensive. The facts in this case are not, however, sufficiently clear at this time for the formulation of a ruling on this matter.

In sum, the court holds that Utah does have a right of access to state school trust lands. That right is subject to federal regulation when its exercise requires the crossing of federal property. Such regulation cannot, however, prohibit access or be so restrictive as to make economic development competitively unprofitable. Further, the court holds that BLM may regulate federal public land so as to prevent impairment of wilderness characteristics. Such authority is, however, subject to uses which were existing on October 21, 1976. These uses must have been actually existing on that date. Cotter's right to gain access was not an existing use on October 21, 1976. Therefore, Cotter's activity may be regulated so as to prevent wilderness impairment. But such regulation cannot be so restrictive as to constitute a taking.

* * *

NOTES

1. The opinion looked in part to the Tenth Circuit's opinion in Utah v. Kleppe, later reversed in Andrus v. Utah, 446 U.S. 500 (1980), supra at page 62. Does the reversal in that case affect this holding?

2. The Solicitor's Opinion cited in the principal case was sharply attacked. See Hall, Mineral Exploration and Development in BLM Wilderness Areas, 21 Ariz.L.Rev. 351 (1979); Ray & Carver, Section 603 of the Federal Land Policy and Management Act: An Analysis of the BLM's Wilderness Study Policy, 21 Ariz.L.Rev. 373 (1979). The latter authors conclude:

> Both the Solicitor's Opinion and the actual management policies instituted by the current administration display no real effort to ascertain some sort of objective truth as to the intent of Congress underlying the terms of FLPMA. Rather, a conscious policy of preferring wilderness use has been adopted by the Interior Department, and the Solicitor has issued an opinion interpreting FLPMA which resembles an advocate's brief more than a dispassionate, unbiased evaluation.

> * * *

> The net effect of the Opinion has been to draw a clear line between the policy priorities of the Department and the interest of mining and mineral leasing operators. No matter how the Department attempts to sugar-coat its administration of section 603 in its WSA Guidelines, it has been locked into defense of the uncompromising legal position enunciated by its solicitor. That position sacrifices all uses of the public lands to the goal of preserving suitability for wilderness designation, at least until such time as specific areas are designated by the inventory process as being unsuitable for wilderness. Because so much land is involved, and because large potential reserves of minerals are believed to lie within such lands (particularly in the case of oil and gas in the Overthrust Belt), the conflict will not be subject to deferral or avoidance on an administrative level.

> The gauntlet has been thrown and enough is at stake to insure that it will be taken up. Although Congress stated in FLPMA its express disapproval of the *Midwest Oil Company* decision, the Solicitor's Opinion has revitalized the doctrine confirmed by that case. A case similar to *Midwest Oil Company* will undoubtedly result. Its outcome will determine whether Congress was at last successful in FLPMA in accomplishing its expressed purpose to "exercise its constitutional authority to withdraw or otherwise designate or dedicate Federal Lands for specified purposes."

The issues raised in the Solicitor's Opinion then returned to court in the following opinion.

ROCKY MOUNTAIN OIL AND GAS ASSOCIATION v. WATT

United States Court of Appeals, Tenth Circuit, 1982.
696 F.2d 734.

SEYMOUR, Circuit Judge.

In this case, plaintiff Rocky Mountain Oil and Gas Association (RMOGA) challenged the Department of the Interior's interpretation of section 603(c) of the Federal Land Policy and Management Act of 1976, 43 U.S.C. § 1782(c) (1976) (FLPMA or Act), as it relates to oil and gas activity on public lands under federal lease. RMOGA sought declaratory and injunctive relief barring Interior's application of a "nonimpairment" standard of protection for wilderness values when it considers lessees' applications to conduct exploration and development activities in Bureau of Land Management Wilderness Study Areas. Several environmental groups sought and were granted permission to intervene as party defendants. The district court granted RMOGA's motion for summary judgment, concluding that Interior's interpretation of section 603 was erroneous as a matter of law, and vacating Interior's programs promulgated under that section. On appeal, we hold that the trial court erred in its interpretation of section 603. Accordingly, we reverse.

I.

BACKGROUND

A. *The Federal Land Policy and Management Act*

* * *

The FLPMA is a complex statute, containing many interdependent sections in order to provide the BLM with a versatile framework for its management efforts. Consequently, individual provisions must be examined in the overall context of the Act. Section 603, at issue in this case, lies at the heart of the Act's land inventory and management processes. Therefore, we undertake a short examination of the FLPMA's purposes and inventory procedures before construing section 603.

The national policy declared in the FLPMA stands in marked contrast to the many older public land statutes that provided for the wholesale disposition of the public lands. The FLPMA requires the retention of public lands in public ownership unless, through the Act's extensive land use planning procedures, disposition of a parcel of land is found to be in the national interest, FLPMA § 102(a)(1), 43 U.S.C. § 1701(a)(1). * * *

The FLPMA requires Interior to recognize competing values. To accomplish this legislative directive within a finite land base, it is necessary to realize that the Act provides a comprehensive statement of congressional policies. It represents an attempt by Congress to balance the use of the public lands by interests as diverse as the lands themselves. Accordingly, Congress provided that the BLM should manage the public lands by using the Act's procedures in a dynamic, evolving manner to accommodate these competing demands.[3] Congress directed the BLM to manage the public lands on a "multiple use" basis, id. §§ 102(a)(7), 302(a), 43 U.S.C. §§ 1701(a)(7), 1732(a), "making the most judicious use of the land *for some or all* of [the public land] resources" and using "some land for *less than all* of the resources," where appropriate, id. § 103(c), 43 U.S.C. § 1702(c). Thus, under sections 102(a)(7)–(8), (12), and 302(a), the BLM need not permit all resource uses on a given parcel of land.[4]

The FLPMA contains comprehensive inventorying and land use planning provisions to ensure that the "proper multiple use mix of retained public lands" be achieved. H.Rep. No. 1163 U.S.Code Cong. & Admin.News 1976, 6176. Section 201(a) directs the Secretary to prepare and maintain an inventory of all public lands and their values. 43 U.S.C. § 1711(a). The Secretary also is required to review those roadless areas in excess of 5,000 acres identified in the inventory process as having "wilderness characteristics described in the Wilderness Act," and to recommend such areas as suitable or unsuitable for preservation as wilderness. FLPMA § 603(a), 43 U.S.C. § 1782(a).

Several sections of the Act prescribe management standards for the BLM. In general, the BLM is to prevent unnecessary or undue degradation of the public lands. Id. § 302(b), 43 U.S.C. § 1732(b). * * * Section 603(c) establishes the standards for lands under wilderness review. During the review period, and until Congress determines otherwise, Interior is required to manage the lands under review

> "in a manner so as not to impair the suitability of such areas for preservation as wilderness, subject, however, to the continuation of existing mining and grazing uses and mineral leasing in the manner and degree in which the same was being conducted on October 21, 1976: *Provided,* That, in managing the public lands the Secretary shall by regulation or otherwise take any action required to prevent unnecessary or undue degradation of the lands and their resources or to afford environmental protection."

43 U.S.C. § 1782(c).

B. Administrative Interpretation and Policy

Interior interpreted section 603(c) as requiring all activities not protected under the section's "grandfather" clause to be regulated so as

---

3. See, e.g., FLPMA § 103(c), 43 U.S.C. § 1702(c) (management to allow periodic adjustments in use to meet changing needs and conditions); id. § 201(a), 43 U.S.C. § 1711(a) (Secretary to maintain a continuing inventory of all public lands and resources and to update it to reflect changes and new values).

4. "If all the competing demands reflected in FLPMA were focused on one particular piece of public land, in many instances only one set of demands could be

satisfied. A parcel of land cannot both be preserved in its natural character and mined. Thus, it would be impossible for BLM to carry out the purposes of the Act if each particular management decision were evaluated separately. It is only by looking at the overall use of the public lands that one can accurately assess whether or not BLM is carrying out the broad purposes of the statute."

Utah v. Andrus, 486 F.Supp. 995, 1003 (D.Utah 1979).

not to impair a Wilderness Study Area's (WSA's) suitability as wilderness. BLM Wilderness Review—Section 603, Federal Land Policy and Management Act, 86 Interior Dec. 91, 99, 101–02, 109–11 (1978) (hereinafter cited as Solicitor's Opinion). The Solicitor interpreted the grandfather clause as exempting from the nonimpairment standard the actual uses of an area as they existed on the date of the Act's passage. Thus, mining and grazing activities, and activities on mineral leases, are considered permissible within a WSA to the extent that such operations were actually occurring on October 21, 1976. Under the Solicitor's interpretation, grandfathered uses are themselves subject to regulation to prevent unnecessary or undue degradation of the WSA and its resources, and to protect the environment.

Pursuant to the Solicitor's Opinion, the BLM developed the Wilderness Inventory Handbook and the Interim Management Policy and Guidelines for Lands Under Wilderness Review (IMP). These documents set out Interior's management policies concerning section 603's wilderness review, and detail Interior's interpretation of the nonimpairment standard.[7]

In 1978, Interior initiated its wilderness review program. Initially, a "wilderness inventory" process is used to identify those roadless areas of 5,000 acres or more and those roadless islands that may have wilderness characteristics. An "intensive inventory" is then performed on those areas. Areas identified at this stage as meeting section 603's requirements are designated "Wilderness Study Areas." WSAs are then studied to determine whether they will be recommended as suitable or unsuitable for wilderness designation. From the initial "inventory" of all public lands to the final formal recommendation stage, all lands still being considered in the process are managed under the nonimpairment standard.

C. The Trial Court's Decision

The trial court found the Solicitor's Opinion to be contrary to section 603 of the FLPMA. Rocky Mountain Oil & Gas Association v.

---

7. Interior set forth its interpretation of the nonimpairment standard in detail in the IMP, following the guidelines of the Solicitor's Opinion. Activities that protect or enhance the land's wilderness values, or that provide the minimum necessary public facilities for enjoyment of wilderness values, are considered nonimpairing. Bureau of Land Management, U.S. Dep't of the Interior, Interim Management Policy and Guidelines for Lands Under Wilderness Review 10 (1979). Interior considers any other activity nonimpairing if:

"a. It is temporary [as defined in the IMP].

"b. Any temporary impacts caused by the activity [are] capable of being reclaimed to a condition of being substantially unnoticeable in the wilderness study area * * * as a whole by the

time the Secretary is scheduled to send his recommendations on that area to the President. * * * [I]n areas not yet scheduled for wilderness study, [the area must be reclaimable within four years of] approval of the activity. * * *

" * * *

"c. When the activity is terminated, and after any needed reclamation is complete, the area's wilderness values [will] not have been degraded so far, compared with the area's [other] values * * *, as to significantly constrain the Secretary's recommendation with respect to the area's suitability or nonsuitability for preservation as wilderness."

The draft IMP stated that an activity was "temporary" if the land was capable of being rehabilitated within five years.

Andrus, 500 F.Supp. 1338, 1344 (D.Wyo.1980). Stating that section 603 was clear and unequivocal on its face, the court apparently construed the language of the grandfather clause to mean that all mineral leasing activity, including activity on leases granted before and after the FLPMA was enacted, was insulated from the nonimpairment standard. The court held that although the FLPMA embodied congressional concern for several policies and interests, the Solicitor's interpretation completely sacrificed mineral development for environmental concerns and thus was "statutorily erroneous."

The trial court also examined Interior's policy of including Wilderness Protection Stipulations in leases issued after 1978. These stipulations stated that the area being leased was a WSA to which the nonimpairment standard would apply, putting potential lessees on notice that development of the lease might be precluded. The court found this system of offering leases on which development might be prohibited to be "clearly an unconstitutional taking, and * * * blatantly unfair to lessees."

Finally, the court found Interior's position to be "counterproductive to public interest." The court ordered the Solicitor's Opinion, the Wilderness Inventory Handbook, and the Interim Management Policy and Guidelines for Lands Under Wilderness Review vacated and set aside.

* * *

III.

THE NONIMPAIRMENT STANDARD

The FLPMA provides a method and a statutory mandate to examine BLM lands for wilderness characteristics, and, where appropriate, to incorporate the lands into the wilderness system. Section 603(a) of the FLPMA requires the Secretary to review roadless areas of five thousand acres or more and roadless islands, identified during the section 201(a) inventory as having wilderness characteristics, and to recommend them to the President as suitable or nonsuitable for preservation. Section 603(c) dictates the management protocol for such areas during the review period, the nub of the present controversy.

In analyzing section 603(c), we must bear in mind several precepts of statutory construction. * * *

With these concepts in mind, we begin our statutory tour. Section 603(c) states that:

"During the period of review of such areas and until Congress has determined otherwise, *the Secretary shall continue to manage such lands* according to his authority under this Act and other applicable law *in a manner so as not to impair the suitability of such areas for preservation as wilderness, subject,* however, *to the continuation of existing mining and grazing uses and mineral leasing in the manner and degree in which the same was being conducted on October 21, 1976:*

Provided, That, in managing the public lands the Secretary
shall by regulation or otherwise take any action required to
prevent unnecessary or undue degradation of the lands and
their resources or to afford environmental protection."

43 U.S.C. § 1782(c) (emphasis added).

Interior construes section 603(c) as requiring the application of the
nonimpairment standard to activities on oil and gas leases. Solicitor's
Opinion, supra. Under Interior's interpretation, only actual development operations occurring on the ground as of October 21, 1976, are
protected by the section's grandfather clause.[17] And even that
grandfathered activity is subject to regulation "to prevent unnecessary
or undue degradation * * * or to afford environmental protection."

The district court found that the statutory language was clear and
unambiguous on its face, and directly contrary to Interior's interpretation. The court apparently construed the nonimpairment standard as
inapplicable to mineral leasing as a whole, distinguishing between the
protection afforded to mining and grazing activities, and that afforded
to mineral leasing activities. Under the court's interpretation, although mining and grazing evidently would be subject to the nonimpairment standard, "mineral leasing" would not. *All* mineral leasing
activities, both physical on-lease development and the actual letting of
leases, would be exempt. Mineral leasing apparently should be continued by the Secretary "in the manner and degree in which [the Secretary was conducting it] on October 21, 1976."

We disagree both with the trial court's characterization of section
603(c) as clear and unambiguous, and with its interpretation of the
section as it pertains to mineral leasing. The court's opinion fails
totally to consider the import of Congress' use of "existing" to modify
the three listed exemptions. The opinion also fails to provide a persua-

---

17. On July 20, 1981, the Solicitor issued an opinion modifying the September
5, 1978 Opinion that we address here. See
The BLM Wilderness Review and Valid
Existing Rights, Op.Solic., Dep't of the Interior (July 20, 1981) (hereinafter cited as
1981 Opinion). In the 1981 Opinion, Interior changed its stance regarding leases
issued prior to October 21, 1976 on which
no development operations had commenced
as of that date. While recognizing the
applicability of the § 603(c) nonimpairment standard, the opinion states that the
application of that standard to pre-FLPMA
leases may be limited in some instances
because of § 701(h) of the FLPMA, 43
U.S.C. § 1701 note, which provides that
"[a]ll actions by the Secretary concerned
under this Act shall be subject to valid
existing rights." 1981 Opinion at 4–5.
The opinion notes that a review of each
lease or approval document will be necessary to determine the scope of any such
pre-existing rights held by the lessee. Id.
The opinion also states that it "formalizes

and is consistent with" Interior's position
on appeal before us. Id. at 1 n. 1.

Intervenors argue that we should address "the Secretary's decision not to apply
the nonimpairment policy to pre-1976
leases," claiming they will be collaterally
estopped by the district court's judgment
from contesting that policy in another forum. We decline Intervenors' invitation.
The 1981 Opinion was issued after the trial
court's opinion was rendered, and perforce
was not before that court. The 1981 Opinion rejects the district court's rationale and
is based instead upon an analysis of
§ 701(h). We are reversing and vacating
all of the judgment below, holding that
§ 603(c)'s nonimpairment standard "remains the norm," 1981 Opinion at 4, with
respect to *all* mineral leases *regardless* of
their date of issuance. Accordingly, Intervenors will not be estopped from contesting
in subsequent litigation what they perceive
to be Interior's § 701(h) position. Whether
§ 701(h) saves a particular lease is an issue
that is not before us.

sive rationale for making a distinction, based on the statutory language, between the treatment to be given "mining and grazing uses" and "mineral leases."

Initially, we note that the grandfather clause in its entirety reads "subject, however, to the continuation of existing mining and grazing uses and mineral leasing in the manner and degree in which the same was being conducted on October 21, 1976." FLPMA § 603(c). The clause contains no internal punctuation indicating that Congress sought to treat "mining and grazing uses," and "mineral leasing" differently, and the legislative history of the Act belies such a construction.

Most of section 603(c), including the nonimpairment standard and the grandfather clause, was originally section 311 of H.R. 13777, 94th Cong., 2d Sess., 122 Cong.Rec. 23,465 (1976). The House Report on H.R. 13777 explained that while areas were under wilderness review, they were "to be managed in a manner to preserve their wilderness character, subject to continuation of existing grazing and *mineral uses* and appropriation under the mining laws." H.Rep. No. 1163, supra, at 17 (emphasis added). This language indicates that Congress intended only *existing* mining and grazing uses and *existing* mineral leasing activities to be exempted by the clause.

It likewise appears obvious that all three protected activities are exempt to "the manner and degree in which [they were] being conducted on October 21, 1976." The nonimpairment standard and the grandfather clause originated in section 311 of H.R. 13777, and were enacted into law unchanged. The House Report contemplated that all three activities—grazing uses, mineral uses, and mining law appropriation— would generally be subject to the nonimpairment standard. Id. The legislative history of H.R. 13777's counterpart, S. 507, shows that the Senate had a similar intention. The analogous provisions in the Senate Bill, sections 102(a) and 103(d) of S. 507, 94th Cong., 2d Sess., 122 Cong. Rec. 4036 (1976), directed the Secretary to prepare an inventory of the public lands and to review areas containing wilderness characteristics. The review was "not, of itself, [to] change or prevent change in the management or use of the [lands under review]." Id. § 103(d). The Senate Report on S. 507 explained that the purpose of this language was

> "to insure that * * * the pattern of uses [would not] be frozen, or * * * uses be automatically terminated * * *. On the other hand, the 'of itself' language [was] not meant to be license to continue to allow or disallow uses as if no [review] processes were being conducted. The Committee fully expect[ed] that *the Secretary,* wherever possible, [*would*] make management decisions which will *insure that no future use* or combination of uses *which might be discovered as appropriate in the [review] process* —be they *wilderness,* grazing, * * * etc.—[would] *be foreclosed by any use* or combination of uses

conducted after enactment of S. 507, *but prior to* the *completion* of those processes."

Thus, Congress intended that no activity on the public lands following the Act's passage be allowed to degrade lands containing wilderness values on the date of enactment, precluding their consideration for wilderness suitability before the review process was concluded. A qualified exception to this policy decision was made for "mining and grazing uses and mineral leasing."

We recognize that the statute itself uses the singular "was" rather than the plural "were" in the phrase "in the manner and degree in which the same was being conducted." FLPMA § 603(c). Therefore, an argument can be made that the "manner and degree" language was intended to apply only to "mineral leasing," and hence that mineral leasing was indeed to be treated differently from the other uses. However, this interpretation must be rejected because it is contradictory to the clause's purpose, as evidenced by the legislative history.

We note that both the nonimpairment standard and the grandfather clause originated in a predecessor bill to the FLPMA, H.R. 5441. They were added to insure that the Secretary would preserve the wilderness character of the lands under review, and "to keep the Secretary from changing anything" during the review period. In its original form, the grandfather clause did not mention mineral leasing, but instead read "existing mining and grazing uses in the manner and degree in which the same *had been* conducted." Id. at 103–04 (emphasis added). The phrase was amended in committee on September 22, 1975 to read as it stands presently. There was no discussion concerning the addition of the "mineral leasing" term, or the change to "was."

Because Congress intended the "manner and degree" language to refer both to mining and grazing uses, Utah v. Andrus, 486 F.Supp. 995, 1006 (D.Utah 1979); see H.Rep. No. 1163, supra, at 17; S.Rep. No. 583, supra, at 44–45, 46, *as well as* to mineral leasing, the use of the singular "was" rather than the plural "were" is clearly an error in grammar, and not a signal that mineral leasing was to be accorded different treatment. See also 1 U.S.C. § 1 (1976) (in interpreting congressional legislation, "words importing the singular include and apply to several persons or things").

Further evidence is available demonstrating that Congress is not always mindful of grammatical niceties. A few days prior to the FLPMA's enactment, Congress passed the Act of October 19, 1976, Pub. L. No. 94–557, 90 Stat. 2633. The two statutes are in pari materia; both involve WSAs and establish interim management standards, using strikingly similar language. Consequently, it is proper for us to look to the October 19th Act to aid us in our construction of the FLPMA.

The October 19th Act designated several areas within national forest lands as "wilderness study areas," and directed the Secretary of Agriculture to administer them "to maintain their presently existing wilderness character and potential for inclusion in the [Wilderness System] * * *. Already established *uses* may be permitted to continue * * * in the manner and degree in which the same *was* being conducted on [October 19, 1976]." Id. § 3(d) (emphasis added). The House Report stated that established nonconforming uses could continue,

"such uses not to exceed the manner and degree of such uses on the date of enactment * * *. The term 'manner and degree' means not only types of uses, but implementation of controls to restrict such uses to the time, place and area where already occurring. * * *

"Designation of a wilderness study area does not * * * change already established mining, mineral leasing or grazing activities, in the manner and degree in which same *is* being conducted on date of enactment."

H.Rep. No. 1562, 94th Cong., 2d Sess. 18–19.

In this Act, passed only two days before the FLPMA, Congress also used the singular verb "was" to refer to the plural noun "uses," providing evidence that the use of "was" in section 603(c) is similarly an error in drafting. We consider the October 19th Act, as explained by its legislative history, a persuasive indication of the kind and degree of protection Congress intended section 603(c) to afford to BLM Wilderness Study Areas.

The conclusion that Congress merely erred in its grammar is inescapable. * * * We will not pervert Congress' avowed intent and the manifest meaning of section 603(c). Instead, we conclude that mining and grazing uses and mineral leasing are to be treated identically under the section's grandfather clause, so as to effect the evident purpose of section 603.

The issue still remains whether Congress intended the phrase "mineral leasing" to refer to an activity of the Secretary or to development activities on mineral leases. The district court found that Congress meant to refer to the Secretary's administration of mineral leasing and the letting of leases. Appellants, however, argue that "mineral leasing" should be construed as referring to activity on leases.

The grandfather clause provides a limited exception to the nonimpairment standard for three types of activities: mining and grazing uses and mineral leasing. At first glance, this clause seems to refer to the Secretary's leasing program. Under this view, the clause appears to direct the Secretary to continue leasing in WSAs "in the manner *and degree* * * * being conducted on October 21, 1976" (emphasis added). In this light, the language suggests that the Secretary is to continue to lease at *the same rate* as at enactment. However, mineral leasing has traditionally been a highly discretionary activity of the Secretary. It would be anomalous, to say the least, if Congress now were to constrict the Secretary's exercise of discretion in such an offhand and cursory manner.

In Utah v. Andrus, 486 F.Supp. 995 (D.Utah 1979), the district court examined the import of the grandfather clause as it pertained to mining in WSAs. Following an extensive review of the FLPMA and its legislative history, the court concluded that the clause protected mining and grazing uses to the extent that *actual* on-the-ground activity was taking place on October 21, 1976. The court determined that the statute referred to "*actual* uses, not merely a statutory right to use." Id. at 1006. Otherwise, "there is no way to give meaningful context to the 'manner and degree' language." Id. We agree with that court's interpretation; we believe that Congress intended to limit existing mining and grazing activities to the level of physical activity being undertaken on the FLPMA's date of enactment, and to regulate post-FLPMA activities so as to prevent impairment of wilderness characteristics. The purpose of the WSA management scheme is to maintain the status quo existing October 21, 1976, so that lands then suitable for wilderness consideration will not be rendered unfit for such consideration before the Secretary makes a recommendation and the Congress acts on the recommendation under section 603(a) and (b).

The House Report states that the grandfather clause covers only "existing grazing and *mineral uses* and appropriation under the mining laws." H.Rep. No. 1163, supra, at 17, U.S.Code Cong. & Admin.News 1976, 6191 (emphasis added). The report makes no reference to the Secretary's administration of the leasing program. This strongly suggests Congress meant "mineral leasing" to refer to actual development activity. In addition, the other two grandfathered activities are mining and grazing uses, referring to actual on-the-ground activity. ＊ ＊ ＊

＊ ＊ ＊

One of the prime concerns of Congress in enacting the FLPMA was that BLM lands suitable for wilderness preservation at the date of the Act's passage be given a chance for consideration as wilderness. Under Interior's policy, the wilderness review period will result in only a brief hiatus from potential mineral development for most of the lands concerned. Lands containing oil and gas, and of no wilderness value, will be released from the review unharmed and fully suitable for mineral development. Under RMOGA's interpretation, however, lands suitable for wilderness could be irrevocably altered by development and their wilderness values destroyed. It would be incongruous to limit mining and grazing to pre-FLPMA levels, but give disruptive mineral leasing activities carte blanche.

In light of the language of section 603(c) and its legislative history, we hold that Interior's interpretation of the section's effect on mineral leasing activities, as expressed in the Solicitor's Opinion of September 5, 1978, is reasonable and entitled to deference. Indeed, under our analysis it is compelling. We hold that mineral leasing is subject to the nonimpairment standard of section 603(c), and that the grandfather clause affords protection only to activities on mineral leases in the manner and degree actually occurring on October 21, 1976. We reverse the district court's opinion, and remand for the entry of judgment in accordance with this opinion.

NOTES

1. Is the 1981 Solicitor's Opinion, discussed in note 17, entitled to the same deference that the court accorded to the 1978 Opinion? To what extent does the statute limit administrative discretion?

2. The Department of Interior speeded its wilderness review to release BLM study areas for multiple use management. Interior Secretary Watt deleted three types of areas from review: (1) areas less than 5,000 acres, (2) "split estate" lands (those areas with private subsurface mineral rights), and (3) areas that are contiguous to wilderness-type lands and that cannot stand as wilderness on their own merit. A number of environmental groups promptly filed the following suit.

SIERRA CLUB v. WATT
United States District Court, Eastern District of California, 1985.
608 F.Supp. 305.

KARLTON, Chief Judge.

I

BACKGROUND

A. Federal Land Policy And Management Act

In 1976, Congress enacted the Federal Land Policy and Management Act (FLPMA), to provide "the first comprehensive, statutory statement of purposes, goals and authority for the use and management of about 448 million acres of federally-owned lands administered by the Secretary of Interior through the Bureau of Land Management." S.Rep. No. 583, 94th Cong., 1st sess. 24 (1975). FLPMA reflected a major change in federal policy. Previously, the lands held by the Bureau of Land Management (BLM) (and its predecessor the General Land Office) were viewed as only temporarily within the custody of the United States and it was expected that their ultimate destiny was private ownership.[3] Under FLPMA, however, BLM lands were to be held in permanent federal ownership unless, as a result of land use planning, the disposal of a particular parcel would serve the national interest.

* * *

As the first step in the process of implementing the new national policy the Secretary of Interior (hereinafter "the Secretary") was directed to prepare and maintain an inventory of all public lands and assess "their resource and other values." FLPMA § 201(a), 42 U.S.C. § 1711(a). As part of the process of inventory the Secretary was directed to review roadless areas of 5,000 acres or more and roadless islands of the public lands having wilderness characteristics as described in the Wilderness Act, and to report to the President his recommendation as to the suitability or nonsuitability of each area for

3. See Leshy, Wilderness and Its Discontents—Wilderness Review Comes to the Public Lands, Ariz.St.L.J. 361, 362–63 (1981).

inclusion in the National Wilderness Preservation System. 43 U.S.C. § 1782(a). "Public lands" required to be reviewed under section 603(a) are lands and interests in land owned by the United States and managed by the BLM, excepting Outer Continental Shelf and native trust lands. 43 U.S.C. § 1702(e). This task was to be completed within fifteen years of FLPMA's enactment. The President, in turn, is to make his recommendation to Congress as to the inclusion of these lands in the wilderness system within two years of the receipt of the Secretary's report. Until Congress determines otherwise, the Secretary is to manage these lands

> so as not to impair the suitability of such areas for preservation as wilderness, subject, however, to the continuation of existing mining and grazing uses and mineral leasing in the manner and degree in which the same was being conducted on October 21, 1976: [the date that FLPMA was enacted] *Provided,* That, in managing the public lands the Secretary shall by regulation or otherwise take any action required to prevent unnecessary or undue degradation of the lands and their resources or to afford environmental protection.

43 U.S.C. § 1782(c) (emphasis in original).   *   *   *

B. *Implementation of the Section 603 Wilderness Review*

In order to carry out the wilderness review provisions of section 603(a) and other sections of the Act, including the inventory preparation requirement of section 201, the former Secretary of Interior, Cecil Andrus, established a wilderness review program consisting of three phases: inventory, study, and reporting. During the inventory phase, those roadless areas of the public lands which have wilderness characteristics were identified as "wilderness study areas" (WSA's). The procedure for determining whether an area of the public lands met WSA status was provided in the *"Wilderness Inventory Handbook"* (WIH), a statement of policy, direction, procedures and guidance for the wilderness review program published by the BLM on September 27, 1978. The WIH provided that, with certain exceptions, the wilderness inventory be conducted on *all* public lands administered by the BLM. The WIH prescribes that in choosing areas for section 603 WSA status the factors to be used are:

1. Size. At least 5,000 contiguous roadless acres of public land.

2. Naturalness. The imprint of man's work must be substantially unnoticeable.

3. Either:

    a. An *outstanding* opportunity for solitude, or

    b. An *outstanding* opportunity for a primitive and unconfined type of recreation.

To qualify for wilderness study identification an area of public land must be shown to meet both factors 2 and 3. An island may be of any size.

(emphasis in original).

In addition, the WIH directed that other areas which had wilderness characteristics as defined in (2) and (3) above, but which contained fewer than 5,000 acres, were still eligible for WSA identification if they were either:

1. Contiguous with land managed by another agency which has been formally determined to have wilderness or potential wilderness values, or

2. Contiguous with an area of less than 5,000 acres of other Federal lands administered by an agency with authority to study and preserve wilderness lands, and the combined total is 5,000 acres or more, or

3. Subject to strong public support for such identification and it is clearly and obviously of sufficient size as to make practicable its preservation and use in an unimpaired condition, and of a size suitable for wilderness management.

In further implementation of the statute, the BLM published on December 12, 1979, an *"Interim Management Policy and Guidelines for Lands Under Wilderness Review"* (IMP) which set forth the guidelines under which the BLM would manage the lands subject to wilderness review, but for which the BLM wilderness inventory process had not yet been completed and lands which the BLM has determined to have wilderness characteristics. * * * Under the IMP, lands with wilderness characteristics but less than 5,000 acres in size were to be managed under a modified nonimpairment standard pursuant to section 43 U.S.C. § 1732(b). * * *

FLPMA was passed in October of 1976 and the inventory began in 1978. By November of 1980, the total acreage subject to the Act (173,727,000 acres) had been inventoried. Secretary Andrus, by order of the Federal Register, placed 919 areas totaling 23,772,000 acres in WSA status and he found the balance of land to be without the requisite wilderness characteristics. 45 Fed.Reg. 77,574 (November 14, 1980) (hereinafter "Andrus order").

C. Secretary Watt's December 30, 1982, Order

On December 30, 1982, a new Secretary of Interior, James Watt, published an order in the Federal Register which affected the status of approximately one million acres of public lands then in WSA status. 47 Fed.Reg. 58,372 (December 30, 1982) (hereinafter "Watt order"). The order was in several parts: First, the Secretary ordered that lands in which the United States does not own the subsurface mineral rights (split-estate lands) be removed from the wilderness inventory altogether and that they no longer be managed under the nonimpairment Interim

Management Policy guidelines. After this deletion the state directors were ordered to reexamine the WSA's in which split-estates were located and to determine whether, after deletion of such lands, the remaining WSA's amounted to more than 5,000 acres. If not, they were also to be deleted. Even if the WSA, after deletion of the split estate lands, still amounted to 5,000 acres, the state directors were ordered to reexamine the wilderness status of these areas if the deletion substantially altered the boundary or configuration of the WSA. Specifically, the Secretary ordered that certain WSA's totaling 327,061 acres of split-estate lands in Arizona and New Mexico be deleted immediately. Specific orders as to other states were soon to follow.

Second, the Secretary determined that the less than 5,000 acre lands were not properly considered for wilderness status under FLMPA as a matter of law. He ordered that 158 less than 5,000 acre areas totaling 340,526 acres should be deleted from WSA status. * * *

Third, the Secretary ordered that all roadless areas larger than 5,000 acres found to have wilderness characteristics only in association with, or in conjunction with, contiguous wilderness or wilderness candidate areas administered by the Forest Service, National Park Service, or Fish and Wildlife Service, should be excluded from the wilderness inventory unless they are determined to have wilderness attributes of their own. He ordered that such areas should be reexamined to determine whether such areas still exceed 5,000 acres and have wilderness attributes on their own after exclusion of all areas adjacent to wilderness or wilderness candidate areas administered by other agencies.

The Secretary's action was described in the Federal Register as made pursuant to an Opinion of his Solicitor, dated December 15, 1982. In turn, this Opinion adopted certain interpretations of section 603 of FLPMA, 43 U.S.C. § 1782, enunciated by the Interior Board of Land Appeals in three cases: *Santa Fe Pacific Railroad Co.,* 64 IBLA 27 (1982); *Don Coops,* et al., 61 IBLA 300 (1982); and *Tri-County Cattlemen's Ass'n,* 60 IBLA 305 (1981). In these three opinions, the IBLA held that certain areas of the public lands had been improperly designated as WSA's under section 603 and discussed the applicability of section 603 to public lands generally.

On March 14, 1983, the BLM issued Department of Interior Instruction Memorandum No. 83–188, Change 1, to all State Directors detailing comprehensive procedures to be used in implementing Secretary Watt's order. With respect to the split-estate lands, the State Directors were given two options: (1) to study the lands for forms of protective management other than WSA or (2) to manage the lands for general multiple use development. Under either option, the lands are not to be considered for wilderness status. Until the Director of the BLM approves the State Director's recommendations, these lands are to be managed in a manner so as to prevent unnecessary or undue degradation of the lands. With respect to the areas under 5,000 acres, the Instruction Memorandum directed the State Directors to determine the suitability of each area for: (1) wilderness consideration under section 202 of FLPMA, 43 U.S.C. § 1712; (2) other forms of protective management; or (3) management under a multiple use standard.

While the total figures are necessarily approximate due to changes in inventory, it is clear that the Secretary's order has had a profound effect.[12]

On January 13, 1983, plaintiffs brought this suit. They attack Secretary Watt's order on a variety of grounds. They assert that the Secretary's exclusion of the split-estate lands over 5,000 acres violated FLPMA; that the exclusion of land under 5,000 acres is subject to being set aside as a violation of NEPA; and that the procedure used by the Secretary violated the Administrative Procedure Act. * * *

II

[The court held that plaintiffs had standing, and that plaintiffs were not required to join all owners of mineral interests potentially affected by the action.]

VI

PROPRIETY OF SECRETARY WATT'S ORDER

A. *Split-Estate Lands*

I first turn to an examination of the correctness of the Secretary's withdrawal of the split-estate lands, for these lands form the nub of the controversy.[46] * * *

12. The impact of Watt's order appears to be as follows:

1. 525,000 acres of split-estate lands have been removed from wilderness consideration under section 603 of FLPMA.

2. 100,000 acres of non split-estate lands found to lack wilderness characteristics after deletion of split-estate lands have been recommended for release to multiple use management.

3. 124 of the 158 areas under 5,000 acres have been recommended for no further study as wilderness.

4. Certain WSA's in Nevada, Oregon and Colorado have been released to multiple use management.

5. 138,000 acres of contiguous areas over 5,000 acres determined not to have wilderness attributes on their own have been released to multiple use management.

The cumulative totals are as follows:

Total number of acres (in ten states) removed from wilderness inventory, released from further wilderness study, and released into multiple use other than wilderness .... 1,218,873 acres

Total number of acres (in ten states) removed from wilderness inventory and no longer to be studied for wilderness but recommended for study for protective classifications other than wilderness .... 321,328 acres

Grand Total number of acres (in ten states) removed from wilderness inventory and released from further wilderness study .... 1,540,201 acres

There is some dispute as to the exact acreage affected by the Secretary's decision. As the issues presented by this case are purely legal, this does not affect disposition of the motions.

46. As noted above, the Secretary's withdrawal of these one-half million acres of split-estates triggered the removal of

* * *

Since the Secretary's decision was an interpretative ruling which reversed a previous policy and which required no special expertise beyond legal skills to make, I find as a first matter that the Secretary's decision is entitled to little, if any, deference.[48] I thus examine the decision essentially unfettered by the Secretary's action. I begin with the Secretary's contention that the removal of the split-estate lands from the WSA's was proper because as a matter of statutory interpretation they should never have been included in the first place.

* * *

The statute, section 603(a) of FLPMA, in plain and unadorned language requires the Secretary to review "those roadless areas of five thousand acres or more * * * of the public lands, identified during the inventory * * * as having wilderness characteristics. * * * " 43 U.S.C. § 1782(a). The statute itself provides a definition of public lands:

> (e) The term "public lands" means any land and interest in land owned by the United States within the several States and administered by the Secretary of the Interior through the Bureau of Land Management, without regard to how the United States acquired ownership, except—

> (1) lands located on the Outer Continental Shelf; and

> (2) lands held for the benefit of Indians, Aleuts, and Eskimos.

43 U.S.C. § 1702(e).[51]

To say that the language is straightforward is to state the obvious. To apply the statute to the split-estates over 5,000 acres seems equally straightforward. In such lands, the United States holds the interest in the surface estate while private parties hold the interest in the subsurface estate. Since the interest in the surface estate is an "interest in land owned by the United States," it appears clearly to fall within the definition of public land provided by the statute. Nor does the fact that private parties have an interest in the minerals below the surface appear to preclude their inclusion as WSAs because such a condition is incompatible with the status of wilderness. The definition of wilderness, incorporated into section 603(a), is directed at the surface attributes of public lands. Indeed, this conclusion is wholly consonant with

---

other lands no longer able to satisfy the WSA requirements.

48. Varying degrees of deference are accorded to administrative interpretations, based on such factors as the timing and consistency of the agency's position, and the nature of its expertise. Batterton v. Francis, 432 U.S. 416, 425 n. 9 (1972). Given the fact that Secretary Watt's order in effect reversed Secretary Andrus, any deference to be accorded it is significantly diminished. See Morton v. Ruiz, 415 U.S. 199, 237 (1974).

51. The IBLA majority in *Santa Fe Pacific Railroad Co.* endorses the startling notion of statutory construction that the public lands definition in section 103(e) of FLPMA may be ignored because it precedes the wilderness review provision of section 603 which is found "[F]ive hundred sections beyond that definition." 64 IBLA at 33. The rule of statutory construction is otherwise. * * *

the Wilderness Act, 16 U.S.C. §§ 1131–1136, which section 603(a) of FLPMA specifies is the guide for the wilderness review process of FLPMA. The Wilderness Act expressly allows for the preservation and exploitation of mining claims and interests in wilderness areas.

* * *

The IBLA found and the defendants argue that such an interpretation is too rigid. The defendants suggest that the statute must be read in conjunction with other responsibilities of the Secretary. See *Santa Fe Pacific Railroad Co.*, 64 IBLA at 33. In this regard, they note that section 603(c) requires that management of areas as wilderness during the study period is nonetheless subject to existing mining rights and that section 701(h), 43 U.S.C. § 1701 n. (h), requires the Secretary's conduct be subject to all valid existing rights. From these two provisions, defendants argue that it is incorrect to interpret the statute to include split-estate lands as subject to wilderness evaluation. I consider each statute in turn.

Section 603(c) provides that the "Secretary shall continue to manage such lands * * * so as not to impair the suitability of such areas for preservation as wilderness, subject, however, to the continuation of existing mining and grazing uses and mineral leasing * * *".

Two things seem directly contemplated by this provision; one, the mere fact that mining rights exist does not preclude management as, much less consideration for wilderness status, but two, that under such circumstances, some adjustment of the management practices might be required. Indeed, in the two decisions which have extensively discussed section 603 of FLPMA, split-estates have, at least impliedly, been viewed as falling within the definition of public lands. See Rocky Mountain Oil and Gas Ass'n v. Watt, 696 F.2d 734 (10th Cir.1982); State of Utah v. Andrus, 486 F.Supp. 995 (D.Utah 1979).

Nor do the provisions of section 701(h) require a different conclusion. There the statute requires that "all actions by the Secretary concerned under this Act shall be subject to valid existing rights." 43 U.S.C. § 1701, n. (h). Defendants argue that the subsurface estate carries with it implied easements for development and that the possible extraction of minerals is inconsistent with the protection of wilderness qualities. * * *

* * * The fact that Congress specifically provided for mining activities to continue in WSA's under the provisions of section 603(c), 43 U.S.C. § 1782(c), directly demonstrates that defendants' position is untenable. If Congress had intended that the split-estate lands be excluded from the inventory it would not have expressly provided for the continuance of existing mining activities during the period of review. * * *

* * *

The IBLA in *Santa Fe Pacific Railroad Co.* nevertheless found that the ownership of the subsurface estate constitutes a "vested right" which could not be denied or extinguished by exercise of Secretarial discretion. Whatever validity the IBLA's premise has, it does not follow that such estates may not be studied for wilderness. The flaw in the IBLA majority's reasoning is that the placement of these areas into wilderness review and even eventually into wilderness designation does not deny or extinguish the owner's property right in the subsurface estate. The land may still be mined subject to certain controls under the Wilderness Act or Congress may choose to recompense the owner through exchange or payment. Finally, as the dissent in *Santa Fe Pacific Railroad Co.* notes, placing the land in WSA status may not have any adverse consequences to the owner of the subsurface rights since the Secretary's final recommendations may exclude such lands.

A final basis for the IBLA's decision was that placement of the split-estate lands into the wilderness study under section 603 would be a futile exercise as the lands could never be placed in permanent wilderness status. 64 IBLA at 34. It appears to the court that the IBLA simply misconstrues the statutory scheme and the nature of the wilderness review process. * * * The statutory scheme contemplated executive study but congressional disposition of wilderness issues. Clearly, if Congress elects to include within the wilderness preservation system split-estate lands, it may authorize the purchase or condemnation of the reserved mineral rights in the subsurface estate, or the exchange of reserved mineral rights for other federal lands or mineral interests.

* * *

Nonetheless, defendants have one more string to their bow. They argue that whatever this court's interpretation of the statutory language as it relates to the split-estates might otherwise be, it is precluded by authority binding on this court.

In Columbia Basin Land Protection Ass'n v. Schlesinger, 643 F.2d 585 (9th Cir.1981) the court held, among other things, that privately held lands in which the United States has retained mineral rights are not subject to FLPMA's right-of-way requirements. In resolving the issue the court relied upon previous cases which had interpreted the term "public lands" to mean "land 'subject to sale or other disposal under general laws' [citations omitted]," and does not include " '[a]ll land, to which any claims or rights to others have attached.' " Relying in part upon this premise the court explicated its specific holdings as follows: "We thus hold that privately held lands in which the United States has retained mineral rights are not subject to FLPMA's right-of-way requirements." Then, after restating its reasons, the court articulated its second holding: "Consequently, we hold that the FLPMA right-of-way permit, as issued, is valid." From these holdings defendants argue that I am bound by the Ninth Circuit's public lands definition and that definition precludes inclusion of the split-estate lands.

I begin by observing that the specific holding of *Columbia Basin* confined to its narrowest ambit does not require me to find that the split-estate lands are not subject to inventory or inclusion within the WSA's. *Columbia Basin* dealt with the converse of the issue here;

namely, where private individuals owned the surface but the United States owned the mineral rights. Indeed, the definition of lands excluded from the WSA's by Secretary Andrus in the WIH, excluded lands like those considered in *Columbia Basin* where the United States did not own the surface estate. Thus it may be said that *Columbia Basin's* holding does not directly affect Secretary Andrus' decision.

Such an observation, however, cannot end the discussion. It is clear that the broad language of the court's reasoning does lend support to defendants' position. While it may be argued that limiting *Columbia Basin* to its specific factual context requires no particular outcome in this case, such manipulation of the notions of holding and dicta appears inappropriate. The reasoning was necessary to the decision and cannot be disregarded. As I now explain, however, *Columbia Basin's* premise, that the term "public lands" did not include land in which others owned an interest has been completely undermined by subsequent Supreme Court authority, and can no longer be viewed as binding.

The Supreme Court has recently discussed the historical development of the now thirty-three million acres of split-estate lands in Watt v. Western Nuclear, Inc., 462 U.S. 36 (1983). *Western Nuclear's* reasoning is simply incompatible with the premise that the traditional definition of "public lands" required that the United States own the entire fee. Throughout the opinion the Court recognized that, where the surface was patented but the United States retained mineral interests, the land did not lose its character as public lands. Indeed, the specific issue decided in *Western Nuclear* was whether mining of gravel under such circumstances was a trespass because it was an unauthorized removal of "mineral materials from public lands under the jurisdiction of the Dept. of Interior." The Court resolved the issue in terms of whether gravel was a mineral. Clearly such a resolution was unnecessary if the gravel was not on "public lands." Given this intervening Supreme Court decision, *Columbia Basin's* broad language cannot be followed.

* * *

I therefore conclude that the IBLA misconstrued FLPMA and the Secretary's decision premised upon that construction cannot stand.
* * *

B. Less Than 5,000 Acre Lands

I now turn to an examination of plaintiffs' claims as to the other set of lands at issue in this litigation—the less than 5,000 acre lands. These lands were formally designated as WSA's along with roadless areas of 5,000 acres or more by Secretary Andrus' order. Secretary Andrus announced in that order that his authority to place these lands in wilderness review derived from section 603 of FLPMA. 43 U.S.C. § 1782.

[In a lengthy discussion, the court held that Secretary Watt's order removing the roadless areas of less that 5000 acres from wilderness review was invalid and that they must continue to be managed as wilderness study areas.]

* * *

VII

CONCLUSION

In *California v. Bergland,* I observed that environmental issues inevitably tender a set of conflicting interests and values. 483 F.Supp. at 501 (E.D.Cal.1980). I noted there that "[c]ourts, the least democratic of our political institutions, are ill equipped to strike the balances and tradeoffs for society." What was true then is equally true today. The resolution of these conflicts should not be made by courts, but by the two political branches. Equally true, however, is the requirement that the political branches in resolving such conflicts must obey the law and courts must, in properly tendered lawsuits, determine whether the political branches have done so.

In this much too lengthy opinion,[76] I have determined that the instant case is properly before this court and that in large measure the Secretary failed to follow the law. As to the split-estates, FLPMA closely defines the Secretary's obligations. As to the less than 5,000 acre estates, this opinion acknowledges that the Secretary has very broad authority. Whether Congress was wise in providing the Secretary with such broad authority, or whether the Secretary will exercise his broad discretion wisely is not for this court to say. Nonetheless, it is this court's responsibility to declare the law and then to apply it.

* * *

NOTES

1. Is this an example of hypertechnical judicial review? Of over-zealous administrative lawmaking? Must the BLM at some point comply with California v. Block, 690 F.2d 753 (9th Cir.1982), supra at page 1001?

2. In 1983 the Bear Canyon Wilderness in Montana became the first wilderness area to be managed by the BLM. Before then, the relatively few BLM wilderness acres had been included within larger wildernesses and managed by other agencies. In February 1985, the BLM adopted procedures for management of designated wilderness areas. 43 C.F.R. Pt. 8560 (1985).

3. In Sierra Club v. Clark, 774 F.2d 1406 (9th Cir.1985), the plaintiffs challenged the BLM's interpretation of the non-impairment criteria of section 603(c) of FLPMA. Under the BLM's "Interim Management Policy and Guidelines for Lands Under Wilderness Review" (IMP), impacts "must at a minimum be capable of being reclaimed to a condition substantially unnoticeable in the Wilderness area * * * *as*

---

76. Complexity does not lend itself to brevity without obscurity; how I wish it were otherwise.

a whole by the time the Secretary of the Interior is scheduled to send his recommendation to the President." Id. at 1409 (emphasis by the court). The Sierra Club argued that the non-impairment criteria of section 1603(c) had to be determined on a "parcel-by-parcel basis." The court deferred to the agency's interpretation and cleared the way for the resumption of the Barstow to Las Vegas motorcycle race through the California Desert Conservation Area. Does the BLM's interpretation, which the Court allowed to stand, mean that the larger the wilderness study area, the greater the impact allowed on any one part of it?

4. How many wilderness areas does the nation need? When asked this question, Bob Marshall, Director of Recreation for the Forest Service and one of the founders of the Wilderness Society, countered: "How many Brahms symphonies do we need?" At the other end of the spectrum, "Joe Posewitz, leader of the resource assessment unit of the Montana Department of Fish, Wildlife and Parks [stated that] 'I've yet to hear anybody say they would not go in and drill, even if wildlife conditions call for a complete prohibition against access.'" Edwards, Battle for a Bigger Bob, National Geographic 691–92 (May 1985). Somewhere in the middle is the outdoor-oriented westerner. See Jeff Sher, Roads to Ruin, American Forests 17–19 (April 1985):

> Roads and whether we should continue to build them at our current breakneck pace into the last untouched strongholds of the mountain West, have become a major issue in the West.
>
> The West's remaining roadless lands in most cases are not as spectacular as the areas we already have set aside to please our sense of aesthetics or satisfy our growing thirst for outdoor recreation. They do not quite rival Glacier National Park or Yellowstone. But many of them are spectacular enough that, were they not so near existing parks and wilderness areas, they almost certainly would already have been granted protected status.
>
> Furthermore, many of these lands, partly by virtue of the fact that they are not the most spectacular and well known, do provide the best hunting and fishing and backcountry solitude that remain in the lower 48 states. For that reason, many westerners view preservation of these lands in an untouched state as crucial to the preservation of their outdoor-oriented lifestyle.
>
> On the other hand, these lands also provide an untapped reservoir of timber in many areas of the West where the government owns most of the land and where most of the private timber lands have been cut over. * * * The argument goes: the larger the timber base, the more sustainable jobs there will be in an industry famous for its dramatic ups and downs. Until fairly recently. * * * there was always someplace else to go for hunting and fishing and to evade the drone of the chainsaws and logging trucks.

Now, however, the West has run out of places to go. Only 14.5 million acres of roadless territory exist in Montana and Idaho, our wildest states, outside National Parks and Wilderness areas.

* * *

Whatever the local arguments, the bottom-line issue remains the same, and it isn't really roads at all. The issue is proper land management.

"We're going to have some roads," said Joe Hinson, executive director of the Idaho Forest Industry Council. "Where they are, how they're managed, whether they'll be closed when their immediate use is finished, are all legitimate questions."

Before the questions of proper management can be adequately addressed, however, it must be determined whether the rugged western landscape, no matter how it is managed, is capable of fulfilling all our desires for resources, recreation, and aesthetics. If it cannot, all the management expertise in the world will not be able to stave off some hard decisions about who wins and who loses in the mountain West.

5. The foregoing excerpt is testament, among other things, to the manner in which the wilderness idea increasingly influences policy on lands not designated as wilderness. Somewhat similarly, Arizona Governor Bruce Babbitt, long a student of public land law and policy, made these comments in an address to the 1985 annual meeting of the Sierra Club:

We * * * need a new western land ethic for non wilderness. The old concept of multiple use no longer fits the reality of the new west. It must be replaced by a concept of public use. From this day on, we must recognize the new reality that the highest and best, most productive use of western public land will usually be for public purposes— watershed, wildlife and recreation.

The move to public use is the climax of a long historical process. The Homestead Act of 1865 recognized that public lands should be used to facilitate settlement and development. Seventy years later, having served that purpose, the public domain was closed to homesteading.

The next phase in the evolution of public lands was private resource exploitation. The Mineral Entry Act, the Timber Entry Acts and the Reclamation Act of 1902 put the public lands up for mining, grazing, logging and water development.

We are now at the threshold of the final stage in the evolution of public lands policy. The great urban centers of the west are filled with citizens who yearn for solitude, for camping facilities, for a blank spot on the map, a place to teach a son or daughter to hunt, fish or simply survive and enjoy.

The conflicts between public use and private exploitation—grazing, mining entry, and timber cutting—are becoming more intense each year.

[T]he multiple use concept is not adequate for public land management. Forest Service resources are devoted to accelerated logging while families search in vain for improved campsites on the National Forest. Frivolous and uneconomical mining claims disrupt forest administration and recreational uses. Elk herds are reduced to make way for cattle which provide fewer economic benefits to local communities. Mining, logging and other commercial uses are subsidized while wildlife and recreational uses are ignored.

The time is at hand to go beyond multiple use. Mining entry must be regulated, timber cutting must be honestly subordinated to watershed and wildlife values, and grazing must be subordinated to regeneration and restoration of grasslands. Many of the forest and BLM plans now being circulated ignore the primacy of public values. It is now time to replace neutral concepts of multiple use with a statutory mandate that public lands are to be administered primarily for public purposes.

Multiple use has been the basic statutory mandate on most of the public lands for a quarter century. Will it be substantially replaced by Babbitt's proposed "public use" concept during the next quarter century? During the next half century?

INDEX

†